SO-BYA-922

Business Law and the Legal Environment -- BUS 251

Custom Edition For Bristol Community College

22e

David P. Twomey | Marianne M. Jennings

CENGAGE
Learning·

Australia • Brazil • Japan • Korea • Mexico • Singapore • Spain • United Kingdom • United States

CENGAGE
Learning·

**Business Law and the Legal Environment --
BUS 251: Custom Edition For Bristol
Community College, 22e**

David P. Twomey | Marianne M. Jennings

Anderson's Business Law and the Legal Environment, Comprehensive
Volume, 22nd Edition
David P. Twomey | Marianne M. Jennings
© 2014, 2011, 2008 & 2005 Cengage Learning. All rights reserved.

Senior Project Development Manager:
  Linda deStefano

Market Development Manager:
  Heather Kramer

Senior Production/Manufacturing Manager:
  Donna M. Brown

Production Editorial Manager:
  Kim Fry

Sr. Rights Acquisition Account Manager:
  Todd Osborne

ALL RIGHTS RESERVED. No part of this work covered by the copyright herein
may be reproduced, transmitted, stored or used in any form or by any means
graphic, electronic, or mechanical, including but not limited to photocopying,
recording, scanning, digitizing, taping, Web distribution, information networks,
or information storage and retrieval systems, except as permitted under
Section 107 or 108 of the 1976 United States Copyright Act, without the prior
written permission of the publisher.

For product information and technology assistance, contact us at
Cengage Learning Customer & Sales Support, 1-800-354-9706

For permission to use material from this text or product,
submit all requests online at **cengage.com/permissions**
Further permissions questions can be emailed to
permissionrequest@cengage.com

This book contains select works from existing Cengage Learning resources and
was produced by Cengage Learning Custom Solutions for collegiate use. As such,
those adopting and/or contributing to this work are responsible for editorial
content accuracy, continuity and completeness.

Compilation © 2013 Cengage Learning
ISBN-13: 978-1-285-89301-3

ISBN-10: 1-285-89301-8
Cengage Learning
5191 Natorp Boulevard
Mason, Ohio 45040
USA

Cengage Learning is a leading provider of customized learning solutions with
office locations around the globe, including Singapore, the United Kingdom,
Australia, Mexico, Brazil, and Japan. Locate your local office at:
international.cengage.com/region.
Cengage Learning products are represented in Canada by Nelson Education, Ltd.
For your lifelong learning solutions, visit **www.cengage.com/custom.**
Visit our corporate website at **www.cengage.com.**

Printed in the United States of America

Brief Contents

PART 1

The Legal and Social Environment of Business

© Manuel Gutjahr/iStockphoto.com

1

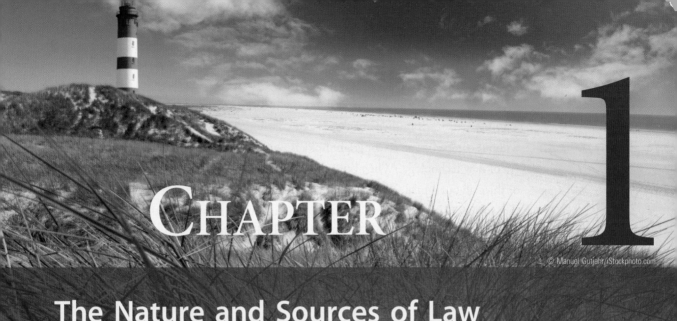

CHAPTER 1

The Nature and Sources of Law

© Manuel Gutjahr/iStockphoto.com

learningoutcomes

After studying this chapter, you should be able to

LO.1 Discuss the nature of law

LO.2 List the sources of law

LO.3 Describe the classifications of law

Why have law? If you have ever been stuck in a traffic jam or jostled in a crowd leaving a stadium, you have observed the need for order to keep those involved moving in an efficient and safe manner. The issues with bloggers' use of others' materials and continuing downloading of music and films without compensation to copyright holders illustrate the need for rules and order in this era of new technology. When our interactions are not orderly, whether at our concerts or through our e-mail, all of us and our rights are affected. The order or pattern of rules that society uses to govern the conduct of individuals and their relationships is called **law**. Law keeps society running smoothly and efficiently.

> **law** – the order or pattern of rules that society establishes to govern the conduct of individuals and the relationships among them.

A. Nature of Law and Legal Rights

Law consists of the body of principles that govern conduct and that can be enforced in courts or by administrative agencies. The law could also be described as a collection or bundle of rights.

1. Legal Rights

> **right** – legal capacity to require another person to perform or refrain from an action.
>
> **duty** – an obligation of law imposed on a person to perform or refrain from performing a certain act.

A **right** is a legal capacity to require another person to perform or refrain from performing an act. Our rights flow from the U.S. Constitution, state constitutions, federal and state statutes, and ordinances at the local levels, including cities, counties, and boroughs. Within these sources of rights are also duties. A **duty** is an obligation of law imposed on a person to perform or refrain from performing a certain act.

Duties and rights coexist. No right exists in one person without a corresponding duty resting on some other person or persons. For example, if the terms of a lease provide that the premises will remain in a condition of good repair so that the tenant can live there comfortably, the landlord has a corresponding duty to provide a dwelling that has hot and cold running water.

2. Individual Rights

The U.S. Constitution gives individuals certain rights. Those rights include the right to freedom of speech, the right to due process or the right to have a hearing before any freedom is taken away, and the right to vote. There are also duties that accompany individual rights, such as the duty to speak in a way that does not cause harm to others. For example, individuals are free to express their opinions about the government or its officials, but they would not be permitted to yell "Fire!" in a crowded theater and cause unnecessary harm to others. The rights given in the U.S. Constitution are rights that cannot be taken away or violated by any statutes, ordinances, or court decisions. These rights provide a framework for the structure of government and other laws.

3. The Right of Privacy

One very important individual legal right is the right of privacy, which has two components. The first is the right to be secure against unreasonable searches and seizures by the government. The Fourth Amendment of the U.S. Constitution

right of privacy – the right to be free from unreasonable intrusion by others.

guarantees this portion of the **right of privacy.**[1] A police officer, for example, may not search your home unless the officer has a reasonable suspicion (which is generally established through a warrant) that your home contains evidence of a crime, such as illegal drugs. If your home or business is searched unlawfully, any items obtained during that unlawful search could be excluded as evidence in a criminal trial because of the Fourth Amendment's exclusionary rule. **For Example,** in the murder trial of O.J. Simpson, Judge Lance Ito excluded some of the evidence the police had obtained from inside Mr. Simpson's Ford Bronco, which was parked on the street outside his home. Judge Ito ruled that the officers should have first obtained a warrant for the locked vehicle, which was not going to be taken anywhere because Mr. Simpson was out of town at that time.

CASE SUMMARY

Searches of Cars When Drivers Are Cuffed

FACTS: Rodney Gant was arrested for driving with a suspended license and handcuffed in the back seat of the squad car of the arresting officers. After handcuffing Mr. Gant, the arresting officers searched his car and found cocaine in the pocket of a jacket lying on the back seat of Gant's vehicle. Mr. Gant was charged with possession of cocaine (as well as driving with a suspended license).

Mr. Gant's lawyer challenged the search of his client's vehicle on the grounds that there were not exigent circumstances. That is, locked in and handcuffed as he was, there was no emergency or reason to believe that Mr. Gant would spring into action and hide, destroy, or swallow the cocaine. As a result, his lawyer argued that the officers needed a warrant. Without the warrant, his lawyer argued, the cocaine could not be used as evidence in the case.

The cocaine evidence was admitted and Mr. Gant was convicted and appealed. The Court of Appeals of Arizona reversed. The United States Supreme Court granted Arizona's petition for *certiorari*, and subsequently vacated and remanded. The Court of Appeals of Arizona remanded for evidentiary hearing on the legality of the warrantless search. On remand, the trial court found no violation. Defendant appealed again. The Court of Appeals of Arizona reversed the decision and the Supreme Court of Arizona affirmed that reversal. Arizona appealed.

DECISION: The court held that the officers needed to impound the vehicle and obtain a warrant in order to search it. Police may search the passenger compartment of a vehicle after such an arrest only if it is reasonable to believe that the person arrested might somehow access the vehicle at the time of the search or that the vehicle contains evidence of the offense of arrest, which, in this case, was a suspended license. Without a warrant to search the vehicle while its owner was handcuffed, the cocaine that was found was not admissible for purposes of prosecuting Mr. Gant on the cocaine charges. Without the cocaine evidence, unless Mr. Gant confesses, that charge had to be dropped. Searches require warrants or a valid exception to the privacy provided under the Fourth Amendment. Affirmed. [***Arizona v. Gant,* 556 U.S. 332 (2009)**]

---

[1] Police officers who record the arrest of a DUI suspect have not violated the suspect's privacy. *State v. Morris,* 214 P.3d 883 (Ut. App. 2009)

A second aspect of the right of privacy protects individuals against intrusions by others. Your private life is not subject to public scrutiny when you are a private citizen. This right is provided in many state constitutions and exists through interpretation at the federal level through the landmark case of *Roe v. Wade,*[2] in which the U.S. Supreme Court established a right of privacy that gives women the right to choose whether to have an abortion.

These two components of the right to privacy have many interpretations. These interpretations are often found in statutes that afford privacy rights with respect to certain types of conduct. **For Example,** a federal statute provides a right of privacy to bank customers that prevents their banks from giving out information about their accounts except to law enforcement agencies conducting investigations. Some laws protect the rights of students. **For Example,** the Family Educational Rights and Privacy Act of 1974 (FERPA, also known as the *Buckley Amendment*) prevents colleges and universities from disclosing students' grades to third parties without the students' permission. From your credit information to your Social Security number, you have great privacy protections.

4. Privacy and Technology

Technology creates new situations that may require the application of new rules of law. Technology has changed the way we interact with each other, and new rules of law have developed to protect our rights. Today, business is conducted by computers, wire transfers of funds, e-mail, electronic data interchange (EDI) order

Ethics & the Law

Twitter, Facebook, Google, and Your Job Application

A study by the social monitoring service, Reppler, found the following about employers:

- 91 percent of the employers polled use social networking sites (Twitter, Facebook, and LinkedIn) to screen prospective employees. Some employers even ask for applicants' passwords as a condition of employment.

- 69 percent say they have rejected a job applicant because of something they saw on one of these social platforms.

- 47 percent of employers do their checks of these social networking sites immediately after receiving their job applications.

- 76 percent of employers check Facebook.

- 53 percent check Twitter.

- 48 percent check LinkedIn.

- 68 percent of employers say that they have hired someone because they liked what they saw on these social networking sites.

One employer commented that these searches are so simple that it would be irresponsible to not do them. Experts tell college students to remember that what may seem to be fun can later come back to haunt you when you begin your professional career. Their advice is to watch what you post and what you write. Discuss privacy rights and whether there is any legal issue when information is posted voluntarily on the Internet. Is there an ethical issue with these types of searches?

Source: Shea Bennett, "91% of Employers Use Twitter, Facebook, and LinkedIn to Screen Job Applicants," **www.alltwitter.com**, October 24, 2011.

[2] 410 U.S. 113 (1973).

placements, and the Internet. We still expect that our communication is private. However, technology also affords others the ability to eavesdrop on conversations and intercept electronic messages. The law has stepped in to reestablish that the right of privacy still exists even in these technologically nonprivate circumstances. Some laws now make it a crime and a breach of privacy to engage in such interceptions of communications.[3] (See Chapter 11)

E-Commerce & Cyberlaw

A University's Access to Your Computer

Scott Kennedy, a computer system administrator for Qualcomm Corporation in San Diego, California, discovered that somebody had obtained unauthorized access (or "hacked into," in popular parlance) the company's computer network. Kennedy contacted the Federal Bureau of Investigation (FBI). Working together, Kennedy and the FBI were able to trace the intrusion to a computer on the University of Wisconsin at Madison network. They contacted Jeffrey Savoy, the University of Wisconsin computer network investigator, who found evidence that someone using a computer on the university network was in fact hacking into the Qualcomm system and that the user had gained unauthorized access to the university's system as well. Savoy traced the source of intrusion to a computer located in university housing, the room of Jerome Heckenkamp, a computer science graduate student at the university. Savoy knew that Heckenkamp had been terminated from his job at the university computer help desk two years earlier for similar unauthorized activity.

While Heckenkamp was online and logged into the university's system, Savoy, along with detectives, went to Heckenkamp's room. The door was ajar, and nobody was in the room. Savoy entered the room and disconnected the network cord that attached the computer to the network. In order to be sure that the computer he had disconnected from the network was the computer that had gained unauthorized access to the university server, Savoy wanted to run some commands on the computer. Detectives located Heckenkamp, explained the situation, and asked for Heckenkamp's password, which Heckenkamp voluntarily provided. Savoy then ran tests on the computer and copied the hard drive without a warrant. When Heckenkamp was charged with several federal computer crimes, he challenged the university's access to his account and Savoy's steps that night, including the copy of the hard drive, as a breach of his privacy. Was Heckenkamp correct? Was his privacy breached?

[*U.S. v. Heckenkamp*, 482 F.3d 1142 (9th Cir. 2007)]

B. Sources of Law

Several layers of law are enacted at different levels of government to provide the framework for business and personal rights and duties. At the base of this framework of laws is constitutional law.

5. Constitutional Law

constitution—a body of principles that establishes the structure of a government and the relationship of the government to the people who are governed.

Constitutional law is the branch of law that is based on the constitution for a particular level of government. A **constitution** is a body of principles that establishes the structure of a government and the relationship of that government to the people who are governed. A constitution is generally a combination of the written document and the practices and customs that develop with the passage of time and the

---

[3] *Luangkhot v. State*, 722 S.E.2d 193 (Ga. App. 2012).

emergence of new problems. In each state, two constitutions are in force: the state constitution and the federal Constitution.

6. Statutory Law

statutory law – legislative acts declaring, commanding, or prohibiting something.

Statutory law includes legislative acts. Both Congress and the state legislatures enact statutory law. Examples of congressional legislative enactments include the Securities Act of 1933 (Chapter 46), the Sherman Antitrust Act (Chapter 5), the bankruptcy laws (Chapter 35), and consumer credit protection provisions (Chapter 33). At the state level, statutes govern the creation of corporations, probate of wills, and the transfer of title to property. In addition to the state legislatures and the U.S. Congress, all cities, counties, and other governmental subdivisions have some power to adopt ordinances within their sphere of operation. Examples of the types of laws found at this level of government include traffic laws, zoning laws, and pet and bicycle licensing laws.

7. Administrative Law

administrative regulations – rules made by state and federal administrative agencies.

Administrative regulations are rules promulgated by state and federal administrative agencies, such as the Securities and Exchange Commission and the National Labor Relations Board. For example, most of your rights related to your wages, hours worked, and overtime pay have been promulgated by the Department of Labor. These regulations generally have the force of statutes.

8. Private Law

private law – the rules and regulations parties agree to as part of their contractual relationships.

Even individuals and businesses create their own laws, or **private law**. Private law consists of the rules and regulations parties agree to as part of their contractual relationships. **For Example,** landlords develop rules for tenants on everything from parking to laundry room use. Employers develop rules for employees on everything from proper computer use to posting pictures and information on bulletin boards located within the company walls. Homeowner associations have rules on everything from your landscaping to the color of your house paint.

9. Case Law, Statutory Interpretation, and Precedent

case law – law that includes principles that are expressed for the first time in court decisions.

Law also includes principles that are expressed for the first time in court decisions. This form of law is called **case law**. Case law plays three very important roles. The first is one of clarifying the meaning of statutes, or providing statutory interpretation. **For Example,** a man who was sentenced to house arrest left his house but still wanted to count the time as part of his sentence.[4] A court decision held that you must actually be in the house to have the time count. The second role that courts play is in creating precedent. When a court decides a new question or problem, its

precedent – a decision of a court that stands as the law for a particular problem in the future.

 decision becomes a **precedent**, which stands as the law in future cases that involve that particular problem.

[4] *Com. v. Stafford,* 29 A.3d 800 (Pa. Super. 2011).

✱ **stare decisis** – "let the decision stand"; the principle that the decision of a court should serve as a guide or precedent and control the decision of a similar case in the future.

Using precedent and following decisions is also known as the doctrine of **stare decisis**. However, the rule of *stare decisis* is not cast in stone. Judges have some flexibility. When a court finds an earlier decision to be incorrect, it overrules that decision. **For Example,** in 1954, the U.S. Supreme Court departed from the general rule of *stare decisis* in *Brown v. Board of Education.*[5] In that case, the Court decided that its 1896 decision *Plessy v. Ferguson,*[6] that held separate facilities for blacks were equal to facilities for whites, was incorrect.

The third role courts play is in developing a body of law that is not statutory but addresses long standing issues. Court decisions do not always deal with new problems or make new rules. In many cases, courts apply rules as they have been for many years, even centuries. These time-honored rules of the community are called the **common law**. **For Example,** most of law that we still follow today in determining real property rights developed in England, beginning in 1066. Statutes sometimes repeal or redeclare the common law rules. Many statutes depend on the common law for definitions of the terms in the statutes.

common law – the body of unwritten principles originally based upon the usages and customs of the community that were recognized and enforced by the courts.

10. Other Forms of Law: Treaties and Executive Orders

Law also includes treaties made by the United States and proclamations and executive orders of the president of the United States or of other public officials.

11. Uniform State Laws

To facilitate the national nature of business and transactions, the National Conference of Commissioners on Uniform State Laws (NCCUSL), composed of representatives from every state, has drafted statutes on various subjects for adoption by the states. The best example of such laws is the Uniform Commercial Code (UCC).[7] (See Chapters 23–31, Chapter 34.) The UCC regulates the sale and lease of goods; commercial paper, such as checks; fund transfers; secured transactions in personal property; banking; and letters of credit. Having the same principles of law on contracts for the sale of goods and other commercial transactions in most of the 50 states makes doing business easier and less expensive. Other examples of uniform laws across the states include the Model Business Corporations Act (Chapter 44), the Uniform Partnership Act (Chapter 42), and the Uniform Residential Landlord Tenant Act (Chapter 51). The Uniform Computer Information Transactions Act (UCITA) as well as the Uniform Electronic Transactions Act (UETA) are two uniform laws that have taken contract law from the traditional paper era to the paperless computer age.

[5] 349 U.S. 294 (1954).
[6] 163 U.S. 537 (1895).
[7] The UCC has been adopted in every state, except that Louisiana has not adopted Article 2, Sales. Guam, the Virgin Islands, and the District of Columbia have also adopted the UCC. The NCCUSL has adopted amendments to Article 8, Investment Securities (1977 and 1994), and Article 9, Secured Transactions (1999, and as amended 2001). There have been new articles of the UCC: Article 2A, Leases, and Article 4A, Funds Transfers. The United Nations Convention on Contracts for the International Sale of Goods (CISG) has been adopted as the means for achieving uniformity in sale-of-goods contracts on an international level. Provisions of CISG were strongly influenced by Article 2 of the UCC.

C. CLASSIFICATIONS OF LAW

✳ 12. Substantive Law vs. Procedural Law

substantive law – the law that defines rights and liabilities.

procedural law – the law that must be followed in enforcing rights and liabilities.

Substantive law creates, defines, and regulates rights and liabilities. The law that determines when a contract is formed is substantive law. **Procedural law** specifies the steps that must be followed in enforcing those rights and liabilities. For example, once that contract is formed, you have rights to enforce that contract, and the steps you take through the court system to recover your damages for a breach of contract are procedural laws. The laws that prohibit computer theft are substantive laws. The prosecution of someone for computer theft follows procedural law.

13. Criminal Law vs. Civil Law

Criminal laws define wrongs against society. **Civil laws** define the rights of one person against another. Criminal law violations carry fines and imprisonment as penalties. Civil laws carry damage remedies for the wronged individual.

Sports & Entertainment Law

MLB and Steroids

On March 17, 2005, former and current major league baseball (MLB) players, Commissioner Bud Selig, and the parents of young baseball players who had taken their own lives after taking steroids testified before the U.S. House of Representatives Government Reform Committee. The House held the hearings to determine whether government regulation of baseball is necessary.

Committee Chair Tom Davis made an opening statement with the following excerpts:

> *Fourteen years ago, anabolic steroids were added to the Controlled Substance Act as a Schedule III drug, making it illegal to possess or sell them without a valid prescription. Today, however, evidence strongly suggests that steroid use among teenagers—especially aspiring athletes—is a large and growing problem.*
>
> *Today we take the committee's first steps toward understanding how we got here, and how we begin turning those numbers around. Down the road, we need to look at whether and how Congress should exercise its legislative powers to further restrict the use and distribution of these substances.*
>
> *Our specific purpose today is to consider MLB's recently negotiated drug policy; how the testing*

> *policy will be implemented; how it will effectively address the use of prohibited drugs by players; and, most importantly, the larger societal and public health ramifications of steroid use.*

Mark McGwire, now a retired MLB player and a record holder, stated during the hearings:

> *Asking me, or any other player, to answer questions about who took steroids in front of television cameras will not solve this problem. If a player answers 'no,' he simply will not be believed. If he answers 'yes,' he risks public scorn and endless government investigations. My lawyers have advised me that I cannot answer these questions without jeopardizing my friends, my family, or myself. I intend to follow their advice.**

Give a list of all the laws, rights, and duties you can find in this information.

*http://reform.house.gov/GovReform/Hearings/EventSingle.aspx? EventID=1637. Click on Mark McGwire

For Example, if you run a red light, you have committed a crime and you will be punished with a fine and points on your license. If you run a red light and strike a pedestrian, you will also have committed a civil wrong of injury to another through your carelessness. Civil laws provide that in addition to taking care of your wrong to society, you must take care of your wrong to the pedestrian and pay damages for the cost of her injuries (see Chapter 8 for more information about recovery of damages for accidents such as this).

14. Law vs. Equity

equity – the body of principles that originally developed because of the inadequacy of the rules then applied by the common law courts of England.

Equity is a body of law that provides justice when the law does not offer an adequate remedy or the application of the law would be terribly unfair. Equity courts developed in England as a means of getting to the heart of a dispute and seeing that justice was done. **For Example,** Christian Louboutin shoes have a distinctive red bottom that is their trademark. Yves Saint Laurent began producing its shoes with a red bottom. Common and statutory law provide for Louboutin to collect damages— the amount the company lost in sales through the copycat efforts of Yves Saint Laurent. However, if the Yves Saint Laurent shoes continue in production, Louboutin is never adequately compensated. Equity provides for an injunction, a court order to stop Yves Saint Laurent from making the red-soled shoes.[8] At one time, the United States had separate law courts and equity courts, but, today, these courts have been combined so that one court applies principles of both law and equity. A party may ask for both legal and equitable remedies in a single court.[9]

For Example, suppose a homeowner contracts to sell his home to a buyer. If the homeowner then refuses to go through with the contract, the buyer has the legal remedy of recovering damages. The rules of equity go further and could require the owner to convey title to the house, an equitable remedy known as *specific performance.* Equitable remedies may also be available in certain contract breaches (see Chapters 2, 12, and 20).

LawFlix

And Justice for All (1979) (R)

An excellent film that gives an overview of the judicial system in Maryland. Rights, precedent, and the role of lawyers are all topics for satire and analysis in the movie.

---

[8] *Christian Louboutin S.A. v. Yves Saint Laurent America, Inc.,* 778 F. Supp. 2d 445 (S.D.N.Y. 2011).
[9] For example, Jennifer Lopez and Marc Anthony filed suit against the manufacturer of a British company that produces baby carriages for using their images on its Web site and in ads without permission; they asked for $5 million in damages as well as an injunction to stop use of their photos and likenesses in the company's ads. *Lopez v. Silver Cross,* 2009 WL 481386 (CD Cal). The case was settled prior to the dissolution of the Lopez and Anthony marriage. The terms of the settlement are not known, but Silver Cross no longer uses the images of Lopez and Anthony in its ads.

MAKE THE CONNECTION

SUMMARY

Law provides rights and imposes duties. One such right is the right of privacy, which affords protection against unreasonable searches of our property and intrusion into or disclosure of our private affairs.

Law consists of the pattern of rules established by society to govern conduct and relationships. These rules can be expressed as constitutional provisions, statutes, administrative regulations, and case decisions. Law can be classified as substantive or procedural, and it can be described in terms of civil or criminal law. Law provides remedies in equity in addition to damages.

The sources of law include constitutions, federal and state statutes, administrative regulations, ordinances, and uniform laws generally codified by the states in their statutes. The courts are also a source of law through their adherence to case precedent under the doctrine of *stare decisis* and through their development of time-honored principles called the common law.

LEARNING OUTCOMES

After studying this chapter, you should be able to clearly explain:

A. Nature of Law and Legal Rights

L0.1 Discuss the nature of law and legal rights
See *Arizona v. Gant*, p. 5.
See Ethics & the Law on p. 6 for a discussion of employers checking Twitter, Facebook, and LinkedIn for information about potential employees.
See E-Commerce & Cyberlaw, p. 7.

B. Sources of Law

L0.2 List the sources of law
See the *For Example* discussion of landlords developing rules for tenants on everything from parking to laundry room use on p. 8.

See the list and explanation of uniform laws on p. 9.
See the Sports & Entertainment Law discussion of steroids in baseball on p. 10.

C. Classifications of Law

L0.3 Describe the classifications of law
See the discussion of law, equity, procedural, substantive, criminal, and civil on pp. 10–11.
See the Christian Louboutin example on its red-bottomed shoe being copied and footnote 9 with the discussion of the Jennifer Lopez/Marc Anthony suit on p. 11.
Explain uniform state laws.

KEY TERMS

administrative
  regulations
case law
civil law
common law
constitution

criminal law
duty
equity
law
precedent
private law

procedural law
right of privacy
right
stare decisis
statutory law
substantive law

QUESTIONS AND CASE PROBLEMS

1. On January 9, 2007, two Springfield, Missouri, Police Department officers made a traffic stop of a vehicle driven by Claude X. The purpose of the stop was to arrest X's passenger, Melissa Owen, who had a pending warrant for check-kiting. Once the officers made visual contact with Owen, the officers stopped X's car and instructed Owen to get out of the car. Ms. Owen did not bring her belongings with her when she got out of the car. One of the officers called dispatch to verify Owen's warrant and requested backup from a K–9 officer. Another officer arrived at the scene with his service dog, Marko. X was told to get out of the car so that it could be searched. X did get out of the car but then also locked it and refused to allow the officers to search. X was handcuffed for obstruction and the officers took away his keys to the car.

   At that time, Marko searched (sniffed) the exterior of X's car. Marko alerted to the car's rear bumper. The officers began to search the trunk of the vehicle and found containers with drugs in them along with a weighing scale. X's lawyer moved to have the evidence excluded because the drugs were found without a warrant. Should the judge exclude the evidence or is it admissible? Be sure to refer to the *Arizona v. Gant* case on p. 5 in developing your answer and explaining why. [*U.S. v. Claude X*, 648 F.3d 599 (8th Cir.)]

2. The Family Educational Rights and Privacy Act (FERPA) protects students' rights to keep their academic records private. What duties are imposed and upon whom because of this protection of rights? Discuss the relationship between rights and duties.

3. List the sources of law.

4. What is the difference between common law and statutory law?

5. Classify the following laws as substantive or procedural:

   a. A law that requires public schools to hold a hearing before a student is expelled.

   b. A law that establishes a maximum interest rate for credit transactions of 24 percent.

   c. A law that provides employee leave for the birth or adoption of a child for up to 12 weeks.

   d. A law that requires the county assessor to send four notices of taxes due and owing before a lien can be filed (attached) to the property.

6. What do uniform laws accomplish? Why do states adopt them? Give an example of a uniform law.

7. Cindy Nathan is a student at West University. While she was at her 9:00 A.M. anthropology class, campus security entered her dorm room and searched all areas, including her closet and drawers. When Cindy returned to her room and discovered what had happened, she complained to the dorm's senior resident. The senior resident said that this was the university's property and that Cindy had no right of privacy. Do you agree with the senior resident's statement? Is there a right of privacy in a dorm room?

8. Professor Lucas Phelps sent the following e-mail to Professor Marlin Jones: "I recently read the opinion piece you wrote for the *Sacramento Bee* on affirmative action. Your opinion is incorrect, your reasoning and analysis are poor, and I am embarrassed that you are a member of the faculty here at Cal State Yolinda." Professor Jones forwarded the note from Professor Phelps to the provost of the university and asked that Professor Phelps be disciplined for using the university e-mail system for harassment purposes. Professor Phelps objected when the provost contacted him: "He had no right to forward that e-mail to you. That was private correspondence. And you have no right of access to my e-mail. I have privacy rights." Do you agree with Professor Phelps? Was there a breach of privacy?

9. Under what circumstances would a court disregard precedent?

10. What is the difference between a statute and an administrative regulation?

11. The Eminem ad for Chrysler that ran during the Super Bowl in February 2011 was rated as one of the best ads for the game. In May 2011, Audi ran an ad at a German auto show that had the "feel" of the Eminem Chrysler "Lose Yourself" ad.

Subsequently, the German auto show ad made its way onto the Internet.

The German ad caught the attention of Eminem and 8 Mile, Eminem's publishing company. They notified Audi that the ad constituted an unauthorized use of their intellectual property. Explain what rights Eminem and 8 Mile have and how the courts can help.

12. Give examples of areas covered by federal laws. Give examples of areas covered by city ordinances. What are the limitations on these two sources of laws? What could the laws at these two levels not do?

13. What is the principle of *stare decisis?*

14. Explain how Twitter, Facebook, and LinkedIn have resulted in the development of new laws and precedent.

15. During the 2001 baseball season, San Francisco Giants player Barry Bonds hit 73 home runs, a new record that broke the one set by Mark McGwire in 2000 (72 home runs). When Mr. Bonds hit his record-breaking home run, the ball went into the so-called cheap seats. Alex Popov was sitting in those seats and had brought along his baseball glove for purposes of catching any hits that might come into the stands.

Everyone sitting in the area agreed that Mr. Popov's glove touched Bonds's home-run ball. Videotape also shows Mr. Popov's glove on the ball. However, the ball dropped and, following a melee among the cheap-seat fans, Patrick Hayashi ended up with Bonds's home-run ball.

Mr. Popov filed suit for the ball, claiming it as his property. Such baseballs can be very valuable. The baseball from Mr. McGwire's record-breaking home run in 2000 sold for $3 million. List those areas of law that will apply as the case is tried and the owner of the baseball is determined.

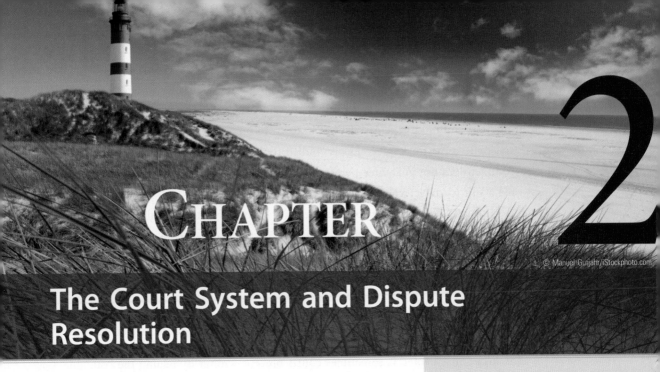

© Manuel Gutjahr/iStockphoto.com

CHAPTER 2

The Court System and Dispute Resolution

learningoutcomes

After studying this chapter, you should be able to

LO.1 Explain the federal and state court systems

LO.2 Describe court procedures

LO.3 List the forms of alternative dispute resolution and distinguish among them

D
espite carefully negotiated and well-written contracts and high safety standards in the workplace or in product design and production, businesses can end up in a lawsuit. **For Example,** you could hire the brightest and most expensive lawyer in town to prepare a contract with another party and believe the final agreement is "bulletproof." However, even a bulletproof contract does not guarantee performance by the other party, and you may have to file a suit to collect your damages.

Business disputes can be resolved in court or through alternative dispute resolution. This chapter covers the structure of the court system and the litigation process as well as the forms of alternative dispute resolution.

A. THE COURT SYSTEM

court – a tribunal established by government to hear and decide matters properly brought to it.

A **court** is a tribunal established by government to hear evidence, decide cases brought before it, and, provide remedies when a wrong has been committed. As discussed in Chapter 1, sometimes courts prevent wrongs by issuing the equitable remedy of an injunction. **For Example,** in March 2012, a federal court issued an injunction against Cardinal Health because it was shipping too much oxycodone to pharmacies in Florida, and the FDA had discovered that the prescriptions were fraudulent. The FDA needed to stop the flow of the drug while it pulled the prescriptions.[1]

1. The Types of Courts

jurisdiction – the power of a court to hear and determine a given class of cases; the power to act over a particular defendant.

Each type of court has the authority to decide certain types or classes of cases. The authority of courts to hear cases is called **jurisdiction**. One form of jurisdiction, **subject matter jurisdiction**, covers the type of cases the court has the authority to hear. Courts that have the authority to hear the original proceedings in a case (the trial court) are called courts of **original jurisdiction**. **For Example,** in a court of original jurisdiction witnesses testify, documents are admitted into evidence, and the jury, in the case of a jury trial, hears all the evidence and then makes a decision.

subject matter jurisdiction – judicial authority to hear a particular type of case.

Other types of subject matter jurisdiction give courts the authority over particular legal topic areas. A court with **general jurisdiction** has broad authority to hear general civil and criminal cases. When a general jurisdiction trial court hears criminal cases, it serves as the trial court for those charged with crimes. General trial courts also have the authority to hear civil disputes, such as breach of contract cases and personal injury lawsuits.

original jurisdiction – the authority to hear a controversy when it is first brought to court.

general jurisdiction – the power to hear and decide most controversies involving legal rights and duties.

A court with **limited or special jurisdiction** has the authority to hear only particular kinds of cases. **For Example,** many states have courts that can hear only disputes in which the damages are $10,000 or less. Other examples of limited or special jurisdiction courts are juvenile courts, probate courts, and domestic relations courts. States vary in the names they give these courts, but these courts of special or limited jurisdiction have very narrow authority for the types of cases they hear. In the federal court system, limited or special jurisdiction courts include bankruptcy courts and the U.S. Tax Court.

limited (special) jurisdiction – the authority to hear only particular kinds of cases.

[1] *Holiday CVS, L.L.C. v. Holder,* 839 F. Supp. 2d 145 (D.D.C. 2012).

appellate jurisdiction – the power of a court to hear and decide a given class of cases on appeal from another court or administrative agency.

appeal – taking a case to a reviewing court to determine whether the judgment of the lower court or administrative agency was correct. (Parties– appellant, appellee)

reversible error – an error or defect in court proceedings of so serious a nature that on appeal the appellate court will set aside the proceedings of the lower court.

affirm – action taken by an appellate court that approves the decision of the court below.

reverse – the term used when the appellate court sets aside the verdict or judgment of a lower court.

remand – term used when an appellate court sends a case back to trial court for additional hearings or a new trial.

A court with **appellate jurisdiction** reviews the work of a lower court. **For Example,** a trial court may issue a judgment that a defendant in a breach of contract suit should pay $500,000 in damages. That defendant could appeal the decision to an appellate court and seek review of the decision itself or even the amount of the damages.[2] An **appeal** is a review of the trial and decision of the lower court. An appellate court does not hear witnesses or take testimony. An appellate court, usually a panel of three judges, simply reviews the transcript and evidence from the lower court and determines whether there has been **reversible error**. A reversible error is a mistake in applying the law or a mistake in admitting evidence that affected the outcome of the case. An appellate court can **affirm** or **reverse** a lower court decision or **remand** that decision for another trial or additional hearings.

CASE SUMMARY

Law and Order on TV and in the Court

FACTS: Andrea Yates was charged with capital murder in the drowning deaths of her five young children. Mrs. Yates had been in and out of treatment facilities, had been taking antidepressants, and was under the care of several experts for her depression. She was also experiencing postpartum depression when she drowned each of her five children in the bathtub at their family home. She then called her husband to ask him to come home and also called 9-1-1.

She entered a "not guilty by reason of insanity" plea, and 10 psychiatrists and two psychologists testified at the trial about Mrs. Yates's mental condition before, during, and after the deaths of the children.

Dr. Parke Dietz, the psychiatrist for the prosecution, testified that he believed Mrs. Yates knew right from wrong and that she was not insane at the time of the drownings. Dr. Dietz had also served as a consultant for the television series *Law and Order* and testified as follows about one of the shows in the series:

> As a matter of fact, there was a show of a woman with postpartum depression who drowned her children in the bathtub and was found insane and it was aired shortly before the crime occurred.

The prosecution used this information about the television show to cross-examine witnesses for Mrs. Yates and also raised its airing in its closing argument to the jury.

The jury found Mrs. Yates guilty. The defense lawyers later discovered that Dr. Dietz was mistaken and that there had been no such *Law and Order* show on postpartum depression. They appealed on the grounds that the evidence was material, prejudiced the jury, and required a new trial.

DECISION: The court held that because Dr. Dietz had testified about the show, that his testimony and the subject matter of the show were a part of the prosecution's examination of defense witnesses, that the prosecution raised the airing of the show in closing arguments, and that the defense had to respond by talking about it meant that the testimony was material. Inasmuch as it was false, there was a reversible error and a retrial was required without the untrue and highly prejudicial evidence. [***Yates v. State,*** 171 S.W.3d 215 (Tex. App. 2005)][3]

---

[2] A case that is sent back for a redetermination of damages is remanded for what is known as *remittur* For example, an appeal of Oracle's $1.3 billion verdict against SAP was sent back for another determination of damages, with the judge indicating $272 million was in the right range. *Oracle USA, Inc. v. SAP AG,* 2012 WL 29095 (N.D. Cal.).

[3] Mrs. Yates was found to be criminally insane in her 2006 retrial and is now institutionalized.

| FIGURE 2-1 | *The Federal Court System* |

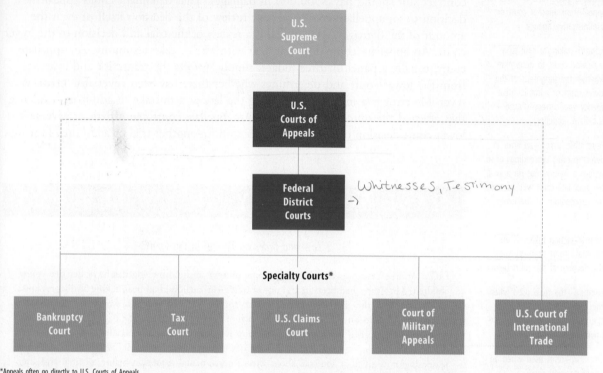

Whitnesses, Testimony →

*Appeals often go directly to U.S. Courts of Appeals.

© Cengage Learning

2. The Federal Court System

The federal court system consists of three levels of courts. Figure 2-1 illustrates federal court structure.

federal district court – a general trial court of the federal system.

(A) FEDERAL DISTRICT COURTS. The **federal district courts** are the general trial courts of the federal system. They are courts of original jurisdiction that hear both civil and criminal matters. Criminal cases in federal district courts are those in which the defendant is charged with a violation of federal law (the U.S. Code). In addition to the criminal cases, the types of civil cases that can be brought in federal district courts include (1) civil suits in which the United States is a party, (2) cases between citizens of different states that involve damages of $75,000 or more, and (3) cases that arise under the U.S. Constitution or federal laws and treaties.

Federal district courts are organized within each of the states. There are 94 federal districts (each state has at least one federal district and there are 89 federal districts in the United States with the remaining courts found in Puerto Rico, Guam, etc.). Judges and courtrooms are assigned according to the caseload in that geographic area of the state.[4] Some states, such as New York and California, have several federal districts because of the population base and the resulting caseload. Figure 2-2 shows the geographic structure of the federal court system, including the appellate circuits.

The federal system has additional trial courts with limited jurisdiction, differing from the general jurisdiction of the federal district courts. These courts include, for

FIGURE 2-2	*The Thirteen Federal Judicial Circuits*

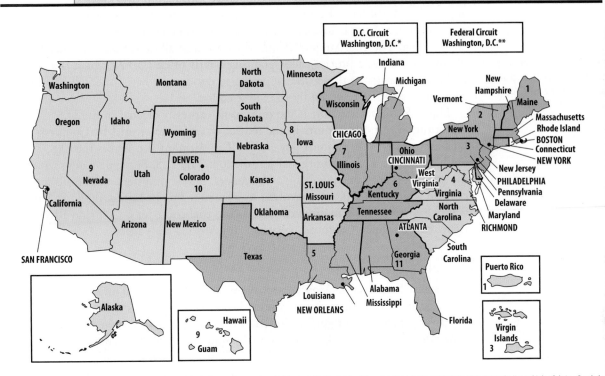

*A sizable portion of the caseload of the D.C. Circuit comes from the federal administrative agencies and offices located in Washington, D.C., such as the Securities and Exchange Commission, the National Labor Relations Board, the Federal Trade Commission, the Secretary of the Treasury, and the Labor Department, as well as appeals from the U.S. District Court of the District of Columbia.

**Rather than being defined by geography like the regional courts of appeals, the Federal Circuit is defined by subject matter, having jurisdiction over such matters as patent infringement cases, appeals from the Court of Federal Claims and the Court of International Trade, and appeals from administrative rulings regarding subject matter such as unfair import practices and tariff schedule disputes.

© Cengage Learning

example, the federal bankruptcy courts, Indian tribal courts, Tax Court, Court of Federal Claims, Court of Veterans Appeals, and the Court of International Trade.

(B) U.S. COURTS OF APPEALS. The final decision in a federal district court can be appealed to a court with appellate jurisdiction. In the federal court system, the federal districts are grouped together geographically into 12 judicial circuits, including one for the District of Columbia. Additionally, a thirteenth federal circuit, called the *Federal Circuit,* hears certain types of appeals from all of the circuits, including specialty cases such as patent appeals. Each circuit has an appellate court called the U.S. Court of Appeals, and the judges for these courts review the decisions of the federal district courts. Generally, a panel of three judges reviews the cases. However, some decisions, called **en banc** decisions, are made by the circuit's full panel of judges. **For Example,** in 2003, the Ninth Circuit heard an appeal on a father's right to challenge the requirement that his daughter recite the Pledge of Allegiance in the public school she attended. The contentious case had so many issues that the Ninth Circuit issued three opinions and the third opinion was issued after the case was heard *en banc.*[5]

en banc—the term used when the full panel of judges on the appellate court hears a case.

3 Judges

---

[5] *Newdow v. U.S. Congress,* 292 F.3d 597 (9th Cir. 2002) (*Newdow I*); *Newdow v. U.S. Congress,* 313 F.3d 500, 502 (9th Cir. 2002) (*Newdow II*); and *Newdow v. U.S. Congress,* 328 F.3d 466, 468 (9th Cir. 2003) (*Newdow III*). The U.S. Supreme Court eventually heard the case. *Elkgrove Unified School District v. Newdow,* 542 U.S. 1 (2004). Another *en banc* hearing occurred at the Ninth Circuit over the issues in the California gubernatorial recall election. The three-judge panel held that the voting methods in California violated the rights of voters and therefore placed a stay on the election. However, the Ninth Circuit then heard the case

(c) **U.S. SUPREME COURT.** The final court in the federal system is the U.S. Supreme Court. The U.S. Supreme Court has appellate jurisdiction over cases that are appealed from the federal courts of appeals as well as from state supreme courts when a constitutional issue is involved in the case or a state court has reversed a federal court ruling. The U.S. Supreme Court does not hear all cases from the federal courts of appeals but has a process called granting a **writ of *certiorari***, which is a preliminary review of those cases appealed to decide whether a case will be heard or allowed to stand as ruled on by the lower courts.[6]

writ of *certiorari* – order by the U.S. Supreme Court granting a right of review by the court of a lower court decision.

The U.S. Supreme Court is the only court expressly created in the U.S. Constitution. All other courts in the federal system were created by Congress pursuant to its Constitutional power. The Constitution also makes the U.S. Supreme Court a court of original jurisdiction. The U.S. Supreme Court serves as the trial court for cases involving ambassadors, public ministers, or consuls and for cases in which two states are involved in a lawsuit. **For Example,** the U.S. Supreme Court has served for a number of years as the trial court for a Colorado River water rights case in which California, Nevada, and Arizona are parties.

3. State Court Systems

(A) **GENERAL TRIAL COURTS.** Most states have trial courts of general jurisdiction that may be called superior courts, circuit courts, district courts, or county courts. These courts of general and original jurisdiction usually hear both criminal and civil cases. Cases that do not meet the jurisdictional requirements for the federal district courts would be tried in these courts. Figure 2-3 illustrates a sample state court system.

(B) **SPECIALTY COURTS.** Most states also have courts with limited jurisdiction, sometimes referred to as *specialty courts.* **For Example,** most states have juvenile courts, or courts with limited jurisdiction over criminal matters that involve defendants who are under the age of 18. Other specialty courts or lesser courts in state systems are probate and family law courts.

(C) **CITY, MUNICIPAL, AND JUSTICE COURTS.** Cities and counties may also have lesser courts with limited jurisdiction, which may be referred to as *municipal courts* or *justice courts*. These courts generally handle civil matters in which the claim made in the suit is an amount below a certain level, such as $5,000 or $10,000. These courts may also handle misdemeanor types of offenses, such as traffic violations or violations of noise ordinances, and the trials for them.

(D) **SMALL CLAIMS COURTS.** Most states also have **small claims courts** at the county or city level. These are courts of limited jurisdiction where parties with small amounts in dispute may come to have a third party, such as a justice of the peace or city judge, review their disputes and determine how they should be resolved. A true small claims court is one in which the parties are not permitted to be represented by counsel. Rather, the parties present their cases to the judge in an informal manner without the strict procedural rules that apply in courts of general jurisdiction. Small claims courts provide a faster and inexpensive means for resolving a dispute that does not involve a large amount of claimed damages.

small claims courts – courts that resolve disputes between parties when those disputes do not exceed a minimal level; no lawyers are permitted; the parties represent themselves.

---

[6] For example, the Supreme Court refused to grant *certiorari* in a Fifth Circuit case on law school admissions at the University of Texas. However, it granted *certiorari* in a later case involving law school admissions at the University of Michigan. *Gratz v. Bollinger,* 539 U.S. 244 (2003). And the court will hear the issue again, in *Fisher v. University of Texas,* 132 S.Ct. 1536 (2012).

FIGURE 2-3	*Sample State Court System*

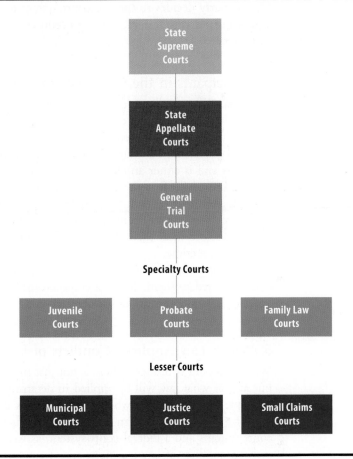

© Cengage Learning

(E) STATE APPELLATE COURTS. Most states also have intermediate-level courts similar to the federal courts of appeals. They are courts with appellate jurisdiction that review the decisions of lower courts in that state. Decisions of the general trial courts in a state would be appealed to these courts.

(F) STATE SUPREME COURTS. The highest court in most states is generally known as the *state supreme court,* but a few states, such as New York, may call their highest court the *court of appeals;* Maine and Massachusetts, for example, call their highest court the *supreme judicial court.* State supreme courts primarily have appellate jurisdiction, but some states' courts do have original jurisdiction, such as in Arizona, where counties in litigation have their trial at the supreme court level. Most state supreme courts also have a screening process for cases. They are required to hear some cases, such as criminal cases in which the defendant has received the death penalty. A decision of a state supreme court is final except in those circumstances in which a federal law or treaty or the U.S. Constitution is involved. Cases with these federal subject matter issues can then be appealed to the U.S. Supreme Court.

✳ B. Court Procedure

Once a party decides to use the court system for resolution of a dispute, that party enters a world with specific rules, procedures, and terms that must be used to have a case proceed.

4. Participants in the Court System

plaintiff – party who initiates a lawsuit.

prosecutor – party who originates a criminal proceeding.

defendant – party charged with a violation of civil or criminal law in a proceeding.

judge – primary officer of the court.

attorney-client privilege – right of individual to have discussions with his/her attorney kept private and confidential.

jury – a body of citizens sworn by a court to determine by verdict the issues of fact submitted to them.

The **plaintiff** is the party that initiates the proceedings in a court of original jurisdiction. In a criminal case in which charges are brought, the party initiating the proceedings would be called the **prosecutor**. The party against whom the civil or criminal proceedings are brought is the **defendant**. A **judge** is the primary officer of the court and is either an elected or an appointed official who presides over the matters brought before the court. Attorneys or lawyers are representatives for the plaintiff and the defendant for purposes of presenting their cases. Lawyers and clients have a privilege of confidentiality known as the **attorney-client privilege**. Lawyers cannot disclose what their clients tell them unless the client is committing, or plans to commit, a crime.

A **jury** is a body of citizens sworn by a court to reach a verdict on the basis of the case presented to them. Jurors are chosen for service based on lists compiled from voter registration and driver's license records.

5. Which Law Applies—Conflicts of Law

When a lawsuit is brought, there is not just the question of where a case will be tried but also of what law will be applied in determining the rights of the parties. The principle that determines when a court applies the law of its own state—the law of the forum—or some foreign law is called *conflict of laws*. Because there are 50 state court systems and a federal court system, as well as a high degree of interstate activity, conflicts of law questions arise frequently.

Some general rules apply. For example, the law of the state in which the court is located governs the case on procedural issues and rules of evidence. In contract litigation, the court applies the law of the state in which the contract was made for determining issues of formation. Performance disputes and damages for nonperformance are generally governed by the law of the state where the contract is to be performed. International contracts follow similar rules. **For Example,** a California court will apply Swiss law to a contract made in Switzerland that is to be performed in that country.

However, it is becoming more common for the parties to specify their choice of law in their contract. In the absence of a law-selecting provision in the contract, there is a growing acceptance of the rule that a contract should be governed by the law of the state that has the most significant contacts with the transaction.

For Example, assume the buyer's place of business and the seller's plant are located in Nebraska, and the buyer is purchasing goods from the seller to resell to Nebraska customers. Many courts will hold that this is a contract governed by the law of Nebraska. In determining which state has the most significant contacts, the court considers the place of contracting, negotiating, and performing; the location of the subject matter of the contract; and the domicile (residence), states of incorporation, and principal place of business of the parties.

6. Initial Steps in a Lawsuit

The following steps in a lawsuit generally apply in cases brought in courts of original jurisdiction. Not every step applies in every case, but understanding litigation steps and terms is important for businesspeople.

complaint – the initial pleading filed by the plaintiff in many actions, which in many states may be served as original process to acquire jurisdiction over the defendant.

(A) COMMENCEMENT OF A LAWSUIT. A lawsuit begins with the filing of a **complaint**. The complaint generally contains a description of the wrongful conduct and a request for damages, such as a monetary amount. **For Example,** a plaintiff in a contract suit would describe the contract, when it was entered into, and when the defendant stopped performance on the contract. A copy of the contract would be attached to the complaint.

process – paperwork served personally on a defendant in a civil case.

(B) SERVICE OF PROCESS. Once the plaintiff has filed the complaint with the proper court, the plaintiff has the responsibility of notifying the defendant that the lawsuit has been filed. The defendant must be served with **process**. Process, often called a *writ, notice,* or *summons,* is delivered to the defendant and includes a copy of the complaint and notification that the defendant must appear and respond to the allegations in the complaint.

answer – what a defendant must file to admit or deny facts asserted by the plaintiff.

motion to dismiss – a pleading that may be filed to attack the adverse party's pleading as not stating a cause of action or a defense.

demurrer – a pleading to dismiss the adverse party's pleading for not stating a cause of action or a defense.

counterclaim – a claim that the defendant in an action may make against the plaintiff.

(C) THE DEFENDANT'S RESPONSE AND THE PLEADINGS. After the defendant is served with process in the case, the defendant is required to respond to or **answer** the complaint within the time provided under the court's rules. In answering the plaintiff's complaint, the defendant has several options. For example, the defendant could make a **motion to dismiss**, which is a request to the court to dismiss the lawsuit on the grounds that, even if everything the plaintiff said in the complaint were true, there is still no right of recovery. A motion to dismiss is also called a **demurrer**.

A defendant could also respond and deny the allegations. **For Example,** in a contract lawsuit, the defendant-seller could say he did not breach the contract but stopped shipment of the goods because the plaintiff-buyer did not pay for the goods in advance as the contract required. A defendant could also **counterclaim** in the answer, which is asking the court for damages as a result of the underlying dispute. **For Example,** the defendant-seller in the contract lawsuit might ask for damages for the plaintiff-buyer's failure to pay as the contract required.

pleadings – the papers filed by the parties in an action in order to set forth the facts and frame the issues to be tried, although, under some systems, the pleadings merely give notice or a general indication of the nature of the issues.

All documents filed in this initial phase of the case are referred to as the **pleadings**. The pleadings are a statement of the case and the basis for recovery if all the facts alleged can be proved.

discovery – procedures for ascertaining facts prior to the time of trial in order to eliminate the element of surprise in litigation.

(D) DISCOVERY. The Federal Rules of Civil Procedure and similar rules in all states permit one party to obtain from the adverse party information about all witnesses, documents, and any other items relevant to the case. **Discovery** requires each side to name its potential witnesses and to provide each side the chance to question those witnesses in advance of the trial. Each party also has the opportunity to examine, inspect, and photograph books, records, buildings, and machines. Even examining the physical or mental condition of a party is part of discovery when it has relevance in the case. The scope of discovery is extremely broad because the rules permit any questions that are likely to lead to admissible evidence.

deposition – the testimony of a witness taken out of court before a person authorized to administer oaths.

Deposition.

A **deposition** is the testimony of a witness taken under oath outside the courtroom; it is transcribed by a court reporter. Each party is permitted to question the witness. If a party or a witness gives testimony at the trial that is inconsistent with her

impeach—using prior inconsistent evidence to challenge the credibility of a witness.

deposition testimony, the prior inconsistent testimony can be used to **impeach** the witness's credibility at trial

Depositions can be taken either for discovery purposes or to preserve the testimony of a witness who will not be available during the trial. Some states now permit depositions to be videotaped. A videotape is a more effective way of presenting deposition testimony than reading that testimony at trial from a reporter's transcript because jurors can see the witness and the witness's demeanor and hear the words as they were spoken, complete with inflection.[7]

Other Forms of Discovery.

interrogatories—written questions used as a discovery tool that must be answered under oath.

request for production of documents—discovery tool for uncovering paper evidence in a case.

Other forms of discovery include medical exams, particularly in cases in which the plaintiff is claiming damages for physical injuries. Written **interrogatories** (questions) and written **requests for production of documents** are discovery requests that can be very time consuming to the answering party and often lead to pretrial legal disputes between the parties and their attorneys as a result of the legal expenses involved.

motion for summary judgment—request that the court decide a case on basis of law only because there are no material issues disputed by the parties.

(E) MOTION FOR SUMMARY JUDGMENT. If a case has no material facts in dispute, either party can file a **motion for summary judgment**. Using affidavits or deposition testimony obtained in discovery, the court can find that there are no factual issues and decide the case as a matter of law. **For Example,** suppose that the parties can agree that they entered into a life insurance contract but dispute whether the policy applies when there is a suicide. The facts are not in dispute; the law on payment of insurance proceeds in the event of a suicide is the issue. Such a case is one that is appropriate for summary judgment.

expert witness—one who has acquired special knowledge in a particular field as through practical experience or study, or both, whose opinion is admissible as an aid to the trier of fact.

(F) DESIGNATION OF EXPERT WITNESSES. In some cases, such as those involving product safety, the parties may want to designate an expert witness. An **expert witness** is a witness who has some special expertise, such as an economist who gives expert opinion on the value of future lost income or a scientist who testifies about the safety of a prescription drug. There are rules for naming expert witnesses as well as for admitting into evidence any studies or documents of the expert.[8] The purpose of these rules is to avoid the problem of what has been called *junk science,* or the admission of experts' testimony and research that has not been properly conducted or reviewed by peers.

7. The Trial

(A) SELECTING A JURY. Jurors drawn for service are questioned by the judge and lawyers to determine whether they are biased or have any preformed judgments about the parties in the case. Jury selection is called *voir dire* **examination**. **For Example,** in the trial of Martha Stewart, the multimedia home and garden diva, it took a great deal of time for the lawyers to question the potential jurors about their prior knowledge concerning the case, which had received nationwide attention and much media coverage. Lawyers have the opportunity to remove jurors who know parties in

***voir dire* examination**—the preliminary examination of a juror or a witness to ascertain fitness to act as such.

---

[7] At the civil trial of O.J. Simpson for the wrongful death of Nicole Brown Simpson and Ronald Goldman, Daniel Petrocelli used a videotape of Mr. Simpson's deposition very effectively in impeaching Mr. Simpson's testimony at trial. Daniel Petrocelli, *Triumph of Justice: The Final Judgment on the Simpson Saga* (New York: Crown, 1998).

[8] *Daubert v. Merrell Dow Pharmaceuticals, Inc.,* 509 U.S. 579 (1993).

opening statements – statements by opposing attorneys that tell the jury what their cases will prove.

admissibility – the quality of the evidence in a case that allows it to be presented to the jury.

direct examination – examination of a witness by his or her attorney.

cross-examination – the examination made of a witness by the attorney for the adverse party.

redirect examination – questioning after cross-examination, in which the attorney for the witness testifying may ask the same witness other questions to overcome effects of the cross-examination.

recross-examination – an examination by the other side's attorney that follows the redirect examination.

the case or who indicate they have already formed opinions about guilt or innocence. The attorneys question the potential jurors to determine if a juror should be *challenged for cause* (e.g., when the prospective juror states he is employed by the plaintiff's company). Challenges for cause are unlimited, but each side can also exercise six to eight peremptory challenges.[9] A peremptory challenge is a challenge that is used to strike (remove) a juror for any reason except on racial grounds.[10]

(B) OPENING STATEMENTS. After the jury is chosen, the attorneys for each of the parties make their **opening statements** to the jury. An opening statement, as one lawyer has explained, makes a puzzle frame for the case so jurors can follow the witnesses and place the pieces of the case—the various forms of evidence—within the frame.

(C) THE PRESENTATION OF EVIDENCE. Following the opening statements, the plaintiff presents his case with witnesses and other evidence. A judge rules on the **admissibility** of evidence. Evidence can consist of documents, testimony, expert testimony, medical information from exams, and even physical evidence.

In the case of testimony, the attorney for the plaintiff conducts **direct examination** of his witnesses during his case, and the defense attorney conducts **cross-examination** of the plaintiff's witnesses. The plaintiff's attorney can then ask questions again of his witnesses in what is called **redirect examination**. Finally, the defense attorney may question the plaintiff's witnesses again in **recross-examination**. The defendant presents her case after the plaintiff's case concludes. During the defendant's case, the lawyer for the defendant conducts direct examination of the defendant's witnesses, and the plaintiff's lawyer can then cross-examine the defendant's witnesses.

Thinking Things Through

Why Do We Require Sworn Testimony?

There is a difference between what people say in conversation (and even what company executives say in speeches and reports) and what they are willing to say under oath. Speaking under oath often means that different information and recollections emerge. The oath is symbolic and carries the penalty of criminal prosecution for perjury if the testimony given is false.

The *Wall Street Journal* has reported that the testimony of executives in the Microsoft antitrust trial and their statements regarding their business relationships outside the courtroom are quite different. For example, the following quotations indicate some discrepancies. Eric Benhamou, the chief executive officer (CEO) of Palm, Inc., said:

We believe that the handheld opportunity remains wide open …. Unlike the PC industry, there is no monopoly of silicon, there is no monopoly of software.

However, at the Microsoft trial, another officer of Palm, Michael Mace, offered the following testimony:

We believe that there is a very substantial risk that Microsoft could manipulate its products and its standards in order to exclude Palm from the marketplace in the future.

[9] The number of peremptory challenges varies from state to state and may also vary within a particular state depending on the type of case. For example, in Arizona, peremptory challenges are unlimited in capital cases.
[10] *Felkner v. Jackson,* 131 S.Ct. 1305 (2011).

Thinking Things Through

Continued

Likewise, Microsoft has taken different positions inside and outside the courtroom. For example, an attorney for Microsoft stated that Microsoft had "zero deployments of its interactive TV middleware products connected to cable systems in the United States." However, Microsoft's marketing materials provide as follows:

Microsoft's multiple deployments around the world now including Charter-show Microsoft TV is ready to

deploy now and set the standard for what TV can be.*

Explain why the executives had differing statements. For more information on the Microsoft antitrust cases, go to **www.usdoj.gov** or **www.microsoft.com**.

*Rebecca Buckman and Nicholas Kulish, "Microsoft Trial Prompts an Outbreak of Doublespeak," Wall Street Journal, April 15, 2002, B1, B3.

---

directed verdict – a direction by the trial judge to the jury to return a verdict in favor of a specified party to the action.

(D) MOTION FOR A DIRECTED VERDICT. A motion for a **directed verdict** asks the court to grant a verdict because even if all the evidence that has been presented by each side were true, there is either no basis for recovery or no defense to recovery. **For Example,** suppose that a plaintiff company presented evidence that an employee who quit working for the company posted on his Facebook page, "I just wasn't happy there." The company might not feel good about the former employee's post, but there is no false statement and no breach of privacy. The evidence is true, but there is no legal right of recovery. The defendant employee would be entitled to a directed verdict. A directed verdict means that the party has not presented enough evidence to show that there is some right of recovery under the law.

summation – the attorney address that follows all the evidence presented in court and sums up a case and recommends a particular verdict be returned by the jury.

(E) CLOSING ARGUMENTS OR SUMMATION. After the witnesses for both parties have been examined and all the evidence has been presented, each attorney makes a closing argument. These statements are also called **summations**; they summarize the case and urge the jury to reach a particular verdict.

mistrial – a court's declaration that terminates a trial and postpones it to a later date; commonly entered when evidence has been of a highly prejudicial character or when a juror has been guilty of misconduct.

(F) MOTION FOR MISTRIAL. During the course of a trial, when necessary to avoid great injustice, the trial court may declare a **mistrial**. A mistrial requires a do-over, a new jury. A mistrial can be declared for jury or attorney misconduct. **For Example,** if a juror were caught fraternizing with one of the lawyers in the case, objectivity would be compromised and the court would most likely declare a mistrial. See also eCommerce & Cyber Law on p. 30 for more information on juror misconduct and case dismissals.

instruction – summary of the law given to jurors by the judge before deliberation begins.

(G) JURY INSTRUCTIONS AND VERDICT. After the summation by the attorneys, the court gives the jurors **instructions** on the appropriate law to apply to the facts presented. The jury then deliberates and renders its verdict. After the jury verdict, the court enters a judgment. If the jury is deadlocked and unable to reach a verdict, known as a hung jury or a mistrial, the case is reset for a new trial at some future date.

judgment n.o.v. – *or non obstante veredicto* (notwithstanding the verdict), a judgment entered after verdict upon the motion of the losing party on the ground that the verdict is so wrong that a judgment should be entered the opposite of the verdict.

(H) MOTION FOR NEW TRIAL; MOTION FOR JUDGMENT N.O.V. A court may grant a **judgment *non obstante veredicto*** or a **judgment *n.o.v.*** (notwithstanding the verdict) if the verdict is clearly wrong as a matter of law. The court can set aside the verdict and enter a judgment in favor of the other party. Perhaps one of the most famous judgments n.o.v. occurred in Boston in 1997 when a judge reversed the murder conviction of nanny Louise Woodward, who was charged with the murder of one of her young charges.

Ethics & the Law

Injustice, Misconduct, and Senator Stevens

The late Senator Ted Stevens (from Alaska) was tried in the fall of 2008 on charges that he lied on his financial disclosure forms by not disclosing the work a contractor performed on his Alaska home. He was convicted just days before the 2008 federal elections and he lost his Senate seat. However, the verdict and all of the charges were dismissed in 2009 on a motion by the U.S. attorney general, Eric Holder, when the Department of Justice discovered that prosecutors withheld exculpatory evidence, evidence that would have helped Senator Stevens. Sadly, Senator Stevens was killed in a plane crash in 2010. A 525-page report released in 2012 concluded that several prosecutors withheld evidence that Mr. Stevens had asked several times to be billed for the work on his home so that he could pay and

make the necessary financial disclosures about its value. Also, one of the witness's background was shaky, something that would have caused his credibility to come into question at the trial. The jury never heard this evidence and neither Senator Stevens nor his lawyers were given the documents and interviews that would have helped his case. No criminal charges will be brought against the prosecutors who withheld the evidence. However, does that mean that their conduct was ethical? What is the obligation of lawyers when they discover evidence that favors the other side in a case?

[*In re Special Proceedings*, 842 F. Supp. 2d 232 (D.D.C. 2012)]

8. Posttrial Procedures

(A) RECOVERY OF COSTS/ATTORNEY FEES. Generally, the prevailing party is awarded costs. Costs include filing fees, service-of-process fees, witness fees, deposition transcript costs, and jury fees. Costs do not include compensation spent by a party for preparing the case or being present at trial, including the time lost from work because of the case and the fee paid to the attorney, although lost wages from an injury are generally part of damages.

Attorney fees may be recovered by a party who prevails if a statute permits the recovery of attorney fees or if the complaint involves a claim for breach of contract and the contract contains a clause providing for recovery of attorney fees.

(B) EXECUTION OF JUDGMENT. After a judgment has been entered or all appeals or appeal rights have ended, the losing party must pay that judgment. The winning party can also take steps to execute, or carry out, the judgment. The **execution** is accomplished by the seizure and sale of the losing party's assets by the sheriff according to a writ of execution or a writ of possession.

Garnishment is a common method of satisfying a judgment. When the judgment debtor is an employee, the appropriate judicial authority in the state garnishes (by written notice to the employer) a portion of the employee's wages on a regular basis until the judgment is paid.

execution–the carrying out of a judgment of a court, generally directing that property owned by the defendant be sold and the proceeds first be used to pay the execution or judgment creditor.

garnishment–the name given in some states to attachment proceedings.

C. ALTERNATIVE DISPUTE RESOLUTION (ADR)

Parties can use means other than litigation to resolve disagreements or disputes. Litigation takes significant time and money, so many businesses use alternative methods for resolving disputes. Those methods include arbitration, mediation, and several other formats. Figure 2-4 provides an overall view of alternative dispute resolution procedures.

arbitration–the settlement of disputed questions, whether of law or fact, by one or more arbitrators by whose decision the parties agree to be bound.

9. Arbitration

In **arbitration**, arbitrators (disinterested persons selected by the parties to the dispute) hear evidence and determine a resolution. Arbitration enables the parties to

| FIGURE 2-4 | *Dispute Resolution Procedures* |

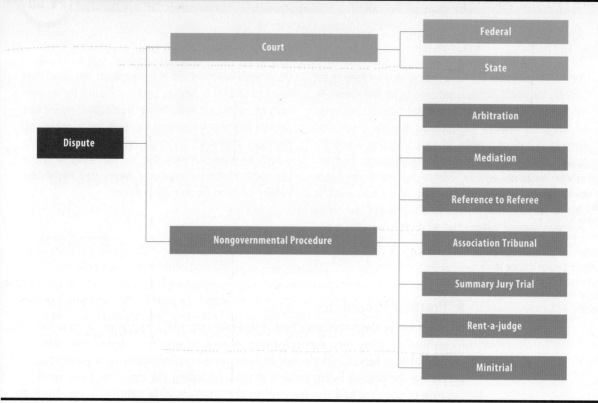

© Cengage Learning

present the facts before trained experts familiar with the industry practices that may affect the nature and outcome of the dispute. Arbitration first reached extensive use in the field of commercial contracts and is encouraged as a means of avoiding expensive litigation and easing the workload of courts.[11]

A number of states have adopted the Uniform Arbitration Act.[12] Under this act and similar statutes, the parties to a contract may agree in advance that all disputes arising under it will be submitted to arbitration. In some instances, the contract will name the arbitrators for the duration of the contract. The uniform act requires a written agreement to arbitrate.[13]

The Federal Arbitration Act[14] provides that an arbitration clause in a contract relating to an interstate transaction is valid, irrevocable, and enforceable. When a contract subject to the Federal Arbitration Act provides for the arbitration of disputes, the parties are bound to arbitrate in accordance with the federal statute even if the agreement to arbitrate would not be binding under state law.

---

[11] *Warfield v. Beth Israel Deaconess Medical Center, Inc.*, 910 N.E.2d 317 (Mass. 2009). Arbitration has existed in the United States since 1920 when New York passed an arbitration statute. For a look at the history of arbitration, see Charles L. Knapp, "Taking Contracts Private: The Quiet Revolution in Contract Law," 71 *Fordham L. Rev.* 761 (2002).

[12] On August 3, 2000, the National Conference of Commissioners on Uniform State Laws unanimously passed major revisions to the Uniform Arbitration Act (UAA). These revisions were the first major changes in 45 years to the UAA, which is the basis of arbitration law in 49 states, although not all states have adopted it in its entirety. Thirty-five states and the District of Columbia have adopted the 1955 version. Only 13 states have adopted the UAA 2000 revisions. Uniform Laws Annotated, Section 1 (2012); see also Donald L. Carpo & John B. LaRocco, "A Comparison of Litigation, Arbitration, and Mediation," 63 *Dispute Resolution J.* 48 (2008).

[13] *Fawzy v. Fawzy*, 973 A.2d 347 (N.J. 2009).

[14] 9 U.S.C §§114 *et seq.*

(A) MANDATORY ARBITRATION. In contrast with statutes that merely regulate arbitration when it is selected voluntarily by the parties, some statutes require that certain kinds of disputes be submitted to arbitration. In some states, by rule or statute, the arbitration of small claims is required.

(B) FINALITY OF ARBITRATION. Most parties provide, within their arbitration agreements, that the decision of the arbitrator will be final. Such a clause is binding on the parties, even when the decision seems to be wrong, and can be set aside only if there is clear proof of fraud, arbitrary conduct, or a significant procedural error.[15]

If the arbitration is mandatory under statute or rule, the losing party generally may appeal such arbitration to a court.[16] The appeal proceeds just as though there had never been any prior arbitration. This new court proceeding is called a **trial *de novo*** and is necessary to preserve the constitutional right to a jury trial. As a practical matter, however, relatively few appeals are taken from arbitration decisions.

> **trial *de novo*** – a trial required to preserve the constitutional right to a jury trial by allowing an appeal to proceed as though there never had been any prior hearing or decision.

10. Mediation

In **mediation**, a neutral person acts as a messenger between opposing sides of a dispute, carrying to each side the latest settlement offer made by the other. The mediator has no authority to make a decision, although in some cases the mediator may make suggestions that might ultimately be accepted by the disputing parties.

> **mediation** – the settlement of a dispute through the use of a messenger who carries to each side of the dispute the issues and offers in the case.

The use of mediation has the advantage of keeping discussions going when the disputing parties have developed such fixed attitudes or personal animosity that direct discussion between them has become impossible.

11. MedArb

In this new form of alternative dispute resolution (ADR), the arbitrator is also empowered to act as a mediator. Beyond just hearing a case, the arbitrator acts as a messenger for the parties on unresolved issues.

12. Reference to a Third Person

Many types of transactions provide for **reference to a third person**, in which a third person or a committee makes an out-of-court determination of the rights of persons. **For Example,** employees and an employer may have agreed as a term of the employment contract that claims of employees under retirement plans will be decided by a designated board or committee. In a sales contract, the seller and buyer can select a third person to determine the price to be paid for goods. Construction contracts often include a provision for disputes to be referred to the architect in charge of the construction with the architect's decision being final.

> **reference to a third person** – settlement that allows a nonparty to resolve the dispute.

These referrals often eliminate the disputes or pursuit of remedies. **For Example,** fire insurance policies commonly provide that if the parties cannot agree on the amount of the loss, each will appoint an appraiser, the two appraisers will appoint a third appraiser, and the three will determine the amount of the loss the insurer is required to pay.

---

[15] *Apache Bohai Corp. LDC v. Texaco China BV*, 480 F.3d 397 (5th Cir. 2007).
[16] *U.S. v. Park Place Associates*, 563 F.3d 907 (9th Cir. 2009).

E-Commerce & Cyberlaw

The Googling Juror

Referred to as the "Google Mistrial," a federal judge in Florida declared a mistrial after a juror told that judge that he had been doing research on the Internet on the drug trial in which he was serving. When the judge declared the mistrial, eight other jurors confessed that they had been doing the same thing.

Judges have long warned jurors about using outside sources, including the Internet, but BlackBerries and iPhones have proven to be mighty tempting for jurors. Some jurors are using Facebook to announce when verdicts are coming. One juror even looked up evidence that had been excluded by the judge in the case. When asked why he violated the judge's order, the juror said simply, "Well, I was curious." Another juror contacted the defendant through Facebook, and another mistrial resulted.

A judge in Arkansas is reviewing a request for a reversal of a $12.6 million jury verdict against a company from one of the company's lawyers based on the court's discovery that one of the jurors was using Twitter to send out postings about how the trial was proceeding. An excerpt from the posting follows:

> "Oh, and nobody buy Stoam. It's bad mojo and they'll probably cease to Exist now that their wallet is $12m lighter … So, Jonathan, what did you do today? Oh nothing really, I just gave away TWELVE MILLION DOLLARS of somebody else's money."*

What is the problem with jurors using these electronic tools during their cases?

*John Schwartz, "As Jurors Turn to Google and Twitter, Mistrials Are Popping Up," *New York Times*, March 18, 2009, p. A1.

13. Association Tribunals

association tribunal – a court created by a trade association or group for the resolution of disputes among its members.

Many disputes never reach the courts because both parties to a dispute belong to a group or an association, and the **association tribunal** created by the group or association disposes of the matter. Trade associations commonly require their members to employ out-of-court methods of dispute settlement. **For Example,** the National Association of Home Builders requires its member builders to employ arbitration. The National Automobile Dealers Association provides for panels to determine warranty claims of customers. The decision of such panels is final as to the builder or dealer, but the consumer can still bring a regular lawsuit after losing before the panel. Members of an association must use the association tribunal, which means they cannot bypass the association tribunal and go directly to a law court.[17]

14. Summary Jury Trial

summary jury trial – a mock or dry-run trial for parties to get a feel for how their cases will play to a jury.

A **summary jury trial** is a dry-run or mock trial in which the lawyers present their claims before a jury of six persons. The object is to get the reaction of a sample jury. No evidence is presented before this jury, and it bases its opinion solely on what the lawyers state. The determination of the jury has no binding effect, but it has value in that it gives the lawyers some idea of what a jury might think if there were an actual trial. This type of ADR has special value when the heart of a case is whether something is reasonable under all circumstances. When the lawyers and their clients see how the sample jury reacts, they may moderate their positions and reach a settlement.

15. Rent-A-Judge

rent-a-judge plan – dispute resolution through private courts with judges paid to be referees for the cases.

Under the **rent-a-judge plan**, the parties hire a judge to hear the case. In many states, the parties voluntarily choose the judge as a "referee," and the judge acts under a statute authorizing the appointment of referees. Under such a statute, the referee hears all evidence just as though there were a regular trial, and the rented judge's determination is binding on the parties unless reversed on appeal if such an appeal (like a court trial) is permitted under the parties' agreement.

16. Minitrial

minitrial – a trial held on portions of the case or certain issues in the case.

When only part of a case is disputed, the parties may stay within the framework of a lawsuit but agree that only the disputed issues will be taken to trial and submitted to a jury. **For Example,** if there is no real dispute over who is liable but the parties disagree as to the damages, the issue of damages alone may be submitted to the jury. This shortened trial is often called a **minitrial**. A minitrial may use a retired judge to make a decision on just the disputed issues. The parties may also specify whether this decision will be binding on the parties. As a practical matter, the evaluation of a case by a neutral person often brings the opposing parties together to reach a settlement.

17. Judicial Triage

judicial triage – court management tool used by judges to expedite certain cases in which time is of the essence, such as asbestos cases in which the plaintiffs are gravely ill.

The court systems, experiencing heavy caseloads, now practice **judicial triage**. Judges examine cases from a timeliness perspective. For example, in asbestos cases, judges are now evaluating plaintiffs on the basis of "how sick they are" and expediting trials for those plaintiffs who are the most ill from the alleged effects of asbestos that are the subject of their suits. The trials of those who do not have medical documentation of current illness are postponed and placed on the inactive docket until the court can get to them or until the plaintiffs become sick. Using triage, one judge has been able to bring to trial 40 percent of all asbestos cases brought since 1992.[18]

18. Contract Provisions

The parties' contract may pave the way for the settlement of future disputes by including clauses that require the parties to use one of the means of ADR. Other provisions in contracts that serve to keep the parties calm with the hope of resolving differences without a lawsuit include waiting periods before a suit can be filed and obligations to continue performing even as they try to resolve differences and issues.

LawFlix

Class Action (1991) (R)

Here is a good movie to illustrate discovery and the ethics of withholding paperwork.

Twelve Angry Men (1957) G

A movie that shows the jury process, rights of parties in court, jury instructions, and group think, all wrapped up in terrific dialogue.

MAKE THE CONNECTION

SUMMARY

Courts have been created to hear and resolve legal disputes. A court's specific power is defined by its jurisdiction. Courts of original jurisdiction are trial courts, and courts that review the decisions of trial courts are appellate courts. Trial courts may have general jurisdiction to hear a wide range of civil and criminal matters, or they may be courts of limited jurisdiction—such as a probate court or the Tax Court—with the subject matter of their cases restricted to certain areas.

The courts in the United States are organized into two different systems: the state and federal court systems. There are three levels of courts, for the most part, in each system, with trial courts, appellate courts, and a supreme court in each. The federal courts are federal district courts, federal courts of appeals, and the U.S. Supreme Court.

In the states, there may be specialized courts, such as municipal, justice, and small claims courts, for trial courts. Within the courts of original jurisdiction, there are rules for procedures in all matters brought before them. A civil case begins with the filing of a complaint by a plaintiff, which is then answered by a defendant. The parties may be represented by their attorneys.

Discovery is the pretrial process used by the parties to find out the evidence in the case. The parties can use depositions, interrogatories, and document requests to uncover relevant information.

The case is managed by a judge and may be tried to a jury selected through the process of *voir dire,* with the parties permitted to challenge jurors on the basis of cause or through the use of their peremptory challenges. The trial begins following discovery and involves opening statements and the presentation of evidence, including the direct examination and cross-examination of witnesses. Once a judgment is entered, the party who has won can collect the judgment through garnishment and a writ of execution.

Alternatives to litigation for dispute resolution are available, including arbitration, mediation, MedArb, reference to a third party, association tribunals, summary jury trials, rent-a-judge plans, minitrials, and judicial triage. Court dockets are relieved and cases consolidated using judicial triage, a process in which courts hear the cases involving the most serious medical issues and health conditions first. Triage is a blending of the judicial and alternative dispute resolution mechanisms.

LEARNING OUTCOMES

After studying this chapter, you should be able to clearly explain:

A. The Court System

LO.1 Explain the federal and state court systems

See Figure 2-1 on p. 18 and accompanying text.
See Figure 2-3 on p. 21 and accompanying text.

B. Court Procedure

LO.2 Describe court procedures
See the discussion of steps in litigation that begins on p. 23.
See the *For Example* discussion of the Martha Stewart *voir dire* example on p. 24.

C. Alternative Dispute Resolution (ADR)

LO.3 List the forms of alternative dispute resolution and distinguish among them
See the discussion of arbitration that begins on p. 27.
See the discussion of other forms of ADR, mediation, minitrials, rent-a-judge, MedArb, judicial triage, and referral to a third party that begins on p. 29.
See the discussion of employee and employer referrals of disputes to a designated board or committee on p. 30.

KEY TERMS

admissibility

affirm

answer

appeal

appellate jurisdiction

arbitration

association tribunal

attorney-client privilege

complaint

counterclaim

court

cross-examination

defendant

demurrer

deposition

direct examination

directed verdict

discovery

en banc

execution

expert witness

federal district courts

garnishment

general jurisdiction

impeach

instructions

interrogatories

judge

judgment *n.o.v.* or judgment *non obstante veredicto*

judicial triage

jurisdiction

jury

limited (special) jurisdiction

mediation

minitrial

mistrial

motion for summary judgment

motion to dismiss

opening statements

original jurisdiction

plaintiff

pleadings

process

prosecutor

recross-examination

redirect examination

reference to a third person

remand

rent-a-judge plan

requests for production of documents

reverse

reversible error

small claims courts

subject matter jurisdiction

summary jury trial

summations

trial *de novo*

voir dire examination

writ of *certiorari*

QUESTIONS AND CASE PROBLEMS

1. List the steps in a lawsuit. Begin with the filing of the complaint, and explain the points at which there can be a final determination of the parties' rights in the case.

2. Explain why a business person would want to use alternative dispute resolution methods. Discuss the advantages. What disadvantages do you see?

3. Ralph Dewey has been charged with a violation of the Electronic Espionage Act, a federal statute that prohibits the transfer, by computer or disk or other electronic means, of a company's proprietary data and information. Ralph is curious. What type of court has jurisdiction? Can you determine which court?

4. Jerry Lewinsky was called for jury duty. When *voir dire* began, Jerry realized that the case involved his supervisor at work. Can Jerry remain as a juror on the case? Why or why not?

5. Carolyn, Elwood, and Isabella are involved in a real estate development. The development is a failure, and Carolyn, Elwood, and Isabella want to have their rights determined. They could bring a lawsuit, but they are afraid the case is so complicated that a judge and jury not familiar with the problems of real estate development would not reach a proper result. What can they do?

6. Larketta Randolph purchased a mobile home from Better Cents Home Builders, Inc., and financed her purchase through Green Tree Financial Corporation. Ms. Randolph signed a standard form contract that required her to buy Vendor's Single Interest insurance, which protects the seller against the costs of repossession in the event of default. The agreement also provided that all disputes arising from the contract would be resolved by binding arbitration. Larketta found that there was an additional $15 in finance charges that were not disclosed in the contract. She and other Green Tree customers filed a class-action suit to recover the fees. Green Tree moved to dismiss the suit because Larketta had not submitted the issue to arbitration. Larketta protests, "But I want the right to go to court!" Does she have that right? What are the

rights of parties under a contract with an arbitration clause? [*Green Tree Financial Corp. v. Randolph*, 531 U.S. 79]

7. John Watson invested $5,000,000 in SmartRead, Inc., a company that was developing an electronic reading device. Within a few months, the $5,000,000 was spent but SmartRead never developed the reading device. John filed suit against directors of SmartRead for their failure to supervise SmartRead's CEO in his operation of the company. The directors used an expert on corporate governance to testify that the directors had done all that they could to oversee the company. The expert did not disclose that he had served as a director of a company and had been found to be negligent in his role there and had been required to pay $370,000 to shareholders. The directors won the case. Is there anything Watson can do?

8. Indicate whether the following courts are courts of original, general, limited, or appellate jurisdiction:

   a. Small claims court

   b. Federal bankruptcy court

   c. Federal district court

   d. U.S. Supreme Court

   e. Municipal court

   f. Probate court

   g. Federal court of appeals

9. The Nursing Home Pension Fund filed suit against Oracle Corporation alleging that Larry Ellison, the company's CEO, misled investors in 2001 about the true financial condition of the company. During the time of the alleged misrepresentation, Mr. Ellison was working with a biographer on his life story and there are videotapes of Mr. Ellison's interviews with his biographer as well as e-mails between the two that discuss Oracle. Could the Nursing Home Pension Fund have access to the tapes and e-mails? Explain how. [*Nursing Home Pension Fund, Local 144 v. Oracle Corp.*, 380 F.3d 1226 (9th Cir.)]

10. Mostek Corp., a Texas corporation, made a contract to sell computer-related products to North American Foreign Trading Corp., a New York corporation. North American used its own purchase order form, on which appeared the statement that any dispute arising out of an order would be submitted to arbitration, as provided in the terms set forth on the back of the order. Acting on the purchase order, Mostek delivered almost all of the goods but failed to deliver the final installment. North American then demanded that the matter be arbitrated. Mostek refused to do so. Was arbitration required? [*Application of Mostek Corp.*, 502 N.Y.S.2d 181 (App. Div.)]

11. Ceasar Wright was a longshoreman in Charleston, South Carolina, and a member of the International Longshoremen's Association (AFL-CIO). Wright used the union hiring hall. The collective bargaining agreement (CBA) of Wright's union provides for arbitration of all grievances. Another clause of the CBA states: "It is the intention and purpose of all parties hereto that no provision or part of this Agreement shall be violative of any Federal or State Law."

    On February 18, 1992, while Wright was working for Stevens Shipping and Terminal Company (Stevens), he injured his right heel and back. He sought permanent compensation from Stevens and settled his claims for $250,000 and another $10,000 in attorney fees. Wright was also awarded Social Security disability benefits.

    In January 1995, Wright, whose doctor had approved his return to work, returned to the hiring hall and asked to be referred for work. Wright did work between January 2 and January 11, 1995, but when the companies realized Wright had been certified as permanently disabled, they deemed him not qualified for longshoreman work under the CBA and refused to allow him to work for them.

    Wright did not file a grievance under the union agreement but instead hired a lawyer and proceeded with a claim under the Americans with Disabilities Act. The district court dismissed the case because Wright had failed to pursue the grievance procedure provided by the CBA. Must Wright pursue the dispute procedure first, or can he go right to court on the basis of his federal rights under the Americans with Disabilities Act? [*Wright v. Universal Maritime Service Corp.*, 525 U.S. 70]

12. Winona Ryder was arrested for shoplifting from Saks Fifth Avenue in California. One of the members of the jury panel for her trial was Peter Guber, a Hollywood executive in charge of the production of three films in which Ms. Ryder starred, including *Bram Stoker's Dracula, The Age of Innocence,* and *Little Women.* If you were the prosecuting attorney in the case, how could you discover such information about this potential juror, and what are your options for excluding him from selection? [Rick Lyman, "For the Ryder Trial, a Hollywood Script," *New York Times*, November 3, 2002, SL-1]

13. Two doctors had a dispute over who was doing how much work at their clinic. Their dispute was submitted to arbitration and the arbitrator held in favor of the less experienced doctor. The senior doctor wants the arbitration set aside. Is it possible for the arbitrator's decision to be set aside?

14. Martha Simms is the plaintiff in a contract suit she has brought against Floral Supply, Inc., for its failure to deliver the green sponge Martha needed in building the floral designs she sells to exclusive home decorators. Martha had to obtain the sponge from another supplier and was late on seven deliveries. One of Martha's customers has been called by Martha's lawyer as a witness and is now on the witness stand, testifying about Martha's late performance and the penalty she charged. The lawyer for Floral Supply knows that Martha's customer frequently waives penalties for good suppliers. How can Floral Supply's lawyer get that information before the jury?

15. What would happen if lawyers for one side withheld evidence in a case? How could the party affected have the problem corrected?

© Manuel Gutjahr/iStockphoto.com

CHAPTER 3

Business Ethics, Social Forces, and the Law

learningoutcomes

After studying this chapter, you should be able to

LO.1 Define business ethics

LO.2 Discuss why ethics are important in business

LO.3 Describe how to recognize and resolve ethical dilemmas

Each day businesspeople work together on contracts and projects. Their completion of the work is partially the result of the laws that protect contract rights. Much of what businesspeople do, however, is simply a matter of their word. Executives arrive at a 9:00 A.M. meeting because they promised they would be there. An employee meets a deadline for an ad display board because she said she would. Business transactions are completed through a combination of the values of the parties and the laws that reflect those values and the importance of one's word in business.

This chapter takes you behind the rules of law to examine the objectives in establishing rules for business conduct. Ethical principles, social norms, and business needs contribute to the standards that govern businesses and their operations.

A. What Is Business Ethics?

ethics – a branch of philosophy dealing with values that relate to the nature of human conduct and values associated with that conduct.

Ethics is a branch of philosophy dealing with values that relate to the nature of human conduct and values associated with that conduct. Balancing the goal of profits with the values of individuals and society is the focus of **business ethics**. Some economists make the point that insider trading is an efficient way to run that market. To an economist, inside information allows those with the best information to make the most money. This view ignores some issues: What about those who trade stock who do not have access to that information? What will happen to the stock market if investors perceive there is not a level playing field? In the U.S. Supreme Court decision *United States v. O'Hagan*[1] on insider trading, Justice Ruth Ginsburg noted, "Investors likely wouldn't invest in a market where trading based on misappropriated nonpublic information is unchecked." The field of business ethics deals with the balance between society's values and the need for businesses to remain profitable.

✳ **business ethics** – balancing the goal of profits with values of individuals and society.

1. The Law as the Standard for Business Ethics

positive law – law enacted and codified by governmental authority.

Philosophers debate the origin of moral and ethical standards as well as which of those standards should be applied. One view of ethics is simply following what codified or **positive law** requires. The test of whether an act is legal is a common moral standard used frequently in business. Codified law, or law created by governmental authority, is used as the standard for ethical behavior. Absent illegality, all behavior is ethical under this simple standard. The phrase "AS IS," on a contract (see Chapter 25 for further discussion), means by law that there are no warranties for the goods being sold. **For Example,** if a buyer purchases a used car and the phrase "AS IS" is in the contract, the seller has no legal obligation, in most states, if the transmission falls apart the day after the buyer's purchase. Following a positive law standard, the seller who refuses to repair the transmission has acted ethically. However, ethical standards are different. We know there was no legal obligation to fix the transmission, but was it fair that the car fell apart the day after it was purchased?

---

[1] 521 U.S. 657 (1997).

2. The Notion of Universal Standards for Business Ethics

Another view of ethics holds that standards exist universally and cannot be changed or modified by law. In many cases, universal standards stem from religious beliefs. In some countries today, the standards for business are still determined by religious tenets. **Natural law** imposes higher standards of behavior than those required by positive law and they must be followed even if those higher standards run contrary to codified law. **For Example,** in the early nineteenth century when slavery was legally permissible in the United States, a positive law standard supported slavery. However, slavery violates the natural law principle of individual freedom and would be unethical. **Civil disobedience** is the remedy natural law proponents use to change positive law.

natural law – a system of principles to guide human conduct independent of, and sometimes contrary to, enacted law and discovered by man's rational intelligence.

civil disobedience – the term used when natural law proponents violate positive law.

Former Supreme Court Justice Sandra Day O'Connor, who was second in her class at Stanford Law School (the late Chief Justice William Rehnquist was first), was offered a job as a receptionist for a law firm while her male classmates were hired as attorneys. At that time, no law prohibited discrimination against women, so law firms' hiring practices, using only a positive law standard, were ethical. However, if the natural law standard of equality is applied, the refusal to hire Sandra O'Connor as a lawyer, a position for which she was qualified, was a violation of the natural law principle of equality and unethical.

3. Ethical Theories and Standards

There are many different views about the correct theory or standard we should apply when we face ethical dilemmas. Some of those theories and standards are covered here.

(A) THE CATEGORICAL IMPERATIVE AND IMMANUEL KANT. Philosopher Immanuel Kant does not allow any resolution of an ethical dilemma in which human beings are used as a means by which others obtain benefits. **Kant's categorical imperative** theory, reduced to simplest terms, is that you cannot use others in a way that gives you a one-sided benefit. Everyone must operate under the same usage rules. In Kant's words, "One ought only to act such that the principle of one's act could become a universal law of human action in a world in which one would hope to live." **For Example,** if you hit a car in a parking lot and damaged it but you could be guaranteed that no one saw you do it, would you leave a note on the other car with contact information? If you answered, "No, because that's happened to me 12 times before and no one left me a note," then you are unhappy with universal behaviors but are unwilling to commit to universal standards of honesty and disclosure to remedy those behaviors.

Kant's categorical imperative – a standard of ethics that requires that we avoid one-sided benefit for us as a result of the conduct or decision

International business presents some interesting Kantian dilemmas. For example, there are some U.S. companies that use suppliers in developing nations. Those suppliers have employees in sweatshop atmospheres who work for pennies per hour. The pennies-per-hour wage seems unjust. However, suppose the company was operating under one of its universal principles: Always pay a fair wage to those who work for it. A "fair wage" in that country might be pennies, and the company owner could argue, "I would work for that wage if I lived in that country." The company owner could also argue, "But, if I lived in the United States, I would not work for that wage, would require a much higher wage, and would want benefits, and we do provide that to all of our U.S. workers."

The company has developed its own ethical standard that is universally applicable, and those who own the company could live with it if it was applied to them, but context is everything under the categorical imperative. The basic question is: Are you comfortable living in a world operating under the standards you have established, or would you deem them unfair or unjust?

There is one more part to Kant's theory: You not only have to be fair but also have to want to do it for all the right reasons. Kant wants you to adopt and accept these ethical standards because you do not want to use other people as a means to your enrichment at their expense.

(B) THE CONTRACTARIANS AND JUSTICE. John Locke and John Rawls developed what is sometimes called the **theory of justice** and sometimes referred to as the **social contract**. Rawls and Locke believe that Kant was wrong in assuming that we could all have a meeting of the minds on what were the good rules for society. Locke and Rawls preferred just putting the rules into place with a social contract. Under this theory we imagine what it would be like if we had no rules or laws at all. If we started with a blank slate, or *tabula rasa* as these philosophers would say, rational people would agree—perhaps in their own self-interest, or perhaps to be fair—that certain universal rules must apply. Rational people, thinking through the results and consequences if there were not rules, would develop rules that would result in fairness. **For Example,** we would probably develop rules such as "Don't take my property without my permission" and "I would like the same rights in court that rich people have even if I am not so rich." Locke and Rawls want us to step back from the emotion of the moment and make universal principles that will survive the test of time.

(C) RIGHTS THEORY. The **rights theory** is also known as an **entitlement theory** and is one of the more modern theories of ethics. Robert Nozick is the key modern-day philosopher on this theory, which has two big elements: (1) everyone has a set of rights, and (2) it is up to the governments to protect those rights. **For Example,** there are rights issues related to sweatshops, abortion, slavery, property ownership and use, justice (as in court processes), animal rights, privacy, and euthanasia. Nozick dealt with all the controversial and emotional issues of ethics including everything from human dignity in suffering to third-trimester abortions.

(D) ETHICAL EGOISM THEORY: AYN RAND AND ATLAS. **Ethical egoism** holds that we all act in our own self-interest and that all of us should limit our judgment to our own ethical egos and not interfere with the exercise of ethical egoism by others. This view holds that everything is determined by self-interest. We act as we do and decide to behave as we do because we have determined that it is in our own self-interest.

Ayn Rand, who wrote books about business and business leaders' decisions in ethical dilemmas, such as *The Fountainhead* and *Atlas Shrugged,* was an ethical egoist. These two famous books made Ms. Rand's point about ethical dilemmas: the world would be better if we did not feel so guilty about the choices we make in ethical dilemmas and just acknowledged that it is all self-interest.

(E) THE UTILITARIAN THEORY: BENTHAM AND MILL. **Utilitarians** resolve ethical dilemmas by doing the most good for the most people. For example, suppose that the FBI has just arrested a terrorist who is clearly a leader in a movement that plans to plant bombs in the nation's trains, subways, and airports. This individual has critical information

---

theory of justice—the Locke and Rawlsian standard for ethics that requires that we all agree on certain universal principles in advance.

social contract—the agreement under Locke and Rawls as to what our ethical standards will be.

rights theory—Nozick's theory of ethics that we all have a set of rights that must be honored and protected by government

entitlement theory—another name for Nozick's theory that we all have certain rights that must be honored and protected by government.

Ethical egoism—theory of ethics that we should all act in our own self-interest; the Ayn Rand theory that separates guilt from acting in our own self-interest

Utilitarians—theory of ethics based on doing the most good for the most people in making decisions about upcoming planned attacks but refuses to speak. A utilitarian would want the greatest good for the greatest number and would feel that harsh interrogation methods would be justified to save thousands of lives. Rights theorists would disagree with using torture to obtain the information because human rights must be protected.

Moral relativists – those who make decisions based on circumstances and not on the basis of any predefined standards.

(F) MORAL RELATIVISTS. Moral relativists resolve ethical dilemmas according to time and place. For example, suppose that you live in a neighborhood in which drug dealers are operating a crystal meth lab or crack house, something that is causing violence in your neighborhood. A relativist would feel justified in committing arson to get rid of the drug house. Another classic example would be a parent stealing a loaf of bread to feed a starving child. Moral relativists resolve ethical dilemmas by weighing competing factors at the moment and then taking the lesser of the evils as the solution. **For Example,** Google and other Internet service providers have agreed to do business in China despite the restrictions the Chinese government places on the use of the Internet and the content of search engines. Such restrictions in the United States would be an unconstitutional violation of our First Amendment. In China, however, government control of information is legal. Google and others testified before Congress that some entry, however restricted, was better for the Chinese people than no access at all. Their decision weighed the conflicting values and concluded that they would use the standard of honoring the law of China despite the censorship.

Thinking Things Through

Corrupt Climates: Good or Bad for Business?

As you examine the following list of countries, those in the column labeled "Least Corrupt" (countries in which government officials are least likely to accept bribes) and those in the column marked "Most Corrupt" (countries in which government officials are most likely to accept bribes), can you comment on the business climates in them? What can you conclude about following the cultural practices of paying bribes? Who is harmed when a company pays bribes?

Least Corrupt (Least Likely to Accept Bribes)

- New Zealand
- Denmark
- Finland
- Sweden
- Singapore
- Norway
- Netherlands
- Australia
- Switzerland
- Canada
- Luxembourg
- Hong Kong
- Iceland

- Germany
- Japan
- Austria
- Barbados
- United Kingdom
- Belgium
- Ireland
- Bahamas
- Chile
- Qatar
- United States
- France
- Santa Lucia

Most Corrupt (Most Likely to Accept Bribes)

- Somalia
- Korea (North)
- Myanmar
- Afghanistan
- Uzbekistan
- Turkmenistan
- Sudan
- Iraq
- Haiti
- Venezuela
- Equatorial Guinea
- Burundi
- Libya

- Democratic Republic of Congo
- Chad
- Yemen
- Kyrgyzstan
- Guinea
- Cambodia
- Zimbabwe
- Paraguay
- Papua New Guinea
- Nepal
- Laos
- Kenya

*From 2011 Transparency International annual survey, **http://www.transparency.org**.

(G) PLATO AND ARISTOTLE: VIRTUE ETHICS. Aristotle and Plato taught that solving ethical dilemmas requires training, that individuals solve ethical dilemmas when they develop and nurture a set of virtues. Aristotle encouraged his students to solve ethical dilemmas using virtues such as honesty, justice, and fairness.

4. The Business Stakeholder Standard of Behavior

stakeholders—those who have a stake, or interest, in the activities of a corporation; stakeholders include employees, members of the community in which the corporation operates, vendors, customers, and any others who are affected by the actions and decisions of the corporation.

stakeholder analysis—the term used when a decision-maker views a problem from different perspectives and measures the impact of a decision on various groups.

Businesses have different constituencies, referred to as **stakeholders**, often with conflicting goals for the business. Shareholders, for example, may share economists' view that earnings, and hence dividends, should be maximized. Members of the community where a business is located are also stakeholders in the business and have an interest in preserving jobs. The employees of the business itself are stakeholders and certainly wish to retain their jobs. Balancing the interests of these stakeholders is a standard used in resolving ethical dilemmas in business.

As Figure 3-1 indicates, stakeholder analysis requires a view of an issue from different perspectives in a transparent way. **Stakeholder analysis** measures the impact of a decision on various groups and then asks whether public disclosure of that decision is defensible. The questions provide insight in a variety of situations and ethical dilemmas. **For Example,** if a lender gives a loan to a debtor without checking income, the lapse seems harmless. But, suppose someone purchases that loan believing the debtor met the standards and the lender verified income. The debtor defaults on the loan. The purchaser has to write down or write off the loan. If enough loans that were not documented go into default, you create the kind of ripples in the real estate and stock markets that occurred in late 2008. Stakeholder analysis helps you to see that the decisions we make in business are not made in isolation or limited in their impact. Figure 3-1 summarizes ethical analysis.

In other ethical dilemmas, a business faces the question of taking voluntary action or simply complying with the law. Some experts maintain that the shareholders' interest is paramount in resolving these conflicts among stakeholders. Others maintain that a business must assume some responsibility for social issues and their

FIGURE 3-1	*Guidelines for Analyzing a Contemplated Action*

1. Define the problem from the decision maker's point of view.
2. Identify who could be injured by the contemplated action.
3. Define the problem from the opposing point of view.
4. Would you (as the decision maker) be willing to tell your family, your supervisor, your CEO, and the board of directors about the planned action?
5. Would you be willing to go before a community meeting, a congressional hearing, or a public forum to describe the action?
6. With full consideration of the facts and alternatives, reach a decision about whether the contemplated action should be taken.

resolution. Economist Milton Friedman expresses his views on resolving the conflicts among stakeholders as follows:

> *A corporate executive's responsibility is to make as much money for the shareholders as possible, as long as he operates within the rules of the game. When an executive decides to take action for reasons of social responsibility, he is taking money from someone else—from the stockholders, in the form of lower dividends; from the employees, in the form of lower wages; or from the consumer, in the form of higher prices. The responsibility of the corporate executive is to fulfill the terms of his contract. If he can't do that in good conscience, then he should quit his job and find another way to do good. He has the right to promote what he regards as desirable moral objectives only with his own money.[2]*

Many businesses feel an obligation to solve social problems because those problems affect their stakeholders. **For Example,** programs such as flextime, job sharing, and telecommuting for work are not legal requirements but voluntary options businesses offer their employees to accommodate family needs. These options are a response to larger societal issues surrounding children and their care but may also serve as a way to retain a quality workforce that is more productive without the worry of poor child care arrangements.

Some businesses are also involved in their communities through employees' volunteer work and companies' charitable donations. For example, a painting company in Phoenix donates paint, and its employees work on weekends painting Habitat for Humanity homes and helping churches get their facilities painted. Apple was able to capture future customers through its donations of computers to schools. Many companies also provide support for employees to participate in volunteer programs in their communities.

Ethics & the Law

Hopping Plankers

Plankers are subway riders who hop the turn styles that is they do not pay. Plankers have a pool that they all contribute to with the funds being used to pay their fines if they are arrested for riding for free. Plankers feel public transportation should be free. Discuss which ethical theories and standards the plankers are following. List the stakeholders in the plankers' actions.

B. Why Is Business Ethics Important?

Ethics and values represent an important part of business success. Business ethics is important for more than the simple justification that "it's the right thing to do." This section covers the significance of ethics in business success.

5. The Importance of Trust

Capitalism succeeds because of trust. Investors provide capital for a business because they believe the business will provide a return on their investment. Customers are willing to purchase products and services from businesses because they believe the businesses will honor their commitments to deliver quality and then stand behind their product or service. Businesses are willing to purchase equipment and hire employees on the assumption that investors will continue to honor their commitment to furnish the necessary funds and will not withdraw their promises or funds. Business investment, growth, and sales are a circle of trust. Although courts provide remedies for breaches of agreements, no economy could grow if it were based solely on positive law and court-mandated performance. It is the reliance on promises, not the reliance on litigation, that produces good business relationships.

6. Business Ethics and Financial Performance

Studies centering on a business's commitment to values and its financial performance suggest that those with the strongest value systems survive and do so successfully. According to the book *Building and Growing a Business Through Good Times and Bad* by Louis Grossman and Marianne Jennings,[3] an in-depth look at companies that paid 100 years of consistent dividends produced a common thread: the companies' commitment to values. All firms studied had focused on high standards for product quality, employee welfare, and customer service.

Poor value choices do have an effect on financial performance. A study of the impact of just breaches of federal law by companies showed that for five years after their regulatory or legal misstep, these companies were still struggling to recover the financial performances they had achieved prior to their legal difficulties.[4]

Over the past few years, there have been devastating stories of companies' fates after ethical lapses. For example, after the congressional hearings revealed that Goldman Sachs took positions in the market that were the opposite of recommendations to its clients, its revenue dropped 18 percent and its share price dropped 32 percent.[5] Columbia Health Care's share price dropped 58 percent and it experienced a 93 percent drop in earnings after it was charged with overbilling for Medicare reimbursements. Its share price dropped from $40 to $18. The nation's largest hospital chain had to spin off 100 hospitals and has paid record fines to settle the charges.[6] When the subprime lender New Century Financial announced that it was finally writing down all the subprime loans it had made that had gone into default but that it had been concealing, it was forced to declare bankruptcy because it was insolvent. On January 1, 2007, New Century had $1.75 billion in market capitalization, but by the middle of March, that figure was $55 million and its stock was delisted by the New York Stock Exchange.

Insurance broker Marsh & McLennan paid $850 million to former clients to settle price-fixing charges brought by then–New York Attorney General Eliot Spitzer. The 134-year-old company saw a drop in both its earnings (64 percent) and its share price (40 percent).[7] The financial crunch resulted in 3,000 employees losing their jobs. AIG, the insurance giant, paid $1.64 billion, to settle charges that it smoothed its earnings over time and was forced to reduce its reported earnings by $1.3 billion.[8] Its $73 share price dropped to $50 before the financial reporting allegations were settled. But AIG continued to underestimate its needed reserves and losses for the subprime mortgage market it had insured. By the fall of 2008, AIG had to be rescued by the federal government with a funds bailout. In 2011, MF Global

[3] Greenwood Press (2002).

[4] Melinda S. Baucus and David A. Baucus, "Paying the Piper: An Empirical Examination of Longer-Term Financial Consequences of Illegal Corporate Behavior," 40 *Academic Management Journal* 129 (1997).

[5] Susanne Craig, "Goldman's Safer Position Eats Deeply Into Its Profits," *New York Times*, July 20, 2011, p. B4.

[6] Lucette Lagnado, "Columbia/HCA Warns of Profit Decline," *Wall Street Journal*, September 10, 1987, A3.

[7] Ian McDonald, "After Spitzer Probe, Marsh CEO Tries Corporate Triage," *Wall Street Journal*, August 29, 2005 A1, A5.

[8] Ian McDonald and Liam Pleven, "AIG Reaches Accord with Regulators, Stock Rises but May Still Be a Bargain," *Wall Street Journal*, February 10, 2006, C1, C4.

had to declare bankruptcy after its risky bets on Greek bonds resulted in $1.6 billion in losses. Over 1,000 employees lost their jobs and the firm is being liquidated.[9]

Ethics & the Law

AIG Bailout and Bonuses

In March 2009, after it received government assistance, AIG announced the payment of $100 million in bonuses to various executives and managers in the company. There was a great hue and cry from regulators, legislators, and the public. However, AIG maintained it was contractually obligated to pay the bonuses. For a time, AIG had to cover its name on its New York office building because of public protests. The executives who received the bonuses received death threats. Evaluate the ethical issues related to the bonus payments. Evaluate the ethical issues in the public response to those bonuses. Be sure to discuss AIG's argument on the legal requirements for the bonuses.

7. The Importance of a Good Reputation

Richard Teerlink, the CEO of Harley-Davidson, once said, "A reputation, good or bad, is tough to shake."[10] A breach of ethics is costly to a firm not only in the financial sense of drops in earnings and possible fines. A breach of ethics also often carries with it a lasting memory that affects the business and its sales for years to come. **For Example,** the Peanut Corporation of America had to declare bankruptcy in 2009 after government officials discovered that its plant was the source of salmonella poisonings among those customers who had eaten peanut products that used Peanut Corporation's base in their production. Records showed that Peanut Corporation continued to produce the product even after salmonella warnings and questions arose. The company's name and image became so damaged that it could not continue to make sales. When an ethical breach occurs, businesses lose that component of trust important to customers' decisions to buy and invest.

8. Business Ethics and Business Regulation: Public Policy, Law, and Ethics

When business behavior results in complaints from employees, investors, or customers, laws or regulations are often used to change the behavior. **For Example,** the bankruptcy of Lehman Brothers, the near-collapse of Bear Stearns, and the losses at Merrill Lynch and AIG in 2008–2009 all resulted from the subprime mortgage financial derivative investment market, a market that had previously been a relatively regulation-free environment. The companies had billions of dollars of exposure because of their sales and purchases of financial instruments that were tied to the subprime mortgage market that ultimately resulted in high rates of foreclosure and nearly worthless loans. Congress, the Securities and Exchange Commission (SEC), and the Federal Reserve all stepped in to regulate virtually all aspects of mortgage transactions, including the lenders and others who were involved in packaging the loans into financial products.

[9] Mike Spector, Aaron Lucchetti, and Liam Pleven, "Corzine Firm's Final Struggles," *Wall Street Journal*, November 5–6, 2011, p. A1.
[10] David K. Wright, *The Harley-Davidson Motor Co.: An Official Ninety-Year History* (Milwaukee: Motorbook International, 1993).

Confusion among consumers about car leasing and its true costs and the fees applicable at the end of the lease terms caused the Federal Reserve (now the Consumer Financial Protection Bureau) to expand its regulation of credit to car leases. Figure 3-2 depicts the relationships among ethics, the social forces of customers and investors, and the laws that are passed to remedy the problems raised as part of the social forces movement.

Businesses that act voluntarily on the basis of value choices often avoid the costs and the sometimes arbitrariness of legislation and regulation. Voluntary change by businesses is less costly and is considered less intrusive.

Businesses that respond to social forces and the movements of the cycle of societal interaction often gain a competitive advantage. Businesses that act irresponsibly and disregard society's views and desire for change speed the transition from value choice to enforceable law. Businesses should watch the cycle of social forces and follow trends there to understand the values attached to certain activities and responses. These values motivate change either in the form of voluntary business activity or legislation. All values that precipitate change have one of several basic underlying goals. These underlying goals are discussed in the following sections.

(A) PROTECTION OF THE STATE. A number of laws exist today because of an underlying goal or value of protection of the state. The U.S Patriot Act and airport security regulations are examples of government programs and regulations created with the protection and security of the state as the goal.

(B) PROTECTION OF THE PERSON. A second social force is protection of the person. Criminal laws are devoted to protection of individuals and their properties. In addition, civil suits permit private remedies for wrongful acts toward people and their property. Over time, the protection of personal rights has expanded to include the rights of privacy and the protection of individuals from defamation. Laws continue to evolve to protect the reputations, privacy, and mental and physical well-being of individuals.

FIGURE 3-2	*The Endless Cycle of Societal Interaction*

© Cengage Learning

Ethics & the Law

Ethics, Trust, and Markets

The cover of *Fortune* magazine from May 14, 2001, featured a picture of Wall Street financial analyst Mary Meeker and the words, "Can we ever trust again?"[*] The inside story focused on the relationship of underwriters, analysts, and brokerage houses with the high-tech companies whose stocks they were touting and selling, knowing there were questionable accounting practices and a lack of earnings at these companies. When the dot-com market bubble burst, the losses to shareholders were catastrophic. Those in the financial markets had too much at stake to be honest with investors. They did not break the law, however.

In 2002, when companies, such as Enron, WorldCom, and Tyco had to take write-downs because of years of overstating earnings, the market once again looked at analysts, wondering how they had failed to catch the accounting issues. The cover of *Fortune* read, "In Search of the Last Honest Analyst."[**]

During 2007, *Fortune* ran a cover with the pictures of the CEOs of the major Wall Street investment firms (such as Merrill Lynch, Bear Stearns, and Lehman Brothers) who had managed to lose trillions of investors' pension and 401(k) plans to risky investments in subprime mortgages that were marketed as low-risk investments. The cover's headline asked, "What Were They Smoking?"[***] In 2011, following the collapse of Jon Corzine's MF Global hedge fund, a headline read, "Trustee Says More Cash Is Missing at MF Global." The estimated loss to investors at the firm was $1.6 billion.[****]

What do these headlines convey about the importance of trust and its role in markets?

[*]"Can We Ever Trust Again?" *Fortune*, May 14, 2001 (cover).
[**]"In Search of the Last Honest Analyst," *Fortune*, June 10, 2002 (cover).

[***]"What Were They Smoking?" *Fortune*, November 26, 2007 (cover).
[****]Michael J. de la Merced and Ben Protess, "Trustee Says More Cash Is Missing at MF Global," *New York Times*, November 22, 2011, p. B1.

(c) PROTECTION OF PUBLIC HEALTH, SAFETY, AND MORALS. Food-labeling regulations are an example of laws grounded in the value of protecting the safety and health of individuals. Food and restaurant inspections, mandatory inoculation, speed limits on roadways, mandatory smoke detectors and sprinkler systems in hotels, and prohibitions on the sale of alcohol to minors are all examples of laws based on the value of safety for the public. Zoning laws that prohibit the operation of adult bookstores and movie theaters near schools and churches are examples of laws based on moral values.

(d) PROTECTION OF PROPERTY: ITS USE AND TITLE. Someone who steals another's automobile is a thief and is punished by law with fines and/or imprisonment. A zoning law that prohibits the operation of a steel mill in a residential area also provides protection for property. A civil suit brought to recover royalties lost because of another's infringement of one's copyrighted materials is based on federal laws that afford protection for property rights in nontangible or intellectual property (see Chapter 10). Laws afford protection of title for all forms of property. The deed recorded in the land record is the legal mechanism for protecting the owner's title. The copyright on a software program or a song protects the creator's rights in that intellectual property. The title documents issued by a department of motor vehicles afford protection of title for the owner of a vehicle.

Those who have title to property are generally free to use the property in any manner they see fit. However, even ownership has restrictions imposed by law. A business may operate a factory on its real property, but if the factory creates a great deal of pollution, adjoining landowners may successfully establish it as a nuisance (see Chapter 49) that interferes with their use and enjoyment of their land.

Environmental laws also emerged as regulation of land use in response to concerns about legal, but harmful, emissions by companies.

(E) PROTECTION OF PERSONAL RIGHTS. The desire for freedom from economic domination resulted in the free enterprise philosophy that exists in the United States today. Individual freedoms and personal rights continue as a focus of value discussions followed by legislation if those individual rights are violated.

(F) ENFORCEMENT OF INDIVIDUAL INTENT. When we voluntarily enter into a contract, we have a responsibility to fulfill the promises made in that agreement. Principles of honesty and the honoring of commitments are the ethical values at the heart of the parties' conduct in carrying out contracts. If, however, the parties do not keep their promises, the law does enforce transactions through sets of rules governing requirements for them. **For Example,** the law will carry out the intentions of the parties to a business transaction through judicial enforcement of contract rights and damages.

(G) PROTECTION FROM EXPLOITATION, FRAUD, AND OPPRESSION. Many laws have evolved because businesses took advantage of others. Minors, or persons under legal age (see Chapter 14), are given special protections under contract laws that permit them to disaffirm their contracts so they are not disadvantaged by excessive commitments without the benefit of the wisdom of age and with the oppressive presence of an adult party.

The federal laws on disclosure in the sales of securities and shareholder relations (see Chapters 45 and 46) were developed following the 1929 stock market crash when many investors lost all they had because of the lack of candor and information by the businesses in which they were investing.

(H) FURTHERANCE OF TRADE. Some laws are the result of social forces seeking to simplify business and trade. Credit laws, regulations, and protections have made additional capital available for businesses and provided consumers with alternatives to cash purchases. The laws on checks, drafts, and notes have created instruments used to facilitate trade.

(I) PROTECTION OF CREDITORS AND REHABILITATION OF DEBTORS. Mortgages, security interests, and surety relationships (see Chapters 32, 34, and 49) are mechanisms created by law to provide creditors the legal mechanisms for collecting their obligations.

When collection techniques became excessive and exploitative, new laws on debtors' rights were enacted. Debtors' prisons were abolished. Congress mandated disclosure requirements for credit contracts. The Fair Debt Collections Practices Act (see Chapter 33) limited collection techniques. The remedy of bankruptcy was afforded debtors under federal law to provide them an opportunity to begin a new economic life when their existing debts reached an excessive level and could no longer be paid in a timely fashion (see Chapter 35).

(J) STABILITY AND FLEXIBILITY. Because of the desire for stability, courts will ordinarily follow former decisions unless there is a strong reason to depart from them. (See Chapter 1 for more discussion of precedent.) Similarly, when no former case bears on the point involved, a court will try to reach a decision that is a logical extension of some former decision or that follows a former decision by analogy rather than strike out on a new path to reach a decision unrelated to the past.

C. How to Recognize and Resolve Ethical Dilemmas

Business managers often find themselves in circumstances in which they are unclear about right and wrong and are confused about how to resolve the dilemmas they face. A recent survey showed that 98 percent of all Fortune 500 companies have codes of ethics designed to help their employees recognize and resolve ethical dilemmas. Nearly 99 percent of those firms provide their employees some form of training in ethics.[11] Almost 80 percent of companies now have an ethics officer. These codes of ethics provide employees information about categories of behavior that constitute ethical breaches. Regardless of the industry, the type of business, or the size of the company, certain universal categories can help managers recognize ethical dilemmas. Figure 3-3 provides a list of those categories.

9. Categories of Ethical Behavior

(A) Integrity and Truthfulness. A famous anonymous quote on truth is, "Circumstances beyond your control will cause the truth to come out, no matter what." As discussed earlier, trust is a key component of business relationships and of the free enterprise system. Trust begins with the belief that honesty is at the heart of relationships. Many contract remedies in law are based on the failure of the parties to be truthful with each other. **For Example,** if you purchase a home that has been certified as termite free but you discover termites in the home shortly after you move in, someone has not been truthful. If you also discover that two termite inspections were conducted and that the first one, which revealed there were termites, was concealed from you, your trust in both the sellers and their exterminators is diminished.

integrity—the adherence to one's values and principles despite the costs and consequences.

   Integrity is the adherence to one's values and principles despite the costs and consequences. **For Example,** an executive contracted with a variety of companies to sell his hard-to-find computer components. When he was approached by one of his largest customers to break a contract with a small customer, the executive refused. The customer assured the executive it would be his last order with the company if he did not get more components. Despite facing the threat of losing a multimillion-

---

FIGURE 3-3	*Categories of Ethical Behavior*

1. Integrity and truthfulness
2. Promise keeping
3. Loyalty—avoiding conflicts of interest
4. Fairness
5. Doing no harm
6. Maintaining confidentiality

---

[11] Jason Lunday, "The Need for More Effective Standards of Conduct," *Corporate Compliance Insights*, June 8, 2010, **http://www.corporatecomplianceinsights.com/the-need-for-more-effective-standards-of-conduct/**

Ethics & the Law

Lying to Get into a Top School

The University of California at Berkeley has implemented a new step in its admission process. The Haas School of Business has begun running background checks on students who have applied to determine whether the information in their applications is correct. The Wharton School implemented a similar procedure and charges applicants a $35 fee for these background checks.

Of the 100 students admitted to Berkeley in the fall of 2003, 5 students were found to have offered false information on their admissions applications. The most common type of false information

was the job titles they held, and the second most common type was their number of years of work experience. Haas admissions officers indicated that had the students not lied, they otherwise met the GMAT score and GPA standards for admission to Haas.

What risk do the students take in lying on their applications? What are the long-term consequences?

Source: "Cheaters Don't Make the Grade at Berkeley Business School," **www.azcentral.com**, March 14, 2003, AP wire reports.

dollar customer, the executive fulfilled his promises to the small purchasers. The executive kept his word on all of his contracts and demonstrated integrity.

(B) PROMISE KEEPING. If we examined the types of things we do in a day, we will find that most of them are based on promises. We promise to deliver goods either with or without a contract. We promise to pay the dentist for our dental work. We promise to provide someone with a ride. Keeping those promises, regardless of whether there is a legal obligation to do so, is a key component of being an ethical person and practicing ethical business. Keeping promises is also evidence of integrity for example.

(C) LOYALTY—AVOIDING CONFLICTS OF INTEREST. An employee who works for a company owes allegiance to that company. Conduct that compromises that loyalty is a **conflict of interest**. **For Example,** suppose that your sister operates her own catering business. Your company is seeking a caterer for its monthly management meetings. You are responsible for these meetings and could hire your sister to furnish the lunches for the meetings. Your sister would have a substantial contract, and your problems with meal logistics would be solved. Nearly all companies have a provision in their codes of ethics covering this situation. An employee cannot hire a relative, friend, or even her own company without special permission because it is a conflict of interest. Your loyalty to your sister conflicts with the loyalty to your employer, which requires you to make the best decision at the best price.

conflict of interest – conduct that compromises an employee's allegiance to that company.

A conflict of interest arises when a purchasing agent accepts gifts from suppliers, vendors, or manufacturers' representatives. The purchasing agent has introduced into the buy-sell relationship an element of *quid pro quo,* or the supplier's expectation that the gift will bring about a return from the agent in the form of a contract. Some companies have zero tolerance for conflicts and establish a complete prohibition on employees accepting any gifts from suppliers and manufacturers. **For Example,** Wal-Mart buyers are not permitted to accept even a cup of coffee from potential merchandise suppliers, and Amgen's buyers can go out to dinner with a supplier only if Amgen pays.

(D) DOING NO HARM. Imagine selling a product that your company's internal research shows presents significant health dangers to its users. Selling the product without disclosure of the information is unfair. There is the additional ethical breach of

Sports & Entertainment Law

Identity Theft and MLB

The Washington Nationals signed Esmailyn "Smiley" Gonzalez (aka Carlos Gonzalez), whom they believed to be a 19-year-old phenomenon, for $1.4 million. Mr. Gonzalez turned out to be a 23-year-old who had presented the Nationals with fake identification when he first signed for the minor leagues, with the ID placing his age at 16. After the Nationals signed, they realized that they did not have a wonder player and that his years left for playing were far less than they had figured. "You know, to say I'm disappointed doesn't begin to describe how I feel. I'm angry. I am very angry. We've been defrauded, and make no mistake—this wasn't a college kid with a fake ID that came in and did this. This was a deliberate, premeditated fraud with a lot more to this story, and we are going to get to the bottom of it. There were many, many people involved in this premeditated fraud."* Some fans and Mr. Gonzalez and his agent did not see any problem because they never misrepresented his skill. They say he was signed because of his skill, not his age. Should the Nationals have been told his real age? Is it fraud or is it an ethical issue? Both? What will the impact be on the sports agent?

*Chico Harlan, "I'm Angry, We've Been Defrauded," *Washington Post*, September 21, 2010.
http://voices.washingtonpost.com/nationalsjournal/2010/09/a_new_development_in_the_smile.html

physical harm to your customers and users. Ford designed and sold its Pinto with a fundamental flaw in the placement of the car's gas tank. Rear-end collisions in which a Pinto was involved resulted, even at very low speeds, in fires that engulfed the car so quickly that occupants could not always escape from it. An internal memo from engineers at Ford revealed that employees had considered doing an analysis of the risk of the tanks versus the cost of redesign but never did. The late Peter Drucker's advice on ethics for businesses is ***primum non nocere***, or "above all, do no harm." Such a rule might have helped Ford.

primum non nocere – above all do no harm.

(E) MAINTAINING CONFIDENTIALITY. Often the success of a business depends on the information or technology that it holds. If the competitive edge that comes from the business's peculiar niche or knowledge is lost through disclosure, so are its profits. Employees not only owe a duty of loyalty to their employers, but they also owe an obligation of confidentiality. Employees should not use, either personally or through a competitor, information they have obtained through their employer's work or research. Providing customer lists or leads is a breach of employees' obligation of confidentiality.

In addition, managers have responsibilities regarding their employees' privacy. Performance evaluations of individual employees are private and should never be disclosed or revealed, even in one-on-one conversations outside the lines of authority and the workplace.

10. Resolving Ethical Dilemmas

Recognizing an ethical dilemma is perhaps the easiest part of business ethics. Resolution of that dilemma is more difficult. The earlier section on stakeholders offers one model for resolution of ethical dilemmas (see Figure 3-1). Other models have been developed to provide managers analytical methods for resolving dilemmas in a timely fashion.

E-Commerce & Cyberlaw

Piggybacking on Wireless Networks

A new issue that has evolved because of technology could require legal steps to stop it. People are "piggybacking" or tapping onto their neighbors' wireless Internet connection. The original subscriber pays a monthly fee for the service, but without security, people located in the area are able to tap into the wireless network, which bogs down the speed of the service. Once limited to geeks and hackers, the practice is now common among the ordinary folk who just want free Internet service.

One college student said, "I don't think it's stealing. I always find [P]eople out there ... aren't protecting their connection, so I just feel free to go ahead and use it."* According to a recent survey, only about 30 percent of the 4,500 wireless networks onto which the surveyors logged were encrypted, and another survey shows that 32 percent of us do engage in Wi-Fi piggybacking.

An apartment dweller said she leaves her connection wide open because "I'm sticking it to the man. I open up my network, leave it wide open for anyone to jump on." One of the users of another's wireless network said, "I feel sort of bad about it, but I do it anyway. It just seems harmless." She said that if she gets caught, I'll just play the dumb card."

Some neighbors offer to pay those with wireless service in exchange for their occasional use rather than paying a wireless company for full-blown service. However, the original subscribers do not really want to run their own Internet service.

Do you think we need new legislation to cover this activity? What do you think of the users' statements? Is their conduct legal? Is it ethical?

*Michael Marriott, "Hey Neighbor, Stop Piggybacking on My Wireless," *New York Times*, March 5, 2006, A1, A23.

(A) BLANCHARD AND PEALE THREE-PART TEST. Dr. Kenneth Blanchard, author of the books on the *One-Minute Manager,* and the late Dr. Norman Vincent Peale developed a model for evaluating ethical breaches that is widely used among Fortune 500 companies.[12] To evaluate situations, ask the following three questions: Is it legal? Is it balanced? How does it make me feel?

In answering the questions on legality, a manager should look to positive law both within and outside the company. If the proposed conduct would violate antitrust laws, the manager's analysis can stop there. If the proposed conduct would violate company policy, the manager's analysis can stop. In the field of business ethics, there is little room for civil disobedience. Compliance with the law is a critical component of a successful ethics policy in any company.

The second question on balance forces the manager to examine the ethical value of fairness. A good follow-up question is, "How would I want to be treated in this circumstance?" Perhaps the decision to downsize must be made, but couldn't the company offer the employees a severance package and outplacement assistance to ease the transition?

The final question of the Blanchard and Peale model is conscience based. Although some managers may employ any tactics to maximize profits, this final question forces a manager to examine the physical impact of a decision: Does it cause sleeplessness or appetite changes? Personalizing business choices often helps managers to see the potential harm that comes from poor ethical choices.

(B) THE FRONT-PAGE-OF-THE-NEWSPAPER TEST. This simple but effective model for ethical evaluation helps a manager visualize the public disclosure of proposed conduct.

[12] Kenneth Blanchard and Norman Vincent Peale, *The Power of Ethical Management* (New York: William Morrow, 1986).

When he temporarily took over as the leader of Salomon Brothers after its bond-trading controversy, Warren Buffett described the newspaper test as follows:

> *Contemplating any business act, an employee should ask himself whether he would be willing to see it immediately described by an informed and critical reporter on the front page of his local paper, there to be read by his spouse, children, and friends. At Salomon, we simply want no part of any activities that pass legal tests but that we, as citizens, would find offensive.*[13]

(c) Laura Nash Model. In her work, business ethicist Laura Nash has developed a series of questions to help businesspeople reach the right decision in ethical dilemmas. These are her questions: Have you defined the problem accurately? How would you define the problem if you stood on the other side of the fence? How did this situation occur in the first place? What is your intention in making this decision? How does the intention compare with the probable results? Whom could your decision or action injure? Can you discuss your decision with the affected parties? Are you confident that your position will be as valid over a long period of time as it seems now? Could you discuss your decision with your supervisor, coworkers, officers, board, friends, and family?

The Nash model requires an examination of the dilemma from all perspectives. Defining the problem and how the problem arose provides the business assistance in avoiding the dilemma again. **For Example,** suppose that a supervisor is asked to provide a reference for a friend who works for her. The supervisor is hesitant because

Ethics & the Law

Pumping Up the SAT Scores for a Good Ranking

Since 2005, Claremont McKenna, ranked #9 on *U.S. News & World Report's* best liberal arts colleges in the country, has been lopping on a few points here and there to its entering students' average SAT score before reporting those numbers to *U.S. News & World Report* and rating organizations such as the Princeton Review. For example, in 2010, its combined median score was reported as 1410, rather than its actual 1400. And its 75th percentile was reported at 1510, when it was, in reality, 1480.

Oops! Turns out the academic world is darn near as competitive as Wall Street when it comes to rankings and ratings. In fact, so competitive are those of the ivory tower that they used the same strategies: cook the books and hope no one notices.

Claremont McKenna's vice president and dean of admissions has been removed from his job title on the college Website. President Pamela B. Gann explained the problem and concluded, "As an institution of higher education with a deep and consistent commitment to the integrity of our academic activities, and particularly, our reporting of institutional data, we take this situation very seriously."

Indeed. Now, if we could just get the rankings and ratings organizations to respond with appropriate outrage. From Robert Franek of the Princeton Review, we have these thoughts, "That is a pretty mild difference in a point score. That said, 10 points, 20 points to a student that isn't getting that score on the SAT could be an important distinction." Yes, but even without the numbers difference, it is an important distinction. Claremont McKenna was not honest, and students who rely on reviews when such an obvious flaw is on the table deserve whatever fate awaits them at an institution that would pull a statistical stunt (however it may have impacted the rankings/ratings). Oh, and Mr. Franek finished with a flourish, "I feel like so many schools have a very clear obligation to college-bound students to report this information honestly." Actually, it would be all schools, not just "so many," and the reporting of correct data is not just a "clear obligation," it is an ethical responsibility.

Daniel E. Slotnik and Richard Pérez-Peña, "College Sats It Exaggerrated SAT Figures for Rating," *New York Times*, Jan. 31, 2012, p. A12.

---

[13] Janet Lowe, *Warren Buffett Speaks: Wit and Wisdom from the World's Greatest Investor* (New York: Wiley, 1997).

the friend has not been a very good employee. The ethical dilemma the manager believes she faces is whether to lie or tell the truth about the employee. The real ethical dilemma is why the supervisor never provided evaluation or feedback indicating the friend's poor performance. Avoiding the problem in the future is possible through candid evaluations. Resolving the problem requires that the supervisor talk to her friend now about the issue of performance and the problem with serving as a reference.

One final aspect of the Nash model that businesspeople find helpful is a question that asks for a perspective on an issue from family and friends. The problem of groupthink in business situations is very real. As businesspeople sit together in a room and discuss an ethical dilemma, they can persuade each other to think the same way. The power of consensus can overwhelm each person's concerns and values. There is a certain fear in bringing up a different point of view in a business meeting. Proper perspective is often lost as the discussion centers around numbers. Therefore, bringing in the views of an outsider is often helpful. **For Example,** when McNeil, the manufacturer of Tylenol, faced the cyanide poisonings from contaminated capsules sold in the Chicago area, it had to make a decision about the existing Tylenol inventory. It was clear to both insiders and outsiders that the poison had not been put in the capsules at McNeil but after delivery to the stores. Despite the huge numbers involved in the recall and the destruction of inventory, the McNeil managers made the decision easily because they viewed the risk to their own families, that is, from the outside. From this standpoint, the issue became a question of human life, not of numbers.[14]

LawFlix

Breaking Away (1979) (PG)

In this story about "cutters" (a nickname for natives of Bloomington, Indiana), a recent high school graduate trains to be a first-class bike rider. He idolizes the Italian world racing team and enters an Indiana race to have the opportunity to compete with them. He does well in the race and manages to catch up and keep pace with the Italian team. As he rides alongside his idols, one of the members of the Italian team places a tire pump in his spoke. His bike crashes, he loses the race and is injured. He becomes disillusioned. Is this experience like business? Do unethical tactics get you ahead? Do nice guys finish last? Are there sanctions for unethical conduct?

Jaws (1975) (PG-13)

The movie that shot Steven Spielberg to directorial legend brings us the classic business dilemma of what to do when you have a high-risk/low-probability event that you know about but about which the public has no knowledge. Do you stop? But what about the economic losses?

Hoosiers (1986) (PG)

Often called the "greatest sports movie ever made," this story of a coach with a history and a small-town team presents several life-defining ethical moments. In one, with advancement to the finals on the table, Coach Norman Dale grapples with whether he should allow one of his injured players to continue when he has no depth on his bench. What do you do when your values are in conflict?

---

[14] "Brief History of Johnson & Johnson" (company pamphlet, 1992).

LawFlix

Continued

The Family Man (2000) (PG-13)

Nicolas Cage plays a Wall Street billionaire who is suddenly given a suburban life in New Jersey with all of its family life and financial constraints. He is forced to examine who he really is and what is important.

MAKE THE CONNECTION

SUMMARY

Business ethics is the application of values and standards to business conduct and decisions. These values originate in various sources from positive (codified) law to natural law to ethical theories and standards and on to stakeholder values. Business ethics is important because trust is a critical component of good business relationships and free enterprise. A business with values will enjoy the additional competitive advantage of a good reputation and, over the long term, better earnings. When businesses make decisions that violate basic ethical standards, they set into motion social forces and cause the area of abuse to be regulated, resulting in additional costs and restrictions for business. Voluntary value choices by businesses position them for a competitive advantage.

The categories of ethical values in business are truthfulness and integrity, promise keeping, loyalty and avoiding conflicts of interest, fairness, doing no harm, and maintaining confidentiality.

Resolution of ethical dilemmas is possible through the use of various models that require a businessperson to examine the impact of a decision before it is made. These models include stakeholder analysis, the Blanchard and Peale test, the front-page-of-the-newspaper test, and the Laura Nash model.

LEARNING OUTCOMES

After studying this chapter, you should be able to clearly explain:

A. What Is Business Ethics?

L0.1 Define business ethics
See the discussion of the definition, balancing the goal of profits with the values of individuals and society, on p. 41–42.

B. Why Is Business Ethics Important?

L0.2 Discuss why ethics are important in business
See "The Importance of Trust" on p. 42.
See "Business Ethics and Financial Performance" on p. 43.
See "The Importance of a Good Reputation" on p. 44.

See Ethics & the Law on market trust on p. 46.

C. How to Recognize and Resolve Ethical Dilemmas

L0.3 Describe how to recognize and resolve ethical dilemmas

See "Integrity and Truthfulness" on p. 48.
See "Promise Keeping" on p. 49.
See "Loyalty—Avoiding Conflicts of Interest" on p. 49.

See "Doing No Harm" on p. 49.
See "Maintaining Confidentiality" on p. 50.
See "Resolving Ethical Dilemmas" on p. 50.
See "Blanchard and Peale Three-Part Test" on p. 51.
See "The Front-Page-of-the-Newspaper Test" on p. 51.
See Ethics & the Law on pumping up SAT scores on p. 52.
See "Laura Nash Model" on p. 52.

KEY TERMS

business ethics
civil disobedience
conflict of interest
entitlement theory
ethics
ethical egoism

integrity
Kant's categorical imperative
moral relativists
natural law
positive law
primum non nocere

rights theory
social contract
stakeholder analysis
stakeholders
theory of justice
utilitarians

QUESTIONS AND CASE PROBLEMS

1. Marty Mankamyer, the president of the United States Olympic Committee (USOC), resigned in early February 2003 following reports in *The Denver Post* that indicated she had demanded a commission from a fellow real estate broker in the Colorado Springs area, the home of the USOC, who had sold property to Lloyd Ward, the CEO of the USOC. Mr. Ward had purchased a 1.3-acre lot in Colorado Springs for $475,000 and had paid the listing broker, Brigette Ruskin, a commission.

   Ms. Mankamyer allegedly demanded a portion of the commission from Ms. Ruskin, and Ms. Ruskin sent her a check. Ms. Mankamyer had shown Mr. Ward and his wife properties in the area when they were being considered for the job and when he was considering taking the job. However, Mrs. Ward indicated that Ms. Mankamyer did not identify herself as a real estate agent and that she assumed that Ms. Mankamyer was showing the properties as a "goodwill gesture."[15] What conflicts of interest do you see here?

2. Ann Elkin, who works for Brill Co., has been sent out to conduct two customer evaluations,

which have gone much more quickly than Ann anticipated. Her supervisor does not expect Ann back until after lunch. It is now 10:30 A.M., and Ann would like to run some personal errands and then go to lunch before returning to work at 1:00 P.M. Should Ann take the time? Would you? Why or why not? Be sure to consider the categories of ethical values and apply one or two models before reaching your conclusion.

3. Fred Sanguine is a New York City produce broker. Ned Santini is a 19-year-old college student who works for Sanguine from 4:00 A.M. until 7:00 A.M. each weekday before he attends classes at Pace University. Fred has instructed Ned on the proper packing of produce as follows: "Look, put the bad and small cherries at the bottom. Do the same with the strawberries and blueberries. Put the best fruit on top and hide the bad stuff at the bottom. This way I get top dollar on all that I sell." Ned is uncomfortable about the instructions, but, as he explains to his roommate, "It's not me doing it. I'm just following orders. Besides, I need the job."

   Should Ned just follow instructions? Is the manner in which the fruit is packed unethical?

---

[15] Richard Sandomir, "U.S. Olympic Chief Resigns in a Furor Over Ethics Issues," *New York Times*, February 5, 2003, A1, C17; Bill Briggs, *Realtor Waving Red Flag*, **www.denverpost.com**, February 4, 2003.

Would you do it? Why or why not? Is anyone really harmed by the practice?

4. Alan Gellen is the facilities manager for the city of Milwaukee and makes all final decisions on purchasing items such as chairs, lights, and other supplies and materials. Alan also makes the final decisions for the award of contracts to food vendors at event sites. Grand Beef Franks has submitted a bid to be one of the city's vendors. Alan went to school with Grand Beef's owner, Steve Grand, who phones Alan and explains that Grand Beef owns a condominium in Maui that Alan could use. Steve's offer to Alan is: "All it would cost you for a vacation is your airfare. The condo is fully stocked with food. Just let me know."

Should Alan take the offer? Would you? Be sure to determine which category of ethical values this situation involves and to apply several models as you resolve the question of whether Alan should accept the invitation.

5. A Dillard's customer brought in a pair of moderately expensive dress shoes, expressing a desire to return them because they just weren't quite right. As the manager processed the order she checked inside the box to be sure that the shoes in the box were the shoes that matched the box – past experience dictated that follow-up on returns. The shoes were the correct ones for the box, but there was another issue. The shoes had masking tape on the bottom – masking tape that was dirty. When the manager returned to the customer she said, "You forgot to remove the masking tape from your shoes." The customer responded, "I only wore them once. That's all I needed them for."

From Neiman Marcus to Saks to Dillard's, managers have to stay one step ahead of customers, or lessees, who buy, or lease for free, dresses and now shoes for one use with premeditated intent to return the merchandise. Stores now place tags strategically so that the dresses cannot be worn without cutting them off and there are no returns if the tags are cut off on formal wear.

Ace Hardware and Home Depot have customers who "buy" a special tool, try to use it once, and then return it. The hardware/home improvement stores are left with opened packaging and used goods by buy-it-temporarily customers.

List some consequences for this behavior by customers.

6. Adam Smith wrote the following in *The Theory of Moral Sentiments*:

In the practice of the other virtues, our conduct should rather be directed by a certain idea of propriety, by a certain taste for a particular tenor of conduct, than by any regard to a precise maxim or rule; and we should consider the end and foundation of the rule, more than the rule itself.[16]

Do you think Adam Smith adhered to positive law as his ethical standard? Was he a moral relativist? Does his quote match stakeholder analysis? What would his ethical posture be on violating the law?

7. A new phenomenon for admissions to MBA programs is hiring consultants to help applicants hone their applications. About 20 percent of those who apply to the top MBA programs have hired consultants at a cost of $150 to $200 per hour to help them say and do the right things to be admitted. The total cost for most who use a consultant is $5,000. The consultants help with personal essays and applications. One admissions officer points out that one function of the consultant is to draw out and emphasize skills that the applicant may not see as important. For example, playing the piano is looked upon favorably because it shows discipline and focus.

However, admissions committees are becoming adept at spotting the applications via consultant because, as the faculty describe it, these essays and applications have a certain "sameness" to them. The Fuqua School at North Carolina suggests that students simply call the admissions office and get comparable advice for free. Is it ethical to use an admissions consultant? When would you cross a line in using the consultant on the essay?

8. "I was very upset that there's that many dishonest people," said Andrea Reuland, the owner of Trigs Shell Station in Minocqua, Wisconsin.

---

[16] Adam Smith, *The Theory of Moral Sentiments* (Arlington House, 1969; originally published in 1769).

She lost $3 per gallon on 586 gallons of gas sold during a 45-minute period when local residents phoned others to come and get gas because an employee had made a mistake and entered the price at 32.9 cents vs. $3.299 per gallon.

Eighty-seven percent of the people who responded to a survey about the incident said they would have done the same thing as the Minocqua residents.

Describe who is affected by what buyers did by not paying the correct price for the gas. Describe a simple test for resolving an ethical dilemma such as this where you can get something for free or very little.

9. The state of Arizona mandates emissions testing for cars before drivers can obtain updated registrations. The state hires a contractor to conduct the emissions tests in the various emissions-testing facilities around the state. In October 1999, the Arizona attorney general announced the arrest of 13 workers at one of the emissions-testing facilities for allegedly taking payoffs of between $50 and $200 from car owners to pass their cars on the emissions tests when those cars fell below emissions standards and would not have been registered. Nearly half of the staff at the emissions facility were arrested.

Why is it a crime for someone working in a government-sponsored facility to accept a payment for a desired outcome? Do the payoffs to the workers really harm anyone?

10. The president and athletic director at the University of California at Los Angeles (UCLA) fired the school's basketball coach because an expense form he had submitted for reimbursement had the names of two students he said had joined him for a recruiting dinner. The students had not been to the dinner. The coach was stunned because he had been at UCLA for eight years and had established a winning program. He said, "And to throw it all away on a meal?" Do you agree with the coach's assessment? Was it too harsh to fire him for one inaccurate expense form? Did the coach commit an ethical breach?

11. When some runners in the New York City Marathon hit the Queensboro Bridge,

temptation sets in and, rather than finishing the last 10 miles through Harlem and the Bronx, they hop a ride on the subway and head toward the finish line at Central Park. A total of 46 runners used the subway solution to finish the race in the 2008 NYC Marathon. When one runner was questioned about his unusual time, he admitted to using the subway and said, "So I skipped a few boroughs. I didn't do anything illegal." How would you respond to his point that he did not break the law? Why should we worry about some runners?

12. David A. Vise, a Pulitzer Prize winner and a reporter for the *Washington Post,* wrote the book *The Bureau and the Mole.* When the book hit the market, Mr. Vise purchased 20,000 copies via Barnes & Noble.com, taking advantage of both free shipping offered by the publisher and a discounted initial price. Mr. Vise's book had already hit the *New York Times'* bestseller list in the week before the purchases. He used the books he purchased to conduct online sales of autographed copies of the books, and then returned 17,500 books and asked for his money back. However, that return of 17,500 books represented more books than a publisher generally runs for a book. Mr. Vise said that he did not intend to manipulate the market or profit from the transactions. He said his only intent was to "increase awareness of *The Bureau and the Mole.*"

Mr. Vise's editor offered to pay Barnes & Noble for any expenses it incurred. Was it ethical to do what Mr. Vise did? Was he within his rights to return the books? What are his remedies? Does Barnes & Noble have any rights?

13. Former Enron Chief Financial Officer Andrew Fastow, in his testimony against his former bosses at their criminal trial for fraud, said, "I thought I was being a hero for Enron. At the time, I thought I was helping myself and helping Enron to make its numbers." Mr. Fastow also added, however, "I lost my moral compass."

Are you able to classify Mr. Fastow into a particular ethical standard or principle?

14. Piper High School in Piper, Kansas, a town located about 20 miles west of Kansas City,

experienced national attention because of questions about students and their term papers for a botany class. Christine Pelton, a high school science teacher, had warned students in her sophomore class not to use papers posted on the Internet for their projects. When their projects were turned in, Ms. Pelton noticed that the writing in some of the papers was well above the students' usual quality and ability. She found that 28 of her 118 students had taken substantial portions of their papers from the Internet. She gave these students a zero grade on their term paper projects with the result that many of the students were going to fail the course for that semester. The students' parents protested, and the school board ordered Ms. Pelton to raise the grades.

She resigned in protest. She received a substantial number of job offers from around the country following her resignation. Nearly half of the high school faculty as well as its principal announced their plans to resign at the end of the year. Several of the parents pointed to the fact that there was no explanation in the Piper High School handbook on plagiarism. They also said that the students were unclear about what could be used, when they had to reword, and when quotations marks were necessary.

The annual Rutgers University survey on academic cheating has revealed that 15 percent of college papers turned in for grades are completely copied from the Internet.

Do you think such copying is unethical? Why do we worry about such conduct? Isn't this conduct just a function of the Internet? Isn't it accepted behavior?

15. Pharmaceutical companies, faced with the uphill battle of getting doctors to take a look at their new products, have created complex systems and programs for enticing doctors to come, sit, and absorb information about the new products.

Following is a list of the various type of benefits and gifts that drug companies have given doctors over the past few years to entice them to consider prescribing their new offerings:

- An event called "Why Cook?" in which doctors were given the chance to review drug studies and product information at a restaurant as their meals were being prepared—they could leave as soon as their meals were ready, and they were treated to appetizers and drinks as they waited

- Events at Christmas tree lots where doctors can come and review materials and pick up a free Christmas tree

- Flowers sent to doctors' offices on Valentine's Day with materials attached

- Manicures as they study materials on new drugs

- Pedicures as they study materials on new drugs

- Free car washes during which they study materials

- Free books with materials enclosed

- Free CDs with materials attached

- Bottles of wine with materials attached

- Events at Barnes & Noble where doctors can browse and pick out a book for themselves for free as long as they also take some materials on a new drug

Some doctors say that they can enjoy dinner on a drug company as often as five times per week. The American Medical Association (AMA) frowns on the "dine-and-dash" format because its rules provide that dinners are acceptable only as long as the doctors sit and learn something from a featured speaker. The AMA also limits gifts to those of a "minimal value" that should be related to their patients, such as note pads and pens with the new drug's name imprinted on them. The chairman of the AMA Committee on Ethics says the following about gifts, "There are doctors who say, 'I always do what's best for my patients, and these gifts and dinners and trips do not influence me.' They are wrong."[17]

In which category of ethical issues do these gifts fall? Do you think doctors act ethically in accepting gifts, meals, and favors? The Food and Drug Administration recently issued rules about such favors and perks. Why?

[17] Chris Adams, "Doctors on the Run Can 'Dine 'n' Dash' in Style in New Orleans," *Wall Street Journal*, May 14, 2001, A1, A6.

© Manuel Gutjahr/iStockphoto.com

CHAPTER 4

The Constitution as the Foundation of the Legal Environment

learningoutcomes

After studying this chapter, you should be able to

LO.1 Describe the U.S. Constitution and the Federal System

LO.2 Explain the relationship between the U.S. Constitution and the States

LO.3 Discuss interpreting and amending the Constitution

LO.4 List and describe the significant federal powers

LO.5 Discuss constitutional limitations on governmental power

T his chapter introduces you to the powers of government and to the protections that you have for your rights. The Constitution of the United States establishes the structure and powers of government but also the limitations on those powers. This Constitution forms the foundation of our legal environment.

A. THE U.S. CONSTITUTION AND THE FEDERAL SYSTEM

By establishing a central government to coexist with the governments of the individual states, the U.S. Constitution created a federal system. In a **federal system,** a central government has power to address national concerns, while the individual states retain the power to handle local concerns.

1. What a Constitution Is

A **constitution** is the written document that establishes the structure of the government and its relationship to the people. The U.S. Constitution was adopted in 1789 by the 13 colonies that had won their independence from King George.[1]

2. The Branches of Government

The U.S. Constitution establishes a **tripartite** (three-part) government: a **legislative branch** (Congress) to make the laws, an **executive branch** (the president) to execute or enforce the laws, and a **judicial branch** (courts) to interpret the laws.[2] The national legislature or Congress is a **bicameral** (two-house) body consisting of the Senate and the House of Representatives. Members of the Senate are popularly elected for a term of six years. Members of the House of Representatives are popularly elected for a term of two years. The president is elected by an electoral college whose membership is popularly elected. The president serves for a term of four years and is eligible for reelection for a second term. Judges of the United States are appointed by the president with the approval of the Senate and serve for life, subject to removal only by impeachment because of misconduct. (See Chapter 2 for a discussion of the federal court system.)

B. THE U.S. CONSTITUTION AND THE STATES

The Constitution created certain powers within the national government that would have been exercised by the individual states, which are given their powers by the people of the state. Figure 4-1 illustrates the delegation of powers. Likewise, the states, as the power-granting authorities, reserved certain powers for themselves.

3. Delegated and Shared Powers

(A) DELEGATED POWERS. The powers given by the states to the national government are described as *delegated powers*. Some of these **delegated powers** are given exclusively

---

federal system – the system of government in which a central government is given power to administer to national concerns while individual states retain the power to administer to local concerns.

constitution – a body of principles that establishes the structure of a government and the relationship of the government to the people who are governed.

tripartite – three-part division (of government).

legislative branch – the branch of government (e.g., Congress) formed to make the laws.

executive branch – the branch of government (e.g., the president) formed to execute the laws.

judicial branch – the branch of government (e.g., the courts) formed to interpret the laws.

bicameral – a two-house form of the legislative branch of government.

delegated powers – powers expressly granted the national government by the Constitution.

---

[1] To examine the U.S. Constitution, go to **www.constitution.org** and click on "Founding Documents," or refer to Appendix 2.
[2] *Free Enterprise Fund v. Public Company Accounting Oversight Board*, 130 S. Ct. 3138 (2010).

vt - Declair war
- coining $

FIGURE 4-1	*Governments of the United States*

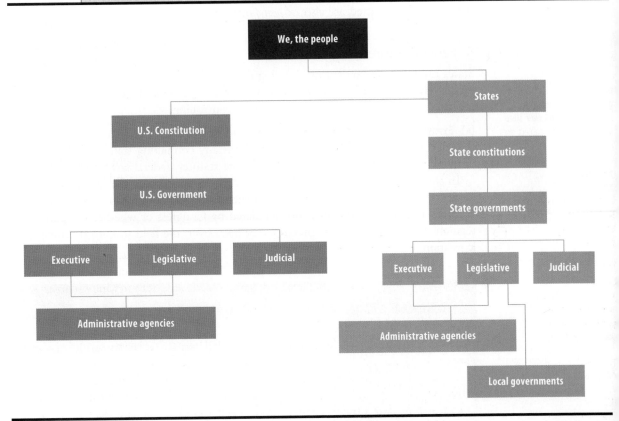

© Cengage Learning

to the national government. **For Example,** the national government alone may declare war or establish a currency.

(B) SHARED POWERS. The powers delegated to the national government that may still be exercised by the states are **shared powers**. **For Example,** the grant of power to the national government to impose taxes did not destroy the state power to tax. In other cases, a state may provide regulation along with, but subject to the supremacy of, federal law. **For Example,** regulation of the use of navigable waterways within a state is an example of joint state and federal regulation.

4. Other Powers

(A) STATE POLICE POWER. The states possess the power to adopt laws to protect the general welfare, health, safety, and morals of the people. This authority is called the **police power. For Example,** states may require that businesses be licensed with state agencies to protect persons dealing with the business. State exercise of the police power may not unreasonably interfere with federal powers.

(B) PROHIBITED POWERS. The Constitution also prohibits both states and the federal government from doing certain things. **For Example,** neither states nor the national government may adopt *ex post facto* **laws,** which make criminal an act that has

shared powers – powers that are held by both state and national governments.

Taxes

police power – the power to govern; the power to adopt laws for the protection of the public health, welfare, safety, and morals.

ex post facto law – a law making criminal an act that was lawful when done or that increases the penalty when done. Such laws are generally prohibited by constitutional provisions.

already been committed but was not criminal when it was committed. Laws that increase the penalty for an act already committed above the penalty in force when the act was committed are also *ex post facto* laws.

5. Federal Supremacy

States cannot enact conflicting state regulation if the congressional intent to regulate exclusively can be inferred from the details of congressional regulation. **Preemption** means that the federal regulatory scheme is controlling.

preemption – the federal government's superior regulatory position over state laws on the same subject area.

(A) EXPRESS FEDERAL REGULATION. The Constitution and statutes passed by Congress are the supreme law of the land. They cancel out any conflicting state law.[3] When a direct conflict exists between federal and state statutes, federal law prevails.

In some cases, however, no obvious conflict occurs because the federal statute covers only part of the subject matter. In such cases, the question becomes whether a state law can regulate the areas not regulated by Congress or whether the partial regulation made by Congress preempts, or takes over, the field so as to preclude state legislation.

CASE SUMMARY

The Folk Singer Who Staged a Protest against Preemption

FACTS: Diana Levine, a folk singer from Vermont, suffered from migraine headaches. She was being administered Wyeth Laboratory's Phenergan through a drip IV. Either because the IV needle entered Levine's artery or the drug escaped from the vein into her surrounding tissue, Ms. Levine developed gangrene. Doctors amputated her right hand and eventually her forearm. Levine could no longer work as a professional musician. Levine filed suit against both the clinic that administered the drug and Wyeth. She was awarded $7.4 million and Wyeth appealed on the grounds that the FDA approval of the drug preempted state tort suits by patients.

DECISION: In a 6 to 3 decision that departed from past precedent on preemption, the U.S. Supreme Court held that federal regulation did not preempt Levine's state tort suit against Wyeth. Wyeth argued that it could not change the label to warn against IV use of Phenergan without first obtaining FDA approval for the change. Wyeth also argued that FDA approval of the drug as safe for use was all that was needed. The Court held that Wyeth could move, when necessary, to change the label with the FDA in a timely fashion and that federal regulation did not preempt responsible follow-up by manufacturers with regard to their drugs. [*Wyeth v. Levine*, 555 U.S. 555 (2009)][4]

(B) SILENCE OF CONGRESS. In some situations, the silence of Congress in failing to cover a particular subject area indicates that Congress does not want any law on the matter. However, when national uniformity is essential, the silence of Congress generally means that the subject has been preempted for practical reasons by Congress and that no state law on the subject may be adopted.

---

[3] U.S. Const., Art VI, cl 2. *Cuomo v Clearinghouse Ass'n, LLC,* 557 U.S. 519 (2009).
[4] For an earlier decision that concluded differently on another preemption case involving medical and FDA issues, see *Riegel v. Medtronic,* 552 U.S. 312 (2008). For a decision reached on generic drug manufacturers' liability under state law, see *Pliva v. Mensing,* 131 S.Ct. 2567 (2011).

(c) **EFFECT OF FEDERAL DEREGULATION.** The fact that the federal government removes the regulations from a regulated industry does not automatically give the states the power to regulate that industry. If under the silence-of-Congress doctrine the states cannot regulate, they are still barred from regulating after deregulation. **For Example,** deregulation of banks in the 1980s did not mean that the states could step in and regulate those banks.[5]

C. INTERPRETING AND AMENDING THE CONSTITUTION

The Constitution as it is interpreted today has changed greatly from the Constitution as originally written. The change has been brought about by interpretation, amendment, and practice.

6. Conflicting Theories

Shortly after the Constitution was adopted, conflict arose over whether it was to be interpreted strictly, so as to give the federal government the least power possible, or broadly, so as to give the federal government the greatest power that the words would permit. These two views may be called the *bedrock view* and the *living-document view,* respectively.

In the **bedrock view,** or strict constructionist or originalist view, the purpose of a constitution is to state certain fundamental principles for all time. In the **living-document view,** a constitution is merely a statement of goals and objectives and is intended to grow and change with time.

Whether the Constitution is to be liberally interpreted under the living-document view or narrowly interpreted under the bedrock view has a direct effect on the Constitution. For the last century, the Supreme Court has followed the living-document view. This view has resulted in strengthening the power of the federal government, permitting the rise of administrative agencies, and expanding the protection of human rights.

One view is not selected to the exclusion of the other. As contradictory as these two views sound, the Constitution remains durable. We do not want a set of New Year's resolutions that will soon be forgotten. At the same time, we know that the world changes, and therefore, we do not want a constitution that will hold us tied in a straitjacket of the past.

In terms of social forces that make the law, we are torn between our desire for stability and our desire for flexibility. We want a constitution that is stable. At the same time, we want one that is flexible.

bedrock view—a strict constructionist interpretation of a constitution.

living-document view— the term used when a constitution is interpreted according to changes in conditions.

7. Amending the Constitution

Constitution has been amended in three ways: (1) expressly, (2) by interpretation, and (3) by practice. Figure 4-2 illustrates these three methods of amendment.

(A) **CONSTITUTIONAL METHOD OF AMENDING.** Article V of the Constitution gives the procedure to be followed for amending the Constitution. Relatively few changes have been made to the Constitution by this formal process, although thousands of

[5] For a discussion of preemption of state regulation of airline advertising when federal regulation of air travel is so pervasive see *New York v. Trans World Airlines*, 556 N.Y.S. 2d 803 (1990) and *Pan American World Airways, Inc. v. Abrams*, 764 F. Supp. 864, 868 (S.D.N.Y. 1991). See also footnote 3 and the *Cuomo* case from 2009.

| **FIGURE 4-2** | *Amending the U.S. Constitution* |

*Article V of the U.S. Constitution specifies the procedure for adopting amendments.

© Cengage Learning

proposals have been made. Since the time of its adoption, there have been only 27 amendments to the Constitution.[6]

(B) AMENDMENT BY JUDICIAL INTERPRETATION. The U.S. Supreme Court has made the greatest changes to the written Constitution by interpreting it. Generally, interpretation is used to apply the Constitution to a new situation that could not have been foreseen when the written Constitution was adopted.

(C) AMENDMENT BY PRACTICE. In practice, the letter of the Constitution is not always followed. Departure from the written Constitution began as early as 1793 when George Washington refused to make treaties as required by the Constitution, by and with the consent of the Senate. Washington began the practice of the president's negotiating a treaty with a foreign country and then submitting it to the Senate for approval. This practice has been followed since that time. Similarly, the electoral college was originally intended to exercise independent judgment in selecting the president, but it now automatically elects the official candidate of the party that elected the majority of the members of the electoral college.

8. The Living Constitution

The living Constitution has the following characteristics.

(A) STRONG GOVERNMENT. One of the characteristics of the new Constitution is strong government. Business enterprises are highly regulated and the economy is controlled through monetary policy.

(B) STRONG PRESIDENT. Instead of being merely an officer who carries out the laws, the president has become the political leader of a party, exerting strong influence on the lawmaking process.

(C) ECLIPSE OF THE STATES. Under constitutional interpretations, all levels of government have powers that they never possessed before, but the center of gravity has shifted from the states to the nation. When the Constitution was adopted in 1789, the federal government was to have only the very limited powers specified in Article I, Section 8, of the Constitution. Whatever regulation of business was permissible was to be imposed by the states. Today, the great bulk of the regulation of business is adopted

[6] Gregory Watson, a University of Texas at Austin student who was doing research for a paper for a class on the U.S. Constitution, ran across a 1789 proposed amendment to the Constitution that had never been ratified by the states. Watson wrote a paper and got a "C," but through a successful letter-writing campaign was able to get the 27th Amendment passed. The amendment reads, "No law, varying the compensation for the services of the Senators and Representatives, shall take effect, until an election of Representatives shall have intervened."

by the federal government through Congress or its administrative agencies. As the U.S. economy moved from the local community stage to the nationwide and then international stages, individual states could no longer provide effective regulation of business. Regulation migrated to the central government.

(D) ADMINISTRATIVE AGENCIES. These units of government were virtually unheard of in 1789, and the Constitution made no mention of them. The vast powers of the new Constitution are exercised to a very large degree by administrative agencies. They are in effect a fourth branch of the government, not provided for in the written Constitution. More importantly, the administrative agencies are the ones that come in contact with the majority of businesspersons and citizens.

Agencies have had a significant amount of power delegated to them. The members and heads of the agencies, boards, or commissions are not elected by the voters (see Chapter 6). They are appointed by the president and, at certain levels of appointment in the agency, must be approved by Congress.

D. FEDERAL POWERS

The federal government possesses powers necessary to administer matters of national concern.

9. The Power to Regulate Commerce

The desire to protect commerce from restrictions and barriers set up by the individual states was a prime factor leading to the adoption of the Constitution of 1789. To protect commerce, Congress was given Article I, Section 8, Clause 3—now known as the **commerce clause**—the power "to regulate commerce with foreign nations, and among the several states, and with the Indian tribes."[7]

commerce clause – that section of the U.S. Constitution allocating business regulation between federal and state governments.

Until 1937, the Supreme Court held that this provision gave Congress the power to control or regulate only that commerce crossing a state line, such as an interstate railway train or an interstate telegraph message.

(A) THE COMMERCE POWER BECOMES A GENERAL WELFARE POWER. In 1937, the Supreme Court began expanding the concept of interstate commerce. By 1946, the power to regulate interstate commerce had become very broad. By that year, the power had expanded to the point that it gave authority to Congress to adopt regulatory laws that were "as broad as the economic needs of the nation."[8] By virtue of this broad interpretation, Congress can regulate manufacturing, agriculture, mining, stock exchanges, insurance, loan sharking, monopolies, and conspiracies in restraint of trade. The far reach of the interstate commerce power is seen in the Freedom of Access to Clinic Entrances Act,[9] which prohibits obstruction of entrances to clinics, as well as in the commerce clause challenges to the Affordable Health Care Act, also known as Obama Care.[10]

The case that was the beginning point in the transition of the commerce clause was *NLRB v. Jones & Laughlin Steel,* 301 U.S. 1 (1937). The "affectation" doctrine

---

[7] For more details on the actual language in the U.S. Constitution, go to **www.constitution.org** and click on "Founding Documents," or refer to Appendix 2.
[8] *American Power & Light Co. v. Securities and Exchange Commission,* 329 U.S. 90 (1946).
[9] 18 USC §248.
[10] *United States v. Wilson,* 73 F.3d 675 (7th Cir. 1995), *cert. denied,* 519 U.S. 806 (1996), Florida ex rel. *National Federation of Independent Business v. Sebelius,* 132 S.Ct. 2566 (2012).

expanded the authority of the federal government under the commerce clause. At that time, the Court concluded, "If it is interstate commerce that feels the pinch, it does not matter how local the squeeze."

(B) The Commerce Clause Today. Today, judicial review of the commerce clause typically finds some connection between the legislation and congressional authority. However, in the past five years, the U.S. Supreme Court has found some areas Congress may not regulate and has placed some limitations on the commerce clause. These constraints on the commerce clause focus on the nature of the underlying activity being regulated. So long as the federal regulation relates to economic/ commercial activity, it is constitutional. If, however, the underlying activity is not economic and has only an economic impact, the Supreme Court has imposed restrictions on congressional authority under the commerce clause. **For Example,** in U.S. v. Morrison, 529 U.S. 598 (2000), the Supreme Court held that the Violence Against Women Act was unconstitutional because the underlying activity being regulated was violence, an activity that was not economic. Regulation of economic activity is required in order to survive constitutional scrutiny under the Commerce Clause.

CASE SUMMARY

If I Don't Buy Something, Is That Economic Activity Congress Can Regulate?

FACTS: Congress passed the Patient Protection and Affordable Care Act (also known as Obama Care) in order to increase the number of Americans covered by health insurance and decrease the cost of health care. One key provision in the law was the individual mandate, which requires most Americans to maintain "minimum essential" health insurance coverage. Attorneys general and businesses from several states challenged this requirement (and other provisions of the law) as being unconstitutional under the Commerce Clause. From a series of federal decisions from the courts below, some finding the law constitutional and others not, the affected parties appealed to the U.S. Supreme Court. The court granted *certiorari* and their cases were consolidated for review.

DECISION: The court faced a new commerce clause issue of whether the federal government could require citizens to purchase a good or service because the lack of health insurance affected commerce. In the 5-4 decision, the court concluded, "The individual mandate, however, does not regulate existing commercial activity. It instead compels individuals to *become* active in commerce by purchasing a product, on the ground that their failure to do so affects interstate commerce. Construing the Commerce Clause to permit Congress to regulate individuals precisely *because* they are doing nothing would open a new and potentially vast domain to congressional authority. Every day individuals do not do an infinite number of things. In some cases they decide not to do something; in others they simply fail to do it. Allowing Congress to justify federal regulation by pointing to the effect of inaction on commerce would bring countless decisions an individual could *potentially* make within the scope of federal regulation, and—under the Government's theory—empower Congress to make those decisions for him." [*National Federation of Independent Business v. Sebelius*, 132 S.Ct. 2566 (2012)] (Note: the law was still upheld)

(c) The Commerce Power as a Limitation on States. The federal power to regulate commerce not only gives Congress the power to act but also prevents states from acting in any way that interferes with federal regulation or burdens interstate commerce. **For Example,** if the federal government establishes safety device regulations for interstate carriers, a state cannot require different devices.

CASE SUMMARY

Minors in Maine and a Major Commerce Clause Decision

FACTS: Maine passed a law that prohibited anyone other than a Maine-licensed tobacco retailer from accepting an order for delivery of tobacco. The law required the retailer to arrange for delivery with a special receipt showing that someone over the age of 18 had received and signed for the tobacco products delivered. Out-of-state shippers and tobacco sellers challenged the law as one that favored Maine tobacco retailers. The state of Maine argued that its law was passed to prevent the public health hazard of minors becoming addicted to tobacco. The federal district court granted summary judgment for the shippers, and the court of appeals affirmed. The state of Maine appealed.

DECISION: In a 9 to 0 decision, the Court held that the Maine law may have been passed with health benefits in mind, but it clearly gave Maine businesses an economic benefit. In addition, other states had managed to fight teen smoking using programs other than discrimination between in-state and out-of-state tobacco retailers. [*Rowe v. New Hampshire Motor Transport Association* **552 U.S. 364 (2008)**]

States may not use their tax power for the purpose of discriminating against interstate commerce. **For Example,** a state cannot impose a higher tax on goods imported from another state than it imposes on the same kind of goods produced in its own territory.

State regulations designed to advance local interests may conflict with the commerce clause. Such regulations are invalid. For example, suppose a state has a health concern about having milk properly processed. One way to address the concern is to require all milk to be processed in-state. Such a regulation clearly favors that state's businesses and imposes a great burden on out-of-state milk producers. Such a regulation would be an unconstitutional exercise of state power because the state could simply require all milk sellers to be licensed. Licensing would allow the state to check the milk-processing procedures of all firms and accomplish the safety goal without imposing such a burden on out-of-state firms.[11]

CASE SUMMARY

Whining about Wine

FACTS: Michigan and New York regulate the sale and importation of alcoholic beverages, including wine, through a three-tier distribution system. Separate licenses are required for producers, wholesalers, and retailers. Both New York and Michigan prohibit out-of-state wine producers from selling their wines directly to consumers there. In-state wineries can sell directly to consumers. The impact of the prohibition on the out-of-state wine producers is that they are required to pay wholesaler fees and thus cannot compete with in-state wine producers on direct-to-consumer sales.

The wine producers challenging the New York and Michigan statutes are small wineries that rely on direct consumer sales as an important part of their businesses. If they did business through wholesalers in the state, the price of their wines would have to be increased to a level that would be noncompetitive.

The district court granted summary judgment for the state of Michigan. The Sixth Circuit Court of Appeals reversed on the grounds that the out-of-state restrictions violated the commerce clause. The state of Michigan appealed. In the New York case, the district court found that the

---

[11] *Minnesota v. Clover Leaf Creamery,* 449 U.S. 456 (1981).

CASE SUMMARY

Continued

out-of-state restrictions violated the commerce clause, and the Second Circuit Court of Appeals reversed and upheld the New York statute as constitutional. The out-of-state wine producers appealed.

DECISION: State laws violate the commerce clause if they treat in-state and out-of-state economic interests differently with the result that one benefits and the other is burdened. The mere fact that a wine producer is not a resident of the state should not foreclose access to markets there. The Michigan statutes prohibiting out-of-state wineries from shipping wine directly to in-state consumers, but permitting in-state wineries to do so if licensed, discriminated against interstate commerce. New York statutes imposing additional burdens on out-of-state wineries seeking to ship wine directly to New York consumers discriminated against interstate commerce. The effect of both statutes was to favor in-state wine producers and create the economic Balkanization that the commerce clause was intended to prevent. Both statutes violated the commerce clause. [*Granholm v. Heald*, 544 U.S. 460 (2005)]

10. The Financial Powers

The financial powers of the federal government include the powers to tax and to borrow, spend, and coin money.

(A) THE TAXING POWER. The federal Constitution provides that "Congress shall have power to lay and collect taxes, duties, imposts and excises, to pay the debts and provide for the common defence and general welfare of the United States."[12] Subject to the express and implied limitations arising from the Constitution, the states may impose such taxes as they desire and as their own individual constitutions and statutes permit. In addition to express constitutional limitations, both national and local taxes are subject to the unwritten limitation that they be imposed for a public purpose. Taxes must also be apportioned. A business cannot be taxed for all of its revenues in all 50 states. There must be apportionment of taxes, and there must be sufficient connection with the state.[13]

CASE SUMMARY

A Quill in Your State Means Taxes in the Coffer

FACTS: Quill is a Delaware corporation with offices and warehouses in Illinois, California, and Georgia. None of its employees works or lives in North Dakota, and Quill owns no property in North Dakota.

Quill sells office equipment and supplies; it solicits business through catalogs and flyers, advertisements in national periodicals, and telephone calls. Its annual national sales exceed $200 million, of which almost $1 million are made to about 3,000 customers in North Dakota. The sixth-largest vendor of office supplies in the state, it delivers all of its merchandise to its North Dakota customers by mail or common carriers from out-of-state locations.

North Dakota requires every "retailer maintaining a place of business in" the state to collect the tax from the consumer and remit it to the state. In 1987, North Dakota amended its statutory definition of the term "retailer" to include "every person who engages in regular or systematic

---

[12] U.S. Const., Art 1, §8, cl 1. To read more of the U.S. Constitution, refer to Appendix 2, or go to **www.constitution.org** and click on "Founding Documents."
[13] *Polar Tankers, Inc. v. City of Valdez, Alaska,* 557 U.S. 1 (2009).

CASE SUMMARY

Continued

solicitation of a consumer market in the state." State regulations in turn define "regular or systematic solicitation" to mean three or more advertisements within a 12-month period.

Quill argued that North Dakota does not have the power to compel it to collect a use tax from its North Dakota customers. North Dakota filed suit to require Quill to pay taxes (as well as interest and penalties) on all such sales made after July 1, 1987. The trial court ruled in Quill's favor. The North Dakota Supreme Court reversed, and Quill appealed.

DECISION: The Court held that the issue is one of whether the company has intentionally placed itself within a state. Whether it does so with offices and salespeople or deluges the citizens with catalogs is irrelevant. So long as the company has voluntarily placed itself within the state, the taxation is neither unfair nor unconstitutional. However, the Court also held that under the Commerce Clause the exercise of the taxing authority placed an undue burden on commerce and retailers such as Quill and that the standard of presence in the state through property or personnel was required to impose taxes. The decision was reversed. [*Quill v. North Dakota,* **504 U.S. 298 (1992)**]

(B) THE SPENDING POWER. The federal government may use tax money and borrowed money "to pay the debts and provide for the common defence and general welfare of the United States."[14]

(C) THE BANKING POWER. The Constitution is liberally interpreted to allow the federal government to create banks and to regulate banks created under state laws. **For Example,** the Federal Reserve System is responsible for this regulatory oversight of banks.

E. CONSTITUTIONAL LIMITATIONS ON GOVERNMENT

The constitutional limitations discussed in the following sections afford protections of rights for both persons and businesses.

11. Due Process

The power of government is limited by both the Fifth and Fourteenth Amendments to the Constitution. Those amendments respectively prohibit the national government and state governments from depriving any person "of life, liberty, or property without due process of law."[15]

(A) WHEN DUE PROCESS RIGHTS ARISE. As a result of liberal interpretation of the Constitution, the **due process clause** now provides a guarantee of protection against the loss of property or rights without the chance to be heard. These amendments also guarantee that all citizens are given the same protections. **For Example,** the Supreme Court has extended the due process clause to protect the record or standing of a student.[16] A student cannot lose credit in a course or be suspended or expelled without some form of a hearing.

Because there are so many areas in which due process rights exist and require a chance to be heard, speeding up due process has resulted in the creation of **quasi-judicial**

due process clause – a guarantee of protection against the loss of property or rights without the chance to be heard.

quasi-judicial proceedings – forms of hearings in which the rules of evidence and procedure are more relaxed but each side still has a chance to be heard.

---

[14] U.S. Const., Art 1, §8, cl 1. See **www.constitution.org**, or Appendix 2.

[15] For more information on the language of the Fifth and Fourteenth Amendments, see the U.S. Constitution in Appendix 2, or go to **www.constitution.org**.

[16] That is, a student cannot be expelled without a chance to have his or her side of the story reviewed.

E-Commerce & Cyberlaw

Internet and Interstate

Collection of sales tax from Internet stores has been a stickler of an issue for businesses, state revenue officials, and the U.S. Supreme Court. All three were grappling with how to collect, what to collect, and whether anybody had any authority to collect. Internet sales represent a large, untapped source of revenue. A study from the Center for Business and Economic Research at the University of Tennessee estimates the lost tax revenue from untaxed Internet sales as $30 billion in 2011.

The merchants involved fell into several different legal groups in terms of their theories on whether tax was owed and whether they should just pay it, with or without the states having the authority to tax:

1. Those stores with physical presences in states (Wal-Mart and J.C. Penney) that just collected sales tax as if they were collecting it in a store in that state where the Internet purchaser was located

2. Those stores without a physical presence (Amazon) that did collect taxes, particularly in those states known for taking a hard-line approach

3. Those stores without a physical presence that do not collect taxes and maintain that it is unconstitutional to do so

4. Those stores with or without a physical presence that have collected taxes but held them until everyone could figure out the legal status of the companies.

What are the constitutional issues in this taxation question?

Note: Amazon.com filed suit in 2011 in nine states challenging their laws on collection of taxes from Amazon when it has no physical presence in those states. In July, 2012, some of the suits were settled. Amazon collected taxes now in Kentucky, New York, North Dakota, Texas, and Washington, and it will collect taxes in eight more states.

Source: Stu Woo, "Amazon Battles States Over Sales Tax," *Wall Street Journal*, August 3, 2011, p. A1.

proceedings. In these types of proceedings, the parties need not go through the complex, lengthy, and formal procedures of a trial (described in Chapter 2). Rather, these proceedings have a hearing officer or administrative law judge (see Chapter 6) who conducts an informal hearing in which the rules of evidence and procedure are relaxed.

For Example, a student taking a grade grievance beyond a faculty member's decision will generally have his case heard by a panel of faculty and students as established by college or university rules. An employer appealing its unemployment tax rate will have the appeal heard by an administrative law judge.

(B) WHAT CONSTITUTES DUE PROCESS? Due process does not require a trial on every issue of rights. Shortcut procedures, such as grade grievance panels, have resulted as a compromise for providing the right to be heard along with a legitimate desire to be expeditious in resolving these issues.

12. Equal Protection of the Law

The Constitution prohibits the states and the national government from denying any person the equal protection of the law.[17] This guarantee prohibits a government from treating one person differently from another when there is no reasonable ground for classifying them differently.

(A) REASONABLE CLASSIFICATION. Whether a classification is reasonable depends on whether the nature of the classification bears a reasonable relation to the wrong to be remedied or to the object to be attained by the law. The judicial trend is to permit

---

[17] U.S. Constitution, Fourteenth Amendment as to the states; modern interpretation of due process clause of the Fifth Amendment as to national government. Congress adopted the Civil Rights Act to implement the concept of equal protection.

the classification to stand as long as there is a rational basis for the distinction made.[18] Whether a rational basis exists is determined by answering whether the lawmaking body has been arbitrary or capricious.

The equal protection clause is the basis of many of the U.S. Supreme Court's most complicated decisions. **For Example,** during the 2000 presidential election, the U.S. Supreme Court faced an issue of equal protection with regard to the challenge then–vice president and presidential candidate Al Gore made to the undervotes in Florida's ballots. However, then–presidential candidate George W. Bush argued that counting the undervotes in some counties and not in others and applying different standards for counting or not counting the infamous dimpled chads, hanging chads, and other undervotes was unconstitutional because it deprived other Florida voters of equal protection because each vote is intended to count equally. Recounts in only some counties while using varying standards resulted in some counties being given greater weight in Florida's presidential election. The U.S. Supreme Court agreed in a 7–2 decision that the recounts were unconstitutional on equal protection grounds.[19] However, the justices split 5–4 on the correct remedy for the unconstitutional recounts.

(B) Improper Classification. Laws that make distinctions in the regulation of business, the right to work, and the right to use or enjoy property on the basis of race, national origin, or religion are invalid. Also invalid are laws that impose restrictions on some, but not all, persons without any justification for the distinction.[20] **For Example,** a state statute taxing out-of-state insurance companies at a higher rate than in-state insurance companies violates the equal protection clause.[21]

✳ 13. Privileges and Immunities

The U.S. Constitution declares that "the citizens of each state shall be entitled to all privileges and immunities of citizens in the several states."[22] The so-called **privileges and immunities clause** means that a person going into another state is entitled to make contracts, own property, and engage in business to the same extent as the citizens of that state. **For Example,** a state cannot bar someone who comes from another state from engaging in local business or from obtaining a hunting or fishing license merely because the person is not a resident of that state.

✳ **privileges and immunities clause** – a clause that entitles a person going into another state to make contracts, own property, and engage in business to the same extent as citizens of that state.

14th Amendment

14. Protection of the Person

The Constitution has no general provision declaring that the government shall not impair rights of persons. The Constitution does not mention the phrase "unalienable right" that was part of the Declaration of Independence.[23] However, the Bill of Rights, the first 10 amendments to the Constitution, does provide protections for freedom of speech, jury trials, and freedom of religion and association.[24] The Bill of Rights provides for the due process protections discussed

---

[18] *Ileto v. Glock, Inc.,* 565 F.3d 1126 (9th Cir. 2006).
[19] *Bush v. Gore,* 531 U.S. 98 (2000).
[20] *Associated Industries of Missouri v. Lohman,* 511 U.S. 641 (1994).
[21] *Metropolitan Life Ins. Co. v. Ward,* 470 U.S. 869 (1985).
[22] U.S. Const., Art IV, §2, cl 1. See **www.constitution.org** and click on "Founding Documents" to access more language of the Constitution, or see Appendix 2.
[23] The term *unalienable right* is employed in reference to natural right, fundamental right, or basic right. Apart from the question of scope of coverage, the adjective *unalienable* emphasizes the fact that the people still possess the right rather than having surrendered or subordinated it to the will of society. The word *alien* is the term of the old common law for transferring title or ownership. Today, we would say *transfer* and, instead of saying unalienable rights, would say *nontransferable* rights. Unalienable rights of the people were therefore rights that the people not only possessed but also could not give up even if they wanted to. Thus, these rights are still owned by everyone. It is important to note that the Declaration of Independence actually uses the word "unalienable" when describing the rights eventually placed in the Constitution as Amendments I–X, the Bill of Rights, not "inalienable."
[24] *North Coast Women's Care Medical Group, Inc. v. San Diego County Superior Court,* 189 P.3d 959 (Ca. 2008).

earlier as well as those that prohibit unlawful searches and seizures. The Second Amendment provides for the right to keep and bear arms, an issue that has resulted in some conflicting decisions that the U.S. Supreme Court has begun to address.[25]

During the last six decades, the Supreme Court has been interpreting the rights in these amendments and has been finding constitutional protection for a wide array of rights of the person that are not expressly protected by the Constitution. **For Example,** judicial interpretations have concluded that the Constitution provides for the right of privacy, the right to marry the person one chooses,[26] protection from unreasonable zoning, protection of parental control, protection from discrimination because of poverty, and protection from gender discrimination.[27]

15. The Bill of Rights and Businesses as Persons

The Bill of Rights provides protections for individuals and also for corporations. **For Example,** the Fourth Amendment (see Chapter 8) provides protections against unreasonable searches. Individuals enjoy that protection in their homes, and corporations enjoy that protection with their files, offices, and business records. Businesses also enjoy freedom of speech protections under the First Amendment. The First Amendment provides that "Congress shall make no law … abridging the freedom of speech …"[28]

The U.S. Supreme Court has clarified the free speech rights of business through classification of the types of business speech. One form of business or commercial speech is advertising. This form of speech in which businesses tout their products is subject to regulation and restriction on form, content, and placement, and such regulation has been deemed constitutional. (See Chapters 25 and 33 for more information on the regulation of advertising.) However, there are other forms of commercial speech. Businesses do have the right to participate in political processes such as creating political action committees and supporting or opposing ballot initiatives. Businesses often take positions and launch campaigns on ballot initiatives that will affect the taxes they will be required to pay. The courts are often balancing the power of corporate political speech, regulation of ads, and the right of corporations as citizens to speak.

CASE SUMMARY

The Case That Caused a Dust-Up between the President and a Justice

FACTS: In January 2008, Citizens United released a film entitled *Hillary: The Movie (Hillary)*, a 90-minute documentary about then-senator Hillary Clinton, who was a candidate in the Democratic Party's 2008 presidential primary elections. Most of the commentators in the film were quite critical of Senator Clinton. *Hillary* was released in theaters and on DVD, but Citizens United wanted to increase distribution by making it available through video-on-demand.

Citizens United produced two 10-second ads and one 30-second ad for *Hillary*. Each ad included a short, pejorative statement about Senator Clinton, followed by the name of the movie and the movie's Web site address. Citizens United wanted to run the advertisements on broadcast and cable television. The Federal Election Commission (FEC) wanted to stop Citizens

---

[25] *District of Columbia v. Heller*, 554 U.S. 570 (2008).

[26] *Akron v. Akron Center for Reproductive Health, Inc.*, 462 U.S. 416 (1983); but see *Colorado v. Hill*, cert. granted, 527 US 1068 (2000). See also *Snyder v. Phelps*, 131 S.Ct. 1207 (2011). For more on commercial speech, see *Greater New Orleans Broadcasting Association, Inc., v. U.S.* 527 U.S. 173 (1999) and *U.S. v. Philip Morris USA Inc.*, 566 F.3d 1095 (D.C. Cir. 2009).

[27] In some cases, the courts have given the due process and equal protection clauses a liberal interpretation in order to find a protection of the person. *Davis v. Passman*, 442 U.S. 228 (1979) (due process); *Grutter v. Bollinger*, 530 U.S. 306 (2003) (equal protection).

[28] To read the full language of the First Amendment, go to Appendix 2, or to **www.constitution.org** and click on "Founding Documents."

CASE SUMMARY

Continued

United from running the ads and Citizens United brought suit, seeking a preliminary injunction against the FEC. The District Court denied Citizens United a preliminary injunction and granted the FEC summary judgment. Citizens United requested and was granted *certiorari*.

DECISION: The court held that the restrictions on running ads were unconstitutional as a prior restraint on speech as well as discrimination between and among speakers. The court held that requirements on disclosure of funding for ads was constitutional, an alternative to a ban on speech that was reasonable and allowed citizens to make their own determinations about the quality/bias of the speech (ads). President Obama spoke harshly of the decision in his State of the Union address in 2011, and Justice Samuel Alito mouthed, "Not true," in response to the president's remarks. [***Citizens United v. Federal Election Commission*, 558 U.S. 310 (2010)**]

Thinking Things Through

Sweating It Out on Free Speech

In 1996, Nike was inundated with allegations about its labor practices in shoe factories around the world. Nike responded to the negative reports and allegations with a series of releases, advertisements, and op-ed pieces in newspapers around the country. *New York Times* columnist Bob Herbert wrote two columns that were sharply critical of Nike's conditions in plants throughout Asia. The columns compared then-CEO Philip Knight's compensation with the $2.20 per day wages of Nike workers in Indonesia.

After the columns appeared, CEO Knight wrote a letter to the editor in response to them. In that letter, he wrote, "Nike has paid, on average, double the minimum wage as defined in countries where its products are produced under contract. History shows that the best way out of poverty for such countries is through exports of light manufactured goods that provide the base for more skilled production."*

Marc Kasky filed suit against Nike in California, alleging that the op-ed pieces and letters in response to negative op-ed pieces about

*Roger Parloff, "Can We Talk?" *Fortune*, September 2, 2002, 102–110.

Nike violated the False Advertising Act of California. The act permits state agencies to take action to fine corporate violators of the act as well as to obtain remedies such as injunctions to halt the ads.

Nike challenged the suit on the grounds that such an interpretation and application of the advertising regulation violated its rights of free speech. The lower court agreed with Kasky and held that the advertising statute applied to Nike's defense of its labor practices, even on the op-ed pages of newspapers. The California Supreme Court, 45 P.3d 243 (Cal. 2002), ruled that Nike could be subject to regulatory sanctions for false advertising. Nike appealed to the U.S. Supreme Court. Should Nike's editorial be protected by the First Amendment? Discuss where this type of speech fits.

The opinion handed down in this case is only one sentence: "The writ of *certiorari* is dismissed as improvidently granted." 539 U.S. 645 (2003). Nike settled the case. Is this letter protected speech? Does the California statute, as applied to Nike's op-ed letters, violate the First Amendment?

LawFlix

The Candidate (1972) (PG)

The movie depicts an idealist running for office who finds himself caught in the political process of fundraising, image-building, and winning. A number of scenes with speeches, fundraising, and principles in conflict provide excellent discussion issues with respect to government structure, the First Amendment, and campaign contributions.

MAKE THE CONNECTION

SUMMARY

The U.S. Constitution created the structure of our national government and gave it certain powers. It also placed limitations on those powers. It created a federal system with a tripartite division of government and a bicameral national legislature.

The national government possesses some governmental powers exclusively, while both the states and the federal government share other powers. In areas of conflict, federal law is supreme.

The U.S. Constitution is not a detailed document. It takes its meaning from the way it is interpreted. In recent years, liberal interpretation has expanded the powers of the federal government. Among the powers of the federal government that directly affect business

are the power to regulate commerce; the power to tax and to borrow, spend, and coin money; and the power to own and operate businesses.

Among the limitations on government that are most important to business are the requirements of due process and the requirement of equal protection of the law. In addition, government is limited by the rights given to individuals such as freedom of speech, freedom of religion, and equal protection. The equal protection concept of the U.S. Constitution prohibits both the federal government and the state governments from treating one person differently from another unless there is a legitimate reason for doing so and unless the basis of classification is reasonable.

LEARNING OUTCOMES

After studying this chapter, you should be able to clearly explain:

A. The U.S. Constitution and the Federal System

LO.1   Describe the U.S. Constitution and the Federal System

See the discussion of the **tripartite** (three-part) government on p. 60.

B. The U.S. Constitution and the States

LO.2   Explain the relationship between the U.S. Constitution and the States

See the discussion of the federal system on p. 60.

See Figure 4-1 for an illustration of the delegation of powers.

C. Interpreting and Amending the Constitution

LO.3   Discuss interpreting and amending the Constitution

See the discussion of the bedrock and constructionist views on p. 63.

D. Federal Powers

LO.4   List and describe the significant federal powers

See the discussion of the commerce power on p. 65.

See the discussion of the taxing power on p. 68.

See the discussion of the banking power on p. 69.

E. Constitutional Limitations on Government

LO.5   Discuss constitutional limitations on governmental power

See the discussion of the Bill of Rights on p. 72.

See the discussion of the Fourth Amendment on p. 72.

See the discussion of due process starting on p. 69.

See the *For Example* discussion of a student taking a grade grievance beyond a faculty member's decision on p. 70.

KEY TERMS

bedrock view	executive branch	police power
bicameral	*ex post facto* laws	preemption
commerce clause	federal system	privileges and immunities clause
constitution	judicial branch	quasi-judicial proceedings
delegated powers	legislative branch	shared powers
due process clause	living-document view	tripartite

QUESTIONS AND CASE PROBLEMS

1. Federal law requires most interstate truckers to obtain a permit that reflects compliance with certain federal requirements. The 1965 version of the law authorized states to require proof that a truck operator had such a permit. By 1991, 39 states had demanded such proof, requiring a $10 per truck registration fee and giving each trucker a stamp to affix to a multistate "bingo card" carried in the vehicle. Finding this scheme inefficient and burdensome, Congress created the current Single State Registration System (SSRS), which allows a trucking company to fill out one set of forms in one state, thereby registering in every participating state through which its trucks travel.

   A subsection of Michigan's Motor Carrier Act imposes on truck companies operating in interstate commerce an annual fee of $100 for each self-propelled motor vehicle operated by or on behalf of the motor carrier. The American Truckers Association (ATA) and others challenged the $100 fee as preempted by the extensive federal regulation of interstate trucking and trucking companies. The ATA and others appealed to the U.S. Supreme Court. What should the U.S. Supreme Court do? Be sure to discuss what portion of the Constitution applies to this issue. [*American Trucking Associations, Inc. v. Michigan Public Service Com'n*, 545 U.S. 429]

2. J.C. Penney, a retail merchandiser, has its principal place of business in Plano, Texas. It operates retail stores in all 50 states, including 10 stores in Massachusetts, and a direct mail catalog business. The catalogs illustrated merchandise available for purchase by mail order. The planning, artwork, design, and layout for these catalogs were completed and paid for outside of Massachusetts, primarily in Texas, and Penney contracted with independent printing companies located outside Massachusetts to produce the catalogs. The three major catalogs were generally printed in Indiana, while the specialty catalogs were printed in South Carolina and Wisconsin. Penney supplied the printers with paper, shipping wrappers, and address labels for the catalogs; the printers supplied the ink, binding materials, and labor. None of these materials was purchased in Massachusetts. Printed catalogs, with address labels and postage affixed, were transported by a common carrier from the printer to a U.S. Postal Service office located outside Massachusetts, where they were sent to Massachusetts addressees via third- or fourth-class mail. Any undeliverable catalogs were returned to Penney's distribution center in Connecticut.

   Purchases of catalog merchandise were made by telephoning or returning an order form to Penney at a location outside Massachusetts, and the merchandise was shipped to customers from a Connecticut distribution center. The Massachusetts Department of Revenue audited Penney in 1995 and assessed a use tax, penalty, and interest on the catalogs that had been shipped into Massachusetts. The position of the department was that there was a tax due of $314,674.62 on the catalogs that were used by Penney's Massachusetts customers. Penney said such a tax was unconstitutional in that it had no control or contact with the catalogs in the state. Can the state impose the tax? Why or why not? [*Commissioner of Revenue v. J.C. Penney Co., Inc.*, 730 N.E.2d 266 (Mass)]

3. Alfonso Lopez, Jr., a 12th-grade student at Edison High School in San Antonio, Texas, went to school carrying a concealed .38-caliber handgun and five bullets. School officials, acting on an anonymous tip, confronted Lopez. Lopez admitted that he had

the gun. He was arrested and charged with violation of federal law, the Gun-Free School Zones Act of 1990. Lopez moved to dismiss his indictment on the grounds that the provision of the Gun-Free School Zones Act with which he was charged was unconstitutional in that it was beyond the power of Congress to legislate controls over public schools. The district court found the statute to be a constitutional exercise of congressional authority.

Lopez was found guilty and sentenced to two years in prison. He appealed and challenged his conviction on the basis of the commerce clause. The Court of Appeals agreed with Lopez, found the Gun-Free School Zones Act an unconstitutional exercise of congressional authority, and reversed the conviction. The U.S. Attorney appealed. Who should win at the U.S. Supreme Court and why? [*United States v. Lopez,* 514 U.S. 549]

4. The University of Wisconsin requires all of its students to pay, as part of their tuition, a student activity fee. Those fees are used to support campus clubs and activities. Some students who objected to the philosophies and activities of some of the student clubs filed suit to have the fees halted. What constitutional basis do you think they could use for the suit? [*Board of Regents of Wisconsin System v. Southworth,* 529 U.S. 217]

5. The Crafts' home was supplied with gas by the city gas company. Because of some misunderstanding, the gas company believed that the Crafts were delinquent in paying their gas bill. The gas company had an informal complaint procedure for discussing such matters, but the Crafts had never been informed that such a procedure was available. The gas company notified the Crafts that they were delinquent and that the company was shutting off the gas. The Crafts brought an action to enjoin the gas company from doing so on the theory that a termination without any hearing was a denial of due process. The lower courts held that the interest of the Crafts in receiving gas was not a property interest protected by the due process clause and that the procedures the gas company followed satisfied the requirements of due

process. The Crafts appealed. Were they correct in contending that they had been denied due process of law? Why or why not? [*Memphis Light, Gas and Water Division v. Craft,* 436 U.S. 1]

6. In 2002, the Williamson family, riding in their 1993 Mazda minivan, was struck head-on by another vehicle. Thanh Williamson was sitting in a rear aisle seat, wearing a lap belt; she died in the accident. Delbert and Alexa Williamson were wearing lap-and-shoulder belts; they survived. Thanh's estate brought suit in a California state court to recover from Mazda for her wrongful death. The basis of the suit was that Mazda should have installed lap-and-shoulder belts on all seats, including the rear aisle seats, and that Thanh died because Mazda equipped her seat with only a lap belt instead. Federal safety requirements do not require lap-and-shoulder belts except for seats located next to doors and windows. Middle seats (aisle) can have a lap belt only. Mazda asked for a dismissal on the grounds that allowing Thanh's estate to recover would contradict federal law and that federal law preempts state tort laws on product liability. The trial court dismissed the suit as preempted by federal law, and the Court of Appeal affirmed. The U.S. Supreme Court granted *certiorari.* What should the court decide and why? [*Williamson v. Mazda Motor of America, Inc.* 131 S. Ct. 1131]

7. Montana imposed a severance tax on every ton of coal mined within the state. The tax varied depending on the value of the coal and the cost of production. It could be as high as 30 percent of the price at which the coal was sold. Montana mine operators and some out-of-state customers claimed that this tax was unconstitutional as an improper burden on interstate commerce. Decide. [*Commonwealth Edison Co. v. Montana,* 453 U.S. 609]

8. Ollie's Barbecue is a family-owned restaurant in Birmingham, Alabama, specializing in barbecued meats and homemade pies, with a seating capacity of 220 customers. It is located on a state highway 11 blocks from an interstate highway and a somewhat greater distance from railroad and bus stations. The restaurant caters to a family and white-collar trade, with a take-out service for

"Negroes." (Note: This term is used by the Court in its opinion in the case.) In the 12 months preceding the passage of the Civil Rights Act, the restaurant purchased locally approximately $150,000 worth of food, $69,683 or 46 percent of which was meat that it bought from a local supplier who had procured it from outside the state. Ollie's has refused to serve Negroes in its dining accommodations since opening in 1927, and since July 2, 1964, it has been operating in violation of the Civil Rights Act. A lower court concluded that if it were required to serve Negroes, it would lose a substantial amount of business. The lower court found that the Civil Rights Act did not apply because Ollie's was not involved in "interstate commerce." Will the commerce clause permit application of the Civil Rights Act to Ollie's? [*Katzenbach v. McClung,* 379 U.S. 294]

9. Ellis was employed by the city of Lakewood. By the terms of his contract, he could be discharged only for cause. After working for six years, he was told that he was going to be discharged because of his inability to generate safety and self-insurance programs, because of his failure to win the confidence of employees, and because of his poor attendance. He was not informed of the facts in support of these conclusions and was given the option to resign. He claimed that he was entitled to a hearing. Is he entitled to one? Why or why not? [*Ellis v. City of Lakewood,* 789 P.2d 449 (Colo. App.)]

10. The Federal Food Stamp Act provided for the distribution of food stamps to needy households. In 1971, section 3(e) of the statute was amended to define households as limited to groups whose members were all related to each other. This was done because of congressional dislike for the lifestyles of unrelated hippies who were living together in hippie communes. Moreno and others applied for food stamps but were refused them because the relationship requirement was not satisfied. An action was brought to have the relationship requirement declared unconstitutional. Is it constitutional? Discuss why or why not. [*USDA v. Moreno,* 413 U.S. 528]

11. New Hampshire adopted a tax law that in effect taxed the income of nonresidents working in New Hampshire only. Austin, a nonresident who worked in New Hampshire, claimed that the tax law was invalid. Was he correct? Explain. [*Austin v. New Hampshire,* 420 U.S. 656]

12. Gladys Mensing and other patients took the generic version of metoclopramide over a long period a time, which resulted in serious neurological damage. Ms. Mensing and others filed suit against the generic manufacturers under the Louisiana Products Liability Act. They alleged that despite mounting evidence of the connection between long-term use of metoclopramide and neurological damage, the manufacturers did not change their labels to provide warnings. The generic drug manufacturers argued that federal statutes and FDA regulations require generic manufacturers to use the same safety standards and labeling as their brand-name counterparts. They argued that it was impossible to simultaneously comply with both federal law and any state tort-law duty that required them to use a different label. What section of the U.S. Constitution will be used to resolve this issue? How will the court decide whether the manufacturers can be held liable? [*PLIVA, Inc. v. Mensing,* 131 S.Ct. 2567]

13. California passed a law that prohibited the sale or rental of "violent video games." The act defined violent video games as games "in which the range of options available to a player includes killing, maiming, dismembering, or sexually assaulting an image of a human being, if those acts are depicted" in a manner that "[a] reasonable person, considering the game as a whole, would find appeals to a deviant or morbid interest of minors." The association of video game manufacturers and developers brought suit, challenging the California statute as an unconstitutional violation of their First Amendment right and a violation of their due process rights because it is so vague. What should the U.S. Supreme Court hold on the constitutionality of the statute and why? [*Brown v. Entertainment Merchants Ass'n,* 131 S.Ct. 2729]

CHAPTER 5

© Manuel Gutjahr/iStockphoto.com

Government Regulation of Competition and Prices

learningoutcomes

After studying this chapter, you should be able to

LO.1 Explain the powers the government has to be sure free markets are working efficiently

LO.2 List the federal statutes that regulate horizontal markets and competition and give examples of each

LO.3 Describe the federal statutes that regulate the supply chain and vertical markets

LO.4 Discuss the remedies available to protect business competition

The government can regulate not just businesses but also business competition and prices. Antitrust laws were passed to help ensure that businesses compete fairly.

A. POWER TO REGULATE BUSINESS

The federal government may regulate any area of business to advance the nation's economic needs.[1] Under the police power, states may regulate all aspects of business so long as they do not impose an unreasonable burden on interstate commerce or any activity of the federal government. (See Chapter 4 for a discussion of the protections and limits of the commerce clause.)

1. Regulation, Free Enterprise, and Deregulation

Milton Friedman, the Nobel economist, has written that government regulation of business interferes with the free enterprise system. Under a true free enterprise system, market forces would provide the necessary protections through the forces of demand and supply. Sometimes, however, the demand response, or market reaction, to problems or services is not rapid enough to prevent harm, and government regulation steps in to stop abuses. The antitrust laws step in when competitors create barriers to market entry or collude on prices or production in order to control prices.

2. Regulation of Unfair Competition

Each of the states and the federal government have statutes and regulations that prohibit unfair methods of competition. Unfair competition is controlled by both statutes and administrative agencies and regulations. The statutes that curb unfair competition are the Sherman Act, the Clayton Act, the Robinson-Patman Act, and the Federal Trade Commission Act.[2] Each of these statutes covers different types of anticompetitive behavior by competitors and each is discussed in the sections below.

B. REGULATION OF HORIZONTAL MARKETS AND COMPETITORS

Antitrust laws regulate the relationships between and among competitors, known as horizontal restraints. The goal of these laws is to be sure that firms that are gaining customers are doing so because they offer better products and better customer service and not because they are manipulating the markets or their prices.

3. Regulation of Prices

Governments, both national and state, may regulate prices. Prices in various forms are regulated, including not only what a buyer pays for goods but also through credit terms and other charges. The Sherman Act is the federal law that regulates anticompetitive behavior among horizontal competitors.

CPA

---

[1] *SKF, USA, Inc. v. Customs and Border Protection*, 556 F.3d 1337 (9th Cir. 2009).
[2] 15 U.S.C. §41 *et seq.* To review the Federal Trade Commission Act, go to **www.ftc.gov**.

CPA

(A) PROHIBITION ON PRICE FIXING. Agreements among competitors, as well as "every contract, combination … or conspiracy" to fix prices, violate Section 1 of the Sherman Act.[3] Known as *horizontal price-fixing,* any agreements to charge an agreed-upon price or to set maximum or minimum prices between or among competitors are *per se*—in, through, or by themselves—a violation of the Sherman Act. Price-fixing can involve competitors agreeing to not sell below a certain price, agreeing on commission rates, agreeing on credit terms, or exchanging cost information. Price is treated as a sensitive element of competition, and discussion among competitors has also been deemed to be an attempt to monopolize. An agreement among real estate brokers to never charge below a 6 percent commission is price-fixing.[4] **For Example,** in 2001, Christie's and Sotheby's auction houses settled an antitrust lawsuit for charging the same commissions for many years.[5]

4. Prevention of Monopolies and Combinations

Monopolies and combinations that restrain trade are prohibited under the federal antitrust laws.

Sherman Antitrust Act – a federal statute prohibiting combinations and contracts in restraint of interstate trade, now generally inapplicable to labor union activity.

(A) THE SHERMAN ACT. The **Sherman Antitrust Act** includes two very short sections that control monopolistic behavior. They provide:

> *[§1] Every contract, combination in the form of trust or otherwise, or conspiracy, in restraint of trade or commerce among the several states, or with foreign nations, is declared to be illegal.*
> *[§2] Every person who shall monopolize or attempt to monopolize, or combine or conspire with any other person or persons to monopolize any part of the trade or commerce among the several states, or with foreign nations, shall be deemed guilty of a felony.*[6]

CPA

The Sherman Act applies not only to buying and selling activities but also to manufacturing and production activities. Section 1 of the Sherman Act applies to agreements, conduct, or conspiracies to restrain trade, which can consist of price-fixing, tying, and monopolization. Section 2 prohibits monopolizing or attempting to monopolize by companies or individuals.

market power – the ability to control price and exclude competitors.

(B) MONOPOLIZATION. To determine whether a firm has engaged in monopolization or attempts to monopolize, the courts determine whether the firm has **market power**, which is the ability to control price and exclude competitors. Market power is defined by looking at both the geographic and product markets. **For Example,** a cereal manufacturer may have 65 percent of the nationwide market for its Crispy Clowns cereal (the product market), but it may have only 10 percent of the Albany, New York, market because of a local competitor, Crunchy Characters. Crispy Clowns may have market power nationally, but in Albany, it would not reach monopoly levels.

Having a large percentage of a market is not necessarily a monopoly.[7] The Sherman Act requires that the monopoly position be gained because of a superior product or consumer preference, not because the company has engaged in purposeful conduct to

---

[3] To view the full language of Section 1 of the Sherman Act, see 15 U.S.C. §1.
[4] *McClain v. Real Estate Board of New Orleans, Inc.,* 441 U.S. 942 (1980).
[5] Carol Vogel and Ralph Blumenthall, "Ex-Chairman of Sotheby's Gets a Year and a Day for Price-Fixing," *New York Times,* April 12, 2002, A26.
[6] 15 U.S.C. §1. Free competition has been advanced by the Omnibus Trade and Competitiveness Act of 1988, 19 U.S.C. §2901 *et seq.*
[7] *Bell Atlantic v. Twombly,* 550 U.S. 544 (2007).

Ethics & the Law

Marsh & McLennan

Marsh & McLennan (MMC) is best known as the world's largest insurance broker with 43,000 employees in its global operations.* MMC had a different way of achieving growth.

MMC should have been obtaining competing bids on employee insurance plans for the companies it represented. However, MMC developed a "pay-to-play" format for obtaining bids that allowed the insurers and MMC to profit. To be sure (1) that the policies were renewed and (2) that the renewal bonus was a given, MMC had all of its insurers agree to roll over on renewals. For example, if Insurer A was up for renewal, Insurers B and C would submit fake and higher bids that MMC would then take to the corporate client and, of course, recommend renewal at the lower rate.

One of the companies to complain about MMC's practices was Munich RE. One of its e-mails to an MMC executive (whose name was blacked out) wrote, "I am not some Goody Two Shoes who believes that truth is absolute, but I have a pretty strict ethical code about being truthful and honest. '[T]hrowing the quote' by artificially high numbers to lose is repugnant... because it is dishonest. [I]... comes awfully close to collusion and price-fixing."

Without admitting or denying guilt, MMC settled antitrust charges by agreeing to drop the commission system and pay $850 million to its clients as a means of compensating for what might have been overcharges. MMC also agreed to hire a new CEO. The value of MMC's shares dropped almost 50 percent within 10 days following the mid-October filing of suit by then New York Attorney General Spitzer against the company.**

MMC hired a new CEO who fired several senior executives despite the fact that there was no evidence that they had broken the law. When asked why he would fire them, Michael G. Cherkasky, a former district attorney in New York, said, "Freedom from criminal culpability is not our standard for executive leadership."***

*Monica Langley and Ianthe Jeanne Dugan, "How a Top Marsh Employee Turned the Tables on Insurers," *Wall Street Journal*, October 23, 204, A1, A9. Some put the number of employees at 60,000. *See also* Gretchen Morgenson, "Who Loses the Most at Marsh? Its Workers," *New York Times*, October 24, 2004, 3–1 (Sunday Business 1) and 9.

**"The Chatter," *New York Times*, November 14, 2004, BU2.
***Ian McDonald, "After Spitzer Probe, Marsh CEO Tries Corporate Triage," *Wall Street Journal*, August 29, 2005, A1.

exclude competitors by other means, such as preventing a competitor from purchasing a factory. **For Example,** perhaps one of the best known monopolization cases involved Microsoft. In the case, the Justice Department alleged that because Microsoft had 90 percent of the market for operating systems, it had and used monopoly power to control and market and did so by refusing to sell its operating system to companies that installed Netscape in lieu of or in addition to the Microsoft Explorer browser.[8] Today, Microsoft has filed antitrust complaints against Google along with Yelp and Expedia, alleging that Google drives those who use its search engine to its own specialized sites that compete with them.

5. Boycotts and Refusals to Deal

Under the Sherman Act, competitors are not permitted to agree not to deal with certain buyers. Boycotts among competitors are *per se* violations of the Sherman Act, which means that there are no defenses to these kinds of controls by competitors on markets. Sometimes boycotts have the best of intentions, but they are still illegal. For example, defense lawyers who went on strike in order to get a higher hourly rate for

[8] *United States v. Microsoft*, 253 F.2d 34 (D.C. Cir. 2001).

public defenders so that the indigent defendants would have quality representation still engaged in an illegal boycott.[9]

6. Mergers among Competitors

The Sherman Antitrust Act does not prohibit bigness. However, Section 7 of the Clayton Act provides that "no corporation … shall acquire the whole or any part of the assets of another corporation … where in any line of commerce in any section of the country, the effect of such acquisition may be substantially to lessen competition, or to tend to create a monopoly." If the Clayton Act is violated through ownership or control of competing enterprises, a court may order the violating defendant to dispose of such interests by issuing a decree called a **divestiture order**.[10] Courts examine market share and relevant markets to determine whether a merger would create a monopoly.

divestiture order – a court order to dispose of interests that could lead to a monopoly.

When large-size enterprises plan to merge, they must give written notice to the FTC and to the head of the Antitrust Division of the Department of Justice. This advance notice gives the department the opportunity to block the merger and thus avoid the loss that would occur if the enterprises merged and were then required to separate.[11] **For Example,** AT&T was required to notify the Justice Department when it proposed acquisition of T-Mobile because AT&T's market share was 37 percent and T-Mobile's was 16 percent. A merger (which was not approved) would have resulted in a company with a 51 percent share of the market.[12]

E-Commerce & Cyberlaw

E-mail's Revelations

In the U.S. Justice Department's case against Microsoft, a lawyer commented, "The Government does not need to put Mr. Gates on the stand because we have his e-mail and memoranda." There were 30 million pages of e-mail used as evidence in the Microsoft trial.

E-mail provides what is known as a *contemporaneous record of events* and has the added bonus that, for whatever psychological reason, those communicating with e-mail tend to be more frank and informal than they would be in a memo. E-mail can also contradict a witness's testimony and serve to undermine credibility. For example, when asked whether he recalled discussions with a subordinate about whether Microsoft should offer to invest in Netscape, Mr. Gates responded in his deposition, "I didn't see that as something that made sense." But Mr. Gates's e-mail included an urging to his subordinates to consider a Netscape alliance: "We could even pay them money as part of the deal, buying a piece of them or something."

E-mail is discoverable, admissible as evidence, and definitely not private. Employees should follow the admonition of one executive whose e-mail was used to fuel a million-dollar settlement by his

company with a former employee: "If you wouldn't want anyone to read it, don't send it in e-mail."

The impact of e-mail in the Microsoft antitrust case on companies and their e-mail policies was widespread. For example, Amazon.com launched a companywide program called "Sweep and Keep," under which employees were instructed to purge e-mail messages no longer needed for conducting business. Amazon.com offered employees who immediately purged their e-mail free lattes in the company cafeteria. The company had a two-part program. The first portion included instructions on document retention and deletion. The second part of the program was on document creation and included the following warning for employees: "Quite simply put, there are some communications that should not be expressed in written form. Sorry, no lattes this time."

Source: Adapted from Marianne M. Jennings, *Business: Its Legal, Ethical and Global Environment,* 8th ed. (Cincinnati, OH: West Legal Studies in Business, 2009), ch. 16.

---

[9] *FTC v. Superior Court Trial Lawyers Ass'n,* 493 U.S. 411 (1990).

[10] *California v. American Stores Co.,* 492 U.S. 1301 (1989).

[11] Antitrust Improvement Act of 1976, 15 U.S.C. §1311 *et seq.*

[12] Thomas Catan and Spencer A. Ante, "U.S. Sues to Stop AT&T Deal," *Wall Street Journal,* September 9, 2011, p. A1.

C. REGULATION OF THE SUPPLY CHAIN AND VERTICAL TRADE RESTRAINTS

7. Price Discrimination

Clayton Act – a federal law that prohibits price discrimination.

Robinson-Patman Act – a federal statute designed to eliminate price discrimination in interstate commerce.

price discrimination – the charging practice by a seller of different prices to different buyers for commodities of similar grade and quality, resulting in reduced competition or a tendency to create a monopoly.

The **Clayton Act** and **Robinson-Patman Act** prohibit price discrimination.[13] **Price discrimination** occurs when a seller charges different prices to different buyers for "commodities of like grade and quality," with the result being reduced competition or a tendency to create a monopoly.[14]

Price discrimination prohibits charging different prices to buyers as related to marginal costs. That is, volume discounts are permissible because the marginal costs are different on the larger volume of goods. However, the Robinson-Patman Act makes it illegal to charge different prices to buyers when the marginal costs of the seller for those goods are the same. Any added incentives or bonuses are also considered part of the price.

For Example, offering one buyer free advertising while not offering it to another as an incentive to buy would be a violation of the Robinson-Patman Act. The Clayton Act makes both the giving and the receiving of any illegal price discrimination a crime.

CPA

State statutes frequently prohibit favoring one competitor by giving a secret discount when the effect is to harm the competition.[15] A state may prohibit either selling below cost to harm competitors or selling to one customer at a secret price that is lower than the price charged other customers when there is no economic justification for the lower price.[16] Some state statutes specifically permit sellers to set prices so that they can match competitive prices, but not to undercut a competitor's prices.[17]

CASE SUMMARY

Getting a Piece of the Pie Market

FACTS: Utah Pie Company is a Utah corporation that for 30 years has been baking pies in its plant in Salt Lake City and selling them in Utah and surrounding states. It entered the frozen pie business in 1957 and was immediately successful with its new line of frozen dessert pies—apple, cherry, boysenberry, peach, pumpkin, and mince.

Continental Baking Company, Pet Milk, and Carnation, all based in California, entered the pie market in Utah. When these companies entered the Utah market, a price war began. In 1958 Utah Pie was selling pies for $4.15 per dozen. By 1961, as all the pie companies competed, it was selling the same pies for $2.75 per dozen. Continental's price went from $5.00 per dozen in 1958 to $2.85 in 1961. Pet's prices went from $4.92 per dozen to $3.46, and Carnation's from $4.82 per dozen to $3.30.

Utah Pie filed suit, charging price discrimination. The district court found for Utah Pie. The Court of Appeals reversed, and Utah Pie appealed.

---

[13] 15 U.S.C. §§1, 2, 3, 7, 8.

[14] 15 U.S.C. §13a. To read the full Clayton Act, go to **www.usdoj.gov** or **www.justice.gov** and plug in "Clayton Act" in a site search.

[15] *Eddins v. Redstone*, 35 Cal. Rptr. 2d 863 (2006).

[16] In *Weyerhaeuser v. Ross-Simons*, 549 U.S. 212 (2007), the U.S. Supreme Court ruled that predatory bidding is also a price discrimination issue. In a monopsony, a buyer tries to control a market by overbidding all its competitors and thereby cornering the market for supplies it needs to produce goods. However, if the bidder is actually just in need of the goods and bids higher for them, there is no anticompetitive conduct.

[17] *Home Oil Company, Inc. v. Sam's East, Inc.*, 252 F. Supp. 2d 1302 (M.D. Ala. 2003).

CASE SUMMARY

Continued

DECISION: There was price discrimination. Pet was selling its pies in Utah through Safeway at prices that were lower than its prices in other markets and also much lower than its own brand pie in the Salt Lake City market. Pet also introduced a 20-ounce economy pie under the Swiss Miss label and began selling the new pie in the Salt Lake market in August 1960 at prices ranging from $3.25 to $3.30 for the remainder of the period. This pie was at times sold at a lower price in the Salt Lake City market than it was sold in other markets. For 7 of the 44 months in question for price discrimination, Pet's prices in Salt Lake were lower than prices charged in the California markets. This was true even though selling in Salt Lake involved a 30- to 35-cent freight cost.

Also, Pet had predatory intent to injure Utah Pie. Pet admitted that it sent into Utah Pie's plant an industrial spy to seek information. Pet suffered substantial losses on its frozen pie sales during the greater part of time involved in this suit. Pet had engaged in predatory tactics in waging competitive warfare in the Salt Lake City market. Coupled with the price discrimination, Pet's behavior lessened competition and violated Robinson-Patman. [*Utah Pie Co. v. Continental Baking Co.*, 386 U.S. 685 (1967)]

Price discrimination is expressly permitted when it can be justified on the basis of (1) a difference in grade, quality, or quantity; (2) the cost of transportation involved in performing the contract; (3) a good-faith effort to meet competition; (4) differences in methods or quantities, that is marginal cost differences; (5) deterioration of goods; or (6) a close-out sale of a particular line of goods. The Robinson-Patman Act[18] reaffirms the right of a seller to select customers and refuse to deal with anyone. The refusal, however, must be in good faith, not for the purpose of restraining trade.

8. Exclusive Dealings and Territories

Sometimes manufacturers have sole outlets. Sole outlets are not *per se* violations. For restrictions on territories and outlets to be legal, there must be enough interbrand competition to justify no intrabrand competition. **For Example,** Coca-Cola can have exclusive distributorships in cities because Pepsi will always be there providing consumers with competitive choices in soft drinks.

9. Resale Price Maintenance

Resale price maintenance is an attempt by manufacturers to control the prices that retailers can charge for their goods. A "suggested retail price" is just that, a suggestion, and is not a violation of the antitrust laws. However, some manufacturers have policies of terminating retailers when they charge too little or charge too much. For example, Apple's iPads are the same price wherever you buy them. Minimum prices are justified in a competitive sense because without them, some retailers would cut the price but not offer the customer service the manufacturer wants for its brand. Retailers who charge more can be stopped by manufacturers who do not want to gouge consumers on prices. The *Khan* and *Leegin* cases illustrate these two principles of legal resale price maintenance.

[18] 15 U.S.C. §§13, 21.

CASE SUMMARY

Bagging Customers for Having Sales

FACTS: Leegin Creative Leather Products, Inc. designs, manufactures, and distributes leather goods and accessories under the brand name "Brighton." The Brighton brand is sold across the United States in over 5,000 retail stores. PSKS, Inc., runs Kay's Kloset, a Brighton retailer in Lewisville, Texas, that carries about 75 different product lines, but was known as the place in that area to go for Brighton.

Leegin's president, Jerry Kohl, who also has an interest in about 70 stores that sell Brighton products, believes that small retailers treat customers better, provide customers more services, and make their shopping experience more satisfactory than do larger, often impersonal retailers. In 1997, Leegin instituted the "Brighton Retail Pricing and Promotion Policy," which banished retailers that discounted Brighton goods below suggested prices.

In December 2002, Leegin discovered that Kay's Kloset had been marking down Brighton's entire line by 20 percent. When Kay's would not stop marking the Brighton products prices down, Leegin stopped selling to the store.

PSKS sued Leegin for violation of the antitrust laws. The jury awarded PSKS $1.2 million in damages and the judge trebled the damages and reimbursed PSKS for its attorney's fees and costs—for a judgment against Leegin of $3,975,000.80. The Court of Appeals affirmed. Leegin appealed.

DECISION: The Court held that the goal of providing customers with information and service through the smaller boutiques was a competitive strategy that offered consumers choices. It was not a *per se* violation for Leegin to require minimum prices. Resale price maintenance increases the choices consumers have by providing them with a full-service retailer. Each case on resale price maintenance requires examination of the market and the effect on competition, but it is not automatically anticompetitive. The decision was reversed. [*Leegin Creative Leather Products, Inc. v. PSKS, Inc.,* **551 U.S. 877 (2007)**]

CASE SUMMARY

Fill It Up: The Price Is Right and Fixed

FACTS: Barkat U. Khan and his corporation entered into an agreement with State Oil to lease and operate a gas station and convenience store owned by State Oil. The agreement provided that Khan would obtain the gasoline supply for the station from State Oil at a price equal to a suggested retail price set by State Oil, less a margin of $3.25 per gallon. Khan could charge any price he wanted, but if he charged more than State Oil's suggested retail price, the excess went to State Oil. Khan could sell the gasoline for less than State Oil's suggested retail price, but the difference would come out of his allowed margin.

After a year, Khan fell behind on his lease payments, and State Oil gave notice of, and began, eviction proceedings. The court had Khan removed and appointed a receiver to operate the station. The receiver did so without the price constraints and received an overall profit margin above the $3.25 imposed on Khan.

Khan filed suit, alleging that the State Oil agreement was a violation of Section 1 of the Sherman Act because State Oil was controlling price. The district court held that there was no

CASE SUMMARY

Continued

per se violation and that Khan had failed to demonstrate antitrust injury. The Court of Appeals reversed, and State Oil appealed.

DECISION: In what was a reversal of prior decisions, the Court held that vertical maximum prices (as in this case in which a retailer was prohibited from charging above a certain amount) are not a *per se* violation of the Sherman Act. The Court noted that benefits can come from retailers' not being able to charge above a certain amount. At a minimum, such controls on maximum prices were not an automatic violation of the Sherman Act and need to be examined in light of what happens to competition. In determining whether such prices might affect competition, the Court noted that maximum prices might have an impact on the survival of inefficient dealers, as was the case here. However, encouraging inefficiency is not the purpose of either the market or the laws on anticompetitive behavior. [*State Oil v. Khan,* **522 U.S. 3 (1997)**]

10. Tying

tying – the anticompetitive practice of requiring buyers to purchase one product in order to get another.

It is a violation of the Sherman Act to force "tying" sales on buyers. **Tying** occurs when the seller makes a buyer who wants to purchase one product buy an additional product that he or she does not want.

The essential characteristic of a tying arrangement that violates Section 1 of the Sherman Act is the use of control over the tying product within the relevant market to compel the buyer to purchase the tied article that either is not wanted or could be purchased elsewhere on better terms. **For Example,** in the Microsoft antitrust case, Microsoft was accused of requiring the purchase and use of its browser as a condition for purchasing its software. The Sherman Act also prohibits professional persons, such as doctors, from using a peer review proceeding to pressure another professional who competes with them in private practice and refuses to become a member of a clinic formed by them.

11. Mergers along the Supply Chain

Vertical mergers occur between firms that have buyer and seller relationships. The Clayton Act also applies to vertical mergers. The test is whether the vertical merger

Sports & Entertainment Law

Celebrity Issues and Antitrust

Public Interest Corporation (PIC) owned and operated television station WTMV-TV in Lakeland, Florida. MCA Television Ltd. (MCA) owns and licenses syndicated television programs. In 1990, the two companies entered into a licensing contract for several first-run television shows. With respect to all but one of these shows, MCA exchanged the licenses on a "barter" basis for advertising time on WTMV. However, MCA conditioned this exchange on PIC's agreeing to license the remaining show, *Harry and the Hendersons,* for cash as well as for barter. *Harry and the Hendersons* was what some in the industry would call a "dog," a show that was not very good that attempted to capitalize on a hit movie. PIC agreed to this

arrangement, although it did not want *Harry and the Hendersons.* The shows that PIC did want were *List of a Lifetime, List of a Lifetime II, Magnum P.I.,* and 17 other miscellaneous features.

The relationship between the parties was strained over nonpayment, poor ratings performance of *Harry,* and other issues. When litigation resulted, PIC alleged that it had been subjected to an illegal tying arrangement. PIC requested damages for MCA's violation of the Sherman Act. What violation do you think occurred?

Source: Adapted from *MCA Television Ltd. v. Public Interest Corp.,* 171 F.3d 1265 (11th Cir. 1998).

will foreclose or lessen competition. **For Example,** the Justice Department took a very close look at whether the merger between Live Nation and Ticketmaster would be anticompetitive because the largest U.S. event promoter was proposing a merger with the largest primary and secondary ticket seller in the world. The merger was eventually approved because there were still thriving smaller ticket sellers.

In addition to controlling business combinations, the federal government protects others. By statute or decision, associations of exporters, marine insurance associations, farmers' cooperatives, and labor unions are exempt from the Sherman Act with respect to agreements between their members. Certain pooling and revenue-dividing agreements between carriers are exempt from the antitrust law when approved by the appropriate federal agency. The Newspaper Preservation Act of 1970 grants an antitrust exemption to operating agreements entered into by newspapers to prevent financial collapse. The Soft Drink Interbrand Competition Act[19] grants the soft drink industry an exemption when it is shown that, in fact, substantial competition exists in spite of the agreements.

The general approach of the U.S. Supreme Court has been that these types of agreements should not be automatically, or *per se*, condemned as a restraint of interstate commerce merely because they create the power or potential to monopolize interstate commerce. It is only when the restraint imposed is unreasonable that the practice is unlawful. The Court applies the rule of reason in certain cases because the practice may not always harm competition.

D. Remedies for Anticompetitive Behavior

12. Criminal Penalties

A violation of either section of the Sherman Act is punishable by fine or imprisonment or both at the discretion of the court. The maximum fine for a corporation is $100 million. A natural person can be fined a maximum of $1,000,000 or imprisoned for a maximum term of ten years or both.

13. Civil Remedies

In addition to these criminal penalties, the law provides for an injunction to stop the unlawful practices.

treble damages—three times the damages actually sustained.

Any individual or company harmed may bring a separate action for **treble damages** (three times the damages actually sustained). In addition to individual suits, there is the possibility that a state could bring a class-action suit if the antitrust violation has resulted in large numbers of buyers paying higher prices. **For Example,** Pilgrim's Pride agreed to pay $26 million in damages to dozens of poultry growers because of its closure of chicken-processing plants in order to bring down the price of chicken.

The attorney general of a state may bring a class-action suit to recover damages on behalf of those who have paid the higher prices. This action is called a *parens patriae* action on the theory that the state is suing as the parent of its people.

---

[19] 15 U.S.C. §3501 *et seq.*

LawFlix

Antitrust (2001) (R)

This movie is based on the story of Bill Gates and Microsoft.

MAKE THE CONNECTION

SUMMARY

Regulation by government has occurred primarily to protect one group from the improper conduct of another group. The police power is the basis for government regulation. Regulation is passed when the free enterprise system fails to control abuses, as when companies engage in unfair methods of competition.

There are horizontal and vertical forms of anticompetitive behavior. The Sherman Act focuses on horizontal anticompetitive behavior such as price-fixing, boycotts, refusals to deal, and monopolization achieved through means other than fair competition.

The Sherman Antitrust Act prohibits price-fixing among competitors, monopolies that do not result from superior skill or products, boycotts, and mergers that lessen competition. The Clayton Act prohibits mergers or the acquisition of the assets of another corporation when this conduct would tend to lessen competition or create a monopoly. The Justice Department requires premerger notification for proposed mergers. Violation of the federal antitrust

statutes subjects the wrongdoer to criminal prosecution and possible civil liability that can include treble damages.

Vertical trade restraints include price discrimination, some exclusive dealings arrangements, resale price maintenance, and some mergers among companies positioned vertically in the supply chain.

Prices have been regulated both by prohibiting setting the exact price or a maximum price and discrimination in pricing. Price discrimination between buyers is prohibited when the effect of such discrimination could tend to create a monopoly or lessen competition. Price discrimination occurs when the prices charged different buyers are different despite the same marginal costs. Another vertical antitrust issue is resale price maintenance. Resale price maintenance is control by the manufacturer of the price of its goods as they flow through the supply chain. Resale price maintenance is not illegal *per se* if the control is for purposes of providing customer service.

LEARNING OUTCOMES

After studying this chapter, you should be able to clearly explain:

A. Power to Regulate Business

LO.1   Explain the powers the government has to be sure free markets are working efficiently
See the *For Example* about Crispy Clowns Cereal on p. 80.

B. Regulation of Horizontal Markets and Competitors

LO.2   List the federal statutes that regulate horizontal markets and competition and give examples of each
See the Christie's and Sotheby's example on p. 80.

See the Marsh & McLennan Ethics & the Law on p. 81.
See the Microsoft monopolization discussion on p. 81.

See the *Leegin* case on resale price maintenance, p. 85.
See the Sports & Entertainment Law feature on tying, p. 86.

C. Regulation of the Supply Chain and Vertical Trade Restraints

LO.3   Describe the federal statutes that regulate the supply chain and vertical markets
See the *Utah Pie* case on predatory pricing, p. 83.
See the *Khan* oil case on price controls, p. 85.

D. Remedies for Anticompetitive Behavior

LO.4   Discuss the remedies available to protect business competition
See a list of the penalties and remedies on p. 87.

KEY TERMS

Clayton Act
divestiture order
market power

price discrimination
Robinson-Patman Act
Sherman Antitrust Act

treble damages
tying

QUESTIONS AND CASE PROBLEMS

1. American Crystal Sugar Co. was one of several refiners of beet sugar in northern California, and it distributed its product in interstate commerce. American Crystal and the other refiners had a monopoly on the seed supply and were the only practical market for the beets. In 1939, all of the refiners began using identical form contracts that computed the price paid to the sugar beet growers using a "factor" common to all the refiners. As a result, all refiners paid the same price for beets of the same quality. Though there was no hard evidence of an illegal agreement, the growers brought suit under the Sherman Act against the refiners, alleging that they conspired to fix a single uniform price among themselves to hold down the cost of the beets. The growers sued for the treble damages available under the Sherman Act. Can they recover? [*Mandeville Island Farms v. American Crystal Sugar Co.,* 334 U.S. 219]

2. Penny Stafford, the owner of Belvi Coffee and Tea Exchange, located in Bellevue, Washington, brought an antitrust suit against Starbucks. She alleged that through its exclusive leases, Starbucks bans other coffee shops from competing. Starbucks has a 73 percent market share, has $8.4 billion in annual sales in the United States, and owns 7,551 of the 21,400 coffeehouses located in the United States. However, if Dunkin' Donuts, Krispy Kreme,

and Tim Hortons are included in the gourmet coffee market, Starbucks holds only 43 percent of the coffee market. Starbucks purchased Seattle's Best Coffee (SBC) in 2003 and Torrefazione Italia the same year. Starbucks then closed one-half of all SBC stores and all of the Torrefazione outlets. Starbucks runs 59 stores within a two-mile radius of downtown Seattle. Stafford said that Starbucks has exclusive leases with landlords so that the landlords cannot lease space in the same building to another coffee shop. Does such an exclusive lease violate any antitrust laws, or are such clauses permitted under the law?

3. David Ungar holds a Dunkin' Donuts franchise. The terms of his franchise agreement require him to use only those ingredients furnished by Dunkin' Donuts. He is also required to buy its napkins, cups, and so on, with the Dunkin' Donuts trademark on them. Is this an illegal tying arrangement? What if Dunkin' Donuts maintains that it needs these requirements to maintain its quality levels on a nationwide basis? [*Ungar v. Dunkin' Donuts of America, Inc.,* 429 U.S. 823]

4. During the 1980s, the NCAA, a voluntary unincorporated association of approximately 1,100 educational institutions, became concerned over the steadily rising costs of maintaining competitive

athletic programs. As a way of containing those costs, the association imposed salary caps on college and university athletic coaches. The caps on salaries as well as limits on number and types of coaches were imposed pursuant to NCAA procedures and members' votes. A group of coaches filed suit, challenging the caps on salaries and hiring as being anticompetitive. The NCAA responded that it had a goal of containing athletic program costs as well as ensuring that entry-level coaching positions were available. Are the salary caps legal under the federal antitrust laws? [*Law v. National Collegiate Athletic Ass'n,* 134 F.3d 1010 (10th Cir.)]

5. Hines Cosmetic Co. sold beauty preparations nationally to beauty shops at a standard or fixed-price schedule. Some of the shops were also supplied with a free demonstrator and free advertising materials. The shops that were not supplied with them claimed that giving the free services and materials constituted unlawful price discrimination. Hines replied that there was no price discrimination because it charged everyone the same. What it was giving free was merely a promotional campaign that was not intended to discriminate against those who were not given anything free. Was Hines guilty of unlawful price discrimination? Explain.

6. Moore ran a bakery in Santa Rosa, New Mexico. His business was wholly intrastate. Meads Fine Bread Co., his competitor, engaged in an interstate business. Meads cut the price of bread in half in Santa Rosa but made no price cut in any other place in New Mexico or in any other state. This price-cutting drove Moore out of business. Moore then sued Meads for damages for violating the Clayton and Robinson-Patman Acts. Meads claimed that the price-cutting was purely intrastate and, therefore, did not constitute a violation of federal statutes. Was Meads correct? Why or why not? [*Moore v. Meads Fine Bread Co.,* 348 U.S. 115]

7. A&P Grocery Stores decided to sell its own brand of canned milk (referred to as *private label* milk). A&P asked its longtime supplier, Borden, to submit an offer to produce the private label milk. Bowman Dairy also submitted a bid, which was lower than Borden's. A&P's Chicago buyer then contacted Borden and said, "I have a bid in my pocket. You people are so far out of line it is not even funny. You are not even in the ballpark." The Borden representative asked for more details but was told only that a $50,000 improvement in Borden's bid "would not be a drop in the bucket." A&P was one of Borden's largest customers in the Chicago area. Furthermore, Borden had just invested more than $5 million in a new dairy facility in Illinois. The loss of the A&P account would result in underutilization of the plant. Borden lowered its bid by more than $400,000. The Federal Trade Commission charged Borden with price discrimination, but Borden maintained it was simply meeting the competition. Did Borden violate the Robinson-Patman Act? Does it matter that the milk was a private label milk, not its normal trade name Borden milk? [*Great Atlantic & Pacific Tea Co., Inc. v. FTC,* 440 U.S. 69]

8. Department 56 is a company that manufactures and sells collectible Christmas village houses and other replica items to allow collectors to create the whimsical "Snow Village" town or "Dickens Christmas." Department 56 has only authorized dealers. Sam's Club, a division of Wal-Mart Stores, Inc., began selling Department 56 pieces from the Heritage Village Collection. Susan Engel, president and CEO of Department 56, refused to sell Department 56 products to Wal-Mart. Does her refusal violate any antitrust laws?

9. Dr. Edwin G. Hyde, a board-certified anesthesiologist, applied for permission to practice at East Jefferson Hospital in Louisiana. An approval was recommended for his hiring, but the hospital's board denied him employment on grounds that the hospital had a contract with Roux & Associates for Roux to provide all anesthesiological services required by the hospital's patients. Dr. Hyde filed suit for violation of antitrust laws. Had the hospital done anything illegal? [*Jefferson Parish Hosp. Dist. No. 2 v. Hyde,* 466 U.S. 2]

10. BRG of Georgia, Inc. (BRG), and Harcourt Brace Jovanovich Legal and Professional Publications (HJB) are the nation's two largest providers of bar review materials and lectures. HJB began offering a Georgia bar review course on a limited basis in 1976 and was in direct, and

often intense, competition with BRG from 1977 to 1979 when the companies were the two main providers of bar review courses in Georgia. In early 1980, they entered into an agreement that gave BRG an exclusive license to market HJB's materials in Georgia and to use its trade name "Bar/Bri." The parties agreed that HJB would not compete with BRG in Georgia and that BRG would not compete with HJB outside of Georgia. Under the agreement, HJB received $100 per student enrolled by BRG and 40 percent of all revenues over $350. Immediately after the 1980 agreement, the price of BRG's course was increased from $150 to more than $400. Is their conduct illegal under federal antitrust laws? [*Palmer v. BRG of Georgia, Inc.,* 498 U.S. 46]

11. Favorite Foods Corp. sold its food to stores and distributors. It established a quantity discount scale that was publicly published and made available to all buyers. The top of the scale gave the highest discount to buyers purchasing more than 100 freight cars of food in a calendar year. Only two buyers, both national food chains, purchased in such quantities, and therefore, they alone received the greatest discount. Favorite Foods was prosecuted for price discrimination in violation of the Clayton Act. Was it guilty?

12. Run America, Inc., manufactures running shoes. Its shoe is consistently rated poorly by *Run Run Run* magazine in its annual shoe review. The number one shoe in *Run Run Run*'s review is the Cheetah, a shoe that Run America has learned is manufactured by the parent company of the magazine. Is this conduct a violation of the antitrust laws? Do you think it is ethical to run the shoe review without disclosing ownership?

13. The Quickie brand wheelchair is the most popular customized wheelchair on the market. Its market share is 90 percent. Other manufacturers produce special-use wheelchairs that fold, that are made of mesh and lighter frames, and that are easily transportable. These manufacturers do not compete with Quickie on customized chairs. One manufacturer of the alternative wheelchairs has stated, "Look, it's an expensive market to be in, that Quickie market. We prefer the alternative chairs without the headaches of customizations."

Another has said, "It is such a drain on cash flow in that market because insurers take so long to pay. We produce chairs that buyers purchase with their own money, not through insurers. Our sales are just like any other product." Quickie entered the market nearly 40 years ago and is known for its quality and attention to detail. Buying a Quickie custom chair, however, takes time, and the revenue stream from sales is slow but steady because of the time required to produce custom wheelchairs. Has Quickie violated the federal antitrust laws with its 90 percent market share? Discuss.

14. Gardner-Denver is the largest manufacturer of ratchet wrenches and their replacement parts in the United States. Gardner-Denver had two different lists of prices for its wrenches and parts. Its blue list had parts that, if purchased in quantities of five or more, were available for substantially less than its white list prices. Did Gardner-Denver engage in price discrimination with its two price lists? [*D. E. Rogers Assoc., Inc. v. Gardner-Denver Co.,* 718 F.2d 1431 (6th Cir.)]

15. The Aspen ski area consisted of four mountain areas. Aspen Highlands, which owned three of those areas, and Aspen Skiing, which owned the fourth, had cooperated for years in issuing a joint, multiple-day, all-area ski ticket. After repeatedly and unsuccessfully demanding an increased share of the proceeds, Aspen Highlands canceled the joint ticket. Aspen Skiing, concerned that skiers would bypass its mountain without some joint offering, tried a variety of increasingly desperate measures to re-create the joint ticket, even to the point of in effect offering to buy Aspen Highland's tickets at retail price. Aspen Highlands refused even that. Aspen Skiing brought suit under the Sherman Act, alleging that the refusal to cooperate was a move by Aspen Highlands to eliminate all competition in the area by freezing it out of business. Is there an antitrust claim here in the refusal to cooperate? What statute and violation do you think Aspen Skiing alleged? What dangers do you see in finding the failure to cooperate to be an antitrust violation? [*Aspen Skiing Co. v. Aspen Highlands Skiing Corp.,* 472 U.S. 585]

© Manuel Gutjahr/iStockphoto.com

CHAPTER 6

Administrative Agencies

learningoutcomes

After studying this chapter, you should be able to

LO.1 Describe the nature and purpose of administrative agencies

LO.2 Discuss the legislative or rulemaking power of administrative agencies

LO.3 Explain the executive or enforcement function of administrative agencies

LO.4 Discuss the judicial power of administrative agencies including the rule on exhaustion of administrative remedies

L
ate in the nineteenth century, a new type of governmental structure began to develop to meet the highly specialized needs of government regulation of business: the administrative agency. The administrative agency is now typically the instrument through which government makes and carries out its regulations.

A. NATURE OF THE ADMINISTRATIVE AGENCY

administrative agency – government body charged with administering and implementing legislation.

Social Security

An **administrative agency** is a government body charged with administering and implementing legislation. An agency may be a department, independent establishment, commission, administration, authority, board, or bureau. Agencies exist on the federal and state levels. One example of a federal agency is the Federal Trade Commission (FTC), whose structure is shown in Figure 6-1.

1. Purpose of Administrative Agencies

Federal administrative agencies are created to carry out general policies specified by Congress. Federal agencies include the Securities Exchange Commission (SEC), the Consumer Product Safety Commission (CPSC), and the Food and Drug Administration (FDA). The law governing these agencies is known as **administrative law**.

administrative law – law governing administrative agencies.

States also have administrative agencies that may have jurisdiction over areas of law affecting business, such as workers' compensation claims, real estate licensing, and unemployment compensation.

2. Uniqueness of Administrative Agencies

Administrative agencies differ from the legislative branch in that those who head up and operate are ordinarily appointed (in the case of federal agencies, by the president of the United States with the consent of the Senate).

| FIGURE 6-1 | *Structure of the Federal Trade Commission* |

© Cengage Learning

FIGURE 6-2   *The Administrative Chain of Command*

© Cengage Learning

In the tripartite structure of legislative, executive, and judicial branches, the judicial branch reviews actions of the executive and legislative branches to ensure that they have not exceeded their constitutional powers. However, governmental agencies combine legislative, executive, and judicial powers (see Figure 6-2). These agencies make the rules, conduct inspections to see that the rules have been or are being obeyed, and determine whether there have been violations of their rules. Because agencies have such broad powers, they are subject to strict procedural rules as well as disclosure requirements (discussed in the following section).

3. Open Operation of Administrative Agencies

The public has ready access to the activity of administrative agencies. That access comes in three ways: (1) open records, (2) open meetings, and (3) public announcement of agency guidelines. The actions and activities of most federal agencies that are not otherwise regulated are controlled by the **Administrative Procedure Act** (APA).[1] Many states have adopted statutes with provisions similar to those of the APA.

Administrative Procedure Act—federal law that establishes the operating rules for administrative agencies.

Freedom of Information Act—federal law permitting citizens to request documents and records from administrative agencies.

(A) OPEN RECORDS. The **Freedom of Information Act**[2] (FOIA) provides that information contained in records of federal administrative agencies is available to citizens on proper request. The primary purpose of this statute is "to ensure that government activities be opened to the sharp eye of public scrutiny."[3] To ensure that members of the public understand how to obtain records, the FOIA provides that "[e]ach agency shall ... publish in the *Federal Register* for the guidance of the public ... the methods whereby the public may obtain

---

[1] Administrative Procedures Act 5 U.S.C. §550 *et seq.*
[2] 5 U.S.C. §552 *et seq.* The Electronic Freedom of Information Act Amendments of 1996 extend the public availability of information to electronically stored data.
[3] *Brady-Lunny v. Massey*, 185 F. Supp. 2d 928 (C.D. Ill. 2007). See also *Better Government Association v. Blagojevich*, 899 N.E.2d 382 (Ill. App. 2008).

information, make submittals or requests, or obtain decisions."[4] There are exceptions to this right of public scrutiny. They prevent individuals and companies from obtaining information that is not necessary to their legitimate interests and might harm the person or company whose information is being sought.[5] State statutes typically exempt from disclosure any information that would constitute an invasion of the privacy of others. However, freedom of information acts are broadly construed, and unless an exemption is clearly given, the information in question is subject to public inspection.[6] Moreover, the person claiming that there is an exemption that prohibits disclosure has the burden of proving that the exemption applies to the particular request made. Exemptions include commercial or financial information not ordinarily made public by the person or company that supplies the information to the agency as part of the agency's enforcement role.[7]

The FOIA's primary purpose is to subject agency action to public scrutiny. Its provisions are liberally interpreted, and agencies must make good-faith efforts to comply with its terms.

open meeting law–law that requires advance notice of agency meeting and public access.

(B) OPEN MEETINGS. Under the Sunshine Act of 1976,[8] called the **open meeting law**, the federal government requires most meetings of major administrative agencies to be open to the public. The Sunshine Act[9] applies to those meetings involving "deliberations" of the agency or those that "result in the joint conduct or disposition of official agency business." The object of this statute is to enable the public to know what actions agencies are taking and to prevent administrative misconduct by having open meetings and public scrutiny. Many states also have enacted Sunshine laws.

(C) PUBLIC ANNOUNCEMENT OF AGENCY GUIDELINES. To inform the public of the way administrative agencies operate, the APA, with certain exceptions, requires that each federal agency publish the rules, principles, and procedures that it follows.[10]

✳ B. LEGISLATIVE POWER OF THE AGENCY

An administrative agency has the power to make laws and does so by promulgating regulations with public input.

4. Agency's Regulations as Law

An agency may adopt regulations within the scope of its authority. The power of an agency to carry out a congressional program "necessarily requires the formulation of policy and the making of rules to fill any gap left by Congress."[11] If the regulation is not authorized by the law creating the agency, anyone affected by it can challenge the regulation on the basis that the agency has exceeded its authority. [See Section 11(c), "Beyond the Jurisdiction of the Agency."]

---

[4] 5 U.S.C. §552(a)(1)(a).

[5] Additional protection is provided by the Privacy Act of 1974, 5 U.S.C. §552a(b); *Doe v. U.S. Dept. of Treasury*, 706 F. Supp. 2d 1 (D.D.C. 2009).

[6] Corporations have limited privacy rights. *FCC v. AT&T Inc.* 131 S.Ct. 1177 (2011).

[7] *Sun-Sentinel Company v. U.S. Dept. of Homeland Security*, 431 F. Supp. 2d 1258 (S.D Fla. 2006). For a state law example, see *Oklahoma Public Employees Ass'n v. State ex rel. Oklahoma Office of Personnel Management*, 267 P.3d 838 (Okla. 2011).

[8] The Government in the Sunshine Act can be found at 5 U.S.C. §552b.

[9] 5 U.S.C. §552b(a)(2).

[10] APA codified at 5 U.S.C. §552. See Section 5(c) of this chapter for a description of the *Federal Register*, the publication in which these agency rules, principles, and procedures are printed.

[11] *National Elec. Mfrs. Ass'n v. U.S. Dept. of Energy*, 654 F.3d 496 (4th Cir. 2011).

An administrative agency cannot act beyond the scope of the authority in the statute that created it or assigned a responsibility to it.[12] However, the authority of an agency is not limited to the technology in existence at the time the agency was created or assigned jurisdiction for enforcement of laws. The sphere in which an agency may act expands with new scientific developments.[13]

CASE SUMMARY

Can An Agency Regulate Hot Air?

FACTS: On October 20, 1999, a group of 19 private organizations (petitioners) filed a rulemaking petition asking EPA to regulate "greenhouse gas emissions from new motor vehicles under §202 of the Clean Air Act." These organizations argued that greenhouse gas emissions have significantly accelerated climate change, and that "carbon dioxide remains the most important contributor to [man-made] forcing of climate change."

Fifteen months after the petition was filed, the EPA requested public comment on "all the issues raised in [the] petition," adding a "particular" request for comments on "any scientific, technical, legal, economic or other aspect of these issues that may be relevant to EPA's consideration of this petition, including whether there was global warming due to carbon emissions." The EPA received more than 50,000 comments over the next five months.

On September 8, 2003, EPA entered an order denying the rulemaking petition because (1) the Clean Air Act does not authorize EPA to issue mandatory regulations to address global climate change; and (2) even if the agency had the authority to set greenhouse gas emission standards, it would be unwise to do so at this time. Massachusetts, other states, and private organizations filed suit challenging the EPA denial as arbitrary and capricious, violative of the APA, and *ultra vires* because of statutory mandates for EPA action.

The court of appeals dismissed the appeal from the agency denial and the Supreme Court granted *certiorari*.

DECISION: The Court held that greenhouse gases were a form of pollution and that the Clean Air Act required the EPA to take steps to curb those emissions. The Court found that any justification the EPA gave for inaction was not supported by either the statutory construction or the evidence on global warming. The decision was a 5 to 4 decision in which the dissent maintained that no matter how strongly we feel about global warming, action is left to the executive and legislative branches, not the courts. The dissent also noted that agencies should be given great deference in making their decisions on whether to regulate certain issues and that the statute did not mandate regulation – it gave the EPA broad discretion and its discretion could include lack of scientific conclusions, deference to the president, or other agencies. [*Massachusetts v. EPA*, 549 U.S. 497 (2007)]

When an agency's proposed regulation deals with a policy question that is not specifically addressed by statute, the agency that was created or given the discretion to administer the statute may establish new policies covering such issues. This power is granted regardless of whether the lawmaker intentionally left such matters to the agency's discretion or merely did not foresee the problem. In either case, the matter is one to be determined within the agency's discretion, and courts defer to agencies'

---

[12] *Zuni Public School Dist. No. 89 v. Department of Educ.*, 550 U.S. 81 (2007).
[13] *United States v. Midwest Video Corp.*, 406 U.S. 649 (1972) (sustaining a commission regulation that provided that "no CATV system having 3,500 or more subscribers shall carry the signal of any television broadcast station unless the system also operates to a significant extent as a local outlet by cablecasting and has available facilities for local production and presentation of programs other than automated services").

policy decisions.[14] **For Example,** the FCC has authority to deal with cell phones and cell phone providers even though when the agency was created, there were only the traditional types of land-line telephones.

Courts regard the administrative agency as holding all powers necessary to effectively perform the duties entrusted to it. When the agency establishes a rational basis for its rule, courts accept the rule and do not substitute their own judgment.[15]

5. Agency Adoption of Regulations

(A) CONGRESSIONAL ENABLING ACT. Before an agency can begin rulemaking proceedings, it must be given jurisdiction by congressional enactment in the form of a statute. **For Example,** Congress has enacted broad statutes governing discrimination in employment practices and has given authority to the Equal Employment Opportunity Commission (EEOC) to establish definitions, rules, and guidelines for compliance with those laws. Sometimes an existing agency is assigned the responsibility for new legislation implementation and enforcement. **For Example,** the Department of Labor has been assigned the responsibility to handle the whistle-blower protection provisions of Sarbanes-Oxley that provide protection against retaliation and/or termination to those who report financial chicanery at their companies. The Department of Labor has been in existence for almost a century, but it was assigned a new responsibility and given new jurisdiction by Congress.

E-Commerce & Cyberlaw

Peer-to-Peer Sharing and the FCC's Authority

Several subscribers to Comcast's Internet services discovered that the company was interfering with their use of peer-to-peer networking applications. The subscribers asked the FCC to regulate the Internet management practices of Comcast. However, the court held that there was no statutory authority that permitted the FCC to regulate the internal practices of communication providers. [*Comcast Corp. v. F.C.C.,* **600 F.3d 642** (C.A.D.C. 2010)]

(B) AGENCY RESEARCH OF THE PROBLEM. After jurisdiction is established, the agency has the responsibility to research the issues and various avenues of regulation for implementing the statutory framework. As the agency does so, it determines the cost and benefit of the problems, issues, and solutions. The study may be done by the agency itself, or it may be completed by someone hired by the agency. **For Example,** before red lights were required equipment in the rear windows of all cars, the Department of Transportation developed a study using taxicabs with the red lights in the rear windows and found that the accident rate for rear-end collisions with taxicabs was reduced dramatically. The study provided justification for the need for regulation as well as the type of regulation itself.

(C) PROPOSED REGULATIONS. Following a study, the agency proposes regulations, which must be published. To provide publicity for all regulations, the **Federal Register Act**[16] provides that proposed administrative regulation be published in the *Federal Register*. This is a government publicatin published five days a week that lists all administrative

Federal Register Act – federal law requiring agencies to make public disclosure of proposed rules, passed rules, and activities.

Federal Register – government publication issued five days a week that lists all administrative regulations, all presidential proclamations and executive orders, and other documents and classes of documents that the president or Congress direct to be published.

---

[14] *Chevron, U.S.A., Inc. v. National Resources Defense Council, Inc.,* 467 U.S. 837 (1984).
[15] *Covad Communications Co. v. FCC,* 450 F.3d 528 (D.C. Cir. 2006).
[16] 44 U.S.C. §1505 *et seq.*

regulations, all presidential proclamations and executive orders, and other documents and classes of documents that the president or Congress directs to be published.

The Federal Register Act provides that printing an administrative regulation in the *Federal Register* is public notice of the contents of the regulation to persons subject to it or affected by it, but in addition, the Regulatory Flexibility Act,[17] passed during the Reagan administration, requires that all proposed rules be published in the trade journals of those trades that will be affected by the proposed rules. **For Example,** any changes in federal regulations on real property closings and escrows have to be published in real estate broker trade magazines. In addition to the public notice of the proposed rule, the agency must also include a "regulatory flexibility analysis" that "shall describe the impact of the proposed rule on small entities."[18] The goal of this portion of the APA was to be certain that small businesses were aware of proposed regulatory rules and their cost impact.

CASE SUMMARY

Seats Belts and Air Bags and Rules, Oh My!

FACTS: The U.S. Department of Transportation (DOT), charged with enforcing the National Traffic and Motor Vehicle Safety Act of 1966 and reducing auto accidents, passed Standard 208 in 1967, which required that all cars be equipped with seat belts. When another study showed the DOT that people did not use the belts, the department began a study of passive restraint systems which showed that these devices—automatic seat belts and air bags—could prevent approximately 12,000 deaths a year and over 100,000 serious injuries.

In 1972, after many hearings and comments, the DOT passed a regulation requiring some type of passive restraint system on all vehicles manufactured after 1975. Because of changes in directors of the DOT and the unfavorable economic climate in the auto industry, the requirements for passive restraints were postponed. In 1981, the department proposed a rescission of the passive restraint rule. After receiving written comments and holding public hearings, the agency concluded there was no longer a basis for reliably predicting that passive restraints increased safety levels or decreased accidents. Furthermore, the agency found it would cost $1 billion to implement the rule, and it was unwilling to impose such substantial costs on auto manufacturers.

State Farm filed suit on the rescission of the rule on the basis that it was arbitrary and capricious. The Court of Appeals held that the rescission was, in fact, arbitrary and capricious. The auto manufacturers appealed.

DECISION: Just as an agency cannot pass regulations without studies, comments, and hearings, an agency cannot withdraw a regulation without going through the same process. In this case, the regulation was eliminated without any prior study of the issues and the impact of its elimination. The withdrawal of a regulation requires the same procedural steps as the promulgation of a rule. [*Motor Vehicles Manufacturers Ass'n v. State Farm Mutual Ins. Co.,* **463 U.S. 29 (1983)**]

(D) PUBLIC COMMENT PERIOD. Following the publication of the proposed rules, the public has the opportunity to provide input on the proposed rules. Called the *public comment period,* this time must last at least 30 days (with certain emergency exceptions) and can consist simply of letters written by those affected that are filed with the agency or of hearings conducted by the agency in Washington, D.C., or at

[17] 5 U.S.C. §601 *et seq.*
[18] 5 U.S.C. §603(a).

FIGURE 6-3	*Steps in Agency Rulemaking*

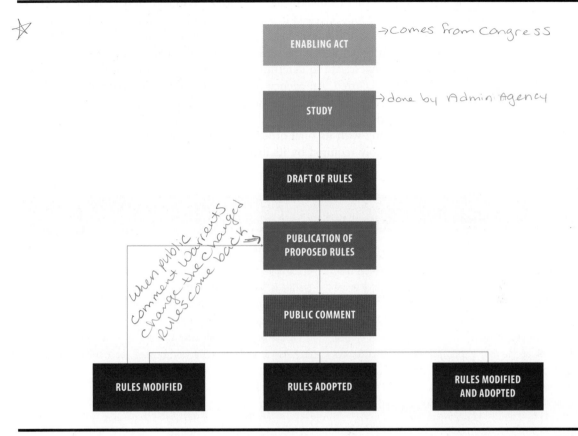

Handwritten annotations:
→ comes from Congress (pointing to ENABLING ACT)
→ done by Admin. Agency (pointing to STUDY)
When public warrants comment change the change rules come back (pointing to PUBLICATION OF PROPOSED RULES)

© Cengage Learning

specified locations around the country. An emergency exemption for the 30-day comment period was made when airport security measures and processes were changed following the September 11, 2001, attacks on the World Trade Center and the Pentagon that used domestic, commercial airliners.

(E) OPTIONS AFTER PUBLIC COMMENT. After receiving the public input on the proposed rule, an agency can decide to pass, or promulgate, the rule. The agency can also decide to withdraw the rule. **For Example,** the EEOC had proposed rules on handling religious discrimination in the workplace. The proposed rules, which would have required employers to police those wearing a cross or other religious symbol, met with so much public and employer protest that they were withdrawn. Finally, the agency can decide to modify the rule based on comments and then promulgate or, if the modifications are extensive or material, modify and put the proposed rule back out for public comment again. A diagram of the rule-making process can be found in Figure 6-3.

C. EXECUTIVE POWER OF THE AGENCY

The modern administrative agency has the power to execute the law and to bring proceedings against violators.

6. Enforcement or Execution of the Law

An agency has the power to investigate, to require persons to appear as witnesses, to require witnesses to produce relevant papers and records, and to bring proceedings against those who violate the law. In this connection, the phrase *the law* embraces regulations adopted by an agency as well as statutes and court decisions.

An agency may investigate to determine whether any violation of the law or of its rules generally has occurred. An agency may also investigate to determine whether additional rules need to be adopted, to ascertain the facts with respect to a particular suspected or alleged violation, and to see whether the defendant in a proceeding before it is complying with its final order. An agency may issue subpoenas to obtain information reasonably required by its investigation.[19]

Ethics & the Law

Joe the Plumber's Privacy

In 1997, the Internal Revenue Service (IRS) disciplined employees who, out of curiosity, were looking up tax returns of famous people to see who made how much income. The IRS fired 23 employees, disciplined 349, and provided counseling for 472. During the 2008 election, the director of the Ohio Department of Job and Family Services ordered employees to look up the child support payment record of Samuel Joseph Wurzelbacher (Joe the Plumber), a man who had raised a controversial issue to then-candidate Barack Obama. Helen Jones-Kelley, the director, was a donor to the Obama campaign. Employees in the office complained about the search, and the director said, "Our practice is when someone is thrust quickly into the public spotlight, we often take a look." The Ohio Inspector General investigated the use of state computers for the search.

Is this practice so bad? What is wrong with just looking at data accessible at work? Why are we concerned about selective research about private citizens? Does it matter that the information was not released to the public?

7. Constitutional Limitations on Administrative Investigation

Although administrative agencies have broad enforcement authority, they remain subject to the constitutional protections afforded individuals and businesses.

(A) INSPECTION OF PREMISES. Agency officials have the right to conduct inspections, pursuant to the warrant protections afforded by the Fourth Amendment (see Chapter 8). However, when violation of the law is dangerous to health and safety, a workplace inspection without advance notice or a search warrant is permitted when such a requirement could defeat the purpose of the inspection.

(B) AERIAL INSPECTION. A search warrant is never required when the subject matter can be seen from a public place. **For Example,** when a police officer walking on a public sidewalk can look through an open window and see illegal weapons, a search warrant is not required to enter the premises and seize the weapons. Using airplanes and helicopters, law enforcement officers can see from the air; an agency, too, can gather information in this manner.[20]

---

[19] *EEOC v. Sidley, Austen, Brown and Wood,* 35 F.3d 696 (7th Cir. 2002).
[20] *Dow Chemical Co. v. United States,* 476 U.S. 1819 (1986).

(c) PRODUCTION OF PAPERS. For the most part, the constitutional guarantee against unreasonable searches and seizures does not afford much protection for papers and records being investigated by an agency. **For Example,** a subpoena to testify or to produce records cannot be opposed on the ground that it is a search and seizure. The constitutional protection is limited to cases of actual physical search and seizure rather than obtaining information by compulsion. Employers must turn over to the Occupational Health and Safety Administration (OSHA) their records on workplace injuries and lost workdays.

The protection afforded by the guarantee against self-incrimination likewise cannot be invoked when a corporate employee or officer in control of corporate records is compelled to produce those records even though he or she would be incriminated by them.[21] The privilege against self-incrimination cannot be invoked if records required to be kept by law are involved.

(d) COMPLIANCE VERIFICATION. To ensure that a particular person or business is obeying the law, including an agency's regulations and orders, the administrative agency may require proof of compliance. At times, the question of compliance may be directly determined by an agency investigation, involving an examination either of a building or plant or of witnesses and documents. An agency may require the regulated person or enterprise to file reports in a specified form.[22]

D. JUDICIAL POWER OF THE AGENCY

Once the investigation of an agency reveals a potential violation of the law, an agency assumes its third role of judicial arbiter to conduct hearings on violations.

8. The Agency as a Specialized Court

An agency, although not a court by law, may be given power to sit as a court and to determine whether any violations of the law or of agency regulations have occurred. The National Labor Relations Board (NLRB) determines whether a prohibited labor practice has been committed. The Federal Trade Commission (FTC) acts as a court to determine whether someone has engaged in unfair competition.

(a) BEGINNING ENFORCEMENT—PRELIMINARY STEPS. Either a private individual or company or an agency may file a written complaint alleging some violation of law or regulation that is within the agency's jurisdiction. This complaint is then served on the company or individual named in the complaint, who then has the opportunity to file an answer to the allegations. There may be other phases of pleading between the parties and the agency, but eventually, the matter comes before the agency to be heard. After a hearing, the agency makes a decision and enters an order either dismissing the complaint or directing remedies or resolutions.

(b) THE ADMINISTRATIVE HEARING. To satisfy the requirements of due process, an agency handling a complaint must generally give notice and hold a hearing at which all

---

[21] *Braswell v. United States,* 487 U.S. 99 (1988); See also *Armstrong v. Guccione,* 470 F.3d 89 (2nd Cir. 2006).
[22] *United States v. Morton Salt Co.,* 338 U.S. 632 (1950).

persons affected may be present. A significant difference between an agency hearing and a court hearing is that there is no right of trial by jury before an agency. **For Example,** a workers' compensation board may decide a claim without any jury. Similarly, a case in which an employer protests the unemployment tax rate assigned to her company by a state agency has no right to a jury trial. The lack of a jury does not deny due process (see Chapter 4). An administrative law judge (ALJ) hears the complaint and has the authority to swear witnesses, take testimony, make evidentiary rulings, and make a decision to recommend to the agency heads for action.

An agency hearing is ordinarily not subject to the rules of evidence. Another difference between an administrative hearing and a judicial determination is that an agency may be authorized to make an initial determination without holding a hearing. If its conclusion is challenged, the agency then holds a hearing. This procedural difference has important practical consequences because the result is that fewer persons go to the trouble of seeking such a hearing, which reduces the number of hearings and the amount of litigation in which an agency becomes involved. The government saves money and time with this abbreviated process.

Civil servants of administrative agencies have greater protections when it comes to due process. The Supreme Court has held that because a civil service employee may be removed only for cause, it is a denial of due process for a statute to authorize an agency to remove the employee without a hearing.[23] Just giving the employee the right to appeal such action is not sufficient. There must be some form of hearing prior to removing the employee to determine that there were not errors in the administrative action.

informal settlements—negotiated disposition of a matter before an administrative agency, generally without public sanctions.

(c) Streamlined Procedure: Consent Decrees. Informal settlements or **consent decrees** are practical devices to cut across the procedures already outlined. In many instances, an alleged wrongdoer informally notified that a complaint has been made is willing to change. An agency's informing an alleged wrongdoer of the charge before filing any formal complaint is sound public relations, as well as expeditious policy. A matter that has already gone into the formal hearing stage may also be terminated by agreement, and a stipulation or consent decree may be filed setting forth the terms of the agreement. The Administrative Dispute Resolution Act of 1990 encourages the streamlining of the regulatory process and authorizes federal agencies to use alternative means of dispute resolution.[24]

consent decrees—informal settlements of enforcement actions brought by agencies.

(d) Form of Administrative Decision. When an administrative agency makes a decision, it usually files an opinion that sets forth findings of facts and reasons for that decision. In some instances, a statute expressly requires this type of opinion, but agencies usually file opinions so that the parties and the court (in the event of an appeal) will understand the agency's action and reasoning.[25]

9. Punishment and Enforcement Powers of Agencies

(a) Penalty. Within the last few decades, agencies have increasingly been given the power to impose a penalty and to issue orders that are binding on a regulated party unless an appeal is taken to a court, which reverses the administrative decision. **For Example,** the Occupational Safety and Health Act of 1970 provides for the

---

[23] *Cleveland Board of Education v. Loudermill,* 470 U.S. 532 (1985); *Darr v. Town of Telluride, Colo.,* 495 F.3d 1243 (10th Cir. 2007).
[24] 5 U.S.C. §571 *et seq.*
[25] *Jordan v. Civil Service Bd., Charlotte,* 570 S.E.2d 912 (N.C. App. 2002).

assessment of civil penalties against employers who fail to end dangerous working conditions when ordered to do so by the administrative agency created by that statute.[26]

(B) CEASE-AND-DESIST ORDER. Environmental protection statutes adopted by states commonly give a state agency the power to assess a penalty for violating environmental protection regulations. As an illustration of the issuance of binding orders, the FTC can issue a **cease-and-desist order** to stop a practice that it decides is improper. This order to stop is binding unless reversed on an appeal.
For Example, the FTC can order a company to stop making claims in ads that have been determined by that agency to be deceptive.

cease-and-desist order – order issued by a court or administrative agency to stop a practice that it decides is improper.

10. Exhaustion of Administrative Remedies

All parties interacting with an agency must follow the procedure specified by the law. No appeal to a court is possible until the agency has acted on the party's matter before it. As a matter of policy, parties are required to exhaust administrative remedies before they may go into court or take an appeal.

As long as an agency is acting within the scope of its authority or jurisdiction, a party cannot appeal before the agency has made a final decision. The fact that the complaining party does not want the agency to decide the matter or is afraid that the agency will reach a wrong decision is not grounds for bypassing the agency by going to court before the agency has acted.

Exceptions to the **exhaustion-of-administrative remedies** requirement are:
(1) available remedies that provide no genuine opportunity for adequate relief;
(2) irreparable injury that could occur if immediate judicial relief is not provided;
(3) an appeal to the administrative agency that would be useless; or (4) a substantial constitutional question that the plaintiff has raised.

exhaustion of administrative remedies – requirement that an agency make its final decision before the parties can go to court.

11. Appeal from Administrative Action and Finality of Administrative Determination

The statute creating the modern administrative agency generally provides that an appeal may be taken from the administrative decision to a particular court. The statute may provide the basis for an appeal. However, judicial precedent holds that courts may review administrative agency decisions on the bases covered in the following sections.

(A) PROCEDURAL ISSUES. If the procedure that an agency is to follow is specified by law, a decision of the agency that was made without following that procedure will be set aside and the matter sent back to the agency to proceed according to the required law.[27] An agency's actions, whether enforcement or rule promulgation, can be set aside if the agency has not followed the procedures required for rule making or, in the case of enforcement, the due process rights of the charged business or individual.

(B) SUBSTANTIVE LAW OR FACT ISSUES. When the question that an agency decides is a question of law, the court on appeal will reverse the agency if the court disagrees with the legal interpretation.[28] Courts tend to accept the agency's interpretation so

---

[26] 29 U.S.C. §651 *et seq.*
[27] *Tingler v. State Board of Cosmetology*, 814 S.W.2d 683 (Mo. App. 1991).
[28] *Wallace v. Iowa State Bd. of Educ.*, 770 N.W.2d 344 (Iowa 2009).

long as it was reasonable even though it was not the only interpretation that could have been made.

A court will not reverse an agency's decision merely because the court would have made a different decision based on the same facts.[29] Because most disputes before an agency are based on questions of fact, the net result is that the agency's decision will be final in most cases.

Courts must give administrative agencies the freedom to do the work delegated to them and should not intervene unless the agency action is clearly unreasonable or arbitrary (see below). The agency action is presumed proper, and a person seeking reversal of the agency action has the burden to prove a basis for reversal.[30]

(c) BEYOND THE JURISDICTION OF THE AGENCY. When the question is whether an administrative action is in harmony with the policy of the statute creating the agency, an appellate court will sustain the administrative action if substantial evidence supports it.

(d) ARBITRARY AND CAPRICIOUS. When an agency changes its prior decisions and customary actions, it must give its reasons. In the absence of such an explanation, a reviewing court cannot tell whether the agency changed its interpretation of the law for a valid reason or has made a mistake. The absence of an explanation means the agency action is arbitrary and requires reversal.[31]

A decision involving agency discretion will not be reversed in the absence of an error of law or a clear abuse of, or the arbitrary or capricious exercise of, discretion. The courts reason that because agency members were appointed on the basis of expert ability, it would be absurd for the court, which is unqualified technically to make a decision in the matter, to step in and determine whether the agency made the proper choice. Courts will not do so unless the agency has clearly acted wrongly, arbitrarily, or capriciously. As a practical matter, an agency's action is rarely found to be arbitrary or capricious. As long as an agency has followed proper procedure, the fact that the court disagrees with the agency's conclusion does not make that conclusion arbitrary or capricious.

CASE SUMMARY

Drilling Down to Arbitrary and Capricious Rules

FACTS: Hornbeck and others (plaintiffs) provide services to support offshore oil and gas drilling, exploration, and production activities in the Gulf of Mexico. Kenneth Salazar is the Secretary of the Department of Interior (DOI), a federal agency that includes the Minerals Management.

Following the BP Deepwater Horizon drilling platform explosion on April 20, 2010, and the resulting devastation and unprecedented disaster, the President asked DOI to conduct a study to determine what steps were needed to be taken to prevent another problem with oil rigs in the Gulf.

DOI did a 30-day study, consulting respected experts from state and federal governments, academic institutions, and industry and advocacy organizations. On May 27, 2010, DOI issued a Report that recommended a six-month moratorium on permits for new wells and an immediate halt to drilling operations on the 33 permitted wells in the Gulf of Mexico. The DOI report also stated that "the recommendations contained in this report have been peer-reviewed by seven experts identified by the National Academy of Engineering." The experts pointedly observed that

[29] *Dorchester Associates LLC v. District of Columbia Bd. of Zoning Adjustment,* 976 A.2d 200 (D.C. 2009).
[30] See note 29.
[31] *Lorillard Tobacco Co. v. Roth,* 786 N.E.2d 7 (N.Y. App. 2003).

CASE SUMMARY

Continued

this statement was misleading and called it a "misrepresentation." Although the experts agreed with the safety recommendations contained in the body of the main Report, five of the National Academy of Engineering experts and three of the other experts publicly stated that they "do not agree with the six month blanket moratorium" on floating drilling. They envisioned a more limited kind of moratorium, but a blanket moratorium was added after their final review and was never agreed to by them. The plaintiffs moved for a preliminary injunction against the moratorium.

DECISION: The court held that the experts balking at the conclusion of the report, the inconsistency of the moratorium with the report information, and the availability of alternatives made the moratorium unlikely to survive a challenge of the action being arbitrary and capricious and issued an injunction. [*Hornbeck Offshore Services, L.L.C. et al. v. Salazar*, 696 F. Supp. 2d (E.D. La. 2010)]

In areas in which economic or technical matters are involved, it is generally sufficient that the agency had a reasonable basis for its decision. A court will not attempt to second-guess the agency about complex criteria with which an administrative agency is intimately familiar. However, if an agency's recommendation parts ways with the underlying factual findings or the conclusions of its experts, then the court is likely to find that the actions of the agency were arbitrary and capricious. The judicial attitude is that for protection from laws and regulations that are unwise, improvident, or out of harmony with a particular school of thought, the people must resort to the ballot box, not to the court.

(E) CONSTITUTIONAL RIGHTS. Challenges to administrative agency rules and actions can also be based in constitutional rights.[32] For example, agency restrictions on language or religious freedom have been successfully challenged in court. EEOC regulations on employees wearing religious jewelry (such as necklaces with crosses) were withdrawn after the agency realized through congressional actions that the regulations could not survive a constitutional challenge.

CASE SUMMARY

The Obscenity Case That Has Been Around As Long As Cher

FACTS: In a case that has been around almost as long as Cher, the U.S. Supreme Court, once again, issued a decision related to three FCC charges against Fox and ABC Television. First, in the 2002 Billboard Music Awards, broadcast by Fox Television, the singer Cher exclaimed during an unscripted acceptance speech: "I've also had my critics for the last 40 years saying that I was on my way out every year. Right. So f * * * 'em." At the 2003 Billboard Music Awards, Nicole Richie made the following unscripted remark while presenting an award: "Have you ever tried to get cow s* * * out of a Prada purse? It's not so f * * *ing simple." The third incident involved an episode of NYPD Blue, a regular television show broadcast by respondent ABC Television Network. The episode, broadcast on February 25, 2003, showed the nude buttocks of

32 *CBS Corp. v. F.C.C.*, 663 F.3d 122 (3rd Cir 2011).

CASE SUMMARY

Continued

an adult female character for approximately seven seconds and for a moment the side of her breast. During the scene, in which the character was preparing to take a shower, a child portraying her boyfriend's son entered the bathroom. A moment of awkwardness followed. The FCC received indecency complaints about all three broadcasts.

After these incidents, but before the FCC issued Notices of Apparent Liability to Fox and ABC, it issued a decision sanctioning NBC for a comment made by the singer Bono during the 2003 Golden Globe Awards. Upon winning the award for Best Original Song, Bono exclaimed: "'This is really, really, f***ing brilliant. Really, really great.'" The FCC found that the use of the F-word was "one of the most vulgar, graphic and explicit descriptions of sexual activity in the English language," and found that "any use of that word or a variation, in any context, inherently" indecent. The FCC then found that both Fox and ABC had violated commission standards for decency.

The networks appealed the findings of indecency and their fines ($1.4 million each). The U.S. Supreme Court (*FCC v. Fox Television Stations, Inc.* (Fox 1), 556 U.S. 502 (2009) held that the FCC's findings were not arbitrary nor capricious and remanded the case for findings related to the network's First Amendment challenges to the fines. On remand, the Court of Appeals found that the FCC indecency policy failed to give broadcasters sufficient notice of what would be considered indecent. The Court of Appeals found that the FCC was inconsistent as to which words it deemed patently offensive. The FCC standard was held to be void for vagueness. The FCC appealed.

DECISION: On appeal the U.S. Supreme Court held that the FCC failed to give Fox or ABC fair notice prior to the broadcasts in question that fleeting expletives and momentary nudity could be found indecent. Therefore, the FCC's standards, as applied to these broadcasts, were vague and void under the First Amendment. The court set aside the FCC's findings as well as its orders and fines against the networks.

The FCC is free to create standards of decency for broadcasting programs. However, the standards must be established in advance of any charges of violations and those standards must be clear and applied consistently. Because the broadcasters would not have understood the standard at the time the violations occurred, the U.S. Supreme Court struck down the standards as void for vagueness. [*F.C.C. v. Fox Television Stations, Inc.*, 132 S.Ct. 2307 (2012)]

(F) ARBITRARY ENFORCEMENT ACTIONS. Because of limited funding and staff, an agency must exercise discretion in deciding which cases it should handle. Ordinarily, a court will not reverse an agency's decision to do nothing about a particular complaint.[33] That is, the courts will not override an agency's decision to do nothing. Exceptions include acting arbitrarily in those enforcement actions as when an agency refuses to act in circumstances in which action is warranted and necessary.

12. Liability of the Agency

The decision of an agency may cause substantial loss to a business by increasing its operating costs or by making a decision that later is shown to be harmful to the economy. An agency is not liable for such loss when it has acted in good faith in the exercise of discretionary powers. An administrator who wrongly denies a person the benefit of a government program is not personally liable to that person.

---

[33] *Heckler v. Chaney*, 470 U.S. 821 (1985).

LawFlix

Clear and Present Danger (1994) PG-13

The struggles of Jack Ryan involve more than Colombian drug lords; he must battle the political appointees and their overstepping of their agency's authority. The relationship between agencies and Congress is also depicted in the film.

MAKE THE CONNECTION

SUMMARY

The administrative agency is unique because it combines the three functions that are kept separate under our traditional governmental system: legislative, executive, and judicial. By virtue of legislative power, an agency adopts regulations that have the force of law, although agency members are not elected by those subject to the regulations. By virtue of the executive power, an agency carries out and enforces the regulations, makes investigations, and requires the production of documents. By virtue of the judicial power, an agency acts as a court to determine whether a violation of any regulation has occurred. To some extent, an agency is restricted by constitutional limitations in inspecting premises and requiring the production of papers. These limitations, however, have a very narrow application in agency actions. When an agency acts as a judge, a jury trial is not required, nor must ordinary courtroom procedures be followed. Typically, an agency gives notice to the person claimed to be acting improperly, and a hearing is then held before the agency. When the agency has determined that there has been a violation, it may order that the violation stop. Under some statutes, the agency may go further and impose a penalty on the violator.

No appeal from an administrative agency's action can be made until every step available before the agency has been taken; that is, the administrative remedy must first be exhausted. An agency's actions can be reversed by a court if the agency exceeded its authority, the decision is not based in law or fact, the decision is arbitrary and capricious, the decision violates the laws or the rights of those affected by the agency's rule or actions, or, finally, the agency violated procedural steps.

Protection from secret government is provided by Sunshine laws that afford the right to know what most administrative agency records contain; by the requirement that most agency meetings be open to the public; by the invitation to the public to take part in rulemaking; and by publicity given, through publication in the *Federal Register* and trade publications, to the guidelines followed by the agency and the regulations it has adopted.

LEARNING OUTCOMES

After studying this chapter, you should be able to clearly explain:

A. Nature of the Administrative Agency

L0.1   Describe the nature and purpose of administrative agencies

See Section A(2) for a discussion of the unique nature of agencies, p. 93.

B. Legislative Power of the Agency

L0.2   Discuss the legislative or rulemaking power of administrative agencies

See the *EPA* case on p. 96.

C. Executive Power of the Agency

L0.3   Explain the executive or enforcement function of administrative agencies

See the *FCC* case on p. 105.

D. Judicial Power of the Agency

L0.4   Discuss the judicial power of administrative agencies including the rule on exhaustion of administrative remedies

See the *Salazar* case on p. 105.

KEY TERMS

administrative agency
administrative law
Administrative Procedure Act
cease-and-desist order

consent decrees
exhaustion-of-administrative
  remedies
Federal Register Act

Federal Register
Freedom of Information Act
informal settlements
open meeting law

QUESTIONS AND CASE PROBLEMS

1. Following the events of September 11, 2001, in which four airplanes crashed as a result of the presence of terrorists on those flights, the FAA concluded that it needed to implement new procedures for airports and flights. The new procedures for security and flights took effect when the airports reopened five days later. Why did the FAA not need to go through the promulgation and public comment processes and time periods to have the new rules take effect?

2. The FDA was challenged by tobacco companies for its new rules that required the tobacco companies to put one of the FDA's 12 picture labels on its packaging. The tobacco companies argued that their First Amendment rights were violated by the rules, forcing them to speak in a certain way using government-mandated materials. The new labels were promulgated by both the FDA and the Department of Health and Human Services (HHS) pursuant to authority granted by Congress in 2009 under the Family Smoking Prevention and Tobacco Control Act.

   Under the law, the following nine textual statements were to be included on cigarette labels:

   WARNING: Cigarettes are addictive.

   WARNING: Tobacco smoke can harm your children.

   WARNING: Cigarettes cause fatal lung disease.

   WARNING: Cigarettes cause cancer.

WARNING: Cigarettes cause strokes and heart disease.

WARNING: Smoking during pregnancy can harm your baby.

WARNING: Smoking can kill you.

WARNING: Tobacco smoke causes fatal lung diseases in nonsmokers.

WARNING: Quitting smoking now greatly reduces serious risks to your health.

The act required that these warnings and graphic labels take up 50 percent of the cigarette package label and 20 percent of all cigarette ads.

   After publishing the proposed rule and receiving more than 1,700 comments, the FDA published its final rule in June 2011. Explain how the tobacco companies could challenge the rules. Discuss whether the rules will be set aside. [In the case of *R.J. Reynolds Tobacco Company et al. v. FDA et al.,* —F.3d —, 2012 WL 3632003 (D.C. Cir.)]

3. The Tacoma-Pierce County Health Department conducted an investigation into the quality of care provided by ambulance service providers in its jurisdiction. On the basis of that investigation, the department issued a set of temporary rules and regulations that established minimum requirements for equipment, drugs, and service availability for ambulance service providers in Pierce County. The *Tacoma News* wanted to publish an article on the matter and sought discovery of everything that had led to the

adoption of the regulations, including all details of the investigation made by the health department. The health department objected to disclosing the names of the persons who had volunteered information on which the department had based its action and the names of the ambulance companies. Were the names subject to a Freedom of Information Act (FOIA) request? [*Tacoma News, Inc. v. Tacoma-Pierce County Health Dept.*, 778 P.2d 1066 (Wash. App.)]

4. Congress adopted a law to provide insurance to protect wheat farmers. The agency in charge of the program adopted regulations to govern applications for this insurance. These regulations were published in the *Federal Register*. Merrill applied for insurance, but his application did not comply with the regulations. He claimed that he was not bound by the regulations because he never knew they had been adopted. Is he bound by the regulations? [*Federal Crop Ins. Corp. v. Merrill*, 332 U.S. 380]

5. Santa Monica adopted a rent control ordinance authorizing the Rent Control Board to set the amount of rents that could be charged. At a hearing before it, the board determined that McHugh was charging his tenants a rent higher than the maximum allowed. McHugh claimed that the action of the board was improper because there was no jury trial. Is McHugh correct? Why or why not? [*McHugh v. Santa Monica Rent Control Board*, 777 P.2d 911 (Cal.)]

6. New York City's charter authorized the New York City Board of Health to adopt a health code that it declared to have the force and effect of law. The board adopted a code that provided for the fluoridation of the public water supply. A suit was brought to enjoin the carrying out of this program on the grounds that it was unconstitutional and that money could not be spent to carry out such a program in the absence of a statute authorizing the expenditure. It was also claimed that the fluoridation program was unconstitutional because there were other means of reducing tooth decay; fluoridation was discriminatory by benefiting only children; it unlawfully imposed medication on children

without their consent; and fluoridation was or may be dangerous to health. Was the code's provision valid? [*Paduano v. City of New York*, 257 N.Y.S.2d 531]

7. What is the *Federal Register*? What role does it play in rulemaking? What is the difference between the *Federal Register* and the Code of Federal Regulations?

8. The Consumer Product Safety Commission is reconsidering a rule it first proposed in 1997 that would require child-resistant caps on household products, including cosmetics. When the rule was first proposed in 1997, it was resisted by the cosmetics industry and abandoned. However, in May 2001, a 16-month-old baby died after drinking baby oil from a bottle with a pull-tab cap.

The proposed rule would cover products such as baby oil and suntan lotion and any products containing hydrocarbons such as cleansers and spot removers. The danger, according to the commission, is simply the inhalation by children, not necessarily the actual ingestion of the products. Five children have died from inhaling such fumes since 1993, and 6,400 children under the age of five were brought into emergency rooms and/or hospitalized for treatment after breathing in hydrocarbons. There is no medical treatment for the inhalation of hydrocarbons.

Several companies in the suntan oil/lotion industry have supported the new regulations. The head of a consumer group has said, "We know these products cause death and injury. That is all we need to know."[34]

What process must the CPSC follow to promulgate the rules? What do you think of the consumer group head's statement? Will that statement alone justify the rulemaking?

9. The *Federal Register* contained the following provision from the Environmental Protection Agency on January 14, 2002:

We, the U.S. Fish and Wildlife Service (Service), announce the re-opening of the comment period on the proposed listing of Lomatium cookii *(Cook's lomatium) and* Limnanthes floccosa ssp. grandiflora *(large-flowered wooly meadowfoam) as*

---

[34] Julian E. Barnes, "Safety Caps Are Considered for Cosmetics," *New York Times*, October 10, 2001, C1, C8.

endangered species under the Endangered Species Act of 1973, as amended (Act). We are re-opening the comment period to provide the public an opportunity to review additional information on the status, abundance, and distribution of these plants, and to request additional information and comments from the public regarding the proposed rule. Comments previously submitted need not be resubmitted as they will be incorporated into the public record as part of this extended comment period; all comments will be fully considered in the final rule.

DATES: We will accept public comments until March 15, 2002.

What was the EPA doing and why? What could those who had concerns do at that point?

10. Macon County Landfill Corp. applied for permission to expand the boundaries of its landfill. Tate and others opposed the application. After a number of hearings, the appropriate agency granted the requested permission to expand. Tate appealed and claimed that the agency had made a wrong decision on the basis of the evidence presented. Will the court determine whether the correct decision was made? [*Tate v. Illinois Pollution Control Board*, 544 N.E.2d 1176 (Ill. App.)]

11. The planning commissioner and a real estate developer planned to meet to discuss rezoning certain land that would permit the real estate developer to construct certain buildings not allowed under the then-existing zoning law. A homeowners association claimed it had the right to be present at the meeting. This claim was objected to on the theory that the state's Open Meetings Act applied only to meetings of specified government units and did not extend to a meeting between one of them and an outsider. Was this objection valid?

12. The Michigan Freedom of Information Act declares that it is the state's policy to give all persons full information about the actions of the government and that "the people shall be informed so that they may participate in the democratic process." The union of clerical workers at Michigan State University requested the trustees of the university to give them the names and addresses of persons making monetary donations to the university. Michigan State objected because the disclosure of addresses was a violation of the right of privacy. Decide. [*Clerical-Technical Union of Michigan State University v. Board of Trustees of Michigan State University*, 475 N.W.2d 373 (Mich.)]

13. The Department of Health and Human Services has proposed new guidelines for the interpretation of federal statutes on gifts, incentives, and other benefits bestowed on physicians by pharmaceutical companies. The areas on which the interpretation focused follow:

- Paying doctors to act as consultants or market researchers for prescription drugs

- Paying pharmacies fees to switch patients to new drugs

- Providing grants, scholarships, and anything more than nominal gifts to physicians for time, information sessions, and so on, on new drugs[35]

The Office of Inspector General is handling the new rules interpretation and has established a public comment period of 60 days. Explain the purpose of the public comment period. What ethical issues do the regulations attempt to address?

14. San Diego Air Sports (SDAS) Center operates a sports parachuting business in Otay Mesa, California. SDAS offers training to beginning parachutists and facilitates recreational jumping for experienced parachutists. It indicates that the majority of SDAS jumps occur at altitudes in excess of 5,800 feet. The jump zone used by SDAS overlaps the San Diego Traffic Control Area (TCA). Although the aircraft carrying the parachutists normally operate outside the TCA, the parachutists themselves are dropped through it. Thus, the air traffic controllers must approve each jump.

In July 1987, an air traffic controller in San Diego filed an Unsatisfactory Condition Report with the Federal Aviation Administration (FAA),

---

[35] See 67 *Federal Register* 62057, October 3, 2002. Go to **www.oig.hhs.gov**. See also Robert Pear, "U.S. Warning to Drug Makers Over Payments," *New York Times*, October 1, 2002, A1, A23; Julie Appleby, "Feds Warn Drugmakers: Gifts to Doctors May Be Illegal," *USA Today*, October 2, 2002, 1A.

complaining of the strain that parachuting was putting on the controllers and raising safety concerns. The report led to a staff study of parachute jumping within the San Diego TCA. This was followed by a letter in March 1988 from the FAA to SDAS, informing SDAS that "[e]ffective immediately parachute jumping within or into the San Diego TCA in the Otay Reservoir Jump Zone will not be authorized." The FAA stated that the letter was final and appealable. SDAS challenged the letter in federal court on grounds that it constituted rulemaking without compliance with required Administrative Procedure Act (APA) procedures. Who is correct in this dispute and why? [*San Diego Air Sports Center, Inc. v. FAA*, 887 F.2d 966 (9th Cir.)]

15. The Endangered Species Act (ESA) charges the National Marine Fisheries Service (a federal agency) with the duty to "ensure" that any proposed action by the Council does not "jeopardize" any threatened or endangered species. The Steller sea lion is on the list of endangered species. The agency developed a North Pacific marine fishery plan that permitted significant harvest of fish by commercial fisheries in the area. Greenpeace, an environmental group, challenged the agency on the grounds that the plan was not based on a sufficient number of biological studies on the impact of the allowed fishing on the Steller sea lion. Greenpeace's biologic opinion concluded that the fishery plan would reduce the level of food for the sea lions by about 40 percent to 60 percent, if the juvenile fish were not counted in that figure. Greenpeace's expert maintained that counting juvenile fish was misleading because they were not capable of reproducing and the government agency's figure was, as a result, much lower at 22 percent. What would Greenpeace need to show to be successful in challenging the agency's fishery plan? [*Greenpeace, American Oceans Campaign v. National Marine Fisheries Service*, 237 F. Supp. 2d 1181 (W.D. Wash.)]

© Manuel Gutjahr/iStockphoto.com

CHAPTER 7

The Legal Environment of International Trade

learningoutcomes

After studying this chapter, you should be able to

LO.1 Explain which country's law will govern an international contract should a dispute arise

LO.2 Identify seven major international organizations, conferences, and treaties that affect the multinational markets for goods, services, and investments

LO.3 List the forms of business organizations for doing business abroad

LO.4 Explain the import protections afforded owners of U.S. intellectual property rights

LO.5 Explain the tariff barriers and nontariff barriers to the free movements of goods across borders

LO.6 Explain U.S. law regarding payment to foreign government officials as a means of obtaining business contracts with other governments, and compare U.S. law to laws and treaties applicable to most First World nations

Them he success or failure of the U.S. firms doing business in foreign countries may well depend on accurate information about the laws and customs of the host countries. In their domestic operations, U.S. business firms compete against imports from other nations. Such imported goods include Canadian lumber, Mexican machinery, Japanese automobiles, German steel, French wine, Chinese textiles, and Chilean copper. To compete effectively, U.S. firms should learn about the business practices of foreign firms. They should be alert to unfair trade practices that will put U.S. firms at a disadvantage. Such practices may include the violation of U.S. antitrust and antidumping laws or violation of international trade agreements. Individuals from all over the world participate in the U.S. securities markets. Special problems exist in the regulation and enforcement of U.S. securities laws involving financial institutions of countries with secrecy laws.

While this chapter focuses on the above aspects of the legal environment of international trade, the American people, nonprofit agencies, American businesses aware of their corporate social responsibilities, and government officials all are very much concerned about the working conditions of the people throughout the world who make the products sold in the United States. **For Example,** in 2012, Apple Inc. joined the Fair Labor Association (FLA), a Washington, D.C.–based nonprofit workers' rights group, and invited the FLA to investigate the performance of its largest suppliers, including Foxconn, China's largest private employer. The FLA report on Foxconn identified some 50 legal violations or policy gaps, including health and safety issues, excessive overtime, and low pay and overtime pay issues, which prompted Foxconn and Apple to agree to new reforms.[1] Nike, Inc., a U.S. apparel company with international operations, is also a participating member of the FLA, agreeing to uphold the FLA Workplace Code of Conduct and Compliance benchmarks.

A. GENERAL PRINCIPLES

Nations enter into treaties and conferences to further international trade. The business world has developed certain forms of organizations for conducting that trade.

1. The Legal Background

Because of the complexity and ever-changing character of the legal environment of international trade, this section will focus on certain underlying elements.

---

[1] Apple Inc.'s reports on supplier responsibility and its supplier list may be accessed at **http://apple.com/suppliersresponsibility/reports.html**.

(A) WHAT LAW APPLIES. When there is a sale of goods within the United States, one law typically applies to the transaction. Some variation may be introduced when the transaction is between parties in different states, but for the most part, the law governing the transaction is the U.S. law of contracts and the Uniform Commercial Code (UCC). In contrast, when an international contract is made, it is necessary to determine whether it is the law of the seller's country or the law of the importer's country that will govern. The parties to an international contract often resolve that question themselves as part of their contract, setting forth which country's law will govern should a dispute arise. Such a provision is called a **choice-of-law clause**.
For Example, U.S. investors Irmgard and Mitchell Lipcon provided capital to underwriters at Lloyd's of London and signed choice-of-law clauses in their investment agreements binding them to proceed in England under English law should disputes arise. When the Lipcons realized that their investments were exposed to massive liabilities for asbestos and pollution insurance claims, they sued in U.S. district court in Florida for alleged U.S. securities acts violations. However, their complaints were dismissed based on the choice-of-law clauses in their contracts. The U.S. court of appeals stated that the Lipcons must "honor their bargains" and attempt to vindicate their claims in English courts under English law. [2]

> **choice-of-law clause** – clause in an agreement that specifies which law will govern should a dispute arise.

The major trading countries of the world have entered into a number of treaties. When their citizens deal with each other and their respective rights are not controlled in their contract, their rights and liabilities are determined by looking at the treaty. These treaties are discussed in Section 7 of this chapter, including the United Nations Convention on Contracts for the International Sale of Goods (CISG), which deals with certain aspects of the formation and performance of international commercial contracts for the sale of goods.

(B) THE ARBITRATION ALTERNATIVE. Traditional litigation may be considered too time consuming, expensive, and divisive to the relationships of the parties to an international venture. The parties, therefore, may agree to arbitrate any contractual disputes that may arise according to dispute resolution procedures set forth in the contract.

Pitfalls exist for U.S. companies arbitrating disputes in foreign lands.
For Example, were a U.S. company to agree to arbitrate a contractual dispute with a Chinese organization in China, it would find that the arbitrator must be Chinese. Also, under Chinese law, only Chinese lawyers can present an arbitration case, even if one party is a U.S. company. Because of situations like this, it is common for parties to international ventures to agree to arbitrate their disputes in neutral countries.

An arbitration agreement gives the parties more control over the decision-making process. The parties can require that the arbitrator have the technical, language, and legal qualifications to best understand their dispute. While procedures exist for the prearbitration exchange of documents, full "discovery" is ordinarily not allowed. The decision of the arbitrator is final and binding on the parties with very limited judicial review possible.

(C) CONFLICTING IDEOLOGIES. Law, for all people and at all times, is the result of the desire of the lawmaker to achieve certain goals. These are the social forces that make the law. In the eyes of the lawmaker, the attainment of these goals is proper and

---

[2] *Lipcon v. Underwriters at Lloyd's, London,* 148 F.2d 1285, 1299 (11th Cir. 1998).

therefore ethical. This does not mean that we all can agree on what the international law should be because different people have different ideas as to what is right. This affects our views as to ownership, trade, and dealings with foreign merchants. **For Example,** a very large part of the world does not share the U.S. dislike of cartels. Other countries do not have our antitrust laws; therefore, their merchants can form a trust to create greater bargaining power in dealing with U.S. and other foreign merchants.

(D) FINANCING INTERNATIONAL TRADE. There is no international currency. This creates problems as to what currency to use and how to make payment in international transactions. Centuries ago, buyers used precious metals, jewels, or furs in payment. Today, the parties to an international transaction agree in their sales contract on the currency to be used to pay for the goods. They commonly require that the buyer furnish the seller a **letter of credit**, which is a commercial device used to guarantee payment to a seller in an international transaction. By this, an issuer, typically a bank, agrees to pay the drafts drawn against the buyer for the purchase price. In trading with merchants in some countries, the foreign country itself will promise that the seller will be paid.

> **letter of credit** – commercial device used to guarantee payment to a seller, primarily in an international business transaction.

2. International Trade Organizations, Conferences, and Treaties

A large number of organizations exist that affect the multinational markets for goods, services, and investments. A survey of major international organizations, conferences, and treaties follows.

(A) GATT AND WTO. The *General Agreement on Tariffs and Trade* 1994 (GATT 1994) is a multilateral treaty subscribed to by 127 member governments, including the United States.[3] It consists of the original 1947 GATT, numerous multilateral agreements negotiated since 1947, the Uruguay Round Agreements, and the agreement establishing the *World Trade Organization* (WTO). On January 1, 1995, the WTO took over responsibility for administrating and policing the objectives of the former GATT administrative structure. Since 1947 and the end of the World War II era, the goal of the GATT has been to liberalize world trade and make it secure for furthering economic growth and human development. The current round of WTO negotiations began in Doha, Qatar, in 2001. As the talks continued in Cancun in 2003 and Hong Kong in 2005 the developed countries and developing countries divided on key issues such as agricultural subsidies. After 10 years, Doha Round negotiations have stalled and, although negotiations continue, the future of the Doha Round remains uncertain.

The GATT is based on the fundamental principles of (1) trade without discrimination and (2) protection through tariffs. The principle of trade without discrimination is embodied in its **most-favored-nation clause**. In treaties between countries, a most-favored-nation clause is one whereby any privilege subsequently granted to a third country in relation to a given treaty subject is extended to the other party to the treaty. In the application and administration of import and export duties and charges under the GATT most-favored-nation clause, all member countries grant each other equal treatment. Thus, no country gives special trading

> **most-favored-nation clause** – clause in treaties between countries whereby any privilege subsequently granted to a third country in relation to a given treaty subject is extended to the other party to the treaty.

---

[3] In December 2011, after 18 years of negotiating membership, Russia became a WTO member and joined the GATT. To secure admission, Russia undertook a series of commitments designed to provide meaningful market access to member countries and a solid legal and administrative framework to guarantee the implementation of contractual commitments.

advantages to another. All member countries are equal and share the benefits of any moves toward lower trade barriers. Exceptions to this basic rule are allowed in certain special circumstances involving regional trading arrangements, such as the European Union (EU) and the North American Free Trade Agreement (NAFTA). Special preferences are also granted to developing countries. The second basic principle is protection for domestic industry, which should be extended essentially through a tariff, not through other commercial measures. The aim of this rule is to make the extent of protection clear and to make competition possible.

Dispute Settlement Body – means, provided by the World Trade Organization, for member countries to resolve trade disputes rather than engage in unilateral trade sanctions or a trade war.

The WTO provides a **Dispute Settlement Body (DSB)** to enable member countries to resolve trade disputes rather than engage in unilateral trade sanctions or a trade war. The DSB appoints panels to hear disputes concerning allegations of GATT agreement violations, and it adopts (or rejects) the panels' decisions. If a GATT agreement violation is found and not removed by the offending country, trade sanctions authorized by a panel may be imposed on that country in an amount equal to the economic injury caused by the violation.

CASE SUMMARY

Philippines Accepts DSB's Rulings. That's the Spirit!

FACTS: On January 14, 2010, the United States requested consultations with the Philippines with respect to the taxation of imported distilled spirits by the Philippines. On January 27, 2010, the European Union joined the consultations. Other third parties thereafter joined. A panel report was circulated on August 15, 2011. On December 21, 2011, the Appellate Body Report was circulated. The report stated in part:

> Before the Panel, the European Union and the United States each brought a complaint with respect to the WTO consistency of the Philippines excise tax on distilled spirits. Under the measure at issue, distilled spirits made from certain designated raw materials ... are subject to a lower specific flat tax rate. Conversely, distilled spirits made from non-designated raw materials are subject to tax rates that are 10 to 40 times higher than those applied to distilled spirits made from designated raw materials. De facto, all Philippine domestic distilled spirits are made from one of the designated raw materials — sugar cane — and are therefore subject to the lower tax rate. The vast majority of imported distilled spirits are made from non-designated raw materials, and are therefore subject to the higher tax rates. Through its excise tax, the Philippines subjects imported distilled spirits made from non-designated raw materials to internal taxes in excess of those applied to "like" domestic distilled spirits made from the designated raw materials, thus acting in a manner inconsistent with Article III:2, first sentence, of the GATT 1994. The Panel also found that the Philippines has acted inconsistently with Article III:2, second sentence, of the GATT 1994 by applying dissimilar taxes on imported distilled spirits and on "directly competitive or substitutable" domestic distilled spirits, so as to afford protection to Philippine production of distilled spirits.

DECISION: At its January 20, 2012, meeting the DSB adopted the Appellate Body Report. At the DSB meeting on February 22, 2012, the Philippines said that it intended to implement the report and recommendations in a manner that respects its WTO obligations. [*United States and Philippines*, DS403, http://wto.org/english/tratop_e/dispu_e/cases_e_/ds403_e.htm F3d. Reprinted by permission.]

(B) CISG. The *United Nations Convention on Contracts for the International Sale of Goods* (CISG or convention) sets forth uniform rules to govern international sales contracts. National law, however, is sometimes required to fill gaps in areas not covered by the CISG. The CISG became effective on January 1, 1988, between the United States and the 60 other nations that had approved it.[4] The provisions of the CISG have been strongly influenced by Article 2 of the UCC.

However, as set forth in Chapter 23 on sales, several distinct differences exist between the convention and the UCC. Excluded from the coverage of the convention under Article 2 are the sale of goods for personal, family, or household uses and the sale of watercraft, aircraft, natural gas, or electricity; letters of credit; and auctions and securities.[5] The CISG is often viewed by foreign entities as a neutral body of law, the utilization of which can be a positive factor in successfully concluding negotiations of a contract. The parties to an international commercial contract may opt out of the convention. However, absent an express "opt-out provision," the CISG is controlling and preempts all state actions.

(c) UNCTAD. The *United Nations Conference on Trade and Development* (UNCTAD) represents the interests of the less developed countries. Its prime objective is the achievement of an international redistribution of income through trade. Through UNCTAD pressure, the developed countries agreed to a system of preferences, with quota limits, for manufactured imports from the developing countries.

(D) EU. The *European Economic Community* (EEC) was established in 1958 by the Treaty of Rome to remove trade and economic barriers between member countries and to unify their economic policies. It changed its name and became the *European Union* (EU) after the Treaty of Maastricht was ratified on November 1, 1993. The Treaty of Rome containing the governing principles of this regional trading group was signed by the original six nations of Belgium, France, West Germany, Italy, Luxembourg, and the Netherlands. Membership expanded by the entry of Denmark, Ireland, and Great Britain in 1973; Greece in 1981; Spain and Portugal in 1986; and Austria, Sweden, and Finland in 1995. Ten countries joined the EU in 2004: Cyprus, the Czech Republic, Estonia, Hungary, Latvia, Lithuania, Malta, Poland, Slovakia, and Slovenia. Bulgaria, Romania, Croatia, and Turkey expect to join in the coming years.

Four main institutions make up the formal structure of the EU. The first, the European Council, consists of the heads of state of the member countries. The council sets broad policy guidelines for the EU. The second, the European Commission, implements decisions of the council and initiates actions against individuals, companies, or member states that violate EU law. The third, the European Parliament, has an advisory legislative role with limited veto powers. The fourth, the European Court of Justice (ECJ) and the lower Court of First Instance make up the judicial arm of the EU. The courts of member states may refer cases involving questions on the EU treaty to these courts.

The Single European Act eliminated internal barriers to the free movement of goods, persons, services, and capital between EU countries. The Treaty on European Union, signed in Maastricht, Netherlands (the Maastricht Treaty), amended the

---

[4] 52 Fed. Reg. 6262.
[5] C.I.S.G. art. 2(a)–(f).

Treaty of Rome with a focus on monetary and political union. It set goals for the EU of (1) single monetary and fiscal policies, (2) common foreign and security policies, and (3) cooperation in justice and home affairs.

(E) NAFTA. The *North American Free Trade Agreement* (NAFTA) is an agreement between Mexico, Canada, and the United States, effective January 1, 1994, that included Mexico in the arrangements previously initiated under the United States–Canada Free Trade Agreement of 1989. NAFTA eliminates all tariffs among the three countries over a 15-year period. Side agreements exist to prevent the exploitation of Mexico's lower environmental and labor standards.

Products are qualified for NAFTA tariff preferences only if they originate in one or more of the three member countries.

CASE SUMMARY

A Reason to Assemble Cars in Mexico

FACTS: DaimlerChrysler assembles trucks in Mexico utilizing sheet metal components manufactured in the United States. The sheet metal is subject to painting in Mexico, consisting of primer coats followed by a color-treated coat and a clear coat, referred to as the top coats. After the assembly is completed, the trucks are shipped to and sold in the United States. The U.S. Customs Service believes the top coats are subject to duty payments. DaimlerChrysler asserts that the entire painting process is duty free. Subheading 9802.00.80 of the Harmonized Tariffs Schedule of the U.S. (HTSUS) provides duty-free treatment for:

> Articles ... assembled abroad in whole or in part of fabricated components, the product of the United States, which (a) were exported in condition ready for assembly without further fabrication, (b) have not lost their physical identity in such articles by change in form, shape or otherwise, and (c) have not been advanced in value or improved in condition abroad except by being assembled and except by operations incidental to the assembly process such as cleaning, lubricating and painting. [emphasis added by the court]

From a judgment by the Court of International Trade in favor of the United States, DaimlerChrysler appealed.

DECISION: Judgment for DaimlerChrysler. Because subheading HTSUS 9802.00.80 unambiguously covers painting operations broadly, DaimlerChrysler's entire painting process, including the application of the top coats, qualifies for duty-free treatment. [**DaimlerChrysler Corp. v. U.S.,** 361 F.3d 1378 (Fed. Cir. 2004)]

Documentation is required in a NAFTA *Certificate of Origin,* except for certain "low-value" items for which the statement of North American origin is recorded on an invoice. NAFTA ensures nondiscriminatory and open markets for a wide range of services and lowers barriers to U.S. investments in both Canada and Mexico. Although NAFTA does not create a common labor market, as does the European Union, the agreement provides temporary access for businesspersons across borders.

(F) REGIONAL TRADING GROUPS OF DEVELOPING COUNTRIES. In recent years, numerous trading arrangements between groups of developing countries have been established.

(G) IMF—WORLD BANK. The *International Monetary Fund* (IMF) was created after World War II by a group of nations meeting in Bretton Woods, New Hampshire.

The Articles of Agreement of the IMF state that its purpose is "to facilitate the expansion and balanced growth of international trade" and to "shorten the duration and lessen the disequilibrium in the international balance of payments of members." The IMF helps to achieve such purposes by administering a complex lending system. A country can borrow money from other IMF members or from the IMF by means of **special drawing rights (SDRs)** sufficient to permit that country to maintain the stability of its currency's relationship to other world currencies. The Bretton Woods conference also set up the *International Bank for Reconstruction and Development* (World Bank) to facilitate the lending of money by capital surplus countries—such as the United States—to countries needing economic help and wanting foreign investments after World War II.

special drawing rights (SDRs) – rights that allow a country to borrow enough money from other International Money Fund (IMF) members to permit that country to maintain the stability of its currency's relationship to other world currencies.

(H) EX-IM BANK. The Export Import Bank (EX-IM Bank) is a United States federal agency that helps U.S. companies sell manufactured goods to foreign firms by providing loan guarantees and some forms of insurance. The bank was reauthorized in 2012, and its financing cap increased from $100 billion to $140 billion. Big exporters like Boeing, General Electric, and Caterpillar were supportive of the reauthorization, asserting that it supports U.S. jobs. Opponents including Delta Airlines opposed the reauthorization, contending that the bank effectively subsidizes foreigners that compete with the U.S. companies. The bank has been self-sustaining, more than covering its operating costs and loan-default experience.

(I) OPEC. The *Organization of Petroleum Exporting Countries* (OPEC) is a producer cartel or combination. One of its main goals was to raise the taxes and royalties earned from crude oil production. Another major goal was to take control over production and exploration from the major oil companies. Its early success in attaining these goals led other nations that export raw materials to form similar cartels. **For Example,** copper and bauxite-producing nations have formed cartels.

3. Forms of Business Organizations

The decision to participate in international business transactions and the extent of that participation depend on the financial position of the individual firm, production and marketing factors, and tax and legal considerations. There are a number of forms of business organizations for doing business abroad.

export sale – direct sale to customers in a foreign country.

(A) EXPORT SALES. A direct sale to customers in a foreign country is an **export sale**. A U.S. firm engaged in export selling is not present in the foreign country in such an arrangement. The export is subject to a tariff by the foreign country, but the exporting firm is not subject to local taxation by the importing country.

agent – person or firm who is authorized by the principal or by operation of law to make contracts with third persons on behalf of the principal.

(B) AGENCY REQUIREMENTS. A U.S. manufacturer may decide to make a limited entry into international business by appointing an agent to represent it in a foreign market. An **agent** is a person or firm with authority to make contracts on behalf of another— the **principal**. The agent will receive commission income for sales made on behalf of the U. S. principal. The appointment of a foreign agent commonly constitutes "doing business" in that country and subjects the U.S. firm to local taxation.

principal – person or firm who employs an agent; the person who, with respect to a surety, is primarily liable to the third person or creditor; property held in trust.

distributor – entity that takes title to goods and bears the financial and commercial risks for the subsequent sale of the goods.

(C) FOREIGN DISTRIBUTORSHIPS. A **distributor** takes title to goods and bears the financial and commercial risks for the subsequent sale. To avoid making a major financial investment, a U.S. firm may decide to appoint a foreign distributor. A U.S. firm may also appoint a foreign distributor to avoid managing a foreign operation with its complicated local business, legal, and labor conditions. Care is required in designing an exclusive distributorship for an EU country lest it would violate EU antitrust laws.

(D) LICENSING. U.S. firms may select licensing as a means of doing business in other countries. **Licensing** involves the transfer of technology rights in a product so that it may be produced by a different business organization in a foreign country in exchange for royalties and other payments as agreed. The technology being licensed may fall within the internationally recognized categories of patents, trademarks, and "know-how" (trade secrets and unpatented manufacturing processes outside the public domain). These intellectual property rights, which are legally protectable, may be licensed separately or incorporated into a single, comprehensive licensing contract. **Franchising**, which involves granting permission to use a trademark, trade name, or copyright under specified conditions, is a form of licensing that is now very common in international business.

licensing—transfer of technology rights to a product so that it may be produced by a different business organization in a foreign country in exchange for royalties and other payments as agreed.

franchising—granting of permission to use a trademark, trade name, or copyright under specified conditions; a form of licensing.

(E) WHOLLY OWNED SUBSIDIARIES. A firm seeking to maintain control over its own operations, including the protection of its own technological expertise, may choose to do business abroad through a wholly owned subsidiary. In Europe the most common choice of foreign business organization, similar to the U.S. corporate form of business organization, is called the *société anonyme* (S.A.). In German-speaking countries, this form is called *Aktiengesellschaft* (A.G.). Small and medium-sized companies in Europe now utilize a newly created form of business organization called the limited liability company (*Gesellschaft mit beschränkter Haftung,* or "GmbH" in Germany; *Società a responsabilità limitata,* or "S.r.l." in Spain). It is less complicated to form but is restrictive for accessing public capital markets.

A corporation doing business in more than one country poses many taxation problems for the governments in those countries where the firm does business. The United States has established tax treaties with many countries granting corporations relief from double taxation. Credit is normally given by the United States to U.S. corporations for taxes paid to foreign governments.

There is a potential for tax evasion by U.S. corporations from their selling goods to their overseas subsidiaries. Corporations could sell goods at less than the fair market value to avoid a U.S. tax on the full profit for such sales. By allowing the foreign subsidiaries located in countries with lower tax rates to make higher profits, a company as a whole would minimize its taxes. Section 482 of the Internal Revenue Code (IRC), however, allows the Internal Revenue Service (IRS) to reallocate the income between the parent and its foreign subsidiary. Intellectual property such as patent rights, internationally held and generating revenues outside the United States, provide a basis for U.S. multinational companies to legally minimize tax liability by shifting income internationally. **For Example,** global companies like Apple, Microsoft, Google, and Facebook may utilize tax avoidance techniques like the "Double Irish with a Dutch Sandwich," relying on transferring profits on international patent royalties to places like Ireland, with routing through the Netherlands, back to an Irish subsidiary, then to a Caribbean tax haven.[6]

---

[6] http://www.nytimes.com/interactive/2012/04/28/business/Double-Irish-With-A-Dutch-Sandwich.html. http://www.npr.org/blogs/money/2010/10/21 /130727655/google-s-tax-tricks-double-irish-and-dutch-sandwich. See also James Barrett and Steven Hadjilogiou, "The Tax Benefits and Obstacles to U.S. Businesses in Transferring Foreign Intellectual Property to Foreign Affiliates," 89 *Fla. B. J.* No. 5, pp. 40–45 (May 2012).

CASE SUMMARY

A Taxing Case

FACTS: E. I. Du Pont de Nemours created a wholly owned Swiss marketing and sales subsidiary: Du Pont International S.A. (DISA). Most of the Du Pont chemical products marketed abroad were first sold to DISA, which then arranged for resale to the ultimate consumer through independent distributors. Du Pont's tax strategy was to sell the goods to DISA at prices below fair market value so that the greater part of the total corporate profit would be realized by DISA upon resale. DISA's profits would be taxed at a much lower level by Switzerland than Du Pont would be taxed in the United States. The IRS, however, under Section 482 of the IRC, reallocated a substantial part of DISA's income to Du Pont, increasing Du Pont's taxes by a considerable amount. Du Pont contended that the prices it charged DISA were valid under the IRC.

DECISION: Judgment for the IRS. The reallocation of DISA's income to Du Pont was proper. Du Pont's prices to DISA were set wholly without regard to the factors that normally enter into the setting of intercorporate prices on an arm's-length basis. For example, there was no correlation of prices to cost. Du Pont set prices for the two years in question based solely on estimates of the greatest amount of profits that could be shifted without causing IRS intervention. [***E.I. Du Pont de Nemours & Co. v. United States***, **608 F.2d 445 (Ct. Cl. 1979)**]

joint venture – relationship in which two or more persons or firms combine their labor or property for a single undertaking and share profits and losses equally unless otherwise agreed.

(F) JOINT VENTURES. A U.S. manufacturer and a foreign entity may form a **joint venture**, whereby the two firms agree to perform different functions for a common result. The responsibilities and liabilities of such operations are governed by contract. **For Example,** General Motors Co. (GM) and its Chinese partner, Shanghai Automotive Industry Corp. (SAIC), formed an auto-making joint venture in 1995, selling 22,000 cars in 1999 and expanding to 2.6 million cars sold in 2011, with a profit of $1.5 billion for GM.[7]

B.   GOVERNMENTAL REGULATION

Nations regulate trade to protect the economic interests of their citizens or to protect themselves in international relations and transactions.

4. Export Regulations

For reasons of national security, foreign policy, or short supply of domestic products, the United States controls the export of goods and technology. The Export Administration Act[8] imposes export controls on goods and technical data from the U.S. Since April 2002, the Bureau of Industry and Security (BIS) of the Department of Commerce has issued Export Administration Regulations to enforce export controls.

Export Administration Regulations effective in 1996 simplify the process and enhance export trade by U.S. citizens.[9] These regulations eliminate the former

---

[7] Sharon Terlep, "GM Seeks Sway in China," *Wall Street Journal*, April 19, 2012, at B3.

[8] The Export Administration Act of 1979 expired in August 1994 and was extended by Executive Orders signed by Presidents Clinton and G. W. Bush. The EAA is now extended annually by presidential notice.

[9] Simplification of Export Regulations, 61 Fed.Reg. 12,714 (1996).

system of general and validated licenses under which every export required a license. Under the 1996 *Simplification Regulations,* no license is required unless the regulations affirmatively require a license. However, when no license is required, the exporter must fill out a Shipper's Export Declaration and attach it to the bill of lading for shipment with the goods being exported.

(A) DETERMINING IF A LICENSE IS NEEDED. To determine whether a product requires a BIS export license, the exporter should review the Commerce Control List (CCL) to see whether the product to be exported is listed. Listed products have Export Control Classification Numbers (ECCNs) that conform to those used by the EU. If a product is on the list, the ECCN code will provide the reason for control, such as national security, missile technology, nuclear nonproliferation, chemical and/or biological weapons, antiterrorism, crime control, short supply, or UN sanctions.[10] The exporter should then consult the Commerce Country Chart to determine whether a license is needed to send the product to its proposed destination. **For Example,** western red cedar is on the Commerce Control List because of the "short supply" of this product. As a result, it is controlled to all destinations, and no reference to the Commerce Country Chart is necessary.

(B) SANCTIONS. Export licenses are required for the export of certain high-technology and military products. a company intending to ship "maraging 350 steel" to a user in Pakistan would find by checking the CCL and the ECCN code for the product that such steel is used in making high-technology products and has nuclear applications. Thus, an export license would be required. Because Pakistan is a nonsignatory nation of the Nuclear Non-Proliferation Treaty, the Department of Commerce would be expected to deny a license application for the use of this steel in a nuclear plant. However, a license to export this steel for the manufacture of high-speed turbines or compressors might be approved. The prospective purchaser must complete a "Statement of Ultimate Consignee and Purchaser" form with the application for an export license. The prospective purchaser must identify the "end use" for the steel and indicate where the purchaser is located and the location in Pakistan where a U.S. embassy official can make an on-site inspection of the product's use. Falsification of the information in the license application process is a criminal offense. Thus, if the exporter of maraging 350 steel asserted that it was to be used in manufacturing high-speed turbines when in fact the exporter knew it was being purchased for use in a nuclear facility, the exporter would be guilty of a criminal offense.[11]

Civil charges may also be brought against U.S. manufacturers who fail to obtain an export license for foreign sales of civilian items that contain any components that have military applications under the Arms Control Export Act. For example. between 2000 and 2003, Boeing Co. shipped overseas 94 commercial jets that carried a gyrochip used as a backup system in determining a plane's orientation in the air. This 2-ounce chip that costs less than $2,000 also has military applications and can be used to stabilize and steer guided missiles. Boeing is asserted to have made false statements on shipping documents to get around the export restrictions. Boeing argued that the

---

[10] *Id.*

[11] See *United States v. Pervez,* 871 F.2d 310 (3d Cir. 1989), on the criminal application of the Export Administration Regulations to an individual who stated a false end use for "maraging 350 steel" (used in the nuclear industry) on his export application to ship this steel to Pakistan.

State Department is without legal authority to regulate its civilian rather than military items. However, Boeing agreed to pay a $15 million fine for the violations.[12]

(c) Expert Assistance. The Department of Commerce's Exporter Assistance Staff provides assistance to exporters needing help in determining whether an export license is needed.[13] Licensed foreign-**freight forwarders** are in the business of handling the exporting of goods to foreign destinations. They are experts on U.S. Department of Commerce export license requirements. Licensed foreign-freight forwarders can attend to all of the essential arrangements required to transport a shipment of goods from the exporter's warehouse to the overseas buyer's specified port and inland destination. They are well versed in all aspects of ocean, air, and inland transportation as well as banking, marine insurance, and other services relating to exporting.

freight forwarder — one who contracts to have goods transported and, in turn, contracts with carriers for such transportation.

5. Protection of Intellectual Property Rights

U.S. laws protect **intellectual property rights**, which consist of trademarks, copyrights, patents, and trade secrets. (See Figure 10-1, p. 215, for a summary of intellectual property law.)

intellectual property rights — trademark, copyright, and patent rights protected by law.

(a) Counterfeit Goods. The importation of counterfeit compact discs, tapes, computer software, and movies into the United States violates U.S. copyright laws. Importing goods, such as athletic shoes, jeans, or watches bearing counterfeits of U.S. companies' registered trademarks violates the Lanham Act. Possible remedies include injunctive relief, seizure and destruction of counterfeit goods that are found in the United States, damages, and attorney fees. U.S. firms injured by counterfeit trademarks may recover triple damages from the counterfeiters.[14]

(b) Patent and Trade Secrets. Importing machines or devices that infringe on U.S. patents not only violates U.S. patent laws but also the Tariff Act of 1930. **For Example,** the United States International Trade Commission (ITC) determined that the importation and sale of personal data and mobile communication devices by High Tech Computer Corp. of Taiwan (HTC) and its U.S. subsidiary HTC, America infringed on two patents of Apple Inc. of Cupertino, California, in violation of Section 337 of the Tariff Act of 1930. It ordered the exclusion of the articles from the United States, but allowed HTC to import refurbished handsets to be provided to consumers as replacement under warranty or insurance contracts until December 13, 2013.[15]

The International Trade Commission has authority under the Tariff Act of 1930 over "unfair methods of competition and unfair acts in the importation of articles into the United States." Accordingly, the ITC is allowed to investigate conduct occurring in a foreign country in the course of a trade secrets misappropriation case, in order to protect domestic industries from injuries arising out of unfair competition in the U.S. domestic marketplace.

---

[12] Associated Press, "Boeing to Pay $15 Million Fine for Export of Military Technology," *The Boston Globe*, April 10, 2006, at E3.

[13] U.S. Export Assistance Centers located in major metropolitan areas throughout the United States provide small or medium-sized firms export assistance. For local centers, see http://archive.sba.gov/aboutsba/sbaprograms/internationaltrade/useac/html.

[14] 15 U.S.C. §1117(b); *Nintendo of America v. NTDEC*, 822 F. Supp. 1462 (D. Ariz. 1993).

[15] *In re Certain Personal Data and Communication Devices and Related Software*, U.S. International Trade Commission Investigation, No. 337-TA-710 (Dec. 19, 2011), http://www.edis.usitc.gov.

CASE SUMMARY

I hear the train a comin'
It's rollin' round the bend. ...*
And it ain't rollin' on cheatin' TianRui wheels!

*Johnny Cash: Folsom Prison Blues

FACTS: Amsted Industries Inc. is a domestic manufacturer of cast steel railway wheels. It owns two secret processes for manufacturing such wheels, the "ABC process" and the "Griffin process." Amsted previously practiced the ABC process at its foundry in Calera, Alabama, but it no longer uses that process in the United States. Instead, Amsted uses the Griffin process at three of its domestic foundries. However, Amsted has licensed the "ABC process" to several firms with foundries in China. TianRui Group Company Limited manufactures cast steel railway wheels in China. TianRui hired nine employees away from one of Amsted's Chinese licensees, Datong ABC Castings Company, Limited. Datong had previously notified those employees through a written employee code of conduct that information pertaining to the ABC process was proprietary and confidential. Each employee had been advised that he had a duty not to disclose confidential information. In the proceedings brought by Amsted before the International Trade Commission (ITC), Amsted alleged that the former Datong employees disclosed information and documents to TianRui that revealed the details of the ABC process and thereby misappropriated Amsted's trade secrets. TianRui partnered with Standard Car Truck Company, Inc., to form the joint venture Barber TianRui Railway Supply, LLC, and has marketed TianRui wheels to United States customers. Other than Amsted, they are the only companies selling or attempting to sell cast steel railway wheels in the United States. The ITC determined that the importation of the articles violated the Tariff Act and issued a limited exclusion order. TianRui appealed to the United States Court of Appeals for the Federal Circuit.

DECISION: The ITC found that the wheels were manufactured using a process that was developed in the United States, protected under domestic trade secret law, and misappropriated abroad. The appeals court was asked to decide whether the ITC's statutory authority over "[u]nfair methods of competition and unfair acts in the importation of articles … into the United States," as provided by section 337(a)(1)(A), allows it to look to conduct occurring in China in the course of a trade secret misappropriation investigation. The ITC has authority to investigate and grant relief based in part on extraterritorial conduct insofar as it is necessary to protect domestic industries from injuries arising out of unfair competition in the domestic marketplace. The imported TianRui wheels would directly compete with wheels domestically produced by the trade secret owner. Such competition constituted an injury to an "industry" within the meaning of section 337(a)(1)(A) of the Tariff Act. [*TianRui Group Co. Ltd. v. I.T.C.*, 661 F.3d 1322 (Fed. Cir. 2011)]

(c) GRAY MARKET GOODS. A U.S. trademark holder may license a foreign business to use its trademark overseas. Exploiting geographic price differentials, a third party may import these foreign-made goods into the United States to compete against the U.S. manufacturer's goods. The foreign made goods are called **gray market goods**. The Copyright Act and the Lanham Act have been utilized with varying degrees of success by U.S. trademark and U.S. copyright owners in their effort to exclude gray market goods from the United States.

gray market goods—foreign-made goods with U.S. trademarks brought into the United States by a third party without the consent of the trademark owners to compete with these owners.

(1) The Copyright Act.

The Copyright Act of 1976 addresses the importation of copyrighted works and may apply to gray market goods. One provision of the act gives the copyright holder the exclusive right to distribute copies of the copyrighted work.[16] Another section, known as the *first sale doctrine*, states that a copyright owner may only influence the price at which their work is sold once; after that the subsequent owners may sell the copyrighted work for as much as they see fit.[17] One type of gray market issue occurs when U.S. manufacturers sell their U.S.-made products overseas at deep discounts, and other firms reimport the products back to the United States for resale. The Supreme Court held that a copyrighted label on the product would not protect a U.S. manufacturer's claim of unauthorized importation because the copyright owner's rights cease upon the original sale to the overseas buyer.[18] However, the "first sale" defense is unavailable to importers who acquire ownership of gray market goods manufactured abroad. **For Example,** Omega, S.A. makes very expensive Seamaster watches in Switzerland that carry a copyrighted logo registered at the U.S. Copyright Office. Costco acquired the Swiss-made watches at a discount through unauthorized channels and sold them for $700.00 below Omega's suggested retail price. In an equally divided 4-4 decision, the Supreme court upheld a Court of Appeal's decision in favor of Omega. That court determined that the phrase "lawfully made under this title" in the section of the act creating the first sale doctrine means "legally made in the United States," thus precluding the first sale defense for importers who acquire ownership of works made abroad.[19]

(2) The Lanham Trademark Act.

A gray market situation also arises when foreign products made by affiliates of U.S. companies have trademarks identical to U.S. trademarks but the foreign products are physically different from U.S. products. The Lanham Act applies.[20] **For Example,** Lever Brothers (Lever U.S.) manufactures a soap under the trademark Shield and a dishwashing liquid under the trademark Sunlight for sale in the United States. A British affiliate, Lever U.K., also makes products using the marks Shield and Sunlight. Because of different needs and tastes of U.S. and U.K. consumers, the products have physical differences. Third parties imported these U.K. products through unauthorized channels into the United States. Because of the confusion and dissatisfaction to American consumers the Customs Service was directed by the court of appeals to exclude the two products from sale in the United States, ruling that Section 42 of the Lanham Act bars importation of physically different foreign goods bearing a trademark identical to a valid U.S. trademark.[21]

(D) OTHER PROTECTIONS. Intellectual property rights are also protected by international treaties, such as the Berne Convention, which protects copyrights; the Patent Cooperation Treaty; and the Madrid System of International Registration of Marks (the Madrid Protocol), a treaty providing for the international registration of marks applicable to more than 60 signatory countries, including the United States.[22]

---

[16] 17 U.S.C. §106(3).

[17] 17 U.S.C. §109(2).

[18] *Quality King v. L'Anza Research*, 523 U.S. 1435 (1998).

[19] *Omega S.A. v. Costco Wholesale Corp.* 541 F.3d 982 (9th Cir. 2008), *aff'd* 131 S.Ct. 565 (2010). Next term, in the case of *John Wiley & Sons v. Kirtsaeng*, 654 F.3d 210 (2d Cir. 2011) *cert. granted*, 80 U.S.L.W. 3365 (U.S. Apr. 16, 2012), the Supreme Court will again consider a "first sale doctrine" defense involving an appeal of a copyright violation by a University of Southern California graduate student who obtained cheaply made foreign-made editions of publisher John Wiley's textbooks from Thailand sources and sold them to American students on eBay.

[20] 15 U.S.C. §1124.

[21] *Lever Brothers Co. v. U.S.*, 981 F.2d 1330 (D.C. Cir. 1993).

[22] The Agreement on Trade-Related Aspects of Intellectual Property (TRIPS) is a WTO agreement that requires WTO members to adhere to certain treaties and guidelines in respecting copyright, trademark, and patent rights. Enforcement of such rights, however, varies, depending on national law.

6. Antitrust

Antitrust laws exist in the United States to protect the U.S. consumer by ensuring the benefits of competitive products from foreign competitors as well as domestic competitors. Competitors' agreements designed to raise the price of imports or to exclude imports from our domestic markets in exchange for not competing in other countries are restraints of trade in violation of our antitrust laws.[23]

The antitrust laws also exist to protect U.S. export and investment opportunities against privately imposed restrictions, whereby a group of competitors seeks to exclude another competitor from a particular foreign market. Antitrust laws exist in other countries where U.S. firms compete. These laws are usually directed not at breaking up cartels to further competition but at regulating them in the national interest.

(A) JURISDICTION. In U.S. courts, the U.S. antitrust laws have a broad extraterritorial reach. Our antitrust laws must be reconciled with the rights of other interested countries as embodied in international law.

(1) The Effects Doctrine.

Judge Learned Hand's decision in *United States v. Alcoa* established the **effects doctrine**.[24] Under this doctrine, U.S. courts assume jurisdiction and apply the antitrust laws to conduct outside of the United States where the activity of the business firms outside the United States has a direct and substantial effect on U.S. commerce. This basic rule has been modified to require that the effect on U.S. commerce also be foreseeable.

(2) The Jurisdictional Rule of Reason.

The jurisdictional rule of reason applies when conduct taking place outside the United States affects U.S. commerce but a foreign state also has a significant interest in regulating the conduct in question. The **jurisdictional rule of reason** balances the vital interests, including laws and policies, of the United States with those of the foreign country involved. This rule of reason is based on **comity**, a principle of international law, that means that the laws of all nations deserve the respect legitimately demanded by equal participants in international affairs.

(B) DEFENSES. Three defenses are commonly raised to the extraterritorial application of U.S. antitrust laws. These defenses are also commonly raised to attack jurisdiction in other legal actions involving international law.

(1) Act-of-State Doctrine.

By the **act-of-state doctrine**, every sovereign state is bound to respect the independence of every other sovereign state, and the courts of one country will not sit in judgment of another government's acts done within its own territory.[25] The act-of-state doctrine is based on the judiciary's concern over its possible interference with the conduct of foreign relations. Such matters are considered to be political, not judicial, questions.

---

effects doctrine – doctrine that states that U.S. courts will assume jurisdiction and will apply antitrust laws to conduct outside of the United States when the activity of business firms has direct and substantial effect on U.S. commerce; the rule has been modified to require that the effect on U.S. commerce also be foreseeable.

jurisdictional rule of reason – rule that balances the vital interests, including laws and policies, of the United States with those of a foreign country.

comity – principle of international and national law that the laws of all nations and states deserve the respect legitimately demanded by equal participants.

act-of-state doctrine – doctrine whereby every sovereign state is bound to respect the independence of every other sovereign state, and the courts of one country will not sit in judgment of another government's acts done within its own territory.

---

[23] *United States v. Nippon Paper Industries Co. Ltd.,* 64 F. Supp. 2d 173 (1999).
[24] 148 F.2d 416 (2d Cir. 1945).
[25] *Underhill v. Hernandez,* 108 U.S. 250, 252 (1897).

(2) The Sovereign Compliance Doctrine.

sovereign compliance
doctrine – doctrine that allows
a defendant to raise as an
affirmative defense to an
antitrust action the fact that the
defendant's actions were
compelled by a foreign state.

The **sovereign compliance doctrine** allows a defendant to raise as an affirmative defense to an antitrust action the fact that the defendant's actions were compelled by a foreign state. To establish this defense, compulsion by the foreign government is required. The Japanese government uses informal and formal contacts within an industry to establish a consensus on a desired course of action. Such governmental action is not a defense for a U.S. firm, however, because the activity in question is not compulsory.

(3) The Sovereign Immunity Doctrine.

sovereign immunity
doctrine – doctrine that states
that a foreign sovereign
generally cannot be sued unless
an exception to the Foreign
Sovereign Immunities Act of
1976 applies.

The **sovereign immunity doctrine** states that a foreign sovereign generally cannot be sued unless an exception to the Foreign Sovereign Immunities Act of 1976 applies.[26] The most important exception covers the commercial conduct of a foreign state.[27] **For Example,** receivers for various insurance companies brought suit against the Vatican City State, contending that the Vatican's conduct fell within the commercial activity exception to the FSIA. Martin Frankel had engaged in a massive insurance fraud scheme, using front organizations to acquire and loot several insurance agencies. Masquerading as "David Rose," a philanthropist, he met Monsignor Emilio Cologiovani and convinced him to create a Vatican-affiliated entity, the St. Francis of Assisi Foundation (SFAF), which was used as part of Frankel's scam. The Court of Appeals held, however, that Cologiovani, acting with only apparent authority of the state, could not trigger the commercial activity doctrine.[28]

(c) LEGISLATION. In response to business uncertainty as to when the antitrust laws apply to international transactions, Congress passed the Foreign Trade Antitrust Improvements Act of 1982. This act, in essence, codified the effects doctrine. The act requires a direct, substantial, and reasonably foreseeable effect on U.S. domestic commerce or exports by U.S. residents before business conduct abroad may come within the purview of U.S. antitrust laws.[29]

(d) FOREIGN ANTITRUST LAWS. Attitudes in different countries vary toward cartels and business combinations. Because of this, antitrust laws vary in content and application. **For Example,** Japan has stressed consumer protection against such practices as price-fixing and false advertising. However, with regard to mergers, stock ownership, and agreements among companies to control production, Japanese law is much less restrictive than U.S. law.

Europe is a major market for U.S. products, services, and investments. U.S. firms doing business in Europe are subject to the competition laws of the EU.[30] The Treaty of Rome uses the term *competition* rather than *antitrust*. Articles 85 and 86 of the Treaty of Rome set forth the basic regulation on business behavior in the EU.[31] Article 85(1) expressly prohibits agreements and concerted practices that

---

[26] See *Verlinden B.V. v. Central Bank of Nigeria*, 461 U.S. 574 (1983).

[27] See *Dole Food Co. v. Patrickson*, 538 U.S. 468 (2003), for a limited discussion of when a foreign state can assert a defense of sovereign immunity under the Foreign Sovereign Immunities Act of 1976 (FSIA). The FSIA allows certain foreign-state commercial entities not entitled to sovereign immunity to have the merits of a case heard in federal court. The U.S. Supreme Court held in the *Dole Food* case that a foreign state must itself own a majority of the shares of a corporation if the corporation is to be deemed an instrumentality of the state under the FSIA, and the instrumentality status is determined at the time of the filing of the complaint.

[28] *Dale v. Cologiovani*, 443 F.3d 425 (5th Cir. 2006).

[29] P.L. 97-290, 96 Stat. 1233, 15 U.S.C. §6(a).

[30] The European Commission is the executive branch of the EU government and performs most of the EU's regulatory work. The Competition Commission oversees antitrust and mergers for the European Commission. New merger regulations took effect on May 1, 2004. The regulations require the Competition Commission to review proposed mergers and prohibit those mergers when the effects may "significantly impede effective competition" (called the *SIEC test*). The U.S. test prohibits mergers when the effect "may substantially lessen competition. ..." 15 U.S.C. §18 (2005). The wording of the EU and U.S. tests is relatively similar.

[31] See *Osakeyhtio v. EEC Commission*, 1988 Common Mkt. Rep. (CCH) ¶ 14,491 for discussion of the extraterritorial reach of the European Commission.

1. even indirectly fix prices of purchases or sales or fix any other trading conditions;

2. limit or control production, markets, technical development, or investment;

3. share markets or sources of supply;

4. apply unequal terms to parties furnishing equivalent considerations, thereby placing one at a competitive disadvantage; or

5. make a contract's formation depend on the acceptance of certain additional obligations that, according to commercial usage, have no connection with the subject of such contracts.

Article 85(3) allows for an individual exemption if the agreement meets certain conditions, such as improving the production or distribution of goods, promoting technical or economic progress, and reserving to consumers a fair share of the resulting economic benefits.

Article 86 provides that it is unlawful for one or more enterprises having a dominant market position within at least a substantial part of the EU to take improper advantage of such a position if trade between the member states may be affected. **For Example,** the European Commission fined computer chip maker Intel $1.45 billion for abusing its dominance in the computer chip market by offering rebates which were conditioned on buying less of a rival's products, or not buying them at all. Intel disagrees with the decision and has appealed the Commission's ruling.[32]

7. Securities and Tax Fraud Regulation in an International Environment

Illegal conduct in the U.S. securities markets, whether this conduct is initiated in the United States or abroad, threatens the vital economic interests of the United States. Investigation and litigation concerning possible violations of the U.S. securities laws often have an extraterritorial effect. Conflicts with the laws of foreign countries may occur.

(A) JURISDICTION. U.S. district courts have jurisdiction over violations of the antifraud provisions of the Securities Exchange Act of 1934 when losses occur from sales to Americans living in the United States.[33] U.S. district courts also have jurisdiction when losses occur to Americans living abroad if the acts occurred in the United States. The antifraud provisions do not apply, however, to losses from sales of securities to foreigners outside the United States unless acts within the United States caused the losses.

(B) IMPACT OF FOREIGN SECRECY LAWS IN SEC ENFORCEMENT. Secrecy laws are confidentiality laws applied to home-country banks. These laws prohibit the disclosure of business records or the identity of bank customers. **Blocking laws** prohibit the disclosure, copying, inspection, or removal of documents located in the enacting country in compliance with orders from foreign authorities. These laws impede, and sometimes foreclose, the SEC's ability to police its securities markets properly.

secrecy laws – confidentiality laws applied to home-country banks.

blocking laws – laws that prohibit the disclosure, copying, inspection, or removal of documents located in the enacting country in compliance with orders from foreign authorities.

---

[32] Intel's appeal was heard before the Luxemburg-based General Court in July of 2012, *Intel v. Commission*, Case T-286109, and it is now awaiting the court's ruling.
[33] *Kauthar Sdn. Bhd. v. Sternberg*, 149 F.3d 659 (7th Cir. 1998).

CASE SUMMARY

The Long Reach of the SEC

FACTS: Banca Della Suizzera Italiana (BSI), a Swiss bank with an office in the United States, purchased certain call options and common stock of St. Joe Minerals Corporation (St. Joe), a New York corporation, immediately prior to the announcement on March 11, 1981, of a cash tender offer by Joseph Seagram & Sons Inc. for all St. Joe common stock at $45 per share. On March 11, 1981, when BSI acted, the stock moved sharply higher in price. BSI instructed its broker to close out the purchases of the options and sell most of the shares of stock, resulting in an overnight profit of $2 million. The SEC noticed the undue activity in the options market and initiated suit against BSI. The SEC, through the Departments of State and Justice, and the Swiss government sought without success to learn the identity of BSI's customers involved in the transactions. The SEC believed that the customers had used inside information in violation of the Securities Exchange Act of 1934. The SEC brought a motion to compel disclosure. BSI objected on the ground that it might be subject to criminal liability under Swiss penal and banking laws if it disclosed the requested information.

DECISION: Judgment for the SEC. BSI made deliberate use of Swiss nondisclosure law to evade the strictures of U.S. securities law against insider trading. Whether acting solely as an agent or also as a principal (something that can be clarified only through disclosure of the requested information), BSI voluntarily engaged in transactions in U.S. securities markets and profited in some measure thereby. It cannot rely on Swiss nondisclosure law to shield this activity. [*SEC v. Banca DellaSuizzera Italiana,* **92 F.R.D. 111 (S.D.N.Y 1981)**]

The SEC is not limited to litigation when a securities law enforcement investigation runs into secrecy or blocking laws. For example, the SEC may rely on the 1977 Treaty of Mutual Assistance in Criminal Matters between the United States and Switzerland.[34] Although this treaty has served to deter the use of Swiss secrecy laws to conceal fraud in the United States, its benefits for securities enforcement have been limited. It applies only where there is a dual criminality—that is, the conduct involved constitutes a criminal offense under the laws of both the United States and Switzerland.

(c) OFFSHORE TAX EVASION. Switzerland and other countries with histories of banking secrecy have yielded to United States and EU pressures to help cut down on tax evaders. The United States and Switzerland have agreed in an amended tax treaty to increase the amount of tax information they share. Swiss banks have been reluctant to provide client information, asserting that it would violate Swiss Privacy laws. **For Example,** Swiss Bank UBS AG admitted that its bankers and managers referred U.S. clients to lawyers and accountants who set up secret offshore entities to conceal assets from the IRS, and it agreed to pay $780 million to settle the federal investigation in the U.S. and the Swiss government's investigations. Subsequently the Swiss Financial Markets Supervising Authority ordered UBS to reveal account details to the U.S. authorities for some 250 customers, asserting that "banking secrecy remains intact," while it "doesn't protect tax fraudsters."[35]

---

[34] 27 U.S.T. 2021.
[35] See "The Swiss Bank UBS Is Set to Open Its Secret Files," *New York Times,* **www.nytimes.com/2009/02/19/business/worldbusiness/19ubs.htm.** See also **http://www.globalpost.com/dispatch/europe/110109/irs-offshore-bank-accounts-tax-cheats-switzerland-ubs.**

8. Barriers to Trade

The most common barrier to the free movement of goods across borders is a tariff. A wide range of nontariff barriers also restricts the free movement of goods, services, and investments. Government export controls used as elements of foreign policy have proven to be a major barrier to trade with certain countries.

(A) TARIFF BARRIERS. A **tariff** is an import or export duty or tax placed on goods as they move into or out of a country. It is the most common method used by countries to restrict foreign imports. The tariff raises the total cost, and thus the price, of an imported product in the domestic market. Thus, the price of a domestically produced product not subject to the tariff is more advantageous.

The U.S. Customs and Border Protection Service (Customs) imposes tariffs on imported goods at the port of entry. The merchandise is classified under a tariff schedule, which lists each type of merchandise and the corresponding duty rate (or percentage). Customs also determines the "computed value" of the imported goods under very precise statutory formulas.[36] The total amount of the duty is calculated by applying the duty percentage to the computed value figure.[37] Customs also has authority to investigate fraudulent schemes to avoid or underpay customs' duties.[38]

> **tariff** – (1) domestically—government-approved schedule of charges that may be made by a regulated business, such as a common carrier or warehouser; (2) internationally—tax imposed by a country on goods crossing its borders, without regard to whether the purpose is to raise revenue or to discourage the traffic in the taxed goods.

CASE SUMMARY

Customs Crunch!

FACTS: Frito-Lay, Inc., owns a Mexican affiliate, Sabritas, S.A. de C.V., and it imports taco shells and *Munchos* potato chips from Mexico to the United States. Customs classified these products as "other bakers' wares" under Section 1905.90.90 of the Tariff Schedule subject to a 10 percent duty rate. Frito-Lay contends before the Court of International Trade that the import of taco shells is properly classified as "bread," which carries duty-free status. It also contends that *Munchos* are properly classified as potato chips and entitled to duty-free treatment.

DECISION: Classification disputes are resolved by (1) ascertaining the proper meaning of the specified terms in the tariff provision; and (2) determining whether the article comes within the meaning of the terms as properly construed. The term "bread" is not specifically defined in the tariff provision or in the legislative history. Customs' food expert, Dr. Pintauro, explained the leavening, loaf forming, and baking process of dough in his definition of bread. Such a narrow definition, however, ignores the reality that flat, fried, usually ethnic breads exist in the U.S. market and are generally accepted forms of bread. Therefore, hard, corn-based taco shells are properly classified as bread under the tariff provisions and are duty-free. *Munchos,* however, are composed of cornmeal, dehydrated potato flakes, and potato starch, while potato chips are produced entirely from sliced raw whole potatoes. As such, Customs properly classified the plaintiffs' *Munchos.* [***Sabritas v. United States,* 998 F. Supp. 1123 (Ct. Int'l Trade 1998)**]

---

[36] See Tariff Act of 1930, as amended, 19 U.S.C. §1401 a(e).

[37] It is common for importers to utilize customs brokers who research the tariff schedules to see whether a product fits unambiguously under one of the Customs Service's classifications. A broker will also research the classifications given to similar products. It may find that a fax switch may be classified as "other telephonic switching apparatus" at a tariff rate of 8.5 percent or "other telegraphic switching apparatus" with a tariff of 4.7 percent. Obviously, the importer desires to pay the lower rate, and the broker with the assistance of counsel will make a recommendation to the Customs Service for the lower rate, and Customs will make a ruling. The decisions of the Customs Service are published in the *Customs Bulletin,* the official weekly publication of the Customs Service. See *Command Communications v. Fritz Cos.,* 36 P.3d 182 (Colo. App. 2001). See also *Estee Lauder, Inc. v. United States,* 815 F. Supp. 2d 1287 (Ct. Int'l Trade 2012), where the importer successfully challenged Custom's classification of a cosmetic product and the court declined to adopt Custom's position because of the flawed analysis and application of the "rule" therefrom, which has been inconsistent and arbitrary.

[38] *U.S. v. Inn Foods, Inc.,* 560 F.3d 1338 (Fed. Cir. 2009).

(B) NONTARIFF BARRIERS. Nontariff barriers consist of a wide range of restrictions that inhibit the free movement of goods between countries. An import quota, such as a limitation on the number of automobiles that can be imported into one country from another, is such a barrier. More subtle nontariff barriers exist in all countries. **For Example,** Japan's complex customs procedures resulted in the restriction of the sale of U.S.-made aluminum baseball bats in Japan. The customs procedures required the individual uncrating and "destruction testing" of bats at the ports of entry. Government subsidies are also nontariff barriers to trade.

One U.S. law—the Turtle Law—prohibits the importation of shrimp from countries that allow the harvesting of shrimp with commercial fishing technology that could adversely affect endangered sea turtles. **For Example,** two U.S. importers sought an exemption, representing that their Brazilian supply of shrimp was caught in the wild by vessels using turtle excluder devices (TEDs). Because Brazil had failed to comply with the U.S. Turtle Law by requiring TEDs on its commercial shrimp fleet, even though it had seven years to do so, the exemption was not granted.[39]

(C) EXPORT CONTROLS AS INSTRUMENTS OF FOREIGN POLICY. U.S. export controls have been used as instruments of foreign policy in recent years. **For Example,** the United States has sought to deny goods and technology of strategic or military importance to unfriendly nations. The United States has also denied goods such as grain, technology, and machine parts, to certain countries to protest or to punish activities considered violative of human rights or world peace.

9. Relief Mechanisms for Economic Injury Caused by Foreign Trade

Certain U.S. industries may suffer severe economic injury because of foreign competition. U.S. law provides protection against unfair competition from foreigners' goods and provides economic relief for U.S. industries, communities, firms, and workers adversely affected by import competition. U.S. law also provides certain indirect relief for U.S. exporters and producers who encounter unfair foreign import restrictions.

dumping—selling goods in another country at less than their fair value.

(A) ANTIDUMPING LAWS AND EXPORT SUBSIDIES. Selling goods in another country at less than their fair value is called **dumping**. The dumping of foreign goods in the United States is prohibited under the Tariff Act of 1930, as amended including the antidumping laws contained in the Uraguay Round Agreement Act of 1994.[40] Proceedings in antidumping cases are conducted by two federal agencies, which separately examine two distinct components. The International Trade Administration (ITA) of the Department of Commerce (commonly referred to in cases as simply "Commerce") investigates whether specified foreign goods are being sold in the United States at less than fair value (LTFV). The International Trade Commission (ITC) conducts proceedings to determine if there is an injury to a domestic industry as a result of such sales. Findings of both LTFV sales and injury must be present before remedial action is taken. Remedial action might include the addition of duties to reflect the difference between the fair value of the goods and the price being charged in the U.S. Commerce and ITC decisions may be appealed to

---

[39] *Earth Island Institute v. Christopher*, 948 F. Supp. 1062 (Ct. Int'l Trade 1996). See *Turtle Island Restoration Network v. Evans*, 284 F.3d 1282 (Fed. Cir. 2002), on the continuing litigation on this topic and the clash between statutory enforcement and political and diplomatic considerations.

[40] 19 U.S.C. §1675b (2000). See *Allegheny Ludlum Corp. v. United States*, 287 F.3d 1365 (Fed. Cir. 2002).

the Court of International Trade. Decisions of this court are reviewable by the U.S. Court of Appeals for the Federal Circuit and then the U.S. Supreme Court.

A settlement may be reached through a suspension agreement, whereby prices are revised to eliminate any LTFV sales and other corrective measures are taken.

American producers have to take the initiative and shoulder the expense of assisting government's enforcement of antidumping laws, and when antidumping laws are violated, producers are entitled to a reward as injured parties.[41]

CASE SUMMARY

Q: P-l-e-a-s-e. We Just Want to Share.

A: No. You're Not on the List.

FACTS: The Byrd Amendment to the Tariff Act, enacted in 2000, requires that antidumping duties collected by Customs be distributed to "affected domestic producers" for "qualifying expenditures." Starting in 1998, the Torrington Company filed a petition with the ITA (Commerce department) and the ITC requesting imposition of antidumping duties on imported antifriction bearings. Through the gathering of extensive data and representation at hearings before Commerce and the ITC, it expended significant economic resources leading to the ITC's material injury determination and Commerce's antidumping duty order on antifriction bearings imported from Japan and several other countries. SKF USA sought to have its name added to the list of affected domestic producers requesting Byrd Amendment distributions for 2005—which request was denied since it had not indicated support for the original petition. SKF USA appealed, raising constitutional issues.

DECISION: Judgment for U.S. Customs and the ITC. The Byrd Amendment is not unconstitutional because it directly advanced substantial governmental interests in preventing dumping by rewarding parties that assisted enforcement of the antidumping statutes. [*SKF USA v. U.S. Customs*, 556 F.3d 1337 (Fed. Cir. 2009)]

The 1979 act also applies to subsidy practices by foreign countries. If subsidized goods are sold in the United States at less than their fair value, the goods may be subject to a countervailing duty.

Canada and Mexico may appeal countervailing duty assessments by the United States to an arbitration panel established under NAFTA. The NAFTA panel, however, can determine only whether the U.S. determinations were made in accordance with U.S. law. An appeal can also be made by member states to the WTO Dispute Settlement Body, which can determine whether the United States breached its obligations under the WTO.

(B) RELIEF FROM IMPORT INJURIES. Title II of the Trade Act of 1974[42] provides relief for U.S. industries, communities, firms, and workers when any one or more of them are substantially adversely affected by import competition. The Department of Commerce, the secretary of labor, and the president have roles in determining eligibility. The relief provided may be temporary import relief through the imposition of a duty or quota on the foreign goods. Workers, if eligible, may obtain

---

[41] The Continued Dumping and Subsidy Offset Act of 2000 (the Byrd Amendment), 19 U.S.C. 1679c(a) (2000).
[42] P.L. 93-618, 88 Stat. 1978, 19 U.S.C. §§2251, 2298.

readjustment allowances, job training, job search allowances, or unemployment compensation.

For Example, trade adjustment assistance, including unemployment compensation and training and relocation allowances, was provided for former employees of Johnson Controls Battery Group plants in Garland, Texas; Bennington, Vermont; and Owosso, Michigan, because surveys of the customers of those plants by the Department of Labor indicated that increased imports of aftermarket batteries, the products produced at these closed plants, caused the shutdowns. Former workers of the closed Louisville battery plant were not provided assistance because this plant produced new car batteries, and the work was shifted to another Johnson Controls plant in the United States.[43]

(c) RETALIATION AND RELIEF AGAINST FOREIGN UNFAIR TRADE RESTRICTIONS. U.S. exporters of agricultural or manufactured goods or of services may encounter unreasonable, unjustifiable, or discriminatory foreign import restrictions. At the same time, producers from the foreign country involved may be benefiting from trade agreement concessions that allow producers from that country access to U.S. markets. Prior trade acts and the Omnibus Trade and Competitiveness Act of 1988 contain broad authority to retaliate against "unreasonable," "unjustifiable," or "discriminatory" acts by a foreign country.[44] The authority to retaliate is commonly referred to as "Section 301 authority." The fear or actuality of the economic sting of Section 301 retaliation often leads offending foreign countries to open their markets to imports. Thus, indirect relief is provided to domestic producers and exporters adversely affected by foreign unfair trade practices.

Enforcement of the act is entrusted to the U.S. trade representative (USTR), who is appointed by the president. Under the 1988 act, mandatory retaliatory action is required if the USTR determines that (1) rights of the United States under a trade agreement are being denied or (2) actions or policies of a foreign country are unjustifiable and a burden or restrict U.S. commerce. The overall thrust of the trade provisions of the 1988 act is to open markets and liberalize trade.

10. Expropriation

A major concern of U.S. businesses that do business abroad is the risk of expropriation of assets by a host government. Firms involved in the extraction of natural resources, banking, communications, or defense-related industries are particularly susceptible to nationalization. Multinational corporations commonly have a staff of full-time political scientists and former Foreign Service officers studying the countries relevant to their operations to monitor and calculate risks of expropriation. Takeovers of U.S.-owned businesses by foreign countries may be motivated by a short-term domestic political advantage or the desire to demonstrate political clout in world politics. Takeovers may also be motivated by long-term considerations associated with planned development of the country's economy.

Treaty commitments, or provisions in other international agreements between the United States and the host country, may serve to narrow expropriation uncertainties. Treaties commonly contain provisions whereby property will not be expropriated except for public benefit and with the prompt payment of just compensation.

One practical way to mitigate the risk of investment loss as a result of foreign expropriation is to purchase insurance through private companies, such as Lloyd's of

---

[43] 20 F. Supp. 2d 1288 (Ct. Int'l Trade 1998). See also *Former Employees of Merrill Corp. v. U.S.*, 387 F. Supp. 2d 1336 (Ct. Int'l Trade 2005).
[44] P.L. 100-418, 102 Stat. 1346, 15 U.S.C. §4727.

London. Commercial insurance is also available against such risks as host governments' arbitrary recall of letters of credit and commercial losses resulting from embargoes.

The Overseas Private Investment Corporation (OPIC) is a U.S. agency under the policy control of the secretary of state. OPIC supports private investments in less developed, friendly countries. OPIC also offers asset protection insurance against risk of loss to plant and equipment as well as loss of deposits in overseas bank accounts to companies that qualify on the basis of the involvement of a "substantial U.S. interest."

11. The Foreign Corrupt Practices Act

The Foreign Corrupt Practices Act of 1977, as amended, prohibits U.S. based companies and foreign companies listed on U.S. stock exchanges from paying anything of value to foreign officials to obtain or retain business with a foreign government. The law is jointly enforced by the Department of Justice and the Securities and Exchange Commission. It requires strict accounting standards and internal control procedures to prevent the hiding of improper payments to foreign officials. The act prohibits any offers, payments, or gifts to foreign officials—or third parties who might have influence with foreign officials—to influence a decision on behalf of the firm making the payment. It provides for sanctions against the company and fines and imprisonment for the employees or agents involved. Moreover, the individuals involved may be responsible for damages as a result of civil actions brought by competitors under federal and state antiracketeering acts.[45]

CASE SUMMARY

You Just Can't Do That!

FACTS: Harry Carpenter, CEO of Kirkpatrick Company, agreed to pay Nigerian government officials a "commission" equal to 20 percent of the contract price if Kirkpatrick obtained the contract to build an aeromedical center in Nigeria. Kirkpatrick was awarded the contract, and the "commission" was paid to the Nigerian officials. A competitor for the project, ETC, International (ETC), learned of the "20 percent commission" and informed U.S. officials. Kirkpatrick and Carpenter pleaded guilty to violations of the Foreign Corrupt Practices Act by paying bribes to get the Nigerian contract. ETC then brought this civil action against Kirkpatrick, Carpenter, and others for damages under the Racketeer Influenced and Corrupt Organizations Act (RICO) and the New Jersey Antiracketeering Act. The district court ruled the suit was barred by the act-of-state doctrine, the Court of Appeals reversed, and the U.S. Supreme Court granted *certiorari*.

DECISION: Judgment for ETC. The act-of-state doctrine does not establish an exception for cases that may embarrass foreign governments. The doctrine merely requires that, in the process of deciding cases, the acts of foreign governments, taken in their own jurisdictions, shall be deemed valid. The doctrine has no application to the present case: The validity of a foreign sovereign act is not at issue because the payment and receipt of bribes are prohibited by Nigerian law. [***Kirkpatrick v. ETC, International,*** **493 U.S. 400 (1990)**]

The act does not apply to payments made to low-level officials for expediting the performance of routine government services.

---

[45] P.L. 95-213, 94 Stat. 1494, 15 U.S.C. §78a nt.

Ethics & the Law

Combating Bribery of Foreign Public Officials in International Business Transactions

Prior to 1999, German law prohibited bribery of domestic public officials (and did not prohibit bribery of foreign officials). Siemens AG, headquartered in Germany and Europe's largest engineering conglomerate, conducts business throughout the world. Employees were allowed to withdraw up to €1 million for bribes from three "cash desks" set up at Siemens's offices to facilitate the obtaining of government contracts throughout the world. And, until 1999, Siemens claimed tax deductions for these bribes, many of which were listed as "useful expenditures."

The Organization for Economic Cooperation and Development (OECD) works on global issues, endeavoring to help member countries sustain economic growth and employment. OECD adopted its Anti-Bribery Convention on November 21, 1997; its regulations came into effect in 1999. In 1999, member countries, including Germany, adopted laws combating bribery of foreign public officials in international business transactions. However, between 2001 and 2004 some $67 million was withdrawn from the Siemens "cash desks." The bribery had continued! Mark Pieth, chairman of the working group on bribery at the OECD, said: "People felt confident that they were doing nothing wrong."* With some 470,000 employee jobs at Siemens depending on the ability to obtain engineering and high-tech contracts throughout the world, were Siemens contracting agents justified in continuing to make "useful expenditures" to save jobs and their company from ruin? How could these expenditures be a bad thing?

On December 11, 2008, Siemens AG pleaded guilty to criminal violations of the United States Foreign Corrupt Practices Act and received a total criminal fine of $450 million. It also reached a settlement with the U.S. Securities and Exchange Commission for violation of the FCPA's antibribery, books and records, and internal control provisions and agreed to pay $350 million in disgorgement of profits. Moreover, it agreed to fines and disgorgement of profits of $569 million to settle an investigation by the Munich Public Prosecutor's Office. Seimens's bribery was a bad thing because bribery and corruption were criminal acts.** Moreover, it allowed the corporation to have an inherently unfair competitive advantage over other contract bidders. The convention helps ensure that public works projects are awarded on the basis of sound economic judgment rather than on the basis of who offers the biggest bribe. The notoriety of the Siemens prosecutions should send a strong and clear message to all trading partners that parties to the convention must not engage in bribery to obtain business deals.*** Siemens's board member Peter Solmssen believes it is a myth that firms have to pay bribes to do business in developing countries, and believes that Siemens can increase sales without paying bribes.

*"The Siemens Scandal: Bavarian Baksheesh," *The Economist*, **www.economist.com/business/ displaystory.cfm?story_id=12814642**.

See also *"SEC Charges Seven Former Siemens Executives with Bribing Leaders in Argentina, News Release,"* SEC 2011-263. On December 13, 2011, the Securities and Exchange Commission charged seven former Siemens executives with violating the Foreign Corrupt Practices Act for their involvement in the company's decade-long bribery scheme to retain a $1 billion government contract to produce national identity cards for Argentine citizens. The scheme lasted from 1996 to early 2007. The SEC's Enforcement Director said: "Corruption erodes public trust and the transparency of our commercial markets, and undermines corporate governance." **http://www.sec .gov./news/press/2011/2011-263.htm.

***The current members of the Anti-Bribery Convention are Argentina, Australia, Austria, Belgium, Brazil, Bulgaria, Canada, Chile, Czech Republic, Denmark, Estonia, Finland, France, Germany, Greece, Hungary, Iceland, Ireland, Israel, Italy, Japan, Korea, Luxemburg, Mexico, Netherlands, New Zealand, Norway, Poland, Portugal, Slovak Republic, Slovenia, South Africa, Spain, Sweden, Switzerland, Turkey, United Kingdom, and the United States.

LawFlix

The In-Laws (1979) (PG)

Review the segment in the film in which money is paid by a dictator for the sale of U.S. currency plates. The dictator's plan is to create worldwide inflation. List the various laws and conventions Peter Falk and Alan Arkin violate through their sale of the plates.

MAKE THE CONNECTION

SUMMARY

The World Trade Organization, a multilateral treaty subscribed to by the United States and most of the industrialized countries of the world, is based on the principle of trade without discrimination. The United Nations Convention on Contracts for the International Sale of Goods provides uniform rules for international sales contracts between parties in contracting nations. The European Union is a regional trading group that includes most of western Europe. The North American Free Trade Agreement involves Mexico, Canada, and the United States and eliminates all tariffs between the three countries over a 15-year period.

U.S. firms may choose to do business abroad by making export sales or contracting with a foreign distributor to take title to their goods and sell them abroad. U.S. firms may also license their technology or trademarks for foreign use. An agency arrangement or the organization of a foreign subsidiary may be required to participate effectively in foreign markets. This results in subjecting the U.S. firm to taxation in the host country. However, tax treaties commonly eliminate double taxation.

The Export Administration Act is the principal statute imposing export controls on goods and technical data.

In choosing the form for doing business abroad, U.S. firms must be careful not to violate the antitrust laws of host countries. Anticompetitive foreign transactions may have an adverse impact on competition in U.S. domestic markets. U.S. antitrust laws have a broad extraterritorial reach. U.S. courts apply a "jurisdictional rule of reason," weighing the interests of the United States against the interests of the foreign country involved in making a decision on whether to hear a case. Illegal conduct may occur in U.S. securities markets. U.S. enforcement efforts sometimes run into foreign countries' secrecy and blocking laws that hinder effective enforcement.

Antidumping laws offer relief for domestic firms threatened by unfair foreign competition. In addition, economic programs exist to assist industries, communities, and workers injured by import competition.

The Foreign Corrupt Practices Act restricts U.S. firms doing business abroad from paying public officials "commissions" for getting business contracts from the foreign governments.

LEARNING OUTCOMES

After studying this chapter, you should be able to clearly explain:

A. General Principles

L0.1   Explain which country's law will govern an international contract should a dispute arise
> See the choice of law example where the U.S. Court required the Lipcons to "honor their bargains" and vindicate their claims in an English Court on p. 114.

L0.2   Identify seven major international organizations, conferences, and treaties that affect the multinational markets for goods, services, and investments
> See the discussion of the GATT-WTO, CISG, UNCTAD, EU, NAFTA, IMF-World Bank, and OPEC beginning on p. 115.

L0.3   List the forms of business organizations for doing business abroad
> See the discussion of export sales, appointing of an agent, foreign distributorships, licensing, subsidiaries, and joint ventures beginning on p. 119.

B. Governmental Regulation

L0.4   Explain the import protections afforded owners of U.S. intellectual property rights
> See the discussion on the legal remedies provided owners of U.S. copyrights and trademarks against counterfeit goods, p. 123.

See the example excluding certain foreign-made mobile phones because the devices infringed on two Apple Inc. patents, p. 123.
See the *TianRui* case whereby the ITC excluded cast steel railway wheels made in a foreign country with misappropriated trade secrets of a U.S. manufacturer, p. 124.
See the application of the U.S. Copyright Act's *first sale doctrine's* to gray market goods, p. 125.
See the *Lever Brothers* example barring importation of physically difficult foreign goods bearing trademarks identical to valid U.S. trademarks, p. 125.

LO.5 Explain the tariff barriers and nontariff barriers to the free movements of goods across borders
See the *Sabritas* case on the applicability of tariff barriers on p. 130.
See the U.S. embargo on all Brazilian shrimp example because of Brazil's failure to require turtle excluder devices on its shrimp boats p. 131.

LO.6 Explain U.S. law regarding payment to foreign government officials as a means of obtaining business contracts with other governments, and compare U.S. law to laws and treaties applicable to most First World nations
See the Ethics & the Law discussion of the tax deductions for "useful expenditures" (bribes) claimed by Siemens AG, p. 135.

KEY TERMS

act-of-state doctrine
agent
blocking laws
choice-of-law clause
comity
Dispute Settlement Body (DSB)
distributor
dumping
effects doctrine

export sale
franchising
freight forwarders
gray market goods
intellectual property rights
joint venture
jurisdictional rule of reason
letter of credit

licensing
most-favored-nation clause
principal
secrecy laws
sovereign compliance doctrine
sovereign immunity doctrine
special drawing rights (SDRs)
tariff

QUESTIONS AND CASE PROBLEMS

1. How does the selling of subsidized foreign goods in the United States adversely affect free trade?

2. Able Time Inc. imported a shipment of watches into the United States. The watches bore the mark "TOMMY," which is a registered trademark owned by Tommy Hilfiger. U.S. Customs seized the watches pursuant to the Tariff Act, which authorizes seizure of any "merchandise bearing a counterfeit mark." Tommy Hilfiger did not make or sell watches at the time of the seizure. Able argues that because Tommy Hilfiger did not make watches at the time of the seizure, the watches it imported were not counterfeit, and the civil penalty imposed by Customs was unlawful. The government argues that the mark was

counterfeit and the Tariff Act does not require the owner of the registered mark to make the same type of goods as those bearing the offending mark. Decide. [*U.S. v. Able Time, Inc.*, 545 F.3d 824 (9th Cir. 2008)].

3. PepsiCo has registered its PEPSI trademarks in the U.S. Patent and Trademark Office. PEPSI products are bottled and distributed in the United States by PepsiCo and by authorized bottlers pursuant to Exclusive Bottling Appointment agreements, which authorize local bottlers to bottle and distribute PEPSI products in their respective territories. Similarly, PepsiCo has appointed local bottlers to bottle and distribute PEPSI products in Mexico within

particular territories. Pacific Produce, Ltd., has been engaged in the sale and distribution within the United States and Nevada of PEPSI products that were manufactured and bottled in Mexico and intended for sale in Mexico ("Mexican product"). The Mexican product sold by Pacific Products in the United States has certain material differences from domestic PEPSI products sold by PepsiCo: (1) it contains inferior paper labels that improperly report nutritional information; (2) it does not comply with the labeling standards followed by PepsiCo in the United States; (3) it is sold in channels of trade different from PepsiCo's authorized distribution channels without "drink by" notice dates on the Mexican product and monitoring on the Mexican product for proper shipment and storage conditions; and (4) it conflicts with the bottle return policies of PepsiCo. The Mexican product with its "Marca Reg" and Spanish language bottle caps is well received by consumers in Pacific Produce distribution channels. Classify the goods being sold by Pacific Produce. State the applicable law governing a dispute between PepsiCo and Pacific Produce. How would you decide this case? [*PepsiCo, Inc. v. Pacific Produce, Ltd.,*70 F. Supp. 2d 1057 (C.D. Cal.)]

4. Ronald Sadler, a California resident, owned a helicopter distribution company in West Germany, Delta Avia. This company distributed U.S.-made Hughes civilian helicopters in western Europe. Sadler's German firm purchased 85 helicopters from Hughes Aircraft Co. After export licenses were obtained in reliance on the purchaser's written assurance that the goods would not be disposed of contrary to the export license, the helicopters were exported to Germany for resale in western Europe. Thereafter, Delta Avia exported them to North Korea, which was a country subject to a trade embargo by the United States. The helicopters were converted to military use. Sadler was charged with violating the Export Administration Regulations. In Sadler's defense, it was contended that the U.S. regulations have no effect on what occurs in the resale of civilian helicopters in another sovereign country. Decide.

5. Mirage Investments Corp. (MIC) planned a tender offer for the shares of Gulf States International Corp. (GSIC). Archer, an officer of MIC, placed purchase orders for GSIC stock through the New York office of the Bahamian Bank (BB) prior to the announcement of the tender offer, making a $300,000 profit when the tender offer was made public. The Bahamas is a secrecy jurisdiction. The bank informed the SEC that under its law, it could not disclose the name of the person for whom it purchased the stock. What, if anything, may the SEC do to discover whether the federal securities laws have been violated?

6. United Overseas, Ltd. (UOL), is a U.K. firm that purchases and sells manufacturers' closeouts in Europe and the Middle East. UOL's representative, Jay Knox, used stationery listing a UOL office in New York to solicit business from Revlon, Inc., in New York. On April 1, 1992, UOL faxed a purchase order from its headquarters in England to Revlon's New York offices for the purchase of $4 million worth of shampoo. The purchase order on its face listed six conditions, none of which referred to a forum selection clause. When Revlon was not paid for the shampoo it shipped, it sued UOL in New York for breach of contract. UOL moved to dismiss the complaint because of a forum selection clause, which it stated was on the reverse side of the purchase order and provided that "the parties hereby agree to submit to the jurisdiction of the English Courts disputes arising out of the contract." The evidence did not show that the reverse side of the purchase order had been faxed with the April 1992 order. Should the court dismiss the complaint based on the "forum selection clause"? Read Chapter 32 on letters of credit and advise Revlon how to avoid similar litigation in the future. [*Revlon, Inc. v. United Overseas, Ltd.,* 1994 WL 9657 (S.D.N.Y)]

7. Reebok manufactures and sells fashionable athletic shoes in the United States and abroad. It owns the federally registered Reebok trademark and has registered this trademark in Mexico as well. Nathan Betech is a Mexican citizen residing in San Diego, California, with business offices there. Reebok believed that Betech was in the business of selling counterfeit Reebok shoes in Mexican border towns, such as Tijuana, Mexico. It sought an injunction in a federal district court in California ordering Betech to cease his

counterfeiting activity and to refrain from destroying certain documents. It also asked the court to freeze Betech's assets pending the outcome of a Lanham Act lawsuit. Betech contended that a U.S. district court has no jurisdiction or authority to enter the injunction for the activities allegedly occurring in Mexico. Decide. [*Reebok Int'l, Ltd. v. Marnatech Enterprises, Inc.,* 970 F.2d 552 (9th Cir.)]

8. Assume that before the formation of the European Union, the lowest-cost source of supply for a certain product consumed in France was the United States. Explain the basis by which, after the EU was formed, higher-cost German producers could have replaced the U.S. producers as the source of supply.

9. A complaint was filed with the U.S. Commerce Department's ITA by U.S. telephone manufacturers AT&T, Comidial Corp., and Eagle Telephones, Inc., alleging that 12 Asian manufacturers of small business telephones, including the Japanese firms Hitachi, NEC, and Toshiba and the Taiwanese firm Sun Moon Star Corp., were dumping their small business phones in the U.S. market at prices that were from 6 percent to 283 percent less than those in their home markets. The U.S. manufacturers showed that the domestic industry's market share had dropped from 54 percent in 1985 to 33 percent in 1989. They asserted that it was doubtful if the domestic industry could survive the dumping. Later, in a hearing before the ITC, the Japanese and Taiwanese respondents contended that their domestic industry was basically sound and that the U.S. firms simply had to become more efficient to meet worldwide competition. They contended that the United States was using the procedures before the ITA and ITC as a nontariff barrier to imports. How should the ITC decide the case? [*American Telephone and Telegraph Co. v. Hitachi,* 6 I.T.C. 1511]

10. Campbell Soup Co. imports tomato paste from a wholly owned Mexican subsidiary, Sinalopasta, S.A. de C.V. It deducted $416,324 from the computed value of goods shipped to the United States, which was the cost of transportation of the finished tomato paste from Sinalopasta's loading dock in Mexico to the U.S. border. The deduction thus lowered the computed value of the goods and the amount of duty to be paid the U.S. government by Campbell Soup Co. United States Customs questioned this treatment of freight costs. Tariff Act §140a(e)(1)(B) requires that profits and general expenses be included in calculating the computed value of goods, which in part quantify the value of the merchandise in the country of production. Is Campbell's position correct? [*Campbell Soup Co., Inc. v. United States,* 107 F.3d 1556 (Fed. Cir.)]

11. Roland Staemphfli was employed as the chief financial officer of Honeywell Bull, S.A. (HB), a Swiss computer company operating exclusively in Switzerland. Staemphfli purportedly arranged financing for HB in Switzerland through the issuance of promissory notes. He had the assistance of Fidenas, a Bahamian company dealing in commercial paper. Unknown to Fidenas, the HB notes were fraudulent. The notes were prepared and forged by Staemphfli, who lost all of the proceeds in a speculative investment and was convicted of criminal fraud. HB denied responsibility for the fraudulently issued notes when they came due. Fidenas's business deteriorated because of its involvement with the HB notes. It sued HB and others in the United States for violations of U.S. securities laws. HB defended, arguing that the U.S. court did not have jurisdiction over the transactions in question. Decide. [*Fidenas v. Honeywell Bull, S.A.,* 606 F.2d 5 (2d Cir.)]

12. Marc Rich & Co., A.G., a Swiss commodities trading corporation, refused to comply with a grand jury subpoena requesting certain business records maintained in Switzerland and relating to crude oil transactions and possible violations of U.S. income tax laws. Marc Rich contended that a U.S. court has no authority to require a foreign corporation to deliver to a U.S. court documents located abroad. The court disagreed and imposed fines, froze assets, and threatened to close a Marc Rich wholly owned subsidiary that did business in the state of New York. The fines amounted to $50,000 for each day the company failed to

comply with the court's order. Marc Rich appealed. Decide. [*Marc Rich v. United States,* 707 U.S. 633 (2d Cir.)]

13. U.S. Steel Corp. formed Orinoco Mining Co., a wholly owned corporation, to mine large deposits of iron ore that U.S. Steel had discovered in Venezuela. Orinoco, which was incorporated in Delaware, was subject to Venezuela's maximum tax of 50 percent on net income. Orinoco was also subject to U.S. income tax, but the U.S. foreign tax credit offset this amount. U.S. Steel purchased the ore from Orinoco in Venezuela. U.S. Steel formed Navios, Inc., a wholly owned subsidiary, to transport the ore. Navios, a Liberian corporation, was subject to a 2.5 percent Venezuelan excise tax and was exempt from U.S. income tax. Although U.S. Steel was Navios's primary customer, it charged other customers the same price it charged U.S. Steel. U.S. Steel's investment in Navios was $50,000. In seven years, Navios accumulated nearly $80 million in cash but had not paid any dividends to U.S. Steel. The IRS used IRC §482 to allocate $52 million of Navios's income to U.S. Steel. U.S. Steel challenged this action, contending Navios's charges to U.S. Steel were at arm's length and the same it charged other customers. Decide. [*United States Steel Corp. v. Commissioner,* 617 F.2d 942 (2d Cir.)]

14. National Computers, Inc., a U.S. firm, entered into a joint venture with a Chinese computer manufacturing organization, TEC. A dispute arose over payments due the U.S. firm under the joint venture agreement with TEC. The agreement called for disputes to be arbitrated in China, with the arbitrator being chosen from a panel of arbitrators maintained by the Beijing arbitration institution, Cietac. What advantages and disadvantages exist for the U.S. firm under this arbitration arrangement? Advise the U.S. firm on negotiating future arbitration agreements with Chinese businesses.

15. Sensor, a Netherlands business organization wholly owned by Geosource, Inc., of Houston, Texas, made a contract with C.E.P. to deliver 2,400 strings of geophones to Rotterdam by September 20, 1982. The ultimate destination was identified as the USSR. Thereafter, in June 1982, the president of the United States prohibited shipment to the USSR of equipment manufactured in foreign countries under license from U.S. firms. The president had a foreign policy objective of retaliating for the imposition of martial law in Poland, and he was acting under regulations issued under the Export Administration Act of 1979. Sensor, in July and August of 1982, notified C.E.P. that as a subsidiary of a U.S. corporation, it had to respect the president's embargo. C.E.P. filed suit in a district court of the Netherlands asking that Sensor be ordered to deliver the geophones. Decide. [*Compagnie Européenne des Pétroles v. Sensor Nederland,* 22 I.L.M. 66]

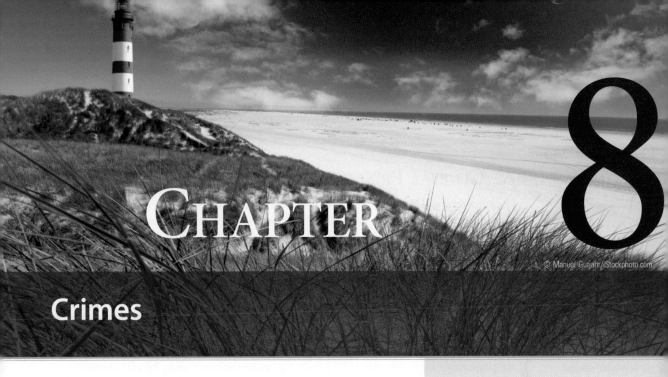

Chapter 8

Crimes

© Manuel Gutjahr/iStockphoto.com

learningoutcomes

After studying this chapter, you should be able to

LO.1 Discuss the nature and classification of crimes

LO.2 Describe the basis of criminal liability

LO.3 Identify who is responsible for criminal acts

LO.4 Explain the penalties for crimes and the sentencing for corporate crimes

LO.5 List examples of white-collar crimes and their elements

LO.6 Describe the common law crimes

LO.7 Discuss crimes related to computers

LO.8 Describe the rights of businesses charged with crimes and the constitutional protections afforded them

S ociety sets certain standards of conduct and punishes a breach of those standards as a crime. This chapter introduces the means by which government protects people and businesses from prohibited conduct.

A. GENERAL PRINCIPLES

Detailed criminal codes and statutes define crimes and specify their punishment. Crimes vary from state to state but still show the imprint of a common law background through similar elements and structure.

1. Nature and Classification of Crimes

crime–violation of the law that is punished as an offense against the state or government.

misdemeanor–criminal offense with a sentence of less than one year that is neither treason nor a felony.

felony–criminal offense that is punishable by confinement in prison for more than one year or by death, or that is expressly stated by statute to be a felony.

A **crime** is conduct that is prohibited and punished by a government. Crimes are classified as *common law* or *statutory* according to their origin. Offenses punishable by less than one year in prison are called **misdemeanors**. More serious crimes are called **felonies**, including serious business crimes such as bribery and embezzlement, which are punishable by confinement in prison for more than one year. Misdemeanors include weighing goods with uninspected scales or operating without a sales tax license. An act may be a felony in one state and a misdemeanor in another.[1]

2. Basis of Criminal Liability

A crime generally consists of two elements: (1) a mental state (scienter or intent) and (2) an act or omission. Harm may occur as a result of a crime, but harm is not an essential element of a crime.

(A) MENTAL STATE. Mental state, or intent, does not require an awareness or knowledge of guilt. In most crimes, the voluntary commission of the act is sufficient for proving mental state. Ignorance that a law is being broken does not mean there is not mental state. **For Example,** dumping waste without a permit is still a criminal act even when the party releasing the waste did not know about the permit requirement.

(B) ACT OR OMISSION. Specific statutes define the conduct that, when coupled with sufficient mental state, constitutes a crime. **For Example,** writing a check knowing you do not have the funds available is a crime. Likewise, the failure to file your annual income tax returns is also a crime.

3. Responsibility for Criminal Acts

In some cases, persons who did not necessarily commit the criminal act itself are still held criminally responsible for acts committed by others.

(A) CORPORATE LIABILITY. Corporations are held responsible for the acts of their employees. A corporation may also be held liable for crimes based on the failure of its employees to act. In the past decade, some of the nation's largest corporations have paid fines for crimes based on employees' failure to take action or for the

---

[1] Some states further define crimes by seriousness with different degrees of a crime, such as first-degree murder, second-degree murder, and so on. Misdemeanors may be differentiated by giving special names to minor misdemeanors.

CASE SUMMARY

Making Stuff Up for the Grand Jury

FACTS: Kathryn Erickson was the general manager of the Uintah Special Services District (USSD), an entity created to use federal-mineral-lease revenues for road projects. She, along with her secretary, Cheryl McCurdy, administered the USSD from a small office in Vernal, Utah. Ms. Erickson's authority was limited and she was not permitted to enter into or modify contracts for or to expend more than $1,000 of USSD funds, without board approval.

Mitchell Construction was a major contractor for USSD. In 1998, USSD awarded Mitchell Construction a contract to haul gravel from a site called Hamaker Bottoms and another contract to carry out small asphalt-paving projects. Both contracts were to be completed within the 1998 construction year.

During 1999 and 2000 Mitchell Construction continued to perform work on the projects covered by its 1998 contracts with USSD, despite their expiration. It submitted invoices to USSD and was paid for this work.

In June 1999 a federal grand jury began to investigate contracting irregularities at USSD and the Uintah County Road Department and issued a *subpoena duces tecum* to USSD requesting copies of "project contracts, invoices" between USSD and contractors.

While the office was preparing the response for the grand jury subpoena, Ms. McCurdy saw Ms. Erickson prepare a handwritten change order for the Hamaker Bottoms contract and saw Ms. Erickson and Gilman N. Mitchell both sign it. The change order, which was backdated to January 13, 1999, extended the contract through December 31, 2000.

Ms. McCurdy later discovered that two other change orders had been created and backdated. She spent a day copying documents for the grand jury and recording, on a handwritten list, all of the documents that she had copied. However, she left Ms. Erickson in the office while she was working on the list in order to go home for dinner. Ms. Erickson called her and told her not to come back because all the copying was done. Later, Ms. McCurdy found on Ms. Erickson's desk a photocopy of the grand jury document list and saw that two entries not in her handwriting had been added. These entries were for change orders for contracts between Mitchell Construction and USSD. Ms. McCurdy reported the change to the government.

Ms. Erickson and Mr. Mitchell were each indicted by a grand jury in the U.S. District Court for the District of Utah on three counts of obstruction of justice by knowingly falsifying a document with the knowledge and intent that the grand jury would rely on it.

The jury returned a verdict of guilty against both Ms. Erickson and Mr. Mitchell on all three counts. The two appealed.

DECISION: The court affirmed the decision. There are three requirements for conviction of obstruction of justice: (1) There must be a pending judicial proceeding; (2) the defendant must have knowledge or notice of the pending proceeding; and (3) the defendant must have acted corruptly with the specific intent to obstruct or impede the administration of justice. The two had backdated the documents in order to cover up the fact that the contracts had expired. They had continued the contracts without authority and authorized or received payments above the $1,000 limit. They were responding to a grand jury subpoena and gave it false change orders. They did so in order to protect Ms. Erickson's job and Mr. Mitchell's company's contracts and relationship with USSD. [*U.S. v. Erickson,* **561 F.3d 1150 (10th Cir. 2009)**]

actions they did take. **For Example,** Siemens, an international company, paid the largest fine in the history of the Foreign Corrupt Practices Act for paying bribes in order to win contracts in countries around the world, a total of $1.6 billion in fines, including $350 million in the United States.

(B) OFFICERS AND AGENTS OF CORPORATIONS. One of the main differences between nonbusiness and business crimes is that more people in a company can be convicted for the same business crime. For nonbusiness crimes, only those who are actually involved in the act itself can be convicted of the crime. For business crimes, however, managers of firms whose employees commit criminal acts can be held liable if the managers authorized the conduct of the employees or knew about their conduct and did nothing or failed to act reasonably in their supervisory positions to prevent the employees from engaging in criminal conduct. **For Example,** the former security chief for Massey Mines was sentenced to three years in prison after being found guilty of notifying employees in advance of the arrival of federal mine inspectors at the company's mines.[2]

(C) FEDERAL LAWS TARGETING OFFICER AND DIRECTOR CRIMINAL RESPONSIBILITY. Following the Michael Milken and Ivan Boesky junk bond era on Wall Street in 1988, the Insider Trading and Securities Fraud Act of 1988 increased the criminal penalties for officers and directors who violated the law tenfold. In addition, the "white-collar kingpin" law imposed mandatory minimum sentences for corporate officers. Sarbanes-Oxley, which followed the 2000-era dot-com failures increased penalties for officers and directors from 5 years to 20 years, along with an increase in fines by 20 times. Under The Dodd-Frank Wall Street Reform and Consumer Protection Act, the types of white-collar executives covered under criminal laws increased to include brokers, insurers, and any financial services firms.

So-called "honest services" fraud has been refined by Dodd-Frank and court decisions.[3] Executives can no longer be convicted on the basis that something went wrong at their company. Proof of fraud requires something more than an officer just being an officer at the company—there must be active engagement in operations that led to the officer's committing fraud.

CASE SUMMARY

Rats in the Warehouse and a CEO with a Fine

FACTS: Acme Markets, Inc., was a national food retail chain headquartered in Philadelphia. John R. Park was president of Acme, which, in 1970, employed 36,000 people and operated 16 warehouses.

In 1970, the Food and Drug Administration (FDA) forwarded a letter to Park describing, in detail, problems with rodent infestation in Acme's Philadelphia warehouse facility. In December 1971, the FDA found the same types of conditions in Acme's Baltimore warehouse facility. In January 1972, the FDA's chief of compliance for its Baltimore office wrote to Park about the inspection:

> We note with much concern that the old and new warehouse areas used for food storage were actively and extensively inhabited by live rodents. Of even more concern was the observation that such reprehensible conditions obviously existed for a prolonged period of time without any detection, or were completely ignored.
>
> We trust this letter will serve to direct your attention to the seriousness of the problem and formally advise you of the urgent need to initiate whatever measures are necessary to prevent recurrence and ensure compliance with the law.

[2] Ken Maher, "Ex-Massey Official Gets Three Years," *Wall Street Journal*, March 1, 2012, p. A3.
[3] *Skilling v. U.S.* 130 S.Ct. 2896 (2010).

CASE SUMMARY

Continued

After Park received the letter, he met with the vice president for legal affairs for Acme and was assured that he was "investigating the situation immediately and would be taking corrective action."

When the FDA inspected the Baltimore warehouse in March 1972, there was some improvement in the facility, but there was still rodent infestation. Acme and Park were both charged with violations of the federal Food, Drug and Cosmetic Act. Acme pleaded guilty. Park was convicted and fined $500; he appealed.

DECISION: Officers of a corporation can be held criminally liable for the conduct of others within the company if it can be shown that the officers knew of the issue and failed to take the steps necessary to eliminate the criminal activity. In this case, Park had been warned and had been given several opportunities to remedy the problem. Part of his responsibility as an officer is following up to be certain that tasks he has assigned are completed. Failure to follow through can be a basis for criminal liability. [*United States v. Park,* **421 U.S. 658 (1975)**]

(D) PENALTY FOR CRIME: FORFEITURE. When a defendant is convicted of a crime, the court may also declare that the defendant's rights in any property used or gained from a crime (an instrument of that crime) be confiscated. Some types of instruments of the crime are automatically forfeited, such as the tools of a crime. **For Example,** the U.S. government confiscated from confessed $50-billion-Ponzi schemer, Bernie Madoff, everything from his yacht to his bank accounts to his seat on NASDAQ. Confiscation is, in effect, an increased penalty for the defendant's crime.

(E) PENALTIES FOR BUSINESS AND WHITE-COLLAR CRIMES. Most common law criminal penalties were created with "natural" persons in mind, as opposed to "artificial" or corporate persons. A $100,000 fine may be significant to an individual but to a corporation with $3 billion in assets and hundreds of millions in income, such a fine could be viewed as a minimal cost of doing business.

As a result of these fine amount realities, corporate penalties and processes have been reformed. Congress, prosecutors, and the courts are in a continual processes of developing penalties for corporations and white-collar crimes so that the result is both a deterrent effect as well as changes in cultures of corporations to prevent additional violations.

(E)(1) COMPUTING NEW PENALTIES FOR CORPORATIONS. Criminal penalties have been increased to allow judges to fine corporations according to how much a bad decision would cost. For example, if a company develops a faulty product, net earnings could decline 10 to 20 percent. Criminal penalties can be assessed as a percentage of net income.

Rather than using fixed-amount fines for corporations, statutes and courts apply percentage of revenue penalties. **For Example,** a bad decision on a product line would cost a company 10 percent to 20 percent of its earnings. A criminal penalty could be imposed in the same percentage fashion with the idea that the company simply made a bad legal decision that should be reflected in earnings.

(E)(2) CORPORATE INTEGRITY AGREEMENTS. Using a corporate integrity agreement (CIA), judges are able to, in effect, place corporations on probation. Under CIAS, companies are assigned monitors who are on-site and follow up to be sure the company is not committing any further violations. **For Example,** because of environmental law violations, ConEd was assigned a monitor from the National

Resources Defense Council to observe the company's activities. CIAS do not require an admission of guilt, but generally require the payment of a fine and an agreement to "stay clean" for three to five years.

(E)(3) FEDERAL SENTENCING GUIDELINES. Another change in penalties for business and white-collar crimes has been the requirement for mandatory prison sentences for officers and directors who are convicted of crimes committed as they led their corporations. The human element of the corporation is then punished for the crimes that the business committed. The U.S. Sentencing Commission, established by Congress in 1984, has developed both federal sentencing guidelines and a carrot-and-stick approach to fighting business crime. If the managers of a company are involved and working to prevent criminal misconduct in the company and a crime occurs, the guidelines permit sentence reductions for the managers' efforts. If the managers do not adequately supervise conduct and do not encourage compliance with the law, the guidelines require judges to impose harsher sentences and fines. The guidelines, referred to as the **Federal Sentencing Guidelines** (or the *U.S. Sentencing Guidelines*), apply to federal crimes such as securities fraud, antitrust violations, racketeering, theft (embezzlement), Medicare fraud, and other business crimes. The sentencing guidelines permit a judge to place a guilty company on probation, with the length of the probation controlled by whether the company had prevention programs in place.

Federal Sentencing Guidelines—federal standards used by judges in determining mandatory sentence terms for those convicted of federal crimes.

(E)(4) MANDATORY SENTENCES FOR OFFICERS OF CORPORATIONS WHO MASTERMIND CRIMES. Following the collapse of companies such as Enron, WorldCom, and Adelphia, the U.S. Sentencing Commission (USSC) piloted the passage of the 2001 Economic Crime Package: Consolidation, Clarification, and Certainty. Amended guidelines, post-Enron, address the increased corporate and white-collar criminal penalties enacted under Sarbanes-Oxley (SOX) (see (E)(5) for more discussion of SOX), and consider the seriousness of the offense, the company's history of violations, its cooperation in the investigation, the effectiveness of its compliance program (often called an *ethics program*), and the role of senior management in the wrongdoing. Corporate managers found to have masterminded any criminal activity must be sentenced to prison time.[4] Figure 8-1 is a summary of the current penalties for federal crimes. Under a U.S. Supreme Court decision in 2005, *U.S. v. Booker,* judges may only use the guidelines as just that, guidelines; the sentencing ranges are no longer mandatory for judges.[5] Going outside those ranges, however, is carefully reviewed by appellate courts.[6] Federal judges can consider only evidence presented at trial in making their sentencing determinations. They can consider evidence of prior convictions, but only if that evidence was presented at trial or if the defendant has a chance to present evidence about those convictions at the sentencing.[7]

White-Collar Crime Penalty Enhancement Act of 2002—federal reforms passed as a result of the collapses of companies such as Enron; provides for longer sentences and higher fines for both executives and companies.

(E)(5) SARBANES-OXLEY REFORMS TO CRIMINAL PENALTIES. Part of SOX, passed by Congress following the collapses of Enron and WorldCom corporations, was the **White-Collar Crime Penalty Enhancement Act of 2002.**[8] This act increases penalties substantially. **For Example,** the penalties for mail and wire fraud are increased from a maximum of 5 years to a maximum of 20 years. Penalties for violation of pension laws increased from 1 year to 10 years and the fines increased from $5,000 to $100,000.[9] In addition, many

---

[4] *U.S. v. Booker,* 543 U.S. 220 (2005).
[5] *U.S. v. Skilling,* 554 F.3d 529 (5th Cir. 2009).
[6] *Gall v. U.S.,* 552 U.S. 38 (2007).
[7] Miriam H. Baer, "Choosing Punishment," 92 *Boston Univ. Law Rev.* 577 (2010).
[8] 18 U.S.C. §1314 *et seq.*
[9] 18 U.S.C. §§1341 and 1343; 29 U.S.C. §1131.

FIGURE 8-1 | *Roster of White-Collar Criminal Charges*

COMPANY/PERSON	ISSUE	STATUS
Andrew Fastow, former CFO of Enron (2004)	Multimillion-dollar earnings from serving as principal in SPEs of Enron created to keep debts off the company books; significant sales of shares during the time frame preceding company collapse	Resigned as CFO; appeared before Congress and took the Fifth Amendment; entered guilty plea to securities and wire fraud; sentence of 6 years; reduced to five years and 3 months; completed at the end of 2012
Galleon Group (hedge fund 2011) A Goldman Sachs director who fed information to Galleon Group was also convicted of insider trading.	Insider trading charges	Twenty-three executives, including CEO, convicted or entered guilty pleas; Galleon's $3.7 billion fund liquidated; CEO sentenced to 11 years
Bernie Ebbers (2005) Former CEO, WorldCom	Fraud	Convicted; sentenced to 25 years
Computer Associates (2004)	Criminal investigation for securities fraud and obstruction following $2.2 billion restatement in sales	Company paid $225 million fine; former CEO entered guilty plea to felony charges; sentenced to 11 years; Company changed name to CA, Inc.
Countrywide Mortgage (2009)	Insider trading; securities fraud	Former CEO Angelo Mozilo charged with insider trading, CFO and COO charged with failure to disclose firm's relaxed lending standards; settled cases for fines
Enron (2001)	Earnings overstated through mark-to-market accounting; off-the-book/special-purpose entities (SPEs) carried significant amounts of Enron debt not reflected in the financial statements; significant offshore SPEs (881 of 3,000 SPEs were offshore, primarily in Cayman Islands)	Company in bankruptcy; impetus for SOX; CFO Andrew Fastow and others entered guilty pleas; Jeffrey Skilling, former CEO, found guilty
HealthSouth (2003)	$2.7 billion accounting fraud; overstatement of revenues	16 former executives indicted; 5 plead guilty; see Richard Scrushy
KPMG (2006)	Tax shelter fraud	Settled by paying a penalty of $456 million fine in lieu of indictment; 16 former partners and employees indicted; most charges dismissed
L. Dennis Kozlowski, former CEO of Tyco (2003)	Accused of improper use of company funds	Indicted in New York for failure to pay sales tax on transactions in fine art; hung jury on charges of looting Tyco; convicted on retrial with 15–25-year sentence; denied parole in 2012
Bernard Madoff (2009)	Ran a $50-billion Ponzi scheme through Madoff Securities	Entered guilty plea to all charges and refused to cooperate with investigators; 150-year sentence (at age of 71 in 2009, it is the equivalent of a life sentence)
Martha Stewart, CEO of Martha Stewart Living, Omnimedia, Inc., and close friend of Dr. Waksal (2003)	Sold 5,000 shares of ImClone one day before public announcement of negative FDA action on Erbitux	Indicted and convicted, along with her broker at Merrill Lynch, of making false statements and conspiracy; served sentence and probation
Richard Scrushy (2003)	Indicted for fraud and bribery for HealthSouth accounting fraud	Acquitted of all charges related to HealthSouth; convicted of bribing former governor of Alabama
Stanford Securities (2012)	$9 billion Ponzi scheme	CEO convicted of mail, wire, and securities fraud; Laura Pendergest-Holt, the former chief investment officer, entered a

Thinking Things Through

Can a Pharmacy's License Be Revoked for Too Many Cash Sales of Oxycodone?

The Drug Enforcement Administration (DEA) has moved to revoke the controlled medication licenses of two pharmacies because the pharmacies were filling prescriptions for oxycodone (the painkiller) in excess of their monthly allowances for controlled substances. In addition, the DEA alleges that the pharmacies' corporate entities failed to conduct on-site inspections and failed to notice that 42 to 58 percent of all the sales of the substances were cash sales, something that is considered a red flag in the sale and distribution of controlled substances. In addition, the number of prescriptions filled continued to escalate.

The two pharmacies won an injunction against the revocation in federal district court. However, the DEA is hoping to persuade the judge to lift the injunction once it is able to show that the corporations should have known there was a problem. The rate of cash sales at these pharmacies was eight times the national rate for filling prescriptions with cash. Pharmacists at the drug stores, in interviews with the DEA agents, indicated that the customers paying cash for the oxycodone were "shady," and that they suspected that some of the prescriptions were not legitimate. One of the companies adjusted (increased) the levels of

shipment of oxycodone to the pharmacies five times. In one on-site visit by a DEA agent, the following information emerged: one of every three cars that came to the drive-thru window had a prescription for oxycodone; many patients living at the same address had the same prescriptions for oxycodone from the same doctor.

Both companies, CVS and Cardinal Health, have indicated in court filings that they have changed their practices and provided training to pharmacy personnel so that they can spot these types of illegal prescriptions and report suspicious activity. Both pharmacy companies have terminated customers, meaning that they will no longer fill prescriptions for those customers.

The DEA seeks to hold the corporations responsible because of the lack of on-site presence and the failure to follow the numbers for sales and distribution at the pharmacies. Can the corporation be held liable when it was not actually participating in the distribution of the oxycodone?

Source: Timothy W. Martin and Devlin Barrett, "Red Flags Ignored, DEA Says," *Wall Street Journal,* February 21, 2012. p. B1.

federal statutes now require executives to reimburse their companies for any money earned as a result of illegal activity. **For Example,** the former CEO of UnitedHealth Group Inc. was required to pay back $448 billion in profits he had made from stock options that were granted illegally.[10]

(E)(6) CREATIVE PENALTIES FOR WHITE-COLLAR CRIME. Federal judges are developing new types of sentences in order to use those convicted to convince business people to avoid criminal conduct. **For Example,** in 2009, a federal judge required an executive who entered a guilty plea to spend his two years of probation writing a book about what he did and offer guidance to business executives so that they can avoid his missteps. He was required to publish and distribute the book.[11] In 2010, a federal agency agreed to defer penalties if an officer agreed to travel around the country and speak to comapneis and executives about the mistakes he had made in order to help them understand the need for vigilance in stopping missteps that lead to crimes.

4. Indemnification of Crime Victims

Penalties are paid to the government. Typically, the victim of a crime does not benefit from the criminal prosecution and conviction of the wrongdoer, although courts can order that restitution be paid to victims.

[10] S. Almashat et al., "Rapidly Increasing Criminal and Civil Monetary Penalties Against the Pharmaceutical Industry: 1991 to 2010," *Public Citizen's Health Research Group,* December 16, 2010, *available at* **http://www.citizen.org/documents/rapidlyincreasingcriminalandcivilpenalti**
[11] Natasha Singer, "Judge Orders Former Bristol-Myers Executive to Write Book," *New York Times,* June 9, 2009, p. B3.

The Victims of Crime Act of 1984 creates a federal Crime Victims Fund.[12] Using the fines paid into the federal courts as well as other monies, the federal government makes grants to the states to assist them in financing programs to provide assistance for victims of crime.[13] The Victim and Witness Protection Act of 1982 authorizes the sentencing judge in a federal district court to order, in certain cases, that the defendant make restitution (restoration) to the victim or pay the victim the amount of medical expenses or loss of income caused by the crime.[14]

Victims may also be entitled to bring civil actions for recovery of the damages they experience because a crime is committed. **For Example,** a company or individual violating federal antitrust laws is liable to the victim for three times the damages actually sustained.

B. White-Collar Crimes

white-collar crimes – crimes that do not use nor threaten to use force or violence or do not cause injury to persons or property.

White-collar crime is generally considered business crime, the type committed generally in the course of doing business and usually involving some form of deceit used to get gains.

5. Conspiracies

conspiracy – agreement between two or more persons to commit an unlawful act.

The crime of conspiracy is committed before the actual crime; it is the planning of the crime. A **conspiracy** is an agreement between two or more persons to commit an unlawful act or to use unlawful means to achieve an otherwise lawful result. Some conspiracy statutes do require that those charged must have done something to carry out the agreement before the crime of conspiracy is committed.

6. Crimes Related to Production, Competition, and Marketing

(A) Improper Use of Interstate Commerce. The shipment of improper goods or the transmission of improper information in interstate commerce is a federal crime. **For Example,** knowingly shipping food with salmonella would be a violation of the federal law that prohibits shipping adulterated foods, drugs, or cosmetics in interstate commerce.

The Communications Act of 1934, as amended, makes it a crime to manufacture or sell devices knowing their primary use is to unscramble satellite telecasts without having paid for the right to do so.[15]

(B) Securities Crimes. To protect the investing public, both state and federal laws have regulated the issuance and public sale of stocks and bonds. These statutes and the crimes associated with sales of securities are covered in Chapter 46.

7. Money Laundering

The federal government has adopted a Money Laundering Control Act (MLCA).[16] The act prohibits the knowing and willful participation in a financial transaction when

---

[12] 18 U.S.C. §3771. The act was amended in 2004 to include a type of bill of rights for crime victims, including assistance through the newly created Office for Victims of Crime.

[13] 18 U.S.C. §1401 *et seq.*

[14] 18 U.S.C. §3579, as amended by 18 U.S.C. §18.18; see *Hughey v. United States,* 495 U.S. 411 (1990). Some states likewise provide for payment into a special fund. Ex parte *Lewis,* 556 So.2d 370 (Ala. 1989). In 2002, Congress passed another victims' compensation statute, with this one providing relief and assistance to the victims of terrorist attacks in the United States. 42 U.S.C. §10603b.

[15] 47 U.S.C. §705(d)(1), (e)(4), 47 U.S.C. §605 (d)(1), (e)(4); *United States v. Harrell,* 983 F.2d 36 (5th Cir. 1993); but see *DIRECTV, Inc. v. Robson,* 420 F.3d 740 (6th Cir. 2000).

[16] 18 U.S.C. §§1956–1957 (2000). *U.S. v. Prince,* 214 F.3d 740 (6th Cir. 2000).

the transaction is designed to conceal or disguise the source of the funds. The so-called *USA Patriot Act* that was passed on October 26, 2001, less than two months after the destruction of the World Trade Center and the damage to the Pentagon on September 11, 2001, includes a substantial number of changes and amendments to the MLCA and the Bank Secrecy Act (BSA).[17] Both statutes have been used as means to control bribery, tax evasion, and money laundering. Their changes and amendments were designed to curb the funding of terrorist activities in the United States.

The Patriot Act expands the coverage of the law from banks and financial institutions to anyone involved in financial transactions, which includes securities brokers; travel agents; those who close real estate transactions; insurance companies; loan or finance companies; casinos; currency exchanges; check-cashing firms; auto, plane, and boat dealers; and branches and agencies of foreign banks located in the United States. The amendments make even small businesses subject to the requirements of disclosure under MLCA and BSA, such as reporting cash transactions in excess of $10,000.

In addition, the types of accounts covered have been expanded. The accounts covered are not only securities accounts but also money market accounts. Furthermore, banks are now more actively involved in supervising accounts and following through on government information furnished to the bank on suspicious transactions and activities as well as individuals. Banks are required to implement new policies to prevent the types of transactions tagged by the government and conduct internal investigations for suspicious transactions. Because of the required close-watch provisions of these laws, banks and others covered under the federal statutes have developed anti-money-laundering programs. These programs must include a "Know Your Customer" training segment that teaches employees how to spot suspicious customers and transactions.

8. Racketeering

Racketeer Influenced and Corrupt Organizations (RICO) Act—federal law, initially targeting organized crime, that has expanded in scope and provides penalties and civil recovery for multiple criminal offenses, or a pattern of racketeering.

Congress passed the **Racketeer Influenced and Corrupt Organizations (RICO) Act**[18] in 1970 as part of the Organized Crime Control Act. The law was designed primarily to prevent individuals involved in organized crime from investing money obtained through racketeering in legitimate businesses. However, the broad language of the act, coupled with a provision that allows individuals and businesses to sue for treble damages, has resulted in an increasing number of lawsuits against ordinary business persons not associated with organized crime.

(A) CRIMINAL AND CIVIL APPLICATIONS. RICO authorizes criminal and civil actions against persons who use any income derived from racketeering activity to invest in, control, or conduct an enterprise through a pattern of *racketeering activity*.[19] In criminal and civil actions under RICO, a pattern of racketeering activity must be established by

---

[17] 31 U.S.C. §531(h).

[18] 18 U.S.C. §§1961–1968.

[19] §1961. Definitions:

  (1) "Racketeering activity" means any act or threat involving murder, kidnapping, gambling, arson, robbery, bribery, extortion, dealing in obscene matter, dealing in a controlled substance or listed chemical, or sports bribery; counterfeiting; theft from interstate shipment; embezzlement from pension and welfare funds; extortionate credit transactions; fraud; wire fraud; mail fraud; procurement of citizenship or nationalization unlawfully; reproduction of naturalization or citizenship papers; obstruction of justice; tampering with a witness, victim, or an informant; retaliating against a witness, victim, or an informant; false statement in application and use of passport; forgery or false use of passport; fraud and misuse of visas, permits, and other documents; racketeering; unlawful welfare fund payments; laundering of monetary instruments; use of interstate commerce facilities in the commission of murder-for-hire; sexual exploitation of children; interstate transportation of stolen motor vehicles; interstate transportation of stolen property; trafficking in counterfeit labels of phonorecords, computer programs or computer program documentation, or packaging and copies of motion pictures or other audiovisual works; criminal infringement of a copyright; trafficking in contraband cigarettes; and white slave traffic.

proving that at least two acts of racketeering activity—so-called *predicate acts*—have been committed within 10 years.[20] Conviction under RICO's criminal provisions may result in a $25,000 fine and up to 20 years' imprisonment as well as forfeiture of the property involved. A successful civil plaintiff may recover three times the actual damages suffered and attorney fees.[21]

(B) EXPANDING USAGE. Civil RICO actions have been successful against business entities, such as accounting firms, labor unions, insurance companies, commercial banks, and stock brokerage firms. However, under the Private Securities Litigation Reform Act of 1995, securities fraud was eliminated as a **predicate act**, or a qualifying underlying offense, for private RICO actions, absent a prior criminal conviction.[22]

predicate act—qualifying underlying offense for RICO liability.

9. Bribery

Bribery is the act of giving money, property, or any benefit to a particular person to influence that person's judgment in favor of the giver.[23] At common law, the crime was limited to doing such acts to influence a public official.

The giving and the receiving of a bribe constitute separate crimes. In addition, the act of trying to obtain a bribe may be a crime of solicitation of bribery in some states, while in other states bribery is broadly defined to include solicitation of bribes.

10. Commercial Bribery

Commercial bribery is a form of bribery in which an agent for another is paid or given something of value in order to make a decision on behalf of his or her principal that benefits the party paying the agent. **For Example,** a napkin supplier who pays a restaurant agent $500 in exchange for that agent's decision to award the restaurant's napkin contract to that supplier has engaged in commercial bribery.[24]

11. Extortion and Blackmail

Extortion and *blackmail* are crimes in which money is exchanged for either specific actions or restraint in taking action.

(A) EXTORTION. When a public officer makes an illegal demand, the officer has committed the crime of **extortion**. **For Example,** if a health inspector threatens to close down a restaurant on a false sanitation law charge unless the restaurant pays the inspector a sum of money, the inspector has committed extortion. (If the restaurant voluntarily offers the inspector the money to prevent the restaurant from being shut down because of actual violations of the sanitation laws, the crime committed would be bribery.)

extortion—illegal demand by a public officer acting with apparent authority.

(B) BLACKMAIL. In jurisdictions where extortion is limited to the conduct of public officials, a nonofficial commits **blackmail** by making demands that would be extortion if made by a public official. Ordinarily, blackmail is the act of threatening

blackmail—extortion demands made by a nonpublic official.

---

[20] Brian Slocum, "RICO and the Legislative Supremacy Approach to Federal Criminal Lawmaking," 31 *Loyola Univ. Chicago Law Journal* 639 (2000).

[21] *Criminal RICO: 18 U.S.C. 1961–1968: A Manual for Federal Prosecutors.* Washington, D.C.: U.S. Dept. of Justice, Criminal Division, Organized Crime and Racketeering Section, [2009].

[22] 15 U.S.C. §78(a), (n)–(t).

[23] *In re Mangone*, 923 N.Y.S.2d 679 (2011).

[24] Connecticut's commercial bribery statute is a good example. It provides: *A person is guilty of commercial bribery when he confers, or agrees to confer, any benefit upon any employee, agent or fiduciary without the consent of the latter's employer or principal, with intent to influence his conduct in relation to his employer's or principal's affairs.* CGSA §53a-160 (2012). Other examples of commercial bribery statues can be found at Minn. Stat Ann §609.86 (Minnesota 2012); NH Rev Stat §638:8 (New Hampshire 2010); Alaska Stat §11.45.670 (Alaska 2012); and Ala. Code §13A-11-120 (Alabama 2012). Mississippi prohibits commercial bribery as well as sports bribery, which is paying the agent of a sports team in order to influence the outcome of a sporting event. Miss. Code Ann §97-9-10 (2010).

someone with publicity about a matter that would damage the victim's personal or business reputation.

12. Corrupt Influence

Legislative bodies have increasingly outlawed certain practices that exert a corrupting influence on business transactions.

(A) IMPROPER POLITICAL INFLUENCE. At the federal and state levels, it is a crime for one who holds public office to hold a financial interest in or to receive money from an enterprise that seeks to do business with the government. Such conduct is a conflict of interest between the official's duty to citizens and his or her personal financial interests. **For Example,** the former governor of Illinois, Rod Blagojevich, was convicted of seeking funds, fundraisers, and positions in exchange for political favors. To keep officials' conduct transparent, lobbyists must register in Washington, D.C.,[25] and adhere to statutory limits on gifts and contributions to political campaigns. Public officials must file annual disclosure forms about their financial positions as well as provide a disclosure of all gifts and their value.

(B) FOREIGN CORRUPT PRACTICES ACT. The **Foreign Corrupt Practices Act (FCPA)** is a federal criminal statute that applies to businesses whose principal offices are in the United States; it is an antibribery and anticorruption statute covering these companies' international operations.[26] The FCPA prohibits making, authorizing, or promising payments or gifts of money or anything of value with the intent to corrupt. This prohibition applies to payments or gifts designed to influence official acts of foreign officials, parties, party officials, candidates for office, nongovernmental organizations (NGOs), or any person who transmits the gift or money to these types of persons.[27]

The FCPA does not prohibit **grease** or **facilitation payments**. These are payments made only to get officials to perform their normal duties or to perform them in a timely manner. Facilitation payments are those made to (1) secure a permit or a license, (2) obtain paper processing, (3) secure police protection, (4) provide phone, water, or power services, or (5) obtain any other similar action.

Foreign Corrupt Practices Act (FCPA) – federal law that makes it a felony to influence decision makers in other countries for the purpose of obtaining business, such as contracts for sales and services; also imposes financial reporting requirements on certain U.S. corporations.

grease payments – (facilitation payments) legal payments to speed up or ensure performance of normal government duties.

facilitation payments – (grease payments) legal payments to speed up or ensure performance of normal government duties.

13. Counterfeiting

Counterfeiting is making, with fraudulent intent, a document or coin that appears to be genuine but is not because the person making it did not have the authority to make it. It is a federal crime to make, to possess with intent to transfer, or to transfer counterfeit coins, bank notes, or obligations or other securities of the United States. Various states also have statutes prohibiting the making and passing of counterfeit coins and bank notes. These statutes often provide, as does the federal statute, a punishment for the mutilation of bank notes or the lightening (of the weight) or mutilation of coins.

---

[25] Foreign Agents Registration Act, 22 U.S.C. §611 *et seq.*, as amended.
[26] 15 U.S.C. §78dd-1 *et seq.*
[27] A state-owned electric utility is considered an instrumentality of government. *United States v. Aguilar*, 783 F. Supp. 2d 1108 (C.D. Cal. 2011)

Ethics & the Law

Am I My Company's Keeper?

Think about the following statements by the former CEOs of companies that had accounting fraud.

CEO	QUOTE
Ken Lay, Enron	"Enron was an enormous corporation. How could I have known everything going on everywhere in the company?"
Richard Scrushy, HealthSouth	"You have to rely; you have to trust people. You have to believe. You have to delegate . . . I signed off on the information based on what was provided to me. And what I was told."
Bernie Ebbers, WorldCom	"Bernie Ebbers did not know about the accounting decisions of Scott Sullivan to reassign billions of dollars."
John Rigas, Adelphia	"John Rigas had a right to trust and rely on professionals and his own staff to get the financials right."

Are the CEOs responsible for knowing what goes on at their companies? Are they able to find out what is happening? Are they criminally responsible? Are they ethically responsible?

Source: Mike France, "The New Accountability," *BusinessWeek,* July 25, 2004. p. 30 at p. 32.

14. Forgery

Forgery consists of the fraudulent making or material altering of an instrument, such as a check, that attempts to create or changes a legal liability of another person.[28] Ordinarily, **forgery** consists of signing another's name with intent to defraud, but it may also consist of making an entire instrument or altering an existing one. It may result from signing a fictitious name or the offender's own name with the intent to defraud.

> **forgery**—fraudulently making or altering an instrument that apparently creates or alters a legal liability of another.

The issuing or delivery of a forged instrument to another person constitutes the crime of **uttering** a forged instrument. Sending a forged check through the channels of commerce or of bank collection constitutes an uttering of a forged instrument. The act of depositing a forged check into the forger's bank account by depositing it in an automatic teller machine constitutes uttering within the meaning of a forgery statute.[29]

> **uttering**—crime of issuing or delivering a forged instrument to another person.
>
> *cashing the forged check*

15. Perjury

Perjury consists of knowingly giving false testimony in a judicial proceeding after having been sworn to tell the truth. Knowingly making false answers on any form filed with a government typically constitutes perjury or is subjected to the same punishment as perjury. In some jurisdictions, the false answers given in a situation other than in court or the litigation process is called the crime of *false swearing.* The penalties for perjury were increased substantially under SOX.

16. False Claims and Pretenses

Many statutes make it a crime to submit false claims or to obtain goods by false pretenses.

---

[28] Misrepresenting the nature of a document in order to obtain their signature on it is forgery. *State v. Martinez,* 74 Cal. Rptr. 3d 409 (2008).
[29] *Warren v. State,* 711 S.E.2d 108 (Ga. App. 2011).

(A) FALSE CLAIMS. The federal false statement statute makes it a crime to knowingly and willfully make a false material statement about any matter within the jurisdiction of any department or agency of the United States. **For Example,** it is a crime for a contractor to make a false claim against the United States for payment for work that was never performed. It is also a crime to make false statements about income and assets on a student's application for federal financial aid.

(B) OBTAINING GOODS BY FALSE PRETENSES. Almost all states have statutes that forbid obtaining money or goods under false pretenses.[30] An intent to defraud is an essential element of obtaining property by false pretenses.[31]

Examples of false pretense include delivering a check knowing that there is insufficient money in the bank account to cover the check.[32] False representations as to future profits in a business are also forms of false pretenses. Identity theft can be prosecuted under false pretenses statutes.[33]

Failing to perform on a contract is not a false pretense crime unless the contract had been entered into with the intent of not performing it.[34]

(C) UNAUTHORIZED USE OF AUTOMATED TELLER MACHINE. Obtaining money from an automated teller machine (ATM) by the unauthorized use of the depositor's ATM card is a federal crime.

(D) FALSE INFORMATION SUBMITTED TO BANKS. Knowingly making false statements in a loan application to a federally insured bank is a federal crime.[35] It is also a crime for a landowner to put a false value on land transferred to a bank as security for a loan.[36] **For Example,** many of the initial criminal charges in the subprime mortgage market collapse have involved mortgage brokers and appraisers who misrepresented property value or applicants' income in their mortgage applications for federally insured loans.

17. Bad Checks

Under a bad check statute, it is a crime to use or pass a check with the intent to defraud with the knowledge that there are insufficient funds in the bank to pay the check when it is presented for payment. Knowledge that the bad check will not be paid when presented to the bank is an essential element of the crime. The bad check statutes typically provide that if the check is not made good within a specified number of days after payment by the bank is refused, it is presumed that the defendant acted with the intent to defraud.[37] For more information on checks, see Chapters 28 and 31.

18. Credit Card Crimes

It is a crime to steal a credit card and, in some states, to possess the credit card of another person without that person's consent. Using a credit card without the permission of the card owner is the crime of obtaining goods or services by false pretenses or with the intent to defraud. Likewise, a person who continues to use a credit card with the knowledge that it has been canceled is guilty of the crime of

[30] *Mass. v. Cheromcka*, 850 N.E.2d 1088 (Mass. App. 2006).
[31] *State v. Moore*, 903 A.2d 669 (Conn. App. 2006).
[32] *U.S. v. Tudeme*, 457 F.3d 577 (Fed. App. 2006).
[33] *State v. Parker*, 2009 WL 1065988 (Ariz. App. 2009).
[34] *Higginbotham v. State*, 356 S.W.3d 584 (Tex. App. 2011).
[35] 18 U.S.C. §1014. See *United States v. Autorino*, 381 F.3d 48 (2nd Cir. 2004).
[36] *U.S. v. Rizk*, 660 F.3d 1125 (9th Cir. 2011).
[37] *McMillan v. First Nat. Bank of Berwick*, 978 A.2d 370 (Pa. Super. 2009).

obtaining goods by false pretenses. Federal law also makes it a crime to use counterfeit credit cards for purposes of obtaining goods, services, or cash. The statute now covers the use of credit card numbers on the Internet in order to obtain goods and services.[38]

19. Embezzlement

embezzlement – statutory offense consisting of the unlawful conversion of property entrusted to the wrongdoer.

Embezzlement is the fraudulent conversion of another's property or money by a person to whom it has been entrusted.[39] Employees who take or sell their employer's property or funds for personal use have committed the crime of embezzlement. An agent employee commits embezzlement when he receives and keeps payments from third persons—payments the agent should have turned over to the principal. **For Example,** when an insured gives money to an insurance agent to pay the insurance company but the insurance agent uses the money to pay premiums on the policies of other persons, the agent is guilty of embezzlement. Generally, the intent to return the property or money embezzled or does in fact do so is no defense.

20. Obstruction of Justice: Sarbanes-Oxley (SOX)

Another SOX provision clarifies what constitutes obstruction of justice and increases the penalties for such an act. The new section makes it a felony for anyone, including company employees, auditors, attorneys, and consultants,

> to alter, destroy, mutilate, conceal, cover up, falsify or make a false entry with the "intent to impede, obstruct, or influence the investigation or proper administration of any matter within the jurisdiction of any department or agency of the United States."[40]

The statute goes on to address audit records specifically and requires auditors to retain their work papers related to a client's audit for at least five years. Any destruction of documents prior to that time constitutes a felony and carries a penalty of up to 20 years. The statute was passed in response to the conduct of Arthur Andersen, the audit firm for the collapsed Enron Corporation. Many of the firm's audit papers on Enron were destroyed, but the firm and partner-in-charge escaped criminal liability because the government could not establish that the senior managers in Andersen were aware of the shredding.[41]

21. Corporate Fraud: SOX

SOX also created a new form of mail and wire fraud. Ordinarily, mail or wire fraud consists of the use of the mail or telephones for purposes of defrauding someone of money and/or property. However, the SOX form of mail or wire fraud is based on new requirements imposed on corporate officers to certify their financial statements when they are issued. If a corporate officer fails to comply with all requirements for financial statement certification or certifies financial statements that

---

[38] 18 U.S.C. §1029. Fines for credit card fraud were increased in 2002 to levels between $50,000 and $100,000 per offense.

[39] *State v. Henry,* 73 So.3d 958 (La. App. 2011); *Stern v. Epps,* 464 Fed.Appx. 388 (5th Cir. 2012).

[40] 18 U.S.C. §1519. *U.S. v. Hunt,* 526 F.3d 739 (11th Cir. 2008).

[41] *Arthur Andersen LLP v. U.S.,* 544 U.S. 696 (2005). The obstruction conviction of the firm was reversed because of insufficient proof of the firm's actual knowledge of document destruction.

Sports & Entertainment Law

The NBA Referee, Gambling, and Some Tossed Games

Tim Donaghy, a referee for the NBA, entered a guilty plea to two federal felony charges in connection with his bets and tips on NBA games. The charges were conspiracy to engage in wire fraud and transmitting betting information via interstate commerce. Mr. Donaghy picked teams to win in games he was scheduled to referee. Mr. Donaghy committed the equivalent of insider trading on Wall Street by providing outsiders with information about games, players, and referees. He got $5,000 from his tippees for correct picks.

Mr. Donaghy began betting on games in 2003, but in December 2006 began passing along inside information to others who were also charged in the conspiracy. The communication was in code via cell phone. Mr. Donaghy explained at his sentencing that he had a gambling addiction problem and took medication under the treatment of a psychiatrist.

The NBA Commissioner, David Stern, referred to Mr. Donaghy as a "rogue referee," but said that the gambling charges were a wake-up call for the NBA and that it must not be "complacent."*

Mr. Donaghy's missteps were discovered as the federal government was conducting an investigation into the Gambino crime family, based in Brooklyn.

*Roscoe Nance, "Scandal Is a 'Wakeup Call,' Stern Says," *USA Today*, August 16, 2007 p. 1C.

Commissioner Stern said that the NBA would be looking at the checks and balances that the NFL has built into its system including Las Vegas travel prohibitions on referees. The NFL also has significant background checks and ongoing monitoring of its referees.

Mr. Donaghy ran a basketball clinic for developmentally disabled boys in Springfield, PA (Mr. Donaghy's hometown) for almost a decade. He was a graduate of Villanova and had worked his way up to being one of the NBA's top referees, coming through the ranks of refereeing in both high school and the Continental Basketball Association. Mr. Donaghy had a wife and four children. His salary with the NBA during 2006 was $260,000. Mr. Donaghy was sentenced to 15 months in prison. After serving 11 months of his prison term, Mr. Donaghy was released to a halfway house, but was sent back to prison to finish out his term because of violations of the terms of his partial release. He wrote a book about his actions, *Personal Foul: A First-Person Account of the Scandal That Rocked the NBA.*

Why do you think Mr. Donaghy was engaged in gambling? Doesn't his civic activity paint a different picture of his character? Mr. Donaghy said in an interview about his book that what he did was no different from Wall Streeters who engaged in insider trading except, "I didn't affect the economy." How would you analyze his comparison?

---

contain false material information, the officer and company have committed corporate fraud with penalties that range from fines of $1,000,000 and/or 10 years to $5,000,000 and/or 20 years for willful violation of the certification requirements.

22. The Common Law Crimes

In contrast to white-collar crimes, *common law crimes* are crimes that involve the use of force or the threat of force or cause injury to persons or damage to property. The following sections discuss crimes of force and crimes against property that affect businesses.

(A) LARCENY. *Larceny* is the wrongful or fraudulent taking of the personal property of another by any person with fraudulent intent. Shoplifting is a common form of larceny. In many states, shoplifting is made a separate crime. In some states, all forms of larceny and robbery are consolidated into a statutory crime of theft. At common law, there was no crime known as theft.

(B) ROBBERY. *Robbery* is the taking of personal property from the presence of the victim by use of force or fear. Most states have aggravated forms of robbery, such as robbery with a deadly weapon. Snatching a necklace from the neck of the victim involves sufficient force to constitute robbery. When the unlawful taking is not by force or fear, as when the victim does not know that the property is being taken, the offense is larceny, but it cannot be robbery.

Some statutes may be aimed at a particular kind of robbery. **For Example,** carjacking is a federal crime under the Anti-Car Theft Act of 1992.[42]

✳ **(c) BURGLARY.** At common law, *burglary* was the breaking and entering during the night into the dwelling house of another with the intent to commit a felony. Inserting the automatic teller card of another, without their knowledge or permission, into an automatic teller machine set in the wall of the bank may constitute an entry into the bank for the purpose of committing burglary.[43] Some states word their burglary statutes, however, so that there is no burglary in this automatic teller case. This act would be covered by other criminal statutes.

Modern statutes have eliminated many of the elements of the common law definition so that under some statutes it is now immaterial when or whether there was an entry to commit a felony. The elements of breaking and entering are frequently omitted. Under some statutes, the offense is aggravated and the penalty is increased, depending on the place where the offense was committed, such as a bank building, freight car, or warehouse. Related statutory offenses, such as the crime of possessing burglars' tools, have been created.

✳ **(d) ARSON.** At common law, *arson* was the willful and malicious burning of another's dwelling. The law was originally designed to protect human life, although arson has been committed just with the burning of the building even if no one is actually hurt. In most states, arson is a felony, so if someone is killed in the resulting fire, the offense is considered a felony-murder. Under the felony-murder rule, homicide, however unintended, occurring in the commission of a felony is automatically classified as murder. Virtually every state has created a special offense of burning to defraud an insurer.

(e) RIOTS AND CIVIL DISORDERS. Damage to property in the course of a riot or civil disorder is ordinarily covered by other types of crimes such as the crime of larceny or arson. In addition, the act of assembling as a riotous mob and engaging in civil disorders is generally some form of crime in itself under either common law concepts of disturbing the peace or modern antiriot statutes, even without destruction or theft of property. However, statutes on civil disorders must be carefully drawn to avoid infringing on constitutionally protected free speech.

C. CRIMINAL LAW AND THE COMPUTER

In some situations, ordinary crimes cover computer crimes situations. In other situations, new criminal law statutes are required.

23. What Is a Computer Crime?

computer crimes – wrongs committed using a computer or with knowledge of computers.

Generally, the term **computer crime** is used to refer to a crime that can be committed only by a person having some knowledge of the operation of a computer.

---

[42] 18 U.S.C. §2119. See *U.S. v. Bell*, 608 F. Supp. 2d 1257 (Kan. 2009).
[43] *People v. Cardwell*, 137 Cal. Rptr.3d 525 (2012).

Just as stealing an automobile requires knowledge of how to operate and drive a car, so the typical computer crime requires the knowledge of how the computer works.

Because the more serious and costly wrongs relating to computers do not fit into the ordinary definitions of crime, there are now computer-specific criminal statutes: Computer crimes can be committed against the computer, using the computer, or through the computer.

24. The Computer as Victim

A traditional crime may be committed by stealing or intentionally damaging a computer.

(A) THEFT OF HARDWARE. When a computer itself is stolen, the ordinary law relating to theft crimes should apply. Theft of a computer is subject to the same law as the theft of a truck or a desk.

(B) THEFT OF SOFTWARE. When a thief takes software, whether in the form of a program written on paper or a program on a disk or memory stick, something has been taken, but it is not tangible property as larceny requires. Virtually every state makes stealing software a crime. Chapter 11 provides more information on crimes, software, and the Internet.

(c) INTENTIONAL DAMAGE. The computer may be the "victim" of a crime when it is intentionally destroyed or harmed. In the most elementary form of damage, the computer could be harmed if it was smashed with an ax or destroyed in an explosion or a fire. In such cases, the purpose of the intentional damage is to cause the computer's owner the financial loss of the computer and the destruction of the information that is stored in it.

Intentional damage can result from more subtle means. Gaining access to the computer and then erasing or altering the data is also the crime of intentional damage. Likewise, interfering with the air conditioning so computers are damaged or malfunction would also be covered under intentional damage statutes. Planting a bug or virus in the software, causing the program to malfunction or to give incorrect output, is a form of intentional damage. Angry employees, former employees, and competitors have all been convicted of intentional damage.

25. Unauthorized Use of Computers

The unlawful use of a computer belonging to someone else is also a crime in some states. There are specific statutes at the state and federal levels that make it unlawful to use government computers without permission. One of the issues that is critical in criminal prosecution is whether the use was, in fact, "unauthorized." With Wi-Fi networks, the ease of access and openess has proven to be a challenge in prosecution for unauthorized use.[44]

26. Computer Raiding

Taking information from a computer without the consent of the owner is a crime. Whether theft is accomplished by instructing the computer to make a printout of

---

[44] U.S.C. §1030(e)(6); for an article summarizing the issues, see Orin S. Kerr, "Cybercrime's Scope: Interpreting 'Access' and 'Authorization' in Computer Misuse Statutes", 78 *N.Y.U. L. Rev.* 1596, 1632-37 (2003).

stored information or by tapping into its data bank by electronic means is not important. In some states, taking information is known as the crime of "computer trespass."[45]

Both Congress and state legislatures have adopted statutes that make it a crime to gain unauthorized access to a computer or use information so gained to cause harm to the computer or its rightful user.[46] Again, the presence of Wi-Fi when there are unsecured users has complicated prosecutions for taking information.

27. Diverted Delivery by Computer

In many industries, a computer controls the delivery of goods. The person in charge of that computer or someone unlawfully gaining access to it may cause the computer to direct delivery to an improper place. That is, instead of shipping goods to the customers to whom they should go, the wrongdoer diverts the goods to a different place, where the wrongdoer or a confederate receives them.

Instructing the computer to give false directions can cause this fraudulent diversion of goods. Because the computer allows changes in delivery of goods through a mere keystroke, the depth of diversion cases is great. **For Example,** in one case, several hundred loaded freight cars disappeared. In another case, a loaded oil tanker was diverted to unload into a fleet of tank trucks operated by an accomplice of the computer operator.

E-Commerce & Cyberlaw

They Were Bullies: Mean Girls in Cyberspace

It has been called the MySpace suicide case. On May 14, 2008, a federal grand jury indicted Lori Drew, 49, of Missouri, the so-called cyber bully. Ms. Drew had created a MySpace site for Josh Evans, a fictitious teen boy she used as a means of getting information from Megan Meier, a 13-year-old girl with whom Ms. Drew's daughter had had a falling-out. Josh pretended to be interested in Megan, but then said that she was "fat" and that the world would be a better place without her. Megan hanged herself within an hour of receiving the final comments from "Josh."

Ms. Drew was charged with one count of conspiracy and two counts of accessing computers without authorization and was convicted of three lesser charges. However, the judge dismissed the charges because of issues related to the meaning of the term "unauthorized use" and whether the federal statutes could be applied to what Ms. Drew did.

When the indictment was made public, Salvador Hernandez, assistant director of the FBI in Los Angeles, said, "Whether we characterize this tragic case as 'cyber-bullying,' cyberabuse, or illegal computer access, it should serve as a reminder that our children use the Internet for social interaction and that technology has altered the way they conduct their daily activities. As adults, we must be sensitive to the potential dangers posed by the use of the Internet by our children."*

Some states have now passed specific statutes to make cyber-bullying a crime.

Why would the judge not find a criminal violation? Is it a crime to bully over the Internet?

*U.S. v. Lori Drew, 259 F.R.D. 449 (C.D. Cal. 2009).

---

[45] *Washington v. Riley,* 846 P.2d 1365 (Wash. 1993).
[46] The Counterfeit Access Device and Computer Fraud Act of 1984, 18 U.S.C. §1030 *et seq.;* Computer Fraud and Abuse Act of 1986, 18 U.S.C. §1001; Electronic Communications Privacy Act of 1986, 18 U.S.C. §2510; Computer Fraud Act of 1987, 15 U.S.C. §§272, 278, 40 U.S.C. §759; National Information Infrastructure Protection Act, 18 U.S.C. §1030 (protecting confidentiality and integrity on the Internet).

28. Economic Espionage by Computer

Economic Espionage Act (EEA) – federal law that makes it a felony to copy, download, transmit, or in any way transfer proprietary files, documents, and information from a computer to an unauthorized person.

The **Economic Espionage Act (EEA)** is a federal law[47] passed in response to several cases in which high-level executives took downloaded proprietary information from their computers to their new employers. The EEA makes it a felony to steal, appropriate, or take a trade secret as well as to copy, duplicate, sketch, draw, photograph, download, upload, alter, destroy, replicate, transmit, deliver, send, mail, or communicate a trade secret. The penalties for EEA violations are up to $500,000 and 15 years in prison for individuals and $10 million for organizations. When employees take new positions with another company, their former employers are permitted to check the departing employees' computer e-mails and hard drives to determine whether the employees have engaged in computer espionage.

29. Electronic Fund Transfer Crimes

The Electronic Fund Transfers Act (EFTA)[48] makes it a crime to use any counterfeit, stolen, or fraudulently obtained card, code, or other device to obtain money or goods in excess of a specified amount through an electronic fund transfer system. The EFTA also makes it a crime to ship in interstate commerce devices or goods so obtained or to knowingly receive goods that have been obtained by means of the fraudulent use of the transfer system.

Ethics & the Law

Ethics and the Tobacco Class-Action Lawyer

Class-action lawyer Dickie Scruggs was portrayed in the 1999 movie "The Insider," which starred Russell Crowe as Jeffrey Wigand, the tobacco industry whistle-blower who obtained a $206 billion settlement from the tobacco companies (Mr. Scruggs's fee for the case was $1 billion). Almost a decade after the movie that made him a hero came out, Scruggs entered a guilty plea to bribery and was sentenced to five years in prison for his role in an attempt to bribe a federal judge.

Mr. Scruggs was representing insurance claimants against insurers for their damages from Hurricane Katrina. The judge presiding over the case contacted the FBI about a bribery attempt. One of the four lawyers working with Scruggs was approached by the FBI and agreed to wear a wire to catch Scruggs. The content of the tapes revealed both *actus reus* and *scienter*. Zachary Scruggs, Dickie's son, also entered a guilty plea. All of

the remaining lawyers involved in the bribery scheme entered guilty pleas as well.

Those in the legal profession said they did not understand Scruggs's actions because he had the skill to win any case. "He didn't need to cheat," was the comment of a representative from the American Trial Lawyers Association. Scruggs's words at his sentencing were poignant: "I could not be more ashamed to be where I am today, mixed up in a judicial bribery scheme.... I realized I was getting mixed up in it. And I will go to my grave wondering why. I have disappointed everyone in my life—my wife, my family, my son, particularly.... I deeply regret my conduct. It is a scar and a stain on my soul that will be there forever."

Source: Abha Bhattarai, "Class-Action Lawyer Given 5 Years in a Bribery Case," *New York Times,* June 28, 2008, B3.

30. Circumventing Copyright Protection Devices Via Computer

The Digital Millennium Copyright Act (DMCA)[49] makes it a federal offense to circumvent or create programs to circumvent encryption devices that copyright

[47] 18 U.S.C. §1831.
[48] 15 U.S.C. §1693(n).
[49] 17 U.S.C. §512(2010).

holders place on copyrighted material to prevent unauthorized copying.
For Example, circumventing the encryption devices on software or CDs or DVDs is a violation of the DMCA.

For Example, Dmitry Sklyarov, a Russian computer programmer, was the first person to be charged with a violation of the DMCA. Mr. Sklyarov was arrested in early 2002 at a computer show after giving a speech in Las Vegas at the Defcon convention on his product that he had developed to permit the circumvention of security devices on copyrighted materials. His program unlocks password-protected e-books and PDF files. He gave his speech and was returned to Russia in exchange for his agreement to testify in a case that will determine the constitutionality of DMCA.

The No Electronic Theft Act makes it a federal criminal offense to willfully infringe copyrighted material worth more than $1,000 using the Internet or other electronic devices even if the infringer does not profit from others' use of the material. **For Example,** sending along copyrighted articles on the Internet to friends, without permission from the site, would be a violation even though there is no profit.

31. Spamming

More states are addressing the use of computers to send unsolicited e-mails. For 2011, there were 7 trillion pieces of spam sent over the Internet. Criminal regulation began with very narrowly tailored statutes such as one in Washington that made it a crime to send an e-mail with a misleading title line. The specific criminal statutes on spamming are evolving, and Virginia became the first state to pass a criminal antispamming law. The statute prohibits sending "unsolicited bulk electronic mail" or spam and makes the offense a felony based on the level of activity.[50] Thirty-six states and the federal government now have some form of spamming regulation.[51] The penalties range from fines to imprisonment.

D. Criminal Procedure Rights for Businesses

The U.S. Constitution guarantees the protection of individual and corporate rights within the criminal justice system.

32. Fourth Amendment Rights for Businesses

(A) Search and Seizure: Warrants. The **Fourth Amendment** of the U.S. Constitution provides that "the right of the people to be secure in their persons, houses, papers, and effects, against unreasonable searches and seizures, shall not be violated." This amendment protects individual privacy by preventing unreasonable searches and seizures. Before a government agency can seize the property of individuals or businesses, it must obtain a valid **search warrant** issued by a judge or magistrate, based on probable cause, unless an exception to this warrant requirement applies. In other words, there must be good reason to search the location named. The Fourth Amendment applies equally to individuals and corporations. If an improper search is conducted, evidence obtained during the

Fourth Amendment – privacy protection in the U.S. Constitution; prohibits unauthorized searches and seizures.

search warrant – judicial authorization for a search of property where there is the expectation of privacy.

---

[50] *Gordon v. Virtumundo, Inc.*, 575 F.3d 1040 (9th Cir. 2009).
[51] Controlling the Assault of Non–Solicited Pornography and Marketing (CAN–SPAM), 15 U.S.C. §7701.

course of that search may be inadmissible in the criminal proceedings for the resulting criminal charges.[52]

(B) EXCEPTIONS TO THE WARRANT REQUIREMENT. Exceptions to the warrant requirement are emergencies, such as a burning building, and the "plain-view" exception, which allows law enforcement officials to take any property that anyone can see, for no privacy rights are violated when items and property are left in the open for members of the public to see. **For Example,** you have an expectation of privacy in the garbage in your garbage can when it is in your house. However, once you move that garbage can onto the public sidewalk for pickup, you no longer have the expectation of privacy because you have left your garbage out in plain view of the public.

Another exception allows officers to enter when they are needed to give aid because of an ongoing criminal act. **For Example,** officers who are able to see a fight through the windows of a house and resulting injuries can enter to render help. Another exception would be that the person who lives in the property to be searched has given permission for the search.

CASE SUMMARY

Low-Flying Aircraft Bearing Federal Agents with Cameras

FACTS: Dow Chemical (petitioner) operates a 2,000-acre chemical plant at Midland, Michigan. The facility, with numerous buildings, conduits, and pipes, is visible from the air. Dow has maintained ground security at the facility and has investigated flyovers by other, unauthorized aircraft. However, none of the buildings or manufacturing equipment is concealed.

In 1978, the Environmental Protection Agency (EPA) conducted an inspection of Dow. The EPA requested a second inspection, but Dow denied the request. The EPA then employed a commercial aerial photographer to take photos of the plant from 12,000, 3,000, and 1,200 feet. The EPA had no warrant, but the plane was always within navigable air space when the photos were taken.

When Dow became aware of the EPA photographer, it brought suit in federal district court and challenged the action as a violation of its Fourth Amendment rights. The district court found that the EPA had violated Dow's rights and issued an injunction prohibiting further use of the aircraft. The Court of Appeals reversed and Dow appealed.

DECISION: The Court ruled against Dow, finding that the EPA did not need explicit statutory provisions to use methods of observation commonly available to the public. There was no expectation of privacy in an area that was not covered. [***Dow Chemical Co. v. United States,*** **476 U.S. 1819 (1986)]**

(C) BUSINESS RECORDS AND SEARCHES. In many business crimes, the records that prove a crime was committed are not in the hands of the person who committed that crime. Accountants, attorneys, and other third parties may have the business records in their possession. In addition to the Fourth Amendment issues involved in seizing these records (a warrant is still required), there may be protections for the business defendants. The next section covers those protections.

---

[52] See, *Arizona v. Gant,* 556 U.S. 332 (2009) in which the U.S. Supreme Court held that evidence obtained searching the vehicle of a suspect who is handcuffed and locked in a police car cannot be used. A search warrant is needed when the suspect has no access to the evidence to destroy it.

(D) PROTECTIONS FOR PRIVILEGED RECORDS AND DOCUMENTS. All states recognize an attorney-client privilege, which means that an individual's conversations with her lawyer and the notes of those conversations are not subject to seizure unless the privilege is waived. In many of the prosecutions of companies, the Justice Department has asked companies to waive the attorney/client privilege so that it can have access to information that is then used to find other companies that may have participated in criminal activity. Some states recognize an accountant-client privilege and other privileges, such as those between priest and parishioner or doctor and patient. A privileged relationship is one in which the records and notes resulting from the contact between individuals cannot be seized even with a warrant (with some exceptions).

33. Fifth Amendment Self-Incrimination Rights for Businesses

(A) SELF-INCRIMINATION. The words "I take the Fifth" are used to invoke the constitutional protections against self-incrimination provided under the **Fifth Amendment** that prevents compelling a person to be a witness against himself. **For Example,** Mark McGwire, the former St. Louis baseball player, invoked the Fifth Amendment in his testimony during Congressional hearings on steroid use. Edith O'Brien, a lawyer for the collapsed investment fund, MF Global, refused to answer questions before Congress, claiming her right against self-incrimination. The Fifth Amendment protection applies only to individuals; corporations are not given Fifth Amendment protection. A corporation cannot prevent the disclosure of its books and records on the grounds of self-incrimination. The officers and employees of a corporation can assert the Fifth Amendment, but the records of the corporation belong to the corporation, not to them.

Fifth Amendment – constitutional protection against self-incrimination; also guarantees due process.

CASE SUMMARY

A Man's Home Is His Castle, but His Wife Can Still Turn on Him

FACTS: Scott Randolph and his wife, Janet, separated in late May 2001, when she left their Americus, Georgia, home and went to stay with her parents in Canada, taking their son and some belongings. In July, she returned to the Americus house with the child. No one is sure whether she had returned to reconcile or whether she had come to gather her remaining possessions.

On July 6, 2001, Janet called police and told them that there were "items of drug evidence" in the house. Sergeant Murray asked Scott Randolph for permission to search the house, which he refused.

The sergeant turned to Janet for consent to search, which she readily gave. She led the officer upstairs to a bedroom that she identified as Scott's, where the sergeant noticed a section of a drinking straw with a powdery residue he suspected was cocaine. He then left the house to get an evidence bag from his car and to call the district attorney's office, which instructed him to stop the search and apply for a warrant. When Sergeant Murray returned to the house, Janet Randolph withdrew her consent. The police took the straw and the Randolphs to the police station. After getting a search warrant, the police returned to the house and seized further evidence of drug use, which served as the basis of Scott's indictment for possession of cocaine.

Scott Randolph moved to suppress the evidence, as products of a warrantless search. The trial court denied the motion, ruling that Janet had common authority to consent to the search.

CASE SUMMARY

Continued

The Court of Appeals of Georgia reversed, and the Georgia Supreme Court sustained the reversal. The state of Georgia appealed, and the U.S. Supreme Court granted *certiorari*.

DECISION: The Court held that "a man's home is his castle" and that when he objects to a search, his spouse could not overrule his decision. Co-ownership of property does not necessarily mean that individuals are willing to waive their rights of privacy for purposes for warrantless searches. The dissent argued that sharing necessarily means waiving privacy. The fact that they are betrayed by a spouse, roommate, or others does not affect the consent exception to the Fourth Amendment because underlying that protection is the right to privacy and that right has been waived through the shared ownership or living arrangement. [*Gerogia v. Randolph* 547 **U.S. 103 (2006)**]

Miranda warnings – warnings required to prevent self-incrimination in a criminal matter.

(B) MIRANDA RIGHTS. The famous **Miranda warnings** come from a case interpreting the extent of Fifth Amendment rights. In *Miranda v. Arizona*,[53] the U.S. Supreme Court ruled that certain warnings must be given to persons who face custodial interrogation for the purposes of possible criminal proceedings. The warnings consist of an explanation to individuals that they have the right to remain silent; that if they do speak, anything they say can be used against them; that they have the right to have an attorney present; and that if they cannot afford an attorney, one will be provided for them. Failure to give the *Miranda* warnings means that any statements, including a confession, obtained while the individual was being interrogated cannot be used as evidence against that individual. The prosecution will have to rely on evidence other than the statements made in violation of *Miranda,* if such evidence exists.

34. Due Process Rights for Businesses

due process – the constitutional right to be heard, question witnesses, and present evidence.

Also included in the Fifth Amendment is the language of due process. **Due process** is the right to be heard, question witnesses, and present evidence before any criminal conviction can occur. Due process in criminal cases consists of an initial appearance at which the charges and the defendant's rights are outlined; a preliminary hearing or grand jury proceeding in which the evidence is determined to be sufficient to warrant a trial; an arraignment for entering a plea and setting a trial date when the defendant pleads innocent; a period of discovery for obtaining evidence; and a trial at which witnesses for the prosecution can be cross-examined and evidence presented to refute the charges. In addition to these procedural steps, the **Sixth Amendment**

Sixth Amendment – the U.S. constitutional amendment that guarantees a speedy trial.

guarantees that the entire process will be completed in a timely fashion because this amendment guarantees a speedy trial.

---

[53] 384 U.S. 436 (1966).

CASE SUMMARY

I Confess, but without *Miranda* You Can't Use It against Me

FACTS: Dickerson confessed to robbing a bank at a field office of the Federal Bureau of Investigation (FBI). At the time he confessed, he was not a suspect, was free to leave, and was not in custody. He was not, however, given his *Miranda* warnings before the FBI agents interrogated him about the robbery. Dickerson's lawyer moved to have his confession excluded from his trial because it was obtained in violation of *Miranda.* The federal district court suppressed the confession. The Court of Appeals reversed, noting that while the warnings had not been given, the confession was clearly voluntary. Dickerson appealed.

DECISION: The U.S. Supreme Court held that the confession could not be used because Dickerson had not been given his warnings. The judicial decision is complex because it focuses on the difference between questioning in custody and the need to give *Miranda* warnings even when there is no custody of the person. The majority of the Court ruled that *Miranda* warnings must still be given as a way to prevent those being questioned from unknowingly waiving their rights. [***Dickerson v. U.S.*, 530 U.S. 428 (2000)**]

LawFlix

Double Jeopardy (2000) R

Ashley Judd plays a woman on the run for false charges of killing her husband. But her husband faked his death and then she finds and kills him – can she be tried again?

Columbo (Seasons 1–6)

Detective Columbo is the bumbling, brilliant sleuth who crosses a few Fourth and Fifth Amendment lines here and there.

MAKE THE CONNECTION

SUMMARY

When a person does not live up to the standards set by law, this punishable conduct, called *crime,* may be common law or statutory in origin. Crimes are classified as *felonies,* which generally carry greater sentences and more long-term consequences, and *misdemeanors.*

Employers and corporations may be criminally responsible for their acts and the acts of their employees. The federal sentencing guidelines provide parameters for sentences for federal crimes and allow judges to consider whether the fact that a business promotes compliance with the law is a reason to reduce a sentence.

White-collar crimes include those relating to financial fraud. Sarbanes-Oxley reforms increased the penalties for financial fraud and added fraudulent financial statement certification as a crime. Other white-collar crimes include bribery, extortion, blackmail, and corrupt influence in politics and in business. Also included as white-collar crimes are counterfeiting, forgery, perjury, making false claims against the government, obtaining goods or money by false pretenses, using bad checks, false financial reporting, and embezzlement. The common law crimes include those that involve injury to person and/or property, such as arson and murder.

Statutes have expanded the area of criminal law to meet situations in which computers are involved. Both federal and state statutes make the unauthorized taking of information from a computer a crime. The diversion of deliveries of goods and the transfer of funds, the theft of software, and the raiding of computers are made crimes to some extent by federal laws. Newer federal statutes that apply to computers are the Economic Espionage Act, which prohibits downloading or copying information via computer to give to a competitor, and the Digital Millennium Copyright Act that prohibits circumventing or designing programs to circumvent encryption devices.

Criminal procedure is dictated by the Fourth, Fifth, and Sixth Amendments. The Fourth Amendment protects against unreasonable searches, the Fifth Amendment protects against self-incrimination and provides due process, and the Sixth Amendment guarantees a speedy trial.

LEARNING OUTCOMES

After studying this chapter, you should be able to clearly explain:

A. General Principles

LO.1 Discuss the nature and classification of crimes

See the discussion of crimes and misdemeanors on p. 142.

LO.2 Describe the basis of criminal liability
See the *For Example*, discussion of dumping waste and intent on p. 142.
See *U.S. v. Erickson* on p. 143.

LO.3 Identify who is responsible for criminal acts
See *U.S. v. Park* on p. 144.
See Thinking Things Through on p. 148.
See Ethical Issue on p. 153, Am I My Company's Keeper?

LO.4 Explain the penalties for crimes and the sentencing for corporate crimes
See the discussion of the sentencing guidelines and the various cases related to them on p. 146.

B. White-Collar Crimes

LO.5 List examples of white-collar crimes and their elements

See the discussion that begins on p. 149.
See the Sports & Entertainment Law discussion of the NBA referee on p. 156.

LO.6 Describe the common law crimes
See the discussion that begins on p. 156.
See the E-Commerce & Cyberlaw discussion of cyber-bullying on p. 159.

C. Criminal Law and the Computer

LO.7 Discuss crimes related to computers
See the discussion that begins on p. 157.

D. Criminal Procedure Rights for Businesses

LO.8 Describe the rights of businesses charged with crimes and the constitutional protections afforded them

See the *Dow* case on p. 162.
See the *Dickerson* case on p. 165.

KEY TERMS

blackmail	due process	facilitation payments
computer crime	Economic Espionage Act (EEA)	Federal Sentencing Guidelines
conspiracy	embezzlement	felonies
crime	extortion	Fifth Amendment

Foreign Corrupt Practices Act
  (FCPA)
forgery
Fourth Amendment
grease payments
Miranda warnings

misdemeanors
predicate act
Racketeer Influenced and Corrupt
  Organizations (RICO) Act
search warrant
Sixth Amendment

uttering
white-collar crime
White-Collar Crime Penalty
  Enhancement Act of 2002

QUESTIONS AND CASE PROBLEMS

1. Bernard Flinn operated a business known as Harvey
Investment Co., Inc./High Risk Loans. Flinn
worked as a loan broker, matching those who came
to him with lenders willing to loan them money
given their credit history and the amount involved.
From 1982 through 1985, Flinn found loans for
five people. Indiana requires that persons engaged in
the business of brokering loans obtain a license from
the state. Flinn was prosecuted for brokering loans
without having a license. He raised the defense that
he did not know that a license was required and
that, accordingly, he lacked the criminal intent to
broker loans without having a license. Does Flinn
have a good defense?
[*Flinn v. Indiana,* 563 N.E.2d 536 (Ind.)]

2. H. J., Inc., and other customers of Northwestern
Bell Corp. alleged that Northwestern Bell had
furnished cash and tickets for air travel, plays, and
sporting events and had offered employment to
members of the Minnesota Public Utilities
Commission in exchange for favorable treatment
in rate cases before the commission. A Minnesota
statute makes it a felony to bribe public officials.
H. J. and other customers brought suit against
Northwestern for violating the criminal bribery
statute. Can the customers bring a criminal action?
[*H. J., Inc. v. Northwestern Bell Corp.,*
420 N.W.2d 673 (Minn. App.)]

3. Baker and others entered a Wal-Mart store shortly
after 3:00 A.M. by cutting through the metal door
with an acetylene torch. They had moved some of
the merchandise in the store to the rear door, but
the police arrived before the merchandise could be
taken from the store. Baker was prosecuted for
larceny. He raised the defense that he was not guilty
of larceny because no merchandise had ever left the
store. Is there enough intent and action for a crime?
[*Tennessee v. Baker,* 751 S.W.2d 154 (Tenn. App.)]

4. Gail drove her automobile after having had dinner
and several drinks. She fell asleep at the wheel and
ran over and killed a pedestrian. Prosecuted for
manslaughter, she raised the defense that she did
not intend to hurt anyone and because of the drinks
did not know what she was doing. Was this a valid
defense?

5. Dr. Doyle E. Campbell, an ophthalmologist,
established his practice in southern Ohio in 1971.
Many of Dr. Campbell's patients are elderly
people who qualify for federal Medicare benefits
and state Medicaid benefits. Under the existing
financing system, a doctor who treats a Medicare
patient is required to submit a "Medicare Health
Insurance Claim Form" (HCFA Form 1500). The
doctor is required to certify that "the services
shown on this form were medically indicated and
necessary for the health of the patient and were
personally rendered by me or were rendered
incident to my professional service by my
employees." Claims Dr. Campbell submitted for
his elderly patients ranged from $900 to $950, of
which $530 to $680 were covered by the
Medicare program. The government alleged that
Dr. Campbell billed Medicare for several
treatments that were either not performed or not
necessary. Dr. Campbell was charged with fraud
for the paperwork he submitted. Has he
committed a crime? [*United States v. Campbell,*
845 F.2d 1374 (6th Cir.)]

6. In the late 1980s, Life Energy Resources, Ltd.
(LER), a New York corporation, was a multilevel
marketing network. LER's marketing plan
provided that members of the general public
could purchase its products only through an
official LER distributor or by becoming LER
distributors themselves. Each potential distributor
had to be sponsored by an existing distributor and

was required to sign a distributorship agreement with LER stating that he or she would not make medical claims or use unofficial literature or marketing aids to promote LER products.

Ballistrea and his partner Michael Ricotta were at the top of the LER distribution network. Two products sold by LER were the REM SuperPro Frequency Generator (REM) and the Lifemax Miracle Cream (Miracle Cream). The REM, which sold for $1,350 to distributors, was a small box powered by electricity that ran currents through the feet and body of the user.

Ballistrea and Ricotta distributed literature and audiotapes to many potential downstream distributors and customers—some of whom were undercover government agents—touting the REM and the Miracle Cream. Other literature claimed that the Miracle Cream could alleviate the discomforts of premenstrual syndrome and reverse the effects of osteoporosis. The Food and Drug Administration charged Ballistrea and Ricotta with violating federal law for making medical claims concerning LER products. Their defense is that they never sold any of the products. They simply earned commissions as part of the marketing scheme and could not be held criminally liable on the charges. Are they correct? [*United States v. Ballistrea*, 101 F.3d 827 (2d Cir.)]

7. Carriage Homes, Inc. was a general contractor that built multifamily residential and land-development projects in Minnesota. John Arkell was Carriage Homes' chief executive officer, president, and sole shareholder. Carriage Homes built Southwinds, a condominium development of 38 residential units in Austin, Minnesota. The foundation elevations of some of the Southwinds units were lower than permitted under the State Building Code, causing storm water to pool in the units' driveways and garages. The city of Austin's development director sent Arkell a series of seven letters in 1999 and 2001 concerning the elevation problems, and Arkell gave the letters to the project managers, who failed to resolve the problems.

Minnesota makes a violation of the State Building Code a misdemeanor. On May 30, 2001, the state charged Carriage Homes and Arkell with three misdemeanor counts each, alleging a violation of the Uniform Building Code (UBC).

Carriage Homes pleaded guilty and was sentenced to a $1,000 fine. But Arkell pleaded not guilty, asserting that he could not be held criminally responsible for the violation. After a bench trial, the district court found Arkell guilty. He was sentenced to pay a fine, pay restitution to the condominium owners, and serve 90 days in jail, with 80 days stayed pending his compliance with sentencing conditions. Mr. Arkell appealed on the grounds that the employees and subcontractors had simply not followed his orders and he was not responsible for their failures. Is he correct? [*State v. Arkell*, 657 N.W.2d 883 (Minn. App. 2003)]

8. James Durham runs an art gallery. He has several paintings from unknown artists that he has listed for sale. The paintings always sell at his weekly auction for $20,000 to $50,000 above what James believes them to be worth. James learns that the bidders at the auctions are employed by an olive distributor located near the shipping yards of the city. What concerns should Durham have about the art, the bidders and the large purchase prices?

9. Jennings operated a courier service to collect and deliver money. The contract with his customers allowed him a day or so to deliver the money that had been collected. Instead of holding collections until delivered, Jennings made short-term investments with the money. He always made deliveries to the customers on time, but because he kept the profit from the investments for himself, Jennings was prosecuted for embezzlement. Was he guilty? [*New York v. Jennings*, 504 N.E.2d 1079 (N.Y.)]

10. In April 2006, a DC-9 aircraft landed in the port city of Ciudad del Carmen, located 500 miles east of Mexico City. When the plane's crew began directing security personnel away from the plane, the suspicious activity piqued the curiosity of local law enforcement officials. They decided to search the plane and found 128 suitcases packed with over 56 tons of cocaine. The cocaine was to have been delivered to Toluca, near Mexico City. In investigating the plane and individual involved, law enforcement agents discovered that the plane had been purchased with money that had been laundered through two U.S. banks, Wachovia Corp. and Bank of America Corp. Neither bank

was actually aware that the money was being used to purchase a plane that would then be used for drug trafficking. Are the banks still criminally liable for breaking the rules? Explain why or why not. What if the banks were aware of large sums of money being run through particular customers' accounts? Would that knowledge make a difference?

11. Grabert ran Beck's, an amusement center in Louisiana. He held a license for video gambling machines. Louisiana makes it illegal to allow a minor to play a video gambling machine. A mother came into Grabert's center carrying her 23-month-old baby in her arms. She sat at the video poker machine with her child on her lap and proceeded to play. State troopers witnessed the baby pushing the buttons on the machine at least three times. The Department of Public Safety and Corrections revoked Grabert's video gaming license because a minor had been allowed to play the machines, and Grabert sought judicial review. The trial court reversed, and the department appealed. Has Grabert committed the crime of allowing a minor to engage in gaming? Is this the crime of allowing a minor to gamble? [*Grabert v. Department of Public Safety & Corrections*, 680 So.2d 764 (La. App.) *cert.* denied; *Grabert v. State through Dept. of Public Safety and Corrections*, 685 So.2d 126 (La.)]

12. The Banco Central administered a humanitarian plan for the government of Ecuador. Fernando Banderas and his wife presented false claims that the bank paid. After the fraud was discovered, the bank sued Banderas and his wife for damages for fraud and treble damages under the Florida version of RICO. Banderas and his wife asserted that they were not liable for RICO damages because there was no proof that they were related to organized crime and because the wrong they had committed was merely ordinary fraud. They had not used any racketeering methods. Is involvement with organized crime a requirement for liability under RICO? [*Banderas v. Banco Central del Ecuador*, 461 So.2d 265 (Fla. App.)]

13. Kravitz owned 100 percent of the stock of American Health Programs, Inc. (AHP). To obtain the Philadelphia Fraternal Order of Police as a customer for AHP, Kravitz paid money bribes to persons who he thought were officers of that organization but who in fact were federal undercover agents. He was prosecuted for violating RICO. He was convicted, and the court ordered the forfeiture of all of Kravitz's shares of AHP stock. Can a forfeiture be ordered? [*United States v. Kravitz*, 738 F.2d 102 (3d Cir.)]

14. Howell made long-distance telephone calls through the telephone company's computer-controlled switching system to solicit funding for a nonexistent business enterprise. What crimes did Howell commit? [*New Mexico v. Howell*, 895 F.2d 232 (N.M. App.)]

© Manuel Gutjahr/iStockphoto.com

CHAPTER 9

Torts

learningoutcomes

After studying this chapter, you should be able to

LO.1 Explain the difference between torts and crimes

LO.2 Identify the possible tort theories applicable to transmission of disease cases

LO.3 Distinguish between an assault and a battery

LO.4 Explain the three different torts of invasion of privacy

LO.5 Explain the torts of defamation and defenses

LO.6 Explain the elements of negligence and defenses

LO.7 Explain the tort of strict liability and why very few defenses are avaliable

The law of torts permits individuals and companies to recover from other individuals and companies for wrongs committed against them. Tort law provides rights and remedies for conduct that meets the elements required to establish that a wrong has occurred.

A. GENERAL PRINCIPLES

Civil, or noncriminal, wrongs that are not breaches of contract are governed by tort law. This chapter covers the types of civil wrongs that constitute torts and the remedies available for those wrongs.

1. What Is a Tort?

tort–civil wrong that interferes with one's property or person.

Tort comes from the Latin term *tortus,* which means "crooked, dubious, twisted." Torts are actions that are not straight but are crooked, or civil, wrongs. A tort is an interference with someone's person or property. **For Example,** entering someone's house without his or her permission is an interference and constitutes the tort of trespass. Causing someone's character to be questioned is a wrong against the person and is the tort of defamation. The law provides protection against these harms in the form of remedies awarded after the wrongs are committed. These remedies are civil remedies for the acts of interference by others.

2. Tort and Crime Distinguished

A *crime* is a wrong that arises from a violation of a public duty, whereas a *tort* is a wrong that arises from a violation of a private duty. A crime is a wrong of such a serious nature that the appropriate level of government steps in to prosecute and punish the wrongdoer to deter others from engaging in the same type of conduct. However, whenever the act that is committed as a crime causes harm to an identifiable person, that person may recover from the wrongdoer for monetary damages to compensate for the harm. For the person who experiences the direct harm, the act is called a *tort*; for the government, the same act is called a *crime*.

When the same act is both a crime and a tort, the government may prosecute the wrongdoer for a violation of criminal law, and the individual who experiences the direct harm may recover damages. **For Example,** O. J. Simpson was charged by the state of California with the murder of his ex-wife, Nicole Brown Simpson, and her friend Ron Goldman. A criminal trial was held in which O. J. Simpson was acquitted. Simpson was subsequently sued civilly by the families of Nicole Simpson and Ron Goldman for the tort of wrongful death. The jury in the civil case found Simpson civilly liable and the court ordered him to pay nearly $20 million in damages plus interest. Only $382,000 of this judgment has actually been paid to the families.

3. Types of Torts

intentional tort–civil wrong that results from intentional conduct.

There are three types of torts: intentional torts, negligence, and strict liability. **Intentional torts** are those that occur when wrongdoers engage in intentional conduct. **For Example,** striking another person in a fight is an intentional act and would be the tort of battery and possibly also the crime of battery. Your arm striking another person's nose in a fast-moving crowd of people at a rock concert is not a tort or crime because your arm was pushed unintentionally by the force of the crowd. If you stretched out your arms in that crowd or began to swing your arms about and struck another person, you would be behaving carelessly in a crowd of people; and, although you may not have committed an intentional tort, it is possible that your careless conduct constitutes the tort of **negligence**. Careless actions, or actions taken without thinking through their consequences, constitute negligence. The harm to the other person's nose may not have been intended, but there is liability for these accidental harms under negligence. **For Example,** if you run a red light, hit another car, and injure its driver, you did not intend the result. However, your careless behavior of disregarding a traffic signal resulted in the injury, and you would have liability for your negligence to that driver.

> **negligence** – failure to exercise due care under the circumstances in consequence of which harm is proximately caused to one to whom the defendant owed a duty to exercise due care.

In transmission of disease cases, depending on the facts, both intentional torts and negligence theories may apply. A person who knows or should know that he or she has herpes and fails to disclose that fact, or misrepresents that he or she is disease-free, may be liable to a sexual partner. The torts theories may include negligence, battery, intentional infliction of emotional distress, and fraud. In most cases, the three words "I have herpes" is fair notice of the danger of infection.[1] However, saying it is okay to have sex because the individual was not having an outbreak of the disease is actionable. **For Example,** Thomas R. disclosed to his girlfriend that he had herpes but nevertheless told her that it was "okay" to have sex with him because he was not then experiencing an outbreak of the disease. The jury's finding of negligence and fraudulent concealment in the transmission of the disease was upheld by the appeals court, and the plaintiff was awarded compensatory damages as well as $2.75 million in punitive damages.[2]

> **strict liability** – civil wrong for which there is absolute liability because of the inherent danger in the underlying activity, for example, the use of explosives.

Strict liability is another type of tort that imposes liability without regard to whether there was any intent to harm or any negligence occurred. Strict liability is imposed without regard to fault. Strict or absolute liability is imposed because the activity involved is so dangerous that there must be full accountability. Nonetheless, the activity is necessary and cannot be prohibited. The compromise is to allow the activity but ensure that its dangers and resulting damages are fully covered through the imposition of full liability for all injuries that result. **For Example,** contractors often need to use dynamite to take a roadway through a mountainside or demolish a building that has become a hazard. When the dynamite is used, noise, debris, and possibly dangerous pieces of earth and building will descend on others' land and possibly on people. In most states, contractors are held strictly liable for the resulting damage from the use of dynamite. The activity is necessary and not illegal, but those who use dynamite must be prepared to compensate those who are injured as a result.

Other areas in which there is strict liability for activity include the storage of flammable materials and crop dusting. The federal government and the states have pure food laws that impose absolute liability on manufacturers who fail to meet the statutory standards for their products. Another area of strict liability is *product liability*, which is covered in Chapter 25.

---

[1] *R.A.P. v. B.J.P.*, 428 N.W.2d 103, 108 (Minn. App. 1988).
[2] *Behr v. Redmond*, 123 Cal. Rptr. 3d 97 (Cal. App. 2011).

B. Intentional Torts

4. Assault

An *assault* is intentional conduct that threatens a person with a well-founded fear of imminent harm coupled with the present ability to carry out the threat of harm. **For Example,** the angry assertion "I'm going to kick your butt" along with aggressive movement in the direction of the victim with the intent to carry out the threat is an assault, even though a third person intervenes to stop the intended action. Mere words, however, although insulting, are ordinarily insufficient to constitute an assault.

5. Battery

A *battery* is the intentional, wrongful touching of another person without that person's consent. Thus, a threat to use force is an assault, and the actual use of force is the battery. The single action of striking an individual can be both a crime and a tort. A lawsuit for the tort of battery provides a plaintiff with the opportunity to recover damages resulting from the battery. The plaintiff must prove damages, however.

CASE SUMMARY

An Exchange of Unpleasantries ...

FACTS: Moore and Beye had an altercation after a public meeting regarding airport expansion. Moore owns a ranch near the airport and staunchly opposes expansion. Beye owns a flying service and avidly supports expansion. Moore and Beye exchanged unpleasantries while leaving the meeting. Beye then punched Moore on the left side of the jaw. Moore stumbled but caught himself before falling. He then exclaimed to the crowd, "You saw that. You are my witnesses. I've been assaulted. I want that man arrested." Ravalli County deputies took Beye into custody, and the state charged him with misdemeanor assault. Moore visited the hospital complaining of back and neck pain two days later and contended that he had injured his back while reeling from Beye's punch. He filed a civil complaint against Beye for damages. Moore's evidence mostly concerned his alleged back injury. Beye did not contest that he had punched Moore. His evidence countered that Moore's back problems had existed before the altercation. The judge instructed the jury that Beye had committed a battery as a matter of law and directed that they answer the question, "Was Moore damaged as a result of the battery?" The jury voted 11 to 1 that the battery did not injure Moore, and Moore appealed.

DECISION: Judgment for Beye. Beye presented the testimony of several eyewitnesses and a medical expert that Moore had sustained no damages. Although Moore presented considerable evidence to the contrary, it was not the court's function to agree or disagree with the verdict. Beye presented sufficient evidence to uphold the jury's verdict. [*Moore v. Beye*, **122 P.3d 1212 (Mont. 2005)**]

6. False Imprisonment

False imprisonment is the intentional detention of a person without that person's consent.[3] The detention need not be for any specified period of time, for any detention against one's will is false imprisonment. False imprisonment is often called

false imprisonment – intentional detention of a person without that person's consent; called the *shopkeeper's tort* when shoplifters are unlawfully detained.

[3] *Forgie-Buccioni v. Hannaford Bros. Inc.,* 413 F.3d 175 (1st Cir. 2005).

the *shopkeeper's tort* because so much liability has been imposed on store owners for their unreasonable detention of customers suspected of shoplifting. Requiring a customer to sit in the manager's office or not allowing a customer to leave the store can constitute the tort of false imprisonment. Shop owners do, however, need the opportunity to investigate possible thefts in their stores. As a result, all states have some form of privilege or protection for store owners called a *shopkeeper's privilege*.

The **shopkeeper's privilege** permits the store owner to detain a suspected shoplifter based on reasonable suspicion for a reasonable time without resulting liability for false imprisonment to the accused customer.[4] The privilege applies even if the store owner was wrong about the customer being a shoplifter, so long as the store owner acted based on reasonable suspicions and treated the accused shoplifter in a reasonable manner.

shopkeeper's privilege – right of a store owner to detain a suspected shoplifter based on reasonable cause and for a reasonable time without resulting liability for false imprisonment.

CASE SUMMARY

A Can of Mousse: A Tote Bag of Trouble

FACTS: Patricia Holguin went to Sally's Beauty Supply Store carrying her "eco-friendly canvas shopping tote," a large bag that is conspicuous when used. Upon entering the store, there were no posted signs stating that shopping totes were not allowed. She picked up a can of mousse that was not exactly what she wanted and started to carry it in her tote toward the front counter to ask the cashier a question about it. As she walked toward the front of the store the assistant manager approached her and asked what was in the bag. She was detained by this manager, who told her that once she put the hair mousse in her tote bag, she was shoplifting. Holguin's lawsuit for false imprisonment against the store was dismissed with prejudice by the trial court. This court held that once she placed the merchandise in her bag, the store had probable cause to believe she was shoplifting and had a statutory conditional privilege to detain her, free from civil liability for false imprisonment, because she "willfully concealed merchandise." Holguin appealed.

DECISION: The court of appeals reversed the district court's decision. In general, merchants and their employees have a conditional privilege to detain a person free from civil liability based on probable cause, or reasonable grounds to believe that the individual "willfully concealed" merchandise without paying for it, provided the detention is for a reasonable time and conducted in a reasonable manner. "Willfully concealed," however, requires more than merely putting merchandise out of sight. In self-service stores customers have implied permission to pick up, handle, move, try on, replace, and carry about merchandise within the store. There must be circumstances which reflect that the purpose of the concealment is adverse to the store's right to be paid before the conclusion can be drawn that the merchandise was "willfully concealed" under the statute providing the conditional privilege to detain a customer. Placing the can of mousse in a reusable, personal canvas shopping bag to carry to the front of the store to ask a question, without more, did not constitute "willful concealment." [*Holguin v. Sally's Beauty Supply, Inc.*, 264 P.3d 732 (N. Mex. App. 2011)]

7. Intentional Infliction of Emotional Distress

The **intentional infliction of emotional distress** (IIED) is a tort involving conduct that goes beyond all bounds of decency and produces mental anguish in the harmed individual. This tort requires proof of outrageous conduct and resulting emotional

intentional infliction of emotional distress – tort that produces mental anguish caused by conduct that exceeds all bounds of decency.

---

[4] *Limited Stores, Inc. v. Wilson-Robinson*, 876 S.W.2d 248 (Ark. 1994); see also *Wal-Mart Stores, Inc. v. Binns*, 15 S.W.3d 320 (Ark. 2000).

distress in the victim. **For Example,** Erica Schoen, a 16-year employee of Freightliner, returned to work on light duty after surgery for a work-related shoulder injury. She was assigned to work out of the nurse's station under two employees who intentionally worked her beyond her restrictions, assigned her to humiliating work, repeatedly called her worthless, and used her as a personal servant—ordering her to get snacks, sodas, and lunches for them and not reimbursing her. After five months of this treatment, Erica brought the matter to the human resources manager, who told her, in part, "Nobody wants you. You're worthless. We build trucks down here…." Erica became hysterical and thereafter required psychiatric care. The jury awarded $250,000 for IIED, and it was upheld on appeal because the repetitive misconduct and its duration, ratified by the human resource manager, was intolerable.[5]

✳ 8. Invasion of Privacy

✳

invasion of privacy – tort of intentional intrusion into the private affairs of another.

The right of privacy is the right to be free of unreasonable intrusion into one's private affairs. The tort of **invasion of privacy** actually consists of three different torts: (1) intrusion into the plaintiff's private affairs (for example, planting a microphone in an office or home); (2) public disclosure of private facts (for example, disclosing private financial information, such as a business posting returned checks from customers near its cash register in a public display); and (3) appropriation of another's name, likeness, or image for commercial advantage. This form of invasion of privacy is generally referred to as the *right of publicity.* The elements of this tort are (1) appropriation of the plaintiff's name or likeness for the value associated with it, and not in an incidental manner or for a newsworthy purpose, (2) identification of the plaintiff in the publication, and (3) an advantage or benefit to the defendant. The right to publicity is designed to protect the commercial interest of celebrities in their identities.

For Example, popular and critically acclaimed rock and roll musician Don Henley, the founder and member of the band The Eagles, successfully sued a department store chain that ran an international newspaper advertisement for its Henley shirt, which stated in large letters as the focus of the ad "This is Don's henley." The ad (1) used the value associated with the famous name Don Henley to get consumers to read it, (2) the plaintiff was identifiable in the ad, and (3) the ad was created with the belief that use of the words "Don's henley" would help sell the product.[6]

CASE SUMMARY

Cashing in on Catherine's Vacation

FACTS: Catherine Bosley worked as a television news anchor for WKBN, Channel 27, in Youngstown, Ohio. While on vacation with her husband in Florida, she participated in a "wet t-shirt" contest that was videotaped without her consent by DreamGirls, Inc., and licensed to Marvad Corp., which runs a Web site for adult entertainment through a subscription service on the Internet. Marvad used depictions of her in advertisements to promote the materials and

---

[5] *Schoen v. Freightliner LLC,* 199 P.3d 332 (Or. App. 2008).
[6] *Henley v. Dillard Department Stores,* 46 F. Supp. 2d 587 (N.D. Tex. 1999).

CASE SUMMARY

Continued

services it markets. Web site searches related to Catherine Bosley in 2004 were the most popular search on the World Wide Web. Due to the publicity, she resigned from her position at WKBN and was prevented from seeking other employment. Bosley sought an injunction under the right of publicity theory against the defendants from using her image in any manner that promotes the sale of their goods or services. The defendants contended that an injunction would violate their First Amendment rights.

DECISION: Judgment for Bosley. The First Amendment does not immunize defendants from damages for infringement of the right of publicity. No significant editorial comment or artistic expression involving First Amendment protections applies in this case. If any "speech" interest is involved, it is commercial speech. At its core, the defendants are selling Bosley's image for a profit without her consent. It is in violation of her right of publicity, which protects one's right to be free from the appropriation of one's persona. The injunction sought was granted. [*Bosley v. Wildwett.com,* **310 F. Supp. 2d 914 (N.D. Ohio 2004)**]

Some states refer to the right of publicity as a cause of action for *commercial misappropriation of a name or likeness,* and provide two vehicles a plaintiff can use to protect the economic value of one's name, a common law action or a statutory remedy. The *Schlein* case involved a breach of contract action and an action for commercial misappropriation of his name.

CASE SUMMARY

The Name Game: We Are Discontinuing Your Royalty on the "Schlein Ultra," Dr. Schlein

FACTS: Orthopedic Systems, Inc. (OSI), and Dr. Schlein entered into a contract, whereby OSI would manufacture and sell an unpatented product originally designed by Dr. Schlein called the "Schlein Shoulder Positioner," to be used in arthroscopic shoulder surgery. The contract called for a 5% royalty of the list price less discounts. Over the years OSI's marketing brochures thanked "Allen P. Schlein M.D. for his assistance in the development of the product." OSI paid royalty checks from January 1991 to January 2005, when OSI paid its last royalty payment for the period ending December 2004. In January 2005, OSI sent a letter to Dr. Schlein stating that in light of the fact that there is no patent protection on the product, it would be discontinuing the royalty. From January 2005 until July 29, 2005, OSI continued to market and sell the product using Dr. Schlein's name. OSI sued Dr. Schlein for declaratory relief and reformation of the royalty contract. Dr. Schlein cross-complained for breach of contract and commercial misappropriation of his name. The jury awarded Dr. Schlein $616,043 for failure to pay royalties under the contract. OSI earned $1,220,000 in profits attributed to the use of Dr. Schlein's name during the period from January 1, 2005 to July 31, 2005, after which OSI stopped using Schlein's name. The trial court declined to award the profits to Schlein, and both parties appealed.

DECISION: The statutory remedy of Section 3444(a) requires the payment of the greater of $750, or the actual damages suffered as a result of the unauthorized use, and any profits for the unauthorized use that are attributable to use and are not taken into account in computing actual

CASE SUMMARY

Continued

damages. The legislative history for the minimum $750 award was intended to fill the gap that existed in the common law tort of invasion of privacy as applied to noncelebrities whose names lacked commercial value on the open market. Unlike sports and entertainment stars, noncelebrities often could not prove damages under the common law; therefore, the statute established a concrete remedy for the little man with a minimum payment. An interpretation that limits damages to $750 as an alternative to all other damages would be contrary to the spirit of the statute. Judgment for Dr. Schlein who is entitled as well to the $1,220,000 profits as a result of OSI's unauthorized use of his name. [***Orthopedic Systems, Inc. v. Schlein*, 135 Cal. Rptr. 3d 200 (Cal. App. 2011)**]

✳ 9. Defamation

defamation – untrue statement by one party about another to a third party.

slander – defamation of character by spoken words or gestures.

libel – written or visual *word* defamation without legal justification.

Defamation is an untrue statement by one party about another to a third party. **Slander** is oral or spoken defamation, and **libel** is written (and in some cases broadcast) defamation. The elements for defamation are (1) a statement about a person's reputation, honesty, or integrity that is untrue; (2) publication (accomplished when a third party hears or reads the defamatory statement); (3) a statement directed at a particular person; and (4) damages that result from the statement.[7]

For Example, a false statement by the owner of a business that the former manager was fired for stealing when he was not would be defamation, and the former manager's damages could be his inability to find another position because of the statement's impact on his reputation.

In cases in which the victim is a public figure, such as a Hollywood celebrity or a professional sports player, another element is required, the element of malice, which means that what was said or written was done with the knowledge that the information was false or with reckless disregard for whether it was true or false.

CASE SUMMARY

"I'm a Great Builder," Trump Said, Nonresponsively

FACTS: Timothy O'Brien, the author of *Trump Nation, the Art of Being the Donald,* and his publisher were sued by Donald Trump for defamation. In writing the book in 2005, O'Brien reinterviewed three anonymous sources who lowered their estimates of Trump's net worth at that time to between $150 million and $250 million because of the decreased value of Trump's casino holding at the time he was writing the book. O'Brien, who interviewed Trump, wrote:

---

[7] Regarding damages, where one publishes a slander that imputes to another a communicable disease, or would adversely affect that person's fitness for the proper conduct of a lawful business, trade, or profession, the words are actionable in themselves, and the law implies compensatory damages. Once compensatory damages are established the jury will assess punitive damages to punish the party who committed the wrong and to deter others from committing similar wrongs in the future. See *Tanner v. Ebbole,* 2011 WL 4425540 (Ala. App. 2011) where the jury returned "nominal" compensatory damages of $1 and punitive damages of $100,000 against Paul Averette, the owner of a competing tattoo business, for slanderous statements to several patrons that his competitor Chassity Ebbole had hepatitis, syphilis, gonorrhea, and AIDS and that she used "nasty needles."

CASE SUMMARY

Continued

So I asked around for guidance. Three people with direct knowledge of Donald's finances, people who had worked closely with him for years, told me that they thought his net worth was somewhere between $150 million and $250 million. By anyone's standards this still qualified Donald as comfortably wealthy, but none of these people thought he was remotely close to being a billionaire.

That passage was followed by:

Donald dismissed this as naysaying. "You can go ahead and speak to guys who have four-hundred-pound wives at home who are jealous of me, but the guys who really know me know I'm a great builder," he told me.

This and other statements underestimating Trump's wealth according to Trump's lawsuit were false statements that tended to harm his reputation in the eyes of the community. From summary judgment in favor of O'Brien and the publisher, Trump appealed.

DECISION: Judgment for O'Brien and the publisher. In order to establish a prima facie case of defamation, a plaintiff must show that a defendant communicated to a third person a false statement about the plaintiff that tended to harm the plaintiff's reputation in the eyes of the community or to cause others to avoid him. Because there is no doubt that Trump is a public figure, to be actionable, the alleged defamatory statements by O'Brien must have been published with "actual malice" or reckless disregard for the truth. There is no evidence to support Trump's conclusion that the confidential sources utilized by O'Brien were fictitious. The issue is not whether the book contained false statements or whether O'Brien had ill will toward him as Trump contends, but, rather, whether the book contained defamatory statements made with actual malice. The record does not support this contention. [***Trump v. O'Brien,*** 29 A.3d 1090 (N.J. Super. 2011)]

The defenses to defamation include the truth. If the statement is true, even if it is harmful to the victim, it is not the tort of defamation.[8]

Some statements are privileged, and this privilege provides a full or partial defense to the tort of defamation. **For Example,** members of Congress enjoy an **absolute privilege** when they are speaking on the floor of the Senate or the House because public policy requires a free dialogue on the issues pending in a legislative body. The same absolute privilege applies to witnesses in court proceedings to encourage witnesses with information to come forward and testify. Where a witness granted immunity from prosecution testifies before a governmental agency, the witness is entitled to immunity from defamation lawsuits. **For Example,** Roger Clemens sued his former trainer, Brian McNamee, for defamation, contending that McNamee falsely stated to a congressional committee that Clemens had used steroids during his professional baseball career. This defamation claim was dismissed because McNamee's statements were entitled to absolute immunity on the reasoning that the proper administration of justice requires full disclosure from witnesses without fear of retaliatory lawsuits.[9]

absolute privilege—complete defense against the tort of defamation, as in the speeches of members of Congress on the floor and witnesses in a trial.

---

[8] See *Stark v. Zeta Phi Beta Sorority Inc.*, 587 F. Supp. 2d 170 (D. D.C. 2008).
[9] *Clemens v. McNamee*, 608 F. Supp. 2d 811 (S.D. Tex. 2009). On June 18, 2012, Clemens was acquitted of all six counts of lying to Congress.

qualified privilege – media privilege to print inaccurate information without liability for defamation, so long as a retraction is printed and there was no malice.

The media enjoy a **qualified privilege** for stories that turn out to be false. Their qualified privilege is a defense to defamation so long as the information was released without malice and a retraction or correction is made when the matter is brought to their attention.

A *qualified privilege* to make a defamatory statement in the workplace exists when the statement is made to protect the interests of the private employer on a work-related matter, especially when reporting actual or suspected wrongdoing. **For Example,** Neda Lewis was fired from her job at Carson Oil Company for allegedly stealing toilet paper. The employee in charge of supplies noticed toilet paper was regularly missing from the ladies room, and one evening from a third-floor window overlooking the parking lot, she observed that the plaintiff's bag contained two rolls of toilet paper. She reported the matter to the executive secretary, who reported it to both the president and the CEO of the firm, who decided to fire her. Two other employees were also informed. The employer was able to successfully raise the defense of a qualified privilege to Ms. Lewis' defamation action for "false accusations of theft" since all of the employees involved were participants in the investigation and termination of the employee.[10]

A new statutory privilege has been evolving with respect to letters of recommendation and references given by employers for employees who are applying for jobs at other companies. Most companies, because of concerns about liability for defamation, will only confirm that a former employee did work at their firm and will provide the time period during which the person was employed. However, many employees who had histories that should have been revealed for safety reasons have been hired because no negative information was released. Numerous states now have statutes that provide employers a qualified privilege with respect to references and recommendations. So long as the employer acts in good faith in providing information, there is no liability for defamation to the former employee as a result of the information provided.

10. Product Disparagement

slander of title – malicious making of false statements as to a seller's title.

trade libel – written defamation about a product or service.

product disparagement – false statements made about a product or business.

contract interference – tort in which a third party interferes with others' freedom to contract.

Although the comparison of products and services is healthy for competition, false statements about another's products constitute a form of slander called **slander of title** or libel called **trade libel**; collectively, these are known as **product disparagement**, which occurs when someone makes false statements about another business, its products, or its abilities.[11] The elements of product disparagement are (1) a false statement about a particular business product or about its service in terms of honesty, reputation, ability, or integrity; (2) communication of the statement to a third party; and (3) damages.

11. Wrongful Interference with Contracts

The tort of **contract interference** or (tortious interference with contracts) occurs when parties are not allowed the freedom to contract without interference from third parties. While the elements required to establish the tort of contract interference are complex, a basic definition is that the law affords a remedy when a third party

---

[10] *Lewis v. Carson Oil Co.*, 127 P.3d 1207 (Or. App. 2006).
[11] *Sannerud v. Brantz*, 879 P.2d 341 (Wyo. 1994). See *Suzuki Motor Corp. v. Consumers Union*, 230 F.3d 1110 (9th Cir. 2003), *cert denied* 540 U.S. 983 (2003), for an example of the complexity of a product disparagement action.

intentionally causes another to break a contract already in existence.[12] **For Example,** Nikke Finke, a newspaper reporter who had a contract with the *New York Post* to write stories about the entertainment industry for the *Post's* business section, wrote two articles about a lawsuit involving a literary agent and the Walt Disney Company over merchandising rights to the Winnie-the-Pooh characters. Finke reported that the trial court sanctioned Disney for engaging in "misuse of the discovery process" and acting in "bad faith" and ordered Disney to pay fees and costs of $90,000. Disney's president, Robert Iger, sent a letter to the *Post's* editor-in-chief, Col Allan, calling Finke's reporting an "absolute distortion" of the record and "absolutely false." Approximately two weeks after the Pooh articles were published, the *Post* fired Finke; her editor told her she was being fired for the Pooh articles. She sued Disney on numerous tort theories, including interference with her contract with the *Post*. Disney sought to have the complaint dismissed, which motion was denied by the court. The Court of Appeals concluded that Finke demonstrated a reasonable probability of proving that Iger's allegations that she made false statements in her article were themselves false; and it concluded that a jury could find Disney liable for intentional interference with contractual relations based on circumstantial evidence and negligent interference with contractual relations because it was reasonably foreseeable to Disney that the nature of its accusations against Finke would result in her termination from employment.[13]

12. Trespass

trespass – unauthorized action with respect to person or property.

A **trespass** is an unauthorized action with respect to land or personal property. A *trespass to land* is any unpermitted entry below, on, across, or above the land of another. **For Example,** Joyce Ameral's home abuts the mid-way point of the 240-yard, par-4 ninth hole of the public Middlebrook Country Club. Balls sliced and hooked by golfers have damaged her windows and screens, dented her car, and made her deck too dangerous for daytime use. Her landscapers are forced to wear hard hats when cutting her lawn. In her lawsuit against the country club owner, the court ruled that the projection of golf balls onto Ameral's property constituted a continuing trespass and it enjoined the trespass.[14]

A *trespass to personal property* is the invasion of personal property without the permission of the owner. **For Example,** the use of someone's car without that person's permission is a trespass to personal property.

C. Negligence

The widest range of tort liability today arises in the field of negligence. Accidents happen! Property is damaged, and/or injuries result. The fact that an individual suffers an injury does not necessarily mean that the individual will be able to recover damages for the injury. **For Example,** Rhonda Nichols was shopping in the outdoor garden center at a Lowe's Home Center when a "wild bird" flew into the back of her head, causing injuries. Her negligence lawsuit against Lowe's was dismissed

---

[12] See *Ventas, Inc. v. HCP, Inc.*, 647 F.3d 291 (6th Cir. 2011); *ASDI, Inc. v. Beard Research, Inc.*, 11 A.3d 749 (Del. 2010).
[13] *Finke v. The Walt Disney Co.*, 2 Cal. Rptr. 3d 436 (Cal. App. 2003).
[14] *Ameral v. Pray*, 831 N.E.2d 915 (Mass. App. 2005).

because the owner did not have a duty to protect her from a wild bird attack because it was not reasonably foreseeable.[15] Jane Costa was passively watching a Boston Red Sox baseball game at Fenway Park when a foul ball struck her in the face, causing severe and permanent injuries. Her negligence lawsuit against the Boston Red Sox was unsuccessful because it was held that the owners had no duty to warn Ms. Costa of the obvious danger of foul balls being hit into the stands.[16] Although cases involving injury to spectators at baseball games in other jurisdictions have turned on other tort doctrines, injured fans, like Ms. Costa, are left to bear the costs of their injuries. Only when an injured person can demonstrate the following four elements of negligence is a right to recover established: (1) a duty, (2) breach of duty, (3) causation, and (4) damages.[17] Several defenses may be raised in a negligence lawsuit.

13. Elements of Negligence

(A) DUTY TO EXERCISE REASONABLE CARE. The first element of negligence is a *duty*. There is a general duty of care imposed to act as a reasonably prudent person would in similar circumstances. **For Example,** Gustavo Guzman worked for a sub-contractor as a chicken catcher at various poultry farms where a Tyson Foods employee, Brian Jones, operated a forklift and worked with the catchers setting up cages to collect birds for processing at a Tyson plant. Contrary to Tyson's instructions "never to allow catchers to move behind the forklift or otherwise out of sight," Brian moved his forklift and struck Guzman, who suffered a serious spinal injury. A general contractor, Tyson Foods, owes a duty to exercise reasonable care to a subcontractor's employee, Gustavo Guzman.[18]

Professionals have a duty to perform their jobs at the level of a reasonable professional. For a professional such as an accountant, doctor, lawyer, dentist, or architect to avoid liability for **malpractice**, the professional must perform his or her skill in the same manner as, and at the level of, other professionals in the same field.

Those who own real property have a duty of care to keep their property in a condition that does not create hazards for guests. Businesses have a duty to inspect and repair their property so that their customers are not injured by hazards, such as spills on the floor or uneven walking areas. When customer safety is a concern, businesses have a duty to provide adequate security, such as security patrols in mall parking lots.

(B) BREACH OF DUTY. The second element of negligence is the breach of duty imposed by statute or by the application of the reasonable person standard. The defendant's conduct is evaluated against what a reasonable person would have done under the circumstances. That is, when there is sufficient proof to raise a jury question, the jury decides whether the defendant breached the duty to the injured person from a reasonable person's perspective.[19] **For Example,** the jury in Guzman's lawsuit against Tyson Foods (the *Tyson* case), after weighing all of the facts and

malpractice – when services are not properly rendered in accordance with commonly accepted standards; negligence by a professional in performing his or her skill.

---

[15] *Nichols v. Lowe's Home Center, Inc.,* 407 F. Supp. 2d 979 (S.D. Ill. 2006).

[16] *Costa v. Boston Red Sox Baseball Club,* 809 N.E.2d 1090 (Mass. App. 2004).

[17] *Alfred v. Capital Area Soccer League, Inc.,* 669 S.E.2d 277 (N.C. App. 2008).

[18] *Tyson Foods Inc. v. Guzman,* 116 S.W.3d 233 (Tex. App. 2003). But see *Pippin v. Hill-Rom Co., Inc.,* 615 F.3d 886 (8th Cir. 2010), where a shipper's failure to load cargo onto an independent truck driver's trailer, as required by the transportation contract, did not give rise to a cause of action for negligence, where the driver was injured loading the truck by himself. The shipper owed no duty to the driver, who chose to load the truck by himself.

[19] A breach of duty may be established by the very nature of the harm to the plaintiff. The doctrine of *res ipsa loquitur* ("the event speaks for itself") provides a rebuttable presumption that the defendant was negligent when a defendant owes a duty to the plaintiff, the nature of the harm caused the plaintiff is such that it ordinarily does not happen in the absence of negligence, and the instrument causing the injury was in the defendant's exclusive control. An example of the doctrine is a lawsuit against a surgeon after a surgical device is discovered in a former patient months after the surgery by another physician seeking the cause of the patient's continuing pain subsequent to the operation.

circumstances, determined that Tyson's employee's operation of the forklift constituted a breach of Tyson's duty of care to Guzman.

(c) CAUSATION. A third element of negligence is *causation,* the element that connects the duty and the breach of duty to the injuries to the plaintiff. **For Example,** in Guzman's lawsuit, the forklift operator's careless conduct was the cause in fact of this worker's injuries. A "but for" test for causation is used. *But for* Tyson employee Brian Jones' negligent conduct in moving the forklift under the circumstances surrounding the accident, Guzman would not have been injured.

Once the cause in fact is established, the plaintiff must establish *proximate cause.* That is, it must establish that the harm suffered by the injured person was a foreseeable consequence of the defendant's negligent actions. Foreseeability requires only the general danger to be foreseeable. In the *Tyson* case, the court determined that while there was some evidence that a jury could possibly infer that Tyson could not foresee an accident similar to the one involving Guzman, the evidence was legally sufficient to support the jury's finding that Tyson's negligence was foreseeable and the cause in fact of Guzman's injuries.

The landmark *Palsgraf v. Long Island Rail Road Co.* case established a limitation on liability for unforeseeable or unusual consequences following a negligent act.

CASE SUMMARY

The Scales Tipped on Causation

FACTS: Helen Palsgraf lived in Brooklyn. On a summer's day, she purchased tickets to travel to Rockaway Beach on the Long Island Rail Road (LIRR) with her two daughters. She was standing on a platform on the LIRR's East New York station when two men ran to catch another train. One of the men made it onto the train, but the other man, who was carrying a package, was unsteady as the train was about to pull out of the station. The LIRR conductor pulled him up, while the LIRR platform guard pushed him in the train, but in the process, he dropped the package. It contained fireworks and exploded! The concussion from the explosion caused the scales located next to Mrs. Palsgraf to fall over, striking and injuring her. Mrs. Palsgraf sued LIRR for the negligence of the two employees who had assisted the passenger with the package to board the train. A jury awarded her $6,000, which was upheld 3-2 by the Appellate Division. Thereafter the state's highest court considered the railroad's appeal.

DECISION: Recovery for negligence is not available unless there has been some violation of a right. Helen Palsgraf was too remote in distance from the accident for any invasion of rights. To reach a different decision would mean that there could be no end to those who might be harmed. By helping someone onto a moving train, the train employees can anticipate that the passenger himself might be injured, that other passengers might be injured, and that those around the immediate scene might be injured. But Mrs. Palsgraf was too remote for her injuries to be reasonably foreseeable as a consequence of the action of helping a passenger onto a moving train. She was 25 to 30 feet away from the scene, and the explosion cannot be called the proximate cause of her concussion and other injuries. [*Palsgraf v. Long Island R.R. Co.,* **162 N.E. 99 (N.Y. 1928)**]

(d) DAMAGES. The plaintiff in a personal injury negligence lawsuit must establish the actual losses caused by the defendant's breach of duty of care and is entitled to be made whole for all losses. The successful plaintiff is entitled to compensation for (1) past and future pain and suffering (mental anguish), (2) past and future physical impairment, (3) past and future medical care, and (4) past and future loss of earning capacity. Life and work life expectancy are critical factors to consider in assessing damage involving permanent disabilities with loss of earning capacity. Expert witnesses are utilized at trial to present evidence based on worklife tables and present value tables to deal with these economic issues. The jury considers all of the evidence in the context of the elements necessary to prove negligence and all defenses raised, and it renders a verdict. **For Example,** in the *Tyson* case, the defendant presented evidence and argued that Gustavo Guzman was himself negligent regarding the accident. The jury found that both parties were negligent and attributed 80 percent of the fault to Tyson and 20 percent to Guzman (this is called *comparative negligence* and is discussed in the following section). The jury awarded Guzman $931,870.51 in damages ($425,000.00 for past physical pain and mental anguish, $150,000.00 for future physical pain and mental anguish, $10,000.00 for past physical impairment, $10,000.00 for future physical impairment, $51,870.51 for past medical care, $5,000.00 for future medical care, $70,000.00 for past lost earning capacity, and $210,000.00 for future lost earning capacity). After deducting 20 percent of the total jury award for Guzman's own negligence, the trial court's final judgment awarded Guzman $745,496.41.

In some situations, the independent actions of two defendants occur to cause harm. **For Example,** Penny Shipler was rendered a quadriplegic as a result of a Chevrolet S-10 Blazer rollover accident. She sued the driver Kenneth Long for negligence and General Motors for negligent design of the Blazer's roof. She was awarded $18.5 million in damages. Because two causes provided a single indivisible injury, the two defendants were held jointly and severally liable.[20] Under *joint and several liability,* each defendant may be held liable to pay the entire judgment. However, should one defendant pay the entire judgment, that party may sue the other for "contribution" for its proportionate share.

In some cases in which the breach of duty was shocking, plaintiffs may be awarded *punitive damages.* However, punitive (also called *exemplary*) damages are ordinarily applied when the defendant's tortious conduct is attended by circumstances of fraud, malice, or willful or wanton conduct.[21]

✱ 14. Defenses to Negligence

(A) CONTRIBUTORY NEGLIGENCE. A plaintiff who is also negligent gives the defendant the opportunity to raise the defense of **contributory negligence**, which the defendant establishes by utilizing the elements of negligence previously discussed, including the plaintiff's duty to exercise reasonable care for his or her own safety, the breach of that duty, causation, and harm. Under common law, the defense of contributory negligence, if established, is a complete bar to recovery of damages from the defendant.

The *Hardesty case* involves the application of the contributory negligence defense.

✱ **contributory negligence**— negligence of the plaintiff that contributes to injury and at common law bars from recovery from the defendant although the defendant may have been more negligent than the plaintiff.

---

[20] *Shipler v. General Motors Corp.,* 710 N.W.2d 807 (Neb. 2006).
[21] See *Eden Electrical, Ltd. v. Amana Co.,* 370 F.3d 824 (8th Cir. 2004); and *University of Colorado v. American Cyanamid Co.,* 342 F.3d 1298 (Fed. Cir. 2003).

CASE SUMMARY

Keep Your Eye on the Ball in Sports: Keep Your Eye on the 300-Pound Boxes in Trucking

FACTS: Lawrence Hardesty is an over-the-road tractor-trailer truck driver who picked up a load of stadium seating equipment for the NFL stadium under construction in Baltimore. The equipment was packaged in large corrugated cardboard boxes weighing several hundred pounds. The shipper, American Seating Co., loaded the trailer while Hardesty remained in the cab of his truck doing "paperwork" and napping. Considerable open space existed between the boxes and the rear door of the trailer. The evidence showed that Hardesty failed to properly examine the load bars used to secure the boxes from movement during transit. When Hardesty arrived at the Baltimore destination, he opened the rear trailer door and boxes at the end of the trailer fell out and injured him. Hardesty brought a personal injury negligence action against the shipper. American Seating Co. responded that Hardesty was contributorily negligent, thus barring his negligence claim.

DECISION: Judgment for American Seating Co. because the claim is barred by Hardesty's contributory negligence. His decision to ignore the loading process by remaining in his truck, oblivious to the manner and means of the loading of the trailer, coupled with his own failure to examine the load bars sufficiently to confirm that they would "adequately secure" the cargo, together with his decision, in the face of his prior omissions, to open the doors of the trailer upon his arrival in Baltimore while standing within the zone of danger created by the possibility (of which he negligently failed to inform himself) of injury from cargo falling out of the trailer, cohered to rise to the level of a cognizable breach of duty—contributory negligence. [*Hardesty v. American Seating Co.*, 194 F. Supp. 2d 447 (D. Md. 2002)]

The contributory negligence defense has given way to the defense of comparative negligence in most states.

(B) COMPARATIVE NEGLIGENCE. Because contributory negligence produced harsh results with no recovery of damages for an injured plaintiff, most states have adopted a fairer approach to handling situations in which both the plaintiff and the defendant are negligent; it is called *comparative negligence*. Comparative negligence is a defense that permits a negligent plaintiff to recover some damages but only in proportion to the defendant's degree of fault.[22] **For Example,** in the *Tyson* case, both the defendant and the plaintiff were found to be negligent. The jury attributed 80 percent of the fault for the plaintiff's injury to Tyson and 20 percent of the fault to the plaintiff, Guzman. While Guzman's total damages were $931,870, they were reduced by 20 percent, and the final judgment awarded Guzman was $745,496.

Some comparative negligence states refuse to allow the plaintiff to recover damages if the plaintiff's fault was more than 50 percent of the cause of the harm.[23]

(C) ASSUMPTION OF THE RISK. The assumption of the risk defense has two categories. *Express assumption of the risk* involves a written exculpatory agreement under which a plaintiff acknowledges the risks involved in certain activities and releases the defendant from prospective liability for personal injuries sustained as a result of the

---

[22] *City of Chicago v. M/V Morgan*, 375 F.3d 563 (7th Cir. 2004).
[23] *Davenport v. Cotton Hope Plantation*, 482 S.E.2d 569 (S.C. App. 1997).

defendant's negligent conduct. Examples include ski lift tickets, white water rafting contracts, permission for high school cheerleading activities, and parking lot claim checks. In most jurisdictions these agreements are enforceable as written. However, in some jurisdictions they may be considered unenforceable because they violate public policy. **For Example,** Gregory Hanks sued the Powder Ridge Ski Resort for negligence regarding serious injuries he sustained while snowtubing at the defendant's facility. He had signed a release which explicitly provided that the snowtuber: *["fully] assume[s] all risks associated with [s]nowtubing,* even if due to the NEGLIGENCE" of the defendants [emphasis in original]. The Supreme Court of Connecticut found that the release was unenforceable because it violated the public policy by shifting the risk of negligence to the weaker bargainer.[24]

Implied primary assumption of the risk arises when a plaintiff has impliedly consented, often in advance of any negligence by the defendant, to relieve a defendant of a duty to the plaintiff regarding specific known and appreciated risks. It is a subjective standard, one specific to the plaintiff and his or her situation. **For Example,** baseball mom Delinda Taylor took her two boys to a Seattle Mariners baseball game and was injured during the pregame warm-up when a ball thrown by José Mesa got past Freddie Garcia, striking Taylor in the face and causing serious injuries. The defendant baseball team successfully raised the affirmative defense of implied primary assumption of the risk by showing that Mrs. Taylor had full subjective understanding of the specific risk of getting hit by a thrown baseball, and she voluntarily chose to encounter that risk.[25] Riding in a motorcycle procession on a Los Angeles freeway qualifies as an application of the implied primary assumption of the risk doctrine regarding involvement in a traffic collision.[26]

A number of states have either abolished the defense of assumption of the risk, reclassifying the defense as comparative negligence so as not to completely bar a plaintiff's recovery of damages, or have eliminated the use of the assumption of the risk terminology and handle cases under the duty, breach of duty, causation, and harm elements of negligence previously discussed.[27]

(D) IMMUNITY. Governments are generally immune from tort liability.[28] This rule has been eroded by decisions and in some instances by statutes, such as the Federal Tort Claims Act. Subject to certain exceptions, this act permits the recovery of damages from the United States for property damage, personal injury, or death action claims arising from the negligent act or omission of any employee of the United States under such circumstances that the United States, if a private person, would be liable to the claimant in accordance with the law of the place where the act or omission occurred. A rapidly growing number of states have abolished governmental immunity, although many still recognize it.

Until the early 1900s, charities were immune from tort liability, and children and parents and spouses could not sue each other. These immunities are fast disappearing. **For Example,** if a father's negligent driving of his car causes injuries to his minor child passenger, the child may recover from the father for his injuries.[29]

---

[24] *Hanks v. Powder Ridge,* 885 A.2d 734 (Conn. 2005).

[25] *Taylor v. Baseball Club of Seattle,* 130 P.3d 835 (Wash. App. 2006).

[26] *Amezcua v. Los Angeles Harley-Davidson,* 132 Cal. Rptr. 3d 567 (Cal. App. 2011).

[27] See, for example, *Costa v. The Boston Red Sox Baseball Club,* 809 N.E.2d 1090 (Mass. App. 2004), where the court cites state precedent that "... the abolishment of assumption of the risk as an affirmative defense did not alter the plaintiff's burden ... to prove the defendant owed [the plaintiff] a duty of care ... and thus left intact the open and obvious damages rule, which operates to negate the existence of a duty to care."

[28] *Kirby v. Macon County,* 892 S.W.2d 403 (Tenn. 1994).

[29] *Cates v. Cates,* 588 N.E.2d 330 (Ill. App. 1992); see also *Doe v. McKay,* 700 N.E.2d 1018 (Ill. 1998).

Sports & Entertainment Law

Liability for Injuries under the Sports Exception Doctrine

Charles "Booby" Clark played football for the Cincinnati Bengals as a running back on offense. Dale Hackbart played defensive free safety for the Denver Broncos. As a consequence of an interception by the Broncos, Hackbart became an offensive player, threw a block, and was watching the play with one knee on the ground when Clark "acting out of anger and frustration, but without a specific intent to injure," stepped forward and struck a blow to the back of Hackbart's head and neck, causing a serious neck fracture. Is relief precluded for injuries occurring during a professional football game? The answer is no. While proof of mere negligence is insufficient to establish liability during such an athletic contest, liability must instead be premised on heightened proof of reckless or intentional conduct on the part of the defendant. In the *Hackbart* case, the court determined that if the evidence established that the injury was the result of acts of Clark that were in reckless disregard of Hackbart's safety, Hackbart is entitled to damages.* Why didn't Hackbart pursue recovery under negligence law, contending that Clark had a general duty of care to act as a reasonably prudent person would in similar circumstances? Because football and other contact sports contain within the rules of the games inherent *unreasonable* risks of harm, a negligence theory is not applicable. What contact sports do you believe qualify under this "sports exception" doctrine for which proof of negligence is insufficient to establish liability for injuries sustained during the athletic contest? Is softball a contact sport for players? What about coaching or officiating decisions made in the middle of a fast-moving game?**

PGA golfer Walter Mallin sued PGA golfer John Paesani for injuries that Mallin sustained while competing in a PGA golf tournament when Paesani drove a golf ball that struck Mallin in the head on his right temple. Paesani contends that the "sports exception" doctrine applies and the negligence case must be dismissed. How would you decide this case?***

*Hackbart v. Cincinnati Bengals, Inc., 601 F.2d 516 (10th Cir. 1979).

**See *Guillo v. DeKamp Junction, Inc.,* 959 N.E.2d 215 (Ill. App. 2011).
****Mallin v. Paesani,* 892 A.2d 1043 (Conn. Super, 2005).

✳ D. Strict Liability

The final form of tort liability is known as *strict liability*. When the standards of strict liability apply, very few defenses are available. Strict liability was developed to provide guaranteed protection for those who are injured by conduct the law deems both serious and inexcusable.

Thinking Things Through

Torts and Public Policy

Over a decade ago, a jury awarded 81-year-old Stella Liebeck nearly $3 million because she was burned after she spilled a cup of McDonald's coffee on her lap. Based on these limited facts, a national discussion ensued about a need for tort reform, and to this day "Stella Awards" are given on Web sites for apparently frivolous or excessive lawsuits. Consider the following additional facts and the actual damages awarded Stella Liebeck. Decide whether her recovery was just.

- McDonald's coffee was brewed at 195 to 205 degrees.

- McDonald's quality assurance manager "was aware of the risk [of burns] ... and had no plans to turn down the heat."

Thinking Things Through

Continued

- Mrs. Liebeck spent seven days in the hospital with third degree burns and had skin grafts. Gruesome photos of burns of the inner thighs, groin, and buttocks were entered as evidence.

- The compensatory damages were $200,000, which were reduced to $160,000 because Mrs. Liebeck was determined to be 20 percent at fault.

- The jury awarded $2.7 million in punitive damages. The trial court judge reduced this amount to $480,000.

- The total recovery at the trial court for Mrs. Liebeck was $640,000. Both parties appealed, and a settlement was reached at what is believed to be close to the $640,000 figure.

Tort remedies have evolved because of public policy incentives for the protection of individuals from physical, mental, and economic damage. Tort remedies provide economic motivation for individuals and businesses to avoid conduct that could harm others.

The amount of the compensation and the circumstances in which compensation for torts should be paid are issues that courts, juries, and legislatures review. Many legislatures have examined and continue to review the standards for tort liability and damages.

The U.S. Supreme Court devoted several decisions in recent years to dealing with excessive punitive damages in civil litigation, and it has set "guideposts" to be used by courts in assessing punitive damages.* In *State Farm Mutual Automobile Insurance Co. v. Campbell*, compensatory damages for the plaintiffs at the trial court level were $1 million, and punitive damages, based in part on evidence that State Farm's nationwide policy was to underpay claims regardless of merit to enhance profits, were assessed at $145 million. The Supreme Court concluded that the facts of *Campbell* would likely justify a punitive damages award only at or near the amount of compensatory damages. Thus, even those who act very badly as State Farm Insurance did have a constitutionally protected right under the Due Process Clause of the Fourteenth Amendment to have civil law damages assessed in accordance with the Supreme Court's guideposts.

BMW of North America v. Gore, 517 U.S. 559 (1996); *Cooper Industries v. Leatherman Tool Group, Inc.*, 532 U.S. 424 (2001); *State Farm Insurance v. Campbell*, 538 U.S. 408 (2003); *Exxon Shipping Co. v. Baker*, 128 S. Ct. 2605, 2621 (2008).

15. What Is Strict Liability?

Strict liability is an absolute standard of liability imposed by the law in circumstances the courts or legislatures have determined require a high degree of protection. When strict liability is imposed, the result is that the company or person who has caused injury or damages by the conduct will be required to compensate for those damages in an absolute sense. Few, if any, defenses apply in a situation in which the law imposes a strict liability standard. **For Example,** as noted earlier in the chapter, engaging in ultrahazardous activities, such as using dynamite to excavate a site for new construction, results in strict liability for the contractor performing the demolition. Any damages resulting from the explosion are the responsibility of that contractor, so the contractor is strictly liable.

16. Imposing Strict Liability

Strict liability arises in a number of different circumstances, but the most common are in those situations in which a statutory duty is imposed and in product liability. **For Example,** at both the state and federal levels, there are requirements for the use, transportation, and sale of radioactive materials, as well as the disposal of biomedical materials and tools. Any violation of these rules and regulations would result in strict liability for the company or person in violation.

Product liability, while more fully covered in Chapter 25, is another example of strict liability. A product that is defective through its design, manufacture, or instructions and that injures someone results in strict liability for the manufacturer.

LawFlix

Class Action (1991) (R)

This movie depicts the magnitude of damages and recovery when multiple injuries occur. The film provides insights on tort reform and the ethics of lawyers. You can learn about the magnitude of discovery and evidence.

Notting Hill (1999) (PG-13)

A story of famous star gets guy, dumps guy, gets guy back, dumps guy again, and then guy dumps famous star, and on and on. But, the guy owns a bookstore that sells travel books and he has a shoplifter. Hugh Grant, as the guy, illustrates perfection in exercising the shopkeeper's privilege.

MAKE THE CONNECTION

SUMMARY

A *tort* is a civil wrong that affords recovery for damages that result. The three forms of torts are intentional torts, negligence, and strict liability. A tort differs from a crime in the nature of its remedy. Fines and imprisonment result from criminal violations, whereas money damages are paid to those who are damaged by conduct that constitutes a tort. An action may be both a crime and a tort, but the tort remedy is civil in nature.

Selected intentional torts are false imprisonment, defamation, product disparagement, contract interference or tortious interference, and trespass. False imprisonment is the detention of another without his or her permission. False imprisonment is often called the *shopkeeper's tort* because store owners detain suspected shoplifters. Many states provide a privilege to store owners if they detain shoplifting suspects based on reasonable cause and in a reasonable manner. Defamation is slander (oral) or libel (written) and consists of false statements about another that damage the person's reputation or integrity. Truth is

an absolute defense to defamation, and there are some privileges that protect against defamation, such as those for witnesses at trial and for members of Congress during debates on the floor. There is a developing privilege for employers when they give references for former employees. Invasion of privacy is intrusion into private affairs; public disclosure of private facts; or appropriation of someone's name, image, or likeness for commercial purposes.

To establish the tort of negligence, one must show that there has been a breach of duty in the form of a violation of a statute or professional competency standards or of behavior that does not rise to the level of that of a reasonable person. That breach of duty must have caused the foreseeable injuries to the plaintiff, and the plaintiff must be able to quantify the damages that resulted. Possible defenses to negligence include contributory negligence, comparative negligence, and assumption of risk.

Strict liability is absolute liability with few defenses.

LEARNING OUTCOMES

After studying this chapter, you should be able to clearly explain:

A. General Principles

L0.1 Explain the difference between torts and crimes

See the discussion on wrongs that are a violation of a private duty as torts, and wrongs that are a violation of a public duty of crimes, p. 171.
See the O.J. Simpson example of his acquittal of the crime of murder and his civil liability for the torts of wrongful death on p. 171.

L0.2 Identify the possible tort theories applicable to transmission of disease cases
See the transmission of herpes example on p. 172.

B. Intentional Torts

L0.3 Distinguish between an assault and a battery

See the "kick your butt" threat example of an assault on p. 173.

L0.4 Explain the three different torts of invasion of privacy
See the discussion of the intrusion into a person's private affairs, public disclosure of private facts, and right to publicity torts beginning on p. 175.
See the *Schlein* case involving commercial misappropriation of one's name on pp. 176–177.

L0.5 Explain the torts of defamation and defenses
See the discussion of slander, libel, and trade libel beginning on p. 177.
See the discussion of the requirement of the enhanced element of malice for cases in which the victim is a public figure, p. 177.

C. Negligence

L0.6 Explain the elements of negligence and defenses

See the discussion of the elements of negligence: duty, breach of duty, and causation and damages beginning on p. 181.
See the discussion of the defenses of contributory negligence, comparative negligence, assumption of risk, and immunity beginning on p. 183.

D. Strict Liability

L0.7 Explain the tort of strict liability and why very few defenses are avaliable
See the dynamite excavation example, holding the contractor liable for any damages with no defenses because of the hazardous activity, p. 187.

KEY TERMS

absolute privilege
contract interference
contributory negligence
defamation
false imprisonment
intentional infliction of
  emotional distress

intentional torts
invasion of privacy
libel
malpractice
negligence
product disparagement
qualified privilege

shopkeeper's privilege
slander
strict liability
tort
trade libel
trespass

QUESTIONS AND CASE PROBLEMS

1. Christensen Shipyards built a 155-foot yacht for Tiger Woods at its Vancouver, Washington, facilities. It used Tiger's name and photographs relating to the building of the yacht in promotional materials for the shipyard without seeking his permission. Was this a right of publicity tort because Tiger could assert that his name and photos were used to attract attention to the shipyard to obtain commercial advantage? Did the shipyard have a First Amendment right to present the truthful facts regarding their building of the yacht and the owner's identity as promotional materials? Does the fact that the yacht was named *Privacy* have an impact on this case? Would it make a difference as to the outcome of this case if the contract for building the yacht had a clause prohibiting the use of Tiger's name or photo without his permission?

2. ESPN held its Action Sports and Music Awards ceremony in April, at which celebrities in the fields of extreme sports and popular music such as rap and heavy metal converged. Well-known musicians Ben Harper and James Hetfield were there, as were popular rappers Busta Rhymes and LL Cool J. Famed motorcycle stuntman Evel Knievel, who is commonly thought of as the "father of extreme sports," and his wife Krystal were photographed. The photograph depicted Evel, who was wearing a motorcycle jacket and rose-tinted sunglasses, with his right arm around Krystal and his left arm around another young woman. ESPN published the photograph on its "extreme sports" Web site with a caption that read "Evel Knievel proves that you're never too old to be a pimp." The Knievels brought suit against ESPN, contending that the photograph and caption were defamatory because they accused Evel of soliciting prostitution and implied that Krystal was a prostitute. ESPN contends that the caption was a figurative and slang usage and was not defamatory as a matter of law. Decide. [*Knievel v. ESPN*, 393 F.3d 1068 (9th Cir.)]

3. While snowboarding down a slope at Mammoth Mountain Ski Area (Mammoth), 17-year-old David Graham was engaged in a snowball fight with his 14-year-old brother. As he was "preparing to throw a snowball" at his brother, David slammed into Liam Madigan, who was working as a ski school instructor for Mammoth, and injured him. Madigan sued Graham for damages for reckless and dangerous behavior. The defense contended that the claim was barred under the doctrine of assumption of the risk, applicable in the state, arising from the risk inherent in the sport that allows for vigorous participation and frees a participant from a legal duty to act with due care. Decide. [*Mammoth Mountain Ski Area v. Graham*, 38 Cal. Rptr. 3d 422 (Cal. App.)]

4. Following a visit to her hometown of Coalinga, Cynthia wrote "An Ode to Coalinga" (Ode) and posted it in her online journal on MySpace.com. Her last name did not appear online. Her page included her picture. The Ode opens with "The older I get, the more I realize how much I despise Coalinga" and then proceeds to make a number of extremely negative comments about Coalinga and its inhabitants. Six days later, Cynthia removed the Ode from her journal. At the time, Cynthia was a student at UC Berkeley, and her parents and sister were living in Coalinga. The Coalinga High School principal, Roger Campbell, submitted the Ode to the local newspaper, the *Coalinga Record*, and it was published in the Letters to the Editor section, using Cynthia's full name. The community reacted violently to the Ode, forcing the family to close its business and move. Cynthia and her family sued Campbell and the newpaper on the right-of-privacy theory of public disclosure of private facts. What are the essential element of this theory? Was Cynthia and her family's right of privacy violated? [*Moreno v. Hanford Sentinel, Inc.*, 91 Cal. Rptr. 3d 858 (Cal. App.)]

5. JoKatherine Page and her 14-year-old son Jason were robbed at their bank's ATM at 9:30 P.M. one evening by a group of four thugs. The thieves took $300, struck Mrs. Page in the face with a gun, and ran. Mrs. Page and her son filed suit against the bank for its failure to provide

adequate security. Should the bank be held liable? [*Page v. American National Bank & Trust Co.,* 850 S.W.2d 133 (Tenn.)]

6. A Barberton Glass Co. truck was transporting large sheets of glass down the highway. Elliot Schultz was driving his automobile some distance behind the truck. Because of the negligent way that the sheets of glass were fastened in the truck, a large sheet fell off the truck, shattered on hitting the highway, and then bounced up and broke the windshield of Shultz's car. He was not injured but suffered great emotional shock. He sued Barberton to recover damages for this shock. Barberton denied liability on the ground that Schultz had not sustained any physical injury at the time or as the result of the shock. Should he be able to recover? [*Schultz v. Barberton Glass Co.,* 447 N.E.2d 109 (Ohio)]

7. Mallinckrodt produces nuclear and radioactive medical pharmaceuticals and supplies. Maryland Heights Leasing, an adjoining business owner, claimed that low-level radiation emissions from Mallinckrodt damaged its property and caused a loss in earnings. What remedy should Maryland Heights have? What torts are involved here? [*Maryland Heights Leasing, Inc. v. Mallinckrodt, Inc.,* 706 S.W.2d 218 (Mo. App.)]

8. An owner abandoned his van in an alley in Chicago. In spite of repeated complaints to the police, the van was allowed to remain in the alley. After several months, it was stripped of most of the parts that could be removed. Jamin Ortiz, age 11, was walking down the alley when the van's gas tank exploded. The flames from the explosion set fire to Jamin's clothing, and he was severely burned. Jamin and his family brought suit brought against the city of Chicago to recover damages for his injuries. Could the city be held responsible for injuries caused by property owned by someone else? Why or why not? [*Ortiz v. Chicago,* 398 N.E.2d 1007 (Ill. App.)]

9. Carrigan, a district manager of Simples Time Recorder Co., was investigating complaints of mismanagement of the company's Jackson office. He called at the home of Hooks, the secretary of that office, who expressed the opinion that part of the trouble was caused by the theft of parts and equipment by McCall, another employee. McCall was later discharged and sued Hooks for slander. Was she liable? [*Hooks v. McCall,* 272 So.2d 925 (Miss.)]

10. Defendant no. 1 parked his truck in the street near the bottom of a ditch on a dark, foggy night. Iron pipes carried in the truck projected nine feet beyond the truck in back. Neither the truck nor the pipes carried any warning light or flag, in violation of both a city ordinance and a state statute. Defendant no. 2 was a taxicab owner whose taxicab was negligently driven at an excessive speed. Defendant no. 2 ran into the pipes, thereby killing the passenger in the taxicab. The plaintiff brought an action for the passenger's death against both defendants. Defendant no. 1 claimed he was not liable because it was Defendant no. 2's negligence that had caused the harm. Was this defense valid? [*Bumbardner v. Allison,* 78 S.E.2d 752 (N.C.)]

11. Carl Kindrich's father, a member of the Long Beach Yacht Club before he died, expressed a wish to be "buried at sea." The Yacht Club permitted the Kindrich family the use of one of its boats, without charge, for the ceremony, and Mr. Fuller—a good friend of Carl's father—piloted the boat. Portable stairs on the dock assisted the attendees in boarding. Upon returning, Fuller asked for help to tie up the boat. The steps were not there, and Carl broke his leg while disembarking to help tie up the boat. Carl sued the Yacht Club for negligence in failing to have someone on the dock to ensure that the portable steps were available. The Yacht Club contended that it was not liable because Carl made the conscious decision to jump from the moving vessel to the dock, a primary assumption of risk in the sport of boating. The plaintiff contended that he was not involved in the sport of boating, and at most his actions constituted minimal comparative negligence, the type which a jury could weigh in conjunction with the defendant's negligence in assessing damages. Decide. [*Kindrich v. Long Beach Yacht Club,* 84 Cal. Rptr. 3d 824 (Cal. App.)]

12. Hegyes was driving her car when it was negligently struck by a Unjian Enterprises truck. She was injured, and an implant was placed in her body to counteract the injuries. She sued Unjian, and the case was settled. Two years later Hegyes became pregnant. The growing fetus pressed against the implant, making it necessary for her doctor to deliver the child 51 days prematurely by Cesarean section. Because of its premature birth, the child had a breathing handicap. Suit was brought against Unjian Enterprises for the harm sustained by the child. Was the defendant liable? [*Hegyes v. Unjian Enterprises, Inc.*, 286 Cal. Rptr. 85 (Cal. App.)]

13. Kendra Knight took part in a friendly game of touch football. She had played before and was familiar with football. Michael Jewett was on her team. In the course of play, Michael bumped into Kendra and knocked her to the ground. He stepped on her hand, causing injury to a little finger that later required its amputation. She sued Michael for damages. He defended on the ground that she had assumed the risk. Kendra claimed that assumption of risk could not be raised as a defense because the state legislature had adopted the standard of comparative negligence. What happens if contributory negligence applies? What happens if the defense of comparative negligence applies?

14. A passenger on a cruise ship was injured by a rope thrown while the ship was docking. The passenger was sitting on a lounge chair on the third deck when she was struck by the weighted end of a rope thrown by an employee of Port Everglades, where the boat was docking. These ropes, or heaving lines, were being thrown from the dock to the second deck, and the passenger was injured by a line that was thrown too high.

    The trial court granted the cruise line's motion for directed verdict on the ground there was no evidence that the cruise line knew or should have known of the danger. The cruise line contended that it had no notice that this "freak accident" could occur. What is the duty of a cruise ship line to its passengers? Is there liability here? Does it matter that an employee of the port city, not the cruise lines, caused the injury? Should the passenger be able to recover? Why or why not? [*Kalendareva v. Discovery Cruise Line Partnership*, 798 So.2d 804 (Fla. App.)]

15. Blaylock was a voluntary psychiatric outpatient treated by Dr. Burglass, who became aware that Blaylock was violence prone. Blaylock told Dr. Burglass that he intended to do serious harm to Wayne Boynton, Jr., and shortly thereafter he killed Wayne. Wayne's parents then sued Dr. Burglass on grounds that he was liable for the death of their son because he failed to give warning or to notify the police of Blaylock's threat and nature. Was a duty breached here? Should Dr. Burglass be held liable? [*Boynton v. Burglass*, 590 So.2d 446 (Fla. App.)]

© Manuel Gutjahr/iStockphoto.com

CHAPTER 10

Intellectual Property Rights and the Internet

learningoutcomes

After studying this chapter, you should be able to

LO.1 Explain the spectrum of distinctiveness used to classify trademarks and explain why distinctiveness is important

LO.2 Explain how personal names can acquire trademark protection

LO.3 List the remedies available for improper use of trademarks

LO.4 Explain what is and is not copyrightable; explain the fair use defense

LO.5 Explain the "new and not obvious" requirement necessary to obtain a patent

LO.6 List and explain the defensive measures employers take to preserve confidential business information

LO.7 Explain the extent of protection provided owners of software ntellectual property comes in many forms: the writing by an author or the software developed by an employee, the new product or process developed by an inventor, the company name Hewlett-Packard, and the secret formula used to make Coca-Cola. Federal law provides rights to owners of these works, products, company names, and secret formulas that are called *copyrights, patents, trademarks,* and *trade secrets.* State laws provide protection for trade secrets. These basic legal principles are also applicable in an Internet and e-commerce context. This chapter discusses the federal and state laws governing intellectual property rights and their Internet context.

A. TRADEMARKS AND SERVICE MARKS

The Lanham Act, a federal law, grants a producer the exclusive right to register a trademark and prevent competitors from using that mark. This law helps assure a producer that it, not an imitating competitor, will reap the financial, reputation-related rewards of a desirable product. And trademarks reduce consumers' search costs, allowing them to make decisions that more closely coincide with their preferences.

1. Introduction

A mark is any word, name, symbol, device, or combination of these used to identify a product or service.[1] If the mark identifies a product, such as an automobile or soap, it is called a **trademark**. If it identifies a service, such as an airline or dry cleaner, it is called a **service mark**.

trademark – mark that identifies a product.

service mark – mark that identifies a service.

The owner of a mark may obtain protection from others using it by registering the mark in accordance with federal law at the United States Patent and Trademark Office (USPTO) in Washington, D.C.[2] To be registered, a mark must distinguish the goods or services of the applicant from those of others. Under the federal Lanham Act, a register, called the Principal Register, is maintained for recording such marks. Inclusion on the Principal Register grants the registrant the exclusive right to use the mark. Challenges may be made to the registrant's right within five years of registration, but after five years, the right of the registrant is incontestable.

A mark may be "reserved" before starting a business by filing an application for registration on the basis of the applicant's good-faith intent to use the mark. Once the mark is used in trade, then the USPTO will actually issue the registration with a priority date retroactive to the date the application was filed. The applicant has a maximum period of 36 months to get the business started and demonstrate that the mark is in "use in commerce."

---

[1] 15 U.S.C. §1127.
[2] Lanham Act, 15 U.S.C. §§1050–1127.

2. International Registration

Under the Madrid System of International Registration of Marks (the Madrid Protocol), the United States became a party to a treaty providing for the international registration of marks in November 2003. Now U.S. companies that sell products and provide services in foreign countries may register their marks and obtain protection for them in more than 60 signatory countries by filing a single application in English for each mark with the U.S. Patent and Trademark Office.[3] Before the mark can be the subject of an international application, it must have already been registered or applied for with the U.S. Patent and Trademark Office (USPTO). A change in ownership of a mark can be accomplished by a single filing. Renewal is required every 10 years by paying a single renewal fee.

3. Registrable Marks

distinctiveness—capable of serving the source-identifying function of a mark.

Trademark law categorizes marks along a spectrum of **distinctiveness**, based on their capacity to serve a source-identifying function. A mark is classified as (1) coined or fanciful (most distinctive), (2) arbitrary, (3) suggestive, (4) descriptive, and (5) generic (least distinctive). **For Example,** the mark EXXON is fanciful because it was designed by its owner to designate petroleum and related products. The name CENGAGE is a coined creation of the owner of this trademark and has no other meaning in English, but it serves to distinguish the products of its owner from all others. The mark APPLE for computers, an arbitrary mark, consists of a word in common usage that is arbitrarily applied in such a way that it is not descriptive or suggestive. The mark COPPERTONE for suntan lotion is a suggestive mark—requiring some imagination to reach a conclusion about the nature of the product. Coined or fanciful, arbitrary, and suggestive marks may be registered on the Principal Register under the Lanham Act without producing any actual evidence of the source-identifying attribution or the public perception of these marks.

acquired distinctiveness— through advertising, use and association, over time, an ordinary descriptive word or phase has taken on a new source-identifying meaning and functions as a mark in the eyes of the public.

secondary meaning—is a legal term signifying the words in question have taken on a new meaning with the public, capable of serving a source-identifying function of a mark.

Descriptive marks are those that convey an immediate idea of the ingredients, qualities, or characteristics of the goods or service, such as SPORTS ILLUSTRATED for a sports magazine. Because descriptive marks are not inherently capable of serving as source identifiers, such marks may only be registered on the Principal Register after the owner has provided sufficient evidence to establish that the public associates the term or phrase not only with a specific feature or quality, but also with a single commercial source. When a descriptive phrase becomes associated with a single commercial source, the phrase is said to possess "**acquired distinctiveness**" or "**secondary meaning,**" and therefore functions as a trademark. **For Example,** when the public perceives the phrase SPORTS ILLUSTRATED as a particular sports magazine in addition to its primary meaning as a description of a specific feature or element, the phrase has "acquired distinctiveness" or "secondary meaning" and may receive trademark protection.

---

[3] Signatory countries include most U.S. trading partners with the exception of Canada and Mexico.

CASE SUMMARY

No Hogging Generic Terms

FACTS: Beginning in the late 1960s and thereafter, the word *hog* was used by motorcycle enthusiasts to refer to large motorcycles. Into the early 1980s, motorcyclists came to use the word *hog* when referring to Harley-Davidson (Harley) motorcycles. In 1981, Harley itself began using *hog* in connection with its merchandise. In 1983, it formed Harley Owners Group, used the acronym H.O.G., and registered the acronym in conjunction with various logos in 1987. Since 1909, Harley has used variations of its bar-and-shield logo. Ronald Grottanelli opened a motorcycle repair shop under the name The Hog Farm in 1969. At some point after 1981, he sold products such as Hog Wash engine degreaser and a Hog Trivia board game. Grottanelli had used variants of Harley's bar-and-shield logo since 1979 on signs and T-shirts, dropping the name Harley-Davidson from the bar of the logo in 1982 after receiving a letter of protest from the company. He continued to use the bar-and-shield, however, and featured a drawing of a pig wearing sunglasses and a banner with the words "Unauthorized Dealer." From a judgment for Harley for infringement of the bar-and-shield trademark and an injunction prohibiting the use of the word *hog* in reference to some of his products and services, Grottanelli appealed.

DECISION: *Hog* was a generic word in the language as applied to large motorcycles before segments of the public began using it to refer to Harley-Davidson motorcycles. Neither a manufacturer nor the public can withdraw from the language a generic term, already applicable to a category of products, and accord it trademark significance as long as the term retains some generic meaning. It was an error to prohibit Grottanelli from using the word *hog*. Harley must rely on a portion of its trademark to identify the brand of motorcycles, for example, Harley Hogs. Grottanelli was properly enjoined from using the bar-and-shield logo. Grottanelli's mark uses Harley's mark in a somewhat humorous manner to promote his own products, which is not a permitted trademark parody use. The use of the prefix "UN" before "AUTHORIZED DEALER" is no defense. The courts have ordinarily found the use of such disclaimers insufficient to avoid liability for infringement. [***Harley-Davidson, Inc. v. Grottanelli*, 164 F.3d 987 (2d Cir. 1999)**]

Generic terms that describe a "genus" or class of goods such as soap, car, cola, or rosé wine are never registrable because they do not have a capacity to serve as a source identifier.

Ordinarily geographic terms are not registrable on the Principal Register. **For Example,** BOSTON BEER was denied trademark protection because it was a geographic term.[4] However, if a geographic term has acquired a secondary meaning, it would be registrable. **For Example,** the geographic term *Philadelphia* has acquired secondary meaning when applied to cream cheese products.

A personal name can acquire trademark protection if the name has acquired secondary meaning. **For Example,** the name "Paul Frank" is a personal name and as a trademark had acquired significant recognition and fame in the sale of t-shirts, clothing, and accessories designed by Paul Frank Sunich. Mr. Sunich had a falling out with Paul Frank Industries Inc. (PFI), and started his own t-shirt business using his own personal name, Paul Frank Sunich. The court rejected Mr. Sunich's contention that he had a right to use his full name as a trademark, because it was likely to cause consumer confusion with the established famous mark, and the court preliminarily enjoined him from using his "Paul Frank Sunich" mark with the sale of clothing or accessories. It did, however, permit him to use his full name, Paul Frank Sunich, in signatures, business meetings, and other such contexts where the name did not

4 *Boston Beer Co. v. Slesar Bros. Brewing Co.*, 9 F.3d 812 (1st Cir. 1994).

resemble a trademark or trade name, and did not appear on goods similar to those sold by PFI. Where Mr. Sunich's full name was used, there also had to be some clear explanation that Mr. Sunich was no longer affiliated with PFI. For example, his use of the Web site domain name ***www.paulfranksunich.com*** was not enjoined so long as it maintained a message explaining that Mr. Sunich no longer worked for or with PFI.[5]

With a limited number of colors available for use by competitors, along with possible shade confusion, courts had held for some 90 years that color alone could not function as a trademark. The U.S. Supreme Court has overturned this rule, and now if a color serves as a symbol that distinguishes a firm's goods and identifies their source without serving any other significant function, it may, sometimes at least, meet the basic legal requirements for use as a trademark.[6] **For Example,** Owens-Corning Fiberglass Corp. has been allowed to register the color pink as a trademark for its fiberglass insulation products.

4. Remedies for Improper Use of Marks

A person who has the right to use a mark may obtain an injunction prohibiting a competitor from imitating or duplicating the mark. The basic question in such litigation is whether the general public is likely to be confused by the mark of the defendant and to believe wrongly that it identifies the plaintiff's mark.[7] If there is this danger of confusion, the court will enjoin the defendant from using the particular mark.

In some cases, the fact that the products of the plaintiff and the defendant did not compete in the same market was held to entitle the defendant to use a mark that would have been prohibited as confusingly similar if the defendant manufactured the same product as the plaintiff. **For Example,** it has been held that Cadillac, as applied to boats, is not confusingly similar to Cadillac as applied to automobiles; therefore, its use cannot be enjoined.[8]

In addition to broad injunctive relief, the prevailing party may recover lost profits and other actual damages. In cases of willful violations, the court has full discretion to award the plaintiff up to treble damages. In "exceptional cases" the court has discretion to award attorney's fees.

5. Abandonment of Exclusive Right to Mark

An owner who has an exclusive right to use a mark may lose that right. If other persons are permitted to use that mark, it loses its exclusive character and is said to pass into the English language and become generic. Examples of formerly enforceable marks that have made this transition into the general language are *aspirin*, *thermos*, *cellophane*, and *shredded wheat*. Nonuse for three consecutive years is prima facie evidence of abandonment.[9]

6. Trade Dress Protection

Firms invest significant resources to develop and promote the appearance of their products and the packages in which these products are sold so that they are clearly recognizable by consumers.

---

[5] *Paul Frank Industries Inc. v. Paul Sunich*, 502 F. Supp. 2d 1094 (C.D. Cal. 2007).

[6] *Qualitex Co. v. Jacobson Products Co., Inc.*, 514 U.S. 159 (1995).

[7] *Resource Lenders, Inc. v. Source Solutions, Inc.*, 404 F. Supp. 2d 1232 (E.D. Cal. 2005).

[8] *General Motors Corp. v. Cadillac Marine and Boat Co.*, 226 F. Supp. 716 (W.D. Mich. 1964). See also *Amstar Corp. v. Domino's Pizza Inc.*, 615 F.2d 252 (5th Cir. 1980), where the mark Domino as applied to pizza was not held to be confusingly similar to Domino as applied to sugar.

[9] *Doeblers' Pennsylvania Hybrids, Inc. v. Doebler*, 442 F.3d 812 (3rd Cir. 2006).

trade dress – product's total image including its overall packaging look.

Trade dress involves a product's total image and, in the case of consumer goods, includes the overall packaging look in which each product is sold.

When a competitor adopts a confusingly similar trade dress, it dilutes the first user's investment and goodwill and deceives consumers, hindering their ability to distinguish between competing brands. The law of trade dress protection was initially settled by the U.S. Supreme Court in 1992,[10] and courts have subsequently become more receptive to claims of trade dress infringement under Section 43(a) of the Lanham Act. To prevail, a plaintiff must prove that its trade dress is distinctive and nonfunctional and the defendant's trade dress is confusingly similar to the plaintiff's.[11] **For Example,** Jose Cuervo International was found to have infringed upon Maker's Mark Distillery's red dripping-wax-seal trade dress element used on its bourbon bottles when it used a similar element on its tequila bottles. The court held that the wax seal was not functional because there was more than one way to seal a bottle. The strength of the mark and the likelihood of the confusion were additional factors supporting the court's decision.[12]

7. Limited Lanham Act Protection of Product Design

Trade dress originally included only the packaging and "dressing" of a product, but in recent years, federal courts of appeals' decisions have expanded trade dress to encompass the design of a product itself. Some manufacturers have been successful in asserting Section 43(a) Lanham Act protection against "knockoffs"—that is, copies of their furniture designs, sweater designs, and handbag designs. In this context Samara Brothers, Inc., discovered that Wal-Mart Stores, Inc., had contacted a supplier to manufacture children's outfits based on photographs of Samara garments, and Wal-Mart was selling these so-called knockoffs. Samara sued Wal-Mart, claiming infringement of unregistered trade dress under Section 43(a) of the Lanham Act. The matter progressed to the U.S. Supreme Court, which considered whether a product's design can be distinctive and, therefore, protectable under Section 43(a) of the Lanham Act. The Court set aside the trial court's decision in favor of Samara Brothers and concluded that a product's design is not inherently distinctive and can only meet the "distinctiveness" element required in a Section 43(a) case by a showing of secondary meaning. That is, the manufacturer must show that the design has come to be known by the public as identifying the product in question and its origin. The matter was remanded for further proceeding consistent with the Court's decision.[13]

It is clear from the Supreme Court's *Wal-Mart Stores, Inc. v. Samara Bros, Inc.* decision that ordinarily only famous designers whose works are widely recognized by the public by their design alone, such as certain Tommy Hilfiger and Ralph Lauren garments, Dooney & Bourke handbags, and Movado watches, will be able to successfully pursue Section 43(a) trade dress protection for their designs against knockoff versions of their work sold under Wal-Mart or other private labels. Of course if a manufacturer's design is copied along with the manufacturer's labels or logo, the makers and sellers of these counterfeit goods are always in clear violation of the Lanham Act.[14] As discussed later, design patents also have limited applicability and protect new and nonobvious ornamental features of a product.

[10] *Two Pesos, Inc. v. Taco Cabana, Inc.*, 505 U.S. 763 (1992).
[11] *Clicks Billiards v. Sixshooters, Inc.*, 251 F.3d 1252 (9th Cir. 2001); and *Woodsland Furniture, LLC v. Larsen*, 124 P.3d, 1016 (Idaho 2005).
[12] *Maker's Mark Distillery, Inc. v. Jose Cuervo International*, 679 F.3d 410 (6th Cir. 2012).
[13] *Wal-Mart Stores, Inc. v. Samara Bros, Inc.*, 529 U.S. 205 (2000).
[14] See *Gucci America Inc. v. Tyrell-Miller*, 678 F. Supp. 2d 117 (S.D.N.Y. 2008), where the court assessed Ms. Miller damages of $200,000 for each of the 15 trademark violations incurred for selling counterfeit Gucci handbags on her Web site.

8. Prevention of Dilution of Famous Marks

The Federal Trademark Dilution Act of 1995 (FTDA
against the "commercial use" of another's famous mark
in a "dilution of the distinctive quality of the mark."
discordant uses, such as Du Pont shoes, Buick aspirin
ordinary trademark infringement action, a dilution a
competition and likelihood of confusion. The act wa
that a plaintiff need not prove actual injury to the economic va
mark to prevail in the lawsuit. In addition, the revised act permits truthful
comparative advertising and a "fair use" defense for parodying a famous mark.[16]

9. Internet Domain Names and Trademark Rights

An *Internet domain name* is a unique address by which an Internet resource can be
identified and found by a Web browser accessing the Internet. Examples of
commercial Internet domain names are "Amazon.com," "Priceline.com," and the
publisher of this book, "Cengage.com." These domain names match the names of
their respective businesses, and these domain names are also trademarks.

Any unused domain name can be registered on a first-come, first-served basis for a
rather modest fee, so long as the name differs from a previously registered name by at
least one character. **For Example,** Facebook, Inc., was allowed to bring a trademark
dilution claim against Teachbook.com LLC, alleging that the TEACHBOOK mark
"impairs the distinctiveness of the FACEBOOK mark."[17]

In 2012 the Internet Corporation for Assigned Names and Numbers (ICANN)
initiated a process for selecting entities to manage new Web address endings,
including, .app, .home, .music, and .fun. Trademark owners were allowed to file
objections against applications if the name sought was confusingly similar to the
objector's own trademark.

(A) CYBERSQUATTERS. Cybersquatters are individuals who register and set up domain
names on the Internet that are identical, or confusingly similar, to existing
trademarks that belong to others or are the personal names of famous persons. The
cybersquatter hopes to sell or "ransom" the domain name to the trademark owner or
the famous individual.

Because the extent of the legal remedies available to famous companies or famous
individuals who have been victims of cybersquatters has not always been certain,
Congress passed the Federal Anticybersquatting Consumer Protection Act (ACPA)[18]
in 1999 to prohibit the practice of cybersquatting and cyberpiracy and to provide
clear and certain remedies. However, to be successful in a ACPA lawsuit, the plaintiff
must prove that the name is famous and that the domain name was registered in bad
faith.[19] Remedies include (1) injunctive relief preventing the use of the name,
(2) forfeiture of the domain name, and (3) attorney fees and costs. In addition,

> **cybersquatters** – term for
> those who register and set up
> domain names on the Internet
> for resale to the famous users of
> the names in question.

---

[15] 15 U.S.C. §125(c)(1).

[16] Trademark Dilution Revision Act (2005).

[17] *Facebook, Inc. v. Teachbook.com LLC,* 819 F. Supp. 2d 764 (N.D. Ill. 2011).

[18] Pub. L. 106, 113 Stat. 1536, 15 U.S.C. §1051.

[19] A plaintiff must meet the burden of proof, however, that its mark is "famous," in order to come within the protection of the ACPA, with the courts requiring the marks
be highly distinctive and thus well known throughout the country. Among the marks courts have ruled not to be distinctive are "Blue Man Group," the performing group;
"Clue," the board game; and "Trek," for bicycles. In contrast, marks that have been ruled famous include "Nike," "Pepsi," and "Victoria's Secret." See *Philbrick v. eNom
Inc.,* 593 F. Supp. 2d 352, 367 (D. N.H. 2009). But see *DSPT International, Inc. v. Nahum,* 624 F.3d 1213 (9th Cir. 2010), where a former employee's actions of removing
access to the Internet Web site at a domain name containing the employer's trademark, and withholding the domain name from the employer to obtain leverage in a dispute
with the employer, constituted "cyberpiracy" under the language of Anti-Cybersquatting Protection Act.

trademark owners may obtain damages and the profits that cybersquatters made from the use of the name.

A safe harbor exists under the ACPA for defendants who both "believed and had reasonable grounds to believe that the use of the domain name was fair use or otherwise lawful."[20] A defendant who acts even partially in bad faith in registering a domain name is not entitled to the shelter of the safe harbor provision.

For Example, Howard Goldberg, the president of Artco, is an operator of Web sites that sell women's lingerie and other merchandise. He registered a domain name **http://www.victoriassecrets.net** to divert consumers to his Web sites to try to sell them his goods. The court rejected his ACPA safe harbor defense that he intended in good faith to have customers compare his company's products with those of Victoria's Secret. The fact that Victoria's Secret is a distinctive or famous mark deserving of the highest degree of trademark protection, coupled with the fact that the defendant added a mere *s* to that mark and gave false contact information when he requested the domain name, indicates that he and his company acted in bad faith and intended to profit from the famous mark.[21]

(B) DISPUTE AVOIDANCE. To avoid the expense of trademark litigation, it is prudent to determine whether the Internet domain name selected for your new business is an existing registered trademark or an existing domain name owned by another. Commercial firms provide comprehensive trademark searches for less than $500. Determining whether a domain name is owned by another may be done online at **www.internic.net/whois.html**.

The Internet Corporation for Assigned Names and Numbers (ICANN) provides fast-track arbitration procedures to protect trademark owners from conflicting online

E-Commerce & Cyberlaw

Metatags describe the contents of a Web site using keywords. Some search engines search metatags to identify Web sites related to a search. In *Playboy Enterprises, Inc. (PEI) v. WELLES,** PEI sued "Playmate of the year 1981" Terri Welles for using that and other phrases involving PEI's trademarks on her Internet Web site metatags. Some search engines that use their own summaries of Web sites, or that search the entire text of sites, would be likely to identify Welles's site as relevant to a search for "Playboy" or "Playmate," thus allowing Welles to trade on PEI's marks, PEI asserted. Remembering that the purpose of a trademark is not to provide a windfall monopoly to the mark owner but to prevent confusion over the source of products or services, the court applied a three-factor test for normative use to this case: (1) the product or service must be one not readily identifiable without the use of the mark, (2)

only so much of the mark may be used as reasonably necessary to identify the product or service, and (3) the user must not suggest sponsorship or endorsement by the trademark holder.

Welles had no practical way of describing herself without using the trademark terms. The court stated, "We can hardly expect someone searching for Welles's site...to describe Welles without referring to Playboy—as the nude model selected by Mr. Hefner's organization."

The court stated that there is no descriptive substitute for the trademarks used in Welles's metatags, and to preclude their use would inhibit the free flow of information on the Internet, which is not a goal of trademark law. Moreover, the metatag use was reasonable use to identify her products and services and did not suggest sponsorship, thus satisfying the second and third elements of the court's test.

*Playboy Enterprises, Inc. v. Welles, 279 F.3d 796 (9th Cir. 2002). See ESS Entertainment 2000, Inc. v. Rockstar Videos Inc., 547 F.3d 1095 (9th Cir. 2008).

---

[20] U.S.C. §1125(d)(1)(B)(ii).
[21] *Victoria's Secret Stores v. Artco,* 194 F. Supp. 2d 204 (S.D. Ohio 2002).

domain names under the auspices of the World Intellectual Property Organization (WIPO). **For Example,** Victoria's Secret stores arbitrated the "victoriassecrets.net" domain name held by Howard Goldberg's company, and the arbitration panel transferred the ownership of the name to Victoria's Secret stores. Victoria's Secret stores subsequently brought an action against Goldberg and Artco for damages and injunctive relief under trademark law and the ACPA.

B. COPYRIGHTS

copyright – exclusive right given by federal statute to the creator of a literary or an artistic work to use, reproduce, and display the work.

A **copyright** is the exclusive right given by federal statute to the creator of a literary or an artistic work to use, reproduce, and display the work. Under the international treaty called the *Berne Convention*, copyright of the works of all U.S. authors is protected automatically in all Berne Convention nations that have agreed under the treaty to treat nationals of other member countries like their own nationals.

A copyright prevents not the copying of an idea but only the copying of the way the idea is expressed.[22] That is, the copyright is violated when there is a duplication of the words, pictures, or other form of expression of the creator but not when there is just use of the idea those words, pictures, or other formats express.

The Copyright Act does not apply extraterritorially. However, if the infringement is completed in the United States and the copied work is then disseminated overseas, there is liability under the act for the resulting extraterritorial damages. **For Example,** the Los Angeles News Service (LANS), an independent news organization, produced two copyrighted videotapes of the beating of Reginald Denny during the Los Angeles riots of April 1992, and LANS licensed them to NBC for use on the *Today Show* in New York. Visnews taped the works and transmitted them by satellite to Reuters in London, which provided copies to its overseas subscribers. The infringement by Visnews occurred in New York, and Visnews was liable for the extraterritorial damages that resulted from the overseas dissemination of the work.[23]

It is a violation of U.S. copyright law for satellite carriers to capture signals of network stations in the United States and transmit them abroad. **For Example,** PrimeTime's satellite retransmission of copyrighted NFL football games to satellite dish owners in Canada was held to be a violation of U.S. copyright law, notwithstanding testimony of PrimeTime's CEO that a law firm in Washington, D.C., told him that U.S. law did not pertain to the distribution of products in Canada. The NFL was awarded $2,557,500 in statutory damages.[24]

10. Duration of Copyright

Article 1, Section 8, of the U.S. Constitution empowered Congress to

> *promote the Progress of Science and useful Arts, by securing for limited times to Authors and Inventors the exclusive Right to their respective Writings and Discoveries.*

The first U.S. copyright statute was enacted soon after in 1790 and provided protection for any "book, map or chart" for 14 years, with a privilege to renew for an additional 14 years. In 1831, the initial 14-year term was extended to 28 years, with a

---

[22] *Attia v. New York Hospital*, 201 F.3d 50 (2d Cir. 2000).
[23] *Los Angeles News Service v. Reuters*, 149 F.3d 987 (9th Cir. 1998).
[24] *National Football League v. PrimeTime 24 Joint Venture*, 131 F. Supp. 2d 458 (S.D.N.Y. 2001).

privilege for an additional 14 years. Under the 1909 Copyright Act, the protection period was for 28 years, with a right of renewal for an additional 28 years.

The Copyright Act of 1976 set the duration of a copyright at the life of the creator of the work plus 50 years. Under the Sonny Bono Copyright Term Extension Act of 1998, the duration has been extended to the life of the creator plus 70 years.[25] If a work is a "work made for hire"—that is, a business pays an individual to create the work—the business employing the creator registers the copyright. Under the 1998 Extension Act, such a copyright has been extended by 20 years and now runs for 120 years from creation or 95 years from publication of the work, whichever period is shorter. After a copyright has expired, the work is in the public domain and may be used by anyone without cost.[26]

11. Copyright Notice

Prior to March 1, 1989, the author of an original work secured a copyright by placing a copyright notice on the work, consisting of the word *copyright* or the symbol©, the year of first publication, and the name or pseudonym of the author. The author was also required to register the copyright with the Copyright Office. Under the Berne Convention Implementation Act of 1988,[27] a law that adjusts U.S. copyright law to conform to the Berne Convention, it is no longer mandatory that works published after March 1, 1989, contain a notice of copyright. However, placing a notice of copyright on published works is strongly recommended. This notice prevents an infringer from claiming innocent infringement of the work, which would reduce the amount of damages owed. To bring a copyright infringement suit for a work of U.S. origin, the owner must have submitted two copies of the work to the Copyright Office in Washington, D.C., for registration.

12. What Is Copyrightable?

Copyrights protect literary, musical, dramatic, and artistic work. Protected are books and periodicals; musical and dramatic compositions; choreographic works; maps; works of art, such as paintings, sculptures, and photographs; motion pictures and other audiovisual works; sound recordings; architectural works; and computer programs.

The work must be original, independently created by the author, and possess at least some minimal degree of creativity.[28] **For Example,** William Darden, a Web page designer, challenged the Copyright Office's denial of a copyright registration for a series of existing maps with some changes in the nature of shading, coloring, or font. A court found that the Copyright Office acted within its discretion when it denied Darden's registration with the finding by the examiner from the Visual Arts Section that the maps were "representations of the preexisting census maps in which the creative spark is utterly lacking or so trivial as to be virtually nonexistent."[29]

13. Copyright Ownership and the Internet

Businesses today commonly use offsite programming services to create copyrightable software, with the delivery of code over the Internet. As set forth previously, when a

[25] P.L. 105-298, 112 Stat. 2827, 17 U.S.C. §302(b).

[26] Without the Sonny Bono Extension Act of 1998, the copyright on Mickey Mouse, created by Walt Disney Co. in 1928, was set to expire in 2003 and enter the public domain. Pluto, Goofy, and Donald Duck would have followed soon after.

[27] P.L. 100-568, 102 Stat. 2854, 17 U.S.C. §101 et seq.

[28] *Feist Publications Inc. v. Rural Telephone Services Co.*, 499 U.S. 340 (1991).

[29] *Darden v. Peters*, 402 F. Supp. 2d 638 (E.D. N.C. 2005).

business pays an employee to create a copyrightable work, it is a "work for hire" and the business employing the creator owns and may register the copyright. On the other hand, if a freelancer is employed offsite to create software for a fixed fee without a contract setting forth the ownership of the work, the freelancer owns the work product and the company utilizing the freelancer has a license to use the work product but does not have ownership of it. To avoid disputes about ownership of custom software, a written contract that addresses these ownership and license questions is necessary.

14. Rights of Copyright Holders

A copyright holder has the exclusive right to (1) reproduce the work; (2) prepare derivative works, such as a script from the original work; (3) distribute copies of recordings of the work; (4) publicly perform the work, in the case of plays and motion pictures; and (5) publicly display the work, in the case of paintings, sculptures, and photographs. **For Example,** David LaChapelle is a photographer and director with a worldwide reputation for his unique body of work in fashion and editorial photography, defined by its saturating, vibrant colors and theatrical, often surreal composition. He charges up to $1 million to direct/produce a music video. "Def Jam" released a music video for Rihanna's song "S&M." Prospective directors of the music video had been asked by Rihanna or persons acting on her behalf to make a "LaChapelle-esque music video." LaChapelle contends that the defendants used protected expressions from eight of his photographs in the video and that an ordinary observer might find Rihanna's "Presence" to be substantially similar to LaChapelle's protectable expression in "Noisy Fame." Accordingly, the district court denied the defendant's motion to dismiss the copyright infringement case.[30]

The copyright owner may assign or license some of the rights listed and will receive royalty payments as part of the agreement. The copyright law also ensures royalty payments. **For Example,** Jessie Riviera is a songwriter whose songs are sung at public performances and are recorded by performers on records, tapes, and CDs. Jessie is entitled to royalties from the public performance of her works. Such royalties are collected by two performing rights societies, the American Society of Composers, Authors, and Publishers (ASCAP) and Broadcast Music, Inc. (BMI), which act on behalf of the copyright holders. Jessie is also entitled to so-called mechanical royalties that refer to the royalty stream derived from "mechanically" reproduced records, tapes, and CDs.[31] The principal payers of mechanical royalties are record companies, and the rates are set by the Copyright Royalty Tribunal.

In addition to rights under the copyright law and international treaties, federal and state laws prohibit record and tape piracy.

15. Limitation on Exclusive Character of Copyright

A limitation on the exclusive rights of copyright owners exists under the principle of *fair use*, which allows limited use of copyrighted material in connection with criticism, news reporting, teaching, and research. Four important factors to consider when judging whether the use made in a particular case is fair use include the following:

[30] *LaChapelle v. Fenty*, 812 F. Supp. 2d 434 (S.D.N.Y. 2011).
[31] The ASCAP was formed in 1914 by eminent American composers including Victor Herbert and John Philip Sousa. BMI was formed in 1939. Public performance royalties collected by these societies exceed $1.5 billion per year and are distributed according to elaborate formulas.

1. The purpose and character of the use, including whether such use is of a commercial nature or is for nonprofit educational purposes[32]

2. The nature of the copyrighted work

3. The amount and substantiality of the portion used in relation to the copyrighted work as a whole

4. The effect of the use on the potential market for or value of the copyrighted work[33]

CASE SUMMARY

Fair Use or Not Fair Use—That Is the Question

FACTS: The American Geophysical Union and 82 other publishers of scientific and technical journals brought a class-action lawsuit against Texaco, claiming that Texaco's unauthorized photocopying of articles from their journals constituted a copyright infringement. Texaco's defense was that the copying was fair use under Section 107 of the Copyright Act of 1976. To avoid extensive discovery, the parties agreed to focus on one randomly selected Texaco scientist, Dr. Donald Chickering, who had photocopies of eight articles from the *Journal of Catalysis* in his files. The trial court judge held that the copying of the eight articles did not constitute fair use, and Texaco appealed.

DECISION: Judgment for the publishers. Applying the four statutory standards to determine whether Texaco's photocopying of the scientific journal articles was fair use, three of the four factors favor the publishers. The first factor, purpose and character of use, favors the publishers because the purpose of Texaco's use was to multiply the number of copies for the benefit of its scientists, which is the same purpose for which additional subscriptions are normally sold. The second factor, the nature of the copyrighted work, which in this case is scientific articles, favors Texaco. The third factor, the amount and substantiality of the portion used, favors the publishers because Texaco copied the entire works. The fourth factor, effect on the potential market or value of the work, favors the publishers because they have shown substantial harm due to lost licensing revenue and lost subscription revenue. The aggregate assessment is that the photocopying was not fair use. [*American Geophysical Union v. Texaco Inc.*, **60 F.3d 913 (2d Cir. 1995)**]

First Amendment privileges of freedom of speech and the press are preserved through the doctrine of *fair use*, which allows for use of portions of another's copyrighted work for matters such as comment and criticism. Parodies and caricatures are the most penetrating forms of criticism and are protected under the fair use doctrine. Moreover, while injunctive relief is appropriate in the vast majority of copyright infringement cases because the infringements are simply piracy, in the case of parodies and caricatures where there are reasonable contentions of fair use, preliminary injunctions to prevent publication are inappropriate. The copyright owner can be adequately protected by an award of damages should infringement be found. **For Example,** Suntrust Bank, the trustee of a trust that holds the copyright to Margaret Mitchell's *Gone with the Wind*, one of the all-time best-selling books in

[32] In *Princeton University Press v. Michigan Document Services, Inc.*, 99 F.3d 1381 (6th Cir. 1996), a commercial copyshop reproduced "coursepacks" and sold them to students attending the University of Michigan. The court refused to consider the "use" as one for nonprofit educational purposes because the use challenged was that of the copyshop, a for-profit corporation that had decided to duplicate copyrighted material for sale to maximize its profits and give itself a competitive edge over other copyshops by declining to pay the royalties requested by the holders of the copyrights.

[33] See fair use analysis in *Perfect 10 v. Amazon.com, Inc.*, 487 F.3d 701, 719–725 (9th Cir. 2007).

the world, obtained a preliminary injunction preventing Houghton Mifflin Co. from publishing Alice Randall's *The Wind Done Gone*. The Randall book is an irreverent parody that turns old ideas upside down. The Court of Appeals set aside the injunction of the federal district court because Houghton Mifflin had a viable fair use defense.[34]

16. Secondary Liability for Infringement

An entity that distributes a device with the object of promoting its use to infringe copyrights as shown by clear expression or other active steps taken to foster the resulting acts of infringement is liable for these acts of infringement by third parties, regardless of the device's lawful uses. **For Example,** Grokster, Ltd., and StreamCast Networks, Inc., distributed free software products that allow all computer users to share electronic files through peer-to-peer networks, so called because users' computers communicate directly with each other, not through central servers. When these firms distributed their free software, each clearly voiced the objective that the recipients use the software to download copyrighted works. These firms derived profits from selling advertising space and streaming ads to the software users. Liability for infringement was established under the secondary liability doctrines of contributory or vicarious infringement.[35]

While copyright holders have historically chosen to litigate against the provider of new technologies rather than the users of the technology, the law is clear that copyright holders may sue individual infringers. **For Example,** Sony and other recording companies successfully sued Goucher College student Joel Tenenbaum for willfully downloading and distributing 30 copyrighted works, and the court assessed statutory damages at $675,000.[36]

Ethics & the Law

The Death of Journalism?

Washington Post columnist Ian Shapira wrote a column entitled "How Gawker Ripped off My Newspaper Story."* He had written a profile on Washington-based "business coach" Anne Loehr, an expert on how people in their 20s and late teens behave in the workplace. He conducted an extensive phone interview with Loehr, attended one of her "Get Wise with Gen Ys" sessions and spent an additional day writing the story. Shapira is provided a living wage, health care, and retirement benefits by *The Post*. Gawker's eight-paragraph posting condensed Loehr's biography with a link to Shapira's story, and utilized Loehr's own words on various points of interest, followed by a "cut and paste" of Shapira's "stuff." It ended with the hyperlinked words "*Washington Post.*"

The newspaper industry is in financial peril. Is there a line that can be drawn between the "fair use" doctrine allowing appropriate quoting and linking, and "parasitic" free-rider Web sites? Shapira asserts that current law allows "the Gawker's of the world to appropriate others' work, repurpose it, and sell ads against it with no payment to or legal recourse for the company that [paid the originator of the story]." Should the copyright law be amended to require those who sell ads against heavily excerpted articles to pay a fee to the originator? Is this payment the ethical thing to do?

*http://www.washingtonpost.com/wp-dyn/content/article/2009/07/31/AR2009073102476.html

---

[34] *Suntrust Bank v. Houghton Mifflin Co.*, 268 F.3d 1257 (11th Cir. 2001). See also *Brownmark Films, LLC. v. Comedy Partners*, 800 F. Supp. 2d 991 (E.D. Wis. 2011), where the federal district court dismissed a copyright infringement lawsuit against the South Park defendants on the basis of fair use defense, in an episode lampooning viral video crazes.

[35] *Metro-Goldwyn-Mayer Studios, Inc. v. Grokster, Ltd.*, 545 U.S. 913 (2005).

[36] *Sony v. Tenenbaum*, 660 F.3d 487 (1st Cir. 2011).

17. Digital Millennium Copyright Act

The Digital Millennium Copyright Act of 1998 (DMCA)[37] was enacted to curb the pirating of software and other copyrighted works, such as books, films, videos, and recordings, by creating civil and criminal penalties for anyone who circumvents encryption software. The law also prohibits the manufacture, import, sale, or distribution of circumvention devices.

Title II of the DMCA provides a "safe harbor" for Internet Service Providers (ISP) from liability for direct, vicarious, and contributory infringement of copyrights provided the ISP (1) does not have actual knowledge of the infringing activity or expeditiously removed access to the problematic material upon obtaining knowledge of infringing activity, (2) does not receive financial benefit directly attributable to the infringing activity, and (3) responded expeditiously upon notification of the claimed infringement.

C. Patents

Under Article 1, Section 8, of the U.S. Constitution, the founding fathers of our country empowered Congress to promote the progress of science by securing for limited times to inventors the exclusive rights to their discoveries. Federal patent laws established under Article 1, Section 8, protect inventors just as authors are protected under copyright law authorized by the same section of the U.S. Constitution.

Thomas Jefferson was the first administrator of the United States' patent system and was the author of the Patent Act of 1793. During his time of administrating the system Jefferson saw clearly the difficulty of deciding what should be patentable. Years after drafting the 1793 Act, he explained that in that Act "the whole was turned over to the judiciary, to be matured into a system, under which everyone might know when his actions were safe and lawful."[38] In practice Congress has left wide latitude for judicial construction of patent law, entrusting the courts to keep pace with advancing industrial and technological developments.

18. Types, Duration, and Notice

There are three types of patents, the rights to which may be obtained by proper filing with the United States Patent and Trademark Office (USPTO) in Washington, D.C. The types and duration of patents are as follows.

(A) Utility Patents. Inventions classified as *utility* or *functional patents* grant inventors of any new and useful process, machine, manufacture, or composition of matter or any new and useful improvement of such devices the right to obtain a patent.[39] Prior to 1995, utility patents had a life of 17 years from the date of grant. Under the Uruguay Round Trade Agreement Act, effective June 8, 1995, the duration of U.S. utility patents was changed from 17 years from the date of grant to 20 years from the date of filing to be consistent with the patent law of World Trade Organization (WTO) member states.

---

[37] 17 U.S.C. §1201.
[38] See *Graham v. John Deere Co. of Kansas City*, 383 U.S.1, 10 (1966).
[39] 35 U.S.C. §101.

(B) DESIGN PATENTS. A second kind of patent exists under U.S. patent law that protects new and nonobvious ornamental features that appear in connection with an article of manufacture.[40] These patents are called *design patents* and have a duration of 14 years. In order to establish design patent infringement, the patent holder has the difficult task of proving, by a preponderance of the evidence, that an ordinary observer (and not the eye of an expert) taking into account the prior art would believe the accused design to be the same as the patented design.[41] **For Example,** the Court of Appeals for the Federal Circuit (CAFC) held that defendant Swisa's Nail Buffer, which features buffer surfaces on all four of its sides, was not "the same as" and thus did not infringe on Egyptian Goddess, Inc.'s patented nail buffer design, which features buffer surfaces on three of its four sides.[42]

(C) PLANT PATENTS. A third type of patent, called a *plant patent*, protects the inventors of asexually reproduced new varieties of plants. The duration is 20 years from the date of filing, the same duration applied to utility patents.

(D) NOTICE. The owner of a patent is required to mark the patented item or device using the word *patent* and must list the patent number on the device to recover damages from an infringer of the patent.

(E) THE AMERICA INVENTS ACT. Federal patent law was amended in 2011 by the America Invents Act (AIA).[43] Section 3 of the Act defines the effective filing date of a claimed invention as the actual filing date of the patent or application for a patent, replacing the current "first to invent" system with a "first to file system." The purpose of this change is to provide the inventor with greater certainty regarding the scope of protection and to promote international uniformity by harmonizing the U.S. patent system with systems used in Europe and other countries with which the United States conducts trade. The AIA provides the option of an expedited patent examination process, with the goal of processing applications within 12 months, as opposed to the ordinary processing period of three to four years. The USPTO fee for this service is an extra $4,800, with a 50% reduction for "small entity" inventors. Under the Act, the USPTO will also speed up the application process, at no additional cost, for inventions that reduce greenhouse emissions or provide energy conservation.

Challenges to patent grants can be made for up to nine months after the patent is granted. The post-grant review is made by a patent examiner.

19. Patentability

Section 101 of the 1952 Patent Act recognizes four categories of subject matter for patent eligibility: (1) processes, (2) machines, (3) manufactures, and (4) compositions of matter. However, even if a claim may be deemed to fit one of these categories, it may not be patent eligible. Phenomena of nature, though just discovered; mental processes; and abstract intellectual concepts are not patentable

---

[40] 35 U.S.C. §173.
[41] *Gorham v. White*, 81 U.S. 511 (1871).
[42] *Egyptian Goddess, Inc. v. SWISA, Inc.*, 545 F.3d 665 (Fed. Cir. 2008).
[43] Pub. L. 112-29, H.R. 1249 enacted September 16, 2011, and effective as of March 16, 2013. Amended 35 U.S.C. §102.

because they are the basic tools of scientific and technological work.[44] **For Example,** Prometheus Laboratories Inc. patented steps for testing the proper dosage level of drug treatments for individuals with gastrointestinal diseases. The Mayo Clinic developed its own test to determine toxicity-risk levels similar to that of Prometheus, and Prometheus sued Mayo for patent infringement. The Supreme Court held that the Prometheus patents were not patent eligible because they were merely instructions to apply the laws of nature.[45]

Once it is established that an invention is patent eligible, a patent may be obtained if the invention is something that is *new and not obvious* to a person of ordinary skill and knowledge in the art or technology to which the invention is related. Whether an invention is new and not obvious in its field may lead to highly technical proceedings before a patent examiner, the USPTO's Board of Patent Appeals, and the U.S. Court of Appeals for the Federal Circuit (CAFC).

For Example, Thomas Devel's application for a patent on complementary DNA (cDNA) molecules encoding proteins that stimulated cell division was rejected by a patent examiner as "obvious" and the rejection was affirmed by the USPTO's Board of Patent Appeals. However, after a full hearing before the CAFC, which focused on the state of research in the field as applied to the patent application, Devel's patent claims were determined to be "not invalid because of obviousness."[46]

Once approved by the Patent and Trademark Office, a patent is presumed valid.[47] However, a defendant in a patent infringement lawsuit may assert a patent's invalidity as a defense to an infringement claim by showing the invention as a whole would have been obvious to a person of ordinary skill in the art when the invention was patented. This showing is called **prior art**. **For Example,** Ron Rogers invented and patented a tree-trimming device that is essentially a chain saw releasably mounted on the end of a telescoping pole. Rogers sued Desa International, Inc. (DIA) for patent infringement after DIA introduced the Remington Pole Saw, a chain saw releasably mounted on the end of a telescoping pole. DIA provided evidence of prior art, citing four preexisting patents dealing with "trimming tools on extension poles" that correlated with Rogers's patent. The court nullified Rogers's patent because it concluded the DIA had met its heavy burden of proof that releasably mounting a lightweight chain saw on the end of a telescoping pole assembly to trim trees would be obvious to a person of ordinary skill in the art.[48]

Patent law has expanded to include human-made microorganisms as patent-eligible subject matter, since such compositions are not nature's handiwork, but the inventor's own work.

prior art—a showing that an invention as a whole would have been obvious to a person of ordinary skill in the art when the invention was patented.

[44] *Gottschalk v. Benson*, 409 U.S. 63, 67 (1972).

[45] *Mayo Collaborative Services v. Prometheus Laboratories, Inc.*, 132 S.Ct. 1289, 1301 (2012). The Court explained in part its rationale: [E]ven though rewarding with patents those who discover new laws of nature and the like might well encourage their discovery, those laws and principles, considered generally, are "the basic tools of scientific and technological work." … And so there is a danger that the grant of patents that tie up their use will inhibit future innovation premised upon them, a danger that becomes acute when a patented process amounts to no more than an instruction to "apply the natural law," or otherwise forecloses more future invention than the underlying discovery could reasonably justify.

[46] *In re Devel*, 51 F.3d 1552 (Fed. Cir. 1995).

[47] See *Microsoft Corp. v. i4i Limited Partnership*, 131 S.Ct. 2238 (2011), where the Supreme Court determined that defenses to patent infringement claims must be proven by clear and convincing evidence.

[48] See *KRS International Co. v. Teleflex, Inc.*, 500 U.S. 398 (2007) for the Supreme Court's recent "obviousness" patent decision, where the Court held that mounting an available sensor on a fixed pivot point of the prior art pedal was a design step well within the grasp of a person of ordinary skill in the relevant art and that the benefit of doing so would be obvious.

CASE SUMMARY

Crude Life Forms Can Be Patented

FACTS: Chakrabarty was a microbiologist. He found a way of creating a bacterium that would break down crude oil. This could not be done by any bacteria that exist naturally. His discovery had a great potential for cleaning up oil spills. When he applied for a patent for this process, the commissioner of patents refused to grant it because what he had done was not a "manufacture" or "composition of matter" within the meaning of the federal statute and because a patent could not be obtained on something that was living. Chakrabarty appealed.

DECISION: Judgment for Chakrabarty. Discovering a way to produce a living organism that is not found in nature is within the protection of the patent laws. The fact that this kind of invention was not known when the patent laws were first adopted has no effect on the decision. The patent laws are to be interpreted according to the facts existing when an application for a patent is made. [*Diamond v. Chakrabarty*, 447 U.S. 303 (1980)]

20. Patentable Business Methods

A 1998 Court of Appeals for the Federal Circuit (CAFC) decision recognized "business methods" as a patent-eligible "process" under Section 101 of the Patent Act.[49] A burgeoning number of business-method patents followed, with the U.S. Supreme Court referencing in its *eBay v. MercExchange* decision the "potential vagueness and suspect validity of some of these patents." A pure business-method patent consists basically of a series of steps related to performing a business process. **For Example,** Patent No. 6,846,131 sets forth a method of doing business with steps for Producing Revenue from Gypsum-Based Refuse Sites. So-called junk patents have also been issued as business-method patents. **For Example,** Patent No. 4,022,227, Method of Concealing Baldness, contains a series of steps for combing one's hair that amount to what is best known as a *comb-over*. Business methods are often in the form of software programs and encompass e-commerce applications.

Recent decisions of the U.S. Court of Appeals for the Federal Circuit, which specializes in patent issues, contained a much more restrictive approach to evaluating the patentability of business methods under Section 101 of the Patent Act.[50] The Supreme Court, however, declined to impose limitations on the Patent Act that are inconsistent with the Act's text.

CASE SUMMARY

Not So Fast Everybody, on the "Machine-or-Transformation" Test

FACTS: Bernard Bilski challenged the denial of his patent application for a method of hedging risk in the field of commodities trading in the energy market based on patent-eligible subject matter. The key claims are claims 1 and 4. Claim 1 describes a series of steps instructing how to hedge risk. Claim 4 puts the concept articulated in claim 1 into a simple mathematical formula. On

---

[49] *State Street Bank v. Signature Financial Group*, 149 F.3d 1368 (Fed. Cir. 1998).
[50] See *In re Bilski*, 545 F.3d 943 (Fed. Cir. 2008) (*en banc*).

CASE SUMMARY

Continued

appeal to the Federal Circuit Court of Appeals (*en banc*), it applied a "machine-or-transformation" test:

> *"A claimed process is surely patent-eligible under §101 if: (1) it is tied to a particular machine or apparatus, or (2) it transforms a particular article into a different state or thing."*

The court determined that Bilski's "business method" of hedging risk in the field of commodities trading was not patent eligible because it was neither "tied to a machine or apparatus," nor did it transform anything. The Supreme Court granted review of the decision.

DECISION: The Court of Appeals incorrectly concluded that this Court has endorsed the machine-or-transformation test as the exclusive test. This Court's precedents establish that the machine-or-transformation test is a useful and important clue, an investigative tool, for determining whether some claimed inventions are processes under §101. It may well provide a sufficient basis for evaluating processes similar to those in the Industrial Age—for example, inventions grounded in a physical or other tangible form. But there are reasons to doubt whether the test should be the sole criterion for determining the patentability of inventions in the Information Age. It would create uncertainty as to the patentability of software, advanced diagnostic medicine techniques, and inventions based on linear programming, data compression, and the manipulation of digital signals.

The argument that business methods are categorically outside of §101's scope is undermined by the fact that federal law explicitly contemplates the existence of at least some business method patents.

In light of Court precedents, however, it is clear that Bilski's application is not a patentable "process." Claims 1 and 4 in his application explain the basic concept of hedging, or protecting against risk: Hedging is a fundamental economic practice long prevalent in our system of commerce and taught in any introductory finance class. The concept of hedging, described in claim 1 and reduced to a mathematical formula in claim 4, is an unpatentable abstract idea. Allowing petitioners to patent risk hedging would pre-empt use of this approach in all fields and would effectively grant a monopoly over an abstract idea. [***Bilski v. Kappos,*** 130 S. Ct. 3218 (2010)]

Believing that many business-method patents are obvious to persons of ordinary skill in their respective fields and have a chilling effect on consumer and public interests, a number of organizations have filed multiple reexamination requests with the USPTO to invalidate these patents.[51]

21. Infringement

The patent owner has the exclusive right to make, use, or sell the invention. The owner may bring suit for patent infringement for unauthorized use of a patent and obtain appropriate monetary damages and injunctive relief.[52] The Patent Act provides for the enhancement of damages upon proof of willful infringement and the award of reasonable attorney's fees in "exceptional cases."[53]

---

[51] See Electronic Frontier Foundation, Patent Busting Project at **www.eff.org/patent/wanted** (April 2009).

[52] See also *Global-Tech Appliances, Inc. v. SEB S.A.,* 131 S.Ct. 2060 (2011), where induced infringement of a patent is also actionable. Global-Tech Appliances, Inc., located in Hong Kong, developed a cool-touch deep fryer for Sunbeam Products by copying the "T-Fal" fryer in violation of SEB's U.S. patent. The Supreme Court agreed that the evidence was sufficient for a jury to find that Global-Tech willfully blinded itself to the infringing nature of the sales it encouraged Sunbeam to make.

[53] See *In re Seagate Technology, LLC,* 497 F.3d 1360 (Fed. Cir. 2007), where the CAFC set a higher "willfulness" standard, requiring at least a showing of objective recklessness on the part of the infringer.

Under the act, the owner has "the right to exclude others from making, using, offering for sale or selling the invention."[54] In *eBay, Inc. v. MercExchange, LLC*, the U.S. Supreme Court dealt with the question of whether the patent holder had the right to obtain the permanent injunctive relief of stopping a business entity from "using" the patented technology in addition to obtaining damages for the patent violation. The threat of a court order may be used to seek high and often unreasonable licensing fees. Major technology companies contended that trial courts should consider multiple factors in deciding whether to issue a permanent injunction.

CASE SUMMARY

"Squeeze Play" Averted

FACTS: eBay and its subsidiary half.com operate popular Internet Web sites that allow private sellers to list goods they wish to sell at either an auction or a fixed price (its "Buy It Now" feature). MercExchange, LLC, sought to license its business-method patent to eBay, but no agreement was reached. In MercExchange's subsequent patent infringement suit, a jury found that its patent was valid, eBay had infringed the patent, and $29.5 million in damages were appropriate. However, the District Court denied MercExchange's motion for permanent injunctions against patent infringement absent exceptional circumstances. MercExchange appealed. The Federal Circuit Court of Appeals reversed, and the U.S. Supreme Court granted *certiorari*.

DECISION: Judgment against MercExchange's position. The traditional four-factor test of equity applied by courts when considering whether to award permanent injunctive relief to a prevailing plaintiff applies to disputes arising under the Patent Act. That test requires a plaintiff to demonstrate that (1) it has suffered an irreparable injury, (2) remedies available at law are inadequate to compensate for that injury, (3) considering the balance of hardships between the plaintiff and defendant, a remedy in equity is warranted, and (4) the public interest would not be disserved by a permanent injunction. The decision to grant or deny such relief is an act of equitable discretion by the district court, reviewable on appeal for abuse of discretion. The Federal Circuit's ruling was vacated and remanded to the district court to apply the four-factor test. [A concurring opinion written by Justice Kennedy and joined by Justices Stevens, Souter, and Breyer stated that "an industry has developed in which firms use patents not as a basis for producing and selling goods but, instead, primarily for obtaining licensing fees. For these firms, an injunction, and the potentially serious sanctions arising from its violation, can be employed as a bargaining tool to charge exorbitant fees to companies that seek to buy licenses to practice the patent." Such may be considered under the four-factor test.] [*eBay, Inc. v. MercExchange, LLC,* **547 U.S. 388 (2006)**]

Under the Supreme Court's "doctrine of equivalents," infringers may not avoid liability for patent infringement by substituting insubstantial differences for some of the elements of the patented product or process. The test for infringement requires an essential inquiry: Does the accused product or process contain elements identical or equivalent to each claimed element of the patented invention?[55]

---

[54] 35 U.S.C. §154(a)(1).
[55] *Warner-Jenkinson v. Hilton Davis Chemical Co.*, 520 U.S. 17 (1997). But see *Festo Corp. v. Shoketsu*, 493 F.3d 1368 (Fed. Cir. 2007).

D. Secret Business Information

A business may have developed information that is not generally known but that cannot be protected under federal law, or a business may want to avoid the disclosure required to obtain a patent or copyright protection of computer software. As long as such information is kept secret, it will be protected under state law relating to trade secrets.[56]

22. Trade Secrets

trade secret – any formula, device, or compilation of information that is used in one's business and is of such a nature that it provides an advantage over competitors who do not have the information.

A **trade secret** may consist of any formula, device, or compilation of information that is used in one's business and is of such a nature that it provides an advantage over competitors who do not have the information. It may be a formula for a chemical compound, a process of manufacturing, treating, or preserving materials. **For Example,** shortly before he departed employment with Siemens, salesman J. J. David e-mailed the wiring schematics for the company's reverse osmosis water desalination units (R.O. units) to his future co-founder of Revo Water Systems, LLC, and also requested and was allowed to observe and assist in the construction of a unit. Two years later a Siemens technician discovered that a Revo unit was a copy of the Siemens R.O. units. Siemens successfully sued David and Revo for breach of the confidentiality agreement David had signed with Siemens. The measure of damages for misappropriation of a trade secret is the profit derived from the misappropriation of the trade secret, which in this case amounted to $908,160 over a 40-month period.[57]

To a limited extent, courts will protect certain confidential customer lists. However, courts will not protect customer lists if customer identities are readily ascertainable from industry or public sources or if products or services are sold to a wide group of purchasers based on their individual needs.[58]

23. Loss of Protection

When secret business information is made public, it loses the protection it had while secret. This loss of protection occurs when the information is made known without any restrictions. In contrast, there is no loss of protection when secret information is shared or communicated for a special purpose and the person receiving the information knows that it is not to be made known to others.

When a product or process is unprotected by a patent or a copyright and is sold in significant numbers to the public, whose members are free to resell to whomever they choose, competitors are free to reverse engineer (start with the known product and work backward to discover the process) or copy the article. **For Example,** Crosby Yacht Co., a boatbuilder on Cape Cod, developed a hull design that is not patented. Maine Boatbuilders, Inc. (MBI), purchased one of Crosby's boats and copied the hull by creating a mold from the boat it purchased. MBI is free to build and sell boats utilizing the copied hull.

---

[56] The Uniform Trade Secrets Act was officially amended in 1985. It is now in force in Alabama, Alaska, Arizona, Arkansas, California, Colorado, Connecticut, Delaware, Florida, Georgia, Hawaii, Idaho, Illinois, Indiana, Iowa, Kansas, Kentucky, Louisiana, Maine, Minnesota, Mississippi, Montana, Nebraska, Nevada, New Hampshire, New Mexico, North Dakota, Ohio, Oklahoma, Oregon, Rhode Island, South Carolina, South Dakota, Utah, Vermont, Virginia, Washington, West Virginia, and Wisconsin. Trade secrets are protected in all states either under the uniform act or common law and under both criminal and civil statutes.

[57] *Siemens Water Technologies Corp. v. Revo Water Systems*, 74 So.3d 824 (La. App. 2011).

[58] *Xpert Automation Systems Corp. v. Vibromatic Co.*, 569 N.E.2d 351 (Ind. App. 1990).

24. Defensive Measures

Employers seek to avoid the expense of trade secret litigation by limiting disclosure of trade secrets to employees with a "need to know." Employers also have employees sign nondisclosure agreements, and they conduct exit interviews when employees with confidential information leave, reminding the employees of the employer's intent to enforce the nondisclosure agreement. In addition, employers have adopted industrial security plans to protect their unique knowledge from "outsiders," who may engage in theft, trespass, wiretapping, or other forms of commercial espionage.

25. Criminal Sanctions

Under the federal Industrial Espionage Act of 1996,[59] knowingly stealing, soliciting, or obtaining trade secrets by copying, downloading, or uploading via electronic means or otherwise with the intention that it will benefit a foreign government or agent is a crime. This act also applies to the stealing or purchasing of trade secrets by U.S. companies or individuals who intend to convert trade secrets to the economic benefit of anyone other than the owner. The definition of trade secret is closely modeled on the Uniform Trade Secrets Act and includes all forms and types of financial, business, scientific, technical, economic, and engineering information. The law requires the owner to have taken "reasonable and proper" measures to keep the information secret. Offenders are subject to fines of up to $500,000 or twice the value of the proprietary information involved, whichever is greater, and imprisonment for up to 15 years.

Corporations may be fined up to $10,000,000 or twice the value of the secret involved, whichever is greater. In addition, the offender's property is subject to forfeiture to the U.S. government, and import-export sanctions may be imposed.

E.   PROTECTION OF COMPUTER SOFTWARE AND MASK WORKS

Computer programs, chip designs, and mask works are protected from infringement with varying degrees of success by federal statutes, restrictive licensing, and trade secrecy.

CPA   ## 26. Copyright Protection of Computer Programs

Under the Computer Software Copyright Act of 1980,[60] a written program is given the same protection as any other copyrighted material regardless of whether the program is written in source code (ordinary language) or object code (machine language). **For Example,** Franklin Computer Corp. copied certain operating-system computer programs that had been copyrighted by Apple Computer, Inc. When Apple sued Franklin for copyright infringement, Franklin argued that the object code on which its programs had relied was an uncopyrightable "method of operation." The Third Circuit held that computer programs, whether in source code or in object code embedded on ROM chips, are protected under the act.[61]

---

[59] P.L. 104–294, 18 U.S.C. §1831 et seq. (1996).
[60] Act of December 12, 1980, P.L. 96–517, 94 Stat. 3015, 17 U.S.C. §§101, 117.
[61] *Apple Computer Inc. v. Franklin Computer Corp.*, 714 F.2d 1240 (3d Cir. 1983).

In determining whether there is a copyright violation under the Computer Software Copyright Act, courts will examine the two programs in question to compare their structure, flow, sequence, and organization. Moreover, the courts in their infringement analysis look to see whether the most *significant* steps of the program are similar rather than whether most of the program's steps are similar. To illustrate a copyright violation, substantial similarity in the structure of two computer programs for dental laboratory record-keeping was found—even though the programs were dissimilar in a number of respects—because five particularly important subroutines within both programs performed almost identically."[62]

The protection afforded software by the copyright law is not entirely satisfactory to software developers because of the distinction made by the copyright law of protecting expressions but not ideas. Also, Section 102(b) of the 1980 Computer Software Copyright Act does not provide protection for "methods of operation." A court has allowed a competitor to copy the identical menu tree of a copyrighted spreadsheet program because it was a noncopyrightable method of operation.[63]

As set forth previously, the Digital Millennium Copyright Act of 1998 was enacted to curb the pirating of a wide range of works, including software.

CPA

27. Patent Protection of Programs

Patents have been granted for computer programs; for example, a method of using a computer to translate from one language to another has been held patentable.

The disadvantage of patenting a program is that the program is placed in the public records and may thus be examined by anyone. This practice poses a potential danger that the program will be copied. To detect patent violators and bring legal action is difficult and costly.[64]

28. Trade Secrets

While primary protection for computer software is found in the Computer Software Copyright Act, industry also uses trade secret law to protect computer programs. When software containing trade secrets is unlawfully appropriated by a former employee, the employee is guilty of trade secret theft.[65]

29. Restrictive Licensing

To retain greater control over proprietary software, it is common for the creator of the software to license its use to others rather than selling it to them. Such licensing agreements typically include restrictions on the use of the software by the licensee and give the licensor greater protection than that provided by copyright law. These restrictions commonly prohibit the licensee from providing, in any manner whatsoever, the software to third persons or subjecting the software to reverse engineering.[66]

---

[62] *Whelen Associates v. Jaslow Dental Laboratory*, 797 F.2d 1222 (3d Cir. 1986).

[63] *Lotus Development Corp. v. Borland International Inc.*, 49 F.3d 807 (1st Cir. 1995), aff'd, 516 U.S. 233 (1996).

[64] The USPTO has adopted guidelines for the examination of computer-related inventions, 61 C.F.R. §§7478–7502.

[65] The National Conference of Commissioners on Uniform State Laws (NCCUSL) has promulgated a new uniform law, the Uniform Computer Information Transactions Act (UCITA), to govern contracts involving the sale, licensing, maintenance, and support of computer software and books in digital form. This uniform act had been identified as Article 2B and was part of the comprehensive revisions to Article 2 of the Uniform Commercial Code. The act is supported by software publishers and opposed by software developers and buyers. The act can be obtained from the NCCUSL at **www.nccusl.org.** Information for and against the UCITA can be found at **www. ucitaonline.com.** The act has been adopted by Maryland and Virginia.

[66] See *Fonar Corp. v. Domenick*, 105 F.3d 99 (2d Cir. 1997).

FIGURE 10-1	*Summary Comparison of Intellectual Property Rights*

TYPE OF INTELLECTUAL PROPERTY	TRADEMARKS	COPYRIGHTS	PATENTS	TRADE SECRETS
PROTECTION	WORDS, NAMES, SYMBOLS, OR DEVICES USED TO IDENTIFY A PRODUCT OR SERVICE	ORIGINAL CREATIVE WORKS OF AUTHORSHIP, SUCH AS WRITINGS, MOVIES, RECORDS, AND COMPUTER SOFTWARE	UTILITY, DESIGN, AND PLANT PATENTS	ADVANTAGEOUS FORMULAS, DEVICES, OR COMPILATION OF INFORMATION
APPLICABLE STANDARD	IDENTIFIES AND DISTINGUISHES A PRODUCT OR SERVICE	ORIGINAL CREATIVE WORKS IN WRITING OR IN ANOTHER FORMAT	NEW AND NONOBVIOUS, ADVANCED IN THE ART	NOT READILY ASCERTAINABLE, NOT DISCLOSED TO THE PUBLIC
WHERE TO APPLY	PATENT AND TRADEMARK OFFICE	REGISTER OF COPYRIGHTS	PATENT AND TRADEMARK OFFICE	NO PUBLIC REGISTRATION NECESSARY
DURATION	INDEFINITE SO LONG AS IT CONTINUES TO BE USED	LIFE OF AUTHOR PLUS 70 YEARS, OR 95 YEARS FROM PUBLICATION FOR "WORKS FOR HIRE"	UTILITY AND PLANT PATENTS, 20 YEARS FROM DATE OF APPLICATION; DESIGN PATENTS, 14 YEARS	INDEFINITE SO LONG AS SECRET IS NOT DISCLOSED TO PUBLIC

© Cengage Learning

30. Semiconductor Chip Protection

mask work—specific form of expression embodied in a chip design, including the stencils used in manufacturing semiconductor chip products.

semiconductor chip product—product placed on a piece of semiconductor material in accordance with a predetermined pattern that is intended to perform electronic circuitry functions.

The Semiconductor Chip Protection Act (SCPA) of 1984[67] created a new form of industrial intellectual property by protecting mask works and the semiconductor chip products in which they are embodied against chip piracy. A **mask work** refers to the specific form of expression embodied in chip design, including the stencils used in manufacturing semiconductor chip products. A **semiconductor chip product** is a product placed on a piece of semiconductor material in accordance with a predetermined pattern that is intended to perform electronic circuitry functions. These chips operate microwave ovens, televisions, computers, robots, X-ray machines, and countless other devices. This definition of semiconductor chip products includes such products as analog chips, logic function chips like microprocessors, and memory chips like RAMS and ROMs.

[67] P.L. 98-620, 98 Stat. 3347, 17 U.S.C. §901.

(A) DURATION AND QUALIFICATIONS FOR PROTECTION. The SCPA provides the owner of a mask work fixed in semiconductor chip products the exclusive right for 10 years to reproduce and distribute the products in the United States and to import them into the United States. The protection of the act applies only to those works that, when considered as a whole, are not commonplace, staple, or familiar in the semiconductor industry.

(B) LIMITATION ON EXCLUSIVE RIGHTS. Under the SCPA's reverse engineering exemption, competitors may not only study mask works but may also use the results of that study to design their own semiconductor chip products embodying their own original masks even if the masks are substantially similar (but not substantially identical) so long as their products are the result of substantial study and analysis, not merely the result of plagiarism.

Innocent infringers are not liable for infringements occurring before notice of protection is given them and are liable for reasonable royalties on each unit distributed after notice has been given them. However, continued purchase of infringing semiconductors after notice has been given can result in penalties of up to $250,000.

(C) REMEDIES. The SCPA provides that an infringer will be liable for actual damages and will forfeit its profits to the owner. As an alternative, the owner may elect to receive statutory damages of up to $250,000 as determined by a court. The court may also order destruction or other disposition of the products and equipment used to make the products. **For Example,** Altera Corporation manufactures programmable logic devices. It was successful in the lawsuit against its competitor Clear Logic, Inc., which works from a different business model. Altera was successful in its lawsuit against Clear Logic under the SCPA, asserting that Clear Logic had copied the layout design of its registered mask works. It also was successful in its claim that Clear Logic induced breach of software licenses with Altera customers. Damages were assessed at $36 million.[68]

LawFlix

The Jerk (1979) (R)

Steve Martin invents a special handle for eyeglasses that is mass marketed by a businessman who gives him a percentage of the royalties from sales. Should Martin be paid?

MAKE THE CONNECTION

SUMMARY

Property rights in trademarks, copyrights, and patents are acquired as provided primarily in federal statutes. A trademark or service mark is any word, symbol, design, or combination of these used to identify a product (in the case of a trademark) or a service (in the case of a service mark). Terms will fall into

[68] *Altera Corp. v. Clear Logic Inc.,* 424 F.3d 1079 (9th Cir. 2005).

one of four categories: (1) generic, (2) descriptive, (3) suggestive, or (4) arbitrary or fanciful. Generic terms are never registrable. However, if a descriptive term has acquired a secondary meaning, it is registrable. Suggestive and arbitrary or fanciful marks are registrable as well. If there is likelihood of confusion, a court will enjoin the second user from using a particular mark.

A copyright is the exclusive right given by federal statute to the creator of a literary or an artistic work to use, reproduce, or display the work for the life of the creator and 70 years after the creator's death.

A patent gives the inventor an exclusive right for 20 years from the date of application to make, use,

and sell an invention that is new and useful but not obvious to those in the business to which the invention is related. Trade secrets that give an owner an advantage over competitors are protected under state law for an unlimited period so long as they are not made public.

Protection of computer programs and the design of computer chips and mask works is commonly obtained, subject to certain limitations, by complying with federal statutes, by using the law of trade secrets, and by requiring restrictive licensing agreements. Many software developers pursue all of these means to protect their proprietary interests in their programs.

LEARNING OUTCOMES

After studying this chapter, you should be able to clearly explain:

A. Trademarks and Service Marks

L0.1 Explain the spectrum of distinctiveness used to classify trademarks and explain why distinctiveness is important

> See the Cengage example, a coined most distinctive mark, p. 195.
> See the Sports Illustrated example, a descriptive mark with acquired distinctiveness, p. 195.
> See the *Harley Davidson* case where H.O.G. was found to be generic and not distinctive at all, p. 196.

L0.2 Explain how personal names can acquire trademark protection

> See the Paul Frank example on p. 196.

L0.3 List the remedies available for improper use of trademarks

> See the applicable remedies of injunctive relief, lost profits, and attorney's fees, p. 197.

B. Copyrights

L0.4 Explain what is and is not copyrightable; explain the fair use defense

> See the discussion on what is copyrightable on p. 202.
> See the Darden example of a denial of a copyright because of lack of creativity, p. 202.

> See the *Wind Done Gone* example of fair use parody p. 205.

C. Patents

L0.5 Explain the "new and not obvious" requirement necessary to obtain a patent

> See the cDNA "not obvious" example on p. 208.
> See the mounted chainsaw "obvious" example on p. 208.
> See the *Bilski* decision where a patent application was found to be an unpatentable abstract idea not entitled to a grant of monopoly, p. 210.

D. Secret Business Information

L0.6 List and explain the defensive measures employers take to preserve confidential business information

> See the discussion on signing and enforcing nondisclosure agreements on p. 212.

E. Protection of Computer Software and Mask Works

L0.7 Explain the extent of protection provided owners of software

> See the Apple Computer example on p. 213.

KEY TERMS

acquired distinctiveness

copyright

cybersquatters

distinctiveness

mask work

prior art

secondary meaning

semiconductor chip product

service mark

trade dress

trade secret

trademark

QUESTIONS AND CASE PROBLEMS

1. China is a signatory country to the Madrid Protocol on the international registration of trademarks. Starbucks opened its first café in China in 1999 and has added outlets in numerous locations including Shanghai and at the Great Wall and the imperial palace in Beijing. Xingbake Café Corp. Ltd. has imitated the designs of Starbuck's cafés in its business coffee café locations in Shanghai. *Xing* (pronounced "Shing") means star, and *bake*, or "bak kuh" is pronounced like "bucks." Does the Seattle, Washington, Starbucks Corporation have standing to bring suit in China against Xingbake Café Corp. Ltd? If so, on what theory? Decide.

2. Cable News Network with its principal place of business in Atlanta, Georgia, is the owner of the trademark CNN in connection with providing news and information services to people worldwide through cable and satellite television networks, Web sites, and news services. Its services are also available worldwide on the Internet at the domain name CNN.com. Maya Online Broadband Network (Maya HK) is a Chinese company. It registered the domain name CNNEWS.com with Network Solutions, Inc. The CNNews.com Web site was designed to provide news and information to Chinese-speaking individuals worldwide, making significant use of the terms *CNNews* and *CNNews.com* as brand names and logos that the Atlanta company contends resembles its logos. Maya HK has admitted that CNNews in fact stands for China Network News abbreviated as CNN. The Atlanta company had notified Maya HK of its legal right to the CNN mark before the Chinese company registered the CNNews.com domain name. Does the federal Anticybersquatting Consumer Protection Act apply to this case? If so, does a "safe harbor" exist under the ACPA for Maya HK in

that most people who access its Web site in China have never heard of CNN? Decide. [*Cable News Network v. CNN News.com,* 177 F. Supp. 2d 506 (E.D. Va.)]

3. Sara Bostwick hired Christian Oth, Inc., to be her wedding photographer. The parties' written contract granted ownership of the copyright in all images created to Oth. Oth posted the wedding photos on its Web site. Bostwick e-mailed Oth to remove the photos from the Web site. Oth failed to do so and Bostwick sued, claiming that she had the sole and exclusive right to control her own wedding photos. Is she correct? [*Bostwick v. Christian Oth, Inc.* 936 N.Y.S.2d 176 (A.D.)]

4. Jim and Eric work for Media Technical Services (MTS) at Cramer University in Casper, Wyoming. For "expenses" of $5, Jim and Eric used MTS facilities after hours to burn discs of Pearl Jam's CD *Vitology* for 25 friends or friends of friends from school. When Mrs. Mullen, who is in charge of MTS, discovered this and confronted them, Jim, a classics major, defended their actions, telling her, "It's *de minimis*… I mean, who cares?" Explain to Jim and Eric the legal and ethical ramifications of their actions.

5. Sullivan sold t-shirts with the name *Boston Marathon* and the year of the race imprinted on them. The Boston Athletic Association (BAA) sponsors and administers the Boston Marathon and has used the name *Boston Marathon* since 1917. The BAA registered the name *Boston Marathon* on the Principal Register. In 1986, the BAA entered into an exclusive license with Image, Inc., to use its service mark on shirts and other apparel. Thereafter, when Sullivan continued to sell shirts imprinted with the name *Boston Marathon*, the BAA sought an injunction. Sullivan's defense was that the general public was

not being misled into thinking that his shirts were officially sponsored by the BAA. Without this confusion of source, he contended, no injunction should be issued. Decide. [*Boston Athletic Ass'n v. Sullivan,* 867 F.2d 22 (1st Cir.)]

6. The University of Georgia Athletic Association (UGAA) brought suit against beer wholesaler Bill Laite for marketing Battlin' Bulldog Beer. The UGAA claimed that the cans infringed its symbol for its athletic teams. The symbol, which depicted an English Bulldog wearing a sweater with a G and the word BULLDOGS on it, had been registered as a service mark. Soon after the beer appeared on the market, the university received telephone calls from friends of the university who were concerned that Battlin' Bulldog Beer was not the sort of product that should in any way be related to the University of Georgia. The university's suit was based on the theory of false designation of origin in violation of the Lanham Act. Laite contended that there was no likelihood of confusion because his bulldog was different from the university's and his cans bore the disclaimer "Not associated with the University of Georgia." Decide. [*University of Georgia Athletic Ass'n v. Laite,* 756 F.2d 1535 (11th Cir.)]

7. Twentieth Century Fox (Fox) owned and distributed the successful motion picture *The Commitments.* The film tells the story of a group of young Irish men and women who form a soul music band. In the film, the leader of the band, Jimmy, tries to teach the band members what it takes to be successful soul music performers. Toward that end, Jimmy shows the band members a videotape of James Brown's energetic performance of the song "Please, Please, Please." This performance came from Brown's appearance in 1965 on a television program called the *TAMI Show.* Portions of the 1965 performance are shown in *The Commitments* in seven separate "cuts" for a total of 27 seconds. Sometimes the cuts are in the background of a scene, and sometimes they occupy the entire screen. Brown's name is not mentioned at all during these relatively brief cuts. His name is mentioned

only once later in the film, when Jimmy urges the band members to abandon their current musical interests and tune in to the great soul performers, including James Brown: "Listen, from now on I don't want you listening to Guns & Roses and The Soup Dragons. I want you on a strict diet of soul. James Brown for the growls, Otis Redding for the moans, Smokey Robinson for the whines, and Aretha for the whole lot put together." Would it be fair use under U.S. copyright law for Fox to use just 27 seconds of James Brown cuts in the film without formally obtaining permission to use the cuts? Advise Fox as to what, if anything, would be necessary to protect it from a lawsuit. [See *Brown v. Twentieth Century Fox Film Corp.,* 799 F. Supp. 166 (D. D.C.)]

8. The Greenwich Bank & Trust Co. (GB&T) opened in 1998 and by 2008 had expanded to a total of four branches in the Greenwich, Connecticut, community of 62,000 residents. A competitor using the name Bank of Greenwich (BOG) opened in December 2006. GB&T's parent entity sued BOG for trademark violation under the Lanham Act. BOG argued that GB&T's service mark is generic and is simply not entitled to Lanham Act protection because it combines the generic term "bank" and the geographic term "Greenwich." GB&T asserted that it had been the only bank in Greenwich using the word *Greenwich* in its name and had done so exclusively for nine years. It asserted that a geographic term is entitled to protection if it acquires secondary meaning. GB&T introduced evidence regarding its advertising expenditures, sales success, and length of exclusivity of use along with evidence of actual consumer confusion. Decide. [*Connecticut Community Bank v. The Bank of Greenwich,* 578 F. Supp. 2d 405 (D. Conn.)].

9. The U.S. Polo Association (USPA) is a not-for-profit corporation that is the governing body of the sport of polo in the United States. It has been in existence since 1890 and derives the majority of its revenue from royalties obtained from licensing its trademarks. It owns more than 900 trademarks worldwide, including marks bearing

the words "U.S. Polo Assn." with the depiction of two polo players for licensees on products sold in the apparel category. In 2009 it produced 10,000 units of a men's fragrance using packaging featuring its logo as used on apparel. Since 1978 PRL (Polo Ralph Lauren) and its licensee of PRL trademarks, L'Oreal, have used the mark known as the "Polo Player" logo on men's fragrances with its logo containing one player. The fragrance has been sold for 32 years and it was voted into the industry's Hall of Fame. PRL sued USPA. What must PRL establish to prevail in an action for trademark infringement? How would you decide this case? [*United States Polo Assn. v. PRL USA Holdings, Inc.,* 800 F. Supp. 2d 515 (S.D.N.Y.)]

10. Diehr devised a computerized process for curing rubber that was based on a well-known mathematical formula related to the cure time, and he devised numerous other steps in his synthetic rubber-curing process. The patent examiner determined that because abstract ideas, the laws of nature, and mathematical formulas are not patentable subject matter, the process in this case (based on a known mathematical formula) was also not patentable. Diehr contended that all of the steps in his rubber-curing process were new and not obvious to the art of rubber curing. He contended also that he did not seek an exclusive patent on the mathematical formula, except for its use in the rubber-curing process. Decide. [*Diamond v. Diehr,* 450 U.S. 175]

11. Aries Information Systems, Inc., develops and markets computer software specifically designed to meet the financial accounting and reporting requirements of such public bodies as school districts and county governments. One of Aries's principal products is the POBAS III accounting program. Pacific Management Systems Corporation was organized by Scott Dahmer, John Laugan, and Roman Rowan for marketing a financial accounting and budgeting system known as FAMIS. Dahmer, Laugan, and Rowan were Aries employees before, during, and shortly after they organized Pacific. As employees, they each gained access to Aries's software materials

(including the POBAS III system) and had information about Aries's existing and prospective clients. Proprietary notices appeared on every client contract, source code list, and magnetic tape. Dahmer, Laugan, and Rowan signed an Employee Confidential Information Agreement after beginning employment with Aries. While still employees of Aries, they submitted a bid on behalf of Pacific to Rock County and were awarded the contract. Pacific's FAMIS software system is substantially identical to Aries's proprietary POBAS III system. Aries sued Pacific to recover damages for misappropriation of its trade secrets. Pacific's defense was that no "secrets" were misappropriated because many employees knew the information in question. Decide. [*Aries Information Systems, Inc. v. Pacific Management Systems Corp.,* 366 N.W.2d 366 (Minn. App.)]

12. The plaintiff, Herbert Rosenthal Jewelry Corporation, and the defendant, Kalpakian, manufactured jewelry. The plaintiff obtained a copyright registration of a jeweled pin in the shape of a bee. Kalpakian made a similar pin. Rosenthal sued Kalpakian for infringement of copyright registration. Kalpakian raised the defense that he was only copying the idea, not the way the idea was expressed. Was he liable for infringement of the plaintiff's copyright? [*Herbert Rosenthal Jewelry Corp. v. Kalpakian,* 446 F.2d 738 (9th Cir.)]

13. Mineral Deposits, Ltd. (MD, Ltd.), an Australian company, manufactures the Reichert Spiral, a device used for recovering gold particles from sand and gravel. The spiral was patented in Australia, and MD, Ltd., had applied for a patent in the United States. Theodore Zigan contacted MD, Ltd., stating he was interested in purchasing up to 200 devices for use in his gravel pit. MD, Ltd., agreed to lend Zigan a spiral for testing its efficiency. Zigan made molds of the spiral's components and proceeded to manufacture 170 copies of the device. When MD, Ltd., found out that copies were being made, it demanded the return of the spiral. MD, Ltd., also sought lost profits for the 170 spirals manufactured by Zigan. Recovery was sought on a theory of misappropriation of trade secrets.

Zigan offered to pay for the spiral lent him by MD, Ltd. He argued that trade secret protection was lost by the public sale of the spiral. What ethical values are involved? Was Zigan's conduct a violation of trade secret law? [*Mineral Deposits, Ltd. v. Zigan,* 773 P.2d 609 (Colo. App.)]

14. Village Voice Media, owners of the famous *Village Voice* newspaper in New York City, sent a letter to *The Cape Cod Voice,* a year-old publication located in Orleans, Massachusetts, objecting to the use of the word *Voice* in the title of its publication. It warned that the Cape Cod publication could cause "confusion as to the source affiliation with the famous Village Voice marks." The publisher of *The Cape Cod Voice* responded that "small places have a right to their own voices." The use of the word *Voice* was thus in dispute between these parties. Would you classify it as generic, descriptive, suggestive, arbitrary, or fanciful? How would you resolve this controversy? [*Cape Cod Times* Business Section, Amy Zipkin, *The New York Times,* October 16, 2004, G-1].

CPA QUESTIONS

1. Multicomp Company wishes to protect software it has developed. It is concerned about others copying this software and taking away some of its profits. Which of the following is true concerning the current state of the law?

   a. Computer software is generally copyrightable.

   b. To receive protection, the software must have a conspicuous copyright notice.

   c. Software in human readable source code is copyrightable but machine language object code is not.

   d. Software can be copyrighted for a period not to exceed 20 years.

2. Which of the following is not correct concerning computer software purchased by Gultch Company from Softtouch Company? Softtouch originally created this software.

   a. Gultch can make backup copies in case of machine failure.

   b. Softtouch can typically copyright its software for at least 75 years.

   c. If the software consists of compiled computer databases, it cannot be copyrighted.

   d. Computer programs are generally copyrightable.

3. Using his computer, Professor Bell makes 15 copies (to distribute to his accounting class) of a database in some software he has purchased for his personal research. The creator of this software is claiming copyright. Which of the following is correct?

   a. This is an infringement of copyright, since he bought the software for personal use.

   b. This is not an infringement of copyright, since databases cannot be copyrighted.

   c. This is not an infringement of copyright because the copies were made using a computer.

   d. This is not an infringement of copyright because of the fair use doctrine.

4. Intellectual property rights included in software may be protected under which of the following?

   a. Patent law

   b. Copyright law

   c. Both of the above

   d. None of the above

© Manuel Gutjahr/iStockphoto.com

CHAPTER 11

Cyberlaw

learningoutcomes

After studying this chapter, you should be able to

LO.1 Define cyberlaw

LO.2 Discuss the employment issues in cyberspace

LO.3 Explain user issues in cyberspace

LO.4 Discuss appropriation and other forms of unfair competition in cyberspace

LO.5 List and explain the contract issues in cyberspace

A. Types of Legal Issues in Cyberspace

1. What Is Cyberlaw?

cyberlaw – laws and precedent applicable to Internet transactions and communications.

Even though the law that is applied to resolve the problems of the new technologies and the new economy that have developed and grown on the Internet is often referred to as **cyberlaw,** you need not fear that you will be required to learn a whole new body of law. There have been and will continue to be changes in the law to accommodate new ways of doing business, but there has also been and will continue to be reliance on the fundamental principles that underlie our laws and the rights they protect. This chapter simply examines the issues and concerns in cyberspace and covers their resolution through a brief overview of new and existing laws. This chapter provides a framework for the challenges of legal issues in **cyberspace**.

cyberspace – World Wide Web and Internet communication.

2. What Are the Issues in Cyberlaw?

The legal issues of cyberspace can be broken down into four main areas: employment issues, user issues, appropriation and competition issues, and contract issues. Within each of these four areas of existing law are a number of new legal issues that have arisen because of the nature of cyberspace and the conduct of business there. That various cyberlaw issues can be grouped into traditional areas of law demonstrates the not-so-new nature of cyberlaw.

B. Employment Issues in Cyberspace

The lines between our jobs and personal lives are increasingly blurred. Just three years ago, the focus in the case law was on employee use of company e-mail systems to send personal messages. Today, personal blogs, social media profiles (such as Facebook), Tweets, and other online activities by employees result in increasing challenges for employers as they try to protect company information and balance employee rights and privacy.[1] Blogging has often resulted in employees disclosing private and/or negative information about their companies. Tweeting is instant and ongoing communication that could reveal, prematurely, information that the company does not want public. E-mails, Internet surfing, and blogging require a delicate balancing of rights and interests.[2]

3. Employers Are Accountable for Employee Electronic Content

Employers are held responsible for the content of employee e-mails and employers must have access and control rights over employee information that is released publicly through various electronic means. For example, e-mails that contain off-color jokes or suggestive comments create an atmosphere of harassment. (See Chapter 40 for more information on sexual harassment).[3] Employers are also responsible when employees use e-mail or the Internet at work to violate intellectual

---

[1] In 2009, Facebook had over one billion users and accounted for 72 percent of online social networking including MySpace, Twitter, and LinkedIn. Nicholas Carlson, Chart of the Day: How Many Users Does Twitter Really Have? *Business Insider*, March 31, 2011. **www.businessinsder.com/**.

[2] A survey found that 72 percent of businesses use social media for marketing purposes. Robert Ball, "Social Media Marketing: What's the Payoff for Your Business," *Huffington Post*, February 24, 2011. **www.huffingtonpost.com**.

[3] See *Garrity v. John Hancock Mut. Life Ins. Co.*, 2002 WL 974676 (D. Mass. 2002) (memorandum opinion), in which an employer's termination of an employee for sending an e-mail entitled, "The Top Ten Reasons Cookie Dough Is Better Than Men" was upheld on grounds that such content created an atmosphere of harassment. An employer was held liable for its failure to take action against an employee who used a company computer to post nude photographs of his daughter. *Doe v. XYC Corp.*, 887 A.2d 1156 (N.J. Super. Ct. 2005).

property rights. Employers are also held accountable when employees use e-mails and blogs to defame fellow employees or competitors, vendors, or even customers.

Employee e-mail is spontaneous, candid, and discoverable. As a result, the content of employees' e-mail is often fertile territory for prosecutors who can find evidence of intent in employee e-mails and blogs. For example, in 2008, investigators uncovered e-mails of employees at Standard & Poor's, the investment rating agency, that indicated that while the employee/analysts were rating debt instruments as AAA, they were also having their doubts about them. One employee wrote, "These deals could have been structured by cows and we would still rate them."[4] Another e-mail read, "Rating agencies continue to create [an] even bigger monster—the CDO market. Let's hope we are all wealthy and retired by the time this house of cards falters."[5] These candid e-mails were a foundation for settlements paid by the analysts' firms and resulted in general reforms of the analyst industry.

E-mails provide a contemporaneous record of events that often defy our recollections. **For Example,** in 2011 the indictment of former Penn State assistant football coach, Jerry Sandusky, for child sexual abuse, resulted in questions about whether university officials had failed to report past incidents of Mr. Sandusky's inappropriate involvement with children. The late and then–head football coach, Joe Paterno, denied any knowledge of a 1998 incident in the football program showers with a young boy. However, subsequent investigation uncovered e-mails that contradicted Coach Paterno's recollection. On May 13, 1998, Tim Curley, the university's athletic director, sent an e-mail to Gary Schultz, a university vice president of finance and operations, with the caption, "Jerry," and this message, "Anything new in this department? Coach is anxious to now where it stands."[6] Mr. Curley also requested updates on May 18 and May 30, 1998. As a result, Mr. Curley and Mr. Schultz were charged with perjury regarding their testimony of not knowing about previous incidents and Coach Paterno and Penn State were disciplined by the NCAA. The e-mail era means our own words often determine our consequences.

4. Employer Monitoring: What's Legal

Because they are held accountable for what employees do in cyberspace, employers use various methods for monitoring employees including using key-stroking software that allows the employer to see those messages employees typed but did not send, using blocking software that limits sites employees can visit, monitoring and searching e-mails, checking blogs for content, and examining items posted on Facebook, Twitter, and YouTube.

There were some efforts in the early days of cyberspace to apply existing law to ensure e-mail privacy. The Electronic Communications Privacy Act of 1986 (ECPA) prohibits the unauthorized access of "live" communications, as when someone uses a listening device to intercept a telephone conversation. However, e-mail and social media are stored information, and the question of this act's application for resolving the privacy issue is doubtful.[7] ECPA also has an exception for consensual interception. The Stored Communication Act (SCA) prohibits the unauthorized interception of

---

[4] Summary Report of Issues Identified in the Commission's Examination of Select Credit Rating Agencies, July 8, 2008.

[5] Ibid.

[6] Freeh Sporkin Sullivan, LLP, Report of the Special Investigative Counsel Regarding the Actions of the Pennsylvania State University Related to the Child Sexual Abuse Committed by Gerald A. Sandusky (2012), at p. 4.

[7] "Every circuit court to have considered the matter has held that an 'intercept' under the ECPA must occur contemporaneously with transmission." See *Fraser v. Nationwide Mut. Ins. Co.,* 352 F.3d 107, 113 (3d Cir. 2003).

CASE SUMMARY

Shared Drive + Shared Access = NO PRIVACY

FACTS: In February 2003, while serving as a civilian contractor, Michael D. King resided in a dormitory at the Prince Sultan Air Base in Saudi Arabia. During his stay in the dormitory, King kept his personal laptop computer in his room and connected it to the base network. All users of the base network signed agreements indicating that they understood their communications over and use of the base network were subject to monitoring.

An enlisted airman was searching the base network for music files when he came across King's computer on the network. The airman was able to access King's hard drive because it was a "shared" drive. The airman discovered a pornographic movie and text files "of a pornographic nature." The airman reported his discovery to a military investigator who in turn referred the matter to a computer specialist. This specialist located King's computer and hard drive on the base network and verified the presence of pornographic videos and explicit text files on the computer. She also discovered a folder on the hard drive labeled "pedophilia."

Military officials seized King's computer and also found CDs containing child pornography.

Two years later, the government obtained an indictment charging King with possession of child pornography. After his arrest, the government searched his residence pursuant to a search warrant and found additional CDs and hard drives containing over 30,000 images of child pornography.

King entered a guilty plea and was sentenced to 108 months in prison. King then appealed his conviction on the grounds that there had been an illegal search and seizure of his computer and files.

DECISION: The court held that there was no Fourth Amendment violation because the investigators did not search King's files or computer initially to discover the pornographic materials. They merely had to access the universally accessible files of the military base. King had no expectation of privacy in whatever was posted on the shared drive. The search of his home computer and files in his room was with a warrant that was based on probable cause obtained from public access to the files. [*U.S. v. King*, 509 F.3d 1338 (11th Cir. 2007)]

electronic communications, generally meaning stored communication, not ongoing communication such as text messaging, tweeting, and instant messaging. However, the courts have held consistently that employees give consent to such monitoring, and there are no statutory violations when employers do live listening, interception, or recovery of sent communication that is stored and available electronically.[8] When employers have informal policies or policies that allow employees to reimburse their employers for private use of text services, the courts have held that monitoring and disclosure of those messages is a violation of the law.

5. Employer Screening of Applicants

If the employer will be doing prehiring monitoring, such as looking at MySpace.com and Facebook—and/or "Googling" the applicant's name—the applicant must be told of this monitoring at the time of the application. The information that we post on publicly available sites is not considered private, so employers, as long as they are maintaining consistent standards for all applicants, can examine what you have posted on the Internet.

Employers are also using Google and other Internet sources to track employee work excuses. One company's human resources official was on the phone with the

---

[8] For detailed information on this issue, see Patricia Sanchez Abril, Avner Levin, and Alissa Del Riego "Blurred Boundaries: Social Media Privacy and the Twenty-First-Century Employee," 49 *American Business Law Journal* 63 (2012).

company employment lawyer seeking to determine what action could be taken against an employee who was absent frequently but who claimed he was absent to care for his ill grandmother. While they were talking, the lawyer "Googled" the employee's name and found that he was being arraigned in federal court.

Schools, employment counselors, and lawyers are offering the following warnings about the dangers of social media and e-mail postings:[9]

1. Nothing is private on the Internet. People can see everything.

2. Be careful what you blog.

3. Protect your identity when in chat rooms.

4. Assume that everything you write and post will be seen.

5. You can clean up your name on Google using several services, but having no hits at all can lead to suspicions.

6. Think before you write, blog, post, or do anything on the Internet.

Ethics & the Law

When Social Media Get Back at Employers

A teacher posts negative information about her high school students on her Facebook page.

A flight attendant posts provocative pictures of herself in her airline's uniform on her Facebook page.

Medical students post information about their patients on their Facebook pages.

Domino's employees post a video on YouTube that shows them putting mucus on Domino's food as they prepare it.

Discuss the ethical obligations of employees to their employers when they are posting information on their Facebook pages.

CASE SUMMARY

Text Me, If You Dare

FACTS: Jeff Quon, a sergeant and member of the city of Ontario's SWAT team, "texted" Sergeant Steve Trujillo, dispatcher April Florio, and his wife Jerilyn Quon (Respondents) using Arch Wireless text-messaging services that were provided for him through the city of Ontario's contract with Arch.

Ontario Police Department (The city) (OPD) (Petitioners) had no official policy directly addressing the use of text messaging. However, the city did have a general "Computer Usage, Internet, and E-mail Policy" applicable to all employees. The policy provided that all software, programs, networks, Internet, e-mail, and other systems were to be used only for city of Ontario–related business. The policy also indicated that usages were monitored and recorded.

Quon attended a meeting during which SWAT team members and others were told that text messages would fall under the city's policy as public information and be therefore eligible for auditing.

---

[9] From Michelle Conlin, "You Are What You Post," *Business Week*, March 27, 2006, pp. 52–53. For a discussion of research on blogging, see Rainie, "The State of Blogging," Pew Internet and American Life Project, November 2005; available at **www.pewinternet.org/pdfs/PIP_blogging_data.pdf**, and **www.technorati.com**.

CASE SUMMARY

Continued

Under the city's contract each pager was allotted 25,000 characters, after which the city had to pay overage charges. Quon's supervisor, Duke, told him that he was over by more than 15,000 characters and that he should reimburse the city for the overage charges so that he (the supervisor) would not have to audit the transmission and see how many messages were non–work related. Quon refused to pay and was told to cut down on his transmissions.

When Quon and another officer again exceeded the 25,000-character limit, his supervisor, Duke, stated that he was "tired of being a bill collector with guys going over the allotted amount of characters on their text pagers." Ontario's chief of police then requested an audit of the text messages.

Because city officials were not able to access the text messages themselves, they requested and obtained the messages from Arch Wireless. The audit of the messages revealed abuse of on-the-clock time through sheer numbers of personal texts and their sexually explicit content.

The officers were disciplined and subsequently challenged the discipline by claiming violation of their Fourth Amendment rights. The trial court found that there was a Fourth Amendment violation, but granted Arch Wireless a summary judgment on Quon's claims of invasion of privacy. The Ninth Circuit held that the search was unreasonable and the city appealed.

DECISION: The court held that even if Quon had a reasonable expectation of privacy in his text messages, the city did not necessarily violate the Fourth Amendment by obtaining and reviewing the transcripts. The search here was reasonable because there were "reasonable grounds for suspecting that the search [was] necessary for a non investigatory work-related purpose."

Quon was told that his messages were subject to auditing. As a law enforcement officer, he would or should have known that his actions were likely to come under legal scrutiny, and that this might entail an analysis of his on-the-job communications. Under the circumstances, a reasonable employee would be aware that sound management principles might require the audit of messages to determine whether the pager was being appropriately used.

The judgment of the Court of Appeals for the Ninth Circuit was reversed. [*City of Ontario v. Quon*, 130 S.Ct. 2619 (2010)]

6. Employers' Right of Access to Employee E-Mails and Internet Use

Because employers are accountable for the content of employee e-mail, it is not a breach of privacy for employers to monitor employee e-mail and Internet usage. Monitoring the content of employee e-mails is important for keeping companies out of legal difficulties. However, employees may believe they have an expectation of privacy in their e-mails, even when those e-mails are sent from work. That belief may spring from the tort standards that protect private lives, communications, and information. The tort of **invasion of privacy,** or intrusion into private affairs, has application to cyberspace communication. Internet disclosure, without permission, of private information is a breach of privacy. Employers generally require employees to sign a document in which they acknowledge that by working at the company and using the company's e-mail and server that they have waived their right to privacy. Former Sun Microsoft Systems CEO, Scott McNealy, summed up employee rights to privacy when it comes to Internet use: "You have zero privacy. Get over it."[10]

Employers can monitor electronic communications from employees that are marked as private; e-mails that are sent from home and from private computers that

invasion of privacy–tort of intentional intrusion into the private affairs of another.

[10] A. Michael Froomkin, "The Death of Privacy," 52 *Stanford Law Review*, 1461, 1462 (2000). Presented at the *Cyberspace and Privacy: A New Legal Paradigm? Symposium*, Stanford, CA, 2000.

use the company server; e-mails that do not involve company business; text messages sent using company phones; and tweets sent over company iPhones, BlackBerries, and other phone communication systems. Employees should be careful when using their work laptops for private communications. Courts have reached different conclusions, for example, on whether employees waive their attorney-client privilege when using their work computers or employer-issued cell phones to communicate with their employers.[11]

CASE SUMMARY

The E-Mail Detailed Pregnancy

FACTS: Gina Holmes began working for Paul Petrovich as his executive assistant in early June 2004. The employee handbook, which Ms. Holmes read and signed, contained the following warnings, "[e]mployees who use the Company's Technology Resources to create or maintain personal information or messages have no right of privacy with respect to that information or message," and, "E-mail is not private communication, because others may be able to read or access the message. E-mail may best be regarded as a postcard rather than as a sealed letter…." The handbook also states that the company may "inspect all files or messages … at any time for any reason at its discretion."

Ms. Holmes told Petrovich in July 2004 that she was pregnant and that her due date was December 7, 2004. During her pregnancy, Ms. Holmes was put off when coworkers asked her questions about maternity leave and made "belly-monitoring" comments. She asked "[t]hat little group of hens" to stop, and they complied. Ms. Holmes discussed her belly getting big and baby names with Mr. Petrovich and felt the discussions were inappropriate but never said anything about being offended.

On Friday morning, August 6, 2004, Mr. Petrovich and Ms. Holmes discussed her maternity leave, which he assumed would start December 7. A few hours later Ms. Holmes e-mailed back that she estimated starting her maternity leave around November 15. Mr. Petrovich responded, "I need some honesty. How pregnant were you when you interviewed with me and what happened to six weeks? You have rights for sure and I am not going to do anything to violate any laws, but I feel taken advantage of and deceived for sure."

Ms. Holmes responded by explaining that she disclosed her pregnancy as soon as the tests from her amniocentesis came back that everything was "normal" with the baby. An amnio cannot be performed until the fourth month of pregnancy. Ms. Holmes added, "I am 39 years old, and therefore, there was a chance that there could be something 'wrong' or 'abnormal' with the baby. If there had been, I had decided not to carry the baby to term. That is a very personal choice, and not something that I wanted to have to share with people at work; so in order to avoid that, I waited until I knew that everything was o.k. before telling anyone I was pregnant. I've also had 2 miscarriages at 3 months into my pregnancy, and could not bear having to share that with coworkers again, as I have in the past. I feel that I have the right to make these decisions, and there is no deceipt[sic] or dishonesty involved with this. [t]here is no requirement in a job interview or application to divulge if you are pregnant or not; in fact, I believe it's considered unethical to even inquire as to such."

Mr. Petrovich forwarded the e-mail exchange to other employees who would need to be aware of the staffing and payroll issues.

On Monday morning, August 9, 2004, Holmes sent an e-mail to Petrovich indicating that she was very flexible and that she wanted to "work out the bumps along the way." Mr. Petrovich replied that he was pleased with her work and commitment to the job and concluded, "I want you to stay. It will work."

[11] *Scott v. Beth Israel Med. Ctr.*, 847 N.Y.S.2d 436 (2007).

CASE SUMMARY

Continued

On August 10, 2004, Ms. Holmes used the company computer to e-mail an attorney, Joanna Mendoza. Ms. Holmes asked for a referral to an attorney specializing in labor law, specifically relating to pregnancy discrimination. Ms. Holmes forwarded a few of Mr. Petrovich's e-mails.

At 4:42 p.m. on the same day, Ms. Mendoza e-mailed Ms. Holmes that she should delete their attorney-client communications from her work computer because her employer might claim a right to access it.

On August 11, 2004, after her lunch with Ms. Mendoza, Ms. Holmes e-mailed Mr. Petrovich saying that she had cleared her things from her desk and would not be returning to work.

In September of 2005, Ms. Holmes filed a lawsuit against Mr. Petrovich and his company for sexual harassment, retaliation, wrongful termination in violation of public policy, violation of the right to privacy, and intentional infliction of emotional distress. She alleged that she was constructively terminated.

DECISION: The court held that there were not enough facts to find that Ms. Holmes's work environment was objectively hostile. The court also found that her supervisor did not take actions that constituted an "adverse employment action" as required for proving retaliation. The court also found that the attorney-client privilege did not apply to Ms. Holmes's e-mails sent to her lawyer using her company computer. The e-mails sent by Holmes to her attorney regarding possible legal action against her employer did not constitute "'confidential communication between client and lawyer'" because Holmes used a computer of the defendant company to send the e-mails even though (1) she had been told of the company's policy that its computers were to be used only for company business and that employees were prohibited from using them to send or receive personal e-mail, (2) she had been warned that the company would monitor its computers for compliance with this company policy and thus might "inspect all files and messages … at any time," and (3) she had been explicitly advised that employees using company computers to create or maintain personal information or messages "have no right of privacy with respect to that information or message." [***Holmes v. Petrovich Development Company, LLC,*** **191 Cal.App.4th 1047, 119 Cal.Rptr.3d 878 (Cal. App. 2011)**]

NOTE: The court did allow the case on intentional infliction of emotional distress and breach of privacy to continue with respect to the forwarded e-mail Mr. Petrovich sent to the group of employees.

E-Commerce & Cyberlaw

Top Ten Tips for Employer Regulation of Social Media and E-Mail Content

1. Create policies for e-mail and social media use by employees.

2. Train employees on the policies and post the policies.

3. Be sure all employees have a copy of the policies.

4. Have employees sign off on the policies every year.

5. Help employees understand what can happen as a result of misuse of e-mail and social networking outlets.

6. Enforce your policies.

7. Explain that you cooperate with law enforcement agencies on e-mail and social media content.

8. Update policies as avenues for social media change and expand.

9. Have an electronic retention policy and train employees on retention of e-mails and other postings.

10. Tell employees that you monitor all sites and uses of company computers, phones, and social media accounts.

C. User Issues in Cyberspace

A second series of issues in cyberlaw is the use of information that Web sites have gleaned from their users.

7. Use of User Information

Each time you are online, there is the possibility that someone is gathering information about you—what you buy, what you are interested in, and even those to whom you are linked. **For Example,** if you use an airline's Web site to book your travel arrangements, that Web site has a profile of your travel habits. The airline knows how frequently you travel and where you travel. That type of targeted customer information is something other Web sites and retailers are willing to pay dearly for because they know their product is being considered by those most likely to purchase it. If you use Amazon.com to buy books, that Web site has relevant information about the types of books you read, your interests, and even some indications about your income level based on your spending habits.

Even though this issue of privacy may seem new and peculiar to cyberspace, it is, in fact, a rather old issue that has long been a concern of credit card companies. These companies' use and sale of information about their customers are restricted. Customers must be given the right to refuse such use of their names and other information for sale as part of lists for target marketing. Some state attorneys general are utilizing these credit card privacy rights to enforce privacy rights against Web site owners who sell information about their users. The Federal Trade Commission (FTC) has begun to take positions on all Internet issues that are identical to its stances on other types of commerce issues. **For Example,** if catalog companies are required to provide notice to customers about delays in shipment of goods to customers, Internet companies must comply with the same notification rules.

8. Identifying Users: Screen Names, Privacy, and Freedom of Speech

Another privacy issue that has arisen is whether plaintiffs in suits for defamation can successfully subpoena Internet Service Providers (ISPs) to obtain the identity of individuals who post statements in chat rooms and across the Internet, make defamatory remarks over the Internet, facilitate the downloading of music through their sites, and even allow the sharing of exam information that is proprietary. Music companies' actions against individuals who download music but do not pay for their songs requires the discovery of the identity of those who are doing the downloading. Can the music companies require the ISPs to disclose the names of their customers for purposes of preventing copyright infringement? There are now clear standards for determining disclosure of identity that tend to favor disclosure.[12] However, the courts have been very careful to distinguish releasing identity information when there is no illegal activity and what is posted on the Internet or Tweets is simply an expression of opinion. The key to releasing identity of posters is whether the posters were engaged in illegal or harmful activity. There is a difference between posting a nasty opinion and posting false information. Posting false information requires ISPs to disclose identity. Nasty opinions enjoy some First Amendment protection. Access to ISP identity information for illegal or actionable behavior on the Internet is now relatively routine.[13]

---

[12] *Columbia Pictures, Inc. v. Bunnell*, 245 F.R.D. 443 (C.D. Cal. 2007). However, the duty to preserve such information for discovery is still up in the air. *Healthcare Advocates, Inc. v. Harding, Earley, Follner & Frailey*, 497 F. Supp. 2d 627 (E.D. Pa. 2007).

[13] See, e.g., *Laface Records, LLC v. Atlantic Recording Corp.*, 2007 WL 4286189, (W.D. Mich. 2007).

CASE SUMMARY

Dissed on a Blog by Taxcut *et al.*

FACTS: The local police chief and officers (Daniel P. Varrenti, Brian Winant, Adam Mesiti, and Stephen Mesiti) (plaintiffs) filed suit against Gannett Co. (specifically its newspaper, the *Democrat & Chronicle*, a newspaper for Brockport, New York) and four John/Jane Does (defendants) who posted allegedly defamatory comments about the officers. The four posters are known online as "Taxcut," "brockportonian," "BkptStar," and "TaxpayerBWare."

The alleged defamatory statements were posted between January 17, 2011 and January 20, 2011, in response to two articles that were posted on the *Democrat & Chronicle's* Web site, one of which was "Brockport, Sweden and Clarkson Feud Over Fire, Ambulance Services." The following comments were posted by the four on January 17, 2011 and January 18, 2011:

> Tom MudGun is Tom MudGun by any other name, and he smells as foul as the venom he dispenses. Now. According to Mr. Varrenti, we had almost 16,000 calls for service in Brockport. We have about 8,000 residents. That's 2 calls per resident. Have you made your call today? Chief V counts as a call for service every time an officer touches a doorknob, every call received for any reason, and I believe every time an officer waves at you. My! Crime has sure soared in Broke-port since Mr. V was hired. Mr. V has a 10 year, million dollar contract with Broke-port. He has found the pot of gold at the end of the rainbow. Just call him "The Million Dollar Dan."
>
> Regarding the competence of Broke-port's 100K a year cops, consider the following, Broke-port cops don't stop for pedestrians.
>
> Officer Masseti broke into a home thru a basement window (without a warrant) and arrested the residents. The case was thrown out of court, and no discipline given to officer. Why?
>
> Officers beat up a deaf kid because he could not hear their commands. Could that be a liability?
>
> "The Million Dollar Dan" could reign in over time, but he has a sweet heart deal with the cops. They both look the other way and ignore their mutual misdeeds.
>
> We don't need cops who harass and intimidate taxpayers who complain about the high cost, and we don't want them to manipulate elections so they can control the village board.

In response to the second article, "Municipalities Discuss Forming Fire District," "BkptStar," wrote the following comment on January 20, 2011:

> Dear Loone,
>
> If BPD is the best in the county, we are all in real trouble. They are sure not the cheapest. Why Varrenti didn't discipline the officers that beat up a deaf kid because he could not hear their commands? Why is Varrenti allowing his cops to rake in all the overtime they want?

In addition, "brockportonian" and "TaxpayerBWare," wrote the following series of comments on January 20, 2011, in response to the second article, "Municipalities Discuss Forming Fire District":

> Mesiti is the least of the ones there to worry about. Someone should check into the cover ups, yes plural, of trouble the current union president got into. And, I wonder how much money was donated to the campaigns of the three blind mice by Broke-port police officers. THAT would be interesting to find out. It would definitely show allegiance.
>
> Replying to brockportonian: Regarding cover ups and the current union president, Brian Winant, are you referring to marijuana? Evidently the investigation will turn up more than the hours that they actually work. We keep hearing about all the overtime worked. I understand that their time sheets will be available to the public soon. If there are

CASE SUMMARY

Continued

more cover ups regarding the corruption that has been allowed by the chif, million dollar dan, laughing all the way to the bank, I can't wait.
"brockportonian":
No, I am not talking about marijuana; that would be the least of their worries. Maybe the MCSO deputies who had to deal with the problem child would cooperate if forced through an investigation. What a shame, Brockport's good cop gone bad; hiding behind the badge. I feel sorry for the reputation he is giving all the other officers. I am sure they aren't like him. He sure puts on a good show.

The court was asked to order Gannett to provide any identifying information regarding the four anonymous John/Jane Doe defendants so that the suit for defamation could proceed.

DECISION: The court refused to require the release of the identity of the four bloggers because their statements, taken in context, were not defamatory because they were clearly expressions of opinion. Isolated statements could not be considered defamation when it was clear they were expressing opinions. Also, the court noted that Internet communication is more freewheeling and requires a higher level of protection. [*Varrenti v. Gannett Co., Inc.*, 929 N.Y.S.2d 671 (2011)]

9. The Cloud and Privacy

Cloud computing is another technological development that has resulted in complex legal issues. With cloud computing (such as Google Docs), the information companies have could be intermingled with other users. In addition, the information is completely within the hands of a third party. One of the benefits of cloud computing is that companies have instantaneous access to computer processing services for a fee, something that does not require substantial capital expense and allows for rapid growth. However, legal rights, in terms of access to information, privacy rights, and information retireval remain unresolved.[14]

10. Cookies and Privacy

Technology has permitted companies to plant "cookies" on the computers of those who are using certain Internet sites. With those "cookies" in place, the Web site owner has a way to track the computer owner's activity. At least one court has held that a Web site operator's placing cookies on a user's computer is a violation of an unauthorized access statute that would provide the computer owner a right of action for that breach of the statute and privacy.[15]

11. Statutory Protections for Privacy in Cyberspace

Several federal laws and some state laws provide privacy protections, although somewhat limited, for Internet users. The Privacy Act of 1974 controls the use of information gathered about consumers, but it applies only to government-collected

---

[14] Shannon M. Curreri, Note, *Developments in the Law: Defining "Document" in the Digital Landscape of Electronic Discovery*, 38 *Loy. L.A. L. Rev.* 1541 (2005).
[15] In re *Intuit Privacy Litigation*, 138 F. Supp. 2d 1272 (C.D. Cal. 2001); see also In re *Toys R Us, Inc., Privacy Litig.*, 2001 WL 34517252 (N.D. Cal.), in which the court reached a different conclusion. However, tapping into sites to gain competitive or proprietary information is a breach of privacy. *Creative Computing v. Getloaded.com LLC*, 386 F.3d 930 (9th Cir. 2004). See also *Rich v. City of Jacksonville*, 2010 WL 4403095 (M.D.Fla.)

data such as information gathered by the Social Security Administration or the Internal Revenue Service. Furthermore, there are exceptions for the agencies for "routine use."[16] Some segments of the Computer Fraud and Abuse Act (CFAA) and the ECPA provide privacy protection for certain types of communications, such as financial information and its use and transfer.[17] These privacy laws are not general protections but address specific issues. For example, the Children's Online Privacy Protection Act (COPPA) targets online informational privacy but applies only to Web sites that collect information from children.[18]

Numerous state laws on privacy exist; the problem comes in enforcing those laws against Web site sponsors who have no presence in the state. (See the discussion of jurisdiction in Chapter 2.)

D. Appropriation and Other Forms of Unfair Competition in Cyberspace

The competition on the Internet is intense. Competitors have many opportunities for expanding their customer bases. However, they still must expand their businesses within the legal standards that apply to competition, regardless of where that competition occurs.

12. Appropriation Online

appropriation – taking of an image, likeness, or name for commercial advantage.

The tort of **appropriation** involves taking an image, likeness, or name for purposes of commercial advantage. A business cannot use someone's name or likeness for advertising or endorsement without permission. The use of that name or image in cyberspace does not change the nature of the protection that this form of the privacy tort provides. **For Example,** the use of Tiger Woods's name or picture on the Web site of a yacht company, without his permission, is appropriation, even if Mr. Woods actually owns one of the company's yachts. A screen saver program that uses a likeness of Richard, the million-dollar winner on the CBS television program *Survivor,* without his permission violated his privacy rights. The use of his likeness for the Conniver screen saver program with the *Survivor* logo was appropriation.

13. Unfair Methods of Competition in Cyberspace

Concealed identity bloggers can wreak havoc on competitors. **For Example,** John Mackey, the CEO of Whole Foods, using the name Rahodeb (his wife's name, Deborah, jumbled), posted over 1,000 messages in chat rooms that were dedicated to stock trading. During the period that Mr. Mackey was posting messages, W-hole Foods stock quadrupled in value. The messages were flattering to Whole Foods and negative about Wild Oats, a competitor. On February 24, 2005, Mackey posted the following comment about Wild Oats CEO Perry Odak: "Perhaps the OATS Board will wake up and dump Odak and bring in a visionary and highly competent CEO [like Mackey]." Referred to as "sock-puppeting," this common practice also raises ethical issues.

[16] 5 U.S.C. §552a (2011).
[17] 18 U.S.C. §1030 and 18 U.S.C. §§2510–2520, 2701 (2011). *LVRC Holdings LLC v. Brekka,* 581 F.3d 1127 (9th Cir. 2009)
[18] 15 U.S.C. §§6501–6506.

Ethics & the Law

The Blogger Who Kissed and Told on Capitol Hill

Jessica Cutler, a staff member for Senator Mike DeWine, began a blog that detailed her sexual encounters with various government officials in Washington, D.C. Ms. Cutler did not identify anyone by name in her blog, but the level of detail in her posts had most of Washington figuring out who was who in the Cutler blog. Ms. Cutler was fired for "misusing an office computer." What ethical issues exist in Ms. Cutler's public revelations? Was it legal for the senator to terminate her employment? What advice could you offer employers that would come from this experience? What about defamation if her partners are not identified by name?

Source: April Witt, "Blog Interrupted," *Washington Post*, Apr. 15, 2004, W12.

E. CONTRACT ISSUES IN CYBERSPACE

14. Formation of Contracts in Cyberspace

contract – binding agreement based upon the genuine assent of the parties, made for a lawful object, between competent parties, in the form required by law, and generally supported by consideration.

Formation of a **contract** in cyberspace is simply the result of the desire for speed and better communication in business. If you wanted to form a contract with a New York seller 20 years ago and you were in Los Angeles, you drafted a proposal and mailed it to the seller. The back-and-forth negotiations took time through the mail. Then overnight delivery service arrived to speed up your cross-country negotiations. Next came faxes and their instantaneous exchanges of terms and negotiations. The amount of paperwork involved in transactions was still unchanged. Paperless contracts were born with the availability of electronic digital interchange (EDI). EDI is simply the electronic exchange of business forms. Contracts are formed using purchase orders and invoices submitted via computer.[19]

With the Internet, e-mail, and the ability to attach documents, cyberspace has provided business yet another method for forming contracts. And while the method is different, the rules for formation have not changed. The same laws that apply when contracts are formed in a business office govern the formation of contracts in cyberspace: there must be offer and acceptance.

Some issues that arise in contract formation in the new economy are, for example, whether a contract is formed when someone downloads a program from the Internet. The person may have paid for the program by credit card and simply downloaded it on the computer. Acceptance occurs when the click occurs—a contract is formed.[20] (See Chapters 12–17 for more information on contracts in cyberspace.)

E-sign – signature over the Internet.

The Electronic Signatures in Global and National Commerce Act (called **E-sign**) is a federal law that recognizes digital signatures as authentic for purposes of contract formation. Even though E-sign recognizes the validity of electronic signatures, state laws regulate the authenticity and security of signatures. The Uniform Electronic Transactions Act (UETA) and the Uniform Computer Information Transaction Act (UCITA) are two model laws drafted to allow states to adopt a uniform position. UETA is a uniform law that 46 states plus the District of Columbia have adopted.[21] Two states have adopted UCITA.[22]

---

[19] L. J. Kutten, Bernard D. Reams, and Allen E. Strehler, *Electronic Contracting Law* (Clark Boardman, 1991).

[20] A.V. *v. iParadigms, Ltd. Liability Co.,* 544 F. Supp. 2d 473 (E.D. Va. 2008).

[21] Forty-six jurisdictions have adopted UETA. The states that have not adopted it are Georgia, Illinois, New York, and Washington.

[22] Maryland Commercial Law §§22-101 to 22-816, and Virginia Code §§59.1-501.1 to 59.1-509.2. Both laws can be found online: **www.uetaonline.com** and **www.ucitaonline.com**.

15. Misrepresentation and Fraud in Cyberspace

misrepresentation – false statement of fact, although made innocently without any intent to deceive.

The types of **misrepresentation** and fraud on the Internet range from promises of delivery not fulfilled to promises of performance not met. The majority of the fraud complaints received by the FBI relate to Internet auctions. These issues are not new legal issues; only the form of misrepresentation or fraud has changed. **For Example,** seven retailers signed a consent decree with the FTC, which required them to pay fines totaling $1.5 million to settle a complaint against them for late delivery of Christmas merchandise ordered over the Web. Macys.com, Toysrus.com, and CDNOW. The consent decree that was the retailers signed based on the FTC mail-and-telephone rule requiring retailers to let customers know when they do not have a product or that there will be a delay in the shipment. The existing notification rule was simply applied to Internet transactions.

Thinking Things Through

Twitter, Social Reponsibility, the First Amendment, and Making Money

It's a tight rope task. The task is dealing with what account holders post on Twitter even as Twitter tries to make money as well as deal with governments in other countries that are not as tolerant of criticism and dissent as our First Amendment allows. For example, during the London Olympics, a Twitter account holder and British journalist, Guy Adams, was tweeting criticisms of NBC's coverage of the games. However, NBC is a Twitter partner. Mr. Adams' account was suspended after a Twitter employee working in the partnerships area of the company told NBC to file a complaint.

Hell hath no fury like those who wish to preserve their unalienable right to tweet. Their outrage caused Twitter's general counsel to apologize, restore the account, and explain that Mr. Adams' account was suspended because he had included an NBC executive's email address in his tweet, something that violates Twitter user policies.

Twitter's general counsel, Alexander Macgillivray, works diligently to balance Twitter's basic policy of not scrutinizing tweets along with the need to work with other country's government, and continue to make money through its partnerships, such as the one with NBC.

The basics of its international policy are that it does not remove any tweets unless someone asks and only if the tweet violates a country's laws. In addition, Twitter has some universal rules such as suspending the accounts of those who pretend to tweet as someone else. In one case this summer, several accounts were suspended because the tweeters pretended to be the prime minister of India.

In the United States, Twitter does not experience government censorship, which leaves the tweeters to post what they wish, within user guidelines. However, the concern is that with its corporate partnerships, Twitter is beholden to those partners who may, as NBC did, request review of posts or even suspension of accounts for posting negative thoughts about those partners.

The other legal issues Twitter faces relate to, for example, defamation (libel) in the written posts. Posts often contain defamatory information, but Twitter enjoys a sort of quasi privilege that allows it to escape liability if it removes the post upon request.

What if Twitter allows its partners to have tweets removed? What happens when Twitter removes tweets because of government demands? Can Twitter balance the interests of its stakeholders?

search engine – Internet service used to locate Web sites.

In marketing **search engines,** some companies have misrepresented the capabilities of their products or have failed to disclose the methods they use to give preference to certain links and their order of listing when the search engine is used. The remedy for such misrepresentations and fraud on the Internet is the same as the remedy in situations with paper contracts. Misrepresentation and fraud are defenses to formation and entitle the party who was misled or defrauded to rescind the agreement and/or collect money damages.

In addition to contract remedies available for misrepresenting the nature of the search engine product and capabilities, a small group of search engine companies has proposed a code of ethics for search engine firms. Headed by Mike Adams, founder and owner of WebSeed.com, the rules are called "Search Engine Promotion Code of Ethics." Adams says that his industry needs reform and gave the following example of Dotsubmit.com, a former company that claimed it would submit its clients' Web sites to 10,000 search engines. Other problems include the lack of limitations on the number of pages from any domain, which means there is so much space used that consumers have difficulty finding what they are looking for.

Key provisions of the search engine code of ethics cover claims about search engine performance as well as the honoring of submission guidelines that impose requirements on Web sites seeking to be listed.

16. Tax Issues on Contracts in Cyberspace

The U.S. Constitution requires that there be some "nexus" between the taxing authority and the business paying the tax (see Chapter 4 for more information on constitutional issues in taxation), and many questions arise about the constitutionality of taxing Internet sales because of the lack of "bricks and mortar" in these businesses. Some Internet retailers are located in one state and have no contact, physically, with any other states. Their only contact is through the computers of their customers, who may be located in all 50 states. Is it constitutional for Colorado to tax a New Jersey company operating out of a small office in Trenton? Courts will simply apply the standards of fairness and allocation that they have relied on in other eras as businesses grew in reach even though their physical locations did not change.

The Internet Tax Freedom Act (ITFA)[23] has been renewed. The ITFA provides that states and local governments cannot tax Internet access. Contrary to popular belief, ITFA does not suspend sales taxes on transactions over the Internet. To tax Internet sales, the seller must have some physical presence in the state or a pattern of distribution and doing business there. **For Example,** Nordstrom might not have stores located in a particular state, but it would be required to collect sales taxes from sales to residents of that state if it had warehouse facilities in that state. Refer to Chapter 3 for a full discussion of the Internet and sales tax. Online retailers have been negotiating tax rates and procedures with states. However, several states have passed laws that require those who purchase merchandise over the Internet declare the amount of goods they purchased and then pay sales tax on those goods on their state income tax returns.

LawFlix

The Net (1995) (PG-13)

In a movie that was ahead of its time, a computer programmer becomes a victim of identity theft when she holds too much information about the software companies for which she has done consulting work.

The Social Network (2010) (PG-13)

The film presents a fascinating picture of the start of Facebook and the resulting contract and intellectual property disputes that arose after the company became successful.

---

[23] 47 U.S.C. §151, originally enacted in 1998, and as amended 2010.

MAKE THE CONNECTION

SUMMARY

The term *cyberlaw* seems to indicate a new body of law that exists or is being created to manage all of the legal issues of the cybereconomy, cyberspace, and cybertechnology. Even though some new criminal statutes have been enacted to address specific types of computer crimes, the law, with its great flexibility, has been able to easily adapt to address many of the legal issues that affect the new economy in cyberspace.

There are four areas of issues in cyberlaw. The first area covers the rights of employers and employees in the workplace cyberspace. Employers are responsible for the content of their Web pages as well as for what employees send out via e-mail, Twitter, and Facebook. Employers have the right to monitor all communications from employees from their work computers. Employers can also use the social media devices for screening potential employees as long as they use the screening for all employees.

Cyberspace also presents legal issues for users such as when and if their anonymous identity online can be revealed by those who provide Internet services. If users are engaged in illegal or tortious activity online, then their identity can be revealed for litigation purposes. If, however, their right to free expression of opinion has been exercised, they can be protected. There are also statutory protections for privacy and required disclosures from retailers who are using information gleaned from users' online activity.

The third area deals with appropriation and competition in cyberspace. The use of trademarks and tradenames that are deceptive can be stopped through injunction for appropriation. In addition, anonymous postings of defamatory information about a competitor can also be halted by an injunction.

The final area that affects users relates to the formation of contracts and issues related to online fraud as well as who pays taxes on goods purchased from online retailers.

LEARNING OUTCOMES

After studying this chapter, you should be able to clearly explain:

A. Define Cyberlaw

L0.1   Explain how we develop cyberlaw See p. 223 for an introduction and explanation

B. Discuss employment issues in cyberspace

Review the list of best practices for employers on monitoring employee electronic communication on p. 229

Study the *Quon* case on employer access to texts on p. 226

L0.2   Discuss the issue of defamation on the Web

See the Ethics & the Law discussion of the blogger who kissed and told, p. 234
See Twitter Thinking Things Through on p. 235

C. Explain User Issues in Cyberspace

L0.3   Refer to the discussion of cookies, p. 232. Discuss the *U.S. v. King* military cloud case on p. 225

D. Discuss Appropriation and Other Forms of Unfair Competition in Cyberspace

L0.4   See the Tiger Woods example on p. 233. Refer to the Whole Foods CEO's conduct on p. 233

E. List and Explain the Contract Issues in Cyberspace

L0.5   Explain the obligations of service providers to reveal identity and content
See the *Gannett* case on pp. 231–232

KEY TERMS

appropriation	cyberspace	misrepresentation
contract	E-sign	search engines
cyberlaw	invasion of privacy	

QUESTIONS AND CASE PROBLEMS

1. Discuss whether employees would have the right of privacy in the following e-mail situations:

   a. E-mail sent in a company in which there is no warning given about the lack of privacy in e-mails. [*Smyth v. Pillsbury*, 914 F. Supp. 97 (E.D. Pa.)]

   b. An e-mail sent to coworkers from home using the employee's AOL account.

   c. An e-mail sent from a laptop while the employee is traveling for the company.

   d. An e-mail sent to a coworker over a company Internet system in a company in which the employer has promised privacy in e-mail. [*Commonwealth v. Proetto*, 771 A.2d 823 (Pa. Super.Ct.).]

   e. Employer monitoring of the e-mails of any employee when those e-mails were stored in a file folder marked "Personal." [*McLaren v. Microsoft Corp.*, 1999 WL 339015 (Tex. App.)]

   f. Employees using company e-mail for union organization purposes. [*Pratt & Whitney*, National Labor Relations Board General Counsel Advisory Memorandum Cases 12-CA-18446, 12-CA-18722, 12-CS-18863]

2. The *New York Times* discovered that 24 of the employees in its payroll processing center were sending "inappropriate and offensive e-mail in violation of corporate policy." Do the employees have any right to privacy with regard to the jokes they send over their e-mail accounts at work? Applying what you have learned about the nature of cyberlaw, determine whether, under existing sexual harassment laws, a company could be held liable for harassment via e-mails.

3. Colleges and universities continue to work to help students understand that what they post on the Web is not private information and can often have unintended consequences. The following examples resulted in student disciplinary proceedings:

   - Several students at Ohio State University boasted on Facebook (a networking/socializing site) that they had stormed the field after Ohio State beat Penn State and had taken part in what erupted into a riot. Law enforcement officials were able to trace the students through the university system, and 50 Ohio State students were referred to the office of judicial affairs.
   - Students at the University of Mississippi stated on an open site that they wanted to have sex with a professor.
   - A student at Fisher College threatened to take steps to silence a campus police officer.

   Another problem with the open sites is that the students are posting personal information with which stalkers and others can access them. These nefarious individuals can then easily obtain students' cell phone numbers, addresses, whereabouts, and other information.

   The most popular college site, Facebook, indicates that students spend an average of 17 minutes per day on the site. A great deal of information can be conveyed during that time period. Students do so without thinking through the possibility that outsiders with bad intentions could be seeking and using information about them that is posted there.

   What legal and ethical issues do you see in the types of comments that students make on these sites and in the sites themselves? Why and how can the colleges and universities obtain information from these sites without a warrant?

4. On July 24, 2002, the Recording Industry Association of America (RIAA) served its first subpoena to obtain the identity of a Verizon subscriber alleged to have made more than 600 copyrighted songs available for downloading over the Internet through peer-to-peer file transfer software provided by KaZaA. Verizon claimed that because RIAA's subpoena related to material transmitted over Verizon's network—rather than stored on it—it fell outside the scope of the subpoena power. Should the subpoena be quashed as Verizon requests, or should it be honored? [In re *Verizon Internet Services, Inc.*, 257 F. Supp. 2d 244 (D.D.C.)]

5. Glenayre Electronics announced to its employees that it could inspect the laptops it furnished for its employees to use. An employee challenged the inspection of his laptop as a violation of his privacy. Could the company search the laptops? [*Muick v. Glenayre Electronics*, 280 F.3d 741 (7th Cir.)]

6. A state university provided a written notice to employees that their computers could be monitored and added a splash screen with the same notice that appears on the computers each time employees start their computers. Has the university done enough to allow monitoring without invading employee privacy? Would it make any difference if the employees had a password for their e-mail access and computer access? What about state public records law? Would employee e-mails be subject to public disclosure because the e-mails would be considered public record? [*U.S. v. Angevine*, 281 F.3d 1130 (10th Cir.)]

7. A hospital filed suit against an individual who began a blog that included disparaging information about the hospital, its physicians, and the results for patients who were treated there. The hospital wants the court to require the cable company to identify the blogger. What will the hospital have to show in order to get the blogger's identity revealed? [In re *Does 1–10*, 242 S.W.3d 805 (Tex. App.)]

8. Sony and others own the copyrights and exclusive licenses to their various sound recordings. Without permission, 40 unidentified individuals (called Does) used "Fast Track," an online media distribution system—or "peer to peer" ("P2P") file-copying network—to download hundreds or thousands of copyrighted sound recordings. Sony was able to identify Cablevision as the Internet service provider (ISP) to which the Does subscribed. Sony did so by using a publicly available database to trace the Internet Protocol (IP) address for each Doe. As a condition of providing its Internet service, Cablevision requires its subscribers to agree to its "Terms of Service" under which "[t]ransmission or distribution of any material in violation of any applicable law or regulation is prohibited. This includes, without limitation, material protected by copyright, trademark, trade secret or other intellectual property right used without proper authorization." On January 26, 2004, the court issued an order granting Sony the right to serve a subpoena upon Cablevision to obtain the identity of each Doe by requesting the name, address, telephone number, e-mail address, and Media Access Control address for each defendant. On February 23, 2004, Cablevision complied with the subpoena and provided relevant information about the Jane and John Does. [*Sony Music Entertainment Inc. v. Does*, 326 F. Supp. 2d 56 (S.D.N.Y.)]

9. Immunomedics, Inc., has discovered sensitive information about its technology posted on various Web sites and chat rooms. The information is so proprietary that it could have come only from company employees, all of whom have signed agreements not to disclose such information. Those who posted the information used screen names, and Immunomedics has asked the court to issue a subpoena to the ISP so that it can determine the identity of those posting the information and recover for breach of contract and trade secret infringement. Should the court issue the subpoena? [*Immunomedics, Inc. v. Does 1–10*, 775 A.2d 773 (N.J. Super.)]

10. Jane Doe filed a complaint against Richard Lee Russell and America Online (AOL) to recover for alleged emotional injuries suffered by her son, John Doe. Doe claimed that in 1994, Russell lured John Doe, who was then 11 years old, and two other minor males to engage in sexual activity with each other and with Russell. She asserted that Russell photographed and videotaped these acts and used AOL's chat rooms to market the photographs and videotapes and to sell a videotape. In her six-count complaint, Doe claimed that AOL violated criminal statutes and that AOL was negligent *per se* in distributing an advertisement offering "a visual depiction of sexual conduct involving [John Doe]" and by allowing Russell to sell or arrange to sell child pornography, thus aiding in the sale and distribution of child pornography, including obscene images of John Doe. Does Mrs. Doe have a cause of action? What laws discussed in this chapter apply? [*Doe v. America Online, Inc.*, 783 So.2d 1010 (Fla.)]

11. Customers of a chat room are using the chat room, Maphia, for access to each other and to transfer Sega games to each other. They are able to avoid paying the $19 to $60 the games cost for purchase in the stores. The users say they are simply transferring files and that there is no crime. The chat room says it cannot stop customers from interacting. Do you think there are any civil or criminal law violations in their conduct? [*Sega Enterprises, Ltd. v. Maphia*, 857 F. Supp. 679 (N.D.Cal.)]

PART 2

Contracts

© Manuel Gutjahr/iStockphoto.com

© Manuel Gutjahr/iStockphoto.com

CHAPTER 12

Nature and Classes of Contracts: Contracting on the Internet

A. Nature of Contracts

1. DEFINITION OF A CONTRACT
2. ELEMENTS OF A CONTRACT
3. SUBJECT MATTER OF CONTRACTS
4. PARTIES TO A CONTRACT
5. HOW A CONTRACT ARISES
6. INTENT TO MAKE A BINDING AGREEMENT
7. FREEDOM OF CONTRACT

B. Classes of Contracts

8. FORMAL AND INFORMAL CONTRACTS
9. EXPRESS AND IMPLIED CONTRACTS
10. VALID AND VOIDABLE CONTRACTS AND VOID AGREEMENTS
11. EXECUTED AND EXECUTORY CONTRACTS
12. BILATERAL AND UNILATERAL CONTRACTS
13. QUASI CONTRACTS

C. Contracting on the Internet

learningoutcomes

After studying this chapter, you should be able to

LO.1 Explain the meaning and importance of privity of a contract

LO.2 Describe the way in which a contract arises

LO.3 Distinguish between bilateral and unilateral contracts

LO.4 Explain the reasoning behind quasi-contract recovery

LO.5 Explain how Internet contracts involve the same types of issues as offline contracts.

P ractically every business transaction affecting people involves a contract.

A. NATURE OF CONTRACTS

This introductory chapter will familiarize you with the terminology needed to work with contract law. In addition, the chapter introduces quasi contracts, which are not true contracts but obligations imposed by law.

1. Definition of a Contract

contract–a binding agreement based on the genuine assent of the parties, made for a lawful object, between competent parties, in the form required by law, and generally supported by consideration.

A **contract** is a legally binding agreement.[1] By one definition, "a contract is a promise or a set of promises for the breach of which the law gives a remedy, or the performance of which the law in some way recognizes as a duty."[2] Contracts arise out of agreements, so a contract may be defined as an agreement creating an obligation.

The substance of the definition of a contract is that by mutual agreement or assent, the parties create enforceable duties or obligations. That is, each party is legally bound to do or to refrain from doing certain acts.

2. Elements of a Contract

The elements of a contract are (1) an agreement (2) between competent parties (3) based on the genuine assent of the parties that is (4) supported by consideration, (5) made for a lawful objective, and (6) in the form required by law, if any. These elements will be considered in the chapters that follow.

3. Subject Matter of Contracts

The subject matter of a contract may relate to the performance of personal services, such as contracts of employment to work developing computer software or to play professional football. A contract may provide for the transfer of ownership of property, such as a house (real property) or an automobile (personal property), from one person to another.

promisor–person who makes a promise.

promisee–person to whom a promise is made.

obligor–promisor.

obligee–promisee who can claim the benefit of the obligation.

privity–succession or chain of relationship to the same thing or right, such as privity of contract, privity of estate, privity of possession.

privity of contract–relationship between a promisor and the promisee.

4. Parties to a Contract

The person who makes a promise is the **promisor**, and the person to whom the promise is made is the **promisee**. If the promise is binding, it imposes on the promisor a duty or obligation, and the promisor may be called the **obligor**. The promisee who can claim the benefit of the obligation is called the **obligee**. The parties to a contract are said to stand in **privity** with each other, and the relationship between them is termed **privity of contract**. **For Example,** when the state of North Carolina and the architectural firm of O'Brien/Atkins Associates executed a contract for the construction of a new building at the University of North Carolina, Chapel Hill, these parties were

[1] The Uniform Commercial Code defines *contract* as "the total legal obligation which results from the parties' agreement as affected by [the UCC] and any other applicable rules of law." U.C.C. §1–201(11).
[2] Restatement (Second) of Contracts §1.

in privity of contract. However, a building contractor, RPR & Associates, who worked on the project did not have standing to sue on the contract between the architect and the state because the contractor was not in privity of contract.[3]

In written contracts, parties may be referred to by name. More often, however, they are given special names that better identify each party. For example, consider a contract by which one person agrees that another may occupy a house upon the payment of money. The parties to this contract are called *landlord* and *tenant*, or *lessor* and *lessee*, and the contract between them is known as a *lease*. Parties to other types of contracts also have distinctive names, such as *vendor* and *vendee* for the parties to a sales contract, *shipper* and *carrier* for the parties to a transportation contract, and *insurer* and *insured* for the parties to an insurance policy.

A party to a contract may be an individual, a partnership, a limited liability company, a corporation, or a government.[4] One or more persons may be on each side of a contract. Some contracts are three-sided, as in a credit card transaction, which involves the company issuing the card, the holder of the card, and the business furnishing goods and services on the basis of the credit card.

If a contract is written, the persons who are the parties and who are bound by it can ordinarily be determined by reading what the document says and seeing how it is signed. A contract binds only the parties to the contract. It cannot impose a duty on a person who is not a party to it. Ordinarily, only a party to a contract has any rights against another party to the contract.[5] In some cases, third persons have rights on a contract as third-party beneficiaries or assignees. A person cannot be bound, however, by the terms of a contract to which that person is not a party. **For Example,** in approximately 1995 Jeff and Mark Bass signed Marshall B. Mathers III, better known as rapper Eminem, to an exclusive record deal with FBT Productions LLC (FBT), their production company. In 2000 Aftermath Records entered into a direct contractual relationship with Eminem, transferring Eminem's recording services from FBT directly to Aftermath. Under the contract FBT became a "passive income participant," retaining a right to royalty income from Eminem's recordings. A dispute occurred regarding percentages of royalties due. Aftermath entered into an agreement with Eminem in 2009, setting the royalties for Eminem's *Recovery* and *Relapse* albums, asserting that all royalties, including royalties owed FBT were dictated by this 2009 agreement. FBT was not a party to the 2009 agreement and as such cannot be bound by it. A contract cannot bind a nonparty. Therefore, Aftermath was required to pay FBT royalties for the two albums at a higher rate in accordance with an earlier agreement.[6]

CPA

5. How a Contract Arises

A contract is based on an agreement. An agreement arises when one person, the **offeror**, makes an offer and the person to whom the offer is made, the **offeree**, accepts. There must be both an offer and an acceptance. If either is lacking, there is no contract.

offeror – person who makes an offer.

offeree – person to whom an offer is made.

---

[3] *RPR & Associates v. O'Brien/Atkins Associates, P.A.*, 24 F. Supp. 2d 515 (M.D. N.C. 1998). See also *Roof Techs Int. Inc. v. State*, 57 P.3d 538, (Kan. App. 2002), where a layer of litigation was avoided regarding lawsuits involving the renovation of the Farrell Library at Kansas State University. The state was the only party in privity of contract with the architectural firm and would thus have to bring claims against the architectural firm on behalf of all of the contractors. Two subcontractors, the general contractor, and the owner of the library, the state of Kansas, used a settlement and liquidation agreement assigning all of the state's claims against the architect to the general contractor.

[4] See *Purina Mills, LLC v. Less*, 295 F. Supp. 2d 1017 (N.D. Iowa 2003) in which the pig-seller plaintiff, which converted from a corporation to a limited liability company (LLC) while the contract was in effect, was a proper party in interest and could maintain a contract action against defendant buyers.

[5] *Hooper v. Yakima County*, 904 P.2d 1193 (Wash. App. 1995).

[6] *F.B.T. Productions, LLC v. Aftermath Records*, 2011 WL 5174766 (C.D. Cal. Oct. 31, 2011).

6. Intent to Make a Binding Agreement

Because a contract is based on the consent of the parties and is a legally binding agreement, it follows that the parties must have an intent to enter into an agreement that is binding. Sometimes the parties are in agreement, but their agreement does not produce a contract. Sometimes there is merely a preliminary agreement, but the parties never actually make a contract, or there is merely an agreement as to future plans or intentions without any contractual obligation to carry out those plans or intentions.

7. Freedom of Contract

In the absence of some ground for declaring a contract void or voidable, parties may make such contracts as they choose. The law does not require parties to be fair, or kind, or reasonable, or to share gains or losses equitably.

B. Classes of Contracts

formal contracts – written contracts or agreements whose formality signifies the parties' intention to abide by the terms.

Contracts may be classified according to their form, the way in which they were created, their binding character, and the extent to which they have been performed.

CPA

8. Formal and Informal Contracts

Contracts can be classified as formal or informal.

contract under seal – contract executed by affixing a seal or making an impression on the paper or on some adhering substance such as wax attached to the document.

(A) Formal Contracts. **Formal contracts** are enforced because the formality with which they are executed is considered sufficient to signify that the parties intend to be bound by their terms. Formal contracts include (1) **contracts under seal** where a person's signature or a corporation's name is followed by a scroll, the word *seal*, or the letters *L.S.*;[7] (2) contracts of record, which are obligations that have been entered before a court of record, sometimes called a **recognizance**; and (3) negotiable instruments.

CPA

recognizance – obligation entered into before a court to do some act, such as to appear at a later date for a hearing. Also called a *contract of record*.

(B) Informal Contracts. All contracts other than formal contracts are called **informal** (or simple) **contracts** without regard to whether they are oral or written. These contracts are enforceable, not because of the form of the transaction but because they represent agreement of the parties.

informal contract – simple oral or written contract.

9. Express and Implied Contracts

Simple contracts may be classified as express *contracts* or *implied contracts* according to the way they are created.

express contract – agreement of the parties manifested by their words, whether spoken or written.

(A) Express Contracts. An **express contract** is one in which the terms of the agreement of the parties are manifested by their words, whether spoken or written.

implied contract – contract expressed by conduct or implied or deduced from the facts.

(B) Implied Contracts. An **implied contract** (or, as sometimes stated, a *contract implied in fact*) is one in which the agreement is shown not by words, written or spoken, but by the acts and conduct of the parties.[8] Such a contract arises when (1) a person renders services under circumstances indicating that payment for them is expected and

---

[7] Some authorities explain *L.S.* as an abbreviation for *locus sigillum* (place for the seal).
[8] *Lindquist Ford, Inc. v. Middleton Motors, Inc.*, 557 F.3d 469, 481 (7th Cir. 2009). See also *Dynegy Marketing and Trade v. Multiut Corp.*, 648 F.3d 506 (7th Cir. 2011).

| FIGURE 12-1 | *Contractual Liability* |

© Cengage Learning

(2) the other person, knowing such circumstances, accepts the benefit of those services. **For Example,** when a building owner requests a professional roofer to make emergency repairs to the roof of a building, an obligation arises to pay the reasonable value of such services, although no agreement has been made about compensation.

An implied contract cannot arise when there is an existing express contract on the same subject.[9] However, the existence of a written contract does not bar recovery on an implied contract for extra work that was not covered by the contract.

CPA 10. Valid and Voidable Contracts and Void Agreements

Contracts may be classified in terms of enforceability or validity.

valid contract—agreement that is binding and enforceable.

(A) VALID CONTRACTS. A **valid contract** is an agreement that is binding and enforceable.

voidable contract—agreement that is otherwise binding and enforceable but may be rejected at the option of one of the parties as the result of specific circumstances.

(B) VOIDABLE CONTRACTS. A **voidable contract** is an agreement that is otherwise binding and enforceable, but because of the circumstances surrounding its execution or the lack of capacity of one of the parties, it may be rejected at the option of one of the parties. **For Example,** a person who has been forced to sign an agreement that that person would not have voluntarily signed may, in some instances, avoid the contract.

void agreement—agreement that cannot be enforced.

(C) VOID AGREEMENTS. A **void agreement** is without legal effect. An agreement that contemplates the performance of an act prohibited by law is usually incapable of enforcement; hence it is void. Likewise, it cannot be made binding by later approval or ratification.

11. Executed and Executory Contracts

Contracts may be classified as *executed contracts* and *executory contracts* according to the extent to which they have been performed.

[9] *Pepsi-Cola Bottling Co. of Pittsburgh, Inc., v. PepsiCo, Inc.,* 431 F.3d 1241 (10th Cir. 2000).

executed contract – agreement that has been completely performed.

(A) EXECUTED CONTRACTS. An **executed contract** is one that has been completely performed. In other words, an executed contract is one under which nothing remains to be done by either party.[10] A contract may be executed immediately, as in the case of a cash sale, or it may be executed or performed in the future.

executory contract – agreement by which something remains to be done by one or both parties.

(B) EXECUTORY CONTRACTS. In an **executory contract**, something remains to be done by one or both parties.[11] **For Example,** on July 10, Mark agreed to sell to Chris his Pearl drum set for $600, the terms being $200 upon delivery on July 14, with $200 to be paid on July 21, and the final $200 being due July 28. Prior to the July 14 delivery of the drums to Chris, the contract was entirely executory. After the delivery by Mark, the contract was executed as to Mark and executory as to Chris until the final payment was received on July 28.

12. Bilateral and Unilateral Contracts

In making an offer, the offeror is in effect extending a promise to do something, such as pay a sum of money, if the offeree will do what the offeror requests. Contracts are classified as *bilateral* or *unilateral*. Some bilateral contracts look ahead to the making of a later contract. Depending on their terms, these are called *option contracts* or *first-refusal contracts*.

CPA

bilateral contract – agreement under which one promise is given in exchange for another.

(A) BILATERAL CONTRACT. If the offeror extends a promise and asks for a promise in return and if the offeree accepts the offer by making the promise, the contract is called a **bilateral contract**. One promise is given in exchange for another, and each party is bound by the obligation. **For Example,** when the house painter offers to paint the owner's house for $3,700 and the owner promises to pay $3,700 for the job, there is an exchange of promises, and the agreement gives rise to a bilateral contract.

unilateral contract – contract under which only one party makes a promise.

Reward for your lost dog must preform

(B) UNILATERAL CONTRACT. In contrast with a bilateral contract, the offeror may promise to do something or to pay a certain amount of money only when the offeree does an act.[12] Examples of where **unilateral contracts** commonly appear are when a reward is offered, a contest is announced, or changes are made and disseminated in an employee manual. The offeree does not accept the offer by express agreement, but rather by performance.

CASE SUMMARY

Unilateral Contract: Pretty Good Bonus!

FACTS: Aon Risk Services, Inc. (ARS Arkansas), and Combined Insurance Companies are subsidiaries of Aon Corporation. The parent corporation issued an "Interdependency Memo" dated February 2000, which encouraged ARS brokerage offices to place insurance business with Aon-affiliated companies. It also set up a bonus pool for revenues generated under the plan, with Combined agreeing to pay "30% of annualized premium on all life products over 15-year term plus 15% 1st year for all other products." John Meadors saw the memo in February 2000, and believed it would entitle him to this compensation over and above his employment contract.

---

[10] *Marsh v. Rheinecker,* 641 N.E.2d 1256 (Ill. App. 1994).
[11] *DiGennaro v. Rubbermaid, Inc.,* 214 F. Supp. 2d 1354 (S.D. Fla. 2002).
[12] See *Young v. Virginia Birth-Related Neurological Injury Compensation Program,* 620 S.E.2d 131 (Va. App. 2005).

CASE SUMMARY

Continued

Meadors put Combined in touch with Dillard's Department Stores and on March 24, 2000, Dillard's and Combined executed a five-year agreement whereby Dillard's employees could purchase life, disability, and other insurance policies through workplace enrollment. When Meadors did not receive bonus-pool money generated by the transaction, he sued his employer for breach of a unilateral contract. The employer's defense was that the memo was not sufficiently definite to constitute an offer.

DECISION: Judgment for Meadors for $2,406,522.60. A unilateral contract is composed of an offer that invites acceptance in the form of actual performance. For example, in the case of a reward, the offeree accepts by performing the particular task, such as the capture of the fugitive for which the reward is offered. In this case the offer contained in the Interdependency Memo set out specific percentages of provisions that would go into the bonus pool, and required that the pool be distributed annually. It was sufficiently definite to constitute an offer. Meadors was responsible for the production of the Dillard's account, and was entitled to the bonus promised in the memo. [*Aon Risk Services Inc. v. Meadors*, 267 S.W.3d 603 (Ark. App. 2007)]

(c) Option and First-Refusal Contracts. The parties may make a contract that gives a right to one of them to enter into a second contract at a later date. If one party has an absolute right to enter into the later contract, the initial contract is called an **option contract**. Thus, a bilateral contract may be made today giving one of the parties the right to buy the other party's house for a specified amount. This is an option contract because the party with the privilege has the freedom of choice, or option, to buy or not buy. If the option is exercised, the other party to the contract must follow the terms of the option and enter into the second contract. If the option is never exercised, no second contract ever arises, and the offer protected by the option contract merely expires.

In contrast with an option contract, a contract may merely give a **right of first refusal**. This imposes only the duty to make the first offer to the party having the right of first refusal.

option contract – contract to hold an offer to make a contract open for a fixed period of time.

right of first refusal – right of a party to meet the terms of a proposed contract before it is executed, such as a real estate purchase agreement.

13. Quasi Contracts

In some cases, a court will impose an obligation even though there is no contract.[13] Such an obligation is called a **quasi contract**, which is an obligation imposed by law.

(a) Prevention of Unjust Enrichment. A quasi contract is not a true contract reflecting all of the elements of a contract set forth previously in this chapter. The court is not seeking to enforce the intentions of the parties contained in an agreement. Rather, when a person or enterprise receives a benefit from another, even in the absence of a promise to pay for the benefit, a court may impose an obligation to pay for the reasonable value of that benefit, to avoid *unjust enrichment*. The spirit behind the law of unjust enrichment is to apply the law "outside the box" and fill in the cracks where common civil law and statutes fail to achieve justice.[14]

quasi contract – court-imposed obligation to prevent unjust enrichment in the absence of a contract.

[13] *Thayer v. Dial Industrial Sales, Inc.*, 85 F. Supp. 2d 263 (S.D.N.Y. 2000).
[14] *Hernandez v. Lopez*, 103 Cal. Rptr.3d 376, 381 (Cal. App. 2009).

| FIGURE 12-2 | *Contract* |

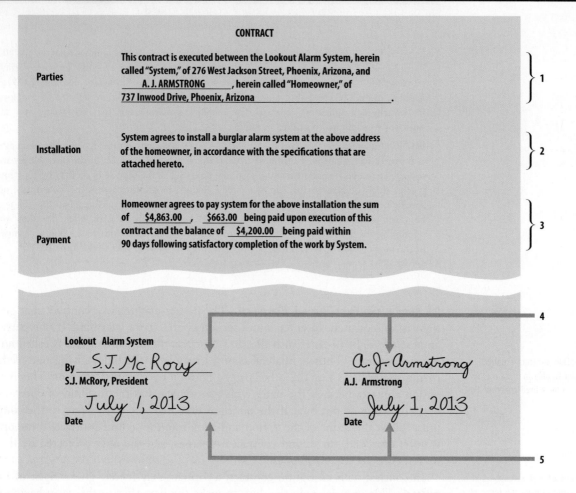

CONTRACT

Parties

This contract is executed between the Lookout Alarm System, herein called "System," of 276 West Jackson Street, Phoenix, Arizona, and _____A. J. ARMSTRONG_____, herein called "Homeowner," of 737 Inwood Drive, Phoenix, Arizona   .

$\Big\}$ 1

Installation

System agrees to install a burglar alarm system at the above address of the homeowner, in accordance with the specifications that are attached hereto.

$\Big\}$ 2

Payment

Homeowner agrees to pay system for the above installation the sum of __$4,863.00__, __$663.00__ being paid upon execution of this contract and the balance of __$4,200.00__ being paid within 90 days following satisfactory completion of the work by System.

$\Big\}$ 3

4

Lookout Alarm System

By _S.J. McRory_
S.J. McRory, President

July 1, 2013
Date

a. J. armstrong
A.J. Armstrong

July 1, 2013
Date

5

Note that this contract includes the following important information: (1) the name and address of each party, (2) the promise or consideration of the seller, (3) the promise or consideration of the buyer, (4) the signature of the two parties, and (5) the date.

✳ A successful claim for unjust enrichment usually requires (1) a benefit conferred on the defendant, (2) the defendant's knowledge of the benefit, and (3) a finding that it would be unjust for the defendant to retain the benefit without payment. The burden of proof is on the plaintiff to prove all of the elements of the claim. **For Example,** Hiram College sued Nicholas Courtad for $6,000 plus interest for tuition and other expenses. Because no evidence of a written contract was produced, the court considered it an unjust enrichment claim by the college. Courtad had attended classes for a few weeks and had not paid his tuition due to a problem with his financial aid package. Because he did not receive any credit hours toward a degree, which is the ultimate benefit of attending college, the court found that he did not receive a benefit and that a finding of unjust enrichment was not appropriate.[15]

[15] *Hiram College v. Courtad,* 834 N.E.2d 432 (Ohio App. 2005).

Sometimes a contract may be unenforceable because of a failure to set forth the contract in writing in compliance with the statute of frauds. In other circumstances, no enforceable contract exists because of a lack of definite and certain terms. Yet in both situations, one party may have performed services for the benefit of the other party and the court will require payment of the reasonable value of services to avoid the unjust enrichment of the party receiving the services without paying for them. These damages are sometimes referred to as *restitution damages*. Some courts refer to this situation as an action or recovery in **quantum meruit** (as much as he or she deserved).

quantum meruit – as much as deserved; an action brought for the value of the services rendered the defendant when there was no express contract as to the purchase price.

For Example, Arya Group, Inc. (Arya), sued the entertainer Cher for unjust enrichment. In June 1996, Cher negotiated an oral agreement with Arya to design and construct a house on her Malibu property for $4,217,529. The parties' oral agreement was set forth in a written contract with an August 1997 date and was delivered to Cher in October 1997. She never signed it. However, between June 1996 and November 1997, Arya performed and received payment for a number of services discharged under the unsigned contract. In August 1997, Cher requested Arya to meet with a home designer named Bussell who had previously worked with Cher on a Florida project, and Arya showed Bussell the plans and designs for the Malibu property and introduced her to his subcontractors. In November 1997, Cher terminated her agreement with Arya without paying the balance then due, as asserted by Arya, of $415,169.41. Arya claims that Cher and Bussell misappropriated the plans and designs Arya had prepared. Cher and the other defendants demurred to Arya's unjust enrichment complaint, pointing out that construction contracts must be evidenced in a writing signed by both parties under state law in order to be enforceable in a court of law. The appeals court determined that Arya's noncompliance with the state law requiring a signed written contract did not absolutely foreclose Arya from seeking damages for unjust enrichment if he could prove the assertions in the complaint that Cher was a sophisticated homeowner with previous involvement in residential construction who had legal representation in negotiating the agreement with Arya, and that Cher would be unjustly enriched if she were not required to compensate Arya for the reasonable value of the work already performed.[16]

CASE SUMMARY

No Free Rides

FACTS: PIC Realty leased farmland to Southfield Farms. After Southfield harvested its crop, it cultivated the land in preparation for the planting in the following year. However, its lease expired, so it did not plant that crop. It then sued PIC for reimbursement for the reasonable value of the services and materials used in preparing the land because this was a benefit to PIC. There was evidence that it was customary for landlords to compensate tenants for such work.

DECISION: Southfield was entitled to recover the reasonable value of the benefit conferred upon PIC. This was necessary in order to prevent the unjust enrichment of PIC. [*PIC Realty Corp. v. Southfield Farms, Inc.*, 832 S.W.2d 610 (Tex. App. 1992)]

[16] *Arya Group, Inc. v. Cher*, 91 Cal. Rptr. 2d 815 (Cal. App. 2000). See also *Fischer v. Flax*, 816 A.2d 1 (2003).

A situation may arise over the mistaken conference of a benefit. **For Example,** Nantucket Island has a few approved colors for houses in its historic district. Using the approved gray color, Martin Kane and his crew began painting Sheldon Adams's house in the historic district as the result of a mistaken address. Adams observed the initiation of the work from his office across the street but did nothing to stop the painters. At the end of the day when the work was done, Adams refused to pay for the work, saying, "I signed no contract and never approved this work." The law deems it inequitable that Adams should have received the benefit of this work, having observed the benefit being conferred and knowing that the painters expected payment. Adams would be unjustly enriched if he were allowed to retain the benefit without payment for the reasonable value of the work. If Adams did not have knowledge that the work was being done and thus that payment was expected, quasi-contractual liability would not be imposed.

The mistake that benefits the defendant may be the mistake of a third party.

(B) Preclusion by an Express Contract. Courts award relief based on quasi-contractual principles, implying by law a contract where one did not exist in fact. Thus, where an express contract exists, it precludes an unjust enrichment claim.

CASE SUMMARY

When in Doubt, Write It Out

FACTS: Facing financial turbulence, Philippine Airlines (PAL) sought to renegotiate its aircraft lease contract (ALC) with World Airlines (WA). WA refused to negotiate with PAL. PAL retained John Sununu, the former Governor of New Hampshire and the former Chief of Staff to President George H. W. Bush and Sununu's partner Victor Frank to represent it. Sununu and Frank sent a contract proposal to PAL, which included a proposed "success fee" of $600,000 if they persuaded WA to accept a modification of the lease contract. PAL gave Sununu and Frank a verbal go-ahead but did not sign the proposed contract. Thereafter PAL sent a contract that was different from that proposed by Sununu and Frank, containing a success fee of 4 percent of savings if they were able to reach a settlement to reduce the remaining obligation of PAL to WA in accordance with either of two very specific settlement offers. Caught up in the actual intense settlement negotiations with WA on behalf of PAL Sununu and Frank signed the contract. Thereafter, they were successful in obtaining an amendment to the lease contract, saving PAL $12.8 million. PAL refused to pay a success fee of $520,000 because the actual settlement did not meet the contractual criteria, which was limited to just the two specific settlement offers. Sununu and Frank sued PAL for unjust enrichment and other contract theories.

DECISION: Judgment for PAL. Sununu and Frank conferred a benefit on PAL through their efforts to persuade WA to negotiate with PAL; and PAL accepted and retained the benefit for the renegotiated lease. There can be no claim, however, for unjust enrichment when an express contract exists between two parties. A court awards relief based on quasi-contractual principles, implying by law a contract, only where one did not exist in fact. The court stated:

> To grant PAL's summary judgment motion is not to condone its conduct. The airline can rightly be accused of stinginess for enforcing the formalistic terms of the contract in spite of the plaintiffs' earnest efforts on its behalf.... PAL may have violated Sununu and Frank's trust, but it did not violate the law.

CASE SUMMARY

Continued

... Sununu and Frank seem to have done their best to serve their client, but they made a reckless bet by trusting PAL. They were accustomed to handshake deals in which personal relationships count for more than legal documents, so they made little effort to put their understanding with PAL on paper. When they ran into a client who didn't play by the same rules, they paid the price.

The lesson is one that should be taught in law and business schools across America: When in doubt, write it out.

[*Sununu v. Philippine Airlines, Inc.*, 792 F. Supp. 2d 39 (D. D.C. 2011)]

Thinking Things Through

Twelve Years of Litigation

Brown University accepted the bid of Marshall Contractors, Inc. (Marshall), to build the Pizzitola Sports Facility on its Providence, Rhode Island, campus. The parties intended to execute a formal written contract. Brown decided to pay $7,157,051 for the project, but Marshall sought additional payment for items it deemed extras and not contemplated in its bid. Because the parties were unable to agree on the scope of the project as compared to the price Brown was willing to pay, they never executed the formal written contract. Nevertheless, in the context of this disagreement over terms and price, construction began in May 1987. When the parties could not resolve their disagreements as the project neared completion in January 1989, Marshall sued Brown University, seeking to recover the costs for what it deemed "changes." Brown asserted that an implied-in-fact contract existed for all work at the $7,157,051 figure because the contractor went ahead with the project knowing the money Brown would pay. The litigation ended up in the Supreme Court of Rhode Island, and in 1997, the court concluded that no express or implied-in-fact contract had ever been reached by the parties concerning the scope of the project and what costs were to be included in the price stipulated by Brown. The case was remanded to the trial court for a new trial. After a trial on the theories of *quantum meruit* and unjust enrichment, a jury awarded Marshall $1.2 million dollars, which was some $3.1 million less than Marshall sought. Brown University appealed, and on November 21, 2001, the Supreme Court of Rhode Island affirmed the jury verdict for the contractor, determining that the proper measure of damages on unjust

enrichment and *quantum meruit* theories was "the reasonable value of the work done."*

In May 1987 when the parties could not reach agreement enabling the execution of a formal written contract, thinking things through at that point in time should have exposed the potential for significant economic uncertainties to both parties in actually starting the building process under such circumstances. In the spring of 1987 when all parties were unable to reach agreement, mediation or expedited arbitration by construction experts may well have resolved the controversy and yielded an amicable written contract with little or no delay to the project. Instead, the unsettled cost issues during the building process could have had an adverse impact on the "job chemistry" between the contractor and the owner, which may have adversely affected the progress and quality of the job. The 12 years of litigation that, with its economic and human resource costs, yielded just $1.2 million for the contractor was a no-win result for both sides. A primary rule for all managers in projects of this scope is to make sure the written contracts are executed before performance begins! Relying on "implied-in-fact" or quasi-contract legal theories is simply a poor management practice.

*ADP Marshall, Inc. v. Brown University, 784 A2d 309 (R.I. 2001).

(c) EXTENT OF RECOVERY. When recovery is allowed in quasi contract, the plaintiff recovers the reasonable value of the benefit conferred on the defendant,[17] or the fair and reasonable[18] value of the work performed, depending on the jurisdiction and the circumstances of the case itself. The customary method of calculating damages in construction contract cases is actual job costs plus an allowance for overhead and profits minus amount paid.[19]

C. CONTRACTING ON THE INTERNET

Doing business online for consumers is very similar to doing business through a catalog purchase or by phone. Before placing an order, a buyer is commonly concerned about the reputation of the seller. The basic purchasing principle of *caveat emptor* still applies: buyer beware! The Internet provides valuable tools to allow a buyer to research the reputation of the seller and its products. Online evaluations of companies and their products can be found at Web sites, such as Consumer Reports (**www.consumerreports.org**), Consumers Digest (**www .consumersdigest.com**), or the Better Business Bureau (**www.bbb.org**). E-consumers may have access to categorized histories of comments by other e-consumers, such as Planet Feedback ratings at **www.planetfeedback.com**.

The intellectual property principles set forth in Chapter 10—as well as the contractual principles, the law of sales, and privacy laws you are about to study—all apply to e-commerce transactions. When you are purchasing an item online, you must carefully read all of the terms and conditions set forth on the seller's Web site when assessing whether to make a contemplated purchase. The proposed terms may require that any disputes be litigated in a distant state or be resolved through arbitration with restricted remedies, or there may be an unsatisfactory return policy, warranty limitations, or limitation of liability. Generally, the Web site terms become the contract of the parties and are legally enforceable.

The laws you have studied that prevent deceptive advertising by brick-and-mortar businesses also apply to Internet sites.[20] If an in-state site is engaging in false advertising, you may be able to exercise consumer protection rights through your state's attorney general's office, or you may find some therapeutic relief by reporting the misconduct to the Internet Scambusters site (**www.scambusters.com**).

From a seller's perspective, it is exceedingly helpful to have as much information as possible on your potential customers' buying habits. Federal law prohibits the collection of personal information from children without parental consent, and some states restrict the unauthorized collection of personal information. European Union countries have strict laws protecting the privacy of consumers. Sellers intending to collect personal information should obtain the consent of their customers, make certain that children are excluded, and make sure that the information is stored in a secure environment.

Advanced encryption technology has made the use of credit card payments through the Internet very safe. No computer system connected to the Internet is

---

[17] *Ramsey v. Ellis*, 484 N.W.2d 331 (Wis. 1992).

[18] *ADP Marshall, Inc. v. Brown University*, 784 A.2d 309 (R.I. 2001).

[19] *Miranco Contracting, Inc. v. Perel*, 871 N.Y.S.2d 310 (A.D. 2008).

[20] See *MADCAP I, LLC v. McNamee*, 712 N.W.2d 16 (Wis. App. 2005) in which the court found genuine issues of material fact as to whether a business Web site falsely represented the size and nature of its business to induce the public to purchase products and services described on its Web site in violation of the state's fraudulent representations statute.

totally secure however. In the worst-case scenario, credit card issuers will not charge a user for more than the first $50 of unauthorized activity.

Internet contracts involve the same types of issues that are addressed in contracts offline but with certain technology-related nuances. The parties to the e-contracts must still negotiate their obligations in clear and unambiguous language, including such terms as quantity, quality, and price as well as warranties, indemnification responsibilities, limitations on liability, and termination procedures. The federal Electronic Signatures in Global and National Commerce Act (E-Sign) and the Uniform Electronic Transactions Act (UETA) mandate parity between paper and electronic contracts. The basic legal rules that govern contracts offline are the very same rules that govern online contracts, and basic civil procedure rules apply. **For Example,** California buyer Paul Boschetto bought a 1964 Ford Galaxy that had been advertised on eBay to be "in awesome condition" from a Milton, Wisconsin resident, J. Hansing, for $34,106. On delivery Boschetto discovered that the car had rust, extensive dents, and would not start. His lawsuit against Hansing in U.S. District Court in California was dismissed for lack of personal jurisdiction.[21] (The formation of a contract with a nonresident defendant was not, standing alone, sufficient to create personal jurisdiction in California.)

Boxes identifying special Internet e-commerce topics are strategically placed throughout these chapters.

LawFlix

Paper Moon (1973) (PG)

In this movie for which Tatum O'Neal was given an Oscar, the ongoing issue between Annie and her alleged father is her recoupment of the money she says he promised. Discuss the contract issues (voidable [minor], formation, unilateral vs. bilateral, express, informal, etc.).

MAKE THE CONNECTION

SUMMARY

A contract is a binding agreement between two or more parties. A contract arises when an offer is accepted with contractual intent (the intent to make a binding agreement).

Contracts may be classified in a number of ways according to form, the way in which they were created, validity, and obligations. With respect to form, a contract may be either informal or formal, such as those under seal or those appearing on the records of courts. Contracts may be classified by the way they were created as those that are expressed by words— written or oral—and those that are implied or deduced from conduct. The question of validity requires distinguishing between contracts that are valid, those that are voidable, and those that are not contracts at all but are merely void agreements. Contracts can be distinguished on the basis of the obligations created as executed contracts, in which

---

[21] *Boschetto v. Hansing*, 539 F.3d 1011 (9th Cir. 2008).

everything has been performed, and executory contracts, in which something remains to be done. The bilateral contract is formed by exchanging a promise for a promise, so each party has the obligation of thereafter rendering the promised performance. In the unilateral contract, which is the doing of an act in exchange for a promise, no further performance is required of the offeree who performed the act.

In certain situations, the law regards it as unjust for a person to receive a benefit and not pay for it.

In such a case, the law of quasi contracts allows the performing person to recover the reasonable value of the benefit conferred on the benefited person even though no contract between them requires any payment. Unjust enrichment, which a quasi contract is designed to prevent, sometimes arises when there was never any contract between the persons involved or when there was a contract, but for some reason it was avoided or held to be merely a void agreement.

LEARNING OUTCOMES

After studying this chapter, you should be able to clearly explain:

A. Nature of Contracts

L0.1   Explain the meaning and importance of privity of a contract

See the example of the subcontractor, RPR & Associates, who worked on a project but could not sue the owner for payment, pp. 244–245.

See the example involving rapper Eminem, FBT, and Aftermath Records, where FBT was not a party to the contract and thus not bound by it, p. 245.

L0.2   Describe the way in which a contract arises

See the discussion on offer and acceptance on p. 245.

See the example of the Nantucket painters on p. 252.

See the *AON Risk Services* case where an insurance agent won his case based on a unilateral contract theory, pp. 248–249.

L0.4   Explain the reasoning behind quasi-contract recovery

See the example whereby Cher had to pay a home designer for certain work even though there was no contract, p. 251.

C. Contracting on the Internet

L0.5   Explain how Internet contracts involve the same types of issues as offline contracts

See the eBay example on p. 255.

B. Classes of Contracts

L0.3   Distinguish between bilateral and unilateral contracts

KEY TERMS

bilateral contract	obligee	*quantum meruit*
contract	obligor	quasi contract
contract under seal	offeree	recognizance
executed contract	offeror	right of first refusal
executory contract	option contract	unilateral contracts
express contract	privity	valid contract
formal contract	privity of contract	void agreement
implied contract	promisee	voidable contract
informal contract	promisor	

QUESTIONS AND CASE PROBLEMS

1. What is a contract?

2. Fourteen applicants for a city of Providence, Rhode Island, police academy training class each received from the city a letter stating that it was a "conditional offer of employment" subject to successful completion of medical and psychological exams. The 14 applicants passed the medical and psychological exams. However, these applicants were replaced by others after the city changed the selection criteria. Can you identify an offer and acceptance in this case? Can you make out a bilateral or unilateral contract? [*Ardito et al. v. City of Providence*, 213 F. Supp. 2d 358 (D.R.I.)]

3. Compare an implied contract with a quasi contract.

4. The Jordan Keys law firm represented the Greater Southeast Community Hospital of Washington, D.C., in a medical malpractice suit against the hospital. The hospital was self-insured for the first $1,000,000 of liability and the St. Paul Insurance Co. provided excess coverage up to $4,000,000. The law firm was owed $67,000 for its work on the malpractice suit when the hospital went into bankruptcy. The bankruptcy court ordered the law firm to release its files on the case to St. Paul to defend under the excess coverage insurance, and the Jordan Keys firm sued St. Paul for its legal fees of $67,000 expended prior to the bankruptcy under an "implied-in-fact contract" because the insurance company would have the benefit of all of its work. Decide. [*Jordan Keys v. St. Paul Fire*, 870 A.2d 58 (D.C.)]

5. Beck was the general manager of Chilkoot Lumber Co. Haines sold fuel to the company. To persuade Haines to sell on credit, Beck signed a paper by which he promised to pay any debt the lumber company owed Haines. He signed this paper with his name followed by "general manager." Haines later sued Beck on this promise, and Beck raised the defense that the addition of "general manager" showed that Beck, who was signing on behalf of Chilkoot, was not personally liable and did not intend to be bound by the paper. Was Beck liable on the paper? [*Beck v. Haines Terminal and Highway Co.*, 843 P.2d 1229 (Alaska)]

6. *A* made a contract to construct a house for *B*. Subsequently, *B* sued *A* for breach of contract. *A* raised the defense that the contract was not binding because it was not sealed. Is this a valid defense? [*Cooper v. G. E. Construction Co.*, 158 S.E.2d 305 (Ga. App.)]

7. Edward Johnson III, the CEO and principal owner of the world's largest mutual fund company, Fidelity Investments, Inc., was a longtime tennis buddy of Richard Larson. In 1995, Johnson asked Larson, who had construction experience, to supervise the construction of a house on Long Pond, Mount Desert Island, Maine. Although they had no written contract, Larson agreed to take on the project for $6,700 per month plus lodging. At the end of the project in 1997, Johnson made a $175,000 cash payment to Larson, and he made arrangements for Larson to live rent-free on another Johnson property in the area called Pray's Meadow in exchange for looking after Johnson's extensive property interests in Maine. In the late summer of 1999, Johnson initiated a new project on the Long Pond property. Johnson had discussions with Larson about doing this project, but Larson asked to be paid his former rate, and Johnson balked because he had already hired a project manager. According to Johnson, at a later date he again asked Larson to take on the "shop project" as a favor and in consideration of continued rent-free use of the Pray's Meadow home. Johnson stated that Larson agreed to do the job "pro bono" in exchange for the use of the house, and Johnson acknowledged that he told Larson he would "take care" of Larson at the end of the project, which could mean as much or as little as Johnson determined. Larson stated that Johnson told him that he would "take care of" Larson if he would do the project and told him to "trust the Great Oracle" (meaning Johnson, the highly successful businessperson). Larson sought payment in March 2000 and asked Johnson for "something on account" in April. Johnson offered

Larson a loan. In August during a tennis match, Larson again asked Johnson to pay him. Johnson became incensed, and through an employee, he ended Larson's participation in the project and asked him to vacate Pray's Meadow. Larson complied and filed suit for payment for work performed at the rate of $6,700 per month. Did Larson have an express contract with Johnson? What legal theory or theories could Larson utilize in his lawsuit? How would you decide this case if you believed Larson's version of the facts? How would you decide the case if you believed Johnson's version of the facts? [*Larson v. Johnson,* 196 F. Supp. 2d 38 (D. Me. 2002)]

8. While Clara Novak was sick, her daughter Janie helped her in many ways. Clara died, and Janie then claimed that she was entitled to be paid for the services she had rendered her mother. This claim was opposed by three brothers and sisters who also rendered services to the mother. They claimed that Janie was barred because of the presumption that services rendered between family members are gratuitous. Janie claimed that this presumption was not applicable because she had not lived with her mother but had her own house. Was Janie correct? [*In re Estate of Novak,* 398 N.W.2d 653 (Minn. App.)]

9. Dozier and his wife, daughter, and grandson lived in the house Dozier owned. At the request of the daughter and grandson, Paschall made some improvements to the house. Dozier did not authorize these, but he knew that the improvements were being made and did not object to them. Paschall sued Dozier for the reasonable value of the improvements, but Dozier argued that he had not made any contract for such improvements. Was he obligated to pay for such improvements?

10. When Harriet went away for the summer, Landry, a house painter, painted her house. He had a contract to paint a neighbor's house but painted Harriet's house by mistake. When Harriet returned from vacation, Landry billed her for $3,100, which was a fair price for the work. She refused to pay. Landry claimed that she had a quasi-contractual liability for that amount.
Was he correct?

11. Margrethe and Charles Pyeatte, a married couple, agreed that she would work so that he could go to law school and that when he finished, she would go back to school for her master's degree. After Charles was admitted to the bar and before Margrethe went back to school, the two were divorced. She sued Charles, claiming that she was entitled to quasi-contractual recovery of the money that she had paid for Charles's support and law school tuition. He denied liability. Was she entitled to recover for the money she spent for Charles's maintenance and law school tuition? [*Pyeatte v. Pyeatte,* 661 P.2d 196 (Ariz. App.)]

12. Carriage Way was a real estate development of approximately 80 houses and 132 apartments. The property owners were members of the Carriage Way Property Owners Association. Each year, the association would take care of certain open neighboring areas, including a nearby lake, that were used by the property owners. The board of directors of the association would make an assessment or charge against the property owners to cover the cost of this work. The property owners paid these assessments for a number of years and then refused to pay any more. In spite of this refusal, the association continued to take care of the areas in question. The association then sued the property owners and claimed that they were liable for the benefit that had been conferred on them. Were the owners liable? [*Board of Directors of Carriage Way Property Owners Ass'n v. Western National Bank,* 487 N.E.2d 974 (Ill. App.)]

13. When improvements or buildings are added to real estate, the real estate tax assessment is usually increased to reflect the increased value of the property. Frank Partipilo and Elmer Hallman owned neighboring tracts of land. Hallman made improvement to his land, constructing a new building and driveway on the tract. The tax assessor made a mistake about the location of the boundary line between Partipilo's and Hallman's land and thought the improvements were made on Partipilo's property. Instead of increasing the taxes on Hallman's land, the assessor wrongly increased the taxes on Partipilo's land. Partipilo paid the increased taxes for three years. When he

learned why his taxes had been increased, he sued Hallman for the amount of the increase that Partipilo had been paying. Hallman raised the defense that he had not done anything wrong and that the mistake had been the fault of the tax assessor. Decide. [*Partipilo v. Hallman*, 510 N.E.2d 8 (Ill.App.)]

14. When a college student complained about a particular course, the vice president of the college asked the teacher to prepare a detailed report about the course. The teacher did and then demanded additional compensation for the time spent in preparing the report. He claimed that the college was liable to provide compensation on an implied contract. Was he correct? [*Zadrozny v. City Colleges of Chicago*, 581 N.E.2d 44 (Ill. App.)]

15. Smith made a contract to sell automatic rifles to a foreign country. Because the sale of such weapons to that country was illegal under an act of Congress, the U.S. government prosecuted Smith for making the contract. He raised the defense that because the contract was illegal, it was void and there is no binding obligation when a contract is void; therefore, no contract for which he could be prosecuted existed. Was he correct?

CPA QUESTIONS

1. Kay, an art collector, promised Hammer, an art student, that if Hammer could obtain certain rare artifacts within two weeks, Kay would pay for Hammer's postgraduate education. At considerable effort and expense, Hammer obtained the specified artifacts within the two-week period. When Hammer requested payment, Kay refused. Kay claimed that there was no consideration for the promise. Hammer would prevail against Kay based on:

   a. Unilateral contract.

   b. Unjust enrichment.

   c. Public policy.

   d. Quasi contract.

© Manuel Gutjahr/iStockphoto.com

CHAPTER 13

Formation of Contracts: Offer and Acceptance

learningoutcomes

After studying this chapter, you should be able to

LO.1 Decide whether an offer contains definite and certain terms

LO.2 Explain the exceptions the law makes to the requirement of definiteness

LO.3 Explain all the ways an offer can be terminated

LO.4 Explain what constitutes the acceptance of an offer

LO.5 Explain the implications of failing to read a clickwrap agreement

A *contract* consists of enforceable obligations that have been voluntarily assumed. Thus, one of the essential elements of a contract is an agreement. This chapter explains how the basic agreement arises, when there is a contract, and how there can be merely unsuccessful negotiations without a resulting contract.

A. REQUIREMENTS OF AN OFFER

offer–expression of an offeror's willingness to enter into a contractual agreement.

An **offer** expresses the willingness of the offeror to enter into a contractual agreement regarding a particular subject. It is a promise that is conditional upon an act, a forbearance (a refraining from doing something one has a legal right to do), or a return promise.

CPA

1. Contractual Intention

To make an offer, the offeror must appear to intend to create a binding obligation. Whether this intent exists is determined by objective standards.[1] This intent may be shown by conduct. **For Example,** when one party signs a written contract and sends it to the other party, such action is an offer to enter into a contract on the terms of the writing.

There is no contract when a social invitation is made or when an offer is made in obvious jest or excitement. A reasonable person would not regard such an offer as indicating a willingness to enter into a binding agreement. The test for a valid, binding offer is whether it induces a reasonable belief in the offeree that he or she can, by accepting it, bind the offeror, as developed in the *Wigod* case.

CASE SUMMARY

A Valid Offer!

FACTS: The U.S. Department of the Treasury implemented the federal Home Affordable Mortgage Program (HAMP) to help homeowners avoid foreclosure amidst the sharp decline in the nation's housing market in 2008. In 2009, Wells Fargo Bank issued Lori Wigod a four-month "trial" loan modification under a Trial Period Plan (TPP). After the trial period, if the borrower complied with all of the terms of the TPP agreement, including making all required payments and providing all required documentation, and if the borrower's representations remained true and correct, the servicer, Well Fargo, had to offer a permanent mortgage modification. Wigod alleged that she complied with these requirements and that Wells Fargo refused to grant a permanent modification. Wells Fargo contended that the TPP contained no valid offer.

DECISION: Judgment for Wigod. A person can prevent his submission from being treated as an offer by using suitable language conditioning the formation of a contract on some further step, such as approval by corporate headquarters. It is when the promisor conditions a promise on *his*

---

[1] *Glass Service Co. v. State Farm Mutual Automobile Ins. Co.,* 530 N.W.2d 867 (Minn. App. 1995).

CASE SUMMARY

Continued

own future action or approval that there is no binding offer. Here, the TTP spelled out two conditions precedent to Wells Fargo's obligation to offer a permanent modification. Wigod had to comply with the requirements of the TPP, and her financial representations had to be true and accurate. These conditions had to be satisfied by the promisee (Wigod). Here a reasonable person in Wigod's position would read the TPP as a default offer that she could accept so long as she satisfied the two conditions. [*Wigod v. Wells Fargo Bank,* **673 F.3d 547 (7th Cir. 2012)**]

(A) INVITATION TO NEGOTIATE. The first statement made by one of two persons is not necessarily an offer. In many instances, there may be a preliminary discussion or an invitation by one party to the other to negotiate or to make an offer. Thus, an inquiry by a school as to whether a teacher wished to continue the following year was merely a survey or invitation to negotiate and was not an offer that could be accepted. Therefore, the teacher's affirmative response did not create a contract.

Ordinarily, a seller sending out circulars or catalogs listing prices is not regarded as making an offer to sell at those prices. The seller is merely indicating a willingness to consider an offer made by a buyer on those terms. The reason for this rule is, in part, the practical consideration that because a seller does not have an unlimited supply of any commodity, the seller cannot possibly intend to make a contract with everyone who sees the circular. The same principle is applied to merchandise that is displayed with price tags in stores or store windows and to most advertisements. An advertisement in a newspaper is ordinarily considered an invitation to negotiate and is not an offer that can be accepted by a reader of the paper.[2] However, some court decisions have construed advertisements as offers that called for an act on the part of the customer thereby forming a unilateral contract, such as the advertisement of a reward for the return of lost property.

Quotations of prices, even when sent on request, are likewise not offers unless the parties have had previous dealings or unless a trade custom exists that would give the recipient of the quotation reason to believe that an offer was being made. Whether a price quotation is to be treated as an offer or merely an invitation to negotiate is a question of the intent of the party giving the quotation.[3]

(B) AGREEMENT TO MAKE A CONTRACT AT A FUTURE DATE. No contract arises when the parties merely agree that at a future date they will consider making a contract or will make a contract on terms to be agreed on at that time. In such a case, neither party is under any obligation until the future contract is made. Unless an agreement is reached on all material terms and conditions and nothing is left to future negotiations, a contract to enter a contract in the future is of no effect. **For Example,** Hewitt Associates provided employee benefits administrative services to Rollins, Inc. under a contract negotiated in 2001 to run through 2006. Prior to its expiration, the

---

[2] *Zanakis-Pico v. Cutter, Dodge, Inc.,* 47 P.2d 1222 (Haw. 2002).
[3] Statutes prohibiting false or misleading advertising may require adherence to advertised prices.

parties negotiated—seeking to agree to a multiyear extension of the 2001 agreement. They agreed to all of the material terms of the contract, except that Rollins balked at a $1.8 million penalty clause. Rollins's employees told Hewitt that the extension "was going to be signed." However, Rollins did not sign and the 2001 agreement expired. Hewitt's contention that the agreement was enforceable at the moment Rollins told Hewitt it was going to sign the new agreement was rejected by the court, stating that an agreement to reach an agreement is a contradiction in terms and imposes no obligation on the parties.[4]

2. Definiteness

An offer, and the resulting contract, must be definite and certain.[5] If an offer is indefinite or vague or if an essential provision is lacking,[6] no contract arises from an attempt to accept it. The reason is that courts cannot tell what the parties are to do. Thus, an offer to conduct a business for as long as it is profitable is too vague to be a valid offer. The acceptance of such an offer does not result in a contract that can be enforced. Statements by a bank that it was "with" the debtors and would "support" them in their proposed business venture were too vague to be regarded as a promise by the bank to make necessary loans to the debtors.

CASE SUMMARY

What Is the Meaning of an Agreement for a "Damn Good Job"?

FACTS: Larry Browneller made an oral contract with Hubert Plankenhorn to restore a 1963 Chevrolet Impala convertible. The car was not in good condition. Hubert advised the owner that his work would not yield a car of "show" quality because of the condition of the body, and he accordingly believed that the owner merely wanted a presentable car. Larry, on the other hand, having told Hubert that he wanted a "damn good job," thought this statement would yield a car that would be competitive at the small amateur car shows he attended. When the finished car had what Larry asserted were "waves" in the paint as a result of an uneven surface on the body, Larry brought suit against Hubert for breach of the oral contract.

DECISION: There was clearly a misunderstanding between the parties over the quality of work that could and would be obtained. *Quality* was a material term of the oral contract between the parties, on which there was no shared understanding. Accordingly, a court will not find an individual in breach of a term of the contract where the term did not exist. [***In re Plankenhorn,* 228 B.R. 638 (N.D. Ohio 1998)**]

The fact that minor, ministerial, and nonessential terms are left for future determination does not make an agreement too vague to be a contract.[7]

---

[4] *Hewitt Associates, LLC v. Rollins, Inc.,* 669 S.E.2d 551 (Ga. App. 2008).

[5] *Norton v. Correctional Medicare, Inc.,* 2010 WL 4103016 (N.D.N.Y. Oct. 18, 2010).

[6] *Peace v. Doming Holdings Inc.,* 554 S.E.2d 314 (Ga. App. 2001).

[7] *Hsu v. Vet-A-Mix, Inc.,* 479 N.W.2d 336 (Iowa App. 1991). But see *Ocean Atlantic Development Corp. v. Aurora Christian Schools, Inc.,* 322 F.3d 983 (7th Cir. 2003), where letter offers to purchase (OTP) real estate were signed by both parties, but the offers conditioned the purchase and sale of each property upon the subsequent execution of a purchase and sale agreement. The court held that the parties thus left themselves room to walk away from the deal under Illinois law, and the OTPs were not enforced.

CASE SUMMARY

Offer to Purchase Is Controlling Legal Document

FACTS: John McCarthy executed an offer to purchase (OTP) real estate on a preprinted form generated by the Greater Boston Real Estate Board. The OTP contained a description of the property, the price to be paid, deposit requirements, limited title requirements, and the time and place for closing. The OTP required the parties to execute the applicable Standard Form Purchase and Sale Agreement recommended by the Greater Boston Real Estate Board that, when executed, was to be the agreement between the parties. An unnumbered paragraph immediately above the signature line stated: "NOTICE: This is a legal document that creates binding obligations. If not understood, consult an attorney." The seller, Ann Tobin, signed the OTP. While lawyers for the parties exchanged drafts of a purchase and sale agreement (PSA), a much higher offer for the property was made to Tobin by the Diminicos. Because she had not yet signed the purchase and sale agreement, Tobin accepted the Diminicos's offer and executed a purchase and sales agreement with them. Before that deal closed, McCarthy filed an action for specific performance of the OTP. McCarthy contended he and Tobin intended to be bound by the OTP and that the execution of a PSA was merely a formality. Tobin contended the OTP language contemplated the execution of a final written document, thus clearly indicating that the parties had not agreed to all material aspects of the transaction, and thus the parties did not intend to be bound until the PSA was signed. From a judgment for Tobin and the Diminicos, McCarthy appealed.

DECISION: Judgment for McCarthy. Although the provisions of the purchase and sale agreement can be the subject of negotiation, norms exist for their customary resolution. The inference that the OTP was legally binding is bolstered by the notice printed on the form. McCarthy and Tobin were alerted to the fact that the OTP "creates binding obligations." The OTP employed familiar contractual language. It stated that McCarthy "hereby offers to buy" the property, and Tobin's signature indicates that "this Offer is hereby accepted." The OTP also details the amount to be paid and when, describes the property bought, and specifies for how long the offer was open. This was a firm offer, the acceptance of which bound Tobin to sell and McCarthy to buy the subject property. [***McCarthy v. Tobin*, 706 N.E.2d 629 (Mass. 1999)**]

Thinking Things Through

The Rules of Negotiations

Business agreements are often reached after much discussion, study, and posturing by both sides. Many statements may be made by both sides about the price or value placed on the subject of the transaction. Withholding information or presenting selective, self-serving information may be perceived by a party to the negotiations as protective self-interest. Does the law of contracts apply a duty of good faith and fair dealing in the negotiation of contracts? Does the Uniform Commercial Code provide for a general duty of good faith in the negotiation of contracts? Are lawyers under an ethical obligation to inform opposing counsel of relevant facts? The answer to all of these questions is no.

The Restatement (Second) of Contracts applies the duty of good faith and fair dealing to the performance and enforcement of contracts,

not their negotiation*; so also does the UCC.** The American Bar Association's Model Rules of Professional Conduct, Rule 4.1 Comment 1 requires a lawyer to be "truthful" when dealing with others on a client's behalf, but it also states that generally a lawyer has "no affirmative duty to inform an opposing party of relevant facts."*** Comment 2 to Rule 4.1 contains an example of a "nonmaterial" statement of a lawyer as "estimates of price or value placed on the subject of a transaction."

The legal rules of negotiations state that—in the absence of fraud, special relationships, or statutory or contractual duties—negotiators are

*Restatement (Second) of Contracts §105, comment (c).
**Uniform Commercial Code §1-203.
***American Bar Association Model Rule of Professional Conduct 4.1(a) Comment 1.

Thinking Things Through

Continued

not obligated to divulge pertinent information to the other party to the negotiations. The parties to negotiations themselves must demand and analyze pertinent information and ultimately assess the fairness of the proposed transaction. Should a party conclude that the elements of a final proposal or offer are excessive or dishonest, that party's legal option is to walk away from the deal. Generally, the party has no basis to bring a lawsuit for lack of good faith and fair dealing in negotiations.

However, THINKING THINGS THROUGH, the ethical standards for negotiations set forth in Chapter 3 indicate that establishing a

reputation for trustworthiness, candor, and reliability often leads to commercial success for a company's continuing negotiations with its customers, suppliers, distributors, lenders, unions, and employees.*

*For a contrary example, consider the following story. The Atlanta Braves baseball team's general manager Frank Wren negotiated with free agent baseball player Rafael Furcal's agent Paul Kinzer. When all terms had been negotiated, Kinzer asked for a written terms-of-agreement sheet signed by the Braves, which to Wren meant an agreement had been reached. Kinzer took the sheet to the L.A. Dodgers, who then reached an agreement to sign the shortstop. Braves President John Schuerholz said, "The Atlanta Braves will no longer do business with that company—ever. I told Arn Tellem that we can't trust them to be honest and forthright." "Braves GM Blasts Furcal's Agents," Associated Press, *The Boston Globe*, December 20, 2008, C-7.

The law does not favor the destruction of contracts because that would go against the social force of carrying out the intent of the parties.[8] Consequently, when it is claimed that a contract is too indefinite to be enforced, a court will do its best to find the intent of the parties and thereby reach the conclusion that the contract is not too indefinite. **For Example,** boxing promoter Don King had both a Promotional Agreement and a Bout Agreement with boxer Miguel Angel Gonzalez. The Bout Agreement for a boxing match with Julio Cesar Chavez gave King the option to promote the next four of Gonzalez's matches. The contract made clear that if Gonzalez won the Chavez match, he would receive at least $75,000 for the next fight unless the parties agreed otherwise, and if he lost, he would receive at least $25,000 for the subsequent fight unless otherwise agreed. The agreement did not explicitly state the purse for the subsequent match in the event of a draw. The Chavez match ended in a draw, and Gonzalez contended that this omission rendered the contract so indefinite that it was unenforceable. The court disagreed, stating that striking down a contract as indefinite and in essence meaningless is at best a last resort. The court held that although the contract was poorly drafted, the Promotional Agreement contained explicit price terms for which a minimum purse for fights following a draw may be inferred.[9] A court may not, however, rewrite the agreement of the parties in order to make it definite.

(A) DEFINITE BY INCORPORATION. An offer and the resulting contract that by themselves may appear "too indefinite" may be made definite by reference to another writing. **For Example,** a lease agreement that was too vague by itself was made definite because the parties agreed that the lease should follow the standard form with which both were familiar. An agreement may also be made definite by reference to the prior dealings of the parties and to trade practices.

[8] *Mears v. Nationwide Mut., Inc. Co.,* 91 F.3d 1118 (8th Cir. 1996).
[9] *Gonzalez v. Don King Productions, Inc.,* 17 F. Supp. 2d 313 (S.D.N.Y. 1998); see also *Echols v. Pelullo,* 377 F.3d 272 (3rd Cir. 2004).

FIGURE 13-1	*Offer and Acceptance*

© Cengage Learning

(B) IMPLIED TERMS. Although an offer must be definite and certain, not all of its terms need to be expressed. Some omitted terms may be implied by law. **For Example,** an offer "to pay $400" for a certain Movado timepiece does not state the terms of payment. A court, however, would not condemn this provision as too vague but would hold that it required that cash be paid and that the payment be made on delivery of the watch. Likewise, terms may be implied from conduct. As an illustration, when borrowed money was given to the borrower by a check on which the word *loan* was written, the act of the borrower in endorsing the check constituted an agreement to repay the amount of the check.

(C) "BEST EFFORTS" CLAUSES. While decades ago it was generally accepted that a duty defined only in terms of "best efforts" was too indefinite to be enforced, such a view is no longer widely held. **For Example,** Thomas Hinc, an inventor, executed a contract with Lime-O-Sol Company (LOS) for LOS to produce and distribute Hinc's secret ingredient Stain Remover. Under the contract, Hinc was to receive $10 per gallon sold. The contract contained a clause obligating both parties to use their "best efforts" to market the product "in a manner that seems appropriate." Ultimately, LOS never produced, marketed, or sold Stain Remover for the duration of the contract. The court rejected the defense that the "best efforts" provision was vague and unenforceable stating "[b]est efforts, as commonly understood, means, at the very least *some* effort. It certainly does not mean *zero* effort—the construction LOS urges here to escape any obligation under its contract." [10]

(D) DIVISIBLE CONTRACTS. When the agreement consists of two or more parts and calls for corresponding performances of each part by the parties, the agreement is a **divisible contract**. Thus, in a promise to buy several separate articles at different

divisible contract—agreement consisting of two or more parts, each calling for corresponding performances of each part by the parties.

[10] *Hinc v. Lime-O-Sol Company,* 382 F.3d 716 (7th Cir. 2004).

prices at the same time, the agreement may be regarded as separate or divisible promises for the articles.

(E) EXCEPTIONS TO DEFINITENESS. The law has come to recognize certain situations in which the practical necessity of doing business makes it desirable to have a contract, yet the situation is such that it is either impossible or undesirable to adopt definite terms in advance. In these cases, the indefinite term is often tied to the concept of good-faith performance or to some independent factor that will be definitely ascertainable at some time in the future. The indefinite term might be tied to market price, cost to complete, production, or sales requirements. Thus, the law recognizes binding contracts in the case of a **requirements contract**—that is, a contract to buy all requirements of the buyer from the seller.[11] **For Example,** an agreement between Honeywell International Inc. and Air Products and Chemicals Inc. whereby Air Products would purchase its total requirements of wet process chemicals from Honeywell was held to be an enforceable requirements contract. [12] The law also recognizes as binding an **output contract**—that is, the contract of a producer to sell the entire production or output to a given buyer. These are binding contracts even though they do not state the exact quantity of goods that are to be bought or sold.

requirements contract—contract to buy all requirements of the buyer from the seller.

output contract—contract of a producer to sell its entire production or output to a given buyer.

CASE SUMMARY

GM—In the Driver's Seat on Quantity and Timing!

FACTS: Automodular entered into a series of purchase orders that obligated Delphi to purchase and Automodular to provide all of Delphi's requirements deliverable to the original equipment manufacturer (OEM), General Motors. Automodular receives directions from the OEM's final assembly plants, regardless of whether Automodular is under contract to the OEM or Delphi. The purchase orders ("Contracts") incorporated Delphi's terms that the Buyer, GM, could require Automodular to implement changes to the specifications or design of the goods or to the scope of any services covered by the Contracts. GM informed Automodular that it needed fewer components and directed Automodular to, among other requirements, reduce shifts, change the assembly line speed, and change the length of workers' shifts. As a result, Automodular requested a price increase per unit assembled from Delphi because Automodular believed that such an increase was warranted pursuant to the Contract's change-in-scope provision. Delphi, however, refused to negotiate any price increase and the matter was litigated.

DECISION: Judgment for Delphi. In a requirements contract, the parties do not fix a quantity term, but instead, the quantity will be the buyer's needs of a specific commodity over the contract's life. Section 2.5 of the Contract states in relevant part that "[d]eliveries will be made in the quantities, on the dates, and at the times specified by Buyer in this Contract or any subsequent releases or instructions Buyer issues under this Contract," and that "[i]f the requirements of Buyer's customers or market, economic or other conditions require changes in delivery schedules, Buyer may change the rate of scheduled shipments or direct temporary suspension of scheduled shipments without entitling [Automodular] to a price adjustment or other compensation." This provision demonstrates the intent of the parties to allow the buyer to effectively control the timing and quantity of deliveries without entitling Automodular to an adjustment in price. [*In re Delphi Corp.,* 2009 WL 803598 (S.D.N.Y. 2009)]

---

[11] *Simcala v. American Coal Trade, Inc.,* 821 So.2d 197 (Ala. 2001).
[12] *Honeywell International Inc. v. Air Products and Chemicals, Inc.,* 872 A.2d 944 (Sup. Ct. Del. 2005).

CPA

3. Communication of Offer to Offeree

An offer must be communicated to the offeree. Otherwise, the offeree cannot accept even though knowledge of the offer has been indirectly acquired. Internal management communications of an enterprise that are not intended for outsiders or employees do not constitute offers and cannot be accepted by them. Sometimes, particularly in the case of unilateral contracts, the offeree performs the act called for by the offeror without knowing of the offer's existence. Such performance does not constitute an acceptance. Thus, without knowing that a reward is offered for information leading to the arrest of a particular criminal, a person may provide information that leads to the arrest of the criminal. In most states, if that person subsequently learns of the reward, the reward cannot be recovered.[13]

Not only must the offer be communicated but also it must be communicated by the offeror or at the offeror's direction.

CPA

B. Termination of Offer

An offeree cannot accept a terminated offer. Offers may be terminated by revocation, counteroffer, rejection, lapse of time, death or disability of a party, or subsequent illegality.

CPA

4. Revocation of Offer by Offeror

Ordinarily, an offeror can revoke the offer before it is accepted. If this is done, the offeree cannot create a contract by accepting the revoked offer. **For Example,** Bank of America (BOA) contended that it had reached a valid settlement agreement on December 17, 2010, with Jonathan Davidoff concerning his lawsuit against BOA seeking damages for slander of credit and breach of contract. At 3:08 P.M. on December 17, 2010, Davidoff revoked his offer to settle the matter. A few minutes later BOA counsel sent by e-mail the settlement agreements signed by the defendants and asked if Mr. Davidoff would "rescind his rejection." Davidoff clearly revoked the settlement offer prior to BOA's delivery of acceptance of the offer and no contract was formed.[14]

An ordinary offer may be revoked at any time before it is accepted even though the offeror has expressly promised that the offer will be good for a stated period and that period has not yet expired.

The fact that the offeror expressly promised to keep the offer open has no effect when no consideration was given for that promise.

(A) What Constitutes a Revocation? No particular form or words are required to constitute a revocation. Any words indicating the offeror's termination of the offer are sufficient. A notice sent to the offeree that the property that is the subject of the offer has been sold to a third person is a revocation of the offer. A customer's order for goods, which is an offer to purchase at certain prices, is revoked by a notice to the seller of the cancellation of the order, provided that such notice is communicated before the order is accepted.

[handwritten: "actual" notice is required]

---

[13] With respect to the offeror, it should not make any difference, as a practical matter, whether the services were rendered with or without knowledge of the existence of the offer. Only a small number of states have adopted this view, however.

[14] *Davidoff v. Bank of America,* 2011 WL 999564 (S.D. Fla. Oct. 18, 2010).

[handwritten margin note: - Can be delivered to the agent]

(B) COMMUNICATION OF REVOCATION. A revocation of an offer is ordinarily effective only when it is made known to the offeree.[15] Until it is communicated to the offeree, directly or indirectly, the offeree has reason to believe that there is still an offer that may be accepted, and the offeree may rely on this belief. A letter revoking an offer made to a particular offeree is not effective until the offeree receives it. It is not a revocation when the offeror writes it or even when it is mailed or dispatched. A written revocation is effective, however, when it is delivered to the offeree's agent or to the offeree's residence or place of business under such circumstances that the offeree may be reasonably expected to be aware of its receipt.

It is ordinarily held that there is a sufficient communication of the revocation when the offeree learns indirectly of the offeror's revocation. This is particularly true in a land sale when the seller-offeror, after making an offer to sell the land to the offeree, sells the land to a third person and the offeree indirectly learns of such sale. The offeree necessarily realizes that the seller cannot perform the original offer and therefore must be considered to have revoked it.

If the offeree accepts an offer before it is effectively revoked, a valid contract is created.

(c) OPTION CONTRACTS. An *option contract* is a binding promise to keep an offer open for a stated period of time or until a specified date. An option contract requires that the promisor receive consideration—that is, something, such as a sum of money—as the price for the promise to keep the offer open. In other words, the option is a contract to refrain from revoking an offer.

(D) FIRM OFFERS. As another exception to the rule that an offer can be revoked at any time before acceptance, statutes in some states provide that an offeror cannot revoke an offer prior to its expiration when the offeror makes a firm offer. A **firm offer** is an offer that states that it is to be irrevocable, or irrevocable for a stated period of time. Under the Uniform Commercial Code, this doctrine of firm offer applies to a merchant's signed, written offer to buy or sell goods but with a maximum of three months on its period of irrevocability.[16]

firm offer – offer stated to be held open for a specified time, which must be so held in some states even in the absence of an option contract, or under the UCC, with respect to merchants.

5. Counteroffer by Offeree

The offeree rejects the offer when she ignores the original offer and replies with a different offer.[17] If the offeree purports to accept an offer but in so doing makes any change to the terms of the offer, such action is a **counteroffer** that rejects the original offer. An "acceptance" that changes the terms of the offer or adds new terms is a rejection of the original offer and constitutes a counteroffer.[18]

counteroffer – proposal by an offeree to the offeror that changes the terms of, and thus rejects, the original offer.

Ordinarily, if *A* makes an offer, such as to sell a used automobile to *B* for $3,000, and *B* in reply makes an offer to buy at $2,500, the original offer is terminated. *B* is in effect indicating refusal of the original offer and in its place is making a different offer. Such an offer by the offeree is known as a *counteroffer*. No contract arises unless the original offeror accepts the counteroffer.

Counteroffers are not limited to offers that directly contradict the original offers. Any departure from or addition to the original offer is a counteroffer even though the original offer was silent on the point added by the counteroffer.

[15] *MD Drilling and Blasting, Inc. v. MLS Construction, LLC,* 889 A.2d 850 (Conn. App. 2006).
[16] U.C.C. §2-205.
[17] *Bourque v. FDIC,* 42 F.3d 704 (1st Cir. 1994).
[18] *McLaughlin v. Heikkila,* 697 N.W.2d 231 (Minn. App. 2005).

6. Rejection of Offer by Offeree

If the offeree rejects the offer and communicates this rejection to the offeror, the offer is terminated. Communication of a rejection terminates an offer even though the period for which the offeror agreed to keep the offer open has not yet expired. It may be that the offeror is willing to renew the offer, but unless this is done, there is no longer any offer for the offeree to accept.

7. Lapse of Time

When the offer states that it is open until a particular date, the offer terminates on that date if it has not yet been accepted. This is particularly so when the offeror declares that the offer shall be void after the expiration of the specified time. Such limitations are strictly construed. **For Example,** Landry's Restaurant Minnesota Inc. extended a written, signed offer to Starlite L.P. to lease Starlite's real estate for a period of 20 years. The written offer stated that if a fully executed acceptance of the lease is not returned to Landry's Minnesota Inc. within six days of the written offer dated April 30, 1998, "the offer to lease … shall be deemed withdrawn and this lease shall be deemed null and void." Starlite signed and returned the lease agreement on May 11, 1998, five days after the May 6 deadline. Landry's Minnesota occupied the property and built a restaurant on it but vacated the property after nine years. Starlite sued the restaurant's parent corporation, Landry's Restaurants Inc., as guarantor of the lease, seeking payment for past due and ongoing rent. Starlite's lawsuit was not successful as no valid lease agreement existed because no contract could be properly formed when acceptance occurred after the written offer had expired.[19]

If the offer contains a time limitation for acceptance, an attempted acceptance after the expiration of that time has no effect and does not give rise to a contract.[20] When a specified time limitation is imposed on an option, the option cannot be exercised after the expiration of that time, regardless of whether the option was exercised within what would have been held a reasonable time if no time period had been specified.

If the offer does not specify a time, it will terminate after the lapse of a reasonable time. What constitutes a reasonable time depends on the circumstances of each case—that is, on the nature of the subject matter, the nature of the market in which it is sold, the time of year, and other factors of supply and demand. If a commodity is perishable or fluctuates greatly in value, the reasonable time will be much shorter than if the subject matter is of a stable value. An offer to sell a harvested crop of tomatoes would expire within a very short time. When a seller purports to accept an offer after it has lapsed by the expiration of time, the seller's acceptance is merely a counteroffer and does not create a contract unless the buyer accepts that counteroffer.

8. Death or Disability of Either Party

If either the offeror or offeree dies or becomes mentally incompetent before the offer is accepted, the offer is automatically terminated. **For Example,** Chet Wilson offers to sell his ranch to Interport, Inc., for $2.5 million. Five days later, Chet

---

[19] *Starlite Limited Partnership v. Landry's Restaurants, Inc.,* 780 N.W.2d 396 (Minn. App. 2010).
[20] *Century 21 Pinetree Properties, Inc. v. Cason,* 469 S.E.2d 458 (Ga. App. 1996).

is killed in an aviation accident. Interport, Inc., subsequently writes to Chet Wilson Jr., an adult, that his father's offer is accepted. No contract is formed because the offer made by Chet died with him.

CPA

9. Subsequent Illegality

If the performance of the contract becomes illegal after the offer is made, the offer is terminated. **For Example,** if an offer is made to sell six semiautomatic handguns to a commercial firing range for $550 per weapon but a new law prohibiting such sales is enacted before the offer is accepted, the offer is terminated.

CPA

C. Acceptance of Offer

acceptance – unqualified assent to the act or proposal of another; as the acceptance of a draft (bill of exchange), of an offer to make a contract, of goods delivered by the seller, or of a gift or deed.

An **acceptance** is the assent of the offeree to the terms of the offer. Objective standards determine whether there has been an agreement of the parties.

10. What Constitutes an Acceptance?

No particular form of words or mode of expression is required, but there must be a clear expression that the offeree agrees to be bound by the terms of the offer. If the offeree reserves the right to reject the offer, such action is not an acceptance.[21]

11. Privilege of Offeree

Ordinarily, the offeree may refuse to accept an offer. If there is no acceptance, by definition there is no contract. The fact that there had been a series of contracts between the parties and that one party's offer had always been accepted before by the other does not create any legal obligation to continue to accept subsequent offers.

CPA

12. Effect of Acceptance

The acceptance of an offer creates a binding agreement or contract,[22] assuming that all of the other elements of a contract are present. Neither party can subsequently withdraw from or cancel the contract without the consent of the other party. **For Example,** James Gang refused to honor an oral stock purchase agreement he made with Moshen Sadeghi under terms he assented to and that were announced on the record to a court as a mutual settlement of a dispute. Gang was not allowed subsequently to withdraw from the agreement, because it was an enforceable contract.[23]

CPA

13. Nature of Acceptance

An *acceptance* is the offeree's manifestation of intent to enter into a binding agreement on the terms stated in the offer. Whether there is an acceptance depends on whether the offeree has manifested an intent to accept. It is the objective or outward appearance that is controlling rather than the subjective or unexpressed intent of the offeree.[24]

---

[21] *Pantano v. McGowan*, 530 N.W.2d 912 (Neb. 1995).
[22] *Ochoa v. Ford*, 641 N.E.2d 1042 (Ind. App. 1994).
[23] *Sadeghi v. Gang*, 270 S.W.3d 773 (Tex. App. 2008).
[24] *Cowan v. Mervin Mewes, Inc.*, 546 N.W.2d 104 (S.D. 1996).

In the absence of a contrary requirement in the offer, an acceptance may be indicated by an informal "okay," by a mere affirmative nod of the head, or in the case of an offer of a unilateral contract, by performance of the act called for.

The acceptance must be absolute and unconditional. It must accept just what is offered.[25] If the offeree changes any terms of the offer or adds any new term, there is no acceptance because the offeree does not agree to what was offered.

When the offeree does not accept the offer exactly as made, the addition of any qualification converts the "acceptance" into a counteroffer, and no contract arises unless the original offeror accepts such a counteroffer.

CPA 14. Who May Accept?

Only the person to whom an offer is directed may accept it. If anyone else attempts to accept it, no agreement or contract with that person arises.

If the offer is directed to a particular class rather than a specified individual, anyone within that class may accept it. If the offer is made to the public at large, any member of the public at large having knowledge of the existence of the offer may accept it.

When a person to whom an offer was not made attempts to accept it, the attempted acceptance has the effect of an offer. If the original offeror is willing to accept this offer, a binding contract arises. If the original offeror does not accept the new offer, there is no contract.

CASE SUMMARY

There's No Turning Back

FACTS: As a lease was about to expire, the landlord, CRA Development, wrote the tenant, Keryakos Textiles, setting forth the square footage and the rate terms on which the lease would be renewed. Keryakos sent a reply stating that it was willing to pay the proposed rate but wanted different cancellation and option terms in the renewal contract. CRA rejected Keryakos's terms, and on learning this, Keryakos notified CRA that it accepted the terms of its original letter. CRA sought to evict Keryakos from the property, claiming that no lease contract existed between it and Keryakos.

DECISION: The lease contract is governed by ordinary contract law. When the tenant offered other terms in place of those made by the landlord's offer, the tenant made a counteroffer. This had the effect of rejecting or terminating the landlord's offer. The tenant could not then accept the rejected offer after the tenant's counteroffer was rejected. Therefore, there was no contract. [*Keryakos Textiles, Inc. v. CRA Development, Inc.*, **563 N.Y.S.2d 308 (App. Div. 1990)**]

CPA 15. Manner and Time of Acceptance

The offeror may specify the manner and time for accepting the offer. When the offeror specifies that there must be a written acceptance, no contract arises when the offeree makes an oral acceptance. If the offeror calls for acceptance by a specified time and date, a late acceptance has no legal effect, and a contract is not formed. Where no time is specified in the offer, the offeree has a reasonable period of time to accept the offer. After the time specified in the offer or a reasonable period of time

---

[25] *Jones v. Frickey*, 618 S.E.2d 29 (Ga. App. 2005).

expires (when no time is specified in the offer), the offeree's power to make a contract by accepting the offer "lapses."

When the offeror calls for the performance of an act or of certain conduct, the performance thereof is an acceptance of the offer and creates a unilateral contract.

When the offeror has specified a particular manner and time of acceptance, generally, the offeree cannot accept in any other way. The basic rule applied by the courts is that the offeror is the master of the offer![26]

CPA **(A) Silence as Acceptance.** In most cases, the offeree's silence and failure to act cannot be regarded as an acceptance. Ordinarily, the offeror is not permitted to frame an offer in such a way as to make the silence and inaction of the offeree operate as an acceptance. Nor can a party to an existing contract effect a modification of that agreement without the other party's actual acceptance or approval. **For Example,** H. H. Taylor made a contract with Andy Stricker, a civil engineer, to design a small hotel. The parties agreed on an hourly rate with "total price not to exceed $7,200," and required that additional charges be presented to Taylor prior to proceeding with any changes. Andy was required to dedicate more hours to the project than anticipated but could not present the additional charges to Taylor because Taylor would not return his phone calls. He billed Taylor $9,035 for his services. Taylor's failure to act in not returning phone calls is not a substitute for the assent needed to modify a contract. Stricker is thus only entitled to $7,200. [27]

(B) Unordered Goods and Tickets. Sometimes a seller writes to a person with whom the seller has not had any prior dealings, stating that unless notified to the contrary, the seller will send specified merchandise and the recipient is obligated to pay for it at stated prices. There is no acceptance if the recipient of the letter ignores the offer and does nothing. The silence of the person receiving the letter is not an acceptance, and the sender, as a reasonable person, should recognize that none was intended.

This rule applies to all kinds of goods, books, magazines, and tickets sent through the mail when they have not been ordered. The fact that the items are not returned does not mean that they have been accepted; that is, the offeree is required neither to pay for nor to return the items. If desired, the recipient of the unordered goods may write "Return to Sender" on the unopened package and put the package back into the mail without any additional postage. The Postal Reorganization Act provides that the person who receives unordered mailed merchandise from a commercial sender has the right "to retain, use, discard, or dispose of it in any manner the recipient sees fit without any obligation whatsoever to the sender."[28] It provides further that any unordered merchandise that is mailed must have attached to it a clear and conspicuous statement of the recipient's right to treat the goods in this manner.

CPA 16. Communication of Acceptance

Acceptance by the offeree is the last step in the formation of a bilateral contract. Intuitively, the offeror's receipt of the acceptance should be the point in time when the contract is formed and its terms apply. When the parties are involved in face-to-face negotiations, a contract is formed upon the offeror's receipt of the

---

[26] See *1-800 Contacts, Inc. v. Weigner,* 127 P.3d 1241 (Utah App. 2005).
[27] *Stricker v. Taylor,* 975 P.2d 930 (Or. App. 1999).
[28] Federal Postal Reorganization Act §3009.

E-Commerce & Cyberlaw

Contract Formation on the Internet

It is not possible for an online service provider or seller to individually bargain with each person who visits its Web site. The Web site owner, therefore, as offeror, places its proposed terms on its Web site and requires visitors to assent to these terms in order to access the site, download software, or purchase a product or service.

In a written contract, the parties sign a paper document indicating their intention to be bound by the terms of the contract. Online, however, an agreement may be accomplished by the visitor-offeree simply typing the words "I Accept" in an onscreen box and then clicking a "send" or similar button that indicates acceptance. Or the individual clicks an "I Agree" or "I Accept" icon or check box. Access to the site is commonly denied those who do not agree to the terms. Such agreements have come to be known as *clickwrap* agreements and in the case of software license agreements, *SLAs*. The agreements contain fee schedules and other financial terms and may contain terms such as a notice of the proprietary nature of the material contained on the site and of any limitations on the use of the site and the downloading of software. Moreover, the clickwrap agreements may contain limitations on liability, including losses associated with the use of downloaded software or products or services purchased from the site.

To determine whether a clickwrap agreement is enforceable, courts apply traditional principles of contract law and focus on whether the plaintiffs had reasonable notice of and manifested assent to the clickwrap agreement. Failure to read an enforceable clickwrap agreement, as with any binding contract, will not excuse compliance with its terms.

In *Specht v. Netscape Communications Corp.,** the Internet users were urged to click on a button to download free software, but the offer did not make clear to the user that clicking the download button would signify assent to restrictive contractual terms and conditions. The court, in its 2002 decision, declined to enforce this clickwrap agreement. Internet sellers and service providers generally learned from the *Specht* decision, and most clickwrap agreements now provide sufficient notice and means for clear assent. For example, in *Feldman v. Google, Inc.,*** decided in 2007, the user was unsuccessful in challenging the terms of Google's "AdWords" Program clickwrap agreement. In order to activate an AdWords account, the user had to visit a Web page that displayed the agreement in a scrollable text box. The text of the agreement was immediately visible to the user, as was a prominent admonition in boldface to read the terms and conditions carefully, and with instructions to indicate assent if the user agreed to the terms.

Unlike the impermissible agreement in *Specht*, the user here had to take affirmative action and click the "Yes, I agree to the above terms and conditions" button in order to proceed to the next step. Clicking "Continue" without clicking the "Yes" button would have returned the user to the same Web page. If the user did not agree to all of the terms, he could not have activated his account, placed ads, or incurred charges.

*306 F.3d 17 (2d Cir. 2002).
***Feldman v. Google, Inc.,* 513 F. Supp. 2d 229 (E.D. Pa. 2007). See also *A.V. v. Iparadigms, LLC,* 554 F. Supp. 2d 473 (E.D. Va. 2008).

---

acceptance. When the offeror hears the offeree's words of acceptance, the parties may shake hands, signifying their understanding that the contract has been formed.

CPA   **(A) MAILBOX RULE.** When the parties are negotiating at a distance from each other, special rules have developed as to when the acceptance takes effect based on the commercial expediency of creating a contract at the earliest period of time and the protection of the offeree. Under the so-called *mailbox rule,* a properly addressed, postage-paid mailed acceptance takes effect when the acceptance is placed into the control of the U.S. Postal Service[29] or, by judicial extension, is placed in the control of a private third-party carrier such as Federal Express or United Parcel Service.[30] That is, the acceptance is effective upon dispatch even before it is received by the offeror.

---

[29] See *Adams v. Lindsell,* 106 Eng. Rep. 250 (K.B. 1818). Common law jurisdictions have unanimously adopted the mailbox rule, as has the Restatement (Second) of Contracts §63, and the U.C.C [see U.C.C §1-201(26),(38)].

[30] But see *Baca v. Trejo,* 902 N.E.2d 1108 (Ill App. 2009) whereby an Illinois Court determined that a statute deeming a document to be filed with a state court on the date shown by the U.S. Postal Service cancellation mark—the mailbox rule—does not apply to documents consigned to a private carrier, UPS. The court reasoned that courts should not have the task of deciding which carriers are acceptable.

CASE SUMMARY

When the Mailbox Bangs Shut

FACTS: The Thoelkes owned land. The Morrisons mailed an offer to the Thoelkes to buy their land. The Thoelkes agreed to this offer and mailed back a contract signed by them. While this letter was in transit, the Thoelkes notified the Morrisons that their acceptance was revoked. Were the Thoelkes bound by a contract?

DECISION: The acceptance was effective when mailed, and the subsequent revocation of the acceptance had no effect. [*Morrison v. Thoelke*, 155 So. 2d 889 (Fla. App. 1963)]

The offeror may avoid the application of this rule by stating in the offer that acceptance shall take effect upon receipt by the offeror.

CPA

(B) Determining the Applicable Means of Communication. The modern rule on the selection of the appropriate medium of communication of acceptance is that unless otherwise unambiguously indicated in the offer, it shall be construed as inviting acceptance in any manner and by any medium reasonable under the circumstances.[31] A medium of communication is normally reasonable if it is one used by the offeror or if it is customary in similar transactions at the time and place the offer is received. Thus, if the offeror uses the mail to extend an offer, the offeree may accept by using the mail. Indeed, acceptance by mail is ordinarily reasonable when the parties are negotiating at a distance even if the offer is not made by mail.

CASE SUMMARY

Just Be Reasonable

FACTS: Maria Cantu was a special education teacher under a one-year contract with the San Benito School District for the 1990–1991 school year. On Saturday, August 18, just weeks before fall-term classes were to begin, she hand delivered a letter of resignation to her supervisor. Late Monday afternoon the superintendent put in the mail a properly stamped and addressed letter to Cantu accepting her offer of resignation. The next morning at 8:00, before the superintendent's letter reached her, Cantu hand delivered a letter withdrawing her resignation. The superintendent refused to recognize the attempted rescission of the resignation.

DECISION: Cantu was wrong. The resignation became binding when the acceptance of the resignation was mailed. The fact that the offer to resign had been delivered by hand did not require that the offer be accepted by a hand delivery of the acceptance. The use of mail was reasonable under the circumstances, and therefore the mailing of the acceptance made it effective. [*Cantu v. Central Education Agency*, 884 S.W.2d 563 (Tex. App. 1994)]

CPA

(C) Telephone and Electronic Communication of Acceptance. Although telephonic communication is very similar to face-to-face communication, most U.S. courts, nevertheless, have applied the mailbox rule, holding that telephoned acceptances are effective where and when dispatched.

---

[31] Restatement (Second) of Contracts §30; U.C.C. §2-206(1) (a).

The courts have yet to address the applicability of the mailbox rule to e-mail. However, when the offeree's server is under the control of an independent entity, such as an online service provider, and the offeree cannot withdraw the message, it is anticipated that the courts will apply the mailbox rule, and acceptance will take effect on proper dispatch. In the case of companies that operate their own servers, the acceptance will take effect when the message is passed onto the Internet.

Facsimile transmissions are substantially instantaneous and could be treated as face-to-face communications. However, it is anticipated that U.S. courts, when called upon to deal with this issue, will apply the mailbox acceptance-upon-dispatch rule as they do with telephoned acceptances.

 (D) EFFECTS OF THE MAILBOX RULE. If an offer requires that acceptance be communicated by a specific date and the acceptance is properly dispatched by the offeree on the final date, the acceptance is timely and the contract is formed, even though the offeror actually receives the acceptance well after the specified date has passed. **For Example,** by letter dated February 18, 1999, Morton's of Chicago mailed a certified letter to the Crab House accepting the Crab House's offer to terminate its restaurant lease. The Crab House, Inc., sought to revoke its offer to terminate the lease in a certified letter dated February 18, 1999 and by facsimile transmission to Morton's dated February 19, 1999. On February 22, 1999, the Crab House received Morton's acceptance letter; and on the same date Morton's received Crab House's letter revoking the offer to terminate the lease. Acceptance of an offer is effective upon dispatch to the Postal Service, and the contract springs into existence at the time of the mailing. Offers, revocations, and rejections are generally effective only upon the offeree's receipt. Morton's dispatch of its acceptance letter on February 18 formed an agreement to terminate the lease, and the fax dispatched on February 19 was too late to revoke the offer to terminate the lease. [32]

17. Auction Sales

At an auction sale, the statements made by the auctioneer to draw forth bids are merely invitations to negotiate. Each bid is an offer, which is not accepted until the auctioneer indicates that a particular offer or bid is accepted. Usually, this is done by the fall of the auctioneer's hammer, indicating that the highest bid made has been accepted.[33] Because a bid is merely an offer, the bidder may withdraw the bid at any time before it is accepted by the auctioneer.

Ordinarily, the auctioneer who is not satisfied with the amounts of the bids that are being made may withdraw any article or all of the property from the sale. Once a bid is accepted, however, the auctioneer cannot cancel the sale. In addition, if it had been announced that the sale was to be made "without reserve," the property must be sold to the person making the highest bid regardless of how low that bid may be.

In an auction "with reserve," the auctioneer takes bids as agent for the seller with the understanding that no contract is formed until the seller accepts the transaction.[34]

---

[32] *Morton's of Chicago v. Crab House Inc.,* 746 N.Y.S.2d 317 (2002). *Kass v. Grais,* 2007 WL 2815498 (N.Y. Sup. Sept. 4, 2007).

[33] *Dry Creek Cattle Co. v. Harriet Bros. Limited Partnership,* 908 P.2d 399 (Wyo 1995).

[34] *Marten v. Staab,* 543 N.W.2d 436 (Neb. 1996). Statutes regulate auctions and auctioneers in all states. For example, state of Maine law prohibits an auctioneer from conducting an auction without first having a written contract with the consignor of any property to be sold, including (1) whether the auction is with reserve or without reserve, (2) the commission rate, and (3) a description of all items to be sold. See *Street v. Board of Licensing of Auctioneers,* 889 A.2d 319 ([Me.] 2006).

LawFlix

Funny Farm (1988) (PG)

Near the end of this Chevy Chase movie, two couples face a formation issue as one couple attempts to purchase a home. An offer, presented around a friendly kitchen table setting, is declined by the sellers. Do the buyers' threats to sue the sellers have any legal basis? While the buyers had made a special trip to see the land and felt that since they were offering more than the asking price that they had a contract, the sellers were free to reject the offer. Listing a house for a price is not an offer; it is an invitation for an offer.

MAKE THE CONNECTION

SUMMARY

Because a contract arises when an offer is accepted, it is necessary to find that there was an offer and that it was accepted. If either element is missing, there is no contract.

An offer does not exist unless the offeror has contractual intent. This intent is lacking if the statement of the person is merely an invitation to negotiate, a statement of intention, or an agreement to agree at a later date. Newspaper ads, price quotations, and catalog prices are ordinarily merely invitations to negotiate and cannot be accepted.

An offer must be definite. If an offer is indefinite, its acceptance will not create a contract because it will be held that the resulting agreement is too vague to enforce. In some cases, an offer that is by itself too indefinite is made definite because some writing or standard is incorporated by reference and made part of the offer. In some cases the offer is made definite by implying terms that were not stated. In other cases, the indefinite part of the offer is ignored when that part can be divided or separated from the balance of the offer.

Assuming that there is in fact an offer that is made with contractual intent and that it is sufficiently definite, it still does not have the legal effect of an offer unless it is communicated to the offeree by or at the direction of the offeror.

In some cases, there was an offer but it was terminated before it was accepted. By definition, an attempted acceptance made after the offer has been terminated has no effect. The offeror may revoke the ordinary offer at any time. All that is required is the showing of the intent to revoke and the communication of that intent to the offeree. The offeror's power to revoke is barred by the existence of an option contract under common law or a firm offer under the Uniform Commercial Code. An offer is also terminated by the express rejection of the offer or by the making of a counteroffer, by the lapse of the time stated in the offer or of a reasonable time when none is stated, by the death or disability of either party, or by a change of law that makes illegal a contract based on the particular offer.

When the offer is accepted, a contract arises. Only the offeree can accept an offer, and the acceptance must be of the offer exactly as made without any qualification or change. Ordinarily, the offeree may accept or reject as the offeree chooses.

The acceptance is any manifestation of intent to agree to the terms of the offer. Ordinarily, silence or failure to act does not constitute acceptance. The recipient of unordered goods and tickets may dispose of the goods or use the goods without such action constituting an acceptance. An acceptance does not exist until the words or conduct demonstrating assent to the offer is communicated to the offeror. Acceptance by mail takes effect at the time and place when and where the letter is mailed or the fax is transmitted.

In an auction sale, the auctioneer asking for bids makes an invitation to negotiate. A person making a bid is making an offer, and the acceptance of the highest bid by the auctioneer is an acceptance of that offer and gives rise to a contract. When the auction sale is without reserve, the auctioneer must accept the highest bid. If the auction is not expressly without reserve, the auctioneer may refuse to accept any of the bids.

LEARNING OUTCOMES

After studying this chapter, you should be able to clearly explain:

A. Requirements of an Offer

L0.1 Decide whether an offer contains definite and certain terms

> See the *Plankenhorn* case for the meaning of a "damn good job" on p. 263.
> See the legal impact of a party's statement that the contract "was going to be signed" in the *Hewitt* example on pp. 262–263.
> See the *Wigod* case that discusses the test for a valid, binding offer, pp. 261–262.

B. Termination of an Offer

L0.2 Explain the exceptions the law makes to the requirement of definiteness

> See the *Delphi* case on requirements contracts, p. 267.

L0.3 Explain all the ways an offer can be terminated

> See the discussion of revocation, counteroffer, rejection, lapse of time, death or disability of a party, or subsequent illegality, starting on p. 268.

> See the *Davidoff* example of a revocation communicated to the offeree prior to acceptance, p. 268.
> See the *Landry's Restaurants* example that illustrates the effect of an "acceptance" signed just a few days after the written offer had expired, p. 270.

C. Acceptance of an Offer

L0.4 Explain what constitutes the acceptance of an offer

> See the *Sadeghi* example where acceptance of an offer created a binding contract, p. 271.
> See the *Keryakos Textiles* case on the impact of a counteroffer, p. 272.

L0.5 Explain the implications of failing to read a clickwrap agreement

> See the *Feldman* case as an example of an enforceable clickwrap agreement containing notice and manifested assent, p. 274.

KEY TERMS

acceptance	firm offer	requirements contract
counteroffer	offer	
divisible contract	output contract	

QUESTIONS AND CASE PROBLEMS

1. Bernie and Phil's Great American Surplus store placed an ad in the *Sunday Times* stating, "Next Saturday at 8:00 A.M. sharp, 3 brand new mink coats worth $5,000 each will be sold for $500 each! First come, First served." Marsha Lufklin was first in line when the store opened and went directly to the coat department, but the coats identified in the ad were not available for sale. She identified herself to the manager and pointed out that she was first in line in conformity with the store's advertised offer and that she was ready to pay the $500 price set forth in the store's offer. The manager responded that a newspaper ad is just an invitation to negotiate and that the store decided to withdraw "the mink coat promotion." Review the text on unilateral contracts in Section 12(B) of Chapter 12. Decide.

2. Brown made an offer to purchase Overman's house on a standard printed form. Underneath Brown's signature was the statement: "ACCEPTANCE ON REVERSE SIDE." Overman did not sign the offer on the back but sent Brown a letter accepting the offer. Later, Brown refused to perform the contract, and Overman sued him for breach of contract. Brown claimed there was no contract because the offer had not been accepted in the manner specified by the offer. Decide. [*Overman v. Brown*, 372 N.W.2d 102 (Neb.)]

3. Katherine mailed Paul an offer with definite and certain terms and that was legal in all respects stating that it was good for 10 days. Two days later she sent Paul a letter by certified mail (time stamped by the Postal Service at 1:14 P.M.) stating that the original offer was revoked. That evening Paul e-mailed acceptance of the offer to Katherine. She immediately phoned him to tell him that she had revoked the offer that afternoon, and he would surely receive it in tomorrow's mail. Was the offer revoked by Katherine?

4. Nelson wanted to sell his home. Baker sent him a written offer to purchase the home. Nelson made some changes to Baker's offer and wrote him that he, Nelson, was accepting the offer as amended. Baker notified Nelson that he was dropping out of the transaction. Nelson sued Baker for breach of contract. Decide. What social forces and ethical values are involved? [*Nelson v. Baker*, 776 S.W.2d 52 (Mo. App.)]

5. Lessack Auctioneers advertised an auction sale that was open to the public and was to be conducted with reserve. Gordon attended the auction and bid $100 for a work of art that was worth much more. No higher bid, however, was made. Lessack refused to sell the item for $100 and withdrew the item from the sale. Gordon claimed that because he was the highest bidder, Lessack was required to sell the item to him. Was he correct?

6. Willis Music Co. advertised a television set at $22.50 in the Sunday newspaper. Ehrlich ordered a set, but the company refused to deliver it on the grounds that the price in the newspaper ad was a mistake. Ehrlich sued the company. Was it liable? Why or why not? [*Ehrlich v. Willis Music Co.*, 113 N.E.2d 252 (Ohio App.)]

7. When a movement was organized to build Charles City College, Hauser and others signed pledges to contribute to the college. At the time of signing, Hauser inquired what would happen if he should die or be unable to pay. The representative of the college stated that the pledge would then not be binding and that it was merely a statement of intent. The college failed financially, and Pappas was appointed receiver to collect and liquidate the assets of the college corporation. He sued Hauser for the amount due on his pledge. Hauser raised the defense that the pledge was not a binding contract. Decide. What ethical values are involved? [*Pappas v. Hauser*, 197 N.W.2d 607 (Iowa)]

8. A signed a contract agreeing to sell land he owned but reserved the right to take the hay from the land until the following October. He gave the contract form to B, a broker. C, a prospective buyer, agreed to buy the land and signed the contract but crossed out the provision regarding the hay crop. Was there a binding contract between A and C?

9. A. H. Zehmer discussed selling a farm to Lucy. After a 40-minute discussion of the first draft of a contract, Zehmer and his wife, Ida, signed a second draft stating: "We hereby agree to sell to W. O. Lucy the Ferguson farm complete for $50,000 title satisfactory to buyer." Lucy agreed to purchase the farm on these terms. Thereafter, the Zehmers refused to transfer title to Lucy and claimed they had made the contract for sale as a joke. Lucy brought an action to compel performance of the contract. The Zehmers claimed there was no contract. Were they correct? [*Lucy v. Zehmer*, 84 S.E.2d 516 (Va. App.)]

10. Wheeler operated an automobile service station, which he leased from W. C. Cornitius, Inc. The lease ran for three years. Although the lease did not contain any provision for renewal, it was in fact renewed six times for successive three-year terms. The landlord refused to renew the lease for a seventh time. Wheeler brought suit to compel the landlord to accept his offer to renew the lease. Decide. [*William C. Cornitius, Inc. v. Wheeler*, 556 P.2d 666 (Or.)]

11. Buster Cogdill, a real estate developer, made an offer to the Bank of Benton to have the bank

provide construction financing for the development of an outlet mall, with funds to be provided at prime rate plus two percentage points. The bank's president Julio Plunkett thanked Buster for the proposal and said, "I will start the paperwork." Did Cogdill have a contract with the Bank of Benton? [*Bank of Benton v. Cogdill*, 454 N.E.2d 1120 (Ill. App.)]

12. Ackerley Media Group, Inc., claimed to have a three-season advertising Team Sponsorship Agreement (TSA) with Sharp Electronics Corporation to promote Sharp products at all Seattle Supersonics NBA basketball home games. Sharp contended that a valid agreement did not exist for the third season (2000–2001) because a material price term was missing, thus resulting in an unenforceable "agreement to agree." The terms of the TSA for the 2000–2001 third season called for a base payment of $144,200 and an annual increase "not to exceed 6% [and] to be mutually agreed upon by the parties." No "mutually agreed" increase was negotiated by the parties. Ackerley seeks payment for the base price of $144,200 only. Sharp contends that since no price was agreed upon for the season, the entire TSA is unenforceable, and it is not obligated to pay for the 2000–2001 season. Is Sharp correct? [*Ackerley Media Group, Inc. v. Sharp Electronics Corp.*, 170 F. Supp. 2d 445 (S.D.N.Y.)]

13. L. B. Foster invited Tie and Track Systems Inc. to submit price quotes on items to be used in a railroad expansion project. Tie and Track responded by e-mail on August 11, 2006, with prices for 9 items of steel ties. The e-mail concluded, "The above prices are delivered/ Terms of Payment—to be agreed/Delivery—to be agreed/We hope you are successful with your bid. If you require any additional information please call." Just 3 of the 9 items listed in Tie and Track's price quote were "accepted" by the project. L. B. Foster demanded that Tie and Track provide the items at the price listed in the quote. Tie and Track refused. L. B. Foster sued for breach of contract. Did the August 11 e-mail constitute an offer, acceptance of which could bind the supplier to a contract? If so, was there a valid acceptance? [*L. B. Foster v. Tie and Track Systems, Inc.*, 2009 WL 900993 (N.D. Ill.)]

14. On August 15, 2003, Wilbert Heikkila signed an agreement with Kangas Realty to sell eight parcels of Heikkila's property. On September 8, 2003, David McLaughlin met with a Kangas agent who drafted McLaughlin's offer to purchase three of the parcels. McLaughlin signed the offer and gave the agent checks for each parcel. On September 9 and 10, 2003, the agent for Heikkila prepared three printed purchase agreements, one for each parcel. On September 14, 2003, David's wife, Joanne McLaughlin, met with the agent and signed the agreements. On September 16, 2003, Heikkila met with his real estate agent. Writing on the printed agreements, Heikkila changed the price of one parcel from $145,000 to $150,000, the price of another parcel from $32,000 to $45,000, and the price of the third parcel from $175,000 to $179,000. Neither of the McLaughlins signed an acceptance of Heikkila's changes to the printed agreements before Heikkila withdrew his offer to sell. The McLaughlins learned that Heikkila had withdrawn his offer on January 1, 2004, when the real estate agent returned the checks to them. Totally shocked at Heikkila's conduct, the McLaughlins brought action to compel specific performance of the purchase agreement signed by Joanne McLaughlin on their behalf. Decide. [*McLaughlin v. Heikkila*, 697 N.W.2d 231 (Minn. App.)]

CPA QUESTIONS

1. Able Sofa, Inc., sent Noll a letter offering to sell Noll a custom-made sofa for $5,000. Noll immediately sent a telegram to Able purporting to accept the offer. However, the telegraph company erroneously delivered the telegram to Abel Soda, Inc. Three days later, Able mailed a

letter of revocation to Noll, which was received by Noll. Able refused to sell Noll the sofa. Noll sued Able for breach of contract. Able:

a. Would have been liable under the deposited acceptance rule only if Noll had accepted by mail.

b. Will avoid liability since it revoked its offer prior to receiving Noll's acceptance.

c. Will be liable for breach of contract.

d. Will avoid liability due to the telegraph company's error (Law, #2, 9911).

2. On September 27, Summers sent Fox a letter offering to sell Fox a vacation home for $150,000. On October 2, Fox replied by mail agreeing to buy the home for $145,000. Summers did not reply to Fox. Do Fox and Summers have a binding contract?

a. No, because Fox failed to sign and return Summers's letter.

b. No, because Fox's letter was a counteroffer.

c. Yes, because Summers's offer was validly accepted.

d. Yes, because Summers's silence is an implied acceptance of Fox's letter (Law, #2, 0462).

3. On June 15, Peters orally offered to sell a used lawn mower to Mason for $125. Peters specified that Mason had until June 20 to accept the offer. On June 16, Peters received an offer to purchase the lawn mower for $150 from Bronson, Mason's neighbor. Peters accepted Bronson's offer. On June 17, Mason saw Bronson using the lawn mower and was told the mower had been sold to Bronson. Mason immediately wrote to Peters to accept the June 15 offer. Which of the following statements is correct?

a. Mason's acceptance would be effective when received by Peters.

b. Mason's acceptance would be effective when mailed.

c. Peters's offer had been revoked and Mason's acceptance was ineffective.

d. Peters was obligated to keep the June 15 offer open until June 20. (Law, #13, 3095).

© Manuel Gutjahr/iStockphoto.com

CHAPTER 14

Capacity and Genuine Assent

learningoutcomes

After studying this chapter, you should be able to

LO.1 Define contractual capacity

LO.2 Explain the extent and effect of avoidance of a contract by a minor

LO.3 Distinguish unilateral mistakes and mutual mistakes

LO.4 Explain the difference between intentional misrepresentation, negligent misrepresentation, and puffery

LO.5 Explain the difference between undue influence and duress

A *contract* is a binding agreement. This agreement must be made between parties who have the capacity to do so. They must also truly agree so that all parties have really consented to the contract. This chapter explores the elements of contractual capacity of the parties and the genuineness of their assent.

A. CONTRACTUAL CAPACITY

Some persons lack contractual capacity, a lack that embraces both those who have a status incapacity, such as minors, and those who have a factual incapacity, such as persons who are insane.

✳ 1. Contractual Capacity Defined

contractual capacity – ability to understand that a contract is being made and to understand its general meaning.

Contractual capacity is the ability to understand that a contract is being made and to understand its general meaning. However, the fact that a person does not understand the full legal meaning of a contract does not mean that contractual capacity is lacking. Everyone is presumed to have capacity unless it is proven that capacity is lacking or there is status incapacity.[1] **For Example,** Jacqueline, aged 22, entered into a contract with Sunrise Storage Co. but later claimed it was not binding because she did not understand several clauses in the printed contract. The contract was binding. No evidence supported her claim that she lacked capacity to contract or to understand its subject. Contractual capacity can exist even though a party does not understand every provision of the contract.

✳ **(A) STATUS INCAPACITY.** Over the centuries, the law has declared that some classes of persons lack contractual capacity. The purpose is to protect these classes by giving them the power to get out of unwise contracts. Of these classes, the most important today is the class identified as minors.

Until recent times, some other classes were held to lack contractual capacity in order to discriminate against them. Examples are married women and aliens.

CASE SUMMARY

We Really Mean Equal Rights

FACTS: An Alabama statute provided that a married woman could not sell her land without the consent of her husband. Montgomery made a contract to sell land she owned to Peddy. Montgomery's husband did not consent to the sale. Montgomery did not perform the contract and Peddy sued her. The defense was raised that the contract was void and could not be enforced because of the statute. Peddy claimed that the statute was unconstitutional.

DECISION: The statute was unconstitutional. Constitutions, both federal and state, guarantee all persons the equal protection of the law. Married women are denied this equal protection when they are treated differently than married men and unmarried women. The fact that such unequal treatment had once been regarded as proper does not justify its modern continuation. [*Peddy v. Montgomery*, 345 So. 2d 988 (Ala. 1991)]

[1] *In re Adoption of Smith*, 578 So 2d 988 (La. App. 1991).

Still other classes, such as persons convicted of and sentenced for a felony, were held to lack contractual capacity in order to punish them. Today, these discriminatory and punitive incapacities have largely disappeared. Married women have the same contractual capacity as unmarried persons.

By virtue of international treaties, the discrimination against aliens has been removed.

(B) FACTUAL INCAPACITY. A *factual incapacity* contrasts with incapacity imposed because of the class or group to which a person belongs. A factual incapacity may exist when, because of a mental condition caused by medication, drugs, alcohol, illness, or age, a person does not understand that a contract is being made or understand its general nature. However, mere mental weakness does not incapacitate a person from contracting. It is sufficient if the individual has enough mental capacity to understand, to a reasonable extent, the nature and effect of what he is doing.[2]

2. Minors

Minors may make contracts.[3] To protect them, however, the law has always treated minors as a class lacking contractual capacity.

(A) WHO IS A MINOR? At common law, any person, male or female, under 21 years of age was a minor. At common law, minority ended the day before the twenty-first birthday. The "day before the birthday" rule is still followed, but the age of majority has been reduced from 21 years to 18 years.

CPA   **(B) MINOR'S POWER TO AVOID CONTRACTS.** With exceptions that will be noted later, a contract made by a minor is voidable at the election of the minor. **For Example,** Adorian Deck, a minor, created a Twitter feed titled "@OMGFacts." The feed collected and republished interesting and trivial facts from other sources on the Internet. It was subscribed to by over 300,000 Twitter users, including some celebrities. Spatz, Inc. entered into a joint venture with Deck as described in a written contract signed by both parties, under which Spatz would expand the Twitter feed into a suite of Internet products, including a Website and a Youtube.com video channel. In an "OMG-moment" prior to his 18th birthday, Deck notified Spatz, Inc. that he wished to disaffirm the parties' agreement. This disaffirmation by a minor rescinded the entire contract, rendering it a nullity.[4] The minor may affirm or ratify the contract on attaining majority by performing the contract, by expressly approving the contract, or by allowing a reasonable time to lapse without avoiding the contract.

CPA   *(1) What Constitutes Avoidance?*
A minor may avoid or *disaffirm* a contract by any expression of an intention to repudiate the contract. Any act inconsistent with the continuing validity of the contract is also an avoidance.

CPA   *(2) Time for Avoidance.*
A minor can disaffirm a contract only during minority and for a reasonable time after attaining majority. After the lapse of a reasonable time, the contract is deemed ratified and cannot be avoided by the minor.

---

[2] *Fisher v. Schefers,* 656 N.W.2d 591 (Minn. App. 2003).
[3] *Buffington v. State Automobile Mut. Ins. Co.,* 384 S.E.2d 873 (Ga. App. 1989).
[4] *Deck v. Spatz, Inc.,* 2011 WL 775067 (E.D. Cal. Sept. 27, 2011).

CPA

(3) Minor's Misrepresentation of Age.

Generally, the fact that the minor has misrepresented his or her age does not affect the minor's power to disaffirm the contract. Some states hold that such fraud of a minor bars contract avoidance. Some states permit the minor to disaffirm the contract in such a case but require the minor to pay for any damage to the property received under the contract.

In any case, the other party to the contract may disaffirm it because of the minor's fraud.

CPA

(C) RESTITUTION BY MINOR AFTER AVOIDANCE. When a minor disaffirms a contract, the question arises as to what the minor must return to the other contracting party.

(1) Original Consideration Intact.

When a minor still has what was received from the other party, the minor, on avoiding the contract, must return it to the other party or offer to do so. That is, the minor must put things back to the original position or, as it is called, restore the **status quo ante**.

status quo ante — original positions of the parties.

(2) Original Consideration Damaged or Destroyed.

What happens if the minor cannot return what has been received because it has been spent, used, damaged, or destroyed? The minor's right to disaffirm the contract is not affected. The minor can still disaffirm the contract and is required to return only what remains. The fact that nothing remains or that what remains is damaged does not bar the right to disaffirm the contract. In states that follow the common law rule, minors can thus refuse to pay for what has been received under a contract or can get back what had been paid or given even though they do not have anything to return or return property in a damaged condition. There is, however, a trend to limit this rule.

(D) RECOVERY OF PROPERTY BY MINOR ON AVOIDANCE. When a minor disaffirms a contract, the other contracting party must return the money received. Any property received from the minor must also be returned. If the property has been sold to a third person who did not know of the original seller's minority, the minor cannot get the property back. In such cases, however, the minor is entitled to recover the property's monetary value or the money received by the other contracting party.

CPA

(E) CONTRACTS FOR NECESSARIES. A minor can disaffirm a contract for necessaries but must pay the reasonable value for furnished necessaries.

(1) What Constitutes Necessaries?

Originally, **necessaries** were limited to those things absolutely necessary for the sustenance and shelter of the minor. Thus limited, the term would extend only to food, clothing, and lodging. In the course of time, the rule was relaxed to extend generally to things relating to the health, education, and comfort of the minor. Thus, the rental of a house used by a married minor is a necessary.

necessaries — things indispensable or absolutely necessary for the sustenance of human life.

(2) Liability of Parent or Guardian.

When a third person supplies the parents or guardian of a minor with goods or services that the minor needs, the minor is not liable for these necessaries because the third person's contract is with the parent or guardian, not with the minor.

When necessary medical care is provided a minor, a parent is liable at common law for the medical expenses provided the minor child. However, at common law, the child can be held contractually liable for her necessary medical expenses when the parent is unable or unwilling to pay.

CASE SUMMARY

The Concussion and Legal Repercussions

FACTS: Sixteen-year-old Michelle Schmidt was injured in an automobile accident and taken to Prince George's Hospital. Although the identities of Michelle and her parents were originally unknown, the hospital provided her emergency medical care for a brain concussion and an open scalp wound. She incurred hospital expenses of $1,756.24. Ms. Schmidt was insured through her father's insurance company. It issued a check to be used to cover medical expenses. However, the funds were used to purchase a car for Ms. Schmidt. Since she was a minor when the services were rendered, she believed that she had no legal obligation to pay. After Ms. Schmidt attained her eighteenth birthday and failed to pay the hospital, it brought suit against her.

DECISION: Judgment for the hospital. The prevailing modern rule is that minors' contracts are voidable except for necessaries. The doctrine of necessaries states that a minor may be held liable for necessaries, including medical necessaries when parents are unwilling to pay. The court concluded that Ms. Schmidt's father demonstrated a clear unwillingness to pay by using the insurance money to purchase a car rather than pay the hospital. The policy behind the necessaries exception is for the benefit of minors because the procurement of such is essential to their existence, and if they were not permitted to bind themselves, they might not be able to obtain the necessaries. [*Schmidt v. Prince George's Hospital*, 784 A.2d 1112 (Md. 2001)]

CPA (F) **RATIFICATION OF FORMER MINOR'S VOIDABLE CONTRACT.** A former minor cannot disaffirm a contract that has been ratified after reaching majority.[5]

CPA *(1) What Constitutes Ratification?*
Ratification consists of any words or conduct of the former minor manifesting an intent to be bound by the terms of a contract made while a minor.

CPA *(2) Form of Ratification.*
Generally, no special form is required for ratification of a minor's voidable contract, although in some states a written ratification or declaration of intention is required.

CPA *(3) Time for Ratification.*
A person can disaffirm a contract any time during minority and for a reasonable time after that but, of necessity, can ratify a contract only after attaining majority. The minor must have attained majority, or the ratification would itself be regarded as voidable.

(G) **CONTRACTS THAT MINORS CANNOT AVOID.** Statutes in many states deprive a minor of the right to avoid an educational loan;[6] a contract for medical care; a contract made

---

[5] *Fletcher v. Marshall*, 632 N.E.2d 1105 (Ill. App. 1994).

[6] A Model Student Capacity to Borrow Act makes educational loans binding on minors in Arizona, Mississippi, New Mexico, North Dakota, Oklahoma, and Washington. This act was reclassified from a uniform act to a model act by the Commissioners on Uniform State Law, indicating that uniformity was viewed as unimportant and that the matter was primarily local in character.

while running a business; a contract approved by a court; a contract made in performance of a legal duty; and a contract relating to bank accounts, insurance policies, or corporate stock.

(H) LIABILITY OF THIRD PERSON FOR A MINOR'S CONTRACT. The question arises as to whether parents are bound by the contract of their minor child. The question of whether a person cosigning a minor's contract is bound if the contract is avoided also arises.

(1) Liability of Parent.

Ordinarily, a parent is not liable on a contract made by a minor child. The parent may be liable, however, if the child is acting as the agent of the parent in making the contract. Also, the parent is liable to a seller for the reasonable value of necessaries supplied by the seller to the child if the parent had deserted the child.

(2) Liability of Cosigner.

When the minor makes a contract, another person, such as a parent or a friend, may sign along with the minor to make the contract more acceptable to the third person.

With respect to the other contracting party, the cosigner is bound independently of the minor. Consequently, if the minor disaffirms the contract, the cosigner remains bound by it. When the debt to the creditor is actually paid, the obligation of the cosigner is discharged.

If the minor disaffirms a sales contract but does not return the goods, the cosigner remains liable for the purchase price.

3. Mentally Incompetent Persons

A person with a mental disorder may be so disabled as to lack capacity to make a contract. An individual seeking to avoid the consequences of a contract due to incompetency must demonstrate that at the time the agreement was executed he or she was suffering from a mental illness or defect, which rendered the party incapable of comprehending the nature of the transaction, or that by reason of mental illness the party was unable to control his or her conduct.[7] **For Example,** a guardian established that Ms. Brunson suffered from a mental illness at the time the challenged mortgage documents were executed, and the contract was set aside by the court.[8] However, where a guardian's evidence was insufficient to demonstrate that at the time two mortgage transactions occurred, one in 1999 for $212,000 and a second in 2003 for $7,628.08, that Mr. and Mrs. Haedrich were incompetent or that Washington Mutual Bank knew or was put on notice of their purported incapacity, the court refused to vacate the judgments of foreclosure.[9]

(A) EFFECT OF INCOMPETENCY. An incompetent person may ordinarily avoid a contract in the same manner as a minor. Upon the removal of the disability (that is, upon becoming competent), the formerly incompetent person can either ratify or disaffirm the contract.

A mentally incompetent person or his estate is liable for the reasonable value of all necessaries furnished that individual.

---

[7] *Horrell v. Horrell,* 900 N.Y.S. 2d 666 (2d Dept. 2010).
[8] *In re* Doar, 900 N.Y.S. 2d 593 (Sup. Ct. Queens Co., Dec. 18, 2009).
[9] *JP Morgan Chase Bank v. Haedrich,* 918 N.Y.S. 2d 398 (Sup. Ct. Nassau County, Oct. 15, 2010).

A current trend in the law is to treat an incompetent person's contract as binding when its terms and the surrounding circumstances are reasonable and the person is unable to restore the other contracting party to the status quo ante.

CASE SUMMARY

Friends Should Tell Friends about Medical Leaves

FACTS: Wilcox Manufacturing Group, Inc., did business under the name of Superior Automation Co., and Howard Wilcox served as Superior's president. As part of a loan "lease agreement" of $50,000 executed on December 5, 2000, Superior was to repay Marketing Services of Indiana (MSI) $67,213.80 over the course of 60 months. Wilcox gave a personal guarantee for full and prompt payment. Wilcox had been a patient of psychiatrist Dr. Shaun Wood since May 21, 1999, and was diagnosed as suffering from bipolar disorder during the period from June 2000 to January 2001. On June 9, 2000, Wilcox told Dr. Wood he was having problems functioning at work, and Dr. Wood determined that Wilcox was experiencing lithium toxicity, which lasted for 10 months, during which time he suffered from impaired cognitive functions that limited his capacity to understand the nature and quality of his actions and judgments. Superior made monthly payments though to October 28, 2003, and the balance owed at that time was $33,031.37. MSI sued Wilcox personally and the corporation for breach of contract. The defendants raise the defense of lack of capacity and contend that they are not liable on the loan signed by the corporate president when he was incapacitated.

DECISION: Judgment for MSI. The acts or deeds of a person of unsound mind whose condition has not been judicially ascertained and who is not under guardianship are voidable and not absolutely void. The acts are subject to ratification or disaffirmance on removal of the disability. The latest Wilcox could have been experiencing the effects of lithium toxicity was October 2001. Wilcox thus regained his capacity by that date. No attempt was made to disaffirm the contract. Rather, monthly payments continued to be made for a year and one-half before the payments ceased. The contract was thus ratified by the conduct of the president of Superior after he recovered his ability to understand the nature of the contract. [*Wilcox Manufacturing, Inc., v. Marketing Services of Indiana, Inc.*, 832 N.E.2d 559 (Ind. App. 2005)]

(B) APPOINTMENT OF GUARDIAN. If a court appoints a guardian for the incompetent person, a contract made by that person before the appointment may be ratified or, in some cases, disaffirmed by the guardian. If the incompetent person makes a contract after a guardian has been appointed, the contract is void and not merely voidable.

✳ 4. Intoxicated Persons

The capacity of a party to contract and the validity of the contract are not affected by the party's being impaired by alcohol at the time of making the contract so long as the party knew that a contract was being made.

If the degree of intoxication is such that a person does not know that a contract is being made, the contract is voidable by that person. On becoming sober, the individual may avoid or rescind the contract. However, an unreasonable delay in taking steps to set aside a known contract entered into while intoxicated may bar the intoxicated person from asserting this right.[10]

[10] *Diedrich v. Diedrich*, 424 N.W.2d 580 (Minn. App. 1988).

Excessive intoxication is a viable defense to contracts arising between casinos and their patrons. Thus, when a casino comes to court to enforce a marker debt against a patron, it seeks to enforce a contractual debt, and the patron is entitled to raise the common law defense that his capacity to contract was impaired by voluntary intoxication.[11]

The courts treat impairment caused by the use of drugs the same as impairment caused by the excessive use of alcohol.

CPA   ## B. MISTAKE

The validity of a contract may be affected by the fact that one or both of the parties made a mistake. In some cases, the mistake may be caused by the misconduct of one of the parties.

5. Unilateral Mistake

A *unilateral mistake*—that is, a mistake by only one of the parties—as to a fact does not affect the contract when the mistake is unknown to the other contracting party.[12] When a contract is made on the basis of a quoted price, the validity of the contract is not affected by the fact that the party furnishing the quotation made a mathematical mistake in computing the price if there was no reason for the other party to recognize that there had been a mistake.[13] The party making the mistake may avoid the contract if the other contracting party knew or should have known of the mistake.

CASE SUMMARY

Bumper Sticker: "Mistakes Happen!" (or words to that effect)

FACTS: Lipton-U City, LLC (Lipton), and Shurgard Storage Centers discussed the sale of a self-storage facility for approximately $7 million. Lipton became concerned about an existing environmental condition and as a result, the parties agreed to a lease with an option to buy rather than an outright sale. The contract specified a 10-year lease with an annual rent starting at $636,000 based on a property valuation of $7 million. Section 2.4 of the contract contained the purchase option. Shurgard representatives circulated an e-mail with a copy to Lipton representatives that a purchase option price would be based on six months of *annualized* net operating income. When the lease was submitted to Lipton, inexplicably any language regarding multiplying by 2 or annualizing the net income was omitted. Donn Lipton announced to his attorneys that the lease reflected his successful negotiation of a purchase option based on six months of *unannualized* net operating income. Eight months after signing the lease, Lipton sought to exercise the purchase option under Section 2.4 and stated a price of $2,918,103. Shurgard rejected the offer and filed suit for rescission, citing the misunderstanding about the price terms.

DECISION: Judgment for Shurgard. Under state law, if a material mistake made by one party is known to the other party or is of such a character or circumstances that the other party should

---

[11] See *Adamar of New Jersey v. Luber*, 2011 WL1325978 (D. N.J. Mar. 30, 2011).
[12] *Truck South Inc. v. Patel*, 528 S.E.2d 424 (S.C. 2000).
[13] *Procan Construction Co. v. Oceanside Development Corp.*, 539 N.Y.S.2d 437 (App. Div. 2d 1989).

CASE SUMMARY

Continued

know of it, the mistaken party has a right to rescission. Lipton knew or should have known of the mistake of the lessor (Shurgard) in believing that the purchase price would be based on a full year of net operating income rather than six months of net operating income. Lipton was notified by e-mail that the six-month figure was to be annualized and knew that the property was valued at approximately $7 million. [***Shurgard Storage Centers v. Lipton-U City, LLC.,* 394 F.3d 1041 (8th Cir. 2005)**]

6. Mutual Mistake *as to a fact*

When both parties enter into a contract under a mutually mistaken understanding concerning a basic assumption of fact or law on which the contract is made, the contract is voidable by the adversely affected party if the mistake has a material effect on the agreed exchange.[14]

A contract based on *a mutual mistake in judgment* is not voidable by the adversely affected party. **For Example,** if both parties believe that a colt is not fast enough to develop into a competitive race horse and effect a sale accordingly, when the animal later develops into the winner of the Preakness as a three-year-old, the seller cannot rescind the contract based on mutual mistake because the mutual mistake was a mistake in judgment. In contrast, when two parties to a contract believe a cow to be barren at the time they contract for its sale, but before delivery of the animal to the buyer, it is discovered that the assumption was mistaken, such is a mutual mistake of fact making the contract void.[15]

7. Mistake in the Transcription or Printing of the Contract: Reformation

In some instances, the parties make an oral agreement, and in the process of committing it to writing or printing it from a manuscript, a phrase, term, or segment is inadvertently left out of the final, signed document. The aggrieved party may petition the court to **reform** the contract to reflect the actual agreement of the parties. However, the burden of proof is heightened to clear and convincing evidence that such a mistake was made. **For Example,** Jewell Coke Co. used an illustration to explain a complex pricing formula in its negotiations with the ArcelMittal steel mill in Cleveland, Ohio, for a long-term contract for the supply of blast furnace coke. The multiplier in the illustration was the actual intent of the parties, according to ArcelMittal, but during the drafting process the multiplier was accidently inverted, resulting in an overpayment of $100,000,000 when discovered, and which potentially could result in an overpayment of over $1 billion over the life of the contract. If proven, the court will reform the contract to reflect the intentions of the parties at the time the contract was made.[16]

> **reformation** – remedy by which a written instrument is corrected when it fails to express the actual intent of both parties because of fraud, accident, or mistake.

---

[14] See *Browning v. Howerton,* 966 P.2d 367 (Wash. App. 1998).
[15] See *Sherwood v. Walker,* 66 Mich. 568 (1887).
[16] *ArcelMittal Cleveland, Inc. v. Jewell Coke Co.,* 750 F. Supp. 2d 839 (N.D. Ohio 2010).

FIGURE 14-1	*Avoidance of Contract*

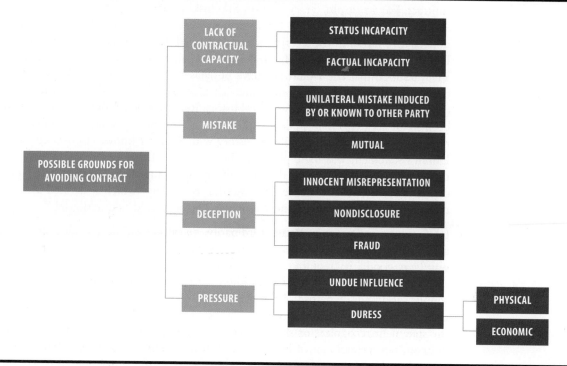

© Cengage Learning

✳ C. Deception

One of the parties may have been misled by a fraudulent statement. In such situations, there is no true or genuine assent to the contract, and it is voidable at the innocent party's option.

8. Intentional Misrepresentation

Fraud is a generic term embracing all multifarious means that human ingenuity can devise and that are resorted to by one individual to get advantage over another. It is classified in the law as a *tort*. However, where a party is induced into making a contract by a material misrepresentation of fact, this form of fraudulent activity adversely affects the genuineness of the assent of the innocent party, and this type of fraud is the focus of our discussion in the chapters on contracts.

✳ 9. Fraud

fraud – making of a false statement of a past or existing fact, with knowledge of its falsity or with reckless indifference as to its truth, with the intent to cause another to rely thereon, and such person does rely thereon and is harmed thereby.

Fraud is the making of a material misrepresentation (or false statement) of fact with (1) knowledge of its falsity or reckless indifference to its truth, (2) the intent that the listener rely on it, (3) the result that the listener does so rely, and (4) the consequence that the listener is harmed.[17]

---

[17] *Maack v. Resource Design & Construction, Inc.*, 875 P.2d 570 (Utah 1994); *Bortz v. Noon*, 729 A.2d 555 (Pa. 1999).

To prove fraud, there must be a material misrepresentation of fact. Such a misrepresentation is one that is likely to induce a reasonable person to assent to a contract. **For Example,** Traci Hanson-Suminski purchased a used Honda Civic from Arlington Acura for $10,899. On a test drive with salesperson Mike Dobin, Traci noticed a vibration in the steering wheel and asked if the car had been in an accident. Dobin said, "No, it's fine." The dealer put new tires on the car and Traci bought it. Traci testified that she would not have purchased the car if she had known it had been in an accident. Eight months later when she sought to trade the car for another car, she was shown a Carfax Vehicle History Report which indicated the car had been in an accident. The dealer testified that all its sales associates are trained to respond to questions about vehicle history with "I don't know." It asserted that Dobin's statement was mere puffery. The court found that Dobin's statement was a material misrepresentation of the car's history, inducing the plaintiff to purchase the car. It rejected outright the dealer's assertion of puffery, which it defined as meaningless superlatives that no reasonable person would take seriously.[18]

(A) **STATEMENT OF OPINION OR VALUE.** Ordinarily, matters of opinion of value or opinions about future events are not regarded as fraudulent. Thus, statements that a building was "very good," it "required only normal maintenance," and the "deal was excellent" were merely matters of opinion. Therefore, a court considered the sophistication and expertise of the parties and the commercial setting of the transaction and enforced the contract "as is." The theory is that the person hearing the statement recognizes or should recognize that it is merely the speaker's personal opinion, not a statement of fact. A statement that is mere sales talk cannot be the basis of fraud liability. **For Example,** CEO Bernard Ellis sent a memo to shareholders of his Internet-related services business some four days before the expiration of a lockup period during which these shareholders had agreed not to sell their stock. In the memo, he urged shareholders not to sell their stock on the release date because in the event of a massive sell-off "our stock could plummet." He also stated, "I think our share price will start to stabilize and then rise as our company's strong performance continues." Based on Ellis's "strong performance" statement, a major corporate shareholder did not sell. The price of the stock fell from $40 a share to 29 cents a share over the subsequent nine-month period. The shareholder sued Ellis for fraud, seeking $27 million in damages. The court held that the first half of the sentence in question was framed as a mere opinion as to future events and thus was nonactionable; and as to the characterization of the company's performance as "strong," such a self-congratulatory comment constituted mere puffery on which no reasonable investor would rely.[19]

A statement of opinion may be fraudulent when the speaker knows of past or present facts that make the opinion false. **For Example,** Biff Williams, the sales manager of Abrasives International (AI), sold an exclusive dealership selling AI products to Fred Farkas for $100,000 down and a 3 percent royalty on all gross proceeds. Williams told Farkas, "You have the potential to earn $300,000 to $400,000 a year in this territory." He later added, "We have four dealerships making that kind of money today." Farkas was thus persuaded by the business potential of the territory and executed the purchase contract. He later found out AI had a total of

[18] *Hanson-Suminski v. Rohrman Midwest Motors Inc.,* 858 N.E.2d 194 (Ill. App. 2008).
[19] *Next Century Communications v. Ellis,* 318 F.3d 1023 (11th Cir. 2003).

just four distributorships at that time, and the actual earnings of the highest producer was $43,000. Assertions of opinions about the future profit potential alone may not amount to fraud, but the assertion of present fact—that four dealerships were presently earning $300,000 to $400,000 a year—was a material misstatement of fact that made the forecast sales potential for Farkas's territory a material misstatement of fact as well. Because there were reliance and damages, Farkas can rescind the contract based on fraud and recover all damages resulting from it.[20]

(B) RELIANCE ON STATEMENT. A fraudulent statement made by one party has no importance unless the other party relies on the statement's truth. **For Example,** after making thorough tests of Nagel Company's pump, Allstate Services Company ordered 100 pumps. It later sued Nagel on the ground that advertising statements made about the pumps were false. Allstate Services cannot impose fraud liability on Nagel for the advertisements, even if they were false, because it had not relied on them in making the purchase but had acted on the basis of its own tests.

If the alleged victim of the fraud knew that the statements were false because the truth was commonly known, the victim cannot rely on the false statements. When the statements of a seller are so "indefinite and extravagant" that reasonable persons would not rely on them, the statements cannot be the basis of a claim of fraud.[21] Trusting the honesty of salespersons or their disarming statements, an individual may knowingly agree in writing that no representations have been made to him or her, while at the same time believing and relying upon representation, which in fact have been made and in fact are false, but for which the individual would not have made the agreement. However, purchasers cannot assert justifiable reliance on statements made by sellers that directly contradict clear and specific terms of their written contracts.

CASE SUMMARY

Are Disclaimer of Reliance Clauses a License to Lie?

FACTS: David Sarif and seven other purchasers (Purchasers) each bought a unit at the 26-story Twelve Atlantic Station (Twelve) condominiums in 2005 and 2006. They sued the developers and the brokers for fraud in the inducement and negligent misrepresentation. They alleged that at the time of their purchases, the developers were advertising "spectacular city views" of Atlanta while they had already undertaken to develop the 46-story Atlantic Station tower directly across the street, and that their brokers were advising the Purchasers that any future development to the south of Twelve would be low- to mid-rise office buildings. Purchasers allege that they paid substantial premiums for their views of the city from the southside of the building, which is now blocked by the 46-story building. Each Purchaser signed an agreement containing a provision

---

[20] The Federal Trade Commission and state agencies have franchise disclosure rules that will penalize the franchisor in this case. See Chapter 41.

[21] *Eckert v. Flair Agency, Inc.*, 909 P.2d 1201 (Okla App. 1995) (seller's statement that house would never be flooded again). But see *Italian Cowboy Partners, Ltd. v. Prudential Insurance*, 341 S.W. 3d 323 (Tex. 2011) where a split decision of the Texas Supreme Court determined that the following contract language was not a disclaimer of reliance to negate the "justifiable reliance" element of a fraud claim.

    Tenant acknowledges that neither Landlord nor Landlord's agents, employees or contractors have made any representations or promises with respect to the Site, the Shopping Center or this lease except as expressly set forth herein.

The court determined that the property manager's representations to the future tenant that the building was problem free; no problems had been experienced by the prior tenant; and the building was a perfect restaurant site were false statements of fact known to be false when made. Testimony indicated that the manager herself had personally experienced a sewer gas odor in the prior tenant's restaurant she described as "almost unbearable" and "ungodly."

CASE SUMMARY

Continued

stating that "[t]he views from and natural light available to the Unit may change over time due to, among other circumstances, additional development and the removal or addition of landscaping"; a disclaimer at the top of the first page as required by the Georgia Condominium Act stating that "ORAL REPRESENTATIONS CANNOT BE RELIED UPON AS CORRECTLY STATING THE REPRESENTATIONS OF SELLER"; an express disclaimer in which Purchasers affirmed that they did not rely upon any representations or statements of the brokers; and a comprehensive merger clause.

DECISION: Set forth in the written contract of the parties, all of the Purchasers signed agreements that expressly stated that views may change over time, and oral representations of the sellers could not be relied on. Justifiable reliance is an essential element of a fraud or negligent misrepresentation claim. Since the Purchasers are estopped from relying on representations outside their agreements, they cannot sustain a case that requires justifiable reliance. [*Novare Group, Inc. v. Sarif,* 718 S.E.2d 304 (Ga. 2011)]

(c) **PROOF OF HARM.** For an individual to recover damages for fraud, proof of harm to that individual is required. The injured party may recover the actual losses suffered as a result of the fraud as well as punitive damages when the fraud is gross or oppressive. The injured party has the right to have the court order the rescission or cancellation of the contract that has been induced by fraud.[22]

10. Negligent Misrepresentation

While fraud requires the critical element of a known or recklessly made falsity, a claim of negligent misrepresentation contains similar elements except it is predicated on a negligently made false statement. That is, the speaker failed to exercise due care regarding material information communicated to the listener but did not intend to deceive. When the negligent misrepresentation of a material fact that the listener relies on results in harm to the listener, the contract is voidable at the option of the injured party. If fraud is proven, as opposed to misrepresentation, recovery of punitive damages in addition to actual damages can occur. Because it may be difficult to prove the intentional falsity required for fraud, it is common for a lawsuit to allege both a claim of fraud and a claim of negligent misrepresentation. **For Example,** Marshall Armstrong worked for Fred Collins, owner of Collins Entertainment, Inc., a conglomerate that owns and operates video games. Collins Entertainment's core product video poker was hurt by a court ruling that prohibited cash payouts, which adversely affected its business and resulted in a debt of $13 to $20 million to SouthTrust bank. Chief operating officer Armstrong, on his own time, came up with the idea of modifying bingo machines as a new venture. To exploit this idea, Collins agreed to form a corporation called Skillpins Inc., that was unencumbered by the SouthTrust debt and to give Armstrong a 10 percent ownership interest. After a period, with some 300 Skillpins machines producing income, Armstrong discovered the revenues from the new venture on the debt-laden Collins

[22] *Paden v. Murray,* 523 S.E.2d 75 (Ga. App. 2000).

Entertainment profit and loss statement, not that of Skillpins, Inc. Armstrong's suit for both fraud and intentional misrepresentation was successful. In addition to actual damages, he received $1.8 million in punitive damages for fraud.[23]

11. Nondisclosure

Under certain circumstances, nondisclosure serves to make a contract voidable, especially when the nondisclosure consists of active concealment.

(A) GENERAL RULE OF NONLIABILITY. Ordinarily, a party to a contract has no duty to volunteer information to the other party. **For Example,** if Fox does not ask Tehan any questions, Tehan is not under any duty to make a full statement of material facts. Consequently, the nondisclosure of information that is not asked for does not impose fraud liability or impair the validity of a contract.

CASE SUMMARY

Welcome to the Seesaw: Buyer versus Seller

FACTS: Dalarna Management Corporation owned a building constructed on a pier on a lake. There were repeated difficulties with rainwater leaking into the building, and water damage was visible in the interior of the building. Dalarna made a contract to sell the building to Curran. Curran made several inspections of the building and had the building inspected twice by a licensed engineer. The engineer reported there were signs of water leaks. Curran assigned his contract to Puget Sound Service Corporation, which then purchased the building from Dalarna. Puget Sound spent approximately $118,000 attempting to stop the leaks. Puget Sound then sued Dalarna for damages, claiming that Dalarna's failure to disclose the extent of the water leakage problem constituted fraud.

DECISION: Judgment for Dalarna. Curran was aware there was a water leakage problem, and therefore the burden was on the buyer to ask questions to determine the extent of the problem. There was no duty on the seller to volunteer the extent of the water damage merely because it had been a continuing problem that was more than just a simple leak. The court reached this conclusion because the law "balances the harshness of the former rule of caveat emptor [let the buyer beware] with the equally undesirable alternative of courts standing in loco parentis [in the place of a parent] to parties transacting business." [***Puget Sound Service Corp. v. Dalarna Management Corp., 752 P.2d 1353 (Wash. App. 1988)***]

(B) EXCEPTIONS. The following exceptions to the general rule of nonliability for nondisclosure exist.

(1) Unknown Defect or Condition.

A duty may exist in some states for a seller who knows of a serious defect or condition to disclose that information to the other party where the defect or condition is unknown to the other person and is of such a nature that it is unlikely that the other person would discover it. However, a defendant who had no knowledge of the defect cannot be held liable for failure to disclose it.[24]

---

[23] *Armstrong v. Collins,* 621 S.E.2d 368 (S.C. App. 2005).
[24] *Nesbitt v. Dunn,* 672 So 2d 226 (La. App. 1996).

(2) Confidential Relationship.

confidential relationship—relationship in which, because of the legal status of the parties or their respective physical or mental conditions or knowledge, one party places full confidence and trust in the other.

If parties stand in a **confidential relationship**, failure to disclose information may be regarded as fraudulent. **For Example,** in an attorney-client relationship,[25] the attorney has a duty to reveal anything that is material to the client's interest when dealing with the client. The attorney's silence has the same legal consequence as a knowingly made false statement that there was no material fact to be told the client.

(3) Active Concealment.

Nondisclosure may be more than the passive failure to volunteer information. It may consist of a positive act of hiding information from the other party by physical concealment, or it may consist of knowingly or recklessly furnishing the wrong information. Such conduct constitutes fraud. **For Example,** when Nigel wanted to sell his house, he covered the wooden cellar beams with plywood to hide extensive termite damage. He sold the house to Kuehne, who sued Nigel for damages on later discovering the termite damage. Nigel claimed he had no duty to volunteer information about the termites, but by covering the damage with plywood, he committed active fraud as if he had made a false statement that there were no termites.

D. PRESSURE

What appears to be an agreement may not in fact be voluntary because one of the parties entered into it as the result of undue influence or physical or economic duress.

CPA 12. Undue Influence

An aged parent may entrust all business affairs to a trusted child; a disabled person may rely on a nurse; a client may follow implicitly whatever an attorney recommends. The relationship may be such that for practical purposes, one person is helpless in the hands of the other. When such a confidential relationship exists, it is apparent that the parent, the disabled person, or the client is not exercising free will in making a contract suggested by the child, nurse, or attorney but is merely following the will of the other person. Because of the great possibility of unfair advantage, the law presumes that the dominating person exerts **undue influence** on the other person whenever the dominating person obtains any benefit from a contract made with the dominated person. The contract is then voidable. It may be set aside by the dominated person unless the dominating person can prove that, at the time the contract was made, no unfair advantage had been taken.

undue influence—influence that is asserted upon another person by one who dominates that person.

The class of confidential relationships is not well defined. It ordinarily includes the relationships of parent and child, guardian and ward, physician and patient, and attorney and client, and any other relationship of trust and confidence in which one party exercises a control or influence over another.

Whether undue influence exists is a difficult question for courts (ordinarily juries) to determine. The law does not regard every influence as undue.

An essential element of undue influence is that the person making the contract does not exercise free will. In the absence of a recognized type of confidential relationship, such as that between parent and child, courts are likely to take the

[25] *In re Boss Trust*, 487 N.W.2d 256 (Minn. App. 1992).

attitude that the person who claims to have been dominated was merely persuaded and there was therefore no undue influence.

CASE SUMMARY

Cards and Small Talk Sometimes Make the Sale

FACTS: John Lentner owned the farm adjacent to the Schefers. He moved off the farm to a nursing home in 1999. In the fall of 2000, Kristine Schefers visited Lentner at the nursing home some 15 times, engaging in small talk and watching him play cards. In the spring of 2001, Lentner agreed to sell his farm to Kristine and her husband Thomas for $50,000 plus $10,000 for machinery and tools. Kristine drove Lentner to the bank to get the deed from his safe deposit box. She also took him to the abstractor who drafted the transfer documents. Soon after the sale, Earl Fisher was appointed special conservator of Lentner. Fisher sought to set aside the transaction, asserting that Kristine's repeated visits to the nursing home and her failure to involve Lentner's other family members in the transaction unduly influenced Lentner.

DECISION: Judgment for Thomas and Kristine Schefers. Undue influence is shown when the person making the contract ceased to act of his own free volition and became a mere puppet of the wielder of that influence. Mere speculation alone that Lentner was a "puppet" acting according to the wishes of Schefers is insufficient to set aside the sale. Undue influence was not established. [*Fisher v. Schefers*, 656 N.W.2d 592 (Minn. App. 2003)]

CPA

13. Duress

> **physical duress**—threat of physical harm to person or property.
>
> **economic duress**—threat of financial loss.
>
> **duress**—conduct that deprives the victim of free will and that generally gives the victim the right to set aside any transaction entered into under such circumstances.

A party may enter into a contract to avoid a threatened danger. The danger threatened may be a physical harm to person or property, called **physical duress**, or it may be a threat of financial loss, called **economic duress**.

(A) PHYSICAL DURESS. A person makes a contract under **duress** when there is such violence or threat of violence that the person is deprived of free will and makes the contract to avoid harm. The threatened harm may be directed either at a near relative of the contracting party or against the contracting party. If a contract is made under duress, the resulting agreement is voidable at the victim's election.

Agreements made to bring an end to mass disorder or violence are ordinarily not binding contracts because they were obtained by duress.

One may not void a contract on grounds of duress merely because it was entered into with great reluctance and proves to be very disadvantageous to that individual.[26]

(B) ECONOMIC DURESS. Economic duress is a condition in which one is induced by a wrongful act or threat of another to make a contract under circumstances that deprive one of the exercise of his own free will.[27] **For Example,** Richard Case, an importer of parts used to manufacture high-quality mountain bicycles, had a contractual duty to supply Katahdin Manufacturing Company's needs for specifically manufactured stainless steel brakes for the 2013 season. Katahdin's president, Bill Read, was in constant contact with Case about the delay in delivery of the parts and the adverse consequences it was having on Katahdin's relationship with its retailers.

---

[26] *Miller v. Calhoun/Johnson Co.*, 497 S.E.2d 397 (Ga. App. 1998).
[27] *Hurd v. Wildman, Harrold, Allen, and Dixon*, 707 N.E.2d 609 (Ill. App. 1999).

Near the absolute deadline for meeting orders for the 2013 season, Case called Read and said, "I've got the parts in, but I'm not sure I'll be able to send them to you because I'm working on next year's contracts, and you haven't signed yours yet." Case's 2014 contract increased the cost of parts by 38 percent. Read signed the contract to obtain the delivery but later found a new supplier and gave notice to Case of this action. The defense of economic duress would apply in a breach of contract suit brought by Case on the 2014 contract because Case implicitly threatened to commit the wrongful act of not delivering parts due under the prior contract, and Katahdin Company had no means available to obtain parts elsewhere to prevent the economic loss that would occur if it did not receive those parts.

LawFlix

Jerry Maguire (1996) (R)

Consider the marriage proposal, its validity, and Dorothy's later statement, "I did this. I made this happen. And the thing is, I can do something about it." What was Maguire's state of mind at the time of the proposal? Consider its possible hypothetical nature and the issues of whether it was a joke and the possible presence of undue influence (the young boy).

Matilda (1996)(PG)

A brilliant little girl with a strong moral compass who tries to instruct her family on many things erudite and her father specifically on what constitutes misrepresentation in selling used cars.

MAKE THE CONNECTION

SUMMARY

An agreement that otherwise appears to be a contract may not be binding because one of the parties lacks contractual capacity. In such a case, the contract is ordinarily voidable at the election of the party who lacks contractual capacity. In some cases, the contract is void. Ordinarily, contractual incapacity is the inability, for mental or physical reasons, to understand that a contract is being made and to understand its general terms and nature. This is typically the case when it is claimed that incapacity exists because of insanity, intoxication, or drug use. The incapacity of minors arises because society discriminates in favor of that class to protect them from unwise contracts.

The age of majority is 18. Minors can disaffirm most contracts. If a minor received anything from the other party, the minor, on avoiding the contract, must return what had been received from the other party if the minor still has it.

When a minor disaffirms a contract for a necessary, the minor must pay the reasonable value of any benefit received.

Minors only are liable for their contracts. Parents of a minor are not liable on the minor's contracts merely because they are the parents. Frequently, an adult enters into the contract as a coparty of the minor and is then liable without regard to whether the minor has avoided the contract.

The contract of an insane person is voidable to much the same extent as the contract of a minor. An important distinction is that if a guardian has been appointed for the insane person, a contract made by the insane person is void, not merely voidable.

An intoxicated person lacks contractual capacity if the intoxication is such that the person does not understand that a contract is being made.

The consent of a party to an agreement is not genuine or voluntary in certain cases of mistake, deception, or pressure. When this occurs, what appears to be a contract can be avoided by the victim of such circumstances or conduct.

As to mistake, it is necessary to distinguish between unilateral mistakes that are unknown to the other contracting party and those that are known. Mistakes that are unknown to the other party usually do not affect the binding character of the agreement. A unilateral mistake of which the other contracting party has knowledge or has reason to know makes the contract avoidable by the victim of the mistake.

The deception situation may be one of negligent misrepresentation or fraud. The law ordinarily does not attach any significance to nondisclosure. Contrary to this rule, there is a duty to volunteer information when a confidential relationship exists between the possessor of the knowledge and the other contracting party.

When concealment goes beyond mere silence and consists of actively taking steps to hide the truth, the conduct may be classified as fraud. A statement of opinion or value cannot ordinarily be the basis for fraud liability.

The voluntary character of a contract may be lacking because the agreement had been obtained by pressure. This may range from undue influence through the array of threats of extreme economic loss (called *economic duress*) to the threat of physical force that would cause serious personal injury or damage to property (called *physical duress*). When the voluntary character of an agreement has been destroyed by deception, or pressure, the victim may avoid or rescind the contract or may obtain money damages from the wrongdoer.

LEARNING OUTCOMES

After studying this chapter, you should be able to clearly explain:

A. Contractual Capacity

LO.1 Define contractual capacity
See the example where Jacqueline, age 22, did not understand parts of a storage contract, p. 283.

LO.2 Explain the extent and effect of avoidance of a contract by a minor.
See the *Adorian Deck* example where the creator of a Twitter feed, a minor, disaffirmed his joint venture contract, p. 284.
See the *Prince George's Hospital* case where a minor had to pay for medical necessaries, p. 286.

B. Mistake

LO.3 Distinguish unilateral mistakes and mutual mistakes
See the *Shurgard Storage* case where the "other party" should have known of the unilateral mistake, p. 289.
See the *Jewell Coke Co.* example of a remedy for a billion dollar mistake, p. 290.

See the example of the mutual mistake of fact regarding the fertility of a cow on p. 290.

C. Deception

LO.4 Explain the difference between intentional misrepresentation, negligent misrepresentation, and puffery

See the example of the purchase of the used Honda where the misrepresentation was found to be fraud not puffery on p. 292.
See the *Novare Group, Inc.* decision on the enforceability of disclaimer-of-liability clauses, pp. 293–294.

D. Pressure

LO.5 Explain the difference between undue influence and duress
See the *Fisher v. Schefers* undue influence litigation, p. 297.
See the Katahdin bicycle example on economic duress, p. 297.

KEY TERMS

confidential relationship	fraud	status quo ante
contractual capacity	necessaries	undue influence
duress	physical duress	
economic duress	reformation	

QUESTIONS AND CASE PROBLEMS

1. Lester purchased a used automobile from MacKintosh Motors. He asked the seller if the car had ever been in a wreck. The MacKintosh salesperson had never seen the car before that morning and knew nothing of its history but quickly answered Lester's question by stating: "No. It has never been in a wreck." In fact, the auto had been seriously damaged in a wreck and, although repaired, was worth much less than the value it would have had if there had been no wreck. When Lester learned the truth, he sued MacKintosh Motors and the salesperson for damages for fraud. They raised the defense that the salesperson did not know the statement was false and had not intended to deceive Lester. Did the conduct of the salesperson constitute fraud?

2. Helen, age 17, wanted to buy a Harley-Davidson "Sportster" motorcycle. She did not have the funds to pay cash but persuaded the dealer to sell the cycle to her on credit. The dealer did so partly because Helen said that she was 22 and showed the dealer an identification card that falsely stated her age as 22. Helen drove the motorcycle away. A few days later, she damaged it and then returned it to the dealer and stated that she disaffirmed the contract because she was a minor. The dealer said that she could not because (1) she had misrepresented her age and (2) the motorcycle was damaged. Can she avoid the contract?

3. Paden signed an agreement dated May 28 to purchase the Murrays' home. The Murrays accepted Paden's offer the following day, and the sale closed on June 27. Paden and his family moved into the home on July 14, 1997. Paden had the home inspected prior to closing. The report listed four minor repairs needed by the home, the cost of which was less than $500. Although these repairs had not been completed at the time of closing, Paden decided to go through with the purchase. After moving into the home, Paden discovered a number of allegedly new defects, including a wooden foundation, electrical problems, and bat infestation. The sales agreement allowed extensive rights to inspect the property. The agreement provided:

> Buyer...shall have the right to enter the property at Buyer's expense and at reasonable times...to thoroughly inspect, examine, test, and survey the Property.... Buyer shall have the right to request that Seller repair defects in the Property by providing Seller within 12 days from Binding Agreement Date with a copy of inspection report(s) and a written amendment to this agreement setting forth the defects in the report which Buyer requests to be repaired and/or replaced.... If Buyer does not timely present the written amendment and inspection report, Buyer shall be deemed to have accepted the Property "as is."

Paden sued the Murrays for fraudulent concealment and breach of the sales agreement. If Mr. Murray told Paden on May 26 that the house had a concrete foundation, would this be fraud? Decide. [*Paden v. Murray*, 523 S.E.2d 75 (Ga. App.)]

4. High-Tech Collieries borrowed money from Holland. High-Tech later refused to be bound by the loan contract, claiming the contract was not binding because it had been obtained by duress. The evidence showed that the offer to make the loan was made on a take-it-or-leave-it basis. Was the defense of duress valid? [*Holland v. High-Tech Collieries, Inc.*, 911 F. Supp. 1021 (N.D. W.Va.)]

5. Thomas Bell, a minor, went to work in the Pittsburgh beauty parlor of Sam Pankas and

agreed that when he left the employment, he would not work in or run a beauty parlor business within a 10-mile radius of downtown Pittsburgh for a period of two years. Contrary to this provision, Bell and another employee of Pankas's opened a beauty shop three blocks from Pankas's shop and advertised themselves as Pankas's former employees. Pankas sued Bell to stop the breach of the noncompetition, or restrictive, covenant. Bell claimed that he was not bound because he was a minor when he had agreed to the covenant. Was he bound by the covenant? [*Pankas v. Bell*, 198 A.2d 312 (Pa.)]

6. Aldrich and Co. sold goods to Donovan on credit. The amount owed grew steadily, and finally Aldrich refused to sell any more to Donovan unless Donovan signed a promissory note for the amount due. Donovan did not want to but signed the note because he had no money and needed more goods. When Aldrich brought an action to enforce the note, Donovan claimed that the note was not binding because it had been obtained by economic duress. Was he correct? [*Aldrich & Co. v. Donovan*, 778 P.2d 397 (Mont.)]

7. James Fitl purchased a 1952 Mickey Mantle Topps baseball card from baseball card dealer Mark Strek for $17,750 and placed it in a safe deposit box. Two years later, he had the card appraised, and he was told that the card had been refinished and trimmed, which rendered it valueless. Fitl sued Strek and testified that he had relied on Strek's position as a sports card dealer and on his representations that the baseball card was authentic. Strek contends that Fitl waited too long to give him notice of the defects that would have enabled Strek to contact the person who sold him the card and obtain relief. Strek asserts that he therefore is not liable. Advise Fitl concerning possible legal theories that apply to his case. How would you decide the case? [See *Fitl v. Strek*, 690 N.W.2d 605 (Neb.)]

8. Willingham proposed to obtain an investment property for the Tschiras at a "fair market price," lease it back from them, and pay the Tschiras a guaranteed return through a management contract. Using a shell corporation, The

Wellingham Group bought a commercial property in Nashville for $774,000 on December 14, and the very same day sold the building to the Tschiras for $1,985,000. The title insurance policy purchased for the Tschiras property by Willingham was for just $774,000. Willingham believes that the deal was legitimate in that they "guaranteed" a return on the investment. The Tschiras disagree. In a lawsuit against Willingham, what theory will the Tschiras rely on? Decide. [*Tschiras v. Willingham*, 133 F.3d 1077 (6th Cir.)]

9. Blubaugh was a district manager of Schlumberger Well Services. Turner was an executive employee of Schlumberger. Blubaugh was told that he would be fired unless he chose to resign. He was also told that if he would resign and release the company and its employees from all claims for wrongful discharge, he would receive about $5,000 in addition to his regular severance pay of approximately $25,000 and would be given job-relocation counseling. He resigned, signed the release, and received about $40,000 and job counseling. Some time thereafter, he brought an action claiming that he had been wrongfully discharged. He claimed that the release did not protect the defendants because the release had been obtained by economic duress. Were the defendants protected by the release? [*Blubaugh v. Turner*, 842 P.2d 1072 (Wyo.)]

10. Sippy was thinking of buying Christich's house. He noticed watermarks on the ceiling, but the agent showing the house stated that the roof had been repaired and was in good condition. Sippy was not told that the roof still leaked and that the repairs had not been able to stop the leaking. Sippy bought the house. Some time later, heavy rains caused water to leak into the house, and Sippy claimed that Christich was liable for damages. What theory would he rely on? Decide. [*Sippy v. Christich*, 609 P.2d 204 (Kan. App.)]

11. Pileggi owed Young money. Young threatened to bring suit against Pileggi for the amount due. Pileggi feared the embarrassment of being sued and the possibility that he might be thrown into bankruptcy. To avoid being sued, Pileggi executed a promissory note to pay Young the

amount due. He later asserted that the note was not binding because he had executed it under duress. Is this defense valid? [*Young v. Pileggi*, 455 A.2d 1228 (Pa. Super.)]

12. Office Supply Outlet, Inc., a single-store office equipment and supply retailer, ordered 100 model RVX-414 computers from Compuserve, Inc. A new staff member made a clerical error on the order form and ordered a quantity that was far in excess of what Office Supply could sell in a year. Office Supply realized the mistake when the delivery trucks arrived at its warehouse. Its manager called Compuserve and explained that it had intended to order just 10 computers. Compuserve declined to accept the return of the extra machines. Is the contract enforceable? What additional facts would allow the store to avoid the contract for the additional machines?

13. The Printers International Union reached agreement for a new three-year contract with a large regional printing company. As was their practice, the union negotiators then met with Sullivan Brothers Printers, Inc., a small specialty shop employing 10 union printers, and Sullivan Brothers and the union agreed to follow the contractual pattern set by the union and the large printing company. That is, Sullivan Brothers agreed to give its workers all of the benefits negotiated for the employees of the large printing company. When the contract was typed, a new benefit of 75 percent employer-paid coverage for a dental plan was inadvertently omitted from the final contract the parties signed. The mistake was not discovered until six months after the contract took effect. Sullivan Brothers Printers, Inc. is reluctant to assume the additional expense. It contends that the printed copy, which does not cover dental benefits, must control. The union believes that clear and convincing evidence shows an inadvertent typing error. Decide.

14. The city of Salinas entered into a contract with Souza & McCue Construction Co. to construct a sewer. City officials knew unusual subsoil conditions (including extensive quicksand) existed that would make performance of the contract unusually difficult. This information was not disclosed when city officials advertised for bids. The advertisement for bids directed bidders to examine carefully the site of the work and declared that the submission of a bid would constitute evidence that the bidder had made an examination. Souza & McCue was awarded the contract, but because of the subsoil conditions, it could not complete on time and was sued by Salinas for breach of contract. Souza & McCue counterclaimed on the basis that the city had not revealed its information on the subsoil conditions and was thus liable for the loss. Was the city liable? [*City of Salinas v. Souza & McCue Construction Co.*, 424 P.2d 921 (Cal. App. 3d)]

15. Vern Westby inherited a "ticket" from Anna Sjoblom, a survivor of the sinking of the *Titanic*, which had been pinned to the inside of her coat. He also inherited an album of postcards, some of which related to the *Titanic*. The ticket was a one-of-a-kind item in good condition. Westby needed cash and went to the biggest antique dealer in Tacoma, operated by Alan Gorsuch and his family, doing business as Sanford and Sons, and asked about the value of these items. Westby testified that after Alan Gorsuch examined the ticket, he said, "It's not worth nothing." Westby then inquired about the value of the postcard album, and Gorsuch advised him to come back later. On Westby's return, Gorsuch told Westby, "It ain't worth nothing." Gorsuch added that he "couldn't fetch $500 for the ticket." Since he needed money, Westby asked if Gorsuch would give him $1,000 for both the ticket and the album, and Gorsuch did so.

Six months later, Gorsuch sold the ticket at a nationally advertised auction for $110,000 and sold most of the postcards for $1,200. Westby sued Gorsuch for fraud. Testimony showed that Gorsuch was a major buyer in antiques and collectibles in the Puget Sound area and that he would have had an understanding of the value of the ticket. Gorsuch contends that all elements of fraud are not present since there was no evidence that Gorsuch intended that Westby rely on the alleged representations, nor did Westby rely on such. Rather, Gorsuch asserts, it was an arm's-length transaction and Westby had access to the same information as Gorsuch. Decide. [*Westby v. Gorsuch*, 50 P.3d 284 (Wash. App.)]

CPA QUESTIONS

1. A building subcontractor submitted a bid for construction of a portion of a high-rise office building. The bid contained material computational errors. The general contractor accepted the bid with knowledge of the errors. Which of the following statements best represents the subcontractor's liability?

   a. Not liable, because the contractor knew of the errors.

   b. Not liable, because the errors were a result of gross negligence.

   c. Liable, because the errors were unilateral.

   d. Liable, because the errors were material (5/95, Law, #17, 5351).

2. Egan, a minor, contracted with Baker to purchase Baker's used computer for $400. The computer was purchased for Egan's personal use. The agreement provided that Egan would pay $200 down on delivery and $200 thirty days later. Egan took delivery and paid the $200 down payment. Twenty days later, the computer was damaged seriously as a result of Egan's negligence. Five days after the damage occurred and one day after Egan reached the age of majority, Egan attempted to disaffirm the contract with Baker. Egan will:

   a. Be able to disaffirm despite the fact that Egan was *not* a minor at the time of disaffirmance.

   b. Be able to disaffirm only if Egan does so in writing.

   c. Not be able to disaffirm because Egan had failed to pay the balance of the purchase price.

   d. Not be able to disaffirm because the computer was damaged as a result of Egan's negligence (11/93, Law, #21, 4318).

© Manuel Gutjahr/iStockphoto.com

CHAPTER 15

Consideration

W ill the law enforce every promise? Generally, a promise will not be enforced unless something is given or received for the promise.

A. General Principles

As a general rule, one of the elements needed to make an agreement binding is consideration.

1. Consideration Defined and Explained

consideration – promise or performance that the promisor demands as the price of the promise.

Consideration is what each party to a contract gives up to the other in making their agreement.

(A) Bargained-for Exchange. *Consideration* is the bargained-for exchange between the parties to a contract. In order for consideration to exist, something of value must be given or promised in return for the performance or promise of performance of the other.[1] The value given or promised can be money, services, property, or the forbearance of a legal right.

For Example, Beth offers to pay Kerry $100 for her used skis, and Kerry accepts. Beth has promised something of value, $100, as consideration for Kerry's promise to sell the skis, and Kerry has promised Beth something of value, the skis, as consideration for the $100. If Kerry offered to *give* Beth the used skis and Beth accepted, these parties would have an agreement but not an enforceable contract because Beth did not provide any consideration in exchange for Kerry's promise of the skis. There was no *bargained-for exchange* because Kerry was not promised anything of value from Beth.

(B) Benefit-Detriment Approach. Some jurisdictions analyze consideration from the point of view of a *benefit-detriment approach,* defining *consideration* as a benefit received by the promisor or a detriment incurred by the promisee.

As an example of a unilateral contract analyzed from a benefit-detriment approach to consideration, Mr. Scully, a longtime summer resident of Falmouth, states to George Corfu, a college senior, "I will pay you $3,000 if you paint my summer home." George in fact paints the house. The work of painting the house by George, the promisee, was a legal detriment to him. Also, the painting of the house was a legal benefit to Scully, the promisor. There was consideration in this case, and the agreement is enforceable.

2. Gifts

Promises to make a gift are unenforceable promises under the law of contracts because of lack of consideration, as illustrated previously in the scenario of Kerry promising to give her used skis to Beth without charge. There was no bargained-for exchange because Kerry was not promised anything of value from Beth. A completed gift, however, cannot be rescinded for lack of consideration.[2]

---

[1] *Brooksbank v. Anderson,* 586 N.W.2d 789 (Minn. App. 1998).
[2] *Homes v. O'Bryant,* 741 So.2d 366 (Miss. App. 1999).

Charitable subscriptions by which individuals make pledges to finance the construction of a college building, a church, or another structure for charitable purposes are binding to the extent that the donor (promisor) should have reasonably realized that the charity was relying on the promise in undertaking the building program. Some states require proof that the charity has relied on the subscription.[3]

CASE SUMMARY

You Can't Back Out Now

FACTS: Salsbury was attempting to establish a new college, Charles City College. Salsbury obtained a pledge from Northwestern Bell Telephone Company to contribute to the college. When the company did not pay, Salsbury sued the company. The company raised the defense that there was no consideration for its promise and that nothing had been done by the college in reliance on the promise.

DECISION: Judgment for Salsbury. As a matter of public policy, a promise of a charitable contribution is binding even though there is no consideration for the promise and without regard for whether the charity had done any acts in reliance on the promise. The company was therefore liable on its promise to contribute. [*Salsbury v. Northwestern Bell Telephone Co.*, **221 N.W.2d 609 (Iowa 1974)**]

An agreement to give property for the consideration of love and affection does not transfer the property to the donee nor secure for the donee a right to sue to compel the completion of the contract. Love and affection alone have not been recognized as consideration for a contract.

CASE SUMMARY

What's Love Got to Do with It...

FACTS: Amber Williams and Frederick Ormsby lived together in a nonmarital relationship in a house deeded to Ormsby in 2004. The couple separated and attended couples counseling. Amber refused to move back into the house unless Frederick granted her a one-half interest in the property. On June 2, 2005, they signed a document purportedly making themselves equal partners in the home. Amber ended the relationship in September 2007, and she sought specific performance of the June 2, 2005 contract giving her a half-interest in the property. Frederick defended that "love and affection is insufficient consideration for a contract."

DECISION: Judgment for Ormsby. The only consideration offered by Amber for the June 2, 2005 agreement was her resumption of a romantic relationship with Frederick. Essentially this agreement amounts to a gratuitous promise by Frederick to give Amber an interest in property based solely on the consideration of love and affection. This June 2005 document is not an enforceable contract because it fails for want of consideration. [*Williams v. Ormsby*, **966 N.E.2d 255 (Ohio 2012)**]

---

[3] *King v. Trustees of Boston University*, 647 N.E.2d 1176 (Ma. 1995).

3. Adequacy of Consideration

Ordinarily, courts do not consider the adequacy of the consideration given for a promise. The fact that the consideration supplied by one party is slight when compared with the burden undertaken by the other party is immaterial. It is a matter for the parties to decide when they make their contract whether each is getting a fair return. In the absence of fraud or other misconduct, courts usually will not interfere to make sure that each side is getting a fair return.

CASE SUMMARY

Who's to Say?

FACTS: On the death of their aunt, a brother and sister became the owners of shares of stock of several corporations. They made an agreement to divide these shares equally between them, although the sister's shares had a value approximately seven times those of the brother. The brother died before the shares were divided. The sister then claimed that the agreement to divide was not binding because the consideration for her promise was not adequate.

DECISION: The value of stock cannot be determined precisely. It may change with time. In addition, the value that one person may see can be different than that seen by another. The court therefore will not make a comparison of the value that each party was to receive under the agreement. It was sufficient that a promise was exchanged for a promise. The adequacy of the consideration would not be examined. This sister was therefore bound by her promise to divide the shares. [*Emberson v. Hartley*, 762 P.2d 364 (Wash. App. 1988)]

Because the adequacy of consideration is ignored, it is immaterial that consideration is so slight that the transaction is in part a "gift." However, the Internal Revenue Service may view a given transaction as part consideration, part gift, and assess a gift tax as appropriate.

The fact that the consideration turns out to be disappointing does not affect the binding character of the contract. Thus, the fact that a business purchased by a group of investors proves unprofitable does not constitute a failure of consideration that releases the buyers from their obligation to the seller.

CASE SUMMARY

Expectations versus Consideration

FACTS: Aqua Drilling Company made a contract to drill a well for the Atlas Construction Company. It was expected that this would supply water for a home being constructed by Atlas. Aqua did not make any guarantee or warranty that water would be produced. Aqua drilled the well exactly as required by the contract, but no water was produced. Atlas refused to pay. It asserted that the contract was not binding on the theory that there had been a failure of consideration because the well did not produce water.

DECISION: The contract was binding. Atlas obtained the exact performance required by the contract. While Atlas had expected that water would be obtained, Aqua did not make any guarantee or warranty that this would be so. Hence, there was no failure of consideration. [*Atlas Construction Co., Inc. v. Aqua Drilling Co.*, 559 P.2d 39 (Wyo. 1977)]

4. Forbearance as Consideration

In most cases, consideration consists of the performance of an act such as providing a service, or the making of a promise to provide a service or goods, or paying money.[4] Consideration may also consist of **forbearance**, which is refraining from doing an act that an individual has a legal right to do, or it may consist of a promise of forbearance. In other words, the promisor may desire to buy the inaction or a promise of inaction of the other party.

The giving up of any legal right can be consideration for the promise of the other party to a contract. Thus, the relinquishment of a right to sue for damages will support a promise for the payment of money given in return for the promise to relinquish the right, if such is the agreement of the parties.

The promise of a creditor to forbear collecting a debt is consideration for the promise of the debtor to modify the terms of the transaction.

forbearance – refraining from doing an act.

5. Illusory Promises

In a bilateral contract, each party makes a promise to the other. For a bilateral contract to be enforceable, there must be *mutuality of obligation.* That is, both parties must have created obligations to the other in their respective promises. If one party's promise contains either no obligation or only an apparent obligation to the other, this promise is an **illusory promise**. The party making such a promise is not bound because he or she has made no real promise. The effect is that the other party, who has made a real promise, is also not bound because he or she has received no consideration. It is said that the contract fails for lack of mutuality.

illusory promise – promise that in fact does not impose any obligation on the promisor.

For Example, Mountain Coal Company promises to sell Midwest Power Company all the coal it may order for $48 per ton for the year 2013, and Midwest Power agrees to pay $48 for any coal it orders from Mountain Coal. Mountain Coal in its promise to Midwest Power has obligated itself to supply all coal ordered at a stated price. However, Midwest Power's promise did not obligate it to buy any coal whatsoever from Mountain Coal (note that it was not a requirements contract). Because Midwest has no obligation to Mountain Coal under its promise, there is no mutuality of obligation, and Midwest cannot enforce Mountain Coal's promise when the market price of coal goes to $55 a ton in the winter of 2013 as the result of severe weather conditions.

Consider as well the example of the Jacksonville Fire soccer team's contract with Brazilian soccer star Edmundo. Edmundo signed a contract to play for the Jacksonville franchise of the new International Soccer League for five years at $25 million. The extensive document signed by Edmundo set forth the details of the team's financial commitment and the details of Edmundo's obligations to the team and its fans. On page 4 of the document, the team inserted a clause reserving the right "to terminate the contract and team obligations at any time in its sole discretion." During the season, Edmundo received a $40 million five-year offer to play for Manchester United of the English Premier League, which he accepted. Because Jacksonville had a free way out of its obligation by the unrestricted cancellation provision in the contract, it thus made its promises to Edmundo illusory. Edmundo was not bound by the Jacksonville contract as a result of a lack of mutuality and was free to sign with Manchester United.

---

[4] *Prenger v. Baumhoer,* 914 S.W.2d 413 (Mo. App. 1996).

cancellation provision – crossing out of a part of an instrument or a destruction of all legal effect of the instrument, whether by act of party, upon breach by the other party, or pursuant to agreement or decree of court.

(A) CANCELLATION PROVISIONS. Although a promise must impose a binding obligation, it may authorize a party to cancel the agreement under certain circumstances on giving notice by a certain date. Such a provision does not make this party's promise illusory, for the party does not have a free way out and is limited to living up to the terms of the **cancellation provision**. **For Example,** actress Zsa Zsa Gabor made a contract with Hollywood Fantasy Corporation to appear at a fantasy vacation in San Antonio, Texas, on May 2–4, for a $10,000 appearance fee plus itemized (extravagant) expenses. The last paragraph of the agreement stated: "It is agreed that if a significant acting opportunity in a film comes up, Ms. Gabor will have the right to cancel her appearance in San Antonio by advising Hollywood Fantasy in writing by April 15, 1991." Ms. Gabor sent a telegram on April 15, 1991, canceling her appearance. During the May 2 through 4 period, Ms. Gabor's only acting activity was a 14-second cameo role during the opening credits of *Naked Gun 2½*. In a lawsuit for breach of contract that followed, the jury saw this portion of the movie and concluded that Ms. Gabor had not canceled her obligation on the basis of a "significant acting opportunity," and she was held liable for breach of contract.[5]

(B) CONDITIONAL PROMISES. A *conditional promise* is a promise that depends on the occurrence of a specified condition in order for the promise to be binding. **For Example,** Mary Sparks, in contemplation of her signing a lease to take over a restaurant at Marina Bay, wanted to make certain that she had a highly qualified chef to run the restaurant's food service. She made a contract with John "Grumpy" White to serve as executive chef for a one-year period at a salary of $150,000. The contract set forth White's responsibilities and was conditioned on the successful negotiation of the restaurant lease with Marina Bay Management. Both parties signed it. Although the happening of the condition was within Mary's control because she could avoid the contract with Grumpy White by not acquiring the restaurant lease, she limited her future options by the contract with White. Her promise to White was not illusory because after signing the contract with him, if she acquired the restaurant lease, she was bound to hire White as her executive chef. Before signing the contract with White, she was free to sign any chef for the position. The contract was enforceable.

CPA B. SPECIAL SITUATIONS

The following sections analyze certain common situations in which a lawsuit turns on whether the promisor received consideration for the promise sued on.

6. Preexisting Legal Obligation

Ordinarily, doing or promising to do what one is already under a legal obligation to do is not consideration.[6] Similarly, a promise to refrain from doing what one has no legal right to do is not consideration. This preexisting duty or legal obligation can be based on statute, on general principles of law, on responsibilities of an office held, or on a preexisting contract.

[5] *Hollywood Fantasy Corp. v. Gabor*, 151 F.2d 203 (5th Cir. 1998).
[6] *Willamette Management Associates, Inc. v. Palczynski*, 38 A.3d 1212 (Conn. App. 2012).

For Example, Officer Mary Rodgers is an undercover police officer in the city of Pasadena, California, assigned to weekend workdays. Officer Rodgers promised Elwood Farnsworth that she would diligently patrol the area of the Farnsworth estate on weekends to keep down the noise and drinking of rowdy young persons who gathered in this area, and Mr. Farnsworth promised to provide a $500 per month gratuity for this extra service. Farnsworth's promise is unenforceable because Officer Rodgers has a preexisting official duty as a police officer to protect citizens and enforce the antinoise and public drinking ordinances.

CPA (A) **COMPLETION OF CONTRACT.** Suppose that a contractor refuses to complete a building unless the owner promises a payment or bonus in addition to the sum specified in the original contract, and the owner promises to make that payment. The question then arises as to whether the owner's promise is binding. Most courts hold that the second promise of the owner is without consideration.

CASE SUMMARY

You're Already Under Contract

FACTS: Crookham & Vessels had a contract to build an extension of a railroad for the Little Rock Port Authority. It made a contract with Larry Moyer Trucking to dig drainage ditches. The ditch walls collapsed because water would not drain off. This required that the ditches be dug over again. Larry Moyer refused to do this unless extra money was paid. Crookham & Vessels agreed to pay the additional compensation, but after the work was done, it refused to pay. Larry Moyer sued for the extra compensation promised.

DECISION: Judgment against Moyer. Moyer was bound by its contract to dig the drainage ditches. Its promise to perform that obligation was not consideration for the promise of Crookham & Vessels to pay additional compensation. Performance of an obligation is not consideration for a promise by a party entitled to that performance. The fact that performance of the contract proved more difficult or costly than originally contemplated does not justify making an exception to this rule. [*Crookham & Vessels, Inc. v. Larry Moyer Trucking, Inc.,* 699 S.W.2d 414 (Ark. App. 1985)]

If the promise of the contractor is to do something that is not part of the first contract, then the promise of the other party is binding. **For Example,** if a bonus of $5,000 is promised in return for the promise of a contractor to complete the building at a date earlier than that specified in the original agreement, the promise to pay the bonus is binding.

CPA *(1) Good-Faith Adjustment*
A current trend is to enforce a second promise to pay a contractor a higher amount for the performance of the original contract when there are extraordinary circumstances caused by unforeseeable difficulties and when the additional amount promised the contractor is reasonable under the circumstances.

CASE SUMMARY

"You Had a Preexisting Legal Obligation," Said the Public Guardian, Mr. Angel.

FACTS: John Murray was director of finance of the city of Newport. A contract was made with Alfred Maher to remove trash. Later, Maher requested that the city council increase his compensation. Maher's costs were greater than had been anticipated because 400 new dwelling units had been put into operation. The city council voted to pay Maher an additional $10,000 a year. After two such annual payments had been made, Angel and other citizens of the city sued Murray and Maher for a return of the $20,000. They said that Maher was already obligated by his contract to perform the work for the contract sum, and there was, accordingly, no consideration for the payment of the increased compensation. From a decision in favor of the plaintiffs, the city and Maher appealed.

DECISION: Judgment for the city and Maher. When a promise modifying an original contract is made before the contract is fully performed on either side due to unanticipated circumstances that prompt the modification, and the modification is fair and equitable, such a good faith adjustment will be enforced. The unanticipated increase in the number of new units from 20 to 25 per year to 400 units in the third year of this five-year contract, which prompted the additional yearly payments of $10,000, was a voluntary good faith adjustment. It was not a "hold up" by a contractor refusing to complete an unprofitable contract unless paid additional compensation, where the preexisting duty rule would apply. [*Angel v. Murray*, 322 A.2d 630 (R.I. 1974)]

(2) Contract for Sale of Goods

When the contract is for the sale of goods, any modification made in good faith by the parties to the contract is binding without regard to the existence of consideration for the modification.

CPA

(B) COMPROMISE AND RELEASE OF CLAIMS. The rule that doing or promising to do what one is already legally bound to do is not consideration applies to a part payment made in satisfaction of an admitted or *liquidated debt*. Thus, a promise to pay part of an amount that is admittedly owed is not consideration for a promise to discharge the balance. It will not prevent the creditor from demanding the remainder later. **For Example,** John owes Mark $100,000, which was due on March 1, 2010. On March 15, John offers to pay back $80,000 if Mark will agree to accept this amount as the discharge of the full amount owed. Mark agrees to this proposal, and it is set forth in writing signed by the parties. However, Mark later sues for the $20,000 balance. Mark will be successful in the lawsuit because John's payment of the $80,000 is not consideration for Mark's promise to discharge the full amount owed because John was doing only what he had a preexisting legal duty to do.

If the debtor pays the part payment before the debt is due, there is consideration because, on the day when the payment was made, the creditor was not entitled to demand any payment. Likewise, if the creditor accepts some article (even of slight value) in addition to the part payment, consideration exists.

A debtor and creditor may have a bona fide dispute over the amount owed or whether any amount is owed. Such is called an *unliquidated debt*. In this case, payment by the debtor of less than the amount claimed by the creditor is consideration for the latter's agreement to release or settle the claim. It is generally regarded as sufficient if the claimant believes in the merit of the claim.[7]

(c) PART-PAYMENT CHECKS. When there is a good-faith dispute about the amount of a debt and the debtor tenders a check that states on its face "paid in full" and references the transaction in dispute, but the amount of the check is less than the full amount the creditor asserts is owed, the cashing of the check by the creditor discharges the entire debt.

(d) COMPOSITION OF CREDITORS. In a **composition of creditors**, the various creditors of one debtor mutually agree to accept a fractional part of their claims in full satisfaction of the claims. Such agreements are binding and are supported by consideration. When creditors agree to extend the due date of their debts, the promise of each creditor to forbear is likewise consideration for the promise of other creditors to forbear.

composition of creditors – agreement among creditors that each shall accept a part payment as full payment in consideration of the other creditors doing the same.

7. Past Consideration

A promise based on a party's past performance lacks consideration.[8] It is said that **past consideration** is no consideration. **For Example,** Fred O'Neal came up with the idea for the formation of the new community bank of Villa Rica and was active in its formation. Just prior to the execution of the documents creating the bank, the organizers discussed that once the bank was formed, it would hire O'Neal, giving him a three-year contract at $65,000 the first year, $67,000 the second year, and $70,000 the third. In a lawsuit against the bank for breach of contract, O'Neal testified that the consideration he gave in exchange for the three-year contract was his past effort to organize the bank. The court stated that past consideration generally will not support a subsequent promise and that the purported consideration was not rendered to the bank, which had not yet been established when his promotion and organization work took place.[9] The presence of a bargained-for exchange is not present when a promise is made in exchange for a past benefit.[10]

past consideration – something that has been performed in the past and which, therefore, cannot be consideration for a promise made in the present.

8. Moral Obligation

In most states, promises made to another based on "moral obligation" lack consideration and are not enforceable.[11] They are considered gratuitous promises and unenforceable. **For Example,** while on a fishing trip, Tom Snyder, a person of moderate means, met an elderly couple living in near-destitute conditions in a rural area of Texas. He returned to the area often, and he regularly purchased groceries for the couple and paid for their medical needs. Some two years later, the couple's son, David, discovered what Tom had been doing and promised to reimburse Snyder for what he had furnished his parents. This promise, based on a moral obligation, is unenforceable. A "past consideration" analysis also renders David's promise as unenforceable.

---

[7] *F. H. Prince & Co. v. Towers Financial Corp.*, 656 N.E.2d 142 (Ill. App. 1995).

[8] *Smith v. Locklear*, 906 So.2d 1273 (Fla. App. 2005).

[9] *O'Neal v. Home Town Bank of Villa Rica*, 514 S.E.2d 669 (Ga. App. 1999).

[10] But see *United Resource Recovery Corp v. Ranko Venture Management Inc.*, 854 F. Supp. 2d 645 (S.D.N.Y. 2008) where a past work agreement was unenforceable because it was based on past consideration—however, the individual could recover under a signed consulting agreement for which no compensation had been paid. See also *Travis v. Paepke*, 3 So.3d 131 (Miss. App. 2009).

[11] *Production Credit Ass'n of Manaan v. Rub*, 475 N.W.2d 532 (N.D. 1991). As to the Louisiana rule of moral consideration, see *Thomas v. Bryant*, 596 So.2d 1065 (La. App. 1992).

Ethics & the Law

Alan Fulkins, who owns a construction company that specializes in single-family residences, is constructing a small subdivision with 23 homes. Tretorn Plumbing, owned by Jason Tretorn, was awarded the contract for the plumbing work on the homes at a price of $4,300 per home.

Plumbing contractors complete their residential projects in three phases. Phase one consists of digging the lines for the plumbing and installing the pipes that are placed in the foundation of the house. Phase two consists of installing the pipes within the walls of the home, and phase three is installing of the surface plumbing, such as sinks and tubs. However, industry practice dictates that the plumbing contractor receive one-half of the contract amount after completion of phase one.

Tretorn completed the digs of phase one for Fulkins and received payment of $2,150. Tretorn then went to Fulkins and demanded an additional $600 per house to complete the work. Fulkins said, "But you already have a contract for $4,300!" Tretorn responded, "I know, but the costs are killing me. I need the additional $600."

Fulkins explained the hardship of the demand, "Look, I've already paid you half. If I hire someone else, I'll have to pay them two-thirds for the work not done. It'll cost me $5,000 per house."

Tretorn responded, "Exactly. I'm a bargain because the additional $600 I want only puts you at $4,900. If you don't pay it, I'll just lien the houses and then you'll be stuck without a way to close the sales. I've got the contract all drawn up. Just sign it and everything goes smoothly."

Should Fulkins sign the agreement? Does Tretorn have the right to the additional $600? Was it ethical for Tretorn to demand the $600? Is there any legal advice you can offer Fulkins?

FIGURE 15-1 | *Consideration and Promises*

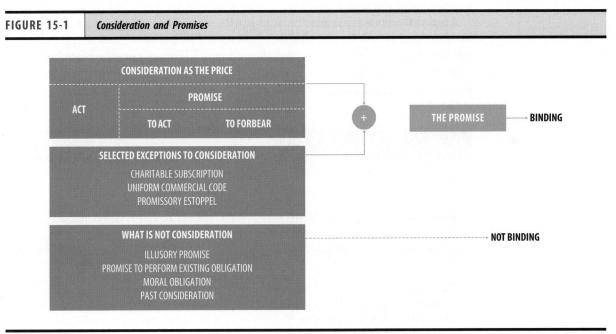

© Cengage Learning

✳ C. EXCEPTIONS TO THE LAWS OF CONSIDERATION

The ever-changing character of law clearly appears in the area of consideration as part of the developing law of contracts.

9. Exceptions to Consideration

By statute or decision, traditional consideration is not required in these situations:

(A) CHARITABLE SUBSCRIPTIONS. Where individuals made pledges to finance the construction of buildings for charitable purposes, consideration is lacking according to technical standards applied in ordinary contract cases. For public policy reasons, the reliance of the charity on the pledge in undertaking the project is deemed a substitute for consideration.

(B) UNIFORM COMMERCIAL CODE. In some situations, the Uniform Commercial Code abolishes the requirement of consideration. **For Example,** under the Code, consideration is not required for (1) a merchant's written, firm offer for goods stated to be irrevocable, (2) a written discharge of a claim for an alleged breach of a commercial contract, or (3) an agreement to modify a contract for the sale of goods. [12]

(C) PROMISSORY ESTOPPEL. Under the doctrine of **promissory estoppel**, a promisor may be prevented from asserting that his or her promise is unenforceable because the promisee gave no consideration for the promise. This doctrine, sometimes called the *doctrine of detrimental reliance,* is applicable when (1) the promisor makes a promise that lacks consideration, (2) the promisor intends or should reasonably expect that the promisee will rely on the promise, (3) the promisee in fact relies on the promise in some definite and substantial manner, and (4) enforcement of the promise is the only way to avoid injustice. [13]

Damages recoverable in a case of promissory estoppel are not the profits that the promisee expected, but only the amount necessary to restore the promisee to the position he or she would have been in had the promisee not relied on the promise. [14]

Legal difficulties often arise because parties take certain things for granted. Frequently, they will be sure that they have agreed to everything and that they have a valid contract. Sometimes, however, they do not. The courts are then faced with the problem of leaving them with their broken dreams or coming to their rescue when promissory estoppel can be established.

reliance

promissory estoppel – doctrine that a promise will be enforced although it is not supported by consideration when the promisor should have reasonably expected that the promise would induce action or forbearance of a definite and substantial character on the part of the promised and injustice can be avoided only by enforcement of the promise.

CASE SUMMARY

Brits Rescued by Promissory Estoppel

FACTS: Portman Lamborghini, Ltd. (Portman), was owned by Chaplake Holdings, Ltd., a United Kingdom company, which was owned by David Jolliffe and David Lakeman as equal shareholders. Between 1984 and 1987, Portman sold approximately 30 new Lamborghinis each year through its exclusive concession contract with the car maker. It was then the largest Lamborghini dealer in the world since Lamborghini's production was just 250 cars per year. These cars sold at a retail price between $200,000 and $300,000. In 1987, Chrysler Corporation bought Lamborghini, and its chairman, Lee Iacocca, presented a plan to escalate production to 5,000 units within five years. The plan included the introduction of a new model, the P140, with a retail price of $70,000. Between 1987 and 1991, *all* of the Chrysler/Lamborghini top executives with whom Jolliffe and Lakeman and their top advisors came in contact provided the same message to them: Chrysler was committed to the Expansion Plan, and in order for Portman to retain its exclusive U.K. market, it must expand its operational capacity from 35 cars in 1987 to 400 cars by 1992. Accordingly, Portman acquired additional financing, staff, and facilities and

---

[12] U.C.C. §2-209(1).

[13] *Neuhoff v. Marvin Lumber and Cedar Co.,* 370 F.3d 197 (1st Cir. 2004).

[14] *Medistar Corp. v. Schmidt,* 267 S.W.3d 150 (Tex. App. 2008).

CASE SUMMARY

Continued

built a new distribution center. An economic downturn in the United States and major development and production problems at Lamborghini led Chrysler to reduce its expansion investment by two-thirds. Factory production delays eroded Portman's profitability and success, and it entered into receivership in April 1992. Suit was brought on behalf of the Portman and Chaplake entities on a promissory estoppel theory against Chrysler, a Delaware corporation.

DECISION: Judgment for Portman and Chaplake on the promissory estoppel theory. (1) A promise was made by Chrysler that the Lamborghini line would expand tenfold and that Portman would retain its exclusivity deal *only* if it expanded its operational capacity. (2) The promisor, Chrysler, should have reasonably expected that Portman would rely on this promise. (3) Lakeman and Jolliffe were given the same message and promise by *all* of the top executives involved, and it was therefore not unreasonable for them to rely upon the promises made by these executives and to undertake the detriment of major expansion activity that would have been unnecessary but for the Expansion Plan and the role they were promised. (4) The prevention of injustice is the "fundamental idea" underlying the doctrine of promissory estoppel, and injustice can be avoided in this case only by the enforcement of Chrysler's promise. Portman is entitled to £ 569,321 for its costs to implement its Expansion Plan, and Chaplake is entitled to £ 462,686 for its investment in Portman's expansion. [*Chrysler Corp. v. Chaplake Holdings, Ltd.,* **822 A.2d 1024 (Del. 2003)**]

LawFlix

Baby Boom (1987) (PG)

Review the scene near the end of the movie when Diane Keaton is presented with an offer for the purchase of her company, Country Baby. List the elements of consideration that Food Giant is paying for the company. Explain what Ms. Keaton's consideration is in exchange.

MAKE THE CONNECTION

SUMMARY

A promise is not binding if there is no consideration for the promise. Consideration is what the promisor requires as the price for his promise. That price may be doing an act, refraining from the doing of an act, or merely promising to do or to refrain. In a bilateral contract, it is necessary to find that the promise of each party is supported by consideration. If either promise is not so supported, it is not binding, and the agreement of the parties is not a contract. Consequently, the agreement cannot be enforced. When a promise is the consideration, it must be a binding promise. The binding character of a promise is not affected by the circumstance that there is a condition precedent to the performance promised. A promise to do what one is already obligated to do is not consideration, although some exceptions are made. Such exceptions include the rendering of a partial performance or a modified performance accepted as a good-faith adjustment to a changed situation, a compromise and release of claims, a part-payment check, and a compromise of creditors. Because consideration is the price that is given to obtain the promise, past benefits conferred on the promisor cannot be consideration.

A promise to refrain from doing an act can be consideration. A promise to refrain from suing or asserting a particular claim can be consideration. When consideration is forbearance to assert a claim, it is immaterial whether the claim is valid as long as the claim has been asserted in the good-faith belief that it was valid.

When the promisor obtains the consideration specified for the promise, the law is not ordinarily concerned with the value or adequacy of that consideration.

Under the doctrine of promissory estoppel a court may enforce a promise lacking consideration where it is the only way to avoid injustice.

LEARNING OUTCOMES

After studying this chapter, you should be able to clearly explain:

A. General Principles—Consideration

LO.1   Explain what constitutes consideration
See the *Williams v. Ormsby* case, which determined that love and affection is not recognized as consideration, p. 306.
See the "bargained for exchange" example involving Beth and Kerry, p. 305.
See the "benefit-detriment" approach to consideration example, p. 305.
See the discussion on forbearance as consideration on p. 308.

B. Special Situations

LO.2   Distinguish between a "preexisting legal obligation" and "past consideration"
See the preexisting duty example involving Officer Rodgers on p. 310.
See the *Angel v. Murray* case involving a good-faith adjustment exception to the preexisting duty rule, p. 311.

See the example involving Fred O'Neal where he found out the past consideration is no consideration rule, p. 312.

LO.3   Explain why promises based on moral obligations lack consideration
See the example of the gratuitous deeds of Tom Snyder on p. 312.

C. Exceptions to The Laws of Consideration

LO.4   List the exceptions to the requirement of consideration
See the discussion on charitable subscriptions, the UCC, and promissory estoppel on p. 314.

LO.5   Explain the "fundamental idea" underlying promissory estoppel
See the *Chaplake Holdings* case where the court enforced Chrysler's promise in order to correct an injustice, pp. 314–315.

KEY TERMS

cancellation provision	forbearance	past consideration
composition of creditors	illusory promise	promissory estoppel
consideration		

QUESTIONS AND CASE PROBLEMS

1. Sarah's house caught on fire. Through the prompt assistance of her neighbor Odessa, the fire was quickly extinguished. In gratitude, Sarah promised to pay Odessa $1,000. Can Odessa enforce this promise?

2. William E. Story agreed to pay his nephew, William E. Story II, a large sum of money (roughly equivalent to $50,000 in 2007 dollars) "if he would refrain from drinking liquor, using tobacco, swearing, and playing cards or billiards for money until he should come to be 21 years of age." William II had been using tobacco and occasionally drank liquor but refrained from using these stimulants over several years until he was 21 and also lived up to the other requirements of his uncle's offer. Just after William II's 21st birthday, Story acknowledged that William II had fulfilled his part of the bargain and advised that the money would be invested for him with interest. Story died, and his executor, Sidway, refused to pay William II because he believed the contract between Story and William II was without consideration. Sidway asserted that Story received no benefit from William II's performance and William II suffered no detriment (in fact, by his refraining from the use of liquor and tobacco, William II was not harmed but benefited, Sidway asserted). Is there any theory of consideration that William II can rely on? How would you decide this case? [*Hamer v. Sidway*, 124 N.Y. 538]

3. Dale Dyer, who was employed by National By-Products, Inc., was seriously injured at work as the result of a job-related accident. He agreed to give up his right to sue the employer for damages in consideration of the employer's giving him a lifetime job. The employer later claimed that this agreement was not binding because Dyer's promise not to sue could not be consideration for the promise to employ on the ground that Dyer in fact had no right to sue. Dyer's only remedy was to make a claim under workers' compensation. Was the agreement binding? [*Dyer v. National By-Products, Inc.*, 380 N.W.2d 732 (Iowa)]

4. Charles Sanarwari retained Stan Gissel to prepare his income tax return for the year 2006. The parties agreed on a fee of $400. Charles had done a rough estimate based on last year's return and believed he would owe the IRS approximately $2,000. When Stan's work was completed, it turned out that Charles would receive a $2,321 tax refund. Stan explained how certain legitimate advantages were used to reduce Charles's tax obligation. Charles paid for Stan's services and was so pleased with the work that he promised to pay Stan an additional $400 for the excellent job on the tax return when he received his tax refund. Thereafter, Stan and Charles had a falling out over a golf tournament where Charles was late for his tee time and Stan started without him, causing Charles to lose an opportunity to win the club championship. Stan was not paid the $400 promised for doing an excellent job on the tax return, and he sued Charles as a matter of principle. Decide.

5. Medistar is a real estate development company specializing in the development of medical facilities. Dr. Schmidt, the team physician for the San Antonio Spurs basketball team, sought to develop "The Texas Center for Athletes" medical center next to the Spurs facility and urged Medistar to obtain the real estate and develop the project on his group's behalf. Medistar spent more than $1 million and thousands of man-hours on the project from 2000 to July 12, 2004 when Dr. Schmidt's new group of investors purchased the property next to the Spur's facility for the project; subsequently, Medistar was informed that it would have no role in the project. Medistar asserts that it relied on Dr. Schmidt's assurances that it would be the developer of the project—and after four years and the $1 million in time and expenses it spent, it is unconscionable to be excluded from the project. Dr. Schmidt and associates contend that Medistar has presented no contractual agreement tying it to any legal obligation to Medistar. Is there a viable legal theory available to Medistar? If so what is the remedy? [*Medistar v. Schmidt*, 267 S.W.3d 150 (Tex. App.)]

6. Fedun rented a building to Gomer, who did business under the name of Mike's Cafe. Later, Gomer was about to sell the business to Brown and requested Fedun to release him from his liability under the lease. Fedun agreed to do so. Brown sold the business shortly thereafter. The balance of the rent due by Gomer under the original lease agreement was not paid, and Fedun sued Gomer on the rent claim. Could he collect after having released Gomer? [*Fedun v. Mike's Cafe,* 204 A.2d 776 (Pa. Super.)]

7. Alexander Proudfoot Co. was in the business of devising efficiency systems for industry. It told Sanitary Linen Service Co. that it could provide an improved system for Sanitary Linen that would save Sanitary Linen money. It made a contract with Sanitary Linen to provide a money-saving system. The system was put into operation, and Proudfoot was paid the amount due under the contract. The system failed to work and did not save money. Sanitary Linen sued to get the money back. Was it entitled to do so? [*Sanitary Linen Service Co. v. Alexander Proudfoot Co.,* 435 F.2d 292 (5th Cir.)]

8. Sears, Roebuck and Co. promised to give Forrer permanent employment. Forrer sold his farm at a loss to take the job. Shortly after beginning work, he was discharged by Sears, which claimed that the contract could be terminated at will. Forrer claimed that promissory estoppel prevented Sears from terminating the contract. Was he correct? [*Forrer v. Sears, Roebuck & Co.,* 153 N.W.2d 587 (Wis.)]

9. Kemp leased a gas filling station from Baehr. Kemp, who was heavily indebted to Penn-O-Tex Oil Corp., transferred to it his right to receive payments on all claims. When Baehr complained that the rent was not paid, he was assured by the corporation that the rent would be paid to him. Baehr did not sue Kemp for the overdue rent but later sued the corporation. The defense was raised that there was no consideration for the promise of the corporation. Decide. [*Baehr v. Penn-O-Tex Corp.,* 104 N.W.2d 661 (Minn.)]

10. Bogart owed several debts to Security Bank & Trust Co. and applied to the bank for a loan to pay the debts. The bank's employee stated that he would take the application for the loan to the loan committee and "within two or three days, we ought to have something here, ready for you to go with." The loan was not made. The bank sued Bogart for his debts. He filed a counterclaim on the theory that the bank had broken its contract to make a loan to him and that promissory estoppel prevented the bank from going back on what the employee had said. Was this counterclaim valid?

11. Kelsoe worked for International Wood Products, Inc., for a number of years. One day Hernandez, a director and major stockholder of the company, promised Kelsoe that the corporation would give her 5 percent of the company's stock. This promise was never kept, and Kelsoe sued International for breach of contract. Had the company broken its contract? [*Kelsoe v. International Wood Products, Inc.,* 588 So.2d 877 (Ala.)]

12. Kathy left her classic 1978 Volkswagen convertible at Freddie's Service Station, requesting a "tune-up." When she returned that evening, Freddie's bill was $374. Kathy stated that Firestone and Sears advertise tune-ups for $70, and she asked Freddie, "How can you justify this bill?" Freddie responded, "Carburator work." Kathy refused to pay the bill and left. That evening, when the station closed, she took her other set of keys and removed her car, after placing a check in the station's mail slot. The check was made out to Freddie's Service Station for $200 and stated on its face: "This check is in full payment of my account with you regarding the tune-up today on my 1978 Volkswagen convertible." Freddie cashed the check in order to meet his business expenses and then sued Kathy for the difference owed. What result?

13. On the death of their mother, the children of Jane Smith gave their interests in their mother's estate to their father in consideration of his payment of $1 to each of them and his promise to leave them the property on his death. The father died without leaving them the property. The children sued their father's second wife to obtain the property in accordance with the agreement. The second wife claimed that the agreement was not a binding contract because

the amount of $1 and future gifts given for the children's interests were so trivial and uncertain. Decide.

14. Radio Station KSCS broadcast a popular music program. It announced that it would pay $25,000 to any listener who detected that it did not play three consecutive songs. Steve Jennings listened to and heard a program in which two songs were followed by a commercial program. He claimed the $25,000. The station refused to pay on the ground that there was no consideration for its promise to pay that amount. Was the station liable? [*Jennings v. Radio Station KSCS,* 708 S.W.2d 60 (Tex. App.)]

15. Hoffman wanted to acquire a franchise for a Red Owl grocery store. (Red Owl was a corporation that maintained a system of chain stores.) An agent of Red Owl informed Hoffman and his wife that if they would sell their bakery in Wautoma, acquire a certain tract of land in Chilton (another Wisconsin city), and put up $6,000, they would be given a franchise. In reliance on the agent's promise, Hoffman sold his business and acquired the land in Chilton, but he was never granted a franchise. He and his wife sued Red Owl. Red Owl raised the defense that there had been only an assurance that Hoffman would receive a franchise, but because there was no promise supported by consideration, there was no binding contract to give him a franchise. Decide. [*Hoffman v. Red Owl Stores, Inc.,* 133 N.W.2d 267 (Wis.)]

© Manuel Gutjahr/iStockphoto.com

Chapter 16

Legality and Public Policy

learningoutcomes

After studying this chapter, you should be able to

LO.1 Explain the general contract principles on "illegality"

LO.2 Explain the implied obligation on all parties of good faith and fair dealing

LO.3 Understand that it is only in unusual situations that a contract provision will be unenforceable because it is unconscionable

LO.4 Explain the rationale for requiring licenses to carry on as a business, trade, or profession

LO.5 Distinguish between noncompete clauses after the sale of a business and noncompete clauses in employment contracts court will not enforce a contract if it is illegal, contrary to public policy, or unconscionable.

A. GENERAL PRINCIPLES

An agreement is illegal either when its formation or performance is a crime or a tort or when it is contrary to public policy or unconscionable.

1. Effect of Illegality

Ordinarily, an illegal agreement is void. When an agreement is illegal, the parties are usually not entitled to the aid of the courts. Examples of illegal contracts where the courts have left the parties where they found them include a liquor store owner not being allowed to bring suit for money owed for goods (liquor) sold and delivered on credit in violation of statute and an unlicensed home improvement contractor not being allowed to enforce his contract for progress payments due him. If the illegal agreement has not been performed, neither party can sue the other to obtain performance or damages. If the agreement has been performed, neither party can sue the other to obtain damages or to set the agreement aside.[1]

CASE SUMMARY

The Illegal Paralegal

FACTS: Brian Neiman was involved in the illegal practice of law for over seven years. Having been found guilty of illegally practicing law, he sought to collect disability benefits under his disability insurance policy with Provident Life due to an alleged bipolar disorder, the onset of which occurred during the pendency of criminal and bar proceedings against him. Neiman contends that his bipolar disorder prevents him from working as a paralegal. Provident contends that Neiman should not be indemnified for the loss of income generated from his illegal practice of law.

DECISION: Because all of Neiman's income was derived from the unlawful practice of law in the seven years preceding his claim, as a matter of public policy, a court will not enforce a disability benefits policy that compensates him for his loss of income he was not entitled to earn. Neiman's own wrongdoing caused the contract to be void. Accordingly, Neiman was *in pari delicto* [equally guilty], if not more at fault than the insurance company, in causing the contract to be void and will recover neither benefits nor the premiums he paid. The court must leave the parties where it found them. [***Neiman v. Provident Life & Accident Insurance Co.***, **217 F. Supp. 2d 1281 (S.D. Fla. 2002)**]

Even if a contract appears to be legal on its face, it may be unenforceable if it was entered into for an illegal purpose. **For Example,** if zoning regulations in the special-purpose district of Washington, D.C., require that only a professional can lease space in a given building, and the rental agent suggests that two nonprofessionals take out the lease in their attorney's name, but all parties realize

---

[1] *Sabia v. Mattituck Inlet Marina, Inc.,* 805 N.Y.S.2d 346 (A.D. 2005).

that the premises will be used only by the nonprofessionals, then the lease in question is illegal and unenforceable.[2]

2. Exceptions to Effect of Illegality

To avoid hardship, exceptions are made to the rules stated in Section 1.

(A) PROTECTION OF ONE PARTY. When the law that the agreement violates is intended to protect one of the parties, that party may seek relief. **For Example,** when, in order to protect the public, the law forbids the issuance of securities by certain classes of corporations, a person who has purchased them may recover the money paid.

(B) UNEQUAL GUILT. When the parties are not ***in pari delicto***—equally guilty—the least guilty party is granted relief when public interest is advanced by doing so. **For Example,** when a statute is adopted to protect one of the parties to a transaction, such as a usury law adopted to protect borrowers, the person to be protected will not be deemed to be *in pari delicto* with the wrongdoer when entering into a transaction that the statute prohibits.

in pari delicto – equally guilty; used in reference to a transaction as to which relief will not be granted to either party because both are equally guilty of wrongdoing.

3. Partial Illegality

An agreement may involve the performance of several promises, some of which are illegal and some legal. The legal parts of the agreement may be enforced provided that they can be separated from the parts that are illegal.

When the illegal provision of a contract may be ignored without defeating the contract's basic purpose, a court will merely ignore the illegal provision and enforce the balance of the contract. Consequently, when a provision for the payment of an attorney's fee in a car rental agreement was illegal because a local statute prohibited it, the court would merely ignore the fee provision and enforce the balance of the contract.[3]

If a contract is susceptible to two interpretations, one legal and the other illegal, the court will assume that the legal meaning was intended unless the contrary is clearly indicated.

4. Crimes and Civil Wrongs

An agreement is illegal, and therefore void, when it calls for the commission of any act that constitutes a crime. To illustrate, one cannot enforce an agreement by which the other party is to commit an assault, steal property, burn a house, or kill a person. A contract to obtain equipment for committing a crime is illegal and cannot be enforced. Thus, a contract to manufacture and sell illegal slot machines is void.

An agreement that calls for the commission of a civil wrong is also illegal and void. Examples are agreements to slander a third person; defraud another; infringe another's patent, trademark, or copyright; or fix prices.

5. Good Faith and Fairness

Every contract has an implied obligation that neither party shall do anything that will have the effect of destroying or injuring the right of the other party to receive the

---

[2] *McMahon v. A, H, & B*, 728 A.2d 656 (D.C. 1999).
[3] *Harbour v. Arelco, Inc.*, 678 N.E.2d 381 (Ind. 1997).

good faith—absence of knowledge of any defects or problems.

fruits of the contract. This means that in every contract there exists an implied covenant of **good faith** and fair dealing. **For Example,** Katy Lesser entered into a 10-year lease of retail space to operate a natural food store in South Burlington, Vermont. Her business prospered and in April of 1999 she signed a lease for additional space. For five years, the landlord continually rebuffed her efforts to meet and discuss plans to renovate the 1999 space to expand the grocery store, motivated solely by a desire to pressure the tenant to pay a portion of his legal fees in an unrelated zoning case. The court found that the landlord breached the obligation of good faith and fair dealing, causing the 1999 space to be essentially unusable from 1999 to 2004. The court awarded the tenant the rent she paid for this period less a storage fee adjustment.[4]

6. Unconscionable Clauses

Ordinarily, a court will not consider whether a contract is fair or unfair, is wise or foolish, or operates unequally between the parties. **For Example,** the Kramper Family Farm agreed to sell 17.59 acres of land to Dakota Industrial Development, Inc. (DID), for $35,000 per acre if the buyer constructed a paved road along the property by December 31. The contract also provided that if the road was not completed by the date set forth in the contract, the price per acre would be $45,000. When the road was not completed by the December 31 date, Family Farm sued DID for the additional $10,000 per acre. DID defended that to apply the contract according to its plain language would create an unconscionable result and was an unenforceable penalty provision contrary to public policy. The court refused to allow DID to escape its contractual obligations on the pretext of unconscionability and public policy arguments. The parties are at liberty to contract as they see fit, the court concluded, and generally, a court will not inquire into the adequacy of consideration inasmuch as the value of property is a matter of personal judgment by the parties to the contract. In this case, the price consisted of either $45,000 per acre, or $35,000 per acre with the road by a certain date.[5]

However, in certain unusual situations, the law may hold a contract provision unenforceable because it is too harsh or oppressive to one of the parties. This principle may be applied to invalidate a clause providing for the payment by one party of an excessive penalty on the breaking of a contract or a provision inserted by the dominant party that it shall not be liable for the consequences of intentional torts, fraud, or gross negligence. This principle is extended in connection with the sale of goods to provide that "if the court ... finds the contract or any clause of the contract to have been unconscionable at the time it was made, the court may refuse to enforce the contract, or it may enforce the remainder of the contract without the unconscionable clause, or it may so limit the application of any unconscionable clause as to avoid any unconscionable result."[6]

(A) What Constitutes Unconscionability? A provision in a contract that gives what the court believes is too much of an advantage over a buyer may be held void as unconscionable.

---

[4] *Century Partners, LP v. Lesser Goldsmith Enterprises,* 958 A.2d 627 (Vt. 2008).
[5] *Kramper Family Farm v. Dakota Industrial Development, Inc.,* 603 N.W.2d 463 (Neb. App. 1999).
[6] U.C.C. §2-302(1).

(B) DETERMINATION OF UNCONSCIONABILITY. Some jurisdictions analyze unconscionability as having two separate elements: procedural and substantive. Both elements must be present for a court to refuse to enforce a contract provision. Other jurisdictions analyze unconscionability by considering the doctrine of adhesion and whether the clause in question is unduly oppressive.

Procedural unconscionability has to do with matters of freedom of assent resulting from inequality of bargaining power and the absence of real negotiations and meaningful choice or a surprise resulting from hiding a disputed term in an unduly long document or fine print. Companywide standardized form contracts imposed on a take-it-or-leave-it basis by a party with superior bargaining strength are called **contracts of adhesion**, and they may sometimes be deemed procedurally unconscionable.

Substantive unconscionability focuses on the actual terms of the contract itself. Such unconscionability is indicated when the contract terms are so one-sided as to shock the conscience or are so extreme as to appear unconscionable according to the mores and business practices of the time and place.

The U.S. Supreme Court has made clear that arbitration is an acceptable forum for the resolution of employment disputes between employees and their employers, including employment-related claims based on federal and state statutes.[7] The controlling arbitration agreement language is commonly devised and implemented by the employer. Under the Federal Arbitration Act (FAA), the employer can obtain a court order to stay court proceedings and compel arbitration according to the terms of the controlling arbitration agreement. The Supreme Court also made clear that in agreeing to arbitration of a statutory claim, a party does not forgo substantive rights afforded by the statute. In a growing number of court decisions, in effect employers are finding that courts will not enforce arbitration agreements in which the employer has devised an arbitration agreement that functions as a thumb on the employer's side of the scale.[8]

When a court finds that a contract or any clause of a contract was unconscionable at the time it was made, it may enforce the remainder of the contract without the unconscionable clause or refuse to enforce the entire agreement if the agreement is permeated by unconscionability. **For Example,** Sandra Menefee sued Geographic Expeditions, Inc. (GeoEx), for the wrongful death of her son while on a GeoEx expedition up Mount Kilimanjaro. GeoEx moved to compel arbitration under the parties' limitation of liability contract. The arbitration provision was found by the court to be procedurally and substantively unconscionable. GeoEx contended that the court should have severed the objectionable provisions and enforced the remainder of the arbitration clause. The court refused to do so because GeoEx designed its arbitration clause to impose arbitration not simply as an alternative to litigation, but as an inferior forum that would give it an advantage. In addition to limiting the plaintiffs' recovery, the agreement required them to indemnify GeoEx for its legal costs and fees if they pursued any claims covered by the release agreement, compounded by the requirement that plaintiffs pay half of any mediation fees and mediate and arbitrate in San Francisco, GeoEx's choice of venue, far from the plaintiffs' home in Colorado.[9]

contract of adhesion – contract offered by a dominant party to a party with inferior bargaining power on a take-it-or-leave-it basis.

---

[7] *Gilmer v. Interstate/Johnson Lane Corp.,* 500 U.S. 20 (1991); *Circuit City Stores, Inc. v. Adams,* 532 U.S. 105 (2001).
[8] See *Vassi/Kouska v. Woodfield Nissan Inc.,* 830 N.E.2d 619 (Ill. App. 2005).
[9] *Lhotka v. Geographic Expeditions, Inc.,* 104 Cal. Rptr. 3d 844 (Cal. App. 2010).

B. Agreements Affecting Public Welfare

Agreements that may harm the public welfare are condemned as contrary to public policy and are not binding. Agreements that interfere with public service or the duties of public officials, obstruct legal process, or discriminate against classifications of individuals may be considered detrimental to public welfare and, as such, are not enforceable.

7. Agreements Contrary to Public Policy

A given agreement may not violate any statute but may still be so offensive to society that the courts feel that enforcing the contract would be contrary to public policy.

public policy – certain objectives relating to health, morals, and integrity of government that the law seeks to advance by declaring invalid any contract that conflicts with those objectives even though there is no statute expressly declaring such a contract illegal.

Public policy cannot be defined precisely but is loosely described as protection from that which tends to be injurious to the public or contrary to the public good or which violates any established interest of society. Contracts that may be unenforceable as contrary to public policy frequently relate to the protection of the public welfare, health, or safety; to the protection of the person; and to the protection of recognized social institutions. **For Example,** a woman entered into a services contract with a male in exchange for financial support. The record disclosed, however, that the association between the parties was one founded upon the exchange of money for sex. The court determined that the agreement for financial support in exchange for illicit sexual relations was violative of public policy and thus was unenforceable.[10] Courts are cautious in invalidating a contract on the ground that it is contrary to public policy because courts recognize that, on the one hand, they are applying a very vague standard and, on the other hand, they are restricting the freedom of the contracting parties to contract freely as they choose.[11]

8. Gambling, Wagers, and Lotteries

lottery – any plan by which a consideration is given for a chance to win a prize; it consists of three elements: (1) there must be a payment of money or something of value for an opportunity to win, (2) a prize must be available, and (3) the prize must be offered by lot or chance.

Gambling contracts are illegal. Largely as a result of the adoption of antigambling statutes, wagers or bets are generally illegal. Private **lotteries** involving the three elements of prize, chance, and consideration (or similar affairs of chance) are also generally held illegal. In many states, public lotteries (lotteries run by a state government) have been legalized by statute. Raffles are usually regarded as lotteries.

CASE SUMMARY

Horseplay Prohibited

FACTS: Robert Bovard contracted to sell American Horse Enterprises, Inc., to James Ralph. When Ralph did not make payments when due, Bovard brought suit against him. The trial judge raised the question whether the contract was void for illegality. American Horse Enterprises was predominantly engaged in manufacturing devices for smoking marijuana and tobacco, and to a lesser degree in manufacturing jewelry. When the contract was made, there was no statute prohibiting the manufacture of any of these items, but there was a statute making it illegal to possess, use, or transfer marijuana.

---

[10] *Anonymous v. Anonymous*, 740 N.Y.S.2d 341 (App. Div. 2002).
[11] *Beacon Hill Civic Ass'n v. Ristorante Toscano, Inc.*, 662 N.E.2d 1015 (Mass. 1996).

CASE SUMMARY

Continued

DECISION: Although the question of illegality had not been raised by the parties, the trial judge had the duty to question the validity of the contract when it appeared that the contract might be illegal. Although there was no statute expressly making the contract illegal, the statute prohibiting the possession and sale of marijuana manifested a public policy against anything that would further the use of marijuana. It was therefore against public policy to make the devices used in smoking marijuana or to sell a business that engaged in such manufacture. The sales contract was therefore contrary to public policy and void and could not be enforced. [*Bovard v. American Horse Enterprises, Inc.*, 247 Cal. Rptr. 340 (Cal. App. 1988)]

In some states, bingo games, lotteries, and raffles are legalized by statute when the funds raised are used for a charitable purpose.

Sales promotion schemes calling for the distribution of property according to chance among the purchasers of goods are held illegal as lotteries without regard to whether the scheme is called a *guessing contest,* a *raffle,* or a *gift.*

Giveaway plans and games are lawful so long as it is not necessary to buy anything or give anything of value to participate. If participation is free, the element of consideration is lacking, and there is no lottery.

An activity is not gambling when the result is solely or predominantly a matter of skill. In contrast, it is gambling when the result is solely a matter of luck. Rarely is any activity 100 percent skill or 100 percent luck.

C. REGULATION OF BUSINESS

Local, state, and national laws regulate a wide variety of business activities and practices.

9. Effect of Violation

Whether an agreement made in connection with business conducted in violation of the law is binding or void depends on how strongly opposed the public policy is to the prohibited act. Some courts take the view that the agreement is not void unless the statute expressly specifies this. In some instances, a statute expressly preserves the validity of the contract. **For Example,** if someone fails to register a fictitious name under which a business is conducted, the violator, after registering the name as required by statute, is permitted to sue on a contract made while illegally conducting business.

10. Statutory Regulation of Contracts

To establish uniformity or to protect one of the parties to a contract, statutes frequently provide that contracts of a given class must follow a statutory model or must contain specified provisions. **For Example,** statutes commonly specify that particular clauses must be included in insurance policies to protect the persons insured and their beneficiaries. Other statutes require that contracts executed in connection with credit buying and loans contain particular provisions designed to protect the debtor.

Consumer protection legislation gives the consumer the right to rescind the contract in certain situations. Laws relating to truth in lending, installment sales, and home improvement contracts commonly require that an installment-sale contract specify the cash price, the down payment, the trade-in value (if any), the cash balance, the insurance costs, and the interest and finance charges.

CPA * ## 11. Licensed Callings or Dealings

Statutes frequently require that a person obtain a license, certificate, or diploma before practicing certain professions, such as law and medicine.[12] A license may also be required before carrying on a particular business or trade, such as that of a real estate broker, stockbroker, hotel keeper, or pawnbroker.

If a license is required to protect the public from unqualified persons, a contract made by an unlicensed person is unenforceable. **For Example,** a corporation that does not hold a required real estate broker's license cannot sue to recover fees for services as a broker. An unlicensed insurance broker who cannot recover a fee because of the absence of a license cannot evade the statutory requirement by having a friend who is a licensed broker bill for the services and collect the payment for him.

CASE SUMMARY

How Much for a Brokerage License? How Much Commission Was Lost?

FACTS: Thompson Halbach & Associates, Inc., an Arizona corporation, entered into an agreement with Meteor Motors, Inc., the owner of Palm Beach Acura, to find a buyer for the dealership, and Meteor agreed to pay a 5 percent commission based on the closing price of the sale. Working out of Scottsdale, Arizona, Thompson solicited potential Florida purchasers for the Florida business by phone, fax, and e-mail. Among those contacted was Craig Zinn Automotive Group, which ultimately purchased Palm Beach Acura from Meteor Motors for $5,000,000. Thompson was not paid its $250,000 commission and brought suit against Meteor for breach of contract. Meteor defended that Thompson was an unlicensed broker and that a state statute declares a contract for a commission with an unlicensed broker to be invalid. Thompson responded that the Florida state statue did not apply because it worked out of Scottsdale.

DECISION: Judgment for Meteor. The Florida statute clearly applies to a foreign broker who provides brokerage activities in Florida. Thompson solicited potential Florida purchasers for the Florida business and that purchaser was a Florida corporation. [*Meteor Motors v. Thompson Halbach & Associates,* **914 So.2d 479 (Fla. App. 2005)**]

In some states an unlicensed contractor can neither enforce a home improvement contract against an owner, nor seek recovery in *quantum meruit.* **For Example,** a contractor who performed work on Adam Gottbetter's apartment in New York City and was not paid for its work was barred from pursuing its claim against the owner.[13]

---

[12] *Hakimi v. Cantwell,* 855 N.Y.S.2d 273 (App. Div. 2008).
[13] *Orchid Construction Corp. v. Gottbetter,* 932 N.Y.S.2d 100 (A.D. 2011).

CPA

12. Contracts in Restraint of Trade

An agreement that unreasonably restrains trade is illegal and void on the ground that it is contrary to public policy. Such agreements take many forms, such as a combination to create a monopoly or to obtain a corner on the market or an association of merchants to increase prices. In addition to the illegality of the agreement based on general principles of law, statutes frequently declare monopolies illegal and subject the parties to various civil and criminal penalties.[14]

CPA

13. Agreements Not to Compete

In the absence of a valid restrictive covenant, the seller of a business may compete with the buyer, or an ex-employee may solicit customers of the former employer.

A noncompetition covenant may be held invalid because of vagueness concerning the duration and geographic area of the restriction.[15] Moreover, if the agreement not to compete is not properly executed in accordance with state law, it will not be enforced. **For Example,** Holly Martinez worked for Avis Rent-A-Car at the New Bern, North Carolina, airport. When hired, she printed her name on the top of the form containing an agreement not to compete but did not sign it. On December 17, she resigned her position to return to school, saying that she planned to get a part-time job. The next day, she began working for Hertz Rent-A-Car at the counter adjacent to the Avis counter. Avis was unsuccessful in obtaining a restraining order to prevent Holly from working for its competitor because the agreement was not signed as required by state law.[16]

CPA

(A) SALE OF BUSINESS. When a going business is sold, it is commonly stated in the contract that the seller shall not go into the same or a similar business again within a certain geographic area or for a certain period of time, or both. In early times, such agreements were held void because they deprived the public of the service of the person who agreed not to compete, impaired the latter's means of earning a livelihood, reduced competition, and exposed the public to monopoly. To modern courts, the question is whether, under the circumstances, the restriction imposed on one party is reasonably necessary to protect the other party. If the restriction is reasonable, it is valid and enforceable. **For Example,** when Scott Gaddy, the majority stockholder of GWC Insurance Brokers, sold his business to Alliant for $4.1 million he agreed to refrain from competing in the insurance business in California for five years. Under California law, contracts not to compete are void, except for noncompetition covenants in connection with the sale of a business. The reason for the exception is to prevent the seller from depriving the buyer of the full value of the acquisition, including the sold company's goodwill. The court enforced the covenant against Gaddy.[17]

(B) EMPLOYMENT CONTRACT. Restrictions to prevent competition by a former employee are held valid when reasonable and necessary to protect the interest of the former employer. **For Example,** a noncompete clause executed by Dr. Samuel Keeley that prohibited his "establishing a competing cardiovascular surgery practice within a 75-mile radius of Albany, Georgia, for a period of two years following the date of

---

[14] Sherman Antitrust Act, 15 U.S.C. §§1–7; Clayton Act, 15 U.S.C. §§12–27; Federal Trade Commission Act, 15 U.S.C. §§41–58.

[15] *Vukovich v. Coleman*, 789 N.E.2d 520 (Ind. App. 2003).

[16] *New Hanover Rent-A-Car, Inc. v. Martinez*, 525 S.E.2d 487 (N.C. App. 2000).

[17] 72 Cal. Rptr. 3d 259 (Cal. App. 2008).

termination" was upheld in court and did not include more territory than necessary to protect the professional corporation's business interests.[18]

Public policy requires that noncompetition covenants be strictly construed in favor of freedom of action of the employee.[19] A restrictive covenant is not binding when it places a restriction on the employee that is broader than reasonably necessary to protect the employer. **For Example,** Illinois manufacturer Arcor's noncompete clause, which had a restricted area of "the United States and Canada" precluding competition by a former employee for a one-year period, was found to be unenforceable as an industrywide ban that constituted a "blanket prohibition on competition."[20] In determining the validity of a restrictive covenant binding an employee, the court balances the aim of protecting the legitimate interests of the employer with the right of the employee to follow gainful employment and provide services required by the public and other employers.

Thinking Things Through

Noncompete Clauses, Cause for Concern?

Some 10 states do not enforce noncompete clauses in employment contracts, according to the research of Matt Marx who has dedicated his doctoral studies at Harvard to this topic. The states are (from west to east): California, Washington, Nevada, Montana, North Dakota, Minnesota, Oklahoma, West Virginia, and Connecticut. (New York and Oregon have significantly limited their applicability). Marx had naively signed a two-year noncompete agreement out of MIT at SpeechWorks, a voice recognition start-up, and when he wanted to leave and continue in the voice recognition field, his options were to sit out the two-year noncompete period or go to work at a California firm, which he did. He is now researching whether enforcing noncompetes in a state can spur inventors, engineers, and entrepreneurs to move elsewhere to pursue development of their ideas.*

Does a state's innovation suffer when noncompete clauses handcuff employees to an employer, or force employees to take an unpaid leave for the noncompete period before continuing in their field with a new or start-up employer? THINKING THINGS THROUGH, prospective employees should carefully consider the impact noncompetes would have on their lives, and if they must sign one, carefully negotiate its duration and scope.**

*See Scott Kirsner, "Why 'Noncompete' Means 'Don't Thrive,'" *Boston Globe*, December 30, 2007, E-1; Scott Kirsner, "Start-ups Stifled by Noncompetes," *Boston Globe*, June 21, 2009, G-1.

**For a comprehensive study of the strength of noncompetition enforcement rankings by state, see Norman D. Bishara, "Fifty Ways to Leave Your Employer: Relative Enforcement of Covenants Not to Compete, Trends and Implications for Employee Mobility Policy," 13 *U. Pa. J. Bus. L.* 751 (2011).

(c) Effect of Invalidity. When a restriction of competition agreed to by the parties is invalid because its scope as to time or geographic area is too great, how does this affect the contract? Some courts trim the restrictive covenant down to a scope they deem reasonable and require the parties to abide by that revision.[21] This rule is nicknamed the "blue-pencil rule." **For Example,** Julie Murray signed a noncompete agreement, which was validly assigned to the purchaser of the Accounting Center of Lucas County, Inc. When the new owner changed from an hourly wage to commission pay for her tax preparation work, she objected and was terminated. The court found the 24-month noncompete restriction exceeded what was reasonable to

---

[18] *Keeley v. CSA, P.C.,* 510 S.E.2d 880 (Ga. App. 1999).

[19] Noncompetition covenants are not valid in California. However, confidentiality agreements protecting trade secrets are enforceable in that state.

[20] *Arcor, Inc. v. Haas,* 842 N.E.2d 265 (Ill. App. 2005).

[21] *Unisource Worldwide, Inc. v. Valenti,* 196 F. Supp. 2d 269 (E.D.N.Y. 2002).

protect the employer's legitimate business interests, and modified the time period to one year.[22] In the *Arcor* case, the court refused to "blue pencil" the covenant because to render the clause reasonable, the court would in effect be writing a new agreement, which is inappropriate.[23]

Ethics & the Law

William Stern and his wife were unable to have children because the wife suffered from multiple sclerosis and pregnancy posed a substantial health risk. Stern's family had been killed in the Holocaust, and he had a strong desire to continue his bloodline.

The Sterns entered into a surrogacy contract with Mary Beth Whitehead through the Infertility Center of New York (ICNY). William Stern and the Whiteheads (husband and wife) signed a contract for Mary Beth to be artificially inseminated and carry Stern's child to term, for which Stern was to pay Mary Beth $10,000 and ICNY $7,500.

Mary Beth was successfully artificially inseminated in 1985, and Baby M was born on March 27, 1986. To avoid publicity, the parents of Baby M were listed as "Mr. and Mrs. Whitehead," and the baby was called Sara Elizabeth Whitehead. On March 30, 1986, Mary Beth turned Baby M over to the Sterns at their home. They renamed the little girl Melissa.

Mary Beth became emotionally distraught and was unable to eat or sleep. The Sterns were so frightened by her behavior that they allowed her to take Baby M for one week to help her adjust. The Whiteheads took the baby and traveled throughout the East, staying in 20 different hotels and motels. Florida authorities found Baby M with Mary Beth's parents and returned her to the Sterns.

Mary Beth said the contract was one to buy a baby and was against public policy and therefore void. She also argued that the contract violated state laws on adoption and the severance of parental rights. The Sterns brought an action to have the contract declared valid and custody awarded to them.

Should the contract be valid or void? What types of behavior would be encouraged if the contract were declared valid? Is it ethical to "rent a womb"? Is it ethical to sell a child? See ***In re Baby M***, 537 A.2d 15 (N.J. 1988).

Other courts refuse to apply the blue-pencil rule and hold that the restrictive covenant is void or that the entire contract is void.[24] There is also authority that a court should refuse to apply the blue-pencil rule when the restrictive covenant is manifestly unfair and would virtually keep the employee from earning a living.

CASE SUMMARY

Overlybroad and Unenforceable

FACTS: Justin Shaffer while an employee of the Home Paramount Pest Control Companies Inc. (Home Paramount) signed an employment agreement (the Provision) providing that:

> *The Employee will not engage directly or indirectly or concern himself/herself in any manner whatsoever in the carrying on or conducting the business of exterminating, pest control, termite control and/or fumigation services as an owner, agent, servant, representative, or employee, and/or as a member of a partnership and/or as an officer, director or stockholder of any corporation, or in any manner whatsoever, in any city, cities, county or counties in the state(s) in which the Employee works and/or in which the*

[22] *Murray v. Accounting Center of Lucas County, Inc.*, 898 N.E.2d 89 (Ohio App. 2008).

[23] *Arcor, Inc. v. Haas*, 842 N.E.2d 265 (Ill. App. 2005).

[24] *SWAT 24 v. Bond*, 759 So.2d 1047 (La. App. 2000). Under California law, any "contract by which anyone is restrained from engaging in a lawful profession, trade or business is to that extent void." Cal B&P Code §16600. A noncompete provision is permitted, however, when "necessary to protect the employer's trade secrets." See *Lotona v. Aetna U.S. Healthcare Inc.*, 82 F. Supp. 2d 1089 (C.D. Cal. 1999), where Aetna was liable for wrongful termination when it fired a California employee for refusing to sign a noncompete agreement.

CASE SUMMARY

Continued

Employee was assigned during the two (2) years next preceding the termination of the Employment Agreement and for a period of two (2) years from and after the date upon which he/she shall cease for any reason whatsoever to be an employee of [Home Paramount].

Shaffer resigned from Home Paramount in 2009 and became an employee of Connor's Termite and Pest Control Inc. Home Paramount sued Shaffer and Connor's, claiming that Shaffer's employment by Connor's violated the provision. The defendants contended the provision was overboard and unenforceable.

DECISION: A noncompetition provision is enforceable if it "is narrowly drawn to protect the employer's legitimate business interest, is not unduly burdensome on the employee's ability to earn a living, and is not against public policy." The employer bears the burden of proving each of these factors. When evaluating whether the employer has met that burden a court considers together the "function, geographic scope, and duration" elements of the restriction. In this case, the provision prohibits Shaffer from working for Connor's or any other business in the pest control industry in any capacity. It bars him from engaging even indirectly, or concerning himself in any manner whatsoever, in the pest control business, even as a passive stockholder of a publicly traded international conglomerate with a pest control subsidiary. The clear overbreadth of the function here cannot be saved by the narrow tailoring of geographic scope and duration. The provision is therefore unenforceable. [***Home Paramount Pest Control Companies, Inc. v. Shaffer,*** 718 S.E.2d 762 (Va. 2011)]

14. Usurious Agreements

usury–lending money at an interest rate that is higher than the maximum rate allowed by law.

Usury is committed when money is loaned at a higher rate of interest than the law allows. Most states prohibit by statute charging more than a stated amount of interest. These statutes provide a maximum annual contract rate of interest that can be exacted under the law of a given state. In many states, the usury law does not apply to loans made to corporations.

Thinking Things Through

Legality and Public Policy

Karl Llewellyn, the principal drafter of the law that governs nearly all sales of goods in the United States—the Uniform Commercial Code (UCC)—once wrote, "Covert tools are never reliable tools." He was referring to unfairness in a contract or between the contracting parties.

The original intent of declaring certain types of contracts void because of issues of imbalance was based in equity. Courts stepped in to help parties who found themselves bound under agreements that were not fair and open in both their written terms and the communications between the parties. One contracts scholar wrote that the original intent could be described as courts stepping in to help "presumptive sillies like sailors and heirs..." and others who, if not crazy, are "pretty peculiar."

However, as the sophistication of contracts and commercial transactions increased, the importance of accuracy, honesty, and fairness increased. Unconscionability is a contracts defense that permits courts to intervene where contracts, if enforced, would "affront the sense of decency." UNCONSCIONABILITY is a term of ethics or moral philosophy used by courts to prevent exploitation and fraud.

When a lender incurs expenses in making a loan, such as the cost of appraising property or making a credit investigation of the borrower, the lender will require the borrower to pay the amount of such expenses. Any fee charged by a lender that goes beyond the reasonable expense of making the loan constitutes "interest" for the purposes of determining whether the transaction is usurious.[25]

Penalites for violating usury laws vary from state to state, with a number of states restricting the lender to the recovery of the loan but no interest whatsoever; other states allow recovery of the loan principal and interest up to the maximum contract rate. Some states also impose a penalty on the lender such as the payment of double the interest paid on a usurious loan.

CASE SUMMARY

Would You Recommend Karen Canzoneri as an Investment Advisor?

FACTS: Karen Canzoneri entered into two agreements with Howard Pinchuck. Under the first agreement, Canzoneri advanced $50,000 to be repaid at 12 percent per month for 12 consecutive months "as an investment profit." The second agreement required "$36,000 to be repaid on or before 6/1/01 with an investment profit of $36,000, total being $72,000." The annualized rate of return for the first transaction was 144 percent and for the second transaction was 608 percent. The civil penalty for violating the state's maximum interest rate of 25 percent per annum is forfeiture of the entire principal amount. Canzoneri contends that the transactions were investments not subject to the usury law.

DECISION: Judgment for Pinchuck. The four elements of a usurious transaction are present: (1) the transaction was a loan, (2) the money loaned required that it be returned, (3) an interest rate higher than allowed by law was required, and (4) a corrupt intention to take more than the legal rate for the use of the money loaned exists. Even though the terms called for "profit," not "interest," the courts looked to the substance, not the form of the transaction. [*Pinchuck v. Canzoneri*, **920 So.2d 713 (Fla. App. 2006)**]

LawFlix

Midnight Run (1988) (R)

Is the contract Robert DeNiro has for bringing in Charles Grodin, an embezzler, legal? Discuss the issues of consideration and ethics as the bail bondsman puts another bounty hunter on the case and DeNiro flees from law enforcement agents in order to collect his fee. And finally, discuss the legality of DeNiro's acceptance of money from Grodin and his release of Grodin at the end of the movie.

---

[25] *Lentimo v. Cullen Center Bank and Trust Co.,* 919 S.W.2d 743 (Tex. App. 1996).

MAKE THE CONNECTION

SUMMARY

When an agreement is illegal, it is ordinarily void and no contract arises from it. Courts will not allow one party to an illegal agreement to bring suit against the other party. There are some exceptions to this, such as when the parties are not equally guilty or when the law's purpose in making the agreement illegal is to protect the person who is bringing suit. When possible, an agreement will be interpreted as being lawful. Even when a particular provision is held unlawful, the balance of the agreement may be saved so that the net result is a contract minus the clause that was held illegal.

The term *illegality* embraces situations in unconscionable contract clauses in which the courts hold that contract provisions are unenforceable because they are too harsh or oppressive to one of the parties to a transaction. If the clause is part of a standard form contract drafted by the party having superior bargaining power and is presented on a take-it-or-leave-it basis (a contract of adhesion) and the substantive terms of the clause itself are unduly oppressive, the clause will be found to be unconscionable and not enforced.

Whether a contract is contrary to public policy may be difficult to determine because public policy is not precisely defined. That which is harmful to the public welfare or general good is contrary to public policy. Contracts condemned as contrary to public policy include those designed to deprive the weaker party of a benefit that the lawmaker desired to provide, agreements injuring public service, and wagers and private lotteries. Statutes commonly make the wager illegal as a form of gambling. The private lottery is any plan under which, for a consideration, a person has a chance to win a prize.

Illegality may consist of the violation of a statute or administrative regulation adopted to regulate business. An agreement not to compete may be illegal as a restraint of trade except when reasonable in its terms and when it is incidental to the sale of a business or to a contract of employment.

The charging by a lender of a higher rate of interest than allowed by law is usury. Courts must examine transactions carefully to see whether a usurious loan is disguised as a legitimate transaction.

LEARNING OUTCOMES

After studying this chapter, you should be able to clearly explain:

A. General Principles

L0.1 Explain the general contract principles on "illegality"

See the unenforceable illegal lease to nonprofessionals example on pp. 321–322. See the example where a contract to manufacture and sell illegal slot machines is void, p. 322.

L0.2 Explain the implied obligation on all parties of good faith and fair dealing

See the example of the Vermont landlord who deprived a tenant of her rights under a lease, p. 323.

B. Agreements Affecting Public Welfare

L0.3 Understand that it is only in unusual situations that a contract provision will be unenforceable because it is unconscionable

See the *Kramper Family Farm* example where the court refused to consider whether the contract was fair or unfair, wise or foolish, p. 323.
But see the *Geographic Expeditions* case that illustrates an unconscionable arbitration clause, p. 324.

C. Regulation of Business

L0.4 Explain the rationale for requiring licenses to carry on as a business, trade, or profession

See the discussion requiring licenses to protect the public from unqualified persons, p. 327.

L0.5 Distinguish between noncompete clauses in the sale of a business and noncompete clauses in employment contracts

See the example where the California court enforced a five-year noncompete clause against the seller of a business, p. 328.
See the example involving Julie Murray's noncompete clause and why it was

modified from 24 months to one year, pp. 329–330.
See the *Home Paramount Pest Control* case that illustrates a trend barring enforcement of overlybroad noncompetition clauses, pp. 330–331.

KEY TERMS

contracts of adhesion	*in pari delicto*	public policy
good faith	lotteries	usury

QUESTIONS AND CASE PROBLEMS

1. When are the parties to an illegal agreement *in pari delicto?*

2. John Iwen sued U.S. West Direct because of a negligently constructed yellow pages advertisement. U.S. West Direct moved to stay litigation and compel arbitration under the yellow pages order form, which required advertisers to resolve all controversies through arbitration, but allowed U.S. West (the publisher) to pursue judicial remedies to collect amounts due it. Under the arbitration provision, Iwen's sole remedy was a pro rata reduction or refund of the cost of the advertisement. The order form language was drafted by U.S. West Direct on a take-it-or-leave-it basis and stated in part:

   > *Any controversy or claim arising out of or relating to this Agreement, or breach thereof, other than an action by Publisher for the collection of amounts due under this Agreement, shall be settled by final, binding arbitration in accordance with the Commercial Arbitration rules of the American Arbitration Association.*

   If forced to arbitration, Iwen would be unable to recover damages for the negligently constructed yellow pages ad, nor could he recover damages for infliction of emotional distress and punitive damages related to his many efforts to adjust the matter with the company, which were ignored or rejected. Must Iwen have his case resolved through arbitration rather than a court of law? [*Iwen v. U.S. West Direct*, 977 P.2d 989 (Mont.)]

3. Sutcliffe Banton, dba Nemard Construction, furnished labor and materials (valued at $162,895) for improving Vicky Deafeamkpor's New York City residential property. She paid only $41,718, leaving $121,987 unpaid. Banton sued her and the jury awarded $90,000 in damages. Deafeamkpor moved for an order setting aside the jury's verdict because Banton was not properly licensed by New York City. Under NYC Code an unlicensed contractor may neither enforce a home improvement contract against an owner or recover in *quantum meruit*. The jury heard all the evidence regarding the materials and labor expended on Deafeamkpor's residence and concluded that the plaintiff performed satisfactory work valued at $90,000 for which he was not paid. Should the court allow the owner to take advantage of Banton and his employees and suppliers? What public policy would support such an outcome? Decide. [*Nemard Construction Corp. v. Deafeamkpor*, 863 N.Y.S.2d 846]

4. Eugene McCarthy left his position as director of sales for Nike's Brand Jordan division in June 2003 to become vice president of U.S. footwear sales and merchandising at Reebok, one of Nike's competitors. Nike sought a preliminary injunction to prevent McCarthy from working for Reebok for a year, invoking a noncompete agreement McCarthy had signed in Oregon in 1997 when Nike had promoted him to his earlier position as a regional footwear sales manager. The agreement stated in pertinent part:

During EMPLOYEE'S employment by NIKE… and for one (1) year thereafter, ("the Restriction Period"), EMPLOYEE will not directly or indirectly… be employed by, consult for, or be connected in any manner with, any business engaged anywhere in the world in the athletic footwear, athletic apparel or sports equipment and accessories business, or any other business which directly competes with NIKE or any of its subsidiaries or affiliated corporations.

McCarty contends that such a contract is a restraint of trade and should not be enforced. Nike contends that the agreement is fair and should be enforced. Decide. [*Nike, Inc. v. McCarthy*, 379 F.3d 576 (9th Cir.)]

5. Ewing was employed by Presto-X-Co., a pest exterminator. His contract of employment specified that he would not solicit or attempt to solicit customers of Presto-X for two years after the termination of his employment. After working several years, his employment was terminated. Ewing then sent a letter to customers of Presto-X stating that he no longer worked for Presto-X and that he was still certified by the state. Ewing set forth his home address and phone number, which the customers did not previously have. The letter ended with the statement, "I thank you for your business throughout the past years." Presto-X brought an action to enjoin Ewing from sending such letters. He raised the defense that he was prohibited only from soliciting and there was nothing in the letters that constituted a seeking of customers. Decide. What ethical values are involved? [*Presto-X-Co. v. Ewing*, 442 N.W.2d 85 (Iowa)]

6. The Minnesota adoption statute requires that any agency placing a child for adoption make a thorough investigation and not give a child to an applicant unless the placement is in the best interests of the child. Tibbetts applied to Crossroads, Inc., a private adoption agency, for a child to adopt. He later sued the agency for breach of contract, claiming that the agency was obligated by contract to supply a child for adoption. The agency claimed that it was required only to use its best efforts to locate a child and was not required to supply a child to Tibbetts unless it found him to be a suitable parent. Decide. [*Tibbetts v. Crossroads, Inc.*, 411 N.W.2d 535 (Minn. App.)]

7. Siddle purchased a quantity of fireworks from Red Devil Fireworks Co. The sale was illegal, however, because Siddle did not have a license to make the purchase, which the seller knew because it had been so informed by the attorney general of the state. Siddle did not pay for the fireworks, and Red Devil sued him. He defended on the ground that the contract could not be enforced because it was illegal. Was the defense valid? [*Red Devil Fireworks Co. v. Siddle*, 648 P.2d 468 (Wash. App.)]

8. Onderdonk entered a retirement home operated by Presbyterian Homes. The contract between Onderdonk and the home required Onderdonk to make a specified monthly payment that could be increased by the home as the cost of operations increased. The contract and the payment plan were thoroughly explained to Onderdonk. As the cost of operations rose, the home continually raised the monthly payments to cover these costs. Onderdonk objected to the increases on the ground that the increases were far more than had been anticipated and that the contract was therefore unconscionable. Was his objection valid?

9. Smith was employed as a salesman for Borden, Inc., which sold food products in 63 counties in Arkansas, 2 counties in Missouri, 2 counties in Oklahoma, and 1 county in Texas. Smith's employment contract prohibited him from competing with Borden after leaving its employ. Smith left Borden and went to work for a competitor, Lady Baltimore Foods. Working for this second employer, Smith sold in 3 counties of Arkansas. He had sold in 2 of these counties while he worked for Borden. Borden brought an injunction action against Smith and Lady Baltimore to enforce the noncompete covenant in Smith's former contract. Was Borden entitled to the injunction? [*Borden, Inc. v. Smith*, 478 S.W.2d 744 (Ark.)]

10. All new employees of Circuit City Stores were required to sign a Dispute Resolution Agreement

(DRA) mandating that employees submit all employment-related disputes to arbitration. Under the DRA Circuit City was not obligated to arbitrate its claims against employees and may bring lawsuits against employees. Remedies are limited under the DRA, including one year back pay limit and a two-year front pay limit, with cap on punitive damages of an amount up to the greater of the amount of back pay and front pay awarded or $5,000. In a civil lawsuit under state law a plaintiff is entitled to all forms of relief. The DRA requires that employees split the cost of the arbitrator's fees with the employer. An individual is not required to pay for the services of a judge. Adams filed a sexual harassment case against his employer in state court. Circuit City filed a petition in federal court to compel arbitration. Decide. [*Circuit City Stores, Inc. v. Adams*, 274 F.3d 889 (9th Cir.)]

11. Vodra was employed as a salesperson and contracting agent for American Security Services. As part of his contract of employment, Vodra signed an agreement that for three years after leaving this employment, he would not solicit any customer of American. Vodra had no experience in the security field when he went to work for American. To the extent that he became known to American's customers, it was because of being American's representative rather than because of his own reputation in the security field. After some years, Vodra left American and organized a competing company that solicited American's customers. American sued him to enforce the restrictive covenant. Vodra claimed that the restrictive covenant was illegal and not binding. Was he correct? [*American Security Services, Inc. v. Vodra*, 385 N.W.2d 73 (Neb.)]

12. Potomac Leasing Co. leased an automatic telephone system to Vitality Centers. Claudene Cato signed the lease as guarantor of payments. When the rental was not paid, Potomac Leasing brought suit against Vitality and Cato. They raised the defense that the rented equipment was to be used for an illegal purpose—namely, the random sales solicitation by means of an automatic telephone in violation of state statute; that this purpose was known to Potomac

Leasing; and that Potomac Leasing could therefore not enforce the lease. Was this defense valid? [*Potomac Leasing Co. v. Vitality Centers, Inc.*, 718 S.W.2d 928 (Ark.)]

13. The English publisher of a book called *Cambridge* gave a New York publisher permission to sell that book any place in the world except in England. The New York publisher made several bulk sales of the book to buyers who sold the book throughout the world, including England. The English publisher sued the New York publisher and its customers for breach of the restriction prohibiting sales in England. Decide.

14. A state law required builders of homes to be licensed and declared that an unlicensed contractor could not recover compensation under a contract made for the construction of a residence. Although Annex Construction, Inc., did not have a license, it built a home for French. When he failed to pay what was owed, Annex sued him. He raised the defense that the unlicensed contractor could not recover for the contract price. Annex claimed that the lack of a license was not a bar because the president of the corporation was a licensed builder and the only shareholder of the corporation, and the construction had been properly performed. Was Annex entitled to recover?

15. Yarde Metals, Inc., owned six season tickets to New England Patriots football games. Gillette Stadium, where the games are played, had insufficient men's restrooms in use for football games at that time, which was the subject of numerous newspaper columns. On October 13, 2002, a guest of Yarde Metals, Mikel LaCroix, along with others, used available women's restrooms to answer the call of nature. As LaCroix left the restroom, however, he was arrested and charged with disorderly conduct. The Patriots organization terminated all six of Yarde's season ticket privileges, incorrectly giving as a reason that LaCroix was ejected "for throwing bottles in the seating section." Yarde sued, contending that "by terminating the plaintiff's season tickets for 2002 and for the future arbitrarily, without cause and based on

false information," the Patriots had violated the implicit covenant of good faith and fair dealing of the season tickets contract. The back of each Patriots ticket states:

> *This ticket and all season tickets are revocable licenses. The Patriots reserve the right to revoke such licenses, in their sole discretion, at any time and for any reason.*

How would you decide this case? [*Yarde Metals, Inc. v. New England Patriots Ltd.*, 834 N.E.2d 1233 (Mass. App.)]

CPA QUESTIONS

1. West, an Indiana real estate broker, misrepresented to Zimmer that West was licensed in Kansas under the Kansas statute that regulates real estate brokers and requires all brokers to be licensed. Zimmer signed a contract agreeing to pay West a 5 percent commission for selling Zimmer's home in Kansas. West did not sign the contract. West sold Zimmer's home. If West sued Zimmer for nonpayment of commission, Zimmer would be:

   a. Liable to West only for the value of services rendered.

   b. Liable to West for the full commission.

   c. Not liable to West for any amount because West did not sign the contract.

   d. Not liable to West for any amount because West violated the Kansas licensing requirements (5/92, Law, #25).

2. Blue purchased a travel agency business from Drye. The purchase price included payment for Drye's goodwill. The agreement contained a covenant prohibiting Drye from competing with Blue in the travel agency business. Which of the following statements regarding the covenant is *not* correct?

   a. The restraint must be *no* more extensive than is reasonably necessary to protect the goodwill purchased by Blue.

   b. The geographic area to which it applies must be reasonable.

   c. The time period for which it is to be effective must be reasonable.

   d. The value to be assigned to it is the excess of the price paid over the seller's cost of all tangible assets (11/87, Law, #2).

© Manuel Gutjahr/iStockphoto.com

CHAPTER 17

Writing, Electronic Forms, and Interpretation of Contracts

learningoutcomes

After studying this chapter, you should be able to

LO.1 Explain when a contract must be evidenced by a writing

LO.2 Explain the effect of noncompliance with the statute of frauds

LO.3 Explain the parol evidence rule and the exceptions to this rule

LO.4 Understand the basic rule of contract construction that a contract is enforced according to its terms

LO.5 State the rules for interpreting ambiguous terms in a contract

A. Statute of Frauds

1. VALIDITY OF ORAL CONTRACTS
2. CONTRACTS THAT MUST BE EVIDENCED BY A WRITING
3. NOTE OR MEMORANDUM
4. EFFECT OF NONCOMPLIANCE

B. Parol Evidence Rule

5. EXCLUSION OF PAROL EVIDENCE
6. WHEN THE PAROL EVIDENCE RULE DOES NOT APPLY

C. Rules of Construction and Interpretation

7. INTENTION OF THE PARTIES
8. WHOLE CONTRACT
9. CONTRADICTORY AND AMBIGUOUS TERMS
10. IMPLIED TERMS
11. CONDUCT AND CUSTOM
12. AVOIDANCE OF HARDSHIP

W hen must a contract be written? What is the effect of a written contract? These questions lead to the statute of frauds and the parol evidence rule.

A. STATUTE OF FRAUDS

A *contract* is a legally binding agreement. Must the agreement be evidenced by a writing?

1. Validity of Oral Contracts

In the absence of a statute requiring a writing, a contract may be oral or written. Managers and professionals should be more fully aware that their oral communications, including telephone conversations and dinner or breakfast discussions, may be deemed legally enforceable contracts. **For Example,** suppose that Mark Wahlberg, after reviewing a script tentatively entitled *The Bulger Boys*, meets with Steven Spielberg to discuss Mark's playing mobster James "Whitey" Bulger in the film. Steven states, "You *are* 'Whitey,' Marky! The nuns at Gate of Heaven Grammar School in South Boston—or maybe it was St. Augustine's—they don't send for the Boston Police when they are troubled about drug use in the schools; they send for you to talk to the kids. Nobody messes with you, and the kids know it. This is true stuff, I think, and this fugitive's brother Bill comes out of the Southie projects to be president of U Mass." Mark likes the script. Steven and Mark block out two months of time for shooting the film this fall. They agree on Mark's usual fee and a "piece of the action" based on a set percentage of the net income from the film. Thereafter, Mark's agent does not like the deal. He believes there are better scripts for Mark. Incredibly brutal things are coming out about "Whitey" and his ties to drug dealers that tarnish the script. And with Hollywood accounting, a percentage of the "net" take is usually of little value. However, all of the essential terms of a contract have been agreed on, and such an oral agreement would be legally enforceable. As set forth in the following text, no writing is required for a services contract that can be performed within one year after the date of the agreement.

Certain contracts, on the other hand, must be evidenced by a writing to be legally enforceable. These contracts are covered by the **statute of frauds**.[1]

Because many oral contracts are legally enforceable, it is a good business practice in the preliminary stages of discussions to stipulate that no binding agreement is intended to be formed until a written contract is prepared and signed by the parties.

statute of frauds—statute that, in order to prevent fraud through the use of perjured testimony, requires that certain kinds of transactions be evidenced in writing in order to be binding or enforceable.

---

[1] The name is derived from the original Statute of Frauds and perjuries, which was adopted in 1677 and became the pattern for similar legislation in America. The 17th section of that statute governed the sale of goods, and its modern counterpart is §2-201 of the U.C.C. The 4th section of the English statute provided the pattern for U.S. legislation with respect to contracts other than for the sale of goods described in this section of the chapter. The English statute was repealed in 1954 except as to land sale and guarantee contracts. The U.S. statutes remain in force, but the liberalization by U.C.C. §2-201 of the pre-Code requirements with respect to contracts for the sale of goods lessens the applicability of the writing requirement. Additional movement away from the writing requirement is seen in the 1994 Revision of Article 8, Securities, which abolishes the statute of frauds provision of the original U.C.C. §8-319 and goes beyond by declaring that the one-year performance provision of the statute of frauds is not applicable to contracts for securities. U.C.C. §8-113 [1994 Revision].

2. Contracts That Must be Evidenced by a Writing

The statute of frauds requires that certain kinds of contracts be evidenced by a writing or they cannot be enforced. This means that either the contract itself must be in writing and signed by both parties or there must be a sufficient written memorandum of the oral contract signed by the person being sued for breach of contract. A *part performance* doctrine or exception to the statute of frauds may exist when the plaintiff's part performance is "unequivocally referable" to the oral agreement.[2]

(A) AGREEMENT THAT CANNOT BE PERFORMED WITHIN ONE YEAR AFTER THE CONTRACT IS MADE. A writing is required when the contract, by its terms or subject matter, cannot be performed within one year after the date of the agreement. An oral agreement to supply a line of credit for two years cannot be enforced because of the statute of frauds.

CASE SUMMARY

Not a Good Move, Doctor

FACTS: Despite not having an executed employment agreement, Dr. William Bithoney sold his home in New York and moved to Atlanta in early October in anticipation of his October 15 start work date as an executive at Grady Memorial Hospital. But the night before his anticipated start, he was informed that Grady's governing body, the Fulton-DeKalb Hospital Authority, did not approve his hiring and would not permit him to commence work. He sued the Authority for breach of an oral contract for severance, claiming that he and Grady's CEO, Otis Story, had agreed that he would receive "a severance payment of 15 months salary if Grady terminated his employment without cause." Bithoney had received a draft employment contract from Grady, which included a provision that, in the event Bithoney was terminated without cause, he would receive "full severance payment," which would be "payable for 15 months from the effective date of said termination."

DECISION: Judgment for the hospital. If the oral severance agreement were to be paid in a lump sum after termination, the oral agreement would not fall within the statute of frauds. Because the draft employment agreement provided that the severance "shall be payable for 15 months from the effective date of said termination," it was found to be a 15-month payment term barred by the statute of frauds. [*Bithoney v. Fulton-DeKalb Hospital Authority,* **721 S.E.2d 577 (Ga. App. 2011)**]

The year runs from the time the oral contract is made rather than from the date when performance is to begin. In computing the year, the day on which the contract was made is excluded.

No *part performance* exception exists to validate an oral agreement not performable within one year. **For Example,** Babyback's Foods negotiated a multiyear oral agreement to comarket its barbecue meat products with the Coca-Cola Co. nationwide and arranged to have several coolers installed at area grocery stores in Louisville under the agreement. Babyback's faxed to Coca-Cola a contract that summarized the oral agreement but Coca-Cola never signed it. Because Coca-Cola

[2] *Carey & Associates v. Ernst,* 802 N.Y.S.2d 160 (A.D. 2005).

| FIGURE 17-1 | Hurdles in the Path of a Contract |

WRITING REQUIRED

STATUTE OF FRAUDS	EXCEPTIONS
MORE THAN ONE YEAR TO PERFORM SALE OF LAND ANSWER FOR ANOTHER'S DEBT OR DEFAULT PERSONAL REPRESENTATIVE TO PAY DEBT OF DECEDENT FROM PERSONAL FUNDS PROMISE IN CONSIDERATION OF MARRIAGE SALE OF GOODS FOR $500 OR MORE MISCELLANEOUS	PART PERFORMANCE PROMISOR BENEFIT DETRIMENTAL RELIANCE
PAROL EVIDENCE RULE	**EXCEPTIONS**
EVERY COMPLETE, FINAL WRITTEN CONTRACT	INCOMPLETE CONTRACT AMBIGUOUS TERMS FRAUD, ACCIDENT, OR MISTAKE TO PROVE EXISTENCE OR NONBINDING CHARACTER OF CONTRACT MODIFICATION OF CONTRACT ILLEGALITY

© Cengage Learning

did not sign and no part performance exception exists for an oral agreement not performable within one year, Babyback's lawsuit was unsuccessful.[3]

When no time for performance is specified by the oral contract and complete performance could "conceivably occur" within one year, the statute of frauds is not applicable to the oral contract.[4]

When a contract may be terminated at will by either party, the statute of frauds is not applicable because the contract may be terminated within a year. **For Example,** David Ehrlich was hired as manager of Gravediggaz pursuant to an oral management agreement that was terminable at will by either Ehrlich or the group. He was entitled to receive 15 percent of the gross earnings of the group and each of its members, including rap artist Robert Diggs, professionally known as RZA, for all engagements entered into while he was manager under this oral agreement. Such an at-will contract is not barred by the statute of frauds.[5]

---

[3] *Coca-Cola Co. v. Babyback's International Inc.*, 841 N.E.2d 557 (Ind. 2006).
[4] *El Paso Healthcare System v. Piping Rock Corp.*, 939 S.W.2d 695 (Tex. App. 1997).
[5] See *Ehrlich v. Diggs*, 169 F. Supp. 2d 124 (E.D.N.Y. 2001). See also *Sterling v. Sterling*, 800 N.Y.S.2d 463 (A.D. 2005), in which the statute of frauds was no bar to an oral partnership agreement, deemed to be at will, that continued for an indefinite period of time.

(1) Oral Extension of a Contract.

A contract in writing, but not required to be so by the statute of frauds because it is terminable at will, may be varied by a new oral contract, even if the original written contract provided that it should not be varied except by writing. However, the burden of proof on the party asserting the oral modification is a heavy one. The modification must be shown by "clear, unequivocal and convincing evidence, direct or implied." **For Example,** John Boyle is the sole shareholder of numerous entertainment-related companies called the Cellar Door Companies, valued at some $106,000,000. Through these companies, he controls much of the large concert business at outdoor amphitheaters in Virginia and North Carolina. Bill Reid worked for Boyle beginning in 1983 as president of one of Boyle's companies. Boyle conducted financial affairs with an "air of informality." Reid proposed to Boyle the need for an amphitheater in Virginia Beach, and Boyle promised him a "33 percent interest" "if he pulled it off." As a result of Reid's efforts, the 20,000-seat Virginia Beach Amphitheater opened in 1996. The Supreme Court of Virginia determined that clear and convincing evidence did support the oral modification of Reid's written contract, including the following excerpt from the Court's opinion:

> *Thomas J. Lyons, Jr., Boyle's friend for over 35 years, testified on behalf of Reid. Lyons and his wife attended a concert in July 1996 at the newly constructed Virginia Beach Amphitheater as guests of Boyle and his wife. Lyons complimented Boyle for the excellent work and effort that Reid had undertaken in making the amphitheater a reality. According to Lyons, Boyle stated: "Well that's why he's my partner… that's why he owns 35 percent in this—in the Amphitheater or this project." After Lyons finished his testimony, the chancellor remarked on the record that Boyle stood up from his seat and "hugged" Lyons, even though Lyons had just provided testimony detrimental to Boyle.*

Reid was thus entitled to a judgment equivalent to the value of his interest in the project, $3,566,343. [6]

(B) Agreement to Sell or a Sale of an Interest in Land. All contracts to sell land, buildings, or interests in land, such as mortgages, must be evidenced by a writing. [7] Leases are also interests in land and must be in writing, except in some states where leases for one year or less do not have to be in writing. [8] **For Example,** if Mrs. O'Toole orally agrees to sell her house to the Gillespies for $250,000 and, thereafter, her children convince her that she could obtain $280,000 for the property if she is patient, Mrs. O'Toole can raise the defense of the statute of frauds should she be sued for breach of the oral agreement. Under the *part performance doctrine,* an exception exists by which an oral contract for the sale of land will be enforced by a court of equity in a suit for specific performance if the buyer has taken possession of the land under an oral contract and has made substantial improvements, the value of which cannot easily be ascertained, or has taken possession and paid part of the purchase price.

---

[6] *Reid v. Boyle,* 527 S.E.2d 137 (Va. 2000).

[7] *Magnum Real Estate Services, Inc. v. Associates, LLC,* 874 N.Y.S.2d 435 (A.D. 2009).

[8] See, however, *BBQ Blues Texas, Ltd. v. Affiliated Business,* 183 S.W.3d 543 (Tex. App. 2006), in which Eddie Calagero of Affiliated Business and the owners of BBQ Blues Texas, Ltd., entered an oral commission agreement to pay a 10 percent commission if he found a buyer for the restaurant, and he did so. The oral agreement was held to be outside the statute of frauds because the activity of finding a willing buyer did not involve the transfer of real estate. The second contract between the buyer and seller of the restaurant, which involved the transfer of a lease agreement, was a separate and distinct agreement over which Calagero had no control.

(c) Promise to Answer for the Debt or Default of Another. If an individual *I* promises a creditor *C* to pay the debt of *D* if *D* does not do so, *I* is promising to answer for the debt of another. Such a promise is sometimes called a **suretyship** contract, and it must be in writing to be enforceable. *I*, the promisor, is obligated to pay only if *D* does not pay. *I*'s promise is a *collateral* or *secondary* promise, and such promises must be in writing under the statute of frauds.[9]

suretyship – undertaking to pay the debt or be liable for the default of another.

(1) Main Purpose of Exception.

When the main purpose of the promisor's promise to pay the debt of another is to benefit the promisor, the statute of frauds is not applicable, and the oral promise to pay the debt is binding.

For Example, an individual *I* hires a contractor *C* to repair *I*'s building, and the supplier *S* is unwilling to extend credit to *C*. In an oral promise by *I* to pay *S* what is owed for the supplies in question if *C* does not pay, *I* is promising to pay for the debt of another, *C*. However, the *main purpose* of *I*'s promise was not to aid *C* but to get his own house repaired. This promise is not within the statute of frauds.[10]

CASE SUMMARY

"I Personally Guarantee" Doesn't Mean I'm Personally Liable, Does It?

FACTS: Joel Burgower owned Material Partnerships Inc. (MPI), which supplied Sacos Tubulares del Centro, S.A. de C.V. (Sacos), a Mexican bag manufacturer, essential materials to make its products. When MPI was not paid for shipments, it insisted that Jorge Lopez, Sacos's general manager, personally guarantee all past and future obligations to MPI. In a letter to Burgower dated September 25, 1998, Lopez wrote:

> I... want to certify you [sic] that I, personally, guaranty all outstanding [sic] and liabilities of Sacos Tubulares with Material Partnerships as well as future shipments.

Lopez drafted the letter himself and signed it over the designation "Jorge Lopez Venture, General Manager."

After receiving the September 25th letter, MPI resumed shipping product to Sacos, sending additional shipments valued at approximately $200,000. MPI subsequently received one payment of approximately $60,000 from Sacos. When Sacos did not pay for the additional shipments, MPI stopped shipping to it. The Sacos plant closed, and MPI brought suit in a Texas court against Lopez, claiming he was individually liable for the corporate debt of more than $900,000 under the terms of the personal guarantee. Lopez contended that he signed the letter in his capacity as general manager of Sacos as a corporate guarantee and that it was not an enforceable personal guarantee. MPI contended that the letter was a clear personal guarantee.

DECISION: The essential terms of a guarantee agreement required by the statute of frauds were present in this case. Lopez stated in his September 25th letter that "I, personally, guaranty," manifesting an intent to guarantee, and described the obligation being guaranteed as "all outstandings and liabilities of Sacos," as well as "future shipments." Lopez's signature over his corporate office does not render the document ambiguous because the clear intent was expressed in the word "personally." [***MPI v. Jorge Lopez Ventura,*** **102 S.W.2d 252 (Tex. App. 2003)**]

---

[9] See *Martin Printing, Inc. v. Sone*, 873 A.2d 232 (Conn. App. 2005), in which James Kuhe, in writing, personally guaranteed Martin Printing, Inc., to pay for printing expenses of *Pub Links Golfer Magazine*, if his corporation, Abbey Inc., failed to do so. When Abbey, Inc., failed to pay, the court enforced Kuhe's promise to pay.

[10] See *Christian v. Smith*, 759 N.W.2d 447 (Neb. 2008).

personal representative – administrator or executor who represents decedents under UPC.

executor, executrix – person (man, woman) named in a will to administer the estate of the decedent.

administrator, administratrix – person (man, woman) appointed to wind up and settle the estate of a person who has died without a will.

decedent – person whose estate is being administered.

(D) PROMISE BY THE EXECUTOR OR ADMINISTRATOR OF A DECEDENT'S ESTATE TO PAY A CLAIM AGAINST THE ESTATE FROM PERSONAL FUNDS. The **personal representative** (**executor** or **administrator**) has the duty of handling the affairs of a deceased person, paying the debts from the proceeds of the estate and distributing any balance remaining. The executor or administrator is not personally liable for the claims against the estate of the **decedent**. If the personal representative promises to pay the decedent's debts with his or her own money, the promise cannot be enforced unless it is evidenced by a writing.

If the personal representative makes a contract on behalf of the estate in the course of administering the estate, a writing is not required. The representative is then contracting on behalf of the estate. Thus, if the personal representative employs an attorney to settle the estate or makes a burial contract with an undertaker, no writing is required.

(E) PROMISES MADE IN CONSIDERATION OF MARRIAGE. Promises to pay a sum of money or give property to another in consideration of marriage must be in writing under the statute of frauds.

For Example, if Mr. John Bradley orally promises to provide Karl Radford $20,000 on Karl's marriage to Mr. Bradley's daughter Michelle—and Karl and Michelle marry—the agreement is not enforceable under the statute of frauds because it was not in writing.

Prenuptial or *antenuptial* agreements are entered into by the parties before their marriage. After full disclosure of each party's assets and liabilities, and in some states, income,[11] the parties set forth the rights of each partner regarding the property and, among other things, set forth rights and obligations should the marriage end in a separation or divorce. Such a contract must be in writing.

For Example, when Susan DeMatteo married her husband M. J. DeMatteo in 1990, she had a 1977 Nova and $5,000 in the bank. M. Joseph DeMatteo was worth as much as $112 million at that time, and he insisted that she sign a prenuptial agreement before their marriage. After full disclosure of each party's assets, the prenuptial agreement was signed and videotaped some five days before their marriage ceremony. The agreement gave Susan $35,000 a year plus cost-of-living increases, as well as a car and a house, should the marriage dissolve. After the couple divorced, Susan argued before the state's highest court that the agreement was not "fair or reasonable" because it gave her less than 1 percent of her former husband's wealth. The court upheld the agreement, however, pointing out that Susan was fully informed about her fiancé's net worth and was represented by counsel.[12] When there is full disclosure and representation, prenuptial agreements, like other contracts, cannot be set aside unless they are unconscionable, which in a domestic relations setting means leaving a former spouse unable to support herself or himself.

(F) SALE OF GOODS. As will be developed in Chapter 23, Nature and Form of Sales, contracts for the sale of goods priced at $500 or more must ordinarily be in writing under UCC §2-201.[13]

---

[11] See FLA. STAT. §732–702 (2).
[12] *DeMatteo v. DeMatteo*, 762 N.E.2d 797 (Mass. 2002). See also *Waton v. Waton*, 887 So.2d 419 (Fla. App. 2004).
[13] As will be presented in Chapter 23, under Revised Article 2, §2-201, the $500 amount is increased to $5,000. This revision has not yet been adopted by any states.

(G) Promissory Estoppel. The statute of frauds may be circumvented when the party seeking to get around the statute of frauds is able to prove an enhanced promissory estoppel. While one element of a routine promissory estoppel case requires that the promisee rely on the promise in some definite and substantial manner, an enhanced level of reasonable reliance is necessary in order to have enhanced promissory estoppel, along with proof of an unconscionable injury or unjust enrichment. **For Example,** an Indiana bakery, Classic Cheesecake Inc., was able to interest several hotels and casinos in Las Vegas in buying its products. On July 27, 2004, its principals sought a loan from a local branch office of J. P. Morgan Chase Bank in order to establish a distribution center in Las Vegas. On September 17, local bank officer Dowling told Classic that the loan was a "go." When credit quality issues surfaced, Dowling continued to make assurances that the loan would be approved. On October 12, however, she told Classic that the loan had been turned down. Classic claimed that the bank's breach of its oral promise to make the loan and Classic's detrimental reliance on the promise caused it to lose more than $1 million. The Indiana statute of frauds requires agreements to lend money to be in writing. Classic contended that the oral agreement in this case must be enforced on the basis of promissory estoppel and the company's unconscionable injury. Judge Posner of the Seventh Circuit upheld the dismissal of the claim, writing (in part):

> ...For the plaintiff to treat the bank loan as a certainty because they were told by the bank officer whom they were dealing with that it would be approved was unreasonable, especially if, as the plaintiffs' damages claim presupposes, the need for the loan was urgent. Rational businessmen know that there is many a slip 'twixt cup and lips,' that a loan is not approved until it is approved, that if a bank's employee tells you your loan application will be approved that is not the same as telling you it has been approved, and that if one does not have a loan commitment in writing yet the need for the loan is urgent one had better be negotiating with other potential lenders at the same time....[14]

CPA 3. Note or Memorandum

The statute of frauds requires a writing to evidence those contracts that come within its scope. This writing may be a note or memorandum as distinguished from a contract.[15] The statutory requirement is, of course, satisfied if there is a complete written contract signed by both parties.

(A) Signing. The note or memorandum must be signed by the party sought to be bound by the contract. **For Example,** in the previous scenario involving Mark Wahlberg and Steven Spielberg, suppose the parties agreed to do the film according to the same terms but agreed to begin shooting the film a year from next April, and Mark wrote the essential terms on a napkin, dated it, and had Steven sign it "to make sure I got it right." Mark then placed the napkin in his wallet for his records. Because the contract could not be performed within one year after the date of the agreement, a writing would be required. If Steven thereafter decided not to pursue the film, Mark could enforce the contract against him because the napkin-note had been signed by the party to be bound or "sought to be charged," Steven. However, if Mark later decided not to appear in the film, the agreement to do the film could not

---

[14] *Classic Cheesecake Co. Inc. v. J. P. Morgan Chase Bank*, 546 F.3d 839 (7th Cir. 2008).
[15] *McLinden v. Coco*, 765 N.E.2d 606 (Ind. App. 2002).

be enforced against Mark because no writing existed signed by Mark, the party sought to be charged.

Some states require that the authorization of an agent to execute a contract coming within the statute of frauds must also be in writing. In the case of an auction, it is usual practice for the auctioneer to be the agent of both parties for the purpose of signing the memorandum.

E-Commerce & Cyberlaw

Electronic Signatures in the Internet Age

A SIGNATURE authenticates a writing by identifying the signers through their distinctive marks. The act of signing a document calls to the attention of the signing parties the legal significance of their act and expresses authorization and assent to the body of the signed writing. An ELECTRONIC SIGNATURE, including technology having digital or wireless capabilities, means any electronic sound, symbol, or process attached to, or logically associated with, a contract or other electronic record and executed with the intent to sign the record. An ELECTRONIC RECORD means any contract or other record created or stored in an electronic medium and retrievable in a perceivable form.

Conducting business electronically over the Internet has many advantages for consumers, businesses, and governments by allowing the instant purchase of goods, information, and services, and the reduction of sales, administrative, and overhead expenses. To facilitate the expansion of electronic commerce and place electronic signatures and electronic contracts on an equal footing with written signatures and paper contracts, Congress enacted a federal electronic signatures law.

Under the Electronic Signatures in Global and National Commerce Act (E-Sign),* electronically signed contracts cannot be denied legal effect because the signatures are in electronic form, nor can they be denied legal effect because they are delivered electronically. Contracts or documents requiring a notarized signature can be satisfied by the electronic signatures of the notaries coupled with the enclosure of all other required information as part of the record.

One of the goals of E-Sign was to spur states to enact the Uniform Electronic Transactions Act (UETA). Under E-Sign, a state may "modify, limit or supersede" the provisions of the federal act by enacting UETA "as approved and recommended for enactment in all the states" by the National Conference of Commissioners on Uniform State Laws or enacting a law that is consistent with E-Sign.** Thus, for those states that enacted the official version of UETA or one consistent with E-Sign,

the federal law is superseded by the state law. UETA is similar to E-Sign. It specifies that e-signatures and e-records can be used in contract formation, in audits, and as evidence. Selective differences between E-Sign and UETA are identified below. **For Example,** inventor Stewart Lamle sued toy maker Mattel, Inc., for breach of contract. The U.S. Court of Appeals for the Federal Circuit remanded the case for trial after resolving the motions before it. The facts reveal that after a June 11, 1997, meeting of the parties, Mattel employee Mike Bucher sent an e-mail dated June 26 to Lamle, which set forth the terms agreed to in principle at the meeting with the salutation "Best regards, Mike Bucher" appearing at the end of the e-mail. The court resolved the issue of whether an e-mail is a writing "subscribed by the party to be charged or the party's agent" in Lamle's favor. The court stated that under the UETA, the e-signature satisfies the state's (California's) Statute of Frauds. Because the e-mail was sent in 1997 prior to the effective date on the UETA, January 1, 2000, an evaluation of state common law was necessary. The court stated that it could see no meaningful difference between a typewritten signature on a telegram, which is sufficient to be a signature under state law, and the typed signature on the June 26 e-mail. It concluded that the e-mail satisfies the Statute of Frauds, assuming that there was a binding oral agreement on June 11. ***

(a) General Rule of Parity. E-Sign provides for parity of electronic and paper signatures, contracts, and records. Electronic signatures and contracts satisfy the statute of frauds to the same extent they would if embodied as paper contracts with handwritten signatures. Internet contracts are neither more nor less valid, legal, and binding than are offline paper contracts. The rules are the same! The UETA is comparable to E-Sign in that it treats e-signatures and e-records as if they were handwritten.****

(b) Identity Verification. Neither E-Sign nor UETA is a digital signature law in that neither requires security procedures or a

---

*Pub. L. 106-229, 114 Stat. 464, 15 U.S.C. §7001.

**§102(a) and 102(a)(2). Forty-eight states and the District of Columbia have enacted the UETA in some form.

***Lamle v. Mattel, Inc., 394 F.3d 1355 (Fed. Cir. 2005); see also Payoutone v. Coral Mortgage Bankers, 602 F. Supp. 2d 1219 (D. Colo. 2009).

****UETA §7(a) and 7(b).

E-Commerce & Cyberlaw

Continued

certification authority for the verification of electronic signatures. The parties themselves determine how they will verify each other's identity. Some options are a credit card, a password or PIN, public-key cryptographic exchange of digital signatures, or biometric signatures.

(c) Exceptions. The E-Sign Act exempts documents and records on trust and estate law so that it does not cover wills, codicils, and testamentary trusts or commercial law matters such as checks, negotiable instruments, and letters of credit. The act also does not cover court documents and cancellation of health and life insurance. Generally, the UETA also does not apply to these documents and records set forth previously.

(d) Consumer Protection and Notice and Consent Requirements. Consumer protection laws remain intact under E-Sign. Protections exist for consumers to consent to receiving electronic contracts, records, and documents; and businesses must tell consumers of their right to receive hardcopy documents.

Consumers must consent to receiving documents electronically or confirm consent electronically. For example, a consumer and a business may have negotiated terms of a contract by telephone and agreed to execute their agreement by e-mail. The consumer is then sent an e-mail that contains a consent disclosure, which contains a hypertext markup language (HTML) link the consumer can use to test her ability to view the contract in HTML. The consumer then returns the e-mail message to the business, thereby confirming electronically her consent to use this electronic means.

The UETA, like E-Sign, defers to existing substantive law regarding consumer protection.

(e) Time and Place of Sending and Receipt. E-Sign does not contain a provision addressing basic contract requirements such as sending and delivery, leaving such matters to existing contract law. However, the UETA provides that an electronic record is sent when it (1) is properly directed to an information processing system designated or used by the recipient to receive such records and from which the recipient may recover that record; (2) is in a form that the recipient's system is able to process; and (3) enters an information processing system that is in the control of the recipient but outside the control of the sender. An electronic record is received when (1) it enters an information processing system designated or used by the recipient to receive such records and from which the recipient is able to obtain the record and (2) it is in a form that the recipient's system can process.*

(f) Errors. Unlike E-Sign, which leaves matters relating to errors to be resolved by existing state contract law, UETA creates a system for dealing with errors. For example, when Marv Hale clicks on "buy" to make an online purchase of 12 bottles of Napa Valley Supreme Chardonnay at $12.90 per bottle, the computer will produce the equivalent of an invoice that includes the product's name, description, quantity, and price to enable Marv to avoid possible error when forming the electronic contract. This procedure gives the buyer an opportunity to identify and immediately correct an error. When such a procedure is not in effect and an error is later discovered, prompt notice to the other party can cure the error under Section 10 of the UETA.**

*UETA §15.
**UETA §10(2)(A)-(C).

The signature may be an ordinary one or any symbol that is adopted by the party as a signature. It may consist of initials, figures, or a mark. In the absence of a local statute that provides otherwise, a signature may be made by pencil, pen, typewriter, print, or stamp. As will be discussed, electronic signatures have parity with on-paper signatures.

(B) CONTENT. The note or memorandum must contain all of the essential terms of the contract so the court can determine just what was agreed. If any essential term is missing, the writing is not sufficient. A writing evidencing a sale of land that does not describe the land or identify the buyer does not satisfy the statute of frauds.

The subject matter must be identified either within the writing itself or in other writings to which it refers. A deposit check given by the buyer to the seller does not take an oral land sales contract out of the statute of frauds. This is so because the check does not set forth the terms of the sale.

The note or memorandum may consist of one writing or of separate papers, such as letters, or a combination of such papers. Separate writings cannot be considered together unless they are linked. Linkage may be express reference in each writing to the other or by the fact that each writing clearly deals with the same subject matter.

4. Effect of Noncompliance

The majority of states hold that a contract that does not comply with the statute of frauds is not enforceable.[16] If an action is brought to enforce the contract, the defendant can raise the defense that the alleged contract is not enforceable because it is not evidenced by a writing, as required by the statute of frauds.

(A) RECOVERY OF VALUE CONFERRED. In most instances, a person who is prevented from enforcing a contract because of the statute of frauds is nevertheless entitled to recover from the other party the value of any services or property furnished or money given under the oral contract. Recovery is not based on the terms of the contract but on a quasi-contractual obligation. The other party is to restore to the plaintiff what was received in order to prevent unjust enrichment at the plaintiff's expense. **For Example,** when an oral contract for services cannot be enforced because of the statute of frauds, the person performing the work may recover the reasonable value of the services rendered.

(B) WHO MAY RAISE THE DEFENSE OF NONCOMPLIANCE? Only a party to the oral contract may raise a defense that it is not binding because there is no writing that satisfies the statute of frauds. Third persons, such as an insurance company or the Internal Revenue Service, cannot claim that a contract is void because the statute of frauds was not satisfied.

B. PAROL EVIDENCE RULE

When the contract is evidenced by a writing, may the contract terms be changed by the testimony of witnesses?

5. Exclusion of Parol Evidence

The general rule is that parol or extrinsic evidence will not be allowed into evidence to add to, modify, or contradict the terms of a written contract that is fully integrated or complete on its face.[17] Evidence of an alleged earlier oral or written agreement within the scope of the fully integrated written contract or evidence of an alleged contemporaneous oral agreement within the scope of the fully integrated written contract is inadmissible as *parol evidence.*

Parol evidence is admissible, however, to show fraud, duress, or mistake and under certain other circumstances to be discussed in the following paragraphs.

The **parol evidence rule** is based on the theory that either there never was an oral agreement or, if there was, the parties abandoned it when they reached the stage in negotiations of executing their written contract. The social objective of the parol evidence rule is to give stability to contracts and to prevent the assertion of terms

parol evidence rule – rule that prohibits the introduction into evidence of oral or written statements made prior to or contemporaneously with the execution of a complete written contract, deed, or instrument, in the absence of clear proof of fraud, accident, or mistake causing the omission of the statement in question.

---

[16] The U.C.C. creates several statutes of frauds of limited applicability, in which it uses the phrase "not enforceable": §1-206 (sale of intangible personal property); §2-201 (sale of goods); and §8-319 (sale of securities).

[17] *Mayday v. Grathwohl,* 805 N.W.2d 285 (Minn. App. 2011).

that did not exist or did not survive the bargaining of the parties so as to reach inclusion in the final written contract.

For Example, *L* (landlord), the owner of a new development containing a five-store mall, discusses leasing one of the stores to *T* (tenant), who is viewing the property with his sister *S*, a highly credible poverty worker on leave from her duties in Central America. *L*, in the presence of *S*, agrees to give *T* the exclusive right to sell coffee and soft drinks in the five-store mall. Soon *L* and *T* execute a detailed written lease for the store, which makes no provision for *T's* exclusive right to sell soft drinks and coffee in the mall. Subsequently, when two of the mall's new tenants begin to sell soft drinks and coffee, *T* brings suit against *L* for the breach of the oral promise granting him exclusive rights to sell soft drinks and coffee. *T* calls *S* as his first witness to prove the existence of the oral promise. *L*, through his attorney, will object to the admission of any evidence of a prior oral agreement that would add to or amend the fully integrated written lease, which set forth all restrictions on the landlord and tenant as to uses of the premises. After study of the matter, the court, based on the parol evidence rule, will not hear testimony from either *S* or *T* about the oral promise *L* made to *T*. In order to preserve his exclusive right to sell the drinks in question, *T* should have made certain that this promise was made part of the lease. His lawsuit will not be successful.

6. When the Parol Evidence Rule Does Not Apply

The parol evidence rule will not apply in certain cases. The most common of these are discussed in the following paragraphs.

ambiguous – having more than one reasonable interpretation.

(A) AMBIGUITY. If a written contract is **ambiguous** or may have two or more different meanings, parol evidence may generally be admitted to clarify the meaning.[18]

Parol evidence may also be admitted to show that a word used in a contract has a special trade meaning or a meaning in the particular locality that differs from the common meaning of that word.

(B) FRAUD, DURESS, OR MISTAKE. A contract apparently complete on its face may have omitted a provision that should have been included. Parol evidence may be admitted to show that a provision was omitted as the result of fraud, duress, or mistake and to further show what that provision stated. Parol evidence is admissible to show that a provision of the written contract was a mutual mistake even though the written provision is unambiguous. When one party claims to have been fraudulently induced by the other to enter into a contract, the parol evidence rule does not bar proof that there was a fraud. **For Example,** the parol evidence rule does not bar proof that the seller of land intentionally misrepresented that the land was zoned to permit use as an industrial park. Such evidence does not contradict the terms of the contract but shows that the agreement is unenforceable. [19]

(C) MODIFICATION OF CONTRACT. The parol evidence rule prohibits only the contradiction of a complete written contract. It does not prohibit proof that the contract was thereafter modified or terminated.

---

[18] *Berg v. Hudesman*, 801 P.2d 222 (Wash. 1990). This view is also followed by U.C.C. §2-202(a), which permits terms in a contract for the sale of goods to be "explained or supplemented by a course of dealing or usage of trade... or by course of performance." Such evidence is admissible not because there is an ambiguity but "in order that the true understanding of the parties as to the agreement may be reached." Official Code Comment to §2-202.
[19] *Edwards v. Centrex Real Estate Corp.*, 61 Cal. Rptr. 518 (Cal. App. 1997).

CASE SUMMARY

All Sail and No Anchor

FACTS: On April 2, 1990, Christian Bourg hired Bristol Boat Co., Inc., and Bristol Marine Co. (defendants) to construct and deliver a yacht on July 1, 1990. However, the defendants did not live up to their promises and the contract was breached. On October 22, 1990, the defendants executed a written settlement agreement whereby Bourg agreed to pay an additional sum of $135,000 for the delivery of the yacht and to provide the defendants a loan of $80,000 to complete the construction of the vessel. Referencing the settlement agreement, the defendants at the same time executed a promissory note obliging them to repay the $80,000 loan plus interest in annual installments due on November 1 of each year, with the final payment due on November 1, 1994. The court stated in presenting the facts: "However, like the yacht itself, the settlement agreement soon proved to be just another hole in the water into which the plaintiff threw his money." Bourg sued the defendants after they failed to make certain payments on the note, and the court granted a motion for summary judgment in favor of Bourg for $59,081. The defendants appealed.

DECISION: Judgment for Bourg. Because the defendants' affidavit recites that an alleged oral side agreement was entered into at the same time as the settlement agreement and promissory note—the oral side agreement allegedly stated "that the note would be paid for by services rendered by the defendants"—the oral side agreement would have constituted a contemporaneous modification that would merge into the integrated promissory note and settlement agreement and thus be barred from admission into evidence under the parol evidence rule. Although parties to an integrated written contract can modify their understanding by a subsequent oral pact, to be legally effective, there must be evidence of mutual assent to the essential terms of the modification and adequate consideration. Here the defendants adduced no competent evidence of either mutual assent to particular terms or a specific consideration that would be sufficiently definite to constitute an enforceable subsequent oral modification to the parties' earlier written agreements. Thus, legally this alleged oral agreement was all sail and no anchor. [***Bourg v. Bristol Boat Co.,* 705 A.2d 969 (R.I. 1998)**]

C. RULES OF CONSTRUCTION AND INTERPRETATION

In interpreting contracts, courts are aided by certain rules.

7. Intention of the Parties

When persons enter into an agreement, it is to be presumed that they intend for their agreement to have some effect. A court will strive to determine the intent of the parties and to give effect to it. A contract, therefore, is to be enforced according to its terms.[20] A court cannot remake or rewrite the contract of the parties under the pretense of interpreting.[21]

No particular form of words is required, and any words manifesting the intent of the parties are sufficient. In the absence of proof that a word has a peculiar meaning or that it was employed by the parties with a particular meaning, a common word is given its ordinary meaning.

---

[20] See *Greenwald v. Kersh,* 621 S.E.2d 463 (Ga. App. 2005).
[21] *Abbot v. Schnader, Harrison, Segal & Lewis, LLP,* 805 A.2d 547 (Pa. Super. 2002).

(A) MEANING OF WORDS. Ordinary words are to be interpreted according to their ordinary meaning.[22] **For Example,** when a contract requires the gasoline dealer to pay the supplier for "gallons" supplied, the term *gallons* is unambiguous and does not require that an adjustment of the gallonage be made for the temperature.[23] When a contract calls for a businessperson to pay a builder for the builder's "costs," the term *costs* is unambiguous, meaning actual costs, not a lesser amount based on the builder's bid.[24]

If there is a common meaning to a term, that meaning will be followed even though the dictionary may contain additional meanings. If technical or trade terms are used in a contract, they are to be interpreted according to the area of technical knowledge or trade from which the terms are taken.

(B) INCORPORATION BY REFERENCE. The contract may not cover all of the agreed terms. The missing terms may be found in another document. Frequently, the parties executing the contract for storage will simply state that a storage contract is entered into and that the contract applies to the goods listed in the schedule attached to and made part of the contract. Likewise, a contract for the construction of a building may involve plans and specifications on file in a named city office. The contract will simply state that the building is to be constructed according to those plans and specifications that are "incorporated herein and made part of this contract." When there is such an **incorporation by reference**, the contract consists of both the original document and the detailed statement that is incorporated in it.

When a contract refers to another document, however, the contract must sufficiently describe the document or so much of it as is to be interpreted as part of the contract.

> **incorporation by reference**—contract consisting of both the original or skeleton document and the detailed statement that is incorporated in it.

the blueprints

CASE SUMMARY

Specificity Required

FACTS: Consolidated Credit Counseling Services, Inc. (Consolidated), sued Affinity Internet, Inc., doing business as SkyNet WEB (Affinity), for breach of its contract to provide computer and Web-hosting services. Affinity moved to compel arbitration, and Consolidated argued that the contract between the parties did not contain an arbitration clause. The contract between the parties stated in part: "This contract is subject to all of SkyNet WEB's terms, conditions, user and acceptable use policies located at **http://www.skynetweb.com/company/legal/legal.php**." By going to the Web site and clicking to paragraph 17 of the User Agreement, an arbitration provision can be found. The contract itself, however, makes no reference to an agreement to arbitrate, nor was paragraph 17 expressly referred to or described in the contract. Nor was a hard copy of the information on the Web site either signed by or furnished to Consolidated.

DECISION: Judgment for Consolidated. Mere reference to another document is not sufficient to incorporate that document into the contract absent specificity describing the portion of the writing to apply to the contract. [*Affinity Internet v. Consolidated Credit*, **920 So.2d 1286 (Fla. App. 2006)**]

---

[22] *Thorton v. D.F.W. Christian Television, Inc.*, 925 S.W.2d 17 (Tex. App. 1995).
[23] *Hopkins v. BP Oil, Inc.*, 81 F.3d 1070 (11th Cir. 1996).
[24] *Batzer Construction, Inc. v. Boyer*, 125 P.3d 773 (Or. App. 2006).

8. Whole Contract

The provisions of a contract must be construed as a whole in such a way that every part is given effect.

Every word of a contract is to be given effect if reasonably possible. The contract is to be construed as a whole, and if the plain language of the contract thus viewed solves the dispute, the court is to make no further analysis.[25]

CASE SUMMARY

When You Permanently Reduced the Shipping Spots to Zero, You "Terminated" the Contract, Silly

FACTS: C.A. Acquisition Newco LLC is a successor in interest to Cyphermint, Inc. ("CI"), a New York corporation specializing in software development for self-service kiosks. DHL Express (USA), Inc., is an Ohio corporation with a principal place of business in Florida. It is a division of DHL International GmBH, a Deutsche Post Company and express carrier of documents and freight. Until 2008, DHL provided express pick-up and delivery, including same-day air delivery of letters and packages throughout the United States.

DHL entered into an agreement with Cyphermint, hoping to expand its customer base by offering domestic shipping services in retail locations, such as Walgreens and OfficeMax, via kiosks, or "Shipping Spots." Customers were able to use the kiosks' touch screen to pay for shipping costs and print shipping labels. The contract provided for an initial three-year term (August 1, 2006, through July 31, 2009) that automatically renewed for two more years unless either party gave notice of its election not to renew 90 days before the end of the initial contract. Under the contract, Cyphermint agreed to provide interactive software, enabling customers to use DHL's services from the shipping spots. Section 10.5 of the contract governs termination fees:

There shall be no termination fees for any termination by either party, irrespective of the reason for such termination, except for a "Material Breach" or as provided pursuant to the "Statement of Work" (SOW).

The SOW contains the following provision concerning termination fees:

Should DHL terminate this agreement for any reason other than a material breach by Cyphermint before its termination date DHL agrees to compensate CI in the amount of $50,000 per month for each month remaining in the initial term.

In November 2008, DHL decided to end all domestic delivery service within the United States. CI requested early termination fees under Section 10.5 of the contract of $413,333.33. DHL refused to pay, contending that Section 2.8 of the contract gave DHL the discretion to control the number and placement of the shipping spots, and when it ended U.S. domestic operations, it exercised its discretion to reduce shipping spots to zero.

DECISION: Judgment for CI. In reviewing a document, a court must consider the document as a whole, rather than attempting to isolate certain parts of it. Even if the court were to accept DHL's argument that Section 2.8 gave it blanket authority to reduce or eliminate the shipping spot project altogether, the outcome would remain the same. The relevant provision in the contract provides for termination fees without regard to whether the termination was authorized. The only restriction placed on the recovery of such fees is that they will not be available in the case of a material breach by Cyphermint. DHL failed to explain how reducing the shipping spots to zero was in any way different from "terminating" the contract. [***C.A. Acquisition Newco, LLC v. DHL Express (USA), Inc.,*** **795 F. Supp. 2d 140 (D. Mass. 2011)**]

---

[25] *Covensky v. Hannah Marine Corp.,* 903 N.E.2d 422 (Ill. App. 2009).

9. Contradictory and Ambiguous Terms

One term in a contract may conflict with another term, or one term may have two different meanings. It is then necessary for the court to determine whether there is a contract and, if so, what the contract really means.

CASE SUMMARY

Who Pays the Piper?

FACTS: Olander Contracting Co., developer Gail Wachter, and the City of Bismarck, North Dakota, entered into a water and sewer construction contract including, among other things, connecting a 10-inch sewer line from Wachter's housing development to the city's existing 36-inch concrete sewer main and installing a manhole at the connection, to be paid for by Wachter. Olander installed the manhole, but it collapsed within a few days. Olander installed a second manhole, with a large base supported by pilings, but it too failed a few days after it was installed. Olander then placed a rock bedding under the city's sewer main, replaced 78 feet of the existing concrete pipe with PVC pipe, and installed a manhole a third time on a larger base. Olander sued Wachter and the City of Bismarck for damages of $456,536.25 for extra work it claims it was required to perform to complete its contract. Both defendants denied they were responsible for the amount sued under the contract. The jury returned a special verdict, finding that Olander performed "extra work/unforeseen work… for which it is entitled to be compensated in excess of the contract price" in the amount of $220,849.67, to be paid by the City of Bismarck. Appeals were taken.

DECISION: Judgment for Olander. The trial judge properly made the initial determination that the contract language was ambiguous. That is, the language used by the parties could support good arguments for the positions of both parties. This resolved a question of law. Once this determination had been made, the judge allowed extrinsic evidence from all parties as to what they meant when they negotiated the contract. This evidence related to the questions of fact, which were left to the jury. Testimony was taken from the parties who negotiated the contract, and testimony was also heard about the role of each of the parties in the actual construction of the manhole, the cause for the collapses, and why the contractor had to replace the city's existing concrete pipe with PVC pipe and the city's role in making this determination. The jury then fulfilled its role answering the question whether or not Olander had performed extra work in the affirmative, concluding that the city was required to pay for it. [*Olander Contracting v. Wachter*, **643 N.W.2d 29 (2002)**]

If the language within the four corners of the contract is unambiguous, the parties' intentions are determined from the plain meaning of the words, used in the contract, as a matter of law, by the judge. A contract term or provision is *ambiguous* if it is capable of more than one reasonable interpretation, because of the uncertain meaning of terms or missing terms. A finding of ambiguity is justified only if the language of the contract reasonably supports the competing interpretations.[26] It is the role of the judge—a question of law—to initially determine whether a contract is ambiguous. If the contract is ambiguous, it is the role of the jury—a question of fact—to determine which party's position is correct with the aid of extrinsic evidence.

---

[26] *QEP Energy Co. v. Sullivan*, 444 Fed. Appx. 284 (10th Cir. 2011).

(A) Nature of Writing. When a contract is partly a printed form or partly type-written and partly handwritten and the written part conflicts with the printed or typewritten part, the written part prevails. When there is a conflict between a printed part and a typewritten part, the latter prevails. Consequently, when a clause typewritten on a printed form conflicts with what is stated by the print, the conflicting print is ignored and the typewritten clause controls. This rule is based on the belief that the parties had given greater thought to what they typed or wrote for the particular contract as contrasted with printed words already in a form designed to cover many transactions. Thus, a typewritten provision to pay 90 cents per unit overrode a preprinted provision setting the price as 45 cents per unit.

When there is a conflict between an amount or quantity expressed both in words and figures, as on a check, the amount or quantity expressed in words prevails. Words control because there is less danger that a word will be wrong than a number.

(B) Ambiguity. A contract is ambiguous when the intent of the parties is uncertain and the contract is capable of more than one reasonable interpretation.[27] The background from which the contract and the dispute arose may help in determining the intention of the parties. **For Example,** when suit was brought in Minnesota on a Canadian insurance policy, the question arose whether the dollar limit of the policy referred to Canadian or U.S. dollars. The court concluded that Canadian dollars were intended. Both the insurer and the insured were Canadian corporations; the original policy, endorsements to the policy, and policy renewals were written in Canada; over the years, premiums had been paid in Canadian dollars; and a prior claim on the policy had been settled by the payment of an amount computed on the basis of Canadian dollars.

(C) Strict Construction Against Drafting Party. An ambiguous contract is interpreted strictly against the party who drafted it.[28] **For Example,** an insurance policy containing ambiguous language regarding coverage or exclusions is interpreted against the insurer and in favor of the insured when two interpretations are reasonably possible. This rule is a secondary rule that may be invoked only after all of the ordinary interpretive guides have been exhausted. The rule basically assigns the risk of an unresolvable ambiguity to the party creating it.[29]

10. Implied Terms

In some cases, a court will imply a term to cover a situation for which the parties failed to provide or, when needed, to give the contract a construction or meaning that is reasonable.

The court often implies details of the performance of a contract not expressly stated in the contract. In a contract to perform work, there is an implied promise to use such skill as is necessary to properly perform the work. When a contract does not specify the time for performance, a reasonable time is implied.

In every contract, there is an implied obligation that neither party shall do anything that will have the effect of destroying or injuring the right of the other party to receive the fruits of the contract. This means that in every contract there

---

[27] *Kaufman & Stewart v. Weinbrenner Shoe Co.,* 589 N.W.2d 499 (Minn. App. 1999).
[28] *Idaho Migrant Council, Inc. v. Warila,* 89 P.2d 39 (Wyo. 1995).
[29] *Premier Title Co. v. Donahue,* 765 N.E.2d 513 (Ill. App. 2002).

good faith – absence of knowledge of any defects or problems.

exists an implied covenant of **good faith** and fair dealing. When a contract may reasonably be interpreted in different ways, a court should make the interpretation that is in harmony with good faith and fair dealing. **For Example,** when a contract is made subject to the condition that one of the parties obtain financing, that party must make reasonable, good-faith efforts to obtain financing. The party is not permitted to do nothing and then claim that the contract is not binding because the condition has not been satisfied. Likewise, when a contract requires a party to obtain government approval, the party must use all reasonable means to obtain it.[30]

The Uniform Commercial Code imposes an obligation of good faith in the performance or enforcement of every contract.[31]

11. Conduct and Custom

The conduct of the parties and the customs and usages of a particular trade may give meaning to the words of the parties and thus aid in the interpretation of their contract.

(A) CONDUCT OF THE PARTIES. The conduct of the parties in carrying out the terms of a contract is the best guide to determine the parties' intent. When performance has been repeatedly tendered and accepted without protest, neither party will be permitted to claim that the contract was too indefinite to be binding. **For Example,** a travel agent made a contract with a hotel to arrange for trips to the hotel. After some 80 trips had already been arranged and paid for by the hotel at the contract price without any dispute about whether the contract obligation was satisfied, any claim by the travel agent that it could charge additional fees must be rejected.

usage of trade – language and customs of an industry.

(B) CUSTOM AND USAGE OF TRADE. The customs and **usages of trade** or commercial activity to which the contract relates may be used to interpret the terms of a contract.[32] **For Example,** when a contract for the construction of a building calls for a "turn-key construction," industry usage is admissible to show what this means: a construction in which all the owner needs to do is to turn the key in the lock to open the building for use and in which all construction risks are assumed by the contractor.[33]

Custom and usage, however, cannot override express provisions of a contract that are inconsistent with custom and usage.

12. Avoidance of Hardship

As a general rule, a party is bound by a contract even though it proves to be a bad bargain. If possible, a court will interpret a contract to avoid hardship. Courts will, if possible, interpret a vague contact in a way to avoid any forfeiture of a party's interest.

When hardship arises because the contract makes no provision for the situation that has occurred, the court will sometimes imply a term to avoid the hardship.

---

[30] *Kroboth v. Brent,* 625 N.Y.S.2d 748 (A.D. 1995).
[31] U.C.C. §§1-201(19), 1-203.
[32] *Affiliated FM Ins. Co. v. Constitution Reinsurance Corp.,* 626 N.E.2d 878 (Mass. 1994).
[33] *Blue v. R.L. Glossen Contracting, Inc.,* 327 S.E.2d 582 (Ga. App. 1985).

LawFlix

The Santa Clause (1996) (PG)

When Scott Calvin (Tim Allen) tries on a Santa suit, he discovers that he has assumed all of Santa's responsibility. Calvin tries to challenge his acceptance of the terms of the agreement. Analyze the problems with offer, acceptance, and terms in very fine print (a magnifying glass is required). Do the terms of the suit contract apply when Calvin did not know them at the time he put on the suit?

MAKE THE CONNECTION

SUMMARY

An oral agreement may be a contract unless it is the intention of the parties that they should not be bound by the agreement without a writing executed by them. Certain contracts must be evidenced by a writing, however, or else they cannot be enforced. The statutes that declare this exception are called *statutes of frauds.* Statutes of frauds commonly require that a contract be evidenced by writing in the case of (1) an agreement that cannot be performed within one year after the contract is made, (2) an agreement to sell any interest in land, (3) a promise to answer for the debt or default of another, (4) a promise by the executor or administrator of a decedent's estate to pay a claim against the estate from personal funds, (5) a promise made in consideration of marriage, and (6) a contract for the sale of goods for a purchase price of $500 or more.

To evidence a contract to satisfy a statute of frauds, there must be a writing of all essential terms. The writing must be signed by the defendant against whom suit is brought for enforcement of the contract.

If the applicable statute of frauds is not satisfied, the oral contract cannot be enforced. To avoid unjust enrichment, a plaintiff barred from enforcing an oral contract may in most cases recover from the other contracting party the reasonable value of the benefits conferred by the plaintiff on the defendant.

When there is a written contract, the question arises whether that writing is the exclusive statement of the parties' agreement. If the writing is the complete and final statement of the contract, parol evidence as to matters agreed to before or at the time the writing was signed is not admissible to contradict the writing. This is called the *parol evidence rule.* In any case, the parol evidence rule does not bar parol evidence when (1) the writing is ambiguous, (2) the writing is not a true statement of the agreement of the parties because of fraud, duress, or mistake, or (3) the existence, modification, or illegality of a contract is in controversy.

Because a contract is based on the agreement of the parties, courts must determine the intent of the parties manifested in the contract. The intent that is to be enforced is the intent as it reasonably appears to a third person. This objective intent is followed.

In interpreting a contract, ordinary words are to be given their ordinary meanings. If trade or technical terms have been used, they are interpreted according to their technical meanings. The court must consider the whole contract and not read a particular part out of context. When different writings are executed as part of the same transaction, or one writing refers to or incorporates another, all of the writings are to be read together as the contract of the parties.

When provisions of a contract are contradictory, the court will try to reconcile or eliminate the conflict. If this cannot be done, the conclusion may be that there is no contract because the conflict makes the agreement indefinite as to a material matter. In some cases, conflict is solved by considering the form of conflicting terms. Handwriting prevails over typing and a printed form, and typing prevails over a printed form. Ambiguity will be eliminated in some cases by the admission of parol evidence or by interpreting the provision strictly against the party preparing the contract, particularly when that party has significantly greater bargaining power.

LEARNING OUTCOMES

After studying this chapter, you should be able to clearly explain:

A. Statute of Frauds

L0.1 Explain when a contract must be evidenced by a writing

See the discussion and examples beginning on p. 339.

L0.2 Explain the effect of noncompliance with the statute of frauds

See the *Bithoney* case where a doctor's oral contract for severance was barred by the statute of frauds, p. 340

See the example in which an oral contract cannot be enforced because it is not in writing, but the plaintiff may recover the reasonable value of the services rendered, p. 348.

B. Parol Evidence Rule

L0.3 Explain the parol evidence rule and the exceptions to this rule

See the example in which the tenant is not allowed to call a witness to testify about a prior oral agreement that would add to and alter the written lease, p. 349.

See the exceptions based on ambiguity, fraud, duress, and mistake discussed on p. 349.

C. Rules of Construction and Interpretation

L0.4 Understand the basic rule of contract construction that a contract is enforced according to its terms

See the example of the interpretation of the word "costs" on p. 351.

See the *DHL Express* case that illustrates the judicial common sense of interpreting the contract as a whole rather than a strained construction contrary to the contract's intent, p. 352.

L0.5 State the rules for interpreting ambiguous terms in a contract

See the discussion on the nature of the writing beginning on p. 354.

KEY TERMS

administrator
ambiguous
decedent
executor

good faith
incorporation by reference
parol evidence rule
personal representative

statute of frauds
suretyship
usages of trade

QUESTIONS AND CASE PROBLEMS

1. Kelly made a written contract to sell certain land to Brown and gave Brown a deed to the land. Thereafter, Kelly sued Brown to get back a 20-foot strip of the land. Kelly claimed that before making the written contract, it was agreed that Kelly would sell all of his land to Brown to make it easier for Brown to get a building permit, but after that was done, the 20-foot strip would be reconveyed to Kelly. Was Kelly entitled to the 20-foot strip? What ethical values are involved? [*Brown v. Kelly*, 545 So.2d 518 (Fla. App.)]

2. Martin made an oral contract with Cresheim Garage to work as its manager for two years. Cresheim wrote Martin a letter stating that the oral contract had been made and setting forth all of its terms. Cresheim later refused to recognize the contract. Martin sued Cresheim for breach of

the contract and offered Cresheim's letter in evidence as proof of the contract. Cresheim claimed that the oral contract was not binding because the contract was not in writing and the letter referring to the contract was not a contract but only a letter. Was the contract binding?

3. Lawrence loaned money to Moore, who died without repaying the loan. Lawrence claimed that when he mentioned the matter to Moore's widow, she promised to pay the debt. She did not pay it, and Lawrence sued her on her promise. Does she have any defense? [*Moore v. Lawrence*, 480 S.W.2d 941 (Ark.)]

4. Jackson signed an agreement to sell 79 acres of land to Devenyns. Jackson owned 80 acres and was apparently intending to keep for himself the acre on which his home was located. The written agreement also stated that "Devenyns shall have the option to buy on property _____," but nothing was stated in the blank space. Devenyns sued to enforce the agreement. Was it binding? [*In re Jackson's Estate*, 892 P.2d 786 (Wyo.)]

5. Boeing Airplane Co. contracted with Pittsburgh–Des Moines Steel Co. for the latter to construct a supersonic wind tunnel. R.H. Freitag Manufacturing Co. sold materials to York-Gillespie Co., which subcontracted to do part of the work. To persuade Freitag to keep supplying materials on credit, Boeing and the principal contractor both assured Freitag that he would be paid. When Freitag was not paid by the subcontractor, he sued Boeing and the contractor. They defended on the ground that the assurances given Freitag were not written. Decide. What ethical values are involved? [*R.H. Freitag Mfg. Co. v. Boeing Airplane Co.*, 347 P.2d 1074 (Wash.)]

6. Louise Pulsifer owned a farm that she wanted to sell and ran an ad in the local newspaper. After Russell Gillespie agreed to purchase the farm, Pulsifer wrote him a letter stating that she would not sell it. He sued her to enforce the contract, and she raised the defense of the statute of frauds. The letter she had signed did not contain any of the terms of the sale. Gillespie, however, claimed that the newspaper ad could be combined with her letter to satisfy the statute of frauds. Was he correct? [*Gillespie v. Pulsifer*, 655 S.W.2d 123 (Mo.)]

7. In February or March, Corning Glass Works orally agreed to retain Hanan as management consultant from May 1 of that year to April 30 of the next year for a present value fee of $200,000. Was this agreement binding? Is this decision ethical? [*Hanan v. Corning Glass Works*, 314 N.Y. S.2d 804 (A.D.)]

8. Catherine (wife) and Peter (husband) Mallen had lived together unmarried for some four years when Catherine got pregnant and a marriage was arranged. Peter asked Catherine to sign a prenuptial agreement. Although his financial statement attached to the agreement did not state his income at $560,000 per year, it showed he was wealthy, and she had lived with him for four years and knew from their standard of living that he had significant income. Catherine contends that failure to disclose Peter's income was a nondisclosure of a material fact when the agreement was drawn up and that accordingly the agreement is not valid. Peter contends that he fully disclosed his net worth and that Catherine was well aware of his significant income. Further, he contends that disparities in the parties' financial status and business experience did not make the agreement unconscionable. Decide. [*Mallen v. Mallen*, 622 S.E.2d 812 (Ga. Sup. Ct.)]

9. Panasonic Industrial Co. (PIC) created a contract making Manchester Equipment Co., Inc. (MECI), a nonexclusive wholesale distributor of its products. The contract stated that PIC reserved the unrestricted right to solicit and make direct sales of the products to anyone, anywhere. The contract also stated that it contained the entire agreement of the parties and that any prior agreement or statement was superseded by the contract. PIC subsequently began to make direct sales to two of MECI's established customers. MECI claimed that this was a breach of the distribution contract and sued PIC for damages. Decide. What ethical values are involved? [*Manchester Equipment Co. Inc. v. Panasonic Industrial Co.*, 529 N.Y.S.2d 532 (App. Div.)]

10. A contract made for the sale of a farm stated that the buyer's deposit would be returned "if for any

reason the farm cannot be sold." The seller later stated that she had changed her mind and would not sell, and she offered to return the deposit. The buyer refused to take the deposit back and brought suit to enforce the contract. The seller contended that the "any reason" provision extended to anything, including the seller's changing her mind. Was the buyer entitled to recover? [*Phillips v. Rogers*, 200 S.E.2d 676 (W. Va.)]

11. Integrated, Inc., entered into a contract with the state of California to construct a building. It then subcontracted the electrical work to Alec Fergusson Electrical Contractors. The subcontract was a printed form with blanks filled in by typewriting. The printed payment clause required Integrated to pay Fergusson on the 15th day of the month following the submission of invoices by Fergusson. The typewritten part of the contract required Integrated to pay Fergusson "immediately following payment" (by the state) to the general contractor. When was payment required? [*Integrated, Inc. v. Alec Fergusson Electrical Contractors*, 58 Cal. Rptr. 503 (Cal. App.)]

12. Norwest Bank had been lending money to Tresch to run a dairy farm. The balance due the bank after several years was $147,000. The loan agreement stated that Tresch would not buy any new equipment in excess of $500 without the express consent of the bank. Some time later, Tresch applied to the bank for a loan of $3,100 to purchase some equipment. The bank refused to make the loan because it did not believe the new equipment would correct the condition for which it would be bought and would not result in significant additional income. Tresch then sued the bank, claiming that its refusal to make the loan was a breach of the implied covenant of good faith and fair dealing. Decide. [*Tresch v. Norwest Bank of Lewistown*, 778 P.2d 874 (Mont.)]

13. Physicians Mutual Insurance Co. issued a policy covering Brown's life. The policy declared that it did not cover any deaths resulting from "mental disorder, alcoholism, or drug addiction." Brown was killed when she fell while intoxicated. The insurance company refused to pay because of the quoted provision. Her executor, Savage, sued the insurance company. Did the insurance company have a defense? [*Physicians Mutual Ins. Co. v. Savage*, 296 N.E.2d 165 (Ind. App.)]

14. The Dickinson Elks Club conducted an annual Labor Day golf tournament. Charbonneau Buick-Pontiac offered to give a new car as a prize to anyone making "a hole in one on hole no. 8." The golf course of the club was only nine holes. To play 18 holes, the players would go around the course twice, although they would play from different tees or locations for the second nine holes. On the second time around, what was originally the eighth hole became the seventeenth hole. Grove was a contestant in the tournament. He scored 3 on the no. 8 hole, but on approaching it for the second time as the seventeenth hole, he made a hole in one. He claimed the prize car from Charbonneau. The latter claimed that Grove had not won the prize because he did not make the hole in one on the eighth hole. Decide. [*Grove v. Charbonneau Buick-Pontiac, Inc.*, 240 N.W.2d 8533 (N.D.)]

15. Tambe Electric Inc. entered into a written agreement with Home Depot to provide copper wire to Tambe at a price set forth in the writing, and allowing the contractor the option of paying for the wire over a period of time. Home Depot did not fulfill this written agreement and Tambe sued for $68,598, the additional cost it had to subsequently pay to obtain copper wire for its work. Home Depot defended that it had made an oral condition precedent requiring payment in full by Tambe at the time it accepted the price quoted in the written agreement. Decide. [*Tambe Electric v. Home Depot*, 856 N.Y.S.2d 373]

CPA QUESTIONS

1. Which of the following statements is true with regard to the statute of frauds?

   a. All contracts involving consideration of more than $500 must be in writing.

   b. The written contract must be signed by all parties.

   c. The statute of frauds applies to contracts that can be fully performed within one year from the date they are made.

   d. The contract terms may be stated in more than one document.

2. With regard to an agreement for the sale of real estate, the statute of frauds:

   a. Requires that the entire agreement be in a single writing.

   b. Requires that the purchase price be fair and adequate in relation to the value of the real estate.

   c. Does *not* require that the agreement be signed by all parties.

   d. Does *not* apply if the value of the real estate is less than $500.

3. In negotiations with Andrews for the lease of Kemp's warehouse, Kemp orally agreed to pay one-half of the cost of the utilities. The written lease, later prepared by Kemp's attorney, provided that Andrews pay all of the utilities. Andrews failed to carefully read the lease and signed it. When Kemp demanded that Andrews pay all of the utilities, Andrews refused, claiming that the lease did not accurately reflect the oral agreement. Andrews also learned that Kemp intentionally misrepresented the condition of the structure of the warehouse during the negotiations between the parties. Andrews sued to rescind the lease and intends to introduce evidence of the parties' oral agreement about sharing the utilities and the fraudulent statements made by Kemp. Will the parol evidence rule prevent the admission of evidence concerning each of the following?

	Oral agreement regarding who pays the utilities	Fraudulent statements by Kemp
a.	Yes	Yes
b.	No	Yes
c.	Yes	No
d.	No	No

CHAPTER 18

Third Persons and Contracts

© Manuel Gutjahr/iStockphoto.com

learningoutcomes

After studying this chapter, you should be able to

LO.1 Explain the two types of intended third-party beneficiaries

LO.2 Explain why an incidental beneficiary does not have the right to sue as a third-party beneficiary

LO.3 Define an assignment

LO.4 Explain the general rule that a person entitled to receive money under a contract may generally assign that right to another person

LO.5 List the nonassignable rights to performance

A. Third-Party Beneficiary Contracts

Generally, only the parties to a contract may sue on it. However, in some cases a third person who is not a party to the contract may sue on the contract.

CPA

1. Definition

✳ **intended beneficiary** – third person of a contract whom the contract is intended to benefit.

✳ **third-party beneficiary** – third person whom the parties to a contract intend to benefit by the making of the contract and to confer upon such person the right to sue for breach of contract.

When a contract is intended to benefit a third person, such a person is an **intended beneficiary** and may bring suit on and enforce the contract. In some states, the right of the intended **third-party beneficiary** to sue on the contract is declared by statute. **For Example,** Ibberson Co., the general contractor hired by AgGrow Oils, LLC to design and build an oilseed processing plant, contracted with subcontractor Anderson International Corp. to supply critical seed processing equipment for the project. Anderson's formal proposal to Ibberson identified the AgGrow Oils Project, and the proposal included drawings of the planned AgGrow plant. Under state law, this contract made between the contractor and subcontractor for the express benefit of the third-party AgGrow Oils could be enforced by the intended third-party beneficiary AgGrow Oils. The project was a failure. AgGrow was successful in the lawsuit against Anderson under the Anderson-Ibberson contract, having the standing to sue as an intended third-party beneficiary of that contract.[1]

✗ **(a) Creditor Beneficiary.** The intended beneficiary is sometimes classified as a *creditor beneficiary* when the promisee's primary intent is to discharge a duty owed to the third party.[2] **For Example,** when Max Giordano sold his business, Sameway Laundry, to Harry Phinn, he had three years of payments totaling $14,500 owing to Davco, Inc., on a commercial Davco shirt drying and pressing machine purchased in 2006. Max (the promisee) made a contract with Harry to sell the business for a stipulated sum. A provision in this contract selling the business called for Harry (the promisor) to make the Davco machine payments when due over the next three years. Should Harry fail to make payments, Davco, Inc., as an intended creditor beneficiary under the contract between Max and Harry, would have standing to sue Harry for breach of the payment provision in the contract.

CPA

(b) Donee Beneficiary. The second type of intended beneficiary is a *donee beneficiary* to whom the promisee's primary intent in contracting is to give a benefit. A life insurance contract is such an intended third-party beneficiary contract. The promisee-insured pays premiums to the insurer under the contract of insurance so that, upon the death of the insured, the promisor-insurer would pay the sum designated in the contract to the beneficiary. The beneficiary's rights vest upon the insured's death, and the beneficiary can sue the insurance company upon the insured's death even though the insurance company never made any agreement directly with the beneficiary.

(c) Necessity of Intent. A third person does not have the status of an intended third-party beneficiary unless it is clear at the time the contract was formed that the parties intended to impose a direct obligation with respect to the third person.[3] In

---

[1] *AgGrow Oils, LLC v. National Union Fire Ins.*, 420 F.3d 751 (8th Cir. 2005).
[2] The Restatement (Second) of Contracts §302 substitutes "intended beneficiary" for the terms "creditor" and "donee" beneficiary. However, some courts continue to use the classifications of creditor and donee third-party beneficiaries. Regardless of the terminology, the law continues to be the same. See *Continental Casualty v. Zurich American Insurance*, 2009 WL 455285 (D.C. Or. 2009).
[3] *American United Logistics, Inc. v. Catellus*, 319 F.3d 921 (7th Cir. 2003).

determining whether there is intent to benefit a third party, the surrounding circumstances as well as the contract may be examined.[4] There is a strong presumption that the parties to a contract intend to benefit only themselves.[5]

CASE SUMMARY

The Pest Control Case

FACTS: Admiral Pest Control had a standing contract with Lodging Enterprises to spray its motel every month to exterminate pests. Copeland, a guest in the motel, was bitten by a spider. She sued Admiral on the ground that she was a third-party beneficiary of the extermination contract.

DECISION: Judgment against Copeland. There was no intent manifested in the contract that guests of the motel were beneficiaries of the contract. The contract was made by the motel to protect itself. The guests were incidental beneficiaries of that contract and therefore could not sue for its breach. [*Copeland v. Admiral Pest Control Co.*, 933 P.2d 937 (Okla. App. 1996)]

(D) DESCRIPTION. It is not necessary that the intended third-party beneficiary be identified by name. The beneficiary may be identified by class, with the result that any member of that class is a third-party beneficiary. **For Example,** a contract between the promoter of an automobile stock car race and the owner of the racetrack contains a promise by the owner to pay specified sums of money to each driver racing a car in certain races. A person driving in one of the designated races is a third-party beneficiary and can sue the owner on the contract for the promised compensation.

2. Modification or Termination of Intended Third-Party Beneficiary Contract

Can the parties to the contract modify or terminate it so as to destroy the right of the intended third-party beneficiary? If the contract contains an express provision allowing a change of beneficiary or cancellation of the contract without the consent of the intended third-party beneficiary, the parties to the contract may destroy the rights of the intended beneficiary by acting in accordance with that contract provision.[6]

For Example, Roy obtained a life insurance policy from Phoenix Insurance Company that provided the beneficiary could be changed by the insured. Roy named his son, Harry, as the beneficiary. Later, Roy had a falling out with Harry and removed him as beneficiary. Roy could do this because the right to change the beneficiary was expressly reserved by the contract that created the status of the intended third-party beneficiary.

---

[4] See *Becker v. Crispell-Snyder, Inc.*, 763 N.W.2d 192 (Wis. App. 2009) for an example of complex circumstances surrounding a third-party beneficiary contract. The town of Somers, Wisconsin, entered into a contract with engineering firm Crispell-Snyder (C-S) because it needed an engineering firm to oversee a new subdivision to be developed by the Beckers. Under this contract C-S would submit bills to the town for overseeing the development, and the town would pay C-S through a line of credit from the Beckers. The court held that the Beckers were third-party beneficiaries entitled to sue C-S for overcharging change orders.

[5] *Barney v. Unity Paving, Inc.*, 639 N.E.2d 592 (Ill. App. 1994).

[6] A common form of reservation is the life insurance policy provision by which the insured reserves the right to change the beneficiary. Section 142 of the Restatement (Second) of Contracts provides that the promisor and the promise may modify their contract and affect the right of the third-party beneficiary thereby unless the agreement expressly prohibits this or the third-party beneficiary has changed position in reliance on the promise or has manifested assent to it.

In addition, the rights of an intended third-party beneficiary are destroyed if the contract is discharged or ended by operation of law, for example, through bankruptcy proceedings.

3. Limitations on Intended Third-Party Beneficiary

Although the intended third-party beneficiary rule gives the third person the right to enforce the contract, it obviously gives no more rights than the contract provides. That is, the intended third-party beneficiary must take the contract as it is. If there is a time limitation or any other restriction in the contract, the intended beneficiary cannot ignore it but is bound by it.

If the contract is not binding for any reason, that defense may be raised against the intended third-party beneficiary suing on the contract.[7]

CPA 4. Incidental Beneficiaries

Not everyone who benefits from the performance of a contract between other persons is entitled to sue as a third-party beneficiary. If the benefit was intended, the third person is an intended beneficiary with the rights described in the preceding sections. If the benefit was not intended, the third person is an *incidental beneficiary*. **For Example,** real estate developer Ocean Atlantic Corp. purchased a series of bonds from American Southern Insurance Co. for the purpose of guaranteeing the performance of public improvement in a subdivision it was developing in Yorkville, Illinois. The bonds representing the surety contract between Ocean Atlantic and American Southern were issued in favor of the City of Yorkville. Ocean Atlantic hired subcontractor Aurora Blacktop, Inc., to perform several improvements, but the project stalled and Aurora was never paid for its work. Aurora lacked standing as a third-party beneficiary to enforce the subdivision bonds against American Southern because the contractual obligations ran only to the city. Aurora was deemed an incidental beneficiary rather than a third-party beneficiary.[8]

Whether or not a third party is an *intended* or *incidental* beneficiary, therefore, comes down to determining whether or not a reasonable person would believe that the promisee intended to confer on the beneficiary an enforceable benefit under the contract in question. The intent must be clear and definite or expressed in the contract itself or in the circumstances surrounding the contract's execution.

CASE SUMMARY

Third Party Must Be Identified in the Four Corners of the Contract

FACTS: Novus International, Inc., manufactures a poultry-feed supplement named Alimet at its plant in Chocolate Bayou, Texas. A key component of Alimet is the chemical MMP. Novus contracted with Union Carbide to secure MMP from Carbide's plant in Taft, Louisiana.

---

[7] *XL Disposal Corp. v. John Sexton Contractors Co.,* 659 N.E.2d 1312 (Ill. App. 1995).
[8] *City of Yorkville v. American Southern Insurance Co.,* 654 F.3d 713 (7th Cir. 2011).

CASE SUMMARY

Continued

Sometime later, Carbide entered into a major rail-transportation contract with the Union Pacific Railroad (UP). The rail contract consisted of nearly 100 pages. Exhibit 2 of the contract delineated inbound and outbound shipments to and from all of Carbide's Texas and Louisiana facilities. Among the hundreds of shipments listed in Exhibit 2 were three outbound MMP shipments from Taft, Louisiana, to Chocolate Bayou, Texas. These shipments were described as "Taft outbound liquid chemicals." Due to difficulties that arose from its merger with the Southern Pacific Railroad, UP experienced severe disruptions in its rail service over parts of two years and was unable to transport sufficient MMP to Chocolate Bayou. As a result, Novus had to utilize more expensive methods of transportation to obtain Alimet. It sued UP to recover the increased costs of premium freight resulting from UP's breach of its rail contract with Carbide. UP asserts that Novus did not have standing to sue; and Novus contends that it had standing to sue as an intended third-party beneficiary.

DECISION: Judgment for UP. Third-party beneficiary claims succeed or fail according to the provisions of the contact upon which suit is brought. The intention to confer a direct benefit on a third party must be clearly and fully spelled out in the four corners of the contract. Otherwise, enforcement of the contract by a third party must be denied. After reviewing the rail contract, no intent to confer a direct benefit on Novus is evident. Novus is never named in the contract, and all obligations flow between UP and Carbide. Nor is it stated anywhere in the contract that the parties are contracting for the benefit of Carbide's customers. Novus, thus, is an incidental beneficiary without standing to sue. [*Union Pacific Railroad v. Novus International, Inc.,* **113 S.W.3d 418 (Tex. App. 2003)**]

---

right – legal capacity to require another person to perform or refrain from an action.

duty – obligation of law imposed on a person to perform or refrain from performing a certain act.

assignment – transfer of a right; generally used in connection with personal property rights, as rights under a contract, commercial paper, an insurance policy, a mortgage, or a lease. (Parties—assignor, assignee.)

obligor – promisor.

debtor – buyer on credit (i.e., a borrower).

obligee – promisee who can claim the benefit of the obligation.

assignor – party who assigns contract rights to a third party.

assignee – third party to whom contract benefits are transferred.

B. ASSIGNMENTS

The parties to a contract have both rights and duties. Can rights be transferred or sold to another person or entity? Can duties be transferred to another person?

5. Definitions

Contracts create **rights** and **duties** between the parties to the contract. An **assignment** is a transfer of contractual rights to a third party. The party owing a duty or debt under the contract is the **obligor** or **debtor**, and the party to whom the obligation is owed is the **obligee**. The party making the assignment is the **assignor**. The third party to whom the assignment is made is the **assignee**. **For Example,** Randy Marshall and Marilee Menendez own Huntington Beach Board (HBB) Company, LLC, a five-employee start-up company making top-of-the line surfboards. Marilee was able to sell 100 Duke Kahanamoku–inspired "longboards" to Watersports, Inc., a large retail sporting goods chain, for $140 per board. However, the best payment terms she could obtain were payment in full in 90 days. A contract containing these terms was executed, and the goods were delivered. To meet internal cash flow needs, HBB assigned its right to receive the $14,000 payment from the buyer to West Coast Financial Associates (Associates) and received $12,800 cash from Associates on execution of the assignment documents. Notice was given at that time to Watersports, Inc., of the assignment. The right to receive the payment due in 90 days under the sales contract has thus been transferred by the

FIGURE 18-1 | *Surfboard Transaction Diagram*

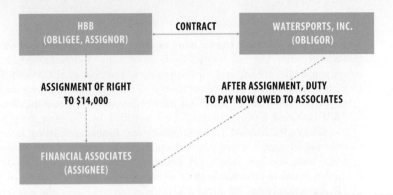

© Cengage Learning

seller HBB (assignor) to the third party, Associates (the assignee), to whom the buyer, Watersports, Inc. (obligor), now owes the duty of payment. Under the law of assignments, Associates, the assignee, now has direct rights against the obligor, Watersports, Inc. (See Figure 18-1.)

6. Form of Assignment

Generally, an assignment may be in any form. Statutes, however, may require that certain kinds of assignments be in writing or be executed in a particular form. Any words, whether written or spoken, that show an intention to transfer or assign will be given the effect of an assignment.[9]

7. Notice of Assignment

An assignment, if otherwise valid, takes effect the moment it is made. The assignee should give immediate notice of the assignment to the obligor, setting forth the obligor's duty to the assignee, in order to prevent improper payment.[10]

CASE SUMMARY

When You Find Yourself in a Hole, NationsBank, Stop Digging

FACTS: L & S General Contractors, LLC (L & S), purchased a book-entry certificate of deposit (CD 005) in the principal amount of $100,000 from NationsBank, N.A. L & S later assigned CD 005 to Credit General Insurance Company (Credit General) as collateral security for performance and payment bonds on a Howard Johnson construction project. Credit General forwarded to NationsBank a written notice of the assignment that stated, "Please hold this account as assigned to use until demanded or released by us." NationsBank recorded the assignment and executed a written acknowledgment. When CD 005 matured, L & S rolled over

---

[9] *JBM Investments, LLC v. Callahan Industries, Inc.*, 667 S.E.2d 429 (Ga. App. 2008).
[10] In some cases, an assignee will give notice of the assignment to the obligor in order to obtain priority over other persons who claim the same right or in order to limit the defenses that the obligor may raise against the assignee. U.C.C. §9-318.

CASE SUMMARY

Continued

the proceeds into a short-term certificate of deposit (CD 058) and, upon maturity, rolled over the proceeds of CD 058 into another short-term certificate of deposit (CD 072).

The bank book entries of CD 058 and CD 072 recorded L & S as the only principal/payee and did not reflect Credit General's assignment interest. NationsBank admitted its failure to show Credit General as assignee on the rollover book entries for CD 058 and CD 072 was a mistake.

Upon maturity, L & S withdrew the proceeds of CD 072 without the knowledge or consent of Credit General. Later Credit General made written demand on NationsBank for the proceeds of CD 005, and NationsBank informed Credit General that CD 005 had been redeemed and refused payment. Credit General sued NationsBank for wrongful payment of proceeds. NationsBank argues that the assignment was limited in time to the completion of the Howard Johnson project.

DECISION: Judgment for the assignee, Credit General. Upon notice and acknowledgment of the assignment, NationsBank incurred a legal duty to pay the account proceeds only to the assignee, Credit General, in whom the account was vested by the terms of the assignment. The assignment was absolute and unambiguous on its face and clearly was not limited as NationsBank proposes. The assignment language controls. [**Credit General Insurance Co. v. NationsBank, 299 F.3d 943 (8th Cir. 2002)**]

If the obligor is notified in any manner that there has been an assignment and that any money due must be paid to the assignee, the obligor's obligation can be discharged only by making payment to the assignee.

If the obligor is not notified that there has been an assignment and that the money due must be paid to the assignee, any payment made by the obligor to the assignor reduces or cancels that portion of the debt. The only remedy for the assignee is to sue the assignor to recover the payments that were made by the obligor.

The Uniform Consumer Credit Code (UCCC) protects consumer-debtors making payments to an assignor without knowledge of the assignment[11] and imposes a penalty for using a contract term that would destroy this protection of consumers.[12]

8. Assignment of Right to Money

Assignments of contracts are generally made to raise money. **For Example,** an automobile dealer assigns a customer's credit contract to a finance company and receives cash for it. Sometimes assignments are made when an enterprise closes and transfers its business to a new owner.

A person entitled to receive money, such as payment for goods sold to a buyer or for work done under a contract, may generally assign that right to another person.[13] A **claim** or **cause of action** against another person may be assigned. Isaac Hayes, an Academy Award®–winning composer, producer, and the original voice of Chef in

claim – right to payment.

cause of action – right to damages or other judicial relief when a legally protected right of the plaintiff is violated by an unlawful act of the defendant.

[11] U.C.C.C. §2.412.
[12] U.C.C.C. §5.202.
[13] *Pravin Banker Associates v. Banco Popular del Peru,* 109 F.3d 850 (2d Cir. 1997).

the television series South Park, assigned his copyright interests in several musical works in exchange for royalties from Stax Records.[14] A contractor entitled to receive payment from a building's owner can assign that right to a bank as security for a loan or can assign it to anyone else.

For Example, Celeste owed Roscoe Painters $5,000 for painting her house. Roscoe assigned this claim to the Main Street Bank. Celeste later refused to pay the bank because she had never consented to the assignment. The fact that Celeste had not consented is irrelevant. Roscoe was the owner of the claim and could transfer it to the bank. Celeste, therefore, is obligated to pay the assignee, Main Street Bank.

(A) FUTURE RIGHTS. By the modern rule, future and expected rights to money may be assigned. Thus, prior to the start of a building, a building contractor may assign its rights to money not yet due under an existing contract's payment on completion-phase schedule.

(B) PURPOSE OF ASSIGNMENT. The assignment of the right to money may be a complete transfer of the right that gives the assignee the right to collect and keep the money. In contrast, the assignment may be held for security. In this case, the assignee may hold the money only as a security for some specified obligation.

(C) PROHIBITION OF ASSIGNMENT OF RIGHTS. A clear and specific contractual prohibition against the assignment of rights is enforceable at common law. However, the UCC favors the assignment of contracts, and express contractual prohibitions on assignments are ineffective against (1) the assignment of rights to payment for goods or services, including accounts receivable,[15] and (2) the assignment of the rights to damages for breach of sales contracts.[16]

9. Nonassignable Rights

If the transfer of a right would materially affect or alter a duty or the rights of the obligor, an assignment is not permitted.[17]

(A) ASSIGNMENT INCREASING BURDEN OF PERFORMANCE. When the assignment of a right would increase the burden of the obligor in performing, an assignment is ordinarily not permitted. To illustrate, if the assignor has the right to buy a certain quantity of a stated article and to take such property from the seller's warehouse, this right can be assigned. However, if the sales contract stipulates that the seller should deliver to the buyer's premises and the assignee's premises are a substantial distance from the assignor's place of business, the assignment would not be given effect. In this case, the seller would be required to give a different performance by providing greater transportation if the assignment were permitted.

(B) PERSONAL SERVICES. Contracts for personal services are generally not assignable. **For Example,** were golf instructor David Ledbetter to sign a one-year contract to provide instruction for professional golfer Davis Love III, David Ledbetter could not assign his first assistant to provide the instruction, nor could Davis Love assign a protégé to receive instruction from Ledbetter. Professional athletes and their agents

---

[14] *Hayes v. Carlin America, Inc.,* 168 F. Supp. 2d 154 (S.D.N.Y 2001).
[15] U.C.C. §9-318(4). This section of the U.C.C. is applicable to most common commercial assignments.
[16] U.C.C. §2-210(2).
[17] *Aslakson v. Home Savings Ass'n,* 416 N.W.2d 786 (Minn. App. 1987) (increase of credit risk).

FIGURE 18-2	*Limitations on Transfer of Rights and Duties*

ASSIGNMENT OF RIGHT TO MONEY	ASSIGNMENT OF RIGHT TO PERFORMANCE	DELEGATION OF DUTIES
GENERALLY NO LIMITATION	INCREASE OF BURDEN PERSONAL SERVICES CREDIT TRANSACTION	PERSONAL OR NONSTANDARDIZED PERFORMANCE

© Cengage Learning

commonly deal with assignment or trading rights of the athletes in their contracts with professional sports franchises.

There is a split among jurisdictions regarding whether employee noncompetition covenants are assignable to the new owner of a business absent employee consent. That is, some courts permit a successor employer to enforce an employee's noncompetition agreement as an assignee of the original employer. However, a majority of states that have considered this issue have concluded that restrictive covenants are personal in nature and not assignable. **For Example,** in September 2000, Philip Burkhardt signed a noncompetition agreement with his employer, NES Trench Shoring. On June 30, 2002, United Rentals Purchased NES with all contracts being assigned to United Rentals. Burkhardt stayed on with the new owner for five weeks and thereafter went to work for Traffic Control Services, a direct competitor of United. United was unsuccessful in its action to enforce the noncompetition covenant Burkhardt had signed with NES. Burkhardt's covenant with NES did not contain a clause allowing the covenant to be assigned to a new owner, and the court refused to enforce it, absent an express clause permitting assignment.[18]

(c) Credit Transaction. When a transaction is based on extending credit, the person to whom credit is extended cannot assign any rights under the contract to another. **For Example,** Jack Aldrich contracted to sell his summer camp on Lake Sunapee to Pat Norton for $200,000, with $100,000 in cash due at the closing and the balance due on an installment basis secured by a mortgage on the property to be executed by Norton. Several days later, Norton found a more desirable property, and her sister Meg was very pleased to take over the Sunapee contract. Pat assigned her rights to Meg. Jack Aldrich, having received a better offer after contracting with Pat, refused to consent to the assignment. In this situation, the assignment to Meg is prohibited because the assignee, Meg, is a different credit risk even though the property to serve as security remained unchanged.

CPA 10. Rights of Assignee

Unless restricted by the terms of the assignment or applicable law, the assignee acquires all the rights of the assignor.[19]

[18] *Traffic Control Sources, Inc. v. United Rentals Northwest, Inc.,* 87 P.3d 1054 (Nev. 2004).
[19] *Puget Sound National Bank v. Washington Department of Revenue,* 868 P.2d 127 (Wash. 1994).

An assignee stands exactly in the position of the assignor. The assignee's rights are no more or less than those of the assignor. If the assigned right to payment is subject to a condition precedent, that same condition exists for the assignee. **For Example,** when a contractor is not entitled to receive the balance of money due under the contract until all bills of suppliers of materials have been paid, the assignee to whom the contractor assigns the balance due under the contract is subject to the same condition. As set forth previously, in some states the assignee of a business purchasing all of the assets and rights of the business has the right to enforce a confidentiality and noncompetition agreement against a former employee of the assignor, just as though it were the assignor.[20]

11. Continuing Liability of Assignor

The making of an assignment does not relieve the assignor of any obligation of the contract. In the absence of a contrary agreement, an assignor continues to be bound by the obligations of the original contract. **For Example,** boatbuilder Derecktor NY's assignment of obligations to a Connecticut boatbuilder did not release it from all liabilities under its boatbuilding contract with New York Water Taxi (NYWT); and NYWT was allowed to proceed against Derecktor NY for breach of contract–design and breach of contract–workmanship.[21]

When a lease is assigned, the assignee becomes the principal obligor for rent payments, and the leasee becomes a surety toward the lessor for the assignee's performance. **For Example,** Tri-State Chiropractic (TSC) held a five-year lease on premises at 6010 East Main Street in Columbus, Ohio. Without the leasor's consent, TSC assigned that lease to Dr. T. Wilson and Buckeye Chiropractic, LLC, prior to the expiration of the lease. TSC continues to be liable for rent as surety during the term of the lease, even if the leasor (owner) had consented to the assignment or accepted payment from the assignee.[22] In order to avoid liability as a surety, TSC would have to obtain a discharge of the lease by **novation**, in which all three parties agree that the original contract (the lease) would be discharged and a new lease between Dr. Wilson and the owner would take effect. A novation allows for the discharge of a contractual obligation by the substitution of a new contract involving a new party.[23]

novation–substitution for an old contract with a new one that either replaces an existing obligation with a new obligation or replaces an original party with a new party.

12. Liability of Assignee

It is necessary to distinguish between the question of whether the obligor can assert a particular defense against the assignee and the question of whether any person can sue the assignee. Ordinarily, the assignee is not subject to suit by virtue of the fact that the assignment has been made.

(A) CONSUMER PROTECTION LIABILITY OF ASSIGNEE. The assignee of the right to money may have no direct relationship to the original debtor except with respect to receiving payments. Consumer protection laws in most states, however, may subject the assignee to some liability for the assignor's misconduct.

---

[20] *Artromick International, Inc. v. Koch,* 759 N.E.2d 385 (Ohio App. 2001).
[21] *New York Trans Harbor, LLC v. Derecktor Shipyards,* 841 N.Y.S.2d 821 (2007).
[22] *Schottenstein Trustees v. Carano,* 2000 WL 1455425 (Ohio. App. 2000).
[23] *Willamette Management Association, Inc. v. Palczynski,* 38 A.3d 1212 (Conn. App. 2012).

CASE SUMMARY

The Pool and the Agreement Will Not Hold Any Water

FACTS: Homeowner Michael Jackson entered into a contract with James DeWitt for the construction of an in-ground lap pool. The contract provided for a 12 ft. by 60 ft. pool at an estimated cost of $21,000. At the time the contract was signed, Jackson paid DeWitt $11,400 in cash and financed $7,500 through a Retail Installment Security Agreement (RISA). Associates Financial Services Company (Associates) provided DeWitt with all of the forms necessary to document the financing of the home improvements. Consumer requests for financing were subject to Associates's approval, which was given for Jackson's lap pool. When the RISA was completed, DeWitt assigned it to Associates. Jackson made two monthly payments of $202.90 and a final payment of $7,094.20 while the lap pool was still under construction. When the pool was filled, it failed to hold water and Jackson had the pool and deck removed. Jackson sued DeWitt for breach of contract. He asserted that all valid claims and defenses he had against DeWitt were also valid against the assignee, Associates. Jackson sought the return of the $7,500 he had financed from Associates. The trial court held that because Jackson had paid the entire balance of the loan before Associates knew of Jackson's claim, he could not obtain relief from Associates under the consumer protection law, section ATCP 110.06 of the Wisconsin Administrative Code. Jackson appealed this decision.

DECISION: Judgment for Jackson. As one commentator has noted, "ch. ATCP 110 deals with virtually a laundry list of unfair or deceptive home improvement practices that have resulted from substantial financial losses to home owners over the years. Jeffries, 57 MARQ. L. REV at 578." Associates is an assignee of a "home improvement contract" that is governed by section ATCP 110.06. The regulation provides that "[e]very assignee of a home improvement contract takes subject to all claims and defenses of the buyer or successors in interest." Therefore, as the assignee of the RISA, Associates is subject to any claims without regard to the negotiability of the contract. [*Jackson v. DeWitt,* **592 N.W.2d 262 (Wis. App. 1999)**]

(B) DEFENSES AND SETOFFS. The assignee's rights are no greater than those of the assignor.[24] If the obligor could successfully defend against a suit brought by the assignor, the obligor will also prevail against the assignee.

The fact that the assignee has given value for the assignment does not give the assignee any immunity from defenses that the other party, the obligor, could have asserted against the assignor. The rights acquired by the assignee remain subject to any limitations imposed by the contract.

13. Warranties of Assignor

implied warranty – warranty that was not made but is implied by law.

When the assignment is made for a consideration, the assignor is regarded as providing an **implied warranty** that the right assigned is valid. The assignor also warrants that the assignor is the owner of the claim or right assigned and that the assignor will not interfere with the assignee's enforcement of the obligation.

14. Delegation of Duties

delegation of duties – transfer of duties by a contracting party to another person who is to perform them.

A **delegation of duties** is a transfer of duties by a contracting party to another person who is to perform them. Under certain circumstances, a contracting party

---

[24] *Shoreline Communications, Inc. v. Norwich Taxi, LLC,* 797 A.2d 1165 (Conn. App. 2002).

FIGURE 18-3 | *Can a Third Person Sue on a Contract?*

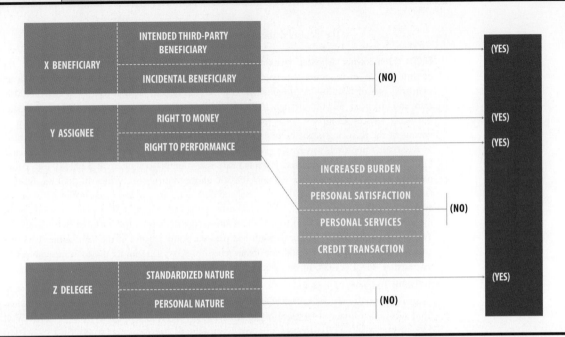

© Cengage Learning

may obtain someone else to do the work. When the performance is standardized and nonpersonal, so that it is not material who performs, the law will permit the **delegation** of the performance of the contract. In such cases, however, the contracting party remains liable in the case of default of the person doing the work just as though no delegation had been made.[25]

delegation – transfer to another of the right and power to do an act.

CASE SUMMARY

Who's Liable for $871,069 In Damages? Not Me. I Wasn't Even There!

FACTS: The Emersons contracted with Martin Winters, the owner of Winters Roofing Company, to install a new roof on their home. When the new roof leaked, Winters agreed to fix the problems. Without the knowledge of the Emersons, Winters hired a subcontractor, Bruce Jacobs, to perform the repair work. Jacobs's use of a propane torch in repairing the roof resulted in a fire that caused $871,069 in damages to the house and personal property. Federal Insurance Co. sued Winters to recover sums it paid the Emersons for damages resulting from the fire. Winters defended that Federal had sued the wrong party because Winters did not participate in the repair work but had subcontracted the work out to Jacobs and was neither at the job site nor supervised Jacobs's work.

DECISION: Judgment for the plaintiff. Winters, based on his contract with the Emersons, had an implied duty under the contract to install the roof properly, skillfully, diligently, and in a workmanlike manner. The delegation of these duties to Jacobs did not serve to release Winters from liability implicit in the original content. [*Federal Insurance Co. v. Winters,* 354 S.W. 3d 287 (Tenn. 2011)]

[25] *Orange Bowl Corp. v. Warren,* 386 S.E.2d 293 (S.C. App. 1989).

A contract may prohibit a party owing a duty of performance under a contract from delegating that duty to another.[26] **For Example,** Tom Joyce of Patriot Plumbing Co. contracts to install a new heating system for Mrs. Lawton. A notation on the sales contract that Tom Joyce will do the installation prohibits Patriot Plumbing from delegating the installation to another equally skilled plumber or to another company if a backlog of work occurs at Patriot Plumbing.

If the performance of a party to a contract involves personal skill, talents, judgment, or trust, the delegation of duties is barred unless consented to by the person entitled to the performance. Examples include performance by professionals such as physicians, dentists, lawyers, consultants, celebrities, artists, and craftpersons with unusual skills.

(A) INTENTION TO DELEGATE DUTIES. An assignment of rights does not in itself delegate the performance of duties to the assignee. In the absence of clear language in the assignment stating that duties are or are not delegated, all circumstances must be examined to determine whether there is a delegation. When the total picture is viewed, it may become clear what was intended. The fact that an assignment is made for security of the assignee is a strong indication there was no intent to delegate to the assignee the performance of any duty resting on the assignor.[27]

CASE SUMMARY

Duties Were Delegated Too, Dude

FACTS: Smith, who owned the Avalon Apartments, a condominium, sold individual apartments under contracts that required each purchaser to pay $15 a month extra for hot and cold water, heat, refrigeration, taxes, and fire insurance. Smith assigned his interest in the apartment house under various contracts to Roberts. When Roberts failed to pay the taxes on the building, the purchasers of the individual apartments sued to compel Roberts to do so.

DECISION: Judgment against Roberts. In the absence of a contrary indication, it is presumed that an assignment of a contract delegates the performance of the duties as well as transfers the rights. Here, there was no indication that a package transfer was not intended, and the assignee was therefore obligated to perform in accordance with the contract terms. [*Radley v. Smith and Roberts*, 313 P.2d 465 (Utah 1957)]

(B) DELEGATION OF DUTIES UNDER THE UCC. With respect to contracts for the sale of goods, "an assignment of 'the contract' or of 'all my rights under the contract' or an assignment in similar general terms is an assignment of rights and, unless the language or the circumstances (as in an assignment for security) indicate the contrary, it is a delegation of performance of the duties of the assignor, and its acceptance by the assignee constitutes a promise … to perform those duties. This promise is enforceable by either the assignor or the other party to the original contract."[28]

[26] See *Physical Distribution Services, Inc. v. R. R. Donnelley*, 561 F.3d 792 (8th Cir. 2009).
[27] *City National Bank of Fort Smith v. First National Bank and Trust Co. of Rogers*, 732 S.W.2d 489 (Ark. App. 1987).
[28] U.C.C. §2-210(4).

LawFlix

It Could Happen to You (1996) (PG)

Discuss the legal, ethical and contract issues involved in the first portion of the film in which a police officer (Nicholas Cage) promises to split a lottery ticket with a coffee shop waitress (Bridget Fonda) as her tip because he does not have enough money. The lottery ticket (purchased by Cage and his wife, Rosie Perez) is a winner, and Cage wrestles with his obligation to tell Fonda. You could discuss whether there was an assignment or whether Fonda was added as a third-party beneficiary after the fact.

MAKE THE CONNECTION

SUMMARY

Ordinarily, only the parties to contracts have rights and duties with respect to such contracts. Exceptions are made in the case of third-party beneficiary contracts and assignments.

When a contract shows a clear intent to benefit a third person or class of persons, those persons are called *intended third-party beneficiaries*, and they may sue for breach of the contract. A third-party beneficiary is subject to any limitation or restriction found in the contract. A third-party beneficiary loses all rights when the original contract is terminated by operation of law or if the contract reserves the right to change the beneficiary and such a change is made.

In contrast, an incidental beneficiary benefits from the performance of a contract, but the conferring of this benefit was not intended by the contracting parties. An incidental beneficiary cannot sue on the contract.

An assignment is a transfer of a right; the assignor transfers a right to the assignee. In the absence of a local statute, there are no formal requirements for an assignment. Any words manifesting the intent to transfer are sufficient to constitute an assignment. No consideration is required. Any right to money may be assigned, whether the assignor is entitled to the money at the time of the assignment or will be entitled or expects to be entitled at some time in the future.

A right to a performance may be assigned except when (1) it would increase the burden of performance, (2) the contract involves the

performance of personal services, or (3) the transaction is based on extending credit.

When a valid assignment is made, the assignee has the same rights—and only the same rights—as the assignor. The assignee is also subject to the same defenses and setoffs as the assignor had been.

The performance of duties under a contract may be delegated to another person except when a personal element of skill or judgment of the original contracting party is involved. The intent to delegate duties may be expressly stated. The intent may also be found in an "assignment" of "the contract" unless the circumstances make it clear that only the right to money was intended to be transferred. The fact that there has been a delegation of duties does not release the assignor from responsibility for performance. The assignor is liable for breach of the contract if the assignee does not properly perform the delegated duties. In the absence of an effective delegation or the formation of a third-party beneficiary contract, an assignee of rights is not liable to the obligee of the contract for its performance by the assignor.

Notice is not required to effect an assignment. When notice of the assignment is given to the obligor together with a demand that future payments be made to the assignee, the obligor cannot discharge liability by payment to the assignor.

When an assignment is made for a consideration, the assignor makes implied warranties that the right assigned is valid and that the assignor owns that right and will not interfere with its enforcement by the assignee.

LEARNING OUTCOMES

After studying this chapter, you should be able to clearly explain:

A. Third-Party Beneficiary Contracts

LO.1 Explain the two types of intended third-party beneficiaries

See the Sameway Laundry example that illustrates how the "intended creditor beneficiary" can sue the buyer, p. 362. See the text discussion explaining that a life insurance contract is an "intended" donee third-party beneficiary contract, p. 362.

LO.2 Explain why an incidental beneficiary does not have the right to sue as a third-party beneficiary

See the *City of Yorkville* example, in which a subcontractor was an incidental beneficiary with no standing to sue on performance bonds because the obligation ran only to the city, p. 364.

B. Assignments

LO.3 Define an assignment

See the text discussion explaining that an assignment is the transfer of contractual rights to a third party, p. 365. See the *Huntington Beach Board* example that discusses the assignee's direct rights against the obligor, pp. 365–366.

LO.4 Explain the general rule that a person entitled to receive money under a contract may generally assign that right to another person

See the example of an automobile dealer assigning a customer's credit contract to a finance company in order to raise cash to buy more inventory, p. 367.

LO.5 List the nonassignable rights to performance

See the text discussion regarding increase of burden, personal services, and credit transactions beginning on p. 368.

KEY TERMS

assignee	delegation of duties	obligee
assignment	delegation	obligor
assignor	duties	rights
cause of action	implied warranty	third-party beneficiary
claim	intended beneficiary	
debtor	novation	

QUESTIONS AND CASE PROBLEMS

1. Give an example of a third-party beneficiary contract.

2. A court order required John Baldassari to make specified payments for the support of his wife and child. His wife needed more money and applied for Pennsylvania welfare payments. In accordance with the law, she assigned to Pennsylvania her right to the support payments from her husband. Pennsylvania then increased her payments. Pennsylvania obtained a court order directing John, in accordance with the terms of the assignment from his wife, to make the support-order payments directly to the Pennsylvania Department of Public Welfare. John refused to pay on the ground that he had not been notified of the assignment or the hearing directing him to make payment to the assignee. Was he correct? [*Pennsylvania v. Baldassari*, 421 A.2d 306 (Pa. Super.)]

3. Lee contracts to paint Sally's two-story house for $2,500. Sally realizes that she will not have sufficient money, so she transfers her rights under this agreement to her neighbor Karen, who has a three-story house. Karen notifies Lee that Sally's

contract has been assigned to her and demands that Lee paint Karen's house for $2,500. Is Lee required to do so?

4. Assume that Lee agrees to the assignment of the house-painting contract to Karen as stated in question 3. Thereafter, Lee fails to perform the contract to paint Karen's house. Karen sues Sally for damages. Is Sally liable?

5. Jessie borrows $1,000 from Thomas and agrees to repay the money in 30 days. Thomas assigns the right to the $1,000 to Douglas Finance Co. Douglas sues Jessie. Jessie argues that she had agreed to pay the money only to Thomas and that when she and Thomas had entered into the transaction, there was no intention to benefit Douglas Finance Co. Are these objections valid?

6. Washington purchased an automobile from Smithville Motors. The contract called for payment of the purchase price in installments and contained the defense preservation notice required by the Federal Trade Commission regulation. Smithville assigned the contract to Rustic Finance Co. The car was always in need of repairs, and by the time it was half paid for, it would no longer run. Washington canceled the contract. Meanwhile, Smithville had gone out of business. Washington sued Rustic for the amount she had paid Smithville. Rustic refused to pay on the grounds that it had not been at fault. Decide.

7. Helen obtained an insurance policy insuring her life and naming her niece Julie as beneficiary. Helen died, and about a year later the policy was found in her house. When Julie claimed the insurance money, the insurer refused to pay on the ground that the policy required that notice of death be given to it promptly following the death. Julie claimed that she was not bound by the time limitation because she had never agreed to it, as she was not a party to the insurance contract. Is Julie entitled to recover?

8. Lone Star Life Insurance Co. agreed to make a long-term loan to Five Forty Three Land, Inc., whenever that corporation requested one. Five Forty Three wanted this loan to pay off its short-term debts. The loan was never made, as it was never requested by Five Forty Three, which owed the Exchange Bank & Trust Co. on a short-term debt. Exchange Bank then sued Lone Star for breach of its promise on the theory that the Exchange Bank was a third-party beneficiary of the contract to make the loan. Was the Exchange Bank correct? [*Exchange Bank & Trust Co. v. Lone Star Life Ins. Co.*, 546 S.W.2d 948 (Tex. App.)]

9. The New Rochelle Humane Society made a contract with the city of New Rochelle to capture and impound all dogs running at large. Spiegler, a minor, was bitten by some dogs while in her schoolyard. She sued the school district of New Rochelle and the Humane Society. With respect to the Humane Society, she claimed that she was a third-party beneficiary of the contract that the Humane Society had made with the city. She claimed that she could therefore sue the Humane Society for its failure to capture the dogs that had bitten her. Was she entitled to recover? [*Spiegler v. School District of the City of New Rochelle*, 242 N.Y.S.2d 430]

10. Zoya operated a store in premises rented from Peerless. The lease required Zoya to maintain liability insurance to protect Zoya and Peerless. Caswell entered the store, fell through a trap door, and was injured. She then sued Zoya and Peerless on the theory that she was a third-party beneficiary of the lease requirement to maintain liability insurance. Was she correct? [*Caswell v. Zoya Int'l*, 654 N.E.2d 552 (Ill. App.)]

11. Henry was owed $10,000 by Jones Corp. In consideration of the many odd jobs performed for him over the years by his nephew, Henry assigned the $10,000 claim to his nephew Charles. Henry died, and his widow claimed that the assignment was ineffective so that the claim was part of Henry's estate. She based her assertion on the ground that the past performance rendered by the nephew was not consideration. Was the assignment effective?

12. Industrial Construction Co. wanted to raise money to construct a canning factory in Wisconsin. Various persons promised to subscribe the needed amount, which they agreed

to pay when the construction was completed. The construction company assigned its rights and delegated its duties under the agreement to Johnson, who then built the cannery. Vickers, one of the subscribers, refused to pay the amount that he had subscribed on the ground that the contract could not be assigned. Was he correct?

13. The Ohio Department of Public Welfare made a contract with an accountant to audit the accounts of health care providers who were receiving funds under the Medicaid program. Windsor House, which operated six nursing homes, claimed that it was a third-party beneficiary of that contract and could sue for its breach. Was it correct? [*Thornton v. Windsor House, Inc.,* 566 N.E.2d 1220 (Ohio)]

CPA QUESTIONS

1. On August 1, Neptune Fisheries contracted in writing with West Markets to deliver to West 3,000 pounds of lobster at $4.00 a pound. Delivery of the lobsters was due October 1, with payment due November 1. On August 4, Neptune entered into a contract with Deep Sea Lobster Farms that provided as follows: "Neptune Fisheries assigns all the rights under the contract with West Markets dated August 1 to Deep Sea Lobster Farms." The best interpretation of the August 4 contract would be that it was:

   a. Only an assignment of rights by Neptune.

   b. Only a delegation of duties by Neptune.

   c. An assignment of rights and a delegation of duties by Neptune.

   d. An unenforceable third-party beneficiary contract.

2. Graham contracted with the city of Harris to train and employ high school dropouts residing in Harris. Graham breached the contract. Long, a resident of Harris and a high school dropout, sued Graham for damages. Under the circumstances, Long will:

   a. Win, because Long is a third-party beneficiary entitled to enforce the contract.

   b. Win, because the intent of the contract was to confer a benefit on all high school dropouts residing in Harris.

   c. Lose, because Long is merely an incidental beneficiary of the contract.

   d. Lose, because Harris did not assign its contract rights to Long.

3. Union Bank lent $200,000 to Wagner. Union required Wagner to obtain a life insurance policy naming Union as beneficiary. While the loan was outstanding, Wagner stopped paying the premiums on the policy. Union paid the premiums, adding the amounts paid to Wagner's loan. Wagner died, and the insurance company refused to pay the policy proceeds to Union. Union may:

   a. Recover the policy proceeds because it is a creditor beneficiary.

   b. Not recover the policy proceeds because it is a donee beneficiary.

   c. Not recover the policy proceeds because it is not in privity of contract with the insurance company.

   d. Not recover the policy proceeds because it is only an incidental beneficiary.

© Manuel Gutjahr/iStockphoto.com

CHAPTER 19

Discharge of Contracts

learningoutcomes

After studying this chapter, you should be able to

LO.1 List the three types of conditions that affect a party's duty to perform

LO.2 Explain the on-time performance rule

LO.3 Explain the adequacy of performance rules

LO.4 Explain four ways a contract can be discharged by agreement of the parties

LO.5 State the effect on a contract of the death or disability of one of the contracting parties

LO.6 Explain when impossibility or impracticability may discharge a contract

I n the preceding chapters, you studied how a contract is formed, what a contract means, and who has rights under a contract. In this chapter, attention is turned to how a contract is ended or discharged. In other words, what puts an end to the rights and duties created by a contract?

A. Conditions Relating to Performance

As developed in the body of this chapter, the ordinary method of discharging obligations under a contract is by performance. Certain promises may be less than absolute and instead come into effect only upon the occurrence of a specified event, or an existing obligation may be extinguished when an event happens. These are conditional promises.

1. Classifications of Conditions

When the occurrence or nonoccurrence of an event, as expressed in a contract, affects the duty of a party to the contract to perform, the event is called a **condition**. Terms such as *if, provided that, when, after, as soon as, subject to,* and *on the condition that* indicate the creation of a condition.[1] Conditions are classified as *conditions precedent, conditions subsequent,* and *concurrent conditions.*

(A) Condition Precedent. A **condition precedent** is a condition that must occur before a party to a contract has an obligation to perform under the contract.
For Example, a condition precedent to a contractor's (MasTec's) obligation to pay a subcontractor (MidAmerica) under a "pay-if-paid" by the owner (PathNet) clause in their subcontract agreement is the receipt of payment by MasTec from PathNet. The condition precedent—payment by the owner—did not occur due to bankruptcy, and therefore MasTec did not have an obligation to pay MidAmerica.[2]

> **condition** – stipulation or prerequisite in a contract, will, or other instrument.

> **condition precedent** – event that if unsatisfied would mean that no rights would arise under a contract.

CASE SUMMARY

A Blitz on Offense?

FACTS: Richard Blitz owns a piece of commercial property at 4 Old Middle Street. On February 2, 1998, Arthur Subklew entered into a lease with Blitz to rent the rear portion of the property. Subklew intended to operate an auto sales and repair business. Paragraph C of the lease was a zoning contingency clause that stated, "Landlord [plaintiff] will use Landlord's best efforts to obtain a written verification that Tenant can operate [an] Auto Sales and Repair Business at the demised premises. If Landlord is unable to obtain such commitment from the municipality, then this agreement shall be deemed null and void and Landlord shall immediately return deposit

---

[1] *Harmon Cable Communications v. Scope Cable Television, Inc.,* 468 N.W.2d 350 (Neb. 1990).
[2] *MidAmerica Construction Management, Inc. v. MasTec North America, Inc.,* 436 F.3d 1257 (10th Cir. 2006). But see *International Engineering Services, Inc. v. Scherer Construction Co.,* 74 So.3d 53 (Fla. App. 2011), where a "pay-when-paid" provision was found to be ambiguous, resulting in the general contractor being liable for the payment to the subcontractor.

CASE SUMMARY

Continued

monies to Tenant." The zoning board approved the location only as a general repair business. When Subklew refused to occupy the premises, Blitz sued him for breach of contract.

DECISION: Judgment for Subklew. A condition precedent is a fact or event that the parties intend must exist before there is right to a performance. If the condition is not fulfilled, the right to enforce the contract does not come into existence. Blitz's obligation to obtain written approval of a used car business was a condition precedent to the leasing agreement. Since it was not obtained, Blitz cannot enforce the leasing agreement. [*Blitz v. Subklew,* 810 A.2d 841 (**Conn. App. 2002**)]

(B) CONDITION SUBSEQUENT. The parties to a contract may agree that a party is obligated to perform a certain act or pay a certain sum of money, but the contract contains a provision that relieves the obligation on the occurrence of a certain event. That is, on the happening of a **condition subsequent**, such an event extinguishes the duty to thereafter perform. **For Example,** Chad Newly served as the weekend anchor on *Channel 5 News* for several years. The station manager, Tom O'Brien, on reviewing tapes in connection with Newly's contract renewal, believed that Newly's speech on occasion was slightly slurred, and he suspected that it was from alcohol use. In the parties' contract discussions, O'Brien expressed his concerns about an alcohol problem and offered help. Newly denied there was a problem. O'Brien agreed to a new two-year contract with Newly at $167,000 for the first year and $175,000 for the second year with other benefits subject to "the condition" that the station reserved the right to make four unannounced drug-alcohol tests during the contract term; and should Newly test positive for drugs or alcohol under measurements set forth in the contract, then all of Channel 5's obligations to Newly under the contract would cease. When Newly subsequently failed a urinalysis test three months into the new contract, the happening of this event extinguished the station's obligation to employ and pay him under the contract. Conditions subsequent are strictly construed, and where ambiguous, are construed against forfeiture.[3]

condition subsequent – event whose occurrence or lack thereof terminates a contract.

Sports & Entertainment Law

Endorsement Contracts

Sports marketing involves the use of famous athletes to promote the sale of products and services in our economy. Should an athlete's image be tarnished by allegations of immoral or illegal conduct, a company could be subject to financial losses and corporate embarrassment. Endorsement contracts may extend for multiyear periods, and should a "morals" issue arise, a company would be well served to have had a broad morals clause in its contract that would allow the company at its sole discretion to summarily terminate the endorsement contract. Representatives of athletes, on the other hand, seek narrow contractual language that allows for termination of endorsement contracts only upon the indictment for a crime, and they seek the right to have an arbitrator, as opposed to the employer, make the determination as to whether the morals clause was violated. NBA player Latrell Spreewell's endorsement contract with Converse Athletic

---

[3] *Cardone Trust v. Cardone*, 8 A.3d 1 (N.H. 2010).

Sports & Entertainment Law

Continued

Shoe Co. was terminated by the company following his altercation with his coach P.J. Carlisimo; John Daly's endorsement contract with Callaway Golf was terminated by the company when he violated his good conduct clause that restricted gambling and drinking activities; and six-time Pro Bowl football player Chad Johnson (aka "Ochocinco") lost his endorsement deal with Zico Coconut Water after he was arrested in a domestic battery case involving his wife. And, Nike, RadioShack and other sponsors ended their relationships with cyclist Lance Armstrong after a report detailing doping charges was issued by the U.S. Anti-Doping Agency.

Can the courts be utilized to resolve controversies over whether a "morals clause" has been violated? If so, is the occurrence of a morals clause violation a condition precedent or a condition subsequent?

(c) CONCURRENT CONDITION. In most bilateral contracts, the performances of the parties are *concurrent conditions*. That is, their mutual duties of performance under the contract are to take place simultaneously. **For Example,** concerning a contract for the sale and delivery of certain goods, the buyer must tender to the seller a certified check at the time of delivery as set forth in the contract, and the seller must tender the goods to the buyer at the same time.

B. DISCHARGE BY PERFORMANCE

When it is claimed that a contract is discharged by performance, questions arise as to the nature, time, and sufficiency of the performance.

2. Normal Discharge of Contracts

A contract is usually discharged by the performance of the terms of the agreement. In most cases, the parties perform their promises and the contract ceases to exist or is thereby discharged. A contract is also discharged by the expiration of the time period specified in the contract.[4]

3. Nature of Performance

Performance may be the doing of an act or the making of payment.

tender – goods have arrived, are available for pickup, and buyer is notified.

(A) TENDER. An offer to perform is known as a **tender**. If performance of the contract requires the doing of an act, the refusal of a tender discharges the party offering to perform and is a basis for that party to bring a lawsuit.

A valid tender of payment consists of an unconditional offer of the exact amount due on the date when due. A tender of payment is not just an expression of willingness to pay; it must be an actual offer to perform by making payment of the amount owed.

(B) PAYMENT. When the contract requires payment, performance consists of the payment of money.

---

[4] *Washington National Ins. Co. v. Sherwood Associates*, 795 P.2d 665 (Utah App. 1990).

(1) Application of Payments.

If a debtor owes more than one debt to the creditor and pays money, a question may arise as to which debt has been paid. If the debtor specifies the debt to which the payment is to be applied and the creditor accepts the money, the creditor is bound to apply the money as specified.[5] Thus, if the debtor specifies that a payment is to be made for a current purchase, the creditor may not apply the payment to an older balance.

(2) Payment by Check.

Payment by commercial paper, such as a check, is ordinarily a conditional payment. A check merely suspends the debt until the check is presented for payment. If payment is then made, the debt is discharged; if not paid, the suspension terminates, and suit may be brought on either the debt or the check. Frequently, payment must be made by a specified date. It is generally held that the payment is made on time if it is mailed on or before the final date for payment.

CASE SUMMARY

The Mailed-Check Payment

FACTS: Thomas Cooper was purchasing land from Peter and Ella Birznieks. Cooper was already in possession of the land but was required to pay the amount owed by January 30; otherwise, he would have to vacate the property. The attorney handling the transaction for the Birznieks told Cooper that he could mail the payment to him. On January 30, Cooper mailed to the attorney a personal check drawn on an out-of-state bank for the amount due. The check arrived at the Birznieks' attorney's office on February 1. The Birznieks refused to accept the check on the grounds that it was not a timely payment and moved to evict Cooper from the property.

DECISION: Because of the general custom to regard a check mailed to a creditor as paying the bill that is owed, payment was made by Cooper on January 30 when he mailed the check. Payment was therefore made within the required time even though received after the expiration of the required time. [*Birznieks v. Cooper*, **275 N.W.2d 221 (Mich. 1979)**]

4. Time of Performance

When the date or period of time for performance is specified in the contract, performance should be made on that date or within that time period.

(A) NO TIME SPECIFIED. When the time for performance is not specified in the contract, an obligation to perform within a reasonable time is implied.[6] The fact that no time is specified neither impairs the contract on the ground that it is indefinite nor allows an endless time in which to perform. What constitutes a reasonable time is determined by the nature of the subject matter of the contract and the facts and circumstances surrounding the making of the contract.

(B) WHEN TIME IS ESSENTIAL. If performance of the contract on or within the exact time specified is vital, it is said that "time is of the essence." Time is of the essence when

[5] *Oakes Logging, Inc. v. Green Crow, Inc.*, 832 P.2d 894 (Wash. App. 1992).
[6] *First National Bank v. Clark*, 447 S.E.2d 558 (W. Va. 1994).

the contract relates to property that is perishable or that is fluctuating rapidly in value. When a contract fixes by unambiguous language a time for performance and where there is no evidence showing that the parties did not intend that time should be of the essence, failure to perform within the specified time is a breach of contract entitling the innocent party to damages. **For Example,** Dixon and Gandhi agreed that Gandhi would close on the purchase of a motel as follows: "Closing Date. The closing shall be held … on the date which is within twenty (20) days after the closing of Nomura Financing." Gandhi did not close within the time period specified, and Dixon was allowed to retain $100,000 in prepaid closing costs and fees as liquidated damages for Gandhi's breach of contract.[7]

(c) WHEN TIME IS NOT ESSENTIAL. Unless a contract so provides, time is ordinarily not of the essence, and performance within a reasonable time is sufficient. In the case of the sale of property, time is not regarded as of the essence when there has not been any appreciable change in the market value or condition of the property and when the person who delayed does not appear to have done so for the purpose of speculating on a change in market price.

(d) WAIVER OF ESSENCE OF TIME LIMITATION. A provision that time is of the essence may be waived. It is waived when the specified time has expired but the party who could complain requests the delaying party to take steps necessary to perform the contract.

5. Adequacy of Performance

When a party renders exactly the performance called for by the contract, no question arises as to whether the contract has been performed. In other cases, there may not have been a perfect performance, or a question arises as to whether the performance satisfies the standard set by the contract.

CPA

substantial performance–equitable rule that if a good-faith attempt to perform does not precisely meet the terms of the agreement, the agreement will still be considered complete if the essential purpose of the contract is accomplished.

(a) SUBSTANTIAL PERFORMANCE. Perfect performance of a contract is not always possible when dealing with construction projects. A party who in good faith has provided **substantial performance** of the contract may sue to recover the payment specified in the contract.[8] However, because the performance was not perfect, the performing party is subject to a counterclaim for the damages caused the other party. When a building contractor has substantially performed the contract to construct a building, the contractor is responsible for the cost of repairing or correcting the defects as an offset from the contract price.[9]

The measure of damages under these circumstances is known as "cost of completion" damages.[10] If, however, the cost of completion would be unreasonably disproportionate to the importance of the defect, the measure of damages is the diminution in value of the building due to the defective performance.

Whether there is substantial performance is a question of degree to be determined by all of the facts, including the particular type of structure involved, its intended purpose, and the nature and relative expense of repairs.

For Example, a certain building contractor (BC) and a certain owner (O) made a contract to construct a home overlooking Vineyard Sound on Martha's Vineyard according to plans and specifications that clearly called for the use of General

---

[7] *Woodhull Corp. v.Saibaba Corp.,* 507 S.E.2d 493 (Ga. App. 1998).

[8] *Gala v. Harris,* 77 So.3d 1065 (La. App. 2012).

[9] Substantial performance is not a defense to a breach of contract claim, however. See *Bentley Systems Inc. v. Intergraph Corp.,* 922 So.2d 61 (Ala. 2005).

[10] *Hammer Construction Corp. v. Phillips,* 994 So.2d 1135 (Fla. App. 2008).

| FIGURE 19-1 | *Causes of Contract Discharge* |

© Cengage Learning

Plumbing Blue Star piping. The contract price was $1,100,000. Upon inspecting the work before making the final $400,000 payment and accepting the building, O discovered that BC had used Republic piping throughout the house. O explained to BC that his family had made its money by investing in General Plumbing, and he, therefore, would not make the final payment until the breach of contract was remedied. BC explained that Republic pipes were of the same industrial grade and quality as the Blue Star pipes. Moreover, BC estimated that it would cost nearly $300,000 to replace all of the pipes because of the destruction of walls and fixtures necessary to accomplish such a task. BC may sue O for $400,000 for breach of contract, claiming he had substantially performed the contract, and O may counterclaim for $300,000, seeking an offset for the cost of remedying the breach. The court will find in favor of the contractor and will not allow the $300,000 offset but will allow a "nominal" offset of perhaps $100 to $1,000 for the amount by which the Republic pipes diminished the value of the building. To have required the pipes to be replaced would amount to economic waste.[11]

When a contractor does not substantially perform its obligations under a contract, not only will the contractor not prevail in a breach of contract claim against a homeowner for extra work beyond the contract price but the contractor is liable for the reasonable cost of making the contractor's work conform to the contract. **For Example,** Superior Wall and Paver, LLC sued homeowners Pamela and Mark Gacek for $14,350 it claimed was still owed Superior as extra work, for concrete pavers it installed in the driveway of their residence. The Gaceks had previously paid the $45,000 contract price. The Gackes counterclaimed for $60,500 for the reasonable cost of making the contractor's work conform to the contract. The evidence established that Superior did not install a proper base of 3" to 4" of crushed limestone before installing the pavers as required by the contract, which caused the pavers to move, creating gaps between the pavers and causing water to flow into the garage. To correct the problem the pavers needed to be removed and the area excavated and replaced with a crushed limestone base before again installing the pavers. Superior claimed it had substantially performed the contract as a fully usable driveway, and the proper remedy, if any, was the diminution of the market value of the Gaceks' property due to any defective performance. Superior asserted the cost of redoing the entire job would be economic waste. The court determined that Superior had not substantially performed the contract and awarded the homeowners the cost of making Superior's work conform to the contract by having the job redone, rejecting Superior's assertion of economic waste.[12]

In most jurisdictions, the willfulness of the departure from the specifications of the contract does not by itself preclude some recovery for the contractor on the "cost of completion" basis but rather is a factor in consideration of whether there was substantial performance by the contractor.[13]

(B) Fault of Complaining Party. A party cannot complain that a performance was defective when the performance follows the terms of the contract required by the complaining party. Thus, a homeowner who supplied the specifications for poured cement walls could not hold a contractor liable for damages when the walls that were poured in exact compliance with those specifications proved defective.

(c) Performance to the Satisfaction of the Contracting Party or a Third Party. Sometimes an agreement requires performance to the satisfaction, taste, or judgment of the other party to the contract. When the contract specifically stipulates that the performance must satisfy the contracting party, the courts will ordinarily enforce the plain meaning of the language of the parties and the work must satisfy the contracting party—subject, of course, to the requirement that dissatisfaction be made in good faith. **For Example,** the Perrones' written contract to purchase the Hills' residence contained a clause making performance subject to inspection to the

---

[11] See *Jacob & Youngs, Inc. v. Kent,* 230 N.Y. 239 (1921).
[12] *Superior Wall and Paver, LLC. v. Gacek,* 73 So.3d 43 (Ala. App. 2011).
[13] But see *USX Corp. v. M. DeMatteo Construction Co.,* 315 F.3d 43 (1st Cir. 2002), for application of a common law rule that prohibits a construction contractor guilty of a willful breach of contract from maintaining any suit on the contract against the other party.

Perrones' satisfaction. During the house inspection, the inspector found a piece of wood in a crawl space that appeared to have been damaged by termites and had possibly been treated some 18 years before with chlordane. At the end of the inspection Mr. Perrone indicated that he would perform on the contract. Thereafter, he went on the Internet and found that chlordane is a highly toxic pesticide now banned from use as a termite treatment. As a result, the Perrones rescinded the contract under the buyer satisfaction clause. The Hills sued, believing that speculation about a pesticide treatment 18 years ago was absurd. They contended that the Perrones had breached the contract without a valid reason. The court decided for the Perrones, since they exercised the "satisfaction clause" in good faith.[14] Good-faith personal satisfaction is generally required when the subject matter of the contract is personal, such as interior design work, tailoring, or the painting of a portrait.

With respect to things mechanical or routine performances, courts require that the performance be such as would satisfy a reasonable person under the circumstances.

When work is to be done subject to the approval of an architect, engineer, or another expert, most courts apply the reasonable person test of satisfaction.

C. Discharge by Action of Parties

Contracts may be discharged by the joint action of both contracting parties or, in some cases, by the action of one party alone.

6. Discharge by Unilateral Action

Ordinarily, a contract cannot be discharged by the action of either party alone. In some cases, however, the contract gives one of either party the right to cancel the contract by unilateral action, such as by notice to the other party. Insurance policies covering loss commonly provide that the insurer may cancel the policy upon giving a specified number of days' notice.

(A) Consumer Protection Rescission. A basic principle of contract law is that once made, a contract between competent persons is a binding obligation. Consumer protection legislation introduces into the law a contrary concept—that of giving the consumer a chance to think things over and to rescind the contract. Thus, the federal Consumer Credit Protection Act (CCPA) gives the debtor the right to rescind a credit transaction within three business days when the transaction would impose a lien on the debtor's home. **For Example,** a homeowner who mortgages his or her home to obtain a loan may cancel the transaction for any reason by notifying the lender before midnight of the third full business day after the loan is made.[15]

A Federal Trade Commission regulation gives the buyer three business days in which to cancel a home-solicited sale of goods or services costing more than $25.[16]

---

[14] *Hill v. Perrones*, 42 P.3d 210 (Kan. App. 2002).
[15] If the owner is not informed of this right to cancel, the three-day period does not begin until that information is given. Consumer Credit Protection Act §125, 15 U.S.C. §1635(a), (e), (f).
[16] C.F.R. §429.1.

7. Discharge by Agreement

A contract may be discharged by the operation of one of its provisions or by a subsequent agreement. Thus, there may be a discharge by (1) the terms of the original contract, such as a provision that the contract should end on a specified date; (2) a mutual cancellation, in which the parties agree to end their contract; (3) a mutual **rescission**, in which the parties agree to annul the contract and return both parties to their original positions before the contract had been made; (4) the **substitution** of a new contract between the same parties; (5) a novation or substitution of a new contract involving a new party;[17] (6) an **accord and satisfaction**; (7) a release; or (8) a **waiver**.

rescission – action of one party to a contract to set the contract aside when the other party is guilty of a breach of the contract.

substitution – substitution of a new contract between the same parties.

accord and satisfaction – agreement to substitute for an existing debt some alternative form of discharging that debt, coupled with the actual discharge of the debt by the substituted performance.

waiver – release or relinquishment of a known right or objection.

(A) Substitution. The parties may decide that their contract is not the one they want. They may then replace it with another contract. If they do, the original contract is discharged by substitution.[18]

(B) Accord and Satisfaction. When the parties have differing views as to the performance required by the terms of a contract, they may agree to a different performance. Such an agreement is called an *accord*. When the accord is performed or executed, there is an accord and satisfaction, which discharges the original obligation. To constitute an accord and satisfaction, there must be a bona fide dispute, a proposal to settle the dispute, and performance of the agreement.

CASE SUMMARY

A Full Court Press to No Avail

FACTS: In September 2002, La Crosse Litho Supply, LLC (La Crosse) entered into a distribution agreement with MKL Pre-Press Electronics (MKL) for the distribution of a printing system. La Crosse purchased a 7000 System unit from MKL for its end user Printing Plus. MKL technicians were to provide service and training for the unit. The 7000 System at Printing Plus failed on three occasions, and ultimately repairs were unsuccessful. On September 30, 2003, La Crosse canceled the distribution agreement. On October 2, 2003, La Crosse sent a letter to MKL's sales vice president Bill Landwer setting forth an itemized accounting of what it owed MKL Pre-Press with deductions for the purchase price of the failed 7000 System and other offsets. MKL sent a subsequent bill for repairs and services, to which La Crosse objected and stated that it would not pay. MKL's attorney sent a demand letter for $26,453.31. La Crosse's president, Randall Peters, responded by letter dated December 30, 2003, explaining that with an offset for training and warranty work it had performed, "we are sending you the final payment in the amount of $1,696.47." He added, "[w]ith this correspondence, we consider all open issues between La Crosse Litho Supply and MKL Pre-Press closed." Enclosed with the letter was a check for $1,696.47 payable to MKL Pre-Press. In the remittance portion of the check, under the heading "Ref," was typed "FINAL PAYM." The check was endorsed and deposited on either January 26 or 27, 2004. MKL sued La Crosse for $24,756.84. La Crosse defended that the tender and subsequent deposit of the check for $1,696.47 constituted an accord and satisfaction. Jill Fleming, MKL's office manager, stated that it was her duty to process checks and that she did not read Peters' letter. From a judgment for La Crosse, MKL appealed.

---

[17] *Eagle Industries, Inc. v. Thompson*, 900 P.2d 475 (Or. 1995). In a few jurisdictions, the term *novation* is used to embrace the substitution of any new contract, whether between the original parties or not.
[18] *Shawnee Hospital Authority v. Dow Construction, Inc.*, 812 P.2d 1351 (Okla. 1990).

CASE SUMMARY

Continued

DECISION: Judgment for La Crosse. There was an honest dispute as to the amount owed, as evident from the exchange of letters. La Crosse tendered an amount with the explicit understanding that it was the "final payment" of all demands, and the creditor MKL's acceptance and negotiation of a check for that amount constitutes an accord and satisfaction. Ms. Fleming had the authority to endorse checks and deposit them, and her doing so can and should be imputed to her employer, thereby constituting an accord and satisfaction. [*MKL Pre-Press Electronics v. La Crosse Litho Supply, LLC*, 840 N.E.2d 687 (Ill. App. 2005)]

D. DISCHARGE BY EXTERNAL CAUSES

Circumstances beyond the control of the contracting parties may discharge the contract.

8. Discharge by Impossibility

To establish impossibility a party must show (1) the unexpected occurrence of an intervening act; (2) that the risk of the unexpected occurrence was not allocated by agreement or custom; and (3) that the occurrence made performance impossible. The doctrine of impossibility relieves nonperformance only in extreme circumstances.[19] The party asserting the defense of impossibility bears the burden of proving "a real impossibility and not a mere inconvenience or unexpected difficulty."[20] Moreover, courts will generally only excuse nonperformance where performance is objectively impossible—that is, incapable performance by anyone. Financial inability to perform a contract that a party voluntarily entered into will rarely, if ever, excuse nonperformance. **For Example,** Ms. Robinson was employed by East Capital Community Development Group under a written employment contract for one year, but was terminated early for lack of funding. The contract did not reference that her continued employment was contingent on continued grant funding. The contract was objectively capable of performance. The defense of impossibility was rejected by the court.[21]

(A) DESTRUCTION OF PARTICULAR SUBJECT MATTER. When parties contract expressly for, or with reference to, a particular subject matter, the contract is discharged if the subject matter is destroyed through no fault of either party. When a contract calls for the sale of a wheat crop growing on a specific parcel of land, the contract is discharged if that crop is destroyed by blight.

On the other hand, if there is merely a contract to sell a given quantity of a specified grade of wheat, the seller is not discharged when the seller's crop is destroyed by blight. The seller had made an unqualified undertaking to deliver wheat of a specified grade. No restrictions or qualifications were imposed as to the source. If the seller does not deliver the goods called for by the contract, the contract is broken, and the seller is liable for damages.

---

[19] *Island Development Corp. v. District of Columbia*, 933 A.2d 340, 350 (D.C. 2007).
[20] *Bergmann v. Parker*, 216 A.2d 581 (D.C. 1966).
[21] *East Capital View Community Development Corp. v. Robinson*, 941 A.2d 1036 (D.C. 2008).

(B) Change of Law. A contract is discharged when its performance is made illegal by a subsequent change in the law. Thus, a contract to construct a nonfireproof building at a particular place is discharged by the adoption of a zoning law prohibiting such a building within that area. Mere inconvenience or temporary delay caused by the new law, however, does not excuse performance.

(C) Death or Disability. When the contract obligates a party to render or receive personal services requiring peculiar skill, the death, incapacity, or illness of the party that was either to render or receive the personal services excuses both sides from a duty to perform. It is sometimes said that "the death of either party is the death of the contract."

The rule does not apply, however, when the acts called for by the contract are of such a character that (1) the acts may be as well performed by others, such as the promisor's personal representatives, or (2) the contract's terms contemplate continuance of the obligations after the death of one of the parties. **For Example,** Lynn Jones was under contract to investor Ed Jenkins to operate certain Subway sandwich shops and to acquire new franchises with funding provided by Jenkins. After Jenkins's death, Jones claimed he was no longer bound under the contract and was free to pursue franchise opportunities on his own. The contract between Jones and Jenkins expressed that it was binding on the parties' "heirs and assigns" and that the contract embodied property rights that passed to Jenkins's widow. The agreement's provisions thus established that the agreement survived the death of Jenkins, and Jones was therefore obligated to remit profits from the franchise he acquired for himself after Jenkins's death.[22]

(D) Act of Other Party. Every contract contains "an implied covenant of good faith and fair dealing." As a result of this covenant, a promisee is under an obligation to do nothing that would interfere with the promisor's performance. When the promisee prevents performance or otherwise makes performance impossible, the promisor is discharged from the contract. Thus, a subcontractor is discharged from any obligation when it is unable to do the work because the principal contractor refuses to deliver the material, equipment, or money required by the subcontract. When the default of the other party consists of failing to supply goods or services, the duty may rest on the party claiming a discharge of the contract to show that substitute goods or services could not be obtained elsewhere.

9. Developing Doctrines

Commercial impracticability and frustration of purpose may excuse performance.

(A) Commercial Impracticability. The doctrine of *commercial impracticability* was developed to deal with the harsh rule that a party must perform its contracts unless it is absolutely impossible. However, not every type of impracticability is an excuse for nonperformance. **For Example,** I. Patel was bound by his franchise agreement with Days Inn, Inc., to maintain his 60-room inn on old Route 66 in Lincoln, Illinois, to at least minimum quality assurance standards. His inn failed five consecutive quality inspections over two years, with the inspector noting damaged guest rooms, burns in the bedding, and severely stained carpets. Patel's defense when his franchise was canceled after the fifth failed inspection was that bridge

---

[22] *Jenkins Subway, Inc. v. Jones,* 990 S.W.2d 713 (Tenn. App. 1998).

repairs on the road leading from I-55 to his inn had adversely affected his business and made it commercially impractical to live up to the franchise agreement. The court rejected his defense, determining that while the bridge work might have affected patronage, it had no effect on his duty to comply with the quality assurance standards of his franchise agreement.[23] Commercial impracticability is available only when the performance is made impractical by the subsequent occurrence of an event whose nonoccurrence was a basic assumption on which the contract was made.[24]

The defense of commercial impractability will not relieve sophisticated business entities from their contractual obligations due to an economic downturn, even one as drastic and severe as the recent recession. **For Example,** real estate developer Beemer Associates was not excused under this doctrine of commercial impracticability from performance of its construction loan payment obligation of $5,250,000 plus interest and fees where unanticipated changes in the financial and real estate markets made it unable to secure tenants at the expected rate.[25] Economic downturns and other market shifts do not constitute unanticipated circumstances in a market economy.[26]

(B) FRUSTRATION OF PURPOSE DOCTRINE. Because of a change in circumstances, the purpose of the contract may have no value to the party entitled to receive performance. In such a case, performance may be excused if both parties were aware of the purpose and the event that frustrated the purpose was unforeseeable.[27]

For Example, National Southern Bank rents a home near Willowbend Country Club on the southeastern shore of North Carolina for $75,000 a week to entertain business guests at the Ryder Cup matches scheduled for the week in question. Storm damage from Hurricane David the week before the event caused the closing of the course and the transfer of the tournament to another venue in a different state. The bank's duty to pay for the house may be excused by the doctrine of *frustration of purpose,* because the transfer of the tournament fully destroyed the value of the home rental, both parties were aware of the purpose of the rental, and the cancellation of the golf tournament was unforeseeable.

CASE SUMMARY

Relief for Broken Dreams

FACTS: John J. Paonessa Company made a contract with the state of Massachusetts to reconstruct a portion of highway. Paonessa then made a contract with Chase Precast Corporation to obtain concrete median barriers for use in the highway. Thereafter, the state highway department decided that such barriers would not be used. Paonessa therefore had no reason to go through with the contract to purchase the barriers from Chase because it could not use them and could not get paid for them by the state. Chase sued Paonessa for the profit Chase would have made on the contract for the barriers.

---

[23] *Days Inn of America, Inc. v. Patel,* 88 F. Supp. 2d 928 (C.D. Ill. 2000).

[24] See Restatement (Second) of Contracts §261; U.C.C. §2-615.

[25] *LSREF2 Baron, LLC v. Beemer,* 2011 WL 6838163 (M.D. Fla. Dec. 29, 2011).

[26] *Flathead-Michigan I, LLC v. Peninsula Dev., LLC,* 2011 WL 940048 (E.D. Mich. March 16, 2011).

[27] The defense of frustration of purpose, or commercial frustration, is very difficult to invoke because the courts are extremely reluctant to allow parties to avoid obligations to which they have agreed. See *Wal-Mart Stores, Inc. v. AIG Life Insurance Co.,* 872 A.2d 611 (Del. Ch. 2005), denying application of the commercial frustration doctrine when the supervening event, the invalidation of hundreds of millions in tax deductions by the IRS, was reasonably foreseeable and could have been provided for in the contract.

CASE SUMMARY

Continued

DECISION: Judgment for Paonessa. The change to the highway construction plan made by the State Department of Highways made the barriers worthless. There was accordingly a frustration of the purpose for which the contract had been made to purchase the barriers. Therefore, the contract for the median barriers was discharged by such frustration of purpose and did not bind Paonessa. [*Chase Precast Corp. v. John J. Paonessa Co., Inc.,* **566 N.E.2d 603 (Mass. 1991)**]

(c) COMPARISON TO COMMON LAW RULE. The traditional common law rule refuses to recognize commercial impracticability or frustration of purpose. By the common law rule, the losses and disappointments against which commercial impracticability and frustration of purpose give protection are merely the risks that one takes in entering into a contract. Moreover, the situations could have been guarded against by including an appropriate condition subsequent in the contract. A condition subsequent declares that the contract will be void if a specified event occurs.[28] The contract also could have provided for a readjustment of compensation if there was a basic change of circumstances. The common law approach also rejects these developing concepts because they weaken the stability of a contract.

An indication of a wider recognition of the concept that "extreme" changes of circumstances can discharge a contract is found in the Uniform Commercial Code. The UCC provides for the discharge of a contract for the sale of goods when a condition that the parties assumed existed, or would continue, ceases to exist.[29]

(d) FORCE MAJEURE. To avoid litigation over impossibility and impractability issues, modern contracting parties often contract around the doctrine of impossibility, specifying the failures that will excuse performance in their contracts. The clauses in which they do this are called *force majeure*—uncontrollable event—clauses. And they are enforced by courts as written.

CASE SUMMARY

WEPCO Was Not Railroaded, It Was *Force Majeured!*

FACTS: WEPCO, an electric utility, sued the Union Pacific Railroad Co. alleging that the railroad breached the *force majeure* provision of the parties' long-term coal-hauling contract, which ran from 1999 to 2005. The provision at issue provides that if the railroad is prevented by "an event of Force Majeure" from reloading its empty cars (after it has delivered coal to WEPCO) with iron ore destined for Geneva, Utah, it can charge the higher rate that the contract makes applicable to shipments that do not involve backhauling. The rate for coal shipped from one of the Colorado coal mines to WEPCO was specified as $13.20 per ton if there was a backhaul shipment but $15.63 if there was not. The iron ore that the railroad's freight trains would have

---

[28] *Wermer v. ABI,* 10 S.W.3d 575 (Mo. App. 2000).
[29] U.C.C. §2-615.

CASE SUMMARY

Continued

picked up in Minnesota was intended for a steel mill in Utah. The steel company was bankrupt when the parties signed the contract. In November 2001 the steel mill shut down, and closed for good in February 2004. Two months later the railroad wrote WEPCO to declare "an event of Force Majeure" and that henceforth it would be charging WEPCO the higher rate applicable to shipments without a backhaul. WEPCO sued the railroad for breach of the force majeure provision in the contract.

DECISION: Judgment for the railroad. The provision dealt with the foreseeable situation of the steel mill shutdown and the possibility of hauling back to the mine empty coal cars, thereby generating no revenue. The contract clause is enforced as written. [***Wisconsin Electric Power Co. v. Union Pacific Railroad Co.,*** **557 F.3d 504 (7th Cir. 2009)**]

10. Temporary Impossibility

Ordinarily, a temporary impossibility suspends the duty to perform. If the obligation to perform is suspended, it is revived on the termination of the impossibility. If, however, performance at that later date would impose a substantially greater burden on the party obligated to perform, some courts discharge the obligor from the contract.

After the September 11, 2001, terrorist attack on the World Trade Center, New York City courts followed wartime precedents that had developed the law of temporary impossibility. Such impossibility, when of brief duration, excuses performance until it subsequently becomes possible to perform rather than excusing performance altogether. Thus, an individual who was unable to communicate her cancellation of travel 60 days prior to her scheduled travel as required by her contract, which needed to occur on or before September 14, 2001, could expect relief from a cancellation penalty provision in the contract based on credible testimony of attempted phone calls to the travel agent on and after September 12, 2001, even though the calls did not get through due to communication problems in New York City.[30]

(A) WEATHER. Acts of God, such as tornadoes, lightning, and floods, usually do not terminate a contract even though they make performance difficult. Thus, weather conditions constitute a risk that is assumed by a contracting party in the absence of a contrary agreement. Consequently, extra expense sustained by a contractor because of weather conditions is a risk that the contractor assumes in the absence of an express provision for additional compensation in such a case. **For Example,** Danielo Contractors made a contract to construct a shopping mall for the Rubicon Center, with construction to begin November 1. Because of abnormal cold and blizzard conditions, Danielo was not able to begin work until April 1 and was five months late in completing the construction of the project. Rubicon sued Danielo for breach of contract by failing to perform on schedule. Danielo is liable. Because the contract

---

[30] See *Bugh v. Protravel International, Inc.,* 746 N.Y.S.2d 290 (Civ. Ct. N.Y.C. 2002).

included no provision covering delay caused by weather, Danielo bore the risk of the delay and resulting loss.

Modern contracts commonly contain a "weather clause" and reflect the parties' agreement on this matter. When the parties take the time to discuss weather issues, purchasing insurance coverage is a common resolution.

11. Discharge by Operation of Law

operation of law – attaching of certain consequences to certain facts because of legal principles that operate automatically as contrasted with consequences that arise because of the voluntary action of a party designed to create those consequences.

A contract is discharged by **operation of law** by (1) an alteration or a material change made by a party, (2) the destruction of the written contract with intent to discharge it, (3) bankruptcy, (4) the operation of a statute of limitations, or (5) a contractual limitation.

(A) BANKRUPTCY. As set forth in the chapter on bankruptcy, even though all creditors have not been paid in full, a discharge in **bankruptcy** eliminates ordinary contract claims against the debtor.

CPA

bankruptcy – procedure by which one unable to pay debts may surrender all assets in excess of any exemption claim to the court for administration and distribution to creditors, and the debtor is given a discharge that releases him from the unpaid balance due on most debts.

statute of limitations – statute that restricts the period of time within which an action may be brought.

(B) STATUTE OF LIMITATIONS. A **statute of limitations** provides that after a certain number of years have passed, a contract claim is barred. The time limitation provided by state statutes of limitations varies widely. The time period for bringing actions for breach of an oral contract is two to three years. The period may differ with the type of contract—ranging from a relatively short time for open accounts (ordinary customers' charge accounts) to four years for sales of goods.[31] A somewhat longer period exists for bringing actions for breach of written contracts (usually four to ten years). **For Example,** Prate Installations, Inc., sued homeowners Richard and Rebecca Thomas for failure to pay for a new roof installed by Prate. Prate had sent numerous invoices to the Thomases over a four-year period seeking payment to no avail. The Thomases moved to dismiss the case under a four-year limitation period. However, the court concluded that the state's ten-year limitations period on written contracts applied.[32] The maximum period for judgments of record is usually 10 to 20 years.

A breach of contract claim against a builder begins to run when a home's construction is substantially complete. **For Example,** a breach of contract claim against home builder Stewart Brockett was time barred under a state's six-year statute of limitations for breach of contract actions inasmuch as the home in question was substantially completed in September 2001 and the breach of contract action commenced on June 17, 2008.[33]

(C) CONTRACTUAL LIMITATIONS. Some contracts, particularly insurance contracts, contain a time limitation within which suit must be brought. This is in effect a private statute of limitations created by the agreement of the parties.

A contract may also require that notice of any claim be given within a specified time. A party who fails to give notice within the time specified by the contract is barred from suing on the contract.

A contract provision requiring that suit be brought within one year does not violate public policy, although the statute of limitations would allow two years in the absence of such a contract limitation.[34]

---

[31] U.C.C. §2-725(1).
[32] *Prate Installations, Inc. v. Thomas,* 842 N.E.2d 1205 (Ill. App. 2006).
[33] *New York Central Mutual Fire Insurance Co. v. Gilder Oil Co.,* 936 N.Y.S. 2d 815 (Sup.Ct. A.D. 2011).
[34] *Keiting v. Skauge,* 543 N.W.2d 565 (Wis. App. 1995).

LawFlix

Uncle Buck (1989) (PG-13)

John Candy plays ne'er-do-well Uncle Buck who promises to go to work at his girlfriend's tire store and marry her. When his brother calls in the middle of the night seeking help with his children, Buck tells his girlfriend (Chenise) that he can no longer honor his promise because he must go to the suburbs to care for his brother's children while his brother and sister-in-law travel to Indiana to be with his sister-in-law's very ill father. Discuss Buck's excuse. Is it impossibility? Does the change in circumstances excuse Buck?

MAKE THE CONNECTION

SUMMARY

A party's duty to perform under a contract can be affected by a condition precedent, which must occur before a party has an obligation to perform; a condition subsequent, that is, a condition or event that relieves the duty to thereafter perform; and concurrent conditions, which require mutual and often simultaneous performance.

Most contracts are discharged by performance. An offer to perform is called a *tender of performance*. If a tender of performance is wrongfully refused, the duty of the tenderer to perform is terminated. When the performance called for by the contract is the payment of money, it must be legal tender that is offered. In actual practice, it is common to pay and to accept payment by checks or other commercial paper.

When the debtor owes the creditor on several accounts and makes a payment, the debtor may specify which account is to be credited with the payment. If the debtor fails to specify, the creditor may choose which account to credit.

When a contract does not state when it is to be performed, it must be performed within a reasonable time. If time for performance is stated in the contract, the contract must be performed at the time specified if such time is essential (is of the essence). Ordinarily, a contract must be performed exactly in the manner specified by the contract. A less-than-perfect performance is allowed if it is a substantial performance and if damages are allowed the other party.

A contract cannot be discharged by unilateral action unless authorized by the contract itself or by statute, as in the case of consumer protection rescission.

Because a contract arises from an agreement, it may also be terminated by an agreement. A contract may also be discharged by the substitution of a new contract for the original contract; by a novation, or making a new contract with a new party; by accord and satisfaction; by release; or by waiver.

A contract is discharged when it is impossible to perform. Impossibility may result from the destruction of the subject matter of the contract, the adoption of a new law that prohibits performance, the death or disability of a party whose personal action was required for performance of the contract, or the act of the other party to the contract. Some courts will also hold that a contract is discharged when its performance is commercially impracticable or there is frustration of purpose. Temporary impossibility, such as a labor strike or bad weather, has no effect on a contract. It is common, though, to include protective clauses that excuse delay caused by temporary impossibility.

A contract may be discharged by operation of law. This occurs when (1) the liability arising from the contract is discharged by bankruptcy, (2) suit on the contract is barred by the applicable statute of limitations, or (3) a time limitation stated in the contract is exceeded.

LEARNING OUTCOMES

After studying this chapter, you should be able to clearly explain:

A. Conditions Relating to Performance

L0.1 List the three types of conditions that affect a party's duty to perform
See the "pay-if-paid" condition-precedent example on p. 379.
See the TV anchor's "failed urinalysis test" condition-subsequent example on p. 380.

B. Discharge by Performance

L0.2 Explain the on-time performance rule
See the "mailed payment" example on p. 382.
See the "time is of the essence" example on p. 383.

L0.3 Explain the adequacy of performance rules
See the application of the substantial performance rule to the nonconforming new home piping example, pp. 383–385.

See the effect of failure to substantially perform a contract in the *Superior Wall and Paver* case, p. 385.

C. Discharge by Action of Parties

L0.4 Explain four ways a contract can be discharged by agreement of the parties
See the text discussion on rescission, cancellation, substitution, and novation on p. 387.

D. Discharge by External Causes

L0.5 State the effect on a contract of the death or disability of one of the contracting parties
See the Subway Sandwich Shops example on p. 389.

L0.6 Explain when impossibility or impracticability may discharge a contract
See the Ryder Cup frustration-of-purpose example on p. 390.

KEY TERMS

accord and satisfaction
bankruptcy
condition
condition precedent
condition subsequent

operation of law
rescission
statute of limitations
substantial performance
substitution

tender
waiver

QUESTIONS AND CASE PROBLEMS

1. CIT entered into a sale/leaseback contract with Condere Tire Corporation for 11 tire presses at Condere's tire plant in Natchez, Mississippi. Condere ceased making payments on these presses owned by CIT, and Condere filed for Chapter 11 bankruptcy. CIT thereafter contracted to sell the presses to Specialty Tires Inc., for $250,000. When the contract was made, CIT, Condere, and Specialty Tire believed that CIT was the owner of the presses and was entitled to immediate possession. When CIT attempted to gain access to the presses to have them shipped, Condere changed its position and

refused to allow the equipment to be removed from the plant. When the presses were not delivered, Specialty sued CIT for damages for nondelivery of the presses, and CIT asserted the defense of impracticability. Decide. [*Specialty Tires, Inc. v. CIT*, 82 F. Supp. 2d 434 (W.D. Pa.)]

2. Lymon Mitchell operated a Badcock Home Furnishings dealership, under which as dealer he was paid a commission on sales and Badcock retained title to merchandise on display. Mitchell sold his dealership to another and to facilitate the sale, Badcock prepared a summary of

commissions owed with certain itemized offsets it claimed that Mitchell owed Badcock. Mitchell disagreed with the calculations, but he accepted them and signed the transfer documents closing the sale on the basis of the terms set forth in the summary and was paid accordingly. After pondering the offsets taken by Badcock and verifying the correctness of his position, he brought suit for the additional funds owed. What defense would you expect Badcock to raise? How would you decide the case? Explain fully. [*Mitchell v. Badcock Corp.*, 496 S.E.2d 502 (Ga. App.)]

3. American Bank loaned Koplik $50,000 to buy equipment for a restaurant about to be opened by Casual Citchen Corp. The loan was not repaid, and Fast Foods, Inc., bought out the interest of Casual Citchen. As part of the transaction, Fast Foods agreed to pay the debt owed to American Bank, and the parties agreed to a new schedule of payments to be made by Fast Foods. Fast Foods did not make the payments, and American Bank sued Koplik. He contended that his obligation to repay $50,000 had been discharged by the execution of the agreement providing for the payment of the debt by Fast Foods. Was this defense valid? [*American Bank & Trust Co. v. Koplik*, 451 N.Y.S.2d 426 (A. D.)]

4. Metalcrafters made a contract to design a new earth-moving vehicle for Lamar Highway Construction Co. Metalcrafters was depending on the genius of Samet, the head of its research department, to design a new product. Shortly after the contract was made between Metalcrafters and Lamar, Samet was killed in an automobile accident. Metalcrafters was not able to design the product without Samet. Lamar sued Metalcrafters for damages for breach of the contract. Metalcrafters claimed that the contract was discharged by Samet's death. Is it correct?

5. The Tinchers signed a contract to sell land to Creasy. The contract specified that the sales transaction was to be completed in 90 days. At the end of the 90 days, Creasy requested an extension of time. The Tinchers refused to grant an extension and stated that the contract was terminated. Creasy claimed that the 90-day

clause was not binding because the contract did not state that time was of the essence. Was the contract terminated? [*Creasy v. Tincher*, 173 S.E.2d 332 (W. Va.)]

6. Christopher Bloom received a medical school scholarship created by the U.S. Department of Health and Human Services to increase the number of doctors serving rural areas. In return for this assistance, Bloom agreed to practice four years in a region identified as being underserved by medical professionals. After some problem with his postgraduation assignment, Bloom requested a repayment schedule from the agency. Although no terms were offered, Bloom tendered to the agency two checks totaling $15,500 and marked "Final Payment." Neither check was cashed, and the government sued Bloom for $480,000, the value of the assistance provided. Bloom claimed that by tendering the checks to the agency, his liability had been discharged by an accord and satisfaction. Decide. [*United States v. Bloom*, 112 F.3d 200 (7th Cir.)]

7. Dickson contracted to build a house for Moran. When it was approximately 25 percent to 40 percent completed, Moran would not let Dickson work any more because he was not following the building plans and specifications and there were many defects. Moran hired another contractor to correct the defects and finish the building. Dickson sued Moran for breach of contract, claiming that he had substantially performed the contract up to the point where he had been discharged. Was Dickson correct? [*Dickson v. Moran*, 344 So.2d 102 (La. App.)]

8. A lessor leased a trailer park to a tenant. At the time, sewage was disposed of by a septic tank system that was not connected with the public sewage system. The tenant knew this, and the lease declared that the tenant had examined the premises and that the landlord made no representation or guarantee as to the condition of the premises. Some time thereafter, the septic tank system stopped working properly, and the county health department notified the tenant that he was required to connect the septic tank system with the public sewage system or else the

department would close the trailer park. The tenant did not want to pay the additional cost involved in connecting with the public system. The tenant claimed that he was released from the lease and was entitled to a refund of the deposit that he had made. Was he correct? [*Glen R. Sewell Street Metal v. Loverde*, 451 P.2d 721 (Cal. App.)]

9. Oneal was a teacher employed by the Colton Consolidated School District. Because of a diabetic condition, his eyesight deteriorated so much that he offered to resign if he would be given pay for a specified number of "sick leave" days. The school district refused to do this and discharged Oneal for nonperformance of his contract. He appealed to remove the discharge from his record. Decide. What ethical values are involved? [*Oneal v. Colton Consolidated School District*, 557 P.2d 11 (Wash. App.)]

10. Northwest Construction, Inc., made a contract with the state of Washington for highway construction. Part of the work was turned over under a subcontract to Yakima Asphalt Paving Co. The contract required that any claim be asserted within 180 days. Yakima brought an action for damages after the expiration of 180 days. The defense was that the claim was too late. Yakima replied that the action was brought within the time allowed by the statute of limitations and that the contractual limitation of 180 days was therefore not binding. Was Yakima correct?

11. The Metropolitan Park District of Tacoma gave Griffith a concession to run the district's parks. The agreement gave the right to occupy the parks and use any improvements found therein. The district later wished to set this agreement aside because it was not making sufficient money from the transaction. While it was seeking to set the agreement aside, a boathouse and a gift shop in one of the parks were destroyed by fire. The district then claimed that the concession contract with Griffith was discharged by impossibility of performance. Was it correct? [*Metropolitan Park District of Tacoma v. Griffith*, 723 P.2d 1093 (Wash.)]

12. Suburban Power Piping Corp., under contract to construct a building for LTV Steel Corp., made a subcontract with Power & Pollution Services, Inc., to do some of the work. The subcontract provided that the subcontractor would be paid when the owner (LTV) paid the contractor. LTV went into bankruptcy before making the full payment to the contractor, who then refused to pay the subcontractor on the ground that the "pay-when-paid" provision of the subcontract made payment by the owner a condition precedent to the obligation of the contractor to pay the subcontractor. Was the contractor correct? [*Power & Pollution Services, Inc. v. Suburban Power Piping Corp.*, 598 N.E.2d 69 (Ohio App.)]

13. Ellen borrowed money from Farmers' Bank. As evidence of the loan, she signed a promissory note by which she promised to pay to the bank in installments the amount of the loan together with interest and administrative costs. She was unable to make the payments on the scheduled dates. She and the bank then executed a new agreement that gave her a longer period of time for making the payments. However, after two months, she was unable to pay on this new schedule. The bank then brought suit against her under the terms of the original agreement. She raised the defense that the original agreement had been discharged by the execution of the second agreement and could not be sued on. Decide.

14. Beeson Company made a contract to construct a shopping center for Sartori. Before the work was fully completed, Sartori stopped making the payments to Beeson that the contract required. The contract provided for liquidated damages of $1,000 per day if Beeson failed to substantially complete the project within 300 days of the beginning of construction. The contract also provided for a bonus of $1,000 for each day Beeson completed the project ahead of schedule. Beeson stopped working and sued Sartori for the balance due under the contract, just as though it had been fully performed. Sartori defended on the ground that Beeson had not substantially completed the work. Beeson proved that Sartori had been able to rent most of the stores in the

center. Was there substantial performance of the contract? If so, what would be the measure of damages? [*J.M. Beeson Co. v. Sartori*, 553 So.2d 180 (Fla. App.)]

15. New Beginnings provides rehabilitation services for alcohol and drug abuse to both adults and adolescents. New Beginnings entered into negotiation with Adbar for the lease of a building in the city of St. Louis, and subsequently entered into a three-year lease. The total rent due for the three-year term was $273,000. After the lease was executed, the city denied an occupancy permit because Alderman Bosley and residents testified at a hearing in vigorous opposition to the presence of New Beginnings in the neighborhood. A court ordered the permit issued. Alderman Bosley thereafter contacted the chair of the state's appointment committee and asked her to pull the agency's funding. He received no commitment from her on this matter. After a meeting with the state director of Alcohol and Drug Abuse where it was asserted that the director said the funding would be pulled if New Beginnings moved into the Adbar location, New Beginnings's board decided not to occupy the building. Adbar brought suit for breach of the lease, and New Beginnings asserted it was excused from performance because of commercial impracticability and frustration of purpose. Do you believe the doctrine of commercial impracticability should be limited in its application so as to preserve the certainty of contracts? What rule of law applies to this case? Decide. [*Adbar v. New Beginnings*, 103 S.W.2d 799 (Mo. App.)]

CPA QUESTIONS

1. Parc hired Glaze to remodel and furnish an office suite. Glaze submitted plans that Parc approved. After completing all the necessary construction and painting, Glaze purchased minor accessories that Parc rejected because they did not conform to the plans. Parc refused to allow Glaze to complete the project and refused to pay Glaze any part of the contract price. Glaze sued for the value of the work performed. Which of the following statements is correct?

   a. Glaze will lose because Glaze breached the contract by not completing performance.

   b. Glaze will win because Glaze substantially performed and Parc prevented complete performance.

   c. Glaze will lose because Glaze materially breached the contract by buying the accessories.

   d. Glaze will win because Parc committed anticipatory breach.

2. Ordinarily, in an action for breach of a construction contract, the statute of limitations time period would be computed from the date the contract is:

   a. Negotiated.

   b. Breached.

   c. Begun.

   d. Signed.

3. Which of the following will release all original parties to a contract but will maintain a contractual relationship?

	Novation	Substituted contract
a.	Yes	Yes
b.	Yes	No
c.	No	Yes
d.	No	No

© Manuel Gutjahr/iStockphoto.com

Chapter 20

Breach of Contract and Remedies

learningoutcomes

After studying this chapter, you should be able to

LO.1 Explain what constitutes a breach of contract and an anticipatory breach of contract

LO.2 Describe the effect of a waiver of a breach

LO.3 Explain the range of remedies available for breach of contract

LO.4 Explain when liquidated damages clauses are valid and invalid

LO.5 State when liability-limiting clauses and releases are valid

W

hat can be done when a contract is broken?

A. WHAT CONSTITUTES A BREACH OF CONTRACT?

The question of remedies does not become important until it is first determined that a contract has been violated or breached.

1. Definition of Breach

breach – failure to act or perform in the manner called for in a contract.

A **breach** is the failure to act or perform in the manner called for by the contract. When the contract calls for performance, such as painting an owner's home, the failure to paint or to paint properly is a *breach of contract*. If the contract calls for a creditor's forbearance, the creditor's action in bringing a lawsuit is a breach of the contract.

2. Anticipatory Breach

anticipatory breach – promisor's repudiation of the contract prior to the time that performance is required when such repudiation is accepted by the promisee as a breach of the contract.

When the contract calls for performance, a party may make it clear before the time for performance arrives that the contract will not be performed. This is referred to as an **anticipatory breach**.

anticipatory repudiation – repudiation made in advance of the time for performance of the contract obligations.

(A) ANTICIPATORY REPUDIATION. When a party expressly declares that performance will not be made when required, this declaration is called an **anticipatory repudiation** of the contract. To constitute such a repudiation, there must be a clear, absolute, unequivocal refusal to perform the contract according to its terms. **For Example,** Procter & Gamble (P&G) sought payment on four letters of credit issued by a Serbian bank, Investbanka. P&G presented two letters by June 8, prior to their expiration dates, with the necessary documentation for payment to Beogradska Bank New York, Investbanka's New York agent. A June 11 letter from Beogradska Bank broadly and unequivocally stated that the bank would not pay the letters of credit. Two additional letters of credit totaling $20,000 issued by Investbanka that expired by June 30 were not thereafter submitted to the New York agent bank by P&G. However, a court found that the bank had anticipatorily breached its obligations under those letters of credit by its broad renouncements in the June 11 letter, and judgments were rendered in favor of P&G.[1]

CASE SUMMARY

Splitting Tips—Contract Price Less Cost of Completion

FACTS: Hartland Developers, Inc., agreed to build an airplane hangar for Robert Tips of San Antonio for $300,000, payable in three installments of $100,000, with the final payment due upon the completion of the building and the issuance of a certificate of completion by the engineer representing Tips. The evidence shows that Tips's representative, Mr. Lavelle,

---

[1] *Procter & Gamble v. Investbanka*, 2000 WL 520630 (S.D.N.Y. 2000).

CASE SUMMARY

Continued

instructed Hartland to cease work on the building because Tips could no longer afford to make payments. Hartland ceased work as instructed before the final completion of the building, having been paid $200,000 at the time. He sued Tips for breach of contract. On May 6, 1996, the trial court allowed Hartland the amount owing on the contract, $100,000, less the cost of completing the building according to the contract, $65,000, plus attorney fees and prejudgment interest. Tips appealed, pointing out, among other assertions, that he was required to spend $23,000 to provide electrical outlets for the hangar, which were contemplated in the contract.

DECISION: Judgment for Tips, subject to offsets. The trial judge based his damages assessment on anticipatory repudiation of contract. The evidence that Tips's representative, Lavelle, instructed Hartland to cease work on the project because Tips no longer could afford to make payments was sufficient to support this finding. However, Tips is entitled to an offset for electrical connections of $23,000 under a breach of contract theory. [*Tips v. Hartland Developers, Inc.,* **961 S.W.2d 618 (Tex. App. 1998)**]

A refusal to perform a contract that is made before performance is required unless the other party to the contract does an act or makes a concession that is not required by the contract, is an anticipatory repudiation of the contract.[2]

A party making an anticipatory repudiation may retract or take back the repudiation if the other party has not changed position in reliance on the repudiation. However, if the other party has changed position, the party making the anticipatory repudiation cannot retract it. **For Example,** if a buyer makes another purchase when the seller declares that the seller will not perform the contract, the buyer has acted in reliance on the seller's repudiation. The seller will therefore not be allowed to retract the repudiation.

(B) ANTICIPATORY REPUDIATION BY CONDUCT. The anticipatory repudiation may be expressed by conduct that makes it impossible for the repudiating party to perform subsequently. **For Example,** while the Town of Mammoth Lakes, California, was claiming a willingness to move forward with a hotel/condominium project under its contract with the developer, in actuality, the evidence established that town officials refused to move forward and actively sought to undermine the developer's rights under the development contract. The court affirmed a judgment of $30 million in damages and attorneys' fees.[3]

B. WAIVER OF BREACH

The breach of a contract may have no importance because the other party to the contract waives the breach.

---

[2] *Chamberlain v. Puckett Construction*, 921 P.2d 1237 (Mont. 1996).

[3] *Mammoth Lakes Land Acquisition, LLC v. Town of Mammoth Lakes*, 120 Cal. Rptr. 3d 797 (Cal. Ct. of App. 3d Dist. 2010).

3. Cure of Breach by Waiver

The fact that one party has broken a contract does not necessarily mean that there will be a lawsuit or a forfeiture of the contract. For practical business reasons, one party may be willing to ignore or waive the breach. When it is established that there has been a **waiver** of a breach, the party waiving the breach cannot take any action on the theory that the contract was broken. The waiver, in effect, erases the past breach. The contract continues as though the breach had not existed.

The waiver may be express or it may be implied from the continued recognition of the existence of the contract by the aggrieved party.[4] When the conduct of a party shows an intent to give up a right, it waives that right.[5]

waiver—release or relinquishment of a known right or objection.

4. Existence and Scope of Waiver

It is a question of fact whether there has been a waiver.

CASE SUMMARY

Have You Driven a Ford Lately, Jennifer?

FACTS: In 1995, Northland Ford Dealers, an association of dealerships, offered to sponsor a "hole in one" contest at Moccasin Creek Country Club. A banner announced that a hole in one would win a car but gave no other details, and the local dealer parked a Ford Explorer near the banner. Northland paid a $4,602 premium to Continental Hole-In-One, Inc., to ensure the award of the contest prize. The insurance application stated in capital letters that "ALL AMATEUR MEN AND WOMEN WILL UTILIZE THE SAME TEE." And Continental established the men/women yardage for the hole to be 170 yards, but did not make this known to the participants. Jennifer Harms registered for the tournament and paid her entrance fee. At the contest hole, she teed off from the amateur women's red marker, which was a much shorter distance to the pin than the 170 yards from the men's marker—and she made a hole in one. When she inquired about the prize, she was told that because of insurance requirements, all amateurs had to tee off from the amateur men's tee box, and because she had not done so, she was disqualified. Harms, a collegiate golfer at Concordia College, returned there to complete her last year of athletic eligibility and on graduation sued Northland for breach of contract. Northland contends that under NCAA rules, accepting a prize or agreeing to accept a prize would have disqualified Harms from NCAA competition. It also asserts that her continuation of her NCAA competition evinced intent to waive acceptance of the car.

DECISION: Judgment for Harms. Northland must abide by the rules it announced, not by the ones it left unannounced that disqualified all amateur women from the contest. This was a vintage unilateral contract with performance by the offeree as acceptance. Harms earned the prize when she sank her winning shot. Waiver is a volitional relinquishment, by act or word, of a known existing right conferred in law or contract. Harms could not disclaim the prize; it was not hers to refuse. She was told her shot from the wrong tee disqualified her. One can hardly relinquish what was never conferred. Northland's waiver defense is devoid of merit. [*Harms v. Northland Ford Dealers*, **602 N.W.2d 58 (S.D. 1999)**]

(A) EXISTENCE OF WAIVER. A party may express or declare that the breach of a contract is waived. A waiver of a breach is more often the result of an express forgiving of a

---

[4] *Huger v. Morrison*, 809 So.2d 1140 (La. App. 2002).
[5] *Stronghaven Inc. v. Ingram*, 555 S.E.2d 49 (Ga. App. 2001).

breach. Thus, a party allowing the other party to continue performance without objecting that the performance is not satisfactory waives the right to raise that objection when sued for payment by the performing party.

For Example, a contract promising to sell back a parcel of commercial property to Jackson required Jackson to make a $500 payment to Massey's attorney on the first of the month for five months, December through April. It was clearly understood that the payments would be "on time without fail." Jackson made the December payment on time. New Year's Day, a holiday, fell on a Friday, and Jackson made the second payment on January 4. He made $500 payments on February 1, March 1, and March 31, respectively, and the payments were accepted and a receipt issued on each occasion. However, Massey refused to convey title back to Jackson because "the January 4 payment was untimely and the parties' agreement had been breached." The court held that the doctrine of waiver applied due to Massey's acceptance of the late payment and the three subsequent payments without objection, and the court declared that Jackson was entitled to possession of the land.[6]

(b) Scope of Waiver. The waiver of a breach of contract extends only to the matter waived. It does not show any intent to ignore other provisions of the contract.

(c) Antimodification Clause. Modern contracts commonly specify that the terms of a contract shall not be deemed modified by waiver as to any breaches. This means that the original contract remains as agreed to. Either party may therefore return to, and insist on, compliance with the original contract.

In the example involving Jackson and Massey's contract, the trial court reviewed the contract to see whether the court was restricted by the contract from applying the waiver. It concluded: "In this case, the parties' contract did not contain any terms that could prevent the application of the doctrine of waiver to the acceptance of late payments."[7]

5. Reservation of Rights

It may be that a party is willing to accept a defective performance but does not wish to surrender any claim for damages for the breach. **For Example,** Midwest Utilities, Inc., accepted 20 carloads of Powder River Basin coal (sometimes called *Western coal*) from its supplier, Maney Enterprises, because its power plants were in short supply of coal. Midwest's requirements contract with Maney called for Appalachian coal, a low-sulfur, highly efficient fuel, which is sold at a premium price per ton. Midwest, in accepting the tendered performance with a **reservation of rights**, gave notice to Maney that it reserved all rights to pursue damages for the tender of a nonconforming shipment.

reservation of rights – assertion by a party to a contract that even though a tendered performance (e.g., a defective product) is accepted, the right to damages for nonconformity to the contract is reserved.

remedy – action or procedure that is followed in order to enforce a right or to obtain damages for injury to a right.

C. Remedies for Breach of Contract

One or more **remedies** may be available to the innocent party in the case of a breach of contract. There is also the possibility that arbitration or a streamlined out-of-court alternative dispute resolution procedure is available or required for determining the rights of the parties.

---

[6] *Massey v. Jackson*, 726 So.2d 656 (Ala. App. 1998).
[7] *Id.* at 659.

| FIGURE 20-1 | **What Follows the Breach** |

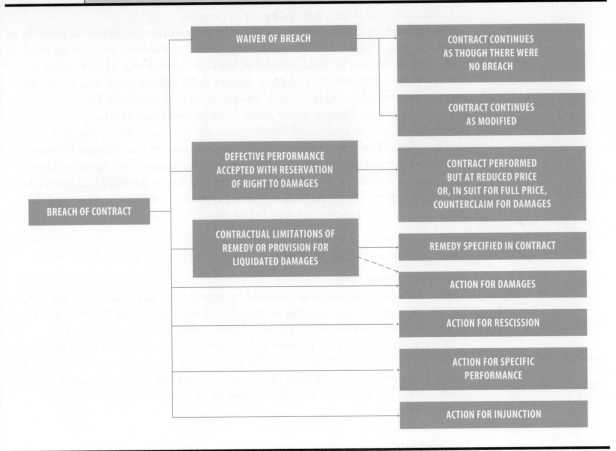

© Cengage Learning

6. Remedies Upon Anticipatory Repudiation

When an anticipatory repudiation of a contract occurs, the aggrieved person has several options. He may (1) do nothing beyond stating that performance at the proper time will be required, (2) regard the contract as having been definitively broken and bring a lawsuit against the repudiating party without waiting to see whether there will be proper performance when the performance date arrives, or (3) regard the repudiation as an offer to cancel the contract. This offer can be accepted or rejected. If accepted, there is a discharge of the original contract by the subsequent cancellation agreement of the parties.

7. Remedies in General and the Measure of Damages

Courts provide a *quasi-contractual* or *restitution* remedy in which a contract is unenforceable because it lacked definite and certain terms or was not in compliance with the statute of frauds, yet one of the parties performed services for the other. The measure of damages in these and other quasi-contract cases is the reasonable value of the services performed, not an amount derived from the defective contract.

In cases when a person retains money or when a contemplated contract is not properly formed and no work is performed, the party retaining the benefit is obligated to make restitution to the person conferring the benefit. **For Example,** Kramer Associates, Inc. (KAI), a Washington D.C., consulting firm, accepted $75,000 from a Ghana-based corporation, Ikam, Ltd., to secure financing for a Ghana development project. No contract was ever executed, and KAI did virtually nothing to secure financing for the project. Restitution of the $75,000 was required.[8]

When there is a breach of contract, the regular remedy is an award of *monetary damages*. In unusual circumstances, when monetary damages are inadequate, the injured party may obtain **specific performance**, whereby the court will order that the contract terms be carried out.

The measure of monetary damages when there has been a breach of contract is the sum of money that will place the injured party in the same position that would have been attained if the contract had been performed.[9] That is, the injured party will be given the *benefit of the bargain* by the court. As seen in the *Tips v. Hartland Developers* case, the nonbreaching party, Hartland, was awarded the contract price less the cost of completion of the project, which had the effect of giving the builder the benefit of the bargain.

8. Monetary Damages

Monetary damages are commonly classified as compensatory damages, nominal damages, and punitive damages. **Compensatory damages** compensate the injured party for the damages incurred as a result of the breach of contract. Compensatory damages have two branches, *direct damages* and *consequential* (or *special*) *damages*.

Injured parties that do not sustain an actual loss because of a breach of contract are entitled to a judgment of a small sum of money such as $1; these damages are called **nominal damages**.

Damages in excess of actual loss, imposed for the purpose of punishing or making an example of the defendant, are known as **punitive damages** or *exemplary damages*. In contract actions, punitive damages are not ordinarily awarded.[10]

(A) DIRECT AND CONSEQUENTIAL DAMAGES. **Direct damages** (sometimes called *general damages*) are those that naturally flow from the given type of breach of contract involved and include *incidental damages*, which are extra expenditures made by the injured party to rectify the breach or mitigate damages. **Consequential damages** (sometimes called *special damages*) are those that do not necessarily flow from the type of breach of contract involved but happen to do so in a particular case as a result of the injured party's particular circumstances.[11]

---

specific performance – action brought to compel the adverse party to perform a contract on the theory that merely suing for damages for its breach will not be an adequate remedy.

compensatory damages – sum of money that will compensate an injured plaintiff for actual loss.

nominal damages – nominal sum awarded the plaintiff in order to establish that legal rights have been violated although the plaintiff in fact has not sustained any actual loss or damages.

punitive damages – damages, in excess of those required to compensate the plaintiff for the wrong done, that are imposed in order to punish the defendant because of the particularly wanton or willful character of wrongdoing; also called *exemplary damages*.

direct damages – losses that are caused by breach of a contract.

consequential damages – damages the buyer experiences as a result of the seller's breach with respect to a third party, also called *special damages*.

---

[8] *Kramer Associates, Inc. v. IKAM, Ltd.*, 888 A.2d 247 (D.C. 2005).
[9] *Leingang v. City of Mandan*, 468 N.W.2d 397 (N.D. 1991).
[10] A party who is not awarded actual damages but wins nominal damages can be considered a "prevailing party" for the purposes of a contractual attorney fee-shifting provision. *Brock v. King*, 629 S.E.2d 829 (Ga. App. 2006).
[11] See *Powell Electrical Systems, Inc. v. Hewlett Packard Co.*, 356 S.W.3d 113 (Tex. App. 2011).

CASE SUMMARY

Who Pays the Expenses?

FACTS: Jerry Birkel was a grain farmer. Hassebrook Farm Service, Inc., made a contract with Jerry to sell to him and install a grain storage and drying bin. Jerry traded in his old dryer to the seller. The new equipment did not work properly, and Jerry had to pay other persons for drying and storing his grain. Jerry sued Hassebrook for damages and claimed the right to be repaid what he had paid to others for drying and storage.

DECISION: Jerry was entitled to recover what he had paid others for drying and storage. Because Jerry had traded in his old dryer to the seller, it was obvious to the seller that if the new equipment did not work properly, Jerry would be forced to pay for alternative drying and storage to prevent the total loss of his crops. The cost of such an alternative was therefore within the seller's contemplation when the contract was made, and so the buyer could recover this cost as an element of damages for the seller's breach of contract. [*Birkel v. Hassebrook Farm Service, Inc.*, 363 N.W.2d 148 (Neb. 1985)]

Consequential damages may be recovered only if it was reasonably foreseeable to the defendant that the kind of loss in question could be sustained by the nonbreaching party if the contract were broken.

For Example, in early August, Spencer Adams ordered a four-wheel-drive GMC truck with a rear-end hydraulic lift for use on his Aroostook County, Maine, potato farm. The contract price was $58,500. He told Brad Jones, the owner of the dealership, that he had to have the truck by Labor Day so he could use it to bring in his crop from the fields before the first frost, and Brad nodded that he understood. The truck did not arrive by Labor Day as promised in the written contract. After a two-week period of gradually escalating recriminations with the dealership, Adams obtained the same model GMC truck at a dealership 40 minutes away in Houlton but at the cost of $60,500. He was also able to rent a similar truck from the Houlton dealer for $250 for the day while the new truck was being prepared. Farmhands had used other means of harvesting, but because of the lack of the truck, their work was set back by five days. As a result of the delays, 30 percent of the crop was still in the fields when the first frost came, causing damages expertly estimated at $320,000. The *direct damages* for the breach of contract in this case would be the difference between the contract price for the truck of $58,500 and the market price of $60,500, or $2,000. These direct damages naturally flow from the breach of contract for the purchase of a truck. Also, the *incidental damages* of $250 for the truck rental are recoverable direct damages. The $320,000 loss of the potato crop was a consequence of not having the truck, and this sum is arguably recoverable by Spencer Adams as *consequential or special damages*. Adams notified Brad Jones of the reason he needed to have the truck by Labor Day, and it should have been reasonably foreseeable to Jones that loss of a portion of the crop could occur if the truck contract was breached. However, because of Spencer Adams's obligation to mitigate damages (as discussed below), it is unlikely that Adams will recover the full consequential damages. Truck rental availability or the lack of availability within the rural area, alternative tractor usage, and the actual harvesting methods used by Adams all relate to the mitigation issue to be resolved by the jury.

✱ **(B) MITIGATION OF DAMAGES.** The injured party is under the duty to mitigate damages if reasonably possible.[12] In other words, damages must not be permitted to increase if an increase can be prevented by reasonable efforts. This means that the injured party must generally stop any performance under the contract to avoid running up a larger bill. The duty to mitigate damages may require an injured party to buy or rent elsewhere the goods that the wrongdoer was obligated to deliver under the contract. In the case of breach of an employment contract by the employer, the employee is required to seek other similar employment. The wages earned from other employment must be deducted from the damages claimed. The discharged employee, however, is not required to take employment of less-than-comparable work.

(1) Effect of Failure to Mitigate Damages.

The effect of the requirement of mitigating damages is to limit recovery by the nonbreaching party to the damages that would have been sustained had this party mitigated the damages where it was possible to do so. **For Example,** self-described "sports nut" Gary Baker signed up for a three-year club-seat "package" that entitled him and a companion to tickets for 41 Boston Bruins hockey games and 41 Boston Celtics basketball games at the New Boston Garden Corporation's Fleet Center for approximately $18,000 per year. After one year, Baker stopped paying for the tickets, thinking that he would simply lose his $5,000 security deposit. Baker, a CPA, tried to work out a compromise settlement to no avail. New Boston sued Baker for breach of contract, seeking the balance due on the tickets of $34,866. At trial, Baker argued to the jury that although he had breached his contract, New Boston had an obligation to mitigate damages, for example, by treating his empty seats and those of others in the same situation as "rush seats" shortly before game time and selling them at a discount. New Boston argued that just as a used luxury car cannot be returned for a refund, a season ticket cannot be canceled without consequences. The jury accepted Baker's position on mitigation and reduced the amount owed New Boston by $21,176 to $13,690.[13]

✱ ## 9. Rescission

When one party commits a material breach of the contract, the other party may rescind the contract; if the party in default objects, the aggrieved party may bring an action for rescission. A breach is *material* when it is so substantial that it defeats the object of the parties in making the contract.[14]

An injured party who rescinds a contract after having performed services may recover the reasonable value of the performance rendered under restitutionary or quasi-contractual damages. Money paid by the injured party may also be recovered. **For Example,** the Sharabianlous signed a purchase agreement to buy a building owned by Berenstein Associates for $2 million. Thereafter the parties learned of environmental contamination on the property. Faced with uncertainty about the scope of the problem and the cost of the cleanup, the deal fell through and litigation ensued. The trial court rescinded the agreement based on mutual

---

[12] *West Pinal Family Health Center, Inc. v. McBride*, 785 P.2d 66 (Ariz. 1989).
[13] Sacha Pfeiffer, "Disenchanted Fan Scores Win in Ticket Fight," *Boston Globe*, August 28, 1999, at B4.
[14] *Greentree Properties, Inc. v. Kissee*, 92 S.W.3d 289 (Mo. App. 2003).

mistake of fact because neither party knew the full extent of the environmental hazard at the property. Damages available to parties upon mistake are more limited than those available in cases in which rescission is based on fault. The Sharabianlous were awarded $61,423.82 in expenses and an order returning their $115,000 deposit.[15]

The purpose of rescission is to restore the injured party to the position occupied before the contract was made. However, the party seeking restitutionary damages must also return what this party has received from the party in default.

For Example, Pedro Morena purchased real estate from Jason Alexander after Alexander had assured him that the property did not have a flooding problem. In fact, the property regularly flooded after ordinary rainstorms. Morena was entitled to the return of the purchase price and payment for the reasonable value of the improvements he made to the property. Alexander was entitled to a setoff for the reasonable rental value of the property during the time Morena was in possession of this property.

✱ 10. Action for Specific Performance

Under special circumstances, an injured party may obtain the equitable remedy of specific performance, which compels the other party to carry out the terms of a contract. Specific performance is ordinarily granted only if the subject matter of the contract is "unique," thereby making an award of money damages an inadequate remedy. Contracts for the purchase of land will be specifically enforced.[16]

Specific performance of a contract to sell personal property can be obtained only if the article is of unusual age, beauty, unique history, or other distinction. **For Example,** Maurice owned a rare Revolutionary War musket that he agreed to sell to Herb. Maurice then changed his mind because of the uniqueness of the musket. Herb can sue and win, requesting the remedy of specific performance of the contract because of the unique nature of the goods.

When the damages sustained by the plaintiff can be measured in monetary terms, specific performance will be refused. Consequently, a contract to sell a television station will not be specifically enforced when the buyer had made a contract to resell the station to a third person; the damages caused by the breach of the first contract would be the loss sustained by being unable to make the resale, and such damages would be adequate compensation to the original buyer.[17]

Ordinarily, contracts for the performance of personal services are not specifically ordered. This is because of the difficulty of supervision by the court and the restriction of the U.S. Constitution's Thirteenth Amendment prohibiting involuntary servitude except as criminal punishment.

✱ 11. Action for an Injunction

When a breach of contract consists of doing an act prohibited by the contract, a possible remedy is an **injunction** against doing the act. **For Example,** when the obligation in an employee's contract is to refrain from competing after resigning

✱ **injunction** – order of a court of equity to refrain from doing (negative injunction) or to do (affirmative or mandatory injunction) a specified act. Statute use in labor disputes has been greatly restricted.

---

[15] *Sharabianlou v. Karp*, 105 Cal. Rptr. 3d 300 (Cal. App. 2010).
[16] *English v. Muller*, 514 S.E.2d 195 (Ga. 1999).
[17] *Miller v. LeSea Broadcasting, Inc.*, 87 F.3d 224 (7th Cir. 1996).

from the company and the obligation is broken by competing, a court may order or enjoin the former employee to stop competing. Similarly, when a vocalist breaks a contract to record exclusively for a particular label, she may be enjoined from recording for any other company. This may have the indirect effect of compelling the vocalist to record for the plaintiff.

12. Reformation of Contract by a Court

At times, a written contract does not correctly state the agreement already made by the parties. When this occurs, either party may seek to have the court reform or correct the writing to state the agreement actually made.

A party seeking reformation of a contract must clearly prove both the grounds for reformation and what the agreement actually was. This burden is particularly great when the contract to be reformed is written. This is so because the general rule is that parties are presumed to have read their written contracts and to have intended to be bound by them when they signed the contracts.

When a unilateral mistake is made and it is of such consequence that enforcing the contract according to its terms would be unreasonable, a court may reform the contract to correct the mistake.

CASE SUMMARY

Will a Court Correct a Huge Mistake?

FACTS: New York Packaging Corp. (NYPC) manufactured plastic sheets used by Owens Corning (OC) at its asphalt plants throughout the country as dividers to separate asphalt containers and prevent them from sticking to one another. Janet Berry, a customer service representative at Owens Corning, called and received a price from NYPC of "$172.50 per box," with a box containing 200 plastic sheets. Ms. Berry put the information into OC's computer systems, which in turn generated a purchase order. She mistakenly believed that the unit of measurement designated as "EA" on the purchase order was per box when it in fact was per sheet. As a result, the purchase orders likewise reflected a price of $172.50 per sheet rather than per box. The computer automatically calculated the total price of the purchase order and faxed it to NYPC as $1,078,195, without Ms. Berry seeing the huge total price. NYPC filled the order, which included overrun sheets, and billed OC $1,414,605.60. NYPC sought payment at the contract price of $172.50 per sheet. It points out that the purchase order contained a "no oral modification" clause and, by its terms, the order was binding when NYPC accepted. The buyer contends that NYPC is attempting to take advantage of this huge and obvious mistake and that the contract should be reformed.

DECISION: Ms. Berry made a unilateral mistake that was, or should have been, known by NYPC. OC used the sheets after its offer to return them to NYPC was refused. Therefore, the contract could not be rescinded. The drafting error in this case was so huge that to enforce the written contract would be unconscionable. Accordingly, the unit of measurement is amended to read "per box" rather than "EA"; the "Order Qty" is amended to read "41 boxes of 200 sheets per box"; and the overall price is modified to read $7,072.50, not $1,078,195. [*In re Owens Corning et al., Debtors in Possession*, 291 B.R. 329 (2003)]

D. CONTRACT PROVISIONS AFFECTING REMEDIES AND DAMAGES

The contract of the parties may contain provisions that affect the remedies available or the recovery of damages.

13. Limitation of Remedies

The contract of the parties may limit the remedies of the aggrieved parties. **For Example,** the contract may give one party the right to repair or replace a defective item sold or to refund the contract price. The contract may require both parties to submit any dispute to arbitration or another streamlined out-of-court dispute resolution procedure.

14. Liquidated Damages

The parties may stipulate in their contract that a certain amount should be paid in case of a breach. This amount is known as liquidated damages and may be variously measured by the parties. When delay is possible, **liquidated damages** may be a fixed sum, such as $1,000 for each day of delay. When there is a total default, damages may be a percentage of the contract price or the amount of the down payment.

liquidated damages –
provision stipulating the amount of damages to be paid in the event of default or breach of contract.

liquidated damages clause –
specification of exact compensation in case of a breach of contract.

(A) VALIDITY. To be valid, a **liquidated damages clause** must satisfy two requirements: (1) The situation must be one in which it is difficult or impossible to determine the actual damages and (2) the amount specified must not be excessive when compared with the probable damages that would be sustained.[18] The validity of a liquidated damages clause is determined on the basis of the facts existing when the clause was agreed to.

CASE SUMMARY

Can We Freeze the Damages?

FACTS: Manny Fakhimi agreed to buy an apartment complex for $697,000 at an auction from David Mason. Fakhimi was obligated to put up 10 percent of the agreed-to price at the auction as a deposit. The agreement signed by Fakhimi allowed Mason to keep this deposit should Fakhimi fail to come up with the remaining 90 percent of the auction price as liquidated damages for the default. Shortly after the auction, Fakhimi heard a rumor that the military base located near the apartment complex might be closing. Fakhimi immediately stopped payment on the check and defaulted on the agreement. Mason sued Fakhimi for the liquidated damages specified in the sales contract.

DECISION: Because of the difficulty of forecasting the loss that might be caused by the breach of a real estate purchase contract, it is held that a liquidated damage clause of 10 percent of the sale price is valid and is not a penalty. The fact that the damages sustained thereafter were less than 10 percent does not convert the 10 percent into an unreasonable forecast. The 10 percent clause remained valid as it would have remained had the damages on resale been more than 10 percent. [*Mason v. Fakhimi*, **865 P.2d 333 (Neb. 1993)**]

---

[18] *Southeast Alaska Construction Co. v. Alaska*, 791 P.2d 339 (Alaska 1990).

(B) EFFECT. When a liquidated damages clause is held valid, the injured party cannot collect more than the amount specified by the clause. The defaulting party is bound to pay such damages once the fact is established that there has been a default. The injured party is not required to make any proof as to damages sustained, and the defendant is not permitted to show that the damages were not as great as the liquidated sum.

(C) INVALID CLAUSES. If the liquidated damages clause calls for the payment of a sum that is clearly unreasonably large and unrelated to the possible actual damages that might be sustained, the clause will be held to be void as a penalty. **For Example,** a settlement agreement between 27 plaintiffs seeking recovery for injuries resulting from faulty breast implants and the implants' manufacturer, Dow Corning Corp., called for seven $200,000 payments to each plaintiff. The agreement also called for a $100 per day payment to each plaintiff for any time when the payments were late as "liquidated damages." The court held that the $100 per day figure was not a reasonable estimate of anticipated damages. Rather, it was an unenforceable "penalty" provision.[19]

When a liquidated damages clause is held invalid, the effect is merely to erase the clause from the contract, and the injured party may proceed to recover damages for breach of the contract. Instead of recovering the liquidated damages amount, the injured party will recover whatever actual damages he can prove. **For Example,** Richard Goldblatt and his wife Valerie breached a five-year restrictive covenant in a settlement agreement with the medical devices corporation that Goldblatt had cofounded, C.P. Motion, Inc. A liquidated damages provision in the settlement agreement that obligated Goldblatt and his wife to pay $250,000 per breach of the restrictive covenant was unenforceable as a penalty clause. The appeals court set aside a $4,969,339 judgment against the Goldblatts, determining that the parties could have agreed to arrive at actual damages by calculating a percentage of lost profits of specific lost clients or reclaiming any profits gained by the breaching parties. Because the liquidated damages clause was a penalty provision, C.P. Motion, Inc., may only recover the actual damages filed and proven at trial.[20]

15. Attorneys' Fees

Attorneys' fees are a very significant factor in contract litigation. In Medistar Corporation's suit against Dr. David Schmidt, the jury awarded it $418,069 in damages under its promissory estoppel claim and in addition thereto the trial court judge allowed Medistar to recover $408,412 for its attorneys' fees. A state statute allows recovery of attorneys' fees for the prevailing party in a breach of partnership claim. On appeal the recovery of $408,412 in attorneys' fees was reversed since the jury awarded zero damages on Medistars' breach of partnership claim. The net result after payment of attorneys' fees—and not counting attorneys' fees for the appeal— was $9657 for Medistar, after four years of "successful" litigation.[21]

---

[19] *Bear Stearns v. Dow Corning Corp.*, 419 F.3d 543 (6th Cir. 2005). See *RKR Motors Inc. v. Associated Uniform Rentals*, 995 So.2d 588 (Fla. App. 2008).
[20] *Goldblatt v. C. P. Motion, Inc.*, 77 So.3d 798 (Fla. App. 2011).
[21] *Medistar Corp. v. Schmidt*, 267 S.W.3d 150 (Tex. App. 2008).

The so-called "American rule" states that each party is responsible for its own attorneys' fees in the absence of an express contractual or statutory provision to the contrary.[22] Even in the event of a valid contractual provision for attorneys' fees, a trial court has the discretion to exercise its equitable control to allow only such sum as is reasonable, or the court may properly disallow attorneys' fees altogether on the basis that such recovery would be inequitable. **For Example,** although Evergreen Tree Care Services was awarded some monetary damages in its breach of contract suit against JHL, Inc., it was unsuccessful in its claim for attorneys' fees under a provision for attorneys' fees in the contract because the trial court exercised its equitable discretion, finding that both parties to the litigation came to court with "unclean hands," and that Evergreen failed to sufficiently itemize and exclude fees to discovery abuses.[23]

16. Limitation of Liability Clauses

A contract may contain a provision stating that one of the parties shall not be liable for damages in case of breach. Such a provision is called an **exculpatory clause**, or when a monetary limit to damages for breach of contract is set forth in the contract, it may be referred to as a **limitation-of-liability clause**.

exculpatory clause – provision in a contract stating that one of the parties shall not be liable for damages in case of breach; also called a *limitation-of-liability clause*.

limitation-of-liability clause – provision in a contract stating that one of the parties shall not be liable for damages in case of breach; also called an *exculpatory clause*.

(A) CONTENT AND CONSTRUCTION. If an exculpatory clause or a limitation-of-liability clause limits liability for damages caused only by negligent conduct, liability is neither excluded nor limited if the conduct alleged is found to be grossly negligent, willful, or wanton. **For Example,** Security Guards Inc. (SGI) provided services to Dana Corporation, a truck frame manufacturer under a contract that contained a limitation-of-liability clause capping losses at $50,000 per occurrence for damages "caused solely by the negligence" of SGI or its employees. When a critical alarm was activated by a fire in the paint shop at 5:39 P.M., the SGI guard on duty did not follow appropriate procedures, which delayed notification to the fire department for 15 minutes. Royal Indemnity Co., Dana's insurer, paid Dana $16,535,882 for the fire loss and sued SGI for $7 million, contending that the SGI guard's actions were grossly negligent and caused the plant to suffer increased damages. The court held that if SGI were to be found grossly negligent, the liability would not be limited to $50,000, and a jury could find damages far exceeding that amount.[24]

(B) VALIDITY. As a general rule, experienced businesspersons are free to allocate liability in their contracts as they see fit. They have freedom to contract—even to make bad bargains or relinquish fundamental rights. However, courts in most states will not enforce a contract provision that *completely exonerates* a party from gross negligence or intentional acts.

(c) RELEASES. Release forms signed by participants in athletic and sporting events declaring that the sponsor, proprietor, or operator of the event shall not be liable for injuries sustained by participants because of its negligence are generally binding.[25] The *Cheley Colorado Camps* decision is such a case.

---

[22] *Centimark v. Village Manor Associates, Ltd.,* 967 A.2d 550 (Conn. App. 2009).

[23] *Stafford v. JHL, Inc.,* 194 P.3d 315 (Wyo. 2008). See also *FNBC v. Jennessey Group, LLC,* 759 N.W.2d 808 (Iowa App. 2008).

[24] *Royal Indemnity Co. v. Security Guards, Inc.,* 255 F. Supp. 2d 497 (E.D. Pa. 2003).

[25] But see *Woodman v. Kera, LLC,* 760 N.W.2d 641 (Mich. App. 2008) where the Court of Appeals of Michigan held that a preinjury waiver signed by a parent on behalf of a five-year-old child was invalid.

CASE SUMMARY

How to Handle a Risky Business

FACTS: Chelsea Hamill attended Camp Cheley for three years. Before attending camp each summer her parents signed a liability/risk release form. In July 2004, when Hamill was 15 years old, she fell off a Cheley horse and broke her arm. Chelsea brought a negligence and gross negligence lawsuit against the summer camp. Hamill's mother testified at her deposition that she voluntarily signed the release after having "skimmed" it. At her deposition, the mother testified as follows:

> Attorney: And, you know, you knew that someone such as Christopher Reeve had been tragically injured falling off a horse?
>
> Ms. Hamill: Yes.
>
> Attorney: Did you personally know Mr. Reeve?
>
> Ms. Hamill: Yes.
>
> Attorney: And so you were aware that there were significant risks associated with horseback riding?
>
> Ms. Hamill: Yes.
>
> Attorney: And you were aware that your daughter was going to be doing a significant amount of horseback riding?
>
> Ms. Hamill: Yes.

Hamill's mother's interpretation of the release was that prospective negligent claims were not waived. The camp disagreed. The release stated in part:

> I, on behalf of myself and my child, hereby release and waive *any claim of liability against Cheley* ... occurring to my child while he/she participates in any and all camp programs and activities.
>
> I give my permission for my child to participate in all camp activities, including those described above. I acknowledge and assume the risks involved in these activities, and for any damages, illness, *injury or death* ... resulting from such risks for myself and my child.
>
> *(Emphasis Added.)*

DECISION: Judgment for Camp Cheley. The release did not need to include an exhaustive list of particularized injury scenarios to be effective. Hamill's mother had more than sufficient information to allow her to assess the extent of injury possible in horseback riding and to make an "informed" decision before signing the release. The mother was informed of the intent to release "all claims," including prospective negligence claims. While exculpatory agreements are not a bar to civil liability for gross negligence, the record is devoid of evidence of gross negligence. [*Hamill v. Cheley Colorado Camps, Inc.*, 262 P.3d 945 (Colo. App. 2011)]

LawFlix

The Goodbye Girl (1977) (PG)

Richard Dreyfuss plays Elliott Garfield, a struggling Shakespearean actor who lands in New York with a sublease on an apartment still occupied by divorcee Marsha Mason and her daughter. The two work out living arrangements, split rent and food, and deal with the issue of whether Mason has any rights. Review all aspects of contracts as the characters discuss subleases, rent payment, living arrangements, and food costs.

MAKE THE CONNECTION

SUMMARY

When a party fails to perform a contract or performs improperly, the other contracting party may sue for damages caused by the breach. What may be recovered by the aggrieved person is stated in terms of being direct or consequential damages. Direct damages are those that ordinarily will result from the breach. Direct damages may be recovered on proof of causation and amount. Consequential damages can be recovered only if, in addition to proving causation and amount, it is shown that they were reasonably within the contemplation of the contracting parties as a probable result of a breach of the contract. The right to recover consequential damages is lost if the aggrieved party could reasonably have taken steps to avoid such damages. In other words, the aggrieved person has a duty to mitigate or reduce damages by reasonable means.

In any case, the damages recoverable for breach of contract may be limited to a specific amount by a liquidated damages clause.

In a limited number of situations, an aggrieved party may bring an action for specific performance to compel the other contracting party to perform the acts called for by the contract. Specific performance by the seller is always obtainable for the breach of a contract to sell land or real estate on the theory that such property has a unique value. With respect to other contracts, specific performance will not be ordered unless it is shown that there was some unique element present so that the aggrieved person would suffer a damage that could not be compensated for by the payment of money damages.

The aggrieved person also has the option of rescinding the contract if (1) the breach has been made concerning a material term and (2) the aggrieved party returns everything to the way it was before the contract was made.

Although there has been a breach of the contract, the effect of this breach is nullified if the aggrieved person by word or conduct waives the right to object to the breach. Conversely, an aggrieved party may accept a defective performance without thereby waiving a claim for breach if the party makes a reservation of rights. A reservation of rights can be made by stating that the defective performance is accepted "without prejudice," "under protest," or "with reservation of rights."

LEARNING OUTCOMES

After studying this chapter, you should be able to clearly explain:

A. What Constitutes a Breach of Contract

L0.1 Explain what constitutes a breach of contract and an anticipatory breach of contract
See the illustration of a painting contractor's failure to properly paint a house, p. 400.
See the *Tips* case in which damages are assessed for anticipatory repudiation of a contract, pp. 400–401.
See the *Mammoth Lakes* example involving anticipatory repudiation by conduct, p. 401.

B. Waiver of Breach

L0.2 Describe the effect of a waiver of a breach
See the application of the waiver doctrine as applied in the Massey example on p. 403.

C. Remedies for Breach of Contract

L0.3 Explain the range of remedies available for breach of contract
See Figure 20-1, "What Follows the Breach," on p. 404.
See the *Spencer Adams* example involving a range of monetary damages on p. 406.

See the *Pedro Morena* example involving rescission of a contract on p. 408.
See the rare Revolutionary War musket example of specific performance, p. 408.

D. Contract Provisions Affecting Remedies and Damages

LO.4   Explain when liquidated damages clauses are valid and invalid
See the Dow Corning faulty breast implants settlement agreement example

in which liquidated damages of a $100 per day late payment were found to be unenforceable penalty provision, p. 411.

LO.5   State when liability-limiting clauses and releases are valid
See the *Cheley Camps* case that illustrates how the camp successfully raised a signed parental exculpatory release as a defense in a horseback riding injury case, p. 413.

KEY TERMS

anticipatory breach
anticipatory repudiation
breach
compensatory damages
consequential damages
direct damages

exculpatory clause
injunction
limitation-of-liability clause
liquidated damages
liquidated damages clause
nominal damages

punitive damages
remedies
reservation of rights
specific performance
valid
waiver

QUESTIONS AND CASE PROBLEMS

1. The Forsyth School District contracted with Textor Construction, Inc., to build certain additions and alter school facilities, including the grading of a future softball field. Under the contract, the work was to be completed by August 1. Various delays occurred at the outset of the project attributable to the school district, and the architect's representative on the job, Mr. Hamilton, told Textor's vice president, William Textor, not to be concerned about a clause in the contract of $250 per day liquidated damages for failure to complete the job by August 1. Textor sued the school district for breach of contract regarding payment for the grading of the softball field, and the District counterclaimed for liquidated damages for 84 days at $250 per day for failure to complete the project by the August 1 date. What legal basis exists for Textor to defend against the counter-claim for failure to complete the job on time? Was it ethical for the school district to bring this counterclaim based on the facts before you? [*Textor Construction, Inc. v. Forsyth R-III School District*, 60 S.W.3d 692 (Mo. App.)]

2. Anthony makes a contract to sell a rare painting to Laura for $100,000. The written contract specifies that if Anthony should fail to perform the contract, he will pay Laura $5,000 as liquidated damages. Anthony fails to deliver the painting and is sued by Laura for $5,000. Can she recover this amount?

3. Rogers made a contract with Salisbury Brick Corp. that allowed it to remove earth and sand from land he owned. The contract ran for four years with provision to renew it for additional four-year terms up to a total of 96 years. The contract provided for compensation to Rogers based on the amount of earth and sand removed. By an unintentional mistake, Salisbury underpaid Rogers the amount of $863 for the months of November and December 1986. Salisbury offered this amount to Rogers, but he refused to accept it and claimed that he had been underpaid in other months. Rogers claimed that he was entitled to rescind the contract. Was he correct? [*Rogers v. Salisbury Brick Corp.*, 882 S. E.2d 915 (S.C.)]

4. A contractor departed from the specifications at a number of points in a contract to build a house. The cost to put the house in the condition called for by the contract was approximately $14,000. The contractor was sued for $50,000 for breach of contract and emotional distress caused by the breach. Decide.

5. Protein Blenders, Inc., made a contract with Gingerich to buy from him the shares of stock of a small corporation. When the buyer refused to take and pay for the stock, Gingerich sued for specific performance of the contract on the ground that the value of the stock was unknown and could not be readily ascertained because it was not sold on the general market. Was he entitled to specific performance? [*Gingerich v. Protein Blenders, Inc.*, 95 N.W.2d 522 (Iowa)]

6. The buyer of real estate made a down payment. The contract stated that the buyer would be liable for damages in an amount equal to the down payment if the buyer broke the contract. The buyer refused to go through with the contract and demanded his down payment back. The seller refused to return it and claimed that he was entitled to additional damages from the buyer because the damages that he had suffered were more than the amount of the down payment. Decide. [*Waters v. Key Colony East, Inc.*, 345 So.2d 367 (Fla. App.)]

7. Kuznicki made a contract for the installation of a fire detection system by Security Safety Corp. for $498. The contract was made one night and canceled at 9:00 the next morning. Security then claimed one-third of the purchase price from Kuznicki by virtue of a provision in the contract that "in the event of cancellation of this agreement… the owner agrees to pay $33^{1/3}$ percent of the contract price, as liquidated damages." Was Security Safety entitled to recover the amount claimed? [*Security Safety Corp. v. Kuznicki*, 213 N.E.2d 866 (Mass.)]

8. FNBC is a business brokerage firm that assits in the purchase and sale of businesses. Jennings and Hennessey were independent contractors working for FNBC. They left FNBC, and FNBC sued them for breach of their contracts with FNBC. The trial court issued a permanent injuction prohibiting the former contractors from using proprietary information and the court awarded attorneys' fees under a clause in the contract that would obligate Jennings and Hennessey to indemnify FNBC against claims "brought by persons not a party to the provision." Jennings and Hennessey appealed the decision on attorneys' fees. Decide. [*FNBC v. Jennessey Group, LLC*, 759 N.W.2d 808 (Iowa App.)]

9. Melodee Lane Lingerie Co. was a tenant in a building that was protected against fire by a sprinkler and alarm system maintained by the American District Telegraph Co. (ADT). Because of the latter's fault, the controls on the system were defective and allowed the discharge of water into the building, which damaged Melodee's property. When Melodee sued ADT, its defense was that its service contract limited its liability to 10 percent of the annual service charge made to the customer. Was this limitation valid? [*Melodee Lane Lingerie Co. v. American District Telegraph Co.*, 218 N.E.2d 661 (N.Y.)]

10. JRC Trading Corp (JRC) bought computer software and hardware from Progressive Data Systems (PDS) for $167,935, which it paid in full, to track movement of its trucks with inventory and to process transactions. The purchase agreement also called for a $7,500 per year licensing fee for an 18-year period, and it stated that in the event of default PDS could "accelerate and declare all obligations of Customer as a liquidated sum." A dispute arose between the parties, and when the case was litigated the only actual contract charges owed PDS were the license fees of $7,500 for two years. The application of the liquidated damages clause would yield an additional $120,000 cash for PDS for the future fees for 16 years without any reduction for expenses or the present cash value for the not-yet-earned fees. JRC contends that actual damages were clearly ascertainable and that the liquidated damages clause was a penalty provision that should not be enforced. Progressive argued that the court must interpret the contract as written, stating that the court has no power to

rewrite the contract. Decide. [*Jefferson Randolf Corp. v. PDS*, 553 S.E.2d 304 (Ga. App.)]

11. Ken Sulejmanagic, aged 19, signed up for a course in scuba diving taught by Madison at the YMCA. Before the instruction began, Ken was required to sign a form releasing Madison and the YMCA from liability for any harm that might occur. At the end of the course, Madison, Ken, and another student went into deep water. After Ken made the final dive required by the course program, Madison left him alone in the water while he took the other student for a dive. When Madison returned, Ken could not be found, and it was later determined that he had drowned. Ken's parents sued Madison and the YMCA for negligence in the performance of the teaching contract. The defendants raised the defense that the release Ken signed shielded them from liability. The plaintiffs claimed that the release was invalid. Who was correct? [*Madison v. Superior Court*, 250 Cal. Rptr. 299 (Cal. App.)]

12. Wassenaar worked for Panos under a three-year contract stating that if the contract were terminated wrongfully by Panos before the end of the three years, he would pay as damages the salary for the remaining time that the contract had to run. After three months, Panos terminated the contract, and Wassenaar sued him for pay for the balance of the contract term. Panos claimed that this amount could not be recovered because the contract provision for the payment was a void penalty. Was this provision valid? [*Wassenaar v. Panos*, 331 N.W.2d 357 (Wis.)]

13. Soden, a contractor, made a contract to build a house for Clevert. The sales contract stated that "if either party defaults in the performance of this contract," that party would be liable to the other for attorneys' fees incurred in suing the defaulter. Soden was 61 days late in completing the contract, and some of the work was defective.

In a suit by the buyer against the contractor, the contractor claimed that he was not liable for the buyer's attorneys' fees because he had made only a defective performance and because "default" in the phrase quoted meant "nonperformance of the contract." Was the contractor liable for the attorneys' fees? [*Clevert v. Soden*, 400 S.E.2d 181 (Va.)]

14. Protection Alarm Co. made a contract to provide burglar alarm security for Fretwell's home. The contract stated that the maximum liability of the alarm company was the actual loss sustained or $50, whichever was the lesser, and that this provision was agreed to "as liquidated damages and not as a penalty." When Fretwell's home was burglarized, he sued for the loss of approximately $12,000, claiming that the alarm company had been negligent. The alarm company asserted that its maximum liability was $50. Fretwell claimed that this was invalid because it bore no relationship to the loss that could have been foreseen when the contract was made or that in fact "had been sustained." Decide.

15. Shepherd-Will made a contract to sell Emma Cousar:

> 5 acres of land adjoining property owned by the purchaser and this being formerly land of Shepherd-Will, Inc., located on north side of Highway 223. This 5 acres to be surveyed at earliest time possible at which time plat will be attached and serve as further description on property.

Shepherd-Will owned only one 100-acre tract of land that adjoined Emma's property. This tract had a common boundary with her property of 1,140 feet. Shepherd-Will failed to perform this contract. Emma sued for specific performance of the contract. Decide. [*Cousar v. Shepherd-Will, Inc.*, 387 S.E.2d 723 (S.C. App.)]

CPA QUESTIONS

1. Master Mfg., Inc., contracted with Accur Computer Repair Corp. to maintain Master's computer system. Master's manufacturing process depends on its computer system operating properly at all times. A liquidated damages clause in the contract provided that

Accur pay $1,000 to Master for each day that Accur was late responding to a service request. On January 12, Accur was notified that Master's computer system had failed. Accur did not respond to Master's service request until January 15. If Master sues Accur under the liquidated damages provision of the contract, Master will:

a. Win, unless the liquidated damage provision is determined to be a penalty.

b. Win, because under all circumstances liquidated damages provisions are enforceable.

c. Lose, because Accur's breach was *not* material.

d. Lose, because liquidated damage provisions violate public policy (5/93, Law, #25).

2. Jones, CPA, entered into a signed contract with Foster Corp. to perform accounting and review services. If Jones repudiates the contract prior to the date performance is due to begin, which of the following is *not* correct?

a. Foster could successfully maintain an action for breach of contract after the date performance was due to begin.

b. Foster can obtain a judgment ordering Jones to perform.

c. Foster could successfully maintain an action for breach of contract prior to the date performance is due to begin.

d. Foster can obtain a judgment for the monetary damages it incurred as a result of the repudiation (5/89, Law, #35).

3. Which of the following concepts affect(s) the amount of monetary damages recoverable by the nonbreaching party when a contract is breached?

	Forseeability of damages	Mitigation of damages
a.	Yes	Yes
b.	Yes	No
c.	No	Yes
d.	No	No

CHAPTER 22

Legal Aspects of Supply Chain Management

© Manuel Gutjahr/iStockphoto.com

learningoutcomes

After studying this chapter, you should be able to

LO.1 Identify and explain all of the features of a negotiable warehouse receipt

LO.2 List and explain the differences between the three types of motor carriers of goods

LO.3 Explain a common carrier's liability for loss or damage to goods

LO.4 Identify and explain the role of each of the persons or business entities involved in the sale of goods on consignment

LO.5 Describe a hotelkeeper's liability for loss of a guest's property

A ll bailments are not created equal. Because of the circumstances under which possession of the bailed property is transferred, the law imposes special duties in some cases on warehouses, common carriers, factors, and hotelkeepers. Documents of title facilitate the transportation, storage, and financing of goods in commerce.

A. WAREHOUSES

The storage of goods in a warehouse is a special bailment.

1. Definitions

warehouse – entity engaged in the business of storing the goods of others for compensation.

A **warehouse** is an entity engaged in the business of storing the goods of others for compensation. **Public warehouses** hold themselves out to serve the public generally, without discrimination.

public warehouses – entities that serve the public generally without discrimination.

A building is not essential to warehousing. Thus, an enterprise that stores boats outdoors on land is engaged in warehousing, for it is engaged in the business of storing goods for hire.

2. Rights and Duties of Warehouses

The rights and duties of a warehouse are for the most part the same as those of a bailee under a mutual benefit bailment.[1] A warehouse is not an insurer of goods. A warehouse is liable for loss or damage to goods stored in its warehouse when the warehouse is negligent.[2]

(A) STATUTORY REGULATION. The rights and duties of warehouses are regulated by the UCC, Article 7. Article 7 was revised in 2003 and 32 states have adopted the revised version.[3] The purpose of revision was to provide a framework for the future development of electronic documents of title and to update the article for modern times in light of state, federal, and international developments, including the need for medium and gender neutrality. For example, the term utilized to designate a person engaged in storing goods for hire under Article 7 is *warehouseman*.[4] The revised act uses the term *warehouse*.[5] In addition, most states have passed warehouse acts defining the rights and duties of warehouses and imposing regulations. Regulations govern charges and liens, bonds for the protection of patrons, maintenance of storage facilities in a suitable and safe condition, inspections, and general methods of transacting business.

specific lien – right of a creditor to hold particular property or assert a lien on particular property of the debtor because of the creditor's having done work on or having some other association with the property, as distinguished from having a lien generally against the assets of the debtor merely because the debtor is indebted to the lien holder.

(B) LIEN OF WAREHOUSE. The public warehouse has a lien against the goods for reasonable storage charges.[6] It is a **specific lien** in that it attaches only to the property on which the

---

[1] U.C.C. §7-204.

[2] General contract principles also apply. For example, in *Williamson v. Strictland & Smith Inc.*, 673 S.E.2d 858 (Ga. App. 2009), a warehouser successfully sued an onion farmer for breach of contract when the warehouser was unable to fill a large order because the majority of the farmer's onions stored at the warehouse were rotten.

[3] Revised Article 7 (2003) has been adopted by Alabama, Arizona, Arkansas, California, Colorado, Connecticut, Delaware, Hawaii, Idaho, Illinois, Indiana, Iowa, Kansas, Maryland, Minnesota, Mississippi, Montana, Nebraska, Nevada, New Hampshire, New Jersey, New Mexico, North Carolina, North Dakota, Oklahoma, Pennsylvania, Rhode Island, Tennessee, Texas, Utah, Virginia, and West Virginia. For more modern statutory drafting, the revised edition converts subparagraph designations from numbers to letters. For example, U.C.C. §7-307(1) is designated as Rev. U.C.C. §7-307(a).

[4] U.C.C. §7-102(1)(h).

[5] Rev. U.C.C. §7-102(a)(13).

[6] U.C.C. §7-209(1). The warehouse's lien provision of the UCC is constitutional as a continuation of the common law lien.

charges arose and cannot be asserted against any other property of the same owner in the possession of the warehouse. However, the warehouse may make a lien carry over to other goods by noting on the receipt for one lot of goods that a lien is also claimed for charges on the other goods. The warehouse's lien for storage charges may be enforced by sale after due notice has been given to all persons who claim any interest in the stored property.

3. Warehouse Receipts

A **warehouse receipt** is a written acknowledgment or record of an acknowledgment by a warehouse (bailee) that certain property has been received for storage from a named person called a **depositor** (bailor). The warehouse receipt is a memorandum of the contract between the **issuer**, the warehouse that prepares the receipt, and the depositor. No particular form is required, but usually the receipt (record) will provide:

(1) the location of the warehouse where the goods are stored, (2) the date of issuance of the receipt, (3) the consecutive number of the receipt, (4) information on the negotiability of the receipt, (5) the rate of storage and handling charges, (6) a description of the goods or the packages containing them, and (7) a statement of any liabilities incurred for which the warehouse claims a lien or security interest.[7]

A warehouse receipt (as well as a bill of lading, discussed at a later point in this chapter) is considered a **document of title**—that is, a document that in the regular course of business or financing is treated as evidence that a person is entitled to receive, hold, and dispose of the document and the goods it covers.[8] Under revised Article 7 of the UCC, the term *record* is used in the definition of document of title, reflecting the present commercial reality of the use of electronic records as documents of title, in addition to traditional "written" documents of title inscribed on a tangible medium.[9] The person holding a warehouse receipt or the person specified in the receipt is entitled to the goods represented by the receipt. A warehouse receipt as a document of title can be bought or sold and can be used as security for a loan.

4. Rights of Holders of Warehouse Receipts

The rights of the holders of warehouse receipts differ depending on whether the receipts are nonnegotiable or negotiable.

CPA

(A) NONNEGOTIABLE WAREHOUSE RECEIPTS. A warehouse receipt in which it is stated that the goods received will be delivered to a specified person is a **nonnegotiable warehouse receipt**. A transferee of a nonnegotiable receipt acquires only the title and rights that the transferor had actual authority to transfer. Therefore, the transferee's rights may be defeated by a good-faith purchaser of the goods from the transferor of the receipt.

(B) NEGOTIABLE WAREHOUSE RECEIPTS. A warehouse receipt stating that the goods will be delivered "to the bearer" or "to the order of" any named person is a **negotiable warehouse receipt**.

(1) Negotiation.
If the receipt provides for the delivery of the goods "to the bearer," the receipt may be negotiated by transfer of the document. If the receipt provides for delivery of the

---

warehouse receipt–receipt issued by the warehouse for stored goods. Regulated by the UCC, which clothes the receipt with some degree of negotiability.

depositor–person, or bailor, who gives property for storage.

issuer–warehouse that prepares a receipt of goods received for storage.

document of title–document treated as evidence that a person is entitled to receive, hold, and dispose of the document and the goods it covers.

nonnegotiable warehouse receipt–receipt that states the covered goods received will be delivered to a specific person.

negotiable warehouse receipt–receipt that states the covered goods will be delivered "to the bearer" or "to the order of."

---

[7] U.C.C. §7-202(2)(a)–(i).
[8] U.C.C. §1-201(15).
[9] Rev. U.C.C. §1-201(b)(16). An "electronic" document of title is evidenced by a record consisting of information stored in an electronic medium. A "tangible" document of title is evidenced by a record consisting of information that is inscribed on a tangible medium.

goods "to the order of" a named individual, the document must be indorsed[10] and delivered by that person in order for the document to be negotiated.

(2) Due Negotiation.

If a receipt is duly negotiated, the person to whom it is negotiated may acquire rights superior to those of the transferor. A warehouse receipt is "duly negotiated" when the holder purchases the document in good faith without notice of any defense to it, for value, in an ordinary transaction in which nothing appears improper or irregular.[11] The holder of a duly negotiated document acquires title to the document and title to the goods.[12] The holder also acquires the direct obligation of the issuer to hold or deliver the goods according to the terms of the warehouse receipt. The rights of a holder of a duly negotiated document cannot be defeated by the surrender of the goods by the warehouse to the depositor.[13]

It is the duty of the warehouse to deliver the goods only to the holder of the negotiable receipt and to cancel this receipt on surrendering the goods.[14]

The rights of a purchaser of a warehouse receipt by due negotiation are not cut off by the fact that (1) an original owner was deprived of the receipt in "bearer" form by misrepresentation, fraud, mistake, loss, theft, or conversion or (2) a bona fide purchaser bought the goods from the warehouse.

A purchaser of a warehouse receipt who takes by due negotiation does not cut off all prior rights. If the person who deposited the goods with the warehouse did not own the goods or did not have power to transfer title to them, the purchaser of the receipt is subject to the title of the true owner. Accordingly, when goods are stolen and delivered to a warehouse and a warehouse receipt is issued for them, the owner of the goods prevails over the due-negotiation purchaser of the warehouse receipt.

Study Figure 22-1, and note all of the features of a negotiable warehouse receipt in the context of the following. **For Example,** Latham and Loud (L&L) sporting goods manufacturers' representatives in Cleveland, Ohio, hijacked a truckload of ice skates from Bartlett Shoe and Skate Company of Bangor, Maine. L&L warehoused the skates at the Northern Transfer Company warehouse, and received a negotiable warehouse receipt. Jack Preston, a large sporting goods retailer who had had previous business dealings with L&L and believed it to be operated by honest individuals, made a bona fide purchase of the receipt. Bartlett, the true owner, discovered that the skates were at Northern's warehouse and informed Northern of the hijacking. Northern delivered the skates to Bartlett; Latham and Loud have fled the country. Preston believed he was entitled to delivery of the skates because he

---

[10] The spelling *endorse* is commonly used in business. The spelling *indorse* is used in the U.C.C.

[11] U.C.C. §7-501(4).

[12] U.C.C. §7-502(1).

[13] For electronic documents of title, Revised Article 7, Section 7-106, includes a list of how a party becomes a holder, and the result is that Article 7 creates a new concept of "control." That is, a holder who has control of a document of title (as evidenced by a record that may be electronic) has all the rights of a holder. The Revised Article states:

   a. A person has control of an electronic document of title if a system employed for evidencing the transfer of interests in the electronic document reliably establishes that person as the person to which the electronic document was issued or transferred,

   b. A system satisfies subsection (a) and a person is deemed to have control of an electronic document of title, if the electronic document is created, stored, and assigned in such a manner that:

     1. a single authoritative copy of the document exists which is unique, identifiable, and, except as otherwise provided in paragraphs (4), (5), and (6), unalterable.

     2. the authoritative copy identifies the person asserting control as:

       A. the person to which the document was issued; or

       B. if the authoritative copy indicates that the document has been transferred, the person to which the document was most recently transferred;

     3. the authoritative copy is communicated to and maintained by the person asserting control or its designated custodian;

     4. copies or amendments that add or change an identified assignee of the authoritative copy can be made only with the consent of the person asserting control;

     5. each copy of the authoritative copy and any copy of a copy is readily identifiable as a copy that is not the authoritative copy; and

     6. any amendment of the authoritative copy is readily identifiable as authorized or unauthorized.

[14] U.C.C. §7-403(3).

FIGURE 22-1	*Negotiable Warehouse Receipt*

Front of receipt

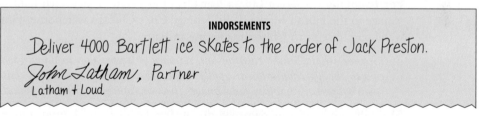

Reverse side

(1) Warehouse, (2) depositor, (3) goods, (4) warehouse's lien, (5) negotiable delivery terms, (6) warehouse's authorized agent. A negotiable warehouse receipt contains a promise to deliver the goods to the bearer or to the order of the depositor, unlike a nonnegotiable warehouse receipt, which promises only to deliver them to the depositor.

© Cengage Learning

acquired the negotiable receipt by due negotiation and informed Northern of his status before delivery of the skates to Bartlett. He contemplated legal action against Northern. Preston, however, is not entitled to the skates. Ordinarily, a purchaser of a warehouse receipt obtained by due negotiation takes title to the document and title to the goods. However, an exception exists in the case of theft. Thus, because of the theft by L&L, Preston's rights have been cut off by the true owner in this case. When conflicting claims exist, the warehouse can protect itself by instituting proceedings under UCC §7-603 to ascertain the validity of the conflicting claims.

CPA

(c) Warranties. The transferor of a negotiable or nonnegotiable warehouse receipt makes certain implied warranties for the protection of the transferee. These warranties are that (1) the receipt is genuine, (2) its transfer is rightful and effective, and (3) the transferor has no knowledge of any facts that impair the validity or worth of the receipt.[15]

5. Field Warehousing

Ordinarily, stored goods are placed in a warehouse belonging to the warehouse company. In other instances, the owner of goods, such as a manufacturer, keeps the goods in the owner's own storage area or building. The warehouse may then take exclusive control over the area in which the goods are stored and issue a receipt for the goods just as though they were in the warehouse. Such a transaction has the same legal effect with respect to other persons and purchasers of the warehouse receipts as though the property were in fact in the warehouse. This practice is called **field warehousing** because the goods are not taken to the warehouse but remain "in the field."

> **field warehousing** – stored goods under the exclusive control of a warehouse but kept on the owner's premises rather than in a warehouse.

The purpose of field warehousing is to create warehouse receipts that the owner of the goods may pledge as security for loans. The owner could, of course, have done this by actually placing the goods in a warehouse, but this would have involved the expense of transportation and storage.

CPA

6. Limitation of Liability of Warehouses

A warehouse may limit liability by a provision in the warehouse receipt specifying the maximum amount for which the warehouse can be held liable. This privilege is subject to two qualifications. First, the customer must be given the choice of storing the goods without such limitation if the customer pays a higher storage rate, and, second, the limitation must be stated for each item or for each unit of weight.[16] **For Example,** Chisholm Ltd., a Canadian Corporation, delivered ham products for storage to the Fulton Market Cold Storage Co.'s Chicago warehouse. Fulton issued a warehouse receipt to Chisholm, stating in part:

> Section 10(e): "in the event of loss, damage or destruction to stored goods for which the warehouseman is legally liable, storer declares and agrees that the warehouseman's liability for damages shall be limited to 50¢ per pound." (id.)

The ham products were damaged due to freezer burn and Fulton sought to "work with" Chisholm to resolve the claim. When Chisholm would not budge off its demand for full compensation for the damage, Fulton reverted to the "fifty cents per pound" limitation of liability clause of the warehouse receipt. The limitation of liability clause based on the unit of weight of "50¢ per pound" was enforced by the court.[17]

General contract law determines whether a limitation clause is a part of the contract between the warehouse and the customer. **For Example,** warehouse Eastern Warehousing, Inc., and customer Delavau, Inc., executed a comprehensive contract for storage of a nutritional supplement after extensive negotiations between Eastern's chief operating officer and Delavau's president. The goods were damaged due to a

---

[15] U.C.C. §7-507. These warranties are in addition to any that may arise between the parties by virtue of the fact that the transferor is selling the goods represented by the receipt to the transferee. See Chapter 25 for a discussion of seller's warranties.

[16] U.C.C. §7-204(2); *Lobel v. Samson Moving & Storage, Inc.*, 737 N.Y.S.2d 24 (A.D. 2002).

[17] *Chisholm, Ltd. v. Fulton Cold Storage Company LCC*, 2011 WL 6182347 (N.D. Ill. Dec. 13, 2011).

leaking warehouse roof. Eastern was unsuccessful in its argument that the contract was formed when the goods were subsequently delivered to the warehouse and a preprinted warehouse receipt containing a limitation-of-liability provision was given to the customer's driver. The court ruled that the terms of the receipt were not part of the contract of the parties, and awarded Delavau $1,358,601 in damages.[18]

B. Common Carriers

The purpose of a bailment may be transportation. In this case, the bailee may be a common carrier.

7. Definitions

carrier – individual or organization undertaking the transportation of goods.

consignor – (1) person who delivers goods to the carrier for shipment, (2) party with title who turns goods over to another for sale.

consignee – (1) person to whom goods are shipped, (2) dealer who sells goods for others.

common carrier – carrier that holds out its facilities to serve the general public for compensation without discrimination.

contract carrier – carrier that transports on the basis of individual contracts that it makes with each shipper.

private carrier – carrier owned by the shipper, such as a company's own fleet of trucks.

A **carrier** of goods is an individual or organization undertaking the transportation of goods regardless of the method of transportation or the distance covered. The **consignor** or shipper is the person who delivers goods to the carrier for shipment. The **consignee** is the person to whom the goods are shipped and to whom the carrier should deliver the goods.

A carrier may be classified as a common carrier, a contract carrier, or a private carrier. A **common carrier** holds itself out as willing to furnish transportation for compensation without discrimination to all members of the public who apply, assuming that the goods to be carried are proper and facilities of the carrier are available. A **contract carrier** transports goods under individual contracts, and a **private carrier** is owned and operated by the shipper. **For Example,** a truck fleet owned and operated by an industrial firm is a private carrier. Common carrier law or special bailment law applies to common carriers, ordinary bailment law to contract carriers, and the law of employment to private carriers.

The Federal Motor Carrier Safety Administration is the successor agency to the Interstate Commerce Commission and was created under the Interstate Commerce Commission Termination Act (ICCTA).[19] Under the ICCTA, Congress merged the separate classifications of common and contract carrier into one classification termed "motor carrier." However, as is seen in the *Fortunoff* case, the fundamental distinction between the types of carriage remains explicit in the act.

CASE SUMMARY

The Distinction Continues

FACTS: M. Fortunoff of Westbury operates a chain of department stores in New York and New Jersey. In March of 1997, the company entered into a contract with Frederickson Motor Express, whereby the carrier agreed "as contract carrier and independent contractor ... to transfer shipments ... as authorized in Carrier's contract carrier permit ... issued by the ICC." The contract further provided: "Although carrier is authorized to operate ... as a common carrier, each and every shipment tendered to carrier by shipper ... shall be deemed to be a tender to carrier as a motor contract carrier...."

---

[18] *Delavau v. Eastern American Trading & Warehousing, Inc.*, 810 A.2d 672 (Pa. Super. 2002).
[19] 49 U.S.C. §13906 (a)(3) (2000) (amended 2005).

CASE SUMMARY

Continued

Fortunoff's goods were damaged in transit, prompting it to make a claim against Frederickson. When the carrier went out of business, Fortunoff asserted the same claim against the carrier's insurer, Peerless Insurance Co., for $13,249.42 under the BMC-32 indorsement (the mandatory attachment to all common carrier insurance policies), which was part of Frederickson's insurance policy. From a judgment for Fortunoff, on the ground that the ICCTA mandated the extension of BMC-32 indorsements to all motor carriers, Peerless appealed.

DECISION: Judgment against the shipper, Fortunoff. Historically, many trucking companies obtained both a common carrier certificate and a contract carrier permit, meaning they were authorized to operate as either type of carrier. If the carrier agreed to transport a shipper's goods according to standard terms and at a fixed rate (i.e., without an individually negotiated contract) on a nonrecurring basis, the transportation was conducted under the carrier's common carrier certificate. Accordingly, common carrier rules, including the cargo liability insurance and the BMC-32 indorsement requirement, applied. If the carrier and the shipper wished to negotiate a bilateral contract for an ongoing course of shipping services, the carrier was required to operate under its contract carrier permit, and no cargo insurance was necessary.

Requiring cargo liability insurance for common carriage but not contract carriage is not an arbitrary distinction. Instead, it makes economic sense because of the different types of services performed and the customers served by common carriage. Although the ICCTA abolished the licensing distinction between common and contract carriers, it did so in large part because most carriers had a common carrier certificate and a contract carrier permit and provided both types of service anyway. But the functional distinction between the two types of carriage survives and is still highly relevant to deciding which motor carriers must have cargo liability insurance. The administrative agency's decision to require BMC-32 cargo insurance only when performing common carriage service is consistent with the ICCTA. The district court's ruling is reversed. [*M. Fortunoff of Westbury Corp. v. Peerless Ins. Co.*, 432 F.3d 127 (2nd Cir. 2005)]

8. Bills of Lading

bill of lading – document issued by a carrier reciting the receipt of goods and the terms of the contract of transportation. Regulated by the Federal Bills of Lading Act or the UCC.

airbill – document of title issued to a shipper whose goods are being sent via air.

When the carrier accepts goods for shipment or forwarding, the carrier ordinarily issues to the shipper a **bill of lading** in the case of land or water transportation or an **airbill** for air transportation. This instrument is a document of title and provides rights similar to those provided by a warehouse receipt. A bill of lading is both a receipt for the goods and a memorandum of a contract stating the terms of carriage. Title to the goods may be transferred by a transfer of the bill of lading made with that intention.

Bills of lading for intrastate shipments are governed by the Uniform Commercial Code. For interstate shipments, bills of lading are regulated by the Federal Bills of Lading Act (FBLA).[20]

CPA **(A) CONTENTS OF BILL OF LADING.** The form of the bill of lading is regulated in varying degrees by administrative agencies. Prior to the revisions to Article 7, negotiable bills of lading were printed on yellow paper, and nonnegotiable or straight bills of lading were printed on white paper. This color-coding may continue as commercial practice for those documents reduced to written form, but new commercial practices will evolve regarding the use of "records.[21]

---

[20] 49 U.S.C. §81 *et seq.*
[21] The U.C.C. contains no provision regulating the form of the bill of lading and the use of records, including electronic tracking, now covered under Revised Article 7. This means that new commercial practices will evolve.

As against the good faith transferee of the bill of lading, a carrier is bound by the recitals in the bill as to the contents, quantity, or weight of goods.[22] This means that the carrier must produce the goods that are described or pay damages for failing to do so. This rule is not applied if facts appear on the face of the bill that should keep the transferee from relying on the recital.

negotiable bill of lading — document of title that by its terms calls for goods to be delivered "to the bearer" or "to the order of" a named person.

nonnegotiable bill of lading — see *straight bill of lading.*

straight (or nonnegotiable) bill of lading — document of title that consigns transported goods to a named person.

(B) NEGOTIATION. A bill of lading is a **negotiable bill of lading** when by its terms the goods are to be delivered "to the bearer" or "to the order of" a named person.[23] Any other bill of lading, such as one that consigns the goods to a named person, is a **nonnegotiable** or **straight bill of lading**. Like transferees of warehouse receipts who take by due negotiation, holders of bills of lading who take by due negotiation ordinarily also acquire title to the bills and title to the goods represented by them.

Rights of a transferee are defeated by the true owner, however, when a thief delivers the goods to the carrier and then negotiates the bill of lading. The thief had no title to the goods at any time.

CASE SUMMARY

International Intrigue

FACTS: Banque de Depots, a Swiss bank, sued Bozel, a Brazilian corporation, for money owed the bank. Banque obtained a writ of attachment from the court against goods being shipped by Bozel from Rio de Janeiro through the port of New Orleans for transit to purchasers located in three states. Bozel claimed that the writ of attachment must be dissolved because the cargo was shipped under negotiable bearer bills of lading and the bills of lading had been sent to U.S. banks for collection from the purchasers.

DECISION: Judgment for Bozel. The writ of attachment must be dissolved. Goods shipped pursuant to a negotiable bill of lading cannot be seized unless the bill of lading is surrendered to the carrier or impounded by a court. On the day of the seizure of the cargo under the writ, the negotiable bills of lading were outstanding. The bills of lading were not in the hands of the carrier, and their negotiation had not been enjoined by the court. The law protects holders of duly negotiated bills of lading from purchasing such bills and then finding out that the goods have been seized by judicial process. The holder of a duly negotiated bill of lading acquires title to the document and title to the goods described in the document. [*Banque de Depots v. Bozel*, **569 So.2d 40 (La. App. 1990)**]

(C) WARRANTIES. By transferring for value a bill of lading, whether negotiable or nonnegotiable, the transferor makes certain implied warranties to the transferee. The transferor impliedly warrants that (1) the bill of lading is genuine, (2) its transfer is rightful and is effective to transfer the goods represented by it, and (3) the transferor has no knowledge of facts that would impair the validity or worth of the bill of lading.[24]

9. Rights of Common Carrier

A common carrier of goods has the right to make reasonable and necessary rules for the conduct of its business. It has the right to charge such rates for its

---

[22] U.C.C. §7-301(1).
[23] U.C.C. §7-104(1)(a).
[24] U.C.C. §7-507; F.B.L.A., 49 U.S.C. §§114, 116. When the transfer of the bill of lading is part of a transaction by which the transferor sells the goods represented thereby to the transferee, there will also arise the warranties that are found in other sales of goods.

services to yield it a fair return on the property devoted to the business of transportation.

As security for unpaid transportation and service charges, a common carrier has a lien on goods that it transports. The carrier's lien also secures demurrage, the costs of preservation of the goods, and the costs of sale to enforce the lien.[25]

10. Duties of Common Carrier

A common carrier is required (1) to receive and carry proper and lawful goods of all persons who offer them for shipment as long as the carrier has space, (2) to furnish facilities that are adequate for the transportation of freight in the usual course of business and to furnish proper storage facilities for goods awaiting shipment or awaiting delivery after shipment, (3) to follow the directions given by the shipper, (4) to load and unload goods delivered to it for shipment, but the shipper or consignee may assume this duty by contract or custom, and (5) to deliver the goods in accordance with the shipment contract.

Goods must be delivered at the usual place of delivery at the specified destination. When goods are shipped under a negotiable bill of lading, the carrier must not deliver the goods without obtaining possession of the bill, properly indorsed. When goods are shipped under a straight bill of lading, the carrier may deliver the goods to the consignee or the consignee's agent without receiving the bill of lading unless notified by the shipper to deliver the goods to someone else. If the carrier delivers the goods to the wrong person, the carrier is liable for breach of contract and for the tort of conversion.

CPA ## 11. Liabilities of Common Carrier

When goods are delivered to a common carrier for immediate shipment and while they are in transit, the carrier is absolutely liable for any loss or damage to the goods unless it can prove that the loss or damage was due solely to one or more of the following excepted causes: (1) an act of God, meaning a natural phenomenon that is not reasonably foreseeable, (2) an act of a public enemy, such as the military forces of an opposing government, as distinguished from ordinary robbers, (3) an act of a public authority, such as a health officer removing goods from the carrier, (4) an act of the shipper, such as fraudulent labeling or defective packing, or (5) the inherent nature of the goods, such as those naturally tending to spoil or deteriorate.

CASE SUMMARY

Landstar Learns the Hard Way

FACTS: Tempel Steel Corporation shipped a large machine press from Minster, Ohio, to Monterrey, Mexico, by Landstar Inway, Inc., a common carrier. Landstar issued Tempel a through bill of lading for this service. It then hauled the press to the U.S. border, where it hired a customs broker who utilized a local carrier, Teresa de Jesus Ortiz Obregon, to move the cargo through U.S. and Mexican customs to interchange with a Mexican carrier. It was determined

[25] U.C.C. §7-307(1); F.B.L.A., 49 U.S.C. §105.

CASE SUMMARY

Continued

that Obregon failed to secure the press properly and drove too fast, causing $300,000 damage to the press. Tempel sued Landstar to recover for this damage. Landstar defended that it was not responsible for causalities in Mexico and that the loss was the fault of Obregon.

DECISION: Landstar is financially responsible for the entire movement by having entered a competitive bid to transport goods from Ohio through to Mexico and having issued a through bill of lading. Tempel is thus entitled to hold Landstar liable for the damage, and Landstar then bears the responsibility for seeking compensation from the carrier actually responsible for the loss. Although Landstar had every legal right to issue a bill of lading that stopped at the U.S. border, it did not do so. Landstar must accept the legal consequences of the issuance of the through bill of lading without limitation of liability for losses. [*Temple Steel Corp. v. Landstar Inway, Inc.*, 211 F.3d 1029 (7th Cir. 2000)]

(A) CARRIER'S LIABILITY FOR DELAY. A carrier is liable for losses caused by its failure to deliver goods within a reasonable time. **For Example,** J.B. Hunt Transport, Inc., "lost" a shipment of boxed Christmas cards specially packaged for Target Stores, Inc., by the shipper, Paper Magic, Inc. The goods were shipped on October 16, 1998, and the invoice valued them at $130,080.48. Hunt located the shipment on February 5, 1999, and Target refused the goods because it was well after Christmas and the goods were worthless to Target. The cards were worthless to Paper Magic because they were packaged with Target's private label. The court found that awarding the shipper the invoice value was a permissible award under the Carmack Amendment to the Interstate Commerce Act.[26]

The carrier, however, is not liable for every delay. The shipper assumes the risk of ordinary delays incidental to transporting goods.

(B) LIMITATION OF LIABILITY OF CARRIER. In the absence of a constitutional or statutory prohibition, a common carrier generally has the right to limit its liability by contract.

Common carriers operating interstate may limit their liability for the negligent loss of consigned items to a stated dollar amount, such as $100 per package. Shippers, however, must be given a reasonable opportunity to select excess liability coverage for the higher value of their shipment, with payment of higher freight charges.[27]

The Carmack Amendment to the Interstate Commerce Act governs the liability of carriers for loss or damage in the interstate shipment of goods.[28] Shippers displeased with liability limitations permitted carriers under the Carmack Amendment may not sue a carrier under any state statute if the statute in any way enlarges the responsibility of a carrier for loss or damage to the goods.[29] The Carmack Amendment provides the exclusive remedy for loss or damage, and its purpose is to provide uniformity in the disposition of claims brought under a bill of

---

[26] *The Paper Magic Group, Inc. v. J.B. Hunt Transport, Inc.*, 318 F.3d 458 (3d Cir. 2003). See also *National Hispanic Circus, Inc. v. Rex Trucking*, 414 F.3d 546 (5th Cir. 2005).

[27] In *Sassy Doll Creations Inc. v. Watkins Motor Lines Inc.*, 331 F.3d 834 (11th Cir. 2003), the carrier was held liable for the full value of a lost shipment of perfume, $28,273.60, rather than $10,000.00, the carrier's established limitation of its liability. The bill of lading prepared by the carrier contained a declared value box, which the shipper filled in. However, the document did not contain any space for requesting excess liability coverage and thus did not give the shipper a reasonable opportunity to select a higher level of coverage as required by the Carmack Amendment to the Interstate Commerce Act.

[28] 49 U.S.C. §11707.

[29] *Dugan v. FedEx Corp.*, 2002 WL 31305208 (C.D. Cal. Sept. 26, 2002).

lading or waybill. An insurer, as a subrogee of the owner or shipper, has standing to sue the carrier under a bill of lading.[30]

CASE SUMMARY

Actual Damage to Cargo, $165,000: Carrier Only Has to Pay $819.71: Can That Be Right?

FACTS: On March 11, 2009, a Straight Bill of Lading (BOL) was issued by Con-way Freight, Inc., for a shipment of cargo from Canada to the United States. The BOL identified the shipper as the Tronosjet Maintenance, Inc., and the consignee as Montex Drilling, Fort Worth, Texas. The "SPECIAL AGREEMENT" box for declaring value and agreeing to pay for excess liability was blank. The BOL identified the cargo as three crates of landing gear. On March 13, 2009, the cargo was picked up in St. John, New Brunswick, Canada. On March 17, 2009, the cargo was transloaded to another trailer, carried from Canada across the border to the United States. On March 19, 2009, the cargo was transloaded to another trailer and physical damage to the crates was noted. On March 23, 2009, the damaged cargo was delivered to Montex Drilling in Fort Worth, Texas. Tronosjet seeks to recover $165,000 as full damages under the Carmack Amendment. Con-way claims that it owes just $819.71 because the claim is subject to the limitation of liability set forth in the BOL and Tariff CNWY 199.

DECISION: Judgment for Con-way. In 1995, under the ICC Termination Act, Congress required that carriers "provide to the shipper, on request of the shipper, a written or electronic copy of the rate, classification, rules, and practices upon which any rate applicable to a shipment, or agreed to between the shipper and the carrier, is based. The BOL under which the cargo shipped stated that "the shipment is received subject to Tariff CNWY–199, Carrier's pricing schedules, terms, conditions, and rules maintained at Carrier's general offices in effect on the date of issue of this Bill of Lading." Because Tronosjet does not dispute that Con-way not only maintained a tariff that incorporated both the limitation of liability at issue and a separate excess valuation charge for full liability, but also published that tariff on its Web site, and incorporated the tariff by reference into the BOL at issue, the court concluded that Con-way has presented undisputed evidence showing that Con-way had established rates for different levels of liability and would have made these rates available to Tronosjet upon request. Moreover, both the BOL and the applicable Con-way tariff clearly state that absent a declared value, Con-way's liability is limited. The court concluded that the shipper had sufficient notice of the limitation of liability and sufficient opportunity to reject that limitation by declaring the value of the shipment and agreeing to pay excess liability charges.
[*Tronosjet v. Con-way Freight, Inc.*, 2011 WL 3322800 (S.D. Tex. Aug. 2, 2011)]

(c) NOTICE OF CLAIM. The bill of lading and applicable government regulations may require that a carrier be given notice of any claim for damages or loss of goods within a specified time, generally within nine months.

(d) COD SHIPMENT. A common carrier transporting goods under a COD (cash on delivery) shipment may not make delivery of the goods without first receiving payment. If it does, it is liable to the shipper for any resulting loss. Thus, if a FedEx or UPS driver were to accept a bad check from a consignee on a COD shipment, the carrier would be liable to the shipper for the amount owed.

There are two forms of COD payments in addition to cash—certified and cashier's checks.

[30] *Onebeacon Insurance Co. v. Haas Industries, Inc.,* 634 F.3d 1092 (9th Cir. 2011).

CASE SUMMARY

Cashier's Check Is King

FACTS: ABF Freight Systems, Inc., accepted a certified check for a COD fee owed upon delivery of 511 cartons of shoes to the location designated in the bill of lading. It turned out that the bank certification stamped on the face of the check was a forgery. The bill of lading included the specification that delivery be "COD Cashier's Check" and that ABF collect payment on behalf of Imports, Ltd. Imports sued ABF for $53,180.90, the full value of the COD payment. From a judgment for Imports for the full amount plus interest, ABF appealed.

DECISION: Judgment for Imports, Ltd. The primary difference between a bank certified check and a cashier's check is in the ease with which one can create a fraudulent instrument. To forge a cashier's check, one would need to replicate all of the other features of the bank's form. To forge a bank check, on the other hand, one need only have a writing on the check indicating that the check is "certified." Imports had a right to believe that a cashier's check is a better form of payment than a certified check. The agreement that ABF would accept only a cashier's check reflected this belief. ABF broke its contract with Imports by accepting a bank certified check rather than a cashier's check for the COD payment. [*Imports, Ltd. v. ABF Freight Systems, Inc.*, 162 F.3d 528 (8th Cir. 1998)]

(E) REJECTED SHIPMENTS. When a common carrier tenders delivery of consigned goods to a consignee that refuses to accept the delivery, the carrier is no longer a common carrier but becomes a warehouse. When the carrier-turned-warehouse receives new shipping instructions from the owner, its status again changes to that of a common carrier.

(F) COMPLEXITIES IN INTERCONTINENTAL AND DOMESTIC SHIPPING. In intercontinental ocean-to-inland shipping, carriers may or may not know whether they are dealing with an intermediary, such as a freight forwarding company rather than a cargo owner, or what legal obligations the cargo owner and intermediary have agreed upon. Moreover, the number of times goods change hands in the course of this intermodal transportation of goods adds to the complexities regarding liability limitations and other bills-of-lading issues such as forum selection clauses. **For Example,** James Kirby, Ltd, an Australian manufacturer, hired International Cargo Control (ICC) to arrange for the delivery of machinery from Australia to Huntsville, Alabama. The bill of lading that ICC issued to Kirby designated Savannah, Georgia, as the discharge port and Huntsville, Alabama, as the ultimate destination, and set ICC's liability limitation lower than the cargo's true value, using the default liability rule in the Carriage of Goods by Sea Act (COGSA) of $500 per package for the sea leg and a higher amount for the land leg. The bill also contained what is known as the "Himalaya Clause," which extends liability limitations to downstream carriers and contractors. When ICC hired a German shipping company, Hamburg Süd, to transport the containers, Hamburg Süd issued its own bill of lading to ICC. That bill of lading also adopted COGSA's default rule, extended it to any land damages, and extended it in a Himalaya Clause to "all agents … (including inland) carriers …." Hamburg Süd hired Norfolk Southern Railway (NS) to transport the machinery some 366 miles from Savannah to Huntsville. The train derailed, causing some $1.5 million in damages. Kirby sued NS for the full value of its loss, and NS, claiming the protections of the ICC and Hamburg Süd bills of lading, asserted that it owed just $500 per container. The U.S. Supreme Court held that "when it comes to liability limitations for negligence resulting in damage, an intermediary [ICC and Hamburg Süd] can negotiate reliable and enforceable agreements with the carrier it engages,"[31] thus upholding NS's limited liability of $500 per container. U.S. courts have also recognized the rule that a freight forwarder has a limited agency to bind a cargo owner to a forum selection clause by accepting a carrier's bill of lading.[32] The COGSA governs the terms of bills of lading by ocean carriers engaged in foreign trade. It does not limit the parties' ability to adopt forum-selection clauses.

CASE SUMMARY

China Cargo; Oklahoma Derailment: Tokyo Trial

FACTS: Regal-Beloit Corp. and other cargo owners delivered goods to Kawasaki Kisen Kaisha Ltd. ("K" Line) for shipping from China to inland United States destinations. "K" Line issued through bills of lading covering both the ocean and inland ports of transport. The bills of lading contained a "Himalaya Clause," which extends the bills' defenses and liability limitations to subcontractors; permitted "K" Line to subcontract to complete the journey; provided that the entire journey through to inland destinations is governed by the Carriage of Goods by Sea Act (COGSA) and contained a forum selection clause that designated a Tokyo, Japan, court as the venue for litigating any dispute. "K" Line subcontracted with Union Pacific Railroad for rail shipment to inland destinations. Upon arrival at the Port of Long Beach, the containers were loaded onto a Union Pacific train, which derailed in Tyrone, Oklahoma, destroying the cargo. The Carmack Amendment to the ICC Act governs the terms of bills of lading issued by domestic rail carriers and limits the parties ability to choose the venue of their lawsuit. The cargo owners assert that the Tokyo forum-selection clause is thus inapplicable, and that they can bring suit against the Union Pacific in the United States under the Carmack Amendment. The district court dismissed the case, ruling that the forum-selection clause was binding. The Court of Appeals reversed, and "K" Line and Union Pacific appealed to the U.S. Supreme Court.

DECISION: Judgment for "K" Line and Union Pacific. The Carmack Amendment does not apply to a shipment originating overseas through a single bill of lading. Applying Carmack to international import shipping transport would undermine COGSA's purpose "to facilitate efficient contracting in contracts for carriage by sea." If two different bills of lading regimes applied to the same through shipments, it would seem to require rail carriers to open containers to check if damage had been done at sea, undermining international container-based transport. [*Kawasaki Kisen Kaisha Ltd. v. Regal-Beloit Corp.*, 130 S.Ct. 2433 (2010)]

C. FACTORS AND CONSIGNMENTS

factor—bailee to whom goods are consigned for sale.

A **factor** is a special type of bailee who sells consigned goods as though the factor were the owner of those goods.

12. Definitions

selling on consignment—entrusting a person with possession of property for the purpose of sale.

Entrusting a person with the possession of property for the purpose of sale is commonly called **selling on consignment**.[33] The owner who consigns the goods

[31] *Norfolk Southern Ry. Co. v. Kirby*, 543 U.S. 1433 (2004).
[32] *Maersk Sealand v. Ocean Express Miami (Quality Print)*, 550 F. Supp. 2d 484 (S.D.N.Y. 2008).
[33] *Amoco Oil Co. v. DZ Enterprises, Inc.*, 607 F. Supp. 595 (S.D.N.Y. 1985).

for sale is the *consignor*. The person or agent to whom they are consigned is the factor or *consignee*; this individual may also be known as a **commission merchant**. A consignee's compensation is known as a **commission** or **factorage**. **For Example,** *consignor* Rolly Tasker Sails Co., Ltd. (RTS) would ship sails from Thailand to the *consignee*, Bacon & Associates of Annapolis, Maryland, with a bill of lading and an "invoice price" for each sail. Mrs. Bacon would then set her "retail fair market value price." Once a set of sails was sold, Mrs. Bacon would deposit a check to the consignor's account at Alex Brown Co. at the invoice price. Her *commission* was the difference between the retail price and the invoice price. This arrangement began in 1971, but began to unravel 27 years later. RTS was successful in its breach of *consignment agreement* lawsuit against Bacon for $345,327 in damages and $78,660 in interest.[34]

commission merchant – bailee to whom goods are consigned for sale.

commission or factorage – consignee's compensation.

13. Effect of Factor Transaction

In a sale on consignment, the property remains the property of the owner-consignor, and the consignee acts as the agent of the owner to pass the owner's title to the buyer. A consignment sale is treated as a sale or return under Article 2 of the Uniform Commercial Code (UCC), and the factor-consignee has full authority to sell the goods for the consignor and can pass title to those goods. Thus, creditors of the consignee can obtain possession of the goods and have a superior right to them over the consignor. If, however, the owner-consignor complies with the security interest and perfection provisions of Article 9 of the UCC (Chapter 34), there is public notice of the consignment, and the goods will be subject to the claims of the owner's creditors, but not to those of the factor-consignee.[35]

If the consignor is not the owner, as when a thief delivers stolen goods to the factor, a sale by the factor passes no title and is an unlawful **conversion**.

conversion – act of taking personal property by a person not entitled to it and keeping it from its true owner or prior possessor without consent.

D. HOTELKEEPERS

A hotelkeeper has a bailee's liability with respect to property specifically entrusted to the hotelkeeper's care. In addition, the hotelkeeper has special duties with respect to a guest's property brought into the hotel. The rules governing the special relationship between a hotelkeeper and a guest arose because of the special needs of travelers.

14. Definitions

The definitions of *hotelkeeper* and *guest* exclude lodging of a more permanent character, such as that provided by boardinghouse keepers to boarders.

(A) HOTELKEEPER. A **hotelkeeper** is an operator of a hotel, motel, or tourist home or anyone who is regularly engaged in the business of offering living accommodations

hotelkeeper – one regularly engaged in the business of offering living accommodations to all transient persons.

---

[34] *Bacon & Associates, Inc. v. Rolly Tasker Sails Co. Ltd. (Thailand)*, 841 A.2d 53 (Md. App. 2004).

[35] Revised Article 2 (1999) modifies the rules on consignments slightly in that all transactions are treated as sales or return or sales on approval unless steps are taken to identify a transaction as a consignment and to comply with state laws on consignment. The new U.C.C. §2-326(a), (b), and (c) provides as follows:

The provisions of this subsection are applicable even though an agreement purports to reserve title to the person making delivery until payment or resale or uses such words as "on consignment" or "on memorandum." However, this subsection is not applicable if the person making delivery

a. complies with an applicable law providing for a consignor's interest or the like to be evidenced by a sign, or

b. establishes that the person conducting the business is generally known by his creditors to be substantially engaged in selling the goods of others, or

c. complies with the filing provisions of the Article on Second Transactions (Article 9).

to transient persons. In the early law, the hotelkeeper was called an *innkeeper* or a *tavernkeeper*.

guest—transient who contracts for a room or site at a hotel.

(B) Guest. A **guest** is a transient. The guest need not be a traveler or come from a distance. A person living within a short distance of a hotel who engages a room at the hotel and remains there overnight is a guest.

In contrast, a person who enters a hotel at the invitation of a guest or attends a dance or a banquet given at the hotel is not a guest. Similarly, the guest of a registered occupant of a motel room who shares the room with the occupant without the knowledge or consent of the management is not a guest of the motel because there is no relationship between that person and the motel.

15. Duration of Guest Relationship

The relationship of guest and hotelkeeper does not begin until a person is received as a guest by the hotelkeeper. The guest–hotelkeeper relationship does not automatically end when the hotel bill is paid.[36]

The relationship terminates when the guest leaves or ceases to be a transient, as when the guest arranges for a more or less permanent residence at the hotel. The transition from the status of guest to the status of boarder or lodger must be clearly indicated. It is not established by the mere fact that one remains at the hotel for a long period, even though it runs into months.

Circumstances arise when a hotel assumes an obligation to deliver packages to a guest from a person who is not a guest of the hotel. The hotelkeeper has a bailee's liability for the care of such packages. **For Example,** Richard St. Angelo, vice president of sales for jewelry manufacturer Don-Linn Inc., left two boxes of jewelry prototypes at the front desk of the Westin Hotel with instructions to deliver the boxes to the hotel's guest from Dillard's Inc., a national department store. This delivery took place. Thereafter, a Dillard's representative notified St. Angelo that Dillard's review of the products was complete and he could pick up the boxes at the hotel but specified no location. St. Angelo and the Westin staff later searched for the boxes, but they were never found. The manufacturer's lawsuit against the Westin asserting a breach of bailment was not successful. St. Angelo was not a guest at the Westin, thus the obligation assumed for the care of the packages initially left at the Westin was not as a hotelkeeper but a bailee. When the Westin surrendered the packages to Dillard's group, it completed its bailment agreement. No bailment or any other legal obligation between Don-Linn and the Westin was shown to exist with regard to the return of the jewelry prototypes.[37]

16. Hotelkeeper's Liability for Guest's Property

With respect to property expressly entrusted to the hotelkeeper's care, the hotelkeeper has a bailee's liability. At common law, the hotelkeeper was absolutely liable for damage to, or loss of, a guest's property unless the hotelkeeper could show

---

[36] *Garrett v. Impac Hotels, LLC,* 87 S.W.3d 870 (Mo. App. 2002).
[37] *Don-Linn Jewelry Co. v. The Westin Hotel Co.,* 877 A.2d 621 (R.I. 2005).

that the damage or loss was caused solely by an act of God, a public enemy, an act of a public authority, the inherent nature of the property, or the fault of the guest.[38]

In most states, statutes limit or provide a method of limiting the common law liability of a hotelkeeper. The statutes may limit the extent of liability, reduce the liability of a hotelkeeper to that of an ordinary bailee, or permit the hotelkeeper to limit liability by contract or by posting a notice of the limitation. Some statutes relieve the hotelkeeper from liability when the guest has not complied with directions for depositing valuables with the hotelkeeper.[39] A hotelkeeper must substantially comply with such statutes in order to obtain their protection.

CASE SUMMARY

Conspicuous Notice Necessary to Avoid Liability

FACTS: While traveling from Florida to Connecticut, Mr. and Mrs. Ippolito stopped in Walterboro, South Carolina, and paid for a room at a Holiday Inn. At the hotel, Mr. Ippolito signed a registration card on which was written, "The management is not responsible for any valuables not secured in safety deposit boxes provided at the front office." In addition to the language on the registration card, notice that the hotel had safety deposit boxes available for guests' valuables was also printed on the pouch that enclosed the key-card to the Ippolitos' room. After bringing their luggage to the room, the Ippolitos walked to a nearby restaurant, and they returned approximately 40 minutes later. Upon their return, they noticed that pieces of their luggage, which contained jewelry valued at over $500,000 and approximately $8,000 in cash, were missing. The Ippolitos sued the innkeeper, alleging that their property loss resulted from "... the negligence, gross negligence, reckless, willful, wanton and careless action ..." of Innkeeper, including "... failing to post proper notices as required under South Carolina law."

The state's innkeeper statute requires the innkeeper to post notice in a "conspicuous manner" in the room occupied by the guest, and the guest must deposit money and jewels in the office safe. The Ippolitos testified that they did not see any notice of safety deposit boxes posted in their room. Police officer Sadler testified that, although he made no mention of it in his police report, he saw a notice posted on the back of the hotel room door indicating that the innkeeper had safety deposit boxes available. The jury awarded the Ippolitos $350,000 in actual damages. However, the jury found that the Ippolitos were 40 percent comparatively negligent, and reduced the award to $210,000. The hotel appealed.

DECISION: Judgment for the Ippolitos. Whether guests observed a conspicuous notice in the room regarding availability of safety deposit boxes is a question for the jury where there is a conflict in testimony. The jury believed the Ippolitos' testimony of a lack of conspicuous notice. If an innkeeper fails to post such a notice, the innkeeper's liability is not limited. [*Ippolito v. Hospitality Management Associates*, 575 S.E.2d 562 (S.C. App. 2003)]

17. Hotelkeeper's Lien

The hotelkeeper has a lien on the baggage of guests for the agreed charges or, if no express agreement was made, for the reasonable value of the accommodations furnished. Statutes permit the hotelkeeper to enforce this lien by selling the goods of

---

[38] *Cook v. Columbia Sussex Corp.,* 807 S.W.2d 567 (Tenn. App. 1991).

[39] *Chappone v. First Florence Corp.,* 504 S.E.2d 761 (Ga. App. 1998). But see *World Diamond Inc. v. Hyatt Corp.,* 699 N.E.2d 980 (Ohio App. 1997), where the court held that when special arrangements have been made between the innkeeper and the guest, the innkeeper is liable for the loss of any property so received when the loss is caused by the innkeeper's negligence.

the guests at a public sale. The lien of the hotelkeeper is terminated by (1) the guest's payment of the hotel charges, (2) any conversion of the guest's goods by the hotelkeeper, or (3) final return of the goods to the guest.

18. Boarders or Lodgers

The hotelkeeper owes only the duty of an ordinary bailee of personal property under a mutual benefit bailment to those persons who are permanent boarders or lodgers rather than transient guests.

A hotelkeeper has no lien on property of boarders or lodgers, as distinguished from guests, in the absence of an express agreement creating such a lien. A number of states, however, have adopted legislation giving a lien to keepers of boardinghouses or lodging houses.

LawFlix

Nine to Five (1980) (PG)

At the heart of the twists and turns in this boss/secretary caper are the warehouse receipts an executive is using to embezzle from his company. Analyze what the executive was doing with the documents.

MAKE THE CONNECTION

SUMMARY

A warehouse stores the goods of others for compensation and has the rights and duties of a bailee in an ordinary mutual benefit bailment. A warehouse issues a warehouse receipt to the depositor of the goods. This receipt is a document of title that ordinarily entitles the person in possession of the receipt to receive the goods. The warehouse receipt can be bought, sold, or used as security to obtain a loan. A nonnegotiable warehouse receipt states that the goods received will be delivered to a specified person. A negotiable warehouse receipt states that the goods will be delivered "to the bearer" or "to the order of" a named person. If a negotiable warehouse receipt is duly negotiated, the transferee may acquire rights superior to those of the transferor. A warehouse may limit its liability for loss or damage to goods resulting from its own negligence to an agreed valuation of the property stated in the warehouse receipt, provided the depositor is given the right to

store the goods without the limitation at a higher storage rate.

A common carrier of goods is in the business of transporting goods received from the general public. It issues to the shipper a bill of lading or an airbill. Both of these are documents of title and provide rights similar to those provided by a warehouse receipt. A common carrier is absolutely liable for any loss or damage to the goods unless the carrier can show that the loss was caused solely by an act of God, an act of a public enemy, an act of a public authority, an act of the shipper, or the inherent nature of the goods. The carrier may limit its liability in the same manner as a warehouse.

A factor is a special type of bailee who has possession of the owner's property for the purpose of sale. The factor, or consignee, receives a commission on the sale.

A hotelkeeper is in the business of providing living accommodations to transient persons called guests. Subject to exceptions, at common law, hotelkeepers were absolutely liable for loss or damage to their guests' property. Most states, however, provide a method of limiting this liability. A hotelkeeper has a lien on the property of the guest for the agreed charges.

LEARNING OUTCOMES

After studying this chapter, you should be able to clearly explain:

A. Warehousers

L0.1 Identify and explain all of the features of a negotiable warehouse receipt

See the example of the bona fide purchase of a warehouse receipt of 4,000 pairs of ice skates on pp. 446–447.
See Figure 22-1.

B. Common Carriers

L0.2 List and explain the differences between the three types of motor carriers of goods

See the *Fortunoff* case and distinctions made between "common" and "contract" carriers, pp. 449–450.

L0.3 Explain a common carrier's liability for loss or damage to goods

See the *Tronosjet* case applying the Carmack Amendment rule on carrier liability, p. 454.

C. Factors and Consignments

L0.4 Identify and explain the role of each of the persons or business entities involved in the sale of goods on consignment

See the Rolly Tasker Sails example involving breach of a consignment agreement on p. 457.

D. Hotelkeepers

L0.5 Describe a hotelkeeper's liability for loss of a guest's property

See the *Ippolito* case for a discussion of the common law rule on liability for loss of a guest's property and application of a statutory exemption, p. 459.

KEY TERMS

airbill	depositor	nonnegotiable bill of lading
bill of lading	document of title	nonnegotiable warehouse receipt
carrier	factorage	private carrier
commission merchant	factor	public warehouses
commission	field warehousing	selling on consignment
common carrier	guest	specific lien
consignee	hotelkeeper	straight bill of lading
consignor	issuer	warehouse
contract carrier	negotiable bill of lading	warehouse receipt
conversion	negotiable warehouse receipt	

QUESTIONS AND CASE PROBLEMS

1. What social forces are involved in the rule of law governing the liability of a common carrier for loss of freight?

2. American Cyanamid shipped 7,000 vials of DPT—a vaccine for immunization of infants and children against diphtheria, pertussis, and tetanus—from its Pearl River, New York, facility to the U.S. Defense Department depot in Mechanicsburg, Pennsylvania, by New Penn Motor Express, a common carrier. Cyanamid's bill

of lading included a "release value," which stated the value of the property was declared as not exceeding $1.65 per pound. Cyanamid's shipment weighed 1,260 pounds. The bill of lading accepted by New Penn on picking up the DPT vaccine on February 6 also clearly stated that the shipment contained drugs and clearly warned to "protect from freezing." The bill further recited "rush … must be delivered by February 8, 1989." New Penn permitted the vaccine to sit in an unheated uninsulated trailer while it gathered enough other merchandise to justify sending a truck to Mechanicsburg. The DPT vaccine was delivered on February 10 in worthless condition, having been destroyed by the cold. New Penn admitted it owed $2,079 in damages pursuant to the bill of lading ($1.65 × 1,260 lb.). Cyanamid claimed that the actual loss was much greater, $53,936.75. It stated that because New Penn breached its contract with Cyanamid, it could not invoke the benefits of that same contract, namely, the release value clause.

Was it ethical for New Penn to hold the vaccine while waiting for enough merchandise to justify the trip? How would you decide the case? [*American Cyanamid Co. v. New Penn Motor Express, Inc.*, 979 F.2d 301 (3d Cir.)]

3. Compare the liens of carriers, warehouses, and hotels in terms of being specific.

4. Compare the limitations of the liability of a warehouse and of a hotelkeeper.

5. Compare warehouse receipts and bills of lading as to negotiability.

6. Doyle Harms applied to his state's Public Utilities Commission for a Class B permit authorizing performance as a common carrier. Doyle testified that it was not his intention to haul in a different direction than he was already going, stating in part:

> No way, that's not what I'm asking for. I've got enough business of my own, it's just the times when you get done with a sale at the end of the day and you've got a half load and somebody else has a half load, then you'd be able to help each other out. It's kind of the name of the game in my mind.

He also testified that the application was so he could haul cattle for his own customers. State law defines a common carrier as "a motor carrier which holds itself out to the general public as engaged in the business of transporting persons or property in intrastate commerce which it is accustomed to and is capable of transporting from place to place in this state, for hire." Its property is "devoted to the public service." Should Doyle Harms be issued a common carrier permit? [*In re Harms*, 491 N.W.2d 760 (S.D.)]

7. Motorola manufactured cell phones for Nextel of Mexico at its facility in Plantation, Florida. Nextel used Westwind International to arrange transportation of the cell phones. Westwind utilized Transpro Logistics to administer the transportation process and Transpro entered a Broker Transportation Agreement (BTA) with Werner Enterprises, a common carrier, to transport the phones from Florida to Texas on a regular basis. The BTA incorporated Werner's tariff giving shippers the option of selecting Carmack Liability full-value coverage or the carrier's limitation of liability of a maximum of $200,000 per truckload shipment. In its contract with Nextel, Westwind notified Nextel that third-party carriers might limit their liability for loss, and stated that it would request excess valuation coverage only upon specific written instructions from Nextel. Nextel simply relied on Westwind to handle shipping issues. On October 8, 2004, a shipment of 7,958 cell phones valued at $1,251,673 was stolen from one of Werner's trucks. Werner contended it owed a maximum liability of $200,000 under its tariff. Nextel's insurer, Ace Seguros SA, sued Werner for the full value of the shipment, contending that contracts downstream by Westwind and Transpro cannot be imputed back to Nextel—and that the cargo owner Nextel had not been given the opportunity to choose between two or more levels of liability as required by the Carmack Amendment. Can intermediaries like Westwind and/or Transpro negotiate an enforceable agreement with a carrier it engages? Was Nextel given a reasonable opportunity to choose between two or more levels of liability? Decide. [*Werner Enterprises, Inc. v. Ace Seguros SA*, 554 F.3d 1319 (11th Cir.)]

8. Richard Schewe and others placed personal property in a building occupied by Winnebago County Fair Association, Inc. Prior to placing their property in the building, they signed a "Storage Rental Agreement" prepared by the County Fair Association, which stated: "No liability exists for damage or loss to the stored equipment from the perils of fire… ." The property was destroyed by fire. Suit was brought against the County Fair Association to recover damages for the losses on the theory of negligence of a warehouse. The County Fair Association claimed that the language in the storage agreement relieved it of all liability. [*Allstate Ins. Co. v. Winnebago County Fair Ass'n, Inc.*, 475 N.E.2d 230 (Ill. App.)]

9. Buffett sent a violin to Strotokowsky by International Parcel Service (IPS), a common carrier. Buffett declared the value of the parcel at $500 on the pick-up receipt given him by the IPS driver. The receipt also stated: "Unless a greater value is declared in writing on this receipt, the shipper hereby declares and agrees that the released value of each package covered by this receipt is $100.00, which is a reasonable value under the circumstance surrounding the transportation." When Strotokowsky did not receive the parcel, Buffett sued IPS for the full retail value of the violin—$2,000. IPS's defense was that it was liable for just $100. Decide.

10. Glen Smith contracted with Dave Watson, a common carrier, to transport 720 hives of live bees along with associated equipment from Idabel, Oklahoma, to Mandan, North Dakota. At 9:00 A.M. on May 24, 1984, while en route, Watson's truck skidded off the road and tipped over, severely damaging the cargo. Watson notified Smith about what had happened, and Smith immediately set out for the scene of the accident. He arrived at 6:00 P.M. with two bee experts and a Bobcat loader. They were hindered by the turned-over truck on top of the cargo, and they determined that they could not safely salvage the cargo that evening. The next day, an insurance adjuster determined that the cargo was a total loss. The adjuster directed a bee expert, Dr. Moffat, to conduct the cleanup; Moffat was allowed to keep the salvageable cargo, valued at $12,326, as compensation. Smith sued

Watson for damages. Watson denied liability and further contended that Smith failed to mitigate damages. Decide. [*Smith v. Watson*, 406 N.W.2d 685 (N.D.)]

11. Garrett and his wife checked into the St. Louis Airport North Holiday Inn on March 29, taking advantage of the hotel's "Park and Fly" package, which provided one night of lodging to individuals, provided a shuttle service to Lambert International Airport, and allowed individuals to keep a vehicle on the hotel's parking lot for up to two weeks. When the Garretts returned from their vacation on April 17, they discovered that their vehicle was stolen. They sued the hotel, contending that a special relationship of an innkeeper and guest was created by the "Park and Fly" marketing package, and that the hotel's knowledge of criminal activity on its parking lot created a duty to warn the Garretts, which it failed to do. What status did the Garretts have with the hotel regarding the protection of their vehicle after boarding the plane on their vacation trip? Was there a bailment of the vehicle under the "Park and Fly" marketing package? [*Garrett v. IMPAC Hotels Inc.*, 87 S.W.3d 870 (Mo. App.)]

12. On March 30, Emery Air Freight Corp. picked up a shipment of furs from Hopper Furs, Inc. Hopper's chief of security filled in certain items in the airbill. In the box entitled ZIP Code, he mistakenly placed the figure "61,045," which was the value of the furs. The ZIP Code box was immediately above the Declared Value box. The airbill contained a clause limiting liability to $10 per pound of cargo lost or damaged unless the shipper makes a declaration of value in excess of the amount and pays a higher fee. A higher fee was not charged in this case, and Gerald Doane signed the airbill for the carrier and took possession of the furs. The furs were lost in transit by Emery, and Hopper sued for the value of the furs, $61,045. Emery's offer to pay $2,150, the $10-per-pound rate set forth in the airbill, was rejected. Hopper claimed that the amount of $61,045, which was mistakenly placed in the ZIP Code box, was in fact part of the contract set forth in the airbill and that Emery, on reviewing the contract, must have

realized a mistake was made. Decide. [*Hopper Furs, Inc. v. Emery Air Freight Corp.*, 749 F.2d 1261 (8th Cir.)]

13. When de Lema, a Brazilian resident, arrived in New York City, his luggage consisted of three suitcases, an attaché case, and a cylindrical bag. The attaché case and the cylindrical bag contained jewels valued at $300,000. De Lema went from JFK Airport to the Waldorf Astoria Hotel, where he gave the three suitcases to hotel staff in the garage, and then he went to the lobby to register. The assistant manager, Baez, summoned room clerk Tamburino to assist him. De Lema stated, "The room clerk asked me if I had a reservation. I said, 'Yes. The name is José Berga de Lema.' And I said, 'I want a safety deposit box.' He said, 'Please fill out your registration.' " While de Lema was filling out the registration form, paying $300 in cash as an advance, and Tamburino was filling out a receipt for that amount, de Lema had placed the attaché case and the cylindrical bag on the floor. A woman jostled de Lema, apparently creating a diversion, and when he next looked down, he discovered that the attaché case was gone. De Lema brought suit against the hotel for the value of the jewels stolen in the hotel's lobby. The hotel maintained a safe for valuables and posted notices in the lobby, garage, and rooms as required by the New York law that modifies a hotelkeeper's common law liability. The notices stated in part that the hotel was not liable for the loss of valuables that a guest had neglected to deliver to the hotel for safekeeping. The hotel's defense was that de Lema had neglected to inform it of the presence of the jewels and to deliver the jewels to the hotel. Is the hotel liable for the value of the stolen jewels? [*De Lema v. Waldorf Astoria Hotel, Inc.*, 588 F. Supp. 19 (S.D.N.Y.)]

14. Frosty Land Foods shipped a load of beef from its plant in Montgomery, Alabama, to Scott Meat Co. in Los Angeles via Refrigerated Transport Co. (RTC), a common carrier. Early Wednesday morning, December 7, at 12:55 A.M., two of RTC's drivers left the Frosty Land plant with the load of beef. The bill of lading called for delivery at Scott Meat on Friday, December 9, at 6:00 A.M. The RTC drivers arrived in Los Angeles at approximately 3:30 P.M. on Friday, December 9. Scott notified the drivers that it could not process the meat at that time. The drivers checked into a motel for the weekend, and the load was delivered to Scott on Monday, December 12. After inspecting 65 of the 308 carcasses, Scott determined that the meat was in off condition and refused the shipment. On Tuesday, December 13, Frosty Land sold the meat, after extensive trimming, at a loss of $13,529. Frosty Land brought suit against RTC for its loss. Decide. [*Frosty Land Foods v. Refrigerated Transport Co.*, 613 F.2d 1344 (5th Cir.)]

15. Tate hired Action-Mayflower Moving & Storage to ship his belongings. Action prepared a detailed inventory of Tate's belongings, loaded them on its truck, and received the belongings at its warehouse, where they would be stored until Tate asked that they be moved. Months later, a dispute arose, and Tate asked Action to release his property to a different mover. Tate had prepaid more than enough to cover all charges to this point. Action refused to release the goods and held them in storage. After allowing storage charges to build up for 15 months, Action sold Tate's property under the warehouser's public sale law. Tate sued Action for damages. Decide. [*Tate v. Action-Mayflower Moving & Storage, Inc.*, 383 S.E.2d 229 (N.C. App.)]

CPA QUESTIONS

1. A common carrier bailee generally would avoid liability for loss of goods entrusted to its care if the goods are:

   a. Stolen by an unknown person.

   b. Negligently destroyed by an employee.

   c. Destroyed by the derailment of the train carrying them due to railroad employee negligence.

   d. Improperly packed by the party shipping them.

2. Under a nonnegotiable bill of lading, a carrier who accepts goods for shipment must deliver the goods to:

   a. Any holder of the bill of lading.

   b. Any party subsequently named by the seller.

   c. The seller who was issued the bill of lading.

   d. The consignee of the bill of lading.

3. Under the UCC, a warehouse receipt:

   a. Is negotiable if, by its terms, the goods are to be delivered to bearer or to the order of a named person.

   b. Will not be negotiable if it contains a contractual limitation on the warehouse's liability.

   c. May qualify as both a negotiable warehouse receipt and negotiable commercial paper if the instrument is payable either in cash or by the delivery of goods.

   d. May be issued only by a bonded and licensed warehouser.

4. Under the Documents of Title Article of the UCC, which of the following acts may limit a common carrier's liability for damages to the goods in transit?

   a. Vandalism.

   b. Power outage.

   c. Willful acts of third person.

   d. Providing for a contractual dollar liability limitation.

© Manuel Gutjahr/iStockphoto.com

CHAPTER 23

Nature and Form of Sales

learningoutcomes

After studying this chapter, you should be able to

LO.1 ▶ Define a sale of goods and explain when UCC Article 2 applies to contracts

LO.2 ▶ Distinguish between an actual sale of goods and other types of transactions in goods

LO.3 ▶ Describe how contracts are formed under Article 2, and list the differences in formation standards between the UCC and common law

LO.4 ▶ Explain when a contract for the sale of goods must be in writing

LO.5 ▶ List and explain the exceptions to the requirement that certain contracts be in writing

LO.6 ▶ Discuss the purpose of the United Nations Convention on Contracts for the International Sale of Goods

C hapters 12 through 20 examined the common law of contracts. That source of contract law applies to contracts whose subject matter is land or services. However, there is another source of contract law, **Article 2** of the Uniform Commercial Code (UCC).

Article 2 – section of Uniform Commercial Code that governs contracts for the sale of goods.

Article 2 was revised substantially by the National Conference of Commissioners on Uniform State Laws (NCCUSL) and the American Law Institute (ALI) in August 2003. Because no state has adopted Revised Article 2, its future remains a question. Revised Article 2 is covered only briefly in this chapter and Chapters 24–27.

UCC Article 2 governs the sale of everything from boats to televisions to compact discs and applies to contracts for the sale of goods. Article 2 exists as a result of the work of businesspeople, commercial transactions lawyers, and legal experts who together have developed a body of contract law suitable for the fast pace of business. Article 2 continues to be refined and modified to ensure seamless laws for transactions in goods across the country.[1]

A. NATURE OF SALES

A *sale of goods* is defined under Article 2 as transfer of title to tangible personal property for a price.[2] This price may be a payment of money, an exchange of other property, or the performance of services.

The parties to a sale are the person who owns the goods, the seller or vendor, and the person to whom the title is transferred, the buyer or vendee.

CPA

1. Subject Matter of Sales

goods – anything movable at the time it is identified as the subject of a transaction.

Goods, as defined under the UCC, consist of all forms of tangible personal property, including specially manufactured goods—everything from a fan to a painting to a yacht.[3] Article 2 does not cover (1) investment securities, such as stocks and bonds, the sale of which is regulated by Article 8 of the UCC; (2) insurance policies, commercial paper, such as checks, and promissory notes because they are regulated under Articles 3 and 4 of the UCC; and (3) real estate, such as houses, factories, farms, and land itself.[4]

---

[1] The UCC Article 2 (prior to the 2003 revisions) has been adopted in 49 states plus the Virgin Islands and the District of Columbia. Louisiana adopted only Article 1; 1990 Revision of Article 3; 1990 Amendments to Article 4; Article 4A (Funds Transfers); 1995 Revision of Articles 5 and 7; 1994 Revision of Article 8; and 2000 Revision of Article 9. The newest revisions of Article 2 were reconciled in July, 2003. The changes in Revised Article 2 are noted briefly throughout this chapter and Chapters 24–27.

[2] UCC §2-105(1). *General Mills Operations, LLC v. Five Star Custom Foods, Ltd.*, 798 F. Supp. 2d 1148 (D. Minn. 2011); *M K Intern., Inc. v. Central Oil & Supply Corp.*, 87 So.3d 165 (La.App. 2012).

[3] *State v. Cardwell*, 718 A.2d 594 (Conn. 1998) (concert tickets are goods); *In re Grede Foundries, Inc.*, 435 B.R. 593 (W.D. Wisc. 2010) (electricity is a good); *Leal v. Holtvogh*, 702 N.E.2d 1246 (Ohio App. 1998) (transfer of part interest in a horse is a good); *Bergeron v. Aero Sales*, 134 P.3d 964 (Or. App. 2006) (jet fuel is a good); *Rite Aid Corp. v. Levy-Gray*, 894 A.2d 563 (Md. 2006) (prescription drug is a good); *Willis Mining v. Noggle*, 509 S.E.2d 731 (Ga. App. 1998) (granite blocks are goods); *Sterling Power Partners, L.P. v. Niagra Mohawk Power Corp.*, 657 N.Y.S.2d 407 (1997) (electricity is a good); *Gladhart v. Oregon Vineyard Supply Co.*, 994 P.2d 134 (Or. App. 1999) (grape plants bought from nursery are goods); *Dantzler v. S.P. Parks, Inc.*, 40 UCC Rep.Serv.2d 955 E.D. Pa. 1988) (purchase of ticket to amusement ride is not transaction in goods); *Rossetti v. Busch Entm't Corp.*, 87 F. Supp. 2d (E.D. Pa. 2000) (computer software programs are goods); and *Saxton v. Pets Warehouse, Inc.*, 691 N.Y.S.2d 872 (1999) (dog is a good).

[4] However, Article 2 does apply to the sale of rare coins. *Bowers and Merena Auctions, LLC, v. James Lull*, 386 B.R. 261, 65 UCC Rep. Ser. 2d 194 (Haw. 2008).

(A) NATURE OF GOODS. Article 2 applies not only to contracts for the sale of familiar items of personal property, such as automobiles or chairs, but also to the transfer of commodities, such as oil, gasoline, milk, and grain.[5]

(B) EXISTING AND FUTURE GOODS. Goods that are already manufactured or crops already grown and owned by the seller at the time of the transaction are called **existing goods**. All other goods are called **future goods**, which include both goods that physically exist but are not owned by the seller and goods that have not yet been produced, as when a buyer contracts to purchase custom-made office furniture.

> **existing goods** – goods that physically exist and are owned by the seller at the time of a transaction.
>
> **future goods** – goods that exist physically but are not owned by the seller and goods that have not yet been produced.

2. Sale Distinguished from Other Transactions

Other types of transactions in goods are not covered by Article 2 because they are not transfers of title to the goods.

(A) BAILMENT. A **bailment** is not a sale because only possession is transferred to a **bailee**. Title to the property is not transferred. (For more information on bailments, their nature, and the rights of the parties, see Chapter 21.) A lease of goods, such as an automobile, is governed by Article 2A of the UCC, which is covered later in Section D of this chapter.

> **bailment** – relationship that exists when personal property is delivered into the possession of another under an agreement, express or implied, that the identical property will be returned or will be delivered in accordance with the agreement. (Parties—bailor, bailee)
>
> **bailee** – person who accepts possession of a property.

(B) GIFT. A **gift** is a gratuitous (free) transfer of the title to property. The Article 2 definition of a sale requires that the transfer of title be made for a price. Gifts are not covered under Article 2.[6]

> **gift** – title to an owner's personal property voluntarily transferred by a party not receiving anything in exchange.

(C) CONTRACT FOR SERVICES. A contract for services, such as a contract for painting a home, is not a sale of goods and is not covered under Article 2 of the UCC. Contracts for services are governed by common law principles.

(D) CONTRACT FOR GOODS AND SERVICES. If a contract calls for both rendering services and supplying materials to be used in performing the services, the contract is classified according to its dominant element. **For Example,** a homeowner may purchase a security system. The homeowner is paying for the equipment that is used in the system as well as for the seller's expertise and installation of that system. Is the homeowner's contract governed by Article 2, or is it a contract for services and covered under the common law of contracts?

If the service element dominates, the contract is a service contract and is governed by common law rather than Article 2. If the goods make up the dominant element of the contract, then the parties' rights are determined under Article 2.[7] In the home security system contract example, the question requires comparing the costs of the system's parts versus the costs of its installation. In some contracts, the equipment costs are minimal, and installation is key for the customer. In more sophisticated security systems, the installation is a small portion of the overall contract price, and the contract would be governed by the UCC.[8]

---

[5] UCC §2-105(1)–(2). *Venmar Ventilation, Inc. v. Von Weise USA, Inc.*, 68 UCC Serv. 2d 373 (D. Minn. 2009); *Marcus Dairy, Inc. v. Rollin Dairy Corp.*, 67 UCC Rep. Serv. 2d 777 (D. Conn. 2008).

[6] The adoption of a dog from an animal shelter is not the sale of goods. *Slodov v. Animal Protective League*, 628 N.E.2d 117 (Oh. App. 1993).

[7] Trees and shrubs as part of a landscaping contract are sales of goods. *Kaitz v. Landscape Creations, Inc.*, 2000 Mass.App.Div. 140, 2000 WL 694274 (Mass.App.Div.), 42 UCC Rep.Serv.2d 691.

[8] *TK Power, Inc. v. Textron, Inc.*, 433 F. Supp. 2d 1058 (N.D. Cal. 2006), see also *Lesiak v. Central Valley Ag Co-op., Inc.*, 808 N.W.2d 67 (Neb. 2012) (a contract for the sale and application of herbicide was primarily a contract for the sale of the herbicide and was governed by the UCC).

CASE SUMMARY

Dirt Is Cheap, But It Is Still a Good

FACTS: Paramount, a civil engineering firm and general contractor, submitted a bid to construct runway improvements at the Atlanta Hartsfield–Jackson International Airport. Paramount included DPS's quote for supplying the fill dirt for the project in its bid. DPS's written quote described its work as "furnish[ing] and haul[ing]/deliver[ing] borrow dirt from DPS's location to the job site," and specifically excluded the provision of "traffic control, dust control, security and escort services" from the scope of work. The quote provides that the dirt would be delivered for a price of "$140/Truck Load."

After Paramount was awarded the airport project, it contacted DPS about the amount of dirt and numbers of trucks that it would need for the airport project. DPS believed that the parties had a contract, and it sent a letter to Paramount confirming that it was "holding approximately 45,000 [cubic yards] of borrow dirt ready to be hauled in to your project once we receive [the] 10–day notice from you." Paramount did not respond.

Over the next two months, DPS sent other letters to Paramount, but Paramount did not respond. After executives from the two companies met, Paramount sent the following:

> [Y]ou insisted that we give commitment to you for buying the dirt before you will give us price [for other work]. This really was a surprise to us. … Also please note that we have never committed to buy all the fill materials from you. In the last meeting you were informed that we intend to purchase some materials from you and it may be through other subcontractors. Our decisions will be conveyed to you as soon as possible.

Ultimately, Paramount bought the dirt it needed from another vendor. DPS sued Paramount for breach of contract. The jury found for DPS. Paramount appealed arguing that the UCC did not apply and a more formal contract was needed.

DECISION: The court held that the sale of dirt was the predominant purpose of the contract. The price was based on the quantity of dirt delivered and the language used was for sale of dirt, not hauling of dirt. Further, the seller severed the dirt from the land, something that means the seller was selling a good. The UCC applied, and there was a valid contract. [***Paramount Contracting Co. v. DPS Industries, Inc.*, 709 S.E.2d 288 (Ga.App. 2011)**]

One of the critical issues under Article 2 that has resulted from technological advances is whether Article 2 covers computer software included with the sale of a computer, thus subjecting software manufacturers to warranty liability and the damage provisions of the UCC.[9] Whether software would be covered under Article 2 was the most spirited debate in the 2003 revision process.[10] Under the final draft, Revised Article 2 does not cover "information," but information is not defined. Several state legislatures have addressed this issue by modifying their versions of the UCC with a section that establishes that "goods" does not cover the sale of "information" not associated with "goods."[11]

---

[9] *Multi-Tech Systems, Inc. v. Floreat, Inc.*, 47 UCC Rep. Serv. 2d 924 (D. Minn. 2002).

[10] Section 2-103(1)(k) of Revised Article 2 defines goods as follows: *all things movable at the time of identification to a contract for sale. The term includes future goods, specially manufactured goods, the unborn young of animals, growing crops, and other identified things attached to realty as described in §2-107. The term does not include information, the money in which the price is to be paid, investment securities under Article 8, the subject matter of foreign exchange transactions and choses in action.*

[11] Up through 2002, the UCC revisions included provisions on computer information. However, the original amendments to Section 2-102 (4) and (5) never made their way into the final version of UCC 2-102. We are left only with the comment partially quoted here. The comment basically says "it depends" as to whether Article 2 applies, with the dependency on the nature of the contract.

CPA

3. Formation of Sales Contracts

(A) NECESSARY DETAIL FOR FORMATION. To streamline business transactions, Article 2 of the UCC does not have standards as rigid as the formation standards of common law contracts.

Under the UCC, a contract can be formed even though one or more terms are left open so long as the parties clearly intend to contract.[12] The minimum terms required for formation of an agreement under the UCC are the subject matter and quantity (if there is more than one).[13] **For Example,** an agreement that described "the sale of my white Scion" would be sufficient, but an agreement to purchase "some white Scions" would require a quantity in order to qualify for formation.[14] Other provisions under Article 2 can cover any missing terms so long as the parties are clear on their intent to contract. Article 2 has provisions that cover price, delivery, time for performance, payment, and other details of performance in the event the parties agree to a sale but have not discussed or reduced to writing their desires in these areas.[15]

(B) THE MERCHANT VERSUS NONMERCHANT PARTIES. Because Article 2 applies to all transactions in goods, it is applicable to sales by both **merchants** and nonmerchants,[16] including consumers. In most instances, the UCC treats all buyers and sellers alike. However, some sections in Article 2 are applicable only to merchants, and as a result, there are circumstances in which merchants are subject to different standards and rules. Generally, these areas of different treatment reflect the UCC's recognition that merchants are experienced, have special knowledge of the relevant commercial practices, and often need to have greater flexibility and speed in their transactions. The sections that have different rules for merchants and nonmerchants are noted throughout Chapters 24–27.

merchant – seller who deals in specific goods classified by the UCC.

CPA

(c) OFFER. Just as in common law, the **offer** is the first step in formation of a sales contract under Article 2.[17] The common law contract rules on offers are generally applicable in sales contract formation with the exception of the **firm offer**[18] provision, which is a special rule on offers applicable only to merchants: A firm offer by a merchant cannot be revoked if the offer (1) expresses an intention that it will be kept open, (2) is in a writing, and (3) is signed by the merchant.[19]

offer – expression of an offeror's willingness to enter into a contractual agreement.

firm offer – offer stated to be held open for a specified time, under the UCC, with respect to merchants.

The period of irrevocability in a merchant's firm offer cannot exceed three months. If no specific time is given in the merchant's firm offer for its duration, it remains irrevocable only for a reasonable time. A firm offer need not have consideration to be irrevocable for a period of three months. **For Example,** a rain check given by a store on advertised merchandise is a merchant's firm offer. The rain check guarantees that you will be able to purchase two bottles of Windex at $1.99 each for a period specified in the rain check.

---

[12] 5 UCC §2-204(3); *Cargill v. Jorgenson Farms,* 719 N.W.2d 226 (Minn. App. 2006). This provision on formation assumes that the agreement the parties do have provides "a reasonably certain basis for giving an appropriate remedy." Price quotations are not considered offers. *Ace American Ins. Co. v. Wendt, LLP,* 724 F. Supp. 2d 899 (N.D. Ill. 2010).

[13] See also, *H.P.B.C., Inc. v. Nor-Tech Powerboats, Inc.,* 946 So.2d 1108 (Fla. App. 2006).

[14] *Griffith v. Clear Lakes Trout Co., Inc.,* 200 P.3d 1162, 67 UCC Rep. Ser. 2d 883 (Idaho 2009).

[15] For information on terms, see UCC §§2-305 (price), 2-307 to 2-308 (delivery), 2-310 (payment), and 2-311 (performance).

[16] *Merchant* is defined in UCC §2-104(1). An operator of a turkey farm is not a merchant with regard to heaters used on turkey farms, only for the turkeys themselves. *Jennie-O-Foods, Inc. v. Safe-Glo Prods. Corp.,* 582 N.W.2d 576 (Minn. App. 1998).

[17] A purchase order is generally considered an offer, but it must have enough information to meet the minimum standards for an offer. *Biotech Pharmacal, Inc. v. International Business Connections, LLC,* 184 S.W.3d 447 (Ark. Ct. App. 2004). *Westlaw E.C. Styberg Engineering Co. v. Eaton Corp.,* 492 F.3d 912 (7th Cir. 2007).

[18] Firm offers are covered in UCC §2-205.

[19] A quotation is a firm offer. *Rich Products Corp. v. Kemutec, Inc.,* 66 F. Supp. 2d 937 (E.D. Wis. 1999), but see *Boydstun Metal Works, Inc. v. Cottrell, Inc.,* 519 F. Supp. 2d 1119 (D. Or. 2007).

For nonmerchants' offers and offers in which the parties want firm offer periods that exceed three months, there must be consideration. In these situations, the parties must create an option contract just like those used in common law contracts (see Chapters 12 and 13).

(D) ACCEPTANCE—MANNER. Unlike the common law rules on acceptance, which control with great detail the method of **acceptance**, the UCC rules on acceptance are much more flexible. Under Article 2, an acceptance of an offer may be in any manner and by any medium that is reasonable under the circumstances.[20] Acceptance can occur through written communication or through performance, as when a seller accepts an offer for prompt shipment of goods by simply shipping the goods.[21] However, just as under common law, Article 2 requires that if the offer specifies the manner or medium of acceptance, the offer can be accepted only in that manner.

> **acceptance** – unqualified assent to the act or proposal of another; as the acceptance of an offer to make a contract.

CPA

(E) ACCEPTANCE—TIMING. The timing rules of the common law for determining when a contract has been formed are used to determine the formation of a contract under Article 2 with one slight modification. The **mailbox rule** applies under the UCC not just for the use of the same method of communication as that used by the offeror, but also applies when the offeree uses any reasonable method of communication. Under the common law, the offeree had to use the same method of communication in order to have the mailbox rule of acceptance apply. However, a UCC offeree can use any reasonable method for communicating acceptance and still enjoy the priority timing of the mailbox rule, something that makes an acceptance effective when it is sent. **For Example,** suppose that Feather-Light Brownies sent a letter offer to Cane Sugar Suppliers offering to buy 500 pounds of confectioner's sugar at $1 per pound. Cane Sugar Suppliers faxes back an acceptance of the letter offer. Cane Sugar Suppliers' acceptance is effective when it sends the fax.

> **mailbox rule** – timing for acceptance tied to proper acceptance.

Ethics & the Law

Restocking at Overstock

Cynthia Hines purchased an ElectroluxOxygen 3 Ultra Canister vacuum from Overstock.com, an online retailer that sells closeout goods. Ms. Hines returned the vacuum and was refunded her full amount, less a $30 restocking fee. She filed suit for breach of contract because she said that Overstock.com advertises that you can return merchandise at no cost and that Overstock.com did not disclose the restocking fee.

However, Overstock.com states that its Web site includes the following, "All retail purchases from Overstock are conducted through Overstock's Internet website. When an individual accesses the website, he or she accepts Overstock's terms. conditions and policies, which govern all of Overstock's customer purchases."

However, users were not required to click on the terms and conditions or to scroll all the way through the terms and conditions in order to use the site. It was possible, then, for a user to miss all the terms, such as a restocking fee.

Evaluate whether the restocking fee was part of the contract. Was it ethical for Overstock.com to impose the terms without users being aware of those terms? Discuss whether Overstock.com should have done more to disclose the restocking charge or put the notice in a different place.*

*Hines v. Overstock.com, Inc., 668 F. Supp. 2d 362 (E.D.N.Y. 2009)

---

[20] UCC §2-206(1). Governs acceptance methods. See *Ardus Medical, Inc. v. Emanuel County Hospital Authority*, 558 F. Supp. 2d 1301 (D. Ga. 2008).
[21] UCC §2-206(1)(b). Shipment of coal in response to an offer is acceptance. *Central Illinois Public Service Co. v. Atlas Minerals, Inc.*, 146 F.3d 448 (7th Cir. 1998). When the buyer and the seller have exchanged two purchase orders and three invoices that set forth price per pound of resin, quantity of resin, place and time of shipment, delivery charges, and the buyer's obligation to pay interest, they have formed a contract. *Bro-Tech Corp. v. Purity Water Co. of San Antonio, Inc.*, 681 F. Supp. 2d 791 (W.D. Tex. 2010).

CPA

mirror image rule – common law contract rule on acceptance that requires language to be absolutely the same as the offer, unequivocal and unconditional.

(F) ACCEPTANCE—LANGUAGE. Under the common law, the **mirror image rule** applies to acceptances. To be valid acceptances under common law, the language of the acceptance must be absolute, unconditional, and unequivocal; that is, the acceptance under common law must be the mirror image of the offer in order for a contract to be formed. However, the UCC has liberalized this rigid rule and permits formation even in circumstances when the acceptance includes terms that vary from the offer. The following sections explain the UCC rules on differing terms in acceptances. These rules for additional terms in acceptance were eliminated under Revised Article 2.[22]

(1) Additional Terms in Acceptance—Nonmerchants.

Under Article 2, unless an offer expressly specifies that an offer to buy or sell goods must be accepted exactly as made, the offeree may accept an offer and at the same time propose an additional term or terms. The additional term or terms in the acceptance does not result in a rejection as it would under common law. A contract is formed with the terms of the original offer. The additional terms are proposals for addition to the contract and may or may not be accepted by the other party.[23] **For Example,** Joe tells Susan, "I'll sell you my X-box for $150," and Susan responds, "I'll take it. The "Call of Duty" game is included." Susan has added an additional term in her acceptance. At this point, Joe and Susan have a contract for the sale of the X-box for $150. Whether the "Call of Duty" game is included is up to Joe; Joe is free to accept Susan's proposal or reject it, but his decision does not control whether he has a contract. There is a contract because Susan has made a definite statement of acceptance. To avoid being bound by a contract before she is clear on the terms, Susan should make an inquiry before using the language of acceptance, such as "Would you include the "Call of Duty" game as part of the sale?" Susan's inquiry is not an acceptance and leaves the original offer still outstanding, which she is free to accept or reject.

(2) Additional Terms in Acceptance—Merchants.

Under Article 2, the use of additional terms in acceptances by merchants is treated slightly differently. The different treatment of merchants in acceptances is the result of a commercial practice known as the **battle of the forms**, which results because a buyer sends a seller a purchase order for the purchase of goods. The seller sends back an invoice to the buyer. Although the buyer and seller may agree on the front of their documents that the subject matter of their contracts is 500 treadmills, the backs of their forms have details on the contracts, often called *boilerplate language*, that will never match. Suppose, for example, that the seller's invoice adds a payment term of "10 days same as cash." Is the payment term now a part of the parties' agreement? The parties have a meeting of the minds on the subject matter of the contract but now have a slight difference in performance terms.

battle of the forms – merchants' exchanges of invoices and purchase orders with differing boilerplate terms.

Under Article 2, in a transaction between merchants, the additional term or terms sent back in an acceptance become part of the contract if the additional term or terms do not materially alter the offer and the offeror does not object in a timely fashion.[24] **For Example,** returning to the Joe and Susan example, suppose that they are both now secondary market video game merchants negotiating for the sale and

---

[22] However, Revised Article 2 has not been adopted widely by the states.
[23] See the Ethics & Law feature on Restocking and Overstock.com.
[24] UCC §2-207(2).

FIGURE 23-1	*Terms in Contracts under UCC Article §2-207*

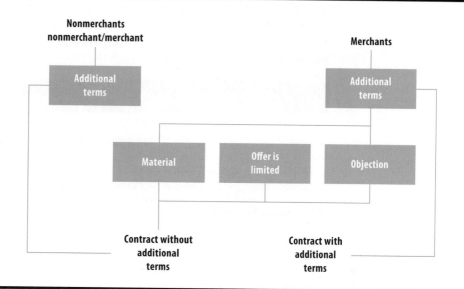

© Cengage Learning

purchase of a used X-box. They would have a contract, and the "Call of Duty" game would be included as part of the sale. Joe could, however, avoid the problem by adding a limitation to his offer, such as "This offer is limited to these terms." With that limitation, Susan would have a contract, but the contract would not include the "Call of Duty" game. Joe could also object immediately to Susan's proposal for the "Call of Duty" game and still have a contract without this additional term.[25]

If the proposed additional term in the acceptance is material, a contract is formed, but the material additional term does not become a part of the contract.[26] **For Example,** if Susan added to her acceptance the statement, "Game system carries one-year warranty," she has probably added a material term because the one-year warranty for a used game system would be unusual in the secondary market and costly for Joe.[27] Again, Joe can avoid this problem by limiting his offer so as to strike any additional terms, whether material or immaterial.

The most significant changes under Revised Article 2 deal with §2-207. Because there were so many confusing circumstances with additional terms, the effect of the new §2-207 is to leave the issues of what is or is not included in a contract to the courts. However, because so many businesses and individuals are using the Internet to contract, they are working out their terms through ongoing and immediate exchanges and questions. The result has been a significant reduction in the number of §2-207 cases.[28]

Figure 23-1 is a graphic picture of the rules on acceptance and contract terms under current Article 2 when additional terms are proposed.

---

[25] *Oakley Fertilizer, Inc. v. Continental Ins. Co.*, 276 S.W.3d 342 (Mo. App. 2009). Revised UCC Article 2 makes changes in the way these additional terms operate. When there is a record of an agreement, with no objection, the terms in the record are the terms of the contract.

[26] Damage limitations clauses are considered material. *Belden Inc. v. American Electronic Components, Inc.*, 885 N.E.2d 751 (Ind. App. 2008). Forum selection clauses are also material. *Hugo Boss Fashions, Inc. v. Sam's European Tailoring, Inc.*, 742 N.Y.S.2d 1 (2002).

[27] A statute of limitations of one year added to the acceptance of an offer is considered a material change because it limits so severely the amount of time for bringing suit on the contract. *American Tempering, Inc. v. Craft Architectural Metals Corp.*, 483 N.Y.S.2d 304 (1985).

[28] Francis J. Mootz III, "After the Battle of the Forms: Commercial Contracting in the Electronic Age," 4 *Journal of Law & Policy for the Information Society* 271, Summer, 2008.

Even without all the UCC provisions on contract terms, an offeror may expressly or by conduct agree to a term added by the offeree to its acceptance of the offer. The offeror may agree orally or in writing to the additional term. There can be acceptance of the additional term by conduct of the parties if the parties just perform their obligations under the contract with knowledge that the term has been added by the offeree.[29]

CASE SUMMARY

The Helium That Tanked

FACTS: On July 3, 2007, SVC–West, L.P. (SVC) did time-share presentations at hotels and ordered helium tanks quite often for balloons. SVC placed a rush order with C9 Ventures (C9) for eight helium-filled tanks used to inflate festive balloons. C9 accepted the order and later that day delivered the tanks.

On the reverse of the invoice was an indemnification provision requiring SVC to indemnify C9 for any loss arising out of the use or possession of the helium-filled tanks. C9 later picked up the tanks, and, weeks later, SVC paid the invoice. SVC had obtained helium-filled tanks from C9 on prior occasions.

The invoice was on a single piece of paper, on the reverse side of which was a section entitled "INDEMNITY/HOLD HARMLESS" (boldface omitted), which stated in part: "Customer agrees to indemnify[,] defend and hold harmless C9 … from and against any and all liability, claims, judgments, attorneys fees and cost of … every[ ] kind and nature, including, but not limited to injuries or death to persons and damage to property, arising out of the use, maintenance, instruction, operation, possession, ownership or Rental & Decor of the items rented, however cause[d], except claims or litigation arising through the solo [sic] gross negligence or willful misconduct of C9…." The reverse side of the invoice also included a section entitled "LEGAL FEES," which provided, in essence, that in an action to enforce "this Rental & Decor Agreement," the prevailing party would be entitled to recover attorney fees.

Before then, C9 had presented the same or similar invoice to SVC 10 times, but had received the signature of an SVC employee only six times. SVC never attempted to substitute its own form agreement for C9's form.

C9 typically delivered the tanks in the morning when no SVC guests were present, but on July 3, C9's employee, Ernesto Roque, did not arrive at the SVC premises to make the delivery until about 5:00 P.M. Roque asked SVC employee, Zayra Renteria, where to place the eight helium-filled tanks. Renteria, who was expecting the delivery during her shift, instructed Roque to bring the tanks up to the mezzanine level of the resort, at which point she would inform him where to place them. Roque wrote the following on the invoice, "[N]obody would sign all running around in lobby nobody knew who . . . After accident nobody got signatures." Roque stacked five to seven tanks against the walls next to the service elevator. He was in the process of bringing up another tank when a young boy, whose parents were attending the time-share presentation, ran up to the tanks and hugged one of them, pulling it over. The tank, which was about five feet tall and weighed 130 pounds, fell on the boy's hand. He was hospitalized and underwent surgery for his injuries.

SVC and C9 each paid the boy's family to settle a lawsuit brought to recover for his injuries. C9 filed a cross-complaint against SVC to enforce the indemnification provision on the back of the unsigned invoice. The trial court found for C9 and SVC appealed.

DECISION: The question: Is the indemnification provision on the back of the unsigned invoice enforceable against SVC? SVC and C9 entered into an oral contract when C9 accepted SVC's

CASE SUMMARY

Continued

telephone order for eight helium-filled tanks. Under section 2-207, additional terms proposed in an acceptance or confirmation may become terms of the contract in certain situations. The oral contract between SVC and C9, however, was a lease of personal property (the helium-filled tanks), and not a sale of goods under the California Uniform Commercial Code.

The terms on the back of the unsigned invoice would have become part of the parties' oral contract only if SVC agreed to those terms. SVC did not agree to those terms by course of dealing or course of performance, or under basic contract law.

However, even if this were a transaction in goods governed by the California Uniform Commercial Code then the issue turns on whether SVC is a merchant. If SVC is not a merchant, the terms of the invoice are considered to be mere proposals for additional terms, which SVC did not accept. However, an indemnification provision is deemed a material alteration to an agreement as a matter of law, so an indemnification provision on the back of the invoice would not, under section 2-207, become part of the contract between SVC and C9.

Reversed. [*C9 Ventures v. SVC-West, L.P.*, 202 Cal.App.4th 1483, 136 Cal.Rptr.3d 550 (Cal. App. 2012)]

(3) Conflicting Terms in Acceptance.

In some situations, the offeree has not added a different term from the original offer but has instead proposed terms that contradict the terms of the offer. **For Example,** a buyer's purchase order may require the seller to offer full warranty protection, whereas the seller's invoice may include a disclaimer of all warranties. The buyer's purchase order may include a clause that provides "payment in 30 days same as cash," whereas the seller's invoice may include a term that has "10 days same as cash." Once again, it is clear that the parties intended to enter into a contract, and the subject matter is also clear. The task for Article 2 becomes one of establishing the rules that determine the terms of a contract when both sides have used different forms. However, if there are conflicting terms on the basic requirements (such as price) for formation, the courts may conclude that the parties have not met minds.[30]

When a term of an acceptance conflicts with a term of an offer but it is clear that the parties intended to be bound by a contract, the UCC still recognizes the formation of a contract. The terms that are conflicting cancel each other and are ignored. The contract then consists of the terms of the offer and acceptance that agree. **For Example,** if one party's contract form provided for full warranty protection and the other party's form provided for no warranty protection, the terms cancel each other out, and the parties' contract includes only those warranties provided under Article 2 (see Chapter 25 for a discussion of those warranties).

(G) DEFENSES TO FORMATION. Article 2 incorporates the common law defenses to formation of contracts by reference to the common law defenses in §1-103 (see Chapter 14 for a full discussion of those defenses). **For Example,** a party to a

---

[30] *Howard Const. Co. v. Jeff-Cole Quarries, Inc.*, 669 S.W.2d 221 (Mo. App. 1984), where the acceptance changed the price, there was not an acceptance but a counteroffer.

contract who can establish that the other party engaged in fraud to get the contract formed may cancel the contract and recover for losses that result from any damages for goods already delivered or payment already made.

(1) Unconscionability.

The UCC includes an additional contract defense for parties to a sale contract called *unconscionability*.[31] This section permits a court to refuse to enforce a sales contract that it finds to be **unconscionable**, which is generally defined as grossly unfair.[32] A court may also find a clause or portions of a contract to be unconscionable and refuse to enforce those clauses or sections.[33]

(2) Illegality.

At common law, a contract is void if its subject matter itself is illegal, such as a contract for hire to murder someone. Under the UCC, a contract for the sale of heroin would be void. Likewise, a contract for the sale of a recalled or banned toy would be void.

(3) The Effect of Illegal Sale.

An illegal sale or contract to sell cannot be enforced. As a general rule, courts will not aid either party in recovering money or property transferred under an illegal agreement.

4. Terms in the Formed Contract

As noted earlier, contracts can be formed under Article 2 with terms of performance still missing or open. A contract is formed with just the quantity agreed on, but there are issues that must be resolved if the contract is to be completed. Article 2 has provisions for such missing terms.

CPA

(A) PRICE. If the price for the goods is not expressly fixed by the contract, the price may be an open term, whereby the parties merely indicate how the price should be determined at a later time. In the absence of any reference to price, the price will be a reasonable price at the time of the delivery of the goods, which is generally the market price.[34]

Parties often use formulas for determining price in sales of goods. The price itself is missing from the contract until the formula is applied at some future time. The so-called **cost plus** formula for determining price has been used a great deal, particularly in commercial contracts. Under this formula, the buyer pays the seller the seller's costs for manufacture or obtaining the goods plus a specified percentage as profit.

The UCC allows contracts that expressly provide that one of the parties may determine the price. In such a case, that party must act in good faith, another requirement under the UCC that applies to merchants and nonmerchants in the formation and performance of their contracts.[35]

unconscionable – unreasonable, not guided or restrained by conscience and often referring to a contract grossly unfair to one party because of the superior bargaining powers of the other party.

cost plus – method of determining the purchase price or contract price equal to the seller's or contractor's costs plus a stated percentage as the profit.

[31] UCC §2-302. Teri J. Dobbins, "Losing Faith: Extracting the Implied Covenant of Good Faith from (Some) Contracts, 84 *Oregon Law Rev* 227 (2005). *U.S. Welding, Inc. v. Battelle Energy Alliance, LLC*, 728 F. Supp. 2d 1110 (D.Idaho 2010).
[32] Disparity in bargaining power is an issue but is not controlling. In *Intrastate Piping & Controls, Inc. v. Robert-James Sales, Inc.*, 39 UCC Rep. Serv. 2d 347 (Ill. Cir. Ct. 1999), a clause limiting remedies to replacement of defective pipe with no additional damages was upheld because while the seller was a large, national business and the buyer a small, local business, the contract merely incorporated industry practice in terms of remedies.
[33] An example would be voiding exorbitant interest charges but enforcing the underlying sale.
[34] UCC §2-305(1) provides, "the price is a reasonable price at the time for delivery."
[35] Good faith requires that the party act honestly and, in the case of a merchant, also requires that the party follow reasonable commercial standards of fair dealing that are recognized in the trade. UCC §§1-201(1)(a), 2-103(1)(b).

CPA

output contract – contract of a producer to sell its entire production or output to a buyer.

requirements contract – contract in which the buyer buys its needs (requirements) from the seller.

(B) OUTPUT AND REQUIREMENTS CONTRACTS. The **output contract** and the **requirements contract**[36] do not specify the quantity to be sold or purchased. Instead, the contract amount is what the seller produces or the buyer requires. **For Example,** a homeowner may contract to purchase propane fuel for her winter heating needs. The propane company agrees to sell her the amount of propane she needs, which will vary from year to year according to the winter weather, her time at home, and other factors. Although the open quantity in contracts such as these introduces an element of uncertainty, such sales contracts are valid but subject to two limitations: (1) The parties must act in good faith and (2) the quantity offered or demanded must not be unreasonably disproportionate to prior output or requirements or to a stated estimate. With these restrictions, the homeowner will obtain all of the propane she needs for heating but could not use her particularly beneficial price under her open-quantity contract to purchase additional propane to sell to others.

(C) INDEFINITE DURATION TERM. When the sales contract is a continuing contract, such as one calling for periodic delivery of coal, but no time is set for the life of the contract, the contract runs for a reasonable time. It may be terminated by notice from either party to the other party.

CPA

(D) CHANGES IN TERMS: MODIFICATION OF CONTRACT. An agreement to modify a contract for the sale of goods is binding even though the modification is not supported by consideration.[37] The modification is valid so long as the agreement is voluntary. **For Example,** suppose that Chester's Drug Store has agreed to purchase 300 bottles of vitamins from Pro-Life, Inc., at a price of $3.71 per bottle. Pro-Life has experienced substantial cost increases from its suppliers and asks Chester to pay $3.74 per bottle. Chester is not required to agree to such a price increase because it has a valid contract for the lower price. If Chester agrees to the price increase, however, the agreement for the higher price is valid despite the lack of additional consideration on the part of Pro-Life. Chester may agree to the higher price because Pro-Life's price is still much lower than its competitors and Chester has a longstanding relationship with Pro-Life and values its customer service. However, Pro-Life could not threaten to cut off Chester's supply in order to obtain the price increase because that would be a breach of contract and would also be duress that would invalidate Chester's consent to the higher price. (See Chapter 14 for a discussion of duress.)

parol evidence rule – rule that prohibits the introduction in evidence of oral or written statements made prior to or contemporaneously with the execution of a complete written contract, deed, or instrument, in the absence of fraud, accident, or mistake.

(E) CONTRADICTING TERMS: PAROL EVIDENCE RULE. The **parol evidence rule** (see Chapter 17 for a complete discussion) applies to the sale of goods, with the slight modification that a writing is not presumed to represent the entire contract of the parties unless the court specifically decides that it does.[38] If the court so decides, parol evidence is not admissible to add to or contradict the terms of the writing. **For Example,** suppose that Ralph Rhodes and Tana Preuss negotiate the sale of Ralph's 1965 Mustang to Tana. During their discussions, Ralph agrees to pay for an inspection and for new upholstery for the car. However, Tana and Ralph sign a simple sales contract that includes only a description of the Mustang and the price. Tana cannot enforce the two provisions because she failed to have them written into their final agreement. The parol evidence rule requires the parties to be certain that

---

[36] UCC §2-306; *XTO Energy Inc. v. Smith Production Inc.*, 282 S.W.3d 672 (Tex. App. 2009); *ABC Metals & Recycling Co., Inc. v. Highland Computer Forms, Inc.*, 771 N.W.2d 651 (Iowa App. 2009).
[37] UCC §2-209(1); *Horbach v. Kacz Marek*, 934 F. Supp. 981 (N.D. Ill. 1996), aff'd, 388 F.3d 969 (7th Cir. 2002).
[38] UCC §2-202.

everything they want is in their agreement before they sign. The courts cannot referee disputes over collateral agreements the parties fail to put in writing.

If the court decides that the writing was not intended to represent the entire contract, the writing may be supplemented by additional extrinsic evidence, including the proof of additional terms as long as these terms are not inconsistent with the written terms. Parol evidence may also be admitted to interpret contract terms or show what the parties meant by their words. The parol evidence rule also does not prohibit the proof of fraud, misrepresentation, and any other defenses in formation.

(F) INTERPRETING CONTRACT TERMS: COURSE OF DEALING AND USAGE OF TRADE. The patterns of doing business the parties develop through their prior contractual transactions, or **course of dealing**, become part of their contract.[39] These patterns may be used to find what was intended by the express provisions in their contract and to supply otherwise missing terms. **For Example,** if the parties had 10 previous agreements and payment was always made on the 30th day following delivery, that conduct could be used to interpret the meaning of a clause "payment due in 30 days" when the start of the 30 days is not specifically agreed to in the contract.

In addition, the customs of the industry, or **usage of trade**, are adopted by courts in their interpretation of contract terms. **For Example,** suppose that a contract provides for the sale of mohair. There are two types of mohair: adult and kid. Because adult mohair is cheaper and easier to find, industry custom provides that unless the parties specifically place the term *kid* with the term *mohair* in the contract, the contract is one for the sale of adult mohair. Under Article 2, the court need not find that a contract is ambiguous or incomplete in order to examine the parties' pattern of previous conduct as well as industry custom.[40]

course of dealing–pattern of performance between two parties to a contract.

usage of trade–language and customs of an industry.

5. Bulk Transfers

Bulk transfer law, Article 6 of the UCC, was created to deal with situations in which sellers of businesses fail to pay the creditors of the business and instead use the proceeds of the sale for their own use.

In 1989, the NCCUSL recommended that UCC Article 6 be repealed because it was obsolete and had little value in the modern business world. At the same time, the commissioners adopted a revised version of Article 6 (Alternative B) for adoption by those states that desired to retain the concept for bulk sales. Rather than relying on the bulk sales law, the trend is for suppliers to use UCC Article 9, Secured Transactions, for protection (see Chapter 34).

B. FORM OF SALES CONTRACT

A contract for the sale of goods may be oral or written. However, under the UCC, certain types of contracts must be evidenced by a record or they cannot be enforced in court.

---

[39] UCC §2-208. Under Revised Article 2, §2-208 is eliminated for those states that have adopted Revised Article 1 because Revised Article 1 contains the definition for course of performance.

[40] Revised §2-202 provides different rules for the use of extrinsic evidence but still includes "course of performance, course of dealing, or usage of trade" as sources for interpretation of contract terms.

CPA

6. Amount

Whenever the sales price of goods is $500 or more, the sales contract must be evidenced by a record to be enforceable. Under Revised Article 2, this amount has been increased to $5,000.[41] The section of the UCC that establishes this requirement is known as the **statute of frauds**. (For more details on the statute of frauds and its role in common law contracts, see Chapter 17.)

statute of frauds—statute that, to prevent fraud through the use of perjured testimony, requires that certain kinds of contracts be in writing to be binding or enforceable.

7. Nature of the Writing Required

The requirement for a record for a contract may be satisfied by a complete written contract signed by both parties. Under Article 2, so that the state laws will be consistent with federal laws on electronic signatures (see Chapter 11), the requirement of a writing has been changed to the requirement of a "record." Under Article 2, two merchants can reduce their agreement to a record in much simpler fashion because the detail required under common law is not required to satisfy the UCC standards.

(A) TERMS. To satisfy the UCC statute of frauds, the record must indicate that there has been a completed transaction covering certain goods. Specifically, the record must (1) indicate that a sale or contract to sell has been made and (2) state the quantity of goods involved.[42] Any other missing terms may be supplied by reference to Code sections (discussed earlier) or shown by parol evidence.

(B) SIGNATURE. The record must be signed or authenticated by the person who is being held to the contract or by the authorized agent of that person. Whatever form of authentication is being used must be put in place in the record with the intention of authenticating the record. The authentication may consist of initials or may be a printed, stamped, electronic, or typewritten signature placed with the intent to authenticate.[43] **For Example,** when you enter into a contract as part of an online transaction, you are generally asked to check a box that states that you understand you are entering into a contract. Once you check that box, a pop-up appears that explains that you are about to charge your credit card or account and that you have agreed to the purchase. These steps are used to authenticate your electronic version of a signature.

The UCC statute of frauds does provide an important exception to the signature requirement for merchants that enables merchants to expedite their transactions. This exception allows merchants to create a confirmation memorandum of their oral agreement as evidence of an agreement. A merchant's *confirmation memorandum* is a letter, memo, or electronic document signed or authenticated by one of the two merchant parties to an oral agreement.[44] This memorandum can be used by either party to enforce the contract. **For Example,** suppose that Ralph has orally agreed to purchase 1,000 pounds of T-bone steak from Jane for $5.79 per pound. Jane sends Ralph a signed memo that reads, "This is to confirm our telephone conversation earlier today. I will sell you 1,000 pounds of T-bone @ $5.79 per pound." Either Ralph or Jane can use the memo to enforce the contract.

---

[41] Under Revised Article 2, the new amount of $5,000 is found at UCC Rev Art 2, §2-201.

[42] *Kelly-Stehney & Assoc., Inc. v. McDonald's Indus. Products, Inc.*, 693 N.W.2d 394 (Mich. 2005).

[43] UCC §§1-201(39), 2-201; *CQ, Inc. v. TXU Min. Co., LP*, 565 F.3d 268 (5th Cir. 2009). Revised Article 2 permits electronic forms and signature and "record" includes e-mail, EDI transmissions, faxes, and printouts of screen pages reflecting transactions.

[44] *Siesta Sol, LLC v. Brooks Pharmacy, Inc.*, 617 F. Supp. 2d 38 (D. R.I. 2007); *In re Sunbelt Grain WKS, LLC*, 406 B.R. 918 (D. Kan. 2009).

A confirming memo, in various forms of communication, sent by one merchant to another results in a binding and enforceable contract that satisfies the statute of frauds. Such a confirmation binds the nonsigning or nonauthenticating merchant, just as if he had signed the letter or a contract. A merchant can object when he receives the confirmation memo, but he must do so immediately because the confirming memo takes effect in 10 days if there is no objection.[45] This confirmation procedure makes it necessary for merchants to watch their communications and all forms of correspondence and to act within 10 days of receiving a confirmation.

CASE SUMMARY

It's Elementary: A Crayon-Scrawled Contract Is Good Enough for the Statute of Frauds

FACTS: Michelle Rosenfeld, an art dealer, went to artist Jean-Michel Basquiat's apartment on October 25, 1982. While she was there, Basquiat agreed to sell her three paintings for $4,000 each, and she picked out three. Basquiat asked for a cash deposit of 10 percent; Rosenfeld left the loft but returned later with $1,000 in cash, which she paid to Basquiat. When she asked for a receipt, he insisted on drawing up a contract and got down on the floor and wrote it out in crayon on a large piece of paper, remarking that someday this contract would be worth money. The handwritten document listed the three paintings, bore Rosenfeld's signature and Basquiat's signature, and stated: "$12,000—$1,000 DEPOSIT ¼ Oct 25 82." Rosenfeld later returned to Basquiat's loft to discuss delivery, but Basquiat convinced her to wait for at least two years so that he could show the paintings at exhibitions. After Basquiat's death, the estate argued that there was no contract because the statute of frauds made the agreement unenforceable. The estate contended that a written contract for the sale of goods must include the date of delivery. From a judgment in favor of the estate, Rosenfeld appealed.

DECISION: The contract for the sale of three paintings is governed by the UCC, and its statute of frauds applies to "transactions in goods for $500 which must be in writing or they are unenforceable. All that is required for a writing is that it provide some basis for believing that there is a real transaction." The writing supplied in this case indicated the price, the date, the specific paintings involved, and that Rosenfeld paid a deposit. It also bore the signatures of the buyer and seller and satisfied the requirements of UCC §2-201. Because the writing, scrawled in crayon by Jean-Michel Basquiat on a large piece of paper, easily satisfied the requirements of §2-201 of the UCC, the alleged contract is valid. [*Rosenfeld v. Basquiat*, 78 F.3d 84 (2nd Cir. 1996)]

(c) PURPOSE OF EXECUTION. A writing or record can satisfy the statute of frauds even though it was not made for that purpose. For example, if a buyer writes to the seller to complain that the goods have not been delivered, there is proof of the contract because the buyer's complaint indicates that there was some kind of understanding or an acknowledgment that there was a sale of those goods.

(d) PARTICULAR WRITINGS. Formal contracts, bills of sale, letters, and telegrams are common forms of writings that satisfy the record requirement.[46] E-mails, faxes, EDI communications, and verifications through screen printouts will generally satisfy the

---

[45] A confirmation memo is not effective when there is no underlying agreement or the parties did not agree on the terms. *Cargill Inc. v. Jorgenson Farms*, 719 N.W.2d 226 (Minn. App. 2009).
[46] Contract terms can be pieced together from invoices sent over the period of the agreement and that the buyer paid. *Fleming Companies, Inc. v. Krist Oil Co.*, 324 F. Supp. 2d 933 (W.D. Wi. 2001).

requirement as to record and authentication so long as they meet minimum formation standards and comply with the requirement of the UCC to specify any quantity. Two or more records grouped together may constitute a record that will be sufficient to satisfy the UCC statute of frauds.[47]

CASE SUMMARY

A Real Basket Case

FACTS: The Greenbrier Basket Company (GBC), a goods distributor, was selling woven baskets to The Pampered Chef (TPC). The ordering process would begin with TPC e-mailing GBC an offer to fill an order. GBC would then go to TPC's Web site and fill out the purchase order using TPC's purchase order management system and would click on the Accept P.O. button at the end of the terms and conditions field.

TPC sent Mark Beal (a GBC employee) an e-mail with an attachment showing him how to use TPC's purchase order management system, including the following:

Clicking on the Accept P.O. button will cause the terms and conditions of the purchase order to pop-up. The user should review these terms and conditions and click the Accept P.O. button at the bottom of the pop-up screen…. If the purchase order is not acceptable in it's [sic] current form, the user may click on the Reject and Request Changes button. This causes a pop-up window to appear where the user may enter a free-form text describing the reason for rejecting the purchase order and request changes that would make the purchase order acceptable.

Clause 17 of the Terms and Conditions in TPC's purchase management order system provided that all disputes on contracts would be resolved in federal district court in Illinois.

When disputes over orders and payments arose, GBC filed suit against TPC in Kansas for breach of contract. TPC moved to dismiss the suit for improper venue.

DECISION: TPC's e-mails containing purchase order information constituted an offer to buy baskets. The e-mails consisted of information about the quantity of baskets to be bought, price, shipment information, and delivery dates. They also provided that to accept the P.O., GBC should go via Internet to TPC's Web site.

GBC was under a duty to read and understand the terms and conditions prior to clicking the Accept P.O. button because this was the formal acceptance required by TPC's offer to purchase baskets. Failure to read or understand the terms and conditions is not a valid reason to set those provisions aside.

A meeting of the minds requirement is proved when the minds of the parties met on the same matter and agreed upon the terms of the contract. GBC agreed upon these terms and conditions published on TPC's Web site by clicking the Accept P.O. button.

The case was dismissed in Kansas and transferred to Illinois. [*Home Basket Co., LLC v. Pampered Chef, Ltd.*, **55 UCC Rep. Serv. 2d 792 (D. Kan. 2005)**]

8. Effect of Noncompliance

A sales agreement that does not satisfy the statute of frauds cannot be enforced. However, the oral contract itself is not unlawful and may be voluntarily performed by the parties.

---

[47] *ReMapp Intern. Corp. v. Comfort Keyboard Co., Inc.*, 560 F.3d 628 (7th Cir. 2009). Letters grouped together satisfy UCC §2-201. *Pepsi-Cola Co. v. Steak 'N Shake, Inc.*, 981 F. Supp. 1149 (S.D. Ind. 1997). Letters and faxes also satisfy the writing requirement. *Den Norske Stats Oljeselskap*, 992 F. Supp. 913 (S.D. Tex. 1998), aff'd, 161 F.3d 8 (5th Cir. 1998).

9. Exceptions to Requirement of a Writing

The absence of a writing does not always mean that a sales contract is unenforceable. Article 2 provides some exceptions for the enforceability of certain oral contracts.

CPA **(A) SPECIALLY MANUFACTURED GOODS.** No record is required when the goods are specially made for the buyer and are of such an unusual nature that they are not suitable for sale in the ordinary course of the seller's business. **For Example,** a manufacturer who builds a stair lift for a two-story home cannot resell the $8,000 device to someone else because it is specially built for the stairs in the buyer's home. The manufacturer could enforce the oral contract against the buyer despite the price being in excess of $500 ($5,000 under Revised Article 2).

For this nonresellable goods exception to apply, the seller must have made a substantial beginning in manufacturing the goods or, if a distributor is the seller, in procuring them before the buyer indicates she will not honor the oral contract.[48]

The stair lift manufacturer, for example, must have progressed to a point beyond simply ordering materials for construction of the lift because those materials could be used for any lift.

CPA **(B) RECEIPT AND ACCEPTANCE.** An oral sales contract may be enforced if it can be shown that the goods were delivered by the seller and were both received and accepted by the buyer even if the amount involved is over $500 ($5,000 Revised) and there is no record. The receipt and acceptance of the goods by the buyer makes the contract enforceable despite the statute of frauds issue. The buyer must actually receive and accept the goods. If only part of the goods have been received and accepted, the contract may be enforced only insofar as it relates to those goods received and accepted.[49] **For Example,** suppose that Wayne ordered 700 baseball jackets at a price of $72 each from Pamela. The order was taken over the telephone, and Wayne emphasized urgency. Pamela shipped the 320 jackets she had on hand and assured Wayne the remainder would be finished during the next two weeks. Wayne received the 320 jackets and sold them to a golf tournament sponsor. Wayne refused to pay Pamela because the contract was oral. Wayne must pay for the 320 jackets, but Pamela will not be able to recover for the remaining 380 jackets she manufactured.

CPA **(c) PAYMENT.** An oral contract may be enforced if the buyer has made full payment. In the case of partial payment for divisible units of goods, a contract may be enforced only with respect to the goods for which payment has been made and accepted. In the Pamela and Wayne example, if the circumstances were changed so that Pamela agreed to ship only if Wayne sent payment, then Pamela, upon accepting the payment, would be required to perform the contract for the amount of payment received. If partial payment is made for indivisible goods, such as an automobile, a partial payment avoids the statute of frauds and is sufficient proof to permit enforcement of the entire oral contract.

(D) ADMISSION. An oral contract may be enforced against a party if that party admits in pleadings, testimony, or otherwise in court that a contract for sale was made. The contract, however, is not enforceable beyond the quantity of goods admitted.[50]

---

[48] *Golden State Porcelain Inc. v. Swid Powell Design Inc.,* 37 UCC Rep. Serv. 2d (N.Y. 1999). Where manufacture has not begun, this exception to the statute of frauds does not apply. *EMSG Sys. Div., Inc. v. Miltope Corp.,* 37 UCC Rep. Serv. 2d 39 (E.D.N.C. 1998).

[49] *Allied Grape Growers v. Bronco Wine Co.,* 249 Cal.Rptr. 872 (Ct. App. 1988).

[50] *Delta Stat, Inc. v. Michael's Carpet World,* 666 S.E.2d 331 (Va. 2008).

Thinking Things Through

Chipping Away at the Contract Terms for Wood Chips

Beginning in the mid-1980s GP and WHI entered into a series of one-year contracts under which WHI supplied wood chips to GP's particle board plant in Gaylord, Michigan. The contract was automatically renewed unless either party gave written notice 60 days before the end of the term. The contracts also permitted either party to terminate a contract at any time with 90 days' notice.

WHI and GP signed a new contract on May 20, 2005 (2005 contract). The contract had a three-year term and a provision for subsequent renewal. It included an early termination clause that permitted either party to terminate the contract after 90 days notice. The contract also contained a clause stating that GP intended to purchase 125,000 tons of wood chips per year but was not required to purchase any minimum quantity.

During the negotiations for the 2005 contract, GP represented that the early termination clause and nonbinding volume clauses were merely generic requirements from GP's legal department and would have no effect on GP's performance. WHI also alleges that both before and after the 2005 contract was signed, GP represented (1) that the

early termination clause was subordinate to the clause stating GP's intent to purchase 125,000 tons of wood chips per year, (2) that GP would not exercise the early termination provision during the contract's initial three-year term, and (3) that the contract would be automatically renewed unless WHI defaulted.

In March 2006, GP informed WHI that it was closing the Gaylord plant. It also terminated the 2005 contract and suspended further deliveries of wood chips to the plant. The parties dispute the date on which the decision to close the Gaylord plant was made. WHI alleges that GP knew it would close the plant by October 2004, but repeatedly represented to WHI that there were no plans to close the plant.*

WH1 filed suit for breach of contract. GP has responded that the negotiation terms are irrelevant because they were not part of the contract terms and they could not be used as evidence for a breach of contract suit. Who is correct? Is there a breach? Or is there a written contract that does not contain protection for WH1 in the event of a plant closure?

*Woodland Harvesting, Inc. v. Georgia Pacific Corporation, 693 F. Supp. 2f 732 (E.D. Mich. 2010)

10. Noncode Requirements

In addition to the UCC requirements for contracts that must be evidenced by a record, other statutes may impose requirements. **For Example,** state consumer protection legislation commonly requires that there be a detailed contract and that a copy of it be given to the consumer.

11. Bill of Sale

bill of sale–writing signed by the seller reciting that the personal property therein described has been sold to the buyer.

Regardless of the requirement of the statute of frauds, the parties may wish to execute a writing as evidence or proof of the sale. Through custom, this writing has become known as a **bill of sale**, but it is neither a bill nor a contract. It is merely a receipt or writing signed by the seller reciting the transfer to the buyer of the title to the described property. A bill of sale can be used as proof of an otherwise oral agreement.

C. Uniform Law for International Sales

Contracts for the International Sale of Goods (CISG)–uniform international contract code contracts for international sale of goods.

The United Nations Convention on **Contracts for the International Sale of Goods (CISG)** applies to contracts between parties in the United States and parties in the other nations that have ratified the convention.[51] The provisions of this convention

[51] 52 Fed. Reg. 6262 (1987). While the list of adopting countries is always increasing, those countries involved in NAFTA, GATT, and the European Union (EU) (see Chapter 7) have adopted the CISG. For complete text, commentary, and case law on CISG, go to **www.cisg.law.pace.edu**.

or international agreement have been strongly influenced by Article 2 of the UCC. The international rules of the convention automatically apply to contracts for the sale of goods if the buyer and seller have places of business in different countries that have ratified the convention. The parties may, however, choose to exclude the convention provisions in their sales contract.

12. Scope of the CISG

The CISG does not govern all contracts between parties in the countries that have ratified it. The CISG does not apply to goods bought for personal, family, or household use.[52] The CISG also does not apply to contracts in which the predominant part of the obligations of the party who furnishes the goods consists of the supply of labor or other services. The CISG has five chapters and 101 articles, and the articles have no titles to them. There is a limited body of case law interpreting the CISG because so many of the decisions under the CISG come through arbitration and other forms of dispute resolution, typical of international commercial arrangements.

D. LEASES OF GOODS

Leases of goods represent a significant part of both contract law and the economy. There are more than $628 billion worth of lease transactions in the United States each year, an amount equal to roughly one-third of all capital investment each year in the United States.[53] One-fourth of all vehicles in the United States are leased. Article 2A of the UCC codifies the law of leases for tangible movable goods. Article 2A applies to any transaction, regardless of form, that creates a lease of personal property or fixtures. Many of the provisions of Article 2 were carried over but changed to reflect differences in style, leasing terminology, or leasing practices.[54] As a practical matter, leases will be of durable goods, such as equipment and vehicles of any kind, computers, boats, airplanes, and household goods and appliances. A **lease** is "a transfer of the right to possession and use of goods for a term in return for consideration."[55]

lease – agreement between the owner of property and a tenant by which the former agrees to give possession of the property to the latter for payment of rent. (Parties—landlord or lessor, tenant or lessee)

13. Types of Leases

Article 2A regulates consumer leases, commercial leases, finance leases, nonfinance leases, and subleases. These categories may overlap in some cases, such as when there is a commercial finance lease.

consumer lease – lease of goods by a natural person for personal, family, or household use.

(A) CONSUMER LEASE. A **consumer lease** is made by a merchant lessor regularly engaged in the business of leasing or selling the kinds of goods involved. A consumer lease is made to a natural person (not a corporation) who takes possession of the goods primarily for personal, family, or household use. Each state places a cap on the amount considered a consumer lease. Section 2A-103(f) simply provides that the

---

[52] The UNIDROIT Principles are often used as guidelines for resolving issues in international consumer contracts. M. J. Bonell, "The CISG, European Contract Law and the Development of a World Contract Law," 56 *American Journal of Comparative Law*, 1–28 (2008).

[53] *Equipment Leasing & Finance Foundation Economic Outlook* (2012).

[54] Forty-nine states (Louisiana has not adopted Article 2A), the District of Columbia, and the Virgin Islands have adopted all or some portions of Article 2A. Not all states have adopted the 1997 version of Article 2A, and some have adopted only selected portions of the 1997 version.

[55] UCC §2A-103(1)(j). The definition of what constitutes a lease is the subject of continuing examination by the UCC Article 2A drafters and the American Law Institute.

state should place its own amount in this section with the admonition to place the cap at a level that ensures that vehicle leases will be covered under the law. During the period from 2002 to 2007, there were a number of suits brought by individuals injured in auto accidents against the leasing companies of the drivers who were driving their leased autos at the time they caused an accident. Many states were holding the leasing companies liable for those accidents because they were title holders of the cars. As a result, leasing companies stopped doing business in certain states because of the liability exposure.

In response, the federal government passed legislation that preempted all state laws and limited the liability of vehicle leasing companies to a basic level of liability that was limited to mandatory insurance coverage standards.[56]

nonconsumer lease – lease that does not satisfy the definition of a consumer lease; also known as a *commercial lease.*

(B) COMMERCIAL LEASE. When a lease does not satisfy the definition of a consumer lease, it may be called a **nonconsumer** or a **commercial lease**. **For Example,** a contractor's one-year rental of a truck to haul materials is a commercial lease.

commercial lease – any nonconsumer lease.

finance lease – three-party lease agreement in which there is a lessor, a lessee, and a financier.

(C) FINANCE LEASE. A **finance lease** is a three-party transaction involving a lessor, a lessee, and a supplier. Instead of going directly to a supplier for goods, the customer goes to a financier and tells the financier where to obtain the goods and what to obtain. The financier then acquires the goods and either leases or subleases the goods to its customer. The financier-lessor is in effect a paper channel, or conduit, between the supplier and the customer-lessee. The customer-lessee must approve the terms of the transaction between the supplier and the financier-lessor.[57]

14. Form of Lease Contract

The lease must be evidenced by a record if the total of the payments under the lease will be $1,000 or more. The record must be authenticated by the party against whom enforcement is sought. The record must describe the leased goods, state the term of the lease, and indicate that a lease contract has been formed.[58]

15. Warranties

Under Article 2A, the lessor, except in the case of finance leases, makes all usual warranties that are made by a seller in a sale of goods. In a finance lease, however, the real parties in interest are the supplier, who supplies the lessor with the goods, and the lessee, who leases the goods. The lessee looks to the supplier of the goods for warranties. Any warranties, express or implied, made by the supplier to the lessor are passed on to the lessee, who has a direct cause of action on them against the supplier regardless of the lack of privity.[59] **For Example,** if a consumer leased an auto and the auto had a defective steering mechanism that resulted in injury to the consumer, the consumer would have a cause of action against the auto manufacturer.

---

[56] See, e.g., *Oliveira v. Lombardi,* 794 A.2d 453 (R.I. 2002). The federal law did not affect all of the suits that were pending at the time of the passage of the federal law. Those suits were permitted to proceed as long as they had been filed by the end of 2005. Those suits have concluded. Future recovery will be limited to mandatory policy requirements.

[57] UCC §2A-103(1)(g). One of the evolving issues in lease financing is the relationship of the parties, the use of liens, and the role of Article 9 security interests (see Chapter 34). The NCCUSL has created Uniform Certificate of Title Act (UCOTA) that makes the interrelationships of lien laws, Article 2, and Article 9 clear. UCOTA was available for adoption by the states in 2006. As of 2012, only three states had adopted the law.

[58] UCC §2-201(b).

[59] UCC §2A-209.

E-Commerce & Cyberlaw

The Deal with Dell

Dell Computer customers purchased computers through the Dell Web site. There were "Terms and Conditions" on the Web site that included terms and conditions such as the requirement that contract disputes be submitted to arbitration in Illinois and the sales tax provisions related to the purchase of computers and service contracts.

Dell maintains that customers have three separate opportunities to review the terms and conditions agreement: (1) by selecting a hyperlink on the Dell Web site, (2) by reading the terms that were included in the acknowledgment/invoice that was sent to customers after they placed their orders, or (3) by reviewing the copy of the terms Dell included in the packaging of its computer products. The court found

that the terms and conditions had to be understood PRIOR to the purchase and that the "Terms and Conditions" tab was not conspicuous on the Dell Web site. From this case and other materials in the chapter, you learn that there are best practices for Internet contracting: (1) Require customers to click on terms and conditions PRIOR to buying; (2) Require customers to physically scroll down through the terms before being allowed to purchase; (3) Notify customers along the way as they are loading their electronic carts that there are terms and conditions and place click points for them to study those terms and conditions; and (4) Posting terms and conditions on your Web site is not enough for those terms and conditions to be part of the contract.

16. Default

The lease agreement and provisions of Article 2A determine whether the lessor or lessee is in default. If either the lessor or the lessee is in default under the lease contract, the party seeking enforcement may obtain a judgment or otherwise enforce the lease contract by any available judicial or nonjudicial procedure. Neither the lessor nor the lessee is entitled to notice of default or notice of enforcement from the other party. Both the lessor and the lessee have rights and remedies similar to those given to a seller in a sales contract.[60] If the lessee defaults, the lessor is entitled to recover any rent due, future rent, and incidental damages.[61] (See Chapter 27 for more information on remedies.)

LawFlix

Beethoven (1992)(G)

Charles Grodin plays a fussy father who has founded and runs an air freshener company. Part of the plot centers on an investment in the company by some venture capitalists who are interested in using Grodin's company as a supplier. There are contract negotiations as well as issues of warranty and liability.

---

[60] UCC §§2A-501, 2A-503; *Mitchell v. Ford Motor Credit Co.*, 702 F. Supp. 2d 1356 (M.D. Fla. 2010).
[61] UCC §2A-529.

MAKE THE CONNECTION

SUMMARY

Contracts for services and real estate are governed by the common law. Contracts for the sale of goods are governed by Article 2 of the UCC. *Goods* are defined as anything movable at the time they are identified as the subject of the transaction. Goods physically existing and owned by the seller at the time of the transaction are *existing goods*.

A *sale of goods* is the transfer of title to tangible personal property for a price. A *bailment* is a transfer of possession but not title and is therefore not a sale. A *gift* is not a sale because no price is paid for the gift. A contract for services is an ordinary contract and is not governed by the UCC. If a contract calls for both the rendering of services and the supplying of goods, the contract is classified according to its dominant element.

The common law contract rules for intent to contract apply to the formation of contracts under the UCC. However, several formation rules under the UCC differ from common law contract rules. A merchant's firm offer is irrevocable without the payment of consideration. The UCC rules on additional terms in an acceptance permit the formation of a contract despite the changes. These proposals for new terms are not considered counteroffers under the UCC. The terms that are included are determined by detailed rules. If the transaction is between nonmerchants, a contract is formed without the additional terms, which the original offeror is free to accept or reject. If the transaction is between merchants, the additional terms become part of the contract if those terms do not materially alter the offer and no objection is made to them. There is no distinction between merchant and nonmerchant for additional terms under Revised Article 2 and the terms issues is left to the courts.

The same defenses available to formation under common law are incorporated in Article 2. In addition, the UCC recognizes unconscionability as a defense to formation.

The UCC does not require the parties to agree on every aspect of contract performance for the contract

to be valid. Provisions in Article 2 will govern the parties' relationship in the event their agreement does not cover all terms. The price term may be expressly fixed by the parties. The parties may make no provision as to price, or they may indicate how the price should be determined later. In output or requirements contracts, the quantity that is to be sold or purchased is not specified, but such contracts are nevertheless valid. A sales contract can be modified even though the modification is not supported by consideration. The parol evidence rule applies to a sale of goods in much the same manner as to ordinary contracts. However, the UCC permits the introduction of evidence of course of dealing and usage of trade for clarification of contract terms and performance.

The UCC's statute of frauds provides that a sales contract for $500 ($5,000 under Revised Article 2) or more must be evidenced by a record. The UCC's merchant's confirmation memorandum allows two merchants to be bound to an otherwise oral agreement by a memo or letter signed by only one party that stands without objection for 10 days. Several exceptions to the UCC statute of frauds exist: when the goods are specially made or procured for the buyer and are nonresellable in the seller's ordinary market; when the buyer has received and accepted the goods; when the buyer has made either full or partial payment; and when the party against whom enforcement is sought admits in court pleadings or testimony that a contract for sale was made.

Uniform rules for international sales are applicable to contracts for sales between parties in countries that have ratified the CISG. Under the CISG, a contract for the sale of goods need not be in any particular form and can be proven by any means.

Article 2A of the UCC regulates consumer leases, commercial leases, finance leases, nonfinance leases, and subleases of tangible movable goods. A lease subject to Article 2A must be in writing if the lease payments will total $1,000 or more.

LEARNING OUTCOMES

After studying this chapter, you should be able to clearly explain:

A. Nature and Legality

L0.1 Define a sale of goods and explain when UCC Article 2 applies to contracts
> See *Paramount Contracting Co. v. DPS Industries, Inc.*, on p. 469.

L0.2 Distinguish between an actual sale of goods and other types of transactions in goods
> See footnotes 3 and 4 for examples.

L0.3 Describe how contracts are formed under Article 2, and list the differences in formation standards between the UCC and common law
> See the *For Example*, discussion of Joe and Susan's X-box transaction on p. 472.
> See the *Greenbrier* basket case on p. 481.
> See the *C9 v. SVC* case on pp. 474–475.

B. Form of Sales Contract

L0.4 Explain when a contract for the sale of goods must be in writing
> See the *Basquiat* case on p. 480.

L0.5 List and explain the exceptions to the requirement that certain contracts be in writing
> See the *For Example*, discussion of Wayne and the baseball jackets on p. 482.

C. Uniform Law for International Sales

L0.6 Discuss the purpose of the United Nations Convention on Contracts for the International Sale of Goods
> See the discussion of the CISG on pp. 483–484.

KEY TERMS

acceptance
Article 2
bailee
bailment
battle of the forms
bill of sale
commercial lease
consumer lease
Contracts for the International
  Sale of Goods (CISG)

cost plus
course of dealing
existing goods
finance lease
firm offer
future goods
gift
goods
lease
mailbox rule

merchants
mirror image rule
nonconsumer lease
offer
output contract
parol evidence rule
requirements contract
statute of frauds
unconscionable
usage of trade

QUESTIONS AND CASE PROBLEMS

1. Triple H Construction Co. contracted with Hunter's Run Stables, Inc., to erect a horse barn and riding arena on Hunter's Run's property in Big Flats, New York. Hunter's Run got a guarantee in its contract with Triple H that "such design with the span so shown will support its weight and will withstand natural forces including but not limited to snow load and wind." Hunter's Run also got the following guarantee from Rigidply, the manufacturer of the rafters: "Rigidply ... hereby guarantees that the design to be used for the construction of a horse barn by Triple H ... will support the weight of such barn and to snow load and wind as per

drawings." The barn was completed in 1983 and collapsed under the weight of snow in 1994. Hunter's Run has sued Triple H for UCC Article 2 remedies. Does Article 2 apply? [*Hunter's Run Stables, Inc. v. Triple H, Inc.*, 938 F. Supp. 166 (W.D.N.Y.)]

2. R-P Packaging manufactured cellophane wrapping material that was used by Kern's Bakery in packaging its product. Kern's decided to change its system for packaging cookies from a tied bread bag to a tray covered with printed cellophane wrapping. R-P took measurements to determine the appropriate size for the cellophane

wrapping and designed the artwork to be printed on the wrapping. After agreeing that the artwork was satisfactory, Kern placed a verbal order for the cellophane at a total cost of $13,000. When the printed wrapping material was received, Kern complained that it was too short for the trays and the art work was not centered. The material, however, conformed exactly to the order placed by Kern. Kern returned the material to R-P by overnight express. R-P sued Kern. Kern claimed that because there was no written contract, the suit was barred by the statute of frauds. What result? [*Flowers Baking Co. v. R-P Packaging, Inc.,* 329 S.E.2d 462 (Va.)]

3. Smythe wrote to Lasco Dealers inquiring about the price of a certain freezer. Lasco wrote her a letter, signed by its credit manager, stating that Smythe could purchase the freezer in question during the next 30 days for $400. Smythe wrote back the next day ordering a freezer at that price. Lasco received Smythe's letter the following day, but Lasco wrote a response letter stating that it had changed the price to $450. Smythe claims that Lasco could not change its price. Is she correct?

4. Mrs. Downing was fitted for dentures by a dentist, Dr. Cook. After she received her dentures, Mrs. Downing began experiencing mouth pain that she attributed to Dr. Cook's manufacture of dentures that did not fit her properly. Mrs. Downing filed suit against Dr. Cook for breach of warranty under Article 2 of the UCC. Dr. Cook defended on the grounds that his denture work was a service and therefore not covered under Article 2 warranties. The trial court found for Mrs. Downing, and Dr. Cook appealed. Is Dr. Cook correct? Are the dentures a contract for services or goods? [*Cook v. Downing,* 891 P.2d 611 (Oka. App.)] Would silicone breast implants be covered by the UCC Article 2 warranties? Does implantation of silicone gel implants constitute a sale of goods by the surgeon? [*In re Breast Implant Product Liability Litigation,* 503 S.E.2d 445 (S.C.)]

5. Meyers was under contract with Henderson to install overhead doors in a factory that Henderson was building. Meyers obtained the disassembled doors from the manufacturer. His contract with Henderson required Meyers to furnish all labor, materials, tools, and equipment to satisfactorily complete the installation of all overhead doors. Henderson felt the doors were not installed properly and paid less than one-half of the contract price after subtracting his costs for correcting the installation. Because of a business sale and other complications, Meyers did not sue Henderson for the difference in payment until five years later. Henderson raised the defense that because the contract was for the sale of goods, it was barred by the Code's four-year statute of limitations. Meyers claimed that it was a contract for services and that suit could be brought within six years. Who is correct? Why? [*Meyers v. Henderson Construction Co.,* 370 A.2d 547 (N.J. Super.)]

6. Valley Trout Farms ordered fish food from Rangen. Both parties were merchants. The invoice that was sent with the order stated that a specified charge—a percentage common in the industry—would be added to any unpaid bills. Valley Trout Farms did not pay for the food and did not make any objection to the late charge stated in the invoice. When sued by Rangen, Valley Trout Farms claimed that it had never agreed to the late charge and therefore was not required to pay it. Is Valley Trout Farms correct? [*Rangen, Inc. v. Valley Trout Farms, Inc.,* 658 P.2d 955 (Idaho)]

7. LTV Aerospace Corp. manufactured all-terrain vehicles for use in Southeast Asia. LTV made an oral contract with Bateman under which Bateman would supply the packing cases needed for the vehicles' overseas shipment. Bateman made substantial beginnings in the production of packing cases following LTV's specifications. LTV thereafter stopped production of its vehicles and refused to take delivery of any cases. When Bateman sued for breach of contract, LTV argued that the contract could not be enforced because there was no writing that satisfied the statute of frauds. Was this a valid defense? [*LTV Aerospace Corp. v. Bateman,* 492 S.W.2d 703 (Tex. App.)]

8. Syrovy and Alpine Resources, Inc., entered into a "Timber Purchase Agreement." Syrovy agreed to

sell and Alpine agreed to buy all of the timber produced during a two-year period. The timber to be sold, purchased, and delivered was to be produced by Alpine from timber on Syrovy's land. Alpine continued harvesting for one year and then stopped after making an initial payment. Syrovy sued Alpine. Alpine alleged there was no contract because the writing to satisfy the statute of frauds must contain a quantity term. Decide. [*Syrovy v. Alpine Resources, Inc.*, 841 P.2d 1279 (Wash. App.)]

9. A subcontractor agreed to remove and dispose of cabinets from a public housing project. When a dispute arose, one party argued that the UCC applied, and the other argued that it was the common law contract. Explain who is correct and why. [*J.O. Hooker's Sons v. Roberts Cabinet*, 683 So. 2d 396]

10. Fastener Corp. sent a letter to Renzo Box Co. that was signed by Ronald Lee, Fastener's sales manager, and read as follows: "We hereby offer you 200 type #14 Fastener bolts at $5 per bolt. This offer will be irrevocable for ten days." On the fifth day, Fastener informed Renzo it was revoking the offer, alleging that there was no consideration for the offer. Could Fastener revoke? Explain.

11. Richard, a retailer of video equipment, telephoned Craft Appliances and ordered a $1,000 videotape recorder for his business. Craft accepted Richard's order and sent him a copy of the purchase memorandum that stated the price, quantity, and model ordered and that was stamped "order accepted by Craft." Richard, however, did not sign or return the purchase memorandum and refused to accept delivery of the recorder when Craft delivered it to him three weeks later. Craft sued Richard, who raised the statute of frauds as a defense. Will Richard prevail? Why or why not?

12. REMC furnished electricity to Helvey's home. The voltage furnished was in excess of 135 volts and caused extensive damage to his 110-volt household appliances. Helvey sued REMC for breach of warranty. Helvey argued that providing electrical energy is not a transaction in goods but a furnishing of services, so that he had six years to sue

REMC rather than the UCC's four-year statute of limitations, which had expired. Was it a sale of goods or a sale of services? Identify the ethical principles involved in this case. [*Helvey v. Wabash County REMC*, 278 N.E.2d 608 (Ind. App.)]

13. U.S. Surgical manufactures medical surgical instruments and markets the instruments to hospitals. The packaging for U.S. Surgical's disposable medical instruments is labeled "for single use only." As an example, one label contains the following language: "Unless opened or damaged, contents of package are sterile. DO NOT RESTERILIZE. For multiple use during a SINGLE surgical procedure. DISCARD AFTER USE."

Orris provides a service to the hospitals that purchase U.S. Surgical's disposable instruments. After the hospitals use or open the instruments, Orris cleans, resterilizes, and/or resharpens the instruments for future use and returns them to the hospitals from which they came.

U.S. Surgical filed suit asserting that reprocessing, repackaging, and reuse of its disposable instruments constituted a violation of its patent and trademark rights. Orris says that U.S. Surgical did not prohibit hospitals from reusing the instruments and it was not doing anything that violated the contracts U.S. Surgical had with the hospitals. U.S. Surgical says the language on the packaging was an additional terms that the hospitals accepted by opening the packages and using the instruments. Who is correct? [*U.S. Surgical Corp. v. Orris, Inc.*, 5 F. Supp. 2d 1201 (D. Kan.); aff'd, 185 F.3d 885 (10th Cir.) and 230 F.3d 1382 (Fed. Cir.)]

14. Flora Hall went to Rent-A-Center in Milwaukee and signed an agreement to make monthly payments of $77.96 for 19 months in exchange for Rent-A-Center's allowing her to have a Rent-A-Center washer and dryer in her home. In addition, the agreement required Hall to pay tax and a liability waiver fee on the washer and dryer. The total amount she would pay under the agreement was $1,643.15. The agreement provided that Hall would return the washer and dryer at the end of the 19 months, or she could, at that time, pay $161.91 and own the washer

and dryer as her own. Is this a sales contract? Is this a consumer lease? At the time Hall leased her washer and dryer, she could have purchased a set for about $600. What do you think about the cost of her agreement with Rent-A-Center? Is it unconscionable? Refer to Chapter 33, and determine whether any other consumer laws apply. Must this contract be in writing? [*Rent-A-Center, Inc. v. Hall*, 510 N.W.2d 789 (Wis.)]

15. Click2Boost, Inc. (C2B) entered into an Internet marketing agreement with the New York Times (NYT) on May 10, 2002, for C2B to solicit subscribers for home delivery of the New York Times newspaper through "pop up ads" at Internet Web sites with which C2B maintained "[m]arketing [a]lliances." The agreement required NYT to pay C2B a fee or commission for each home delivery subscription C2B submitted to NYT. NYT paid C2B more than $1.5 million in subscription submission fees from May 2002 to September 2003, but most of the subscriptions were ended, so NYT terminated the C2B agreement on September 16, 2003.

In October 2003, Wall Street Network (WSN) took over C2B and filed suit for breach of contract against NYT. WSN said that NYT had breached the agreement by terminating it before September 30, 2003, because the contract was one for goods and C2B had furnished those goods. WSN wanted damages under the UCC for breach of a contract because the pop-up ads were sold independently as goods. NYT argued that the contract was one for services for furnishing subscribers, something C2B did not do successfully. WSN countered that the customers generated from the pop-up ads were what was being sold, just like selling a list of names, something that would be considered a good. The trial court granted the NYT summary judgment and WSN appealed. Should WSN win the case? Why or why not? [*Wall Street Network, Ltd. v. New York Times Company*, 164 Cal. App. 4th 1171, 80 Cal. Rptr. 3d 6, 66 UCC Rep. Serv. 2d 261]

CPA QUESTIONS

1. Webstar Corp. orally agreed to sell Northco, Inc., a computer for $20,000. Northco sent a signed purchase order to Webstar confirming the agreement. Webstar received the purchase order and did not respond. Webstar refused to deliver the computer to Northco, claiming that the purchase order did not satisfy the UCC statute of frauds because it was not signed by Webstar. Northco sells computers to the general public, and Webstar is a computer wholesaler. Under the UCC Sales Article, Webstar's position is:

   a. Incorrect, because it failed to object to Northco's purchase order.

   b. Incorrect, because only the buyer in a sale-of-goods transaction must sign the contract.

   c. Correct, because it was the party against whom enforcement of the contract is being sought.

   d. Correct, because the purchase price of the computer exceeded $500.

2. On May 2, Lace Corp., an appliance wholesaler, offered to sell appliances worth $3,000 to Parco, Inc., a household appliances retailer. The offer was signed by Lace's president and provided that it would not be withdrawn before June 1. It also included the shipping terms: "F.O.B.—Parco's warehouse." On May 29, Parco mailed an acceptance of Lace's offer. Lace received the acceptance June 2. Which of the following is correct if Lace sent Parco a telegram revoking its offer and Parco received the telegram on May 25?

   a. A contract was formed on May 2.

   b. Lace's revocation effectively terminated its offer on May 25.

   c. Lace's revocation was ineffective because the offer could not be revoked before June 1.

   d. No contract was formed because Lace received Parco's acceptance after June 1.

3. Bond and Spear orally agreed that Bond would buy a car from Spear for $475. Bond paid Spear a $100 deposit. The next day, Spear received an offer of $575, the car's fair market value. Spear immediately notified Bond that Spear would not sell the car to Bond and returned Bond's $100. If Bond sues Spear and Spear defends on the basis of the statute of frauds, Bond will probably:

   a. Lose, because the agreement was for less than the fair market value of the car.

   b. Win, because the agreement was for less than $500.

   c. Lose, because the agreement was not in writing and signed by Spear.

   d. Win, because Bond paid a deposit.

4. Cookie Co. offered to sell Distrib Markets 20,000 pounds of cookies at $1.00 per pound, subject to certain specified terms for delivery. Distrib replied in writing as follows: "We accept your offer for 20,000 pounds of cookies at $1.00 per pound, weighing scale to have valid city certificate." Under the UCC:

   a. A contract was formed between the parties.

   b. A contract will be formed only if Cookie agrees to the weighing scale requirement.

   c. No contract was formed because Distrib included the weighing scale requirement in its reply.

   d. No contract was formed because Distrib's reply was a counteroffer.

5. Under the Sales Article of the UCC, which of the following requirements must be met for a writing to be an enforceable contract for the sale of goods?

   a. The writing must contain a term specifying the price of the goods.

   b. The writing must contain a term specifying the quantity of the goods.

   c. The writing must contain the signatures of all parties to the writing.

   d. The writing must contain the signature of the party seeking to enforce the writing.

6. Card communicated an offer to sell Card's stereo to Bend for $250. Which of the following statements is correct regarding the effect of the communication of the offer?

   a. Bend should immediately accept or reject the offer to avoid liability to Card.

   b. Card is not obligated to sell the stereo to Bend until Bend accepts the offer.

   c. Card is required to mitigate any loss Card would sustain in the event Bend rejects the offer.

   d. Bend may not reject the offer for a reasonable period of time.

CHAPTER 28

Kinds of Instruments, Parties, and Negotiability

© Manuel Gutjahr/iStockphoto.com

learningoutcomes

After studying this chapter, you should be able to

LO.1 Explain the importance and function of negotiable instruments

LO.2 Name the parties to negotiable instruments

LO.3 Describe the concept of negotiability and distinguish it from assignability

LO.4 List the requirements for a negotiable instrument

commercial paper – written, transferable, signed promise or order to pay a specified sum of money; a negotiable instrument.

For convenience and as a way to facilitate transactions, businesses began to accept certain kinds of paper called **commercial paper** or negotiable instruments as substitutes for money or as a means of offering credit. Negotiable commercial paper is special paper created for the special purpose of facilitating transfer of funds and payment. In addition, the use of this special paper for special purposes can create additional rights in a special person status known as a *holder in due course.* Although the details on holders in due course are covered in Chapters 29 and 30, it is important to understand that one of the purposes of the use of special paper is to allow parties to achieve the special status of holder in due course and its protections and rights. Taking each component of negotiable instruments in step-by-step sequences, from their creation to the rights associated with each, and to their transfer, helps in understanding how commercial paper is used for special purposes in order to create rights for special persons.

A. TYPES OF NEGOTIABLE INSTRUMENTS AND PARTIES

Article 3 of the Uniform Commercial Code (UCC) defines the types of negotiable instruments and the parties for each.[1] Article 3 of the UCC was last amended in 2002 with those reforms adopted in some states and under consideration in others.[2] Those changes are explained in each of the relevant sections.

1. Definition

negotiable instruments – drafts, promissory notes, checks, and certificates of deposit that, in proper form, give special rights as "negotiable commercial paper."

Section 3-104(a)(1) and (2) of the UCC defines a **negotiable instrument** as "an unconditional promise or order to pay a fixed amount of money, ... if it (1) is payable to bearer or order...; (2) is payable on demand or at a definite time; and (3) does not state any other undertaking or instruction ... to do any act in addition to the payment of money...."[3] A *negotiable instrument* is a record of a signed promise or order to pay a specified sum of money.[4] The former requirement that the instrument be in writing to be valid has been changed to incorporate requirements of UETA (Uniform Electronic Transactions Act) and E-Sign (Electronic Signatures in Global and National Commerce Act of 2000). Many lenders now use electronic promissory notes.[5] In addition, we now have electronic checks, or those check withdrawals from your account that you authorize over the phone or via the Internet.

Instruments are negotiable when they contain certain elements required by the UCC. These elements are listed and explained in Section 5 of this chapter. However, even those instruments that do not meet the requirements for negotiability may still be referred to by their UCC names or classifications.

---

[1] The law covering negotiable instruments has been evolving and changing. The latest version of Article 3 was adopted in 1990. The 1990 version of Article 3 had been adopted in all 50 states by August 1999. States with variations are Alabama, Georgia, Montana, Ohio, South Dakota, and Wisconsin. The earlier version was called UCC-Commercial Paper, and the 1990 version is called UCC-Negotiable Instruments.
[2] As of April 2012, 49 states and the District of Columbia had adopted the 2002 changes to Article 3.
[3] UCC §3-104(a)(1) and (2).
[4] See UCC §3-104.
[5] Electronic Signatures in Global and National Commerce Act, 15 U.S.C. §7001 (Supp. 2011).

CPA

2. Kinds of Instruments

There are two categories of negotiable instruments: (1) promises to pay, which include promissory notes and certificates of deposit,[6] and (2) orders to pay, including drafts and checks.

(A) PROMISSORY NOTES. A **promissory note** is a written promise made and signed by the maker to pay a *sum certain* in money to the holder of the instrument.[7] (See Figure 28-1.)

(B) CERTIFICATES OF DEPOSIT. A **certificate of deposit (CD)** is a promise to pay issued by a bank.[8] Through a CD, a bank acknowledges the customer's deposit of a specific sum of money and promises to pay the customer that amount plus interest when the certificate is surrendered.

(c) DRAFTS. A **draft, or bill of exchange**, is an order by one party to pay a sum of money to a second party. (See Figure 28-2.) The party who gives the order is called the *drawer*, and the party on whom the order to pay is drawn is the *drawee*.[9] The party to whom payment is to be made is the *payee*. The drawer may also be named as the payee, as when a seller draws a draft naming a buyer as the drawee. The draft is then used as a means to obtain payment for goods delivered to that buyer. A drawee is not bound to pay a draft simply because the drawer has placed his name on it. However, the drawee may agree to pay the draft by accepting it, which then attaches the drawee's liability for payment.

(D) CHECKS. Under UCC §3-104(f), *check* means "a draft, other than a documentary draft, payable on demand and drawn on a bank."[10] A **check** is an order by a depositor (the drawer) on a bank or credit union (the drawee) to pay a sum of money to the order of another party (the payee).[11]

---

promissory note – unconditional promise in writing made by one person to another, signed by the maker engaging to pay on demand, or at a definite time, a sum certain in money to order or to bearer. (Parties—maker, payee)

certificate of deposit (CD) – promise-to-pay instrument issued by a bank.

draft or bill of exchange – an unconditional order in writing by one person upon another, signed by the person giving it, and ordering the person to whom it is directed to pay upon demand or at a definite time a sum certain in money to order or to bearer.

check – order by a depositor on a bank to pay a sum of money to a payee; a bill of exchange drawn on a bank and payable on demand.

FIGURE 28-1	*Promissory Note*

> **MARCH 31, 2013**
>
> Six months after date debtor undersigned hereby promises to pay to the order of Galactic Games, Inc., three thousand six hundred dollars with interest at the rate of 5.9%. This note is secured by the Video Arcade game purchased with its funds.
>
> In the event of default, all sums due hereunder may be collected. Debtor agrees to pay all costs of collection including, but not limited to, attorney fees, costs of repossession, and costs of litigation.
>
> /s/ JOHN R. HALDEHAND
>
> VIDEO ARCADE, INC.

© Cengage Learning

---

[6] UCC §3-104(j).
[7] *IFC Credit Corp. v. Specialty Optical Systems, Inc.*, 252 S.W.3d 761 (Tex. App. 2008).
[8] UCC §3-104(j).
[9] UCC §3-103(a)(2)–(3).
[10] UCC §3-104(f).
[11] *Id.*

FIGURE 28-2	*Draft*

TO: *Topa Fabrics, Inc.*   *March 17,*   20 *13*
     1700 W. Lincoln
     Marina Del Rey, CA

Thirty days from date   PAY TO THE ORDER OF
Malden Mills, Inc.

THE SUM OF   *sixteen thousand and ⁿᵒ/100 ―――――* DOLLARS

ACCEPTED BY: *Aaron Johnson*
_____   *Malden Mills, Inc.*

DATE

© Cengage Learning

In addition to the ordinary checks just described, there are also cashier's checks, teller's checks, traveler's checks, and bank money orders. A **cashier's check** is a draft drawn by a bank on itself. UCC §3-104(g) defines a cashier's check as "a draft with respect to which the drawer and drawee are the same bank or branches of the same bank."[12] A **teller's check** is a draft drawn by a bank on another bank in which it has an account.[13] A **traveler's check** is a check that is payable on demand, provided it is countersigned by the person whose signature was placed on the check at the time the check was purchased.[14] Money orders are issued by both banks and nonbanks. A **money order** drawn by a bank is also a check.[15]

3. Parties to Instruments

A note has two original parties: the *maker* and the *payee*.[16] A draft or a check has three original parties: the *drawer*, the *drawee*, and the *payee*. The names given to the parties to these instruments are important because the liability of the parties varies depending on the parties' roles. The rights and liabilities of the various parties to negotiable instruments are covered in Chapters 29 and 30.

A **party** to an instrument may be a natural person, an artificial person such as a corporation, or an unincorporated enterprise such as a government agency.

(A) Maker. The **maker** is the party who writes or creates a promissory note, thereby promising to pay the amount specified in the note.

(B) Drawer. The **drawer** is the party who writes or creates a draft or check.

(C) Drawee. The **drawee** is the party to whom the draft is addressed and who is ordered to pay the amount of money specified in the draft. The bank is the drawee

cashier's check – draft drawn by a bank on itself.

teller's check – draft drawn by a bank on another bank in which it has an account.

traveler's check – check that is payable on demand provided it is countersigned by the person whose specimen signature appears on the check.

money order – draft issued by a bank or a nonbank.

party – person involved in a legal transaction; may be a natural person, an artificial person (e.g., a corporation), or an unincorporated enterprise (e.g., a governmental agency).

maker – party who writes or creates a promissory note.

drawer – person who writes out and creates a draft or bill of exchange, including a check.

drawee – person to whom the draft is addressed and who is ordered to pay the amount of money specified in the draft.

---

[12] UCC §3-104(g).
[13] UCC §3-104(h).
[14] UCC §3-104(i).
[15] *Com. v. Pantalion*, 957 A.2d 1267 (Pa. Super. 2008). Some items are held to be checks for purposes other than Article 3 negotiability. For example, in *In re Armstrong* 291 F.3d 517 (8th Cir. 2002), the court held that gambling markers were checks for purposes of the state's "bad check" law.
[16] UCC §3-103(a)(5).

on a check, and the credit union is the drawee on a share draft. Again, a drawee on a draft has no responsibility under the draft until it has accepted that instrument.

payee – party to whom payment is to be made.

(D) PAYEE. The **payee** is the person named in the instrument to receive payment. **For Example,** on a check with the words "Pay to the order of John Jones," the named person, John Jones, is the payee.

The payee has no rights in the instrument until the drawer or the maker has delivered it to the payee. Likewise, the payee is not liable on the instrument in any way until the payee transfers the instrument to someone else.

(E) ACCEPTOR. When the drawee of a draft has indicated by writing or record a willingness to pay the amount specified in the draft, the drawee has accepted liability and is called the **acceptor**.[17]

acceptor – drawee who has accepted the liability of paying the amount of money specified in a draft.

(F) SECONDARY OBLIGOR (ACCOMMODATION PARTY). When a party who is not originally named in an instrument allows her name to be added to it for the benefit of another party in order to add strength to the collectability of the instrument, that party becomes a secondary obligor (formerly called an **accommodation party**) and assumes a liability role.[18] Revised Article 3 now refers to drawer, indorsers, and accommodation parties as "secondary obligors."[19]

accommodation party – person who signs an instrument to lend credit to another party to the paper.

CPA

B. NEGOTIABILITY

An instrument is a form of contract that, if negotiable, affords certain rights and protections for the parties. **Negotiability** is the characteristic that distinguishes commercial paper and instruments from ordinary contracts or what makes such paper and instruments special paper.[20] That an instrument is negotiable means that certain rights and protections may be available to the parties to the instrument under Article 3. A **nonnegotiable instrument's** terms are enforceable, but the instrument is treated simply as a contract governed by contract law.[21]

negotiability – quality of an instrument that affords special rights and standing.

nonnegotiable instrument – contract, note, or draft that does not meet negotiability requirements of Article 3.

4. Definition of Negotiability

If an instrument is negotiable, it is governed by Article 3 of the UCC, and it may be transferred by negotiation. This form of transfer permits the transferee to acquire rights greater than those afforded assignees of contracts under contract law. The quality of negotiability in instruments creates opportunities for transfers and financings that streamline payments in commerce. Transfers can be made with assurance of payment without the need for investigation of the underlying contract. The process of negotiation is covered in Chapter 29. For more information on the rights of assignees of contracts, refer to Chapter 18.

---

[17] UCC §3-103(a)(1).
[18] UCC §3-419; *In re TML, Inc.*, 291 B.R. 400, 50 UCC Rep. Serv.2d 511 (W.D. Mich. 2003).
[19] Revised Article 3, §3-103(12), has the following definition of a secondary obligor on an instrument: "an indorser, a drawer, an accommodation party, or any other party to the instrument that has a right of recourse against another party to the instrument...." This definition was changed to be consistent with the Restatement of Surety.
[20] UCC §3-104.
[21] Loan-and-supply contract is not a negotiable instrument. *Quality Oil, Inc. v. Kelley Partners, Inc.*, 657 F.3d 609 (7th Cir. 2011). A note payable when "lessee is granted possession of the premises" is not a negotiable instrument, but it is an enforceable contract. *Schiffer v. United Grocers, Inc.*, 989 P.2d 10 (Or. 1999). A deed of trust is not a negotiable instrument. *Arnold v. Palmer*, 686 S.E.2d 725 (W.Va. 2009).

E-Commerce & Cyberlaw

The Check Is in the Internet

The Check Clearing for the 21st Century Act ("Check 21") allows banks to use electronic images of checks as full and complete records of transactions, the same status formerly used only for paper checks that had been canceled. You can also pay your monthly credit card bills by preauthorizing your credit card company to withdraw the amount you specify from your account. With the bank's routing number and your account number, the company can obtain payment on the due date or any date you authorize. PayPal allows you to do the same with your bank account when you purchase items on the Internet. Paperless payment is on the increase.

CPA

5. Requirements of Negotiability

To be negotiable, an instrument (1) must be evidenced by a record[22] and (2) must be signed (authenticated under Revised Article 3) by the maker or the drawer, (3) must contain an unconditional promise or order to pay, (4) must pay a sum certain, (5) must be payable in money, (6) must be payable on demand or at a definite time, and (7) must be payable to order or bearer, using what are known as words of negotiability.[23]

(A) A RECORD (WRITING). A negotiable instrument must be evidenced by a record. The requirement of a *record*, under Revised Article 3, is satisfied by handwriting, typing, printing, electronic record, and any other method of making a record. A negotiable instrument may be partly printed and partly typewritten. No particular form is required for an instrument to satisfy the record requirement, although customers of banks may agree to use the banks' forms as part of their contractual agreement with their banks. Telephonic checks are a complete record for purposes of Article 3 rights and obligations.

(B) AUTHENTICATED (SIGNED) BY THE MAKER OR DRAWER. The instrument must be authenticated (signed under old Article 3) by the maker or the drawer. When a signature is used as authentication, it usually appears at the lower right-hand corner of the face of the instrument, but there is no requirement for where the signature must be placed on the instrument.[24]

The authentication may consist of the full name or of any symbol placed with the intent to authenticate the instrument. Other means of authentication that are valid as signatures include initials, figures, and marks. Electronic security devices can be used as a means of authentication for electronic records. A person signing a trade name or an assumed name is liable just as if the signer's own name had been used.

(1) Agent.

An authentication may be made by the drawer or the maker or by his or her authorized agent. **For Example,** Eileen Smith, the treasurer of Mills Company, could sign a note for her company as an agent. No particular form of authorization

---

[22] Revised Article 3. Existing Article 3 requires a writing, but the revisions reflect electronic transactions and the federal mandate for recognizing electronic transactions as valid and on equal footing with paper transactions. The definition of a record is found in Revised UCC §3-103(a)(14), which provides that *record* "means information that is inscribed on a tangible medium or which is stored in an electronic or other medium and is retrievable in perceivable form."

[23] UCC §3-104.

[24] According to Revised UCC §3-103, *authenticate* means (a) to sign or (b) to execute or otherwise adopt a symbol, or encrypt or similarly process a record in whole or in part, with the present intent of the authenticating person to identify the person and adopt or accept a record.

for an agent to authenticate an instrument is required. An authenticating agent should disclose on the instrument (1) the identity of the principal and (2) the fact that the authentication was done in a representative capacity. When this information appears on the face of the instrument, an authorized agent is not liable on it.

The representative capacity of an officer of an organization can be shown by the authentication of the officer along with the title of the office and the organization's name.[25] **For Example,** a signature of "James Shelton, Treasurer, NorWest Utilities, Inc.," or "NorWest Utilities, Inc., by James Shelton, Treasurer," on a note is enough to show Shelton's representative capacity. NorWest Utilities, not Shelton, would be liable on the note.

(2) Absence of Representative Capacity or Identification of Principal.

representative capacity —
action taken by one on behalf of another, as the act of a personal representative on behalf of a decedent's estate, or action taken both on one's behalf and on behalf of others, as a shareholder bringing a representative action.

If an instrument fails to show the **representative capacity** of the person who is authenticating or fails to identify the person, then the individual who authenticates the instrument is personally liable on the instrument to anyone who acquires superior rights, such as the rights of a holder in due course (see Chapter 30). Because the instrument is a final agreement, the parol evidence rule applies, and the party who authenticated is not permitted to introduce extrinsic evidence that might clarify his or her representative capacity. The party who authenticated, in order to avoid personal liability, must indicate on the face of the instrument his or her role in the principal, such as president or vice president. (For more information about the parol evidence rule, see Chapter 17.)

However, an agent is not personally liable on a check that is drawn on the bank account of the principal and authenticated by him or her, even though the agent failed to disclose his or her representative capacity on the check. **For Example,** a check that is already imprinted with the employer's name is not the check of the employee, regardless of whether the employee only authenticates with his or her name or also adds a title such as "Payroll Clerk" or "Treasurer" near the signature.

(c) PROMISE OR ORDER TO PAY. A promissory note must contain a promise to pay money. A mere acknowledgment of a debt, such as a record stating "I.O.U.," is not a promise. A draft or check must contain an order or command to pay money.

(d) UNCONDITIONAL PROMISE OR ORDER. For an instrument to be negotiable, the promise or order to pay must be unconditional.[26]

For Example, when an instrument makes the duty to pay dependent on the completion of the construction of a building, the promise is conditional and the instrument is nonnegotiable. The instrument is enforceable as a contract, but it is not a negotiable instrument given all the rights and protections afforded under Article 3.

An order for the payment of money out of a particular fund is negotiable. The instrument can refer to a particular account or merely indicate a source of reimbursement for the drawee, such as "Charge my expense account." Nor is an instrument conditional when payment is to be made only from an identified fund if the issuer is a government or governmental unit or agency, or when payment is to be made from the assets of a partnership, unincorporated association, trust, or estate.[27] However, the fund noted must in fact exist because payment from a fund to be

---

[25] UCC §3-402. *In re Bedrock Marketing, LLC,* 404 B.R. 939 (D.Utah 2009) and *Arntz v. Valdez,* 2011 WL 3433018, 163 Wash.App. 1003 (Wash. App. 2011).
[26] UCC §3-109(c).
[27] A check issued by a debtor in bankruptcy for payment of court-ordered obligations is not conditional because the involvement of the court or ongoing conditions on debtor's payments. *In re Blasco,* 352 B.R. 888 (Bankr. N.D. Ala. Div. 2006).

created by a future event would be conditional. **For Example,** making an instrument "payable from the account I'll establish when the sale of my house occurs" is conditional because the fund's creation is tied to an event whose time of occurrence is unknown.

The standards for negotiability do not require that the issuer of the instrument be personally obligated to pay it.[28] An instrument's negotiability is not destroyed by a reference to a related document. Section 3-106(b) provides, "A promise or order is not made conditional (i) by a reference to another writing for a statement of rights with respect to collateral, prepayment, or acceleration."[29] **For Example,** if a note includes the following phrase, "This note is secured by a mortgage on the property located at Hilding Lane," the note is still negotiable.[30]

CASE SUMMARY

The Sticky Note That Was a Reminder of Personal Liability

FACTS: Northwest Harvest Products, Inc., fell behind on payments on its account with Major Products Company, Inc. Major requested a note for the debt, and Northwest sent a $78,445.24 note. The chief executive officer of Northwest at that time signed the note "Donald H. Eoll CEO," attached a Post-It fax transmittal memo indicating that the note came from Donald Eoll at Northwest, and sent the note via facsimile. The note was not paid, and Major sued both Eoll and Northwest for the debt. Only the facsimile copy of the note was presented at trial, and the trial court found that the writing on the Post-It note, coupled with the signature, identified Northwest as the principal on the note. The trial court held that Eoll was not personally liable for the debt because he signed the note as an agent for Northwest. Major appealed.

DECISION: The court held that Eoll was personally liable on the note. The Post-It note was separate from the document and anything that Eoll and Major wanted to be part of the promissory note should have been written on the promissory note. Without the Post-it, there is no indication of capacity on the promissory note, which leaves Eoll liable personally on that note. Reversed. [*Major Products Co., Inc. v. Northwest Harvest Products, Inc.,* 979 P.2d 905 (Wash. App. 1999)]

Thinking Things Through

When Your John Hancock Is Enough

Work through the following examples of signatures on negotiable instruments and capacity, and determine whether there would be personal liability on the part of the company executives signing the instruments personal liability.

1. Donald Schaffer owned and operated Grafton Janitorial Service, Inc. On October 6, 1998, Mr. Schaffer obtained a $25,000 line of credit for his company from First Merit Bank by executing a promissory note, which he signed both as "Donald J. Schaffer,

[28] UCC §3-110(c)(1)–(2) (1990); *Ocwen Loan Servicing, LLC v. Branaman,* 554 F. Supp. 2d 645 (N.D. Miss. 2008).

[29] UCC §3-106(b).

[30] Reference to a bill of lading does not affect negotiability. *Regent Corp., U.S.A. v. Azmat Bangladesh, Ltd.,* 686 N.Y.S.2d 24 (1999); However, a reference to a standby agreement does affect negotiability. *In re Sabertooth, LLC,* 443 B.R. 671 (E.D. Pa. 2011).

Thinking Things Through

Continued

President" and "Donald J. Schaffer, Cosigner." The note contains no guarantee provision, and Mr. Schaffer did not sign the note in the capacity as a guarantor. **[*Schaffer v. First Merit Bank, N.A.*, 927 N.E.2d 15 (Ohio App. 2009)]**

2. A corporate guaranty was signed as follows:
THE PRODUCERS GROUP OF FLA., INC. a Florida corporation, by the following officers solely on behalf of the corporation:

/s/ Eddie Beverly, as its President

CORPORATE PRESIDENT Eddie Beverly

/s/ Stephen Edman, as its Secretary

CORPORATE SECRETARY Steve Edman

/s/ John Bauder, as its Treasurer

CORPORATE TREASURER John Bauder

Are the officers personally liable on the gzuaranty? **[*Tampa Bay Economic Development Corp. v. Edman*, 598 So.2d 172 (Fla. App. 1992)]**

---

money – medium of exchange.

(E) **PAYMENT IN MONEY.** A negotiable instrument must be payable in money. **Money** is defined to include any medium of exchange adopted or authorized by the United States, a foreign government, or an intergovernmental organization. The parties to an instrument are free to decide which currency will be used for payment even though their transaction may occur in a different country.[31] **For Example,** two parties in the United States are free to agree that their note will be paid in pesos.

If the order or promise is not for money, the instrument is not negotiable. **For Example,** an instrument that requires the holder to take stock or goods in place of money is nonnegotiable. The instrument is enforceable as a contract, but it cannot qualify as a negotiable instrument for purposes of Article 3 rights.

sum certain – amount due under an instrument that can be computed from its face with only reference to interest rates.

(F) **SUM CERTAIN.** Negotiable instruments must include a statement of a **sum certain**, or an exact amount of money. Without a definite statement as to how much is to be paid under the terms of the instrument, there is no way to determine how much the instrument is worth.

There are some minor variations from sum certain requirement. **For Example,** an instrument is not nonnegotiable because its interest rate provisions include changes in the rate at maturity or because it provides for certain costs and attorney fees to be recovered by the holder in the event of enforcement action or litigation.[32]

In most states, the sum payable under an instrument is certain even though it calls for the payment of a floating or variable interest rate.[33] An instrument is negotiable even though it provides for an interest rate of 1 percent above the prime rate of a named bank. It is immaterial that the exact amount of interest that will be paid cannot be determined at the time the paper is issued because the rate may later change. It is also immaterial that the amount due on the instrument cannot be determined without looking at records outside of the face of the instrument.[34]

---

[31] UCC §3-107. *Means v. Clardy*, 735 S.W.2d 6 (Mo. App. 1987) (payment in cabinets makes a note nonnegotiable).

[32] UCC §3-106. *In re MCB Financial Group, Inc.*, 461 B.R. 914 (N.D. Ga. 2011).

[33] While revised Article 3 permits variable and market rates, notes entered into before the revised act was adopted will be governed under old Article 3; *YYY Corp. v. Gazda*, 761 A.2d 395 (N.H. 2000), *Barnsley v. Empire Mortgage, Ltd. Partnership*, 720 A.2d 63 (N.H. 1998), but see *Bankers Trust (Delaware) v. 236 Beltway Inv.*, 865 F. Supp. 1186 (E.D. Va. 1994)

[34] *SCADIF, S.A. v. First Union Nat. Bank*, 208 F. Supp. 2d 1352 (S.D. Fla. 2002), aff'd, 344 F.3d 1123 (11th Cir. 2003). See also *Bankers Trust v. 236 Beltway Investment*, 865 F. Supp. 1186 (E.D. Va. 1994).

(G) TIME OF PAYMENT. A negotiable instrument must be payable on demand or at a definite time.[35] If an instrument is payable "when convenient," it is nonnegotiable because the day of payment may never arrive. An instrument payable only upon the happening of a particular event that may or may not happen is not negotiable. **For Example,** a provision in a note to pay the sum certain when a person marries is not payable at a definite time because that particular event may never occur. It is immaterial whether the contingency in fact has happened because from an examination of the instrument alone, it still appears to be subject to a condition that might not occur.

(1) Demand.

An instrument is *payable on demand* when it expressly states that it is payable "on demand," at sight, or on presentation. UCC §3-108(a) provides "A promise or order is 'payable on demand' if (i) it states that it is payable on demand or at sight, or otherwise indicates that it is payable at the will of the holder, or (ii) it does not state any time of payment."[36] Presentation occurs when a holder demands payment. Commercial paper is deemed to be payable on demand when no time for payment is stated in the instrument.[37]

(2) Definite Time.

definite time – time of payment computable from the face of the instrument.

The time of payment is a **definite time** if an exact time or times are specified or if the instrument is payable at a fixed time after sight or acceptance or at a time that is readily ascertainable. The time of payment is definite even though the instrument provides for prepayment, for acceleration, or for extensions at the option of a party or automatically on the occurrence of a specified contingency.

CASE SUMMARY

Whenever...Paying When You Can Does Not a Negotiable Instrument Make

FACTS: Gary Vaughn signed a document stating that Fred and Martha Smith were loaning him $9,900. As to when the loan was to be repaid, the document stated, "when you can." Approximately 18 months later, the Smiths sued Vaughn for the entire amount, claiming default on the note as well as unjust enrichment. The Smiths moved for summary judgment. They contended that Vaughn was immediately liable for the entire amount but that they were willing to work out a repayment schedule. Vaughn also moved for summary judgment, arguing that he did not have to repay the Smiths because he did not have the ability to do so. The trial court denied the Smiths' motion and granted Vaughn's. The Smiths appealed.

DECISION: The court held the following: a promissory note that calls for a borrower to repay "when you can" was not payable on demand and was not a negotiable instrument. However, an issue of fact remained as to when a debt payable "when you can" became payable. There were other issues of fact such as whether there was unjust enrichment and whether it was reasonable for the borrower to repay the debt. The language implied that there was an open-ended agreement. The parties might have a contract, but the Smiths could not demand payment as if the instrument were a demand negotiable instrument. Reversed for further factual determinations. [*Smith v. Vaughn,* 882 N.E.2d 941 (Ohio App. 2007)]

---

35 UCC §3-108.
36 UCC §3-108(a).
37 UCC §3-112; *Universal Premium Acceptance Corp. v. York Bank's Trust Co.,* 69 F.3d 695 (3d Cir. 1995); *State v. McWilliams,* 178 P. 3d 121 (Mont. 2008).

(3) Missing Date.

An instrument that is not dated is deemed dated on the day it is issued to the payee. Any holder may add the correct date to the instrument.

(4) Effect of Date on a Demand Instrument.

The date on a demand instrument controls the time of payment, and the paper is not due before its date. Consequently, a check that is postdated ceases to be demand paper and is not properly payable before the date on the check. A bank making earlier payment does not incur any liability for doing so unless the drawer has given the bank a postdated check notice.

(H) WORDS OF NEGOTIABILITY: PAYABLE TO ORDER OR BEARER. An instrument that is not a check must be **payable to order** or **bearer**.[38] This requirement is met by such phrases as "Pay to the order of John Jones," "Pay to John Jones or order," "Pay to bearer," and "Pay to John Jones or bearer." The use of the phrase "to the order of John Jones" or "to John Jones or order" shows that the person executing the instrument had no intention of restricting payment of the instrument to John Jones. These phrases indicate that there is no objection to paying anyone to whom John Jones orders the paper to be paid. Similarly, if the person executing the instrument originally wrote that it will be paid "to bearer" or "to John Jones or bearer," there is no restriction on the payment of the paper to the original payee. However, if the instrument is not a check and it is payable on its face "to John Jones," the instrument is not negotiable.[39] Whether an instrument is bearer or order paper is important because the two instruments are transferred in different ways and because the liability of the transferors can be different.

payable to order–term stating that a negotiable instrument is payable to the order of any person described in it or to a person or order.

bearer–person in physical possession of commercial paper payable to bearer, a document of title directing delivery to bearer, or an investment security in bearer form.

Ethics & the Law

Medicaid Eligibility and Article 3 Negotiability

Kenneth Wilson was hospitalized from January 7, 2007, until his death on February 22, 2007. During the hospitalization, Kenneth's wife, Doris, sold her 100% stock ownership in the Brothers Delivery Service (her husband's company) to her son. The agreement provided that Kenneth, Jr. would pay $62,531 in 60 installments of $1.041.82, starting March 1, 2007. Kenneth Jr. did not sign the promissory note for these terms. Doris never signed the purchase agreement. Doris then applied for Medicaid benefits in order to cover the costs of her husband's hospitalization. Eligibility for Medicaid requires a determination that there are insufficient personal assets to pay the bill. The Division of Social Services concluded that Doris was the owner of a promissory note, a liquid asset, that could be sold to pay the medical bills. Coverage was denied due to excessive resources. Doris argues that there is no negotiable note because the requirements for negotiability are not met. The appellate court agreed because the underlying contract had not been signed by Doris and because there was not, as yet, a promissory note. The purchase agreement did not have words of negotiability and there was no definite time for payment because the note did not yet exist. Discuss whether Doris attained Medicaid eligibility through a legal loophole. Does she actually have assets that could be used to pay at least part of the debt? Should legal definitions allow us to escape an obligation to pay? **[*Estate of Wilson v. Division of Social Services,* 685 S.E.2d 135 (N.C. App. 2009)]**

---

[38] *Unlimited Adjusting Group, Inc. v. Wells Fargo Bank,* 94 Cal. Rptr.3d 672 (Cal. App. 2009).
[39] UCC §3-108.

CASE SUMMARY

The Goal Was a Hockey Team AND a Negotiable Instrument

FACTS: William Kidd served as managing director of Limeco Corporation. Beginning in 2001, negotiations began between Kidd/Limeco (defendants) and R.W. Whitaker and Monty Fletcher (plaintiffs) in connection with what later became a failed effort to purchase a hockey team in Tupelo. Whitaker and Fletcher loaned Limeco $750,000. Whitaker and Fletcher claim that Kidd concealed the fact that Limeco had no assets. Whitaker also loaned Kidd an additional $100,000, with the understanding that Kidd and Limeco would be responsible for paying back the loan that Whitaker had taken out from the Peoples Bank & Trust Company in Tupelo in order to make the loan to Kidd.

On July 1, 2002, the parties entered into what they referred to as promissory notes (referred to as the "Fletcher note" and the "Whitaker note") to memorialize the terms of the loan agreements they had made in early 2002. Both Fletcher and Whitaker, in an effort to secure what they thought were promissory notes, were granted a continuing lien on Limeco's monies, securities, and/or other property for the entire amount of the promissory notes (each in the amount of $375,000).

On December 11, 2003, Whitaker and Fletcher filed separate complaints against Limeco and Kidd for recovery of the more than $850,000 that had never been repaid. The trial court found that the suit had to be dismissed because it was brought after the contracts' statute of limitations had expired. Whitaker and Fletcher argued that the notes were negotiable instruments and that their fraud claim was valid because of the six-year statute of limitations that applied with regard to negotiable instruments.

DECISION: The court held that words of negotiability are an absolute requirement for a negotiable instrument. Without those words, the note is simply a contract, and a suit on a contract required that it be filed within three years. Because Whitaker and Fletcher were over the three years, their suit had to be dismissed. If they had had the words of negotiability, then the suit could have proceeded because it was brought well within the time limits. [***Whitaker v. Limeco Corp.*, 32 So.3d 429 (Miss. 2010)**]

(1) Order Paper.

order paper – instrument payable to the order of a party.

An instrument is payable to order, or **order paper**, when by its terms it is payable to the order of any person described in it ("Pay to the order of K. Read") or to a person or order ("Pay to K. Read or order").

(2) Bearer Paper.

bearer paper – instrument with no payee, payable to cash or payable to bearer.

An instrument is payable to bearer, or **bearer paper**, when it is payable (1) to bearer or the order of bearer, (2) to a specified person or bearer, or (3) to "cash," "the order of cash," or any other designation that does not purport to identify a person or when (4) the last or only indorsement is a blank indorsement (an indorsement that does not name the person to whom the instrument is negotiated). An instrument that does not identify any payee is payable to bearer.[40]

Whether an instrument is bearer or order paper is important for determining how the instrument is transferred (see Chapter 28) and what the liability of the parties under the instrument is. Review Figure 28-3 for more background.

[40] UCC §3-104(d).

CASE SUMMARY

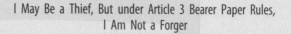

I May Be a Thief, But under Article 3 Bearer Paper Rules, I Am Not a Forger

FACTS: Joshua Herrera found a purse in a dumpster near San Pedro and Kathryn Streets in Albuquerque. Herrera took the purse with him to a friend's house. Either Herrera or his friend called the owner of the purse and the owner retrieved the purse at some point. After the purse was returned to the owner, Herrera returned to the dumpster where he found a check and some other items. The check Herrera found was written out to "Cash" and he thought this meant that he "could get money for [the] check."

When he presented the check to the teller at a credit union to cash it, the teller instructed him to put his name on the payee line next to "Cash." Herrera added "to Joshua Herrera" next to the word "Cash" on the payee line of the check and indorsed the check.

Herrera had pleaded guilty to one count of forgery but moved to have the indictment dismissed on the grounds that adding his name to a bearer instrument was not forgery. He appealed the denial of the motion to dismiss the indictment.

DECISION: The court held that the instrument that Herrera originally found was bearer paper. By adding his named "to Joshua Herrera" to the "Pay to" line after "Cash" did not change the character of the instrument from bearer to order paper. At best, the addition of the words created an ambiguity and under the code interpretations should continue to be treated as bearer paper. Since he did not alter the nature of the instrument or convert it to a different instrument, he could not be charged with forgery. [*New Mexico v. Herrera*, **18 P.3d 326 (N.M. App. 2001);** *cert.* **den. 20 P.3d 810 (N.M. 2001)]**

6. Factors Not Affecting Negotiability

postdate – to insert or place on an instrument a later date than the actual date on which it was executed.

Omitting a date of execution or antedating or **postdating** an instrument has no effect on its negotiability.

collateral – property pledged by a borrower as security for a debt.

Provisions relating to **collateral**, such as specifying the collateral as security for the debt or a promise to maintain, protect, or give additional collateral, do not affect negotiability. **For Example,** the phrase "This note is secured by a first mortgage" does not affect negotiability.

FIGURE 28-3	*Bearer versus Order Paper*

"Pay to the order of ABC Corp."	ORDER
"Pay to the order of Bearer."	BEARER
"Pay to the order of ABC Corp. or Bearer"	BEARER
"Pay to the order of ABC Corp., Bearer"	ORDER
"Pay to the order of John Jones" (note)	ORDER
"Pay to the order of John Jones" (check)	ORDER
"Pay to John Jones" (note)	NONNEGOTIABLE
"Pay to John Jones" (check)	NEGOTIABLE/ORDER
"Pay to the order of John Jones or Bearer"	BEARER
"Pay to cash"	BEARER
"Pay to the order of cash"	BEARER

7. Ambiguous Language

ambiguous – having more than one reasonable interpretation.

The following rules are applied when **ambiguous** language exists in words or descriptions:

1. Words control figures where conflict exists.

2. Handwriting supersedes conflicting typewritten and printed terms.

3. Typewritten terms supersede preprinted terms.

4. If there is a failure to provide for the payment of interest or if there is a provision for the payment of interest but no rate is mentioned, the judgment rate at the place of payment applies from the date of the instrument.[41]

8. Statute of Limitations

Article 3 of the UCC establishes a three-year statute of limitations for most actions involving negotiable instruments. This limitation also applies to actions for the conversion of such instruments and for breach of warranty. There is a six-year statute of limitations for suits on certificates of deposit and accepted drafts.

MAKE THE CONNECTION

SUMMARY

An instrument or piece of commercial paper is a transferable, signed promise or order to pay a specified sum of money that is evidenced by a record. An instrument is negotiable when it contains the terms required by the UCC.

Negotiable instruments have two categories: (1) promises to pay and (2) orders to pay. Checks and drafts are orders to pay. Notes and certificates of deposits are promises to pay. In addition to ordinary checks, there are cashier's checks and teller's checks. A bank money order is a check even though it bears the words *money order*.

The original parties to a note are the maker and the payee. The original parties to a draft are the drawer, the drawee, and the payee. The term *party* may refer to a natural person or to an artificial

person, such as a corporation. Indorsers and accommodation parties are considered secondary obligors.

The requirements of negotiability are that the instrument (1) be evidenced by a record, (2) be signed (authenticated) by the maker or the drawer, and (3) contain a promise or order (4) of an unconditional character (5) to pay in money (6) a sum certain (7) on demand or at a definite time (8) to order or bearer. A check may be negotiable without being payable to order or bearer.

If an instrument meets the requirements of negotiability, the parties have the rights and protections of Article 3. If it does not meet the requirements of negotiability, the rights of the parties are governed under contract law.

---

[41] *In re Blasco*, 352 B.R. 888 (N.D. Ala. 2006).

LEARNING OUTCOMES

After studying this chapter, you should be able to clearly explain:

A. Types of Negotiable Instruments and Parties

LO.1   Explain the importance and function of negotiable instruments

See the discussion of negotiability on p. 585.
See *New Mexico v. Herrera* on p. 593.

LO.2   Name the parties to negotiable instruments

See the list of parties to instruments starting on p. 584.

B. Negotiability

LO.3   Describe the concept of negotiability and distinguish it from assignability

See *Whitaker v. Limeco Corp.* on p. 592 for what can happen if an instrument is not negotiable.

LO.4   List the requirements for a negotiable instrument

See the list of negotiability requirements on p. 586.
See *Smith v. Vaughn* on p. 590.

KEY TERMS

acceptor	definite time	order paper
accommodation party	draft, or bill of exchange	party
ambiguous	drawee	payable to order
bearer	drawer	payee
bearer paper	maker	postdating
cashier's check	money	promissory note
certificate of deposit (CD)	money order	representative capacity
check	negotiability	sum certain
collateral	negotiable instrument	teller's check
commercial paper	nonnegotiable instrument	traveler's check

QUESTIONS AND CASE PROBLEMS

1. Harold H. Heidingsfelder signed a credit agreement as vice president of J. O. H. Construction Co. for a line of credit with Pelican Plumbing Co. The credit agreement contained the following language:

   In consideration of an open account privilege, I hereby understand and agree to the above terms. Should it become necessary to place this account for collection I shall personally obligate myself and my corporation, if any, to pay the entire amount due including service charges (as outlined above terms) thirty-three and one-third (33¹/₃%) attorney's fees, and all costs of collection, including court costs.
   Signed [Harold H. Heidingsfelder]
   Company J. O. H. Construction Co., Inc.

   When J. O. H. Construction failed to make payment, Pelican, claiming it was a holder of a negotiable instrument, sued Heidingsfelder to hold him personally liable for his failure to indicate a representative capacity on the credit agreement. He claims that a credit application is not a negotiable instrument and that he could not be held personally liable. Is he right? [*Pelican Plumbing Supply, Inc. v. J. O. H. Construction Co., Inc.*, 653 So.2d 699 (La.)]

2. Abby Novel signed a note with the following on it: "Glen Gallwitz 1-8-2002 loaned me $5,000 at 6% interest a total of $10,000.00." The note did not contain a payment schedule or a time for repayment.

Abby used the $10,000 as start-up money for her business and says that she orally agreed to repay the loan out of the proceeds from her first 1,000-product sales. Abby did not make any payments. Glen passed away and his son, as executor of his estate, demanded that Abby repay the $10,000 plus 6% interest for a total of $14,958 (the amount due as of April 2010). The trial court granted judgment for the estate. Abby has appealed, alleging that she repaid the note through the care she gave for Glen. The estate maintains that the instrument was a negotiable promissory note and that it is entitled to collect the amount due in cash. Who is correct and why? [*Gallwitz v. Novel*, 2011 WL 303253 (Ohio App.)]

3. Charter Bank of Gainesville had in its possession a note containing the following provision: "This note with interest is secured by a mortgage on real estate, of even date herewith, made by the maker hereof in favor of said payee…. The terms of said mortgage are by this reference made a part hereof." When the bank sued on the note, it said it was a holder of a negotiable instrument. Is this instrument negotiable? [*Holly Hill Acres, Ltd. v. Charter Bank of Gainesville*, 314 So.2d 209 (Fla. App.)]

4. On October 14, 1980, United American Bank of Knoxville made a $1,700,000 loan to Frederic B. Ingram. William F. Earthman, the president of the bank and a beneficiary of the loan, had arranged for the loan and prepared the loan documents. Mr. Ingram and Mr. Earthman were old friends, and Mr. Ingram had loaned Mr. Earthman money in the past. Mr. Ingram was in jail at the time of this loan and was unable to complete the documents for the loan. Mr. Earthman says that Mr. Ingram authorized him to do the loan so long as it did not cost him anything to do it.

Also on October 14, 1980, Mr. Earthman prepared and executed a personal $1,700,000 note to Mr. Ingram, using a standard Commerce Union Bank note form. Mr. Earthman wrote "Frederic B. Ingram" in the space for identifying the lending bank and also filled in another blank stating that the note would be due "Eighteen

Months after Date." With regard to the interest, Mr. Earthman checked a box signifying that the interest would be "At the Bank's 'Prime Rate' plus % per year."

Mr. Earthman then sold both of the notes, which ended up in the hands of third parties (holders in due course) who demanded payment. Mr. Ingram raised the defense that he had not authorized Mr. Earthman to handle the transactions. The third parties said the notes were negotiable instruments and they were entitled to payment without listening to Mr. Ingram's defenses. Mr. Earthman said his note to Mr. Ingram as well as the bank note from Mr. Ingram were not negotiable and that they could both raise defenses to the third parties seeking payment.

Who is correct? What do you think of Mr. Earthman's banking processes and procedures? What ethical issues do you see in these loan transactions? [*Ingram v. Earthman*, 993 S.W.2d 611 (Tenn.)]

5. The state of Alaska was a tenant in a large office building owned by Univentures, a partnership. The state made a lease payment of $28,143.47 to Univentures with state treasury warrant No. 21045102. Charles LeViege, the managing partner of Univentures, assigned the warrant to Lee Garcia. A dispute then arose among the Univentures partners, and the company notified the state that it should no longer pay LeViege the rent. The state placed a stop payment order on the warrant. Garcia claimed that he was a holder of a negotiable instrument and that the state owed him the money. The state claimed that a warrant did not qualify as a negotiable instrument. The warrant was in writing, was signed by the governor of the state, provided a definite sum of $28,143.47, and stated that "it will be deemed paid unless redeemed within two years after the date of issue." The warrant stated that it was "payable to the order of Univentures." Does the warrant meet the requirements for a negotiable instrument? [*National Bank v. Univentures*, 824 P.2d 1377 (Alaska)]

6. Nation-Wide Check Corp. sold money orders through local agents. A customer would purchase

a money order by paying an agent the amount of the desired money order plus a fee. The customer would then sign the money order as the remitter or sender and would fill in the name of the person who was to receive the money following the printed words "Payable to." In a lawsuit between Nation-Wide and Banks, a payee on some of these orders, the question was raised as to whether these money orders were checks and could be negotiable even though not payable to order or to bearer. Are the money orders negotiable instruments? [*Nation-Wide Check Corp. v. Banks*, 260 A.2d 367 (D.C.)]

7. George S. Avery signed a letter regarding the unpaid balance on a $20,000 promissory note owed to Jim Whitworth in the form of a letter addressed to Whitworth stating: "This is your note for $45,000.00, secured individually and by our Company for your security, due February 7, 1984." The letter was signed: "Your friend, George S. Avery." It was typed on stationery with the name of Avery's employer, V & L Manufacturing Co., Inc., printed at the bottom and the words "George Avery, President" printed at the top. Avery says he is not personally liable on the note. The court granted summary judgment for Whitworth and Avery appealed. Who is liable? [*Avery v. Whitworth*, 414 S.E.2d 725 (Ga. App.)]

8. Bellino made a promissory note that was payable in installments and contained the provision that on default of the payment of any installment, the holder had the option to declare the entire balance due and payable on demand. The note was negotiated to Cassiani, who sued Bellino for the full debt when there was a default on the installment. Is a note with an acceleration clause still negotiable? [*Cassiani v. Bellino*, 157 N.E.2d 409 (Mass.)]

9. Atlas Capital, LLC's sole member and manager was Weston Wade Sleater. Mr. Sleater signed two promissory notes totaling $4,000,000 as the maker of the notes. The signature blocks of the notes read, "Weston Wade Sleater & Atlas Marketing Group, L.C.," but the signature was only that of Mr. Sleater. Mr. Sleater is referred to as the maker of the note. Mr. Sleater failed to pay the notes and a bankruptcy trustee brought suit to collect the remaining amount due. Mr. Sleater maintains that the notes are not his, but those of Atlas Capital. Is he correct? Is Mr. Sleater liable on the notes? Discuss the ambiguity issues as well as the way the notes were signed. [*In re Bedrock Marketing*, LLC, 404 B.R. 929 (D. Utah)]

10. Lloyd and Mario Spaulding entered into a contract to purchase property from Richard and Robert Krajcir. The two Spaulding brothers signed a promissory note to the Krajcir brothers with the following language: "The amount of $10,000 [is] to be paid sellers at the time of the initial closing [delivery of the deed]; plus, the principal amount payable to sellers at the time of the final indorsement of the subject H.U.D. loan." In litigation over the note, the Spauldings said it was not a negotiable instrument. The lower court found it to be a negotiable promissory note and the Spaulding partners appealed. Is the note negotiable? [*Krajcir v. Egid*, 712 N.E.2d 917 (Ill. App.)]

11. Is the following instrument negotiable?

I, Richard Bell, hereby promise to pay to the order of Lorry Motors Ten Thousand Dollars ($10,000) upon the receipt of the final distribution from the estate of my deceased aunt, Rita Dorn. This negotiable instrument is given by me as the down payment on my purchase of a 1986 Buick to be delivered in three weeks.

Richard Bell (signature).

12. Smith has in his possession the following instrument:

September 1, 2003
I, Selma Ray, hereby promise to pay Helen Savit One Thousand Dollars ($1,000) one year after date. This instrument was given for the purchase of Two Hundred (200) shares of Redding Mining Corporation, Interest 6%.

Selma Ray (signature).

What is this instrument? Is it negotiable?

13. Master Homecraft Co. received a promissory note with a stated face value from Sally and Tom Zimmerman. The note was payment for

remodeling their home and contained unused blanks for installment payments but contained no maturity date. When Master Homecraft sued the Zimmermans on the note, the couple argued that they should not be liable on the note because it is impossible to determine from its face the amount due or the date of maturity. Decide. [*Master Homecraft Co. v. Zimmerman*, 22 A.2d 440 (Pa.)]

14. A note from Mark Johnson with HealthCo International as payee for $28,979.15 included the following language:

[p]ayable in _____, Successive Monthly Installments of $ Each, and in 11 Successive Monthly Installments of $2,414.92 Each

thereafter, and in a final payment of $2,415.03 thereafter. The first installment being payable on the _____ day of _____ 20 _____, and the remaining installments on the same date of each month thereafter until paid.

Johnson signed the note. Is it negotiable? [*Barclays Bank, P.L.C. v. Johnson*, 499 S.E.2d 769 (N.C. App.)]

15. The text of a handwritten note stated simply that "'I Robert Harrison owe Peter Jacob $25,000 …,' /s/ Robert Harrison." Peter Jacob sought to use the handwritten note as a negotiable promissory note. Can he? [*Jacob v. Harrison*, 49 UCC Rep. Serv. 2d 554 (Del. Super.)]

CPA QUESTIONS

1. A company has in its possession the following instrument:

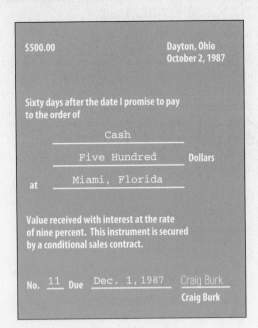

This instrument is:

   a. Not negotiable until December 1, 1987.

   b. A negotiable bearer note.

   c. A negotiable time draft.

   d. A nonnegotiable note because it states that it is secured by a conditional sales contract.

2. The instrument shown here is a:

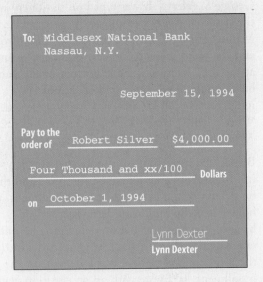

   a. Draft

   b. Postdated check

   c. Trade acceptance

   d. Promissory note

3. Under the commercial paper article of the UCC, for an instrument to be negotiable, it must:

   a. Be payable to order or to bearer.

   b. Be signed to the payee.

c. Contain references to all agreements between the parties.

d. Contain necessary conditions of payment.

4. An instrument reads as follows:

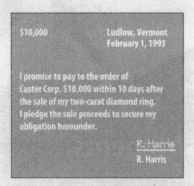

| $10,000 | Ludlow, Vermont February 1, 1993 |

I promise to pay to the order of Custer Corp. $10,000 within 10 days after the sale of my two-carat diamond ring. I pledge the sale proceeds to secure my obligation hereunder.

R. Harris
R. Harris

Which of the following statements correctly describes this instrument?

a. The instrument is nonnegotiable because it is not payable at a definite time.

b. The instrument is nonnegotiable because it is secured by the proceeds of the sale of the ring.

c. The instrument is a negotiable promissory note.

d. The instrument is a negotiable sight draft payable on demand.

5. Which of the following instruments is subject to the provisions of the Negotiable Instruments Article of the UCC?

a. A bill of lading

b. A warehouse receipt

c. A certificate of deposit

d. An investment security

6. Under the Negotiable Instruments Article of the UCC, which of the following statements is correct regarding a check?

a. A check is a promise to pay money.

b. A check is an order to pay money.

c. A check does not need to be payable on demand.

d. A check does not need to be drawn on a bank.

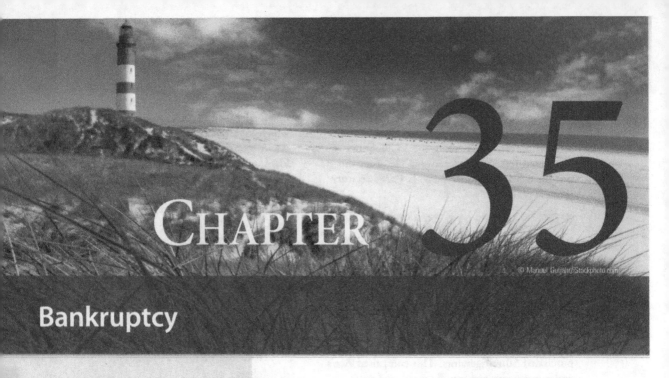

© Manuel Gutjahr/iStockphoto.com

CHAPTER 35

Bankruptcy

learningoutcomes

After studying this chapter, you should be able to

LO.1 List the requirements for the commencement of a voluntary bankruptcy case and an involuntary bankruptcy case

LO.2 Explain the procedure for the administration of a debtor's estate

LO.3 List a debtor's duties and exemptions

LO.4 Explain the significance of a discharge in bankruptcy

LO.5 Explain when a business reorganization plan or an extended-time payment plan might be used

W hat can a person or business do when overwhelmed by debts? Bankruptcy proceedings can provide temporary and sometimes permanent relief from those debts.

A. Bankruptcy Law

Bankruptcy is a statutory proceeding with detailed procedures and requirements.

1. The Federal Law

Bankruptcy law is based on federal statutes that have been refined over the years. In October 2005, the Bankruptcy Abuse Prevention and Consumer Protection Act of 2005 (BAPCPA) took effect.[1] The BAPCPA was passed more than 10 years after the Bankruptcy Reform Commission was created, and the changes in bankruptcy law reflect an expressed congressional desire to curb a 15-year trend of increases in the number of bankruptcies.

Jurisdiction over bankruptcy proceedings is vested in the federal district courts. The district courts have the authority to transfer such matters to courts of special jurisdiction called **bankruptcy courts**.

bankruptcy courts – court of special jurisdiction to determine bankruptcy issues.

2. Types of Bankruptcy Proceedings

The three types of bankruptcy proceedings that existed before the 2005 reforms are still available to individuals and businesses.

CPA

(A) Liquidation or Chapter 7 Bankruptcy. A **Chapter 7 bankruptcy** is one in which all of the debtor's assets (with some exemptions) will be **liquidated** to pay debts. Those debts that remain unpaid or are paid only partially are discharged, with some exceptions. The debtor who declares Chapter 7 bankruptcy begins again with a nearly clean slate.

Chapter 7 bankruptcy – liquidation form of bankruptcy under federal law.

liquidation – process of converting property into money whether of particular items of property or of all the assets of a business or an estate.

Chapter 7 bankruptcy is available to individuals, partnerships, and corporations. However, farmers, insurance companies, savings and loans, municipalities, Small Business Administration companies, and railroads are not entitled to declare Chapter 7 bankruptcy because they are specifically governed by other statutes or specialized sections of the Bankruptcy Code.[2]

Under the BAPCPA, consumers generally cannot go directly to a Chapter 7 liquidation bankruptcy because they must demonstrate that they do not have the means to repay the debts before they can do a Chapter 7 liquidation.[3] The means test, which is discussed later, considers the disposable income that is available after the bankruptcy court has deducted allowable expenses that are listed as part of the means section of the BAPCPA, including items such as health insurance and child support.

[handwritten: → creditor gets nothing]

---

[1] Pub. L. No. 109-8, 119 Stat. 23 (2005); the act is codified at 11 U.S.C. §101 *et seq.*

[2] For example, the Small Business Investment Act governs the insolvency of small business investment companies, 11 U.S.C. §109(b). Municipalities' bankruptcies are governed by Chapter 9 of the Bankruptcy Code, and farmers' bankruptcies are covered under Chapter 12. Following the 2008 market collapse, there were a series of municipal bankruptcies because of excessive debt and pension obligations.

[3] 11 U.S.C. §707(C)(2)(a). There are exceptions to the requirements of establishing no means, such as those who incurred their debts while on active military service.

Ethics & the Law

Bankruptcy Records

According to **www.bankruptcydata.com**, the following are the largest bankruptcies in the history of the United States:

Company	Date	Amount
Lehman Brothers	09/15/2008	$691,000,000 billion
Washington Mutual (WaMu)	09/26/2008	$327,900,000 billion
WorldCom	07/21/2002	$103,900,000 billion
General Motors	06/01/2009	$91,000,000 billion
CIT	11/01/2009	$80,400,000 billion
Enron	12/02/2001	$65,500,000 billion
Conseco	12/02/2002	$61,300,000 billion
MF Global	10/31/2011	$40,500,000 billion
Chrysler	04/20/2009	$39,300,000 billion
Thornburg Mortgage	05/05/2009	$36,500,000 billion

Total bankruptcy filings in the United States from 2005 to 2011 were as follows. Note the significant drop following the 2005 reforms, followed by the spike in 2008 because of the economic crisis.

Year	Total	Nonbusiness	Business
2011	1,410,653	1,362,847	47,806
2010	1,593,081	1,536,799	56,282
2009	1,473,675	1,412,838	60,837
2008	1,117,641	1,074,108	43,533
2007	850,912	822,590	28,322
2006	617,660	597,965	19,695
2005	2,078,415	2,039,214	39,201

Is there an ethical component to declaring bankruptcy? For example, actor Gary Busey's agent referred to bankruptcy as a business strategy. What are the risks of using bankruptcy as a business strategy?

CPA

Chapter 11 bankruptcy— reorganization form of bankruptcy under federal law.

(B) REORGANIZATION OR CHAPTER 11 BANKRUPTCY. Chapter 11 bankruptcy is a way for a debtor to reorganize and continue a business with protection from overwhelming debts and without the requirement of liquidation. Chrysler, General Motors, United Airlines, and Delta are all examples of companies that have gone through Chapter 11 bankruptcies. Stockbrokers, however, are not eligible for Chapter 11 bankruptcy.

CPA

Chapter 13 bankruptcy— proceeding of consumer debt readjustment plan bankruptcy.

(C) CHAPTER 13 BANKRUPTCY OR PAYMENT PLANS OR CONSUMER DEBT ADJUSTMENT PLANS. Chapter 13 of the federal Bankruptcy Code provides consumers an individual form of reorganization. Chapter 13 works with consumer debtors to develop a plan to repay debt. To be eligible for **Chapter 13 bankruptcy**, the individual must owe unsecured debts of less than $360,475 and secured debts of less than $1,081,400 and have regular income.[4] Chapter 13 plays an expanded role in bankruptcy because reforms require debtors with the means to pay their debts to go first into Chapter 13 bankruptcy rather than automatically declaring Chapter 7 bankruptcy.

B. HOW BANKRUPTCY IS DECLARED

Bankruptcy can be declared in different ways. The federal Bankruptcy Code spells out the requirements and process for declaration.

---

[4] 11 U.S.C. §109(e).

CPA

3. Declaration of Voluntary Bankruptcy

voluntary bankruptcy–
proceeding in which the debtor
files the petition for relief.

A **voluntary bankruptcy** is begun when the debtor files a petition with the bankruptcy court. A joint petition may be filed by a husband and wife. When a voluntary case is begun, the debtor must file a schedule of current income and current expenditures unless the court excuses this filing.

means test–new standard
under the Reform Act that
requires the court to find that
the debtor does not have the
means to repay creditors; goes
beyond the past requirement of
petitions being granted on the
simple assertion of the debtor
saying, "I have debts."

Under the 2005 reforms, a court can dismiss an individual debtor's (consumer's) petition for abuse if the debtor does not satisfy the **means test**, which measures the debtor's ability to pay by computing the debtor's disposable income. Only those debtors who fall below their state's median disposable income will be able to continue in a Chapter 7 proceeding. Individual debtors who meet the means test are required to go into Chapter 13 bankruptcy because they have not qualified for Chapter 7 bankruptcy. The formula for applying the means test is as follows:

Debtor's current monthly income less
Allowable expenses under the Bankruptcy Code = Disposable income
Disposable income × 60

The debtor commits bankruptcy abuse if this number is not less than the lower of the following:

- 25 percent of the debtor's unsecured claims or $7,025, whichever is greater; or

- $11,725

A finding of abuse means that the debtor's Chapter 7 voluntary petition is dismissed. Previously, the law required the judge to find "substantial abuse" before dismissing the petition; now the standard reads only "abuse."[5]

Under the BAPCPA, the bankruptcy judge also has the discretion to order the debtor's lawyer to reimburse the trustee for costs and attorney's fees and to assess a civil penalty against the lawyer if the court finds that the lawyer has not acted in good faith in filing the debtor's bankruptcy petition.[6] As part of this change, lawyers must declare themselves (in public ads as well as in any individual meetings with clients) to be "debt relief agencies" or state that they "help people file for relief under the Bankruptcy Code." The Code now requires those who help consumers deal with their creditors to disclose that part of the assistance could include filing for bankruptcy. Lawyers who advertise their credit/bankruptcy expertise are subject to the laws and regulations that apply to debt relief agencies. If the agency/lawyer advises them to do something that causes the court to declare that there has been bankruptcy abuse, the lawyer/debt relief agency is responsible as well. As part of their role as debt counselors, lawyers are prohibited under the changes in the law from advising clients to undertake more debt in contemplation of filing bankruptcy.[7]

Debtors are required to undergo credit counseling (from an approved nonprofit credit counseling agency) within the 180 days prior to declaring a bankruptcy. In addition, the court applies the means test described earlier to determine whether the debtor qualifies for bankruptcy.[8]

---

[5] 11 U.S.C. §707(b). *In re Lapke*, 428 B.R. 839 (8th Cir. 2010). A debtor who increased his federal income tax withholding to 85% prior to filing bankruptcy and earned over $200,000 per year as a pathologist was guilty of bad faith. *In re Laine*, 383 B.R. 166 (D. Kan. 2008).

[6] 11 U.S.C. §707(b)(4).

[7] 11 U.S.C. §§526–528. *Milavetz, Gallop & Milavetz, P.A. v. U.S.*, 130 S.Ct. 1324 (2010).

[8] 11 U.S.C. §109(h)(2). There are exceptions to the counseling requirements; for example, active military duty, disability, and emergencies. 11 U.S.C. 111(a) is the counseling provision. The counseling must be completed prior to filing for bankruptcy or the petition can be dismissed, *In re Ingram*, 460 B.R. 904 (6th Cir. 2011).

There is significant disagreement among the bankruptcy courts about the meaning of "projected income." The disagreement results from the differing situations of the debtors. **For Example,** how do courts deal with debtors who are about to experience a large drop in disposable income? And do courts then consider what happens when debtors' incomes are expected to go up? If the projected income test used is applied, the bankruptcy could be dismissed. Debtors and creditors take different positions depending on which way the income goes, and the courts continue to debate the definition of projected income.[9]

CASE SUMMARY

Disposable Income and Predisposed Not to Pay

FACTS: The Jasses filed for Chapter 13 bankruptcy relief. Their Form B22C indicated that their yearly household aggregate income was $143,403.96 based on income they received during the six-month period before filing. After deducting allowed expenses and deductions from their income, the Jasses' Statement of Current Monthly Income showed a "disposable income" of $3,625.63 per month.

The Jasses filed a Chapter 13 plan, which proposed to return $790.00 per month to unsecured creditors. At the hearing, the trustee objected to confirmation because the Jasses' "disposable income," as calculated on their Form B22C, was $3,625.63, and they proposed to pay only $790.00 to unsecured creditors. The trustee argued that because the Jasses were not proposing to pay their full disposable income of $3,625.63 to unsecured creditors, their plan did not comply with this "disposable income test."

The Jasses argued that the word "projected" in the statute modifies the definition of "disposable income." Mrs. Jass testified that beginning in December 2005, her husband experienced serious medical problems involving injuries to his intestines. She testified that her family incurred $12,000 in medical expenses. In light of these expenses and medical problems, the Jasses argued that their income in the future would not be commensurate with the "disposable income" shown on Form B22C. They argued that the changes under the BAPCPA did not require them to pay unsecured creditors the amount resulting from their Form B22C, so long as they could show that the income and expenses reported on the Form were inadequate representations of their future budget.

DECISION: The court held that the word *projected* modifies *disposable income* and that the Code intended that the disposable income figure be based on "projected income." The court acknowledged that the debtor would need to provide testimony regarding the change in circumstances that would result in a reduction of the income but also noted that without the word *projected* being used, the parties to a bankruptcy would be deprived of the fresh-start purpose the laws were intended to provide. They could not pay more money to creditors than they would be earning and their change in health and financial circumstances meant that they would simply not have the funds available to pay all that the form computed. [*In re Jass*, 340 B.R. 411 (Utah 2006)]

[9] *In re Turner*, 425 B.R. 918 (S.D. Ga. 2010); *In re Hilton*, 395 B.R. 433 (E.D. Wis. 2008); *In re Anstett*, 383 B.R. 380 (D.S.C. 2008); *In re Colclasure*, 383 B.R. 463 (E.D. Ark. 2008); and *In re Justice*, 418 B.R. 342 (W.D. Mo. 2009).

Thinking Things Through

Means Test Justifying the End of Debt

The following excerpt is a hypothetical case an experienced bankruptcy attorney worked through to illustrate the application of the means test.

The Brokes, a married couple in their early 40s, have two children in private schools. They are residents of Memphis, Shelby County, Tennessee; their annual gross income is $86,496. Like many debtors, the Brokes lost their home following an unsuccessful Chapter 13 case three years ago. They now rent a house for $2,000 a month. They owe back federal taxes in the amount of $9,000. They have secured debt on two cars with remaining balances of $10,000 and $6,000 and unsecured, consumer debt totaling $28,000. They desire to seek relief under Chapter 7 of the Bankruptcy Code.

The Brokes' gross monthly income is $7,208. After deducting taxes and other mandatory payroll deductions of $1,509, the couple has $5,699 in monthly income. The means test requires several additional deductions from the Brokes' gross monthly income. Section 707(b)(A)(2)(ii) provides a deduction for living and housing expenses using National Standards and Local Standards and additional Internal Revenue Service (IRS) figures. Allowable living expenses for a family of four in Ura and Ima Brokes' income bracket, based on national standards, total $1,564, while housing and utility figures for Shelby County, Tennessee, allow $1,354. In addition, there are allowable expenses for transportation. Based on IRS figures, the Brokes can subtract national ownership costs of $475 for the first car and $338 for the second, as well as regional operating and public transportation costs of $242 and $336, respectively. They can also deduct their

reasonably necessary health insurance costs, here the sum of $600, and $250 a month for private school tuition. Subtracting all of these figures from the Brokes' monthly income leaves $540.

Under §707(b)(2)(A)(iii), the Brokes can subtract payments on secured debt. The amount contractually due on their two automobiles over the next 60 months is $16,000. After dividing this total by 60 and rounding to the nearest dollar, the monthly allowable deduction for secured debt is $267. Subtracting this amount from $540 leaves $273.

Next come priority claim deductions. The Brokes are not subject to any child support or alimony claims, but they do owe $9,000 in back taxes. Again, dividing this amount by 60 yields a deductible amount of $150. Subtracting this from $273 leaves $123 in disposable monthly income. This figure would be multiplied by 60, amounting to a total of $7,380 in disposable income over the five-year period. Abuse is thus statutorily presumed because the debtors' current monthly income reduced by allowable amounts is not less than either $7,000 (25 percent of their nonpriority unsecured claims of $28,000) or $6,000. The Brokes' Chapter 7 case will therefore be dismissed (or they will be allowed voluntarily to convert their Chapter 7 case to a case under Chapter 13).

Does the means test make it more difficult for debtors to declare bankruptcy?*

*Robert J. Landry III and Nancy Hisey Mardis, "Consumer Bankruptcy Reform: Debtors' Prison without Bars or 'Just Desserts' for Deadbeats?" 36 *Golden Gate U. L. Rev.* 91 (2006). Reprinted with permission.

CPA

4. Declaration of Involuntary Bankruptcy

involuntary bankruptcy— proceeding in which a creditor or creditors file the petition for relief with the bankruptcy court.

(A) ELIGIBILITY. An **involuntary bankruptcy** is begun when creditors file a petition with the bankruptcy court. An involuntary case may be commenced against any individual, partnership, or corporation, except those excluded from filing voluntary petitions. Nonprofit corporations are also exempt from involuntary proceedings.[10]

CPA

(B) NUMBER AND CLAIMS OF PETITIONING CREDITORS. If there are 12 or more creditors, at least 3 of those creditors whose unsecured and undisputed claims total $14,425 or more must sign the involuntary petition.[11] If there are fewer than 12 creditors, excluding employees or insiders (that is, the debtor's relatives, partners, directors, and controlling

---

[10] 11 U.S.C. §303(a). *In re C.W. Min. Co.*, 431 B.R. 307 (Utah 2009). These amounts are adjusted periodically by statutory formulas.

[11] 11 U.S.C. §303. The term "undisputed" was added to this section. *In re Memorial Medical Center, Inc.*, 337 B.R. 388 (D.N.M. 2005).

persons), any creditor whose unsecured claim is at least $14,425 may sign the petition. In the case of involuntary consumer petitions, there is disagreement as to whether the debtor will still be required to complete the credit counseling requirement prior to the granting of the automatic stay.

bona fide–in good faith; without any fraud or deceit.

If a creditor holds security for a claim, only the amount of the claim in excess of the value of the security is counted. The holder of a claim that is the subject of a **bona fide** dispute may not be counted as a petitioning creditor.[12] **For Example,** David, a CPA, is an unsecured creditor of Arco Company for $15,000. Arco has a total of 10 creditors, all of whom are unsecured. Arco has not paid any of the creditors for three months. The debtor has fewer than 12 creditors. Any one of the creditors may file the petition if the unsecured portion of the amount due that creditor is at least $14,425.[13] Because David is owed $15,000 in unsecured debts, he may file the petition alone.

CPA

(c) GROUNDS FOR RELIEF FOR INVOLUNTARY CASE. The mere filing of an involuntary case petition does not result in an order of relief. The debtor may contest the bankruptcy petition. If the debtor does not contest the petition, the court will enter an order of relief if at least one of the following grounds exists: (1) The debtor is generally not paying debts as they become due or (2) within 120 days before the filing of the petition, a custodian has been appointed for the debtor's property.

FIGURE 35-1 | *Declaration of Bankruptcy*

	Chapter 7	Chapter 11	Chapter 13
Trustee	Yes	No	Yes
Eligible persons: Individuals Partnerships Corporations	Yes (consumer restrictions) yes Yes	Yes (individual restrictions) yes Yes	Yes (consumer restrictions) No No
Voluntary	Yes	Yes	Yes
Involuntary	Yes, except for farmers and nonprofits**	Yes, except for farmers and nonprofits	No
Exemptions	S & L's, credit unions, SBA, railroads, municipalities	Same as chapter 7 plus stockbrokers*	Only individuals allowed
Requirements-Voluntary	Debts; means test applies to consumers	Debts; means test applies to consumers	Income plus <$360,475 unsecured debt; <$1,081,400 secured debt
Requirements-Involuntary	<12 = 1/$14,425 ≥12 = 3/$14,425	<12 = 1/$14,425 ≥12 = 3/$14,425	N/a

*Railroads are eligible
**Chapter 9 — Municipalities; Chapter 12 — Farmers

© Cengage Learning

---

[12] 11 U.S.C. §303(b)(1). *In re Ballato*, 252 B.R. 553 (M.D. Fla. 2000).
[13] The amount was $10,000 originally, but the bankruptcy reforms had a built-in clause for increases in this figure.

CPA

automatic stay – order to prevent creditors from taking action such as filing suits or seeking foreclosure against the debtor.

5. Automatic Stay

Just the filing of either a voluntary or an involuntary petition operates as an **automatic stay**, which prevents creditors from taking action, such as filing suits or foreclosure actions, against the debtor.[14] The stay freezes all creditors in their filing date positions so that no one creditor gains an advantage over other creditors. This automatic stay ends when the bankruptcy case is closed or dismissed (for example, on a finding of abuse by the debtor who has failed to survive the means-to-pay test) or when the debtor is granted a discharge. An automatic stay means that all activity by creditors with respect to collection must stop, with some exceptions incorporated for child support and other family support issues under the 2005 reforms. All litigation with the debtor is halted, and any judgments in place cannot be executed.[15]

6. If the Creditors Are Wrong: Rights of Debtor in an Involuntary Bankruptcy

If an involuntary petition is dismissed other than by consent of all petitioning creditors and the debtor, the court may award costs, reasonable attorney fees, or damages to the debtor. The damages are those that were caused by taking possession of the debtor's property. The debtor may also recover damages against any creditor who filed the petition in bad faith.[16]

Figure 35-1 provides a summary of the requirements for declaration of bankruptcy and the standards for relief.

C. ADMINISTRATION OF THE BANKRUPTCY ESTATE

The administration of the bankruptcy estate varies according to the type of bankruptcy declared. This section of the chapter focuses on the process for liquidation or Chapter 7 bankruptcy. Figure 35-2 provides a flowchart view of the Chapter 7 liquidation process.

7. The Order of Relief

order of relief – the order from the bankruptcy judge that starts the protection for the debtor; when the order of relief is entered by the court, the debtor's creditors must stop all proceedings and work through the bankruptcy court to recover debts (if possible). Court finding that creditors have met the standards for bankruptcy petitions.

The **order of relief** is granted by the bankruptcy court and is the procedural step required for the case to proceed in bankruptcy court.[17] An order of relief is entered automatically in a voluntary case and in an involuntary case when those filing the petition have established that the debtor is unable to pay his, her, or its debts as they become due. In consumer cases and Chapter 11 cases that involve an individual, the bankruptcy court must apply the means test to determine whether the individual is eligible for declaring bankruptcy or whether there has been an abuse of the bankruptcy court and system.

[14] 11 U.S.C. §362. *In re Webb*, 2012 WL 1150139 (Ohio) and *In re Wolverine Fire Apparatus Co. of Sherwood Michigan*, 465 B.R. 808 (E.D. Wis. 2012). Proceeding with the foreclosure on a home after a stay is entered is a violation of the stay order. *In re Gonzalez*, 456 B.R. 429 (C.D. Cal. 2011).
[15] The reforms exempt dissolution, custody, child support, and other related litigation from the stay.
[16] *Arizona Public Service v. Apache County*, 857 P. 2d 1339 (Ariz. App. 1993).
[17] 11 U.S.C. §301.

Sports & Entertainment Law

From Millions to Nada: Celebrity Bankruptcies

- Michael Vick, who was one of the highest paid NFL players, filed for bankruptcy in 2008, from prison. Mr. Vick could not afford to pay his bills as well as the fines that were imposed when he entered a guilty plea on charges related to a dog-fighting operation. The former Atlanta Falcons player would not have the fines discharged in bankruptcy, but he was relieved of his other debts related to his personal property.

- MC Hammer, the "Hammer Time" mega star of the early 1990s declared bankruptcy in 1996 with $9.6 million in assets and $13.7 million in debts. Mr. Hammer's problem was that he had salary costs of $500,000 per month in order to maintain his entourage.

- Mike Tyson, the champ, facing sexual harassment charges, and the lawyer fees that go with them, declared bankruptcy in 2003. Today, Mr. Tyson says that he is broke but happy.

- Willie Nelson, Country Western singer, declared bankruptcy in 1990, a necessary result of his owing $16.7 million in taxes because the IRS won its case on Nelson's tax shelters, which were fraudulent. Mr. Nelson also said that he had too many hangers-on that he was supporting. Mr. Nelson was not able to get all of his tax debt discharged because the last three years survive bankruptcy. That is, not all tax debts are fully dischargeable and there is no discharge allowed for tax debts that resulted from fraud.

- Walt Disney, the founder of Disney Films, Disneyland, Disney World, and Disney Entertainment, declared bankruptcy in Kansas City before he moved to Hollywood. Mr. Disney ran a small animation studio there and when his only customer went bankrupt, Mr. Disney tried to continue on, living in his office and eating only canned beans. He eventually gave up, declared bankruptcy, and moved to Hollywood, where his animation skills were welcomed and, as a result, he founded an empire.

- Sir Elton John is the quintessential profligate spender whose purchases landed him in bankruptcy. By the time he declared bankruptcy in 2002, Sir Elton had credit card charges of $400,000 per month. His total debt per month was $2,000,000. He was discharged from most of his credit card and contract debt.

- Sinbad, the comedian, failed to pay taxes on his earnings from *Jingle All the Way*. California's Department of Revenue filed a $2.5 million lien on his home and he and his wife declared bankruptcy shortly after in 2009. Again, California will be paid, but the comedian and his spouse are relieved of other debts.

- Gary Coleman, the 4'8" comedian/actor, simply could not pay all the medical bills related to his various health problems. He was once worth $7,000,000 but declared bankruptcy with $72,000 in debt and no assets. The actor passed away in 2010 and there is an ongoing dispute among relatives over his estate, which grew after his bankruptcy.

What are the causes of bankruptcy? What advice would you give to celebrities and athletes about management of their income and bills?

8. List of Creditors

It is the debtor's responsibility to furnish the bankruptcy court with a list of creditors. Although imposing the responsibility for disclosing debts on the debtor may not seem to be effective, the debtor has an incentive for full disclosure. Those debts not disclosed by the debtor will not be discharged in bankruptcy.

9. Trustee in Bankruptcy

trustee in bankruptcy—impartial person elected to administer the debtor's estate.

The **trustee in bankruptcy** is elected by the creditors. The court or the U.S. trustee will appoint an interim trustee if the creditors do not elect a trustee.

The trustee is the successor to the property rights of the debtor. By operation of law, the trustee automatically becomes the owner of all of the debtor's property in excess of the property to which the debtor is entitled under exemption laws. The trustee holds all of the rights formerly owned by the debtor.

FIGURE 35-2	*Anatomy of Bankruptcy Case*

Voidable preferences

1. 2 yr. Fraud
2. 1 yr. Insolvent ** and unfair
3. 1 yr. Insider
4. 90 days—presumed insolvent**—not ordinary course of business
5. Security for antecedent debt

OK (not voidable)

1. Up to $600 consumer debt
2. Contemporaneous exchange
3. Regular payments
4. Up to $5,850 for non-consumer creditors***

*Means test for consumers
**Insolvent = "Bankruptcy" sense (liabilities > assets)
***Amounts are adjusted annually

© Cengage Learning

CPA   ## 10. The Bankrupt's Estate

All of the debtor's property, with certain exceptions discussed later, is included in the *bankrupt's estate.* Property inherited by the debtor within six months after the filing of the petition also passes to the trustee.

In many cases, when a debtor knows that insolvency is a problem and bankruptcy is imminent, the debtor attempts to hang onto property or reputation by making transfers of assets to friends, relatives, and creditors. However, trustees have the authority to set aside or void (1) transfers by the debtor that a creditor holding a valid claim under state law could have avoided at the commencement of the bankruptcy case, (2) **preferences**, that is, transfers of property by the debtor to a creditor, the effect of which is to enable the creditor to obtain payment of a higher

preferences – transfers of property by a debtor to one or more specific creditors to enable these creditors to obtain payment for debts owed.

percentage of the creditor's claim than the creditor would have received if the debtor's assets had been liquidated in bankruptcy, and (3) statutory liens that became effective against the debtor at the commencement of the bankruptcy.

11. Voidable Preferences

A debtor may not transfer property to prevent creditors from satisfying their legal claims. The trustee may void any such transfer, known as a *fraudulent transfer,* made or obligation incurred by the debtor within two years of bankruptcy when the debtor's actual intent was to hinder, delay, or defraud creditors by doing so.[18]

The trustee may also void certain transfers of property made by a debtor merely because their effect is to make the debtor insolvent or to reduce the debtor's assets to an unreasonably low amount.[19]

CPA

insolvency—excess of debts and liabilities over assets, or inability to pay debts as they mature.

balance sheet test—comparison of assets to liabilities made to determine solvency.

preferential transfers—certain transfers of money or security interests in the time frame just prior to bankruptcy that can be set aside if voidable.

insider—full-time corporate employee or a director or their relatives.

(A) THE INSOLVENT DEBTOR. A debtor is insolvent for purposes of determining voidable transfers when the total fair value of all of the debtor's assets does not exceed the debts owed by the debtor. This test for **insolvency** under voidable transfers is commonly called the **balance sheet test** because it is merely a comparison of assets to liabilities without considering whether the debtor will be able to meet future obligations as they become due. The debtor is presumed to be insolvent in the 90 days prior to declaration of bankruptcy.

(B) PREFERENTIAL TRANSFERS. A transfer of property by the debtor to a creditor may be set aside as **preferential transfers** and the property recovered by the debtor's trustee in bankruptcy if (1) the transfer was made to pay a debt incurred at some earlier time, (2) the transfer was made when the debtor was insolvent and within 90 days before the filing of the bankruptcy petition, and (3) the transfer resulted in the creditor receiving more than the creditor would have received in a liquidation of the debtor's estate. A debtor is presumed to be insolvent on and during the 90 days immediately preceding the date of the filing of the bankruptcy petition.[20]

Transfers made to **insiders** within the 12 months prior to the filing of the petition may be set aside.[21] **For Example,** if a building contractor transferred title to one of his model homes to the company accountant just six months before declaring bankruptcy, the transfer would be a preferential one that would be set aside. However, a transfer by an insider to a noninsider is not subject to recovery by the trustee. The sale of that same model home to a good faith buyer just three days before bankruptcy would be valid. **For Example,** the trustee in the Bernie Madoff case sought to set aside several transfers made to companies and individuals just prior to the time Mr. Madoff admitted that he had an insolvent, $50-billion Ponzi scheme. The trustee used several of the voidable preferences theories to seek a return of funds.

The trustee may not set aside certain transfers by a debtor as preferences. A transaction for present consideration, such as a cash sale, is not set aside.[22] A payment by a debtor in the ordinary course of business, such as the payment of a utility bill, will not be set aside. Under the prior bankruptcy law, a payment was not

---

[18] Prior to the reforms, the time period for fraudulent transfers was one year. *Grochocinski v. Schlossberg,* 402 B.R. 825 (N.D. Ill. 2009).
[19] 11 U.S.C. §548.
[20] 11 U.S.C. §547(f).
[21] 11 U.S.C. §547(b)(4)(B). *In re Manhattan Inv. Fund Ltd.,* 421 B.R. 613 (S.D.N.Y. 2009).
[22] *In re Smith Min. and Material, LLC,* 405 B.R. 589 (W.D. Ky. 2009).

a voidable preference if it was made in the ordinary course of business and it was made according to industry terms and practices. Under the 2005 reforms, the *and* is changed to *or,* and it is now easier for creditors to show that they were not the recipients of a voidable preference. Also under the 2005 reforms, nonconsumer debt payments that have a value of less than $5,850 are not subject to the voidable preference standards. The expectation is that the time and effort spent by bankruptcy trustees and courts will be reduced because of the minimum amount required before a challenge can be made. In nonconsumer debts, transfers of less than $5,850 within the voidable preference period are not considered voidable preferences.

CASE SUMMARY

Favoring Friends and Paying Early and Often

FACTS: Ames Department Stores operated over 400 retail stores throughout the northeastern United States. Promotions and advertising were crucial to Ames' business strategy, and Ames attributed over 50 percent of store revenue to advertised sales. Cellmark was Ames' principal paper supplier for all of these circulars, including the Home Book. Ames was also one of Cellmark's largest customers and top credit exposures.

Between June 1, 2000, and the beginning of the preference period —90 days before Ames filed for Chapter 11 bankruptcy on August 20, 2001—Ames employed an automated accounts payable system created by Oracle to track orders and generate payments to all of its domestic merchandise vendors. During that same period, Ames paid invoices in full at or around the invoice due date, because its computerized payables system automatically printed checks according to payment due date without regard to the identity of the vendor. The computer-generated checks were routinely mailed to vendors within a day or two of being printed. In the three years of the parties' prior dealings, Cellmark issued approximately 300 invoices to Ames.

In May 2001, as Ames' cash was becoming increasingly tight, Ames executives, including CFO Rolando de Aguiar, began holding regular meetings to decide which vendors should be paid. The decisions were based on the identity of the vendor and the needs of Ames' business. By August 2001, in the last three weeks before Ames' Chapter 11 filing, Ames was not issuing any checks to its creditors through a general check run. Instead, Ames issued checks only to pay invoices specifically selected out of the Oracle database and based on specific requests.

Eugene Bankers, Ames' Senior Vice President of Marketing and Advertising, repeatedly inquired about the status of payments to Cellmark.

Bankers communicated to others at Ames that if Ames did not send payment to Cellmark, Ames would not get the circular out, and it would go out of business. Bankers told Cellmark CEO Joe Hoffman that he was "aggressive with [Ames'] finance department to make sure that checks sent were being sent on a continuity [sic] basis to them."

The bankruptcy trustee sought to recover approximately $1.9 million that Ames had made by three checks to Cellmark for four invoices in the two weeks before filing for bankruptcy:

1. a check for $700,000.00 (the "$700,000 Check"), issued on August 6, 2001, that cleared on August 10, 2001;

2. a check for $690,690.52 (the "$691,000 Check"), issued on August 9, 2001, that cleared on August 13, 2001; and

3. a check for $764,918.81 (the "$765,000 Check"), issued on August 13, 2001, that cleared on August 15, 2001.

CASE SUMMARY

Continued

As of the Petition Date, Ames did not owe Cellmark anything.

DECISION: The court applied the test for voidable preferences and concluded that the payments made to Cellmark were not in the ordinary course of business and were made while Ames was insolvent. The court noted that the checks were issued immediately, rather than according to the pattern of the parties over the past few years; that Ames executives overrode their payment system to issue the checks early; and that the executives were aware of how critical Cellmark was to the company continuing to operate. The court noted that Ames did not disclose $200 million in debt on its financial statement and that its assets were not properly valued so that there was little chance it was solvent at the time the payments to Cellmark occurred. [*In re Ames Dept. Stores, Inc.*, 450 B.R. 24 (S.D.N.Y. 2011)]

(c) SELF-SETTLED TRUST. Under the Reform Act, the trustee has the ability to set aside the transfer of property into a "self-settled" (a self-created personal trust) any time within the past 10 years if the trustee can establish that the trust was created with actual intent to hinder, delay, or defraud existing or future creditors.[23] This section was added to address the problem of the many assets of individuals being in personal trusts for which those individuals serve as trustees.

12. Proof of Claim

Bankruptcy law regulates the manner in which creditors present their claims and the way in which the debtor's assets are distributed in payment of these claims.

After the debtor has filed a list of creditors, the court then sends a notice of the bankruptcy proceedings to listed creditors. The creditors who wish to participate in the distribution of the proceeds of the liquidation of the debtor's estate must file a proof of claim. A **claim** is a right to payment, whether liquidated (certain and not disputed), unliquidated, contingent, unmatured, disputed, legal, or equitable. A **proof of claim** is a written statement, signed by the creditor or an authorized representative, setting forth any claim made against the debtor and the basis for it. It must ordinarily be filed within 90 days after the first meeting of creditors.[24] A creditor must file within that time even though the trustee in bankruptcy in fact knows of the existence of the creditor's claim.

claim – creditor's right to payment.

proof of claim – written statement, signed by the creditor or an authorized representative, setting forth any claim made against the debtor and the basis for it.

CPA

13. Priority of Claims

Creditors who hold security for payment, such as a lien or a mortgage on the debtor's property, are less affected by the debtor's bankruptcy. Secured creditors may enforce their security interest to obtain payment of their claims up to the value of their security, the collateral in which they hold an interest. **For Example,** suppose that First Bank holds a mortgage on a company's office building. The mortgage amount is $750,000. The building is sold for $700,000. First Bank is entitled to the $700,000 from the sale. For the remaining portion of the debt, First Bank drops

---

[23] 11 U.S.C. §548(e).
[24] 11 U.S.C. §302(c).

down in priority to wait with the other unsecured creditors for its remaining $50,000. Unsecured creditors with unsecured debts have a statutory order of priority following the secured creditors' rights in their collateral as outlined in the list that appears below.[25] Once the bottom of the priority list is reached, any remaining unsecured creditors share on a *pro rata* basis any remaining assets of the debtor. Any balance remaining after all creditors have been paid goes to the debtor. However, in 98 to 99 percent of all bankruptcies, no unsecured creditors receive any payments, so it is highly unlikely that the debtor would ever receive anything from the bankruptcy litigation of the debtor's property and funds.

The list below is the statutory one for priorities of the unsecured creditors following the payment to any secured creditors from the debtors' pledged property:[26]

1. Allowed claims for debts to a spouse, former spouse, or child of the debtor and for alimony to, maintenance for, or support of such spouse or child (that were obligations at the time of the filing of the bankruptcy petition).

2. Costs and expenses of administration of the bankruptcy case, including fees to trustees, attorneys, and accountants, and the reasonable expenses of creditors in recovering property transferred or concealed by the debtor.

3. Claims arising in the ordinary course of a debtor's business or financial affairs after the commencement of the case but before the order of relief (involuntary).

4. Claims for wages, salaries, or commissions, including vacation, severance, or sick leave pay earned within 180 days before the filing of the petition or the date of cessation of the debtor's business, whichever occurred first, limited, however, to $11,725 for each person.[27]

5. Claims arising for contributions to employee benefit plans, based on services rendered within 180 days before the filing of the petition or when the debtor ceased doing business, whichever occurred first; the maximum amount is $11,725. Under the 2005 reforms (especially in Chapter 11 reorganizations), payments of key-employee retention plans are not permitted unless the plans are "essential" to keeping the key employee at the company that is in bankruptcy. Proving that they are essential requires the key employee actually to have a "bona fide" offer of employment from another company. In addition, there are limits on how much can be paid under key-employee retention plans.

6. Farm producers (up to $5,775) and fishers against debtors who operate grain storage facilities or fish storage or processing facilities, up to $5,775 per claim.

7. Claims by consumer creditors, not to exceed $2,600 for each claimant, arising from the purchase of consumer goods or services when such property or services were not delivered or provided.

8. Certain taxes and penalties due government, such as income and property taxes (there are time limits, for example, three years is the general time limit, with exceptions for fraud).

---

[25] 11 U.S.C. §507(1)–(6). Secured creditors' priority is determined by the priority rules related to Article 9, liens, and mortgages. *In re Black Angus Holdings, LLC*, 434 B.R. 612 (D. Kan. 2010).

[26] 11 U.S.C. §507. *In re Penaran*, 424 B.R. 868 (D. Kan. 2010). Debts owed to government agencies for unlawful receipt of food stamps are grouped in with alimony and support payments. *Wisconsin Dept. of Workforce Development v. Ratliff*, 390 B.R. 607 (E.D. Wis. 2008).

[27] Claims involving wage disputes or discrimination are treated as the claims of unsecured creditors. *In re Trans World Airlines, Inc.*, 322 F.3d 283 (3rd Cir. 2003).

9. All other unsecured creditors.

10. Tort claims for death or personal injury resulting from operation of a vehicle or vessel while intoxicated from alcohol, drug, and other substances.

11. Remainder (if any) to debtor.

Each claim must be paid in full before any lower claim is paid anything. If a class of claims cannot be paid in full, the claims in that case are paid on a *pro rata* basis. **For Example,** suppose that following the payment of all secured creditors, $10,000 is left to be distributed. The accountants who performed work on the bankruptcy are owed $15,000, and the lawyers who worked on it are owed $10,000. Because there is not enough to pay two parties in the same priority ranking, the $10,000 is split proportionately. The accountants will receive 15/25, or 3/5, of the $10,000, or $6,000, and the lawyers will receive 10/25, or 2/5, of the $10,000, or $4,000.

D. Debtor's Duties and Exemptions

Bankruptcy law imposes certain duties on the debtor and provides for specific exemptions of some of the debtor's estate from the claims of creditors.

14. Debtor's Duties

A debtor must file with the court a list of creditors, a schedule of assets and liabilities, and a statement of her financial affairs. The debtor must also appear for examination under oath at the first meeting of creditors.

CPA ### 15. Debtor's Exemptions

A debtor is permitted to claim certain property of the estate in the trustee's possession and keep it free from claims of creditors. Exemptions are provided under federal law, but state laws also provide for exemptions. In 14 states (examples are Massachusetts, New Jersey, Pennsylvania, and Connecticut), debtors can elect either federal or state exemption. In the other states (New York, California, Florida, and Delaware are examples), debtors are permitted to use only the state exemptions.[28] Examples of exempt property from the federal code include wedding rings, property used to earn a living, one VCR, and one car. New York exemptions include "all stoves in the home, one sewing machine, the family Bible, a pew in a public house of worship, enough food for sixty days, a wedding ring, and a watch not exceeding thirty-five dollars in value."[29] California exempts tools of the trade and the family cemetery plot.[30]

The principal exemptions provided by the Bankruptcy Code are the debtor's interest in real or personal property used as a residence.[31] The Reform Act has greatly limited the homestead exemption and, in effect, preempts state law on this debtor exemption. Debtors are required to have lived in the home for two years prior to bankruptcy, and the amount of the homestead exemption would be limited to $146,450.[32] To be able to

[28] 11 U.S.C. §522.

[29] N.Y. C.P.L.R. §5205 (2010).

[30] Cal. Civ. Proc. Code §704.010-704.210 (2009).

[31] A married couple gets a single homestead exemption. Gay couples who have registered under state domestic partner rights statutes are also entitled to only one homestead exemption. *In re Rabin*, 359 B.R. 242 (2007).

[32] The time requirement is at 11 U.S.C. §522(b)(3)(A), and the amount limitation is at 11 U.S.C. §522(o)(1). This amount refers to those who elect state exemptions. In the absence of state exemptions, the federal maximum is $21,625.

use a higher state homestead exemption, the debtor must have lived in the home for 1215 days (40 months).[33] Labeled as the most flagrant abuse of the existing bankruptcy system, debtors have used the homestead exemption to shift their assets into expensive homes to shield everything from bankruptcy. Known as the "mansion loophole," the changes in the Reform Act related to the homestead exemption were among the most debated and the most dramatic.[34] **For Example,** prior to the reforms actor Burt Reynolds declared bankruptcy in Florida and was relieved of millions in debt, but he was able to keep his $2.5 million Valhalla estate there. Corporate raider Paul Bilzerian, who was convicted of securities fraud, also declared bankruptcy in Florida but kept his mansion, the largest home in Hillsborough County, Florida. Former WorldCom CFO Scott Sullivan (who entered a guilty plea to fraud and other charges and is serving a five-year sentence) built a multimillion-dollar home in Florida to gain homestead protections. Wendy Gramm, who sat on Enron's board, purchased 200 acres of land in Texas and constructed a large home with her husband, former senator Phil Gramm, to take advantage of homestead exemptions then available in Texas. However, the Reform Act closed this corporate executive loophole by requiring that the $146,450 exemption apply to debtors who are convicted of securities fraud or bankruptcy fraud.[35]

Other exemptions include payments under a life insurance contract, alimony and child support payments, and awards from personal injury litigation.[36] Under the Reform Act, college savings accounts and IRAs are exempt property under the federal exemptions and can be used even by those debtors who are using state exemptions. The IRA exemption is limited to $1,171,650.[37]

CASE SUMMARY

Setting Aside Money for the Kids Before the Bankruptcy

FACTS: Michael and Alice Werth (debtors) filed a Chapter 7 petition on April 14, 2011, and received a discharge on January 23, 2012. On December 2, 2010, the Werths had opened two 529 accounts for the benefit of Michael Werth's two children by a previous marriage. They deposited $6,000.00 into each account. The accounts are owned by Alice Werth. By the petition date, the accounts held $12,197.12.

Michael Werth is responsible for one-half of the postsecondary educational expenses for his two children pursuant to a 2002 Separation Agreement, subject to certain limitations. As of the petition date, neither of Werth's children had yet graduated from high school.

The bankruptcy trustee moved for an order directing the debtors to turn over the balances in the two 529 education savings accounts.

DECISION: The court held that 529 accounts are exempt property under bankruptcy laws if they were started earlier than a year before the bankruptcy petition is filed. The court also held that even if the obligation to save is part of a divorce decree, the terms of which require the debtor/ex-spouse to provide support for his or her children, it is still not entitled to exemption from creditors' claims unless the obligation was undertaken sooner than one year before bankruptcy. [*In re Werth*, 468 B.R. 412 (D.Kan. 2012)]

---

[33] 11 U.S.C. §522(p)(2)(B).
[34] 11 U.S.C. §522(p).
[35] 11 U.S.C. §522(q).
[36] 11 U.S.C. §522(d) (including automatic adjustments).
[37] 11 U.S.C. §522(n). There are time requirements on college savings (529) accounts in order to obtain the exemption.

Businesses that declare bankruptcy would not have employee pension plan contributions included in their bankruptcy estates. Those contributions would be returned to the employees. The proposed changes are the result of the numerous large corporate bankruptcies, such as the one involving United Airlines and the pensions of its employees.[38]

16. Debtor's Protection against Discrimination

Federal, state, and local law may not discriminate against anyone on the basis of a discharge in bankruptcy. For example, a state cannot refuse to issue a new license to an individual if the license fees on a previous one have been discharged as a debt in the individual's declaration of bankruptcy.

E. DISCHARGE IN BANKRUPTCY

discharge in bankruptcy— order of the bankruptcy court relieving the debtor from obligation to pay the unpaid balance of most claims.

The main objectives of a bankruptcy proceeding are to collect and distribute the debtor's assets and then issue a **discharge in bankruptcy** of the debtor from obligations. The decree terminating the bankruptcy proceeding is generally a discharge that releases the debtor from most debts. Under the BAPCPA, a discharge is available only once every eight years.

17. Denial of Discharge

The court will refuse to grant a discharge if the debtor has (1) within one year of the filing of the petition fraudulently transferred or concealed property with intent to

---

Ethics & the Law

The Skies Are Not So Friendly to Employee Pensions

As part of its Chapter 11 bankruptcy, United Airlines was relieved of its pension liabilities. Employees and unions wonder how a company can be permitted to renege on those benefits when so many protections were built into the law under ERISA. Congressional hearings now reveal that there were loopholes in the accounting processes for pension fund reporting that permitted United, and many others, to report pension numbers that made the pension funds look healthy when they really were not. The loopholes were Enronesque in nature. Companies could spin the pension obligations off the books so that the existing levels of obligations of the plan looked small and the assets very rich. Because of United's pension bailout, Congress changed the accounting for pension plans to avoid the problem of the rosy picture when the funds really need further funding. One interesting approach to protecting pension

plans is to require companies to fund the pension plans according to the numbers they have reported to the SEC in their financials. The numbers reported to the SEC for company pensions are accurate whereas the numbers reported for ERISA purposes are inflated. If United had funded its plans when its SEC numbers indicated it needed to (e.g., in 1998), the plan would have been sufficiently funded. Under ERISA guidelines, it was not required to kick in funds until 2002 when it was grossly underfunded.

Were companies acting ethically on their pension accounting? Were they acting legally?*

*Marry Williams Walsh, "Pension Law Loopholes Helped United Hide Its Troubles," *New York Times*, June 7, 2005, C1.

---

[38] 11 U.S.C. §541(b).

hinder, delay, or defraud creditors, (2) failed to keep proper financial records, (3) made a false oath or account,[39] (4) failed to explain satisfactorily any loss of assets, (5) refused to obey any lawful order of the court or refused to testify after having been granted immunity, (6) obtained a discharge within the last eight years,[40] (7) filed a written waiver of discharge that is approved by the court,[41] or (8) in the case of a consumer debtor, has failed to complete a personal financial management instructional course.[42]

A discharge releases the debtor from the unpaid balance of most debts except for taxes, customs duties, child support obligations, and tax penalties.[43] Student loan obligations are not discharged in bankruptcy unless the loan first became due more than seven years before bankruptcy or unless not allowing a discharge would impose undue hardship on the debtor.

CASE SUMMARY

Your Living Expenses Are Fairly Minimal in Maximum Security

FACTS: Bryan Anthony Looper had over $300,000 in student loans that were used to finance his education at Mercer University where he obtained an A.B., an M.B.A, and another unspecified graduate degree as well as a large number of courses toward his J.D. degree. He did not make payments on these student loans.

In 1996, he was elected assessor for Putnam County, Tennessee, a position he held for two years and four months. He was then convicted of the first-degree murder of state senator Tommy Burks. He exhausted all of his appeals and is currently serving a life sentence without the possibility of parole. The debtor has one dependent, a son born in August 1998. The circuit court for Putnam County, Tennessee, ordered Looper to pay child support of $161.00 per month plus $7,254.20 in medical expenses. Looper did not make any of the court-ordered child support payments and was in arrears by more than $23,515.00.

Looper asked to have his student loans discharged on the basis of his hardship.

DECISION: The court refused to discharge the student loans. Looper had all of his living expenses covered by the Tennessee Department of Corrections. Looper had made no effort to make any payments on any of his student loans and had also not made attempts to try and work with his lenders or apply to programs set up to help with student loans. The court also noted that Looper's circumstances were the result of his choices and conduct, not the result of unforeseen and uncontrollable events. He had three degrees and the capability of earning a living but, through poor choices, produced his own difficult circumstances. [*In re Looper*, **2007 WL 1231700 (Bankr. E.D. Tenn. 2007)**]

In addition, the following debts are not discharged by bankruptcy: (1) loans obtained by use of a false financial statement made with intent to deceive and on which the creditor reasonably relied, (2) debts not scheduled or listed with the

---

[39] The debtor must actually make a false statement. In *In re Mercer*, 211 F.3d 214 (5th Cir. 2000), the debtor ran up $3,186.82 on a credit card she was given by AT&T with a $3,000 credit limit. The credit card was issued to the debtor on a preapproved basis, so there was no fraud, just a great deal of spending. See also *In re Carver*, 418 B.R. 734 (C.D. Ill. 2009) that did not punish a debtor because he was mixed up when he began paying his attorney.

[40] 11 U.S.C. §727(a)(8).

[41] 11 U.S.C. §523.

[42] 11 U.S.C. §727(a)(11). The financial management course requirement applies to both Chapter 7 and Chapter 13 consumer bankruptcies.

[43] Child support obligations enjoy additional protections and priorities in bankruptcy. 11 U.S.C. §507(a).

FIGURE 35-3	*Nondischargeable Debts in Bankruptcy*

1. Taxes within three years of filing bankruptcy petition
2. Liability for obtaining money or property by false pretenses
3. Willful and malicious injuries
4. Debts incurred by driving DWI*
5. Alimony, maintenance, or child support
6. Unscheduled debts (unless actual notice)
7. debts resulting from fraud as a fiduciary (embezzlement)
8. government fines or penalties imposed within three years prior
9. Educational loans due within seven prior years (unless hardship)
10. prior bankruptcy debts in which debtor waived discharge
11. Presumption on luxury goods: $550 goods; $825 cash
12. Reaffirmation agreements — Writing
    — Filed with court
    — Not rescinded prior to discharge

*Includes vessels and aircraft

© Cengage Learning

court in time for allowance, (3) debts arising from fraud while the debtor was acting in a fiduciary capacity or by reason of embezzlement or larceny, (4) alimony and child support, (5) a judgment for willful and malicious injury, (6) a consumer debt to a single creditor totaling more than $5775 for luxury goods or services (within 90 days of the order of relief) and cash advances exceeding $825 based on consumer open-end credit, such as a credit card (within 70 days of the order of relief),[44] (7) damages arising from drunk driving or the operation of vessels and aircrafts by people who are inebriated,[45] (8) loans used to pay taxes (including credit cards),[46] (9) taxes not paid as a result of a fraudulent return, although other unpaid taxes beyond the past three years can be discharged,[47] (10) prebankruptcy fees and assessments owed to homeowners associations, and (11) debts owed to tax-qualified retirement plans. **For Example,** in regard to (5), the finding of malice in *Goldman v. O. J. Simpson* precluded the discharge by bankruptcy of the $8.5 million damage award from Simpson to the families of his murder victims, the Goldmans and Browns. Figure 35-3 has a listing of nondischargeable debts.

F. Reorganization Plans under Chapter 11

In addition to liquidation under Chapter 7, the Bankruptcy Code permits debtors to restructure the organization and finances of their businesses so that they may continue to operate. In these rehabilitation plans, the debtor keeps all of the assets

---

[44] 11 U.S.C. §523(a)(2)(c)(i). (Amounts are adjusted each year).
[45] 11 U.S.C. §523(a)(9).
[46] 11 U.S.C. §523(a)(14A),(14B).
[47] 11 U.S.C. §§1129(a)(9)(c), (D), 1129(b)(2)(B), 1141(d)(6)(B).

(exempt and nonexempt), continues to operate the business, and makes a settlement that is acceptable to the majority of the creditors. This settlement is binding on the minority creditors.

Individuals, partnerships, and corporations in business may all be reorganized under the Bankruptcy Code. The first step is to file a plan for the debtor's reorganization. This plan may be filed by the debtor, any party in interest, or a committee of creditors. If the debtor wishes to move from a Chapter 11 proceeding (in the case of an individual debtor), the debtor must survive the means test that is now a requirement for determining eligibility for bankruptcy.

18. Contents of the Plan

The plan divides ownership interests and debts into those that will be affected by the adoption of the plan and those that will not be. It then specifies what will be done to those interests and claims that are affected. **For Example,** when mortgage payments are too high for the income of a corporation, a possible plan would be to reduce the mortgage payments and give the mortgage holder preferred stock to compensate for the loss sustained.

All creditors, shareholders, and other interest holders within a particular class must be treated the same way. **For Example,** the holders of first mortgage bonds must all be treated similarly. The treatment of the bondholders in the Chrysler and GM bankruptcies was a point of contention and negotiation in those reorganizations.

A plan can also provide for the assumption, rejection, or assignment of executory contracts. The trustee or debtor can, under certain circumstances, suspend performance of a contract not yet fully performed. **For Example,** collective bargaining agreements may be rejected with the approval of the bankruptcy court.[48]

19. Confirmation of the Plan

After the plan is prepared, the court must approve or confirm it. A plan will be confirmed if it has been submitted in good faith and if its provisions are reasonable.[49] After the plan is confirmed, the owners and creditors of the enterprise have only the rights that are specified in the plan. They cannot go back to their original contract positions.

CPA G. PAYMENT PLANS UNDER CHAPTER 13

The Bankruptcy Code also provides for the adoption of extended-time payment plans for individual debtors who have regular income. These debtors must owe unsecured debts of less than $360,475 and secured debts of less than $1,081,400.

An individual debtor who has a regular income may submit a plan for the installment payment of outstanding debts. If the court approves it, the debtor may then pay the debts in the installments specified by the plan even if the creditors had not originally agreed to such installment payments.

[48] 11 U.S.C. §1113.
[49] 11 U.S.C. §1129.

20. Contents of the Plan

The individual debtor plan is, in effect, a budget of the debtor's future income with respect to outstanding debts. The plan must provide for the eventual payment in full of all claims entitled to priority under the Bankruptcy Code. All creditors holding the same kind or class of claim must be treated the same way.

21. Confirmation of the Plan

The plan has no effect until the court approves or confirms it. A plan will be confirmed if it was submitted in good faith and is in the best interests of the creditors.[50] When the plan is confirmed, debts are payable in the manner specified in the plan.

22. Discharge of the Debtor

After all of the payments called for by the plan have been made, the debtor is given a discharge. The discharge releases the debtor from liability for all debts except those that would not be discharged by an ordinary bankruptcy discharge.[51] Under the bankruptcy reforms, the court cannot grant a discharge until the debtor has completed an instructional course concerning personal financial management.[52] If the debtor does not perform under the plan, the creditors can move to transfer the debtor's case to a Chapter 7 proceeding, but they would still face the means test in qualifying for this move to Chapter 7.

MAKE THE CONNECTION

SUMMARY

Jurisdiction over bankruptcy cases is in U.S. district courts, which may refer all cases and related proceedings to adjunct bankruptcy courts.

Three bankruptcy proceedings are available: liquidation (Chapter 7), reorganization (Chapter 11), and extended-time payment (Chapter 13). A liquidation proceeding under Chapter 7 may be either voluntary or involuntary.

A *voluntary case* is commenced by the debtor's filing a petition with the bankruptcy court. A voluntary petition is subject to the means test to determine if the debtor meets the standard for declaring bankruptcy. An involuntary case is commenced by the creditors' filing a petition with the bankruptcy court. If there are 12 or more creditors, at least 3 whose unsecured claims total $14,425 or more must sign the involuntary petition. If there are fewer than 12 creditors, any creditor whose unsecured claim is at least $14,425 may sign the petition. If the debtor contests the bankruptcy petition, it must be shown that the debtor is not paying debts as they become due.

Eligibility for Chapters 7 and 11 bankruptcy excludes railroads, municipalities, and Small Business Administration companies. Individual debtors are restricted on Chapters 7 and 11 filings by their ability to repay. If found to have the means to pay, they go into a Chapter 13 proceeding. Chapter 13 eligibility is limited to consumers with $360,475 in unsecured debt and $1,081,400 in secured debt.

---

[50] 11 U.S.C. §1325.
[51] 11 U.S.C. §1328.
[52] 11 U.S.C. §1328(g)(1).

An automatic stay prevents creditors from taking legal action against the debtor after a bankruptcy petition is filed. The trustee in bankruptcy is elected by the creditors and is the successor to, and acquires the rights of, the debtor. In certain cases, the trustee can avoid transfers of property to prevent creditors from satisfying their claims. Preferential transfers may be set aside. A transfer for a present consideration, such as a cash sale, is not a preference.

Bankruptcy law regulates the way creditors present their claims and how the assets of the debtor are to be distributed in payment of the claims. Some assets of the debtor are exempt from the bankruptcy estate, such as a portion of the value of the debtor's home.

Secured claims are not affected by the debtor's bankruptcy. Unsecured claims are paid in the following order of priority:

1. Support or maintenance for a spouse, former spouse, or child.

2. Costs and expenses of administration of the bankruptcy case.

3. Claims arising in the ordinary course of a debtor's business or financial affairs after the commencement of the case but before the order of relief (involuntary).

4. Claims for wages, salaries, or commissions, including vacation, severance, or sick leave pay earned within 180 days before the filing of the petition or the date of cessation of the debtor's business, limited to $11,725 for each person.

5. Claims arising for contributions (up to $5,850) to employee benefit plans based on services

rendered within 180 days before the filing of the petition or when the debtor ceased doing business.

6. Farm producers (up to $5,775) and fishers against debtors who operate grain storage facilities or fish produce storage or processing facilities, up to $5,775 per claim.

7. Claims by consumer creditors, not to exceed $2,600 for each claimant.

8. Certain taxes and penalties due government units, such as income and property taxes.

9. All other unsecured creditors.

10. Remainder (if any) to debtor.

The decree terminating bankruptcy proceedings is generally a discharge that releases the debtor from most debts. Certain debts, such as income taxes, student loans, loans obtained by use of a false financial statement, alimony, and debts not listed by the debtor, are not discharged.

Under Chapter 11 bankruptcy, individuals, partnerships, and corporations in business may be reorganized so that the business can continue to operate. A plan for reorganization must be approved by the court. Under a Chapter 13 bankruptcy proceeding, individual debtors with a regular income may adopt extended-time payment plans for the payment of debts. A plan for extended-time payment must also be confirmed by the court. Federal, state, and local law may not discriminate against anyone on the basis of a discharge in bankruptcy.

LEARNING OUTCOMES

After studying this chapter, you should be able to clearly explain:

A. Bankruptcy Law

B. How Bankruptcy Is Declared

L0.1 List the requirements for the commencement of a voluntary bankruptcy case and an involuntary bankruptcy case
> See the Sports & Entertainment Law discussion of celebrity bankruptcies on p. 754.

> See discussion of Chapters 7, 11, and 13 on pp. 747–748 and chart on p. 752.

C. Administration of the Bankruptcy Estate

L0.2 Explain the procedure for the administration of a debtor's estate
> See the list of priorities on p. 758.
> See *In re Ames Dept. Stores* on pp. 757–758.

D. Debtor's Duties and Exemptions

LO.3 List a debtor's duties and exemptions
See the discussion of the homestead exemptions on p. 760.
See *In re Werth* case on p. 761.

E. Discharge in Bankruptcy

LO.4 Explain the significance of a discharge in bankruptcy
See *In re Looper* on p. 763.

F. Reorganization Plans under Chapter 11

See Ethics & the Law, The Skies Are Not So Friendly on p. 762.

G. Payment Plans under Chapter 13

LO.5 Explain when a business reorganization plan or an extended-time payment plan might be used
See the Ethics & the Law discussion of United Airlines on p. 762.
See the discussion of Chrysler and GM on p. 765.

KEY TERMS

automatic stay
balance sheet test
bankruptcy courts
bona fide
Chapter 7 bankruptcy
Chapter 11 bankruptcy
Chapter 13 bankruptcy

claim
discharge in bankruptcy
insiders
insolvency
involuntary bankruptcy
liquidated
means test

order of relief
preferences
preferential transfers
proof of claim
trustee in bankruptcy
voluntary bankruptcy

QUESTIONS AND CASE PROBLEMS

1. Hall-Mark regularly supplied electronic parts to Peter Lee. On September 11, 1992, Lee gave Hall-Mark a $100,000 check for parts it had received. Hall-Mark continued to ship parts to Lee. On September 23, 1992, Lee's check was dishonored by the bank. On September 25, 1992, Lee delivered to Hall-Mark a cashier's check for $100,000. Hall-Mark shipped nothing more to Lee after receipt of the cashier's check. On December 24, 1992, Lee filed a voluntary petition for bankruptcy. The trustee filed a complaint to have the $100,000 payment to Hall-Mark set aside as a voidable preference. Hall-Mark said it was entitled to the payment because it gave value to Lee. The trustee said that the payment was not actually made until the cashier's check was delivered on September 25, 1992, and that Hall-Mark gave no further value to Lee after that check was paid. Who was correct? [*In re Lee*, 108 F.3d 239 (9th Cir.)]

2. Orso, who had declared bankruptcy, received a structured tort settlement in a personal injury claim he had pending. The settlement would pay him an annuity each year for 30 years because the claim was the result of an auto accident that left him permanently and severely brain damaged with an IQ of about 70. His ex-wife had a pending claim for $48,000 in arrearages on Orso's $1,000 per month child support payments. His ex-wife wanted the annuity included in the bankruptcy estate. Would this property have been included in Orso's bankruptcy estate? [*In re Orso*, 214 F.3d 637 (5th Cir.)]

3. Harold McClellan sold ice-making machinery to Bobbie Cantrell's brother for $200,000 to be paid in installment payments. McClellan took a security interest in the ice machine but did not perfect it by filing a financing statement. The brother defaulted when he owed $100,000, and McClellan brought suit. With the suit pending, the brother "sold" the ice machine to Bobbie Cantrell for $10. Bobbie then sold the machine to someone for $160,000 and refused to explain what happened to that money. McClellan added Bobbie as a defendant in his suit against her brother. Bobbie then declared bankruptcy. McClellan sought to have the various transfers set aside. The trial court refused to do so, and McClellan appealed. Should the transfers be set

aside? Why or why not? [*McClellan v. Cantrell*, 217 F.3d 890 (7th Cir.)]

4. Okamoto owed money to Hornblower & Weeks-Hemphill, Noyes (a law firm and hereafter Hornblower). Hornblower filed an involuntary bankruptcy petition against Okamoto, who moved to dismiss the petition on the ground that he had more than 12 creditors and the petition could not be filed by only one creditor. Hornblower replied that the other creditors' claims were too small to count and, therefore, the petition could be filed by one creditor. Decide. [*In re Okamoto*, 491 F.2d 496 (9th Cir.)]

5. Jane Leeves declared voluntary Chapter 7 bankruptcy. The trustee included the following property in her bankruptcy estate:

   - Jane's wedding ring

   - Jane's computer for her consulting business that she operated from her home

   - Jane's car payment from a client in the amount of $5,000 that was received 91 days after Jane filed bankruptcy

   After collecting all of Jane's assets, the bankruptcy trustee was trying to decide how to distribute the assets. Jane had the following creditors:

   - Mortgage company—owed $187,000 (the trustee sold Jane's house for $190,000)

   - Expenses of the bankruptcy—$3,000

   - Federal income taxes—$11,000

   - Utility bills—$1,000

   - Office supply store open account—$1,000

   The trustee had $11,500 in cash, including the $3,000 additional cash left from the sale of the house after the mortgage company was paid. How should the trustee distribute this money? What if the amount were $14,500; how should that be distributed?

6. Kentile sold goods over an extended period of time to Winham. The credit relationship began without Winham's being required to furnish a financial statement. After a time, payments were not made regularly, and Kentile requested a financial statement. Winham submitted a statement for the year just ended. Kentile requested a second statement. The second statement was false. Kentile objected to Winham's discharge in bankruptcy because of the false financial statement. Should the discharge be granted? Why or why not?

7. D. Erik Von Kiel obtained loans from the U.S. Department of Health & Human Services so that he could complete his education as an osteopathic physician. He works at the International Academy of Life (IAL) in Orem, Utah, for no salary but receives gifts from IAL that total $150,000 per year, or about $12,787 per month. He pays no taxes on these "gifts" and has received them since 2005. Dr. Von Kiel pays all but $1,000 to his ex-wife and nine children for their support. He has given up his practice, taken a vow of poverty, and works at IAL to concentrate on alternative medicine. He has signed over full authority for the management of his financial affairs to two individuals, who apparently failed to manage wisely. As a result, Dr. Von Kiel filed for bankruptcy in order to be discharged from his HHS loans. HHS says that Dr. Von Kiel should not be discharged because of bad faith. Who is correct and why? [*In re Von Kiel*, 461 B.R. 323 (E.D. Pa.)]

8. Sonia, a retailer, has the following assets: a factory worth $1 million; accounts receivable amounting to $750,000, which fall due in four to six months; and $20,000 cash in the bank. Sonia's sole liability is a $200,000 note falling due today, which she is unable to pay. Can Sonia be forced into involuntary bankruptcy under the Bankruptcy Code?

9. Samson Industries ceased doing business and is in bankruptcy proceedings. Among the creditors are five employees seeking unpaid wages. Three of the employees are owed $3,500 each, and two are owed $1,500 each. These amounts became due within 90 days preceding the filing of the petition. Where, in the priority of claims, will the employees' wage claims fall?

10. Carol Cott, doing business as Carol Cott Fashions, is worried about an involuntary bankruptcy proceeding being filed by her creditors. Her net worth, using a balance sheet

approach, is $8,000 ($108,000 in assets minus $100,000 in liabilities). However, her cash flow is negative, and she has been hard pressed to meet current obligations as they mature. She is in fact some $12,500 in arrears in payments to her creditors on bills submitted during the past two months. Will the fact that Cott is solvent in the balance-sheet sense result in the court's dismissing the creditors' petition if Cott objects to the petition? Explain.

11. On July 1, Roger Walsh, a sole proprietor operating a grocery, was involuntarily petitioned into bankruptcy by his creditors. At that time, and for at least 90 days prior to that time, Walsh was unable to pay current obligations. On June 16, Walsh paid the May electric bill for his business. The trustee in bankruptcy claimed that this payment was a voidable preference. Was the trustee correct? Explain.

12. Steven and Teresa Hornsby are married and have three young children. On May 25, 1993, the Hornsbys filed a voluntary Chapter 7 petition. They had by that date accumulated more than $30,000 in debt, stemming almost entirely from student loans. They wanted a discharge of their student loans on grounds of undue hardship. The Hornsbys attended a succession of small Tennessee state colleges. Both studied business and computers, but neither graduated. Although they received several deferments and forbearances on the loans, they ultimately defaulted before making any payments. Interest had accumulated on the loans to the extent that Steven was indebted to the Tennessee Student Assistance Corporation (TSAC) for $15,058.52, and Teresa was indebted to TSAC for $18,329.15.

Steven was working for AT&T in Dallas, Texas; he made $6.53 per hour, occasionally working limited overtime hours. Teresa was employed by KinderCare Learning Center. Although she had begun work in Tennessee, she had transferred to become the director of a child care facility in Dallas. Teresa was earning $17,500 per year with medical benefits at the time of the hearing. In monthly net income, Steven earned approximately $1,083.33, and Teresa earned

$1,473.33, amounting to $2,556.66 of disposable income per month. The Hornsbys' reported monthly expenses came to $2,364.90. They operated with a monthly surplus of $191.76 to $280.43, depending on whether Steven earned overtime for a particular month. Under the federal bankruptcy laws, are the Hornsbys entitled to a discharge on their student loans? Explain your answer. [*In re Hornsby*, 144 F.3d 433 (6th Cir.)]

13. TLC was an Atlanta rhythm, blues, and hip-hop band that performed at clubs in 1991. The three-woman group signed a recording contract with LaFace Records. The group's first album that LaFace produced, *Oooooooohhh on the TLC Tip*, sold almost 3 million albums in 1992. The group's second album, *Crazysexycool*, also produced by LaFace, sold 5 million albums through June 1996. The two albums together had six top-of-the-chart singles.

LaFace had the right to renew TLC's contract in 1996 following renegotiation of the contract terms. In the industry, royalty rates for unknown groups, as TLC was in 1991, are generally 7 percent of the revenues for the first 500,000 albums and 8 percent for sales on platinum albums (albums that sell over 1 million copies). The royalty rate increases to 9.5 percent for all sales on an eighth album. Established artists in the industry who renegotiate often have royalty rates of 13 percent, and artists with two platinum albums can command an even higher royalty.

The three women in TLC—Tionne Watkins (T-Boz), Lisa Lopes (Left-Eye, who has since died), and Rozonda Thomas (Chili)—declared bankruptcy in July 1995. All three listed debts that exceeded their assets, which included sums owed to creditors for their cars and to Zale's and The Limited for credit purchases. Lopes was being sued by Lloyd's of London, which claimed she owed it $1.3 million it had paid on a policy held by her boyfriend on his home that was destroyed by fire. Lopes pleaded guilty to one count of arson in the destruction of the home but denied that she intended to destroy it. She was sentenced to five years probation and treatment at a halfway house.

Lopes asked that the Lloyd's claim be discharged in her bankruptcy. All three members of TLC asked that their contract with LaFace be discharged in bankruptcy because being bound to their old contract could impede their fresh financial starts.

Did the three women meet the standards for declaring bankruptcy? Evaluate whether Lopes's Lloyd's claim should be discharged. Determine whether the record contract should be discharged.

14. Place the following in order for a bankruptcy proceeding:
    a. Order of relief
    b. Collection of bankrupt's estate
    c. List of creditors
    d. Petition
    e. Evaluation of claims
    f. Voidable preferences
    g. Discharge

15. Three general unsecured creditors are owed $45,000 as follows: *A,* $15,000; *B,* $5,000; and *C,* $25,000. After all other creditors were paid, the amount left for distribution to general unsecured creditors was $9,000. How will the $9,000 be distributed?

CPA QUESTIONS

1. Which of the following statements is correct concerning the voluntary filing of a petition of bankruptcy?

   a. If the debtor has 12 or more creditors, the unsecured claims must total at least $13,475.

   b. The debtor must be solvent.

   c. If the debtor has less than 12 creditors, the unsecured claims must total at least $13,475.

   d. The petition may be filed jointly by spouses (AICPA adapted).

2. On February 28, Master, Inc., had total assets with a fair market value of $1,200,000 and total liabilities of $990,000. On January 15, Master made a monthly installment note payment to Acme Distributors Corp., a creditor holding a properly perfected security interest in equipment having a fair market value greater than the balance due on the note. On March 15, Master voluntarily filed a petition in bankruptcy under the liquidation provisions of Chapter 7 of the federal Bankruptcy Code. One year later, the equipment was sold for less than the balance due on the note to Acme.

   If a creditor challenged Master's right to file, the petition would be dismissed:

   a. If Master had less than 12 creditors at the time of filing.

   b. Unless Master can show that a reorganization under Chapter 11 of the federal Bankruptcy Code would have been unsuccessful.

   c. Unless Master can show that it is unable to pay its debts in the ordinary course of business or as they come due.

   d. If Master is an insurance company.

3. A voluntary petition filed under the liquidation provisions of Chapter 7 of the federal Bankruptcy Code:

   a. Is not available to a corporation unless it has previously filed a petition under the reorganization provisions of Chapter 11 of the federal Bankruptcy Code.

   b. Automatically stays collection actions against the debtor except by secured creditors for collateral only.

   c. Will be dismissed unless the debtor has 12 or more unsecured creditors whose claims total at least $13,475.

   d. Does not require the debtor to show that the debtor's liabilities exceed the fair market value of assets.

4. Which following conditions, if any, must a debtor meet to file a voluntary bankruptcy

petition under Chapter 7 of the federal Bankruptcy Code?

	Insolvency	Three or More Creditors
a.	Yes	Yes
b.	Yes	No
c.	No	Yes
d.	No	No

5. On July 15, 1988, White, a sole proprietor, was involuntarily petitioned into bankruptcy under the liquidation provisions of the Bankruptcy Code. White's nonexempt property has been converted to $13,000 cash, which is available to satisfy the following claims:

Unsecured claim for 1986 state income tax	$10,000
Fee owed to Best & Co., CPAs, for services rendered from April 1, 1988, through June 30, 1988	$6,000
Unsecured claim by Stieb for wages earned as an employee of White during March 1988	$3,000

There are no other claims.

What is the maximum amount that will be distributed for the payment of the 1986 state income tax?

a. $4,000

b. $5,000

c. $7,000

d. $10,000

6. On May 1, 1997, two months after becoming insolvent, Quick Corp., an appliance wholesaler, filed a voluntary petition for bankruptcy under the provisions of Chapter 7 of the federal Bankruptcy Code. On October 15, 1996, Quick's board of directors had authorized and paid Erly $50,000 to repay Erly's April 1, 1996, loan to the corporation. Erly is a sibling of Quick's president. On March 15, 1996, Quick paid Kray $100,000 for inventory delivered that day. Which of the following is not relevant in determining whether the repayment of Erly's loan is a voidable preferential transfer?

a. That Erly is an insider.

b. That Quick's payment to Erly was made on account of an antecedent debt.

c. Quick's solvency when the loan was made by Erly.

d. That Quick's payment to Erly was made within one year of the filing of the bankruptcy petition.

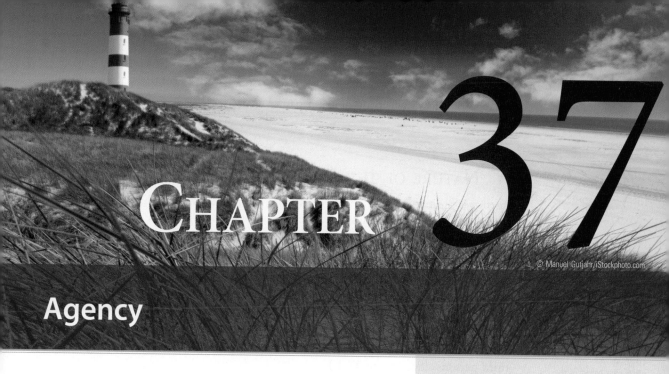

© Manuel Gutjahr/iStockphoto.com

CHAPTER 37

Agency

learningoutcomes

After studying this chapter, you should be able to

LO.1 Explain the difference between an agent and an independent contractor

LO.2 Explain three methods of creating an agency relationship

LO.3 Recognize that third persons who deal with an agent are required to take notice of acts contrary to the interests of the principal

LO.4 List and explain the duties an agent owes the principal

LO.5 Explain how the Uniform Durable Power of Attorney Act changes the common law rule on incapacity of the principal

O ne of the most common business relationships is that of agency. By virtue of the agency device, one person can make contracts at numerous places with many different parties at the same time.

A. NATURE OF THE AGENCY RELATIONSHIP

Agency is ordinarily based on the consent of the parties, and for that reason is called a *consensual relationship*. However, the law sometimes imposes an agency relationship. If consideration is present, the agency relationship is contractual.

1. Definitions and Distinctions

agency – relationship that exists between a person identified as a principal and another by virtue of which the latter may make contracts with third persons on behalf of the principal. (Parties—principal, agent, third person)

Agency is a relationship based on an express or implied agreement by which one person, the **agent**, is authorized to act under the control of and for another, the **principal**, in negotiating and making contracts with third persons.[1] The acts of the agent obligate the principal to third persons and give the principal rights against third persons. (See Figure 37-1.)

The term *agency* is frequently used with other meanings. It is sometimes used to denote the fact that one has the right to sell certain products, such as when a dealer is said to possess an automobile agency. In other instances, the term is used to mean an exclusive right to sell certain articles within a given territory. In these cases, however, the dealer is not an agent in the sense of representing the manufacturer.

agent – person or firm who is authorized by the principal or by operation of law to make contracts with third persons on behalf of the principal.

It is important to be able to distinguish agencies from other relationships because certain rights and duties in agencies are not present in other relationships.

principal – person or firm who employs an agent; person who, with respect to a surety, is primarily liable to the third person or creditor; property held in trust.

(A) EMPLOYEES AND INDEPENDENT CONTRACTORS. Control and authority are characteristics that distinguish ordinary employees and independent contractors from agents.

(1) Employees.

An agent is distinguished from an ordinary employee who is not hired to represent the employer in making contracts with third persons. It is possible, however, for the same person to be both an agent and an employee. **For Example,** the driver for a spring water delivery service is an agent in making contracts between the company and its customers but is an employee with respect to the work of delivering products.

(2) Independent Contractors.

independent contractor – contractor who undertakes to perform a specified task according to the terms of a contract but over whom the other contracting party has no control except as provided for by the contract.

An **independent contractor** is bound by a contract to produce a certain result—for example, to build a house. The actual performance of the work is controlled by the contractor, not the owner. An agent or employee differs from an independent contractor in that the principal or employer has the right to control the agent or employee, but not the contractor, in the performance of the work. **For Example,** Ned and Tracy Seizer contract with Fox Building Company to build a new home on Hilton Head Island, South Carolina, according to referenced plans and specifications. Individuals hired by Fox to work on the home are subject to the authority and control of Fox, the independent contractor, not the Seizers.

---

[1] Restatement (Second) of Agency §1; *Union Miniere, S.A. v. Parday Corp.*, 521 N.E.2d 700 (Ind. App. 1988).

| FIGURE 37-1 | *Agency Relationships* |

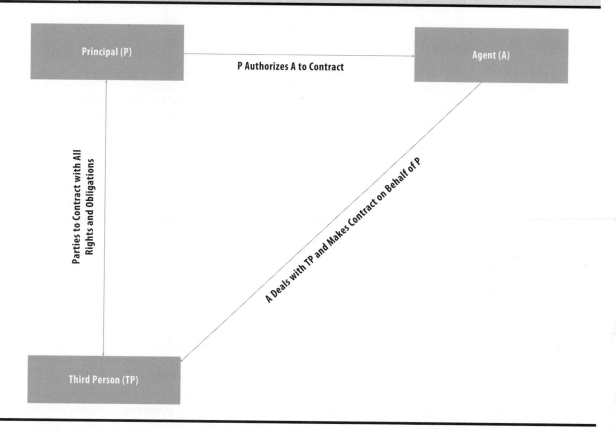

Principal (P)

P Authorizes A to Contract

Agent (A)

Parties to Contract with All Rights and Obligations

A Deals with TP and Makes Contract on Behalf of P

Third Person (TP)

© Cengage Learning

However, Ned and Tracy could decide to build the home themselves, hiring two individuals from nearby Beaufort, Ted Chase and Marty Bromley, to do the work the Seizers will direct each day. Because Ted and Marty would be employees of the Seizers, the Seizers would be held responsible for any wrongs committed by these employees within the scope of their employment. As a general rule, on the other hand, the Seizers are not responsible for the torts of Fox, the independent contractor, and the contractor's employees. A "right to control" test determines whether an individual is an agent, an employee, or an independent contractor.[2]

CASE SUMMARY

Why Some Businesses Use Independent Agents Rather than Employees!

FACTS: Patricia Yelverton died from injuries sustained when an automobile owned and driven by Joseph Lamm crossed the center line of a roadway and struck the automobile driven by Yelverton. Yelverton's executor brought suit against Lamm and Lamm's alleged employer,

[2] *NE Ohio College of Massotherapy v. Burek,* 759 N.E.2d 869 (Ohio App. 2001).

CASE SUMMARY

Continued

Premier Industrial Products Inc. The relationship between Lamm and Premier was governed by a written contract entitled "Independent Agent Agreement," in which Lamm, as "Independent Agent," was given the right to sell Premier's products in a designated territory. The agreement provided that all orders were subject to acceptance by Premier and were not binding on Premier until so accepted. Lamm was paid by commission only. He was allowed to work on a self-determined schedule, retain assistants at his own expense, and sell the products of other companies not in competition with Premier. The executor claimed Lamm was an agent or employee of Premier. Premier stated Lamm was an independent contractor.

DECISION: Judgment for Premier. Lamm had no authority to make contracts for Premier but simply took orders. Therefore, he was not an agent. Lamm was not an employee of Premier. Premier had no right to control the way he performed his work and did not in fact do so. Lamm was an independent contractor. [*Yelverton v. Lamm*, 380 S.E.2d 621 (N.C. App. 1989)]

A person who appears to be an independent contractor may in fact be so controlled by the other party that the contractor is regarded as an agent of, or employee of, the controlling person. **For Example,** Pierce, who was under contract to Brookville Carriers, Inc., was involved in a tractor-trailer/car collision with Rich and others. Pierce owned the tractor involved in the accident on a lease from Brookville but could use it only to haul freight for Brookville; he had no authority to carry freight on his own, and all of his operating authority belonged to Brookville. The "owner/operator" was deemed an employee rather than independent contractor for purposes of assessing the liability of the employer.[3] The separate identity of an independent contractor may be concealed so that the public believes that it is dealing with the principal. When this situation occurs, the principal is liable as though the contractor were an agent or employee.

2. Classification of Agents

special agent–agent authorized to transact a specific transaction or to do a specific act.

A **special agent** is authorized by the principal to handle a definite business transaction or to do a specific act. One who is authorized by another to purchase a particular house is a special agent.

general agent–agent authorized by the principal to transact all affairs in connection with a particular type of business or trade or to transact all business at a certain place.

A **general agent** is authorized by the principal to transact all affairs in connection with a particular type of business or trade or to transact all business at a certain place. To illustrate, a person who is appointed as manager by the owner of a store is a general agent.

universal agent–agent authorized by the principal to do all acts that can lawfully be delegated to a representative.

A **universal agent** is authorized by the principal to do all acts that can be delegated lawfully to a representative. This form of agency arises when a person absent because of being in the military service gives another person a blanket power of attorney to do anything that must be done during such absence.

3 *Rich v. Brookville Carriers, Inc.*, 256 F. Supp. 2d 26 (D. Me. 2003).

CPA

interest in the authority – form of agency in which an agent has been given or paid for the right to exercise authority.

3. Agency Coupled with an Interest

An agent has an **interest in the authority** when consideration has been given or paid for the right to exercise the authority. To illustrate, when a lender, in return for making a loan of money, is given, as security, authority to collect rents due the borrower and to apply those rents to the payment of the debt, the lender becomes the borrower's agent with an interest in the authority given to collect the rents.

interest in the subject matter – form of agency in which an agent is given an interest in the property with which that agent is dealing.

An agent has an **interest in the subject matter** when, for a consideration, she is given an interest in the property with which she is dealing. Hence, when the agent is authorized to sell property of the principal and is given a lien on such property as security for a debt owed to her by the principal, she has an interest in the subject matter.

B. CREATING THE AGENCY

An agency may arise by appointment, conduct, ratification, or operation of law.

express authorization – authorization of an agent to perform a certain act.

4. Authorization by Appointment

The usual method of creating an agency is by **express authorization**; that is, a person is appointed to act for, or on behalf of, another.

In most instances, the authorization of the agent may be oral. However, some appointments must be made in a particular way. A majority of the states, by statute, require the appointment of an agent to be in writing when the agency is created to acquire or dispose of any interest in land. A written authorization of agency is called a **power of attorney**. An agent acting under a power of attorney is referred to as an **attorney in fact**.[4]

power of attorney – written authorization to an agent by the principal.

attorney in fact – agent authorized to act for another under a power of attorney.

5. Authorization by Conduct

Conduct consistent with the existence of an agency relationship may be sufficient to show authorization. The principal may have such dealing with third persons as to cause them to believe that the "agent" has authority. Thus, if the owner of a store places another person in charge, third persons may assume that the person in charge is the agent for the owner in that respect. The "agent" then appears to be authorized and is said to have *apparent authority*, and the principal is estopped from contradicting the appearance that has been created.[5]

CASE SUMMARY

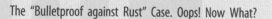

The "Bulletproof against Rust" Case. Oops! Now What?

FACTS: While constructing a hotel in Lincoln City, Oregon, the owner, Todd Taylor, became concerned about possible rusting in the exterior stucco system manufactured by ChemRex that was being installed at the hotel. The general contractor Ramsay-Gerding arranged a meeting with

---

[4] *Lamb v. Scott*, 643 So.2d 972 (Ala. 1994).
[5] *Intersparex Leddin KG v. AL-Haddad*, 852 S.W.2d 245 (Tenn. App. 1992).

CASE SUMMARY

Continued

the owner, the installer, and ChemRex's territory manager for Oregon, Mike McDonald, to discuss Mr. Taylor's concerns. McDonald told those present that the SonoWall system was "bulletproof against rust," and stated that "you're getting a five-year warranty." He followed up with a letter confirming the five-year warranty on parts and labor. A year later rust discoloration appeared, and no one from ChemRex ever fixed the problem. Taylor sued ChemRex for breach of warranty. ChemRex defended that McDonald did not have actual or apparent authority to declare such a warranty.

DECISION: Judgment for Taylor. The evidence indicated that ChemRex clothed Mike McDonald with the title of "territory manager" and gave him the actual authority to visit job sites and resolve problems. Although it denies he had actual authority, ChemRex took sufficient steps to create apparent authority to provide the five-year warranty on the stucco system. [*Taylor v. Ramsay-Gerding Construction Co.*, 196 P.3d 532 (Or. 2008)]

The term *apparent authority* is used when there is only the appearance of authority but no actual authority, and that appearance of authority was created by the principal. The test for the existence of apparent authority is an objective test determined by the principal's outward manifestations through words or conduct that lead a third person reasonably to believe that the "agent" has authority. A principal's express restriction on authority not made known to a third person is no defense.

Apparent authority extends to all acts that a person of ordinary prudence, familiar with business usages and the particular business, would be justified in believing that the agent has authority to perform. It is essential to the concept of apparent authority that the third person reasonably believe that the agent has authority. The mere placing of property in the possession of another does not give that person either actual or apparent authority to sell the property.

CPA 6. Agency by Ratification

An agent may attempt, on behalf of the principal, to do an act that was not authorized, or a person who is not the agent of another may attempt to act as such an agent. Very generally, notification may be express, where the principal explicitly approves the contract, or implied, where the principal does not object to the contract and accepts the contract's benefits. **For Example,** homeowners Schafstall and Alexander went to Lowe's Home Center to purchase a water system. Schafstall completed the purchase and signed the warranty contract for the installation service. The installation failed and resulted in over $100,000 in water damages to the property. Lowe's warranty limited its liability to just the cost of the reinstallation and repair parts for the system. Not only was Schafstall bound by the terms of the contract with its warranty, but Alexander ratified the contract by his presence at the transaction and is thus bound by its terms.[6]

---

[6] *Guideone Insurance Co. v. U.S. Water Systems, Inc. and Lowe's Home Centers*, 950 N.E.2d 1236 (Ind. App. 2011).

(A) Intention to Ratify. Initially, ratification is a question of intention. Just as in the case of authorization, when there is a question of whether the principal authorized the agent, there is a question of whether the principal intended to approve or ratify the action of the unauthorized agent.

The intention to ratify may be expressed in words, or it may be found in conduct indicating an intention to ratify. **For Example,** James Reiner signed a five-year lease of commercial space on 320 West Main Street in Avon, Connecticut, because his father Calvin was away on vacation, and the owner, Robert Udolf, told James that if he did not come in and sign the lease, his father would lose the opportunity to rent the space in question. James was aware that his father had an interest in the space, and while telling Robert several times that he had no authority, James did sign his name to the lease. In fact, his father took occupancy of the space and paid rent for three years and then abandoned the space. James is not liable on the remainder of the lease because the owner knew at the time of signing that James did not have authority to act. Although he did not sign the lease, Calvin ratified the lease signed by James by his conduct of moving into the space and doing business there for three years with full knowledge of all material facts relating to the transaction. The owner, therefore, had to bring suit against Calvin, not James.[7]

CPA **(B) Conditions for Ratification.** In addition to the intent to ratify, expressed in some instances with a certain formality, the following conditions must be satisfied for the intention to take effect as a ratification:

1. The agent must have purported to act on behalf of or as agent for the identified principal.

2. The principal must have been capable of authorizing the act both at the time of the act and at the time it was ratified.

3. The principal must have full knowledge of all material facts.

It is not always necessary, however, to show that the principal had actual knowledge. Knowledge will be imputed if a principal knows of other facts that would lead a prudent person to make inquiries or if that knowledge can be inferred from the knowledge of other facts or from a course of business. **For Example,** Stacey, without authorization but knowing that William needed money, contracted to sell one of William's paintings to Courtney for $298. Stacey told William about the contract that evening; William said nothing and helped her wrap the painting in a protective plastic wrap for delivery. A favorable newspaper article about William's art appeared the following morning and dramatically increased the value of all of his paintings. William cannot recover the painting from Courtney on the theory that he never authorized the sale because he ratified the unauthorized contract made by Stacey by his conduct in helping her wrap the painting with full knowledge of the terms of the sale. The effect is a legally binding contract between William and Courtney.

(c) Effect of Ratification. When an unauthorized act is ratified, the effect is the same as though the act had been originally authorized. Ordinarily, this means that the

[7] *Udolf v. Reiner,* 2000 WL 726953 (Conn. Super. May 19, 2000).

principal and the third party are bound by the contract made by the agent.[8] When the principal ratifies the act of the unauthorized person, such ratification releases that person from the liability that would otherwise be imposed for having acted without authority.

CPA ## 7. Proving the Agency Relationship

The burden of proving the existence of an agency relationship rests on the person who seeks to benefit by such proof. The third person who desires to bind the principal because of the act of an alleged agent has the burden of proving that the latter person was in fact the authorized agent of the principal and possessed the authority to do the act in question.[9]

C. AGENT'S AUTHORITY

When there is an agent, it is necessary to determine the scope of the agent's authority.

8. Scope of Agent's Authority

The scope of an agent's authority may be determined from the express words of the principal to the agent or it may be implied from the principal's words or conduct or from the customs of the trade or business.

(A) EXPRESS AUTHORITY. If the principal tells the agent to perform a certain act, the agent has express authority to do so. Express authority can be given orally or in writing.

(B) INCIDENTAL AUTHORITY. An agent has implied **incidental authority** to perform any act reasonably necessary to execute the express authority given to the agent. **For Example,** if the principal authorizes the agent to purchase goods without furnishing funds to the agent to pay for them, the agent has the implied incidental authority to purchase the goods on credit.[10]

incidental authority – authority of an agent that is reasonably necessary to execute express authority.

(C) CUSTOMARY AUTHORITY. An agent has implied **customary authority** to do any act that, according to the custom of the community, usually accompanies the transaction for which the agent is authorized to act. An agent who has express authority to receive payments from third persons, for example, has the implied customary authority to issue receipts.

customary authority – authority of an agent to do any act that, according to the custom of the community, usually accompanies the transaction for which the agent is authorized to act.

(D) APPARENT AUTHORITY. A person has **apparent authority** as an agent when the principal's words or conduct leads a third person to reasonably believe that the person has that authority and the third person relies on that appearance.[11]

apparent authority – appearance of authority created by the principal's words or conduct.

[8] *Bill McCurley Chevrolet v. Rutz*, 808 P.2d 1167 (Wash. App. 1991).
[9] *Cummings, Inc. v. Nelson*, 115 P.3d 536 (Alaska 2005).
[10] *Badger v. Paulson Investment Co.*, 803 P.2d 1178 (Or. 1991).
[11] *Alexander v. Chandler*, 179 S.W.2d 385 (Mo. App. 2005).

CASE SUMMARY

CSX Gets Railroaded by Albert Arillotta

FACTS: Recovery Express and Interstate Demolition (IDEC) are two separate corporations located at the same business address in Boston. On August 22, 2003, Albert Arillotta, a "partner" at IDEC, sent an e-mail to Len Whitehead, Jr. of CSX Transportation expressing an interest in buying "rail cars as scrap." Arillotta represented himself to be "from interstate demolition and recovery express" in the e-mail. The e-mail address from which he sent his inquiry was **albert@recoveryexpress.com**. Arillotta went to the CSX rail yard, disassembled the cars, and transported them away. Thereafter CSX sent invoices for the scrap rail cars totaling $115,757.36 addressed to IDEC at its Boston office shared with Recovery Express. Whitehead believed Arillotta was authorized to act for Recovery Express, based on the e-mail's domain name, recoveryexpress.com. Recovery claims that Arillotta never worked for it. Recovery's president Thomas Trafton allowed the "fledgling" company to use telephone, fax, and e-mail services at its offices but never shared anything—assets, funds, books of business, or financials with IDEC— CSX sued Recovery for the invoice amount on the doctrine of "apparent authority." IDEC is now defunct. Recovery claims that Arillotta never worked for it and that it is not liable.

DECISION: Judgment for Recovery. Issuance of an e-mail address with Recovery's domain name to an individual who shared office space with Recovery did not give the individual, Albert Arillotta, apparent authority to enter contracts on Recovery's behalf. No reasonable person could conclude that Arillotta had apparent authority on the basis of an e-mail domain name by itself. Given the anonymity of the Internet, the court warned businesses to take additional action to verify a purported agent's authority to make a deal. [**CSX Transportation, Inc. v. Recovery Express, Inc.**, 415 F. Supp. 2d 6 (D. Mass. 2006)]

9. Effect of Proper Exercise of Authority

When an agent with authority properly makes a contract with a third person that purports to bind the principal, there is by definition a binding contract between the principal and the third person. The agent is not a party to this contract. Consequently, when the owner of goods is the principal, the owner's agent is not liable for breach of warranty with respect to the goods "sold" by the agent. The owner-principal, not the agent, was the "seller" in the sales transaction.

CPA

10. Duty to Ascertain Extent of Agent's Authority

A third person who deals with a person claiming to be an agent cannot rely on the statements made by the agent concerning the extent of authority.[12] If the agent is not authorized to perform the act or is not even the agent of the principal, the transaction between the alleged agent and the third person will have no legal effect between the principal and the third person.

Third persons who deal with an agent whose authority is limited to a special purpose are bound at their peril to find out the extent of the agent's authority. An attorney is such an agent. Unless the client holds the attorney out as having greater

[12] *Breed v. Hughes Aircraft Col.*, 35 Fed. App. 864 (Fed. Cir. 2002).

authority than usual, the attorney has no authority to settle a claim without approval from the client.

(A) AGENT'S ACTS ADVERSE TO PRINCIPAL. The third person who deals with an agent is required to take notice of any acts that are clearly adverse to the interest of the principal. Thus, if the agent is obviously using funds of the principal for the agent's personal benefit, persons dealing with the agent should recognize that the agent may be acting without authority and that they are dealing with the agent at their peril.

The only certain way that third persons can protect themselves is to inquire of the principal whether the agent is in fact the agent of the principal and has the necessary authority. **For Example,** Ron Fahd negotiated the sale of a fire truck to the Edinburg Volunteer Fire Company, on behalf of the manufacturer, Danko Company, at a price of $158,000. On Danko forms and letterhead Fahd drafted a "Proposal for Fire Apparatus" and it was signed by the president of the Fire Company and Fahd, as a dealer for Danko. Fahd gave a special $2,000 discount for prepayment of the cost of the chassis. Fahd directed that the prepayment check of $55,000 be made payable to "Ron Fahd Sales" in order to obtain the discount. The Fire Company's treasurer inquired of Fahd why the prepayment check was being made out to Fahd rather than Danko, and he accepted Fahd's answer without contacting Danko to confirm this unusual arrangement. Fahd absconded with the proceeds of the check. The Fire Company sued Danko claiming Fahd had apparent authority to receive the prepayment. While there was some indicia of agency, the court found that the Fire Company had failed to make reasonable inquiry with Danko to verify Fahd's authority to receive the prepayment in Fahd's name, and it rejected the claim that Fahd had apparent authority to accept the prepayment check made out to Fahd as opposed to Danko.[13]

11. Limitations on Agent's Authority

A person who has knowledge of a limitation on the agent's authority cannot ignore that limitation. When the third person knows that the authority of the agent depends on whether financing has been obtained, the principal is not bound by the act of the agent if the financing in fact was not obtained. If the authority of the agent is based on a writing and the third person knows that there is such a writing, the third person is charged with knowledge of limitations contained in it.

(A) "OBVIOUS" LIMITATIONS. In some situations, it may be obvious to third persons that they are dealing with an agent whose authority is limited. When third persons know that they are dealing with a representative of a government agency, they should recognize that such a person will ordinarily have limited authority. Third persons should recognize that a contract made with such an officer or representative may not be binding unless ratified by the principal.

The federal government places the risk on any individual making arrangements with the government to accurately ascertain that the government agent is within the bounds of his or her authority.

---

[13] *Edinburg Volunteer Fire Company v. Danko,* 867 N.Y.S.2d 547 (A.D. 2008).

CASE SUMMARY

Humlen Was Had?

FACTS: The FBI approached Humlen for assistance in securing the conviction of a drug trafficker. Humlen executed an agreement with the FBI to formalize his status as an informant. The agreement he signed contained compensation figures significantly less than those he had been promised by the FBI agents with whom he was dealing. Humlen claims that five agents repeatedly assured him that he would receive the extra compensation they had discussed with him, despite the wording of the contract. It was explained that the agreement had to be "couched" in that way because it was a discoverable document in any future criminal prosecution and thus could be used to destroy his credibility. Based on the information provided by Humlen, an arrest was made, and Humlen sought the remainder of his promised monetary reward from the FBI. The FBI refused to pay him any more than the contract stipulated. When no additional payment was forthcoming, Humlen sued the U.S. government.

DECISION: Judgment for the United States. The government, unlike private parties, cannot be bound by the apparent authority of its agents. When an agent exceeds his or her authority, the government can disavow the agent's words and is not bound by an implied contract. As a general rule, FBI agents lack the requisite actual authority—either express or implied—to contractually bind the United States to remit rewards to confidential informants. Moreover, Humlen's claims directly collide with the plain language of the agreement. [**Humlen v. United States**, 49 Fed. Cl. 497 (2001)]

(B) SECRET LIMITATIONS. If the principal has clothed an agent with authority to perform certain acts but the principal gives secret instructions that limit the agent's authority, the third person is allowed to take the authority of the agent at its face value. The third person is not bound by the secret limitations of which the third person has no knowledge.

D. DUTIES AND LIABILITIES OF PRINCIPAL AND AGENT

The creation of the principal-agent relationship gives rise to duties and liabilities.

12. Duties and Liabilities of Agent during Agency

While the agency relationship exists, the agent owes certain duties to the principal.

(A) LOYALTY. An agent must be loyal or faithful to the principal.[14] The agent must not obtain any secret benefit from the agency. If the principal is seeking to buy or rent property, the agent cannot secretly obtain the property and then sell or lease it to the principal at a profit.

An agent who owns property cannot sell it to the principal without disclosing that ownership to the principal. If disclosure is not made, the principal may avoid the

---

[14] *Patterson Custom Homes v. Bach*, 536 F. Supp. 2d 1026 (E.D. Ill. 2008).

contract even if the agent's conduct did not cause the principal any financial loss. Alternatively, the principal can approve the transaction and sue the agent for any secret profit obtained by the agent.

A contract is voidable by the principal if the agent who was employed to sell the property purchases the property, either directly or indirectly, without full disclosure to the principal.

An agent cannot act as agent for both parties to a transaction unless both know of the dual capacity and agree to it. If the agent does act in this capacity without the consent of both parties, any principal who did not know of the agent's double status can avoid the transaction.

An agent must not accept secret gifts or commissions from third persons in connection with the agency. If the agent does so, the principal may sue the agent for those gifts or commissions. Such practices are condemned because the judgment of the agent may be influenced by the receipt of gifts or commissions.

It is a violation of an agent's duty of loyalty to make and retain secret profits.

CASE SUMMARY

Was Grappolini a "Bad Boy"?

FACTS: Arthur Frigo, an adjunct professor at the Kellogg Graduate School of Management, formed Lucini Italia Co. (Lucini) to import and sell premium extra virgin olive oil and other products from Italy. Lucini's officers hired Guiseppe Grappolini as their olive oil supplier. They also hired him as their consultant. Grappolini signed an exclusivity agreement and a confidentiality agreement acknowledging the confidential nature of Lucini's product development, plans, and strategies. Grappolini was "branded" as a "master cultivator" in Lucini's literature and commercials.

In 1998, Lucini and Grappolini, as his consultant, discussed adding a line of extra virgin olive oils blended with "essential oils," for example, natural extracts such as lemon and garlic. It spent more than $800,000 developing the market information, testing flavors, designing labels and packaging, creating recipes, and generating trade secrets for the new products. Vegetal-Progress s.r.l. (Vegetal) was identified as the only company in Italy that was capable of producing the superior products Lucini sought, and Grappolini was assigned responsibility to obtain an exclusive supply contract with Vegetal.

In direct contravention of his representations to Lucini, Grappolini secretly negotiated an exclusive supply contract for the Grappolini Co., not for Lucini. Moreover, Grappolini Co. began to sell flavored olive oils in the United States, which coincided with Lucini's market research and recipe development that had been disclosed to Grappolini. When Lucini officers contacted Vegetal, they acknowledged that Grappolini was a "bad boy" in procuring the contract for his own company rather than for Lucini, but they would not renege on the contract. Lucini sued Grappolini.

DECISION: Judgment for Lucini. Grappolini was Lucini's agent and owed Lucini a duty to advance Lucini's interests, not his own. When he obtained an exclusive supply agreement with Vegetal for the Grappolini Co. instead of Lucini, he was disloyal and breached his fiduciary duties. As a result, Lucini suffered lost profits and damages of $4.17 million. In addition to these damages, Grappolini was ordered to pay $1,000,000 in punitive damages to deter similar acts in the future. Additionally, a permanent injunction was issued prohibiting Grappolini from using Lucini's trade secrets. [*Lucini Italia Co. v. Grappolini*, 2003 WL 1989605 (N.D. Ill. 2003)]

An agent is, of course, prohibited from aiding the competitors of a principal or disclosing to them information relating to the business of the principal. It is also a breach of duty for the agent to knowingly deceive a principal.[15]

(B) OBEDIENCE AND PERFORMANCE. An agent is under a duty to obey all lawful instructions.[16] The agent is required to perform the services specified for the period and in the way specified. An agent who does not do so is liable to the principal for any harm caused. For example, if an agent is instructed to take cash payments only but accepts a check in payment, the agent is liable for the loss caused the principal if a check is dishonored by nonpayment.

(C) REASONABLE CARE. It is the duty of an agent to act with the care that a reasonable person would exercise under the circumstances. **For Example,** Ethel Wilson applied for fire insurance for her house with St. Paul Reinsurance Co., Ltd., through her agent Club Services Corp. She thought she was fully covered. Unbeknown to her, however, St. Paul had refused coverage and returned her premium to Club Services, who did not refund it to Ms. Wilson or inform her that coverage had been denied. Fire destroyed her garage and St. Paul denied coverage. Litigation resulted, and St. Paul ended up expending $305,406 to settle the Wilson matter. Thereafter, St. Paul successfully sued Club Services Corp. under basic agency law principles that an agent (Club Services) is liable to its principal for all damages resulting from the agent's failure to discharge its duties.[17] In addition, if the agent possesses a special skill, as in the case of a broker or an attorney, the agent must exercise that skill.

(D) ACCOUNTING. An agent must account to the principal for all property or money belonging to the principal that comes into the agent's possession. The agent must, within a reasonable time, give notice of collections made and render an accurate account of all receipts and expenditures. The agency agreement may state at what intervals or on what dates such accountings are to be made. An agent must keep the principal's property and money separate and distinct from that of the agent.

(E) INFORMATION. It is the duty of an agent to keep the principal informed of all facts relating to the agency that are relevant to protecting the principal's interests.[18]

13. Duties and Liabilities of Agent after Termination of Agency

When the agency relationship ends, the duties of the agent continue only to the extent necessary to perform prior obligations. For example, the agent must return to the former principal any property that had been entrusted to the agent for the purpose of the agency. With the exception of such "winding-up" duties, the agency relationship is terminated, and the former agent can deal with the principal as freely as with a stranger.[19]

---

[15] *Koontz v. Rosener*, 787 P.2d 192 (Colo. App. 1990).
[16] *Stanford v. Neiderer*, 341 S.E.2d 892 (Ga. App. 1986).
[17] *St. Paul Reinsurance Co., Ltd. v. Club Services Corp.*, 30 Fed. Appx. 834 (10th Cir. 2002).
[18] Restatement (Second) of Agency §381; *Lumberman's Mutual Ins. Co. v. Franey Muha Alliant Ins.*, 388 F. Supp. 2d 292 (S.D.N.Y. 2005).
[19] *Corron & Black of Illinois, Inc. v. Magner*, 494 N.E.2d 785 (Ill. App. 1986).

14. Duties and Liabilities of Principal to Agent

The principal must perform the contract, compensate the agent for services, make reimbursement for proper expenditures and, under certain circumstances, must indemnify the agent for loss.

(A) EMPLOYMENT ACCORDING TO TERMS OF CONTRACT. When the contract is for a specified time, the principal is obligated to permit the agent to act as agent for the term of the contract. Exceptions are made for just cause or contract provisions that permit the principal to terminate the agency sooner. If the principal gives the agent an exclusive right to act in that capacity, the principal cannot give anyone else the authority to act as agent, nor may the principal do the act to which the exclusive agent's authority relates. **For Example,** if Jill Baker gives Brett Stamos the exclusive right for six months to sell her house, she cannot give another real estate agent the right to sell it during the six-month period or undertake to sell the house herself. If the principal or another agent sells the house, the exclusive agent is entitled to full compensation just as though the act had been performed by the exclusive agent.

(B) COMPENSATION. The principal must pay the agent the agreed compensation.[20] If the parties have not fixed the amount of the compensation by their agreement but intended that the agent should be paid, the agent may recover the customary compensation for such services. If there is no established compensation, the agent may recover the reasonable value of the services rendered.

(1) Repeating Transactions.

In certain industries, third persons make repeated transactions with the principal. In these cases, the agent who made the original contract with the third person commonly receives a certain compensation or percentage of commissions on all subsequent renewal or additional contracts. In the insurance business, for example, the insurance agent obtaining the policyholder for the insurer receives a substantial portion of the first year's premiums and then receives a smaller percentage of the premiums paid by the policyholder in subsequent years.

(2) Postagency Transactions.

An agent is not ordinarily entitled to compensation in connection with transactions, such as sales or renewals of insurance policies, occurring after the termination of the agency even if the postagency transactions are the result of the agent's former activities. However, if the parties' employment contract calls for such compensation, it must be paid. **For Example,** real estate agent Laura McLane's contract called for her to receive $1.50 for every square foot the Atlanta Committee for the Olympic Games, Inc. (ACOG), leased at an Atlanta building; and even though she had been terminated at the time ACOG executed a lease amendment for 164,412 additional square feet, she was contractually entitled to a $246,618 commission.[21]

---

[20] *American Chocolates, Inc. v. Mascot Pecan Co., Inc.,* 592 So.2d 93 (Miss. 1992).
[21] *McLane v. Atlanta Market Center Management Co.,* 486 S.E.2d 30 (Ga. App. 1997).

E. TERMINATION OF AGENCY

An agency may be terminated by the act of one or both of the parties to the agency agreement or by operation of law. When the authority of an agent is terminated, the agent loses all right to act for the principal.

15. Termination by Act of Parties

The duration of the agency relationship is commonly stated in the contract creating the relationship. In most cases, either party has the power to terminate the agency relationship at any time. However, the terminating party may be liable for damages to the other if the termination is in violation of the agency contract.

When a principal terminates an agent's authority, it is not effective until the agent receives the notice. Because a known agent will have the appearance of still being an agent, notice must be given to third persons of the termination, and the agent may have the power to bind the principal and third persons until this notice is given.

16. Termination by Operation of Law

The agency relationship is a personal one, and anything that renders one of the parties incapable of performing will result in the termination of the relationship by operation of law. The death of either the principal or the agent ordinarily terminates the authority of an agent automatically even if the death is unknown to the other.[22]

An agency is also terminated by operation of law on the (1) insanity of the principal or agent, (2) bankruptcy of the principal or agent, (3) impossibility of performance, such as the destruction of the subject matter, or (4) when the country of the principal is at war with that of the agent.

CASE SUMMARY

Missing Out by Minutes

FACTS: William Moore, a fire chief for the city of San Francisco, suffered severe head injuries in a fall while fighting a fire. Moore sued the building owner, Lera, for negligence. The attorneys for the parties held a conference and reached a settlement at 5:15 P.M. Unknown to them, Moore had died at 4:50 P.M. on that day. Was the settlement agreement binding?

DECISION: No. The death of either the principal or the agent terminates the agency. Thus, the death of a client terminates the authority of his agent to act on his behalf. Because Moore died at 4:50 P.M., his attorney no longer had authority to act on his behalf, and the settlement was not enforceable. [***Moore v. Lera Development Inc.*, 274 Cal. Rptr. 658 (Cal. App. 1990)**]

---

[22] *New York Life Ins. Co. v. Estate of Haelen*, 521 N.Y.S.2d 970 (N.Y. Civ. Ct.1987).

17. Disability of the Principal under the UDPAA

The Uniform Durable Power of Attorney Act (UDPAA) permits the creation of an agency by specifying that "this power of attorney shall not be affected by subsequent disability or incapacity of the principal." Alternatively, the UDPAA permits the agency to come into existence upon the disability or incapacity of the principal. For this to be effective, the principal must designate the attorney in fact in writing. The writing must contain words showing the intent of the principal that the authority conferred shall continue notwithstanding the disability or incapacity of the principal. The UDPAA, which has been adopted by most states,[23] changes the common law and the general rule that insanity of the principal terminates the agent's authority to act for the principal. Society today recognizes that it may be in the best interest of a principal and good for the business environment for a principal to designate another as an attorney in fact to act for the principal when the principal becomes incapacitated.[24] It may be prudent to grant durable powers of attorney to different persons for property matters and for health care decisions.

Durable powers of attorney grant only those powers that are specified in the instrument. A durable power of attorney may be terminated by revocation by a competent principal and by the death of the principal.

CASE SUMMARY

Broad Powers ... But There Is a Limit, Lucille

FACTS: On May 31, 2000, Thomas Graham made his niece Lucille Morrison his attorney in fact by executing a durable power of attorney. It was notarized and filed at the Registry of Deeds. The power of attorney granted Lucille broad powers and discretion in Graham's affairs. However, it did not contain express authority to make gifts. On October 26, 2000, Lucille conveyed 11.92 acres of property valued at between $400,000 and $700,000 to herself based on consideration of services rendered to the principal, Thomas Graham. On June 5, 2001, Lucille, as attorney in fact for Graham, conveyed Graham's house in Charlotte to her son Ladd Morrison. On June 20, 2001, she conveyed Graham's Oakview Terrace property to her brother John Hallman for $3,000 to pay for an attorney to defend Graham in a competency proceeding. Thomas Graham died on August 7, 2001, and his estate sued to set aside the deeds, alleging Lucille's breach of fiduciary duties. After a judgment for the defendants, the estate appealed.

DECISION: Judgment for the estate regarding the 11.92 acre parcel of land Lucille conveyed to herself. When an attorney in fact conveys property to herself based on consideration of services rendered to the principal, the consideration must reflect a fair and reasonable price when compared with the market value of the property. There was no testimony regarding the value of Lucille's services compared with the value of the real property. The deed must be set aside. The conveyance of Graham's home to Ladd Morrison was a gift that was not authorized by her power

---

[23] The Uniform Durable Power of Attorney Act has been adopted in some fashion in all states except Connecticut, Florida, Georgia, Illinois, Indiana, Kansas, Louisiana, and Missouri.

[24] The Uniform Probate Code and the Uniform Durable Power of Attorney Act provide for the coexistence of durable powers and guardians or conservators. These acts allow the attorney in fact to continue to manage the principal's financial affairs while the court-appointed fiduciary takes the place of the principal in overseeing the actions of the attorney in fact. See *Rice v. Flood,* 768 S.W.2d 57 (Ky. 1989).

CASE SUMMARY

Continued

of attorney and must be set aside. Lucille had authority to sell the principal's property to John Hallman to obtain funds to pay an attorney to represent the principal. The estate's claim of conversion regarding this sale was denied. [***Estate of Graham v. Morrison***, **607 S.E.2d 295 (N.C. App. 2005)**]

18. Termination of Agency Coupled with an Interest

An agency coupled with an interest is an exception to the general rule as to the termination of an agency. Such an agency cannot be revoked by the principal before the expiration of the interest. It is not terminated by the death or insanity of either the principal or the agent.

19. Protection of Agent from Termination of Authority

The modern world of business has developed several methods of protecting an agent from the termination of authority for any reason.[25]

These methods include the use of an exclusive agency contract, a secured transaction, an escrow deposit, a standby letter of agreement, or a guarantee agreement.

20. Effect of Termination of Authority

If the principal revokes the agency, the authority to act for the principal is not terminated until the agent receives notice of revocation. As between the principal and the agent, the right of the agent to bind the principal to third persons generally ends immediately upon the termination of the agent's authority. This termination is effective without giving notice to third persons.

When the agency is terminated by the act of the principal, notice must be given to third persons. If this notice is not given, the agent may have the power to make contracts that will bind the principal and third persons. This rule is predicated on the theory that a known agent will have the appearance of still being the agent unless notice to the contrary is given to third persons.[26] **For Example,** Seltzer owns property in Boca Raton that he uses for the month of February and leases the remainder of the year. O'Neil has been Seltzer's rental agent for the past seven years, renting to individuals like Ed Tucker under a power of attorney that gives him authority to lease the property for set seasonal and off-season rates.

---

[25] These methods generally replace the concept of an agency coupled with an interest because of the greater protection given to the agent. Typically, the rights of the agent under these modern devices cannot be defeated by the principal, by operation of law, or by claims of other creditors.

[26] See *Stout Street Funding, LLC v. Johnson*, 2012 WL 1994800 (E.D. Pa. June 1, 2012). TRGC terminated its contract with Mabstract to serve as TRGC's closing agent on July 12, 2010, and obtained a court injunction barring Mabstract from engaging in any business on behalf of TRGC on July 15. Stout asserts that it had no actual notice of Mabstract's termination nor were there any red flags when it transmitted $480,000 into an escrow account held by Mabstract for a July 19 real estate transaction, which funds were misappropriated by Mabstract. It asserts that apparent authority lasts until a third party has actual notice of an agent's termination or until the third party has enough information to put that individual on inquiry.

O'Neil's right to bind Seltzer on a rental agreement ended when Seltzer faxed O'Neil a revocation of the power of attorney on March 1. A rental contract with Ed Tucker signed by O'Neil on behalf of Seltzer on March 2 will bind Seltzer, however, because O'Neil still appeared to be Seltzer's agent and Tucker had no notice to the contrary.

When the law requires giving notice in order to end the power of the agent to bind the principal, individual notice must be given or mailed to all persons who had prior dealings with the agent. In addition, notice to the general public can be given by publishing in a newspaper of general circulation in the affected geographic area a statement that the agency has been terminated.

If a notice is actually received, the power of the agent is terminated without regard to whether the method of giving notice was proper. Conversely, if proper notice is given, it is immaterial that it does not actually come to the attention of the party notified. Thus, a member of the general public cannot claim that the principal is bound on the ground that the third person did not see the newspaper notice stating that the agent's authority had been terminated.

MAKE THE CONNECTION

SUMMARY

An agency relationship is created by an express or implied agreement by which one person, the agent, is authorized to make contracts with third persons on behalf of, and subject to, the control of another person, the principal. An agent differs from an independent contractor in that the principal, who controls the acts of an agent, does not have control over the details of performance of work by the independent contractor. Likewise, an independent contractor does not have authority to act on behalf of the other contracting party.

A special agent is authorized by the principal to handle a specific business transaction. A general agent is authorized by the principal to transact all business affairs of the principal at a certain place. A universal agent is authorized to perform all acts that can be lawfully delegated to a representative.

The usual method of creating an agency is by express authorization. However, an agency relationship may be found to exist when the principal causes or permits a third person to reasonably believe that an agency relationship exists. In such a case, the "agent" appears to be authorized and is said to have apparent authority.

An unauthorized transaction by an agent for a principal may be ratified by the principal.

An agent acting with authority has the power to bind the principal. The scope of an agent's authority may be determined from the express words of the principal to the agent; this is called express authority. An agent has incidental authority to perform any act reasonably necessary to execute the authority given the agent. An agent's authority may be implied so as to enable the agent to perform any act in accordance with the general customs or usages in a business or an industry. This authority is often referred to as customary authority.

The effect of a proper exercise of authority by an agent is to bind the principal and third person to a contract. The agent, not being a party to the contract, is not liable in any respect under the contract. A third person dealing with a person claiming to be an agent has a duty to ascertain the extent of the agent's authority and a duty to take notice of any acts that are clearly adverse to the principal's interests. The third person cannot claim that apparent authority existed when that person has notice that the agent's conduct is adverse to the interests of the principal. A third person who has knowledge of limitations on an agent's authority is bound by those limitations. A third person is not bound by secret limitations.

While the agency relationship exists, the agent owes the principal the duties of (1) being loyal, (2) obeying all lawful instructions, (3) exercising reasonable care, (4) accounting for all property or money belonging to the principal, and (5) informing the principal of all facts relating to the agency that are relevant to the principal's interests. An agency relationship can be terminated by act of either the principal or the agent. However, the terminating party may be liable for damages to the other if the termination is in violation of the agency contract.

Because a known agent will have the appearance of still being an agent, notice must be given to third persons of the termination, and the agent may have the power to bind the principal and third persons until this notice is given.

An agency is terminated by operation of law upon (1) the death of the principal or agent, (2) insanity of the principal or agent, (3) bankruptcy of the principal or agent, (4) impossibility of performance, caused, for example, by the destruction of the subject matter, or (5) war.

In states that have adopted the Uniform Durable Power of Attorney Act (UDPAA), an agency may be created that is not affected by subsequent disability or incapacity of the principal. In UDPAA states, the agency may also come into existence upon the "disability or incapacity of the principal." The designation of an attorney in fact under the UDPAA must be in writing.

LEARNING OUTCOMES

After studying this chapter, you should be able to clearly explain:

A. Nature of the Agency Relationship

L0.1 Explain the difference between an agent and an independent contractor
See the Ned and Tracy Seizer example and the "right to control" test, beginning on p. 800.

B. Creating the Agency

L0.2 Explain three methods of creating an agency relationship
See the discussion on the usual method of creating an agency (which is by express authorization), p. 803.
See the *Taylor* case where actual authority to perform some tasks created apparent authority to perform other related tasks, pp. 803–804.
See the agency by ratification example of James and Calvin Reiner on p. 805.

C. Agent's Authority

L0.3 Recognize that third persons who deal with an agent are required to take notice of acts contrary to the interests of the principal

See the example of the Fire Company that failed to verify with the principal an agent's authority to receive a prepayment check of $55,000 made out in the agent's name, p. 808.

D. Duties and Liabilities Of Principal and Agent

L0.4 List and explain the duties an agent owes the principal
See the discussion concerning an agent's duty of loyalty, obedience, reasonable care, accounting, and information beginning on p. 809.

E. Termination of Agency

L0.5 Explain how the Uniform Durable Power of Attorney Act changes the common law rule on incapacity of the principal
See the *Estate of Graham* case on the limits of a durable power of attorney, pp. 814–815.

KEY TERMS

agency	general agent	principal
agent	incidental authority	special agent
apparent authority	independent contractor	universal agent
attorney in fact	interest in the authority	
customary authority	interest in the subject matter	
express authorization	power of attorney	

QUESTIONS AND CASE PROBLEMS

1. How does an agent differ from an independent contractor?

2. Compare authorization of an agent by (a) appointment and (b) ratification.

3. Ernest A. Kotsch executed a durable power of attorney when he was 85 years old, giving his son, Ernie, the power to manage and sell his real estate and personal property "and to do all acts necessary for maintaining and caring for [the father] during his lifetime." Thereafter, Kotsch began "keeping company" with a widow, Margaret Gradl. Ernie believed that the widow was attempting to alienate his father from him, and he observed that she was exerting a great deal of influence over his father. Acting under the durable power of attorney and without informing his father, Ernie created the "Kotsch Family Irrevocable Trust," to which he transferred $700,000, the bulk of his father's liquid assets, with the father as grantor and initial beneficiary and Ernie's three children as additional beneficiaries. Ernie named himself trustee. His father sued to avoid the trust. Ernie defended his action on the ground that he had authority to create the trust under the durable power of attorney. Decide. [*Kotsch v. Kotsch*, 608 So.2d 879 (Fla. App.)]

4. Ken Jones, the number-one-ranked prizefighter in his weight class, signed a two-year contract with Howard Stayword. The contract obligated Stayword to represent and promote Jones in all business and professional matters, including the arrangement of fights. For these services, Jones was to pay Stayword 10 percent of gross earnings. After a year, when Stayword proved unsuccessful in arranging a title match with the champion,

Jones fired Stayword. During the following year, Jones earned $4 million. Stayword sued Jones for $400,000. Jones defended himself on the basis that a principal has the absolute power at any time to terminate an agency relationship by discharging the agent, so he was not liable to Stayword. Was Jones correct?

5. Paul Strich did business as an optician in Duluth, Minnesota. Paul used only the products of the Plymouth Optical Co., a national manufacturer of optical products and supplies with numerous retail outlets and some franchise arrangements in areas other than Duluth. To increase business, Paul renovated his office and changed the sign on it to read "Plymouth Optical Co." Paul did business this way for more than three years—advertised under that name, paid bills with checks bearing the name of Plymouth Optical Co., and listed himself in the telephone and city directories by that name. Plymouth immediately became aware of what Paul was doing. However, because Paul used only Plymouth products and Plymouth did not have a franchise in Duluth, it saw no advantage at that time in prohibiting Paul from using the name and losing him as a customer. Paul contracted with the *Duluth Tribune* for advertising, making the contract in the name of Plymouth Optical Co. When the advertising bill was not paid, the *Duluth Tribune* sued Plymouth Optical Co. for payment. Plymouth's defense was that it never authorized Paul to do business under the name, nor authorized him to make a contract with the newspaper. Decide.

6. Record owned a farm that was managed by his agent, Berry, who lived on the farm. Berry hired

Wagner to bale the hay and told him to bill Record for this work. Wagner did so and was paid by Record. By the summer of the following year, the agency had been terminated by Record, but Berry remained in possession as tenant of the farm and nothing appeared changed. Late in the summer, Berry asked Wagner to bale the hay as he had done the previous year and bill Record for the work. He did so, but Record refused to pay on the ground that Berry was not then his agent. Wagner sued him. Decide. [*Record v. Wagner*, 128 A.2d 921 (N.H.)]

7. Gilbert Church owned Church Farms, Inc., in Manteno, Illinois. Church advertised its well-bred stallion Imperial Guard for breeding rights at $50,000, directing all inquiries to "Herb Bagley, Manager." Herb Bagley lived at Church Farms and was the only person available to visitors. Vern Lundberg answered the ad, and after discussions in which Bagley stated that Imperial Guard would remain in Illinois for at least a two-year period, Lundberg and Bagley executed a two-year breeding rights contract. The contract was signed by Lundberg and by Bagley as "Church Farms, Inc., H. Bagley, Mgr." When Gil Church moved Imperial Guard to Oklahoma prior to the second year of the contract, Lundberg brought suit for breach of contract. Church testified that Bagley had no authority to sign contracts for Church Farms. Decide. [*Lundberg v. Church Farms, Inc.*, 502 N.E.2d 806 (Ill.)]

8. The Holzmans signed an exclusive listing agreement with the Blum real estate brokerage firm. The contract provided that the Holzmans had an obligation to pay a commission "if they enter into a written agreement to sell the property to any person during the term of this exclusive listing agreement." The Holzmans entered into a written agreement to sell their house for $715,000 to the Noravians. On the advice of their attorney, the Holzmans included a default provision in this contract stating that in the event of default by the Holzmans, the Noravians' only remedy would be a refund of their deposit. Subsequently, the Sterns offered $850,000 for the property and the Holzmans

canceled their contract with the Noravians and returned their deposit. After the exclusive listing period expired, the Holzmans executed a contract to sell their property to the Sterns at the offered price of $850,000—with the contract calling for the Holzmans to pay half the real estate fee to Blum and half to a cooperating broker. Blum was paid this fee of $21,500. Blum brought suit against the Holzmans seeking the full commission for the Noravian contract under the exclusive listing agreement. Did Blum have a legal obligation or ethical duty to advise the Holzmans when considering the Sterns' offer that he believed they were obligated to him for the full commission under the Novarian contract? Decide. [*Holzman v. Blum*, 726 A.2d 818 (Md. App.)]

9. Tillie Flinn properly executed a durable power of attorney designating her nephew James C. Flanders and/or Martha E. Flanders, his wife, as her attorney in fact. Seven months later, Martha Flanders went to the Capitol Federal Savings and Loan Association office. She had the durable power of attorney instrument, five certificates of deposit, and a hand-printed letter identifying Martha as an attorney in fact and stating that Tillie wished to cash her five CDs that Martha had with her. At approximately 10:31 A.M., five checks were given to Martha in the aggregate amount of $135,791.34, representing the funds in the five CDs less penalties for early withdrawal. Some of the checks were drawn to the order of Martha individually and some to the order of James and Martha, as individuals. Tillie was found dead of heart disease later that day. The time of death stated on her death certificate was 11:30 A.M. The Flanderses spent the money on themselves. Bank IV, as administrator of Tillie's estate, sued Capitol Federal to recover the amount of the funds paid to the Flanderses. It contended that Capitol Federal breached its duty to investigate before issuing the checks. Capitol Federal contended that it did all that it had a duty to do. Decide. [*Bank IV v. Capitol Federal Savings and Loan Ass'n*, 828 P.2d 355 (Kan.)]

10. Lew owns a store on Canal Street in New Orleans. He paid a person named Mike and

other individuals commissions for customers brought into the store. Lew testified that he had known Mike for less than a week. Boulos and Durso, partners in a wholesale jewelry business, were visiting New Orleans on a business trip when Mike brought them into the store to buy a stereo. While Durso finalized the stereo transaction with the store's manager, Boulos and Mike negotiated to buy 2 cameras, 3 videos, and 20 gold Dupont lighters. Unknown to the store's manager, Mike was given $8,250 in cash and was to deliver the merchandise later that evening to the Marriott Hotel, where Boulos and Durso were staying. Mike gave a receipt for the cash, but it showed no sales tax or indication that the goods were to be delivered. Boulos testified that he believed Mike was the store owner. Mike never delivered the merchandise and disappeared. Boulos and Durso contended that Lew is liable for the acts of his agent, Mike. Lew denied that Mike was his agent, and the testimony showed that Mike had no actual authority to make a sale, to use a cash register, or even to go behind a sales counter. What ethical principle applies to the conduct of Boulos and Durso? Decide. [*Boulos v. Morrison*, 503 So.2d 1(La.)]

11. Martha Christiansen owns women's apparel stores bearing her name in New Seabury, Massachusetts; Lake Placid, New York; Palm Beach, Florida; and Palm Springs, California. At a meeting with her four store managers, she discussed styles she thought appropriate for the forthcoming season, advised them as always to use their best judgment in the goods they purchased for each of their respective stores, and cautioned "but no blue jeans." Later, Jane Farley, the manager of the Lake Placid store, purchased a line of high-quality blue denim outfits (designer jeans with jacket and vest options) from Women's Wear, Inc., for the summer season. The outfits did not sell. Martha refused to pay for them, contending that she had told all of her managers "no blue jeans" and that if it came to a lawsuit, she would fly in three managers to testify that Jane Farley had absolutely no authority to purchase denim outfits and was, in fact, expressly forbidden to do so. Women's Wear sued Martha, and the three managers testified for her. Is the fact that Martha had explicitly forbidden Farley to purchase the outfits in question sufficient to protect her from liability for the purchases made by Farley?

12. Fred Schilling, the president and administrator of Florence General Hospital, made a contract, dated August 16, 1989, on behalf of the hospital with CMK Associates to transfer the capacity to utilize 25 beds from the hospital to the Faith Nursing Home. Schilling, on behalf of the hospital, had previously made a contract with CMK Associates on May 4, 1987. Schilling had been specifically authorized by the hospital board to make the 1987 contract. The hospital refused to honor the 1989 contract because the board had not authorized it. CMK contended that Schilling had apparent authority to bind the hospital because he was president and administrator of the hospital and he had been the person who negotiated and signed a contract with CMK in 1987. Thus, according to CMK, the hospital had held out Schilling as having apparent authority to make the contract. The hospital disagreed. Decide. [*Pee Dee Nursing Home v. Florence General Hospital*, 419 S.E.2d 843 (S.C. App.)]

13. Barbara Fox was the agent of Burt Hollander, a well-known athlete. She discovered that Tom Lanceford owned a 1957 Chevrolet convertible, which had been stored in a garage for the past 15 years. After demonstrating to Lanceford that she was the authorized agent of Hollander, she made a contract with Lanceford on behalf of Hollander to purchase the Chevrolet. Lanceford later discovered that the car was much more valuable than he originally believed, and he refused to deliver the car to Fox. Fox sued Lanceford for breach of contract. Can she recover?

14. Francis Gagnon, an elderly gentleman, signed a power of attorney authorizing his daughter, Joan, "to sell any of my real estate and to execute any document needed to carry out the sale... and to add property to a trust of which I am grantor or beneficiary." This power was given in case Gagnon was not available to take care of

matters personally because he was traveling. When Joan learned that Gagnon intended to sell his Shelburne property to Cosby for $750,000, she created an irrevocable trust naming Gagnon as beneficiary and herself as trustee. Acting then on the basis of the authority set forth in the power of attorney, she conveyed the Shelburne property to herself as trustee of the irrevocable trust, thus blocking the sale to Cosby. When Gagnon learned of this, he demanded that Joan return the Shelburne property to him, but she refused, saying she had acted within the authority set forth in the power of attorney. Did Joan violate any duty owed to Gagnon? Must she reconvey the property to Gagnon? [*Gagnon v. Coombs*, 654 N.E.2d 54 (Mass. App.)]

15. Daniels and Julian were employed by the Marriott Hotel in New Orleans and were close personal friends. One day after work, Daniels and Julian went to Werlein's music store to open a credit account. Julian, with Daniels's authorization and in her presence, applied for credit using Daniels's name and credit history. Later, Julian went to Werlein's without Daniels and charged the purchase of a television set to Daniels's account, executing a retail installment contract by signing Daniels's name. Daniels saw the new television in Julian's home and was informed that it was charged to the Werlein's account. Daniels told Julian to continue making payments. When Werlein's credit manager first contacted Daniels to inform her that her account was delinquent, she claimed that a money order for the television was in the mail. On the second call, she asked for a "payment balance." Some four months after the purchase, she informed Werlein's that she had not authorized the purchase of the television nor ratified the purchase. Werlein's sued Daniels for the unpaid balance. Decide. [*Philip Werlein, Ltd. v. Daniels*, 536 So.2d 722 (La. App.)]

CPA QUESTIONS

1. Generally, an agency relationship is terminated by operation of law in all of the following situations except the:

   a. Principal's death

   b. Principal's incapacity

   c. Agent's renunciation of the agency

   d. Agent's failure to acquire a necessary business license

2. Able, on behalf of Pix Corp., entered into a contract with Sky Corp., by which Sky agreed to sell computer equipment to Pix. Able disclosed to Sky that she was acting on behalf of Pix. However, Able had exceeded her actual authority by entering into the contract with Sky. If Pix wishes to ratify the contract with Sky, which of the following statements is correct?

   a. Pix must notify Sky that Pix intends to ratify the contract.

   b. Able must have acted reasonably and in Pix's best interest.

   c. Able must be a general agent of Pix.

   d. Pix must have knowledge of all material facts relating to the contract at the time it is ratified.

3. Which of the following actions requires an agent for a corporation to have a written agency agreement?

   a. Purchasing office supplies for the principal's business

   b. Purchasing an interest in undeveloped land for the principal

   c. Hiring an independent general contractor to renovate the principal's office building

   d. Retaining an attorney to collect a business debt owed the principal

4. Simmons, an agent for Jensen, has the express authority to sell Jensen's goods. Simmons also has the express authority to grant discounts of up to 5 percent of list price. Simmons sold Hemple a 10 percent discount. Hemple had not

previously dealt with either Simmons or Jensen. Which of the following courses of action may Jensen properly take?

a. Seek to void the sale to Hemple

b. Seek recovery of $50 from Hemple only

c. Seek recovery of $50 from Simmons only

d. Seek recovery of $50 from either Hemple or Simmons

5. Ogden Corp. hired Thorp as a sales representative for nine months at a salary of $3,000 per month plus 4 percent of sales. Which of the following statements is correct?

a. Thorp is obligated to act solely in Ogden's interest in matters concerning Ogden's business.

b. The agreement between Ogden and Thorp formed an agency coupled with an interest.

c. Ogden does not have the power to dismiss Thorp during the nine-month period without cause.

d. The agreement between Ogden and Thorp is not enforceable unless it is in writing and signed by Thorp.

6. Frost's accountant and business manager has the authority to:

a. Mortgage Frost's business property

b. Obtain bank loans for Frost

c. Insure Frost's property against fire loss

d. Sell Frost's business

Appendix 1

In order to determine what the law on a particular question or issue is, it may be necessary to examine (1) compilations of constitutions, treaties, statutes, executive orders, proclamations, and administrative regulations; (2) reports of state and federal court decisions; (3) digests of opinions; (4) treatises on the law; and (5) loose-leaf services. These sources can be either researched traditionally or using fee and/or non-fee-based computerized legal research, accessed through the World Wide Web.

A. COMPILATIONS

In the consideration of a legal problem in business it is necessary to determine whether the matter is affected or controlled by a constitution, national or state; by a national treaty; by an Act of Congress, a state legislature, or a city ordinance; by a decree or proclamation of the President of the United States, a governor, or a mayor; or by a regulation of a federal, state, or local administrative agency.

Each body or person that makes laws, regulations, or ordinances usually compiles and publishes at the end of each year or session all of the matter that it has adopted. In addition to the periodical or annual volumes, it is common to compile all the treaties, statutes, regulations, or ordinances in separate volumes. To illustrate, the federal Anti-Injunction Act may be cited as the Act of March 23, 1932, 47 Stat. 70, 29 U.S.C. § 101 et seq. This means that this law was enacted on March 23, 1932, and that it can be found at page 70 in Volume 47 of the reports that contain all of the statutes adopted by the Congress.

The second part of the citation, 29 U.S.C. § 101 et seq., means that in the collection of all of the federal statutes, which is known as the United States Code, the full text of the statute can be found in the sections of the 29th title beginning with Section 101.

B. COURT DECISIONS

For complicated or important legal cases or when an appeal is to be taken, a court will generally write an opinion, which explains why the court made the decision. Appellate courts as a rule write opinions. The great majority of these decisions, particularly in the case of the appellate courts, are collected and printed. In order to avoid confusion, the opinions of each court are ordinarily printed in a separate set of reports, either by official reporters or private publishers.

In the reference "*Pennoyer v. Neff*, 95 U.S. 714, 24 L. Ed. 565," the first part states the names of the parties. It does not necessarily tell who was the plaintiff and who was the defendant. When an action is begun in a lower court, the first name is that of the plaintiff and the second name that of the defendant. When the case is appealed, generally the name of the person taking the appeal appears on the records of the higher court as the first one and that of the adverse party as the second. Sometimes, therefore, the original order of the names of the parties is reversed.

The balance of the reference consists of two citations. The first citation, 95 U.S. 714, means that the opinion which the court filed in the case of *Pennoyer v. Neff* may be found on page 714 of the 95th volume of a series of books in which are printed officially the opinions of the United States Supreme Court. Sometimes the same opinion is printed in two different sets of volumes. In the example, 24 L.Ed. 565 means that in the 24th volume of another set of books, called Lawyer's Edition, of the United States Supreme Court Reports, the same opinion begins on page 565.

In opinions by a state court there may also be two citations, as in the case of *Morrow v. Corbin*, 122 Tex. 553, 62 S.W.2d 641. This means that the opinion in the lawsuit between Morrow and Corbin may be found in the 122nd volume of the reports of the highest court of Texas, beginning on page 553; and also in Volume 62 of the Southwestern Reporter, Second Series, at page 641.

The West Publishing Company publishes a set of sectional reporters covering the entire United States. They are called "sectional" because each reporter, instead of being limited to a particular court or a particular state, covers the decisions of the courts of a particular section of the country. Thus the decisions of the courts of Arkansas, Kentucky, Missouri, Tennessee, and Texas are printed by the West Publishing company as a group in a sectional reporter called the Southwestern Reporter.[1] Because of the large number of decisions involved, generally only the opinions of the state appellate courts are printed. A number of states[2] have discontinued publication of the opinions of their courts, and those opinions are now found only in the West reporters.

The reason for the "Second Series" in the Southwestern citation is that when there were 300 volumes in the original series, instead of calling the next volume 301, the publisher called it Volume 1, Second Series. Thus 62 S. W.2d Series really means the 362nd volume of the Southwestern Reporter. Six to eight volumes appear in a year for each geographic section.

In addition to these state reporters, the West Publishing Company publishes a Federal Supplement, which primarily reports the opinions of the Federal District Courts; the Federal Reporter, which primarily reports the decisions of the United States Courts of Appeals; and the Supreme Court Reporter, which reports the decisions of the United States Supreme Court. The Supreme Court decisions are also reported in a separate set called the Lawyers' Edition, published by the Lawyers Cooperative Publishing Company.

The reports published by the West Publishing Company and Lawyers Cooperative Publishing Company are unofficial reports, while those bearing the name or abbreviation of the United States or of a state, such as "95 U.S. 714" or "122 Tex. 553" are official reports. This means that in the case of the latter, the particular court, such as the United States Supreme Court, has officially authorized that its decisions be printed and that by federal statute such official printing is made. In the case of the unofficial reporters, the publisher prints the decisions of a court on its own initiative. Such opinions are part of the public domain and not subject to any copyright or similar restriction.

C. Digests of Opinions

The reports of court decisions are useful only if one has the citation, that is, the name and volume number of the book and the page number of the opinion one is seeking. For this reason, digests of the decisions have been prepared. These digests organize the entire field of law under major headings, which are then arranged in alphabetical order. Under each heading, such as "Contracts," the subject is divided into the different questions that can arise with respect to that field. A master outline is thus created on the subject. This outline includes short paragraphs describing what each case holds and giving its citation.

D. Treatises and Restatements

Very helpful in finding a case or a statute are the treatises on the law. These may be special books, each written by an author on a particular subject, such as Williston on Contracts, Bogert on Trusts, Fletcher on Corporations, or they may be general encyclopedias, as in the case of *American Jurisprudence, American Jurisprudence, Second,* and *Corpus Juris Secundum.*

Another type of treatise is found in the restatements of the law prepared by the American Law Institute. Each restatement consists of one or more volumes devoted to a particular phase of the law, such as the Restatement of the Law of Contracts, Restatement of the Law of Agency, and Restatement of the Law of Property. In each restatement, the American Law Institute, acting through special committees of judges, lawyers, and professors of law, has set forth what the law is; and in many areas where there is no law or the present rule is regarded as unsatisfactory, the restatement specifies what the Institute deems to be the desirable rule.

E. Loose-Leaf Services

A number of private publishers, notably Commerce Clearing House and Prentice-Hall, publish loose-leaf books devoted to particular branches of the law. Periodically, the publisher sends to the purchaser a number of pages that set forth any decision, regulation, or statute made or adopted since the prior set of pages was prepared. Such services are unofficial.

F. Computerized Legal Research

National and local computer services are providing constantly widening assistance for legal research. The database in such a system may be opinions, statutes, or administrative regulations stored word for word; or the later history of a particular case giving its full citation and showing whether the case has been followed by other courts; or the text of forms and documents. By means of a

---

[1] The sectional reporters are: Atlantic—A. (Connecticut, Delaware, District of Columbia, Maine, Maryland, New Hampshire, New Jersey, Pennsylvania, Rhode Island, Vermont); Northeastern—N.E. (Illinois, Indiana, Massachusetts, New York, Ohio); N.W. (Iowa, Michigan, Minnesota, Nebraska, North Dakota, South Dakota, Wisconsin); Pacific—P. (Alaska, Arizona, California, Colorado, Hawaii, Idaho, Kansas, Montana, Nevada, New Mexico, Oklahoma, Oregon, Utah, Washington, Wyoming); Southeastern—S.E. (Georgia, North Carolina, South Carolina, Virginia, West Virginia); Southwestern— S.W. (Arkansas, Kentucky, Missouri, Tennessee, Texas); and Southern—So. (Alabama, Florida, Louisiana, Mississippi). There is also a special New York State reporter known as the New York Supplement and a special California State reporter known as the California Reporter.

[2] See, for example, Alaska, Florida, Iowa, Kentucky, Louisiana, Maine, Mississippi, Missouri, North Dakota, Oklahoma, Texas, and Wyoming.

terminal connected to the system, the user can retrieve the legal information at a great saving of time and with the assurance that it is up-to-date.

There are two leading, fee-based systems for computer-aided research. Listed alphabetically, they are LEXIS and WESTLAW.

A specialized service of legal forms for business is provided by Shepard's BUSINESS LAW CASE MANAGEMENT SYSTEM. A monthly fee is required for usage.

Numerous free, private sites offer a lot of legal resources. The federal government offers a variety of case law, regulations, and code enactments, either pending or newly promulgated. To find the most comprehensive source of government-maintained legal information, go to **http://www.house.gov**. The United States Supreme Court has information about both its current term and past terms at **www.supremecourt.gov**. Another website that provides excellent information about current controversies that reach the United States Supreme Court is **www.scotusblog.com**.

State governments provide access to regulations and codes online. As an example, go to the State of California's site, **www.leginfo.legislation.ca.gov**. You can access an array of information about both state and federal government through links at **www.USA.gov**.

We the people of the United States of America, in order to form a more perfect union, establish justice, insure domestic tranquility, provide for the common defense, promote the general welfare, and secure the blessings of liberty to ourselves and our posterity, do ordain and establish this Constitution for the United States of America.

Article I

SECTION 1

All legislative powers herein granted shall be vested in a Congress of the United States, which shall consist of a Senate and House of Representatives.

SECTION 2

1. The House of Representatives shall be composed of members chosen every second year by the people of the several States, and the electors in each State shall have the qualifications requisite for electors of the most numerous branch of the State legislature.

2. No person shall be a representative who shall not have attained to the age of twenty-five years, and been seven years a citizen of the United States, and who shall not, when elected, be an inhabitant of that State in which he shall be chosen.

3. Representatives and direct taxes shall be apportioned among the several States which may be included within this Union, according to their respective numbers, which shall be determined by adding to the whole number of free persons, including those bound to service for a term of years, and excluding Indians not taxed, three fifths of all other persons.[1] The actual enumeration shall be made within three years after the first meeting of the Congress of the United States, and within every subsequent term of ten years, in such manner as they shall by law direct. The number of representatives shall not exceed one for every thirty thousand, but each State shall have at least one representative; and until such enumeration shall be made, the State of New Hampshire shall be entitled to choose three, Massachusetts eight, Rhode Island and Providence Plantations one, Connecticut five, New York six, New Jersey four, Pennsylvania eight, Delaware one, Maryland six, Virginia ten, North Carolina five, South Carolina five, and Georgia three.

4. When vacancies happen in the representation from any State, the executive authority thereof shall issue writs of election to fill such vacancies.

5. The House of Representatives shall choose their speaker and other officers; and shall have the sole power of impeachment.

SECTION 3

1. The Senate of the United States shall be composed of two senators from each State, chosen by the legislature thereof, for six years; and each senator shall have one vote.

2. Immediately after they shall be assembled in consequence of the first election, they shall be divided as equally as may be into three classes. The seats of the senators of the first class shall be vacated at the expiration of the second year, of the second class at the expiration of the fourth year, and of the third class at the expiration of the sixth year, so that one third may be chosen every second year; and if vacancies happen by resignation, or otherwise, during the recess of the legislature of any State, the executive thereof may make temporary appointments until the next meeting of the legislature, which shall then fill such vacancies.[2]

3. No person shall be a senator who shall not have attained to the age of thirty years, and been nine years a citizen of the United States, and who shall not, when elected, be an inhabitant of that State for which he shall be chosen.

4. The Vice President of the United States shall be President of the Senate, but shall have no vote, unless they be equally divided.

5. The Senate shall choose their other officers, and also a president pro tempore, in the absence of the Vice President, or when he shall exercise the office of the President of the United States.

6. The Senate shall have the sole power to try all impeachments. When sitting for that purpose, they shall

[1] See the 14th Amendment.

[2] See the 17th Amendment.

be on oath or affirmation. When the President of the United States is tried, the chief justice shall preside: and no person shall be convicted without the concurrence of two thirds of the members present.

7. Judgment in cases of impeachment shall not extend further than to removal from office, and disqualification to hold and enjoy any office of honor, trust or profit under the United States: but the party convicted shall nevertheless be liable and subject to indictment, trial, judgment and punishment, according to law.

SECTION 4

1. The times, places, and manner of holding elections for senators and representatives, shall be prescribed in each State by the legislature thereof; but the Congress may at any time by law make or alter such regulations, except as to the places of choosing senators.

2. The Congress shall assemble at least once in every year, and such meeting shall be on the first Monday in December, unless they shall by law appoint a different day.

SECTION 5

1. Each House shall be the judge of the elections, returns and qualifications of its own members, and a majority of each shall constitute a quorum to do business; but a smaller number may adjourn from day to day, and may be authorized to compel the attendance of absent members, in such manner, and under such penalties as each House may provide.

2. Each House may determine the rules of its proceedings, punish its members for disorderly behavior, and, with the concurrence of two thirds, expel a member.

3. Each House shall keep a journal of its proceedings, and from time to time publish the same, excepting such parts as may in their judgment require secrecy; and the yeas and nays of the members of either House on any question shall, at the desire of one fifth of those present, be entered on the journal.

4. Neither House, during the session of Congress, shall, without the consent of the other, adjourn for more than three days, nor to any other place than that in which the two Houses shall be sitting.

SECTION 6

1. The senators and representatives shall receive a compensation for their services, to be ascertained by law, and paid out of the Treasury of the United States. They shall in all cases, except treason, felony, and breach of the peace, be privileged from arrest during their attendance at the session of their respective Houses, and in going to and returning from the same; and for any speech or debate in either House, they shall not be questioned in any other place.

2. No senator or representative shall, during the time for which he was elected, be appointed to any civil office under the authority of the United States, which shall have been created, or the emoluments whereof shall have been increased during such time; and no person holding any office under the United States shall be a member of either House during his continuance in office.

SECTION 7

1. All bills for raising revenue shall originate in the House of Representatives; but the Senate may propose or concur with amendments as on other bills.

2. Every bill which shall have passed the House of Representatives and the Senate, shall, before it becomes a law, be presented to the President of the United States; if he approves he shall sign it, but if not he shall return it, with his objections to that House in which it shall have originated, who shall enter the objections at large on their journal, and proceed to reconsider it. If after such reconsideration two thirds of that House shall agree to pass the bill, it shall be sent, together with the objections, to the other House, by which it shall likewise be reconsidered, and if approved by two thirds of that House, it shall become a law. But in all such cases the votes of both Houses shall be determined by yeas and nays, and the names of the persons voting for and against the bill shall be entered on the journal of each House respectively. If any bill shall not be returned by the President within ten days (Sundays excepted) after it shall have been presented to him, the same shall be a law, in like manner as if he had signed it, unless the Congress by their adjournment prevent its return, in which case it shall not be a law.

3. Every order, resolution, or vote to which the concurrence of the Senate and the House of Representatives may be necessary (except on a question of adjournment) shall be presented to the President of the United States; and before the same shall take effect, shall be approved by him, or being disapproved by him, shall be repassed by two thirds of the Senate and House of Representatives, according to the rules and limitations prescribed in the case of a bill.

SECTION 8

The Congress shall have the power

1. To lay and collect taxes, duties, imposts, and excises, to pay the debts and provide for the common defense and general welfare of the United States; but all duties, imposts, and excises shall be uniform throughout the United States;

2. To borrow money on the credit of the United States;

3. To regulate commerce with foreign nations, and among the several States, and with the Indian tribes;

4. To establish a uniform rule of naturalization, and uniform laws on the subject of bankruptcies throughout the United States;

5. To coin money, regulate the value thereof, and of foreign coin, and fix the standard of weights and measures;

6. To provide for the punishment of counterfeiting the securities and current coin of the United States;

7. To establish post offices and post roads;

8. To promote the progress of science and useful arts, by securing for limited times to authors and inventors the exclusive rights to their respective writings and discoveries;

9. To constitute tribunals inferior to the Supreme Court;

10. To define and punish piracies and felonies committed on the high seas, and offenses against the law of nations;

11. To declare war, grant letters of marque and reprisal, and make rules concerning captures on land and water;

12. To raise and support armies, but no appropriation of money to that use shall be for a longer term than two years;

13. To provide and maintain a navy;

14. To make rules for the government and regulation of the land and naval forces;

15. To provide for calling forth the militia to execute the laws of the Union, suppress insurrections and repel invasions;

16. To provide for organizing, arming, and disciplining the militia, and for governing such part of them as may be employed in the service of the United States, reserving to the States respectively, the appointment of the officers, and the authority of training the militia according to the discipline prescribed by Congress;

17. To exercise exclusive legislation in all cases whatsoever, over such district (not exceeding ten miles square) as may, by cession of particular States, and the acceptance of Congress, become the seat of the government of the United States, and to exercise like authority over all places purchased by the consent of the legislature of the State in which the same shall be, for the erection of forts, magazines, arsenals, dockyards, and other needful buildings; and

18. To make all laws which shall be necessary and proper for carrying into execution the foregoing powers, and all other powers vested by this Constitution in the government of the United States, or in any department or officer thereof.

SECTION 9

1. The migration or importation of such persons as any of the States now existing shall think proper to admit, shall not be prohibited by the Congress prior to the year one thousand eight hundred and eight, but a tax or duty may be imposed on such importation, not exceeding ten dollars for each person.

2. The privilege of the writ of habeas corpus shall not be suspended, unless when in cases of rebellion or invasion the public safety may require it.

3. No bill of attainder or ex post facto law shall be passed.

4. No capitation, or other direct, tax shall be laid, unless in proportion to the census or enumeration hereinbefore directed to be taken.[3]

5. No tax or duty shall be laid on articles exported from any State.

6. No preference shall be given by any regulation of commerce or revenue to the ports of one State over those of another: nor shall vessels bound to, or from, one State be obliged to enter, clear, or pay duties in another.

7. No money shall be drawn from the treasury, but in consequence of appropriations made by law; and a regular statement and account of the receipts and expenditures of all public money shall be published from time to time.

8. No title of nobility shall be granted by the United States: and no person holding any office of profit or trust under them, shall, without the consent of the Congress, accept of any present, emolument, office, or title, of any kind whatever, from any king, prince, or foreign State.

SECTION 10

1. No State shall enter into any treaty, alliance, or confederation; grant letters of marque and reprisal; coin money; emit bills of credit; make anything but gold and silver coin a tender in payment of debts; pass any bill of attainder, ex post facto law, or law impairing the obligation of contracts, or grant any title of nobility.

2. No State shall, without the consent of the Congress, lay any imposts or duties on imports or exports, except what may be absolutely necessary for executing its inspection laws: and the net produce of all duties and imposts laid by any State on imports or exports, shall be for the use of the treasury of the United States; and all such laws shall be subject to the revision and control of the Congress.

3. No State shall, without the consent of the Congress, lay any duty of tonnage, keep troops, or ships of war in time of peace, enter into any agreement or compact with another State, or with a foreign power, or engage in war, unless actually invaded, or in such imminent danger as will not admit of delay.

Article II

SECTION 1

1. The executive power shall be vested in a President of the United States of America. He shall hold his office during the term of four years, and, together with the Vice President, chosen for the same term, be elected as follows:

2. Each State shall appoint, in such manner as the legislature thereof may direct, a number of electors, equal to the whole number of senators and representatives to

---

[3] See the 16th Amendment.

which the State may be entitled in the Congress: but no senator or representative, or person holding an office of trust or profit under the United States, shall be appointed an elector.

The electors shall meet in their respective States, and vote by ballot for two persons, of whom one at least shall not be an inhabitant of the same State with themselves. And they shall make a list of all the persons voted for, and of the number of votes for each; which list they shall sign and certify, and transmit sealed to the seat of the government of the United States, directed to the president of the Senate. The president of the Senate shall, in the presence of the Senate and House of Representatives, open all the certificates, and the votes shall then be counted. The person having the greatest number of votes shall be the President, if such number be a majority of the whole number of electors appointed; and if there be more than one who have such majority, and have an equal number of votes, then the House of Representatives shall immediately choose by ballot one of them for President; and if no person have a majority, then from the five highest on the list the said House shall in like manner choose the President. But in choosing the President, the votes shall be taken by States, the representation from each State having one vote; a quorum for this purpose shall consist of a member or members from two thirds of the States, and a majority of all the States shall be necessary to a choice. In every case, after the choice of the President, the person having the greatest number of votes of the electors shall be the Vice President. But if there should remain two or more who have equal votes, the Senate shall choose from them by ballot the Vice President.[4]

3. The Congress may determine the time of choosing the electors, and the day on which they shall give their votes; which day shall be the same throughout the United States.

4. No person except a natural born citizen, or a citizen of the United States, at the time of the adoption of this Constitution, shall be eligible to the office of President; neither shall any person be eligible to that office who shall not have attained to the age of thirty-five years, and been fourteen years a resident within the United States.

5. In the case of removal of the President from office, or of his death, resignation, or inability to discharge the powers and duties of the said office, the same shall devolve on the Vice President, and the Congress may by law provide for the case of removal, death, resignation, or inability, both of the President and Vice President, declaring what officer shall then act as President, and such officer shall act accordingly, until the disability be removed, or a President shall be elected.

6. The President shall, at stated times, receive for his services a compensation, which shall neither be increased nor diminished during the period for which he shall have been elected, and he shall not receive within that period any other emolument from the United States, or any of them.

7. Before he enter on the execution of his office, he shall take the following oath or affirmation:—"I do solemnly swear (or affirm) that I will faithfully execute the office of President of the United States, and will to the best of my ability, preserve, protect and defend the Constitution of the United States."

SECTION 2

1. The President shall be commander in chief of the army and navy of the United States, and of the militia of the several States, when called into the actual service of the United States; he may require the opinion, in writing, of the principal officer in each of the executive departments, upon any subject relating to the duties of their respective office, and he shall have power to grant reprieves and pardons for offenses against the United States, except in cases of impeachment.

2. He shall have power, by and with the advice and consent of the Senate, to make treaties, provided two thirds of the senators present concur; and he shall nominate, and by and with the advice and consent of the Senate, shall appoint ambassadors, other public ministers and consuls, judges of the Supreme Court, and all other officers of the United States, whose appointments are not herein otherwise provided for, and which shall be established by law: but the Congress may by law vest the appointment of such inferior officers, as they think proper, in the President alone, in the courts of law, or in the heads of departments.

3. The President shall have power to fill up all vacancies that may happen during the recess of the Senate, by granting commissions which shall expire at the end of their next session.

SECTION 3

He shall from time to time give to the Congress information of the state of the Union, and recommend to their consideration such measures as he shall judge necessary and expedient; he may, on extraordinary occasions, convene both Houses, or either of them, and in case of disagreement between them with respect to the time of adjournment, he may adjourn them to such time as he shall think proper; he shall receive ambassadors and other public ministers; he shall take care that the laws be faithfully executed, and shall commission all the officers of the United States.

SECTION 4

The President, Vice President, and all civil officers of the United States, shall be removed from office on impeachment for, and conviction of, treason, bribery, or other high crimes and misdemeanors.

[4] Superseded by the 12th Amendment.

Article III

SECTION 1

The judicial power of the United States shall be vested in one Supreme Court, and in such inferior courts as the Congress may from time to time ordain and establish. The judges, both of the Supreme and inferior courts, shall hold their offices during good behavior, and shall, at stated times, receive for their services, a compensation, which shall not be diminished during their continuance in office.

SECTION 2

1. The judicial power shall extend to all cases, in law and equity, arising under this Constitution, the laws of the United States, and treaties made, or which shall be made, under their authority;—to all cases affecting ambassadors, other public ministers and consuls;—to all cases of admiralty and maritime jurisdiction;—to controversies to which the United States shall be a party;—to controversies between two or more States; between a State and citizens of another State;[5]—between citizens of different States;—between citizens of the same State claiming lands under grants of different States, and between a State, or the citizens thereof, and foreign States, citizens or subjects.

2. In all cases affecting ambassadors, other public ministers and consuls, and those in which a State shall be party, the Supreme Court shall have original jurisdiction. In all the other cases before mentioned, the Supreme Court shall have appellate jurisdiction, both as to law and to fact, with such exceptions, and under such regulations as the Congress shall make.

3. The trial of all crimes, except in cases of impeachment, shall be by jury; and such trial shall be held in the State where the said crimes shall have been committed; but when not committed within any State, the trial shall be at such place or places as the Congress may by law have directed.

SECTION 3

1. Treason against the United States shall consist only in levying war against them, or in adhering to their enemies, giving them aid and comfort. No person shall be convicted of treason unless on the testimony of two witnesses to the same overt act, or on confession in open court.

2. The Congress shall have power to declare the punishment of treason, but no attainder of treason shall work corruption of blood, or forfeiture except during the life of the person attainted.

Article IV

SECTION 1

Full faith and credit shall be given in each State to the public acts, records, and judicial proceedings of every other State. And the Congress may by general laws prescribe the manner in which such acts, records and proceedings shall be proved, and the effect thereof.

SECTION 2

1. The citizens of each State shall be entitled to all privileges and immunities of citizens in the several States.[6]

2. A person charged in any State with treason, felony, or other crime, who shall flee from justice, and be found in another State, shall on demand of the executive authority of the State from which he fled, be delivered up to be removed to the State having jurisdiction of the crime.

3. No person held to service or labor in one State under the laws thereof, escaping into another, shall in consequence of any law or regulation therein, be discharged from such service or labor, but shall be delivered up on claim of the party to whom such service or labor may be due.[7]

SECTION 3

1. New States may be admitted by the Congress into this Union; but no new State shall be formed or erected within the jurisdiction of any other State, nor any State be formed by the junction of two or more States, or parts of States, without the consent of the legislatures of the States concerned as well as of the Congress.

2. The Congress shall have power to dispose of and make all needful rules and regulations respecting the territory or other property belonging to the United States; and nothing in this Constitution shall be so construed as to prejudice any claims of the United States, or of any particular State.

SECTION 4

The United States shall guarantee to every State in this Union a republican form of government, and shall protect each of them against invasion; and on application of the legislature, or of the executive (when the legislature cannot be convened) against domestic violence.

Article V

The Congress, whenever two thirds of both Houses shall deem it necessary, shall propose amendments to this Constitution, or, on the application of the legislature of two thirds of the several States, shall call a convention for

---

[5] See the 11th Amendment.

[6] See the 14th Amendment, Sec. 1.
[7] See the 13th Amendment.

proposing amendments, which in either case, shall be valid to all intents and purposes, as part of this Constitution when ratified by the legislatures of three fourths of the several States, or by conventions in three fourths thereof, as the one or the other mode of ratification may be proposed by the Congress; provided that no amendment which may be made prior to the year one thousand eight hundred and eight shall in any manner affect the first and fourth clauses in the ninth section of the first article; and that no State, without its consent, shall be deprived of its equal suffrage in the Senate.

Article VI

1. All debts contracted and engagements entered into, before the adoption of this Constitution, shall be as valid against the United States under this Constitution, as under the Confederation.[8]

2. This Constitution, and the laws of the United States which shall be made in pursuance thereof; and all treaties made, or which shall be made, under the authority of the United States, shall be the supreme law of the land; and the judges in every State shall be bound thereby, anything in the Constitution or laws of any State to the contrary notwithstanding.

3. The senators and representatives before mentioned, and the members of the several State legislatures, and all executive and judicial officers, both of the United States and of the several States, shall be bound by oath or affirmation to support this Constitution; but no religious test shall ever be required as a qualification to any office or public trust under the United States.

Article VII

The ratification of the conventions of nine States shall be sufficient for the establishment of this Constitution between the States so ratifying the same.

Done in Convention by the unanimous consent of the States present the seventeenth day of September in the year of our Lord one thousand seven hundred and eighty-seven, and of the independence of the United States of America the twelfth. In witness whereof we have hereunto subscribed our names.

A. AMENDMENTS

First Ten Amendments passed by Congress Sept. 25, 1789.
Ratified by three-fourths of the States December 15, 1791.

[8] See the 14th Amendment, Sec. 4.

Amendment I

Congress shall make no law respecting an establishment of religion, or prohibiting the free exercise thereof; or abridging the freedom of speech, or of the press; or the right of the people peaceably to assemble, and to petition the government for a redress of grievances.

Amendment II

A well regulated militia, being necessary to the security of a free State, the right of the people to keep and bear arms, shall not be infringed.

Amendment III

No soldier shall, in time of peace be quartered in any house, without the consent of the owner, nor in time of war, but in a manner to be prescribed by law.

Amendment IV

The right of the people to be secure in their persons, houses, papers, and effects, against unreasonable searches and seizures, shall not be violated, and no warrants shall issue, but upon probable cause, supported by oath or affirmation, and particularly describing the place to be searched, and the person or things to be seized.

Amendment V

No person shall be held to answer for a capital, or otherwise infamous crime, unless on a presentment or indictment of a grand jury, except in cases arising in the land or naval forces, or in the militia, when in actual service in time of war or public danger; nor shall any person be subject for the same offense to be twice put in jeopardy of life or limb; nor shall be compelled in any criminal case to be a witness against himself, nor be deprived of life, liberty, or property, without due process of law; nor shall private property be taken for public use without just compensation.

Amendment VI

In all criminal prosecutions, the accused shall enjoy the right to a speedy and public trial, by an impartial jury of the State and district wherein the crime shall have been committed, which district shall have been previously ascertained by law, and to be informed of the nature and cause of the accusation; to be confronted with the witnesses against him; to have compulsory process for obtaining witnesses in his favor, and to have the assistance of counsel for his defense.

Amendment VII

In suits at common law, where the value in controversy shall exceed twenty dollars, the right of trial by jury shall be preserved, and no fact tried by a jury shall be otherwise reexamined in any court of the United States, then according to the rules of the common law.

Amendment VIII

Excessive bail shall not be required, nor excessive fines imposed, nor cruel and unusual punishments inflicted.

Amendment IX

The enumeration in the Constitution of certain rights shall not be construed to deny or disparage others retained by the people.

Amendment X

The powers not delegated to the United States by the Constitution, nor prohibited by it to the States, are reserved to the States respectively, or to the people.

Amendment XI

Passed by Congress March 5, 1794. Ratified January 8, 1798.

The judicial power of the United States shall not be construed to extend to any suit in law or equity, commenced or prosecuted against one of the United States by citizens of another State, or by citizens or subjects of any foreign State.

Amendment XII

Passed by Congress December 12, 1803. Ratified September 25, 1804.

The electors shall meet in their respective States, and vote by ballot for President and Vice President, one of whom, at least, shall not be an inhabitant of the same State with themselves; they shall name in their ballots the person voted for as President, and in distinct ballots the person voted for as Vice President, and they shall make distinct lists of all persons voted for as President and of all persons voted for as Vice President, and of the number of votes for each, which lists they shall sign and certify, and transmit sealed to the seat of the government of the United States, directed to the President of the Senate;—The President of the Senate shall, in the presence of the Senate and House of Representatives, open all the certificates and the votes shall then be counted;—The person having the greatest number of votes for President, shall be the President, if such number be a majority of the whole number of electors appointed; and if no person have such majority, then from the persons having the highest numbers not exceeding three on the list of those voted for as President, the House of Representatives shall choose immediately, by ballot, the President. But in choosing the President, the votes shall be taken by States, the representation from each State having one vote; a quorum for this purpose shall consist of a member or members from two thirds of the States, and a majority of all the States shall be necessary to a choice. And if the House of Representatives shall not choose a President whenever the right of choice shall devolve upon them, before the fourth day of March next following, then the Vice President shall act as President, as in the case of the death or other constitutional disability of the President. The person having the greatest number of votes as Vice President shall be the Vice President, if such number be a majority of the whole number of electors appointed, and if no person have a majority, then from the two highest numbers on the list, the Senate shall choose the Vice President; a quorum for the purpose shall consist of two thirds of the whole number of Senators, and a majority of the whole number shall be necessary to a choice. But no person constitutionally ineligible to the office of President shall be eligible to that of Vice President of the United States.

Amendment XIII

Passed by Congress February 1, 1865. Ratified December 18, 1865.

SECTION 1

Neither slavery nor involuntary servitude, except as punishment for crime whereof the party shall have been duly convicted, shall exist within the United States, or any place subject to their jurisdiction.

SECTION 2

Congress shall have power to enforce this article by appropriate legislation.

Amendment XIV

Passed by Congress June 16, 1866. Ratified July 23, 1868.

SECTION 1

All persons born or naturalized in the United States, and subject to the jurisdiction thereof, are citizens of the

United States and of the State wherein they reside. No State shall make or enforce any law which shall abridge the privileges or immunities of citizens of the United States; nor shall any State deprive any person of life, liberty, or property, without due process of law; nor deny to any person within its jurisdiction the equal protection of the laws.

SECTION 2

Representatives shall be apportioned among the several States according to their respective numbers, counting the whole number of persons in each State, excluding Indians not taxed. But when the right to vote at any election for the choice of electors for President and Vice President of the United States, representatives in Congress, the executive and judicial officers of a State, or the members of the legislature thereof, is denied to any of the male inhabitants of such State, being twenty-one years of age, and citizens of the United States, or in any way abridged, except for participation in rebellion, or other crime, the basis of representation therein shall be reduced in the proportion which the number of such male citizens shall bear to the whole number of male citizens twenty-one years of age in such State.

SECTION 3

No person shall be a senator or representative in Congress, or elector of President and Vice President, or hold any office, civil or military, under the United States, or under any State, who having previously taken an oath, as a member of Congress, or as an officer of the United States, or as a member of any State legislature, or as an executive or judicial officer of any State, to support the Constitution of the United States, shall have engaged in insurrection or rebellion against the same, or given aid or comfort to the enemies thereof. But Congress may by a vote of two thirds of each House, remove such disability.

SECTION 4

The validity of the public debt of the United States, authorized by law, including debts incurred for payment of pensions and bounties for services in suppressing insurrection or rebellion, shall not be questioned. But neither the United States nor any State shall assume or pay any debt or obligation incurred in aid of insurrection or rebellion against the United States, or any claim for the loss or emancipation of any slave; but all such debts, obligations, and claims shall be held illegal and void.

SECTION 5

The Congress shall have power to enforce, by appropriate legislation, the provisions of this article.

Amendment XV

Passed by Congress February 27, 1869. Ratified March 30, 1870.

SECTION 1

The right of citizens of the United States to vote shall not be denied or abridged by the United States or by any State on account of race, color, or previous condition of servitude.

SECTION 2

The Congress shall have power to enforce this article by appropriate legislation.

Amendment XVI

Passed by Congress July 12, 1909. Ratified February 25, 1913.

The Congress shall have power to lay and collect taxes on incomes, from whatever source derived, without apportionment among the several States, and without regard to any census or enumeration.

Amendment XVII

Passed by Congress May 16, 1912. Ratified May 31, 1913.

The Senate of the United States shall be composed of two senators from each State, elected by the people thereof, for six years; and each senator shall have one vote. The electors in each State shall have the qualifications requisite for electors of the most numerous branch of the State legislature.

When vacancies happen in the representation of any State in the Senate, the executive authority of such State shall issue writs of election to fill such vacancies: Provided, That the legislature of any State may empower the executive thereof to make temporary appointments until the people fill the vacancies by election as the legislature may direct.

This amendment shall not be so construed as to affect the election or term of any senator chosen before it becomes valid as part of the Constitution.

Amendment XVIII

Passed by Congress December 17, 1917. Ratified January 29, 1919.

After one year from the ratification of this article, the manufacture, sale, or transportation of intoxicating liquors within, the importation thereof into, or the exportation thereof from the United States and all territory subject to the jurisdiction thereof for beverage purposes is hereby prohibited.

The Congress and the several States shall have concurrent power to enforce this article by appropriate legislation.

This article shall be inoperative unless it shall have been ratified as an amendment to the Constitution by the legislatures of the several States, as provided in the Constitution, within seven years from the date of the submission hereof to the States by Congress.

Amendment XIX

Passed by Congress June 5, 1919. Ratified August 26, 1920.

The right of citizens of the United States to vote shall not be denied or abridged by the United States or by any State on account of sex.

The Congress shall have power by appropriate legislation to enforce the provisions of this article.

Amendment XX

Passed by Congress March 3, 1932. Ratified January 23, 1933.

SECTION 1

The terms of the President and Vice President shall end at noon on the 20th day of January, and the terms of Senators and Representatives at noon on the 3d day of January, of the years in which such terms would have ended if this article had not been ratified; and the terms of their successors shall then begin.

SECTION 2

The Congress shall assemble at least once in every year, and such meeting shall begin at noon on the 3d day of January, unless they shall by law appoint a different day.

SECTION 3

If, at the time fixed for the beginning of the term of the President, the President-elect shall have died, the Vice President-elect shall become President. If a President shall not have been chosen before the time fixed for the beginning of his term, or if the President-elect shall have failed to qualify, then the Vice President-elect shall act as President until a President shall have qualified; and the Congress may by law provide for the case wherein neither a President-elect nor a Vice President-elect shall have qualified, declaring who shall then act as President, or the manner in which one who is to act shall be selected, and such person shall act accordingly until a President or Vice President shall have qualified.

SECTION 4

The Congress may by law provide for the case of the death of any of the persons from whom the House of Representatives may choose a President whenever the right of choice shall have devolved upon them, and for the case of the death of any of the persons from whom the Senate may choose a Vice President whenever the right of choice shall have devolved upon them.

SECTION 5

Sections 1 and 2 shall take effect on the 15th day of October following the ratification of this article.

SECTION 6

This article shall be inoperative unless it shall have been ratified as an amendment to the Constitution by the legislatures of three-fourths of the several States within seven years from the date of its submission.

Amendment XXI

Passed by Congress February 20, 1933. Ratified December 5, 1933.

SECTION 1

The eighteenth article of amendment to the Constitution of the United States is hereby repealed.

SECTION 2

The transportation or importation into any State, Territory, or possession of the United States for delivery or use therein of intoxicating liquors in violation of the laws thereof, is hereby prohibited.

SECTION 3

This article shall be inoperative unless it shall have been ratified as an amendment to the Constitution by conventions in the several States, as provided in the Constitution, within seven years from the date of the submission thereof to the States by the Congress.

Amendment XXII

Passed by Congress March 24, 1947. Ratified February 26, 1951.

SECTION 1

No person shall be elected to the office of the President more than twice, and no person who has held the office of President, or acted as President, for more than two years of a term to which some other person was elected President shall be elected to the office of the President more than once. But this article shall not apply to any person holding the office of President when this article was proposed by the Congress, and shall not prevent any person who may be holding the office of President, or acting as President, during the term within which this article becomes operative from holding the office of President or acting as President during the remainder of such term.

SECTION 2

This article shall be inoperative unless it shall have been ratified as an amendment to the Constitution by the legislatures of three-fourths of the several States within seven years from the date of its submission to the States by the Congress.

Amendment XXIII

Passed by Congress June 16, 1960. Ratified April 3, 1961.

SECTION 1

The District constituting the seat of Government of the United States shall appoint in such manner as the Congress may direct:

A number of electors of President and Vice President equal to the whole number of Senators and Representatives in Congress to which the District would be entitled if it were a State, but in no event more than the least populous State; they shall be in addition to those appointed by the States, but they shall be considered, for the purposes of the election of President and Vice President, to be electors appointed by a State; and they shall meet in the District and perform such duties as provided by the twelfth article of amendment.

SECTION 2

The Congress shall have power to enforce this article by appropriate legislation.

Amendment XXIV

Passed by Congress August 27, 1962. Ratified February 4, 1964.

SECTION 1

The right of citizens of the United States to vote in any primary or other election for President or Vice President, for electors for President or Vice President, or for Senator or Representative in Congress, shall not be denied or abridged by the United States or any State by reason of failure to pay any poll tax or other tax.

SECTION 2

The Congress shall have power to enforce this article by appropriate legislation.

Amendment XXV

Passed by Congress July 6, 1965. Ratified February 23, 1967.

SECTION 1

In case of the removal of the President from office or of his death or resignation, the Vice President shall become President.

SECTION 2

Whenever there is a vacancy in the office of the Vice President, the President shall nominate a Vice President who shall take office upon confirmation by a majority vote of both Houses of Congress.

SECTION 3

Whenever the President transmits to the President pro tempore of the Senate and the Speaker of the House of Representatives his written declaration that he is unable to discharge the powers and duties of his office, and until he transmits to them a written declaration to the contrary, such powers and duties shall be discharged by the Vice President as Acting President.

SECTION 4

Whenever the Vice President and a majority of either the principal officers of the executive departments or of such other body as Congress may by law provide, transmit to the President pro tempore of the Senate and the Speaker of the House of Representatives their written declaration that the President is unable to discharge the powers and duties of his office, the Vice President shall immediately assume the powers and duties of the office as Acting President.

Thereafter, when the President transmits to the President pro tempore of the Senate and the Speaker of the House of Representatives his written declaration that no inability exists, he shall resume the powers and duties of his office unless the Vice President and a majority of either the principal officers of the executive department or of such other body as Congress may by law provide, transmit within four days to the President pro tempore of the Senate and the Speaker of the House of Representatives their written declaration that the President is unable to discharge the powers and duties of his office. Thereupon Congress shall decide the issue, assembling within forty-eight hours for that purpose if not in session. If the Congress, within twenty-one days after receipt of the latter written declaration, or, if Congress is not in session, within twenty-one days after Congress is required to assemble, determines by two-thirds vote of both Houses that the President is unable to discharge the powers and duties of his office, the Vice President shall continue to discharge the same as Acting President; otherwise, the President shall resume the powers and duties of his office.

Amendment XXVI

Passed by Congress March 23, 1971. Ratified July 5, 1971.

SECTION 1

The right of citizens of the United States, who are eighteen years of age or older, to vote shall not be denied or abridged by the United States or by any State on account of age.

Amendment XXVII

Passed by Congress September 25, 1789. Ratified May 18, 1992.

No law, varying the compensation for the services of the Senators and Representatives, shall take effect, until an election of Representatives shall have intervened.

Appendix 3

(Adopted in fifty-two jurisdictions; all fifty States, although Louisiana has adopted only Articles 1, 3, 4, 7, 8, and 9; the District of Columbia; and the Virgin Islands.)

Articles

1. General Provisions
2. Sales
   2A. Leases
3. Negotiable Instruments
4. Bank Deposits and Collections
   4A. Funds Transfers
5. Letters of Credit
6. Repealer of Article 6—Bulk Transfers and [Revised] Article 6—Bulk Sales
7. Warehouse Receipts, Bills of Lading and Other Documents of Title
8. Investment Securities
9. Secured Transactions

ARTICLE 1 GENERAL PROVISIONS

Part 1 Short Title, Construction, Application and Subject Matter of the Act

* * * *

§1—103. SUPPLEMENTARY GENERAL PRINCIPLES OF LAW APPLICABLE

Unless displaced by the particular provisions of this Act, the principles of law and equity, including the law merchant and the law relative to capacity to contract, principal and agent, estoppel, fraud, misrepresentation, duress, coercion, mistake, bankruptcy, or other validating or invalidating cause shall supplement its provisions.

* * * *

§1—201. GENERAL DEFINITIONS

* * * *

(3) "Agreement" means the bargain of the parties in fact as found in their language or by implication from other circumstances including course of dealing or usage of trade or course of performance as provided in this Act (Sections 1—205 and 2—208). Whether an agreement has legal consequences is determined by the provisions of this Act, if applicable; otherwise by the law of contracts (Section 1—103). (Compare "Contract".)

(4) "Bank" means any person engaged in the business of banking.

(5) "Bearer" means the person in possession of an instrument, document of title, or certificated security payable to bearer or indorsed in blank.

(6) "Bill of lading" means a document evidencing the receipt of goods for shipment issued by a person engaged in the business of transporting or forwarding goods, and includes an airbill. "Airbill" means a document serving for air transportation as a bill of lading does for marine or rail transportation, and includes an air consignment note or air waybill.

* * * *

(9) "Buyer in ordinary course of business" means a person that buys goods in good faith, without knowledge that the sale violates the rights of another person in the goods, and in the ordinary course from a person, other than a pawnbroker, in the business of selling goods of that kind. A person buys goods in the ordinary course if the sale to the person comports with the usual or customary practices in the kind of business in which the seller is engaged or with the seller's own usual or customary practices. A person that sells oil, gas, or other minerals at the wellhead or minehead is a person in the business of selling goods of that kind. A buyer in ordinary course of business may buy for cash, by exchange of other property, or on secured or unsecured credit, and may acquire goods or documents of title under a pre-existing contract for sale. Only a buyer that takes possession of the goods or has a right to recover the goods from the seller under Article 2 may be a buyer in ordinary course of business. A person that acquires goods in a transfer in bulk or as security for or in total or partial satisfaction of a money debt is not a buyer in ordinary course of business.

(10) "Conspicuous": A term or clause is conspicuous when it is so written that a reasonable person against whom it is

to operate ought to have noticed it. A printed heading in capitals (as: NON-NEGOTIABLE BILL OF LADING) is conspicuous. Language in the body of a form is "conspicuous" if it is in larger or other contrasting type or color. But in a telegram any stated term is "conspicuous". Whether a term or clause is "conspicuous" or not is for decision by the court.

(11) "Contract" means the total legal obligation which results from the parties' agreement as affected by this Act and any other applicable rules of law. (Compare "Agreement".)

* * * *

(15) "Document of title" includes bill of lading, dock warrant, dock receipt, warehouse receipt or order for the delivery of goods, and also any other document which in the regular course of business or financing is treated as adequately evidencing that the person in possession of it is entitled to receive, hold and dispose of the document and the goods it covers. To be a document of title a document must purport to be issued by or addressed to a bailee and purport to cover goods in the bailee's possession which are either identified or are fungible portions of an identified mass.

* * * *

(17) "Fungible" with respect to goods or securities means goods or securities of which any unit is, by nature or usage of trade, the equivalent of any other like unit. Goods which are not fungible shall be deemed fungible for the purposes of this Act to the extent that under a particular agreement or document unlike units are treated as equivalents.

* * * *

(19) "Good faith" means honesty in fact in the conduct or transaction concerned.

(20) "Holder" with respect to a negotiable instrument, means the person in possession if the instrument is payable to bearer or, in the cases of an instrument payable to an identified person, if the identified person is in possession. "Holder" with respect to a document of title means the person in possession if the goods are deliverable to bearer or to the order of the person in possession.

* * * *

(23) A person is "insolvent" who either has ceased to pay his debts in the ordinary course of business or cannot pay his debts as they become due or is insolvent within the meaning of the federal bankruptcy law.

(24) "Money" means a medium of exchange authorized or adopted by a domestic or foreign government and includes a monetary unit of account established by an intergovernmental organization or by agreement between two or more nations.

(25) A person has "notice" of a fact when

(a) he has actual knowledge of it; or ·

(b) he has received a notice or notification of it; or

(c) from all the facts and circumstances known to him at the time in question he has reason to know that it exists.

* * * *

(37) "Security interest" means an interest in personal property or fixtures which secures payment or performance of an obligation. The term also includes any interest of a consignor and a buyer of accounts, chattel paper, a payment intangible, or a promissory note in a transaction that is subject to Article 9. The special property interest of a buyer of goods on identification of those goods to a contract for sale under Section 2—401 is not a "security interest", but a buyer may also acquire a "security interest" by complying with Article 9. Except as otherwise provided in Section 2—505, the right of a seller or lessor of goods under Article 2 or 2A to retain or acquire possession of the goods is not a "security interest", but a seller or lessor may also acquire a "security interest" by complying with Article 9. The retention or reservation of title by a seller of goods notwithstanding shipment or delivery to the buyer (Section 2—401) is limited in effect to a reservation of a "security interest".

Whether a transaction creates a lease or security interest is determined by the facts of each case; however, a transaction creates a security interest if the consideration the lessee is to pay the lessor for the right to possession and use of the goods is an obligation for the term of the lease not subject to termination by the lessee, and

(a) the original term of the lease is equal to or greater than the remaining economic life of the goods,

(b) the lessee is bound to renew the lease for the remaining economic life of the goods or is bound to become the owner of the goods,

(c) the lessee has an option to renew the lease for the remaining economic life of the goods for no additional consideration or nominal additional consideration upon compliance with the lease agreement, or

(d) the lessee has an option to become the owner of the goods for no additional consideration or nominal additional consideration upon compliance with the lease agreement.

A transaction does not create a security interest merely because it provides that

(a) the present value of the consideration the lessee is obligated to pay the lessor for the right to possession and use of the goods is substantially equal to or is greater than the fair market value of the goods at the time the lease is entered into,

(b) the lessee assumes risk of loss of the goods, or agrees to pay taxes, insurance, filing, recording, or registration fees, or service or maintenance costs with respect to the goods,

(c) the lessee has an option to renew the lease or to become the owner of the goods,

(d) the lessee has an option to renew the lease for a fixed rent that is equal to or greater than the reasonably predictable fair market rent for the use of the goods for the term of the renewal at the time the option is to be performed, or

(e) the lessee has an option to become the owner of the goods for a fixed price that is equal to or greater than the reasonably predictable fair market value of the goods at the time the option is to be performed.

* * * *

(39) "Signed" includes any symbol executed or adopted by a party with present intention to authenticate a writing.

(40) "Surety" includes guarantor.

* * * *

(43) "Unauthorized" signature means one made without actual, implied or apparent authority and includes a forgery.

(44) "Value". Except as otherwise provided with respect to negotiable instruments and bank collections (Sections 3—303, 4—210 and 4—211) a person gives "value" for rights if he acquires them

(a) in return for a binding commitment to extend credit or for the extension of immediately available credit whether or not drawn upon and whether or not a chargeback is provided for in the event of difficulties in collection; or

(b) as security for or in total or partial satisfaction of a pre-existing claim; or

(c) by accepting delivery pursuant to a preexisting contract for purchase; or

(d) generally, in return for any consideration sufficient to support a simple contract.

(45) "Warehouse receipt" means a receipt issued by a person engaged in the business of storing goods for hire.

(46) "Written" or "writing" includes printing, typewriting or any other intentional reduction to tangible form.

* * * *

§1—203. OBLIGATION OF GOOD FAITH

Every contract or duty within this Act imposes an obligation of good faith in its performance or enforcement.

§1—204. TIME; REASONABLE TIME; "SEASONABLY"

(1) Whenever this Act requires any action to be taken within a reasonable time, any time which is not manifestly unreasonable may be fixed by agreement.

(2) What is a reasonable time for taking any action depends on the nature, purpose and circumstances of such action.

(3) An action is taken "seasonably" when it is taken at or within the time agreed or if no time is agreed at or within a reasonable time.

§1—205. COURSE OF DEALING AND USAGE OF TRADE

(1) A course of dealing is a sequence of previous conduct between the parties to a particular transaction which is fairly to be regarded as establishing a common basis of understanding for interpreting their expressions and other conduct.

(2) A usage of trade is any practice or method of dealing having such regularity of observance in a place, vocation or trade as to justify an expectation that it will be observed with respect to the transaction in question. The existence and scope of such a usage are to be proved as facts. If it is established that such a usage is embodied in a written trade code or similar writing the interpretation of the writing is for the court.

(3) A course of dealing between parties and any usage of trade in the vocation or trade in which they are engaged or of which they are or should be aware give particular meaning to and supplement or qualify terms of an agreement.

(4) The express terms of an agreement and an applicable course of dealing or usage of trade shall be construed wherever reasonable as consistent with each other; but when such construction is unreasonable express terms control both course of dealing and usage of trade and course of dealing controls usage trade.

(5) An applicable usage of trade in the place where any part of performance is to occur shall be used in interpreting the agreement as to that part of the performance.

(6) Evidence of a relevant usage of trade offered by one party is not admissible unless and until he has given the other party such notice as the court finds sufficient to prevent unfair surprise to the latter.

* * * *

ARTICLE 2 SALES

§2—102. SCOPE; CERTAIN SECURITY AND OTHER TRANSACTIONS EXCLUDED FROM THIS ARTICLE

Unless the context otherwise requires, this Article applies to transactions in goods; it does not apply to any transaction which although in the form of an unconditional contract to sell or present sale is intended to operate only as a security transaction nor does this Article impair or repeal any statute regulating sales to consumers, farmers or other specified classes of buyers.

§2—103. DEFINITIONS AND INDEX OF DEFINITIONS

(1) In this Article unless the context otherwise requires

(a) "Buyer" means a person who buys or contracts to buy goods.

(b) "Good faith" in the case of a merchant means honesty in fact and the observance of reasonable commercial standards of fair dealing in the trade.

(c) "Receipt" of goods means taking physical possession of them.

(d) "Seller" means a person who sells or contracts to sell goods.

§2—104. DEFINITIONS: "MERCHANT"; "BETWEEN MERCHANTS"; "FINANCING AGENCY"

(1) "Merchant" means a person who deals in goods of the kind or otherwise by his occupation holds himself out as having knowledge or skill peculiar to the practices or goods involved in the transaction or to whom such knowledge or skill may be attributed by his employment of an agent or broker or other intermediary who by his occupation holds himself out as having such knowledge or skill.

§2—105. DEFINITIONS: TRANSFERABILITY; "GOODS"; "FUTURE" GOODS; "LOT"; "COMMERCIAL UNIT"

(1) "Goods" means all things (including specially manufactured goods) which are movable at the time of identification to the contract for sale other than the money in which the price is to be paid, investment securities (Article 8) and things in action. "Goods" also includes the unborn young of animals and growing crops and other identified things attached to realty as described in the section on goods to be severed from realty (Section 2—107).

(2) Goods must be both existing and identified before any interest in them can pass. Goods which are not both existing and identified are "future" goods. A purported present sale of future goods or of any interest therein operates as a contract to sell.

(3) There may be a sale of a part interest in existing identified goods.

(4) An undivided share in an identified bulk of fungible goods is sufficiently identified to be sold although the quantity of the bulk is not determined. Any agreed proportion of such a bulk or any quantity thereof agreed upon by number, weight or other measure may to the extent of the seller's interest in the bulk be sold to the buyer who then becomes an owner in common.

(5) "Lot" means a parcel or a single article which is the subject matter of a separate sale or delivery, whether or not it is sufficient to perform the contract.

(6) "Commercial unit" means such a unit of goods as by commercial usage is a single whole for purposes of sale and division of which materially impairs its character or value on the market or in use. A commercial unit may be a single article (as a machine) or a set of articles (as a suite of furniture or an assortment of sizes) or a quantity (as a bale, gross, or carload) or any other unit treated in use or in the relevant market as a single whole.

* * * *

§2—107. GOODS TO BE SEVERED FROM REALTY: RECORDING

(1) A contract for the sale of minerals or the like (including oil and gas) or a structure or its materials to be removed from realty is a contract for the sale of goods within this Article if they are to be severed by the seller but until severance a purported present sale thereof which is not effective as a transfer of an interest in land is effective only as a contract to sell.

(2) A contract for the sale apart from the land of growing crops or other things attached to realty and capable of severance without material harm thereto but not described in subsection (1) or of timber to be cut is a contract for the sale of goods within this Article whether the subject matter is to be severed by the buyer or by the seller even though it forms part of the realty at the time of contracting, and the parties can by identification effect a present sale before severance.

(3) The provisions of this section are subject to any third party rights provided by the law relating to realty records, and the contract for sale may be executed and recorded as a document transferring an interest in land and shall then constitute notice to third parties of the buyer's rights under the contract for sale.

§2—201. FORMAL REQUIREMENTS; STATUTE OF FRAUDS

(1) Except as otherwise provided in this section a contract for the sale of goods for the price of $500 [some states have increased this amount to $5,000] or more is not enforceable by way of action or defense unless there is some writing sufficient to indicate that a contract for sale has been made between the parties and signed by the party against whom enforcement is sought or by his authorized agent or broker. A writing is not insufficient because it omits or incorrectly states a term agreed upon but the contract is not enforceable under this paragraph beyond the quantity of goods shown in such writing.

(2) Between merchants if within a reasonable time a writing in confirmation of the contract and sufficient against the sender is received and the party receiving it has reason to know its contents, it satisfies the requirements of subsection (1) against such party unless written notice of objection to its contents is given within ten days after it is received.

(3) A contract which does not satisfy the requirements of subsection (1) but which is valid in other respects is enforceable

(a) if the goods are to be specially manufactured for the buyer and are not suitable for sale to others in the ordinary course of the seller's business and the seller, before notice of repudiation is received and under circumstances which reasonably indicate that the goods are for the buyer, has made either a substantial beginning of their manufacture or commitments for their procurement; or

(b) if the party against whom enforcement is sought admits in his pleading, testimony or otherwise in court that a contract for sale was made, but the contract is not enforceable under this provision beyond the quantity of goods admitted; or

(c) with respect to goods for which payment has been made and accepted or which have been received and accepted (Sec. 2—606).

§2—202. FINAL WRITTEN EXPRESSION: PAROL OR EXTRINSIC EVIDENCE

Terms with respect to which the confirmatory memoranda of the parties agree or which are otherwise set forth in a writing intended by the parties as a final expression of their agreement with respect to such terms as are included therein may not be contradicted by evidence of any prior agreement or of a contemporaneous oral agreement but may be explained or supplemented

(a) by course of dealing or usage of trade (Section 1—205) or by course of performance (Section 2—208); and

(b) by evidence of consistent additional terms unless the court finds the writing to have been intended also as a complete and exclusive statement of the terms of the agreement.

* * * *

§2—204. FORMATION IN GENERAL

(1) A contract for sale of goods may be made in any manner sufficient to show agreement, including conduct by both parties which recognizes the existence of such a contract.

(2) An agreement sufficient to constitute a contract for sale may be found even though the moment of its making is undetermined.

(3) Even though one or more terms are left open a contract for sale does not fail for indefiniteness if the parties have intended to make a contract and there is a reasonably certain basis for giving an appropriate remedy.

§2—205. FIRM OFFERS

An offer by a merchant to buy or sell goods in a signed writing which by its terms gives assurance that it will be held open is not revocable, for lack of consideration, during the time stated or if no time is stated for a reasonable time, but in no event may such period of irrevocability exceed three months; but any such term of assurance on a form supplied by the offeree must be separately signed by the offeror.

§2—206. OFFER AND ACCEPTANCE IN FORMATION OF CONTRACT

(1) Unless other unambiguously indicated by the language or circumstances

(a) an offer to make a contract shall be construed as inviting acceptance in any manner and by any medium reasonable in the circumstances;

(b) an order or other offer to buy goods for prompt or current shipment shall be construed as inviting acceptance either by a prompt promise to ship or by the prompt or current shipment of conforming or non-conforming goods, but such a shipment of non-conforming goods does not constitute an acceptance if the seller seasonably notifies the buyer that the shipment is offered only as an accommodation to the buyer.

(2) Where the beginning of a requested performance is a reasonable mode of acceptance an offeror who is not notified of acceptance within a reasonable time may treat the offer as having lapsed before acceptance.

§2—207. ADDITIONAL TERMS IN ACCEPTANCE OR CONFIRMATION

(1) A definite and seasonable expression of acceptance or a written confirmation which is sent within a reasonable time operates as an acceptance even though it states terms additional to or different from those offered or agreed upon, unless acceptance is expressly made conditional on assent to the additional or different terms.

(2) The additional terms are to be construed as proposals for addition to the contract. Between merchants such terms become part of the contract unless:

(a) the offer expressly limits acceptance to the terms of the offer;

(b) they materially alter it; or

(c) notification of objection to them has already been given or is given within a reasonable time after notice of them is received.

(3) Conduct by both parties which recognizes the existence of a contract is sufficient to establish a contract for sale although the writings of the parties do not otherwise establish a contract. In such case the terms of the particular contract consist of those terms on which the writings of the parties agree, together with any supplementary terms incorporated under any other provisions of this Act.

§2—208. COURSE OF PERFORMANCE OR PRACTICAL CONSTRUCTION

(1) Where the contract for sale involves repeated occasions for performance by either party with knowledge of the nature of the performance and opportunity for objection to it by the other, any course of performance accepted or acquiesced in without objection shall be relevant to determine the meaning of the agreement.

(2) The express terms of the agreement and any such course of performance, as well as any course of dealing and usage of trade, shall be construed whenever reasonable as consistent with each other; but when such construction is unreasonable, express terms shall control course of

performance and course of performance shall control both course of dealing and usage of trade (Section 1—205).

(3) Subject to the provisions of the next section on modification and waiver, such course of performance shall be relevant to show a waiver or modification of any term inconsistent with such course of performance.

§2—209. MODIFICATION, RESCISSION AND WAIVER

(1) An agreement modifying a contract within this Article needs no consideration to be binding.

(2) A signed agreement which excludes modification or rescission except by a signed writing cannot be otherwise modified or rescinded, but except as between merchants such a requirement on a form supplied by the merchant must be separately signed by the other party.

(3) The requirements of the statute of frauds section of this Article (Section 2—201) must be satisfied if the contract as modified is within its provisions.

(4) Although an attempt at modification or rescission does not satisfy the requirements of subsection (2) or (3) it can operate as a waiver.

(5) A party who has made a waiver affecting an executory portion of the contract may retract the waiver by reasonable notification received by the other party that strict performance will be required of any term waived, unless the retraction would be unjust in view of a material change of position in reliance on the waiver.

§2—210. DELEGATION OF PERFORMANCE; ASSIGNMENT OF RIGHTS

* * * *

(5) An assignment of "the contract" or of "all my rights under the contract" or an assignment in similar general terms is an assignment of rights and unless the language or the circumstances (as in an assignment for security) indicate the contrary, it is a delegation of performance of the duties of the assignor and its acceptance by the assignee constitutes a promise by him to perform those duties. This promise is enforceable by either the assignor or the other party to the original contract.

§2—301. GENERAL OBLIGATIONS OF PARTIES

The obligation of the seller is to transfer and deliver and that of the buyer is to accept and pay in accordance with the contract.

§2—302. UNCONSCIONABLE CONTRACT OR CLAUSE

(1) If the court as a matter of law finds the contract or any clause of the contract to have been unconscionable at the time it was made the court may refuse to enforce the contract, or it may enforce the remainder of the contract without the unconscionable clause, or it may so limit the application of any unconscionable clause as to avoid any unconscionable result.

(2) When it is claimed or appears to the court that the contract or any clause thereof may be unconscionable the parties shall be afforded a reasonable opportunity to present evidence as to its commercial setting, purpose and effect to aid the court in making the determination.

§2—303. ALLOCATIONS OR DIVISION OF RISKS

Where this Article allocates a risk or a burden as between the parties "unless otherwise agreed", the agreement may not only shift the allocation but may also divide the risk or burden.

§2—304. PRICE PAYABLE IN MONEY, GOODS, REALTY, OR OTHERWISE

(1) The price can be made payable in money or otherwise. If it is payable in whole or in part in goods each party is a seller of the goods which he is to transfer.

(2) Even though all or part of the price is payable in an interest in realty the transfer of the goods and the seller's obligations with reference to them are subject to this Article, but not the transfer of the interest in realty or the transferor's obligations in connection therewith.

§2—305. OPEN PRICE TERM

(1) The parties if they so intend can conclude a contract for sale even though the price is not settled. In such a case the price is a reasonable price at the time for delivery if

(a) nothing is said as to price; or

(b) the price is left to be agreed by the parties and they fail to agree; or

(c) the price is to be fixed in terms of some agreed market or other standard as set or recorded by a third person or agency and it is not so set or recorded.

(2) A price to be fixed by the seller or by the buyer means a price for him to fix in good faith.

(3) When a price left to be fixed otherwise than by agreement of the parties fails to be fixed through fault of one party the other may at his option treat the contract as cancelled or himself fix a reasonable price.

(4) Where, however, the parties intend not to be bound unless the price be fixed or agreed and it is not fixed or agreed there is no contract. In such a case the buyer must return any goods already received or if unable so to do must pay their reasonable value at the time of delivery and the seller must return any portion of the price paid on account.

§2—306. OUTPUT, REQUIREMENTS AND EXCLUSIVE DEALINGS

(1) A term which measures the quantity by the output of the seller or the requirements of the buyer means such actual output or requirements as may occur in good faith, except that no quantity unreasonably disproportionate to any stated estimate or in the absence of a stated estimate to

any normal or otherwise comparable prior output or requirements may be tendered or demanded.

(2) A lawful agreement by either the seller or the buyer for exclusive dealing in the kind of goods concerned imposes unless otherwise agreed an obligation by the seller to use best efforts to supply the goods and by the buyer to use best efforts to promote their sale.

§2—307. DELIVERY IN SINGLE LOT OR SEVERAL LOTS

Unless otherwise agreed all goods called for by a contract for sale must be tendered in a single delivery and payment is due only on such tender but where the circumstances give either party the right to make or demand delivery in lots the price if it can be apportioned may be demanded for each lot.

§2—308. ABSENCE OF SPECIFIED PLACE FOR DELIVERY

Unless otherwise agreed

(a) the place for delivery of goods is the seller's place of business or if he has none his residence; but

(b) in a contract for sale of identified goods which to the knowledge of the parties at the time of contracting are in some other place, that place is the place for their delivery; and

(c) documents of title may be delivered through customary banking channels.

§2—309. ABSENCE OF SPECIFIC TIME PROVISIONS; NOTICE OF TERMINATION

(1) The time for shipment or delivery or any other action under a contract if not provided in this Article or agreed upon shall be a reasonable time.

§2—310. OPEN TIME FOR PAYMENT OR RUNNING OF CREDIT; AUTHORITY TO SHIP UNDER RESERVATION

Unless otherwise agreed

(a) payment is due at the time and place at which the buyer is to receive the goods even though the place of shipment is the place of delivery; and

(b) if the seller is authorized to send the goods he may ship them under reservation, and may tender the documents of title, but the buyer may inspect the goods after their arrival before payment is due unless such inspection is inconsistent with the terms of the contract (Section 2—513).

* * * *

§2—312. WARRANTY OF TITLE AND AGAINST INFRINGEMENT; BUYER'S OBLIGATION AGAINST INFRINGEMENT

(1) Subject to subsection (2) there is in a contract for sale a warranty by the seller that

(a) the title conveyed shall be good, and its transfer rightful; and

(b) the goods shall be delivered free from any security interest or other lien or encumbrance of which the buyer at the time of contracting has no knowledge.

(2) A warranty under subsection (1) will be excluded or modified only by specific language or by circumstances which give the buyer reason to know that the person selling does not claim title in himself or that he is purporting to sell only such right or title as he or a third person may have.

(3) Unless otherwise agreed a seller who is a merchant regularly dealing in goods of the kind warrants that the goods shall be delivered free of the rightful claim of any third person by way of infringement or the like but a buyer who furnishes specifications to the seller must hold the seller harmless against any such claim which arises out of compliance with the specifications.

§2—313. EXPRESS WARRANTIES BY AFFIRMATION, PROMISE, DESCRIPTION, SAMPLE

(1) Express warranties by the seller are created as follows:

(a) Any affirmation of fact or promise made by the seller to the buyer which relates to the goods and becomes part of the basis of the bargain creates an express warranty that the goods shall conform to the affirmation or promise.

(b) Any description of the goods which is made part of the basis of the bargain creates an express warranty that the goods shall conform to the description.

(c) Any sample or model which is made part of the basis of the bargain creates an express warranty that the whole of the goods shall conform to the sample or model.

(2) It is not necessary to the creation of an express warranty that the seller use formal words such as "warrant" or "guarantee" or that he have a specific intention to make a warranty, but an affirmation merely of the value of the goods or a statement purporting to be merely the seller's opinion or commendation of the goods does not create a warranty.

§2—314. IMPLIED WARRANTY: MERCHANTABILITY; USAGE OF TRADE

(1) Unless excluded or modified (Section 2—316), a warranty that the goods shall be merchantable is implied in a contract for their sale if the seller is a merchant with respect to goods of that kind. Under this section the serving for value of food or drink to be consumed either on the premises or elsewhere is a sale.

(2) Goods to be merchantable must be at least such as

(a) pass without objection in the trade under the contract description; and

(b) in the case of fungible goods, are of fair average quality within the description; and

(c) are fit for the ordinary purposes for which such goods are used; and

(d) run, within the variations permitted by the agreement, of even kind, quality and quantity within each unit and among all units involved; and

(e) are adequately contained, packaged, and labeled as the agreement may require; and

(f) conform to the promises or affirmations of fact made on the container or label if any.

(3) Unless excluded or modified (Section 2—316) other implied warranties may arise from course of dealing or usage of trade.

§2—315. IMPLIED WARRANTY: FITNESS FOR PARTICULAR PURPOSE

Where the seller at the time of contracting has reason to know any particular purpose for which the goods are required and that the buyer is relying on the seller's skill or judgment to select or furnish suitable goods, there is unless excluded or modified under the next section an implied warranty that the goods shall be fit for such purpose.

§2—316. EXCLUSION OR MODIFICATION OF WARRANTIES

(1) Words or conduct relevant to the creation of an express warranty and words or conduct tending to negate or limit warranty shall be construed wherever reasonable as consistent with each other; but subject to the provisions of this Article on parol or extrinsic evidence (Section 2—202) negation or limitation is inoperative to the extent that such construction is unreasonable.

(2) Subject to subsection (3), to exclude or modify the implied warranty of merchantability or any part of it the language must mention merchantability and in case of a writing must be conspicuous, and to exclude or modify any implied warranty of fitness the exclusion must be by a writing and conspicuous. Language to exclude all implied warranties of fitness is sufficient if it states, for example, that "There are no warranties which extend beyond the description on the face hereof."

(3) Notwithstanding subsection (2)

(a) unless the circumstances indicate otherwise, all implied warranties are excluded by expressions like "as is", "with all faults" or other language which in common understanding calls the buyer's attention to the exclusion of warranties and makes plain that there is no implied warranty; and

(b) when the buyer before entering into the contract has examined the goods or the sample or model as fully as he desired or has refused to examine the goods there is no implied warranty with regard to defects which an examination ought in the circumstances to have revealed to him; and

(c) an implied warranty can also be excluded or modified by course of dealing or course of performance or usage of trade.

(4) Remedies for breach of warranty can be limited in accordance with the provisions of this Article on liquidation or limitation of damages and on contractual modification of remedy (Sections 2—718 and 2—719).

§2—317. CUMULATION AND CONFLICT OF WARRANTIES EXPRESS OR IMPLIED

Warranties whether express or implied shall be construed as consistent with each other and as cumulative, but if such construction is unreasonable the intention of the parties shall determine which warranty is dominant. In ascertaining that intention the following rules apply:

(a) Exact or technical specifications displace an inconsistent sample or model or general language of description.

(b) A sample from an existing bulk displaces inconsistent general language of description.

(c) Express warranties displace inconsistent implied warranties other than an implied warranty of fitness for a particular purpose.

§2—318. THIRD PARTY BENEFICIARIES OF WARRANTIES EXPRESS OR IMPLIED

Note: If this Act is introduced in the Congress of the United States this section should be omitted. (States to select one alternative.)

Alternative A

A seller's warranty whether express or implied extends to any natural person who is in the family or household of his buyer or who is a guest in his home if it is reasonable to expect that such person may use, consume or be affected by the goods and who is injured in person by breach of the warranty. A seller may not exclude or limit the operation of this section.

Alternative B

A seller's warranty whether express or implied extends to any natural person who may reasonably be expected to use, consume or be affected by the goods and who is injured in person by breach of the warranty. A seller may not exclude or limit the operation of this section.

Alternative C

A seller's warranty whether express or implied extends to any person who may reasonably be expected to use, consume or be affected by the goods and who is injured by breach of the warranty. A seller may not exclude or limit the operation of this section with respect to injury to the person of an individual to whom the warranty extends.

§2—319. F.O.B. AND F.A.S. TERMS

(1) Unless otherwise agreed the term F.O.B. (which means "free on board") at a named place, even though used only in connection with the stated price, is a delivery term under which

    (a) when the term is F.O.B. the place of shipment, the seller must at that place ship the goods in the manner provided in this Article (Section 2—504) and bear the expense and risk of putting them into the possession of the carrier; or

    (b) when the term is F.O.B. the place of destination, the seller must at his own expense and risk transport the goods to that place and there tender delivery of them in the manner provided in this Article (Section 2—503);

    (c) when under either (a) or (b) the term is also F.O.B. vessel, car or other vehicle, the seller must in addition at his own expense and risk load the goods on board. If the term is F.O.B. vessel the buyer must name the vessel and in an appropriate case the seller must comply with the provisions of this Article on the form of bill of lading (Section 2—323).

(2) Unless otherwise agreed the term F.A.S. vessel (which means "free alongside") at a named port, even though used only in connection with the stated price, is a delivery term under which the seller must

    (a) at his own expense and risk deliver the goods alongside the vessel in the manner usual in that port or on a dock designated and provided by the buyer; and

    (b) obtain and tender a receipt for the goods in exchange for which the carrier is under a duty to issue a bill of lading.

(3) Unless otherwise agreed in any case falling within subsection (1)(a) or (c) or subsection (2) the buyer must seasonably give any needed instructions for making delivery, including when the term is F.A.S. or F.O.B. the loading berth of the vessel and in an appropriate case its name and sailing date. The seller may treat the failure of needed instructions as a failure of cooperation under this Article (Section 2—311). He may also at his option move the goods in any reasonable manner preparatory to delivery or shipment.

(4) Under the term F.O.B. vessel or F.A.S. unless otherwise agreed the buyer must make payment against tender of the required documents and the seller may not tender nor the buyer demand delivery of the goods in substitution for the documents.

§2—320. C.I.F. AND C. & F. TERMS

(1) The term C.I.F. means that the price includes in a lump sum the cost of the goods and the insurance and freight to the named destination. The term C. & F. or C.F. means that the price so includes cost and freight to the named destination.

(2) Unless otherwise agreed and even though used only in connection with the stated price and destination, the term C.I.F. destination or its equivalent requires the seller at his own expense and risk to

    (a) put the goods into the possession of a carrier at the port for shipment and obtain a negotiable bill or bills of lading covering the entire transportation to the named destination; and

    (b) load the goods and obtain a receipt from the carrier (which may be contained in the bill of lading) showing that the freight has been paid or provided for; and

    (c) obtain a policy or certificate of insurance, including any war risk insurance, of a kind and on terms then current at the port of shipment in the usual amount, in the currency of the contract, shown to cover the same goods covered by the bill of lading and providing for payment of loss to the order of the buyer or for the account of whom it may concern; but the seller may add to the price the amount of the premium for any such war risk insurance; and

    (d) prepare an invoice of the goods and procure any other documents required to effect shipment or to comply with the contract; and

    (e) forward and tender with commercial promptness all the documents in due form and with any indorsement necessary to perfect the buyer's rights.

(3) Unless otherwise agreed the term C. & F. or its equivalent has the same effect and imposes upon the seller the same obligations and risks as a C.I.F. term except the obligation as to insurance.

(4) Under the term C.I.F. or C. & F. unless otherwise agreed the buyer must make payment against tender of the required documents and the seller may not tender nor the buyer demand delivery of the goods in substitution for the documents.

* * * *

§2—322. DELIVERY "EX-SHIP"

(1) Unless otherwise agreed a term for delivery of goods "ex-ship" (which means from the carrying vessel) or in equivalent language is not restricted to a particular ship and requires delivery from a ship which has reached a place at the named port of destination where goods of the kind are usually discharged.

(2) Under such a term unless otherwise agreed

    (a) the seller must discharge all liens arising out of the carriage and furnish the buyer with a direction which puts the carrier under a duty to deliver the goods; and

    (b) the risk of loss does not pass to the buyer until the goods leave the ship's tackle or are otherwise properly unloaded.

* * * *

§2—324. "NO ARRIVAL, NO SALE" TERM

Under a term "no arrival, no sale" or terms of like meaning, unless otherwise agreed,

(a) the seller must properly ship conforming goods and if they arrive by any means he must tender them on arrival but he assumes no obligation that the goods will arrive unless he has caused the non-arrival; and

(b) where without fault of the seller the goods are in part lost or have so deteriorated as no longer to conform to the contract or arrive after the contract time, the buyer may proceed as if there had been casualty to identified goods (Section 2—613).

* * * *

§2—326. SALE ON APPROVAL AND SALE OR RETURN; RIGHTS OF CREDITORS

(1) Unless otherwise agreed, if delivered goods may be returned by the buyer even though they conform to the contract, the transaction is

(a) a "sale on approval" if the goods are delivered primarily for use, and

(b) a "sale or return" if the goods are delivered primarily for resale.

(2) Goods held on approval are not subject to the claims of the buyer's creditors until acceptance; goods held on sale or return are subject to such claims while in the buyer's possession.

(3) Any "or return" term of a contract for sale is to be treated as a separate contract for sale within the statute of frauds section of this Article (Section 2—201) and as contradicting the sale aspect of the contract within the provisions of this Article or on parol or extrinsic evidence (Section 2—202).

§2—327. SPECIAL INCIDENTS OF SALE ON APPROVAL AND SALE OR RETURN

(1) Under a sale on approval unless otherwise agreed

(a) although the goods are identified to the contract the risk of loss and the title do not pass to the buyer until acceptance; and

(b) use of the goods consistent with the purpose of trial is not acceptance but failure seasonably to notify the seller of election to return the goods is acceptance, and if the goods conform to the contract acceptance of any part is acceptance of the whole; and

(c) after due notification of election to return, the return is at the seller's risk and expense but a merchant buyer must follow any reasonable instructions.

(2) Under a sale or return unless otherwise agreed

(a) the option to return extends to the whole or any commercial unit of the goods while in substantially their original condition, but must be exercised seasonably; and

(b) the return is at the buyer's risk and expense.

§2—328. SALE BY AUCTION

(1) In a sale by auction if goods are put up in lots each lot is the subject of a separate sale.

(2) A sale by auction is complete when the auctioneer so announces by the fall of the hammer or in other customary manner. Where a bid is made while the hammer is falling in acceptance of a prior bid the auctioneer may in his discretion reopen the bidding or declare the goods sold under the bid on which the hammer was falling.

(3) Such a sale is with reserve unless the goods are in explicit terms put up without reserve. In an auction with reserve the auctioneer may withdraw the goods at any time until he announces completion of the sale. In an auction without reserve, after the auctioneer calls for bids on an article or lot, that article or lot cannot be withdrawn unless no bid is made within a reasonable time. In either case a bidder may retract his bid until the auctioneer's announcement of completion of the sale, but a bidder's retraction does not revive any previous bid.

(4) If the auctioneer knowingly receives a bid on the seller's behalf or the seller makes or procures such a bid, and notice has not been given that liberty for such bidding is reserved, the buyer may at his option avoid the sale or take the goods at the price of the last good faith bid prior to the completion of the sale. This subsection shall not apply to any bid at a forced sale.

§2—401. PASSING OF TITLE; RESERVATION FOR SECURITY; LIMITED APPLICATION OF THIS SECTION

Each provision of this Article with regard to the rights, obligations and remedies of the seller, the buyer, purchasers or other third parties applies irrespective of title to the goods except where the provision refers to such title. Insofar as situations are not covered by the other provisions of this Article and matters concerning title became material the following rules apply:

(1) Title to goods cannot pass under a contract for sale prior to their identification to the contract (Section 2—501), and unless otherwise explicitly agreed the buyer acquires by their identification a special property as limited by this Act. Any retention or reservation by the seller of the title (property) in goods shipped or delivered to the buyer is limited in effect to a reservation of a security interest. Subject to these provisions and to the provisions of the Article on Secured Transactions (Article 9), title to goods passes from the seller to the buyer in any manner and on any conditions explicitly agreed on by the parties.

(2) Unless otherwise explicitly agreed title passes to the buyer at the time and place at which the seller completes his performance with reference to the physical delivery of the goods, despite any reservation of a security interest and even though a document of title is to be delivered at a different time or place; and in particular and despite any reservation of a security interest by the bill of lading

(a) if the contract requires or authorizes the seller to send the goods to the buyer but does not require him to deliver them at destination, title passes to the buyer at the time and place of shipment; but

(b) if the contract requires delivery at destination, title passes on tender there.

(3) Unless otherwise explicitly agreed where delivery is to be made without moving the goods,

(a) if the seller is to deliver a document of title, title passes at the time when and the place where he delivers such documents; or

(b) if the goods are at the time of contracting already identified and no documents are to be delivered, title passes at the time and place of contracting.

(4) A rejection or other refusal by the buyer to receive or retain the goods, whether or not justified, or a justified revocation of acceptance revests title to the goods in the seller. Such revesting occurs by operation of law and is not a "sale".

* * * *

§2—403. POWER TO TRANSFER; GOOD FAITH PURCHASE OF GOODS; "ENTRUSTING"

(1) A purchaser of goods acquires all title which his transferor had or had power to transfer except that a purchaser of a limited interest acquires rights only to the extent of the interest purchased. A person with voidable title has power to transfer a good title to a good faith purchaser for value. When goods have been delivered under a transaction of purchase the purchaser has such power even though

(a) the transferor was deceived as to the identity of the purchaser, or

(b) the delivery was in exchange for a check which is later dishonored, or

(c) it was agreed that the transaction was to be a "cash sale", or

(d) the delivery was procured through fraud punishable as larcenous under the criminal law.

(2) Any entrusting of possession of goods to a merchant who deals in goods of that kind gives him power to transfer all rights of the entruster to a buyer in ordinary course of business.

(3) "Entrusting" includes any delivery and any acquiescence in retention of possession regardless of any condition expressed between the parties to the delivery or acquiescence and regardless of whether the procurement of the entrusting or the possessor's disposition of the goods have been such as to be larcenous under the criminal law.

(4) The rights of other purchasers of goods and of lien creditors are governed by the Articles on Secured Transactions (Article 9), Bulk Transfers (Article 6) and Documents of Title (Article 7).

§2—501. INSURABLE INTEREST IN GOODS; MANNER OF IDENTIFICATION OF GOODS

(1) The buyer obtains a special property and an insurable interest in goods by identification of existing goods as goods to which the contract refers even though the goods so identified are non-conforming and he has an option to return or reject them. Such identification can be made at any time and in any manner explicitly agreed to by the parties. In the absence of explicit agreement identification occurs

(a) when the contract is made if it is for the sale of goods already existing and identified;

(b) if the contract is for the sale of future goods other than those described in paragraph (c), when goods are shipped, marked or otherwise designated by the seller as goods to which the contract refers;

(c) when the crops are planted or otherwise become growing crops or the young are conceived if the contract is for the sale of unborn young to be born within twelve months after contracting or for the sale of crops to be harvested within twelve months or the next normal harvest season after contracting whichever is longer.

(2) The seller retains an insurable interest in goods so long as title to or any security interest in the goods remains in him and where the identification is by the seller alone he may until default or insolvency or notification to the buyer that the identification is final substitute other goods for those identified.

(3) Nothing in this section impairs any insurable interest recognized under any other statute or rule of law.

§2—502. BUYER'S RIGHT TO GOODS ON SELLER'S INSOLVENCY

(1) Subject to subsections (2) and (3) and even though the goods have not been shipped a buyer who has paid a part or all of the price of goods in which he has a special property under the provisions of the immediately preceding section may on making and keeping good a tender of any unpaid portion of their price recover them from the seller if:

(a) in the case of goods bought for personal, family, or household purposes, the seller repudiates or fails to deliver as required by the contract; or

(b) in all cases, the seller becomes insolvent within ten days after receipt of the first installment on their price.

(2) The buyer's right to recover the goods under subsection (1)(a) vests upon acquisition of a special property, even if the seller had not then repudiated or failed to deliver.

(3) If the identification creating his special property has been made by the buyer he acquires the right to recover the goods only if they conform to the contract for sale.

As amended in 1999.

§2—503. MANNER OF SELLER'S TENDER OF DELIVERY

(1) Tender of delivery requires that the seller put and hold conforming goods at the buyer's disposition and give the buyer any notification reasonably necessary to enable him to take delivery. The manner, time and place for tender are determined by the agreement and this Article, and in particular

(a) tender must be at a reasonable hour, and if it is of goods they must be kept available for the period reasonably necessary to enable the buyer to take possession; but

(b) unless otherwise agreed the buyer must furnish facilities reasonably suited to the receipt of the goods.

(2) Where the case is within the next section respecting shipment tender requires that the seller comply with its provisions.

(3) Where the seller is required to deliver at a particular destination tender requires that he comply with subsection (1) and also in any appropriate case tender documents as described in subsections (4) and (5) of this section.

(4) Where goods are in the possession of a bailee and are to be delivered without being moved

(a) tender requires that the seller either tender a negotiable document of title covering such goods or procure acknowledgment by the bailee of the buyer's right to possession of the goods; but

(b) tender to the buyer of a non-negotiable document of title or of a written direction to the bailee to deliver is sufficient tender unless the buyer seasonably objects, and receipt by the bailee of notification of the buyer's rights fixes those rights as against the bailee and all third persons; but risk of loss of the goods and of any failure by the bailee to honor the non-negotiable document of title or to obey the direction remains on the seller until the buyer has had a reasonable time to present the document or direction, and a refusal by the bailee to honor the document or to obey the direction defeats the tender.

(5) Where the contract requires the seller to deliver documents

(a) he must tender all such documents in correct form, except as provided in this Article with respect to bills of lading in a set (subsection (2) of Section 2—323); and

(b) tender through customary banking channels is sufficient and dishonor of a draft accompanying the documents constitutes non-acceptance or rejection.

§2—504. SHIPMENT BY SELLER

Where the seller is required or authorized to send the goods to the buyer and the contract does not require him to deliver them at a particular destination, then unless otherwise agreed he must

(a) put the goods in the possession of such a carrier and make such a contract for their transportation as may be reasonable having regard to the nature of the goods and other circumstances of the case; and

(b) obtain and promptly deliver or tender in due form any document necessary to enable the buyer to obtain possession of the goods or otherwise required by the agreement or by usage of trade; and

(c) promptly notify the buyer of the shipment. Failure to notify the buyer under paragraph (c) or to make a proper contract under paragraph (a) is a ground for rejection only if material delay or loss ensues.

* * * *

§2—506. RIGHTS OF FINANCING AGENCY

(1) A financing agency by paying or purchasing for value a draft which relates to a shipment of goods acquires to the extent of the payment or purchase and in addition to its own rights under the draft and any document of title securing it any rights of the shipper in the goods including the right to stop delivery and the shipper's right to have the draft honored by the buyer.

(2) The right to reimbursement of a financing agency which has in good faith honored or purchased the draft under commitment to or authority from the buyer is not impaired by subsequent discovery of defects with reference to any relevant document which was apparently regular on its face.

§2—507. EFFECT OF SELLER'S TENDER; DELIVERY ON CONDITION

(1) Tender of delivery is a condition to the buyer's duty to accept the goods and, unless otherwise agreed, to his duty to pay for them. Tender entitles the seller to acceptance of the goods and to payment according to the contract.

(2) Where payment is due and demanded on the delivery to the buyer of goods or documents of title, his right as against the seller to retain or dispose of them is conditional upon his making the payment due.

§2—508. CURE BY SELLER OF IMPROPER TENDER OR DELIVERY; REPLACEMENT

(1) Where any tender or delivery by the seller is rejected because non-conforming and the time for performance has

not yet expired, the seller may seasonably notify the buyer of his intention to cure and may then within the contract time make a conforming delivery.

(2) Where the buyer rejects a non-conforming tender which the seller had reasonable grounds to believe would be acceptable with or without money allowance the seller may if he seasonably notifies the buyer have a further reasonable time to substitute a conforming tender.

§2—509. RISK OF LOSS IN THE ABSENCE OF BREACH

(1) Where the contract requires or authorizes the seller to ship the goods by carrier

(a) if it does not require him to deliver them at a particular destination, the risk of loss passes to the buyer when the goods are duly delivered to the carrier even though the shipment is under reservation (Section 2—505); but

(b) if it does require him to deliver them at a particular destination and the goods are there duly tendered while in the possession of the carrier, the risk of loss passes to the buyer when the goods are there duly so tendered as to enable the buyer to take delivery.

(2) Where the goods are held by a bailee to be delivered without being moved, the risk of loss passes to the buyer

(a) on his receipt of a negotiable document of title covering the goods; or

(b) on acknowledgment by the bailee of the buyer's right to possession of the goods; or

(c) after his receipt of a non-negotiable document of title or other written direction to deliver, as provided in subsection (4)(b) of Section 2—503.

(3) In any case not within subsection (1) or (2), the risk of loss passes to the buyer on his receipt of the goods if the seller is a merchant; otherwise the risk passes to the buyer on tender of delivery.

(4) The provisions of this section are subject to contrary agreement of the parties and to the provisions of this Article on sale on approval (Section 2—327) and on effect of breach on risk of loss (Section 2—510).

§2—510. EFFECT OF BREACH ON RISK OF LOSS

(1) Where a tender or delivery of goods so fails to conform to the contract as to give a right of rejection the risk of their loss remains on the seller until cure or acceptance.

(2) Where the buyer rightfully revokes acceptance he may to the extent of any deficiency in his effective insurance coverage treat the risk of loss as having rested on the seller from the beginning.

(3) Where the buyer as to conforming goods already identified to the contract for sale repudiates or is otherwise in breach before risk of their loss has passed to him, the seller may to the extent of any deficiency in his effective insurance coverage treat the risk of loss as resting on the buyer for a commercially reasonable time.

§2—511. TENDER OF PAYMENT BY BUYER; PAYMENT BY CHECK

(1) Unless otherwise agreed tender of payment is a condition to the seller's duty to tender and complete any delivery.

(2) Tender of payment is sufficient when made by any means or in any manner current in the ordinary course of business unless the seller demands payment in legal tender and gives any extension of time reasonably necessary to procure it.

(3) Subject to the provisions of this Act on the effect of an instrument on an obligation (Section 3—310), payment by check is conditional and is defeated as between the parties by dishonor of the check on due presentment.

As amended in 1994.

§2—512. PAYMENT BY BUYER BEFORE INSPECTION

(1) Where the contract requires payment before inspection non-conformity of the goods does not excuse the buyer from so making payment unless

(a) the non-conformity appears without inspection; or

(b) despite tender of the required documents the circumstances would justify injunction against honor under this Act (Section 5—109(b)).

(2) Payment pursuant to subsection (1) does not constitute an acceptance of goods or impair the buyer's right to inspect or any of his remedies.

§2—513. BUYER'S RIGHT TO INSPECTION OF GOODS

(1) Unless otherwise agreed and subject to subsection (3), where goods are tendered or delivered or identified to the contract for sale, the buyer has a right before payment or acceptance to inspect them at any reasonable place and time and in any reasonable manner. When the seller is required or authorized to send the goods to the buyer, the inspection may be after their arrival.

(2) Expenses of inspection must be borne by the buyer but may be recovered from the seller if the goods do not conform and are rejected.

(3) Unless otherwise agreed and subject to the provisions of this Article on C.I.F. contracts (subsection (3) of Section 2—321), the buyer is not entitled to inspect the goods before payment of the price when the contract provides

(a) for delivery "C.O.D." or on other like terms; or

(b) for payment against documents of title, except where such payment is due only after the goods are to become available for inspection.

(4) A place or method of inspection fixed by the parties is presumed to be exclusive but unless otherwise expressly

agreed it does not postpone identification or shift the place for delivery or for passing the risk of loss. If compliance becomes impossible, inspection shall be as provided in this section unless the place or method fixed was clearly intended as an indispensable condition failure of which avoids the contract.

* * * *

§2—601. BUYER'S RIGHTS ON IMPROPER DELIVERY

Subject to the provisions of this Article on breach in installment contracts (Section 2—612) and unless otherwise agreed under the sections on contractual limitations of remedy (Sections 2—718 and 2—719), if the goods or the tender of delivery fail in any respect to conform to the contract, the buyer may

    (a) reject the whole; or

    (b) accept the whole; or

    (c) accept any commercial unit or units and reject the rest.

§2—602. MANNER AND EFFECT OF RIGHTFUL REJECTION

(1) Rejection of goods must be within a reasonable time after their delivery or tender. It is ineffective unless the buyer seasonably notifies the seller.

(2) Subject to the provisions of the two following sections on rejected goods (Sections 2—603 and 2—604),

    (a) after rejection any exercise of ownership by the buyer with respect to any commercial unit is wrongful as against the seller; and

    (b) if the buyer has before rejection taken physical possession of goods in which he does not have a security interest under the provisions of this Article (subsection (3) of Section 2—711), he is under a duty after rejection to hold them with reasonable care at the seller's disposition for a time sufficient to permit the seller to remove them; but

    (c) the buyer has no further obligations with regard to goods rightfully rejected.

(3) The seller's rights with respect to goods wrongfully rejected are governed by the provisions of this Article on Seller's remedies in general (Section 2—703).

§2—603. MERCHANT BUYER'S DUTIES AS TO RIGHTFULLY REJECTED GOODS

(1) Subject to any security interest in the buyer (subsection (3) of Section 2—711), when the seller has no agent or place of business at the market of rejection a merchant buyer is under a duty after rejection of goods in his possession or control to follow any reasonable instructions received from the seller with respect to the goods and in the absence of such instructions to make reasonable efforts to sell them for the seller's account if they are perishable or threaten to decline in value speedily. Instructions are not reasonable if on demand indemnity for expenses is not forthcoming.

(2) When the buyer sells goods under subsection (1), he is entitled to reimbursement from the seller or out of the proceeds for reasonable expenses of caring for and selling them, and if the expenses include no selling commission then to such commission as is usual in the trade or if there is none to a reasonable sum not exceeding ten per cent on the gross proceeds.

(3) In complying with this section the buyer is held only to good faith and good faith conduct hereunder is neither acceptance nor conversion nor the basis of an action for damages.

§2—604. BUYER'S OPTIONS AS TO SALVAGE OF RIGHTFULLY REJECTED GOODS

Subject to the provisions of the immediately preceding section on perishables if the seller gives no instructions within a reasonable time after notification of rejection the buyer may store the rejected goods for the seller's account or reship them to him or resell them for the seller's account with reimbursement as provided in the preceding section. Such action is not acceptance or conversion.

§2—605. WAIVER OF BUYER'S OBJECTIONS BY FAILURE TO PARTICULARIZE

(1) The buyer's failure to state in connection with rejection a particular defect which is ascertainable by reasonable inspection precludes him from relying on the unstated defect to justify rejection or to establish breach

    (a) where the seller could have cured it if stated seasonably; or

    (b) between merchants when the seller has after rejection made a request in writing for a full and final written statement of all defects on which the buyer proposes to rely.

(2) Payment against documents made without reservation of rights precludes recovery of the payment for defects apparent on the face of the documents.

§2—606. WHAT CONSTITUTES ACCEPTANCE OF GOODS

(1) Acceptance of goods occurs when the buyer

    (a) after a reasonable opportunity to inspect the goods signifies to the seller that the goods are conforming or that he will take or retain them in spite of their nonconformity; or

    (b) fails to make an effective rejection (subsection (1) of Section 2—602), but such acceptance does not occur until the buyer has had a reasonable opportunity to inspect them; or

(c) does any act inconsistent with the seller's ownership; but if such act is wrongful as against the seller it is an acceptance only if ratified by him.

(2) Acceptance of a part of any commercial unit is acceptance of that entire unit.

§2—607. EFFECT OF ACCEPTANCE; NOTICE OF BREACH; BURDEN OF ESTABLISHING BREACH AFTER ACCEPTANCE; NOTICE OF CLAIM OR LITIGATION TO PERSON ANSWERABLE OVER

(1) The buyer must pay at the contract rate for any goods accepted.

(2) Acceptance of goods by the buyer precludes rejection of the goods accepted and if made with knowledge of a non-conformity cannot be revoked because of it unless the acceptance was on the reasonable assumption that the non-conformity would be seasonably cured but acceptance does not of itself impair any other remedy provided by this Article for non-conformity.

(3) Where a tender has been accepted

(a) the buyer must within a reasonable time after he discovers or should have discovered any breach notify the seller of breach or be barred from any remedy; and

(b) if the claim is one for infringement or the like (subsection (3) of Section 2—312) and the buyer is sued as a result of such a breach he must so notify the seller within a reasonable time after he receives notice of the litigation or be barred from any remedy over for liability established by the litigation.

(4) The burden is on the buyer to establish any breach with respect to the goods accepted.

(5) Where the buyer is sued for breach of a warranty or other obligation for which his seller is answerable over

(a) he may give his seller written notice of the litigation. If the notice states that the seller may come in and defend and that if the seller does not do so he will be bound in any action against him by his buyer by any determination of fact common to the two litigations, then unless the seller after seasonable receipt of the notice does come in and defend he is so bound.

(b) if the claim is one for infringement or the like (subsection (3) of Section 2—312) the original seller may demand in writing that his buyer turn over to him control of the litigation including settlement or else be barred from any remedy over and if he also agrees to bear all expense and to satisfy any adverse judgment, then unless the buyer after seasonable receipt of the demand does turn over control the buyer is so barred.

(6) The provisions of subsections (3), (4) and (5) apply to any obligation of a buyer to hold the seller harmless against infringement or the like (subsection (3) of Section 2—312).

§2—608. REVOCATION OF ACCEPTANCE IN WHOLE OR IN PART

(1) The buyer may revoke his acceptance of a lot or commercial unit whose non-conformity substantially impairs its value to him if he has accepted it

(a) on the reasonable assumption that its non-conformity would be cured and it has not been seasonably cured; or

(b) without discovery of such non-conformity if his acceptance was reasonably induced either by the difficulty of discovery before acceptance or by the seller's assurances.

(2) Revocation of acceptance must occur within a reasonable time after the buyer discovers or should have discovered the ground for it and before any substantial change in condition of the goods which is not caused by their own defects. It is not effective until the buyer notifies the seller of it.

(3) A buyer who so revokes has the same rights and duties with regard to the goods involved as if he had rejected them.

§2—609. RIGHT TO ADEQUATE ASSURANCE OF PERFORMANCE

(1) A contract for sale imposes an obligation on each party that the other's expectation of receiving due performance will not be impaired. When reasonable grounds for insecurity arise with respect to the performance of either party the other may in writing demand adequate assurance of due performance and until he receives such assurance may if commercially reasonable suspend any performance for which he has not already received the agreed return.

(2) Between merchants the reasonableness of grounds for insecurity and the adequacy of any assurance offered shall be determined according to commercial standards.

(3) Acceptance of any improper delivery or payment does not prejudice the party's right to demand adequate assurance of future performance.

(4) After receipt of a justified demand failure to provide within a reasonable time not exceeding thirty days such assurance of due performance as is adequate under the circumstances of the particular case is a repudiation of the contract.

§2—610. ANTICIPATORY REPUDIATION

When either party repudiates the contract with respect to a performance not yet due the loss of which will substantially impair the value of the contract to the other, the aggrieved party may

(a) for a commercially reasonable time await performance by the repudiating party; or

(b) resort to any remedy for breach (Section 2—703 or Section 2—711), even though he has notified the repudiating party that he would await the latter's performance and has urged retraction; and

(c) in either case suspend his own performance or proceed in accordance with the provisions of this Article on the seller's right to identify goods to the contract notwithstanding breach or to salvage unfinished goods (Section 2—704).

§2—611. RETRACTION OF ANTICIPATORY REPUDIATION

(1) Until the repudiating party's next performance is due he can retract his repudiation unless the aggrieved party has since the repudiation cancelled or materially changed his position or otherwise indicated that he considers the repudiation final.

(2) Retraction may be by any method which clearly indicates to the aggrieved party that the repudiating party intends to perform, but must include any assurance justifiably demanded under the provisions of this Article (Section 2—609).

(3) Retraction reinstates the repudiating party's rights under the contract with due excuse and allowance to the aggrieved party for any delay occasioned by the repudiation.

§2—612. "INSTALLMENT CONTRACT"; BREACH

(1) An "installment contract" is one which requires or authorizes the delivery of goods in separate lots to be separately accepted, even though the contract contains a clause "each delivery is a separate contract" or its equivalent.

(2) The buyer may reject any installment which is non-conforming if the non-conformity substantially impairs the value of that installment and cannot be cured or if the non-conformity is a defect in the required documents; but if the non-conformity does not fall within subsection (3) and the seller gives adequate assurance of its cure the buyer must accept that installment.

(3) Whenever non-conformity or default with respect to one or more installments substantially impairs the value of the whole contract there is a breach of the whole. But the aggrieved party reinstates the contract if he accepts a non-conforming installment without seasonably notifying of cancellation or if he brings an action with respect only to past installments or demands performance as to future installments.

§2—613. CASUALTY TO IDENTIFIED GOODS

Where the contract requires for its performance goods identified when the contract is made, and the goods suffer casualty without fault of either party before the risk of loss passes to the buyer, or in a proper case under a "no arrival, no sale" term (Section 2—324) then

(a) if the loss is total the contract is avoided; and

(b) if the loss is partial or the goods have so deteriorated as no longer to conform to the contract

the buyer may nevertheless demand inspection and at his option either treat the contract as voided or accept the goods with due allowance from the contract price for the deterioration or the deficiency in quantity but without further right against the seller.

§2—614. SUBSTITUTED PERFORMANCE

(1) Where without fault of either party the agreed berthing, loading, or unloading facilities fail or an agreed type of carrier becomes unavailable or the agreed manner of delivery otherwise becomes commercially impracticable but a commercially reasonable substitute is available, such substitute performance must be tendered and accepted.

(2) If the agreed means or manner of payment fails because of domestic or foreign governmental regulation, the seller may withhold or stop delivery unless the buyer provides a means or manner of payment which is commercially a substantial equivalent. If delivery has already been taken, payment by the means or in the manner provided by the regulation discharges the buyer's obligation unless the regulation is discriminatory, oppressive or predatory.

§2—615. EXCUSE BY FAILURE OF PRESUPPOSED CONDITIONS

Except so far as a seller may have assumed a greater obligation and subject to the preceding section on substituted performance:

(a) Delay in delivery or non-delivery in whole or in part by a seller who complies with paragraphs (b) and (c) is not a breach of his duty under a contract for sale if performance as agreed has been made impracticable by the occurrence of a contingency the nonoccurrence of which was a basic assumption on which the contract was made or by compliance in good faith with any applicable foreign or domestic governmental regulation or order whether or not it later proves to be invalid.

(b) Where the causes mentioned in paragraph (a) affect only a part of the seller's capacity to perform, he must allocate production and deliveries among his customers but may at his option include regular customers not then under contract as well as his own requirements for further manufacture. He may so allocate in any manner which is fair and reasonable.

(c) The seller must notify the buyer seasonably that there will be delay or non-delivery and, when allocation is required under paragraph (b), of the estimated quota thus made available for the buyer.

* * * *

§2—702. SELLER'S REMEDIES ON DISCOVERY OF BUYER'S INSOLVENCY

(1) Where the seller discovers the buyer to be insolvent he may refuse delivery except for cash including payment for all goods theretofore delivered under the contract, and stop delivery under this Article (Section 2—705).

(2) Where the seller discovers that the buyer has received goods on credit while insolvent he may reclaim the goods upon demand made within ten days after the receipt, but if misrepresentation of solvency has been made to the particular seller in writing within three months before delivery the ten day limitation does not apply. Except as provided in this subsection the seller may not base a right to reclaim goods on the buyer's fraudulent or innocent misrepresentation of solvency or of intent to pay.

(3) The seller's right to reclaim under subsection (2) is subject to the rights of a buyer in ordinary course or other good faith purchaser under this Article (Section 2—403). Successful reclamation of goods excludes all other remedies with respect to them.

§2—703. SELLER'S REMEDIES IN GENERAL

Where the buyer wrongfully rejects or revokes acceptance of goods or fails to make a payment due on or before delivery or repudiates with respect to a part or the whole, then with respect to any goods directly affected and, if the breach is of the whole contract (Section 2—612), then also with respect to the whole undelivered balance, the aggrieved seller may

(a) withhold delivery of such goods;

(b) stop delivery by any bailee as hereafter provided (Section 2—705);

(c) proceed under the next section respecting goods still unidentified to the contract;

(d) resell and recover damages as hereafter provided (Section 2—706);

(e) recover damages for non-acceptance (Section 2—708) or in a proper case the price (Section 2—709);

(f) cancel.

§2—704. SELLER'S RIGHT TO IDENTIFY GOODS TO THE CONTRACT NOTWITHSTANDING BREACH OR TO SALVAGE UNFINISHED GOODS

(1) An aggrieved seller under the preceding section may

(a) identify to the contract conforming goods not already identified if at the time he learned of the breach they are in his possession or control;

(b) treat as the subject of resale goods which have demonstrably been intended for the particular contract even though those goods are unfinished.

(2) Where the goods are unfinished an aggrieved seller may in the exercise of reasonable commercial judgment for the purposes of avoiding loss and of effective realization either complete the manufacture and wholly identify the goods to the contract or cease manufacture and resell for scrap or salvage value or proceed in any other reasonable manner.

§2—705. SELLER'S STOPPAGE OF DELIVERY IN TRANSIT OR OTHERWISE

(1) The seller may stop delivery of goods in the possession of a carrier or other bailee when he discovers the buyer to be insolvent (Section 2—702) and may stop delivery of carload, truckload, planeload or larger shipments of express or freight when the buyer repudiates or fails to make a payment due before delivery or if for any other reason the seller has a right to withhold or reclaim the goods.

(2) As against such buyer the seller may stop delivery until

(a) receipt of the goods by the buyer; or

(b) acknowledgment to the buyer by any bailee of the goods except a carrier that the bailee holds the goods for the buyer; or

(c) such acknowledgment to the buyer by a carrier by reshipment or as warehouseman; or

(d) negotiation to the buyer of any negotiable document of title covering the goods.

(3) ****

(a) To stop delivery the seller must so notify as to enable the bailee by reasonable diligence to prevent delivery of the goods.

(b) After such notification the bailee must hold and deliver the goods according to the directions of the seller but the seller is liable to the bailee for any ensuing charges or damages.

(c) If a negotiable document of title has been issued for goods the bailee is not obliged to obey a notification to stop until surrender of the document.

(d) A carrier who has issued a non-negotiable bill of lading is not obliged to obey a notification to stop received from a person other than the consignor.

§2—706. SELLER'S RESALE INCLUDING CONTRACT FOR RESALE

(1) Under the conditions stated in Section 2—703 on seller's remedies, the seller may resell the goods concerned or the undelivered balance thereof. Where the resale is made in good faith and in a commercially reasonable manner the seller may recover the difference between the resale price and the contract price together with any incidental damages allowed under the provisions of this Article (Section 2—710), but less expenses saved in consequence of the buyer's breach.

(2) Except as otherwise provided in subsection (3) or unless otherwise agreed resale may be at public or private sale including sale by way of one or more contracts to sell or of identification to an existing contract of the seller. Sale may be as a unit or in parcels and at any time and place and on any terms but every aspect of the sale including the method, manner, time, place and terms must be commercially reasonable. The resale must be reasonably identified as referring to the broken contract, but it is not necessary

that the goods be in existence or that any or all of them have been identified to the contract before the breach.

(3) Where the resale is at private sale the seller must give the buyer reasonable notification of his intention to resell.

(4) Where the resale is at public sale

(a) only identified goods can be sold except where there is a recognized market for a public sale of futures in goods of the kind; and

(b) it must be made at a usual place or market for public sale if one is reasonably available and except in the case of goods which are perishable or threaten to decline in value speedily the seller must give the buyer reasonable notice of the time and place of the resale; and

(c) if the goods are not to be within the view of those attending the sale the notification of sale must state the place where the goods are located and provide for their reasonable inspection by prospective bidders; and

(d) the seller may buy.

(5) A purchaser who buys in good faith at a resale takes the goods free of any rights of the original buyer even though the seller fails to comply with one or more of the requirements of this section.

(6) The seller is not accountable to the buyer for any profit made on any resale. A person in the position of a seller (Section 2—707) or a buyer who has rightfully rejected or justifiably revoked acceptance must account for any excess over the amount of his security interest, as hereinafter defined (subsection (3) of Section 2—711).

* * * *

§2—708. SELLER'S DAMAGES FOR NON-ACCEPTANCE OR REPUDIATION

(1) Subject to subsection (2) and to the provisions of this Article with respect to proof of market price (Section 2—723), the measure of damages for non-acceptance or repudiation by the buyer is the difference between the market price at the time and place for tender and the unpaid contract price together with any incidental damages provided in this Article (Section 2—710), but less expenses saved in consequence of the buyer's breach.

(2) If the measure of damages provided in subsection (1) is inadequate to put the seller in as good a position as performance would have done then the measure of damages is the profit (including reasonable overhead) which the seller would have made from full performance by the buyer, together with any incidental damages provided in this Article (Section 2—710), due allowance for costs reasonably incurred and due credit for payments or proceeds of resale.

§2—709. ACTION FOR THE PRICE

(1) When the buyer fails to pay the price as it becomes due the seller may recover, together with any incidental damages under the next section, the price

(a) of goods accepted or of conforming goods lost or damaged within a commercially reasonable time after risk of their loss has passed to the buyer; and

(b) of goods identified to the contract if the seller is unable after reasonable effort to resell them at a reasonable price or the circumstances reasonably indicate that such effort will be unavailing.

(2) Where the seller sues for the price he must hold for the buyer any goods which have been identified to the contract and are still in his control except that if resale becomes possible he may resell them at any time prior to the collection of the judgment. The net proceeds of any such resale must be credited to the buyer and payment of the judgment entitles him to any goods not resold.

(3) After the buyer has wrongfully rejected or revoked acceptance of the goods or has failed to make a payment due or has repudiated (Section 2—610), a seller who is held not entitled to the price under this section shall nevertheless be awarded damages for non-acceptance under the preceding section.

§2—710. SELLER'S INCIDENTAL DAMAGES

Incidental damages to an aggrieved seller include any commercially reasonable charges, expenses or commissions incurred in stopping delivery, in the transportation, care and custody of goods after the buyer's breach, in connection with return or resale of the goods or otherwise resulting from the breach.

§2—711. BUYER'S REMEDIES IN GENERAL; BUYER'S SECURITY INTEREST IN REJECTED GOODS

(1) Where the seller fails to make delivery or repudiates or the buyer rightfully rejects or justifiably revokes acceptance then with respect to any goods involved, and with respect to the whole if the breach goes to the whole contract (Section 2—612), the buyer may cancel and whether or not he has done so may in addition to recovering so much of the price as has been paid

(a) "cover" and have damages under the next section as to all the goods affected whether or not they have been identified to the contract; or

(b) recover damages for non-delivery as provided in this Article (Section 2—713).

(2) Where the seller fails to deliver or repudiates the buyer may also

(a) if the goods have been identified recover them as provided in this Article (Section 2—502); or

(b) in a proper case obtain specific performance or replevy the goods as provided in this Article (Section 2—716).

(3) On rightful rejection or justifiable revocation of acceptance a buyer has a security interest in goods in his

possession or control for any payments made on their price and any expenses reasonably incurred in their inspection, receipt, transportation, care and custody and may hold such goods and resell them in like manner as an aggrieved seller (Section 2—706).

§2—712. "COVER"; BUYER'S PROCUREMENT OF SUBSTITUTE GOODS

(1) After a breach within the preceding section the buyer may "cover" by making in good faith and without unreasonable delay any reasonable purchase of or contract to purchase goods in substitution for those due from the seller.

(2) The buyer may recover from the seller as damages the difference between the cost of cover and the contract price together with any incidental or consequential damages as hereinafter defined (Section 2—715), but less expenses saved in consequence of the seller's breach.

(3) Failure of the buyer to effect cover within this section does not bar him from any other remedy.

§2—713. BUYER'S DAMAGES FOR NON-DELIVERY OR REPUDIATION

(1) Subject to the provisions of this Article with respect to proof of market price (Section 2—723), the measure of damages for non-delivery or repudiation by the seller is the difference between the market price at the time when the buyer learned of the breach and the contract price together with any incidental and consequential damages provided in this Article (Section 2—715), but less expenses saved in consequence of the seller's breach.

(2) Market price is to be determined as of the place for tender or, in cases of rejection after arrival or revocation of acceptance, as of the place of arrival.

§2—714. BUYER'S DAMAGES FOR BREACH IN REGARD TO ACCEPTED GOODS

(1) Where the buyer has accepted goods and given notification (subsection (3) of Section 2—607) he may recover as damages for any non-conformity of tender the loss resulting in the ordinary course of events from the seller's breach as determined in any manner which is reasonable.

(2) The measure of damages for breach of warranty is the difference at the time and place of acceptance between the value of the goods accepted and the value they would have had if they had been as warranted, unless special circumstances show proximate damages of a different amount.

(3) In a proper case any incidental and consequential damages under the next section may also be recovered.

§2—715. BUYER'S INCIDENTAL AND CONSEQUENTIAL DAMAGES

(1) Incidental damages resulting from the seller's breach include expenses reasonably incurred in inspection, receipt,

transportation and care and custody of goods rightfully rejected, any commercially reasonable charges, expenses or commissions in connection with effecting cover and any other reasonable expense incident to the delay or other breach.

(2) Consequential damages resulting from the seller's breach include

    (a) any loss resulting from general or particular requirements and needs of which the seller at the time of contracting had reason to know and which could not reasonably be prevented by cover or otherwise; and

    (b) injury to person or property proximately resulting from any breach of warranty.

§2—716. BUYER'S RIGHT TO SPECIFIC PERFORMANCE OR REPLEVIN

(1) Specific performance may be decreed where the goods are unique or in other proper circumstances.

(2) The decree for specific performance may include such terms and conditions as to payment of the price, damages, or other relief as the court may deem just.

(3) The buyer has a right of replevin for goods identified to the contract if after reasonable effort he is unable to effect cover for such goods or the circumstances reasonably indicate that such effort will be unavailing or if the goods have been shipped under reservation and satisfaction of the security interest in them has been made or tendered. In the case of goods bought for personal, family, or household purposes, the buyer's right of replevin vests upon acquisition of a special property, even if the seller had not then repudiated or failed to deliver.

§2—717. DEDUCTION OF DAMAGES FROM THE PRICE

The buyer on notifying the seller of his intention to do so may deduct all or any part of the damages resulting from any breach of the contract from any part of the price still due under the same contract.

§2—718. LIQUIDATION OR LIMITATION OF DAMAGES; DEPOSITS

(1) Damages for breach by either party may be liquidated in the agreement but only at an amount which is reasonable in the light of the anticipated or actual harm caused by the breach, the difficulties of proof of loss, and the inconvenience or nonfeasibility of otherwise obtaining an adequate remedy. A term fixing unreasonably large liquidated damages is void as a penalty.

(2) Where the seller justifiably withholds delivery of goods because of the buyer's breach, the buyer is entitled to restitution of any amount by which the sum of his payments exceeds

    (a) the amount to which the seller is entitled by virtue of terms liquidating the seller's damages in accordance with subsection (1), or

(b) in the absence of such terms, twenty per cent of the value of the total performance for which the buyer is obligated under the contract or $500, whichever is smaller.

(3) The buyer's right to restitution under subsection (2) is subject to offset to the extent that the seller establishes

(a) a right to recover damages under the provisions of this Article other than subsection (1), and

(b) the amount or value of any benefits received by the buyer directly or indirectly by reason of the contract.

(4) Where a seller has received payment in goods their reasonable value or the proceeds of their resale shall be treated as payments for the purposes of subsection (2); but if the seller has notice of the buyer's breach before reselling goods received in part performance, his resale is subject to the conditions laid down in this Article on resale by an aggrieved seller (Section 2—706).

§2—719. CONTRACTUAL MODIFICATION OR LIMITATION OF REMEDY

(1) Subject to the provisions of subsections (2) and (3) of this section and of the preceding section on liquidation and limitation of damages,

(a) the agreement may provide for remedies in addition to or in substitution for those provided in this Article and may limit or alter the measure of damages recoverable under this Article, as by limiting the buyer's remedies to return of the goods and repayment of the price or to repair and replacement of non-conforming goods or parts; and

(b) resort to a remedy as provided is optional unless the remedy is expressly agreed to be exclusive, in which case it is the sole remedy.

(2) Where circumstances cause an exclusive or limited remedy to fail of its essential purpose, remedy may be had as provided in this Act.

(3) Consequential damages may be limited or excluded unless the limitation or exclusion is unconscionable. Limitation of consequential damages for injury to the person in the case of consumer goods is prima facie unconscionable but limitation of damages where the loss is commercial is not.

§2—720. EFFECT OF "CANCELLATION" OR "RESCISSION" ON CLAIMS FOR ANTECEDENT BREACH

Unless the contrary intention clearly appears, expressions of "cancellation" or "rescission" of the contract or the like shall not be construed as a renunciation or discharge of any claim in damages for an antecedent breach.

§2—721. REMEDIES FOR FRAUD

Remedies for material misrepresentation or fraud include all remedies available under this Article for non-fraudulent breach. Neither rescission or a claim for rescission of the contract for sale nor rejection or return of the goods shall bar or be deemed inconsistent with a claim for damages or other remedy.

§2—722. WHO CAN SUE THIRD PARTIES FOR INJURY TO GOODS

Where a third party so deals with goods which have been identified to a contract for sale as to cause actionable injury to a party to that contract

(a) a right of action against the third party is in either party to the contract for sale who has title to or a security interest or a special property or an insurable interest in the goods; and if the goods have been destroyed or converted a right of action is also in the party who either bore the risk of loss under the contract for sale or has since the injury assumed that risk as against the other;

(b) if at the time of the injury the party plaintiff did not bear the risk of loss as against the other party to the contract for sale and there is no arrangement between them for disposition of the recovery, his suit or settlement is, subject to his own interest, as a fiduciary for the other party to the contract;

(c) either party may with the consent of the other sue for the benefit of whom it may concern.

§2—723. PROOF OF MARKET PRICE: TIME AND PLACE

(1) If an action based on anticipatory repudiation comes to trial before the time for performance with respect to some or all of the goods, any damages based on market price (Section 2—708 or Section 2—713) shall be determined according to the price of such goods prevailing at the time when the aggrieved party learned of the repudiation.

(2) If evidence of a price prevailing at the times or places described in this Article is not readily available the price prevailing within any reasonable time before or after the time described or at any other place which in commercial judgment or under usage of trade would serve as a reasonable substitute for the one described may be used, making any proper allowance for the cost of transporting the goods to or from such other place.

(3) Evidence of a relevant price prevailing at a time or place other than the one described in this Article offered by one party is not admissible unless and until he has given the other party such notice as the court finds sufficient to prevent unfair surprise.

§2—724. ADMISSIBILITY OF MARKET QUOTATIONS

Whenever the prevailing price or value of any goods regularly bought and sold in any established commodity market is in issue, reports in official publications or trade journals or in newspapers or periodicals of general circulation published as the reports of such market shall be admissible in evidence. The circumstances of the preparation of such a report may be shown to affect its weight but not its admissibility.

§2—725. STATUTE OF LIMITATIONS IN CONTRACTS FOR SALE

(1) An action for breach of any contract for sale must be commenced within four years after the cause of action has accrued. By the original agreement the parties may reduce the period of limitation to not less than one year but may not extend it.

(2) A cause of action accrues when the breach occurs, regardless of the aggrieved party's lack of knowledge of the breach. A breach of warranty occurs when tender of delivery is made, except that where a warranty explicitly extends to future performance of the goods and discovery of the breach must await the time of such performance the cause of action accrues when the breach is or should have been discovered.

(3) Where an action commenced within the time limited by subsection (1) is so terminated as to leave available a remedy by another action for the same breach such other action may be commenced after the expiration of the time limited and within six months after the termination of the first action unless the termination resulted from voluntary discontinuance or from dismissal for failure or neglect to prosecute.

(4) This section does not alter the law on tolling of the statute of limitations nor does it apply to causes of action which have accrued before this Act becomes effective.

ARTICLE 2 AMENDMENTS (EXCERPTS)

Part 1 Short Title, General Construction and Subject Matter

* * * *

§2—103. DEFINITIONS AND INDEX OF DEFINITIONS

(1) In this article unless the context otherwise requires

* * * *

(b) "Conspicuous", with reference to a term, means so written, displayed, or presented that a reasonable person against which it is to operate ought to have noticed it. A term in an electronic record intended to evoke a response by an electronic agent is conspicuous if it is presented in a form that would enable a reasonably configured electronic agent to take it into account or react to it without review of the record by an individual. Whether a term is "conspicuous" or not is a decision for the court. Conspicuous terms include the following:

(i) for a person:

(A) a heading in capitals equal to or greater in size than the surrounding text, or in contrasting type, font, or color to the surrounding text of the same or lesser size;

(B) language in the body of a record or display in larger type than the surrounding text, or in contrasting type, font, or color to the surrounding text of the same size, or set off from surrounding text of the same size by symbols or other marks that call attention to the language; and

(ii) for a person or an electronic agent, a term that is so placed in a record or display that the person or electronic agent cannot proceed without taking action with respect to the particular term.

(c) "Consumer" means an individual who buys or contracts to buy goods that, at the time of contracting, are intended by the individual to be used primarily for personal, family, or household purposes.

(d) "Consumer contract" means a contract between a merchant seller and a consumer.

* * * *

(j) "Good faith" means honesty in fact and the observance of reasonable commercial standards of fair dealing.

(k) "Goods" means all things that are movable at the time of identification to a contract for sale. The term includes future goods, specially manufactured goods, the unborn young of animals, growing crops, and other identified things attached to realty as described in Section 2—107. The term does not include information, the money in which the price is to be paid, investment securities under Article 8, the subject matter of foreign exchange transactions, and choses in action.

* * * *

(m) "Record" means information that is inscribed on a tangible medium or that is stored in an electronic or other medium and is retrievable in perceivable form.

(n) "Remedial promise" means a promise by the seller to repair or replace the goods or to refund all or part of the price upon the happening of a specified event.

* * * *

(p) "Sign" means, with present intent to authenticate or adopt a record,

(i) to execute or adopt a tangible symbol; or

(ii) to attach to or logically associate with the record an electronic sound, symbol, or process.

* * * *

Part 2 Form, Formation, Terms and Readjustment of Contract; Electronic Contracting

§2—201. FORMAL REQUIREMENTS; STATUTE OF FRAUDS

(1) A contract for the sale of goods for the price of $5,000 or more is not enforceable by way of action or defense unless there is some record sufficient to indicate that a

contract for sale has been made between the parties and signed by the party against whom which enforcement is sought or by the party's authorized agent or broker. A record is not insufficient because it omits or incorrectly states a term agreed upon but the contract is not enforceable under this subsection beyond the quantity of goods shown in the record.

(2) Between merchants if within a reasonable time a record in confirmation of the contract and sufficient against the sender is received and the party receiving it has reason to know its contents, it satisfies the requirements of subsection (1) against such party the recipient unless notice of objection to its contents is given in a record within 10 days after it is received.

(3) A contract which does not satisfy the requirements of subsection (1) but which is valid in other respects is enforceable

(a) if the goods are to be specially manufactured for the buyer and are not suitable for sale to others in the ordinary course of the seller's business and the seller, before notice of repudiation is received and under circumstances which reasonably indicate that the goods are for the buyer, has made either a substantial beginning of their manufacture or commitments for their procurement; or

(b) if the party against whom which enforcement is sought admits in the party's pleading, or in the party's testimony or otherwise under oath that a contract for sale was made, but the contract is not enforceable under this paragraph beyond the quantity of goods admitted; or

(c) with respect to goods for which payment has been made and accepted or which have been received and accepted (Sec. 2—606).

(4) A contract that is enforceable under this section is not rendered unenforceable merely because it is not capable of being performed within one year or any other applicable period after its making.

* * * *

§2—207. TERMS OF CONTRACT; EFFECT OF CONFIRMATION

If (i) conduct by both parties recognizes the existence of a contract although their records do not otherwise establish a contract, (ii) a contract is formed by an offer and acceptance, or (iii) a contract formed in any manner is confirmed by a record that contains terms additional to or different from those in the contract being confirmed, the terms of the contract, subject to Section 2—202, are:

(a) terms that appear in the records of both parties;

(b) terms, whether in a record or not, to which both parties agree; and

(c) terms supplied or incorporated under any provision of this Act.

* * * *

Part 3 General Obligation and Construction of Contract

* * * *

§2—312. WARRANTY OF TITLE AND AGAINST INFRINGEMENT; BUYER'S OBLIGATION AGAINST INFRINGEMENT

(1) Subject to subsection (2) there is in a contract for sale a warranty by the seller that

(a) the title conveyed shall be good, good and its transfer rightful and shall not, because of any colorable claim to or interest in the goods, unreasonably expose the buyer to litigation; and

(b) the goods shall be delivered free from any security interest or other lien or encumbrance of which the buyer at the time of contracting has no knowledge.

(2) Unless otherwise agreed a seller that is a merchant regularly dealing in goods of the kind warrants that the goods shall be delivered free of the rightful claim of any third person by way of infringement or the like but a buyer that furnishes specifications to the seller must hold the seller harmless against any such claim that arises out of compliance with the specifications.

(3) A warranty under this section may be disclaimed or modified only by specific language or by circumstances that give the buyer reason to know that the seller does not claim title, that the seller is purporting to sell only the right or title as the seller or a third person may have, or that the seller is selling subject to any claims of infringement or the like.

§2—313. EXPRESS WARRANTIES BY AFFIRMATION, PROMISE, DESCRIPTION, SAMPLE; REMEDIAL PROMISE

(1) In this section, "immediate buyer" means a buyer that enters into a contract with the seller.

* * * *

(4) Any remedial promise made by the seller to the immediate buyer creates an obligation that the promise will be performed upon the happening of the specified event.

§2—313A. OBLIGATION TO REMOTE PURCHASER CREATED BY RECORD PACKAGED WITH OR ACCOMPANYING GOODS

(1) This section applies only to new goods and goods sold or leased as new goods in a transaction of purchase in the normal chain of distribution. In this section:

(a) "Immediate buyer" means a buyer that enters into a contract with the seller.

(b) "Remote purchaser" means a person that buys or leases goods from an immediate buyer or other person in the normal chain of distribution.

(2) If a seller in a record packaged with or accompanying the goods makes an affirmation of fact or promise that

relates to the goods, provides a description that relates to the goods, or makes a remedial promise, and the seller reasonably expects the record to be, and the record is, furnished to the remote purchaser, the seller has an obligation to the remote purchaser that:

(a) the goods will conform to the affirmation of fact, promise or description unless a reasonable person in the position of the remote purchaser would not believe that the affirmation of fact, promise or description created an obligation; and

(b) the seller will perform the remedial promise.

(3) It is not necessary to the creation of an obligation under this section that the seller use formal words such as "warrant" or "guarantee" or that the seller have a specific intention to undertake an obligation, but an affirmation merely of the value of the goods or a statement purporting to be merely the seller's opinion or commendation of the goods does not create an obligation.

(4) The following rules apply to the remedies for breach of an obligation created under this section:

(a) The seller may modify or limit the remedies available to the remote purchaser if the modification or limitation is furnished to the remote purchaser no later than the time of purchase or if the modification or limitation is contained in the record that contains the affirmation of fact, promise or description.

(b) Subject to a modification or limitation of remedy, a seller in breach is liable for incidental or consequential damages under Section 2—715, but the seller is not liable for lost profits.

(c) The remote purchaser may recover as damages for breach of a seller's obligation arising under subsection (2) the loss resulting in the ordinary course of events as determined in any manner that is reasonable.

(5) An obligation that is not a remedial promise is breached if the goods did not conform to the affirmation of fact, promise or description creating the obligation when the goods left the seller's control.

§2—313B. OBLIGATION TO REMOTE PURCHASER CREATED BY COMMUNICATION TO THE PUBLIC

(1) This section applies only to new goods and goods sold or leased as new goods in a transaction of purchase in the normal chain of distribution. In this section:

(a) "Immediate buyer" means a buyer that enters into a contract with the seller.

(b) "Remote purchaser" means a person that buys or leases goods from an immediate buyer or other person in the normal chain of distribution.

(2) If a seller in advertising or a similar communication to the public makes an affirmation of fact or promise that

relates to the goods, provides a description that relates to the goods, or makes a remedial promise, and the remote purchaser enters into a transaction of purchase with knowledge of and with the expectation that the goods will conform to the affirmation of fact, promise, or description, or that the seller will perform the remedial promise, the seller has an obligation to the remote purchaser that:

(a) the goods will conform to the affirmation of fact, promise or description unless a reasonable person in the position of the remote purchaser would not believe that the affirmation of fact, promise or description created an obligation; and

(b) the seller will perform the remedial promise.

(3) It is not necessary to the creation of an obligation under this section that the seller use formal words such as "warrant" or "guarantee" or that the seller have a specific intention to undertake an obligation, but an affirmation merely of the value of the goods or a statement purporting to be merely the seller's opinion or commendation of the goods does not create an obligation.

(4) The following rules apply to the remedies for breach of an obligation created under this section:

(a) The seller may modify or limit the remedies available to the remote purchaser if the modification or limitation is furnished to the remote purchaser no later than the time of purchase. The modification or limitation may be furnished as part of the communication that contains the affirmation of fact, promise or description.

(b) Subject to a modification or limitation of remedy, a seller in breach is liable for incidental or consequential damages under Section 2—715, but the seller is not liable for lost profits.

(c) The remote purchaser may recover as damages for breach of a seller's obligation arising under subsection (2) the loss resulting in the ordinary course of events as determined in any manner that is reasonable.

(5) An obligation that is not a remedial promise is breached if the goods did not conform to the affirmation of fact, promise or description creating the obligation when the goods left the seller's control.

* * * *

§2—316. EXCLUSION OR MODIFICATION OF WARRANTIES.

* * * *

(2) Subject to subsection (3), to exclude or modify the implied warranty of merchantability or any part of it in a consumer contract the language must be in a record, be conspicuous and state "The seller undertakes no responsibility for the quality of the goods except as otherwise provided in this contract," and in any other contract the language must mention merchantability and in case of a

record must be conspicuous. Subject to subsection (3), to exclude or modify the implied warranty of fitness the exclusion must be in a record and be conspicuous. Language to exclude all implied warranties of fitness in a consumer contract must state "The seller assumes no responsibility that the goods will be fit for any particular purpose for which you may be buying these goods, except as otherwise provided in the contract," and in any other contract the language is sufficient if it states, for example, that "There are no warranties which extend beyond the description on the face hereof." Language that satisfies the requirements of this subsection for the exclusion and modification of a warranty in a consumer contract also satisfies the requirements for any other contract.

(3) Notwithstanding subsection (2):

(a) unless the circumstances indicate otherwise, all implied warranties are excluded by expressions like "as is", "with all faults" or other language which in common understanding calls the buyer's attention to the exclusion of warranties, makes plain that there is no implied warranty, and in a consumer contract evidenced by a record is set forth conspicuously in the record; and

(b) when the buyer before entering into the contract has examined the goods or the sample or model as fully as desired or has refused to examine the goods after a demand by the seller there is no implied warranty with regard to defects which an examination ought in the circumstances to have revealed to the buyer; and

(c) an implied warranty can also be excluded or modified by course of dealing or course of performance or usage of trade.

* * * *

§2—318. THIRD PARTY BENEFICIARIES OF WARRANTIES EXPRESS OR IMPLIED

(1) In this section:

(a) "Immediate buyer" means a buyer that enters into a contract with the seller.

(b) "Remote purchaser" means a person that buys or leases goods from an immediate buyer or other person in the normal chain of distribution.

Alternative A to subsection (2)

(2) A seller's warranty whether express or implied to an immediate buyer, a seller's remedial promise to an immediate buyer, or a seller's obligation to a remote purchaser under Section 2—313A or 2—313B extends to any natural person who is in the family or household of the immediate buyer or the remote purchaser or who is a guest in the home of either if it is reasonable to expect that the person may use, consume or be affected by the goods and

who is injured in person by breach of the warranty, remedial promise or obligation. A seller may not exclude or limit the operation of this section.

Alternative B to subsection (2)

(2) A seller's warranty whether express or implied to an immediate buyer, a seller's remedial promise to an immediate buyer, or a seller's obligation to a remote purchaser under Section 2—313A or 2—313B extends to any natural person who may reasonably be expected to use, consume or be affected by the goods and who is injured in person by breach of the warranty, remedial promise or obligation. A seller may not exclude or limit the operation of this section.

Alternative C to subsection (2)

(2) A seller's warranty whether express or implied to an immediate buyer, a seller's remedial promise to an immediate buyer, or a seller's obligation to a remote purchaser under Section 2—313A or 2—313B extends to any person that may reasonably be expected to use, consume or be affected by the goods and that is injured by breach of the warranty, remedial promise or obligation. A seller may not exclude or limit the operation of this section with respect to injury to the person of an individual to whom the warranty, remedial promise or obligation extends.

* * * *

Part 5 Performance

* * * *

§2—502. BUYER'S RIGHT TO GOODS ON SELLER'S INSOLVENCY

(1) Subject to subsections (2) and (3) and even though the goods have not been shipped a buyer who that has paid a part or all of the price of goods in which the buyer has a special property under the provisions of the immediately preceding section may on making and keeping good a tender of any unpaid portion of their price recover them from the seller if:

(a) in the case of goods bought by a consumer, the seller repudiates or fails to deliver as required by the contract; or

(b) in all cases, the seller becomes insolvent within ten days after receipt of the first installment on their price.

(2) The buyer's right to recover the goods under subsection (1) vests upon acquisition of a special property, even if the seller had not then repudiated or failed to deliver.

(3) If the identification creating the special property has been made by the buyer, the buyer acquires the right to recover the goods only if they conform to the contract for sale.

* * * *

§2—508. CURE BY SELLER OF IMPROPER TENDER OR DELIVERY; REPLACEMENT

(1) Where the buyer rejects goods or a tender of delivery under Section 2—601 or 2—612 or except in a consumer contract justifiably revokes acceptance under Section 2—608(1)(b) and the agreed time for performance has not expired, a seller that has performed in good faith, upon seasonable notice to the buyer and at the seller's own expense, may cure the breach of contract by making a conforming tender of delivery within the agreed time. The seller shall compensate the buyer for all of the buyer's reasonable expenses caused by the seller's breach of contract and subsequent cure.

(2) Where the buyer rejects goods or a tender of delivery under Section 2—601 or 2—612 or except in a consumer contract justifiably revokes acceptance under Section 2—608(1)(b) and the agreed time for performance has expired, a seller that has performed in good faith, upon seasonable notice to the buyer and at the seller's own expense, may cure the breach of contract, if the cure is appropriate and timely under the circumstances, by making a tender of conforming goods. The seller shall compensate the buyer for all of the buyer's reasonable expenses caused by the seller's breach of contract and subsequent cure.

§2—509. RISK OF LOSS IN THE ABSENCE OF BREACH

(1) Where the contract requires or authorizes the seller to ship the goods by carrier

(a) if it does not require the seller to deliver them at a particular destination, the risk of loss passes to the buyer when the goods are delivered to the carrier even though the shipment is under reservation (Section 2—505); but

(b) if it does require the seller to deliver them at a particular destination and the goods are there tendered while in the possession of the carrier, the risk of loss passes to the buyer when the goods are there so tendered as to enable the buyer to take delivery.

(2) Where the goods are held by a bailee to be delivered without being moved, the risk of loss passes to the buyer

(a) on the buyer's receipt of a negotiable document of title covering the goods; or

(b) on acknowledgment by the bailee to the buyer of the buyer's right to possession of the goods; or

(c) after the buyer's receipt of a non-negotiable document of title or other direction to deliver in a record, as provided in subsection (4)(b) of Section 2—503.

(3) In any case not within subsection (1) or (2), the risk of loss passes to the buyer on the buyer's receipt of the goods.

* * * *

§2—513. BUYER'S RIGHT TO INSPECTION OF GOODS

* * * *

(3) Unless otherwise agreed, the buyer is not entitled to inspect the goods before payment of the price when the contract provides

(a) for delivery on terms that under applicable course of performance, course of dealing, or usage of trade are interpreted to preclude inspection before payment; or

(b) for payment against documents of title, except where such payment is due only after the goods are to become available for inspection.

* * * *

Part 6 Breach, Repudiation and Excuse
* * * *

§2—605. WAIVER OF BUYER'S OBJECTIONS BY FAILURE TO PARTICULARIZE

(1) The buyer's failure to state in connection with rejection a particular defect or in connection with revocation of acceptance a defect that justifies revocation precludes the buyer from relying on the unstated defect to justify rejection or revocation of acceptance if the defect is ascertainable by reasonable inspection

(a) where the seller had a right to cure the defect and could have cured it if stated seasonably; or

(b) between merchants when the seller has after rejection made a request in a record for a full and final statement in record form of all defects on which the buyer proposes to rely.

(2) A buyer's payment against documents tendered to the buyer made without reservation of rights precludes recovery of the payment for defects apparent on the face of the documents.

* * * *

§2—607. EFFECT OF ACCEPTANCE; NOTICE OF BREACH; BURDEN OF ESTABLISHING BREACH AFTER ACCEPTANCE; NOTICE OF CLAIM OR LITIGATION TO PERSON ANSWERABLE OVER

* * * *

(3) Where a tender has been accepted

(a) the buyer must within a reasonable time after the buyer discovers or should have discovered any breach notify the seller; however, failure to give timely notice bars the buyer from a remedy only to the extent that the seller is prejudiced by the failure and

(b) if the claim is one for infringement or the like (subsection (3) of Section 2—312) and the buyer is sued as a result of such a breach the buyer must so notify the seller within a reasonable time after the buyer receives notice of the litigation or be barred from any remedy over for liability established by the litigation.

* * * *

§2—608. REVOCATION OF ACCEPTANCE IN WHOLE OR IN PART

* * * *

(4) If a buyer uses the goods after a rightful rejection or justifiable revocation of acceptance, the following rules apply:

(a) Any use by the buyer that is unreasonable under the circumstances is wrongful as against the seller and is an acceptance only if ratified by the seller.

(b) Any use of the goods that is reasonable under the circumstances is not wrongful as against the seller and is not an acceptance, but in an appropriate case the buyer shall be obligated to the seller for the value of the use to the buyer.

* * * *

§2—612. "INSTALLMENT CONTRACT"; BREACH

* * * *

(2) The buyer may reject any installment which is nonconforming if the non-conformity substantially impairs the value of that installment to the buyer or if the nonconformity is a defect in the required documents; but if the non-conformity does not fall within subsection (3) and the seller gives adequate assurance of its cure the buyer must accept that installment.

(3) Whenever non-conformity or default with respect to one or more installments substantially impairs the value of the whole contract there is a breach of the whole. But the aggrieved party reinstates the contract if the party accepts a non-conforming installment without seasonably notifying of cancellation or if the party brings an action with respect only to past installments or demands performance as to future installments.

* * * *

Part 7 Remedies

§2—702. SELLER'S REMEDIES ON DISCOVERY OF BUYER'S INSOLVENCY

* * * *

(2) Where the seller discovers that the buyer has received goods on credit while insolvent the seller may reclaim the goods upon demand made within a reasonable time after the buyer's receipt of the goods. Except as provided in this subsection the seller may not base a right to reclaim goods on the buyer's fraudulent or innocent misrepresentation of solvency or of intent to pay.

* * * *

§2—705. SELLER'S STOPPAGE OF DELIVERY IN TRANSIT OR OTHERWISE

(1) The seller may stop delivery of goods in the possession of a carrier or other bailee when the seller discovers the buyer to be insolvent (Section 2—702) or when the buyer repudiates or fails to make a payment due before delivery or if for any other reason the seller has a right to withhold or reclaim the goods.

* * * *

§2—706. SELLER'S RESALE INCLUDING CONTRACT FOR RESALE

In an appropriate case involving breach by the buyer, the seller may resell the goods concerned or the undelivered balance thereof. Where the resale is made in good faith and in a commercially reasonable manner the seller may recover the difference between the contract price and the resale price together with any incidental or consequential damages allowed under the provisions of this Article (Section 2—710), but less expenses saved in consequence of the buyer's breach.

* * * *

§2—708. SELLER'S DAMAGES FOR NON-ACCEPTANCE OR REPUDIATION

(1) Subject to subsection (2) and to the provisions of this Article with respect to proof of market price (Section 2—723)

(a) the measure of damages for non-acceptance by the buyer is the difference between the contract price and the market price at the time and place for tender together with any incidental or consequential damages provided in this Article (Section 2—710), but less expenses saved in consequence of the buyer's breach; and

(b) the measure of damages for repudiation by the buyer is the difference between the contract price and the market price at the place for tender at the expiration of a commercially reasonable time after the seller learned of the repudiation, but no later than the time stated in paragraph (a), together with any incidental or consequential damages provided in this Article (Section 2—710), but less expenses saved in consequence of the buyer's breach.

(2) If the measure of damages provided in subsection (1) or in Section 2—706 is inadequate to put the seller in as good a position as performance would have done then the measure of damages is the profit (including reasonable overhead) which the seller would have made from full performance by the buyer, together with any incidental or consequential damages provided in this Article (Section 2—710).

§2—709. ACTION FOR THE PRICE

(1) When the buyer fails to pay the price as it becomes due the seller may recover, together with any incidental or consequential damages under the next section, the price

(a) of goods accepted or of conforming goods lost or damaged within a commercially reasonable time after risk of their loss has passed to the buyer; and

(b) of goods identified to the contract if the seller is unable after reasonable effort to resell them at a reasonable price or the circumstances reasonably indicate that such effort will be unavailing.

* * * *

§2—710. SELLER'S INCIDENTAL AND CONSEQUENTIAL DAMAGES

(1) Incidental damages to an aggrieved seller include any commercially reasonable charges, expenses or commissions incurred in stopping delivery, in the transportation, care and custody of goods after the buyer's breach, in connection with return or resale of the goods or otherwise resulting from the breach.

(2) Consequential damages resulting from the buyer's breach include any loss resulting from general or particular requirements and needs of which the buyer at the time of contracting had reason to know and which could not reasonably be prevented by resale or otherwise.

(3) In a consumer contract, a seller may not recover consequential damages from a consumer.

* * * *

§2—713. BUYER'S DAMAGES FOR NON-DELIVERY OR REPUDIATION

(1) Subject to the provisions of this Article with respect to proof of market price (Section 2—723), if the seller wrongfully fails to deliver or repudiates or the buyer rightfully rejects or justifiably revokes acceptance

(a) the measure of damages in the case of wrongful failure to deliver by the seller or rightful rejection or justifiable revocation of acceptance by the buyer is the difference between the market price at the time for tender under the contract and the contract price together with any incidental or consequential damages provided in this Article (Section 2—715), but less expenses saved in consequence of the seller's breach; and

(b) the measure of damages for repudiation by the seller is the difference between the market price at the expiration of a commercially reasonable time after the buyer learned of the repudiation, but no later than the time stated in paragraph (a), and the contract price together with any incidental or consequential damages provided in this Article (Section 2—715), but less expenses saved in consequence of the seller's breach.

* * * *

§2—725. STATUTE OF LIMITATIONS IN CONTRACTS FOR SALE

(1) Except as otherwise provided in this section, an action for breach of any contract for sale must be commenced within the later of four years after the right of action has accrued under subsection (2) or (3) or one year after the breach was or should have been discovered, but no longer than five years after the right of action accrued. By the original agreement the parties may reduce the period of limitation to not less than one year but may not extend it; however, in a consumer contract, the period of limitation may not be reduced.

(2) Except as otherwise provided in subsection (3), the following rules apply:

(a) Except as otherwise provided in this subsection, a right of action for breach of a contract accrues when the breach occurs, even if the aggrieved party did not have knowledge of the breach.

(b) For breach of a contract by repudiation, a right of action accrues at the earlier of when the aggrieved party elects to treat the repudiation as a breach or when a commercially reasonable time for awaiting performance has expired.

* * * *

ARTICLE 2A LEASES

§2A—102. SCOPE

This Article applies to any transaction, regardless of form, that creates a lease.

§2A—103. DEFINITIONS AND INDEX OF DEFINITIONS

* * * *

(e) "Consumer lease" means a lease that a lessor regularly engaged in the business of leasing or selling makes to a lessee who is an individual and who takes under the lease primarily for a personal, family, or household purpose [, if the total payments to be made under the lease contract, excluding payments for options to renew or buy, do not exceed $___].

* * * *

(g) "Finance lease" means a lease with respect to which:

(i) the lessor does not select, manufacture or supply the goods;

(ii) the lessor acquires the goods or the right to possession and use of the goods in connection with the lease; and

(iii) one of the following occurs:

(A) the lessee receives a copy of the contract by which the lessor acquired the goods or the right to possession and use of the goods before signing the lease contract;

(B) the lessee's approval of the contract by which the lessor acquired the goods or the right to possession and use of the goods is a condition to effectiveness of the lease contract;

(C) the lessee, before signing the lease contract, receives an accurate and complete statement designating the promises and warranties, and any disclaimers of warranties, limitations or modifications of remedies, or liquidated damages, including those of a third party, such as the manufacturer of the goods, provided to the lessor by the person supplying the goods in connection with or as part of the contract by which the lessor acquired the goods or the right to possession and use of the goods; or

(D) if the lease is not a consumer lease, the lessor, before the lessee signs the lease contract, informs the lessee in writing (a) of the identity of the person supplying the goods to the lessor, unless the lessee has selected that person and directed the lessor to acquire the goods or the right to possession and use of the goods from that person, (b) that the lessee is entitled under this Article to any promises and warranties, including those of any third party, provided to the lessor by the person supplying the goods in connection with or as part of the contract by which the lessor acquired the goods or the right to possession and use of the goods, and (c) that the lessee may communicate with the person supplying the goods to the lessor and receive an accurate and complete statement of those promises and warranties, including any disclaimers and limitations of them or of remedies.

* * * *

(h) "Goods" means all things that are movable at the time of identification to the lease contract, or are fixtures (Section 2A—309), but the term does not include money, documents, instruments, accounts, chattel paper, general intangibles, or minerals or the like, including oil and gas, before extraction. The term also includes the unborn young of animals.

(i) "Installment lease contract" means a lease contract that authorizes or requires the delivery of goods in separate lots to be separately accepted, even though the lease contract contains a clause "each delivery is a separate lease" or its equivalent.

(j) "Lease" means a transfer of the right to possession and use of goods for a term in return for consideration, but a sale, including a sale on approval or a sale or return, or retention or creation of a security interest is not a lease. Unless the context clearly indicates otherwise, the term includes a sublease.

(k) "Lease agreement" means the bargain, with respect to the lease, of the lessor and the lessee in fact as found in their language or by implication from other circumstances including course of dealing or usage of trade or course of performance as provided in this Article. Unless the context clearly indicates otherwise, the term includes a sublease agreement.

(l) "Lease contract" means the total legal obligation that results from the lease agreement as affected by this Article and any other applicable rules of law. Unless the context clearly indicates otherwise, the term includes a sublease contract.

* * * *

(o) "Lessee in ordinary course of business" means a person who in good faith and without knowledge that the lease to him [or her] is in violation of the ownership rights or security interest or leasehold interest of a third party in the goods, leases in ordinary course from a person in the business of selling or leasing goods of that kind but does not include a pawnbroker. "Leasing" may be for cash or by exchange of other property or on secured or unsecured credit and includes receiving goods or documents of title under a pre-existing lease contract but does not include a transfer in bulk or as security for or in total or partial satisfaction of a money debt.

(p) "Lessor" means a person who transfers the right to possession and use of goods under a lease. Unless the context clearly indicates otherwise, the term includes a sublessor.

(q) "Lessor's residual interest" means the lessor's interest in the goods after expiration, termination, or cancellation of the lease contract.

* * * *

§2A—104. LEASES SUBJECT TO OTHER LAW

(1) A lease, although subject to this Article, is also subject to any applicable:

(a) certificate of title statute of this State: (list any certificate of title statutes covering automobiles, trailers, mobile homes, boats, farm tractors, and the like);

(b) certificate of title statute of another jurisdiction (Section 2A—105); or

(c) consumer protection statute of this State, or final consumer protection decision of a court of this State existing on the effective date of this Article.

§2A—105. TERRITORIAL APPLICATION OF ARTICLE TO GOODS COVERED BY CERTIFICATE OF TITLE

Subject to the provisions of Sections 2A—304(3) and 2A—305(3), with respect to goods covered by a certificate of title issued under a statute of this State or of another jurisdiction, compliance and the effect of compliance or noncompliance with a certificate of title statute are governed by the law (including the conflict of laws rules) of the jurisdiction issuing the certificate until the earlier of (a) surrender of the certificate, or (b) four months after the goods are removed from that jurisdiction and thereafter until a new certificate of title is issued by another jurisdiction.

* * * *

§2A—108. UNCONSCIONABILITY

(1) If the court as a matter of law finds a lease contract or any clause of a lease contract to have been unconscionable at the time it was made the court may refuse to enforce the lease contract, or it may enforce the remainder of the lease contract without the unconscionable clause, or it may so

limit the application of any unconscionable clause as to avoid any unconscionable result.

(2) With respect to a consumer lease, if the court as a matter of law finds that a lease contract or any clause of a lease contract has been induced by unconscionable conduct or that unconscionable conduct has occurred in the collection of a claim arising from a lease contract, the court may grant appropriate relief.

(3) Before making a finding of unconscionability under subsection (1) or (2), the court, on its own motion or that of a party, shall afford the parties a reasonable opportunity to present evidence as to the setting, purpose, and effect of the lease contract or clause thereof, or of the conduct.

(4) In an action in which the lessee claims unconscionability with respect to a consumer lease:

    (a) If the court finds unconscionability under subsection (1) or (2), the court shall award reasonable attorney's fees to the lessee.

    (b) If the court does not find unconscionability and the lessee claiming unconscionability has brought or maintained an action he [or she] knew to be groundless, the court shall award reasonable attorney's fees to the party against whom the claim is made.

    (c) In determining attorney's fees, the amount of the recovery on behalf of the claimant under subsections (1) and (2) is not controlling.

§2A—109. OPTION TO ACCELERATE AT WILL

(1) A term providing that one party or his [or her] successor in interest may accelerate payment or performance or require collateral or additional collateral "at will" or "when he [or she] deems himself [or herself] insecure" or in words of similar import must be construed to mean that he [or she] has power to do so only if he [or she] in good faith believes that the prospect of payment or performance is impaired.

(2) With respect to a consumer lease, the burden of establishing good faith under subsection (1) is on the party who exercised the power; otherwise the burden of establishing lack of good faith is on the party against whom the power has been exercised.

Part 2 Formation and Construction of Lease Contract

§2A—201. STATUTE OF FRAUDS

(1) A lease contract is not enforceable by way of action or defense unless:

    (a) the total payments to be made under the lease contract, excluding payments for options to renew or buy, are less than $1,000; or

    (b) there is a writing, signed by the party against whom enforcement is sought or by that party's authorized agent, sufficient to indicate that a lease contract has been made between the parties and to describe the goods leased and the lease term.

(2) Any description of leased goods or of the lease term is sufficient and satisfies subsection (1)(b), whether or not it is specific, if it reasonably identifies what is described.

(3) A writing is not insufficient because it omits or incorrectly states a term agreed upon, but the lease contract is not enforceable under subsection (1)(b) beyond the lease term and the quantity of goods shown in the writing.

(4) A lease contract that does not satisfy the requirements of subsection (1), but which is valid in other respects, is enforceable:

    (a) if the goods are to be specially manufactured or obtained for the lessee and are not suitable for lease or sale to others in the ordinary course of the lessor's business, and the lessor, before notice of repudiation is received and under circumstances that reasonably indicate that the goods are for the lessee, has made either a substantial beginning of their manufacture or commitments for their procurement;

    (b) if the party against whom enforcement is sought admits in that party's pleading, testimony or otherwise in court that a lease contract was made, but the lease contract is not enforceable under this provision beyond the quantity of goods admitted; or

    (c) with respect to goods that have been received and accepted by the lessee.

(5) The lease term under a lease contract referred to in subsection (4) is:

    (a) if there is a writing signed by the party against whom enforcement is sought or by that party's authorized agent specifying the lease term, the term so specified;

    (b) if the party against whom enforcement is sought admits in that party's pleading, testimony, or otherwise in court a lease term, the term so admitted; or

    (c) a reasonable lease term.

§2A—202. FINAL WRITTEN EXPRESSION: PAROL OR EXTRINSIC EVIDENCE

Terms with respect to which the confirmatory memoranda of the parties agree or which are otherwise set forth in a writing intended by the parties as a final expression of their agreement with respect to such terms as are included therein may not be contradicted by evidence of any prior agreement or of a contemporaneous oral agreement but may be explained or supplemented:

    (a) by course of dealing or usage of trade or by course of performance; and

(b) by evidence of consistent additional terms unless the court finds the writing to have been intended also as a complete and exclusive statement of the terms of the agreement.

* * * *

§2A—205. FIRM OFFERS

An offer by a merchant to lease goods to or from another person in a signed writing that by its terms gives assurance it will be held open is not revocable, for lack of consideration, during the time stated or, if no time is stated, for a reasonable time, but in no event may the period of irrevocability exceed 3 months. Any such term of assurance on a form supplied by the offeree must be separately signed by the offeror.

§2A—206. OFFER AND ACCEPTANCE IN FORMATION OF LEASE CONTRACT

(1) Unless otherwise unambiguously indicated by the language or circumstances, an offer to make a lease contract must be construed as inviting acceptance in any manner and by any medium reasonable in the circumstances.

(2) If the beginning of a requested performance is a reasonable mode of acceptance, an offeror who is not notified of acceptance within a reasonable time may treat the offer as having lapsed before acceptance.

§2A—207. COURSE OF PERFORMANCE OR PRACTICAL CONSTRUCTION

(1) If a lease contract involves repeated occasions for performance by either party with knowledge of the nature of the performance and opportunity for objection to it by the other, any course of performance accepted or acquiesced in without objection is relevant to determine the meaning of the lease agreement.

(2) The express terms of a lease agreement and any course of performance, as well as any course of dealing and usage of trade, must be construed whenever reasonable as consistent with each other; but if that construction is unreasonable, express terms control course of performance, course of performance controls both course of dealing and usage of trade, and course of dealing controls usage of trade.

(3) Subject to the provisions of Section 2A—208 on modification and waiver, course of performance is relevant to show a waiver or modification of any term inconsistent with the course of performance.

§2A—208. MODIFICATION, RESCISSION AND WAIVER

(1) An agreement modifying a lease contract needs no consideration to be binding.

(2) A signed lease agreement that excludes modification or rescission except by a signed writing may not be otherwise modified or rescinded, but, except as between merchants, such a requirement on a form supplied by a merchant must be separately signed by the other party.

(3) Although an attempt at modification or rescission does not satisfy the requirements of subsection (2), it may operate as a waiver.

(4) A party who has made a waiver affecting an executory portion of a lease contract may retract the waiver by reasonable notification received by the other party that strict performance will be required of any term waived, unless the retraction would be unjust in view of a material change of position in reliance on the waiver.

* * * *

§2A—216. THIRD-PARTY BENEFICIARIES OF EXPRESS AND IMPLIED WARRANTIES

Alternative A

A warranty to or for the benefit of a lessee under this Article, whether express or implied, extends to any natural person who is in the family or household of the lessee or who is a guest in the lessee's home if it is reasonable to expect that such person may use, consume, or be affected by the goods and who is injured in person by breach of the warranty. This section does not displace principles of law and equity that extend a warranty to or for the benefit of a lessee to other persons. The operation of this section may not be excluded, modified, or limited, but an exclusion, modification, or limitation of the warranty, including any with respect to rights and remedies, effective against the lessee is also effective against any beneficiary designated under this section.

Alternative B

A warranty to or for the benefit of a lessee under this Article, whether express or implied, extends to any natural person who may reasonably be expected to use, consume, or be affected by the goods and who is injured in person by breach of the warranty. This section does not displace principles of law and equity that extend a warranty to or for the benefit of a lessee to other persons. The operation of this section may not be excluded, modified, or limited, but an exclusion, modification, or limitation of the warranty, including any with respect to rights and remedies, effective against the lessee is also effective against the beneficiary designated under this section.

Alternative C

A warranty to or for the benefit of a lessee under this Article, whether express or implied, extends to any person who may reasonably be expected to use, consume, or be affected by the goods and who is injured by breach of the warranty. The operation of this section may not be excluded, modified, or limited with respect to injury to the person of an individual to whom the warranty extends, but an exclusion, modification, or limitation of the warranty, including any with respect to rights and remedies, effective against the lessee is also effective against the beneficiary designated under this section.

* * * *

§2A—219. RISK OF LOSS

(1) Except in the case of a finance lease, risk of loss is retained by the lessor and does not pass to the lessee. In the case of a finance lease, risk of loss passes to the lessee.

(2) Subject to the provisions of this Article on the effect of default on risk of loss (Section 2A—220), if risk of loss is to pass to the lessee and the time of passage is not stated, the following rules apply:

(a) If the lease contract requires or authorizes the goods to be shipped by carrier

(i) and it does not require delivery at a particular destination, the risk of loss passes to the lessee when the goods are duly delivered to the carrier; but

(ii) if it does require delivery at a particular destination and the goods are there duly tendered while in the possession of the carrier, the risk of loss passes to the lessee when the goods are there duly so tendered as to enable the lessee to take delivery.

(b) If the goods are held by a bailee to be delivered without being moved, the risk of loss passes to the lessee on acknowledgment by the bailee of the lessee's right to possession of the goods.

(c) In any case not within subsection (a) or (b), the risk of loss passes to the lessee on the lessee's receipt of the goods if the lessor, or, in the case of a finance lease, the supplier, is a merchant; otherwise the risk passes to the lessee on tender of delivery.

§2A—220. EFFECT OF DEFAULT ON RISK OF LOSS

(1) Where risk of loss is to pass to the lessee and the time of passage is not stated:

(a) If a tender or delivery of goods so fails to conform to the lease contract as to give a right of rejection, the risk of their loss remains with the lessor, or, in the case of a finance lease, the supplier, until cure or acceptance.

(b) If the lessee rightfully revokes acceptance, he [or she], to the extent of any deficiency in his [or her] effective insurance coverage, may treat the risk of loss as having remained with the lessor from the beginning.

(2) Whether or not risk of loss is to pass to the lessee, if the lessee as to conforming goods already identified to a

lease contract repudiates or is otherwise in default under the lease contract, the lessor, or, in the case of a finance lease, the supplier, to the extent of any deficiency in his [or her] effective insurance coverage may treat the risk of loss as resting on the lessee for a commercially reasonable time.

* * * *

§2A—304. SUBSEQUENT LEASE OF GOODS BY LESSOR

(1) Subject to Section 2A—303, a subsequent lessee from a lessor of goods under an existing lease contract obtains, to the extent of the leasehold interest transferred, the leasehold interest in the goods that the lessor had or had power to transfer, and except as provided in subsection (2) and Section 2A—527(4), takes subject to the existing lease contract. A lessor with voidable title has power to transfer a good leasehold interest to a good faith subsequent lessee for value, but only to the extent set forth in the preceding sentence. If goods have been delivered under a transaction of purchase the lessor has that power even though:

(a) the lessor's transferor was deceived as to the identity of the lessor;

(b) the delivery was in exchange for a check which is later dishonored;

(c) it was agreed that the transaction was to be a "cash sale"; or

(d) the delivery was procured through fraud punishable as larcenous under the criminal law.

(2) A subsequent lessee in the ordinary course of business from a lessor who is a merchant dealing in goods of that kind to whom the goods were entrusted by the existing lessee of that lessor before the interest of the subsequent lessee became enforceable against that lessor obtains, to the extent of the leasehold interest transferred, all of that lessor's and the existing lessee's rights to the goods, and takes free of the existing lease contract.

(3) A subsequent lessee from the lessor of goods that are subject to an existing lease contract and are covered by a certificate of title issued under a statute of this State or of another jurisdiction takes no greater rights than those provided both by this section and by the certificate of title statute.

§2A—305. SALE OR SUBLEASE OF GOODS BY LESSEE

(1) Subject to the provisions of Section 2A—303, a buyer or sublessee from the lessee of goods under an existing lease contract obtains, to the extent of the interest transferred, the leasehold interest in the goods that the lessee had or had power to transfer, and except as provided in subsection (2) and Section 2A—511(4), takes subject to the existing lease contract. A lessee with a voidable leasehold interest has power to transfer a good leasehold interest to a good faith buyer for value or a good faith sublessee for value, but

only to the extent set forth in the preceding sentence. When goods have been delivered under a transaction of lease the lessee has that power even though:

(a) the lessor was deceived as to the identity of the lessee;

(b) the delivery was in exchange for a check which is later dishonored; or

(c) the delivery was procured through fraud punishable as larcenous under the criminal law.

(2) A buyer in the ordinary course of business or a sublessee in the ordinary course of business from a lessee who is a merchant dealing in goods of that kind to whom the goods were entrusted by the lessor obtains, to the extent of the interest transferred, all of the lessor's and lessee's rights to the goods, and takes free of the existing lease contract.

(3) A buyer or sublessee from the lessee of goods that are subject to an existing lease contract and are covered by a certificate of title issued under a statute of this State or of another jurisdiction takes no greater rights than those provided both by this section and by the certificate of title statute.

* * * *

§2A—501. DEFAULT: PROCEDURE

(1) Whether the lessor or the lessee is in default under a lease contract is determined by the lease agreement and this Article.

(2) If the lessor or the lessee is in default under the lease contract, the party seeking enforcement has rights and remedies as provided in this Article and, except as limited by this Article, as provided in the lease agreement.

(3) If the lessor or the lessee is in default under the lease contract, the party seeking enforcement may reduce the party's claim to judgment, or otherwise enforce the lease contract by self-help or any available judicial procedure or nonjudicial procedure, including administrative proceeding, arbitration, or the like, in accordance with this Article.

(4) Except as otherwise provided in Section 1—106 (1) or this Article or the lease agreement, the rights and remedies referred to in subsections (2) and (3) are cumulative.

(5) If the lease agreement covers both real property and goods, the party seeking enforcement may proceed under this Part as to the goods, or under other applicable law as to both the real property and the goods in accordance with that party's rights and remedies in respect of the real property, in which case this Part does not apply.

§2A—502. NOTICE AFTER DEFAULT

Except as otherwise provided in this Article or the lease agreement, the lessor or lessee in default under the lease contract is not entitled to notice of default or notice of enforcement from the other party to the lease agreement.

§2A—503. MODIFICATION OR IMPAIRMENT OF RIGHTS AND REMEDIES

(1) Except as otherwise provided in this Article, the lease agreement may include rights and remedies for default in addition to or in substitution for those provided in this Article and may limit or alter the measure of damages recoverable under this Article.

(2) Resort to a remedy provided under this Article or in the lease agreement is optional unless the remedy is expressly agreed to be exclusive. If circumstances cause an exclusive or limited remedy to fail of its essential purpose, or provision for an exclusive remedy is unconscionable, remedy may be had as provided in this Article.

(3) Consequential damages may be liquidated under Section 2A—504, or may otherwise be limited, altered, or excluded unless the limitation, alteration, or exclusion is unconscionable. Limitation, alteration, or exclusion of consequential damages for injury to the person in the case of consumer goods is prima facie unconscionable but limitation, alteration, or exclusion of damages where the loss is commercial is not prima facie unconscionable.

(4) Rights and remedies on default by the lessor or the lessee with respect to any obligation or promise collateral or ancillary to the lease contract are not impaired by this Article.

As amended in 1990.

§2A—504. LIQUIDATION OF DAMAGES

(1) Damages payable by either party for default, or any other act or omission, including indemnity for loss or diminution of anticipated tax benefits or loss or damage to lessor's residual interest, may be liquidated in the lease agreement but only at an amount or by a formula that is reasonable in light of the then anticipated harm caused by the default or other act or omission.

(2) If the lease agreement provides for liquidation of damages, and such provision does not comply with subsection (1), or such provision is an exclusive or limited remedy that circumstances cause to fail of its essential purpose, remedy may be had as provided in this Article.

(3) If the lessor justifiably withholds or stops delivery of goods because of the lessee's default or insolvency (Section 2A—525 or 2A—526), the lessee is entitled to restitution of any amount by which the sum of his [or her] payments exceeds:

(a) the amount to which the lessor is entitled by virtue of terms liquidating the lessor's damages in accordance with subsection (1); or

(b) in the absence of those terms, 20 percent of the then present value of the total rent the lessee was obligated to pay for the balance of the lease term, or, in the case of a consumer lease, the lesser of such amount or $500.

(4) A lessee's right to restitution under subsection (3) is subject to offset to the extent the lessor establishes:

(a) a right to recover damages under the provisions of this Article other than subsection (1); and

(b) the amount or value of any benefits received by the lessee directly or indirectly by reason of the lease contract.

§2A—505. CANCELLATION AND TERMINATION AND EFFECT OF CANCELLATION, TERMINATION, RESCISSION, OR FRAUD ON RIGHTS AND REMEDIES

(1) On cancellation of the lease contract, all obligations that are still executory on both sides are discharged, but any right based on prior default or performance survives, and the cancelling party also retains any remedy for default of the whole lease contract or any unperformed balance.

(2) On termination of the lease contract, all obligations that are still executory on both sides are discharged but any right based on prior default or performance survives.

(3) Unless the contrary intention clearly appears, expressions of "cancellation," "rescission," or the like of the lease contract may not be construed as a renunciation or discharge of any claim in damages for an antecedent default.

(4) Rights and remedies for material misrepresentation or fraud include all rights and remedies available under this Article for default.

(5) Neither rescission nor a claim for rescission of the lease contract nor rejection or return of the goods may bar or be deemed inconsistent with a claim for damages or other right or remedy.

§2A—506. STATUTE OF LIMITATIONS

(1) An action for default under a lease contract, including breach of warranty or indemnity, must be commenced within 4 years after the cause of action accrued. By the original lease contract the parties may reduce the period of limitation to not less than one year.

(2) A cause of action for default accrues when the act or omission on which the default or breach of warranty is based is or should have been discovered by the aggrieved party, or when the default occurs, whichever is later. A cause of action for indemnity accrues when the act or omission on which the claim for indemnity is based is or should have been discovered by the indemnified party, whichever is later.

(3) If an action commenced within the time limited by subsection (1) is so terminated as to leave available a remedy by another action for the same default or breach of warranty or indemnity, the other action may be commenced after the expiration of the time limited and within 6 months after the termination of the first action unless the termination resulted from voluntary discontinuance or from dismissal for failure or neglect to prosecute.

(4) This section does not alter the law on tolling of the statute of limitations nor does it apply to causes of action that have accrued before this Article becomes effective.

* * * *

§2A—508. LESSEE'S REMEDIES

(1) If a lessor fails to deliver the goods in conformity to the lease contract (Section 2A—509) or repudiates the lease contract (Section 2A—402), or a lessee rightfully rejects the goods (Section 2A—509) or justifiably revokes acceptance of the goods (Section 2A—517), then with respect to any goods involved, and with respect to all of the goods if under an installment lease contract the value of the whole lease contract is substantially impaired (Section 2A—510), the lessor is in default under the lease contract and the lessee may:

(a) cancel the lease contract (Section 2A—505(1));

(b) recover so much of the rent and security as has been paid and is just under the circumstances;

(c) cover and recover damages as to all goods affected whether or not they have been identified to the lease contract (Sections 2A—518 and 2A—520), or recover damages for nondelivery (Sections 2A—519 and 2A—520);

(d) exercise any other rights or pursue any other remedies provided in the lease contract.

(2) If a lessor fails to deliver the goods in conformity to the lease contract or repudiates the lease contract, the lessee may also:

(a) if the goods have been identified, recover them (Section 2A—522); or

(b) in a proper case, obtain specific performance or replevy the goods (Section 2A—521).

(3) If a lessor is otherwise in default under a lease contract, the lessee may exercise the rights and pursue the remedies provided in the lease contract, which may include a right to cancel the lease, and in Section 2A—519(3).

(4) If a lessor has breached a warranty, whether express or implied, the lessee may recover damages (Section 2A—519(4)).

(5) On rightful rejection or justifiable revocation of acceptance, a lessee has a security interest in goods in the lessee's possession or control for any rent and security that has been paid and any expenses reasonably incurred in their inspection, receipt, transportation, and care and custody and may hold those goods and dispose of them in good faith and in a commercially reasonable manner, subject to Section 2A—527(5).

(6) Subject to the provisions of Section 2A—407, a lessee, on notifying the lessor of the lessee's intention to do so,

may deduct all or any part of the damages resulting from any default under the lease contract from any part of the rent still due under the same lease contract.

§2A—509. LESSEE'S RIGHTS ON IMPROPER DELIVERY; RIGHTFUL REJECTION

(1) Subject to the provisions of Section 2A—510 on default in installment lease contracts, if the goods or the tender or delivery fail in any respect to conform to the lease contract, the lessee may reject or accept the goods or accept any commercial unit or units and reject the rest of the goods.

(2) Rejection of goods is ineffective unless it is within a reasonable time after tender or delivery of the goods and the lessee seasonably notifies the lessor.

* * * *

§2A—512. LESSEE'S DUTIES AS TO RIGHTFULLY REJECTED GOODS

(1) Except as otherwise provided with respect to goods that threaten to decline in value speedily (Section 2A—511) and subject to any security interest of a lessee (Section 2A—508(5)):

(a) the lessee, after rejection of goods in the lessee's possession, shall hold them with reasonable care at the lessor's or the supplier's disposition for a reasonable time after the lessee's seasonable notification of rejection;

(b) if the lessor or the supplier gives no instructions within a reasonable time after notification of rejection, the lessee may store the rejected goods for the lessor's or the supplier's account or ship them to the lessor or the supplier or dispose of them for the lessor's or the supplier's account with reimbursement in the manner provided in Section 2A—511; but

(c) the lessee has no further obligations with regard to goods rightfully rejected.

(2) Action by the lessee pursuant to subsection (1) is not acceptance or conversion.

§2A—513. CURE BY LESSOR OF IMPROPER TENDER OR DELIVERY; REPLACEMENT

(1) If any tender or delivery by the lessor or the supplier is rejected because nonconforming and the time for performance has not yet expired, the lessor or the supplier may seasonably notify the lessee of the lessor's or the supplier's intention to cure and may then make a conforming delivery within the time provided in the lease contract.

(2) If the lessee rejects a nonconforming tender that the lessor or the supplier had reasonable grounds to believe would be acceptable with or without money allowance, the lessor or the supplier may have a further reasonable time to substitute a conforming tender if he [or she] seasonably notifies the lessee.

* * * *

REVISED ARTICLE 3 NEGOTIABLE INSTRUMENTS

Part 1 General Provisions and Definitions

§3—102. SUBJECT MATTER

(a) This Article applies to negotiable instruments. It does not apply to money, to payment orders governed by Article 4A, or to securities governed by Article 8.

(b) If there is conflict between this Article and Article 4 or 9, Articles 4 and 9 govern.

(c) Regulations of the Board of Governors of the Federal Reserve System and operating circulars of the Federal Reserve Banks supersede any inconsistent provision of this Article to the extent of the inconsistency.

§3—103. DEFINITIONS

(a) In this Article:

(1) "Acceptor" means a drawee who has accepted a draft.

(2) "Drawee" means a person ordered in a draft to make payment.

(3) "Drawer" means a person who signs or is identified in a draft as a person ordering payment.

(4) "Good faith" means honesty in fact and the observance of reasonable commercial standards of fair dealing.

(5) "Maker" means a person who signs or is identified in a note as a person undertaking to pay.

(6) "Order" means a written instruction to pay money signed by the person giving the instruction. The instruction may be addressed to any person, including the person giving the instruction, or to one or more persons jointly or in the alternative but not in succession. An authorization to pay is not an order unless the person authorized to pay is also instructed to pay.

(7) "Ordinary care" in the case of a person engaged in business means observance of reasonable commercial standards, prevailing in the area in which the person is located, with respect to the business in which the person is engaged. In the case of a bank that takes an instrument for processing for collection or payment by automated means, reasonable commercial standards do not require the bank to examine the instrument if the failure to examine does not violate the bank's prescribed procedures and the bank's procedures do not vary unreasonably from general banking usage not disapproved by this Article or Article 4.

(8) "Party" means a party to an instrument.

§3—104. NEGOTIABLE INSTRUMENT

(a) Except as provided in subsections (c) and (d), "negotiable instrument" means an unconditional promise or order to pay a fixed amount of money, with or without interest or other charges described in the promise or order, if it:

(1) is payable to bearer or to order at the time it is issued or first comes into possession of a holder;

(2) is payable on demand or at a definite time; and

(3) does not state any other undertaking or instruction by the person promising or ordering payment to do any act in addition to the payment of money, but the promise or order may contain (i) an undertaking or power to give, maintain, or protect collateral to secure payment, (ii) an authorization or power to the holder to confess judgment or realize on or dispose of collateral, or (iii) a waiver of the benefit of any law intended for the advantage or protection of an obligor.

(b) "Instrument" means a negotiable instrument.

(c) An order that meets all of the requirements of subsection (a), except paragraph (1), and otherwise falls within the definition of "check" in subsection (f) is a negotiable instrument and a check.

(d) A promise or order other than a check is not an instrument if, at the time it is issued or first comes into possession of a holder, it contains a conspicuous statement, however expressed, to the effect that the promise or order is not negotiable or is not an instrument governed by this Article.

(e) An instrument is a "note" if it is a promise and is a "draft" if it is an order. If an instrument falls within the definition of both "note" and "draft," a person entitled to enforce the instrument may treat it as either.

(f) "Check" means (i) a draft, other than a documentary draft, payable on demand and drawn on a bank or (ii) a cashier's check or teller's check. An instrument may be a check even though it is described on its face by another term, such as "money order."

(g) "Cashier's check" means a draft with respect to which the drawer and drawee are the same bank or branches of the same bank.

(h) "Teller's check" means a draft drawn by a bank (i) on another bank, or (ii) payable at or through a bank.

(i) "Traveler's check" means an instrument that (i) is payable on demand, (ii) is drawn on or payable at or through a bank, (iii) is designated by the term "traveler's check" or by a substantially similar term, and (iv) requires, as a condition to payment, a countersignature by a person whose specimen signature appears on the instrument.

(j) "Certificate of deposit" means an instrument containing an acknowledgment by a bank that a sum of money has been received by the bank and a promise by the bank to repay the sum of money. A certificate of deposit is a note of the bank.

* * * *

§3—106. UNCONDITIONAL PROMISE OR ORDER

(a) Except as provided in this section, for the purposes of Section 3—104(a), a promise or order is unconditional unless it states (i) an express condition to payment, (ii) that the promise or order is subject to or governed by another writing, or (iii) that rights or obligations with respect to the promise or order are stated in another writing. A reference to another writing does not of itself make the promise or order conditional.

(b) A promise or order is not made conditional (i) by a reference to another writing for a statement of rights with respect to collateral, prepayment, or acceleration, or (ii) because payment is limited to resort to a particular fund or source.

(c) If a promise or order requires, as a condition to payment, a countersignature by a person whose specimen signature appears on the promise or order, the condition does not make the promise or order conditional for the purposes of Section 3—104(a). If the person whose specimen signature appears on an instrument fails to countersign the instrument, the failure to countersign is a defense to the obligation of the issuer, but the failure does not prevent a transferee of the instrument from becoming a holder of the instrument.

(d) If a promise or order at the time it is issued or first comes into possession of a holder contains a statement, required by applicable statutory or administrative law, to the effect that the rights of a holder or transferee are subject to claims or defenses that the issuer could assert against the original payee, the promise or order is not thereby made conditional for the purposes of Section 3—104(a); but if the promise or order is an instrument, there cannot be a holder in due course of the instrument.

§3—107. INSTRUMENT PAYABLE IN FOREIGN MONEY

Unless the instrument otherwise provides, an instrument that states the amount payable in foreign money may be paid in the foreign money or in an equivalent amount in dollars calculated by using the current bank-offered spot rate at the place of payment for the purchase of dollars on the day on which the instrument is paid.

§3—108. PAYABLE ON DEMAND OR AT DEFINITE TIME

(a) A promise or order is "payable on demand" if it (i) states that it is payable on demand or at sight, or otherwise indicates that it is payable at the will of the holder, or (ii) does not state any time of payment.

(b) A promise or order is "payable at a definite time" if it is payable on elapse of a definite period of time after sight or acceptance or at a fixed date or dates or at a time or times readily ascertainable at the time the promise or order is issued, subject to rights of (i) prepayment, (ii) acceleration, (iii) extension at the option of the holder, or (iv) extension to a further definite time at the option of the maker or acceptor or automatically upon or after a specified act or event.

(c) If an instrument, payable at a fixed date, is also payable upon demand made before the fixed date, the instrument is payable on demand until the fixed date and, if demand for payment is not made before that date, becomes payable at a definite time on the fixed date.

§3—109. PAYABLE TO BEARER OR TO ORDER

(a) A promise or order is payable to bearer if it:

(1) states that it is payable to bearer or to the order of bearer or otherwise indicates that the person in possession of the promise or order is entitled to payment;

(2) does not state a payee; or

(3) states that it is payable to or to the order of cash or otherwise indicates that it is not payable to an identified person.

(b) A promise or order that is not payable to bearer is payable to order if it is payable (i) to the order of an identified person or (ii) to an identified person or order. A promise or order that is payable to order is payable to the identified person.

(c) An instrument payable to bearer may become payable to an identified person if it is specially indorsed pursuant to Section 3—205(a). An instrument payable to an identified person may become payable to bearer if it is indorsed in blank pursuant to Section 3—205(b).

§3—110. IDENTIFICATION OF PERSON TO WHOM INSTRUMENT IS PAYABLE

(a) The person to whom an instrument is initially payable is determined by the intent of the person, whether or not authorized, signing as, or in the name or behalf of, the issuer of the instrument. The instrument is payable to the person intended by the signer even if that person is identified in the instrument by a name or other identification that is not that of the intended person. If more than one person signs in the name or behalf of the issuer of an instrument and all the signers do not intend the same person as payee, the instrument is payable to any person intended by one or more of the signers.

(b) If the signature of the issuer of an instrument is made by automated means, such as a check-writing machine, the payee of the instrument is determined by the intent of the person who supplied the name or identification of the payee, whether or not authorized to do so.

(c) A person to whom an instrument is payable may be identified in any way, including by name, identifying number, office, or account number.

§3—111. PLACE OF PAYMENT

Except as otherwise provided for items in Article 4, an instrument is payable at the place of payment stated in the instrument. If no place of payment is stated, an instrument is payable at the address of the drawee or maker stated in the instrument. If no address is stated, the place of payment is the place of business of the drawee or maker. If a drawee or maker has more than one place of business, the place of payment is any place of business of the drawee or maker chosen by the person entitled to enforce the instrument. If the drawee or maker has no place of business, the place of payment is the residence of the drawee or maker.

§3—112. INTEREST

(a) Unless otherwise provided in the instrument, (i) an instrument is not payable with interest, and (ii) interest on an interest-bearing instrument is payable from the date of the instrument.

(b) Interest may be stated in an instrument as a fixed or variable amount of money or it may be expressed as a fixed or variable rate or rates. The amount or rate of interest may be stated or described in the instrument in any manner and may require reference to information not contained in the instrument. If an instrument provides for interest, but the amount of interest payable cannot be ascertained from the description, interest is payable at the judgment rate in effect at the place of payment of the instrument and at the time interest first accrues.

§3—113. DATE OF INSTRUMENT

(a) An instrument may be antedated or postdated. The date stated determines the time of payment if the instrument is payable at a fixed period after date. Except as provided in Section 4—401(c), an instrument payable on demand is not payable before the date of the instrument.

(b) If an instrument is undated, its date is the date of its issue or, in the case of an unissued instrument, the date it first comes into possession of a holder.

§3—114. CONTRADICTORY TERMS OF INSTRUMENT

If an instrument contains contradictory terms, typewritten terms prevail over printed terms, handwritten terms prevail over both, and words prevail over numbers.

§3—115. INCOMPLETE INSTRUMENT

(a) "Incomplete instrument" means a signed writing, whether or not issued by the signer, the contents of which show at the time of signing that it is incomplete but that the signer intended it to be completed by the addition of words or numbers.

(b) Subject to subsection (c), if an incomplete instrument is an instrument under Section 3—104, it may be enforced according to its terms if it is not completed, or according to its terms as augmented by completion. If an incomplete instrument is not an instrument under Section 3—104, but, after completion, the requirements of Section 3—104 are met, the instrument may be enforced according to its terms as augmented by completion.

(c) If words or numbers are added to an incomplete instrument without authority of the signer, there is an alteration of the incomplete instrument under Section 3—407.

(d) The burden of establishing that words or numbers were added to an incomplete instrument without authority of the signer is on the person asserting the lack of authority.

§3—116. JOINT AND SEVERAL LIABILITY; CONTRIBUTION

(a) Except as otherwise provided in the instrument, two or more persons who have the same liability on an instrument as makers, drawers, acceptors, indorsers who indorse as joint payees, or anomalous indorsers are jointly and severally liable in the capacity in which they sign.

(b) Except as provided in Section 3—419(e) or by agreement of the affected parties, a party having joint and several liability who pays the instrument is entitled to receive from any party having the same joint and several liability contribution in accordance with applicable law.

(c) Discharge of one party having joint and several liability by a person entitled to enforce the instrument does not affect the right under subsection (b) of a party having the same joint and several liability to receive contribution from the party discharged.

* * * *

§3—118. STATUTE OF LIMITATIONS

(a) Except as provided in subsection (e), an action to enforce the obligation of a party to pay a note payable at a definite time must be commenced within six years after the due date or dates stated in the note or, if a due date is accelerated, within six years after the accelerated due date.

(b) Except as provided in subsection (d) or (e), if demand for payment is made to the maker of a note payable on demand, an action to enforce the obligation of a party to pay the note must be commenced within six years after the demand. If no demand for payment is made to the maker, an action to enforce the note is barred if neither principal nor interest on the note has been paid for a continuous period of 10 years.

(c) Except as provided in subsection (d), an action to enforce the obligation of a party to an unaccepted draft to

pay the draft must be commenced within three years after dishonor of the draft or 10 years after the date of the draft, whichever period expires first.

(d) An action to enforce the obligation of the acceptor of a certified check or the issuer of a teller's check, cashier's check, or traveler's check must be commenced within three years after demand for payment is made to the acceptor or issuer, as the case may be.

(e) An action to enforce the obligation of a party to a certificate of deposit to pay the instrument must be commenced within six years after demand for payment is made to the maker, but if the instrument states a due date and the maker is not required to pay before that date, the six-year period begins when a demand for payment is in effect and the due date has passed.

(f) An action to enforce the obligation of a party to pay an accepted draft, other than a certified check, must be commenced (i) within six years after the due date or dates stated in the draft or acceptance if the obligation of the acceptor is payable at a definite time, or (ii) within six years after the date of the acceptance if the obligation of the acceptor is payable on demand.

(g) Unless governed by other law regarding claims for indemnity or contribution, an action (i) for conversion of an instrument, for money had and received, or like action based on conversion, (ii) for breach of warranty, or (iii) to enforce an obligation, duty, or right arising under this Article and not governed by this section must be commenced within three years after the [cause of action] accrues.

* * * *

Part 2 Negotiation, Transfer, and Indorsement

§3—201. NEGOTIATION

(a) "Negotiation" means a transfer of possession, whether voluntary or involuntary, of an instrument by a person other than the issuer to a person who thereby becomes its holder.

(b) Except for negotiation by a remitter, if an instrument is payable to an identified person, negotiation requires transfer of possession of the instrument and its indorsement by the holder. If an instrument is payable to bearer, it may be negotiated by transfer of possession alone.

* * * *

§3—203. TRANSFER OF INSTRUMENT; RIGHTS ACQUIRED BY TRANSFER

(a) An instrument is transferred when it is delivered by a person other than its issuer for the purpose of giving to the person receiving delivery the right to enforce the instrument.

(b) Transfer of an instrument, whether or not the transfer is a negotiation, vests in the transferee any right of the transferor to enforce the instrument, including any right as a holder in due course, but the transferee cannot acquire rights of a holder in due course by a transfer, directly or indirectly, from a holder in due course if the transferee engaged in fraud or illegality affecting the instrument.

(c) Unless otherwise agreed, if an instrument is transferred for value and the transferee does not become a holder because of lack of indorsement by the transferor, the transferee has a specifically enforceable right to the unqualified indorsement of the transferor, but negotiation of the instrument does not occur until the indorsement is made.

(d) If a transferor purports to transfer less than the entire instrument, negotiation of the instrument does not occur. The transferee obtains no rights under this Article and has only the rights of a partial assignee.

§3—204. INDORSEMENT

(a) "Indorsement" means a signature, other than that of a signer as maker, drawer, or acceptor, that alone or accompanied by other words is made on an instrument for the purpose of (i) negotiating the instrument, (ii) restricting payment of the instrument, or (iii) incurring indorser's liability on the instrument, but regardless of the intent of the signer, a signature and its accompanying words is an indorsement unless the accompanying words, terms of the instrument, place of the signature, or other circumstances unambiguously indicate that the signature was made for a purpose other than indorsement. For the purpose of determining whether a signature is made on an instrument, a paper affixed to the instrument is a part of the instrument.

(b) "Indorser" means a person who makes an indorsement.

(c) For the purpose of determining whether the transferee of an instrument is a holder, an indorsement that transfers a security interest in the instrument is effective as an unqualified indorsement of the instrument.

(d) If an instrument is payable to a holder under a name that is not the name of the holder, indorsement may be made by the holder in the name stated in the instrument or in the holder's name or both, but signature in both names may be required by a person paying or taking the instrument for value or collection.

§3—205. SPECIAL INDORSEMENT; BLANK INDORSEMENT; ANOMALOUS INDORSEMENT

(a) If an indorsement is made by the holder of an instrument, whether payable to an identified person or payable to bearer, and the indorsement identifies a person to whom it makes the instrument payable, it is a "special indorsement." When specially indorsed, an instrument becomes payable to the identified person and may be negotiated only by the indorsement of that person. The principles stated in Section 3—110 apply to special indorsements.

(b) If an indorsement is made by the holder of an instrument and it is not a special indorsement, it is a "blank indorsement." When indorsed in blank, an instrument becomes payable to bearer and may be negotiated by transfer of possession alone until specially indorsed.

(c) The holder may convert a blank indorsement that consists only of a signature into a special indorsement by writing, above the signature of the indorser, words identifying the person to whom the instrument is made payable.

(d) "Anomalous indorsement" means an indorsement made by a person who is not the holder of the instrument. An anomalous indorsement does not affect the manner in which the instrument may be negotiated.

§3—206. RESTRICTIVE INDORSEMENT

(a) An indorsement limiting payment to a particular person or otherwise prohibiting further transfer or negotiation of the instrument is not effective to prevent further transfer or negotiation of the instrument.

(b) An indorsement stating a condition to the right of the indorsee to receive payment does not affect the right of the indorsee to enforce the instrument. A person paying the instrument or taking it for value or collection may disregard the condition, and the rights and liabilities of that person are not affected by whether the condition has been fulfilled.

(c) If an instrument bears an indorsement (i) described in Section 4—201(b), or (ii) in blank or to a particular bank using the words "for deposit," "for collection," or other words indicating a purpose of having the instrument collected by a bank for the indorser or for a particular account, the following rules apply:

(1) A person, other than a bank, who purchases the instrument when so indorsed converts the instrument unless the amount paid for the instrument is received by the indorser or applied consistently with the indorsement.

(2) A depositary bank that purchases the instrument or takes it for collection when so indorsed converts the instrument unless the amount paid by the bank with respect to the instrument is received by the indorser or applied consistently with the indorsement.

(3) A payor bank that is also the depositary bank or that takes the instrument for immediate payment over the counter from a person other than a collecting bank converts the instrument unless the proceeds of the instrument are received by the indorser or applied consistently with the indorsement.

(4) Except as otherwise provided in paragraph (3), a payor bank or intermediary bank may disregard the indorsement and is not liable if the proceeds of the instrument are not received by the indorser or applied consistently with the indorsement.

(d) Except for an indorsement covered by subsection (c), if an instrument bears an indorsement using words to the effect that payment is to be made to the indorsee as agent, trustee, or other fiduciary for the benefit of the indorser or another person, the following rules apply:

(1) Unless there is notice of breach of fiduciary duty as provided in Section 3—307, a person who purchases the instrument from the indorsee or takes the instrument from the indorsee for collection or payment may pay the proceeds of payment or the value given for the instrument to the indorsee without regard to whether the indorsee violates a fiduciary duty to the indorser.

(2) A subsequent transferee of the instrument or person who pays the instrument is neither given notice nor otherwise affected by the restriction in the indorsement unless the transferee or payor knows that the fiduciary dealt with the instrument or its proceeds in breach of fiduciary duty.

(e) The presence on an instrument of an indorsement to which this section applies does not prevent a purchaser of the instrument from becoming a holder in due course of the instrument unless the purchaser is a converter under subsection (c) or has notice or knowledge of breach of fiduciary duty as stated in subsection (d).

(f) In an action to enforce the obligation of a party to pay the instrument, the obligor has a defense if payment would violate an indorsement to which this section applies and the payment is not permitted by this section.

§3—207. REACQUISITION

Reacquisition of an instrument occurs if it is transferred to a former holder, by negotiation or otherwise. A former holder who reacquires the instrument may cancel indorsements made after the reacquirer first became a holder of the instrument. If the cancellation causes the instrument to be payable to the reacquirer or to bearer, the reacquirer may negotiate the instrument. An indorser whose indorsement is canceled is discharged, and the discharge is effective against any subsequent holder.

Part 3 Enforcement of Instruments

§3—301. PERSON ENTITLED TO ENFORCE INSTRUMENT

"Person entitled to enforce" an instrument means (i) the holder of the instrument, (ii) a nonholder in possession of the instrument who has the rights of a holder, or (iii) a person not in possession of the instrument who is entitled to enforce the instrument pursuant to Section 3—309 or 3—418(d). A person may be a person entitled to enforce the instrument even though the person is not the owner of the instrument or is in wrongful possession of the instrument.

§3—302. HOLDER IN DUE COURSE

(a) Subject to subsection (c) and Section 3—106(d), "holder in due course" means the holder of an instrument if:

(1) the instrument when issued or negotiated to the holder does not bear such apparent evidence of forgery or alteration or is not otherwise so irregular or incomplete as to call into question its authenticity; and

(2) the holder took the instrument (i) for value, (ii) in good faith, (iii) without notice that the instrument is overdue or has been dishonored or that there is an uncured default with respect to payment of another instrument issued as part of the same series, (iv) without notice that the instrument contains an unauthorized signature or has been altered, (v) without notice of any claim to the instrument described in Section 3—306, and (vi) without notice that any party has a defense or claim in recoupment described in Section 3—305(a).

(b) Notice of discharge of a party, other than discharge in an insolvency proceeding, is not notice of a defense under subsection (a), but discharge is effective against a person who became a holder in due course with notice of the discharge. Public filing or recording of a document does not of itself constitute notice of a defense, claim in recoupment, or claim to the instrument.

(c) Except to the extent a transferor or predecessor in interest has rights as a holder in due course, a person does not acquire rights of a holder in due course of an instrument taken (i) by legal process or by purchase in an execution, bankruptcy, or creditor's sale or similar proceeding, (ii) by purchase as part of a bulk transaction not in ordinary course of business of the transferor, or (iii) as the successor in interest to an estate or other organization.

(d) If, under Section 3—303(a)(1), the promise of performance that is the consideration for an instrument has been partially performed, the holder may assert rights as a holder in due course of the instrument only to the fraction of the amount payable under the instrument equal to the value of the partial performance divided by the value of the promised performance.

(e) If (i) the person entitled to enforce an instrument has only a security interest in the instrument and (ii) the person obliged to pay the instrument has a defense, claim in recoupment, or claim to the instrument that may be asserted against the person who granted the security interest, the person entitled to enforce the instrument may assert rights as a holder in due course only to an amount payable under the instrument which, at the time of enforcement of the instrument, does not exceed the amount of the unpaid obligation secured.

(f) To be effective, notice must be received at a time and in a manner that gives a reasonable opportunity to act on it.

(g) This section is subject to any law limiting status as a holder in due course in particular classes of transactions.

§3—303. VALUE AND CONSIDERATION

(a) An instrument is issued or transferred for value if:

(1) the instrument is issued or transferred for a promise of performance, to the extent the promise has been performed;

(2) the transferee acquires a security interest or other lien in the instrument other than a lien obtained by judicial proceeding;

(3) the instrument is issued or transferred as payment of, or as security for, an antecedent claim against any person, whether or not the claim is due;

(4) the instrument is issued or transferred in exchange for a negotiable instrument; or

(5) the instrument is issued or transferred in exchange for the incurring of an irrevocable obligation to a third party by the person taking the instrument.

(b) "Consideration" means any consideration sufficient to support a simple contract. The drawer or maker of an instrument has a defense if the instrument is issued without consideration. If an instrument is issued for a promise of performance, the issuer has a defense to the extent performance of the promise is due and the promise has not been performed. If an instrument is issued for value as stated in subsection (a), the instrument is also issued for consideration.

§3—304. OVERDUE INSTRUMENT

(a) An instrument payable on demand becomes overdue at the earliest of the following times:

(1) on the day after the day demand for payment is duly made;

(2) if the instrument is a check, 90 days after its date; or

(3) if the instrument is not a check, when the instrument has been outstanding for a period of time after its date which is unreasonably long under the circumstances of the particular case in light of the nature of the instrument and usage of the trade.

(b) With respect to an instrument payable at a definite time the following rules apply:

(1) If the principal is payable in installments and a due date has not been accelerated, the instrument becomes

overdue upon default under the instrument for nonpayment of an installment, and the instrument remains overdue until the default is cured.

(2) If the principal is not payable in installments and the due date has not been accelerated, the instrument becomes overdue on the day after the due date.

(3) If a due date with respect to principal has been accelerated, the instrument becomes overdue on the day after the accelerated due date.

(c) Unless the due date of principal has been accelerated, an instrument does not become overdue if there is default in payment of interest but no default in payment of principal.

§3—305. DEFENSES AND CLAIMS IN RECOUPMENT

(a) Except as stated in subsection (b), the right to enforce the obligation of a party to pay an instrument is subject to the following:

(1) a defense of the obligor based on (i) infancy of the obligor to the extent it is a defense to a simple contract, (ii) duress, lack of legal capacity, or illegality of the transaction which, under other law, nullifies the obligation of the obligor, (iii) fraud that induced the obligor to sign the instrument with neither knowledge nor reasonable opportunity to learn of its character or its essential terms, or (iv) discharge of the obligor in insolvency proceedings;

(2) a defense of the obligor stated in another section of this Article or a defense of the obligor that would be available if the person entitled to enforce the instrument were enforcing a right to payment under a simple contract; and

(3) a claim in recoupment of the obligor against the original payee of the instrument if the claim arose from the transaction that gave rise to the instrument; but the claim of the obligor may be asserted against a transferee of the instrument only to reduce the amount owing on the instrument at the time the action is brought.

(b) The right of a holder in due course to enforce the obligation of a party to pay the instrument is subject to defenses of the obligor stated in subsection (a)(1), but is not subject to defenses of the obligor stated in subsection (a)(2) or claims in recoupment stated in subsection (a)(3) against a person other than the holder.

(c) Except as stated in subsection (d), in an action to enforce the obligation of a party to pay the instrument, the obligor may not assert against the person entitled to enforce the instrument a defense, claim in recoupment, or claim to the instrument (Section 3—306) of another person, but the other person's claim to the instrument may be asserted by the obligor if the other person is joined in the action and personally asserts the claim against the person entitled to enforce the instrument. An obligor is not obliged to pay the instrument if the person seeking enforcement of the instrument does not have rights of a holder in due course and the obligor proves that the instrument is a lost or stolen instrument.

(d) In an action to enforce the obligation of an accommodation party to pay an instrument, the accommodation party may assert against the person entitled to enforce the instrument any defense or claim in recoupment under subsection (a) that the accommodated party could assert against the person entitled to enforce the instrument, except the defenses of discharge in insolvency proceedings, infancy, and lack of legal capacity.

§3—306. CLAIMS TO AN INSTRUMENT

A person taking an instrument, other than a person having rights of a holder in due course, is subject to a claim of a property or possessory right in the instrument or its proceeds, including a claim to rescind a negotiation and to recover the instrument or its proceeds. A person having rights of a holder in due course takes free of the claim to the instrument.

§3—307. NOTICE OF BREACH OF FIDUCIARY DUTY

(a) In this section:

(1) "Fiduciary" means an agent, trustee, partner, corporate officer or director, or other representative owing a fiduciary duty with respect to an instrument.

(2) "Represented person" means the principal, beneficiary, partnership, corporation, or other person to whom the duty stated in paragraph (1) is owed.

(b) If (i) an instrument is taken from a fiduciary for payment or collection or for value, (ii) the taker has knowledge of the fiduciary status of the fiduciary, and (iii) the represented person makes a claim to the instrument or its proceeds on the basis that the transaction of the fiduciary is a breach of fiduciary duty, the following rules apply:

(1) Notice of breach of fiduciary duty by the fiduciary is notice of the claim of the represented person.

(2) In the case of an instrument payable to the represented person or the fiduciary as such, the taker has notice of the breach of fiduciary duty if the instrument is (i) taken in payment of or as security for a debt known by the taker to be the personal debt of the fiduciary, (ii) taken in a transaction known by the taker to be for the personal benefit of the fiduciary, or (iii) deposited to an account other than an account of the fiduciary, as such, or an account of the represented person.

(3) If an instrument is issued by the represented person or the fiduciary as such, and made payable to the fiduciary personally, the taker does not have notice of the breach of fiduciary duty unless the taker knows of the breach of fiduciary duty.

(4) If an instrument is issued by the represented person or the fiduciary as such, to the taker as payee, the taker has notice of the breach of fiduciary duty if the instrument is (i) taken in payment of or as security for a debt known by the taker to be the personal debt of the fiduciary, (ii) taken in a transaction known by the taker to be for the personal benefit of the fiduciary, or (iii) deposited to an account other than an account of the fiduciary, as such, or an account of the represented person.

§3—308. PROOF OF SIGNATURES AND STATUS AS HOLDER IN DUE COURSE

(a) In an action with respect to an instrument, the authenticity of, and authority to make, each signature on the instrument is admitted unless specifically denied in the pleadings. If the validity of a signature is denied in the pleadings, the burden of establishing validity is on the person claiming validity, but the signature is presumed to be authentic and authorized unless the action is to enforce the liability of the purported signer and the signer is dead or incompetent at the time of trial of the issue of validity of the signature. If an action to enforce the instrument is brought against a person as the undisclosed principal of a person who signed the instrument as a party to the instrument, the plaintiff has the burden of establishing that the defendant is liable on the instrument as a represented person under Section 3—402(a).

(b) If the validity of signatures is admitted or proved and there is compliance with subsection (a), a plaintiff producing the instrument is entitled to payment if the plaintiff proves entitlement to enforce the instrument under Section 3—301, unless the defendant proves a defense or claim in recoupment. If a defense or claim in recoupment is proved, the right to payment of the plaintiff is subject to the defense or claim, except to the extent the plaintiff proves that the plaintiff has rights of a holder in due course which are not subject to the defense or claim.

§3—309. ENFORCEMENT OF LOST, DESTROYED, OR STOLEN INSTRUMENT

(a) A person not in possession of an instrument is entitled to enforce the instrument if (i) the person was in possession of the instrument and entitled to enforce it when loss of possession occurred, (ii) the loss of possession was not the result of a transfer by the person or a lawful seizure, and (iii) the person cannot reasonably obtain possession of the instrument because the instrument was destroyed, its whereabouts cannot be determined, or it is in the wrongful possession of an unknown person or a person that cannot be found or is not amenable to service of process.

(b) A person seeking enforcement of an instrument under subsection (a) must prove the terms of the instrument and the person's right to enforce the instrument. If that proof is made, Section 3—308 applies to the case as if the person seeking enforcement had produced the instrument. The court may not enter judgment in favor of the person seeking enforcement unless it finds that the person required to pay the instrument is adequately protected against loss that might occur by reason of a claim by another person to enforce the instrument. Adequate protection may be provided by any reasonable means.

§3—310. EFFECT OF INSTRUMENT ON OBLIGATION FOR WHICH TAKEN

(a) Unless otherwise agreed, if a certified check, cashier's check, or teller's check is taken for an obligation, the obligation is discharged to the same extent discharge would result if an amount of money equal to the amount of the instrument were taken in payment of the obligation. Discharge of the obligation does not affect any liability that the obligor may have as an indorser of the instrument.

(b) Unless otherwise agreed and except as provided in subsection (a), if a note or an uncertified check is taken for an obligation, the obligation is suspended to the same extent the obligation would be discharged if an amount of money equal to the amount of the instrument were taken, and the following rules apply:

(1) In the case of an uncertified check, suspension of the obligation continues until dishonor of the check or until it is paid or certified. Payment or certification of the check results in discharge of the obligation to the extent of the amount of the check.

(2) In the case of a note, suspension of the obligation continues until dishonor of the note or until it is paid. Payment of the note results in discharge of the obligation to the extent of the payment.

(3) Except as provided in paragraph (4), if the check or note is dishonored and the obligee of the obligation for which the instrument was taken is the person entitled to enforce the instrument, the obligee may enforce either the instrument or the obligation. In the case of an instrument of a third person which is negotiated to the obligee by the obligor, discharge of the obligor on the instrument also discharges the obligation.

(4) If the person entitled to enforce the instrument taken for an obligation is a person other than the obligee, the obligee may not enforce the obligation to the extent the obligation is suspended. If the obligee is the person entitled to enforce the instrument but no longer has possession of it because it was lost, stolen, or destroyed, the obligation may not be enforced to the extent of the amount payable on the instrument, and to that extent the obligee's rights against the obligor are limited to enforcement of the instrument.

(c) If an instrument other than one described in subsection (a) or (b) is taken for an obligation, the effect is (i) that stated in subsection (a) if the instrument is one on which a bank is liable as maker or acceptor, or (ii) that stated in subsection (b) in any other case.

* * * *

§3—312. LOST, DESTROYED, OR STOLEN CASHIER'S CHECK, TELLER'S CHECK, OR CERTIFIED CHECK.

(1) "Check" means a cashier's check, teller's check, or certified check.

(2) "Claimant" means a person who claims the right to receive the amount of a cashier's check, teller's check, or certified check that was lost, destroyed, or stolen.

(3) "Declaration of loss" means a written statement, made under penalty of perjury, to the effect that (i) the declarer lost possession of a check, (ii) the declarer is the drawer or payee of the check, in the case of a certified check, or the remitter or payee of the check, in the case of a cashier's check or teller's check, (iii) the loss of possession was not the result of a transfer by the declarer or a lawful seizure, and (iv) the declarer cannot reasonably obtain possession of the check because the check was destroyed, its whereabouts cannot be determined, or it is in the wrongful possession of an unknown person or a person that cannot be found or is not amenable to service of process.

(4) "Obligated bank" means the issuer of a cashier's check or teller's check or the acceptor of a certified check.

* * * *

Part 4 Liability of Parties

§3—401. SIGNATURE

(a) A person is not liable on an instrument unless (i) the person signed the instrument, or (ii) the person is represented by an agent or representative who signed the instrument and the signature is binding on the represented person under Section 3—402.

(b) A signature may be made (i) manually or by means of a device or machine, and (ii) by the use of any name, including a trade or assumed name, or by a word, mark, or symbol executed or adopted by a person with present intention to authenticate a writing.

§3—402. SIGNATURE BY REPRESENTATIVE

(a) If a person acting, or purporting to act, as a representative signs an instrument by signing either the name of the represented person or the name of the signer, the represented person is bound by the signature to the same extent the represented person would be bound if the signature were on a simple contract. If the represented person is bound, the signature of the representative is the "authorized signature of the represented person" and the represented person is liable on the instrument, whether or not identified in the instrument.

(b) If a representative signs the name of the representative to an instrument and the signature is an authorized signature of the represented person, the following rules apply:

(1) If the form of the signature shows unambiguously that the signature is made on behalf of the represented person who is identified in the instrument, the representative is not liable on the instrument.

(2) Subject to subsection (c), if (i) the form of the signature does not show unambiguously that the signature is made in a representative capacity or (ii) the represented person is not identified in the instrument, the representative is liable on the instrument to a holder in due course that took the instrument without notice that the representative was not intended to be liable on the instrument. With respect to any other person, the representative is liable on the instrument unless the representative proves that the original parties did not intend the representative to be liable on the instrument.

(c) If a representative signs the name of the representative as drawer of a check without indication of the representative status and the check is payable from an account of the represented person who is identified on the check, the signer is not liable on the check if the signature is an authorized signature of the represented person.

§3—403. UNAUTHORIZED SIGNATURE

(a) Unless otherwise provided in this Article or Article 4, an unauthorized signature is ineffective except as the signature of the unauthorized signer in favor of a person who in good faith pays the instrument or takes it for value. An unauthorized signature may be ratified for all purposes of this Article.

(b) If the signature of more than one person is required to constitute the authorized signature of an organization, the signature of the organization is unauthorized if one of the required signatures is lacking.

(c) The civil or criminal liability of a person who makes an unauthorized signature is not affected by any provision of this Article which makes the unauthorized signature effective for the purposes of this Article.

§3—404. IMPOSTORS; FICTITIOUS PAYEES

(a) If an impostor, by use of the mails or otherwise, induces the issuer of an instrument to issue the instrument to the impostor, or to a person acting in concert with the impostor, by impersonating the payee of the instrument

or a person authorized to act for the payee, an indorsement of the instrument by any person in the name of the payee is effective as the indorsement of the payee in favor of a person who, in good faith, pays the instrument or takes it for value or for collection.

(b) If (i) a person whose intent determines to whom an instrument is payable (Section 3—110(a) or (b)) does not intend the person identified as payee to have any interest in the instrument, or (ii) the person identified as payee of an instrument is a fictitious person, the following rules apply until the instrument is negotiated by special indorsement:

(1) Any person in possession of the instrument is its holder.

(2) An indorsement by any person in the name of the payee stated in the instrument is effective as the indorsement of the payee in favor of a person who, in good faith, pays the instrument or takes it for value or for collection.

(c) Under subsection (a) or (b), an indorsement is made in the name of a payee if (i) it is made in a name substantially similar to that of the payee or (ii) the instrument, whether or not indorsed, is deposited in a depositary bank to an account in a name substantially similar to that of the payee.

(d) With respect to an instrument to which subsection (a) or (b) applies, if a person paying the instrument or taking it for value or for collection fails to exercise ordinary care in paying or taking the instrument and that failure substantially contributes to loss resulting from payment of the instrument, the person bearing the loss may recover from the person failing to exercise ordinary care to the extent the failure to exercise ordinary care contributed to the loss.

§3—405. EMPLOYER'S RESPONSIBILITY FOR FRAUDULENT INDORSEMENT BY EMPLOYEE

(a) In this section:

(1) "Employee" includes an independent contractor and employee of an independent contractor retained by the employer.

(2) "Fraudulent indorsement" means (i) in the case of an instrument payable to the employer, a forged indorsement purporting to be that of the employer, or (ii) in the case of an instrument with respect to which the employer is the issuer, a forged indorsement purporting to be that of the person identified as payee.

(3) "Responsibility" with respect to instruments means authority (i) to sign or indorse instruments on behalf of the employer, (ii) to process instruments received by the employer for book-keeping purposes, for deposit to an account, or for other disposition, (iii) to prepare or process instruments for issue in the name of the employer, (iv) to supply information determining the

names or addresses of payees of instruments to be issued in the name of the employer, (v) to control the disposition of instruments to be issued in the name of the employer, or (vi) to act otherwise with respect to instruments in a responsible capacity. "Responsibility" does not include authority that merely allows an employee to have access to instruments or blank or incomplete instrument forms that are being stored or transported or are part of incoming or outgoing mail, or similar access.

(b) For the purpose of determining the rights and liabilities of a person who, in good faith, pays an instrument or takes it for value or for collection, if an employer entrusted an employee with responsibility with respect to the instrument and the employee or a person acting in concert with the employee makes a fraudulent indorsement of the instrument, the indorsement is effective as the indorsement of the person to whom the instrument is payable if it is made in the name of that person. If the person paying the instrument or taking it for value or for collection fails to exercise ordinary care in paying or taking the instrument and that failure substantially contributes to loss resulting from the fraud, the person bearing the loss may recover from the person failing to exercise ordinary care to the extent the failure to exercise ordinary care contributed to the loss.

(c) Under subsection (b), an indorsement is made in the name of the person to whom an instrument is payable if (i) it is made in a name substantially similar to the name of that person or (ii) the instrument, whether or not indorsed, is deposited in a depositary bank to an account in a name substantially similar to the name of that person.

§3—406. NEGLIGENCE CONTRIBUTING TO FORGED SIGNATURE OR ALTERATION OF INSTRUMENT

(a) A person whose failure to exercise ordinary care substantially contributes to an alteration of an instrument or to the making of a forged signature on an instrument is precluded from asserting the alteration or the forgery against a person who, in good faith, pays the instrument or takes it for value or for collection.

(b) Under subsection (a), if the person asserting the preclusion fails to exercise ordinary care in paying or taking the instrument and that failure substantially contributes to loss, the loss is allocated between the person precluded and the person asserting the preclusion according to the extent to which the failure of each to exercise ordinary care contributed to the loss.

(c) Under subsection (a), the burden of proving failure to exercise ordinary care is on the person asserting the preclusion. Under subsection (b), the burden of proving failure to exercise ordinary care is on the person precluded.

§3—407. ALTERATION

(a) "Alteration" means (i) an unauthorized change in an instrument that purports to modify in any respect the obligation of a party, or (ii) an unauthorized addition of words or numbers or other change to an incomplete instrument relating to the obligation of a party.

(b) Except as provided in subsection (c), an alteration fraudulently made discharges a party whose obligation is affected by the alteration unless that party assents or is precluded from asserting the alteration. No other alteration discharges a party, and the instrument may be enforced according to its original terms.

(c) A payor bank or drawee paying a fraudulently altered instrument or a person taking it for value, in good faith and without notice of the alteration, may enforce rights with respect to the instrument (i) according to its original terms, or (ii) in the case of an incomplete instrument altered by unauthorized completion, according to its terms as completed.

§3—408. DRAWEE NOT LIABLE ON UNACCEPTED DRAFT

A check or other draft does not of itself operate as an assignment of funds in the hands of the drawee available for its payment, and the drawee is not liable on the instrument until the drawee accepts it.

§3—409. ACCEPTANCE OF DRAFT; CERTIFIED CHECK

(a) "Acceptance" means the drawee's signed agreement to pay a draft as presented. It must be written on the draft and may consist of the drawee's signature alone. Acceptance may be made at any time and becomes effective when notification pursuant to instructions is given or the accepted draft is delivered for the purpose of giving rights on the acceptance to any person.

(b) A draft may be accepted although it has not been signed by the drawer, is otherwise incomplete, is overdue, or has been dishonored.

(c) If a draft is payable at a fixed period after sight and the acceptor fails to date the acceptance, the holder may complete the acceptance by supplying a date in good faith.

(d) "Certified check" means a check accepted by the bank on which it is drawn. Acceptance may be made as stated in subsection (a) or by a writing on the check which indicates that the check is certified. The drawee of a check has no obligation to certify the check, and refusal to certify is not dishonor of the check.

§3—410. ACCEPTANCE VARYING DRAFT

(a) If the terms of a drawee's acceptance vary from the terms of the draft as presented, the holder may refuse the acceptance and treat the draft as dishonored. In that case, the drawee may cancel the acceptance.

(b) The terms of a draft are not varied by an acceptance to pay at a particular bank or place in the United States, unless the acceptance states that the draft is to be paid only at that bank or place.

(c) If the holder assents to an acceptance varying the terms of a draft, the obligation of each drawer and indorser that does not expressly assent to the acceptance is discharged.

§3—411. REFUSAL TO PAY CASHIER'S CHECKS, TELLER'S CHECKS, AND CERTIFIED CHECKS

(a) In this section, "obligated bank" means the acceptor of a certified check or the issuer of a cashier's check or teller's check bought from the issuer.

(b) If the obligated bank wrongfully (i) refuses to pay a cashier's check or certified check, (ii) stops payment of a teller's check, or (iii) refuses to pay a dishonored teller's check, the person asserting the right to enforce the check is entitled to compensation for expenses and loss of interest resulting from the nonpayment and may recover consequential damages if the obligated bank refuses to pay after receiving notice of particular circumstances giving rise to the damages.

(c) Expenses or consequential damages under subsection (b) are not recoverable if the refusal of the obligated bank to pay occurs because (i) the bank suspends payments, (ii) the obligated bank asserts a claim or defense of the bank that it has reasonable grounds to believe is available against the person entitled to enforce the instrument, (iii) the obligated bank has a reasonable doubt whether the person demanding payment is the person entitled to enforce the instrument, or (iv) payment is prohibited by law.

§3—412. OBLIGATION OF ISSUER OF NOTE OR CASHIER'S CHECK

The issuer of a note or cashier's check or other draft drawn on the drawer is obliged to pay the instrument (i) according to its terms at the time it was issued or, if not issued, at the time it first came into possession of a holder, or (ii) if the issuer signed an incomplete instrument, according to its terms when completed, to the extent stated in Sections 3—115 and 3—407. The obligation is owed to a person entitled to enforce the instrument or to an indorser who paid the instrument under Section 3—415.

§3—413. OBLIGATION OF ACCEPTOR

(a) The acceptor of a draft is obliged to pay the draft (i) according to its terms at the time it was accepted, even though the acceptance states that the draft is payable "as originally drawn" or equivalent terms, (ii) if the acceptance varies the terms of the draft, according to the terms of the draft as varied, or (iii) if the acceptance is of a draft that is an incomplete instrument, according to its terms when completed, to the extent stated in Sections 3—115 and 3—407. The obligation is owed to a person entitled to

enforce the draft or to the drawer or an indorser who paid the draft under Section 3—414 or 3—415.

(b) If the certification of a check or other acceptance of a draft states the amount certified or accepted, the obligation of the acceptor is that amount. If (i) the certification or acceptance does not state an amount, (ii) the amount of the instrument is subsequently raised, and (iii) the instrument is then negotiated to a holder in due course, the obligation of the acceptor is the amount of the instrument at the time it was taken by the holder in due course.

§3—414. OBLIGATION OF DRAWER

(a) This section does not apply to cashier's checks or other drafts drawn on the drawer.

(b) If an unaccepted draft is dishonored, the drawer is obliged to pay the draft (i) according to its terms at the time it was issued or, if not issued, at the time it first came into possession of a holder, or (ii) if the drawer signed an incomplete instrument, according to its terms when completed, to the extent stated in Sections 3—115 and 3—407. The obligation is owed to a person entitled to enforce the draft or to an indorser who paid the draft under Section 3—415.

(c) If a draft is accepted by a bank, the drawer is discharged, regardless of when or by whom acceptance was obtained.

(d) If a draft is accepted and the acceptor is not a bank, the obligation of the drawer to pay the draft if the draft is dishonored by the acceptor is the same as the obligation of an indorser under Section 3—415(a) and (c).

(e) If a draft states that it is drawn "without recourse" or otherwise disclaims liability of the drawer to pay the draft, the drawer is not liable under subsection (b) to pay the draft if the draft is not a check. A disclaimer of the liability stated in subsection (b) is not effective if the draft is a check.

(f) If (i) a check is not presented for payment or given to a depositary bank for collection within 30 days after its date, (ii) the drawee suspends payments after expiration of the 30-day period without paying the check, and (iii) because of the suspension of payments, the drawer is deprived of funds maintained with the drawee to cover payment of the check, the drawer to the extent deprived of funds may discharge its obligation to pay the check by assigning to the person entitled to enforce the check the rights of the drawer against the drawee with respect to the funds.

§3—415. OBLIGATION OF INDORSER

(a) Subject to subsections (b), (c), and (d) and to Section 3—419(d), if an instrument is dishonored, an indorser is obliged to pay the amount due on the instrument (i) according to the terms of the instrument at the time it was indorsed, or (ii) if the indorser indorsed an incomplete instrument, according to its terms when completed, to the extent stated in Sections 3—115 and 3—407. The obligation of the indorser is owed to a person entitled to enforce the instrument or to a subsequent indorser who paid the instrument under this section.

(b) If an indorsement states that it is made "without recourse" or otherwise disclaims liability of the indorser, the indorser is not liable under subsection (a) to pay the instrument.

(c) If notice of dishonor of an instrument is required by Section 3—503 and notice of dishonor complying with that section is not given to an indorser, the liability of the indorser under subsection (a) is discharged.

(d) If a draft is accepted by a bank after an indorsement is made, the liability of the indorser under subsection (a) is discharged.

(e) If an indorser of a check is liable under subsection (a) and the check is not presented for payment, or given to a depositary bank for collection, within 30 days after the day the indorsement was made, the liability of the indorser under subsection (a) is discharged.

As amended in 1993.

§3—416. TRANSFER WARRANTIES

(a) A person who transfers an instrument for consideration warrants to the transferee and, if the transfer is by indorsement, to any subsequent transferee that:

(1) the warrantor is a person entitled to enforce the instrument;

(2) all signatures on the instrument are authentic and authorized;

(3) the instrument has not been altered;

(4) the instrument is not subject to a defense or claim in recoupment of any party which can be asserted against the warrantor; and

(5) the warrantor has no knowledge of any insolvency proceeding commenced with respect to the maker or acceptor or, in the case of an unaccepted draft, the drawer.

(b) A person to whom the warranties under subsection (a) are made and who took the instrument in good faith may recover from the warrantor as damages for breach of warranty an amount equal to the loss suffered as a result of the breach, but not more than the amount of the instrument plus expenses and loss of interest incurred as a result of the breach.

(c) The warranties stated in subsection (a) cannot be disclaimed with respect to checks. Unless notice of a claim for breach of warranty is given to the warrantor within 30 days after the claimant has reason to know of the breach and

the identity of the warrantor, the liability of the warrantor under subsection (b) is discharged to the extent of any loss caused by the delay in giving notice of the claim.

(d) A [cause of action] for breach of warranty under this section accrues when the claimant has reason to know of the breach.

§3—417. PRESENTMENT WARRANTIES

(a) If an unaccepted draft is presented to the drawee for payment or acceptance and the drawee pays or accepts the draft, (i) the person obtaining payment or acceptance, at the time of presentment, and (ii) a previous transferor of the draft, at the time of transfer, warrant to the drawee making payment or accepting the draft in good faith that:

(1) the warrantor is, or was, at the time the warrantor transferred the draft, a person entitled to enforce the draft or authorized to obtain payment or acceptance of the draft on behalf of a person entitled to enforce the draft;

(2) the draft has not been altered; and

(3) the warrantor has no knowledge that the signature of the drawer of the draft is unauthorized.

(b) A drawee making payment may recover from any warrantor damages for breach of warranty equal to the amount paid by the drawee less the amount the drawee received or is entitled to receive from the drawer because of the payment. In addition, the drawee is entitled to compensation for expenses and loss of interest resulting from the breach. The right of the drawee to recover damages under this subsection is not affected by any failure of the drawee to exercise ordinary care in making payment. If the drawee accepts the draft, breach of warranty is a defense to the obligation of the acceptor. If the acceptor makes payment with respect to the draft, the acceptor is entitled to recover from any warrantor for breach of warranty the amounts stated in this subsection.

(c) If a drawee asserts a claim for breach of warranty under subsection (a) based on an unauthorized indorsement of the draft or an alteration of the draft, the warrantor may defend by proving that the indorsement is effective under Section 3—404 or 3—405 or the drawer is precluded under Section 3—406 or 4—406 from asserting against the drawee the unauthorized indorsement or alteration.

(d) If (i) a dishonored draft is presented for payment to the drawer or an indorser or (ii) any other instrument is presented for payment to a party obliged to pay the instrument, and (iii) payment is received, the following rules apply:

(1) The person obtaining payment and a prior transferor of the instrument warrant to the person making payment in good faith that the warrantor is, or was, at the time the warrantor transferred the instrument, a person entitled to enforce the instrument or

authorized to obtain payment on behalf of a person entitled to enforce the instrument.

(2) The person making payment may recover from any warrantor for breach of warranty an amount equal to the amount paid plus expenses and loss of interest resulting from the breach.

(e) The warranties stated in subsections (a) and (d) cannot be disclaimed with respect to checks. Unless notice of a claim for breach of warranty is given to the warrantor within 30 days after the claimant has reason to know of the breach and the identity of the warrantor, the liability of the warrantor under subsection (b) or (d) is discharged to the extent of any loss caused by the delay in giving notice of the claim.

(f) A [cause of action] for breach of warranty under this section accrues when the claimant has reason to know of the breach.

§3—418. PAYMENT OR ACCEPTANCE BY MISTAKE

(a) Except as provided in subsection (c), if the drawee of a draft pays or accepts the draft and the drawee acted on the mistaken belief that (i) payment of the draft had not been stopped pursuant to Section 4—403 or (ii) the signature of the drawer of the draft was authorized, the drawee may recover the amount of the draft from the person to whom or for whose benefit payment was made or, in the case of acceptance, may revoke the acceptance. Rights of the drawee under this subsection are not affected by failure of the drawee to exercise ordinary care in paying or accepting the draft.

(b) Except as provided in subsection (c), if an instrument has been paid or accepted by mistake and the case is not covered by subsection (a), the person paying or accepting may, to the extent permitted by the law governing mistake and restitution, (i) recover the payment from the person to whom or for whose benefit payment was made or (ii) in the case of acceptance, may revoke the acceptance.

(c) The remedies provided by subsection (a) or (b) may not be asserted against a person who took the instrument in good faith and for value or who in good faith changed position in reliance on the payment or acceptance. This subsection does not limit remedies provided by Section 3—417 or 4—407.

(d) Notwithstanding Section 4—215, if an instrument is paid or accepted by mistake and the payor or acceptor recovers payment or revokes acceptance under subsection (a) or (b), the instrument is deemed not to have been paid or accepted and is treated as dishonored, and the person from whom payment is recovered has rights as a person entitled to enforce the dishonored instrument.

§3—419. INSTRUMENTS SIGNED FOR ACCOMMODATION

(a) If an instrument is issued for value given for the benefit of a party to the instrument ("accommodated party") and another party to the instrument ("accommodation party")

signs the instrument for the purpose of incurring liability on the instrument without being a direct beneficiary of the value given for the instrument, the instrument is signed by the accommodation party "for accommodation."

(b) An accommodation party may sign the instrument as maker, drawer, acceptor, or indorser and, subject to subsection (d), is obliged to pay the instrument in the capacity in which the accommodation party signs. The obligation of an accommodation party may be enforced notwithstanding any statute of frauds and whether or not the accommodation party receives consideration for the accommodation.

* * * *

(e) An accommodation party who pays the instrument is entitled to reimbursement from the accommodated party and is entitled to enforce the instrument against the accommodated party. An accommodated party who pays the instrument has no right of recourse against, and is not entitled to contribution from, an accommodation party.

§3—420. CONVERSION OF INSTRUMENT

(a) The law applicable to conversion of personal property applies to instruments. An instrument is also converted if it is taken by transfer, other than a negotiation, from a person not entitled to enforce the instrument or a bank makes or obtains payment with respect to the instrument for a person not entitled to enforce the instrument or receive payment. An action for conversion of an instrument may not be brought by (i) the issuer or acceptor of the instrument or (ii) a payee or indorsee who did not receive delivery of the instrument either directly or through delivery to an agent or a co-payee.

(b) In an action under subsection (a), the measure of liability is presumed to be the amount payable on the instrument, but recovery may not exceed the amount of the plaintiff's interest in the instrument.

(c) A representative, other than a depositary bank, who has in good faith dealt with an instrument or its proceeds on behalf of one who was not the person entitled to enforce the instrument is not liable in conversion to that person beyond the amount of any proceeds that it has not paid out.

§3—501. PRESENTMENT

(a) "Presentment" means a demand made by or on behalf of a person entitled to enforce an instrument (i) to pay the instrument made to the drawee or a party obliged to pay the instrument or, in the case of a note or accepted draft payable at a bank, to the bank, or (ii) to accept a draft made to the drawee.

(b) The following rules are subject to Article 4, agreement of the parties, and clearing-house rules and the like:

(1) Presentment may be made at the place of payment of the instrument and must be made at the place of

payment if the instrument is payable at a bank in the United States; may be made by any commercially reasonable means, including an oral, written, or electronic communication; is effective when the demand for payment or acceptance is received by the person to whom presentment is made; and is effective if made to any one of two or more makers, acceptors, drawees, or other payors.

(2) Upon demand of the person to whom presentment is made, the person making presentment must (i) exhibit the instrument, (ii) give reasonable identification and, if presentment is made on behalf of another person, reasonable evidence of authority to do so, and (...) sign a receipt on the instrument for any payment made or surrender the instrument if full payment is made.

(3) Without dishonoring the instrument, the party to whom presentment is made may (i) return the instrument for lack of a necessary indorsement, or (ii) refuse payment or acceptance for failure of the presentment to comply with the terms of the instrument, an agreement of the parties, or other applicable law or rule.

(4) The party to whom presentment is made may treat presentment as occurring on the next business day after the day of presentment if the party to whom presentment is made has established a cut-off hour not earlier than 2 P.M. for the receipt and processing of instruments presented for payment or acceptance and presentment is made after the cut-off hour.

§3—502. DISHONOR

(a) Dishonor of a note is governed by the following rules:

(1) If the note is payable on demand, the note is dishonored if presentment is duly made to the maker and the note is not paid on the day of presentment.

(2) If the note is not payable on demand and is payable at or through a bank or the terms of the note require presentment, the note is dishonored if presentment is duly made and the note is not paid on the day it becomes payable or the day of presentment, whichever is later.

(3) If the note is not payable on demand and paragraph (2) does not apply, the note is dishonored if it is not paid on the day it becomes payable.

(b) Dishonor of an unaccepted draft other than a documentary draft is governed by the following rules:

(1) If a check is duly presented for payment to the payor bank otherwise than for immediate payment over the counter, the check is dishonored if the payor bank makes timely return of the check or sends timely notice of dishonor or nonpayment under Section 4—301 or 4—302, or becomes accountable for the amount of the check under Section 4—302.

(2) If a draft is payable on demand and paragraph (1) does not apply, the draft is dishonored if presentment for payment is duly made to the drawee and the draft is not paid on the day of presentment.

(3) If a draft is payable on a date stated in the draft, the draft is dishonored if (i) presentment for payment is duly made to the drawee and payment is not made on the day the draft becomes payable or the day of presentment, whichever is later, or (ii) presentment for acceptance is duly made before the day the draft becomes payable and the draft is not accepted on the day of presentment.

(4) If a draft is payable on elapse of a period of time after sight or acceptance, the draft is dishonored if presentment for acceptance is duly made and the draft is not accepted on the day of presentment.

(c) Dishonor of an unaccepted documentary draft occurs according to the rules stated in subsection (b)(2), (3), and (4), except that payment or acceptance may be delayed without dishonor until no later than the close of the third business day of the drawee following the day on which payment or acceptance is required by those paragraphs.

(d) Dishonor of an accepted draft is governed by the following rules:

(1) If the draft is payable on demand, the draft is dishonored if presentment for payment is duly made to the acceptor and the draft is not paid on the day of presentment.

(2) If the draft is not payable on demand, the draft is dishonored if presentment for payment is duly made to the acceptor and payment is not made on the day it becomes payable or the day of presentment, whichever is later.

(e) In any case in which presentment is otherwise required for dishonor under this section and presentment is excused under Section 3—504, dishonor occurs without presentment if the instrument is not duly accepted or paid.

(f) If a draft is dishonored because timely acceptance of the draft was not made and the person entitled to demand acceptance consents to a late acceptance, from the time of acceptance the draft is treated as never having been dishonored.

§3—503. NOTICE OF DISHONOR

(a) The obligation of an indorser stated in Section 3—415 (a) and the obligation of a drawer stated in Section 3—414 (d) may not be enforced unless (i) the indorser or drawer is given notice of dishonor of the instrument complying with this section or (ii) notice of dishonor is excused under Section 3—504(b).

(b) Notice of dishonor may be given by any person; may be given by any commercially reasonable means, including an oral, written, or electronic communication; and is sufficient if it reasonably identifies the instrument and indicates that the instrument has been dishonored or has not been paid or accepted. Return of an instrument given to a bank for collection is sufficient notice of dishonor.

(c) Subject to Section 3—504(c), with respect to an instrument taken for collection by a collecting bank, notice of dishonor must be given (i) by the bank before midnight of the next banking day following the banking day on which the bank receives notice of dishonor of the instrument, or (ii) by any other person within 30 days following the day on which the person receives notice of dishonor. With respect to any other instrument, notice of dishonor must be given within 30 days following the day on which dishonor occurs.

* * * *

§3—601. DISCHARGE AND EFFECT OF DISCHARGE

(a) The obligation of a party to pay the instrument is discharged as stated in this Article or by an act or agreement with the party which would discharge an obligation to pay money under a simple contract.

(b) Discharge of the obligation of a party is not effective against a person acquiring rights of a holder in due course of the instrument without notice of the discharge.

§3—602. PAYMENT

(a) Subject to subsection (b), an instrument is paid to the extent payment is made (i) by or on behalf of a party obliged to pay the instrument, and (ii) to a person entitled to enforce the instrument. To the extent of the payment, the obligation of the party obliged to pay the instrument is discharged even though payment is made with knowledge of a claim to the instrument under Section 3—306 by another person.

(b) The obligation of a party to pay the instrument is not discharged under subsection (a) if:

(1) a claim to the instrument under Section 3—306 is enforceable against the party receiving payment and (i) payment is made with knowledge by the payor that payment is prohibited by injunction or similar process of a court of competent jurisdiction, or (ii) in the case of an instrument other than a cashier's check, teller's check, or certified check, the party making payment accepted, from the person having a claim to the instrument, indemnity against loss resulting from refusal to pay the person entitled to enforce the instrument; or

(2) the person making payment knows that the instrument is a stolen instrument and pays a person it knows is in wrongful possession of the instrument.

§3—603. TENDER OF PAYMENT

(a) If tender of payment of an obligation to pay an instrument is made to a person entitled to enforce the instrument, the effect of tender is governed by principles of law applicable to tender of payment under a simple contract.

(b) If tender of payment of an obligation to pay an instrument is made to a person entitled to enforce the instrument and the tender is refused, there is discharge, to the extent of the amount of the tender, of the obligation of an indorser or accommodation party having a right of recourse with respect to the obligation to which the tender relates.

(c) If tender of payment of an amount due on an instrument is made to a person entitled to enforce the instrument, the obligation of the obligor to pay interest after the due date on the amount tendered is discharged. If presentment is required with respect to an instrument and the obligor is able and ready to pay on the due date at every place of payment stated in the instrument, the obligor is deemed to have made tender of payment on the due date to the person entitled to enforce the instrument.

§3—604. DISCHARGE BY CANCELLATION OR RENUNCIATION

(a) A person entitled to enforce an instrument, with or without consideration, may discharge the obligation of a party to pay the instrument (i) by an intentional voluntary act, such as surrender of the instrument to the party, destruction, mutilation, or cancellation of the instrument, cancellation or striking out of the party's signature, or the addition of words to the instrument indicating discharge, or (ii) by agreeing not to sue or otherwise renouncing rights against the party by a signed writing.

(b) Cancellation or striking out of an indorsement pursuant to subsection (a) does not affect the status and rights of a party derived from the indorsement.

§3—605. DISCHARGE OF INDORSERS AND ACCOMMODATION PARTIES

(a) In this section, the term "indorser" includes a drawer having the obligation described in Section 3—414(d).

(b) Discharge, under Section 3—604, of the obligation of a party to pay an instrument does not discharge the obligation of an indorser or accommodation party having a right of recourse against the discharged party.

(c) If a person entitled to enforce an instrument agrees, with or without consideration, to an extension of the due date of the obligation of a party to pay the instrument, the extension discharges an indorser or accommodation party having a right of recourse against the party whose obligation is extended to the extent the indorser or accommodation party proves that the extension caused loss to the indorser or accommodation party with respect to the right of recourse.

(d) If a person entitled to enforce an instrument agrees, with or without consideration, to a material modification of the obligation of a party other than an extension of the due date, the modification discharges the obligation of an indorser or accommodation party having a right of recourse against the person whose obligation is modified to the extent the modification causes loss to the indorser or accommodation party with respect to the right of recourse. The loss suffered by the indorser or accommodation party as a result of the modification is equal to the amount of the right of recourse unless the person enforcing the instrument proves that no loss was caused by the modification or that the loss caused by the modification was an amount less than the amount of the right of recourse.

(e) If the obligation of a party to pay an instrument is secured by an interest in collateral and a person entitled to enforce the instrument impairs the value of the interest in collateral, the obligation of an indorser or accommodation party having a right of recourse against the obligor is discharged to the extent of the impairment. The value of an interest in collateral is impaired to the extent (i) the value of the interest is reduced to an amount less than the amount of the right of recourse of the party asserting discharge, or (ii) the reduction in value of the interest causes an increase in the amount by which the amount of the right of recourse exceeds the value of the interest. The burden of proving impairment is on the party asserting discharge.

(f) If the obligation of a party is secured by an interest in collateral not provided by an accommodation party and a person entitled to enforce the instrument impairs the value of the interest in collateral, the obligation of any party who is jointly and severally liable with respect to the secured obligation is discharged to the extent the impairment causes the party asserting discharge to pay more than that party would have been obliged to pay, taking into account rights of contribution, if impairment had not occurred. If the party asserting discharge is an accommodation party not entitled to discharge under subsection (e), the party is deemed to have a right to contribution based on joint and several liability rather than a right to reimbursement. The burden of proving impairment is on the party asserting discharge.

* * * *

(h) An accommodation party is not discharged under subsection (c), (d), or (e) unless the person entitled to enforce the instrument knows of the accommodation or has notice under Section 3—419(c) that the instrument was signed for accommodation.

(i) A party is not discharged under this section if (i) the party asserting discharge consents to the event or conduct that is the basis of the discharge, or (ii) the instrument or a separate agreement of the party provides for waiver of discharge under this section either specifically or by general language indicating that parties waive defenses based on suretyship or impairment of collateral.

* * * *

Revised Article 4 Bank Deposits and Collections

Part 1 General Provisions and Definitions

§4—103. VARIATION BY AGREEMENT; MEASURE OF DAMAGES; ACTION CONSTITUTING ORDINARY CARE

(a) The effect of the provisions of this Article may be varied by agreement, but the parties to the agreement cannot disclaim a bank's responsibility for its lack of good faith or failure to exercise ordinary care or limit the measure of damages for the lack or failure. However, the parties may determine by agreement the standards by which the bank's responsibility is to be measured if those standards are not manifestly unreasonable.

(b) Federal Reserve regulations and operating circulars, clearing-house rules, and the like have the effect of agreements under subsection (a), whether or not specifically assented to by all parties interested in items handled.

* * * *

§4—104. DEFINITIONS AND INDEX OF DEFINITIONS

(1) "Account" means any deposit or credit account with a bank, including a demand, time, savings, passbook, share draft, or like account, other than an account evidenced by a certificate of deposit;

* * * *

(3) "Banking day" means the part of a day on which a bank is open to the public for carrying on substantially all of its banking functions;

(4) "Clearing house" means an association of banks or other payors regularly clearing items;

* * * *

(7) "Draft" means a draft as defined in Section 3 —104 or an item, other than an instrument, that is an order;

(8) "Drawee" means a person ordered in a draft to make payment;

* * * *

(10) "Midnight deadline" with respect to a bank is midnight on its next banking day following the banking day on which it receives the relevant item or notice or from which the time for taking action commences to run, whichever is later;

* * * *

§4—105. "BANK"; "DEPOSITARY BANK"; "PAYOR BANK"; "INTERMEDIARY BANK"; "COLLECTING BANK"; "PRESENTING BANK"

In this Article:

(1) "Bank" means a person engaged in the business of banking, including a savings bank, savings and loan association, credit union, or trust company;

(2) "Depositary bank" means the first bank to take an item even though it is also the payor bank, unless the item is presented for immediate payment over the counter;

(3) "Payor bank" means a bank that is the drawee of a draft;

(4) "Intermediary bank" means a bank to which an item is transferred in course of collection except the depositary or payor bank;

(5) "Collecting bank" means a bank handling an item for collection except the payor bank;

(6) "Presenting bank" means a bank presenting an item except a payor bank.

§4—106. PAYABLE THROUGH OR PAYABLE AT BANK: COLLECTING BANK

(a) If an item states that it is "payable through" a bank identified in the item, (i) the item designates the bank as a collecting bank and does not by itself authorize the bank to pay the item, and (ii) the item may be presented for payment only by or through the bank.

Alternative A

(b) If an item states that it is "payable at" a bank identified in the item, the item is equivalent to a draft drawn on the bank.

Alternative B

(b) If an item states that it is "payable at" a bank identified in the item, (i) the item designates the bank as a collecting bank and does not by itself authorize the bank to pay the item, and (ii) the item may be presented for payment only by or through the bank.

(c) If a draft names a nonbank drawee and it is unclear whether a bank named in the draft is a co-drawee or a collecting bank, the bank is a collecting bank.

§4—107. SEPARATE OFFICE OF BANK

A branch or separate office of a bank is a separate bank for the purpose of computing the time within which and determining the place at or to which action may be taken or notices or orders shall be given under this Article and under Article 3.

§4—108. TIME OF RECEIPT OF ITEMS

(a) For the purpose of allowing time to process items, prove balances, and make the necessary entries on its books to determine its position for the day, a bank may fix an afternoon hour of 2 P.M. or later as a cutoff hour for the handling of money and items and the making of entries on its books.

(b) An item or deposit of money received on any day after a cutoff hour so fixed or after the close of the banking day may be treated as being received at the opening of the next banking day.

§4—109. DELAYS

(a) Unless otherwise instructed, a collecting bank in a good faith effort to secure payment of a specific item drawn on a payor other than a bank, and with or without the approval of any person involved, may waive, modify, or extend time limits imposed or permitted by this [act] for a period not exceeding two additional banking days without discharge of drawers or indorsers or liability to its transferor or a prior party.

(b) Delay by a collecting bank or payor bank beyond time limits prescribed or permitted by this [act] or by instructions is excused if (i) the delay is caused by interruption of communication or computer facilities, suspension of payments by another bank, war, emergency conditions, failure of equipment, or other circumstances beyond the control of the bank, and (ii) the bank exercises such diligence as the circumstances require.

§4—110. ELECTRONIC PRESENTMENT

(a) "Agreement for electronic presentment" means an agreement, clearing-house rule, or Federal Reserve regulation or operating circular, providing that presentment of an item may be made by transmission of an image of an item or information describing the item ("presentment notice") rather than delivery of the item itself. The agreement may provide for procedures governing retention, presentment, payment, dishonor, and other matters concerning items subject to the agreement.

* * * *

§4—111. STATUTE OF LIMITATIONS

An action to enforce an obligation, duty, or right arising under this Article must be commenced within three years after the [cause of action] accrues.

§4—201. STATUS OF COLLECTING BANK AS AGENT AND PROVISIONAL STATUS OF CREDITS; APPLICABILITY OF ARTICLE; ITEM INDORSED "PAY ANY BANK"

(a) Unless a contrary intent clearly appears and before the time that a settlement given by a collecting bank for an item is or becomes final, the bank, with respect to an item, is an agent or sub-agent of the owner of the item and any settlement given for the item is provisional. This provision applies regardless of the form of indorsement or lack of indorsement and even though credit given for the item is subject to immediate withdrawal as of right or is in fact withdrawn; but the continuance of ownership of an item by its owner and any rights of the owner to proceeds of the item are subject to rights of a collecting bank, such as those resulting from outstanding advances on the item and rights of recoupment or setoff. If an item is handled by banks for purposes of presentment, payment, collection, or return, the relevant provisions of this Article apply even though action of the parties clearly establishes that a particular bank has purchased the item and is the owner of it.

(b) After an item has been indorsed with the words "pay any bank" or the like, only a bank may acquire the rights of a holder until the item has been:

(1) returned to the customer initiating collection; or

(2) specially indorsed by a bank to a person who is not a bank.

§4—202. RESPONSIBILITY FOR COLLECTION OR RETURN; WHEN ACTION TIMELY

(a) A collecting bank must exercise ordinary care in:

(1) presenting an item or sending it for presentment;

(2) sending notice of dishonor or nonpayment or returning an item other than a documentary draft to the bank's transferor after learning that the item has not been paid or accepted, as the case may be;

(3) settling for an item when the bank receives final settlement; and

(4) notifying its transferor of any loss or delay in transit within a reasonable time after discovery thereof.

(b) A collecting bank exercises ordinary care under subsection (a) by taking proper action before its midnight deadline following receipt of an item, notice, or settlement. Taking proper action within a reasonably longer time may constitute the exercise of ordinary care, but the bank has the burden of establishing timeliness.

(c) Subject to subsection (a)(1), a bank is not liable for the insolvency, neglect, misconduct, mistake, or default of another bank or person or for loss or destruction of an item in the possession of others or in transit.

* * * *

§4—205. DEPOSITARY BANK HOLDER OF UNINDORSED ITEM

If a customer delivers an item to a depositary bank for collection:

(1) the depositary bank becomes a holder of the item at the time it receives the item for collection if the customer at the time of delivery was a holder of the item, whether or not the customer indorses the item,

and, if the bank satisfies the other requirements of Section 3—302, it is a holder in due course; and

(2) the depositary bank warrants to collecting banks, the payor bank or other payor, and the drawer that the amount of the item was paid to the customer or deposited to the customer's account.

* * * *

§4—207. TRANSFER WARRANTIES

(a) A customer or collecting bank that transfers an item and receives a settlement or other consideration warrants to the transferee and to any subsequent collecting bank that:

(1) the warrantor is a person entitled to enforce the item;

(2) all signatures on the item are authentic and authorized;

(3) the item has not been altered;

(4) the item is not subject to a defense or claim in recoupment (Section 3—305(a)) of any party that can be asserted against the warrantor; and

(5) the warrantor has no knowledge of any insolvency proceeding commenced with respect to the maker or acceptor or, in the case of an unaccepted draft, the drawer.

(b) If an item is dishonored, a customer or collecting bank transferring the item and receiving settlement or other consideration is obliged to pay the amount due on the item (i) according to the terms of the item at the time it was transferred, or (ii) if the transfer was of an incomplete item, according to its terms when completed as stated in Sections 3—115 and 3—407. The obligation of a transferor is owed to the transferee and to any subsequent collecting bank that takes the item in good faith. A transferor cannot disclaim its obligation under this subsection by an indorsement stating that it is made "without recourse" or otherwise disclaiming liability.

(c) A person to whom the warranties under subsection (a) are made and who took the item in good faith may recover from the warrantor as damages for breach of warranty an amount equal to the loss suffered as a result of the breach, but not more than the amount of the item plus expenses and loss of interest incurred as a result of the breach.

(d) The warranties stated in subsection (a) cannot be disclaimed with respect to checks. Unless notice of a claim for breach of warranty is given to the warrantor within 30 days after the claimant has reason to know of the breach and the identity of the warrantor, the warrantor is discharged to the extent of any loss caused by the delay in giving notice of the claim.

(e) A cause of action for breach of warranty under this section accrues when the claimant has reason to know of the breach.

§4—208. PRESENTMENT WARRANTIES

(a) If an unaccepted draft is presented to the drawee for payment or acceptance and the drawee pays or accepts the draft, (i) the person obtaining payment or acceptance, at the time of presentment, and (ii) a previous transferor of the draft, at the time of transfer, warrant to the drawee that pays or accepts the draft in good faith that:

(1) the warrantor is, or was, at the time the warrantor transferred the draft, a person entitled to enforce the draft or authorized to obtain payment or acceptance of the draft on behalf of a person entitled to enforce the draft;

(2) the draft has not been altered; and

(3) the warrantor has no knowledge that the signature of the purported drawer of the draft is unauthorized.

(b) A drawee making payment may recover from a warrantor damages for breach of warranty equal to the amount paid by the drawee less the amount the drawee received or is entitled to receive from the drawer because of the payment. In addition, the drawee is entitled to compensation for expenses and loss of interest resulting from the breach. The right of the drawee to recover damages under this subsection is not affected by any failure of the drawee to exercise ordinary care in making payment. If the drawee accepts the draft (i) breach of warranty is a defense to the obligation of the acceptor, and (ii) if the acceptor makes payment with respect to the draft, the acceptor is entitled to recover from a warrantor for breach of warranty the amounts stated in this subsection.

(c) If a drawee asserts a claim for breach of warranty under subsection (a) based on an unauthorized indorsement of the draft or an alteration of the draft, the warrantor may defend by proving that the indorsement is effective under Section 3—404 or 3—405 or the drawer is precluded under Section 3—406 or 4—406 from asserting against the drawee the unauthorized indorsement or alteration.

(d) If (i) a dishonored draft is presented for payment to the drawer or an indorser or (ii) any other item is presented for payment to a party obliged to pay the item, and the item is paid, the person obtaining payment and a prior transferor of the item warrant to the person making payment in good faith that the warrantor is, or was, at the time the warrantor transferred the item, a person entitled to enforce the item or authorized to obtain payment on behalf of a person entitled to enforce the item. The person making payment may recover from any warrantor for breach of warranty an amount equal to the amount paid plus expenses and loss of interest resulting from the breach.

(e) The warranties stated in subsections (a) and (d) cannot be disclaimed with respect to checks. Unless notice of a claim for breach of warranty is given to the warrantor within 30 days after the claimant has reason to know of the breach and the identity of the warrantor, the warrantor is discharged to the extent of any loss caused by the delay in giving notice of the claim.

(f) A cause of action for breach of warranty under this section accrues when the claimant has reason to know of the breach.

* * * *

§4—211. WHEN BANK GIVES VALUE FOR PURPOSES OF HOLDER IN DUE COURSE

For purposes of determining its status as a holder in due course, a bank has given value to the extent it has a security interest in an item, if the bank otherwise complies with the requirements of Section 3—302 on what constitutes a holder in due course.

As amended in 1990.

§4—212. PRESENTMENT BY NOTICE OF ITEM NOT PAYABLE BY, THROUGH, OR AT BANK; LIABILITY OF DRAWER OR INDORSER

(a) Unless otherwise instructed, a collecting bank may present an item not payable by, through, or at a bank by sending to the party to accept or pay a written notice that the bank holds the item for acceptance or payment. The notice must be sent in time to be received on or before the day when presentment is due and the bank must meet any requirement of the party to accept or pay under Section 3—501 by the close of the bank's next banking day after it knows of the requirement.

(b) If presentment is made by notice and payment, acceptance, or request for compliance with a requirement under Section 3—501 is not received by the close of business on the day after maturity or, in the case of demand items, by the close of business on the third banking day after notice was sent, the presenting bank may treat the item as dishonored and charge any drawer or indorser by sending it notice of the facts.

* * * *

§4—214. RIGHT OF CHARGE-BACK OR REFUND; LIABILITY OF COLLECTING BANK; RETURN OF ITEM

(a) If a collecting bank has made provisional settlement with its customer for an item and fails by reason of dishonor, suspension of payments by a bank, or otherwise to receive settlement for the item which is or becomes final, the bank may revoke the settlement given by it, charge back the amount of any credit given for the item to its customer's account, or obtain refund from its customer, whether or not it is able to return the item, if by its midnight deadline or within a longer reasonable time after it learns the facts it returns the item or sends notification of the facts. If the return or notice is delayed beyond the bank's midnight deadline or a longer reasonable time after it learns the facts, the bank may revoke the settlement, charge back the credit, or obtain refund from its customer, but it is liable for any loss resulting from the delay. These rights to revoke, charge back, and obtain refund terminate if and when a settlement for the item received by the bank is or becomes final.

(b) A collecting bank returns an item when it is sent or delivered to the bank's customer or transferor or pursuant to its instructions.

(c) A depository bank that is also the payor may charge back the amount of an item to its customer's account or obtain refund in accordance with the section governing return of an item received by a payor bank for credit on its books (Section 4—301).

(d) The right to charge back is not affected by:

(1) previous use of a credit given for the item; or

(2) failure by any bank to exercise ordinary care with respect to the item, but a bank so failing remains liable.

(e) A failure to charge back or claim refund does not affect other rights of the bank against the customer or any other party.

(f) If credit is given in dollars as the equivalent of the value of an item payable in foreign money, the dollar amount of any charge-back or refund must be calculated on the basis of the bank-offered spot rate for the foreign money prevailing on the day when the person entitled to the charge-back or refund learns that it will not receive payment in ordinary course.

§4—215. FINAL PAYMENT OF ITEM BY PAYOR BANK; WHEN PROVISIONAL DEBITS AND CREDITS BECOME FINAL; WHEN CERTAIN CREDITS BECOME AVAILABLE FOR WITHDRAWAL

(a) An item is finally paid by a payor bank when the bank has first done any of the following:

(1) paid the item in cash;

(2) settled for the item without having a right to revoke the settlement under statute, clearing- house rule, or agreement; or

(3) made a provisional settlement for the item and failed to revoke the settlement in the time and manner permitted by statute, clearing-house rule, or agreement.

(b) If provisional settlement for an item does not become final, the item is not finally paid.

* * * *

§4—216. INSOLVENCY AND PREFERENCE

(a) If an item is in or comes into the possession of a payor or collecting bank that suspends payment and the item has not been finally paid, the item must be returned by the receiver, trustee, or agent in charge of the closed bank to the presenting bank or the closed bank's customer.

(b) If a payor bank finally pays an item and suspends payments without making a settlement for the item with its customer or the presenting bank which settlement is or becomes final, the owner of the item has a preferred claim against the payor bank.

(c) If a payor bank gives or a collecting bank gives or receives a provisional settlement for an item and thereafter suspends payments, the suspension does not prevent or interfere with the settlement's becoming final if the finality occurs automatically upon the lapse of certain time or the happening of certain events.

(d) If a collecting bank receives from subsequent parties settlement for an item, which settlement is or becomes final and the bank suspends payments without making a settlement for the item with its customer which settlement is or becomes final, the owner of the item has a preferred claim against the collecting bank.

§4—301. DEFERRED POSTING; RECOVERY OF PAYMENT BY RETURN OF ITEMS; TIME OF DISHONOR; RETURN OF ITEMS BY PAYOR BANK

(a) If a payor bank settles for a demand item other than a documentary draft presented otherwise than for immediate payment over the counter before midnight of the banking day of receipt, the payor bank may revoke the settlement and recover the settlement if, before it has made final payment and before its midnight deadline, it

(1) returns the item; or

(2) sends written notice of dishonor or nonpayment if the item is unavailable for return.

(b) If a demand item is received by a payor bank for credit on its books, it may return the item or send notice of dishonor and may revoke any credit given or recover the amount thereof withdrawn by its customer, if it acts within the time limit and in the manner specified in subsection (a).

(c) Unless previous notice of dishonor has been sent, an item is dishonored at the time when for purposes of dishonor it is returned or notice sent in accordance with this section.

(d) An item is returned:

(1) as to an item presented through a clearing house, when it is delivered to the presenting or last collecting bank or to the clearing house or is sent or delivered in accordance with clearing-house rules; or

(2) in all other cases, when it is sent or delivered to the bank's customer or transferor or pursuant to instructions.

§4—302. PAYOR BANK'S RESPONSIBILITY FOR LATE RETURN OF ITEM

(a) If an item is presented to and received by a payor bank, the bank is accountable for the amount of:

(1) a demand item, other than a documentary draft, whether properly payable or not, if the bank, in any case in which it is not also the depositary bank, retains the item beyond midnight of the banking day of

receipt without settling for it or, whether or not it is also the depositary bank, does not pay or return the item or send notice of dishonor until after its midnight deadline; or

(2) any other properly payable item unless, within the time allowed for acceptance or payment of that item, the bank either accepts or pays the item or returns it and accompanying documents.

(b) The liability of a payor bank to pay an item pursuant to subsection (a) is subject to defenses based on breach of a presentment warranty (Section 4—208) or proof that the person seeking enforcement of the liability presented or transferred the item for the purpose of defrauding the payor bank.

§4—303. WHEN ITEMS SUBJECT TO NOTICE, STOP-PAYMENT ORDER, LEGAL PROCESS, OR SETOFF; ORDER IN WHICH ITEMS MAY BE CHARGED OR CERTIFIED

(a) Any knowledge, notice, or stop-payment order received by, legal process served upon, or setoff exercised by a payor bank comes too late to terminate, suspend, or modify the bank's right or duty to pay an item or to charge its customer's account for the item if the knowledge, notice, stop-payment order, or legal process is received or served and a reasonable time for the bank to act thereon expires or the setoff is exercised after the earliest of the following:

(1) the bank accepts or certifies the item;

(2) the bank pays the item in cash;

(3) the bank settles for the item without having a right to revoke the settlement under statute, clearing-house rule, or agreement;

(4) the bank becomes accountable for the amount of the item under Section 4—302 dealing with the payor bank's responsibility for late return of items; or

(5) with respect to checks, a cutoff hour no earlier than one hour after the opening of the next banking day after the banking day on which the bank received the check and no later than the close of that next banking day or, if no cutoff hour is fixed, the close of the next banking day after the banking day on which the bank received the check.

(b) Subject to subsection (a), items may be accepted, paid, certified, or charged to the indicated account of its customer in any order.

§4—401. WHEN BANK MAY CHARGE CUSTOMER'S ACCOUNT

(a) A bank may charge against the account of a customer an item that is properly payable from the account even though the charge creates an overdraft. An item is properly payable if it is authorized by the customer and is in accordance with any agreement between the customer and bank.

(b) A customer is not liable for the amount of an overdraft if the customer neither signed the item nor benefited from the proceeds of the item.

(c) A bank may charge against the account of a customer a check that is otherwise properly payable from the account, even though payment was made before the date of the check, unless the customer has given notice to the bank of the postdating describing the check with reasonable certainty. The notice is effective for the period stated in Section 4—403(b) for stop-payment orders, and must be received at such time and in such manner as to afford the bank a reasonable opportunity to act on it before the bank takes any action with respect to the check described in Section 4—303. If a bank charges against the account of a customer a check before the date stated in the notice of postdating, the bank is liable for damages for the loss resulting from its act. The loss may include damages for dishonor of subsequent items under Section 4—402.

(d) A bank that in good faith makes payment to a holder may charge the indicated account of its customer according to:

(1) the original terms of the altered item; or

(2) the terms of the completed item, even though the bank knows the item has been completed unless the bank has notice that the completion was improper.

§4—402. BANK'S LIABILITY TO CUSTOMER FOR WRONGFUL DISHONOR; TIME OF DETERMINING INSUFFICIENCY OF ACCOUNT

(a) Except as otherwise provided in this Article, a payor bank wrongfully dishonors an item if it dishonors an item that is properly payable, but a bank may dishonor an item that would create an overdraft unless it has agreed to pay the overdraft.

(b) A payor bank is liable to its customer for damages proximately caused by the wrongful dishonor of an item. Liability is limited to actual damages proved and may include damages for an arrest or prosecution of the customer or other consequential damages. Whether any consequential damages are proximately caused by the wrongful dishonor is a question of fact to be determined in each case.

(c) A payor bank's determination of the customer's account balance on which a decision to dishonor for insufficiency of available funds is based may be made at any time between the time the item is received by the payor bank and the time that the payor bank returns the item or gives notice in lieu of return, and no more than one determination need be made. If, at the election of the payor bank, a subsequent balance determination is made for the purpose of reevaluating the bank's decision to dishonor the item, the account balance at that time is determinative of whether a dishonor for insufficiency of available funds is wrongful.

§4—403. CUSTOMER'S RIGHT TO STOP PAYMENT; BURDEN OF PROOF OF LOSS

(a) A customer or any person authorized to draw on the account if there is more than one person may stop payment of any item drawn on the customer's account or close the account by an order to the bank describing the item or account with reasonable certainty received at a time and in a manner that affords the bank a reasonable opportunity to act on it before any action by the bank with respect to the item described in Section 4—303. If the signature of more than one person is required to draw on an account, any of these persons may stop payment or close the account.

(b) A stop-payment order is effective for six months, but it lapses after 14 calendar days if the original order was oral and was not confirmed in writing within that period. A stop-payment order may be renewed for additional six-month periods by a writing given to the bank within a period during which the stop-payment order is effective.

(c) The burden of establishing the fact and amount of loss resulting from the payment of an item contrary to a stop-payment order or order to close an account is on the customer. The loss from payment of an item contrary to a stop-payment order may include damages for dishonor of subsequent items under Section 4—402.

§4—404. BANK NOT OBLIGED TO PAY CHECK MORE THAN SIX MONTHS OLD

A bank is under no obligation to a customer having a checking account to pay a check, other than a certified check, which is presented more than six months after its date, but it may charge its customer's account for a payment made thereafter in good faith.

§4—405. DEATH OR INCOMPETENCE OF CUSTOMER

(a) A payor or collecting bank's authority to accept, pay, or collect an item or to account for proceeds of its collection, if otherwise effective, is not rendered ineffective by incompetence of a customer of either bank existing at the time the item is issued or its collection is undertaken if the bank does not know of an adjudication of incompetence. Neither death nor incompetence of a customer revokes the authority to accept, pay, collect, or account until the bank knows of the fact of death or of an adjudication of incompetence and has reasonable opportunity to act on it.

(b) Even with knowledge, a bank may for 10 days after the date of death pay or certify checks drawn on or before the date unless ordered to stop payment by a person claiming an interest in the account.

§4—406. CUSTOMER'S DUTY TO DISCOVER AND REPORT UNAUTHORIZED SIGNATURE OR ALTERATION

(a) A bank that sends or makes available to a customer a statement of account showing payment of items for the account shall either return or make available to the customer the items paid or provide information in the statement of account sufficient to allow the customer reasonably to identify the items paid. The statement of account provides sufficient information if the item is described by item number, amount, and date of payment.

(b) If the items are not returned to the customer, the person retaining the items shall either retain the items or, if the items are destroyed, maintain the capacity to furnish legible copies of the items until the expiration of seven years after receipt of the items. A customer may request an item from the bank that paid the item, and that bank must provide in a reasonable time either the item or, if the item has been destroyed or is not otherwise obtainable, a legible copy of the item.

(c) If a bank sends or makes available a statement of account or items pursuant to subsection (a), the customer must exercise reasonable promptness in examining the statement or the items to determine whether any payment was not authorized because of an alteration of an item or because a purported signature by or on behalf of the customer was not authorized. If, based on the statement or items provided, the customer should reasonably have discovered the unauthorized payment, the customer must promptly notify the bank of the relevant facts.

(d) If the bank proves that the customer failed, with respect to an item, to comply with the duties imposed on the customer by subsection (c), the customer is precluded from asserting against the bank:

(1) the customer's unauthorized signature or any alteration on the item, if the bank also proves that it suffered a loss by reason of the failure; and

(2) the customer's unauthorized signature or alteration by the same wrongdoer on any other item paid in good faith by the bank if the payment was made before the bank received notice from the customer of the unauthorized signature or alteration and after the customer had been afforded a reasonable period of time, not exceeding 30 days, in which to examine the item or statement of account and notify the bank.

(e) If subsection (d) applies and the customer proves that the bank failed to exercise ordinary care in paying the item and that the failure substantially contributed to loss, the loss is allocated between the customer precluded and the bank asserting the preclusion according to the extent to which the failure of the customer to comply with subsection (c) and the failure of the bank to exercise ordinary care contributed to the loss. If the customer proves that the bank did not pay the item in good faith, the preclusion under subsection (d) does not apply.

(f) Without regard to care or lack of care of either the customer or the bank, a customer who does not within one year after the statement or items are made available to the customer (subsection (a)) discover and report the customer's unauthorized signature on or any alteration on the item is precluded from asserting against the bank the unauthorized signature or alteration. If there is a preclusion under this subsection, the payor bank may not recover for breach or warranty under Section 4—208 with respect to the unauthorized signature or alteration to which the preclusion applies.

§4—407. PAYOR BANK'S RIGHT TO SUBROGATION ON IMPROPER PAYMENT

If a payor has paid an item over the order of the drawer or maker to stop payment, or after an account has been closed, or otherwise under circumstances giving a basis for objection by the drawer or maker, to prevent unjust enrichment and only to the extent necessary to prevent loss to the bank by reason of its payment of the item, the payor bank is subrogated to the rights

(1) of any holder in due course on the item against the drawer or maker;

(2) of the payee or any other holder of the item against the drawer or maker either on the item or under the transaction out of which the item arose; and

(3) of the drawer or maker against the payee or any other holder of the item with respect to the transaction out of which the item arose.

* * * *

ARTICLE 4A FUNDS TRANSFERS

Part 1 Subject Matter and Definitions

§4A—104. FUNDS TRANSFER—DEFINITIONS

(a) "Funds transfer" means the series of transactions, beginning with the originator's payment order, made for the purpose of making payment to the beneficiary of the order. The term includes any payment order issued by the originator's bank or an intermediary bank intended to carry out the originator's payment order. A funds transfer is completed by acceptance by the beneficiary's bank of a payment order for the benefit of the beneficiary of the originator's payment order.

(b) "Intermediary bank" means a receiving bank other than the originator's bank or the beneficiary's bank.

(c) "Originator" means the sender of the first payment order in a funds transfer.

(d) "Originator's bank" means (i) the receiving bank to which the payment order of the originator is issued if the originator is not a bank, or (ii) the originator if the originator is a bank.

§4A—105. OTHER DEFINITIONS

(1) "Authorized account" means a deposit account of a customer in a bank designated by the customer as a source of payment of payment orders issued by the customer to the bank. If a customer does not so designate an account, any account of the customer is an authorized account if payment of a payment order from that account is not inconsistent with a restriction on the use of that account.

(2) "Bank" means a person engaged in the business of banking and includes a savings bank, savings and loan association, credit union, and trust company. A branch or separate office of a bank is a separate bank for purposes of this Article.

(3) "Customer" means a person, including a bank, having an account with a bank or from whom a bank has agreed to receive payment orders.

(4) "Funds-transfer business day" of a receiving bank means the part of a day during which the receiving bank is open for the receipt, processing, and transmittal of payment orders and cancellations and amendments of payment orders.

(5) "Funds-transfer system" means a wire transfer network, automated clearing house, or other communication system of a clearing house or other association of banks through which a payment order by a bank may be transmitted to the bank to which the order is addressed.

(6) "Good faith" means honesty in fact and the observance of reasonable commercial standards of fair dealing.

(7) "Prove" with respect to a fact means to meet the burden of establishing the fact (Section 1—201(8)).

* * * *

§4A—106. TIME PAYMENT ORDER IS RECEIVED

(a) The time of receipt of a payment order or communication cancelling or amending a payment order is determined by the rules applicable to receipt of a notice stated in Section 1—201(27). A receiving bank may fix a cut-off time or times on a funds-transfer business day for the receipt and processing of payment orders and communications cancelling or amending payment orders. Different cut-off times may apply to payment orders, cancellations, or amendments, or to different categories of payment orders, cancellations, or amendments. A cut-off time may apply to senders generally or different cut-off times may apply to different senders or categories of payment orders. If a payment order or communication cancelling or amending a payment order is received after the close of a funds-transfer business day or after the appropriate cut-off time on a funds-transfer business day, the receiving bank may treat the payment order or communication as received at the opening of the next funds-transfer business day.

(b) If this Article refers to an execution date or payment date or states a day on which a receiving bank is required to take action, and the date or day does not fall on a funds-transfer business day, the next day that is a funds- transfer business day is treated as the date or day stated, unless the contrary is stated in this Article.

* * * *

§4A—108. EXCLUSION OF CONSUMER TRANSACTIONS GOVERNED BY FEDERAL LAW

This Article does not apply to a funds transfer any part of which is governed by the Electronic Fund Transfer Act of 1978 (Title XX, Public Law 95—630, 92 Stat. 3728, 15 U.S.C. §1693 et seq.) as amended from time to time.

* * * *

REVISED ARTICLE 9 SECURED TRANSACTIONS

§9—102. DEFINITIONS AND INDEX OF DEFINITIONS

(1) "Accession" means goods that are physically united with other goods in such a manner that the identity of the original goods is not lost.

(2) "Account", except as used in "account for", means a right to payment of a monetary obligation, whether or not earned by performance, (i) for property that has been or is to be sold, leased, licensed, assigned, or otherwise disposed of, (ii) for services rendered or to be rendered, (iii) for a policy of insurance issued or to be issued, (iv) for a secondary obligation incurred or to be incurred, (v) for energy provided or to be provided, (vi) for the use or hire of a vessel under a charter or other contract, (vii) arising out of the use of a credit or charge card or information contained on or for use with the card, or (viii) as winnings in a lottery or other game of chance operated or sponsored by a State, governmental unit of a State, or person licensed or authorized to operate the game by a State or governmental unit of a State. The term includes health-care insurance receivables. The term does not include (i) rights to payment evidenced by chattel paper or an instrument, (ii) commercial tort claims, (iii) deposit accounts, (iv) investment property, (v) letter-of-credit rights or letters of credit, or (vi) rights to payment for money or funds advanced or sold, other than rights arising out of the use of a credit or charge card or information contained on or for use with the card.

* * * *

(5) "Agricultural lien" means an interest, other than a security interest, in farm products:

(A) which secures payment or performance of an obligation for:

(i) goods or services furnished in connection with a debtor's farming operation; or

(ii) rent on real property leased by a debtor in connection with its farming operation;

(B) which is created by statute in favor of a person that:

(i) in the ordinary course of its business furnished goods or services to a debtor in connection with a debtor's farming operation; or

(ii) leased real property to a debtor in connection with the debtor's farming operation; and

(C) whose effectiveness does not depend on the person's possession of the personal property.

(6) "As-extracted collateral" means:

(A) oil, gas, or other minerals that are subject to a security interest that:

(i) is created by a debtor having an interest in the minerals before extraction; and

(ii) attaches to the minerals as extracted; or

(B) accounts arising out of the sale at the wellhead or minehead of oil, gas, or other minerals in which the debtor had an interest before extraction.

(7) "Authenticate" means:

(A) to sign; or

(B) to execute or otherwise adopt a symbol, or encrypt or similarly process a record in whole or in part, with the present intent of the authenticating person to identify the person and adopt or accept a record.

* * * *

(11) "Chattel paper" means a record or records that evidence both a monetary obligation and a security interest in specific goods, a security interest in specific goods and software used in the goods, a security interest in specific goods and license of software used in the goods, a lease of specific goods, or a lease of specific goods and license of software used in the goods. In this paragraph, "monetary obligation" means a monetary obligation secured by the goods or owed under a lease of the goods and includes a monetary obligation with respect to software used in the goods. The term does not include (i) charters or other contracts involving the use or hire of a vessel or (ii) records that evidence a right to payment arising out of the use of a

credit or charge card or information contained on or for use with the card. If a transaction is evidenced by records that include an instrument or series of instruments, the group of records taken together constitutes chattel paper.

(12) "Collateral" means the property subject to a security interest or agricultural lien. The term includes:

(A) proceeds to which a security interest attaches;

(B) accounts, chattel paper, payment intangibles, and promissory notes that have been sold; and

(C) goods that are the subject of a consignment.

(13) "Commercial tort claim" means a claim arising in tort with respect to which:

(A) the claimant is an organization; or

(B) the claimant is an individual and the claim:

(i) arose in the course of the claimant's business or profession; and

(ii) does not include damages arising out of personal injury to or the death of an individual.

* * * *

(19) "Consignee" means a merchant to which goods are delivered in a consignment.

(20) "Consignment" means a transaction, regardless of its form, in which a person delivers goods to a merchant for the purpose of sale and:

(A) the merchant:

(i) deals in goods of that kind under a name other than the name of the person making delivery;

(ii) is not an auctioneer; and

(iii) is not generally known by its creditors to be substantially engaged in selling the goods of others;

(B) with respect to each delivery, the aggregate value of the goods is $1,000 or more at the time of delivery;

(C) the goods are not consumer goods immediately before delivery; and

(D) the transaction does not create a security interest that secures an obligation.

(21) "Consignor" means a person that delivers goods to a consignee in a consignment.

(22) "Consumer debtor" means a debtor in a consumer transaction.

(23) "Consumer goods" means goods that are used or bought for use primarily for personal, family, or household purposes.

(24) "Consumer-goods transaction" means a consumer transaction in which:

(A) an individual incurs an obligation primarily for personal, family, or household purposes; and

(B) a security interest in consumer goods secures the obligation.

(25) "Consumer obligor" means an obligor who is an individual and who incurred the obligation as part of a transaction entered into primarily for personal, family, or household purposes.

(26) "Consumer transaction" means a transaction in which (i) an individual incurs an obligation primarily for personal, family, or household purposes, (ii) a security interest secures the obligation, and (iii) the collateral is held or acquired primarily for personal, family, or household purposes. The term includes consumer-goods transactions.

(27) "Continuation statement" means an amendment of a financing statement which:

(A) identifies, by its file number, the initial financing statement to which it relates; and

(B) indicates that it is a continuation statement for, or that it is filed to continue the effectiveness of, the identified financing statement.

(28) "Debtor" means:

(A) a person having an interest, other than a security interest or other lien, in the collateral, whether or not the person is an obligor;

(B) a seller of accounts, chattel paper, payment intangibles, or promissory notes; or

(C) a consignee.

(29) "Deposit account" means a demand, time, savings, passbook, or similar account maintained with a bank. The term does not include investment property or accounts evidenced by an instrument.

(30) "Document" means a document of title or a receipt of the type described in Section 7—201(2).

(31) "Electronic chattel paper" means chattel paper evidenced by a record or records consisting of information stored in an electronic medium.

(32) "Encumbrance" means a right, other than an ownership interest, in real property. The term includes mortgages and other liens on real property.

(33) "Equipment" means goods other than inventory, farm products, or consumer goods.

(34) "Farm products" means goods, other than standing timber, with respect to which the debtor is engaged in a farming operation and which are:

(A) crops grown, growing, or to be grown, including:

(i) crops produced on trees, vines, and bushes; and

(ii) aquatic goods produced in aquacultural operations;

(B) livestock, born or unborn, including aquatic goods produced in aquacultural operations;

(C) supplies used or produced in a farming operation; or

(D) products of crops or livestock in their unmanufactured states.

(35) "Farming operation" means raising, cultivating, propagating, fattening, grazing, or any other farming, livestock, or aquacultural operation.

* * * *

(39) "Financing statement" means a record or records composed of an initial financing statement and any filed record relating to the initial financing statement.

(40) "Fixture filing" means the filing of a financing statement covering goods that are or are to become fixtures and satisfying Section 9—502(a) and (b). The term includes the filing of a financing statement covering goods of a transmitting utility which are or are to become fixtures.

(41) "Fixtures" means goods that have become so related to particular real property that an interest in them arises under real property law.

(42) "General intangible" means any personal property, including things in action, other than accounts, chattel paper, commercial tort claims, deposit accounts, documents, goods, instruments, investment property, letter-of-credit rights, letters of credit, money, and oil, gas, or other minerals before extraction. The term includes payment intangibles and software.

* * * *

(44) "Goods" means all things that are movable when a security interest attaches. The term includes (i) fixtures, (ii) standing timber that is to be cut and removed under a conveyance or contract for sale, (iii) the unborn young of animals, (iv) crops grown, growing, or to be grown, even if the crops are produced on trees, vines, or bushes, and (v) manufactured homes.

The term also includes a computer program embedded in goods and any supporting information provided in connection with a transaction relating to the program if (i) the program is associated with the goods in such a manner that it customarily is considered part of the goods, or (ii) by becoming the owner of the goods, a person acquires a right to use the program in connection with the goods. The term does not include a computer program embedded in goods that consist solely of the medium in which the program is embedded. The term also does not include accounts, chattel paper, commercial tort claims, deposit accounts, documents, general intangibles, instruments, investment property, letter-of-credit rights, letters of credit, money, or oil, gas, or other minerals before extraction.

* * * *

(46) "Health-care-insurance receivable" means an interest in or claim under a policy of insurance which is a right to payment of a monetary obligation for health-care goods or services provided.

(47) "Instrument" means a negotiable instrument or any other writing that evidences a right to the payment of a monetary obligation, is not itself a security agreement or lease, and is of a type that in ordinary course of business is transferred by delivery with any necessary indorsement or assignment. The term does not include (i) investment property, (ii) letters of credit, or (iii) writings that evidence a right to payment arising out of the use of a credit or charge card or information contained on or for use with the card.

(48) "Inventory" means goods, other than farm products, which:

(A) are leased by a person as lessor;

(B) are held by a person for sale or lease or to be furnished under a contract of service;

(C) are furnished by a person under a contract of service; or

(D) consist of raw materials, work in process, or materials used or consumed in a business.

(49) "Investment property" means a security, whether certificated or uncertificated, security entitlement, securities account, commodity contract, or commodity account.

* * * *

(51) "Letter-of-credit right" means a right to payment or performance under a letter of credit, whether or not the beneficiary has demanded or is at the time entitled to demand payment or performance. The term does not include the right of a beneficiary to demand payment or performance under a letter of credit.

(52) "Lien creditor" means:

(A) a creditor that has acquired a lien on the property involved by attachment, levy, or the like;

(B) an assignee for benefit of creditors from the time of assignment;

(C) a trustee in bankruptcy from the date of the filing of the petition; or

(D) a receiver in equity from the time of appointment.

* * * *

(55) "Mortgage" means a consensual interest in real property, including fixtures, which secures payment or performance of an obligation.

(56) "New debtor" means a person that becomes bound as debtor under Section 9—203(d) by a security agreement previously entered into by another person.

(57) "New value" means (i) money, (ii) money's worth in property, services, or new credit, or (iii) release by a transferee of an interest in property previously transferreed to the transferee. The term does not include an obligation substituted for another obligation.

* * * *

(61) "Payment intangible" means a general intangible under which the account debtor's principal obligation is a monetary obligation.

* * * *

(64) "Proceeds", except as used in Section 9—609 (b), means the following property:

(A) whatever is acquired upon the sale, lease, license, exchange, or other disposition of collateral;

(B) whatever is collected on, or distributed on account of, collateral;

(C) rights arising out of collateral;

(D) to the extent of the value of collateral, claims arising out of the loss, nonconformity, or interference with the use of, defects or infringement of rights in, or damage to, the collateral; or

(E) to the extent of the value of collateral and to the extent payable to the debtor or the secured party, insurance payable by reason of the loss or nonconformity of, defects or infringement of rights in, or damage to, the collateral.

* * * *

(69) "Record", except as used in "for record", "of record", "record or legal title", and "record owner", means information that is inscribed on a tangible medium or which is stored in an electronic or other medium and is retrievable in perceivable form.

* * * *

(72) "Secured party" means:

(A) a person in whose favor a security interest is created or provided for under a security agreement, whether or not any obligation to be secured is outstanding;

(B) a person that holds an agricultural lien;

(C) a consignor;

(D) a person to which accounts, chattel paper, payment intangibles, or promissory notes have been sold;

(E) a trustee, indenture trustee, agent, collateral agent, or other representative in whose favor a security interest or agricultural lien is created or provided for; or

(F) a person that holds a security interest arising under Section 2—401, 2—505, 2—711(3), 2A—508(5), 4 —210, or 5—118.

(73) "Security agreement" means an agreement that creates or provides for a security interest.

* * * *

(78) "Tangible chattel paper" means chattel paper evidenced by a record or records consisting of information that is inscribed on a tangible medium.

(79) "Termination statement" means an amendment of a financing statement which:

(A) identifies, by its file number, the initial financing statement to which it relates; and

(B) indicates either that it is a termination statement or that the identified financing statement is no longer effective.

* * * *

§9—103. PURCHASE-MONEY SECURITY INTEREST; APPLICATION OF PAYMENTS; BURDEN OF ESTABLISHING

(a) In this section:

(1) "purchase-money collateral" means goods or software that secures a purchase-money obligation incurred with respect to that collateral; and

(2) "purchase-money obligation" means an obligation of an obligor incurred as all or part of the price of the collateral or for value given to enable the debtor to acquire rights in or the use of the collateral if the value is in fact so used.

(b) A security interest in goods is a purchase-money security interest:

(1) to the extent that the goods are purchase-money collateral with respect to that security interest;

(2) if the security interest is in inventory that is or was purchase-money collateral, also to the extent that the security interest secures a purchase-money obligation incurred with respect to other inventory in which the secured party holds or held a purchase-money security interest; and

(3) also to the extent that the security interest secures a purchase-money obligation incurred with respect to software in which the secured party holds or held a purchase-money security interest.

(c) A security interest in software is a purchase-money security interest to the extent that the security interest also secures a purchase-money obligation incurred with respect to goods in which the secured party holds or held a purchase-money security interest if:

(1) the debtor acquired its interest in the software in an integrated transaction in which it acquired an interest in the goods; and

(2) the debtor acquired its interest in the software for the principal purpose of using the software in the goods.

(d) The security interest of a consignor in goods that are the subject of a consignment is a purchase-money security interest in inventory.

(e) In a transaction other than a consumer-goods transaction, if the extent to which a security interest is a purchase-money security interest depends on the application of a payment to a particular obligation, the payment must be applied:

(1) in accordance with any reasonable method of application to which the parties agree;

(2) in the absence of the parties' agreement to a reasonable method, in accordance with any intention of the obligor manifested at or before the time of payment; or

(3) in the absence of an agreement to a reasonable method and a timely manifestation of the obligor's intention, in the following order:

(A) to obligations that are not secured; and

(B) if more than one obligation is secured, to obligations secured by purchase-money security interests in the order in which those obligations were incurred.

(f) In a transaction other than a consumer-goods transaction, a purchase-money security interest does not lose its status as such, even if:

(1) the purchase-money collateral also secures an obligation that is not a purchase-money obligation;

(2) collateral that is not purchase-money collateral also secures the purchase-money obligation; or

(3) the purchase-money obligation has been renewed, refinanced, consolidated, or restructured.

(g) In a transaction other than a consumer-goods transaction, a secured party claiming a purchase-money security interest has the burden of establishing the extent to which the security interest is a purchase-money security interest.

(h) The limitation of the rules in subsections (e), (f), and (g) to transactions other than consumer-goods transactions is intended to leave to the court the determination of the proper rules in consumer-goods transactions. The court may not infer from that limitation the nature of the proper rule in consumer-goods transactions and may continue to apply established approaches.

§9—104. CONTROL OF DEPOSIT ACCOUNT

(a) A secured party has control of a deposit account if:

(1) the secured party is the bank with which the deposit account is maintained;

(2) the debtor, secured party, and bank have agreed in an authenticated record that the bank will comply with instructions originated by the secured party directing disposition of the funds in the deposit account without further consent by the debtor; or

(3) the secured party becomes the bank's customer with respect to the deposit account.

(b) A secured party that has satisfied subsection (a) has control, even if the debtor retains the right to direct the disposition of funds from the deposit account.

§9—105. CONTROL OF ELECTRONIC CHATTEL PAPER

A secured party has control of electronic chattel paper if the record or records comprising the chattel paper are created, stored, and assigned in such a manner that:

(1) a single authoritative copy of the record or records exists which is unique, identifiable and, except as otherwise provided in paragraphs (4), (5), and (6), unalterable;

(2) the authoritative copy identifies the secured party as the assignee of the record or records;

(3) the authoritative copy is communicated to and maintained by the secured party or its designated custodian;

(4) copies or revisions that add or change an identified assignee of the authoritative copy can be made only with the participation of the secured party;

(5) each copy of the authoritative copy and any copy of a copy is readily identifiable as a copy that is not the authoritative copy; and

(6) any revision of the authoritative copy is readily identifiable as an authorized or unauthorized revision.

§9—106. CONTROL OF INVESTMENT PROPERTY

(a) A person has control of a certificated security, uncertificated security, or security entitlement as provided in Section 8—106.

(b) A secured party has control of a commodity contract if:

(1) the secured party is the commodity intermediary with which the commodity contract is carried; or

(2) the commodity customer, secured party, and commodity intermediary have agreed that the commodity intermediary will apply any value distributed on account of the commodity contract as directed by the secured party without further consent by the commodity customer.

(c) A secured party having control of all security entitlements or commodity contracts carried in a securities account or commodity account has control over the securities account or commodity account.

§9—107. CONTROL OF LETTER-OF-CREDIT RIGHT

A secured party has control of a letter-of-credit right to the extent of any right to payment or performance by the issuer or any nominated person if the issuer or nominated person has consented to an assignment of proceeds of the letter of credit under Section 5—114(c) or otherwise applicable law or practice.

§9—108. SUFFICIENCY OF DESCRIPTION

(a) Except as otherwise provided in subsections (c), (d), and (e), a description of personal or real property is sufficient, whether or not it is specific, if it reasonably identifies what is described.

(b) Except as otherwise provided in subsection (d), a description of collateral reasonably identifies the collateral if it identifies the collateral by:

(1) specific listing;

(2) category;

(3) except as otherwise provided in subsection (e), a type of collateral defined in [the Uniform Commercial Code];

(4) quantity;

(5) computational or allocational formula or procedure; or

(6) except as otherwise provided in subsection

(c) any other method, if the identity of the collateral is objectively determinable. (c) A description of collateral as "all the debtor's assets" or "all the debtor's personal property" or using words of similar import does not reasonably identify the collateral.

(d) Except as otherwise provided in subsection (e), a description of a security entitlement, securities account, or commodity account is sufficient if it describes:

(1) the collateral by those terms or as investment property; or

(2) the underlying financial asset or commodity contract.

(e) A description only by type of collateral defined in [the Uniform Commercial Code] is an insufficient description of:

(1) a commercial tort claim; or

(2) in a consumer transaction, consumer goods, a security entitlement, a securities account, or a commodity account.

§9-109 SCOPE

* * * *

This article does not apply to:

(1) a landlord's lien, other than an agricultural lien;

(2) a lien, other than an agricultural lien, given by statute or other rule of law for services or materials, but Section 9—333 applies with respect to priority of the lien;

(3) an assignment of a claim for wages, salary, or other compensation of an employee;

(4) a sale of accounts, chattel paper, payment intangibles, or promissory notes as part of a sale of the business out of which they arose;

(5) an assignment of accounts, chattel paper, payment intangibles, or promissory notes which is for the purpose of collection only;

(6) an assignment of a right to payment under a contract to an assignee that is also obligated to perform under the contract;

(7) an assignment of a single account, payment intangible, or promissory note to an assignee in full or partial satisfaction of a preexisting indebtedness;

(8) a transfer of an interest in or an assignment of a claim under a policy of insurance, other than an assignment by or to a health-care provider of a health-care-insurance receivable and any subsequent assignment of the right to payment, but Sections 9—315 and 9—322 apply with respect to proceeds and priorities in proceeds;

(9) an assignment of a right represented by a judgment, other than a judgment taken on a right to payment that was collateral;

(10) a right of recoupment or set-off, but:

(A) Section 9—340 applies with respect to the effectiveness of rights of recoupment or set-off against deposit accounts; and

(B) Section 9—404 applies with respect to defenses or claims of an account debtor;

(11) the creation or transfer of an interest in or lien on real property, including a lease or rents thereunder, except to the extent that provision is made for:

(A) liens on real property in Sections 9—203 and 9—308;

(B) fixtures in Section 9—334;

(C) fixture filings in Sections 9—501, 9—502, 9—512, 9—516, and 9—519; and

(D) security agreements covering personal and real property in Section 9—604;

(12) an assignment of a claim arising in tort, other than a commercial tort claim, but Sections 9—315 and 9—322 apply with respect to proceeds and priorities in proceeds; or

(13) an assignment of a deposit account in a consumer transaction, but Sections 9—315 and 9 —322 apply with respect to proceeds and priorities in proceeds.

* * * *

§9—201. GENERAL EFFECTIVENESS OF SECURITY AGREEMENT

(a) Except as otherwise provided in [the Uniform Commercial Code], a security agreement is effective according to its terms between the parties, against purchasers of the collateral, and against creditors.

(b) A transaction subject to this article is subject to any applicable rule of law which establishes a different rule for consumers and [insert reference to (i) any other statute or regulation that regulates the rates, charges, agreements, and practices for loans, credit sales, or other extensions of credit and (ii) any consumer-protection statute or regulation].

(c) In case of conflict between this article and a rule of law, statute, or regulation described in subsection (b), the rule of law, statute, or regulation controls. Failure to comply with a statute or regulation described in subsection (b) has only the effect the statute or regulation specifies.

(d) This article does not:

(1) validate any rate, charge, agreement, or practice that violates a rule of law, statute, or regulation described in subsection (b); or

(2) extend the application of the rule of law, statute, or regulation to a transaction not otherwise subject to it.

§9—202. TITLE TO COLLATERAL IMMATERIAL

Except as otherwise provided with respect to consignments or sales of accounts, chattel paper, payment intangibles, or promissory notes, the provisions of this article with regard to rights and obligations apply whether title to collateral is in the secured party or the debtor.

§9—203. ATTACHMENT AND ENFORCEABILITY OF SECURITY INTEREST; PROCEEDS; SUPPORTING OBLIGATIONS; FORMAL REQUISITES

(a) A security interest attaches to collateral when it becomes enforceable against the debtor with respect to the collateral, unless an agreement expressly postpones the time of attachment.

(b) Except as otherwise provided in subsections (c) through (i), a security interest is enforceable against the debtor and third parties with respect to the collateral only if:

(1) value has been given;

(2) the debtor has rights in the collateral or the power to transfer rights in the collateral to a secured party; and

(3) one of the following conditions is met:

(A) the debtor has authenticated a security agreement that provides a description of the collateral and, if the security interest covers timber to be cut, a description of the land concerned;

(B) the collateral is not a certificated security and is in the possession of the secured party under Section 9—313 pursuant to the debtor's security agreement;

(C) the collateral is a certificated security in registered form and the security certificate has been delivered to the secured party under Section 8—301 pursuant to the debtor's security agreement; or

(D) the collateral is deposit accounts, electronic chattel paper, investment property, or letter-of-credit rights, and the secured party has control under Section 9—104, 9—105, 9 —106, or 9—107 pursuant to the debtor's security agreement.

(c) Subsection (b) is subject to Section 4—210 on the security interest of a collecting bank, Section 5—118 on the security interest of a letter-of-credit issuer or nominated person, Section 9—110 on a security interest arising under Article 2 or 2A, and Section 9—206 on security interests in investment property.

(d) A person becomes bound as debtor by a security agreement entered into by another person if, by operation of law other than this article or by contract:

(1) the security agreement becomes effective to create a security interest in the person's property; or

(2) the person becomes generally obligated for the obligations of the other person, including the obligation secured under the security agreement, and acquires or succeeds to all or substantially all of the assets of the other person.

(e) If a new debtor becomes bound as debtor by a security agreement entered into by another person:

(1) the agreement satisfies subsection (b)(3) with respect to existing or after-acquired property of the new debtor to the extent the property is described in the agreement; and

(2) another agreement is not necessary to make a security interest in the property enforceable.

(f) The attachment of a security interest in collateral gives the secured party the rights to proceeds provided by Section 9—315 and is also attachment of a security interest in a supporting obligation for the collateral.

(g) The attachment of a security interest in a right to payment or performance secured by a security interest or other lien on personal or real property is also attachment of a security interest in the security interest, mortgage, or other lien.

(h) The attachment of a security interest in a securities account is also attachment of a security interest in the security entitlements carried in the securities account.

(i) The attachment of a security interest in a commodity account is also attachment of a security interest in the commodity contracts carried in the commodity account.

§9—204. AFTER-ACQUIRED PROPERTY; FUTURE ADVANCES

(a) Except as otherwise provided in subsection (b), a security agreement may create or provide for a security interest in after-acquired collateral.

(b) A security interest does not attach under a term constituting an after-acquired property clause to:

(1) consumer goods, other than an accession when given as additional security, unless the debtor acquires rights in them within 10 days after the secured party gives value; or

(2) a commercial tort claim.

(c) A security agreement may provide that collateral secures, or that accounts, chattel paper, payment intangibles, or promissory notes are sold in connection with, future advances or other value, whether or not the advances or value are given pursuant to commitment.

§9—205. USE OR DISPOSITION OF COLLATERAL PERMISSIBLE

(a) A security interest is not invalid or fraudulent against creditors solely because:

(1) the debtor has the right or ability to:

(A) use, commingle, or dispose of all or part of the collateral, including returned or repossessed goods;

(B) collect, compromise, enforce, or otherwise deal with collateral;

(C) accept the return of collateral or make repossessions; or

(D) use, commingle, or dispose of proceeds; or

(2) the secured party fails to require the debtor to account for proceeds or replace collateral.

(b) This section does not relax the requirements of possession if attachment, perfection, or enforcement of a security interest depends upon possession of the collateral by the secured party.

§9—206. SECURITY INTEREST ARISING IN PURCHASE OR DELIVERY OF FINANCIAL ASSET

(a) A security interest in favor of a securities intermediary attaches to a person's security entitlement if:

(1) the person buys a financial asset through the securities intermediary in a transaction in which the person is obligated to pay the purchase price to the securities intermediary at the time of the purchase; and

(2) the securities intermediary credits the financial asset to the buyer's securities account before the buyer pays the securities intermediary.

(b) The security interest described in subsection (a) secures the person's obligation to pay for the financial asset.

* * * *

§9—207. RIGHTS AND DUTIES OF SECURED PARTY HAVING POSSESSION OR CONTROL OF COLLATERAL

(a) Except as otherwise provided in subsection (d), a secured party shall use reasonable care in the custody and preservation of collateral in the secured party's possession. In the case of chattel paper or an instrument, reasonable care includes taking necessary steps to preserve rights against prior parties unless otherwise agreed.

(b) Except as otherwise provided in subsection (d), if a secured party has possession of collateral:

(1) reasonable expenses, including the cost of insurance and payment of taxes or other charges, incurred in the custody, preservation, use, or operation of the collateral are chargeable to the debtor and are secured by the collateral;

(2) the risk of accidental loss or damage is on the debtor to the extent of a deficiency in any effective insurance coverage;

(3) the secured party shall keep the collateral identifiable, but fungible collateral may be commingled; and

(4) the secured party may use or operate the collateral:

(A) for the purpose of preserving the collateral or its value;

(B) as permitted by an order of a court having competent jurisdiction; or

(C) except in the case of consumer goods, in the manner and to the extent agreed by the debtor.

(c) Except as otherwise provided in subsection (d), a secured party having possession of collateral or control of collateral under Section 9—104, 9—105, 9—106, or 9—107:

(1) may hold as additional security any proceeds, except money or funds, received from the collateral;

(2) shall apply money or funds received from the collateral to reduce the secured obligation, unless remitted to the debtor; and

(3) may create a security interest in the collateral.

(d) If the secured party is a buyer of accounts, chattel paper, payment intangibles, or promissory notes or a consignor:

(1) subsection (a) does not apply unless the secured party is entitled under an agreement:

(A) to charge back uncollected collateral; or

(B) otherwise to full or limited recourse against the debtor or a secondary obligor based on the nonpayment or other default of an account debtor or other obligor on the collateral; and

(2) subsections (b) and (c) do not apply.

§9—208. ADDITIONAL DUTIES OF SECURED PARTY HAVING CONTROL OF COLLATERAL

(a) This section applies to cases in which there is no outstanding secured obligation and the secured party is not committed to make advances, incur obligations, or otherwise give value.

(b) Within 10 days after receiving an authenticated demand by the debtor:

(1) a secured party having control of a deposit account under Section 9—104(a)(2) shall send to the bank with which the deposit account is maintained an authenticated statement that releases the bank from any further obligation to comply with instructions originated by the secured party;

(2) a secured party having control of a deposit account under Section 9—104(a)(3) shall:

(A) pay the debtor the balance on deposit in the deposit account; or

(B) transfer the balance on deposit into a deposit account in the debtor's name;

(3) a secured party, other than a buyer, having control of electronic chattel paper under Section 9—105 shall:

(A) communicate the authoritative copy of the electronic chattel paper to the debtor or its designated custodian;

(B) if the debtor designates a custodian that is the designated custodian with which the authoritative copy of the electronic chattel paper is maintained for the secured party, communicate to the custodian an authenticated record releasing the designated custodian from any further obligation to comply with instructions originated by the secured party and instructing the custodian to comply with instructions originated by the debtor; and

(C) take appropriate action to enable the debtor or its designated custodian to make copies of or revisions to the authoritative copy which add or change an identified assignee of the authoritative copy without the consent of the secured party;

(4) a secured party having control of investment property under Section 8—106(d)(2) or 9—106 (b) shall send to the securities intermediary or commodity intermediary with which the security entitlement or commodity contract is maintained an authenticated record that releases the securities intermediary or commodity intermediary from any further obligation to comply with entitlement orders or directions originated by the secured party; and

(5) a secured party having control of a letter-of-credit right under Section 9—107 shall send to each person having an unfulfilled obligation to pay or deliver proceeds of the letter of credit to the secured party an authenticated release from any further obligation to pay or deliver proceeds of the letter of credit to the secured party.

§9—209. DUTIES OF SECURED PARTY IF ACCOUNT DEBTOR HAS BEEN NOTIFIED OF ASSIGNMENT

(a) Except as otherwise provided in subsection (c), this section applies if:

(1) there is no outstanding secured obligation; and

(2) the secured party is not committed to make advances, incur obligations, or otherwise give value.

(b) Within 10 days after receiving an authenticated demand by the debtor, a secured party shall send to an account debtor that has received notification of an assignment to the secured party as assignee under Section 9—406(a) an authenticated record that releases the account debtor from any further obligation to the secured party.

* * * *

§9—301. LAW GOVERNING PERFECTION AND PRIORITY OF SECURITY INTERESTS

Except as otherwise provided in Sections 9—303 through 9—306, the following rules determine the law governing perfection, the effect of perfection or nonperfection, and the priority of a security interest in collateral:

(1) Except as otherwise provided in this section, while a debtor is located in a jurisdiction, the local law of that jurisdiction governs perfection, the effect of perfection or nonperfection, and the priority of a security interest in collateral.

(2) While collateral is located in a jurisdiction, the local law of that jurisdiction governs perfection, the effect of perfection or nonperfection, and the priority of a possessory security interest in that collateral.

(3) Except as otherwise provided in paragraph (4), while negotiable documents, goods, instruments, money, or tangible chattel paper is located in a jurisdiction, the local law of that jurisdiction governs:

(A) perfection of a security interest in the goods by filing a fixture filing;

(B) perfection of a security interest in timber to be cut; and

(C) the effect of perfection or nonperfection and the priority of a nonpossessory security interest in the collateral.

(4) The local law of the jurisdiction in which the wellhead or minehead is located governs perfection, the effect of perfection or nonperfection, and the priority of a security interest in as-extracted collateral.

* * * *

§9—309. SECURITY INTEREST PERFECTED UPON ATTACHMENT

The following security interests are perfected when they attach:

(1) a purchase-money security interest in consumer goods, except as otherwise provided in Section 9—311(b) with respect to consumer goods that are subject to a statute or treaty described in Section 9—311(a);

(2) an assignment of accounts or payment intangibles which does not by itself or in conjunction with other assignments to the same assignee transfer a significant part of the assignor's outstanding accounts or payment intangibles;

(3) a sale of a payment intangible;

(4) a sale of a promissory note;

(5) a security interest created by the assignment of a health-care-insurance receivable to the provider of the health-care goods or services;

(6) a security interest arising under Section 2—401, 2—505, 2—711(3), or 2A—508(5), until the debtor obtains possession of the collateral;

(7) a security interest of a collecting bank arising under Section 4—210;

(8) a security interest of an issuer or nominated person arising under Section 5—118;

(9) a security interest arising in the delivery of a financial asset under Section 9—206(c);

(10) a security interest in investment property created by a broker or securities intermediary;

(11) a security interest in a commodity contract or a commodity account created by a commodity intermediary;

(12) an assignment for the benefit of all creditors of the transferor and subsequent transfers by the assignee thereunder; and

(13) a security interest created by an assignment of a beneficial interest in a decedent's estate; and

(14) a sale by an individual of an account that is a right to payment of winnings in a lottery or other game of chance.

§9—310. WHEN FILING REQUIRED TO PERFECT SECURITY INTEREST OR AGRICULTURAL LIEN; SECURITY INTERESTS AND AGRICULTURAL LIENS TO WHICH FILING PROVISIONS DO NOT APPLY

(a) Except as otherwise provided in subsection (b) and Section 9—312(b), a financing statement must be filed to perfect all security interests and agricultural liens.

(b) The filing of a financing statement is not necessary to perfect a security interest:

(1) that is perfected under Section 9—308(d), (e), (f), or (g);

(2) that is perfected under Section 9—309 when it attaches;

(3) in property subject to a statute, regulation, or treaty described in Section 9—311(a);

(4) in goods in possession of a bailee which is perfected under Section 9—312(d)(1) or (2);

(5) in certificated securities, documents, goods, or instruments which is perfected without filing or possession under Section 9—312(e), (f), or (g);

(6) in collateral in the secured party's possession under Section 9—313;

(7) in a certificated security which is perfected by delivery of the security certificate to the secured party under Section 9—313;

(8) in deposit accounts, electronic chattel paper, investment property, or letter-of-credit rights which is perfected by control under Section 9—314;

(9) in proceeds which is perfected under Section 9—315; or

(10) that is perfected under Section 9—316.

(c) If a secured party assigns a perfected security interest or agricultural lien, a filing under this article is not required to continue the perfected status of the security interest against creditors of and transferees from the original debtor.

§9—311. PERFECTION OF SECURITY INTERESTS IN PROPERTY SUBJECT TO CERTAIN STATUTES, REGULATIONS, AND TREATIES

(a) Except as otherwise provided in subsection (d), the filing of a financing statement is not necessary or effective to perfect a security interest in property subject to:

(1) a statute, regulation, or treaty of the United States whose requirements for a security interest's obtaining priority over the rights of a lien creditor with respect to the property preempt Section 9—310(a);

(2) [list any certificate-of-title statute covering automobiles, trailers, mobile homes, boats, farm tractors, or the like, which provides for a security interest to be indicated on the certificate as a condition or result of perfection, and any non Uniform Commercial Code central filing statute]; or

(3) a certificate-of-title statute of another jurisdiction which provides for a security interest to be indicated on the certificate as a condition or result of the security interest's obtaining priority over the rights of a lien creditor with respect to the property.

* * * *

§9—312. PERFECTION OF SECURITY INTERESTS IN CHATTEL PAPER, DEPOSIT ACCOUNTS, DOCUMENTS, GOODS COVERED BY DOCUMENTS, INSTRUMENTS, INVESTMENT PROPERTY, LETTER-OF-CREDIT RIGHTS, AND MONEY; PERFECTION BY PERMISSIVE FILING; TEMPORARY PERFECTION WITHOUT FILING OR TRANSFER OF POSSESSION

(a) A security interest in chattel paper, negotiable documents, instruments, or investment property may be perfected by filing.

(b) Except as otherwise provided in Section 9—315 (c) and (d) for proceeds:

(1) a security interest in a deposit account may be perfected only by control under Section 9—314;

(2) and except as otherwise provided in Section 9—308(d), a security interest in a letter-of-credit right may be perfected only by control under Section 9—314; and

(3) a security interest in money may be perfected only by the secured party's taking possession under Section 9—313.

(c) While goods are in the possession of a bailee that has issued a negotiable document covering the goods:

(1) a security interest in the goods may be perfected by perfecting a security interest in the document; and

(2) a security interest perfected in the document has priority over any security interest that becomes perfected in the goods by another method during that time.

(d) While goods are in the possession of a bailee that has issued a nonnegotiable document covering the goods, a security interest in the goods may be perfected by:

(1) issuance of a document in the name of the secured party;

(2) the bailee's receipt of notification of the secured party's interest; or

(3) filing as to the goods.

(e) A security interest in certificated securities, negotiable documents, or instruments is perfected without filing or the taking of possession for a period of 20 days from the time it attaches to the extent that it arises for new value given under an authenticated security agreement.

(f) A perfected security interest in a negotiable document or goods in possession of a bailee, other than one that has issued a negotiable document for the goods, remains perfected for 20 days without filing if the secured party makes available to the debtor the goods or documents representing the goods for the purpose of:

(1) ultimate sale or exchange; or

(2) loading, unloading, storing, shipping, transshipping, manufacturing, processing, or otherwise dealing with them in a manner preliminary to their sale or exchange.

(g) A perfected security interest in a certificated security or instrument remains perfected for 20 days without filing if the secured party delivers the security certificate or instrument to the debtor for the purpose of:

(1) ultimate sale or exchange; or

(2) presentation, collection, enforcement, renewal, or registration of transfer.

(h) After the 20-day period specified in subsection (e), (f), or (g) expires, perfection depends upon compliance with this article.

§—313. WHEN POSSESSION BY OR DELIVERY TO SECURED PARTY PERFECTS SECURITY INTEREST WITHOUT FILING

(a) Except as otherwise provided in subsection (b), a secured party may perfect a security interest in negotiable documents, goods, instruments, money, or tangible chattel paper by taking possession of the collateral. A secured party may perfect a security interest in certificated securities by taking delivery of the certificated securities under Section 8—301.

(b) With respect to goods covered by a certificate of title issued by this State, a secured party may perfect a security interest in the goods by taking possession of the goods only in the circumstances described in Section 9—316(d).

(c) With respect to collateral other than certificated securities and goods covered by a document, a secured party takes possession of collateral in the possession of a person other than the debtor, the secured party, or a lessee of the collateral from the debtor in the ordinary course of the debtor's business, when:

(1) the person in possession authenticates a record acknowledging that it holds possession of the collateral for the secured party's benefit; or

(2) the person takes possession of the collateral after having authenticated a record acknowledging that it will hold possession of collateral for the secured party's benefit.

(d) If perfection of a security interest depends upon possession of the collateral by a secured party, perfection occurs no earlier than the time the secured party takes possession and continues only while the secured party retains possession.

(e) A security interest in a certificated security in registered form is perfected by delivery when delivery of the certificated security occurs under Section 8—301 and remains perfected by delivery until the debtor obtains possession of the security certificate.

(f) A person in possession of collateral is not required to acknowledge that it holds possession for a secured party's benefit.

(g) If a person acknowledges that it holds possession for the secured party's benefit:

(1) the acknowledgment is effective under subsection (c) or Section 8—301(a), even if the acknowledgment violates the rights of a debtor; and

(2) unless the person otherwise agrees or law other than this article otherwise provides, the person does not owe any duty to the secured party and is not required to confirm the acknowledgment to another person.

(h) A secured party having possession of collateral does not relinquish possession by delivering the collateral to a person other than the debtor or a lessee of the collateral from the debtor in the ordinary course of the debtor's business if the person was instructed before the delivery or is instructed contemporaneously with the delivery:

(1) to hold possession of the collateral for the secured party's benefit; or

(2) to redeliver the collateral to the secured party.

(i) A secured party does not relinquish possession, even if a delivery under subsection (h) violates the rights of a debtor. A person to which collateral is delivered under subsection (h) does not owe any duty to the secured party and is not required to confirm the delivery to another person unless the person otherwise agrees or law other than this article otherwise provides.

§9—314. PERFECTION BY CONTROL

(a) A security interest in investment property, deposit accounts, letter-of-credit rights, or electronic chattel paper may be perfected by control of the collateral under Section 9—104, 9—105, 9—106, or 9—107.

(b) A security interest in deposit accounts, electronic chattel paper, or letter-of-credit rights is perfected by control under Section 9—104, 9—105, or 9—107 when the secured party obtains control and remains perfected by control only while the secured party retains control.

(c) A security interest in investment property is perfected by control under Section 9—106 from the time the secured party obtains control and remains perfected by control until:

(1) the secured party does not have control; and

(2) one of the following occurs:

(A) if the collateral is a certificated security, the debtor has or acquires possession of the security certificate;

(B) if the collateral is an uncertificated security, the issuer has registered or registers the debtor as the registered owner; or

(C) if the collateral is a security entitlement, the debtor is or becomes the entitlement holder.

§9—315. SECURED PARTY'S RIGHTS ON DISPOSITION OF COLLATERAL AND IN PROCEEDS

(a) Except as otherwise provided in this article and in Section 2—403(2):

(1) a security interest or agricultural lien continues in collateral notwithstanding sale, lease, license, exchange, or other disposition thereof unless the secured party authorized the disposition free of the security interest or agricultural lien; and

(2) a security interest attaches to any identifiable proceeds of collateral.

(b) Proceeds that are commingled with other property are identifiable proceeds:

(1) if the proceeds are goods, to the extent provided by Section 9—336; and

(2) if the proceeds are not goods, to the extent that the secured party identifies the proceeds by a method of tracing, including application of equitable principles, that is permitted under law other than this article with respect to commingled property of the type involved.

(c) A security interest in proceeds is a perfected security interest if the security interest in the original collateral was perfected.

(d) A perfected security interest in proceeds becomes unperfected on the 21st day after the security interest attaches to the proceeds unless:

(1) the following conditions are satisfied:

(A) a filed financing statement covers the original collateral;

(B) the proceeds are collateral in which a security interest may be perfected by filing in the office in which the financing statement has been filed; and

(C) the proceeds are not acquired with cash proceeds;

(2) the proceeds are identifiable cash proceeds; or

(3) the security interest in the proceeds is perfected other than under subsection (c) when the security interest attaches to the proceeds or within 20 days thereafter.

(e) If a filed financing statement covers the original collateral, a security interest in proceeds which remains perfected under subsection (d)(1) becomes unperfected at the later of:

(1) when the effectiveness of the filed financing statement lapses under Section 9—515 or is terminated under Section 9—513; or

(2) the 21st day after the security interest attaches to the proceeds.

§9—316. CONTINUED PERFECTION OF SECURITY INTEREST FOLLOWING CHANGE IN GOVERNING LAW

(a) A security interest perfected pursuant to the law of the jurisdiction designated in Section 9—301(1) or 9—305(c) remains perfected until the earliest of:

(1) the time perfection would have ceased under the law of that jurisdiction;

(2) the expiration of four months after a change of the debtor's location to another jurisdiction; or

(3) the expiration of one year after a transfer of collateral to a person that thereby becomes a debtor and is located in another jurisdiction.

(b) If a security interest described in subsection (a) becomes perfected under the law of the other jurisdiction before the earliest time or event described in that subsection, it remains perfected thereafter. If the security interest does not become perfected under the law of the other jurisdiction before the earliest time or event, it becomes unperfected and is deemed never to have been perfected as against a purchaser of the collateral for value.

(c) A possessory security interest in collateral, other than goods covered by a certificate of title and as-extracted collateral consisting of goods, remains continuously perfected if:

(1) the collateral is located in one jurisdiction and subject to a security interest perfected under the law of that jurisdiction;

(2) thereafter the collateral is brought into another jurisdiction; and

(3) upon entry into the other jurisdiction, the security interest is perfected under the law of the other jurisdiction.

(d) Except as otherwise provided in subsection (e), a security interest in goods covered by a certificate of title which is perfected by any method under the law of another jurisdiction when the goods become covered by a certificate of title from this State remains perfected until the security interest would have become unperfected under the law of the other jurisdiction had the goods not become so covered.

(e) A security interest described in subsection (d) becomes unperfected as against a purchaser of the goods for value and is deemed never to have been perfected as against a purchaser of the goods for value if the applicable requirements for perfection under Section 9—311(b) or 9 —313 are not satisfied before the earlier of:

(1) the time the security interest would have become unperfected under the law of the other jurisdiction had the goods not become covered by a certificate of title from this State; or

(2) the expiration of four months after the goods had become so covered.

(f) A security interest in deposit accounts, letter-of-credit rights, or investment property which is perfected under the law of the bank's jurisdiction, the issuer's jurisdiction, a nominated person's jurisdiction, the securities intermediary's jurisdiction, or the commodity intermediary's jurisdiction, as applicable, remains perfected until the earlier of:

(1) the time the security interest would have become unperfected under the law of that jurisdiction; or

(2) the expiration of four months after a change of the applicable jurisdiction to another jurisdiction.

(g) If a security interest described in subsection (f) becomes perfected under the law of the other jurisdiction before the earlier of the time or the end of the period described in that subsection, it remains perfected thereafter. If the security interest does not become perfected under the law of the other jurisdiction before the earlier of that time or the end of that period, it becomes unperfected and is deemed never to have been perfected as against a purchaser of the collateral for value.

§9—317. INTERESTS THAT TAKE PRIORITY OVER OR TAKE FREE OF SECURITY INTEREST OR AGRICULTURAL LIEN

(a) A security interest or agricultural lien is subordinate to the rights of:

(1) a person entitled to priority under Section 9—322; and

(2) except as otherwise provided in subsection (e), a person that becomes a lien creditor before the earlier of the time:

(A) the security interest or agricultural lien is perfected; or

(B) one of the conditions specified in Section 9—203(b)(3) is met and a financing statement covering the collateral is filed.

(b) Except as otherwise provided in subsection (e), a buyer, other than a secured party, of tangible chattel paper, documents, goods, instruments, or a security certificate takes free of a security interest or agricultural lien if the buyer gives value and receives delivery of the collateral without knowledge of the security interest or agricultural lien and before it is perfected.

(c) Except as otherwise provided in subsection (e), a lessee of goods takes free of a security interest or agricultural lien if the lessee gives value and receives delivery of the collateral without knowledge of the security interest or agricultural lien and before it is perfected.

(d) A licensee of a general intangible or a buyer, other than a secured party, of accounts, electronic chattel paper, general intangibles, or investment property other than a certificated security takes free of a security interest if the licensee or buyer gives value without knowledge of the security interest and before it is perfected.

(e) Except as otherwise provided in Sections 9—320 and 9—321, if a person files a financing statement with respect to a purchase-money security interest before or within 20 days after the debtor receives delivery of the collateral, the security interest takes priority over the rights of a buyer, lessee, or lien creditor which arise between the time the security interest attaches and the time of filing.

§9—318. NO INTEREST RETAINED IN RIGHT TO PAYMENT THAT IS SOLD; RIGHTS AND TITLE OF SELLER OF ACCOUNT OR CHATTEL PAPER WITH RESPECT TO CREDITORS AND PURCHASERS

(a) A debtor that has sold an account, chattel paper, payment intangible, or promissory note does not retain a legal or equitable interest in the collateral sold.

(b) For purposes of determining the rights of creditors of, and purchasers for value of an account or chattel paper from, a debtor that has sold an account or chattel paper, while the buyer's security interest is unperfected, the debtor is deemed to have rights and title to the account or chattel paper identical to those the debtor sold.

§9—319. RIGHTS AND TITLE OF CONSIGNEE WITH RESPECT TO CREDITORS AND PURCHASERS

(a) Except as otherwise provided in subsection (b), for purposes of determining the rights of creditors of, and purchasers for value of goods from, a consignee, while the goods are in the possession of the consignee, the consignee is deemed to have rights and title to the goods identical to those the consignor had or had power to transfer.

(b) For purposes of determining the rights of a creditor of a consignee, law other than this article determines the rights and title of a consignee while goods are in the consignee's possession if, under this part, a perfected security interest held by the consignor would have priority over the rights of the creditor.

§—320. BUYER OF GOODS

(a) Except as otherwise provided in subsection (e), a buyer in ordinary course of business, other than a person buying farm products from a person engaged in farming operations, takes free of a security interest created by the buyer's seller, even if the security interest is perfected and the buyer knows of its existence.

(b) Except as otherwise provided in subsection (e), a buyer of goods from a person who used or bought the goods for use primarily for personal, family, or household purposes takes free of a security interest, even if perfected, if the buyer buys:

    (1) without knowledge of the security interest;

    (2) for value;

    (3) primarily for the buyer's personal, family, or household purposes; and

    (4) before the filing of a financing statement covering the goods.

(c) To the extent that it affects the priority of a security interest over a buyer of goods under subsection (b), the period of effectiveness of a filing made in the jurisdiction in which the seller is located is governed by Section 9—316(a) and (b).

(d) A buyer in ordinary course of business buying oil, gas, or other minerals at the wellhead or minehead or after extraction takes free of an interest arising out of an encumbrance.

(e) Subsections (a) and (b) do not affect a security interest in goods in the possession of the secured party under Section 9—313.

* * * *

§—322. PRIORITIES AMONG CONFLICTING SECURITY INTERESTS IN AND AGRICULTURAL LIENS ON SAME COLLATERAL

(a) Except as otherwise provided in this section, priority among conflicting security interests and agricultural liens in the same collateral is determined according to the following rules:

    (1) Conflicting perfected security interests and agricultural liens rank according to priority in time of filing or perfection. Priority dates from the earlier of the time a filing covering the collateral is first made or the security interest or agricultural lien is first perfected, if there is no period thereafter when there is neither filing nor perfection.

    (2) A perfected security interest or agricultural lien has priority over a conflicting unperfected security interest or agricultural lien.

    (3) The first security interest or agricultural lien to attach or become effective has priority if conflicting security interests and agricultural liens are unperfected.

(b) For the purposes of subsection (a)(1):

    (1) the time of filing or perfection as to a security interest in collateral is also the time of filing or perfection as to a security interest in proceeds; and

    (2) the time of filing or perfection as to a security interest in collateral supported by a supporting obligation is also the time of filing or perfection as to a security interest in the supporting obligation.

(c) Except as otherwise provided in subsection (f), a security interest in collateral which qualifies for priority over a conflicting security interest under Section 9—327, 9—328, 9—329, 9—330, or 9—331 also has priority over a conflicting security interest in:

    (1) any supporting obligation for the collateral; and

    (2) proceeds of the collateral if:

        (A) the security interest in proceeds is perfected;

        (B) the proceeds are cash proceeds or of the same type as the collateral; and

        (C) in the case of proceeds that are proceeds of proceeds, all intervening proceeds are cash proceeds, proceeds of the same type as the collateral, or an account relating to the collateral.

(d) Subject to subsection (e) and except as otherwise provided in subsection (f), if a security interest in chattel paper, deposit accounts, negotiable documents, instruments, investment property, or letter-of-credit rights is perfected by a method other than filing, conflicting perfected security interests in proceeds of the collateral rank according to priority in time of filing.

(e) Subsection (d) applies only if the proceeds of the collateral are not cash proceeds, chattel paper, negotiable documents, instruments, investment property, or letter-of-credit rights.

(f) Subsections (a) through (e) are subject to:

    (1) subsection (g) and the other provisions of this part;

    (2) Section 4—210 with respect to a security interest of a collecting bank;

    (3) Section 5—118 with respect to a security interest of an issuer or nominated person; and

    (4) Section 9—110 with respect to a security interest arising under Article 2 or 2A.

(g) A perfected agricultural lien on collateral has priority over a conflicting security interest in or agricultural lien on the same collateral if the statute creating the agricultural lien so provides.

§9—323. FUTURE ADVANCES

(a) Except as otherwise provided in subsection (c), for purposes of determining the priority of a perfected security interest under Section 9—322(a)(1), perfection of the security interest dates from the time an advance is made to the extent that the security interest secures an advance that:

(1) is made while the security interest is perfected only:

(A) under Section 9—309 when it attaches; or

(B) temporarily under Section 9—312(e), (f), or (g); and

(2) is not made pursuant to a commitment entered into before or while the security interest is perfected by a method other than under Section 9—309 or 9—312(e), (f), or (g).

(b) Except as otherwise provided in subsection (c), a security interest is subordinate to the rights of a person that becomes a lien creditor to the extent that the security interest secures an advance made more than 45 days after the person becomes a lien creditor unless the advance is made:

(1) without knowledge of the lien; or

(2) pursuant to a commitment entered into without knowledge of the lien.

(c) Subsections (a) and (b) do not apply to a security interest held by a secured party that is a buyer of accounts, chattel paper, payment intangibles, or promissory notes or a consignor.

(d) Except as otherwise provided in subsection (e), a buyer of goods other than a buyer in ordinary course of business takes free of a security interest to the extent that it secures advances made after the earlier of:

(1) the time the secured party acquires knowledge of the buyer's purchase; or

(2) 45 days after the purchase.

(e) Subsection (d) does not apply if the advance is made pursuant to a commitment entered into without knowledge of the buyer's purchase and before the expiration of the 45-day period.

(f) Except as otherwise provided in subsection (g), a lessee of goods, other than a lessee in ordinary course of business, takes the leasehold interest free of a security interest to the extent that it secures advances made after the earlier of:

(1) the time the secured party acquires knowledge of the lease; or

(2) 45 days after the lease contract becomes enforceable.

(g) Subsection (f) does not apply if the advance is made pursuant to a commitment entered into without knowledge of the lease and before the expiration of the 45 day period.

§9—324. PRIORITY OF PURCHASE-MONEY SECURITY INTERESTS

(a) Except as otherwise provided in subsection (g), a perfected purchase-money security interest in goods other than inventory or livestock has priority over a conflicting security interest in the same goods, and, except as otherwise provided in Section 9—327, a perfected security interest in its identifiable proceeds also has priority, if the purchase-money security interest is perfected when the debtor receives possession of the collateral or within 20 days thereafter.

(b) Subject to subsection (c) and except as otherwise provided in subsection (g), a perfected purchase-money security interest in inventory has priority over a conflicting security interest in the same inventory, has priority over a conflicting security interest in chattel paper or an instrument constituting proceeds of the inventory and in proceeds of the chattel paper, if so provided in Section 9—330, and, except as otherwise provided in Section 9—327, also has priority in identifiable cash proceeds of the inventory to the extent the identifiable cash proceeds are received on or before the delivery of the inventory to a buyer, if:

(1) the purchase-money security interest is perfected when the debtor receives possession of the inventory;

(2) the purchase-money secured party sends an authenticated notification to the holder of the conflicting security interest;

(3) the holder of the conflicting security interest receives the notification within five years before the debtor receives possession of the inventory; and

(4) the notification states that the person sending the notification has or expects to acquire a purchase-money security interest in inventory of the debtor and describes the inventory.

(c) Subsections (b)(2) through (4) apply only if the holder of the conflicting security interest had filed a financing statement covering the same types of inventory:

(1) if the purchase-money security interest is perfected by filing, before the date of the filing; or

(2) if the purchase-money security interest is temporarily perfected without filing or possession under Section 9—312(f), before the beginning of the 20-day period thereunder.

(d) Subject to subsection (e) and except as otherwise provided in subsection (g), a perfected purchase-money security interest in livestock that are farm products has priority over a conflicting security interest in the same livestock, and, except as otherwise provided in Section 9—327, a perfected security interest in their identifiable proceeds and identifiable products in their unmanufactured states also has priority, if:

(1) the purchase-money security interest is perfected when the debtor receives possession of the livestock;

(2) the purchase-money secured party sends an authenticated notification to the holder of the conflicting security interest;

(3) the holder of the conflicting security interest receives the notification within six months before the debtor receives possession of the livestock; and

(4) the notification states that the person sending the notification has or expects to acquire a purchase-money security interest in livestock of the debtor and describes the livestock.

(e) Subsections (d)(2) through (4) apply only if the holder of the conflicting security interest had filed a financing statement covering the same types of livestock:

(1) if the purchase-money security interest is perfected by filing, before the date of the filing; or

(2) if the purchase-money security interest is temporarily perfected without filing or possession under Section 9—312(f), before the beginning of the 20-day period thereunder.

(f) Except as otherwise provided in subsection (g), a perfected purchase-money security interest in software has priority over a conflicting security interest in the same collateral, and, except as otherwise provided in Section 9—327, a perfected security interest in its identifiable proceeds also has priority, to the extent that the purchase-money security interest in the goods in which the software was acquired for use has priority in the goods and proceeds of the goods under this section.

(g) If more than one security interest qualifies for priority in the same collateral under subsection (a), (b), (d), or (f):

(1) a security interest securing an obligation incurred as all or part of the price of the collateral has priority over a security interest securing an obligation incurred for value given to enable the debtor to acquire rights in or the use of collateral; and

(2) in all other cases, Section 9—322(a) applies to the qualifying security interests.

§9—325. PRIORITY OF SECURITY INTERESTS IN TRANSFERRED COLLATERAL

(a) Except as otherwise provided in subsection (b), a security interest created by a debtor is subordinate to a security interest in the same collateral created by another person if:

(1) the debtor acquired the collateral subject to the security interest created by the other person;

(2) the security interest created by the other person was perfected when the debtor acquired the collateral; and

(3) there is no period thereafter when the security interest is unperfected.

(b) Subsection (a) subordinates a security interest only if the security interest:

(1) otherwise would have priority solely under Section 9—322(a) or 9—324; or

(2) arose solely under Section 2—711(3) or 2A—508(5).

§9—326. PRIORITY OF SECURITY INTERESTS CREATED BY NEW DEBTOR

(a) Subject to subsection (b), a security interest created by a new debtor which is perfected by a filed financing statement that is effective solely under Section 9—508 in collateral in which a new debtor has or acquires rights is subordinate to a security interest in the same collateral which is perfected other than by a filed financing statement that is effective solely under Section 9—508.

(b) The other provisions of this part determine the priority among conflicting security interests in the same collateral perfected by filed financing statements that are effective solely under Section 9—508. However, if the security agreements to which a new debtor became bound as debtor were not entered into by the same original debtor, the conflicting security interests rank according to priority in time of the new debtor's having become bound.

* * * *

§9—330. PRIORITY OF PURCHASER OF CHATTEL PAPER OR INSTRUMENT

(a) A purchaser of chattel paper has priority over a security interest in the chattel paper which is claimed merely as proceeds of inventory subject to a security interest if:

(1) in good faith and in the ordinary course of the purchaser's business, the purchaser gives new value and takes possession of the chattel paper or obtains control of the chattel paper under Section 9—105; and

(2) the chattel paper does not indicate that it has been assigned to an identified assignee other than the purchaser.

(b) A purchaser of chattel paper has priority over a security interest in the chattel paper which is claimed other than merely as proceeds of inventory subject to a security interest if the purchaser gives new value and takes possession of the chattel paper or obtains control of the chattel paper under Section 9—105 in good faith, in the ordinary course of the purchaser's business, and without knowledge that the purchase violates the rights of the secured party.

(c) Except as otherwise provided in Section 9—327, a purchaser having priority in chattel paper under subsection (a) or (b) also has priority in proceeds of the chattel paper to the extent that:

(1) Section 9—322 provides for priority in the proceeds; or

(2) the proceeds consist of the specific goods covered by the chattel paper or cash proceeds of the specific goods, even if the purchaser's security interest in the proceeds is unperfected.

(d) Except as otherwise provided in Section 9—331 (a), a purchaser of an instrument has priority over a security interest in the instrument perfected by a method other than possession if the purchaser gives value and takes possession of the instrument in good faith and without knowledge that the purchase violates the rights of the secured party.

(e) For purposes of subsections (a) and (b), the holder of a purchase-money security interest in inventory gives new value for chattel paper constituting proceeds of the inventory.

(f) For purposes of subsections (b) and (d), if chattel paper or an instrument indicates that it has been assigned to an identified secured party other than the purchaser, a purchaser of the chattel paper or instrument has knowledge that the purchase violates the rights of the secured party.

* * * *

§9—333. PRIORITY OF CERTAIN LIENS ARISING BY OPERATION OF LAW

(a) In this section, "possessory lien" means an interest, other than a security interest or an agricultural lien:

(1) which secures payment or performance of an obligation for services or materials furnished with respect to goods by a person in the ordinary course of the person's business;

(2) which is created by statute or rule of law in favor of the person; and

(3) whose effectiveness depends on the person's possession of the goods.

(b) A possessory lien on goods has priority over a security interest in the goods unless the lien is created by a statute that expressly provides otherwise.

§9—334. PRIORITY OF SECURITY INTERESTS IN FIXTURES AND CROPS

(a) A security interest under this article may be created in goods that are fixtures or may continue in goods that become fixtures. A security interest does not exist under this article in ordinary building materials incorporated into an improvement on land.

(b) This article does not prevent creation of an encumbrance upon fixtures under real property law.

(c) In cases not governed by subsections (d) through (h), a security interest in fixtures is subordinate to a conflicting interest of an encumbrancer or owner of the related real property other than the debtor.

(d) Except as otherwise provided in subsection (h), a perfected security interest in fixtures has priority over a conflicting interest of an encumbrancer or owner of the real property if the debtor has an interest of record in or is in possession of the real property and:

(1) the security interest is a purchase-money security interest;

(2) the interest of the encumbrancer or owner arises before the goods become fixtures; and

(3) the security interest is perfected by a fixture filing before the goods become fixtures or within 20 days thereafter.

(e) A perfected security interest in fixtures has priority over a conflicting interest of an encumbrancer or owner of the real property if:

(1) the debtor has an interest of record in the real property or is in possession of the real property and the security interest:

(A) is perfected by a fixture filing before the interest of the encumbrancer or owner is of record; and

(B) has priority over any conflicting interest of a predecessor in title of the encumbrancer or owner;

(2) before the goods become fixtures, the security interest is perfected by any method permitted by this article and the fixtures are readily removable:

(A) factory or office machines;

(B) equipment that is not primarily used or leased for use in the operation of the real property; or

(C) replacements of domestic appliances that are consumer goods;

(3) the conflicting interest is a lien on the real property obtained by legal or equitable proceedings after the security interest was perfected by any method permitted by this article; or

(4) the security interest is:

(A) created in a manufactured home in a manufactured-home transaction; and

(B) perfected pursuant to a statute described in Section 9—311(a)(2).

(f) A security interest in fixtures, whether or not perfected, has priority over a conflicting interest of an encumbrancer or owner of the real property if:

(1) the encumbrancer or owner has, in an authenticated record, consented to the security interest or disclaimed an interest in the goods as fixtures; or

(2) the debtor has a right to remove the goods as against the encumbrancer or owner.

(g) The priority of the security interest under paragraph (f)(2) continues for a reasonable time if the debtor's right to remove the goods as against the encumbrancer or owner terminates.

(h) A mortgage is a construction mortgage to the extent that it secures an obligation incurred for the construction of an improvement on land, including the acquisition cost of the land, if a recorded record of the mortgage so indicates. Except as otherwise provided in subsections (e) and (f), a security interest in fixtures is subordinate to a construction mortgage if a record of the mortgage is recorded before the goods become fixtures and the goods become fixtures before the completion of the construction. A mortgage has this priority to the same extent as a construction mortgage to the extent that it is given to refinance a construction mortgage.

(i) A perfected security interest in crops growing on real property has priority over a conflicting interest of an encumbrancer or owner of the real property if the debtor has an interest of record in or is in possession of the real property.

* * * *

§9—336. COMMINGLED GOODS

(a) In this section, "commingled goods" means goods that are physically united with other goods in such a manner that their identity is lost in a product or mass.

(b) A security interest does not exist in commingled goods as such. However, a security interest may attach to a product or mass that results when goods become commingled goods.

(c) If collateral becomes commingled goods, a security interest attaches to the product or mass.

(d) If a security interest in collateral is perfected before the collateral becomes commingled goods, the security interest that attaches to the product or mass under subsection (c) is perfected.

(e) Except as otherwise provided in subsection (f), the other provisions of this part determine the priority of a security interest that attaches to the product or mass under subsection (c).

(f) If more than one security interest attaches to the product or mass under subsection (c), the following rules determine priority:

(1) A security interest that is perfected under subsection (d) has priority over a security interest that is unperfected at the time the collateral becomes commingled goods.

(2) If more than one security interest is perfected under subsection (d), the security interests rank equally in proportion to the value of the collateral at the time it became commingled goods.

* * * *

§9—501. FILING OFFICE

(a) Except as otherwise provided in subsection (b), if the local law of this State governs perfection of a security interest or agricultural lien, the office in which to file a financing statement to perfect the security interest or agricultural lien is:

(1) the office designated for the filing or recording of a record of a mortgage on the related real property, if:

(A) the collateral is as-extracted collateral or timber to be cut; or

(B) the financing statement is filed as a fixture filing and the collateral is goods that are or are to become fixtures; or

(2) the office of [ ] [or any office duly authorized by [ ]], in all other cases, including a case in which the collateral is goods that are or are to become fixtures and the financing statement is not filed as a fixture filing.

(b) The office in which to file a financing statement to perfect a security interest in collateral, including fixtures, of a transmitting utility is the office of [ ]. The financing statement also constitutes a fixture filing as to the collateral indicated in the financing statement which is or is to become fixtures.

Legislative Note: The State should designate the filing office where the brackets appear. The filing office may be that of a governmental official (e.g., the Secretary of State) or a private party that maintains the State's filing system.

§9—502. CONTENTS OF FINANCING STATEMENT; RECORD OF MORTGAGE AS FINANCING STATEMENT; TIME OF FILING FINANCING STATEMENT

(a) Subject to subsection (b), a financing statement is sufficient only if it:

(1) provides the name of the debtor;

(2) provides the name of the secured party or a representative of the secured party; and

(3) indicates the collateral covered by the financing statement.

(b) Except as otherwise provided in Section 9—501 (b), to be sufficient, a financing statement that covers as-extracted collateral or timber to be cut, or which is filed as a fixture filing and covers goods that are or are to become fixtures, must satisfy subsection (a) and also:

(1) indicate that it covers this type of collateral;

(2) indicate that it is to be filed [for record] in the real property records;

(3) provide a description of the real property to which the collateral is related [sufficient to give constructive notice of a mortgage under the law of this State if the description were contained in a record of the mortgage of the real property]; and

(4) if the debtor does not have an interest of record in the real property, provide the name of a record owner.

(c) A record of a mortgage is effective, from the date of recording, as a financing statement filed as a fixture filing or as a financing statement covering as-extracted collateral or timber to be cut only if:

(1) the record indicates the goods or accounts that it covers;

(2) the goods are or are to become fixtures related to the real property described in the record or the collateral is related to the real property described in the record and is as-extracted collateral or timber to be cut;

(3) the record satisfies the requirements for a financing statement in this section other than an indication that it is to be filed in the real property records; and

(4) the record is [duly] recorded.

(d) A financing statement may be filed before a security agreement is made or a security interest otherwise attaches.

Legislative Note: Language in brackets is optional. Where the State has any special recording system for real property other than the usual grantor-grantee index (as, for instance, a tract system or a title registration or Torrens system) local adaptations of subsection (b) and Section 9—519(d) and (e) may be necessary. See, e.g., Mass. Gen. Laws Chapter 106, Section 9—410.

§9—503. NAME OF DEBTOR AND SECURED PARTY

(a) A financing statement sufficiently provides the name of the debtor:

(1) if the debtor is a registered organization, only if the financing statement provides the name of the debtor indicated on the public record of the debtor's jurisdiction of organization which shows the debtor to have been organized;

(2) if the debtor is a decedent's estate, only if the financing statement provides the name of the decedent and indicates that the debtor is an estate;

(3) if the debtor is a trust or a trustee acting with respect to property held in trust, only if the financing statement:

(A) provides the name specified for the trust in its organic documents or, if no name is specified, provides the name of the settlor and additional information sufficient to distinguish the debtor from other trusts having one or more of the same settlors; and

(B) indicates, in the debtor's name or otherwise, that the debtor is a trust or is a trustee acting with respect to property held in trust; and

(4) in other cases:

(A) if the debtor has a name, only if it provides the individual or organizational name of the debtor; and

(B) if the debtor does not have a name, only if it provides the names of the partners, members, associates, or other persons comprising the debtor.

(b) A financing statement that provides the name of the debtor in accordance with subsection (a) is not rendered ineffective by the absence of:

(1) a trade name or other name of the debtor; or

(2) unless required under subsection (a)(4)(B), names of partners, members, associates, or other persons comprising the debtor.

(c) A financing statement that provides only the debtor's trade name does not sufficiently provide the name of the debtor.

(d) Failure to indicate the representative capacity of a secured party or representative of a secured party does not affect the sufficiency of a financing statement.

(e) A financing statement may provide the name of more than one debtor and the name of more than one secured party.

§9—504. INDICATION OF COLLATERAL

A financing statement sufficiently indicates the collateral that it covers if the financing statement provides:

(1) a description of the collateral pursuant to Section 9—108; or

(2) an indication that the financing statement covers all assets or all personal property.

As amended in 1999.

* * * *

§9—506. EFFECT OF ERRORS OR OMISSIONS

(a) A financing statement substantially satisfying the requirements of this part is effective, even if it has minor errors or omissions, unless the errors or omissions make the financing statement seriously misleading.

(b) Except as otherwise provided in subsection (c), a financing statement that fails sufficiently to provide the name of the debtor in accordance with Section 9—503(a) is seriously misleading.

(c) If a search of the records of the filing office under the debtor's correct name, using the filing office's standard search logic, if any, would disclose a financing statement that fails sufficiently to provide the name of the debtor in accordance with Section 9—503(a), the name provided does not make the financing statement seriously misleading.

(d) For purposes of Section 9—508(b), the "debtor's correct name" in subsection (c) means the correct name of the new debtor.

* * * *

§9—509. PERSONS ENTITLED TO FILE A RECORD

(a) A person may file an initial financing statement, amendment that adds collateral covered by a financing statement, or amendment that adds a debtor to a financing statement only if:

(1) the debtor authorizes the filing in an authenticated record or pursuant to subsection (b) or (c); or

(2) the person holds an agricultural lien that has become effective at the time of filing and the financing statement covers only collateral in which the person holds an agricultural lien.

(b) By authenticating or becoming bound as debtor by a security agreement, a debtor or new debtor authorizes the filing of an initial financing statement, and an amendment, covering:

(1) the collateral described in the security agreement; and

(2) property that becomes collateral under Section 9—315(a)(2), whether or not the security agreement expressly covers proceeds.

(c) By acquiring collateral in which a security interest or agricultural lien continues under Section 9—315(a)(1), a debtor authorizes the filing of an initial financing statement, and an amendment, covering the collateral and property that becomes collateral under Section 9—315(a)(2).

(d) A person may file an amendment other than an amendment that adds collateral covered by a financing statement or an amendment that adds a debtor to a financing statement only if:

(1) the secured party of record authorizes the filing; or

(2) the amendment is a termination statement for a financing statement as to which the secured party of record has failed to file or send a termination statement as required by Section 9—513(a) or (c), the debtor authorizes the filing, and the termination statement indicates that the debtor authorized it to be filed.

(e) If there is more than one secured party of record for a financing statement, each secured party of record may authorize the filing of an amendment under subsection (d).

§9—510. EFFECTIVENESS OF FILED RECORD

(a) A filed record is effective only to the extent that it was filed by a person that may file it under Section 9—509.

(b) A record authorized by one secured party of record does not affect the financing statement with respect to another secured party of record.

(c) A continuation statement that is not filed within the six-month period prescribed by Section 9—515(d) is ineffective.

* * * *

§9—513. TERMINATION STATEMENT

(a) A secured party shall cause the secured party of record for a financing statement to file a termination statement for the financing statement if the financing statement covers consumer goods and:

(1) there is no obligation secured by the collateral covered by the financing statement and no commitment to make an advance, incur an obligation, or otherwise give value; or

(2) the debtor did not authorize the filing of the initial financing statement.

(b) To comply with subsection (a), a secured party shall cause the secured party of record to file the termination statement:

(1) within one month after there is no obligation secured by the collateral covered by the financing statement and no commitment to make an advance, incur an obligation, or otherwise give value; or

(2) if earlier, within 20 days after the secured party receives an authenticated demand from a debtor.

(c) In cases not governed by subsection (a), within 20 days after a secured party receives an authenticated demand from a debtor, the secured party shall cause the secured party of record for a financing statement to send to the debtor a termination statement for the financing statement or file the termination statement in the filing office if:

(1) except in the case of a financing statement covering accounts or chattel paper that has been sold or goods that are the subject of a consignment, there is no obligation secured by the collateral covered by the financing statement and no commitment to make an advance, incur an obligation, or otherwise give value;

(2) the financing statement covers accounts or chattel paper that has been sold but as to which the account debtor or other person obligated has discharged its obligation;

(3) the financing statement covers goods that were the subject of a consignment to the debtor but are not in the debtor's possession; or

(4) the debtor did not authorize the filing of the initial financing statement.

(d) Except as otherwise provided in Section 9—510, upon the filing of a termination statement with the filing office, the financing statement to which the termination statement relates ceases to be effective. Except as otherwise provided in Section 9—510, for purposes of Sections 9—519(g), 9—522(a), and 9—523(c), the filing with the filing office of a termination statement relating to a financing statement that indicates that the debtor is a transmitting utility also causes the effectiveness of the financing statement to lapse.

* * * *

§9—515. DURATION AND EFFECTIVENESS OF FINANCING STATEMENT; EFFECT OF LAPSED FINANCING STATEMENT

(a) Except as otherwise provided in subsections (b), (e), (f), and (g), a filed financing statement is effective for a period of five years after the date of filing.

(b) Except as otherwise provided in subsections (e), (f), and (g), an initial financing statement filed in connection with a public-finance transaction or manufactured-home transaction is effective for a period of 30 years after the date of filing if it indicates that it is filed in connection with a public-finance transaction or manufactured-home transaction.

(c) The effectiveness of a filed financing statement lapses on the expiration of the period of its effectiveness unless before the lapse a continuation statement is filed pursuant to subsection (d). Upon lapse, a financing statement ceases to be effective and any security interest or agricultural lien that was perfected by the financing statement becomes unperfected, unless the security interest is perfected otherwise. If the security interest or agricultural lien becomes unperfected upon lapse, it is deemed never to have been perfected as against a purchaser of the collateral for value.

(d) A continuation statement may be filed only within six months before the expiration of the five-year period specified in subsection (a) or the 30-year period specified in subsection (b), whichever is applicable.

(e) Except as otherwise provided in Section 9—510, upon timely filing of a continuation statement, the effectiveness of the initial financing statement continues for a period of five years commencing on the day on which the financing statement would have become ineffective in the absence of the filing. Upon the expiration of the five-year period, the financing statement lapses in the same manner as provided in subsection (c), unless, before the lapse, another continuation statement is filed pursuant to subsection (d). Succeeding continuation statements may be filed in the same manner to continue the effectiveness of the initial financing statement.

(f) If a debtor is a transmitting utility and a filed financing statement so indicates, the financing statement is effective until a termination statement is filed.

(g) A record of a mortgage that is effective as a financing statement filed as a fixture filing under Section 9—502(c) remains effective as a financing statement filed as a fixture filing until the mortgage is released or satisfied of record or its effectiveness otherwise terminates as to the real property.

* * * *

§9—601. RIGHTS AFTER DEFAULT; JUDICIAL ENFORCEMENT; CONSIGNOR OR BUYER OF ACCOUNTS, CHATTEL PAPER, PAYMENT INTANGIBLES, OR PROMISSORY NOTES

(a) After default, a secured party has the rights provided in this part and, except as otherwise provided in Section 9—602, those provided by agreement of the parties.

A secured party:

(1) may reduce a claim to judgment, foreclose, or otherwise enforce the claim, security interest, or agricultural lien by any available judicial procedure; and

(2) if the collateral is documents, may proceed either as to the documents or as to the goods they cover.

(b) A secured party in possession of collateral or control of collateral under Section 9—104, 9—105, 9—106, or 9—107 has the rights and duties provided in Section 9—207.

(c) The rights under subsections (a) and (b) are cumulative and may be exercised simultaneously.

(d) Except as otherwise provided in subsection (g) and Section 9—605, after default, a debtor and an obligor have the rights provided in this part and by agreement of the parties.

(e) If a secured party has reduced its claim to judgment, the lien of any levy that may be made upon the collateral by virtue of an execution based upon the judgment relates back to the earliest of:

(1) the date of perfection of the security interest or agricultural lien in the collateral;

(2) the date of filing a financing statement covering the collateral; or

(3) any date specified in a statute under which the agricultural lien was created.

(f) A sale pursuant to an execution is a foreclosure of the security interest or agricultural lien by judicial procedure within the meaning of this section. A secured party may purchase at the sale and thereafter hold the collateral free of any other requirements of this article.

(g) Except as otherwise provided in Section 9—607 (c), this part imposes no duties upon a secured party that is a consignor or is a buyer of accounts, chattel paper, payment intangibles, or promissory notes.

* * * *

§9—604. PROCEDURE IF SECURITY AGREEMENT COVERS REAL PROPERTY OR FIXTURES

(a) If a security agreement covers both personal and real property, a secured party may proceed:

(1) under this part as to the personal property without prejudicing any rights with respect to the real property; or

(2) as to both the personal property and the real property in accordance with the rights with respect to the real property, in which case the other provisions of this part do not apply.

(b) Subject to subsection (c), if a security agreement covers goods that are or become fixtures, a secured party may proceed:

(1) under this part; or

(2) in accordance with the rights with respect to real property, in which case the other provisions of this part do not apply.

(c) Subject to the other provisions of this part, if a secured party holding a security interest in fixtures has priority over all owners and encumbrancers of the real property, the secured party, after default, may remove the collateral from the real property.

(d) A secured party that removes collateral shall promptly reimburse any encumbrancer or owner of the real property, other than the debtor, for the cost of repair of any physical injury caused by the removal. The secured party need not reimburse the encumbrancer or owner for any diminution in value of the real property caused by the absence of the goods removed or by any necessity of replacing them. A person entitled to reimbursement may refuse permission to remove until the secured party gives adequate assurance for the performance of the obligation to reimburse.

* * * *

§9—607. COLLECTION AND ENFORCEMENT BY SECURED PARTY

(a) If so agreed, and in any event after default, a secured party:

(1) may notify an account debtor or other person obligated on collateral to make payment or otherwise render performance to or for the benefit of the secured party;

(2) may take any proceeds to which the secured party is entitled under Section 9—315;

(3) may enforce the obligations of an account debtor or other person obligated on collateral and exercise the rights of the debtor with respect to the obligation of the account debtor or other person obligated on collateral to make payment or otherwise render performance to the debtor, and with respect to any property that secures the obligations of the account debtor or other person obligated on the collateral;

(4) if it holds a security interest in a deposit account perfected by control under Section 9—104(a)(1), may apply the balance of the deposit account to the obligation secured by the deposit account; and

(5) if it holds a security interest in a deposit account perfected by control under Section 9—104(a)(2) or (3), may instruct the bank to pay the balance of the deposit account to or for the benefit of the secured party.

(b) If necessary to enable a secured party to exercise under subsection (a)(3) the right of a debtor to enforce a mortgage nonjudicially, the secured party may record in the office in which a record of the mortgage is recorded:

(1) a copy of the security agreement that creates or provides for a security interest in the obligation secured by the mortgage; and

(2) the secured party's sworn affidavit in recordable form stating that:

(A) a default has occurred; and

(B) the secured party is entitled to enforce the mortgage nonjudicially.

(c) A secured party shall proceed in a commercially reasonable manner if the secured party:

(1) undertakes to collect from or enforce an obligation of an account debtor or other person obligated on collateral; and

(2) is entitled to charge back uncollected collateral or otherwise to full or limited recourse against the debtor or a secondary obligor.

(d) A secured party may deduct from the collections made pursuant to subsection (c) reasonable expenses of collection and enforcement, including reasonable attorney's fees and legal expenses incurred by the secured party.

(e) This section does not determine whether an account debtor, bank, or other person obligated on collateral owes a duty to a secured party.

§9—608. APPLICATION OF PROCEEDS OF COLLECTION OR ENFORCEMENT; LIABILITY FOR DEFICIENCY AND RIGHT TO SURPLUS

(a) If a security interest or agricultural lien secures payment or performance of an obligation, the following rules apply:

(1) A secured party shall apply or pay over for application the cash proceeds of collection or enforcement under Section 9—607 in the following order to:

(A) the reasonable expenses of collection and enforcement and, to the extent provided for by agreement and not prohibited by law, reasonable attorney's fees and legal expenses incurred by the secured party;

(B) the satisfaction of obligations secured by the security interest or agricultural lien under which the collection or enforcement is made; and

(C) the satisfaction of obligations secured by any subordinate security interest in or other lien on the collateral subject to the security interest or agricultural lien under which the collection or enforcement is made if the secured party receives an authenticated demand for proceeds before distribution of the proceeds is completed.

(2) If requested by a secured party, a holder of a subordinate security interest or other lien shall furnish reasonable proof of the interest or lien within a reasonable time. Unless the holder complies, the secured party need not comply with the holder's demand under paragraph (1)(C).

(3) A secured party need not apply or pay over for application noncash proceeds of collection and

enforcement under Section 9—607 unless the failure to do so would be commercially unreasonable. A secured party that applies or pays over for application noncash proceeds shall do so in a commercially reasonable manner.

(4) A secured party shall account to and pay a debtor for any surplus, and the obligor is liable for any deficiency.

(b) If the underlying transaction is a sale of accounts, chattel paper, payment intangibles, or promissory notes, the debtor is not entitled to any surplus, and the obligor is not liable for any deficiency.

§9—609. SECURED PARTY'S RIGHT TO TAKE POSSESSION AFTER DEFAULT

(a) After default, a secured party:

(1) may take possession of the collateral; and

(2) without removal, may render equipment unusable and dispose of collateral on a debtor's premises under Section 9—610.

(b) A secured party may proceed under subsection (a):

(1) pursuant to judicial process; or

(2) without judicial process, if it proceeds without breach of the peace.

(c) If so agreed, and in any event after default, a secured party may require the debtor to assemble the collateral and make it available to the secured party at a place to be designated by the secured party which is reasonably convenient to both parties.

§9—610. DISPOSITION OF COLLATERAL AFTER DEFAULT

(a) After default, a secured party may sell, lease, license, or otherwise dispose of any or all of the collateral in its present condition or following any commercially reasonable preparation or processing.

(b) Every aspect of a disposition of collateral, including the method, manner, time, place, and other terms, must be commercially reasonable. If commercially reasonable, a secured party may dispose of collateral by public or private proceedings, by one or more contracts, as a unit or in parcels, and at any time and place and on any terms.

(c) A secured party may purchase collateral:

(1) at a public disposition; or

(2) at a private disposition only if the collateral is of a kind that is customarily sold on a recognized market or the subject of widely distributed standard price quotations.

(d) A contract for sale, lease, license, or other disposition includes the warranties relating to title, possession, quiet enjoyment, and the like which by operation of law accompany a voluntary disposition of property of the kind subject to the contract.

(e) A secured party may disclaim or modify warranties under subsection (d):

(1) in a manner that would be effective to disclaim or modify the warranties in a voluntary disposition of property of the kind subject to the contract of disposition; or

(2) by communicating to the purchaser a record evidencing the contract for disposition and including an express disclaimer or modification of the warranties.

(f) A record is sufficient to disclaim warranties under subsection (e) if it indicates "There is no warranty relating to title, possession, quiet enjoyment, or the like in this disposition" or uses words of similar import.

§9—611. NOTIFICATION BEFORE DISPOSITION OF COLLATERAL

(a) In this section, "notification date" means the earlier of the date on which:

(1) a secured party sends to the debtor and any secondary obligor an authenticated notification of disposition; or

(2) the debtor and any secondary obligor waive the right to notification.

(b) Except as otherwise provided in subsection (d), a secured party that disposes of collateral under Section 9—610 shall send to the persons specified in subsection (c) a reasonable authenticated notification of disposition.

(c) To comply with subsection (b), the secured party shall send an authenticated notification of disposition to:

(1) the debtor;

(2) any secondary obligor; and

(3) if the collateral is other than consumer goods:

(A) any other person from which the secured party has received, before the notification date, an authenticated notification of a claim of an interest in the collateral;

(B) any other secured party or lienholder that, 10 days before the notification date, held a security interest in or other lien on the collateral perfected by the filing of a financing statement that:

(i) identified the collateral;

(ii) was indexed under the debtor's name as of that date; and

(iii) was filed in the office in which to file a financing statement against the debtor covering the collateral as of that date; and

(C) any other secured party that, 10 days before the notification date, held a security interest in the collateral perfected by compliance with a statute, regulation, or treaty described in Section 9—311(a).

(d) Subsection (b) does not apply if the collateral is perishable or threatens to decline speedily in value or is of a type customarily sold on a recognized market.

(e) A secured party complies with the requirement for notification prescribed by subsection (c)(3)(B) if:

(1) not later than 20 days or earlier than 30 days before the notification date, the secured party requests, in a commercially reasonable manner, information concerning financing statements indexed under the debtor's name in the office indicated in subsection (c)(3)(B); and

(2) before the notification date, the secured party:

(A) did not receive a response to the request for information; or

(B) received a response to the request for information and sent an authenticated notification of disposition to each secured party or other lienholder named in that response whose financing statement covered the collateral.

§9—612. TIMELINESS OF NOTIFICATION BEFORE DISPOSITION OF COLLATERAL

(a) Except as otherwise provided in subsection (b), whether a notification is sent within a reasonable time is a question of fact.

(b) In a transaction other than a consumer transaction, a notification of disposition sent after default and 10 days or more before the earliest time of disposition set forth in the notification is sent within a reasonable time before the disposition.

* * * *

§9—615. APPLICATION OF PROCEEDS OF DISPOSITION; LIABILITY FOR DEFICIENCY AND RIGHT TO SURPLUS

(a) A secured party shall apply or pay over for application the cash proceeds of disposition under Section 9—610 in the following order to:

(1) the reasonable expenses of retaking, holding, preparing for disposition, processing, and disposing, and, to the extent provided for by agreement and not prohibited by law, reasonable attorney's fees and legal expenses incurred by the secured party;

(2) the satisfaction of obligations secured by the security interest or agricultural lien under which the disposition is made;

(3) the satisfaction of obligations secured by any subordinate security interest in or other subordinate lien on the collateral if:

(A) the secured party receives from the holder of the subordinate security interest or other lien an authenticated demand for proceeds before distribution of the proceeds is completed; and

(B) in a case in which a consignor has an interest in the collateral, the subordinate security interest or other lien is senior to the interest of the consignor; and

(4) a secured party that is a consignor of the collateral if the secured party receives from the consignor an authenticated demand for proceeds before distribution of the proceeds is completed.

(b) If requested by a secured party, a holder of a subordinate security interest or other lien shall furnish reasonable proof of the interest or lien within a reasonable time. Unless the holder does so, the secured party need not comply with the holder's demand under subsection (a)(3).

(c) A secured party need not apply or pay over for application noncash proceeds of disposition under Section 9—610 unless the failure to do so would be commercially unreasonable. A secured party that applies or pays over for application noncash proceeds shall do so in a commercially reasonable manner.

(d) If the security interest under which a disposition is made secures payment or performance of an obligation, after making the payments and applications required by subsection (a) and permitted by subsection (c):

(1) unless subsection (a)(4) requires the secured party to apply or pay over cash proceeds to a consignor, the secured party shall account to and pay a debtor for any surplus; and

(2) the obligor is liable for any deficiency.

(e) If the underlying transaction is a sale of accounts, chattel paper, payment intangibles, or promissory notes:

(1) the debtor is not entitled to any surplus; and

(2) the obligor is not liable for any deficiency.

(f) The surplus or deficiency following a disposition is calculated based on the amount of proceeds that would have been realized in a disposition complying with this part to a transferee other than the secured party, a person related to the secured party, or a secondary obligor if:

(1) the transferee in the disposition is the secured party, a person related to the secured party, or a secondary obligor; and

(2) the amount of proceeds of the disposition is significantly below the range of proceeds that a complying disposition to a person other than the secured party, a person related to the secured party, or a secondary obligor would have brought.

(g) A secured party that receives cash proceeds of a disposition in good faith and without knowledge that the receipt violates the rights of the holder of a security interest or other lien that is not subordinate to the security interest or agricultural lien under which the disposition is made:

(1) takes the cash proceeds free of the security interest or other lien;

(2) is not obligated to apply the proceeds of the disposition to the satisfaction of obligations secured by the security interest or other lien; and

(3) is not obligated to account to or pay the holder of the security interest or other lien for any surplus.

* * * *

§9—617. RIGHTS OF TRANSFEREE OF COLLATERAL

(a) A secured party's disposition of collateral after default:

1) transfers to a transferee for value all of the debtor's rights in the collateral;

2) discharges the security interest under which the disposition is made; and

3) discharges any subordinate security interest or other subordinate lien [other than liens created under [cite acts or statutes providing for liens, if any, that are not to be discharged]].

(b) A transferee that acts in good faith takes free of the rights and interests described in subsection (a), even if the secured party fails to comply with this article or the requirements of any judicial proceeding.

(c) If a transferee does not take free of the rights and interests described in subsection (a), the transferee takes the collateral subject to:

(1) the debtor's rights in the collateral;

(2) the security interest or agricultural lien under which the disposition is made; and

(3) any other security interest or other lien.

* * * *

§9—620. ACCEPTANCE OF COLLATERAL IN FULL OR PARTIAL SATISFACTION OF OBLIGATION; COMPULSORY DISPOSITION OF COLLATERAL

(a) Except as otherwise provided in subsection (g), a secured party may accept collateral in full or partial satisfaction of the obligation it secures only if:

(1) the debtor consents to the acceptance under subsection (c);

(2) the secured party does not receive, within the time set forth in subsection (d), a notification of objection to the proposal authenticated by:

(A) a person to which the secured party was required to send a proposal under Section 9—621; or

(B) any other person, other than the debtor, holding an interest in the collateral subordinate to the security interest that is the subject of the proposal;

(3) if the collateral is consumer goods, the collateral is not in the possession of the debtor when the debtor consents to the acceptance; and

(4) subsection (e) does not require the secured party to dispose of the collateral or the debtor waives the requirement pursuant to Section 9—624.

(b) A purported or apparent acceptance of collateral under this section is ineffective unless:

(1) the secured party consents to the acceptance in an authenticated record or sends a proposal to the debtor; and

(2) the conditions of subsection (a) are met.

(c) For purposes of this section:

(1) a debtor consents to an acceptance of collateral in partial satisfaction of the obligation it secures only if the debtor agrees to the terms of the acceptance in a record authenticated after default; and

(2) a debtor consents to an acceptance of collateral in full satisfaction of the obligation it secures only if the debtor agrees to the terms of the acceptance in a record authenticated after default or the secured party:

(A) sends to the debtor after default a proposal that is unconditional or subject only to a condition that collateral not in the possession of the secured party be preserved or maintained;

(B) in the proposal, proposes to accept collateral in full satisfaction of the obligation it secures; and

(C) does not receive a notification of objection authenticated by the debtor within 20 days after the proposal is sent.

(d) To be effective under subsection (a)(2), a notification of objection must be received by the secured party:

(1) in the case of a person to which the proposal was sent pursuant to Section 9—621, within 20 days after notification was sent to that person; and

(2) in other cases:

(A) within 20 days after the last notification was sent pursuant to Section 9—621; or

(B) if a notification was not sent, before the debtor consents to the acceptance under subsection (c).

(e) A secured party that has taken possession of collateral shall dispose of the collateral pursuant to Section 9—610 within the time specified in subsection (f) if:

(1) 60 percent of the cash price has been paid in the case of a purchase-money security interest in consumer goods; or

(2) 60 percent of the principal amount of the obligation secured has been paid in the case of a non-purchase-money security interest in consumer goods.

(f) To comply with subsection (e), the secured party shall dispose of the collateral:

(1) within 90 days after taking possession; or

(2) within any longer period to which the debtor and all secondary obligors have agreed in an agreement to that effect entered into and authenticated after default.

(g) In a consumer transaction, a secured party may not accept collateral in partial satisfaction of the obligation it secures.

* * * *

§9—623. RIGHT TO REDEEM COLLATERAL

(a) A debtor, any secondary obligor, or any other secured party or lienholder may redeem collateral.

(b) To redeem collateral, a person shall tender:

    (1) fulfillment of all obligations secured by the collateral; and

    (2) the reasonable expenses and attorney's fees described in Section 9—615(a)(1).

(c) A redemption may occur at any time before a secured party:

    (1) has collected collateral under Section 9—607;

    (2) has disposed of collateral or entered into a contract for its disposition under Section 9—610; or

    (3) has accepted collateral in full or partial satisfaction of the obligation it secures under Section 9—622.

* * * *

§9—625. REMEDIES FOR SECURED PARTY'S FAILURE TO COMPLY WITH ARTICLE

(a) If it is established that a secured party is not proceeding in accordance with this article, a court may order or restrain collection, enforcement, or disposition of collateral on appropriate terms and conditions.

(b) Subject to subsections (c), (d), and (f), a person is liable for damages in the amount of any loss caused by a failure to comply with this article. Loss caused by a failure to comply may include loss resulting from the debtor's inability to obtain, or increased costs of, alternative financing.

(c) Except as otherwise provided in Section 9—628:

    (1) a person that, at the time of the failure, was a debtor, was an obligor, or held a security interest in or other lien on the collateral may recover damages under subsection (b) for its loss; and

    (2) if the collateral is consumer goods, a person that was a debtor or a secondary obligor at the time a secured party failed to comply with this part may recover for that failure in any event an amount not less than the credit service charge plus 10 percent of the principal amount of the obligation or the time-price differential plus 10 percent of the cash price.

(d) A debtor whose deficiency is eliminated under Section 9—626 may recover damages for the loss of any surplus. However, a debtor or secondary obligor whose deficiency is eliminated or reduced under Section 9—626 may not otherwise recover under subsection (b) for noncompliance with the provisions of this part relating to collection, enforcement, disposition, or acceptance.

(e) In addition to any damages recoverable under subsection (b), the debtor, consumer obligor, or person named as a debtor in a filed record, as applicable, may recover $500 in each case from a person that:

    (1) fails to comply with Section 9—208;

    (2) fails to comply with Section 9—209;

    (3) files a record that the person is not entitled to file under Section 9—509(a);

    (4) fails to cause the secured party of record to file or send a termination statement as required by Section 9—513(a) or (c);

    (5) fails to comply with Section 9—616(b)(1) and whose failure is part of a pattern, or consistent with a practice, of noncompliance; or

    (6) fails to comply with Section 9—616(b)(2).

(f) A debtor or consumer obligor may recover damages under subsection (b) and, in addition, $500 in each case from a person that, without reasonable cause, fails to comply with a request under Section 9—210. A recipient of a request under Section 9—210 which never claimed an interest in the collateral or obligations that are the subject of a request under that section has a reasonable excuse for failure to comply with the request within the meaning of this subsection.

(g) If a secured party fails to comply with a request regarding a list of collateral or a statement of account under Section 9—210, the secured party may claim a security interest only as shown in the list or statement included in the request as against a person that is reasonably misled by the failure.

* * * *

§9—627. DETERMINATION OF WHETHER CONDUCT WAS COMMERCIALLY REASONABLE

(a) The fact that a greater amount could have been obtained by a collection, enforcement, disposition, or acceptance at a different time or in a different method from that selected by the secured party is not of itself sufficient to preclude the secured party from establishing that the collection, enforcement, disposition, or acceptance was made in a commercially reasonable manner.

(b) A disposition of collateral is made in a commercially reasonable manner if the disposition is made:

    (1) in the usual manner on any recognized market;

    (2) at the price current in any recognized market at the time of the disposition; or

(3) otherwise in conformity with reasonable commercial practices among dealers in the type of property that was the subject of the disposition.

(c) A collection, enforcement, disposition, or acceptance is commercially reasonable if it has been approved:

(1) in a judicial proceeding;

(2) by a bona fide creditors' committee;

(3) by a representative of creditors; or

(4) by an assignee for the benefit of creditors.

(d) Approval under subsection (c) need not be obtained, and lack of approval does not mean that the collection, enforcement, disposition, or acceptance is not commercially reasonable.

Copyright 2002 by the American Law Institute and the National Conference of Commissioners on Uniform State Laws. Reproduced with permission.

glossary

A

abate—put a stop to a nuisance; reduce or cancel a legacy because the estate of the decedent is insufficient to make payment in full.

absolute guaranty—agreement that creates an obligation for a guarantor similar to that promised by a surety in suretyship relationships. The ability to demand payment immediately from a guarantor in an absolute guaranty situation distinguishes it from suretyship.

absolute privilege—complete defense against the tort of defamation, as in the speeches of members of Congress on the floor and witnesses in a trial.

abstract of title—history of the transfers of title to a given piece of land, briefly stating the parties to and the effect of all deeds, wills, and judicial proceedings relating to the land.

acceptance—unqualified assent to the act or proposal of another; as the acceptance of a draft (bill of exchange), of an offer to make a contract, of goods delivered by the seller, or of a gift or deed.

acceptor—drawee who has accepted the liability of paying the amount of money specified in a draft.

accommodation party—person who signs an instrument to lend credit to another party to the paper.

accord and satisfaction—agreement to substitute for an existing debt some alternative form of discharging that debt, coupled with the actual discharge of the debt by the substituted performance.

acknowledgment—admission or confirmation, generally of an instrument and usually made before a person authorized to administer oaths, such as a notary public; used to establish that the instrument was executed by the person making the instrument, that it was a voluntary act, or that the instrument is recorded.

acquired distinctiveness—through advertising, use and association, over time, an ordinary descriptive word or phase has taken on a new source identifying meaning and functions as a mark in the eyes of the public.

act-of-state doctrine—doctrine whereby every sovereign state is bound to respect the independence of every other sovereign state, and the courts of one country will not sit in judgment of another government's acts done within its own territory.

adeemed—canceled; as in a specifically bequeathed property being sold or given away by the testator prior to death, thus canceling the bequest.

adjustable rate mortgage (ARM)—mortgage with variable financing charges over the life of the loan.

administrative agency—government body charged with administering and implementing legislation.

administrative law—law governing administrative agencies.

Administrative Procedure Act—federal law that establishes the operating rules for administrative agencies.

administrative regulations—rules made by state and federal administrative agencies.

administrator, administratrix—person (man, woman) appointed to wind up and settle the estate of a person who has died without a will.

admissibility—the quality of the evidence in a case that allows it to be presented to the jury.

adverse possession—hostile possession of real estate, which when actual, visible, notorious, exclusive, and continued for the required time, will vest the title to the land in the person in such adverse possession.

advising bank—bank that tells beneficiary that letter of credit has been issued.

affidavit—statement of facts set forth in written form and supported by the oath or affirmation of the person making the statement setting forth that such facts are true on the basis of actual knowledge or on information and belief. The affidavit is executed before a notary public or other person authorized to administer oaths.

affirm—action taken by an appellate court that approves the decision of the court below.

affirmative action plan (AAP)—plan to have a diverse and representative workforce.

after-acquired goods—goods acquired after a security interest has attached.

agency—the relationship that exists between a person identified as a principal and another by virtue of which the latter may make contracts with third persons on behalf of the principal. (Parties—principal, agent, third person) *agent*—person or firm who is authorized by the principal or by operation of law to make contracts with third persons on behalf of the principal.

airbill—document of title issued to a shipper whose goods are being sent via air.

alteration—unauthorized change or completion of a negotiable instrument designed to modify the obligation of a party to the instrument.

alternative payees—those persons to whom a negotiable instrument is made payable, any one of whom may indorse and take delivery of it.

ambiguous—having more than one reasonable interpretation.

answer—what a defendant must file to admit or deny facts asserted by the plaintiff.

anticipatory breach—promisor's repudiation of the contract prior to the time that performance is required.

anticipatory repudiation—repudiation made in advance of the time for performance of the contract obligations.

antilapse statutes—statutes providing that the children or heirs of a deceased beneficiary may take the legacy in the place of the deceased beneficiary.

apparent authority—appearance of authority created by the principal's words or conduct.

appeal—taking a case to a reviewing court to determine whether the judgment of the lower court or administrative agency was correct. (Parties—appellant, appellee)

appellate jurisdiction—the power of a court to hear and decide a given class of cases on appeal from another court or administrative agency.

appropriation—taking of an image, likeness, or name for commercial advantage.

arbitration—the settlement of disputed questions, whether of law or fact, by one or more arbitrators by whose decision the parties agree to be bound.

Article 2—section of the Uniform Commercial Code that governs contracts for the sale of goods.

articles of copartnership—See *Partnership Agreement*.

articles of incorporation—See *Certificate of Incorporation*.

articles of partnership—See *Partnership Agreement*.

assignee—third party to whom contract benefits are transferred.

assignment—transfer of a right. Generally used in connection with personal property rights, as rights under a contract, commercial paper, an insurance policy, a mortgage, or a lease. (Parties—assignor, assignee)

assignor—party who assigns contract rights to a third party.

association tribunal—a court created by a trade association or group for the resolution of disputes among its members.

assumption—mortgage transfers in which the transferee and mortgagor are liable and the property is subject to foreclosure by the mortgagee if payments are not made.

attestation clause—clause that indicates a witness has observed either the execution of the will or the testator's acknowledgment of the writing as the testator's will.

attorney in fact—agent authorized to act for another under a power of attorney.

attorney-client privilege—right of individual to have discussions with his/her attorney kept private and confidential.

attractive nuisance doctrine—a rule imposing liability upon a landowner for injuries sustained by small children playing on the land when the landowner permits a condition to exist or maintains equipment that a reasonable person should realize would attract small children who could not realize the danger. The rule does not apply if an unreasonable burden would be imposed upon the landowner in taking steps to protect the children.

authorities—corporations formed by government that perform public service.

automatic perfection—perfection given by statute without specific filing or possession requirements on the part of the creditor.

automatic stay—order to prevent creditors from taking action such as filing suits or seeking foreclosure against the debtor.

B

bad check laws—laws making it a criminal offense to issue a bad check with intent to defraud.

bailee—person who accepts possession of a property.

bailee's lien—specific, possessory lien of the bailee upon the goods for work done to them. Commonly extended by statute to any bailee's claim for compensation, eliminating the necessity of retention of possession.

bailment—relationship that exists when personal property is delivered into the possession of another under an agreement, express or implied, that the identical property will be returned or will be delivered in accordance with the agreement. (Parties—bailor, bailee)

bailment for mutual benefit—bailment in which the bailor and bailee derive a benefit from the bailment.

bailor—person who turns over the possession of a property.

balance sheet test—comparison of assets to liabilities made to determine solvency.

bankruptcy—procedure by which one unable to pay debts may surrender all assets in excess of any exemption claim to the court for administration and distribution to creditors, and the debtor is given a discharge that releases him from the unpaid balance due on most debts.

bankruptcy courts—court of special jurisdiction to determine bankruptcy issues.

battle of the forms—merchants' exchanges of invoices and purchase orders with differing boilerplate terms.

bearer—person in physical possession of commercial paper payable to bearer, a document of title directing delivery to bearer, or an investment security in bearer form.

bearer paper—instrument with no payee, payable to cash or payable to bearer.

bedrock view—a strict constructionist interpretation of a constitution.

beneficiary—person to whom the proceeds of a life insurance policy are payable, a person for whose benefit property is held in trust, or a person given property by a will; the ultimate recipient of the benefit of a funds transfer.

beneficiary's bank—the final bank, which carries out the payment order, in the chain of a transfer of funds.

bequest—gift of personal property by will.

best available treatment—in environmental law, a requirement that state-of-the-art methods be used for treating water.

best conventional treatment—in environmental law, a requirement that water be treated with the most commonly used method.

bicameral—a two-house form of the legislative branch of government.

bilateral contract—agreement under which one promise is given in exchange for another.

bill of lading—document issued by a carrier acknowledging the receipt of goods and the terms of the contract of transportation.

bill of sale—writing signed by the seller reciting that the personal property therein described has been sold to the buyer.

blackmail—extortion demands made by a nonpublic official.

blank indorsement—an indorsement that does not name the person to whom the paper, document of title, or investment security is negotiated.

blocking laws—laws that prohibit the disclosure, copying, inspection, or removal of documents located in the enacting country in compliance with orders from foreign authorities.

blue sky laws—state statutes designed to protect the public from the sale of worthless stocks and bonds.

bona fide—in good faith; without any fraud or deceit.

bond—obligation or promise in writing and sealed, generally of corporations, personal representatives, and trustees; fidelity bonds.

bond indenture—agreement setting forth the contractual terms of a particular bond issue.

book value—value found by dividing the value of the corporate assets by the number of shares outstanding.

breach—failure to act or perform in the manner called for in a contract.

breach of the peace—violation of the law in the repossession of the collateral.

brownfields—land that is a designated Superfund cleanup site but which lies fallow because no one is willing to risk liability by buying the property, even when the hazardous waste has been removed or property no one is willing to spend the money to remove the hazardous waste.

bubble concept—method for determining total emissions in one area; all sources are considered in an area.

business ethics—balancing the goal of profits with values of individuals and society.

business judgment rule (BJR)—rule that allows board immunity from liability for corporate acts where there is a reasonable indication that the acts were made in good faith with due care.

bylaws—rules and regulations enacted by a corporation to govern the affairs of the corporation and its shareholders, directors, and officers.

C

cancellation provision—crossing out of a part of an instrument or a destruction of all legal effect of the instrument, whether by act of party, upon breach by the other party, or pursuant to agreement or decree of court.

capital stock—declared money value of the outstanding stock of the corporation.

cargo insurance—insurance that protects a cargo owner against financial loss if goods being shipped are lost or damaged at sea.

carrier—individual or organization undertaking the transportation of goods.

case law—law that includes principles that are expressed for the first time in court decisions.

cashier's check—draft (check) drawn by a bank on itself.

cash surrender value—sum paid the insured upon the surrender of a policy to the insurer.

cash tender offer—general offer to all shareholders of a target corporation to purchase their shares for cash at a specified price.

cause of action—right to damages or other judicial relief when a legally protected right of the plaintiff is violated by an unlawful act of the defendant.

cease-and-desist order—order issued by a court or administrative agency to stop a practice that it decides is improper.

certificate of deposit (CD)—promise to pay instrument issued by a bank.

certificate of incorporation—written approval from the state or national government for a corporation to be formed.

certificate of stock—document evidencing a shareholder's ownership of stock issued by a corporation.

certified check—check for which the bank has set aside in a special account sufficient funds to pay it; payment is made when check is presented regardless of amount in drawer's account at that time; discharges all parties except certifying bank when holder requests certification.

cestui que trust—beneficiary or person for whose benefit the property is held in trust.

CF—cost and freight.

Chapter 11 bankruptcy—reorganization form of bankruptcy under federal law.

Chapter 7 bankruptcy—liquidation form of bankruptcy under federal law.

Chapter 13 bankruptcy—proceeding of consumer debt readjustment plan bankruptcy.

charging order—order by a court, after a business partner's personal assets are exhausted, requiring that the partner's share of the profits be paid to a creditor until the debt is discharged.

charter—grant of authority from a government to exist as a corporation. Generally replaced today by a certificate of incorporation approving the articles of incorporation.

check—order by a depositor on a bank to pay a sum of money to a payee; a draft drawn on a bank and payable on demand.

choice-of-law clause—clause in an agreement that specifies which law will govern should a dispute arise.

chose in action—intangible personal property in the nature of claims against another, such as a claim for accounts receivable or wages.

CIF—cost, insurance, and freight.

civil disobedience—the term used when natural law proponents violate positive law.

civil law—the law that defines the rights of one person against another.

claim—right to payment.

Clayton Act—a federal law that prohibits price discrimination.

Clean Air Act—federal legislation that establishes standards for air pollution levels and prevents further deterioration of air quality.

Clean Water Act—federal legislation that regulates water pollution through a control system.

close corporation—corporation whose shares are held by a single shareholder or a small group of shareholders.

close-connection doctrine—circumstantial evidence, such as an ongoing or a close relationship, that can serve as notice of a problem with an instrument.

COD—cash on delivery.

coinsurance clause—clause requiring the insured to maintain insurance on property up to a stated amount and providing that to the extent that this is not done, the insured is to be deemed a coinsurer with the insurer,

so that the latter is liable only for its proportionate share of the amount of insurance required to be carried.

collateral—property pledged by a borrower as security for a debt.

comity—principle of international and national law that the laws of all nations and states deserve the respect legitimately demanded by equal participants.

commerce clause—that section of the U.S. Constitution allocating the power for business regulation between the federal government and the states.

commercial impracticability—situation that occurs when costs of performance rise suddenly and performance of a contract will result in a substantial loss.

commercial lease—any nonconsumer lease.

commercial paper—written, transferable, signed promise or order to pay a specified sum of money; a negotiable instrument.

commercial unit—standard of the trade for shipment or packaging of a good.

commission merchant—bailee to whom goods are consigned for sale.

commission or factorage—consignee's compensation.

common carrier—carrier that holds out its facilities to serve the general public for compensation without discrimination.

common law—the body of unwritten principles originally based upon the usages and customs of the community that were recognized and enforced by the courts.

common stock—stock that has no right or priority over any other stock of the corporation as to dividends or distribution of assets upon dissolution.

community property—cotenancy held by husband and wife in property acquired during their marriage under the law of some of the states, principally in the southwestern United States.

comparative negligence—defense to negligence that allows plaintiff to recover reduced damages based on his level of fault.

compensatory damages—sum of money that will compensate an injured plaintiff for actual loss.

complaint—the initial pleading filed by the plaintiff in many actions, which in many states may be served as original process to acquire jurisdiction over the defendant.

composition of creditors—agreement among creditors that each shall accept a partial payment as full payment in consideration of the other creditors doing the same.

Comprehensive Environmental Response, Compensation, and Liability Act (CERCLA)—federal law that authorizes the president to issue funds for the cleanup of areas that were once disposal sites for hazardous wastes.

computer crimes—wrongs committed using a computer or with knowledge of computers.

concealment—failure to volunteer information not requested.

condition—stipulation or prerequisite in a contract, will, or other instrument.

condition precedent—event that must take place before the duty to perform under a contract arises.

condition subsequent—event whose occurrence or lack thereof terminates a contract.

condominium—combination of co-ownership and individual ownership.

confidential relationship—relationship in which, because of the legal status of the parties or their respective physical or mental conditions or knowledge, one party places full confidence and trust in the other.

conflict of interest—conduct that compromises an employee's allegiance to that company.

conglomerate—relationship of a parent corporation to subsidiary corporations engaged in diversified fields of activity unrelated to the field of activity of the parent corporation.

consent decrees—informal settlements of enforcement actions brought by agencies.

consequential damages—damages the buyer experiences as a result of the seller's breach with respect to a third party; also called *special damages.*

consideration—promise or performance that the promisor demands as the price of the promise.

consignee—(1) person to whom goods are shipped, (2) dealer who sells goods for others.

consignment—bailment made for the purpose of sale by the bailee. (Parties —consignor, consignee)

consignor—(1) person who delivers goods to the carrier for shipment, (2) party with title who turns goods over to another for sale.

consolidation (of corporations)—combining of two or more corporations in which the corporate existence of each one ceases and a new corporation is created.

conspiracy—agreement between two or more persons to commit an unlawful act.

constitution—a body of principles that establishes the structure of a government and the relationship of the government to the people who are governed.

constructive bailment—bailment imposed by law as opposed to one created by contract, whereby the bailee must preserve the property and redeliver it to the owner.

constructive delivery—See *symbolic delivery.*

constructive eviction—act or omission of the landlord that substantially deprives the tenant of the use and enjoyment of the premises.

consumer—any buyer afforded special protections by statute or regulation.

consumer credit—credit for personal, family, and household use.

consumer goods—goods used or bought primarily for personal, family, or household use.

consumer lease—lease of goods by a natural person for personal, family, or household use.

Consumer Product Safety Improvement Act—federal law that sets standards for the types of paints used in toys; a response to the lead paint found in toys made in China; requires tracking for international production; increases penalties.

contract—a binding agreement based on the genuine assent of the parties, made for a lawful object, between competent parties, in the form required by law, and generally supported by consideration.

contract carrier—carrier that transports on the basis of individual contracts that it makes with each shipper.

contract interference—tort in which a third party interferes with others' freedom to contract.

contract of adhesion—contract offered by a dominant party to a party with inferior bargaining power on a take-it-or-leave-it basis.

contract under seal—contract executed by affixing a seal or making an impression on the paper or on some adhering substance such as wax attached to the document.

contracting agent—agent with authority to make contracts; person with whom the buyer deals.

Contracts for the International Sale of Goods (CISG)—uniform international contract code contracts for international sale of goods.

contractual capacity—ability to understand that a contract is being made and to understand its general meaning.

contribution—right of a co-obligor who has paid more than a proportionate share to demand that the other obligor pay the amount of the excess payment made.

contributory negligence—negligence of the plaintiff that contributes to injury and at common law bars recovery from the defendant although the defendant may have been more negligent than the plaintiff.

conversion—act of taking personal property by a person not entitled to it and keeping it from its true owner or prior possessor without consent.

cooperative—group of two or more persons or enterprises that acts through a common agent with respect to a common objective, such as buying or selling.

copyright—exclusive right given by federal statute to the creator of a literary or an artistic work to use, reproduce, and display the work.

corporation—artificial being created by government grant, which for many purposes is treated as a natural person.

corporation by estoppel—corporation that comes about when parties estop themselves from denying that the corporation exists.

corporation de jure—corporation with a legal right to exist by virtue of law.

correspondent bank—will honor the letter of credit from the domestic bank of the buyer.

cost plus—method of determining the purchase price or contract price equal to the seller's or contractor's costs plus a stated percentage as the profit.

co-sureties—sureties for the same debtor and obligor.

cotenancy—when two or more persons hold concurrent rights and interests in the same property.

Council on Environmental Quality (CEQ)—federal agency that establishes national policies on environmental quality and then recommends legislation to implement these policies.

counterclaim—a claim that the defendant in an action may make against the plaintiff.

counteroffer—proposal by an offeree to the offeror that changes the terms of, and thus rejects, the original offer.

course of dealing—pattern of performance between two parties to a contract.

court—a tribunal established by government to hear evidence, decide cases brought before it, and provide remedies when a wrong has been committed.

covenant against encumbrances—guarantee that conveyed land is not subject to any right or interest of a third person.

covenant of further assurances—promise that the grantor of an interest in land will execute any additional documents required to perfect the title of the grantee.

covenant of quiet enjoyment—covenant by the grantor of an interest in land that the grantee's possession of the land shall not be disturbed.

covenant of right to convey—guarantee that the grantor of an interest in land, if not the owner, has the right or authority to make the conveyance to a new owner.

covenant of seisin—guarantee that the grantor of an interest in land owns the estate conveyed to a new owner.

covenants (or warranties) of title—grantor's covenants of a deed that guarantee such matters as the right to make the conveyance, to ownership of the property, to freedom of the property from encumbrances, or that the grantee will not be disturbed in the quiet enjoyment of the land.

credit transfer—transaction in which a person making payment, such as a buyer, requests payment be made to the beneficiary's bank.

creditor—person (seller or lender) who is owed money; also may be a secured party.

crime—violation of the law that is punished as an offense against the state or government.

criminal law—the law that defines wrongs against society.

cross-examination—the examination made of a witness by the attorney for the adverse party.

cumulative voting—system of voting for directors in which each shareholder has as many votes as the number of voting shares owned multiplied by the number of directors to be elected, and such votes can be distributed for the various candidates as desired.

customary authority—authority of an agent to do any act that, according to the custom of the community, usually accompanies the transaction for which the agent is authorized to act.

cyberlaw—laws and precedent applicable to Internet transactions and communications.

cyberspace—World Wide Web and Internet communication.

cybersquatters—term for those who register and set up domain names on the Internet for resale to the famous users of the names in question.

D

de facto—existing in fact as distinguished from as of right, as in the case of an officer or a corporation purporting to act as such without being elected to the office or having been properly incorporated.

debenture—unsecured bond of a corporation, with no specific corporate assets pledged as security for payment.

debit transfer—transaction in which a beneficiary entitled to money requests payment from a bank according to a prior agreement.

debtor—buyer on credit (i.e., a borrower).

decedent—upon death, person whose estate is being administered.

deed—instrument by which the grantor(owner of land) conveys or transfers the title to a grantee.

defamation—untrue statement by one party about another to a third party.

defendant—party charged with a violation of civil or criminal law in a proceeding.

defined benefit plan—an employer commitment to make specified future payments to participants upon retirement.

defined contribution plan—a plan that provides for an individual account for each plan participant and for benefits based solely on the amount contributed to the participant's account; also known as an *individual account plan*.

definite time—time of payment computable from the face of the instrument.

delegated powers—powers expressly granted the national government by the Constitution.

delegation—transfer to another of the right and power to do an act.

delegation of duties—transfer of duties by a contracting party to another person who is to perform them.

delivery—constructive or actual possession.

demand draft—draft that is payable upon presentment.

demurrer—a pleading to dismiss the adverse party's pleading for not stating a cause of action or a defense.

deposition—the testimony of a witness taken out of court but under oath.

depositor—person, or bailor, who gives property for storage.

derivative (secondary) action—secondary action for damages or breach of contract brought by one or more corporate shareholders against directors, officers, or third persons.

development statement—statement that sets forth significant details of a real estate or property development as required by the federal Interstate Land Sales Act.

devise—gift of real estate made by will.

devisee—beneficiary of a devise.

direct damages—losses that are caused by breach of a contract.

direct examination—examination of a witness by his or her attorney.

directed verdict—a direction by the trial judge to the jury to return a verdict in favor of a specified party to the action.

disability—any incapacity resulting from bodily injury or disease to engage in any occupation for remuneration or profit.

discharge in bankruptcy—order of the bankruptcy court relieving the debtor from obligation to pay the unpaid balance of most claims.

disclosed principal—principal whose identity is made known by the agent as well as the fact that the agent is acting on the principal's behalf.

discovery—procedures for ascertaining facts prior to the time of trial in order

to eliminate the element of surprise in litigation.

dishonor—status when the primary party refuses to pay the instrument according to its terms.

disinherited—excluded from sharing in the estate of a decedent.

Dispute Settlement Body (DSB)—means, provided by the World Trade Organization, for member countries to resolve trade disputes rather than engage in unilateral trade sanctions or a trade war.

distinctiveness—capable of serving the source-identifying function of a mark.

distribution per stirpes—distribution of an estate made in as many equal parts as there are family lines represented in the nearest generation; also known as *stirpital distribution*.

distributor—entity that takes title to goods and bears the financial and commercial risks for the subsequent sale of the goods.

divestiture order—a court order to dispose of interests that could lead to a monopoly.

divisible contract—agreement consisting of two or more parts, each calling for corresponding performances of each part by the parties.

document of title—document treated as evidence that a person is entitled to receive, hold, and dispose of the document and the goods it covers.

domestic corporation—corporation that has been incorporated by the state in question as opposed to incorporation by another state.

dominant tenement—land that is benefited by an easement.

donee—recipient of a gift.

donor—person making a gift.

double indemnity—provision for payment of double the amount specified by the insurance contract if death is caused by an accident and occurs under specified circumstances.

draft or bill of exchange—an unconditional order in writing by one person upon another, signed by the person giving it, and ordering the person to whom it is directed to pay upon demand or at a definite time a sum certain in money to order or to bearer.

drawee—person to whom the draft is addressed and who is ordered to pay the amount of money specified in the draft.

drawer—person who writes out and creates a draft or bill of exchange, including a check.

due diligence—process of checking the environmental history and nature of land prior to purchase.

due process—the constitutional right to be heard, question witnesses, and present evidence.

due process clause—in the Fifth and Fourteenth Amendments, a guarantee of protection from unreasonable procedures and unreasonable laws.

dumping—selling goods in another country at less than their fair value.

duress—conduct that deprives the victim of free will and that generally gives the victim the right to set aside any transaction entered into under such circumstances.

duty—an obligation of law imposed on a person to perform or refrain from performing a certain act.

E

easement—permanent right that one has in the land of another, as the right to cross another's land or an easement of way.

easement by implication—easement not specifically created by deed that arises from the circumstances of the parties and the land location and access.

economic duress—threat of financial loss.

Economic Espionage Act (EEA)—federal law that makes it a felony to copy, download, transmit, or in any-way transfer proprietary files, documents, and information from a computer to an unauthorized person.

economic strikers—union strikers trying to enforce bargaining demands when an impasse has been reached in the negotiation process for a collective bargaining agreement.

effects doctrine—doctrine that U.S. courts will assume jurisdiction and will apply antitrust laws to conduct outside of the United States when the activity of business firms has direct and substantial effect on U.S. commerce; the rule has been modified to require that the effect on U.S. commerce also be foreseeable.

effluent guidelines—EPA standards for maximum ranges of discharge into water.

electronic funds transfer (EFT)—any transfer of funds (other than a transaction originated by a check, draft, or similar paper instrument) that is initiated through an electronic terminal, telephone, computer, or magnetic tape so as to authorize a financial institution to debit or credit an account.

Electronic Funds Transfer Act (EFTA)—federal law that provides consumers with rights and protections in electronic funds transfers.

eleemosynary corporation—corporation organized for a charitable or benevolent purpose.

embezzlement—statutory offense consisting of the unlawful conversion of property entrusted to the wrongdoer.

eminent domain—power of government and certain kinds of corporations to take private property against the objection of the owner, provided the taking is for a public purpose and just compensation is made for it.

emissions offset policy—controls whether new factories can be built in a nonattainment area.

employment-at-will doctrine—doctrine in which the employer has historically been allowed to terminate the employment contract at any time for any reason or for no reason.

en banc—the term used when the full panel of judges on the appellate court hears a case.

encoding warranty—warranty made by any party who encodes electronic information on an instrument; a warranty of accuracy.

Endangered Species Act (ESA)—federal law that identifies and protects species that are endangered from development or other acts that threaten their existence.

endowment insurance—insurance that pays the face amount of the policy if the insured dies within the policy period.

entitlement theory—also known as *rights theory*; Nozick's theory that (1) everyone has a set of rights, and (2) it is up to the governments to protect those rights.

environmental impact statement (EIS)—formal report prepared under NEPA to document findings on the impact of a federal project on the environment.

equitable title—beneficial interest in a trust.

equity—the body of principles that originally developed because of the inadequacy of the rules then applied by the common law courts of England.

escalation clause—provision for the automatic increase of the rent at periodic intervals.

escheat—transfer to the state of the title to a decedent's property when the owner of the property dies intestate and is not survived by anyone capable of taking the property as heir.

E-sign—signature over the Internet.

estate in fee—largest estate possible, in which the owner has absolute and entire interest in the land.

estoppel—principle by which a person is barred from pursuing a certain course of action or of disputing the truth of certain matters.

ethical egoism—Ayn Rand theory of ethics that we should all act in our own best interests.

ethics—a branch of philosophy dealing with values that relate to the nature of human conduct and values associated with that conduct.

ex post facto *law*—a law making criminal an act that was lawful when done or that increases the penalty when done. Such laws are generally prohibited by constitutional provisions.

exculpatory clause—provision in a contract stating that one of the parties is not liable for damages in case of breach; also called *limitation-of-liability clause.*

executed contract—agreement that has been completely performed.

execution—the carrying out of a judgment of a court, generally directing that property owned by the defendant be sold and the proceeds first be used to pay the execution or judgment creditor.

executive branch—the branch of government (e.g., the president) formed to execute the laws.

executor, executrix—person (man, woman) named in a will to administer the estate of the decedent.

executory contract—contract in which something remains to be done by one or both parties.

exhaustion of administrative remedies—requirement that an agency make its final decision before the issue can be taken to court.

existing goods—goods that physically exist and are owned by the seller at the time of a transaction.

exoneration—agreement or provision in an agreement that one party will not be held liable for loss; the right of the surety to demand that those primarily liable pay the claim for which the surety is secondarily liable.

expert witness—one who has acquired special knowledge in a particular field as through practical experience or study, or both, whose opinion is admissible as an aid to the trier of fact.

export sale—direct sale to customers in a foreign country.

express authority—authority of an agent to perform a certain act.

express authorization—authorization of an agent to perform a certain act.

express contract—agreement of the parties manifested by their words, whether spoken or written.

express warranty—statement by the defendant relating to the goods, which statement is part of the basis of the bargain.

extortion—illegal demand by a public officer acting with apparent authority.

F

facilitation payments—(or grease payments) legal payments to speed up or ensure performance of normal government duties.

factor—bailee to whom goods are consigned for sale.

false imprisonment—intentional detention of a person without that person's consent; called the shopkeeper's tort when shoplifters are unlawfully detained.

FAS—free alongside the named vessel.

federal district court—the general trial court of the federal system.

Federal Register—government publication issued five days a week that lists all administrative regulations, all presidential proclamations and executive orders, and other documents and classes of documents that the president or Congress direct to be published.

Federal Register Act—federal law requiring agencies to make public disclosure of proposed rules, passed rules, and activities.

Federal Sentencing Guidelines—federal standards used by judges in determining mandatory sentence terms for those convicted of federal crimes.

federal system—the system of government in which a central government is given power to administer to national concerns while individual states retain the power to administer to local concerns.

fee simple defeasibles—fee simple interest that can be lost if restrictions on its use are violated.

fee simple estate—highest level of land ownership; full interest of unlimited duration.

felony—criminal offense that is punishable by confinement in prison for more than one year or by death, or that is expressly stated by statute to be a felony.

field warehousing—stored goods under the exclusive control of a warehouse but kept on the owner's premises rather than in a warehouse.

Fifth Amendment—constitutional protection against self-incrimination; also guarantees due process.

finance lease—three-party lease agreement in which there is a lessor, a lessee, and a financier.

financing statement—brief statement (record) that gives sufficient information to alert third persons that a particular creditor may have a security interest in the collateral described.

fire insurance policy—a contract that indemnifies the insured for property destruction or damage caused by fire.

firm offer—offer stated to be held open for a specified time, which must be so held in some states even in the absence of an option contract, or under the UCC, with respect to merchants.

first-in-time provision—creditor whose interest attached first has priority in the collateral when two creditors have a secured interest.

first-to-perfect basis—rule of priorities that holds that first in time in perfecting a security interest, mortgage, judgment, lien, or other property attachment right should have priority.

fixture—personal property that has become so attached to or adapted to real estate that it has lost its character as personal property and is part of the real estate.

floating lien—claim in a changing or shifting stock of goods of the buyer.

FOB place of destination—shipping contract that requires seller to deliver goods to buyer.

FOB place of shipment—contract that requires the seller to arrange for shipment only.

forbearance—refraining from doing an act.

forcible entry and detainer—action by the landlord to have the tenant removed for nonpayment of rent.

foreclosure—procedure for enforcing a mortgage resulting in the public sale of the mortgaged property and, less commonly, in merely barring the right of the mortgagor to redeem the property from the mortgage.

foreign corporation—corporation incorporated under the laws of another state.

Foreign Corrupt Practices Act (FCPA)—federal law that makes it a felony to influence decision makers in other countries for the purpose of obtaining business, such as contracts for sales and services; also imposes financial

reporting requirements on certain U.S. corporations.

forged or unauthorized indorsement—instrument indorsed by an agent for a principal without authorization or authority.

forgery—fraudulently making or altering an instrument that apparently creates or alters a legal liability of another.

formal contracts—written contracts or agreements whose formality signifies the parties' intention to abide by the terms.

Fourth Amendment—privacy protection in the U.S. Constitution; prohibits unauthorized searches and seizures.

franchise—(1) privilege or authorization, generally exclusive, to engage in a particular activity within a particular geographic area, such as a government franchise to operate a taxi company within a specified city, or a private franchise as the grant by a manufacturer of a right to sell products within a particular territory or for a particular number of years; (2) right to vote.

franchise agreement—sets forth rights of franchisee to use trademarks, etc., of franchisor.

franchisee—person to whom franchise is granted.

Franchise Rule—rule requiring detailed disclosures and prohibiting certain practices.

franchising—granting of permission to use a trademark, trade name, or copyright under specified conditions; a form of licensing.

franchisor—party granting the franchise.

fraud—making of a false statement of a past or existing fact, with knowledge of its falsity or with reckless indifference as to its truth, with the intent to cause another to rely thereon, and such person does rely thereon and is harmed thereby.

fraud in the inducement—fraud that occurs when a person is persuaded or induced to execute an instrument because of fraudulent statements.

fraud-on-the-market—a theory that in an open and developed securities market, the price of a stock is determined by the information on the company available to the public, and misleading statements will defraud purchasers of stock even if they do not directly rely on these statements.

Freedom of Information Act—federal law permitting citizens to request documents and records from administrative agencies.

freight forwarder—one who contracts to have goods transported and, in turn, contracts with carriers for such transportation.

freight insurance—insures that ship owner will receive payment for transportation charges.

full warranty—obligation of a seller to fix or replace a defective product within a reasonable time without cost to the buyer.

funds transfer—communication of instructions or requests to pay a specific sum of money to the credit of a specified account or person without an actual physical passing of money.

fungible goods—homogeneous goods of which any unit is the equivalent of any other unit.

future goods—goods that exist physically but are not owned by the seller and goods that have not yet been produced.

G

garnishment—the name given in some states to attachment proceedings.

general agent—agent authorized by the principal to transact all affairs in connection with a particular type of business or trade or to transact all business at a certain place.

general corporation code—state's code listing certain requirements for creation of a corporation.

general jurisdiction—the power to hear and decide most controversies involving legal rights and duties.

general legacies—certain sums of money bequeathed to named persons by the testator; to be paid out of the decedent's assets generally without specifying any particular fund or source from which the payment is to be made.

general partnership—partnership in which the partners conduct as co-owners a business for profit, and each partner has a right to take part in the management of the business and has unlimited liability.

general partners—partners who publicly and actively engage in the transaction of firm business.

general partners—partnership in which the partners conduct as co-owners a business for profit, and each partner has a right to take part in the management of the business and has unlimited liability; general partners publicly and actively engage in the transaction of firm business.

gift—title to an owner's personal property voluntarily transferred by a party not receiving anything in exchange.

gift causa mortis—gift, made by the donor in the belief that death was immediate and impending, that is revoked or is revocable under certain circumstances.

good faith—absence of knowledge of any defects or problems; "pure heart and an empty head."

goods—anything movable at the time it is identified as the subject of a transaction.

grantee—new owner of a land conveyance.

grantor—owner who transfers or conveys an interest in land to a new owner.

gratuitous bailment—bailment in which the bailee does not receive any compensation or advantage.

gray market goods—foreign-made goods with U.S. trademarks brought into the United States by a third party without the consent of the trademark owners to compete with these owners.

grease payments—(or facilitation payments) legal payments to speed up or ensure performance of normal government duties.

guarantor—one who undertakes the obligation of guaranty.

guaranty—agreement or promise to answer for a debt; an undertaking to pay the debt of another if the creditor first sues the debtor.

guaranty of collection—form of guaranty in which creditor cannot proceed against guarantor until after proceeding against debtor.

guaranty of payment—absolute promise to pay when a debtor defaults.

guest—transient who contracts for a room or site at a hotel.

H

hearsay evidence—statements made out of court that are offered in court as proof of the information contained in the statements and that, subject to many exceptions, are not admissible in evidence.

holder—someone in possession of an instrument that runs to that person (i.e., is made payable to that person, is indorsed to that person, or is bearer paper).

holder in due course—a holder who has given value, taken in good faith without notice of dishonor, defenses, or that instrument is overdue, and who is afforded special rights or status.

holder through a holder in due course—holder of an instrument who attains holder-in-due-course status because a holder in due course has held it previous to him or her.

holographic will—unwitnessed will written by hand.

homeowners insurance policy—combination of standard fire insurance and comprehensive personal liability insurance.

hotelkeeper—one regularly engaged in the business of offering living accommodations to all transient persons.

hull insurance—insurance that covers physical damage on a freight-moving vessel.

I

identification—point in the transaction when the buyer acquires an interest in the goods subject to the contract.

identified—term applied to particular goods selected by either the buyer or the seller as the goods called for by the sales contract.

identity theft—use of another's credit tools, social security number, or other IDs to obtain cash, goods, or credit without permission.

illusory promise—promise that in fact does not impose any obligation on the promisor.

impeach—using prior inconsistent evidence to challenge the credibility of a witness.

implied contract—contract expressed by conduct or implied or deduced from the facts.

implied warranty—warranty that was not made but is implied by law.

implied warranty of merchantability—group of promises made by the seller, the most important of which is that the goods are fit for the ordinary purposes for which they are sold.

impostor rule—an exception to the rules on liability for forgery that covers situations such as the embezzling payroll clerk.

in pari delicto—equally guilty; used in reference to a transaction as to which relief will not be granted to either party because both are equally guilty of wrongdoing.

incidental authority—authority of an agent that is reasonably necessary to execute express authority.

incidental damages—incurred by the nonbreaching party as part of the process of trying to cover (buy substitute goods) or sell (selling subject matter of contract to another); includes storage fees, commissions, and the like.

income—money earned by the principal, or property in trust, and distributed by the trustee.

incontestability clause—provision that after the lapse of a specified time the insurer cannot dispute the policy on the ground of misrepresentation or fraud of the insured or similar wrongful conduct.

incorporation by reference—contract consisting of both the original or skeleton document and the detailed statement that is incorporated in it.

incorporator—one or more natural persons or corporations who sign and file appropriate incorporation forms with a designated government official.

indemnity—right of a person secondarily liable to require that a person primarily liable pay for loss sustained when the secondary party discharges the obligation that the primary party should have discharged; the right of an agent to be paid the amount of any loss or damage sustained without fault because of obedience to the principal's instructions; an undertaking by one person for a consideration to pay another person a sum of money to indemnify that person when a specified loss is incurred.

indemnity contract—agreement by one person, for consideration, to pay another person a sum of money in the event that the other person sustains a specified loss.

indenture trustee—usually a commercial banking institution, to represent the interests of the bondholders and ensure that the terms and covenants of the bond issue are met by the corporation.

independent contractor—contractor who undertakes to perform a specified task according to the terms of a contract but over whom the other contracting party has no control except as provided for by the contract.

indorsee—party to whom special indorsement is made.

indorsement—signature of the payee on an instrument.

indorser—secondary party (or obligor) on a note.

informal contract—simple oral or written contract.

informal settlements—negotiated disposition of a matter before an administrative agency, generally without public sanctions.

injunction—order of a court of equity to refrain from doing (negative injunction) or to do (affirmative or mandatory injunction) a specified act.

inland marine—insurance that covers domestic shipments of goods over land and inland waterways.

insider—full-time corporate employee or a director or their relatives.

insider information—privileged information on company business only known to employees.

insolvency—excess of debts and liabilities over assets, or inability to pay debts as they mature.

instruction—summary of the law given to jurors by the judge before deliberation begins.

insurable interest—the right to hold a valid insurance policy on a person or property.

insurance—a plan of security against risks by charging the loss against a fund created by the payments made by policyholders.

insurance agent—agent of an insurance company.

insurance broker—independent contractor who is not employed by any one insurance company.

insured—person to whom the promise in an insurance contract is made.

insurer—promisor in an insurance contract.

integrity—the adherence to one's values and principles despite the costs and consequences.

intellectual property rights—trademark, copyright, and patent rights protected by law.

intended beneficiary—third person of a contract whom the contract is intended to benefit.

intentional infliction of emotional distress—tort that produces mental anguish caused by conduct that exceeds all bounds of decency.

intentional tort—civil wrong that results from intentional conduct.

intervivos gift—any transaction that takes place between living persons and creates rights prior to the death of any of them.

interest in the authority—form of agency in which an agent has been given or paid for the right to exercise authority.

interest in the subject matter—form of agency in which an agent is given an interest in the property with which that agent is dealing.

interlineation—writing between the lines or adding to the provisions of a document, the effect thereof depending upon the nature of the document.

intermediary bank—bank between the originator and the beneficiary bank in the transfer of funds.

interrogatories—written questions used as a discovery tool that must be answered under oath.

intestate—condition of dying without a will as to any property.

intestate succession—distribution, made as directed by statute, of a decedent's property not effectively disposed of by will.

invasion of privacy—tort of intentional intrusion into the private affairs of another.

invitee—person who enters another's land by invitation.

involuntary bankruptcy—proceeding in which a creditor or creditors file the petition for relief with the bankruptcy court.

issuer—party who issues a document such as a letter of credit or a document of title such as a warehouse receipt or bill of lading.

J

joint and several liability—disproportionate satisfaction of partnership debt rendering each partner liable for the entire debt with the right to contribution from other partners.

joint liability—apportions partners' responsibility for debt equally.

joint tenancy—estate held jointly by two or more with the right of survivorship as between them, unless modified by statute.

joint venture—relationship in which two or more persons or firms combine their labor or property for a single undertaking and share profits and losses equally unless otherwise agreed.

judge—primary officer of the court.

judgment lien—lien by a creditor who has won a verdict against the landowner in court.

judgment n.o.v. (or non obstante veredicto, *"notwithstanding the verdict"*)— a judgment entered after verdict upon the motion of the losing party on the ground that the verdict is so wrong that a judgment should be entered the opposite of the verdict.

judicial branch—the branch of government (courts) formed to interpret the laws.

judicial triage—court management tool used by judges to expedite certain cases in which time is of the essence, such as asbestos cases in which the plaintiffs are gravely ill.

jurisdiction—the authority of courts to hear and determine a given class of cases; the power to act over a particular defendant.

jurisdictional rule of reason—rule that balances the vital interests, including laws and policies, of the United States with those of a foreign country.

jury—a body of citizens sworn by a court to determine by verdict the issues of fact submitted to them.

K

Kant's categorical imperative—theory of ethical thought that asks individuals to be governed by the same set of rules in all circumstances; whether you are buyer or seller, the standards for full and fair disclosure are the same.

L

land—earth, including all things embedded in or attached thereto, whether naturally or by the act of humans.

landlord—one who leases real property to another.

law—the order or pattern of rules that society establishes to govern the conduct of individuals and the relationships among them.

lease—agreement between the owner of property and a tenant by which the former agrees to give possession of the property to the latter in consideration of the payment of rent. (Parties—landlord or lessor, tenant or lessee)

leasehold estate—interest of a tenant in rented land.

legacy—gift of money made by will.

legal title—title held by the trustee in a trust situation.

legatee—beneficiary who receives a gift of personal property by will.

legislative branch—the branch of government (e.g., Congress) formed to make the laws.

lessee—one who has a possessory interest in real or personal property under a lease; a tenant.

lessor—one who conveys real or personal property by a lease; a landlord.

letter of credit—commercial device used to guarantee payment to a seller, primarily in an international business transaction.

letters of administration—written authorization given to an administrator of an estate as evidence of appointment and authority.

letters testamentary—written authorization given to an executor of an estate as evidence of appointment and authority.

liability insurance—covers the ship owner's liability if the ship causes damage to another ship or its cargo.

libel—written or visual defamation without legal justification.

license—personal privilege to do some act or series of acts upon the land of another, as the placing of a sign there on, not amounting to an ease mentor a right of possession.

licensee—someone on another's premises with the permission of the occupier, whose duty is to warn the licensee of nonobvious dangers.

licensing—transfer of technology rights to a product so that it may be produced by a different business organization in a foreign country in exchange for royalties and other payments as agreed.

lien—claim or right, against property, existing by virtue of the entry of a judgment against its owner or by the entry of a judgment and a levy there under on the property, or because of the relationship of the claimant to the particular property, such as an unpaid seller.

life estate—an estate for the duration of a life.

limitation-of-liability clause—provision in a contract stating that one of the parties shall not be liable for damages in case of breach; also called an *exculpatory clause*.

limited covenant—any covenant that does not provide the complete protection of a full covenant.

limited defenses—defenses available to secondary parties if the presenting party is a holder in due course.

limited liability company (LLC)—a partnership for federal tax treatment and the limited liability feature of the corporate form of business organization.

limited liability partnership (LLP)—partnership in which at least one partner has a liability limited to the loss of the capital contribution made to the partnership.

limited partner—partner who neither takes part in the management of the partnership nor appears to the public to be a general partner.

limited partnership—partnership that can be formed by "one or more general partners and one or more limited partners."

limited (special) jurisdiction—the authority to hear only particular kinds of cases.

limited warranty—any warranty that does not provide the complete protection of a full warranty.

lineals—relationship that exists when one person is a direct descendant of the other; also called *lineal descendants*.

liquidated damages—damages established in advance of breach as an alternative to establishing compensatory damages at the time of the breach.

liquidated damages clause—specification of exact compensation in case of a breach of contract.

liquidation—process of converting property into money whether of particular items of property or of all the assets of a business or an estate.

living trust—trust created to take effect within the lifetime of the settlor; also called *inter vivos* trust.

living will—document by which individuals may indicate that if they become unable to express their wishes and are in an irreversible, incurable condition, they do not want life-sustaining medical treatments.

living-document view—the term when a constitution is interpreted according to changes in conditions.

lottery—any plan by which a consideration is given for a chance to win a prize; it consists of three elements: (1) there must be a payment of money or something of value for an opportunity to win, (2) a prize must be available, and (3) the prize must be offered by lot or chance.

M

mailbox rule—timing for acceptance tied to proper acceptance.

maker—party who writes or creates a promissory note.

malpractice—basis for liability when services are not properly rendered in accordance with commonly accepted standards; negligence by a professional in performing his or her skill.

marine insurance—policies that cover perils relating to the transportation of goods.

market power—the ability to control price and exclude competitors.

market value—price at which a share of stock can be voluntarily bought or sold in the open market.

mask work—specific form of expression embodied in a chip design, including the stencils used in manufacturing semiconductor chip products.

mass picketing—illegal tactic of employees massing together in great numbers to effectively shut down entrances of the employer's facility.

maturity date—date that a corporation is required to repay a loan to a bondholder.

means test—new standard under the Reform Act that requires the court to find that the debtor does not have the means to repay creditors; goes beyond the past requirement of petitions being granted on the simple assertion of the debtor saying, "I have debts."

mechanic's lien—protection afforded by statute to various kinds of laborers and persons supplying materials, by giving them a lien on the building and land that has been improved or added to by them.

mediation—the settlement of a dispute through the use of a messenger who carries to each side of the dispute the issues and offers in the case.

merchant—seller who deals in specific goods classified by the UCC.

merger (of corporations)—combining of corporations by which one absorbs the other and continues to exist, preserving its original charter and identity while the other corporation ceases to exist.

minitrial—a trial held on portions of the case or certain issues in the case.

Miranda warnings—warnings required to prevent self-incrimination in a criminal matter.

mirror image rule—common law contract rule on acceptance that requires language to be absolutely the same as the offer, unequivocal and unconditional.

misdemeanor—criminal offense with a sentence of less than one year that is neither treason nor a felony.

misrepresentation—false statement of fact made innocently without any intent to deceive.

mistrial—a court's declaration that terminates a trial and postpones it to a later date; commonly entered when evidence has been of a highly prejudicial character or when a juror has been guilty of misconduct.

money—medium of exchange.

money order—draft issued by a bank or a nonbank.

moral relativists—group of ethical theorists who believe that ethical choices are determined according to the circumstances and not according to any predetermined set of standards.

mortgage—interest in land given by the owner to a creditor as security for the payment of the creditor for a debt, the nature of the interest depending upon the law of the state where the land is located. (Parties—mortgagor, mortgagee)

most-favored-nation clause—clause in treaties between countries whereby any privilege subsequently granted to a third country in relation to a given treaty subject is extended to the other party to the treaty.

motion for summary judgment—request that the court decide a case on basis of law only because there are no material issues disputed by the parties.

motion to dismiss—a pleading that may be filed to attack the adverse party's pleading as not stating a cause of action or a defense.

N

National Environmental Policy Act (NEPA)—federal law that mandates study of a project's impact on the environment before it can be undertaken by any federal agency.

National Pollutant Discharge Elimination System (NPDES)—federal law that regulates discharge into bodies of water.

natural law—a system of principles to guide human conduct independent of, and sometimes contrary to, enacted law and discovered by man's rational intelligence.

necessaries—things indispensable or absolutely necessary for the sustenance of human life.

negligence—failure to exercise due care under the circumstances in consequence of which harm is proximately caused to one to whom the defendant owed a duty to exercise due care.

negotiability—quality of an instrument that affords special rights and standing.

negotiable bill of lading—document of title that by its terms calls for goods to be delivered "to the bearer" or "to the order of" a named person.

negotiable instruments—drafts, promissory notes, checks, and certificates of deposit that, in proper form, give special rights as "negotiable commercial paper."

negotiable warehouse receipt—receipt that states the covered goods will be delivered "to the bearer" or "to the order of."

negotiation—the transfer of commercial paper by indorsement and delivery by the person to whom it is then payable in the case of order paper and by physical transfer in the case of bearer paper.

Noise Control Act—federal law that controls noise emissions from low-flying aircraft.

nominal damages—nominal sum awarded the plaintiff in order to establish that legal rights have been violated although the plaintiff in fact has not sustained any actual loss or damages.

nonattainment areas—"dirty" areas that do not meet federal standards under the Clean Air Act.

nonconforming use—use of land that conflicts with a zoning ordinance at the time the ordinance goes into effect.

nonconsumer lease—lease that does not satisfy the definition of a consumer lease; also known as a *commercial lease*.

nonnegotiable bill of lading—See *straight bill of lading*.

nonnegotiable instrument—contract, note, or draft that does not meet negotiability requirements of Article 3.

nonnegotiable warehouse receipt—receipt that states the covered goods received will be delivered to a specific person.

notice of dishonor—notice that an instrument has been dishonored; such notice can be oral, written, or electronic but is subject to time limitations.

notice statute—statute under which the last good faith or bona fide purchaser holds the title.

notice-race statute—statute under which the first bona fide purchaser to record the deed holds the title.

novation—substitution for an old contract with a new one that either replaces an existing obligation with a new obligation or replaces an original party with a new party.

nuisance—conduct that harms or prejudices another in the use of land or that harms or prejudices the public.

O

obligee—promisee who can claim the benefit of the obligation.

obligor—promisor.

ocean marine—policies that cover transportation of goods in vessels in international and coastal trade.

offer—expression of an offeror's willingness to enter into a contractual agreement.

offeree—person to whom an offer is made.

offeror—person who makes an offer.

Oil Pollution Act—federal law that assigns cleanup liability for oil spills in U.S. waters.

open meeting law—law that requires advance notice of agency meeting and public access.

opening statements—statements by opposing attorneys that tell the jury what their cases will prove.

operation of law—attaching of certain consequences to certain facts because of legal principles that operate automatically as contrasted with consequences that arise because of the voluntary action of a party designed to create those consequences.

option contract—contract to hold an offer to make a contract open for a fixed period of time.

order of relief—the order from the bankruptcy judge that starts the protection for the debtor; when the order of relief is entered by the court, the debtor's creditors must stop all proceedings and work through the bankruptcy court to recover debts (if possible). Court finding that creditors have met the standards for bankruptcy petitions.

order paper—instrument payable to the order of a party.

original jurisdiction—the authority of courts to hear the original proceedings in a case.

originator—party who originates the funds transfer.

output contract—contract of a producer to sell its entire production or output to a buyer.

outstanding—name for shares of a company that have been issued to stockholders.

overdraft—negative balance in a drawer's account.

P

par value—specified monetary amount assigned by an issuing corporation for each share of its stock.

parol evidence rule—rule that prohibits the introduction into evidence of oral or written statements made prior to or contemporaneously with the execution of a complete written contract, deed, or instrument, in the absence of clear proof of fraud, accident, or mistake causing the omission of the statement in question.

partially disclosed principal—principal whose existence is made known but whose identity is not.

partner—one of two or more persons who jointly own and carry on a business for profit.

partnership—pooling of capital resources and the business or professional talents of two or more individuals (partners) with the goal of making a profit.

partnership agreement—document prepared to evidence the contract of the parties. (Parties—partners or general partners)

party—person involved in a legal transaction; may be a natural person, an artificial person (e.g., a corporation), or an unincorporated enterprise (e.g., a government agency).

past consideration—something that has been performed in the past and which, therefore, cannot be

consideration for a promise made in the present.

payable to order—term stating that a negotiable instrument is payable to the order of any person described in it or to a person or order.

payee—party to whom payment is to be made.

payment order—direction given by an originator to his or her bank or by any bank to a subsequent bank to make a specified funds transfer.

Pension Benefit Guaranty Corporation (PBGC)—a federal insurance plan established by ERISA that protects employees covered under defined benefit plans should the employer go out of business.

per capita—method of distributing estate assets on an equal-per-person basis.

per stirpes—method for distribution of an estate that divides property equally down family lines.

perfected security interest—security interest with priority because of filing, possession, automatic or temporary priority status.

periodic tenancy—tenancy that continues indefinitely for a specified rental period until terminated; often called a month-to-month tenancy.

personal property—property that is movable or intangible, or rights in such things.

personal representative—administrator or executor who represents decedents under the UPC.

physical duress—threat of physical harm to person or property.

plaintiff—the party who initiates a lawsuit.

pleadings—the papers filed by the parties in an action in order to set forth the facts and frame the issues to be tried, although, under some systems, the pleadings merely give notice or a general indication of the nature of the issues.

pledge—bailment given as security for the payment of a debt or the performance of an obligation owed to the pledgee. (Parties—pledgor, pledgee)

police power—the power to govern; the power to adopt laws for the protection of the public health, welfare, safety, and morals.

policy—paper evidencing the contract of insurance.

positive law—law enacted and codified by governmental authority.

possession—exclusive dominion and control of property.

possibility of reverter—nature of the interest held by the grantor after conveying land outright but subject to a condition or provision that may cause the grantee's interest to become forfeited and the interest to revert to the grantor or heirs.

postdate—to insert or place on an instrument a later date than the actual date on which it was executed.

power of attorney—written authorization to an agent by the principal.

precedent—a decision of a court that stands as the law for a particular problem in the future.

predatory lending—a practice on the part of the subprime lending market whereby lenders take advantage of less sophisticated consumers or those who are desperate for funds by using the lenders' superior bargaining positions to obtain credit terms that go well beyond compensating them for their risk.

predicate act—qualifying underlying offense for RICO liability.

preemption—the federal government's superior regulatory position over state laws on the same subject area.

preemptive right—shareholder's right upon the increase of a corporation's capital stock to be allowed to subscribe to such a percentage of the new shares as the shareholder's old shares bore to the former total capital stock.

preferences—transfers of property by a debtor to one or more specific creditors to enable these creditors to obtain payment for debts owed.

preferential transfers—certain transfers of money or security interests in the time frame just prior to bankruptcy that can be set aside if voidable.

preferred stock—stock that has a priority or preference as to payment of dividends or upon liquidation, or both.

prescription—acquisition of a right to use the land of another, as an easement, by making hostile, visible, and notorious use of the land, continuing for the period specified by the local law.

presentment—formal request for payment on an instrument.

price discrimination—the charging practice by a seller of different prices to different buyers for commodities of similar grade and quality, resulting in reduced competition or a tendency to create a monopoly.

prima facie—evidence that, if believed, is sufficient by itself to lead to a particular conclusion.

primary party—party to whom the holder or holder in due course must turn first to obtain payment.

primary picketing—legal presentations in front of a business notifying the public of a labor dispute.

primum non nocere—"above all do no harm."

principal—person or firm who employs an agent; person who, with respect to a surety, is primarily liable to the third person or creditor; property held in trust.

principal debtor—original borrower or debtor.

prior art—a showing that an invention as a whole would have been obvious to a person of ordinary skill in the art when the invention was patented.

private carrier—carrier owned by the shipper, such as a company's own fleet of trucks.

private corporation—corporation organized for charitable and benevolent purposes or for purposes of finance, industry, and commerce.

private law—the rules and regulations parties agree to as part of their contractual relationships.

private nuisance—nuisance that affects only one or a few individuals.

privileges and immunities clause—a clause that entitles a person going into another state to make contracts, own property, and engage in business to the same extent as citizens of that state.

privity—succession or chain of relationship to the same thing or right, such as privity of contract, privity of estate, privity of possession.

privity of contract—relationship between a promisor and the promisee.

privity rule—succession or chain of relationship to the same thing or right, such as privity of contract, privity of estate, privity of possession.

pro rata—proportionately, or divided according to a rate or standard.

probate—procedure for formally establishing or proving that a given writing is the last will and testament of the person who purportedly signed it.

procedural law—the law that specifies the steps that must be followed in enforcing rights and liabilities.

process—paperwork served personally on a defendant in a civil case.

product disparagement—false statements made about a product or business.

profit—right to take a part of the soil or produce of another's land, such as timber or water.

promisee—person to whom a promise is made.

promisor—person who makes a promise.

promissory estoppel—doctrine that a promise will be enforced although it is not supported by consideration when the promisor should have reasonably expected that the promise would induce action or forbearance of a definite and substantial character on the part of the promised and injustice can be avoided only by enforcement of the promise.

promissory note—unconditional promise in writing made by one person to another, signed by the maker engaging to pay on demand, or at a definite time, a sum certain in money to order or to bearer. (Parties—maker, payee)

promoters—persons who plan the formation of the corporation and sell or promote the idea to others.

proof of claim—written statement, signed by the creditor or an authorized representative, setting forth any claim made against the debtor and the basis for it.

property report—condensed version of a property development statement filed with the secretary of HUD and given to a prospective customer at least 48 hours before signing a contract to buy or lease property.

prosecutor—party who originates a criminal proceeding.

prospectus—information provided to each potential purchaser of securities setting forth the key information contained in the registration statement.

proxy—written authorization by a shareholder to another person to vote the stock owned by the shareholder; the person who is the holder of such a written authorization.

public corporation—corporation that has been established for governmental purposes and for the administration of public affairs.

public nuisance—nuisance that affects the community or public at large.

public policy—certain objectives relating to health, morals, and integrity of government that the law seeks to advance by declaring invalid any contract that conflicts with those objectives even though there is no statute expressly declaring such a contract illegal.

public warehouses—entities that serve the public generally without discrimination.

punitive damages—damages, in excess of those required to compensate the plaintiff for the wrong done, that are imposed in order to punish the defendant because of the particularly wanton or willful character of wrongdoing; also called *exemplary damages*.

purchase money security interest (PMSI)—the security interest in the goods a seller sells on credit that become the collateral for the creditor/seller.

Q

qualified indorsement—an indorsement that includes words such as "without recourse" that disclaims certain liability of the indorser to a maker or a drawee.

qualified privilege—media privilege to print inaccurate information without liability for defamation, so long as a retraction is printed and there was no malice.

quantum meruit—"as much as deserved"; an action brought for the value of the services rendered the defendant when there was no express contract as to the purchase price.

quasi contract—court-imposed obligation to prevent unjust enrichment in the absence of a contract.

quasi-judicial proceedings—forms of hearings in which the rules of evidence and procedure are more relaxed but each side still has a chance to be heard.

quasi-public corporation—private corporation furnishing services on which the public is particularly dependent, for example, a gas and electric company.

quitclaim deed—deed by which the grantor purports to give up only whatever right or title the grantor may have in the property without specifying or warranting transfer of any particular interest.

quorum—minimum number of persons, shares represented, or directors who must be present at a meeting in order to lawfully transact business.

R

race statute—statute under which the first party to record the deed holds the title.

race-notice statute—See *notice-race statute*.

Racketeer Influenced and Corrupt Organizations (RICO) Act—federal law, initially targeting organized crime, that has expanded in scope and provides penalties and civil recovery for multiple criminal offenses, or a pattern of racketeering.

real property—land and all rights in land.

recognizance—obligation entered into before a court to do some act, such as to appear at a later date for a hearing. Also called a *contract of record*.

recorder—public official in charge of deeds.

recross-examination—an examination by the other side's attorney that follows the redirect examination.

redemption—buying back of one's property, which has been sold because of a default, upon paying the amount that had been originally due together with interest and costs.

redirect examination—questioning after cross-examination, in which the attorney for the witness testifying may ask the same witness other questions to overcome effects of the cross-examination.

reference to a third person—settlement that allows a nonparty to resolve the dispute.

reformation—remedy by which a written instrument is corrected when it fails to express the actual intent of both parties because of fraud, accident, or mistake.

registered bonds—bonds held by owners whose names and addresses are registered on the books of the corporation.

registration requirements—provisions of the Securities Act of 1933 requiring advance disclosure to the public of a new securities issue through filing a statement with the SEC and sending a prospectus to each potential purchaser.

registration statement—document disclosing specific financial information regarding the security, the issuer, and the underwriter.

remainder interest—land interest that follows a life estate.

remand—term used when an appellate court sends a case back to trial court for additional hearings or a new trial.

remedy—action or procedure that is followed in order to enforce a right or to obtain damages for injury to a right.

rent-a-judge plan—dispute resolution through private courts with judges paid to be referees for the cases.

representative capacity—action taken by one on behalf of another, as the act of a personal representative on behalf of a decedent's estate, or action taken both on one's behalf and on behalf of others, as a shareholder bringing a representative action.

repudiation—result of a buyer or seller refusing to perform the contract as stated.

request for production of documents—discovery tool for uncovering paper or electronic evidence in a case.

requirements contract—contract in which the buyer buys its needs (requirements) from the seller.

rescission—action of one party to a contract to set the contract aside when the other party is guilty of a breach of the contract.

reservation of rights—assertion by a party to a contract that even though a tendered performance (e.g., a defective product) is accepted, the right to damages for nonconformity to the contract is reserved.

Resource Conservation and Recovery Act (RCRA)—federal law that regulates the disposal of potentially harmful substances and encourages resource conservation and recovery.

Resource Recovery Act—early federal solid waste disposal legislation that provided funding for states and local governments with recycling programs.

respondeat superior—doctrine that the principal or employer is vicariously liable for the unauthorized torts committed by an agent or employee while acting within the scope of the agency or the course of the employment, respectively.

restrictive covenants—covenants in a deed by which the grantee agrees to refrain from doing specified acts.

restrictive indorsement—an indorsement that restricts further transfer, such as in trust for or to the use of some other person, is conditional, or for collection or deposit.

reverse—the term used when the appellate court sets aside the verdict or judgment of a lower court.

reverse mortgage—mortgage in which the owners get their equity out of their home over a period of time and return the house to the lender upon their deaths.

reversible error—an error or defect in court proceedings of so serious a nature that on appeal the appellate court will set aside the proceedings of the lower court.

reversionary interest—interest that a lessor has in property that is subject to an outstanding lease.

revoke—testator's act of taking back his or her will and its provisions.

right—legal capacity to require another person to perform or refrain from an action.

right of escheat—right of the state to take the property of a decedent that has not been distributed.

right of first refusal—right of a party to meet the terms of a proposed contract before it is executed, such as a real estate purchase agreement.

right of privacy—the right to be free from unreasonable intrusion by others.

rights theory—Nozick's theory of ethics that (1) everyone has a set of rights, and (2) it is up to the governments to protect those rights.

right to cure—second chance for a seller to make a proper tender of conforming goods.

right-to-work laws—laws restricting unions and employees from negotiating clauses in their collective bargaining agreements that make union membership compulsory.

risk—peril or contingency against which the insured is protected by the contract of insurance.

risk of loss—in contract performance, the cost of damage or injury to the goods contracted for.

Robinson-Patman Act—a federal statute designed to eliminate price discrimination in interstate commerce.

run with the land—concept that certain covenants in a deed to land are deemed to run or pass with the land so that whoever owns the land is bound by or entitled to the benefit of the covenants.

S

Safe Drinking Water Act—a federal law that establishes national standards for contaminants in drinking water.

sale on approval—term indicating that no sale takes place until the buyer approves or accepts the goods.

sale or return—sale in which the title to the property passes to the buyer at the time of the transaction but the buyer is given the option of returning the property and restoring the title to the seller.

search engine—Internet service used to locate Web sites.

search warrant—judicial authorization for a search of property where there is the expectation of privacy.

seasonable—timely.

secondary meaning—a legal term signifying the words in question have taken on a new meaning with the public, capable of serving a source-identifying function of a mark.

secondary parties—called *secondary obligors* under Revised Article 3; parties to an instrument to whom holders turn when the primary party, for whatever reason, fails to pay the instrument.

secondary picketing—picketing an employer with which a union has no dispute to persuade the employer to stop doing business with a party to the dispute; generally illegal under the NLRA.

secrecy laws—confidentiality laws applied to home-country banks.

secured party—person owed the money, whether as a seller or a lender, in a secured transaction in personal property.

secured transaction—credit sale of goods or a secured loan that provides special protection for the creditor.

securities—stocks and bonds issued by a corporation. Under some investor protection laws, the term includes any interest in an enterprise that provides unearned income to its owner.

security agreement—agreement of the creditor and the debtor that the creditor will have a security interest.

security interest—property right that enables the creditor to take possession of the property if the debtor does not pay the amount owed.

self-help repossession—creditor's right to repossess the collateral without judicial proceedings.

self-proved wills—wills that eliminate some formalities of proof by being executed according to statutory requirements.

selling on consignment—entrusting a person with possession of property for the purpose of sale.

semiconductor chip product—product placed on a piece of semiconductor material in accordance with a predetermined pattern that is intended to perform electronic circuitry functions.

service mark—mark that identifies a service.

servient tenement—land that is subject to an easement.

settlor—one who settles property in trust or creates a trust estate.

severalty—ownership of property by one person.

shared powers—powers that are held by both state and national governments.

Sherman Antitrust Act—a federal statute prohibiting combinations and contracts in restraint of interstate trade, now generally inapplicable to labor union activity.

shop right—right of an employer to use in business without charge an invention discovered by an employee during working hours and with the employer's material and equipment.

shopkeeper's privilege—right of a store owner to detain a suspected shoplifter based on reasonable cause and for a reasonable time without resulting liability for false imprisonment.

short-swing profit—profit realized by a corporate insider from selling securities less than six months after purchase.

sinking fund—fixed amount of money set aside each year by the borrowing corporation toward the ultimate payment of bonds.

situational ethics—a flexible standard of ethics that permits an examination of circumstances and motivation before attaching the label of right or wrong to conduct.

Sixth Amendment—the U.S. constitutional amendment that guarantees a speedy trial.

slander—defamation of character by spoken words or gestures.

slander of title—malicious making of false statements as to a seller's title.

small claims courts—courts that resolve disputes between parties when those disputes do not exceed a minimal level; no lawyers are permitted; the parties represent themselves.

social contract—theory of ethics that focuses on social norms; what is ethical is the standard set by implied agreement; for example, we disapprove of people who cut in line ahead of us.

sole or individual proprietorship—form of business ownership in which one individual owns the business.

soliciting agent—salesperson.

sovereign compliance doctrine—doctrine that allows a defendant to raise as an affirmative defense to an antitrust action the fact that the defendant's actions were compelled by a foreign state.

sovereign immunity doctrine—doctrine that states that a foreign sovereign generally cannot be sued unless an exception to the Foreign Sovereign Immunities Act of 1976 applies.

special agent—agent authorized to transact a specific transaction or to do a specific act.

special drawing rights (SDRs)—rights that allow a country to borrow enough money from other International Money Fund (IMF) members to permit that country to maintain the stability of its currency's relationship to other world currencies.

special indorsement—an indorsement that specifies the person to whom the instrument is indorsed.

specific legacies—identified property bequeathed by a testator; also called *specific devises.*

specific lien—right of a creditor to hold particular property or assert a lien on particular property of the debtor because of the creditor's having done work on or having some other association with the property, as distinguished from having a lien generally against the assets of the debtor merely because the debtor is indebted to the lien holder.

specific performance—action brought to compel the adverse party to perform a contract on the theory that merely suing for damages for its breach will not be an adequate remedy.

spendthrift trust—a trust that, to varying degrees, provides that creditors of the beneficiary shall not be able to reach the principal or income held by the trustee and that the beneficiary shall not be able to assign any interest in the trust.

spot zoning—allowing individual variation in zoning.

stakeholder analysis—the term used when a decision maker views a problem from different perspectives and measures the impact of a decision on various groups.

stakeholders—those who have a stake, or interest, in the activities of a corporation; stakeholders include employees, members of the community in which the corporation operates, vendors, customers, and any others who are affected by the actions and decisions of the corporation.

stale check—a check whose date is longer than six months ago.

standby letter—letter of credit for a contractor ensuring he will complete the project as contracted.

stare decisis—"let the decision stand"; the principle that the decision of a court should serve as a guide or precedent and control the decision of a similar case in the future.

status quo ante—original positions of the parties.

statute of frauds—statute that, in order to prevent fraud through the use of perjured testimony, requires that certain kinds of transactions be evidenced in writing in order to be binding or enforceable.

statute of limitations—statute that restricts the period of time within which an action may be brought.

statutory law—laws enacted by a legislative body.

stay (or delay) of foreclosure—delay of foreclosure obtained by the mortgagor to prevent undue hardship.

stirpes—family lines; distribution *per stirpes* refers to the manner in which descendants take property by right of representation.

stock subscription—contract or agreement to buy a specific number and kind of shares when they are issued by the corporation.

stop payment order—order by a depositor to the bank to refuse to make payment of a check when presented for payment.

straight (or nonnegotiable) bill of lading—document of title that consigns transported goods to a named person.

strict liability—civil wrong for which there is absolute liability because of the inherent danger in the underlying activity, for example, the use of explosives.

strict tort liability—product liability theory that imposes liability upon the manufacturer, seller, or distributor of goods for harm caused by defective goods.

subject matter jurisdiction—judicial authority to hear a particular type of case.

sublease—a transfer of the premises by the lessee to a third person, the sublessee or subtenant, for a period of less than the term of the original lease.

sublessee—person with lease rights for a period of less than the term of the original lease (also *subtenant*).

subprime lending market—a credit market that makes loans to high-risk consumers (those who have bankruptcies, no credit history, or a poor credit history), often loaning money to pay off other debts the consumer has due.

subrogation—right of a party secondarily liable to stand in the place of the creditor after making payment to the creditor and to enforce the creditor's right against the party primarily liable in order to obtain indemnity from such primary party.

substantial impairment—material defect in a good.

substantial performance—equitable rule that if a good-faith attempt to perform does not precisely meet the terms of the agreement, the agreement will still be considered complete if the essential purpose of the contract is accomplished.

substantive law—the law that creates, defines, and regulates rights and liabilities.

substitute check—electronic image of a paper check that a bank can create and that has the same legal effect as the original instrument.

substitution—substitution of a new contract between the same parties.

sum certain—amount due under an instrument that can be computed from its face with only reference to interest rates.

summary jury trial—a mock or dry-run trial for parties to get a feel for how their cases will play to a jury.

summation—the attorney address to a jury that is given after all the evidence is presented in court and sums up a case and urges the jury to reach a particular verdict.

Superfund Amendment and Reauthorization Act—federal law that authorizes the EPA to collect cleanup costs from those responsible for the ownership, leasing, dumping, or security of hazardous waste sites.

Superfund sites—areas designated by the EPA for cleanup of hazardous waste.

surety—obligor of a suretyship; primarily liable for the debt or obligation of the principal debtor.

suretyship—undertaking to pay the debt or be liable for the default of another.

symbolic delivery—delivery of goods by delivery of the means of control, such as a key or a relevant document of title, such as a negotiable bill of lading; also called *constructive delivery*.

T

takeover laws—laws that guard against unfairness in corporate takeover situations.

tariff—(1) domestically—government-approved schedule of charges that may be made by a regulated business, such as a common carrier or warehouser; (2) internationally—tax imposed by a country on goods crossing its borders, without regard to whether the purpose is to raise revenue or to discourage the traffic in the taxed goods.

tax lien—lien on property by a government agency for nonpayment of taxes.

teller's check—draft drawn by a bank on another bank in which it has an account.

temporary insider—someone retained by a corporation for professional services on an as-needed basis, such as an attorney, accountant, or investment banker.

temporary perfection—perfection given for a limited period of time to creditors.

tenancy at sufferance—lease arrangement in which the tenant occupies the property at the discretion of the landlord.

tenancy at will—holding of land for an indefinite period that may be terminated at any time by the landlord or by the landlord and tenant acting together.

tenancy by entirety or tenancy by entireties—transfer of property to both husband and wife.

tenancy for years—tenancy for a fixed period of time, even though the time is less than a year.

tenancy in common—relationship that exists when two or more persons own undivided interests in property.

tenancy in partnership—ownership relationship that exists between partners under the Uniform Partnership Act.

tenant—one who holds or possesses real property by any kind of right or title; one who pays rent for the temporary use and occupation of another's real property under a lease.

tender—goods have arrived, are available for pickup, and buyer is notified.

term insurance—policy written for a specified number of years that terminates at the end of that period.

termination statement—document (record), which may be requested by a debtor who has paid in full, stating that a security interest is no longer claimed under the specified financing statement.

testamentary capacity—sufficient mental capacity to understand that a writing being executed is a will and what that entails.

testamentary intent—designed to take effect at death, as by disposing of property or appointing a personal representative.

testamentary trust—trust that becomes effective only when the settlor's will takes effect after death.

testate—condition of leaving a will upon death.

testate distribution—distribution of an estate in accordance with the will of the decedent.

testator, testatrix—man, woman who makes a will.

third-party beneficiary—third person whom the parties to a contract intend to benefit by the making of the contract and to confer upon such person the right to sue for breach of contract.

time draft—bill of exchange payable at a stated time after sight or at a definite time.

tippee—individual who receives information about a corporation from an insider or temporary insider.

tort—civil wrong that interferes with one's property or person.

Toxic Substances Control Act (TOSCA)—first federal law to control the manufacture, use, and disposal of toxic substances.

trade dress—product's total image including its overall packaging look.

trade libel—written defamation about a product or service.

trade name—name under which a business is carried on and, if fictitious, must be registered.

trade secret—any formula, device, or compilation of information that is used in one's business and is of such a nature that it provides an advantage over competitors who do not have the information.

trademark—mark that identifies a product.

transferee—buyer or vendee.

traveler's check—check that is payable on demand provided it is countersigned by the person whose specimen signature appears on the check.

treasury stock—corporate stock that the corporation has reacquired.

treble damages—three times the damages actually sustained.

trespass—an unauthorized action with respect to person or property.

trial de novo—a trial required to preserve the constitutional right to a jury trial by allowing an appeal to proceed as though there never had been any prior hearing or decision.

tripartite—three-part division (of government).

trust—transfer of property by one person to another with the understanding or declaration that such property be held for the benefit of another; the holding of property by the owner in trust for another, upon a declaration of trust, without a transfer to another person. (Parties—settlor, trustee, beneficiary)

trust agreement—instrument creating a trust; also called *deed of trust.*

trust corpus—fund or property that is transferred to the trustee or held by the settlor as the body or subject matter of the trust; also called *trust fund, trust estate,* and *trust res.*

trustee—party who has legal title to estate and manages it.

trustee in bankruptcy—impartial person elected to administer the debtor's estate.

trustor—donor or settlor who is the owner of property and creates a trust in the property.

tying—the anticompetitive practice of requiring buyers to purchase one product in order to get another.

U

ultra vires—act or contract that the corporation does not have authority to do or make.

unconscionable—unreasonable, not guided or restrained by conscience and often referring to a contract grossly unfair to one party because of the superior bargaining powers of the other party.

underwriter—insurer.

undisclosed principal—principal on whose behalf an agent acts without disclosing to the third person the fact of agency or the identity of the principal.

undue influence—influence that is asserted upon another person by one who dominates that person.

Uniform Probate Code (UPC)—uniform statute on wills and administration of estates.

Uniform Simultaneous Death Act—law providing that when survivorship cannot be established, the property of each person shall be disposed of as though he or she had survived the other.

unilateral contract—contract under which only one party makes a promise.

unincorporated association—combination of two or more persons for the furtherance of a common nonprofit purpose.

universal agent—agent authorized by the principal to do all acts that can lawfully be delegated to a representative.

universal defenses—defenses that are regarded as so basic that the social interest in preserving them outweighs the social interest of giving negotiable instruments the freely transferable qualities of money; accordingly, such defenses are given universal effect and may be raised against all holders.

USA Patriot Act—federal law that, among other things, imposes reporting requirements on banks.

usage of trade—language and customs of an industry.

usury—lending money at an interest rate that is higher than the maximum rate allowed by law.

utilitarians—those who support the ethical theory of resolving dilemmas by doing the most good for the most people.

uttering—crime of issuing or delivering a forged instrument to another person.

V

valid—legal.

valid contract—agreement that is binding and enforceable.

value—consideration or antecedent debt or security given in exchange for the transfer of a negotiable instrument or creation of a security interest.

variance—permission of a landowner to use the land in a specified manner that is inconsistent with the zoning ordinance.

vicarious liability—imposing liability for the fault of another.

void agreement—agreement that cannot be enforced.

voidable contract—agreement that is otherwise binding and enforceable but may be rejected at the option of one of the parties as the result of specific circumstances.

voidable title—title of goods that carries with it the contingency of an underlying problem.

voir dire examination—the preliminary examination of a juror or a witness to ascertain fitness to act as such.

voluntary bankruptcy—proceeding in which the debtor files the petition for relief.

voting by proxy—authorizing someone else to vote the shares owned by the shareholder.

voting trust—transfer by two or more persons of their shares of stock of a corporation to a trustee who is to vote the shares and act for such shareholders.

W

waiver—release or relinquishment of a known right or objection.

warehouse—entity engaged in the business of storing the goods of others for compensation.

warehouse receipt—receipt issued by the warehouse for stored goods. Regulated by the UCC, which clothes the receipt with some degree of negotiability.

warranty—promise either express or implied about the nature, quality, or performance of the goods.

warranty against encumbrances—warranty that there are no liens or other encumbrances to goods except those noted by seller.

warranty deed—deed by which the grantor conveys a specific estate or interest to the grantee and makes one or more of the covenants of title.

warranty of habitability—implied warranty that the leased property is fit for dwelling by tenants.

warranty of title—implied warranty that title to the goods is good and transfer is proper.

wasting assets corporation—corporation designed to exhaust or use up the assets of the corporation, such as by extracting oil, coal, iron, and other ores.

way of necessity—grantee's right to use land retained by the grantor for going to and from the conveyed land.

White-Collar Crime Penalty Enhancement Act of 2002—federal reforms passed as a result of the collapses of companies such as Enron; provides for longer sentences and higher fines for both executives and companies.

white-collar crimes—crimes committed generally in the course of doing business and usually involving some form of deceit used to get gains.

whole life insurance—ordinary life insurance providing lifetime insurance protection.

will—instrument executed with the formality required by law by which a person makes a disposition of his or her property to take effect upon death.

writ of certiorari—order by the U.S. Supreme Court granting a right of review by the court of a lower court decision.

wrongfully dishonored—error by a bank in refusing to pay a check.

Z

zoning—restrictions imposed by government on the use of designated land to ensure an orderly physical development of the regulated area.

Opinion cases are in boldface type at the case summary; cited cases are in Roman type.